Venice

VENICE

The Remarkable History of the Lagoon City

DENNIS ROMANO

OXFORD
UNIVERSITY PRESS

Oxford University Press is a department of the University of Oxford. It furthers the University's objective of excellence in research, scholarship, and education by publishing worldwide. Oxford is a registered trade mark of Oxford University Press in the UK and certain other countries.

Published in the United States of America by Oxford University Press
198 Madison Avenue, New York, NY 10016, United States of America.

Library of Congress Cataloging-in-Publication Data
Names: Romano, Dennis, 1951– author.
Title: Venice : the remarkable history of the lagoon city / Dennis Romano.
Description: Oxford ; New York : Oxford University Press, [2024] |
Includes bibliographical references and index. |
Identifiers: LCCN 2023032463 (print) | LCCN 2023032464 (ebook) |
ISBN 9780190859985 (hardback) | ISBN 9780190860004 (epub) |
ISBN 9780197696026
Subjects: LCSH: Venice (Italy)—Civilization. | Venice (Italy)—History.
Classification: LCC DG675.6 .R66 2024 (print) | LCC DG675.6 (ebook) |
DDC 945/.311—dc23/eng/20230908
LC record available at https://lccn.loc.gov/2023032463
LC ebook record available at https://lccn.loc.gov/2023032464

DOI: 10.1093/oso/9780190859985.001.0001

Printed by Sheridan Books, Inc., United States of America

For Mary, Ethan, Philip, Owen, and Rocco
and in memory of
Mary Josephine Vaccaro (1902–1965)

Contents

Illustrations

Plates

Maps

Figures

Timeline of Venetian History

BCE c. 4000	Formation of primordial lagoon
BCE 1100–700	Veneti migrate into the region from the Balkans
BCE 181	Foundation of Aquileia
BCE 131	Via Annia links Adria to Aquileia via Padua
BCE c. 79	Pliny the Elder dubs the route between Ravenna and Altino the "Seven Seas"
BCE c. 1	Lagoon assumes current form
CE 8	Establishment of Roman region of Venetia and Istria
421	March 25: Legendary foundation of Venice
452	Huns under Attila invade Italy
476	End of Roman Empire in the West
537	Cassiodorus's Letter to the Tribunes of the Maritime Provinces
568	Lombard invasion of Italy, further migration into lagoon
580	Exarchate of Ravenna established; Venetia ruled by a *magister militum* (master of troops)
606–7	Split between Aquileia and Grado, each claiming to be the patriarchate
726–7	Iconoclast controversy; revolt against Byzantium; Orso elected first *dux* (doge)
751	Ravenna falls to Lombards; end of Exarchate; doge becomes ruler of the lagoon province
774–6	Bishopric established at Olivolo (Castello)
810	Venetians defeat Charlemagne's son Pepin
811	Doge Agnello Partecipazio moves capital from Malamocco to Rivoalto and builds first ducal palace
828	Saint Mark's relics arrive in Venice
877	Saracens attack Grado and Comacchio
932	Venetians humble Capodistria, destroy rival Comacchio, and assert control over Gulf of Venice
982	Doge Tribuno Menio transfers island of San Giorgio Maggiore to Benedictines

1000	Doge Pietro II Orseolo defeats Narentan pirates, asserts Venetian dominance in middle Adriatic, and wrests concessions from bishop of Treviso
1082	Byzantine emperor issues Golden Bull granting Venetians trade advantages; in exchange Venetians offer naval support to emperor against Normans
1097	Donation of land at Rialto market to government
1100	Venetian participation in First Crusade (1096–1109); Saint Nicholas's relics brought to Venice
1105	Pala d'Oro commissioned by Doge Ordelaffo Falier
1123	Venetians defeat Fatimid navy off coast of Palestine near Ascalon
1143	First evidence of the Venetian commune
1177	Peace of Venice—Doge Sebastiano Ziani mediates peace between Pope Alexander III and Holy Roman emperor Frederick Barbarossa
1192	First extant ducal oath of office
1204	Fourth Crusade conquest of Constantinople
1218	Venice gains full control of Crete
1260s	*Popolo* (common people) excluded from political power
1271–95	Marco Polo journeys to China
1285	First gold ducat minted
1286–1323	Serrata (Closing) of the Greater Council
1310	Querini-Tiepolo Conspiracy; origin of Council of Ten
1321	Savi agli Ordini (Maritime Sages) established to coordinate state-merchant galley system
1355	Conspiracy of Doge Marino Falier
1379–81	Fourth Venetian-Genoese War (War of Chioggia)
1404–6	Venice acquires Padua, Vicenza, and Verona
1423	General Assembly stripped of its last vestiges of power
1426–8	Brescia and Bergamo come under Venetian rule
1453	Sultan Mehmed II conquers Constantinople
1454	Peace of Lodi ends three decades of war with Milan.
1457–8	Doge Francesco Foscari deposed; effort to rein in Council of Ten
1463–79	First Venice-Ottoman War; Ottomans seize Negroponte and make forays into Friuli and the Veneto
1469	First printing press established in Venice
1489	Caterina Corner forced to cede Cyprus to the Republic
1499–1503	Second Venice-Ottoman War; Venice loses Modon and Coron (the "Eyes of the Republic"); end of Venetian naval supremacy in eastern Mediterranean
1500	Jacopo de' Barbari produces bird's-eye view of Venice
1501	Portuguese circumnavigate Cape of Good Hope, sail to India, and disrupt Venetian spice trade

1508	League of Cambrai formed against Venice
1516	Jews allowed to settle in Ghetto; Vittore Carpaccio completes painting of *Lion of Saint Mark* for the office of the State Treasurers
1529	Peace of Bologna; Venice loses Cervia, Ravenna, and Apulian ports; Hapsburgs become predominant power in Italy
1537–40	Third Venice-Ottoman War
1539	Office of State Inquisitors established
1543	Gasparo Contarini's *De magistratibus et republica venetorum* (On the Magistracies and Republic of the Venetians) published
1545	Completion of Sansovino's Loggetta
1569	Final state-merchant galley voyage
1570–73	Fourth Venice-Ottoman War; battle of Lepanto; Cyprus lost to the Ottomans
1573	Painter Paolo Veronese interrogated by Inquisition regarding his painting of the Last Supper
1576	Andrea Palladio receives commission to build the Church of the Santissimo Redentore in thanksgiving for the end of the plague
1580	Courtesan Veronica Franco publishes *Lettere familiari a diversi* (Familiar Letters to Various People)
1595	*Popolo* demand election of Marino Grimani as doge
1606–7	Interdict Crisis; Venice defies papacy
1630	Accademia degli Incogniti established
1631	Foundation stone laid for the Church of the Salute designed by Baldassare Longhena
1637	Teatro Sant'Aponal, first opera house, opens
1645–69	War of Candia (Fifth Venice-Ottoman War); Venice loses Crete
1646	Venice begins selling admission to Greater Council
1654	Arcangela Tarabotti's *Tirannia paterna* (Paternal Tyranny) posthumously published with the title *La semplicità ingannata* (Innocence Deceived)
1677	Amelot de la Houssaye publishes *Histoire du gouvernemente de Venise* (History of the Government of Venice), helps establish negative view of Venice's aristocratic republic
1684–89	First War of the Morea (Sixth Venice-Ottoman War); Venetians blow up Parthenon
1714–18	Second War of the Morea (Seventh Venice-Ottoman War); humiliating losses for Venice
1723	Hospital of the Pietà contracts with Antonio Vivaldi for two concertos per month
1737–82	*Murazzi* (sea walls) built along barrier islands to protect lagoon
1750	Carlo Goldoni debuts sixteen comedies

1797	May 12: Greater Council votes itself out of existence; end of the Republic
1797–98	Democratic Municipal Government
1798–1806	First Austrian Domination
1806–1814	Napoleonic Kingdom of Italy; major infrastructure projects developed
1810	Ateneo Veneto established
1846	Railway bridge linking Venice to mainland opens
1848–9	Venetian Revolutionary Republic led by Daniele Manin
1851–3	John Ruskin publishes *The Stones of Venice*
1866	Venice incorporated into Kingdom of Italy
1869	Work begins on Maritime Station
1882	Cotonificio Veneziano (Venetian Cotton Factory) opens
1895	First Biennale
1902	Collapse of San Marco's bell tower
1915	World War I aerial bombardment of city commences
1917	Giuseppe Volpi orchestrates agreement with the national government for development of Porto Marghera
1932	Inauguration of Venice Film Festival
1943	December 5: Order for arrest of Venetian Jews
1951	City reaches population of 174,969 residents
1966	November 4: Devastating *acqua alta* (high tide)
1968	Completion of Petroleum Tanker Canal from Malamocco mouth to Marghera
1987	UNESCO names Venice a World Heritage Site
1988	Prototype MOSE gate (Modulo Sperimentale Elettromeccanico—Experimental Electromechanical Model) to prevent city flooding installed at lagoon mouth
1997	The group Veneto Serenissimo Governo (Most Serene Venetian Government)commandeers the bell tower of San Marco on bicentenary of Republic's end
2008	Calatrava bridge linking Piazzale Roma and train station opens
2020	MOSE flood gates become operational
2022	Population of Venice drops below 50,000

Venice

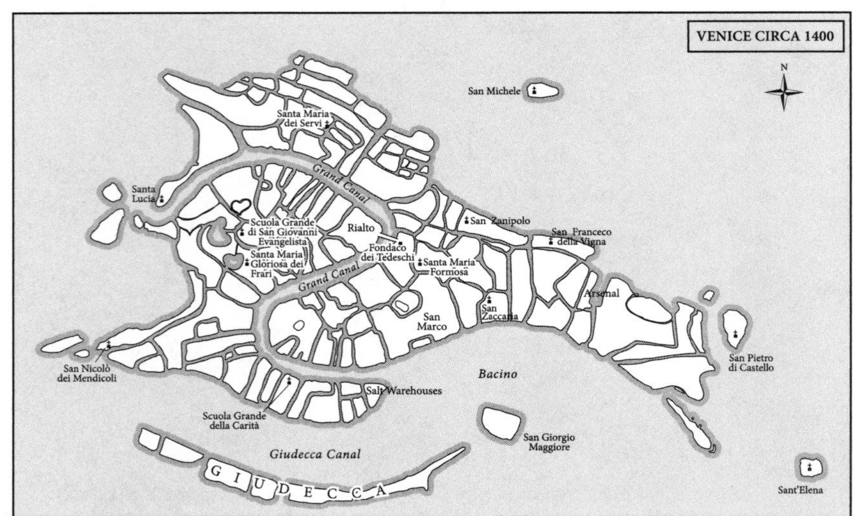

MAP 1 Venice circa 1400

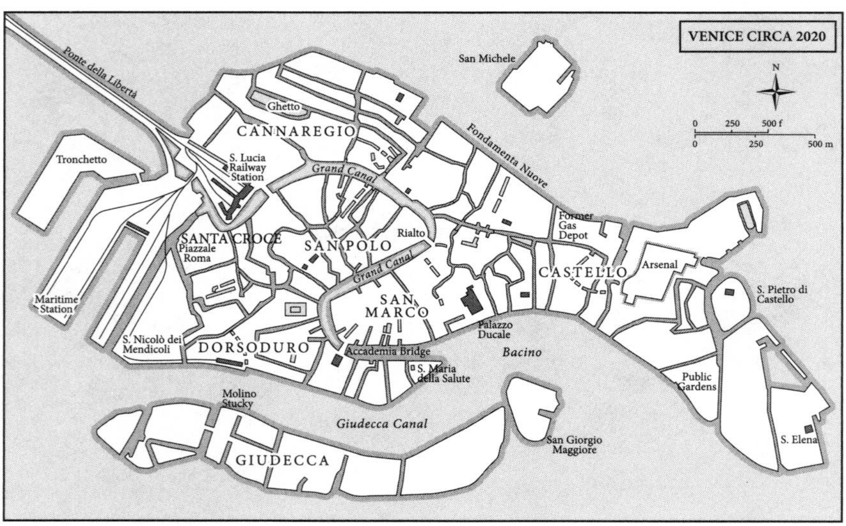

MAP 2 Venice circa 2020

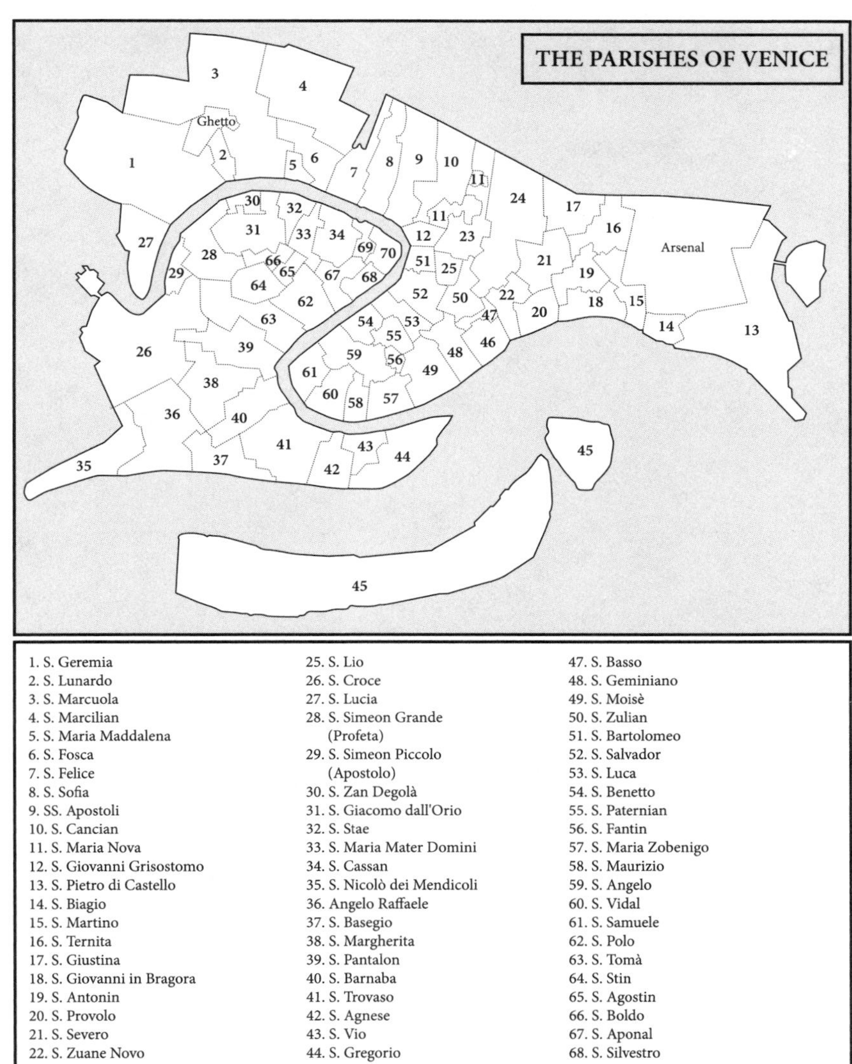
THE PARISHES OF VENICE
Ghetto
Arsenal
1. S. Geremia
2. S. Lunardo
3. S. Marcuola
4. S. Marcilian
5. S. Maria Maddalena
6. S. Fosca
7. S. Felice
8. S. Sofia
9. SS. Apostoli
10. S. Cancian
11. S. Maria Nova
12. S. Giovanni Grisostomo
13. S. Pietro di Castello
14. S. Biagio
15. S. Martino
16. S. Ternita
17. S. Giustina
18. S. Giovanni in Bragora
19. S. Antonin
20. S. Provolo
21. S. Severo
22. S. Zuane Novo
23. S. Marina
24. S. Maria Formosa
25. S. Lio
26. S. Croce
27. S. Lucia
28. S. Simeon Grande (Profeta)
29. S. Simeon Piccolo (Apostolo)
30. S. Zan Degolà
31. S. Giacomo dall'Orio
32. S. Stae
33. S. Maria Mater Domini
34. S. Cassan
35. S. Nicolò dei Mendicoli
36. Angelo Raffaele
37. S. Basegio
38. S. Margherita
39. S. Pantalon
40. S. Barnaba
41. S. Trovaso
42. S. Agnese
43. S. Vio
44. S. Gregorio
45. S. Eufemia
46. S. Marco
47. S. Basso
48. S. Geminiano
49. S. Moisè
50. S. Zulian
51. S. Bartolomeo
52. S. Salvador
53. S. Luca
54. S. Benetto
55. S. Paternian
56. S. Fantin
57. S. Maria Zobenigo
58. S. Maurizio
59. S. Angelo
60. S. Vidal
61. S. Samuele
62. S. Polo
63. S. Tomà
64. S. Stin
65. S. Agostin
66. S. Boldo
67. S. Aponal
68. S. Silvestro
69. S. Matteo
70. S. Giovanni Elemosinario

MAP 3 The Parishes of Venice

Introduction

Situated in the middle of a tidal lagoon, at the northernmost extreme of the Mediterranean Sea, Venice astounds. The improbability of splendid churches and gilded palaces emerging, Venus-like, from the watery depths defies logic and sends observers, native and foreign alike, into ecstatic reveries. For centuries, writers have sought to capture the essence of Venice and its civilization in an image, a metaphor, an allusion. Coming from the solid ground of his native Tuscany, fourteenth-century humanist Francesco Petrarch described marshy Venice as "another world." Francesco Sansovino, Renaissance scholar and chronicler of the city's artistic treasures, characterized Venice and its watery locale as the "impossible in the impossible." Danish writer Hans Christian Andersen pronounced it, appropriately enough, "the city of a fairy tale," while Russian socialist theorist Alexander Herzen considered Venice a "magnificent absurdity" and the decision to build it amid the waves "the madness of genius."[1] What these writers and countless others have sought to convey is that Venice is, simply put, a miracle. Yet since miracles cannot be explained, such musings rob the history of Venice of its lessons and meaning, obscuring the ceaseless work and harsh realities that building a city on water requires.

The truth is that no city on earth has been more profoundly influenced by its natural environment than Venice. Nature endowed it with extraordinary gifts. Venice's location, at a site where numerous rivers originating in the Alps empty into the Adriatic Sea, made it the ideal spot for terrestrial, riverine, and maritime trade routes to intersect. Here, the cities of north and central Europe could be linked to the wealthy metropolises of Constantinople and Alexandria and to the silk and spice routes that lay beyond them. Venice had the potential, if great effort was made, to become a global trade emporium. At the same time, the lagoon had its own treasures to bestow, especially upon its earliest inhabitants. Salt was the original source of Venetian riches, fish the sustenance of life, the surrounding waters its defensive barrier.

But living in a lagoon, especially one as hydrologically dynamic as Venice's, was (and remains) fraught with toil and peril. Every inch of dry land must be wrested with great effort from the shallows, reinforced with embankments, and constantly protected lest it be reclaimed by unrelenting waves.[2] Water imperils Venice from two directions. The mainland rivers carry huge quantities of silt from the nearby mountains, threatening to transform the lagoon into a malaria-ridden swamp and, ultimately, dry land. Only through centuries of effort at building dikes and channeling the rivers into artificial beds were the Venetians able to divert the flow away from the lagoon and maintain its viability. The sea poses a different danger as periodic floods of salt water inundate the city, damaging goods and undermining buildings. If sea level continues to rise, it will eventually render the city uninhabitable. To stem the tide, generations of Venetians have built sea walls to protect the barrier islands from erosion. Originally, they were made of wooden poles backfilled with chunks of stone; later more elaborate curved walls were built to counteract the power of the waves. More recently, rising sea level has prompted the introduction of mobile gates that can shut the lagoon off from the Adriatic when extreme high tides are threatening. Managing the lagoon is the great constant in Venice's history.[3]

Water may be a threat, but it is also Venice's lifeblood, influencing every aspect of life. Lacking land, the very definition of wealth in the Middle Ages, Venetians were compelled to look to trade and commerce for their livelihood. Ships stood at the center of the city's existence and served as formidable projections of Venetian power. They were often named for the families that owned them. One medieval chronicler even included them in his description of Venice's inhabitants.[4] For centuries on end, tens of thousands of Venetians built and maintained the city's merchant marine and naval fleets and supplied its crews. The Arsenal, the Venetian Republic's state-owned shipyard, was a marvel of the preindustrial age. Dante Alighieri captured its frenzied activity as workers crafted new vessels and repaired old ones. In the *Divine Comedy*, he compared the boiling muck torturing the damned in the fifth ditch of Hell's eighth circle to the sticky pitch the Venetians used to seal their ships' hulls.[5]

At the same time, the Venetians' focus on business and trade made them suspect, pariahs even, to their western European neighbors. The aristocrats of mainland Europe questioned the legitimacy of Venetian nobles due to their engagement in trade, which was considered denigrating work suitable only for commoners, and because they failed to participate in the land-based feudal system.[6] Venetians famously (and stereotypically) cut a poor figure on horseback—the very definition of chivalric dignity. Simultaneously, the Catholic Church's doubts whether salvation and money-making were reconcilable—a position popularized by Francis of Assisi in the thirteenth century—combined with Venetians' willingness to trade with Muslims led some to question their allegiance to Christendom. The sea and trade may have made the Venetians rich and powerful, but they also saddled them with enduring stereotypes regarding their cunning and faithlessness.[7]

The city's amphibious environment did much to shape social relations and personal interactions. In the earliest centuries, Venetians traveled between the scattered islands of their archipelago in small boats, but as the city solidified into a compact mass and pedestrian streets developed, residents principally got around by foot. At times nobles employed their private gondolas, themselves potent status symbols, to move about, but they also often walked the city.[8] Foreigner notables were struck by how they did so without a retinue of retainers in tow.[9] Consequently, Venetians of all social backgrounds had frequent face-to-face contact, promoting familiar, if not necessarily cordial, relations. To this day, the streets of Venice are the great social equalizer as people conduct their daily activities on foot.

Water also put its stamp on Venetian festive and ritual life. Much socializing took place in boats, and most of Venice's festivals and celebrations included an aquatic component, the doge's annual marriage to the sea ceremony being the most famous.[10] And when the Venetians built the votive churches of the Santissimo Redentore on the island of the Giudecca and Santa Maria della Salute at the Custom's House Point in thanksgiving for the cessation of plagues, they situated those churches to replicate the arduousness of pilgrimage journeys.[11] To arrive at these temples on the appointed feast days, the faithful had to cross undulating bridges temporarily fashioned from boats lashed together with ropes. Marine entertainments including bridge battles and rowing competitions were mainstays of Venetian life in the early modern era.[12] Regattas and fireworks displays in the Bacino (Basin) of San Marco still are.

Erecting solid buildings on water required innovative construction techniques. Early on, the Venetians found ways to build on the unstable ground they had reclaimed from the lagoon. Piles driven into the mud and planks placed one atop the other served as the foundations for buildings. Eventually these wooden supports were supplemented with Istrian stone whose imperviousness to water made it ideal for preventing the constant upward seepage of saltwater that could damage edifices from within. The Venetians discovered as well that it made sense to orient their buildings so as to protect the lengthy weight-bearing walls from the constant erosion caused by waves. For this reason, as any trip down the Grand Canal makes clear, most

Venetian houses are narrow and long, with their narrow decorative façades fronting the water.[13] And buildings often abut, offering further reinforcement and stability. In these ways, water shaped the very form of the city and the configuration of its squares, streets, and houses.

Less obvious is water's influence on art, although much has been made of the special quality of Venetian light and how it is reflected in the canals and captured in paintings.[14] Water's deleterious impact on frescos—which once adorned the façades of many Renaissance buildings and have succumbed to the damp—favored the adoption of canvas, in ready supply from Venice's sail-making industry. Bolts of canvas were sewn together to create pictures of huge dimension, and artists discovered that applying paint to canvas's rough surface allowed them to create unique textural and coloristic effects.[15]

Water especially shaped the Venetian mindset, offering a sense of security since the lagoon's expanses made the city nearly invulnerable to foreign invasion. Well into the nineteenth century, defensive walls were the hallmark of cities around the world. As a city without walls, Venice was unique. Only twice did enemies nearly breach Venice's aquatic ramparts: in the early ninth century when Charlemagne's son Pepin invaded the lagoon, and in the late fourteenth century when the Genoese captured the southern lagoon town of Chioggia. Even on those occasions the surrounding waters proved salvific. After marching up the barrier islands, Pepin was unable to cross the shoals and capture the then capital at Malamocco, its location today lost in the waters of the lagoon.[16] For their part, the Genoese were thwarted when the Venetians removed channel markers and blocked waterways with sunken ships, preventing the enemy from advancing on Venice itself. "No walls, no gates, no fortifications," proudly proclaimed Renaissance humanist Bernardo Giustinian. For many of his fellow humanists, not walls but the city's rulers, laws, institutions, and citizens constituted the true safeguard of the city.[17] As Petrarch observed, Venice was "ringed by salt waters but more secure with the salt of good counsel."[18]

Most of all, the lagoon fostered the Venetians' sense of identity and of their city's exceptionalism. When they related the story of Saint Mark's dream of the great city that would one day arise in his honor, they located that premonition—what they called Venice's *praedestinatio* (predestination)—as having occurred while the saint was adrift in the lagoon. Venetians took pride in their city's divinely sanctioned watery locale, comparing it at times to the Red Sea that protected the Israelites from pharaoh. They imagined themselves as God's newly chosen.[19] In the nineteenth and twentieth centuries, consternation greeted plans to build rail and automobile causeways linking the city to the mainland. Opponents feared that these bridges would end Venice's splendid isolation, undermine its aquatic orientation, and destroy the very thing that made the city unique. When in 1848 the Venetians revolted against their Austrian overlords, they severed the railway span linking Venice to the mainland village of Marghera in a futile attempt to recreate the watery protection that the city had enjoyed for centuries. By then, however, such defenses were obsolete; advances in ballistics allowed the Austrians to bombard the city from the mainland. In the early twentieth century, the fascists put Venice's aquatic traditions and heritage to their own use. They appropriated Venice's maritime identity to justify Italy's imperialistic designs on the Adriatic Sea, especially the regions around Trieste recently controlled by Austria. In this way, Venice's past was linked to Italy's present.

The precarity of the natural environment, the sense that water and land were constantly in flux, fostered a Venetian obsession with stability, constancy, and order. Theorists and apologists lauded the longevity of the Venetian Republic, arguing that the city's inhabitants had discovered the keys to orderly and stable rule.[20] They celebrated that their regime had outlasted even that of ancient Rome. When change was forced and enshrined in law, lawmakers unfailingly presented it not as innovation but as a return to the rules, precepts, and traditions of the ancestors. The series of ducal portraits that adorn the walls of the Greater Council Hall and the Hall of the Scrutinio in the Ducal Palace were intended to emphasize the centuries-long continuum of dogal rule.[21] Even the predilection for electing extremely elderly men to the dogeship seemed an affirmation of conservatism and stability.[22]

Venetians called all this serenity. They applied the sobriquet Most Serene to their Republic and the title His Serenity to the doge. They emphasized the city's orderliness and social harmony, arguing that there was a concordance of minds, a unity of purpose, that united all Venetians, rich and poor, noble and common, women and men, native born and immigrant.[23] Theirs was a city, they claimed, free of social strife. They were, of course, trying mightily to deny the forces of chaos and flux, human and especially natural, that surrounded them. Venice's foes were only too eager to remind them of their environmental vulnerability. Following the Republic's loss of Cyprus to the Ottoman Turks in 1573, disgruntled Venetian subjects in Spalato (Split) in Dalmatia sang a song whose lyrics recounted that "the Turk is running water that erodes, and . . . the Doge is a sandbank which has been carried away little by little by the river."[24]

Despite the rhetoric of timelessness, change is the other constant of Venice's history. To the modern visitor, this seems counterintuitive since, on the surface at least, Venice seems to have defied time. One of the reasons, indeed the primary reason, that tourists have been flocking to the city since the nineteenth century is to catch a glimpse of what they imagine to be a premodern, preindustrial age.[25] The absence of automobiles, more than anything else, fosters the mistaken perception that Venice is unchanging. Yet today's Venice is not the Venice of the past.

When change is acknowledged in Venice's history, it is often related as a tale of rise, apogee, and fall. Such an approach is seductive, since readers find stories with clear beginnings, middles, and ends compelling. Some histories of Venice are even presented in three volumes to reflect this narrative and end with the collapse of the Venetian Republic in 1797.[26] But adopting such an approach limits the criteria for judging success and failure. In Venice's case, these usually include territorial expansion and maritime commercial might. Examining Venice's history over the longue durée demonstrates that for a time Venice was indeed an economic and political powerhouse, but at other times it was a leader in the creation of new cultural forms like opera and innovations in painting and comic theater. Confining the history of Venice to the period prior to the demise of the Republic in 1797 to make it fit a rise and fall schema neglects important concerns of the nineteenth, twentieth, and twenty-first centuries, including Venice's role in the forging of Italian fascism and environmentally destructive industrialization, debates over modernization versus preservation, and the development of mass tourism—the current foundation of the city's economy.

Rather than charting rise and fall, this book emphasizes major turning points—moments when Venice notably shifted course. While change was ongoing, three centuries—the ninth, thirteenth, and nineteenth—stand out as especially significant. In the ninth century the Venetians forged their unique identity. Following Pepin's defeat, they made the fateful decision to relocate the capital from Malamocco to Rivoalto—to the place today known as Venice. A few years later Venetian merchants stole Saint Mark's relics from Alexandria and brought them to Venice where the doge built a church to house his remains. Venice and Venetian identity were born in the ninth century. During the thirteenth century, the Venetians acquired the bulk of their maritime empire—the network of trading posts and colonies—that allowed the city to become an international emporium at the intersection of Western and Eastern trade routes. In that same century, they worked out the structures of their governmental regime and established the criteria for membership in the ruling class that would preside over the Republic until Napoleon's conquest of the city. The nineteenth century witnessed the most dramatic alterations to the cityscape of any period, including the transfer of port facilities from the Bacino to the Giudecca Canal to better link them to the railway, the planning of the public gardens where the Biennale was eventually housed, the infilling of canals and widening of streets, the building of two additional bridges (besides the Rialto Bridge) across the Grand Canal, and the transformation of private family palaces into hotels. In these ways and others, the cityscape developed to accommodate two hallmarks of the modern world: heavy industry and tourism. The perceived incompatibility of these two visions of Venice's economic future led to furious debates over preservation versus economic rejuvenation, which continue to this day.

What follows is an urban history broadly conceived, as Venice was more than just a city. To write its history entails writing an account of a medieval city-state, an imperial power with vast overseas possessions, a Renaissance regional-state with significant holdings on the Italian mainland, and a provincial capital of the Austrian empire and later the Italian nation-state.

In the central and high Middle Ages, Venice was just one of many city-states that dotted the landscape of northern and central Italy. Like those others, Venice asserted control over its surrounding *contado* (countryside), which in Venice's case was the lagoon and a few tiny strips of land bordering the lagoon. Venice used salt as a weapon in its wars with neighboring city-states as it sought to establish a trade monopoly over the northern Adriatic Sea. What distinguished Venice from its Italian counterparts, Genoa excepted, was that it also possessed a far-reaching empire of overseas possessions that stretched down the eastern coastline of the Adriatic and also included islands and ports in the Ionian and Aegean Seas. Crete was its most prized possession. The wealth extracted from the maritime empire and the vital role that it played in supporting Venetian merchant enterprises made Venice an economic giant among the Italian city-states, one that claimed, thanks to its isolation in the lagoon and Byzantine origins, to be immune from the aggrandizing pretensions of popes and Holy Roman emperors.

During the fourteenth century, bigger city-states like Florence and Milan began to conquer smaller ones, creating regional-states. Venice stepped gingerly into this role, first acquiring nearby Treviso. By the beginning of the fifteenth century, however, Milan's aggressive push eastward compelled the Venetians to meet the challenge by creating a regional-state of their own—one that eventually stretched from Bergamo to Udine, from the Alps to the river Po. The decision to do so was not easy, since many within the ruling class feared that this turn to the mainland would imperil the overseas empire that was under increasing pressure from the Ottoman Turks. Venice was surprisingly successful, leading many of its rivals to fear that it aspired to hegemony over Italy. The turn to the mainland also brought significant cultural changes as Venice slowly shifted emphasis away from its Byzantine heritage to embrace the Renaissance classical revival. In the sixteenth century with the help of architects like Jacopo Sansovino and Andrea Palladio, Venice remade itself as a New Rome.

The fortunes of Venice's mainland and maritime empire ebbed and flowed until finally the city's regional-state resources were unable to compete against much larger monarchic states such as France and England or withstand the repercussions of the shift in global trade networks from the Mediterranean to the Atlantic. Venice lost its independence as it became the capital (along with Milan) of Napoleon's Kingdom of Italy, and later of the province of Venetia under the Austrians. In 1866 Venice became part of the independent Kingdom of Italy. Venetians had to accommodate themselves to their new supporting role. Even today the relationship of Venice to the Italian state remains fraught, with periodic calls for greater autonomy and, in extreme cases, for independence altogether.

The challenges and achievements of Venice's history are told in this book across the Middle Ages, Renaissance, Old Regime, and modern/contemporary periods. Each is marked by distinctive projects and problems. Part I, the Middle Ages, examines the natural environment and the history of the region of Venetia before Venice, the settlement of the lagoon, the legends the Venetians fashioned to explain their origins, and the creation and building of the city. It explores the development of business practices and commercial trade networks and Venice's efforts to assert a trade monopoly over the northern Adriatic. With its 1204 conquest of Constantinople as part of the Fourth Crusade, Venice became an imperial power and laid full claim to its Byzantine cultural inheritance. This ascent of Venice to commercial and colonial prominence was accompanied by dramatic political change. The city evolved from a dukedom, ruled by doges with almost complete monarchic powers, into a commune, and eventually a republic that excluded all but approximately 150 noble families from power. The Venetian Middle Ages concluded in 1381 with the city's triumph over Genoa in the War of Chioggia, which left Venice the undisputed naval power in the eastern Mediterranean.

The Venetian Renaissance, the focus of Part II, spanned 1381 to the early seventeenth century. This is the most renowned period in Venetian history due in no small measure to the accomplishments and lasting fame of painters Titian,

Veronese, and Tintoretto. During the Renaissance the Venetians adopted a new cultural lodestar—the world of classical Greece and Rome. This was partly a response to the acquisition of mainland cities like Verona and Padua that could legitimately claim a classical heritage of their own. Venice aggressively pursued territorial expansion, relying on its commercial might to fund its wars and the mercenary captains who did the fighting. But its ambitions were humbled when the great powers of Europe united against it in the early sixteenth century in the League of Cambrai. Although it emerged at the end of this crisis largely unscathed, Venice found that it was no longer able to compete against its neighboring superpowers, the Hapsburgs and Ottomans. During these same decades, Venetian commercial hegemony suffered serious economic blows after the Portuguese circumnavigated Africa, which led to the disruption of traditional spice routes and the creation of the Atlantic economy. Venice compensated for the losses by pivoting to manufacturing. It became a powerhouse in the production of textiles and luxury products like glass. Venice was also at the forefront of the new technology of printing, becoming the European center of information and communication. Through the new medium of print, writers celebrated the purported perfection of the Venetian regime as Venice came to serve as the model republic in an age of princes. The city's Renaissance ended on a triumphant note with its successful defiance of the papacy in the Interdict Crisis of 1606-7. The Republic cast its rejection of papal pretensions and interference in its dominions as a secular defense of liberty.

The Ancien or Old Regime, from the early seventeenth century to the absorption of Venice into Italy in 1866, examined in Part III, is usually considered a period of stagnation and retrenchment. It was anything but. The seventeenth and eighteenth centuries were among the most culturally dynamic in Venice's long history. The city gained a reputation for libertinism, characterized by its residents' proclivity for gambling, prostitution, Carnival, and coffeehouses. But libertinism also meant free-thinking, especially as practiced in some of its academies. It became a place where accepted truths could be questioned and authority challenged, and where personal virtue was no longer presented solely as a monopoly of nobles. It also perfected a new musical art form—opera—that became a pinnacle of European high culture. Painting witnessed its own eighteenth-century revival with a new triumvirate: Canaletto, Guardi, and Tiepolo.

The end of independence brought other great changes. These included the advancement of Jews into the civic elite, a dramatic and dark reimagining of Venice's aristocratic past, and a new cultural role for Venice as a locus for

Romantic ruminations on ruin, death, and time's passage. Despite daunting problems of economic stagnation and appalling poverty, the groundwork was laid for the development of heavy industry and tourism. Both involved major interventions in the cityscape. The failed Revolution of 1848-9 against the Austrians, when the Venetians created a new Revolutionary Republic, found them looking both backward to their lost aristocratic Republic and forward to their place in a unified Italian state.

Part IV, Modern and Contemporary Venice, considers the period from 1866 to the present. The late nineteenth and early twentieth centuries were marked by momentous changes in the cityscape and ongoing debates over how to revive the economy. The decision was made to relocate heavy industry to nearby Marghera at the mainland edge of the lagoon. Proponents justified this decision by arguing that wherever was the lagoon, there was Venice.[27] But the city was essentially bifurcated, with Porto Marghera dedicated to industry and the historic island city focused on tourism. Such cultural markers of present-day Venice as the Biennale and the Venice Film Festival originated as efforts to bolster tourism, which increasingly shifted to the Lido barrier island.

By the 1960s the environmental and human costs of Porto Marghera's industrialization were becoming apparent, while Venice's increasing vulnerability to rising sea level came dramatically to the fore in the disastrous high tide of November 1966. Following that unprecedented flood, the city took on a new global role as the bellwether of climate change. Contemporary Venice also offers a cautionary tale regarding the social and cultural costs of a tourism monoculture and the commodification of Venice itself. The cultural and social disjuncture between the historic island city and the towns on the mainland that together make up the present-day Metropolitan City of Venice, compounded by an influx of immigrant workers, has provoked renewed calls for greater independence from Italy as well as overt racism and xenophobia. What seems clear is that Venice's future will be as contested and consequential as its past.

The history of Venice is a story of constant adaptation and change, against the backdrop of living on water. To fully convey its rich past, this narrative casts a wide net, incorporating material from official government documents, trial records, chronicles, humanist treatises, maps, inscriptions, censuses, business letters, personal memoirs, wills, fabrics, coins, songs, paintings, sculptures, bridges, ships, and boats. These sources highlight the accomplishments of Venetian women and men of all social classes and backgrounds: noblemen and notaries, abbesses and Arsenal workers, scholars and servant girls, priests and prostitutes, ambassadors and artisans, clerical and lay, Christians and Jews, native born and immigrant, the enslaved and the free. Inevitably the deeds of the wealthy and powerful, their wars and diplomacy, the traditional stuff of history, are disproportionally represented, but that is itself a residual consequence of their power. Nevertheless, these pages bring to the fore the labor and sacrifice of those who facilitated the accomplishments of the great and the good, and, where possible, record their names. Many of the Venetians considered here speak for themselves through quotations from original sources.

Despite this book's size, much has been left out of this history covering more than 2,000 years. Certain topics get a paragraph when they deserve pages; others have been omitted entirely. For coherence, particular themes are traced across the vast sweep of the city's history. These include the transformation of Venice from a trade emporium to a transit port to an industrial port; relations with the nearby Italian mainland and Adriatic Sea; and the evolution of its ruling elite before, during, and after the Republic. Considerable attention is paid to the role of the laboring classes throughout the ages, not just in the Venetian economy and society but more unexpectedly in politics. Accomplishments in art, architecture, and material culture are highlighted, particularly their role in propagating, reinforcing, and, in some instances, contesting prevailing ideologies. The cult of Saint Mark and its part in the creation of Venetian identity looms large, as does the city's complicated and ever-changing relationship to the surrounding waters of the lagoon.

Venice, perhaps more than any other city, has been mythologized.[28] In truth, it is even more fascinating when seen for what it was and is: a constantly evolving urban complex, one made more interesting still by its interplay with the amphibious environment from which it has emerged. With myths swept aside, a fascinating prospect comes into view, just as it does when the fog lifts on the lagoon and Venice shines.

PART I

Medieval Venice

I

Before Venice

ACCOUNTS OF VENICE'S origins are a jumble. Its foundation legends contained myriad elements, some contradictory, yet all sought to explain how a great city had arisen and prospered in the midst of the waves. Typical is the account that Renaissance diarist and chronicler Marino Sanudo presented in his treatise/guidebook *De origine, situ et magistratibus urbis Venetae* (On the Origins, Location, and Magistracies of the City of Venice). He wrote that "the city of Venice first and most powerful in Italy, in the region called Venetia, . . . had its beginnings in the year of our Savior 421 on 25 March according to various chronicles and that is true; and [it was not founded] by shepherds like Rome was, but by noble and powerful men."

Sanudo went on to explain that ancient Venetia was settled by refugees from Troy who established various mainland towns, including nearby Padua. These immigrants and their progeny flourished for many centuries until the incursions of the Huns. Under their leader Attila, the Huns devastated Thrace, Macedonia, Dalmatia, and other lands before entering Italy. When they attacked Aquileia, a Roman town to the east of Venice in Friuli, the residents fled to nearby "barrier islands and built Grado," while those of the town of Altino settled Torcello, Burano, Murano, and other islands. The Paduans took refuge in "the lagoons of the Venetians, which at the time were islands inhabited by fishermen; and those who came were worthy, illustrious, rich, and religious men; and they began to build small dwellings where they could sustain their lives and be safe from the barbarians. And so, in a place surrounded by water called Prealto or Rivoalto they first began to live."

Some Renaissance historians dated these events to the year 456, but Sanudo observed that "other chroniclers, writing of the origins,—and this is the truth—have it that this city began to be built on the island of Rialto and [they] laid the first foundations of the church of San Giacomo, which is still at Rialto, on Friday March 25, 421." He noted that March 25 was the date of Adam's creation, the Archangel Gabriel's annunciation to the Virgin Mary, and Jesus's crucifixion, adding, "It was a day of great meaning and thus our ancestors wanted to choose that day for such [an important] foundation."[1] In trying to explain away one of the most obvious inconsistencies, namely, the year of the city's establishment, Sanudo commented, "It's a marvel that writers don't agree on the date of the foundation, even though it was first founded in 421 and then augmented in 456 almost, one could say, like a refoundation."

Modern historians and archeologists likewise struggle to piece together Venice's beginnings. The former rely on written accounts composed centuries after the actual events themselves. The latter analyze whatever archeological evidence has been uncovered either by chance or by the few digs that have been conducted in the lagoon, an inhospitable environment for excavations.

Yet fretting about the accuracy of the origin stories is to miss their point. Foundation legends are not about getting the facts straight but about providing an inspirational account about who a people are and why. The Venetians wanted to believe that their city had a pedigree as distinguished as that of ancient Rome. So they invented a story that their own city was also founded by successors of refugees from the Trojan War. In addition, the Venetians contended, as Sanudo did, that their city was not founded by rustics like the Roman shepherd twins Romulus and Remus but by distinguished, urbane, and pious men. By telling the story of Venice's Trojan origins (via Paduan evacuees), the Venetians endowed their city with an ancient past, which carried great weight in the Middle Ages and Renaissance.

The claim that the refugees escaped into a barren watery landscape inhabited only by humble fishermen served other purposes too. It substantiated Venice's claim to independence from foreign powers. Since the city had been created on *terra nova* (new land) wrested from the sea, the argument went, it was not subject to claims of sovereignty by any of the successor states to the Roman Empire or even by the pope. Additionally, the flight across the water—not unlike the escape of the Israelites from Pharoah's Egypt—established in Venetian hearts the belief that something truly miraculous occurred when their city was born. They must, they believed, have been specially chosen by God. Venice's supposed foundation on March 25, the feast of the Annunciation, enriched the city with Christian significance and established its special relationship with the Virgin Mary. And by claiming that the city was established on the Vernal Equinox in the Julian calendar, the Venetians imbued their city not only with an auspicious destiny but also with the idea of continual renewal implicit in the equinox.[2]

The foundation stories the Venetians told themselves and others about themselves highlight Venice's geographical location at the northern tip of the Adriatic Sea, the environmental conditions that shaped the city, and the peoples and institutions active in the region at the time. Combined, these indelibly marked the lagoon and its hinterland and impacted the future fortunes of Venice. Accordingly, while most histories of Venice begin with the Hunnish incursion in 452 or with the flight from the Lombard invaders more than a century later, this one begins thousands—even millions—of years earlier. The history of Venice and its people can be fully understood only by taking into account the characteristics of the natural environment of the northern Adriatic and what happened before Venice.

More than a million years ago, what is now called the Adriatic Sea engulfed the entire Po River valley, extending as far west as Milan and Turin. Around 20,000 years ago it receded, so the location where Venice now sits was dry land and hundreds of miles from the coastline.[3] That once dry surface, known as *caranto*, today buried under subsequent layers of sediment and situated from thirteen to twenty-three feet below mean sea level in the lagoon, constitutes the Venetian equivalent of bedrock, although actual bedrock lies deeper still. Buildings in Venice do not float. Rather they rest either on wooden platforms and pilings that compress the sediments below against the *caranto* or, in the case of very large buildings or bridges, on poles cut from ash, oak, and other trees that have been hammered down to the *caranto* itself.[4] The foundation of the massive seventeenth-century church Santa Maria della Salute rests on 1,156,657 such poles that took twenty-six months to drive into place.[5]

Since the end of the last Ice Age, approximately 12,000 years ago, sea levels have been rising and the Adriatic has been advancing. Someday, it may once again swallow up the Po River valley. The Adriatic is not, however, the only aquatic feature influencing the coastline from Ravenna to the Istrian peninsula. Several major rivers, including the Isonzo, Tagliamento, Livenza, Piave, Brenta, Adige, and Po, as well as numerous lesser ones such as the Bacchiglione, Zero, Dese, Sile, Stella, and Natisone carry their waters and immense amounts of silt toward the sea. Circa 23 CE, the Greek geographer Strabo described what is today the Veneto this way: "The whole country is filled with rivers and marshes . . . and this part, furthermore, is also affected by the behavior of the sea."[6] Indeed, the coast of the northern Adriatic is a dynamic contact zone where fresh river water and silt meet the saltwater and wave action of the sea. The result is a constant tug of war, with the silt-laden rivers pushing the land forward and the sea undercutting the advance and creating dunes. The dunes then trap river water behind them to form lagoons, transforming the dunes themselves into barrier islands. Today the two primary lagoons are the lagoon of Grado and the lagoon of Venice.[7] At various weak points along the chain of barrier islands, rivers force their way through the dunes, creating mouths that allow river water to exit to the sea and the tidal flow of sea water in and out of the lagoons.[8] Because of differences in temperature, density, and other factors, the salt and fresh waters do not mix readily. Phases of the moon influence the tidal flow, but high pressure in the Ionian Sea to the south can lead to exceptionally high tides in the northern Adriatic.[9]

Scientists estimate that the present-day Venetian lagunal zone has undergone at least six major transitions in the past 18,000 years as sea level has risen and fallen. They believe that the primordial Venetian lagoon formed about 6,000 years ago, and that the present lagoon assumed its current form around 2,000 years ago.[10] It is likely that small outcroppings that constituted the original nuclei around which the present-day city of Venice coalesced were remnants of an earlier line of coastal dunes.[11] Names such Dorsoduro (hardback) and Rivoalto (high bank) testify to the original character and appearance of what would later become sections of the city. The specifics of the lagoon's evolution remain hotly debated. What is clear is that this is an ever-changing natural environment in which the sea has transgressed and regressed, rivers have shifted course, shoals and islets have appeared and disappeared, outlets to the sea have opened and closed, and dunes have formed and then washed away.[12]

The sea offered the possibility of making a living for those dwelling along the mainland coast, within the lagoons, and on the barrier islands. Shellfish could be harvested year-round, while the spring and summer months provided opportunities for large catches of fish. In the early Middle Ages, prominent families and monasteries acquired fishponds within the lagoons and fish-farming developed, organized to take advantage of the migratory and spawning habits of various species. By contrast, fishing in the open Adriatic resisted privatization. Winter offered ample opportunities for hunting migratory waterfowl.[13] But salt was the most lucrative of the gifts borne by the sea and became the earliest source of Venetian riches.

Venice sits at 45 degrees, 26', 13" latitude, very nearly at the most northerly reach of the Mediterranean Sea and farther north than other western European port cities such as Genoa and Marseille. It is perfectly located for communication between north and central Europe and the Middle East. No less a figure than Napoleon Bonaparte recognized as much, writing, "Venice

FIGURE 1.1 The Northern Adriatic Coastline in the Early Middle Ages.

is the best situated city and commercial port of all. . . . Nature made Venice the mediator for traffic of the Levant, Italy, and southern Germany."[14] But the Venetians would not have been able to take advantage of such a propitious geographical location for trade and communication had it not been for the rivers, which made travel inland simple and cheap, or for the accessible passes across the Alps.

Yet like the sea, the rivers pose a threat. The Greek historian Polybius (died c. 118 BCE) described the Po River valley as a triangle, with the Alps and Apennines constituting the two sides and the Adriatic the base.[15] The slow erosion of these two great mountain ranges creates the silt that the rivers carry toward the sea. Silting has two effects: first, it pushes the coastline farther south and eastward. In Roman times, for example, the great city of Ravenna stood at the edge of the Adriatic, but over the past 3 millennia the shoreline has pushed seaward fifteen miles. As silting continued, the people of Ravenna relocated their harbor to Classis (Classe), closer to the receding sea. Today both Ravenna and Classe are landlocked.[16] Although at present the sea poses the more immediate danger to Venice, at times in the past, the peril came from the many rivers emptying into the Adriatic. The silt they carried risked turning the open-water lagoon into malarial marshland and rendering the mouths or openings into the lagoon shallow and thus unnavigable for large ships, the commercial lifeblood of the Venetians. The second effect of silting is subsidence. The deposited silt, often thousands of feet in depth, is compacting under its own weight. This accounts in large part for the sinking of Venice and indeed for the subsidence of the entire northwestern shore of the Adriatic. This problem is exacerbated by the subduction or overriding of the Adriatic tectonic plate by the Eurasian plate.

The Po River valley slopes slowly and gently toward the east. Because of that gradual decline, once the various branches of the Po and other rivers exit the mountains and foothills, they slow in velocity and meander, creating a water-logged environment, one that has changed substantially due to thousands of years of human effort at reclaiming land by building canals and dikes to control the flow. Before that intervention, the region alternated dry ground and swampland and was naturally prone to disastrous flooding that could radically alter the landscape and property holdings. Paul the Deacon (c. 720s to late 790s CE), the most reliable early source for the history of Venice, relates that in 589 CE terrible floods caused rivers to overflow their banks.[17] It was probably this inundation that forced the Adige River to change course, shifting near Albaredo from its old path that took it toward Montagnana to its present-day course to the southwest.[18]

The pre-Alps and Alps, which rise only sixty miles from Venice, present a formidable but not insurmountable barrier between northern Italy and the rest of Europe. (Plate 1) The Brenner and Reschen passes (4,495 and 4,934 feet, respectively) both offer routes through the mountains into what is today Austria and conveniently link to the Adige watershed. The lowest mountain passes, such as the Predil pass (3,793 feet) lie to the east through the Julian Alps. Once through the Julian Alps, it is easy to reach the Pannonian basin (centered in modern-day Hungary but also incorporating parts of neighboring states) and the Danube. It is no coincidence that this was the route that various invaders including the Huns and Lombards followed as they swept into Italy.

A wind known as the Bora also sweeps out of the Julian Alps at their lowest point near modern-day Trieste. This cold wind from the northeast,

east-northeast, can reach a velocity of sixty miles per hour and is especially pronounced from February to April. In contrast, the hot and humid Sirocco blows from southeast to northwest, is able to reach a velocity of fifty miles per hour, and can dramatically affect Venice's tides.[19] Knowledge of such wind patterns was crucial in the age of navigation by sail.

Finally, Venice sits near the border between the humid subtropical climate zone and the temperate ocean climate zone. For much of the year, the water is warmer than the air; hence Venice draws heat from the sea. Average humidity is high. Inland the climate grows harsher, and snowfall is more frequent.

The geographical situation and climate of the northern Adriatic coastline offered both opportunities and perils for those who chose to make their homes there. It was not a wasteland, as some accounts of Venice's foundation have it, but a place rich in resources for making a living: fish and fowl for consumption; mud, timber, and thatch for construction; and salt for income. Many took up the challenge. The lives those early settlers forged and the habits and customs they developed shaped the patterns of what would become Venice.

The story that Sanudo and others told about the foundation of the church of San Giacomo di Rialto on March 25, 421, was a mere fancy. There was no intentional founding of Venice.[20] Its creation was a slow and continuous process whose origins can be traced to Roman times and even earlier. It involved the establishment of numerous settlements throughout the Venetian lagoon. Only after several centuries did the one founded at Rialto assume primacy over the others and become known as Venice.

Archeologists have discovered evidence of Stone Age settlements on high ground in the Veneto, including the Euganean Hills near Padua and the Berici Hills near Vicenza. Elevated sites continued to be preferred during the Bronze Age, although some villages were also established on low ground near the coast. At many of these sites, such as a late Bronze Age settlement near Caorle on the present-day coastline, the inhabitants constructed their dwellings on boards and pilings because of the damp. The Iron Age (1100–700 BCE) saw the introduction of new peoples, the Veneti, who arrived from the Balkans and bequeathed their name to the region and ultimately to the Venetians as well, and the Etruscans who migrated from central Italy. In the sixth century BCE, the Etruscans established the towns of Adria and Spina in the Po delta near what was at the time the coastline; a century earlier the Veneti had settled the town of Altino at the edge of the Venetian lagoon. These and other towns were situated near the coast and on rivers. They served as entry points for seaborne goods from Greece and southern Italy to move inland. Spina became an important center for Greek manufactures to reach the Po valley as well as the heartland of Etruria (modern-day Tuscany and Umbria). Both Spina and Adria eventually fell victim to silting and were cut off from the sea. Spina disappeared for centuries in the lagoons known as the Valli di Comacchio, only to be rediscovered following land reclamation projects in the 1950s. The invasion of the Gauls or Celts into the Po valley (c. 400 BCE) also played a role in the decline of Adria and Spina as it isolated them from Etruria, the destination for their trade goods.[21]

Allied with the Veneti, the Romans defeated two Celtic tribes—the Boii who had settled the area around modern-day Bologna and the Insubri with their center at Milan—at the Battle of Clastidium (Casteggio) in 222 BCE. This victory set in motion the Roman conquest of the Po valley. The failed attempt by a large group of transalpine Gauls to settle in Friuli, the area east of modern-day Venice, in 181 BCE, led the Roman consul Marcus Claudius Marcellus to establish a colony in the same area at Aquileia.[22]

Aquileia, which was connected by the Natisone River to the small port of Grado, became a major international entrepot in the late Roman Empire. When Consul Marcellus established the colony, he populated it with 3,000 soldier-settlers. During the second century BCE, the Romans created a system of roads linking Aquileia and other cities of Cisalpine (south of the Alps) Gaul. In 148 BCE they constructed the Via Postumia which ran east from Genoa, passing through Verona and other towns before finally reaching Aquileia. In 132 BCE they linked Rimini to Adria by means of the Via Popillia, and a year later built the Via Annia that ran from Adria via Padua and Altino to Aquileia. The Popillia-Annia was a more southerly route than the Postumia. Near Altino, it ran just a short distance from the Venetian lagoon. Its construction indicated a growing Roman interest in the coastal zone. In 48 BCE Roman citizenship was extended to Transpadania (the region north of the Po and south of the Alps), and between 42 and 40 BCE, the town of Iulia Concordia (Concordia) was established just west of Aquileia at the intersection of the Postumia and Annia.[23]

The age of the Julio-Claudian emperors (27 BCE–68 CE) witnessed two important developments that would impact the future city of Venice. First, in 8 CE the Emperor Augustus divided Italy into eleven *regiones* (regions), the tenth of which was the region of Venetia and Istria.[24] The two areas would remain locked in an uneasy relationship that at times involved intertwining political and religious ties until Istria was taken over first by the Lombards

FIGURE 1.2 Mainland Towns and Lagoon Settlements in the Early Middle Ages, with an inset of the Rivoalto (Venice) archipelago, showing the original clusters from which Venice grew and the monasteries defining the Bacino of San Marco. The hatching indicates areas that are today solid land due to either natural siltation or human reclamation efforts. Because of this, the lagoons of Venice and Grado are today separate bodies of water.

and then by the Franks in the eighth century. In the thirteenth century Istria would come under Venetian domination.

Second, the Romans designated Ravenna the headquarters of their Adriatic fleet and constructed a series of canals linking the various rivers of the region to facilitate trade and communication. The Fossa Augusta (Augustan Canal), constructed to connect Ravenna to the Po, is an example. In this period, the Romans, who had strategically favored higher elevation sites in the Veneto hinterland, began to recognize and develop the potential of the northern Adriatic coast. The establishment of Concordia with a link to the sea at Caorle, the growth of Altino on the Sile (perhaps with sea access via the port of San Nicolò, the best-known of the present-day entry points to the Venetian lagoon), and Aquileia with the small landing of Grado are evidence of a concerted effort by the Romans to knit the littoral and the hinterland together. In 46 CE the emperor Claudius constructed the Via Claudia Augusta, which ran from Altino to Merano, over the Reschen Pass, down the Inn River valley to Augsburg, and eventually to the Danube. Another road, likely also built by Claudius, ran from Altino south to Ravenna, following in part the Via Annia and in part a course that bordered the southern half of today's Venetian lagoon. Along the route were three small landings that correspond with the present-day mouths of the lagoon and that linked up with branches of the Brenta and other rivers to carry traffic inland.[25] It was also possible to make the journey from Ravenna to Altino by crossing the "Seven Seas," which according to Pliny the Elder (d. 79 CE) referred to the lagoons near Adria but in time came to refer to the entire system of lagoons, rivulets, and canals between the two cities.[26] From Altino one could continue on to Aquileia by boat or take the overland route along the Annia. Importantly, even in the period of the early Roman Empire, the lagoons were linked to the mainland and included numerous minor settlements. They were not the barren and nearly uninhabited wastelands of the Attila legend.

At the end of the turbulent third century, Emperor Diocletian reorganized the Roman Empire into a tetrarchy or rule by two senior emperors and two junior ones in an effort to create an orderly line of succession to rulership of the empire. Milan, which often served as one of the imperial capitals, acquired new significance, as did Aquileia and Ravenna. Aquileia was the location of a treasury and headquarters of the military official who was charged with supervision of fortifications along the eastern Alps.[27] In the third century, the historian Herodian described the city this way, "Aquileia has always been an important city with a large local population. Sited as it is on the coast, commanding the hinterland of the Illyrian [western Balkan] territories, it has acted as a trading port for Italy by providing sea traders with a market for goods that come from inland by land and river. Similarly, essential goods which cannot be produced in the Illyrian countryside because of the winters, come by sea and are sent from Aquileia up country to the people of the interior. . . . [T]he city is teeming with local citizens, aliens and traders."[28] Aquileia's economy flourished in the fourth century CE as the city took on new prominence as the hub for trade with the eastern Mediterranean, including Syria and Egypt, and with the north, including the Danube basin.[29]

Given its significance as the largest and most important city in northeastern Italy, Aquileia became the center of Christianity in the region. The new religion likely arrived via the Jewish community or through ties to the Christian community in Egyptian Alexandria. Later patriarchs (essentially archbishops) of Aquileia and the Venetians had their own foundational legend of Christianity's arrival there. According to this account, Saint Peter sent Mark the Evangelist and his fellow missionary Hermagoras to spread the faith in Aquileia. While traveling back to Rome, Mark and his companions took shelter from a storm in the Venetian lagoon at the future site of Rialto. During the night, an angel appeared to Mark in a dream and calmed the evangelist with the words "Pax tibi Marce" (Peace to you, Mark). The angel went on to explain that, after much further journeying, Mark would one day find eternal rest in this place.[30] Mark eventually traveled to Egypt and is credited with founding the Alexandrian church. Regardless of the veracity of the account of Mark's mission, it attests to the trade and cultural links between Aquileia and Alexandria.[31]

The angel's apparition to Mark became the subject of a mosaic executed in the basilica of San Marco in the later thirteenth century as well as a late sixteenth-century painting by Jacopo and Domenico Tintoretto for the confraternity of San Marco in Venice. The mosaic emphasizes the supposed

FIGURE 1.3 *The Dream of Saint Mark*, second half of the thirteenth century. Zen Chapel, Basilica of San Marco, Venice. Cameraphoto Arte, Venice/Art Resource, NY.

emptiness of the lagoon at the time of Mark's journey. It shows his bark affixed to a pole at the end of a tiny sandbar on which tufts of vegetation have gained a precarious foothold. Otherwise, there is nothing but water. When it was executed, the space where the mosaic is located served as the sea portal to the basilica, the only place in the church with a clear view of the lagoon beyond. In this way, the mosaic and panorama linked for viewers Mark's predestined past and Venice's providential present.[32]

In contrast to the barren seascape of the mosaic, the lagoon in the Tintoretto painting is inhabited by poor fishermen who eke out a living from

FIGURE 1.4 Jacopo and Domenico Tintoretto, *The Dream of Saint Mark*, 1587–90. Gallerie dell'Accademia, Venice. Photo by Didier Descouens, distributed under a CC-BY-SA-4.0 license via Wikimedia Commons.

the surrounding waters. In the background between Mark and the angel a man appears to be repairing a fish trap while his wife holds a light to illuminate his work. Another man stands near a small fishing vessel surrounded by baskets, probably used to store the catch. On the far left a woman appears to be pulling an implement from the water while an old man draws near the wooden pier in front of the thatched-roof hut. The fragile bit of land on which the hut stands is protected from the waves by wooden poles that have been driven into the mud and bound together with horizontal sticks in a technique known as osier or basketweave work. Such reclamation techniques were still being used in the sixteenth century at the outer edges of the city and throughout the lagoon. Both the mosaicists and the Tintorettos wanted to convey the fragility of the environment that presented itself to Mark and the earliest Venetians, as a way of emphasizing how truly miraculous the city was to have been built in the midst of shoals and mudflats.

However Christianity arrived in Aquileia, by the early fourth century, it was flourishing. In 313, shortly after the conversion of the Roman emperor Constantine to the faith, Bishop Teodoro built a cathedral in Aquileia dedicated to Santa Maria Assunta. Christianity spread to other areas of Venetia and Istria as well, with bishoprics established in places such as Concordia. A letter from Pope Leo the Great indicates that by 442 at the latest, the bishop of Aquileia's authority over other bishops in the region was recognized in Rome.[33]

By that point, Italy had witnessed the first in a series of invasions that would ultimately destroy the Roman Empire in the West, lead to a reconquest of large parts of the peninsula by the surviving Eastern Roman (or Byzantine) Empire, and establish the littoral from Ravenna to Istria as a Byzantine outpost. The barbarian onslaught, prompted in no small measure by climate change in the Eurasian steppe, began in 401 when Alaric, king of the Visigoths, crossed the Julian Alps, besieged Aquileia, and overran Venetia and Istria. He then moved south but was forced in 403 to withdraw from Italy. Just two years later, Italy was invaded by an army led by Radagaisus composed of Ostrogoths, Vandals, Burgundians, and other peoples from beyond the Danube. Radagaisus was defeated by the Romans at Fiesole and executed in 406, but in 408 Alaric launched a second invasion, which ended in 410 in the sack of Rome.

Fear of invasion and the realization that the Alps were not the barrier the Romans had imagined them to be led Emperor Honorius in 402 to move his capital from Milan to Ravenna, which was protected by a lagoon and marshes to its west. Ravenna thus became the terminus for trade and communication with Constantinople, its economic growth and development coming at Aquileia's expense.[34]

After a period of calm, Attila arrived in 452. In Venetia, he and his men conquered Aquileia, Concordia, Altino, Oderzo, and Padua. There is little doubt that some of the residents of these towns sought refuge in the lagoons, but once the Hunnish danger passed, they returned to the mainland to rebuild their lives. But Aquileia never recovered its former glory. Instead, its small port at Grado, protected by its lagoon and fortifications, gained in significance. Over the following decades, the Western Roman emperors found themselves engaged in an endless series of civil wars. It was the Germanic king Odoacer who finally delivered the coup de grâce to the Western Roman Empire when in 476 he deposed Romulus Augustulus and declared himself king of Italy. Even though the Eastern Roman emperor Zeno, with his capital in Constantinople, granted him the title of patrician, relations between the two deteriorated as Odoacer invaded Dalmatia and later attacked the Eastern empire's western provinces. Zeno got his revenge when he appointed the Ostrogothic leader Theodoric king of Italy. In 489 Theodoric invaded Italy; in March 493 he overran Ravenna and had Odoacer killed.[35]

The decline of Aquileia continued under Theodoric as he made Cividale in Friuli and Concordia the centers for the eastern defense. In the western Po valley, Pavia grew in importance as it was easily reachable from Ravenna by boat. Theodoric's thirty-three-year reign as king (493–526) was largely peaceful as he tried to maintain good relations between the Goths who controlled the army and the Romans who continued to monopolize the civil administration. After Theodoric's death, his daughter Amalasuntha served as regent for her young son and continued to pursue a strongly pro-Eastern Roman Empire policy. But plots against her and her eventual murder gave the Byzantine emperor Justinian (reigned 527–65) the excuse he needed to launch a re-conquest of the lost western half of the Roman Empire.

Justinian's war of reconquest, known as the Gothic War (535–54), proved extremely costly. The destruction and chaos caused by it and the accompanying Byzantine fiscal demands led to resentment of Justinian, which was exacerbated by a theological controversy. In May–June 553 Justinian called the Second Council of Constantinople to condemn the so-called Three Chapters—the writings of three theologians—which Justinian and others deemed a revival of Nestorianism, the belief that Christ has two distinct natures, human and divine. Both the Council of Ephesus (431) and the Council of Chalcedon (451) had condemned this position as heretical and affirmed that Christ was but one person both fully human and divine. Pope Virgilius agreed to the condemnation, but the archbishop of Milan and the patriarch of Aquileia refused to go along.[36] It may have been during this controversy that the legend of Mark's foundation of the Aquileian church took shape.[37] By asserting that it was Peter who originally sent Mark on his mission there, the Aquileians affirmed the orthodoxy of their position against, in their view, a renegade pope.

The Gothic War signaled a growing division between inland or mainland Venetia and coastal or maritime Venetia, as evidenced by a preference of the Byzantines for the coastal route when moving their troops since the Goths controlled cities such as Verona farther inland. This division would only deepen and become permanent when the Lombards invaded in 568.[38]

A revealing glimpse into the pre-Lombard situation in Venetia and Istria comes by way of letters that the top civilian administrator at the court of Theodoric and his immediate successors, Flavius Magnus Aurelius Cassiodorus, wrote in the 530s. In them, Cassiodorus was concerned with provisioning the capital Ravenna and the army. In the first letter dated 535 or 536 he sent orders granting the residents of Venetia a reprieve from furnishing supplies to the food storage depots maintained at Concordia, Aquileia, and Cividale. During this time of widespread famine and poor harvest throughout the Po valley, he informed them that they were only required to supply pork, while the residents of Istria, untouched by crop failure, had to send grain.[39] Two years later and facing threats from other Germanic tribes, Cassiodorus informed the residents of Istria of their obligation to supply additional oil, wine, and grain to the court and army but relieved them of the transportation costs. To persuade them to comply, Cassiodorus praised Istria's mild climate, abundant olives, vines, and grain, its oysters and fish farms, its barrier islands that allowed for safe travel by boat, and its villas—stretching, as he put it, like a strand of pearls along the shore.[40]

Cassiodorus's rhetorical skills are on display in his letter to the "tribunes of the maritime provinces," sometimes inaccurately described as the first historical reference to Venice.[41] Venice did not yet exist, although there were likely some minor settlements at its future site. But his letter does paint an evocative picture of life in the lagoons at the time. The tribunes, about whom very little is known, seem to have been the leaders of individual towns, and notable for their property holdings.[42]

The administrator ordered the tribunes to use the nautical resources of Venetia to transport supplies of Istrian wine and oil to Ravenna, deploying flattery to ensure compliance. He noted that the residents were so used to crossing long distances on open sea that the voyage to Ravenna was like little more than crossing through their own home. Moreover, they had the luxury of a second, more secure intracoastal option. He described how shallow-draft boats were pulled by ropes along canals or ditches cut through the marshes so that "viewers from a distance, not seeing the channel of the stream, might think them moving through meadows."

Cassiodorus reminisced about his own visit to the region and his impression of the houses built on islets among the shifting tides, saying, "It is a pleasure to recall the situation of your dwellings.... Venetia long praiseworthy, full of the dwellings of the nobility ... where the alternating tide now reveals and now conceals the surface of the fields by the ebb and flow of its flood. Here like water-fowl have you fixed your home." He lauded the inhabitants' hard work and ingenuity, which allowed them to turn this aquatic landscape into a "firm foundation" upon which to build their homes. They did so, he noted, by weaving thin branches and poles together to create retaining walls and then back-filling the enclosed space with earth.

Cassiodorus also praised the residents and their lifestyle, including a diet primarily of fish. Such moderation allowed them to "escape that vice [of envy] to which all the rest of the world is liable." And he noted their dedication to the salt industry, their one source of wealth. "Your whole attention," he wrote, "is concentrated on your salt-works. Instead of driving the plough or wielding the sickle, you push your rollers. . . . There, it may be said, is the money for your subsistence coined. Every wave is assigned to your craft. Of the quest for gold a man may tire, but everyone desires to find salt." Cassiodorus closed by admonishing the recipients to get their ships, which he described as "tethered, like so many beasts of burden, to your walls," ready to transport the Istrian wine and oil to Ravenna.[43]

Except for the purported lack of envy and enmity among the inhabitants, Cassiodorus's portrait of life on the northern Adriatic littoral corroborates what can be gleaned from other written sources and from archeological evidence. Maritime Venetia was not the sparsely inhabited zone of the Attila legend, home only to few poor fishermen eking out a meager living. Rather it was a region with well-developed salt manufactures and fishing industries, rich timber resources, ships and boats that could traverse either the open sea or intracoastal waterways, a socially differentiated population including both rich and poor, a rudimentary administration in the form of tribunes, and inhabitants experienced in the skills of land reclamation and living in an amphibious environment. Although Cassiodorus did not mention it, the residents presumably had an active religious life, with an apparent affinity for saints who offered protection against the perils of the sea and flood, and a cultural attachment to the Eastern Roman Empire.[44] Many of these qualities and characteristics were legacies of centuries, millenia even, of human interaction with the ever-changing natural environment of the Po valley and the northern Adriatic coast.

Cassiodorus could have been addressing himself to the leaders of any number of settlements between Chioggia and Grado that hugged the coast, lagoons, and barrier islands. But given Venetia's key geographical location as an intersection for trade between north and central Europe and the eastern and southern Mediterranean, it was all but certain that some spot along the northern Adriatic shoreline—perhaps a revivified Aquileia or another already established town—would again become a great international center of trade. At this point, however, further mass migrations of Germanic peoples and Byzantine imperial politics conjoined with geography in the creation of a new town that would assume that role. The rise of Venice proper was still nearly two centuries in the future, but the arduous and circuitous journey to Rialto had already begun.

2

To Rialto

FIVE MILES FROM Venice's Marco Polo airport stand the archeological site and museum of the ancient Roman city of Altino (Altinum in Latin). Strategically located in antiquity at the intersection of the Annia, Popillia, and Claudia Augusta roads, Altino was a thriving town comparable in size to Pompei. Today only a few fragments of streets and building foundations that have been excavated in what are now croplands are visible.[1] Even Marino Sanudo writing in the sixteenth century remarked that "at present there are no vestiges [of the place]."[2] Yet in its prime Altino had all the trappings of a significant Roman town, including theaters, a forum with a temple and shops, basilica, baths, and harbor facilities. Located on a rise only six to ten feet above the surrounding territory, Altino stood near the edge of the Venetian lagoon to which it was connected by a canal running through the town. The nearby Zero, Dese, and Sile rivers allowed for easy communication inland, the Sile leading to Treviso. With the largest theater at least 130 feet in height, Altino would have been visible in the flat alluvial plain from twelve miles away and to ships navigating into the lagoon. It was a commercial port. The museum houses an extraordinary object: a balance engraved with inscriptions in Latin, Attic Greek, and Ptolemaic Egyptian—evidence that the merchant or shopkeeper who used it was familiar with the systems of weights and measures used across the eastern half of the Mediterranean world.

What became of the magnificent buildings that once adorned Altino? Much of the stone and brick was reused at Torcello when Altino was abandoned between the sixth and seventh centuries CE in favor of the new settlement in the lagoon. The relocation to Torcello, which became the lagoon's major commercial center in the early Middle Ages, was not random. The channel of the rivers converging near Altino threaded its way through the lagoon past the outcroppings that became Torcello, Mazzorbo, and Burano before emptying into the sea via one of several mouths that subsequently closed. Two factors led to the abandonment of Altino. One was environmental change. Silting rendered its port less viable. As happened elsewhere, most notably at Ravenna, settlements kept moving to keep pace with the southeastward advance of the land toward the Adriatic. The residents of Altino followed the Sile to Torcello.[3] The second impetus was the invasion of the Lombards in the sixth century. Unlike the Hunnish invasion, which led to a temporary flight into the lagoons, the displacement prompted by the Lombard invaders was permanent. The incursion altered the political and ecclesiastical organization of the Italian peninsula, created social disruption and cleavages, and led over a period of two and a half centuries to the emergence of Rivoalto as the preeminent settlement along the northern Adriatic shoreline. By the year 811, that community can legitimately be referred to as Venice, even if contemporaries did not yet employ that name.

The Lombards were a Germanic people who in the first century CE occupied territory in northwestern Germany. Like several other Germanic tribes, they began a southward migration in the fourth century and by the end of the fifth had established themselves north of the Danube in what is today modern Austria. They saw opportunity in an Italy weakened by Justinian's Gothic War. In 568, when Lombard king Alboin and his men crossed the Julian Alps, they met no resistance from Byzantine forces and easily took Cividale, where they established the first of several duchies, that of Friuli. They also attacked Aquileia. Many of its residents fled as they had done during previous invasions to Grado. Paolino, the patriarch of Aquileia, took his church's treasury, including its most important relics, to Grado. The invasions dealt yet another blow to Aquileia's prosperity.

For their part, the Lombards continued along the Via Postumia and occupied Treviso, Vicenza, and Verona before conquering most of the other important towns north of the Po, including Milan. Pavia resisted until 572, but when it was taken, it became the capital of the new Lombard kingdom of Italy. In subsequent years, the Lombards penetrated farther south, establishing duchies in Benevento and Spoleto. The invasion dramatically exacerbated the division between mainland Venetia and maritime Venetia that had begun during the Gothic War. While the Lombards occupied the interior, the Byzantines continued to control the coastline and lagoons as well as a few inland towns such as Padua and Monselice to the west and Oderzo to the north. On a larger scale the entire Italian peninsula was divided, with the Lombard territories bisected by the lands under the pope and the Byzantines running from Rome to Ravenna. The Byzantines also controlled lands in southern Italy and Sicily.[4]

After Justinian had previously put so much effort and treasure into the reconquest of Italy, the eastern emperors' failure to act in the face of the Lombard threat may seem surprising. But, following the death of Justinian in 565, the Byzantines found themselves confronting more immediate dangers from their traditional enemy, the Persians to the east (and eventually from the Arabs to the south), as well as trouble from the Slavs and Avars to the west. Between 577 and 640 they launched no military enterprises in Italy. Instead, they expected troops already stationed there to hold the line, and to that end, they undertook an important administrative reorganization of the territory. Around the year 580 the title of the deputy or governor sent from Constantinople to Ravenna was changed from prefect (*praefectus*) to exarch (*exarchus*), and the territory under his control, which ran from Ravenna to Istria, became known as the Exarchate of Ravenna. The exarch held both the civilian administrative power of the prefecture and the military power formerly vested in the master of troops (*magister militum*). Venetia, which remained a province of the empire, had its own *magister militum* answering to the exarch. Emperor Maurice, who authorized this reorganization, hoped that the exarch's authority would spur him to meet the Lombard challenge vigorously. He was also counting on local support, which he received. A letter the bishops of the region wrote to him in 590 or 591 expressed their dismay at suffering under the "barbarian [Lombard] yoke" as well as their desire to live once again under "your holy vestige."[5]

For many of them, however, this was not to be. Following a lull in their expansion, the Lombards started attacking towns previously beyond their reach. In 602 Padua fell under their control, forcing its bishop to take temporary refuge at Malamocco, an island in the southern lagoon.[6] Monselice was next. Cremona and Mantua followed in 603. In 616 Concordia was conquered, leaving the old Byzantine administrative center at Oderzo particularly vulnerable. Oderzo finally succumbed in 639. Its inhabitants settled in the town of Civitas Nova Eracliana (referred to as Cittanova or Eraclea after the reigning emperor Heraclius) at the lagoon's edge, which had a direct line of communication with Grado. It became the new administrative center for the Byzantine government in the region. In 641 Altino bore the brunt of the Lombard assault. Another big Lombard push in 642–3 to complete the expulsion of the Byzantines from northern Italy was unsuccessful. Yet all that remained under Byzantine authority in northern Italy were Ravenna, a narrow strip of mainland at the water's edge, the lagoons, and barrier islands running from Ravenna to Grado. With land routes closed, the only safe way to travel around the exarchate was by water.[7] Already one of the constants in Venice's history was in place: the complex and often fraught relationship between the island city and the mainland.

An inscription on the island of Torcello dated 639 offers a tantalizing glimpse into this much-reduced Byzantine province. The plaque commemorates the construction of the Church of Mary Mother of God, which was likely dedicated on September 8, the feast of the birth of Mary. It reads,

> In the name of our lord God Jesus Christ, in the 29th year of the 13th Indiction of the reign of our perpetual lord augustus Heraclius, this church of Holy Mary Mother of God was erected by command of our pious and devout lord Isaac, most excellent exarch and patrician, and by the will of God for his [Isaac's] merits and those of his army; this church was built from the foundations by means of the well-deserving Maurice, the glorious master of troops of the province of Venetia residing in this his place, with fortunate consecration by the holy and most reverend Mauro bishop of this church.[8]

The inscription makes clear that what remained of Venetia was under the command of the master of troops Maurice, who owed his allegiance to Isaac the exarch of Ravenna, who in turn answered to the Byzantine emperor Heraclius. Maurice's choice of Torcello rather than Oderzo as his headquarters suggests how vulnerable the few Byzantine outposts on the mainland had become. Torcello, which was clearly growing in power and economic strength, offered not only protection but also easy communication by water with Ravenna. That Maurice built the church from his own resources is also significant; it indicates that military officials were major property holders in the area and, along with the tribunes or leaders of individual cities, formed the local political and social elite.[9]

Ecclesiastical leaders also took up residence in the lagoons and constituted another corps of elites. The Lombard invasions spurred the flight of church officials and the transfer of their dioceses. In addition to the patriarch of Aquileia's shift to Grado, the bishop of Concordia moved to Caorle, Oderzo's bishop went to Cittanova and Altino's to Torcello. Unlike civil administration in which the lines between Lombard Venetia and Byzantine Venetia were clearly drawn, the loyalties and jurisdictions of churchmen were much more ambiguous and straddled the two realms.[10]

Yet after that initial period in which clergy continued to move easily between the two domains, the border began to harden under the influence of papal, Byzantine, and Lombard politics, complicated by ongoing theological disputes. All the patriarchs of Aquileia in the second half of the sixth century, including the refugee Paolino, adhered to the Nestorian view that Christ had two separate natures, human and divine. This put them at odds with the Byzantine emperor as well as the pope. Matters came to a head in 606–7 when, on the death of patriarch Marciano, it was time to elect a successor. The Grado clergy, that is, those residing in Byzantine territory including Istria, elected Candidiano as their leader, while the clergy at Aquileia and in Lombard territory (under pressure from the Lombard king and the Duke of Friuli) elected the Nestorian Giovanni. "At this time there began to be," wrote Paul the Deacon, "two Patriarchs [of Grado and of Aquileia]."[11] So also were born two contending churches, each claiming to be the true patriarchate and thus the rightful heir to the see purportedly established by Saint Mark himself.

Matters grew even more complicated when in 627–8 Fortunato, who had recently been elected patriarch of Grado, refused to make a formal act of adherence to Rome. Fearing for his safety, he fled to Lombard territory, taking with him the gold, vestments, and other paraphernalia from the treasury of the Grado church. Recognizing the threat that his flight posed to Grado's claim to be the legitimate patriarchate and to Byzantium's religious influence in the area, Emperor Heraclius sent to the new patriarch Primigenio objects designed to replenish the church's treasury, add to its prestige, and bolster its claim to be the true successor to Saint Mark's evangelizing efforts. These gifts apparently included two symbolic thrones, one for Mark, the other for his companion Saint Hermagoras. A gray alabaster throne known as the "Throne of Saint Mark" may be the one originally intended to honor Hermagoras. Created in the eastern Mediterranean, perhaps in Alexandria in the sixth century, it includes depictions of the Cross, the Tree of Life, the Lamb of God, the evangelists, and the rivers of Paradise. This curious object is too small to have served as an actual throne but was instead a reliquary that was designed to hold a piece of the True Cross. In his own effort to strengthen Grado's position, patriarch Primigenio moved the relics of Hermagoras and other saints from Aquileia to Grado, thus emphasizing in a way that contemporaries could clearly understand the shift of authority.[12]

Even when in 699 Aquileia came into communion with Rome, the two churches remained divided, with bishops in Lombard territory adhering to the Aquileian Patriarch and those in Byzantine territory owing allegiance to

ASSERVARENTVR CONCINNAVERVNT
ANTONIO CAPELLO ETIAM TEMPLI QVAESTORE

FIGURE 2.1 Throne of Saint Mark, sixth/early seventh century. Treasury of San Marco, Venice. Cameraphoto Arte, Venice/Art Resource, NY.

Grado's. The problem grew even more complicated when between 768 and 772 the Lombards conquered Istria and incorporated it into their territory. The Lombards were eventually defeated by the Franks, another Germanic tribe that had settled in what became France. During the reign of Louis the Pious, son of the Frankish king Charlemagne, Istria too passed into the jurisdiction of the patriarch of Aquileia who would become the greatest landowner in Friuli and would constantly cause difficulties for the Venetians on their eastern border.[13]

Following the fall of Oderzo in 639 and the transfer of Byzantine administration to Cittanova, the region settled into a period of relative calm for nearly a century. But the reverberations of the events between the Lombard incursion in 569 and Oderzo's conquest in 639 would last for centuries. Most significantly, the Lombards failed to capture the lagoons—either out of disinterest or because they lacked the naval capability to do so. This meant that when the Lombards in turn were conquered by Frankish King Pepin the Short who ceded to Pope Stephen II (752–7) Byzantine imperial territories recently occupied by the Lombards, maritime Venetia was not incorporated into the Papal State.[14] Had that happened, Venice's history would have been very different. Perhaps then some town directly on the Po, such as Ferrara, or more centrally located in the papal enclave might have become the great center of northern Adriatic trade. Similarly, when Emperor Heraclius decided not to include Venetia in his reorganization of the empire into military zones called themes, his decision showed the extent to which the Byzantines too saw the lagoons as peripheral.[15] Certainly, the Greeks had bigger and more serious threats facing them closer to home. So just as the lagoons were a border between fresh- and saltwater, so too were they a buffer zone between greater powers. This pattern would recur throughout Venice's history. The lagoons' marginality to both the Lombards and Byzantines allowed the region's economy to develop relatively undisturbed, permitted a distinct identity to emerge, and let a local elite coalesce and assert itself. This calm would be broken in 726 when yet another theological controversy roiled the Christian world.

The new arena of theological dispute concerned the production and use of images of Christ, Mary, and the saints. While proponents of such paintings and sculptures saw them as useful in the instruction of the illiterate, spurs to prayer and contemplation, and tangible affirmations of Christ's incarnation, opponents, known as iconoclasts, deemed the use of images idolatrous. In 726, Byzantine emperor Leo III adopted the iconoclast position and ordered the wholesale destruction of icons. While some in the Eastern Empire supported the move, it was widely condemned in the West, especially by Pope Gregory II, and provoked a widespread revolt against Byzantine rule, which was encouraged by the Lombards. In Ravenna, the exarch Paul was murdered.

The residents of what remained of the province of Venetia joined the rebellion and in 726 or 727 elected as their *dux* (duke) Orso, from Cittanova, who came from the local elite class of tribunes. Although later writers claimed that two other men had preceded Orso in the post, it is generally accepted that Orso was the first duke or doge of the communities scattered throughout the Venetian lagoon.[16] Orso's office should not be equated with the dogeship as it later came to be known, nor should his election be seen as Venetia's declaration of independence from Byzantium. Indeed, soon after his election, the emperor conferred on Orso the honorific title *hypatos* (consul). And in 735 troops from Venetia used their naval capability to help reinstate the exarch Paul's successor after the Lombards forced him to flee Ravenna.[17]

The situation proved highly fluid, however. In 737 Orso was killed after ten years of rule. For the next five years, Venetia was again governed by masters of troops who were elected on an annual basis and were functionaries of the exarch. The third of these, Deodato, was son of the murdered first duke Orso. When in 742 the last master of troops Giovanni Fabriciaco was blinded and driven from office, a faction within the community elected Deodato as duke. He promptly moved the government of Venetia from Cittanova, on the lagoon's northern edge, to Malamocco in the southern lagoon, which had seen an influx of refugees from Padua. Cittanova sank into oblivion as many of the prominent families moved to the settlement at Rivoalto (Rialto) where one of the channels of the Brenta wound through the lagoon.[18] Regardless of the internecine conflicts that caused it, the displacement of the capital from the fringes of the mainland to the southern lagoon highlighted the maritime nature and orientation of what remained of Byzantine Venetia.

Then in 751, after decades of effort, the Lombards finally took Ravenna, bringing the Byzantine exarchate to an end. With no superior in Italy, the Duke of Venetia answered only to the local community and distant emperor. At this point, some argue, it is legitimate to begin using the term *doge* to refer to the duke or leader of these scattered and increasingly autonomous lagoonal communities.[19] Indeed, one sign of the growing capacity for independent action among the residents of Venetia was their decision to build a fort at Brondolo south of Chioggia to guard the mouth of the Bacchiglione River, as a counterweight to the Lombards, who controlled the nearby mouth of the Adige.[20] Clearly they were intent on safeguarding Malamocco as well as their access to river traffic and trade. When the Lombards took Istria between 768 and 772, yet another vestige of the old order disappeared. The unity of the old Roman region of Venetia and Istria was finally and completely dissolved. The rupture was perhaps best expressed by the emperor's designation of Doge Maurizio I Galbaio (764–97) as "consul and imperial duke of the province of the Venetians."[21]

During the reign of Maurizio I, another decisive step in the rise of Rialto (or what we today call Venice) occurred. Between 774 and 776 a bishopric with a church dedicated to Saint Peter was established on the small island of Olivolo at what is now the southeastern tip of the city, to meet the needs of the burgeoning settlement at Rialto. Olivolo was strategically located midway between Malamocco, the political capital, and Torcello, the lagoon's economic center. Protected from direct assault by ships advancing from the Adriatic by the islands of Certosa and Le Vignole, Olivolo offered a control point for traffic entering the lagoon through the mouth of San Nicolò.[22] For this reason, a castle may have been built there.[23] It eventually lent its name (Castello) to one of the six subdivisions of Venice, as well as to the church—San Pietro di Castello. The island's original name Olivolo (Olivolus) suggests that, even before the bishopric was established there, the site was settled and supported olive cultivation. Several other bishoprics were also established in the lagoons over these centuries; some of them transfers from the mainland, others new foundations. All six bishops (Torcello, Malamocco, Jesolo, Caorle, Cittanova, and Olivolo) answered to the patriarch of Grado.[24]

The Frankish king Charlemagne's conquest of the Lombard kingdom of Italy in 774 ushered in the final act in Rialto's protracted rise to preeminence among the various lagoon communities. Charlemagne's triumph was the product of the alliance between the Franks and the papacy that had begun under his father Pepin and was pursued by the pope to counter the Lombard threat to papal lands. The pope had turned to the Franks for help when his pleas to the Byzantine emperor went unanswered. Pepin and his heirs, known as the Carolingians, in return for papal sanction guaranteed the pontiff control of Rome and promised him all Byzantine-claimed lands in northern and central Italy. Accordingly, in 787 the pope expelled merchants from Venetia from Ravenna and from another former Byzantine possession, five cities along the Adriatic coast known as the Duchy of the Pentapolis. After Charlemagne conquered Istria and northern Dalmatia and placed the Istrian bishops under the patriarch of Aquileia, the residents of Venetia were surrounded. The Byzantines finally awoke to the danger the Frankish-Papal alliance posed to their prestige and authority and to their control of Venetia when on Christmas Day in 800, Pope Leo III crowned Charlemagne as emperor. This represented a direct challenge to Byzantium's claim to be the only true heir to Rome.[25]

Making matters worse, the lagoon community was itself divided and hence extremely vulnerable. While Doge Giovanni Galbaio adhered to a pro-Byzantine policy, others, especially the Grado clergy, adopted a pro-papal and pro-Frankish stance, although these allegiances were strategic and could change quickly.[26] In 802 the doge sent a naval force under the direction of his son and co-regent Maurizio (II) to depose the patriarch of Grado, who, according to some accounts, was thrown from a tower to his death. His successor made his way to Charlemagne's court where he received a series of privileges in favor of the Grado church. Meanwhile the pro-Frankish party in Venetia hatched a plot that led in 804 to the deposition and exile of Giovanni and his son Maurizio and the election of Obelerio from Malamocco as the new doge. Obelerio and his brother (and co-regent) Beato soon traveled to see Charlemagne, as did representatives from Dalmatia. Although the details of the accord that followed are unclear, Venetia was coming increasingly into the Frankish sphere.

At this point, the Byzantine emperor Nicephorus I, fearing the loss of Dalmatia and Venetia, dispatched a fleet under the command of Nicetas to the northern Adriatic. Co-regent doges Obelerio and Beato quickly pivoted back to the Byzantine side, as evidenced by the honorific titles they received from Nicephorus, while the patriarch of Grado fled back to Charlemagne's court. Nicetas and Charlemagne's son Pepin, whom Charlemagne had made King of Italy in 806, reached an agreement not to allow malcontents to use their territories to prepare attacks on the other, but left unresolved the long-term status of Venetia. With his goal of protecting Venetia from an outright Frankish takeover seemingly accomplished, Nicetas sailed back east in late 807.

In 809, however, the Byzantine fleet had to return to the region to respond to the actions of Obelerio and Beato, who had reverted to their pro-Frankish position. After a brief and unsuccessful attack on the Frankish stronghold at Comacchio, the fleet departed again. With that, Pepin saw his chance and, encouraged by the co-regents, attacked Venetia from both land and sea. His troops marched up the barrier islands, taking Chioggia and Pellestrina, but were blocked at Albiola from crossing to the capital at Malamocco.[27] In the meantime, Pepin's ships sailed east and captured Grado before moving to protect Dalmatia. When the Venetians finally grasped the danger to their semi-autonomous status, they mounted a resistance, although it was certainly less heroic than as it was recorded by later chroniclers. Many sought shelter on the islets clustered around Rialto. In the end, it was the reappearance of the Byzantine fleet that forced Pepin to abandon his effort to capture the lagoons.

In the meantime, the Byzantine emperor had sent his representative Arsaphios to meet with Pepin. But after Arsaphios learned of Pepin's death in July 810, he negotiated an agreement with Charlemagne instead. In clarifying the terms of the agreement that had been worked out in 807, both sides made important concessions. For his part, Charlemagne agreed to give up his claim to Venetia and return towns on the Dalmatian coast (but not Istria) that the

Franks had conquered. In essence, he abandoned Carolingian efforts to control the northern Adriatic. For their part, the Byzantines would recognize Charlemagne's title as emperor. Other clauses established procedures for the resolution of various civil and criminal matters and regularized property, river, maritime, and usage rights for inhabitants on both sides of the border. This was especially important in guaranteeing residents of the lagoon the security of their properties on the mainland.

As Arsaphios journeyed back to Constantinople, he took with him Doge Obelerio, who had fled to Charlemagne's court but was turned over to the Byzantines for punishment. While in Venice, Arsaphios oversaw the formal deposition of Obelerio and Beato—the latter was banished to Zara (Zadar)—and the election in 811 of a new doge, Agnello Partecipazio, who was to be assisted by two tribunes. Once in Constantinople, the terms of the agreement were accepted with the proviso that Charlemagne would be acknowledged simply as emperor, not as emperor of the Romans. Follow-up negotiations resulted in a final agreement in 814, the Peace of Aachen, that was concluded between Louis the Pious, Charlemagne's son and successor, and Nicephorus's successor, Michael.

The years between 751 and 814 have been described as the most perilous in Venice's long history—and with good reason.[28] Had Pepin succeeded in conquering Venetia, the lagoons between Chioggia and Grado would have been incorporated into the Carolingian Empire and its successor, the Holy Roman Empire. The region could well have become an obscure backwater on the fringes of Western control. Instead, it was to remain temporarily part of the Eastern Roman Empire and thus subject to the Byzantine emperor. What people at the time could not have known is that this would prove a boon since Venetia was too incidental to Byzantine interests for them to show much concern with it. In fact, once the accord with the Carolingians was reached, the Byzantines never again sent a fleet into the northern Adriatic or directly interfered with Venetian affairs. Venetia was thus marginal to both empires while at the same time a border between them. Its status as a contact point for merchants, coupled with its geographical advantages (protected waterways and proximity to navigable rivers and traversable mountain passes) and natural resources (wood, salt, and fish) put it on the path to independence and economic greatness.

Pepin's failure to capture the lagoons led to an additional change with a lasting impact. In 811, with the election of Agnello Partecipazio, and perhaps at the behest of Byzantine legate Arsaphios, the decision was made to move the capital from Malamocco to the settlement at Rialto. Several factors contributed to the transfer. Rialto's central location in the lagoons meant that it was well protected from attack by both land and sea, a key consideration given the vulnerability of locations in the south, including Malamocco.[29] The desire to start anew surely played a role as well. As the capital of deposed doge Obelerio, Malamocco had too many pro-Frankish associations for it to serve as the center of a community in need of social repair. At Rialto, where refugees from all over the lagoon had taken sanctuary during the crisis, new ties could be forged and old enmities forgotten. Proximity to the settlement, bishopric, and fort at Olivolo was another advantage. So too was the easily navigable deepwater channel, a branch of the Brenta River, that took a dramatic turn there and would become over time the Grand Canal. It was at the Rialto settlement that Doge Partecipazio erected a *palatium* (palace), the predecessor to today's Ducal Palace.[30]

To an observer in the ninth and tenth centuries, the new capital at Rialto appeared as scattered settlements separated by vast expanses of water rather than a compact urban center. But the same processes of land reclamation that Cassiodorus had described in his letter in the 530s were proceeding apace. Slowly bits of land were being wrested from the marshes as retaining walls were constructed and household refuse and silt dredged from water courses were used to build up the land. Over time, a system of primary and secondary canals began to take shape. As the population grew, wooden houses with thatched roofs fronting on the water multiplied. Wood was well suited to the lagoon's building conditions and typical of Carolingian Europe.[31] Orchards and vegetable gardens were planted, fishponds fenced off. Ditches were dug and dikes erected for the evaporation of water and production of salt. Parish churches also built of wood were erected, each church surrounded by a field (*campo*) and a cemetery. Bridges developed extremely slowly and only as bits of reclaimed land grew close enough together to make linking them structurally feasible. The first bridges (documented from 1088) were made of wooden planks; the earliest evidence of a stone bridge is from 1170.[32] In this period water was not a barrier but rather the primary means by which this micro-archipelago was knit together.[33]

Early medieval Venice would also have appeared chaotic and unplanned since there was neither an overall blueprint for development nor any agency directing it. Projects were undertaken at the initiative of individuals, families, neighbors, and religious institutions, in particular Benedictine monasteries.

But the cumulative effect and underlying logic of these individual actions began to become apparent, driven as it was by the need for defense and for the efficient movement of traffic and trade. The islands housing the monasteries of San Servolo (founded circa 810 but documented in 819) and San Giorgio Maggiore (documented in 892 but likely founded earlier), along with the convent of San Zaccaria near the Doge's Palace (founded circa 818 and documented in 829) and the cathedral of San Pietro on the island of Olivolo, began to define the contours of the Bacino di San Marco, which would become the city's primary harbor.[34] The castle at Olivolo offered protection to the Bacino against possible assault from the sea, while the monasteries, rich in mainland estates and properties in the lagoons, could meet traders' demand for grain, salt, and fish, while generating their own demand for imported goods.[35] Into this basin two deep channels, the future Grand Canal and the future Giudecca Canal, also converged. Following these two water courses upstream brought one within sight of the mainland and near where branches of the Brenta emptied into the lagoon. In other words, development was beginning to define a navigational system that would carry goods from the mainland down the rivers, along these major canals, through the Bacino to the mouth at San Nicolò, and then into the Adriatic and vice versa.

Gradually, the scattered islets that bordered the future Grand Canal also began to coalesce into six concentrated settlements. Four (Olivolo, Gemini, Rivoalto, and Canaleclo) developed on the canal's eastern side. Dorsoduro developed on the western side, as did Luprio whose boundaries crossed the canal. In the case of Olivolo (olive orchard), Rivoalto (high bank) and Dorsoduro (hardback), the names reference their original natural features. Gemini probably began as twin islands, while Luprio may refer to a swampy zone, and Canaleclo, the nucleus of the future section of the city called Cannaregio, likely recalls canes that grew in the area. Spinalonga (long-back) and the island of San Giorgio Maggiore started to define the shape of the Giudecca, separated by the canal of the same name from Dorsoduro.[36] By the end of the tenth century, slightly more than twenty parish churches had been established in the small settlements around Rialto.[37]

Having survived the Carolingian assault and escaped the attentions of their Byzantine overlords, the inhabitants of the *dogado* (duchy or dukedom) of Venetia, which constituted little more than the lagoons and barrier islands between Grado and the town of Cavarzere, suddenly found themselves in 811 with a new doge, a new capital, and conditions ripe for economic growth. What they did not know is that they were soon to welcome their supernatural protector as well. Saint Mark, true to the angelic message delivered to him while he was taking refuge in the lagoons, would find his true and proper repose in the new city emerging from the water.

3

Ducal Venice

SOMETIME BETWEEN CHRISTMAS Day 828 and August 829, Doge Giustiniano Partecipazio, son of Doge Agnello Partecipazio, drew up his last will and testament. Giustiniano's route to the dogeship had hardly been smooth. After his father's ascension to the ducal throne in 811, Giustiniano had been dispatched to Constantinople where the emperor honored him with the title consul. But while there, his father named Giustiniano's younger brother Giovanni as co-regent, thus laying the groundwork for Giovanni's eventual succession to the ducal office. When Giustiniano returned to Venice, however, Agnello reversed course, named Giustiniano co-regent, and exiled Giovanni to Zara. From there Giovanni made his way to the court of Louis the Pious, Charlemagne's successor, who at the request of Agnello and Giustiniano sent Giovanni as a hostage to Constantinople. On Agnello's death in 827, Giustiniano became sole doge, but he soon reconciled with Giovanni, who became co-regent and succeeded his brother as doge in 829. About this time, Obelerio, the doge who had been exiled after the defeat of Pepin, returned to the lagoon and made a play for power from his old base at Malamocco. Doge Giovanni showed no mercy: he had Malamocco burned and Obelerio decapitated. Obelerio's head was then dispatched on a gruesome pilgrimage throughout the lagoon. During these years, Giovanni also barely survived a coup d'etat led by the tribune Caroso. But in 836, his luck ran out. Giovanni was accosted by members of the Mastalici family while exiting the church of San Pietro di Castello, tonsured, and forced to end his days as a monk at Grado.[1]

Giustiniano Partecipazio's testament is one of only two Venetian wills to survive from before the twelfth century.[2] Just as his career offers a glimpse into the tumultuous nature of ducal politics, so his will is revealing of the economy and society of ninth-century Venice. The doge had inherited or accumulated a vast amount of wealth, much of it tied up in real estate situated in the lagoon and on the nearby mainland. These properties included pastures, woodlands, gardens, vineyards, fishponds, and bird-hunting grounds. On some of these he had constructed houses and barns where horses, cattle, and pigs were stabled. Serfs, whom he promised to free on his death, worked some of these lands, many of which he pledged as donations to the monasteries of Sant'Ilario and San Zaccaria.[3] Additionally, Giustiniano had as much as 1,200 pounds in movable wealth, including 200 pounds in silver- and gold-plate, as well as "working monies," his way of describing cash that was invested in maritime trade, although he cautioned, "if they [the monies] come back safely from sea." Giustiniano's will shows how, even at this early date, the Venetian economy straddled both land and sea.

The testament also displays Giustiniano's deep concern with earning merit for his soul. He requested that building stone he had at Equilo (Jesolo) be used to complete the construction of the monastery of Sant'Ilario, which was located near the Brenta and thus could control river traffic.[4] By far the most historically significant clause in Giustiniano's will was the following: "Concerning the body of blessed Mark, I wish that my wife build a basilica in his honor within the territory of [the monastery of] San Zaccaria." He ordered that surplus stone from the Sant'Ilario construction site, as well as stone from a house on Torcello, "be used to build the basilica of the blessed Mark the Evangelist." Just a year before Giustiniano dictated his will, Saint Mark's relics had arrived at Rialto in what the Venetians believed was fulfillment of the saint's destiny.

Doge Giustiniano's will offers a fitting introduction to Venice's ducal age, which began with his father Agnello Partecipazio's decision to move the capital to Rialto in 811. During this period the power of the doges was immense and nearly unchecked. Over the course of the ninth and tenth centuries, prominent families, especially the Orseolos and Candianos, competed to attain the dogeship and pass it to their heirs. This was also the most violent period in Venetian history. Of the twenty-nine doges who ruled between 742 and 1032, only eight died of natural causes.[5] Several ended their lives at the edge of a sword or were forced to take monastic vows. Venice was not unique in this respect. The ninth and tenth centuries in Europe were characterized by violence perpetrated by powerful laymen and churchmen alike as they sought to fill the political void left by the weakened later Carolingians. Strongmen based their authority on their possession of land, ties to lesser men, and control of the spiritual charisma thought to reside in the bodies of saints, whose relics were believed to provide direct access to the divine and as such were frequently purloined, exchanged, or given as gifts in order to establish or consolidate relationships of power. Venice's domestic politics remained entangled with international ones as the doges sought allies at the Byzantine court or among Charlemagne's successors. Even so, Venice continued to enjoy working relations with both and to act as a conduit between East and West. More significantly, the doges of this period personally oversaw Venice's efforts to gain control of the northern Adriatic Sea and protect the movement of its ships throughout the rest of the waterway. The resulting growth of the Venetian economy fostered the development of a substantial class of new men who, by demanding a share of power, began slowly reining in the doges and bringing an end to Venice's ducal age.

The advent of Saint Mark's body in 828 was arguably the single most important event in Venice's long history since this otherworldly protector came to stand at the very center of Venetian identity. According to an account already circulating in the tenth century, Mark's *translatio* (transfer), like many such saintly relocations, was the result of theft. Two merchants, Buono da Malamocco and Rustico da Torcello, were on a trading venture to the East when they were forced to land in Muslim Alexandria, which was off limits to Christian merchants. There they met the guardians of the church housing Mark's body, who told them that the temple would soon be stripped of its marble columns and other adornments in order to build a palace. Outraged at the insult to the saint, Buono and Rustico offered to rescue the body, but the custodians balked at the idea of removing Mark from the city where he had died. The Venetians responded by telling them of Mark's mission to Aquileia, an event that made the Venetians Mark's eldest sons and Venice his proper home. Only after persecution by the Muslims did the custodians (a monk and a priest) agree to help orchestrate Mark's escape. To disguise their sacred theft, the men removed Mark's body from its tomb and substituted that of Saint Claudia. However, the sweet odor that emanated from Mark's body when the crypt was opened (saints' bodies were believed to emit a fragrant scent) alarmed the Alexandrians who, rushing to the tomb and seeing the body of Claudia, concluded that nothing was awry. The Venetians covered Mark's body with pork to disguise their precious cargo. This subterfuge succeeded since, when the smugglers were stopped by customs officials, the sight of the pork so disgusted the Muslim guards that they let the Venetians pass. During the voyage home, Mark defended the vessel against demons and shipwreck. When the ship neared Istria, however, Buono and Rustico began to fear that they would be punished for having gone to Alexandria. Yet when Doge Giustiniano learned of their holy contraband, he welcomed the men into the city, rewarded them for their efforts, and deposited Mark's body in the Doge's Palace.[6] A thirteenth-century mosaic over the Porta Sant'Alipio, the far left doorway to the church, shows how later Venetians imagined Mark's entry into the basilica, greeted as he was by the doge and members male and female, clerical and lay, of the community.

Whether the account has any basis in fact is debated, but Mark's arrival undoubtedly strengthened Venice's status on the international stage. Events of the previous year explain the city's urgent need for his fortuitous appearance. In 827 a synod had been called in Mantua to settle the ongoing question of the relationship between the competing patriarchates of Aquileia and Grado. The synod, which was filled with churchmen from the Carolingian-controlled mainland, came down firmly on Aquileia's side. The assembled clergymen declared that it was the true patriarchal seat, and Grado was nothing but a dependent parish. Had the patriarch of Grado and the Venetians accepted the decision, it would have placed the entire Venetian ecclesiastical establishment under Carolingian control and extended Frankish influence into the lagoons. By acquiring the body of Mark, however, the Venetians dramatically

FIGURE 3.1 *The Arrival of Mark's Relics in San Marco*, second half of the thirteenth century. Porta Sant'Alipio, Basilica of San Marco, Venice. O. Böhm, Venice.

emphasized their view that authority had passed from Aquileia to Grado and by extension to Rialto.[7]

The theft offered other international advantages as well. Mark served as a useful counterweight to the papacy. The papal threat to Venice was twofold. First, the Venetians feared, as did all powers in the West, papal encroachment on local ecclesiastical liberties. As early as 982, the Venetians were claiming that the basilica of San Marco was exempt from the normal obligations to "holy mother church."[8] Second, several cities in papal territory, including Ravenna, Rimini, and Ancona, were Venice's business competitors. By acquiring the body of one of the four Evangelists, the Venetians were nearly able to match the prestige the pope enjoyed by virtue of his possession of Saint Peter's body. Mark granted them a degree of independence from Rome.[9]

Some have argued that Mark played a similar role in Venice's relations with Byzantium. According to this view, Mark, who was especially associated with Italy because of his evangelizing efforts in northeastern Italy, replaced Saint Theodore, a Greek soldier saint, as the chief patron of the Venetians. Mark thus enabled the Venetians to separate themselves from their eastern imperial overlords.[10] It is unclear, however, whether Theodore was ever considered Venice's chief patron, despite Venetians' assertions of such in later centuries. Certainly, a chapel dedicated to Theodore stood near the Ducal Palace. It is possible that Theodore's relics were brought to Venice by Nicetas in 806, as part of a broader campaign by emperor Nicephorus I to use saintly remains to bolster his claim to lands bordering the Adriatic, claims that were being challenged by the Franks. During Nicephorus's reign, Saint Tryphon's relics arrived in Cattaro (Kotor) and Saint Anastasia's in Zara.[11] Rather than an attempt to usurp Theodore, the acquisition of Mark's body more likely provided a useful element in the creation of a Venetian identity that only gradually came to see itself as distinct from Byzantium.

Mark's transfer also impacted domestic politics. When his body arrived in Venice, Doge Giustiniano deposited it in the Ducal Palace rather than in the bishop's church in Olivolo or the patriarch's church in Grado. By linking Mark and the doge in this way, he weakened these possible competitors for leadership of the Venetian community. The doge's decision strengthened Rialto's claim to primacy among the various communities within the lagoon, while the identification of the theft's protagonists as Buono from Malamocco and Rustico from Torcello emphasized that Venetians from both the southern and northern parts of the lagoon and towns with traditionally pro-Frankish or pro-Byzantine sympathies were united in their holy heist.[12]

Finally, Giustiniano's decision to deposit the saint's body in the doge's palace had a lasting impact on Venetian urbanism. The palace that his father doge Agnello had established as his residence when he moved the capital to Rialto began life as a fort or castle, replete with corner towers and thick defensive walls. Mark's relics were likely first secured in one of those towers. In his will, Giustiniano asked his wife to build a church to house Mark in the garden belonging to the nearby monastery of San Zaccaria. The site selected stood between the palace and a preexisting church dedicated to Saint Theodore, probably located in what is today the Piazzetta dei Leoncini.

Little is known about the first church of San Marco, although it, like the core of the present church, was likely in the shape of a Greek cross. The

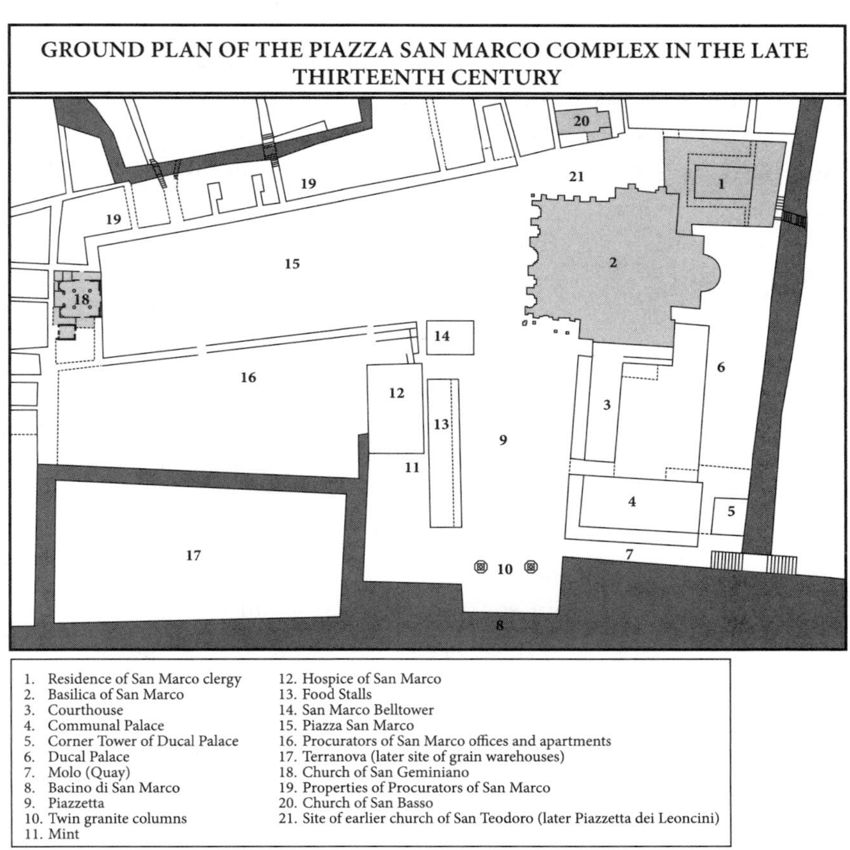

FIGURE 3.2 Ground Plan of the Piazza San Marco complex in the late thirteenth century. Based on the plan in Michela Agazzi, *Platea Sancti Marci: i luoghi marciani dall'XI al XIII secolo e la formazione della piazza* (Venice, 1991), 140–1.

main altar stood in the central crossing, which was topped with a wooden dome. It was modeled on the Apostoleion, the church of the Holy Apostles in Constantinople, rather than on the basilican plan or Latin cross churches commonly found in the region such as the cathedrals of Aquileia, Grado, and Torcello. Built by Constantine and reconstructed by Justinian, the Apostoleion housed the relics of Saints Andrew, Luke, and Timothy as well as the tombs of numerous emperors. Both Giustiniano and Giovanni Partecipazio, who had spent time in the imperial capital, would have been familiar with the Apostoleion and understood that, as "a martyrium, an apostles' church, a dynastic chapel and a state sanctuary," it performed the multiple functions that would be required of a church dedicated to Mark.[13] Parts of the outer walls of the present-day church and the wall that divides the atrium from the nave, with its grand entrance niche, are remnants of that first building.

San Marco, the adjoining church of San Teodoro, the Ducal Palace, and the open field in front of San Marco quickly became the political and sacred center of the Rialto settlement, as well as the axis from which Venice's urban development emanated.[14] In most Italian cities during the central Middle Ages the cathedral and the adjoining bishop's palace served those functions. In Venice, by contrast, the bishop, headquartered in Olivolo/Castello, was some remove from the center of power. Saint Mark and his church were linked to the doge and strengthened ducal power.

While possession of Mark's body conferred an aura of divine sanction on the doges, they had a variety of more practical tools at their disposal to augment their and their families' authority. One of the most effective was co-regency, that is, the naming of a male relative as co-ruler. The practice began with Maurizio I Galbaio who became doge in 765. In the case of the Partecipazio doges, Agnello named his sons Giovanni and then Giustiniano as co-regents, then Giustiniano made Giovanni co-regent. Giovanni Partecipazio's immediate successor, Pietro Tradonico, appointed his son Giovanni as co-regent. Pietro II Orseolo reigned first with his son Giovanni and on Giovanni's death, with Pietro's younger son Ottone. The Venetians likely borrowed the practice from the Byzantium emperors, and the naming of a co-regent was usually among a doge's first actions. The aim was to guarantee a smooth succession and thereby minimize factional strife.[15] Yet by furthering the dynastic ambitions of ducal families, co-regency could stir up resentment among competing families, fueling the very factionalism and succession crises it was intended to prevent.

Once a co-regent was named, he was dispatched almost immediately to Constantinople to garner imperial recognition of his new position. The emperor would publicize his approval by conferring on the co-regent an honorific title usually one step below the title enjoyed by the incumbent doge. In so doing, the emperor signaled his understanding that the co-regent would eventually ascend to the level of the reigning doge. This practice legitimated the doges and their sons, who often came to power through violence, and signaled Venice's ongoing affiliation with Byzantium.[16]

In addition to co-regency, doges tried to guarantee their hold on power through strategic marriages to other families within the community or more significantly with foreign princes. Pietro IV Candiano forced his first wife into the convent of San Zaccaria where he installed her as abbess and then married Waldrada, sister of the powerful and wealthy Marquess Ugo of Tuscany. Doge Pietro II Orseolo used his children to create a vast network of connections. In 1004 his first son (and co-regent) Giovanni married Maria, a member of the Byzantine Argyropoulos family, and sister of a future emperor. Emperor Basil II gave her relics of Saint Barbara which she carried to Venice. They were eventually deposited in the monastery of San Giovanni on Torcello.[17] Pietro's son, Ottone, married the sister of the king of Hungary while his daughter Icela married the king of Croatia's son. Another of Pietro's sons, Domenico, married a relative of Doge Pietro IV Candiano. God-parentage served a similar purpose. Doge Pietro Tradonico became godfather to the daughter of Louis II, king of Italy and Holy Roman emperor. Doge Pietro II Orseolo had close ties to Holy Roman emperor Otto III. Otto served as godfather to Orseolo's son Ottone and attended the baptism of one of Orseolo's daughters. By linking themselves to foreign sovereigns through marital or godparental ties, the doges affirmed their status as princes.[18]

The doges further sought to secure their power by installing their children or other relations in the most important ecclesiastical posts in the lagoon.[19] This was especially crucial since bishoprics and monastic houses had the economic means and prestige to compete with the doges for leadership of the Venetian community. First and foremost, the doges sought to guarantee that the patriarchate of Grado was in friendly hands. The need to do so became especially apparent during the reign of Doge Ottone Orseolo, son of Pietro II. In 1026 a revolt engineered by Domenico Flabiano and the Coloprini family forced Ottone to flee to Constantinople and prompted the election of Pietro Centranico as doge. But Ottone's brother Orso, patriarch of Grado, staged a counter-coup and served as co-regent while awaiting Ottone's return. When Ottone died before making his way back to Venice, Patriarch Orso tried to install another relation, Domenico Orseolo, on the ducal throne. But Domenico Orseolo's reign lasted little more than a day before he was driven from the city, and Domenico Flabiano became the new doge.[20] The bishoprics of Castello and Torcello were other favored posts for ducal sons, while daughters and other female relations were installed as abbesses of San Zaccaria and other convents.

Despite these strategies, none of the doges were able to establish a permanent dynasty and make the office hereditary. Their rivals (sometimes even within the family) were simply too strong and factional affiliations too potent for this to succeed. The animosity between the Orseolo and Candiano families resulted in some extraordinary outbursts of violence, the most dramatic of which involved Pietro IV Candiano.[21] Pietro IV's path to the ducal throne was rocky. His father Pietro III (ruled 942–59) cultivated stronger ties to Italy and the West than to Byzantium. He acquired large estates on the mainland in the vicinity of Chioggia and forged marital ties to *terraferma* (the Venetian term for the mainland) families. Pietro named his son co-regent, but for reasons that are not entirely clear, Pietro the son rebelled against his father and went into exile in Ravenna, where he harassed Venetian ships. However, on Pietro III's death, Pietro was recalled from exile by an assembly of the community and named doge. The convoking of an assembly, a common practice in the Carolingian kingdom of Italy, indicates that Venice's evolving political forms were a hybrid of Byzantine and Carolingian elements.[22]

As ruler, Pietro IV expanded the westward-looking policies of his father, including his marriage to the sister of the Marquess of Tuscany. He brought in foreign troops to serve as his personal bodyguards and dispatched Venetian troops to such places as Ferrara and Oderzo to protect his wife's dowry rights. The arrival of foreign soldiers tied to him was particularly worrisome as it threatened to introduce the personal bonds of the feudal system—those between lords and vassals—into Venetian society.

At the very moment when Pietro was forging closer links to the mainland, the chaos that had characterized the reigns of Charlemagne's successors came to an end with the rise of the German Saxon dynasty and the coronation in 962 of Otto I as Holy Roman emperor. Otto made clear his plan to dominate Italy and perhaps even subsume Venice into the empire. The pact that Otto signed with Venice in 967 weakened the border guarantees of previous treaties and described the money that Venice paid to the emperor as "tribute."[23] Three years later, a reinvigorated Byzantium slapped new restrictions on Venetian merchants. It forbade them from supplying timber and other military supplies to Muslims in Syria and Asia.

At this point, Pietro's opponents had had enough and in 976 launched a revolt against him. After being repelled by the doge's bodyguards, they started a conflagration that quickly got out of control and consumed not only the Ducal Palace and San Marco but also more than 300 houses. As the doge sought to escape the flames, he was accosted by his enemies and, according to the contemporary chronicler John the Deacon exclaimed, "Why, oh brothers, do you want to conspire for my ruin? If I committed errors in words or in public matters, I ask that my life be spared and I promise to satisfy all your desires."[24] Unmoved, the enraged mob killed Pietro on the spot, along with his and Waldrada's infant son.

The Venetians selected as his successor, Pietro I Orseolo, who had a reputation for piety. Whether he was involved in the plot to overthrow Pietro IV Candiano is unclear. During his brief reign, he rebuilt San Marco. Given how quickly the reconstruction was accomplished, it seems likely that the fire had destroyed only the wooden parts of the building not the brick walls.[25] Orseolo stabilized relations with Capodistria (Koper)—a Candiano stronghold—and reached an accord with Candiano's widow Waldrada. But after just two years on the ducal throne, Orseolo fled the city and traveled to the Benedictine monastery of Saint Michael of Cuxa in the French Pyrenees, where he passed the rest of his days and was buried. He was succeeded by Vitale Candiano, whose short reign came to an end when he entered the monastery of Sant'Ilario. He was followed in 979 by Tribuno Menio, who was married to one of Pietro IV Candiano's daughters.

As this dizzying account indicates, Venetian politics in this period were chaotic and characterized by extraordinary violence and instability. Factional conflicts and affiliations and inter- and even intra-familial disputes, often over contested properties along *terraferma* rivers, were given ideological and cultural window dressing by the pro-Ottonian or pro-Byzantine stances of the various parties. The Ottonians posed by the far the greater danger due to their geographic proximity. This became clear during the reign of Tribuno Menio, when Emperor Otto II, egged on by the rebel Coloprini faction, placed severe restrictions on Venetian trade with the mainland. The Coloprini and their allies, anxious to seize power, prepared for a military assault by taking up strategic positions at Padua, Mestre, Ravenna, and on the Adige River. But before the attack could begin, Otto died. Stefano Coloprini, leader of the rebel Venetian faction, died around the same time. Most of the rebels were repatriated, but rancor and suspicion persisted. One day, three of Coloprini's sons were slaughtered by the rival Morosini faction as they made their way home from the Ducal Palace. Doge Menio was eventually forced to abdicate and, like his two immediate predecessors, enter a monastery.[26]

His successor Pietro II Orseolo tried to bring an end to the perpetual violence by banning the incitement of tumults within the Ducal Palace. Part of his effort to pacify society included forging better relations with Emperor Otto III with whom he was particularly close, as well as reaching new agreements with the bishops of Ceneda, Treviso, and Belluno that secured Venetian commercial interests with those nearby territories.[27] In 992, the same year that he signed a new pact with Otto III, Pietro obtained a chrysobull—a decree named for the golden seal attached to it—from the Byzantine emperor Basil II and his co-regent Constantine VIII, which granted Venetian merchants important tariff advantages and protection from abusive officials when trading in Constantinople, in return for Venetian pledges to transport imperial troops to Italy on request.[28] Thus after passing through one of the most tumultuous moments in its history, Venice entered a period of relative stability under Pietro II Orseolo.

Despite these internal divisions and internecine struggles, Venetians in the ninth and tenth centuries were united in their effort to secure control over the Adriatic Sea, particularly the northern section. The doges pursued this goal generation after generation, regardless of whether they came from the Candiano, Orseolo, or other clans, and despite their pro-Byzantine or pro-Carolingian/Ottonian sympathies. Protecting Venetian maritime and trade interests overrode all other concerns.[29]

Competition for control of the Adriatic came from many different fronts. Rival cities bordering the northern gulf aspired to be, like Venice, the entrepôt relaying goods from the eastern Mediterranean to northern and central Europe and vice versa. These included Capodistria and Pola (Pula) on the Istrian peninsula, and Comacchio, a major salt producer, located on the Po delta that could control river traffic.

Others, including various Slavic peoples who had invaded the Balkans in the seventh and eighth centuries and established themselves in the cities along the Dalmatian coast, were vying for control of the middle Adriatic. Like the Venetians, the inhabitants of these cities were engaged in trade, although on a smaller scale. Typically, Venetian ships making their way to Constantinople and other ports in the eastern Mediterranean hugged the eastern shore of the Adriatic. They avoided the western coastline because storms blowing from north or north-east easily ran sailing vessels aground or rendered them unable

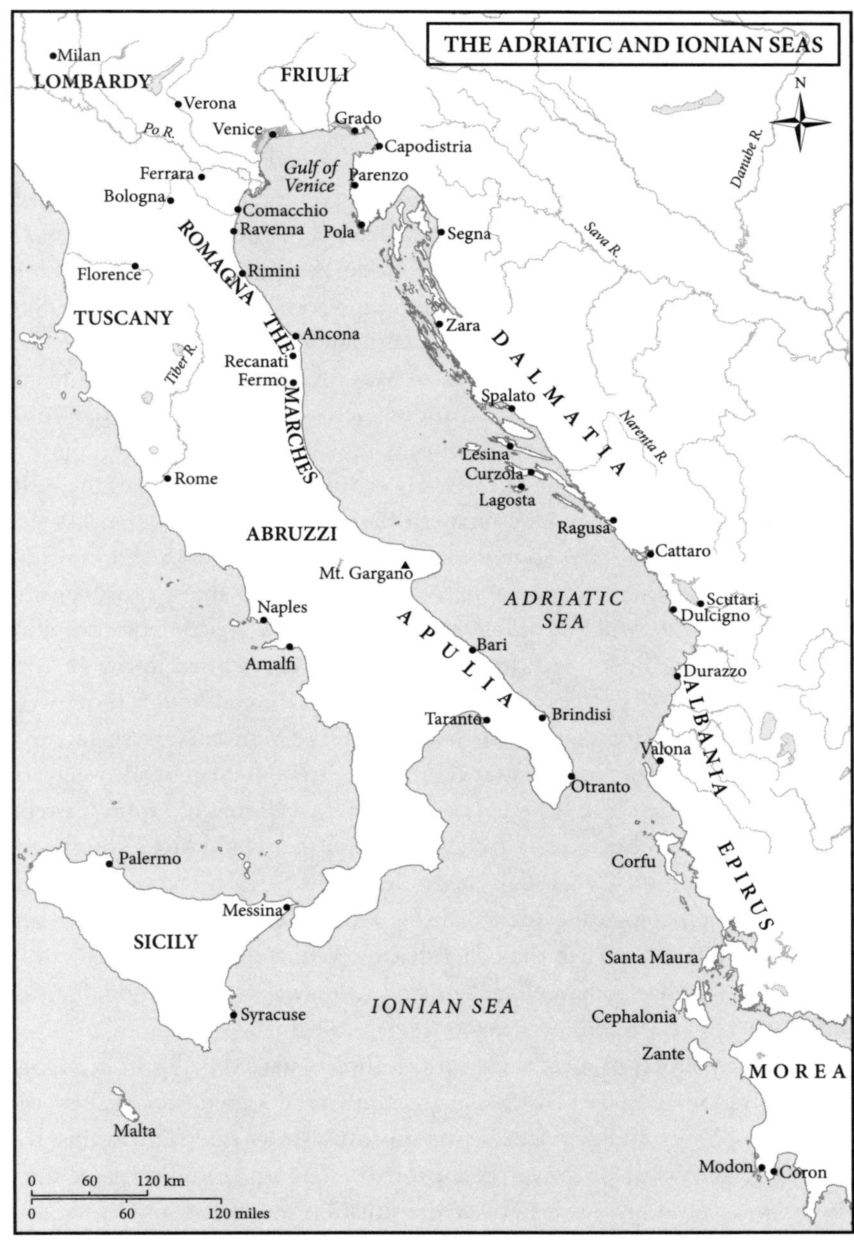

FIGURE 3.3 The Adriatic and Ionian Seas.

to advance. In contrast, the rocky, island-studded eastern coastline—one modern survey counts sixty-six inhabited islands, 659 smaller uninhabited ones and 496 rocks—offered safe havens in storms as well as anchorages for commerce particularly in slaves and for the replenishment of fresh water and other provisions.[30] That same topography provided hideouts and nests for pirates, who were especially prevalent around the mouth of the Narenta River and the nearby islands of Brazza (Brač), Curzola (Korčula), Lesina (Hvar), and Lagosta (Lastova).[31] Pirate raids made passage through the middle Adriatic particularly risky for Venetian shipping. In 846 a group of Slavs even struck as far north as Caorle between Rialto and Grado.

In the lower Adriatic, the Saracens, Muslim adventurers, posed a major threat. They had been rapidly expanding across the entire Mediterranean basin. In 826 a band of Iberian Saracens took Crete. A year later a group originating in Tunisia began their nearly century-long conquest of Sicily. In the 840s they established an emirate in Bari and challenged Byzantium for control of southern Italy. Should they gain control over both shores of the Adriatic, they would then be able to block entry into the sea through the Strait of Otranto which is only forty-five miles wide. Yet their sorties were not confined to the lower Adriatic. In the 840s they raided in the vicinity of Adria and in 875 attacked Grado and Comacchio, although those were the last forays to extend as far north as the Gulf of Venice. Nevertheless, as a precaution against a possible attack on Venice itself by them or the Magyars, Hungarian invaders, the Venetians in 899 built a wall that ran from Castello to Santa Maria Zobenigo and installed a chain that could block ships from entering the Grand Canal. Chronciler John the Deacon recorded this, although no archeological evidence of this wall has ever been found. Perhaps John invented the story in the belief that for Venice to be considered a true *civitas* (city), it had to have, like mainland cities, walls—something that was unnecessary in the middle of a lagoon.[32]

Venetian efforts to meet these various threats started badly. In 839 Doge Pietro Tradonico launched an unsuccessful naval expedition against the Narentan pirates, and then led an even more disastrous campaign against the Saracens, who were able to capture the town of Taranto. A mid-ninth-century Byzantine revival helped to stabilize the situation somewhat, and by 880 the Byzantines had retaken Taranto. For the next century, relations in the lower Adriatic were relatively stable, with the Byzantines controlling southern Italy and the Saracens Sicily. At the same time, the situation in the middle Adriatic worsened. The low point was reached when in 887 Doge Pietro I Candiano, commanding a squadron of twelve ships, was defeated and killed by the Narentans in a naval battle off Macarsca (Makarska). The situation had improved little by 911 when the son of Doge Orso II Partecipazio was held hostage by the king of the Bulgarians, then at war with Byzantium.

The elevation of Pietro II Candiano to the ducal throne in 931 ushered in a more aggressive Adriatic posture on the part of the Venetians, one that proved highly successful. First, he brought Istria to heel. The Istrians, encouraged by their margrave Wintero, had been occupying lands claimed by the patriarch of Grado, sequestering Venetian goods and credit, and harassing Venetian shipping, all in violation of long-standing agreements. Through a combination of economic pressure and military threat, Pietro II forced Capodistria in 932 to accede to a *promissio* (promise) by which the city agreed to restore the recently usurped rights of Venetians and donate to the doge 100 amphoras of wine annually. The following year, Wintero and the rest of Istria agreed to a formal peace treaty. Istria would remain under the margrave and continue as a province of the Kingdom of Italy, but Pietro II had secured Venice's trade and navigation privileges there.[33]

In that same year he turned his attention westward toward Comacchio, which represented an even greater threat to Venice's commercial interests due to its salt production and trade advantages on the Po. The doge used the arrest of some Venetian subjects as the pretext for an assault on this rival city. Its castle was torched and many of the inhabitants massacred. Survivors were brought to Venice where they were forced to swear allegiance. In this way, Venice sought to guarantee its access to the Po and hence to inland trade.[34]

Through these actions, Pietro II Candiano asserted Venetian dominion over the Gulf of Venice. His son Pietro III Candiano would make that domination clear in 944 when he applied an economic blockade against Lupo, patriarch of Aquileia, who was harassing the patriarch of Grado over control of the mouth of the Natisone River. In the end, Lupo agreed not to take up arms against Grado or other Venetian subject lands.[35] Again, Venetian control over the Gulf had been affirmed.

Four years later, in 948, Pietro III launched a flotilla of thirty-three ships against the Dalmatian pirates. As he made his way south, the murder of his grandfather in 887 was surely on his mind. The first foray was unsuccessful, but a second strike forced the Narentans to sign a treaty guaranteeing the Venetians freedom of navigation in return for various gifts. Pietro's action was not in response to an uptick in pirate raids but instead was symptomatic of a more confident and assertive Venetian policy. The treaty ushered in fifty years of relatively good relations between Venice and the Dalmatians.

In 1,000, Doge Pietro II Orseolo made Venetian domination over the middle Adriatic clear to all. He personally led an expedition aimed at suppressing pirates who were harassing not only Venetian trade but also that of the Dalmatian cities themselves. As he proceeded down the coast, he stopped at city after city, all technically under Byzantine dominion, offering protection in return for promises of loyalty. Finally, after reaching an accord with the Prince of Narenta, he isolated the pirates on the islands of Curzola and Lagosta, destroyed their hideouts, and brought them low. On his return to Venice, he assumed the title dux Veneticorum et Dalmaticorum (Duke of the Venetians and Dalmatians).[36] Although the title carried no legal weight since these realms were not incorporated into the Venetian dominion, it signaled Venice's power in the middle Adriatic. Two years later Pietro II Orseolo led an expedition of 100 vessels to assist the Byzantines in their successful effort to protect the Apulian city of Bari from a Saracen siege.

Over the course of the tenth century then, Venice had established its primacy in the Adriatic, though its control lessened the greater the distance from the Gulf of Venice. As Orseolo's expedition along the Dalmatian coast demonstrates, Venice was interested in protecting the movement of ships rather than in acquiring territory. This made sense for an economy increasingly based on the transportation of a variety of goods around the Adriatic and between the eastern Mediterranean and north-central Europe.

Two coin finds—one a hoard uncovered in the foundations of the church of San Lorenzo in 1592; the other specimens discovered in mud excavated along the Rio di Ca' Foscari in the parish of San Tomà in 1934—attest to Venice's precocious development as a point of contact between East and West. The San Lorenzo cache includes more than 400 Arab gold coins minted between 715–6 and 760–61, while the San Tomà find consists of seven Byzantine coins minted between 829 and 842 and one contemporary Arab dirham. They offer mute but compelling testimony to Venice's economic relations with both the Byzantium and Muslim spheres between the eighth and ninth centuries.[37]

Given Venice's status as a Byzantine dependency, its contact with Constantinople is unsurprising. People, goods, and news moved regularly between the two cities. Venetian doges sent their co-regent sons to the eastern capital for imperial sanction, while merchants traveled in search of products, especially precious silks, highly in demand among Western elites. Bishop Liudprand of Cremona, who traveled to Constantinople in 968 on behalf of Emperors Otto I and II, bought luxury silk garments from Venetian and

Amalfitan merchants in the Byzantine capital. Venetian merchants were also acting as couriers carrying letters and news from the Kingdom of Italy, Saxony, and Bavaria to Constantinople.[38] Moving in the opposite direction, Greek workmen and artisans, including stone carvers and mosaicists traveled to Venice, where their handiwork adorned San Marco and other churches. Byzantine shipwrights brought with them knowledge of naval architecture perfected in the eastern Mediterranean. In 840 the emperor sent Theodosius Babutzicus to Venice to supervise the construction of ships to be used against the Saracen occupation of Taranto. The San Tomà coin hoard may have been part of Babutzicus's payroll.[39] Venice's status as a Byzantine province gave its merchants access to ports throughout the eastern imperial realm, including mainland Greece and the Aegean islands as well as the coast of Asia Minor, while the golden bull of 992 gave them a trade advantage over their Italian competitors in Constantinople itself.

Little is known about Venetian ships in this period although in 1002–3 a sizable fleet of warships was sent to assist the Byzantines in protecting Bari. That force was likely recruited from throughout the entire *dogado* from Grado to Cavarzere.[40] Warships were probably modeled on the Byzantine dromon, a galley with two decks of rowers that was also equipped with lateen (triangular) sails, while other ships called *zalandrie*, also based on Byzantine models, were used to transport horses.[41] Compared to the great fleets put to sea by the Saracens, Venetian naval forces remained relatively meager in this period. Merchant ships, which depended entirely on wind for propulsion and did not have crews of oarsmens for defense, sailed only during daylight hours. Because of the danger of pirate attack, ships traveled in convoy until they reached the Ionian Sea at which point, they could sail independently.[42] Flat-bottomed barges and low draft river boats, traveling the Po, Adige, and other watercourses and within the lagoon, vastly outnumbered the ships used for overseas commerce.[43]

As the Arab coins found at San Lorenzo and San Tomà indicate, Venice had extensive trade contact with Muslim centers too, even as the Saracens were contesting Byzantium for control of the eastern Mediterranean.[44] The story of Saint Mark's *translatio* speaks to the presence of Venetian merchants in Alexandria. In return for luxury products like velvets, silks, spices, drugs, precious stones, even pheasant and peacock feathers, the Venetians furnished the Muslims with timber, in abundant supply in the Adriatic region, iron from near Brescia and Carinthia, and weapons, as well perhaps as other items like furs, wax, and livestock that reached Venice via the ancient Amber Trail.[45] Under pressure from Constantinople, Venice agreed in 971 not to supply the Arabs with weapons or timber for ships, but the degree to which its merchants complied is unclear. The same is true of the slave trade. In these centuries, Venetian merchants conducted a lively business in slaves, who were much sought after in the Arab world. Most came from the Balkan interior, where raids produced a steady supply of captives for Venice and cities along the Dalmatian coast. A Venetian order of 960 decreed that ship captains were not to take on board slaves, "either in Venice or in Istria or in Dalmatia or in any other place," but this order was likely violated.[46] It may well be that the emergence of "the European commercial economy" grew out of the slave trade with the Arab world that was centered on Naples, Amalfi, and Venice, with Venice serving as the very epicenter.[47]

If the coin finds point to Venice's economic contacts with the East, then the first coin minted for Venice provides equally compelling evidence of its strong trade connections with the West. Produced around 820, this silver denarius or penny was designed to facilitate trade with Europe which, unlike the Byzantine and Arab worlds, relied on silver currency. One side bore a cross and the name of Emperor Louis the Pious, while on the reverse were inscribed the words "Venecias" or "Venecias moneta." As in so much else, Venice stood quite literally at an intersection, in this case between gold- and silver-based monetary systems.

The pact that the Venetians reached in 840 with Lothar, king of Italy and emperor of the Carolingian Empire, established the terms of the relationship between Venice and its neighbors in the kingdom along an arc of territory running from Istria and Friuli south to Ravenna and Fermo. It granted Venetian merchants freedom to trade along the rivers and in the market towns of the Veneto, the Romagna, and the Marches in return for modest landing fees. For its part, Venice agreed to allow merchants from those territories to trade at various landing stations in the *dogado* on the same terms. The Venetians promised not to use the kingdom as a hunting ground for the slave trade but secured their right to harvest timber and pasture their herds on the mainland. The pact established procedures for the settlement of legal disputes and guaranteed the safe passage of couriers. Both parties agreed to aid one another against the threat of the Slavs. Not long after the pact, Lothar further guaranteed Venetian properties on the mainland.[48]

The pact with Lothar was renewed with slight modifications by subsequent kings until the reign of Otto II, who placed an embargo on Venice. But after his defeat by the Saracens in 983, he renewed the pact and even extended Venetians' trade privileges to include the entire Kingdom of Italy, not just the territories outlined in the original pact.[49] In these years, Venice was especially intent on securing its commercial privileges in the lands immediately bordering the lagoon. In 1000, for example, Pietro II Orseolo wrested significant concessions from the bishop of Treviso, including a third of the income from the city's harbor on the Sile and the right of Venetian merchants to establish shops alongside those of the locals and for the doge to export to Treviso 300 *moggia* (equal to about 2,400 bushels) of salt tax free.[50]

If silks and spices came to Venice from the East, more mundane but equally important products came from these nearby territories. Liudprand of Cremona perfectly captured Venice's intermediary role when in 968 he explained to functionaries in Constantinople how especially fine purple silks were readily available for purchase in the West, despite the fact that they were reserved for high-ranking Byzantine officials and forbidden from export. "Whence do they come to you?" the Byzantines asked him. "Through the Venetian and Amalfitan traders," he replied, "who support their lives with our foodstuffs by bearing such cloth to us."[51] As Liudprand made clear, in exchange for the silks and other Eastern imported goods, the Venetians acquired raw materials they were unable to produce for themselves. For example, Venice imported grain, oil, and timber from Istria—the first two the same products that Ravenna had been requisitioning from Istria in Cassiodorus's time. While truck gardens within the lagoon produced significant amounts of fruits and vegetables, staples such as meat and grain had to come from the *terraferma*.[52] Venice paid for these products with imported goods and with salt, which was used in the preservation of meat and was essential in the diets of both humans and livestock. Salt was being produced on the outer borders of the Rialto settlement (for example, in Castello and Dorsoduro) and especially in the southern part of the lagoon around Chioggia. Powerful families and the great monastic establishments owned these salt pans. Venice also used salt as a weapon. At various times, salt embargos brought recalcitrant neighbors, like the bishops of Treviso and patriarchs of Aquileia, to heel.[53]

Despite all this, the scope and scale of trade during Venice's ducal age should not be overestimated, especially given the paucity of records. While the gains were certainly significant, Venice was not yet the economic powerhouse it would later become. Nevertheless, it is worth asking why, even at this early date, Venice was already outpacing other northern Adriatic towns like Comacchio that enjoyed many of the same geographical advantages. The answer appears to lie in the military expertise of the local elite and especially the doges' ability to meet the naval needs of both the Carolingians and Byzantines. Recall the Byzantine emperor's dispatch of Babutzicus to Venice to help prepare a fleet to sail against the Saracens at Taranto. The Carolingians also called on Venetian naval assistance against the Saracens as well as the Slavs. In return, the Venetians garnered trade privileges that gave them an edge over their north Adriatic competitors. Additionally, they were not hesitant to use their military power to coerce or, in the case of Comacchio, even destroy their neighbors.[54] The early doges frequently personally commanded fleets. Already in Venice's ducal age then, a close collaboration between political and economic leadership was being forged, a pattern that would repeat well into the twentieth century.

Venice's early advances in commerce also impacted society, governance, and administration. In December 982, Doge Tribuno Menio transferred the small island of San Giorgio Maggiore across the Bacino from San Marco to Giovanni Morosini so that he could erect a Benedictine monastery there. The charter granted Morosini and the monks a small church dedicated to Saint George that already existed on the site as well as the surrounding shoals, ponds, vineyards, and mills. It also contained one of the earliest articulations of the composition of Venetian society. Menio stated that he was making the donation with the agreement of "our bishops and the leaders (*primates*) and people (*populus*) of Venice."[55] In addition to the doge and three bishops, 126 men witnessed or signed the document. They included not only men from well-established families—such as Candiano and Orseolo—but also those from families that were only beginning to leave their mark on Venice, including Dandolo, Bragadin, and Contarini. The economic development of the past two centuries had resulted in a considerable expansion of the men who counted in Venetian society. What distinguished them from other European elites whose wealth was tied up almost exclusively in land was the source of their wealth. As the will of Doge Giustiniano Partecipazio made clear, the Venetian elite derived a portion of their riches from trade in which they were directly and personally engaged.

The advancement of new men resonated in the political sphere. Specialists continue to debate what relationship, if any, the old class of tribunes who had served as the leaders of individual settlements within the lagoon had to the *primates*. What is clear is that, starting around the year 900, some men are identified as *iudices* (judges or counselors) who advised the doge and thus represented a first and very imperfect check on ducal power. They may in fact be identical to the *primates*.[56] Regardless, what is noteworthy is the growing number of men with some voice in Venice's affairs, men whose attention and interest were increasingly centered around the Ducal Palace rather than on particular settlements within the lagoon. The *iudices/primates*, along with the doge and the highest ecclesiastical officials, presided over the assembly of the entire community, which also included the *populus*, though they too were men of at least moderate means.[57]

Despite all this, the doges continued to exercise extraordinary power and enjoy many of the perogatives associated with monarchy. The inhabitants of various *dogado* communities owed them donations and services. The residents of Cittanova, for example, had to present the doge with 100 fish annually, as well as gifts of chicken, bread, and wine whenever he went hunting in the Livenza River valley. The fishermen and hunters of Dorsoduro had to offer an annual tribute of fish as well as perform special services. The millers who worked the mills belonging to the monastery of San Giorgio Maggiore were required to perform guard duty at the Ducal Palace. While some of these gifts were useful in sustaining the ducal household, others were purely symbolic as in the case of the head and feet of every boar taken that the inhabitants of Cittanova owed the doge in return for their hunting privileges. Such gifts and services served to bind symbolically the various communities of the *dogado* together through the person of the doge.[58]

Yet the monarchical tendencies of the dogeship were soon to be put in check as Venice evolved from a quasi-hereditary ducal regime into a communal or republican one. That change was precipitated by a rapid acceleration of the economy and Venice's assumption of an ever-larger role in the wider Mediterranean Sea. Radical changes, both commercial and political, were afoot.

4

Between Empires and Beyond-the-Sea

IN DECEMBER 1125, the children of the late Pietro Stagnario—his sons Giovenale, a chaplain at San Marco, and Orio, and his daughters Dorotea and Froiza, a nun at San Lorenzo—fulfilled one of the clauses in their father's last will and testament. Acting on his testamentary wishes, they had a notary draw up a charter freeing Pietro's Croatian slave Dobramiro. According to the charter, Pietro was motivated by divine love and the desire to earn merit for his soul. Dobramiro, for his part, was freed from all servile ties and guaranteed the protection of the law. Giovenale and Orio signed the charter while Dorotea and Froiza, who were illiterate, made their marks on it. Three male witnesses also signed the manumission.[1]

This was not the only appearance of Dobramiro in the sparse records that have survived from twelfth-century Venice. In June 1128, two men went before the notary Orso to testify that a month earlier Romano, a priest and chaplain of San Marco, had loaned to the former enslaved man, now identified as Dobramiro the Dalmatian of the parish of San Provolo, 100 lire for a year at 20 percent interest.[2] Since gaining his freedom, Dobramiro had gotten involved in trade, and over the next few years his business activities, like those of Venice itself, expanded and prospered. In 1135 he was in Corinth where he was dealing in flax and the shipment of olive oil from Sparta to Alexandria. A year after that, he borrowed money that was to be repaid thirty days after the arrival of merchant ships traveling from Corinth to Constantinople. Other elements of his life had changed as well. He had taken his former owner's last name as his own, referring to himself as Dobramiro Stagnario da (from) Dalmatia or simply as Dobramiro Stagnario.[3] He had also sired a son Pangrazio.

Like his father before him, Pangrazio became actively involved in Venice's trade in the eastern Mediterranean. His fortunes progressed to the point that he even served as the *nauclerus* (shipping master) on voyages to

Constantinople and Acre.[4] The *nauclerus* was, along with the ship's scribe, one of the two most important officers on board a merchant vessel, with responsibility not only to the ship's owners, but also to the crew and Venetian government.[5] As *nauclerus*, Pangrazio also likely owned a share of the cargo. His appointment to these posts is a measure of the trust that others placed in him and his increasing fortunes.

Pangrazio fathered three sons, Giovanni, Domenico, and Zaccaria, the latter of whom became one of the wealthiest men in Venice. Zaccaria, who like Pangrazio lived in the precinct of San Giovanni Evangelista, had a shop at Rialto that sold spices and other goods, and property in the Padovano (the countryside around Padua) from which he and his father garnered grain, wine, flax, and other agricultural products in rent.[6] By no means a stay-at-home businessman, he established himself in Constantinople following the conquest of the city by Westerners in the Fourth Crusade. In 1207 he served as councilor in the recently established Venetian colonial government there and in the same year got one of the highest assessments for a forced loan which the home government imposed on its wealthy citizens. He was even related by marriage to the venerable Trevisan family. After September 1219 he disappears from the record. The Stagnario (or Staniario) family, however, continued to prosper, and by the fourteenth century it had been accepted into the ranks of Venice's nobility.[7]

The story of the formerly enslaved Dobramiro Stagnario and his progeny has often been taken as emblematic of Venice itself in the years from the eleventh to the early thirteenth centuries. One historian has said of Zaccaria that he "represented the new man in Venice who climbed to the top because of his business skills."[8] He and his contemporaries were major participants in what is often referred to as the Commercial Revolution of the Middle Ages by which the city emerged as the preeminent mercantile power in the eastern Mediterranean. Venice's success depended on the willingness of individual merchants to take risks and on a concerted and sustained effort by the government to maximize the advantages that geography had bestowed upon the city by vigorously protecting and promoting its merchants' trading interests in the Italian hinterland, the Adriatic, and beyond. To this end, Venice continued its delicate balancing act between the Holy Roman Empire in the West and the Byzantine empire in the East. These efforts were complicated by the emergence of two new powers whose interests competed with those of Venice in the Adriatic—the Norman kings of Sicily and the kings of Hungary—as well as by the city's more direct engagement with affairs in the eastern Mediterranean following the First Crusade.

Dobramiro and his lineage indeed symbolize the great changes taking place in Venice in these centuries, but they should not be made to serve a triumphalist narrative of capitalism's success or Venetian exceptionalism. Dobramiro had an advantage that most men did not. An act drawn up by Pietro Stagnario's daughter Dorotea indicates that Pietro had given Dobramiro a gold ring.[9] This suggests there was a strong emotional attachment between the men that was not typical of most master/enslaved relationships. Perhaps Dobramiro had accompanied Pietro on his own trading ventures and the knowledge that he garnered on those voyages is what allowed him to make such a rapid transition from slave to businessman. Most enslaved persons were never so lucky. At worst they died in bondage; at best they moved into the ranks of the free laboring classes. In addition, Dobramiro was an immigrant—in his case a coerced one. He was one of many thousands of immigrants who shaped Venice throughout its history. These newcomers were products both of Venetian society and their societies of origin. The mixing of experiences, cultures, languages, and customs, together with consciously pursued governmental policies, explains the extraordinary changes taking place in Venice in these centuries, not some innate and quintessentially Venetian aptitude for business.

Around the year 1000, the economy of Europe experienced a period of intense growth that would last for nearly three centuries. Historians disagree about the preconditions for this commercial expansion. A warming of the climate in northern Europe—known as the Medieval Warm Period or Medieval Climate Optimum (c. 950–c. 1300)—which made for a longer growing season; the adoption of new farming techniques; the introduction of innovative technologies, especially in the use of water and wind power; and a greater sense of security fostered by the cessation of periodic raids by Vikings, Magyars, and Saracens, have all been posited as explanations for a rise in agricultural yields. Peasants were no longer producing barely enough food to survive but also a surplus they could use to trade for themselves or their noble landlords skimmed off in the form of increased rents. With that greater income, European nobles had the means to buy luxury products from the eastern Mediterranean that the Italian cities, first Venice and Amalfi, then Pisa and Genoa, were importing. Growing demand fostered increasing supply.[10]

The problem that Venetian merchants, like their counterparts elsewhere, faced was a chronic shortage of capital. Where and how could they find the money to fund their voyages and purchase the goods that consumers wanted? This need for cash led to a variety of innovative business arrangements, many of which derived from Byzantine or Muslim commercial precedents. The simplest way to raise capital was through a loan. In 1136, for example, Dobramiro borrowed forty hyperpers (the hyperper was a Byzantine gold coin) in Corinth from Giovanni da Canal and agreed to repay him fifty hyperpers within thirty days of the arrival of the convoys from Corinth in Constantinople.[11] Twenty percent, as in this case, was the usual interest rate for such loans and indicates just how scarce capital was that lenders could command such high rates. Two generations later, Dobramiro's grandson Zaccaria took advantage of another lending arrangement referred to as a loan for trading. In June 1191, he borrowed 1,000 lire from Giovanni Ghisi to use in his shop at Rialto and to trade "here in Venice." The arrangement was to last a year or more.[12]

The more popular way to raise capital in these centuries was through a temporary partnership called a *colleganza*. In the classic form of this arrangement the stay-at-home partner supplied all the capital and received three-fourths of the profit, while the traveling partner supplied his labor and got one-fourth of the profit. If the traveling partner put up some of the capital, then any profit was divided proportionally. For example, in 1073 Giovanni Lissado, a resident in the part of Venice known as Luprio, reached a *colleganza* arrangement with Sevasto Orefice. Sevasto put up 200 lire, while Giovanni invested 100. With their combined capital of 300 lire, they purchased two shares of the ship that Gosmiro da Molin was taking on a commercial voyage to Thebes. Giovanni agreed to travel with the ship and, in the words of the contract, "work this entire [capital] and to strive the best way I can." Any profit that derived from the voyage was to be divided equally because, although Giovanni put up a lesser share of the money, he supplied all the labor.[13] Since there was nothing to prevent a traveling partner from making simultaneous arrangements with several lenders, he could accumulate significant capital for a venture. Similarly, a lender could form partnerships with multiple men undertaking different voyages and in so doing diversify his investments and minimize his risk. At the time of his death in 1268 Doge Ranieri Zeno was a partner in 132 *colleganza* contracts. The money invested in those contracts constituted nearly one-half of his total wealth. Although in some cases, he suffered a loss (such as in a shipwreck), the average return was around 10 percent.[14]

While the wealthy and powerful like Zeno made extensive use of *colleganze*, those of more modest means could also utilize them. Women, especially widows, invested some of their dowry money or bequests left to them by their husbands or other kin in these contracts.[15] *Colleganze* offered a way for them to participate in the booming commercial sector and grow their capital. More significantly, they provided a means whereby poor men—like Dobramiro at the time of his manumission—with little or no capital but a willingness to undertake the hardships and dangers of overseas voyages could gain a foothold in the new economy. *Colleganze* were a vehicle for upward economic and social mobility, and the profits were great enough in these centuries that many were willing to take the risk. They would continue to increase in popularity until the fourteenth century.[16]

Entering a *colleganza* arrangement involved a lender's extension of both capital and trust. After all, she or he was lending money to someone who would be gone for months or even a year or more and who would, given the nature of communication at the time, be independently making decisions regarding market conditions and what sorts of commodities to purchase. Although most contracts included penalties for noncompliance, the lender was hazarding his or her money based on an assessment of the traveling partner's character and reliability. Any number of factors, including mutual friendships, testimonials of other merchants, and a record of previously successful outcomes, factored into the choice of partners.[17]

Another way to accumulate capital while minimizing the danger of dealing with strangers was to invest with family members. In Venice, brothers frequently held both their movable and immovable wealth in common, in an arrangement known as a *fraterna compagnia* (fraternal company) or simply a *fraterna*. In 1200, for example, the brothers Pietro, Giacomo, and Filippo da Molin held in common not only lands and houses but also a variety of *colleganze*, commission contracts, and other receipts. Living together in a family palace and sharing the costs of ships were other means by which brothers could economize on their expenses and save capital for use in trade.[18]

The first compilation of Venetian civil statutes, which dates to the reign of Doge Enrico Dandolo (1192–1205), contains numerous clauses dealing with such commercial matters as debts and *colleganze*, losses due to shipwreck or theft of a ship, and payments made overseas.[19] The compilation highlights the central place that commerce had assumed in Venetian life and the concerns of merchants. Writing in the thirteenth century, Venetian chronicler Martino da Canal noted the overwhelmingly mercantile character of his native city saying, "Goods flow through this noble city like water from a spring. . . . [F]rom everywhere goods arrive as do merchants, who buy the merchandise they desire and have it transported to their homelands."[20]

Venetian merchants dealt in a remarkable variety of goods. They imported spices, especially pepper, cinnamon, and cloves, to feed a growing Western hunger for these exotic ingredients that were used in foods, medicines, and perfumes. They tried to meet the demand for fine silk and other fabrics that were a Constantinopolitan specialty. But there was also a market north of the Alps for bulkier Mediterranean items like olive oil and figs, as well as for linen cloth that was woven in northern Italian towns. Egyptian alum, which was used to set dye in fabrics, was another much sought after import.

For their part, buyers in the eastern Mediterranean were most interested in purchasing raw materials from the West. Mines in parts of Germany and northern Italy produced gold, silver, iron, and copper that were in short supply in the East. Timber and pitch for shipbuilding were especially scarce and much sought after. Indeed, the chronic shortage of such materials gave the Venetian navy a significant advantage over the Muslim fleet of the Fatimids in Egypt and helps explain how Venice became the predominant naval power in the eastern Mediterranean, following the battle of Ascalon off the coast of Palestine in 1123. Furs and hides were other Western raw materials that had a ready market in the East, as did cotton cloth produced in north Italian towns.[21] Slave-trading, which had helped fuel Venetian trade between the eighth and tenth centuries, slowed as the Balkans and northeastern Europe were Christianized and for that reason were no longer considered legitimate slave-hunting grounds. But the trade would pick up again in the thirteenth century when the Venetians gained access to the Black Sea and slaves from Russia.[22]

Salt remained Venice's most important indigenous product, although production increasingly shifted around the turn of the twelfth century from the northern part of the lagoon (the area around Venice, Torcello, and Murano) to Chioggia in the southern part of the *dogado*, which had easier access to the Po and Adige rivers and hence to the townspeople of northern Italy and the mainland livestock herds that were the primary consumers of Venetian salt. Salt was an important source of income for wealthy Venetian families. As great families replaced monasteries as the primary proprietors of saltworks, they formed a "salt patriciate."[23] By way of example, the sons of Doge Sebastiano Ziani, who were joined together in a *fraterna* between 1170 and 1186, acquired forty-eight salt pans distributed among various saltworks. Wealthy men would contract with builders to construct saltworks consisting of numerous salt pans, which were then rented out to salt workers. The rent was based on the harvest of a set number of days of salt extraction.[24] Salt was also an important source of governmental revenue and a powerful weapon in Venice's ongoing conflicts with mainland towns.

In order to feed its burgeoning population, Venice had to import significant amounts of food, especially cereals. In times of drought and famine, Venice's maritime resources gave it a significant advantage over mainland cities in that its merchants could travel to distant ports, such as those of Sicily or Greece, in search of grain.

The typical merchant ship of this era, referred to as a *navis*, was a round ship and was the property of a single owner or more often a group that jointly financed its construction. The co-owners utilized the cargo space themselves or rented out portions of it to others. The *navis* was equipped with two masts that were rigged with lateen sails; had two decks, a stern castle and forecastle; and was steered with a side rudder. In harbor, it was secured with between ten and twenty anchors, which at the end of the eleventh and early twelfth centuries were rented from their owners for the duration of a voyage.[25] In 1039, for example, a widow named Penelda rented an anchor to Dominicus de Gemino; in 1098 Giovanni Moyranesego, parish priest of San Bartolomeo, rented one to Pietro Iubano from Cannaregio. Commonly made of iron or less frequently of stone, anchors represented a significant investment of capital and even appeared occasionally as items in women's dowries.[26] A *navis* normally carried about 200 tons of cargo in its hold. To protect against pirates and enemy ships, vessels often sailed in convoy, although they were not required to do so. Crews were composed of freemen. Eight to ten years was the lifespan for most round ships. Shipworms, which bored into the wood below the waterline and weakened the integrity of the planking, limited the life expectancy of ships and substantially contributed to maintenance costs as hulls had to be exposed, scraped, and new coats of pitch applied. The worms were yet another environmental factor influencing Venice's maritime fortunes.[27]

The career of traveling merchant Romano Mairano, who was active in the second half of the twelfth century, highlights both the opportunities and perils that Venetian merchants faced in this period. From an apparently modest background, Mairano first appears in 1150 when he repaid a loan in Constantinople. For the next several years, he, like many Venetians, made the Byzantine capital his base of operation. He financed his activities through loans and *colleganze* (as well as the financial backing of his father-in-law) and dealt in commodities like lumber which he shipped to Constantinople. In 1156 he was serving as the *nauclerus* on a vessel traveling between Constantinople and Smryna (Izmir) on the coast of Anatolia. He gradually extended his trade horizons to include Crete, the Crusader States (Western-controlled territories

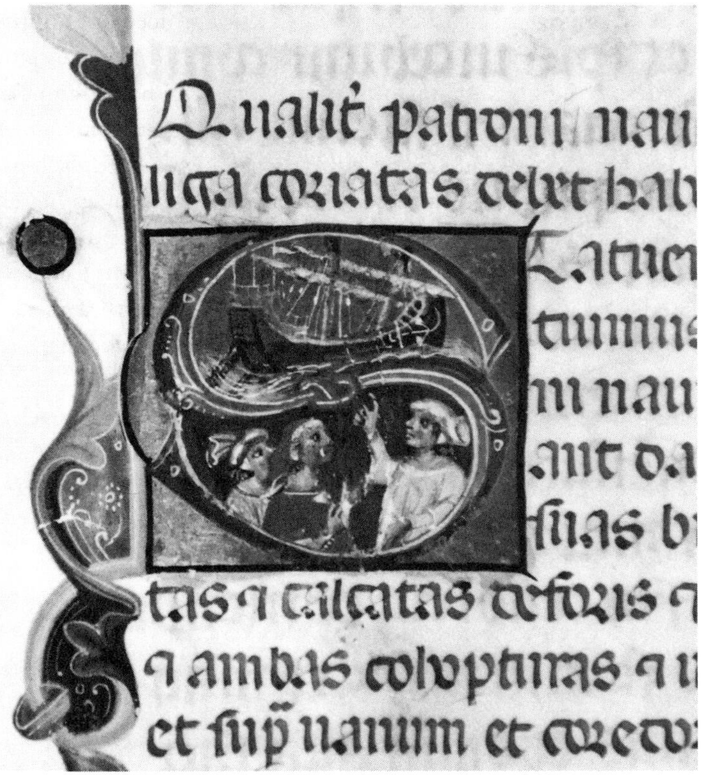

FIGURE 4.1 Two-masted, Lateen-rigged Merchant Round Ship in the illuminated initial "S" in the manuscript *Capitolarium nauticum pro navis*, c. 1255. Biblioteca Querini-Stampalia Ms. Cl. IV Cod. 1 (Mss = 147), folio 84recto. Fondazione Querini-Stampalia, Venice.

in Syria, Lebanon, and Palestine acquired during the First Crusade), and Alexandria and grew wealthy from high profit margins. In 1167, for example, the eight men who loaned him money for a voyage between Constantinople and Alexandria got an astonishing average return of nearly 45 percent. The range of men who were willing to extend him credit was wide and included future doge Sebastiano Ziani, the richest man in Venice. Mairano also became part owner of two ships.

However, the vicissitudes of the market soon became clear. During a period of increasing tension between the Venetians and Byzantines, Mairano gambled on a speedy restoration of good relations. In 1169 he reached an agreement with the patriarch of Grado to oversee for six years the patriarchate's properties and privileges in Constantinople in return for an annual payment of 500 lire. Among the patriarch's privileges was a monopoly on the use of weights and measures and as every transaction had to be weighed, this amounted to a significant income. At the same time, Mairano borrowed heavily from other investors, including Sebastiano Ziani. Then catastrophe struck, as relations between Venice and Byzantium worsened. In March 1171, Emperor Manuel Comnenus ordered the arrest of all Venetian merchants in the capital. Mairano escaped and barely managed to save his newly built ship, the *Maiorando*, from being set afire by the Greeks. But the concessions he had rented from the patriarch were worthless once trade with Constantinople ceased. Still his lenders had to be repaid. Only in 1183 did he manage to pay off the final debt.

Mairano did so by shifting his activities from Constantinople to Alexandria, the Crusader States, and even Messina where Venice had reached an accord with its one-time enemy, the Norman kings of Sicily. In Egypt, he traded in pepper and alum. Always on the lookout for new opportunities, he decided in 1177 to dispatch his new ship to Ceuta in present-day Morocco or to Bougie (Béjaïa) in present-day Algeria. This was unusual since, following the Arab conquest of Sicily in the ninth century, the Venetians had largely avoided the risky western Mediterranean routes and focused instead on Byzantium and the Levant.[28] However, this venture demonstrates that, despite his recent setbacks in Constantinople, Mairano had not lost his penchant for taking chances and seeking new business opportunities. He did not personally sail with the ship which was to be sold upon reaching its destination.

Meanwhile Mairano continued traveling in the eastern Mediterranean, calling in various ports including in Lebanon and Egypt. In 1184, he secured a loan from Pietro Corner, to be repaid with a shipment of pepper. Mairano put up as surety one-half of another new ship that he was having built at the time in a private shipyard in the parish of San Luca. By 1190 he was even back in Constantinople. In one of his last financial dealings, Mairano got a receipt in May 1200 acknowledging that a loan he had procured from the late Pangrazio Michiel had been repaid, along with a share of the profit. Mairano had not utilized the money himself; instead, he had entrusted it to his son Giovanni who used it while on a voyage to Alexandria. After fifty years traveling the Mediterranean, Mairano was allowing the next generation of his family to endure the hardships of travel. However, future generations did not enjoy the benefits of his lifetime of labor since the family died out soon thereafter.[29]

The business success of the Stagnario family and Romano Mairano stemmed from their willingness to work hard, take risks, seek out economic opportunities wherever they might present themselves, and frankly, to enjoy good luck. In no small measure it also resulted from the extraordinary economic advantages that Venetian merchants received in 1082 as concessions from the Byzantine emperor Alexius I Comnenus. In a chrysobull of that year, Alexius made a number of outright grants to the Venetians. Both the doge and the patriarch of Grado received monetary stipends as well as honorific titles that were to be enjoyed in perpetuity. The church of San Marco was awarded three gold coins a year that were to be exacted from each of the properties owned by the Amalfitans in the empire; and twenty pounds of gold were to be awarded annually to Venetian churches. The Venetians got their own neighborhood or quarter in Constantinople. It included shops, houses, a bakery, warehouses, and the church of Saint Akindynos in the Perama market district, as well as three wharves on the Golden Horn, the city's harbor.[30] In this way the Venetians gained a toehold in Constantinople, the largest city by far in the Christian Mediterranean. A major center of trade and silk manufacturing, Constantinople was also rich in churches, saints' relics, and antique sculptures. It enjoyed unparalleled cultural cachet as the "New Rome" and a Christian one at that. In addition to the Constantinopolitan quarter, the Venetians received the church of Saint Andrew in Durazzo (Durrës) and its income. By far the most important provision was the one granting the Venetians extraordinary trade privileges. They were exempted from all customs duties, taxes, and other fees normally due for trading anywhere in the empire, except Crete, Cyprus, and the Black Sea, regardless of the kind of merchandise involved. Furthermore, anyone who challenged the provisions of the chrysobull would face a stiff fine.[31]

This chrysobull gave Venetian merchants a significant economic advantage not only over the Amalfitans, Pisans, and Genoese, but even over Greek merchants themselves. The exemptions from taxes and duties meant that they could consistently undercut their competitors and dominate trade. The Venetians enjoyed these advantages across nearly the entire empire, from Syria to the western Balkans.[32] The agreement sparked Venice's economic takeoff and allowed its merchants over time to perfect a triangular trade between Venice, Constantinople, and Alexandria, laying the foundations for Venice's economic greatness.

In addition, the grant of a section of the city and wharves in Constantinople marked the beginning of Venice's overseas possessions, which would last until the end of the Republic in 1797.[33] Rather than supervising these possessions itself, the Venetian government soon decided to hand over their administration to various ecclesiastical institutions in Venice. One section of the Venetian quarter was entrusted to the church of San Nicolò on the Lido while the rest of the quarter and two wharves were given to San Giorgio Maggiore. In 1107 the church of Saint Akindynos, the bakery, and all the taverns in the district were granted to the patriarchate of Grado. Only the largest wharf remained in governmental hands. By entrusting these possessions to ecclesiastical institutions, the government secured for them a source of revenue. In return, it could rely on the clergy to oversee their supervision. Officials may also have hoped that they were protecting these properties from possible confiscation since it was considered illegal in the West for laymen to expropriate church property. However, the same view did not prevail in the East, and Emperor Alexius no doubt saw the property grants as conditional.[34]

Alexius's reasoning in making such extraordinary concessions to the Venetians lies in the dire international political situation in which the empire found itself. Following the death of Emperor Basil II in 1025, Byzantium entered a long period in which civil authority and the power of the emperor declined and that of the aristocracy grew. The system of military districts known as themes broke down, and revenue fell as tax collection was farmed out to private individuals. Additionally, the empire faced enemies on all sides. By the 1050s Byzantine authority over the western Balkans was being challenged by the Croatians. In 1059 the Croat Cresimir IV took the title king of Croatia and Dalmatia and asserted his authority over Zara, and a decade later the Byzantines ceded maritime Dalmatia to the Croat kingdom. They did so in large part because they faced more serious and dangerous threats on their northern and eastern frontiers. In the north, various Turkic tribes, including the Pechenegs, Cumans, and Oghuzes, were infiltrating the empire along its extensive Danube frontier. And in the east, the Seljuk Turks were on the advance. In 1065 they wrested Armenia from the empire, and then in August 1071 they defeated the Byzantines in the Battle of Manzikert. With that defeat, "the gates of Asia Minor were wide open for the Seljuqs [*sic*] to march in and occupy the heartland of the Byzantine Empire."[35]

In that same disastrous year for the Byzantines, the city of Bari in southern Italy fell to the Normans. These knights from Normandy, descendants of the Vikings, had begun turning up in southern Italy as pilgrims and mercenaries for the Byzantines and Lombards beginning around 1000; and by the 1040s they had managed to gain control over much of Apulia. Under their brilliant and energetic leader Robert Guiscard their advance accelerated. Guiscard found an ally in the papacy, which was increasingly at odds with the Holy

Roman emperor over the papacy's efforts to reform the church by limiting lay control. In 1059 the pope invested Guiscard as Duke of Apulia and Calabria and future lord of Sicily. In 1061 Guiscard began the Norman conquest of Sicily, which was still in Arab (Saracen) hands. Palermo fell in 1071, although Noto, the last Arab stronghold, did not surrender until 1091.

Guiscard's ambitions went beyond southern Italy and Sicily to the Byzantine empire itself. With the support of the pope he launched an invasion in May 1081. His plan was to take the town of Durazzo on the Albanian coast and then follow the ancient Roman Via Egnatia to Thessalonica and ultimately to Constantinople itself. The Venetians were particularly alarmed since, as had been the case with the Saracens two centuries earlier, hostile control of both shores of the southern Adriatic could effectively strangle their trade. They had to protect the natural waterway that was their lifeblood and so, when Alexius asked Doge Domenico Silvo for naval assistance, the doge personally led a fleet consisting of fourteen warships and forty-five support vessels to Durazzo. The Venetian fleet defeated the Norman navy. As William of Apulia, the author of a poem recounting the deeds of Guiscard, remarked of the Venetians, "No people is more valiant than them in naval combat or in the art of navigation."[36] But the Byzantine army, which was led by Alexius himself, was unable to prevent the city from falling to the Normans in 1082.

When Guiscard was summoned back to Italy by Pope Gregory VII, who was being threatened by the Holy Roman emperor Henry IV, his son Bohemond continued the Normans' eastward push. Over the next two years, the Venetians undertook new naval expeditions to Durazzo and Corfu, which they retook from the Normans. In the meantime, the Byzantine army had slowed the Normans' overland advance. But when Guiscard returned in 1084, his navy inflicted a stunning and disastrous defeat on the combined Veneto/Byzantine squadron and recaptured Corfu. Many Venetians were taken prisoner or died (Anna Comnena, the emperor's daughter, put the number of casualties at 13,000), and nine warships were lost. Doge Silvo was made to pay for this debacle. He was forced to abdicate and take monastic vows. The Venetians elected Vitale Falier in his place. A full reprieve from the Norman threat only arrived with Guiscard's unexpected death from disease in July 1085. The chrysobull of 1082 was Alexius's reward to the Venetians for their pledge of assistance during the Norman emergency and an indication of just how dependent Byzantium had become on the Venetian navy.[37]

Venice's relations with its more immediate neighbor, the Holy Roman Empire, had been fraught for much of the eleventh century but were resolved in 1095 with a pact that in many ways served as a Western complement to

Alexius's chrysobull. The source of conflict was the never-ending dispute between Aquileia and Grado. Emperor Conrad II was especially hostile to Venice and wanted to subjugate it. He supported the patriarch of Aquileia Poppone, who in 1044 attacked and devastated Grado. Conrad refused to renew the usual treaty with Venice. However, over the succeeding decades relations between Venice and the empire gradually improved due to their common interest in keeping the Normans out of the Adriatic. In the pact of 1095 Henry IV made a significant concession to the Venetians. They retained the right to travel by land or river anywhere in the Kingdom of Italy, while residents of the kingdom could travel only as far as Venice and not elsewhere in the *dogado* to do business. The clause effectively designated Venice as the required port of call for the kingdom's merchants. This concentrated trade at Rialto.[38] Venice now enjoyed extraordinary commercial advantages from both empires.

The First Crusade, which was preached by pope Urban II the same year as the pact with Henry IV, further projected Venetian naval and commercial power into the eastern Mediterranean. Urban called on the knights of western Europe to assemble in Constantinople and then free the Holy Land, control of which was at the time being contested by the Seljuks Turks and the Fatimid caliphs of Egypt. The Venetians' participation in the crusade, however, was late in coming and only half-hearted since they recognized that the movement of vast numbers of Westerners to the East was likely to allow their competitors, the Pisans and the Genoese, to gain a stronger foothold in a region where they already enjoyed trade advantages. They also feared disruption of their lucrative trade with Fatimid Egypt.

When the swarm of western knights arrived in the Byzantine capital, Alexius did his best to hurry them on their way after extracting from them a loyalty oath and a promise to restore to the empire the lands they captured from the Turks. A combined Byzantine and crusader force managed to take Nicaea. While the emperor's troops engaged in mopping up operations in the region, the crusaders continued their march toward Jerusalem. But the lack of accord between the Greeks and the crusaders became apparent when Guiscard's son Bohemond seized the Syrian town of Antioch for himself and refused to cede it to Alexius. The other crusaders soldiered on toward Jerusalem and managed to capture it in July 1099. In addition to the principality of Antioch, three other Crusader States were established: the County of Edessa, the County of Tripoli, and the Kingdom of Jerusalem. Godfrey de Bouillon was elected king, although his official title was defender of the Holy Sepulcher. He held the kingdom in grant from the church, having done

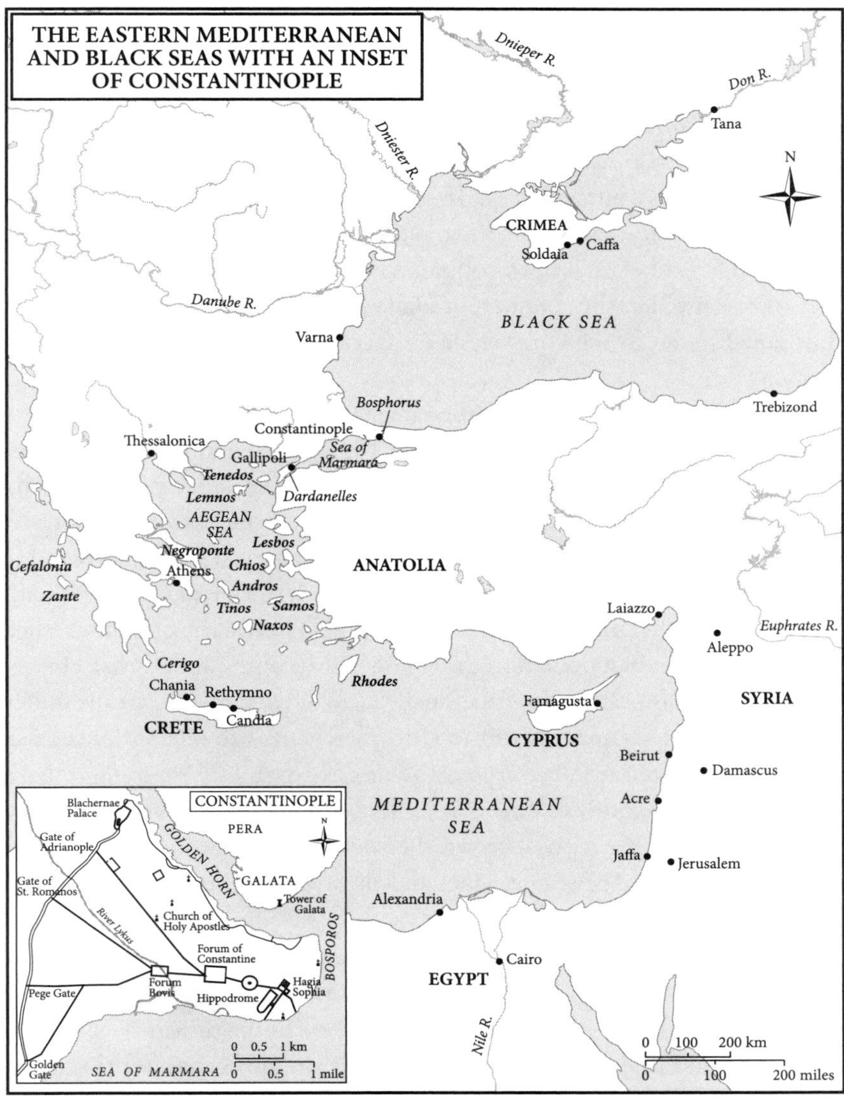

FIGURE 4.2 The Eastern Mediterranean and Black Seas with an inset of Constantinople.

homage to the pope's representative, Daimbert, archbishop of Pisa and Latin patriarch of Jerusalem.[39] Westerners referred to the Crusaders States collectively as Outremer (Beyond- or Over-the Sea).

Not until the summer of 1099, after the Pisans and Genoese had earned commercial privileges for their efforts in aiding the crusaders, did the Venetians decide to act. A flotilla set off under the command of the doge

Vitale I Michiel's son Giovanni and the bishop of Castello Enrico Contarini. They wintered on Rhodes, where they managed to capture numerous Pisan ships. In the spring, they set sail for Outremer, after stopping at Myra in southern Anatolia to purloin the relics of Saint Nicholas. They arrived in Jaffa (Tel Aviv) in June 1100 and agreed to assist Godfrey de Bouillon in his effort to secure the coast, but at a price. In return for two months' assistance, they expected free trade in his realm, a marketplace and church in each city already taken, and a third of each town conquered with their assistance. In the event, they only assisted in the conquest of Haifa before their contract expired and they sailed home, arriving in Venice on December 6, 1100, Saint Nicholas's feast day.[40]

The commercial gains that Venetian merchants secured because of the First Crusade were relatively modest since Byzantium and Egypt, rather than Syria and Palestine, remained their preferred ports of call. By contrast, the acquisition of Nicholas's relics was a major coup. Domestically it mattered because Nicholas, who had lived in the fourth century, was the patron saint of sailors. According to legend, while making a pilgrimage to the Holy Land, Nicholas saved the ship on which he was sailing. As a seafaring nation, Venice naturally coveted a supernatural protector for its ships and crews. His arrival in Venice also carried international weight since Bari, at the time under Norman control, claimed that in 1087 its merchants had secured Nicholas's body and deposited it in the crypt of their cathedral.[41] By claiming to have discovered the real body of Nicholas in Myra (the Baresi had been duped by an imposter), the Venetians asserted that they had received divine sanction for their control of Adriatic sea lanes and the Apulian grain trade against an important south Italian rival.[42]

The Venetians enshrined Nicholas's relics in the Benedictine monastery of San Nicolò on the Lido, close to the opening to the Adriatic that is referred to either as the Bocca del Lido (Lido mouth) or Bocca di San Nicolò (San Nicolò mouth). The monastery had been built and dedicated to the saint in 1053. Its location at the boundary between open sea and lagoon, Venice and abroad, was charged with meaning. For outgoing ships, San Nicolò was their last glimpse of Venice. For returning ships, arrival at San Nicolò meant that they had made it safely home. San Nicolò served as one of the most important entryways to wall-less Venice. Visiting dignitaries were often met there to begin their ceremonial advent into the city. It served as well as the setting for important civic rites and ceremonies. Until 1172 it was the place where newly elected doges were acclaimed and where every spring the sailing season commenced with a blessing of the sea. Devotion to Nicholas united Venetians across social and geographical boundaries. The Ducal Palace housed a chapel dedicated to him, while the parish of San Nicolò dei Mendicoli, a community of fishermen, also enjoyed his patronage. With the parish at the far western edge of Venice, the monastery on the Lido at the eastern extreme, and the Ducal Palace chapel in between, sites dedicated to Nicholas formed an axis radiating his marine protection across the city.[43]

The two decades following the First Crusade saw little Venetian involvement in Outremer because it had to contend with the ongoing Norman threat to the Adriatic as well as the king of Hungary who took control of Croatia and Dalmatia. In the meantime, the Genoese had established trading posts in Acre and elsewhere, and in 1111 Alexius rewarded the Pisans with their own chrysobull granting them trade privileges in the empire and a wharf and quarters in Constantinople. The Venetians under the command of Doge Domenico Michiel did win a major victory over the Egyptian navy off the coast of Ascalon in 1123 and assisted in the capture of Tyre in 1124. However, while returning to Venice they plundered various Greek cities since in 1119 Alexius's successor, his son John II Comnenus, had refused to renew the privileges of Alexius's chrysobull. Among the treasures that the Venetians looted from the Greeks were the relics of Saint Isidore, stolen from Chios. Even before relations soured, the Venetians had offended the Greeks by making off with the relics of Saint Stephen the first martyr from a church in Constantinople and depositing them at the monastery of San Giorgio Maggiore. And in 1126 they looted the relics of Saint Donatus of Epirus from Cephalonia and enshrined them in the church of Santa Maria on Murano, which they rededicated as Santi Maria e Donato. Under pressure, John renewed the chrysobull in August 1126 that soon included access to Crete and Cyprus, important jumping-off points for trade with Egypt and Outremer, respectively.[44]

A Norman resurgence is what had drawn Venice and Constantinople together again. In 1127 Robert Guiscard's nephew Roger, count of Sicily, acquired the Norman lands in southern Italy. In 1130 the pope named him king of Sicily, a realm which he held in vassalage from the pontiff. Utilizing the best elements of Greek, Arab, and Norman administration, Roger created an efficient and highly centralized government with Palermo as his capital.

Like his uncle, Roger had his eye on the Byzantine empire. In 1147 the Normans captured Corfu and raided along the Greek coast. Alarmed by this move, the new Byzantine emperor, Manuel I Comnenus, called on the Venetians for assistance, and in return for their help approved two new chrysobulls that extended their trade privileges and granted them two additional wharves in Constantinople.[45] The Normans were forced to surrender

Corfu in the summer of 1149. During the protracted assault on Corfu, tension between Venetian and Byzantine sailors and soldiers resulted in riotous infighting and the staging of a mock coronation ceremony in which the Venetians crowned an Ethiopian slave as emperor of the Romans. The swarthy complexioned Manuel never forgave this insult to his dignity and would eventually take revenge on the Venetians.[46]

Events in the second half of the twelfth century proved that despite its economic and naval might, Venice remained very much at the mercy of larger powers. It found itself trying to balance the threats posed by two ambitious men: Holy Roman emperor Frederick Barbarossa, who wanted to reestablish imperial authority over the city-states that had arisen in northern and central Italy, and Manuel, who hoped to reassert Byzantine authority over the parts of southern Italy that had been usurped by the Normans.

Manuel was the first to act. In 1155 he directed a fleet to Ancona, which he used as a base from which to attack the Normans. The Venetians feared Byzantine interference so close to their shores and reached an agreement with the new Norman king William I which gave them trading privileges in southern Italy and Sicily as well as Norman recognition that the northern Adriatic—in a line running west from Ragusa (Dubrovnik)—was their sphere. Indeed, Venice's claim to the Adriatic was so generally acknowledged that Muhammad al-Idrisi, a Berber geographer working in the court of Roger II, referred to it in his *Tabula Rogeriana* (The Map of Roger) of 1154 as both the "canal" and "sea of the Venetians." As early as the tenth century, Arab writer ibn Hawqal had called the Adriatic the "Gulf of the Venetians."[47] After some initial successes by the Byzantines, William bested their troops and forced Manuel in 1158 to come to terms.[48]

The two men were drawn together by their common fear of Holy Roman emperor Frederick Barbarossa, who at the Diet of Roncaglia in 1158 made clear his intention to assert his sovereign rights over Italy. These rights had eroded as both sides in the ongoing contest between the empire and the papacy over the relationship of church and state had granted privileges to the city-states or communes of north and central Italy in return for their support. Even though Barbarossa had renewed the pact with Venice in 1154, the Venetians feared that if the *terraferma* came firmly under his control, this would threaten not just commerce but the very existence of Venice.

They had good reason to be concerned. In 1162 Barbarossa destroyed Milan and then set his sights on Venice which was supporting his nemesis,

Pope Alexander III. On the southern border of the *dogado*, a coalition made up of contingents from Ferrara, Padua, and Verona attacked and took Cavarzere.[49] This was neither the first nor the last time that Venice would fight with neighboring city-states over borders, control of river traffic, and Venice's efforts to make itself the obligatory port of call of the region. Twenty years earlier, Venice had gone to war with Padua over possession of the towns of Conche and Fogolana near Cavarzere, prime salt producing areas.[50] At the same time that Venice was facing this threat from the south, the patriarch of Aquileia, Ulrich II of Treffen, attacked Grado. In the end, he was taken prisoner and had to agree to an annual tribute of a bull, twelve pigs, and 300 loaves of bread for his freedom. The defeat of the patriarch and the Friulian nobles who supported him would be commemorated in Venice for centuries in Fat Tuesday celebrations that included the slaughter of a bull and pigs in the Piazzetta in front of the Ducal Palace and the ritual smashing in the Senate Hall of model castles representing the Friulian nobles.[51]

In the end Venice paid Verona, Vicenza, and Padua to abandon Barbarossa's side and adhere to an anti-imperial coalition known as the Veronese League. The financial strain caused by Venice's subvention of the league forced the government to borrow 1,150 silver marks from a group of twelve subscribers who in return for the loan received a guarantee of rents and other income generated at the Rialto market. The subscribers included two future doges—Sebastiano Ziani and Orio Mastropiero—who each contributed about two-twelfths of the total, seven men who proffered one-twelfth each, and three other men who together furnished one-twelfth. The loan is evidence of the formation of the practice of funding the government by borrowing from wealthy individuals that would become a mainstay of Venetian policy for centuries and an important source of income and political power for the lenders.[52] The loans were a lucrative investment opportunity for the subscribers who already constituted the richest members of society.

In 1167 an even broader coalition of north Italian cities, including those that were part of the Veronese League, formed the formidable Lombard League to oppose Barbarossa. Venice offered financial but not military support. The league also had the backing of William of Sicily and Pope Alexander III. When Barbarossa suffered a serious defeat at the Battle of Legnano in 1176 he was forced to seek peace. The negotiations were held in Venice since both sides saw it as a neutral venue. In July 1177, pontiff and emperor were reconciled in San Marco with Doge Sebastiano Ziani looking on.[53] In his later chronicle Doge Andrea Dandolo was careful to note that when Alexander proceeded to the high altar, he was flanked by the emperor and doge, an arrangement that made the three rulers appear visually equivalent.[54] The Venetians would celebrate this so-called Peace of Venice for centuries in art and rituals and use its memory to bolster their claims to sovereignty and independence from the papacy and empire.[55] In the aftermath of the peace, both the pope and emperor granted privileges to various Venetian churches; and Barbarossa renewed his 1154 pact with Venice. This time he granted Venetian merchants total exemption from taxes not simply in the Kingdom of Italy but throughout the entire Holy Roman Empire.[56]

When Barbarossa next returned to Italy in 1183 after having brought rebellious nobles in Germany to heel, he reached a new accord with the Lombard League that granted the cities of northern Italy a degree of autonomy in return for an annual tribute. This meant that despite its pact with Frederick, Venice would now have to deal with each of these cities individually as it tried to assert its commercial privileges and enforce its status as the staple or monopoly port of the northern Adriatic. For his part, Frederick created a new power base for himself in central Italy and reached an accord with the Normans of Sicily. He married his son Henry (VI) to the daughter of Roger

FIGURE 4.3 Attributed to Giustino di Gherardino da Forlì, *The Emperor Frederick Barbarossa and Pope Alexander III Make Peace in Front of San Marco*, from *Storia di Alessandro III*, c. 1370. Venice, Museo Civico Correr, Cod. Correr I 383 (1497). The image emphasizes Doge Sebastiano Ziani's intermediary role and presents him as coequal with the pope and the emperor. Museo Correr, Venice, Italy/Bridgeman Images.

II and aunt of William II. When William died in 1189 without an heir, Henry, who succeeded his father in 1190, was positioned to unite all of Italy under imperial rule, save for Venice and the lands of the church.

If Frederick Barbarossa's ambition had proved a challenge to Venice, Manuel's was much more serious since it went to the very heart of the city's economic interests. In 1167 Manuel defeated King Stephen III of Hungary and asserted his claim that Dalmatia and Croatia were part of the Byzantine empire. There was still a strong pro-Byzantine faction in Ancona. In addition, the Pisans, who enjoyed Manuel's favor, had entered the Adriatic marketplace by signing commercial treaties with Ragusa and Spalato (Split). They could provide the naval support for Manuel's plan to link the eastern and western shores of the Adriatic. Suddenly, it was the Byzantines, not the Normans, who threatened Venice's control of the Adriatic. In an extraordinary reversal, Venice tried to improve relations with Hungary, which it had been fighting during the previous decade for control of Dalmatia.[57]

Then in 1170, in a move that further alienated the Venetians, Manuel granted trade privileges and quarters in Constantinople to Venice's competitors, the Pisans and the Genoese. The Venetians in Constantinople reacted by destroying the newly established Genoese quarter. Fed up with the Venetians, on March 12, 1171, Manuel set a trap. He ordered the arrest not only in Constantinople but throughout the Byzantine empire of all Venetians and the impounding of their merchandise. It was this mass arrest that merchant Romano Mairano barely managed to escape by fleeing on his ship. Most were not so lucky; it is said that 10,000 Venetians were taken prisoner in the capital alone. That figure is surely overblown, since it was a common convention for medieval chroniclers to record a large number as a way of conveying scale.

When news of Manuel's treachery reached Venice, Doge Vitale II Michiel organized a large armada to sail to Constantinople and seek revenge. As the flotilla made its way along the Dalmatian coast various towns, including Zara, again pledged themselves to Venice. The Venetians decided to winter at Chios where illness broke out and took 1,000 lives. Manuel played for time as three different Venetian embassies made their way to the capital for negotiations. After moving around the Aegean but failing to escape the epidemic that was decimating his navy, Doge Michiel was compelled to abandon the campaign. Manuel reportedly wrote a disdainful letter to the doge in which he described how the Venetians, in a reference to the city's origins, "were once a people not even worthy to be named," adding, "you . . . owe what prestige you have to the Romans [i.e., the Byzantines]."[58] The fleet limped home in May 1172. Enraged at the outcome, the Venetians demanded Michiel's head. He was assassinated on the threshold of San Zaccaria, where he had fled to escape an angry mob.

Sebastiano Ziani was elected in his place and again sought unsuccessfully to end the crisis through diplomacy. When that failed, he supported Frederick Barbarossa's 1173 assault on the Byzantine stronghold at Ancona. Ziani was motivated more by a desire to keep an eye on what was happening in this rival Adriatic port than by a wish to support Barbarossa's ambitions. In 1175 Venice reached a new twenty-year accord with William II of Sicily that granted the Venetians significant trade privileges in his kingdom and reaffirmed Norman recognition of the Venetian sphere of influence over the northern and central Adriatic. With Constantinople off limits to them, Venetian merchants shifted the focus of their attention to the Norman kingdom, Alexandria, ports in Syria, and even the western Mediterranean.

The treaty between William and Venice, coupled with Manuel's own crushing defeat by the Seljuk Turks at the battle of Myriocephalon in 1176, finally brought the emperor to the negotiating table; even so, it took several more years for an informal agreement to be reached since the release of prisoners and compensation for losses had to be worked out.[59] When Manuel died in September 1180, the sum of his achievements was meager indeed. He had failed in his efforts to reassert Byzantine hegemony in the West and completely alienated the Venetians, whose naval support the empire had often relied upon. Manuel's twelve-year-old heir Alexius II did not long survive the machinations of his relative Andronicus, who had the boy strangled and assumed the throne for himself. Andronicus rode a wave of anti-western sentiment that was directed at the Pisans and Genoese but not the Venetians, who were only beginning to reappear in the capital. He agreed to terms by which the Venetians would be paid 1,500 pounds of hyperpers as compensation for their losses in 1171. But when in June 1185 the Norman king William launched yet another invasion of the empire and was at the gates of Constantinople, the mob turned on Andronicus and butchered him.

The new emperor Isaac II Angelus managed to repel the Normans and force them back across the Adriatic. He then turned his efforts to getting the Venetians to abandon their treaty with William and reenergizing the anti-Norman Veneto/Byzantine alliance. He did so by granting them three new chrysobulls in 1187. The first reinstated all the previous commercial privileges enjoyed by the Venetians; the second restored the Venetian quarter as it had been defined in 1148; the third laid out the terms of the military alliance between the two powers. This third chrysobull was "more in the nature of a contract between equal partners . . . which emperors in an earlier age would not have countenanced."[60]

Isaac granted a fourth chrysobull in June 1189 when Frederick Barbarossa was on the doorstep of Constantinople as part of his participation in the Third Crusade, which had been called to retake Jerusalem after it fell to the Kurdish general Saladin in 1187. This fourth chrysobull enlarged yet again the Venetians' quarter, granted them further docks, and laid out a new schedule of payments for the losses suffered in the 1171 expulsion. However, the terms of the four chrysobulls were never fully put into effect, and Isaac was deposed by his brother Alexius III. A chrysobull that Alexius granted to the Venetians in 1198 reaffirmed the terms of the 1187 alliance and clarified the legal status of Venetians resident in Constantinople, who were described as *cives extranei* (foreign citizens). By the end of the century, the Venetians were fully back in Constantinople, which had been reduced to the capital of a disintegrating empire.

Over the course of the eleventh and twelfth centuries, Venice had emerged as the major naval power in the eastern Mediterranean. When it served Venetian interests, the city had supported the Byzantine emperor and the crusading movement and had expanded its range of trade to include the entirety of the Byzantine empire (except the Black Sea provinces), the towns of Outremer, and Egypt. Venetian ships called at ports in southern Italy and Sicily too. Its merchants, thanks in large measure to the extraordinary advantages first contained in the chrysobull of 1082, had become the primary carriers of goods between East and West and had grown fabulously wealthy as a result.

Even so, events had shown just how precarious Venice's position remained and how vulnerable its economic well-being was to situations often beyond its control. As the reigns of Frederick Barbarossa and Manuel made clear, Venice truly was caught in a vise between the Holy Roman and Byzantine empires. At any moment, its lands could be invaded, its privileges rescinded, its goods impounded, and its citizens imprisoned or even killed. Closer to home, Venice had to fend off challenges to its control of the Adriatic from the Normans to the south and the Hungarians and the towns of Dalmatia and Croatia to the east. To the west, it had to protect its access to the rivers of the Italian mainland and even the borders of the *dogado* itself against the thriving city-states that had sprung up throughout the Po River valley.

At the same time, the need to navigate the difficult shoals of international power politics combined with the emergence of a large class of new wealthy men—like Mairano and the Stagnarios—revealed both the inadequacy and the unsustainability of a regime that was based on rule by a doge with nearly monarchical power. As Venice threaded its way between empires and expanded beyond the sea, and while its merchants grew rich through the technical business innovations of the Commercial Revolution, a quieter revolution was also taking place. Venice was evolving into a commune, and its doge from a monarch into an elected head of state with carefully circumscribed powers.

5

From Ducal to Communal Venice

IN 1105, DOGE Ordelaffo Falier commissioned from Constantinople a magnificent new screen to adorn the high altar of the church of San Marco. Known as the Pala d'Oro (Golden Altarpiece), it is the most sumptuous of the many luxurious objects that embellish the basilica. (Plate 2) Sylvester Syropoulos, a fifteenth-century Byzantine visitor to Venice, labeled the Pala, encrusted as it is with gold, pearls, precious stones, and multicolored enamels, "the icon of icons."[1] Yet the Pala as it appears today is not Falier's original but one that was altered several times over the centuries.[2]

On the lowest register, flanking the Virgin in the center, are full-length depictions of Doge Falier and the Byzantine empress Irene, a truly odd pairing. The most widely accepted explanation for this is that when the Pala was altered in 1209, five years after Venice conquered Constantinople in the Fourth Crusade, the figure of Irene's husband Alexius I Comnenus was removed, as well as that of his son and co-emperor John II Comnenus. Presumably Alexius and Irene originally flanked the Virgin, and John II and Falier stood next to them in the spaces occupied by the inscription plaques commemorating the fourteenth-century renovation of the Pala. During the 1209 alteration, the image of Irene was retained, possibly since she was a relative of former doge Domenico Silvo's wife, while Falier's portrait was moved closer to the Virgin and augmented with a halo. Angelo Falier, a descendant of Doge Ordelaffo, was a Procurator of San Marco (an administrator of the church) at the time of the alteration. He may have pushed for Falier's more prestigious placement and the addition of the halo, a symbol of imperial dignity.[3]

In the enamel plaque, the earliest extant portrait of a Venetian doge, Falier is shown bearded and mustachioed and standing on a cushion. He is dressed in an elaborate ankle-length cloak of black, green, and silver, and wears black boots. His head is covered with a bejeweled crown and surrounded with a pale blue halo. His left hand appears to be raised in greeting, while in his right he holds a scepter. The inscription, which seems to be original, explains that he is "Ordelaffo Falier, by the grace of God, duke of Venice."

Historians have made much of the fact that Falier holds a scepter, which he received at the altar of Saint Mark according to investiture rites of the time. Yet when Pietro Polani became doge in 1130—only twenty-eight years after Falier's own elevation to the ducal throne—he received not a scepter but a banner. From the late twelfth century until the end of the Republic in 1797, an image of the doge receiving a banner from Saint Mark would be standard imagery on the most important Venetian coins. This seemingly insignificant

FIGURE 5.1 Enamel Portrait of Doge Ordelaffo Falier, early twelfth century. Pala d'Oro (detail), Basilica of San Marco, Venice. Falier holds a scepter, a symbol of power. O. Böhm, Venice.

substitution of a banner for a scepter was anything but. The scepter was a symbol of kingship, of almost unlimited personal power. By contrast, the banner symbolized the commune of the Venetians. The substitution of the banner for the scepter in ducal installation rites and its subsequent depiction on coinage signaled a major change in the very conception of Venetian governance. While Mark remained the ultimate conferrer of authority, the nature of the dogeship had changed. The doge was now the servant, not the master, of the state.[4]

This chapter explores this political transformation that was so fundamental that it could be termed a revolution save for its slow pace and largely bloodless nature. Put simply, Venice evolved from a dukedom, a polity ruled by a semi-monarchical doge, into a commune, a form of collective or republican government based on councils. The impetus for this change was the social transformation sparked by the Commercial Revolution. As more men like Zaccaria Stagnario gained wealth and social standing, they demanded a greater voice in affairs and gradually took up offices and assumed positions of power. This phenomenon was not confined to Venice. In towns throughout central and northern Italy in the late eleventh and early twelfth centuries, communes were emerging as groups of new men displaced the bishops and counts who had controlled civic governance since the decline of Roman imperial administration.[5] What made the Venetian case unique was that the doges, unlike the bishops and counts of the mainland towns, were not excluded from power; instead they were subsumed into the communal structure, although their power to act independently was dramatically curtailed. And as the commune developed, administrative offices and courts proliferated, especially those with responsibilities in the commercial sector.

The cityscape reflected these changes. The church of San Marco was rebuilt for a third and final time, and the piazza in front of it was expanded and transformed. Two new buildings to house courts and councils were added to the Ducal Palace complex. A central marketplace developed at Rialto and came under governmental control. As the population grew, the scattered island nuclei that had constituted the original Rialto settlement archipelago coalesced into a coherent urban space. (Henceforth the Rialto settlement cluster will be referred to as Venice, and Rialto will indicate the part of Venice around the marketplace and bridge as it is known today.) Parishes were incorporated into the administrative apparatus of the city and became part of residents' identity. At the same time, other communities in the lagoon saw their power and influence decline.

In 1071 a cleric named Domenico Tino composed an account of the election and installation of Doge Domenico Silvo. Tino's eyewitness testimony offers an invaluable window onto the governmental structure and composition of the political community on the eve of the commune.[6] According to Tino's report, the electoral process that took place at San Nicolò on the Lido commenced with the clergy, led by the several bishops of the *dogado*, calling on God to deliver to them a doge who was both pleasing to him and suited to the task. While the clergy prayed inside the church, the *popolo* (common people), who had arrived in armed ships from throughout the lagoon, assembled on the beach in front. At a certain point a seemingly spontaneous chant arose from the crowd: "we want and we praise Domenico Silvo [as doge]." Hoisted aloft on the shoulders of *nobiles viri* (noblemen), Silvo was immediately placed on a boat and rowed in procession to San Marco, accompanied by the beating of drums, the clanging of bells, and the singing of a Te Deum (hymn of thanksgiving). Once at the church, Silvo removed his shoes and, escorted by the clergy, entered the church barefoot. At the altar of San Marco, he prostrated himself and then took up the scepter. Exiting the basilica, he proceeded to the Ducal Palace. There he received on oath of loyalty from the people and distributed gifts.[7]

Tino's account shows the Venetian political community in action. All (male) sectors of Venetian society—save the servile—had a role in the new doge's selection. These included the clergy whose task it was to invoke divine assistance in the choice of a suitable candidate. The Concio or Arengo (General Assembly) which was composed of freemen from throughout the lagoon but likely dominated by Venetians, made the actual selection. Yet this was not the divinely inspired choice that Tino made it out to be. Clearly the noblemen, the men who headed society and who served as *iudices* or advisors to the doge, had pre-selected Silvo and made sure that his was the name that the *popolo* started to chant.[8] Additionally, it is worth noting that it was the people who swore an oath to the doge, indicating that they owed loyalty to their sovereign, not the other way around.

The transformation of Venice from a dukedom to a commune was a twofold process. On one hand, it involved reining in ducal power. The emergence of the *iudices* around 900 represented the very first effort to limit the doge's power, followed by a move in 1040, forbidding doges from naming their successors or co-regents.[9] On the other hand, the emergence of the commune involved the development of councils that arrogated to themselves the tasks of governing and represented the intentions of an expanding number of men of wealth and standing, as the growing lists of men who signed their names to decisions of the General Assembly indicate. It also embodied a new conception of the state itself, one in which authority derived from below.

The earliest incontrovertible evidence for the existence of the Venetian commune dates to the reign of Pietro Polani, the first doge to take up the banner. In February 1143, a dispute arose over the processional route to be followed for the celebrations of the feast of the Purification of the Virgin. Worried that the controversy might lead to even greater division, Doge Polani and his kinsman, the bishop of Castello Giovanni Polani, met at the palace with, in the words of the decision, "our *iudices* and those wise men (*viri sapientibus*), who are in charge of the council, which manages in this time the honor and benefit and salvation of our fatherland, which council the *popolo* of Venice are required to obey by oath."[10] By this date then, a new body, a council of an unknown number of wise men, had been created to stand alongside the doge and his *iudices* and assist in their deliberations. Furthermore, the populace was bound by oath to follow the council's decisions. Conflict with Padua in these years over salt-rich territory near Chioggia may have provided the impetus for the creation of this new council.[11] With such a weighty matter at stake, a new governmental body took form. Within a short time, the council became an established component of the government. Rule by councils was the essence of communal governance. When Polani sent legates to Constantinople in 1147, they were empowered to speak for him, as well as for "our entire commune."[12]

The rise of the commune did not, however, signal an immediate decline in ducal might as the power struggles of various elite families indicate. The most prominent of these was the Michiel family which nearly monopolized the dogeship from 1096 to 1172. Pietro Polani was part of this family as son-in-law of his predecessor Domenico Michiel. A particularly fierce struggle erupted between the Polanis (and by extension the Michiels) and the Dandolo family and their allies, the Badoers, over the relationship between church and state. The dispute involved Enrico Dandolo, patriarch of Grado, and Doge Pietro Polani and Giovanni Polani, bishop of Castello. Dandolo, like other patriarchs of Grado, had taken up residence in the patriarch's palace at San Silvestro, close to the Rialto market, rather than in Grado itself. Although the bishop of Castello was technically subordinate to the patriarch, the presence of these two high-ranking churchmen in the same city was a recipe for trouble, particularly when these posts represented power bases for different families. Dandolo was a proponent of the ecclesiastical reform movement advocated by the papacy which aimed at reducing lay control over the church. When Nella Michiel, the abbess of San Zaccaria, died, Doge Polani appointed a replacement whom the nuns duly elected. As was customary, Polani asked the new abbess to swear an oath of loyalty. Polani was simply acting as his predecessors always had, using powerful church positions to augment family power. Inspired by the reform movement, Dandolo fulminated against this governmental encroachment on ecclesiastic liberty and turned to Rome for help.

In the meantime, Doge Polani had agreed to come to the Byzantine emperor Manuel I's aid against a renewed Norman threat to his empire. Dandolo condemned this alliance with the Byzantines since they refused to recognize the primacy of the pope in Christendom, including over the patriarch of Constantinople.[13] In April 1147 Polani retaliated by ordering the expulsion of the Dandolo clan and the destruction of their family stronghold in the parish of San Luca. Dandolo fled to Rome with his relatives and many of the clergy who sided with him. He convinced the pope to excommunicate the doge and place the city under interdict, which meant that the clergy were forbidden to perform the sacraments. Only following Polani's death was peace restored and Dandolo recalled from exile. As a reward for his loyalty, the pope placed the archbishopric of Zara under the authority of the patriarch of Grado. This represented an elevation of the patriarch's prestige but also benefited Venice by strengthening its claim to Dalmatia.

This episode was significant in two ways. The first is in relation to ongoing efforts by certain families, most especially the Michiel/Polanis, to monopolize the dogeship and use church positions to increase their power. Patriarch Dandolo's resistance to Doge Polani is symptomatic of the effort by other elite families to rein in the doges—a movement best exemplified by the rise of the commune itself. Second, the Polani/Dandolo rivalry was part of the effort by the Venetians to work out the relationship between the church and the government. Here the outcome was much more equivocal. In one respect, Dandolo won; the pope increased the dignity of the patriarch by placing Zara under his jurisdiction. But soon, the commune removed the clergy from a direct voice in Venetian governance, something the clergy had heretofore enjoyed as part of the ducal court.[14]

Another crucial step in the evolution of the commune occurred when in 1172 Vitale II Michiel was assassinated at San Zaccaria after the return of his ill-fated naval campaign to punish the emperor Manuel for his expulsion of all Venetians from the empire—an expedition that some members of the council of wise men had resisted. In the wake of Michiel's murder, a fundamental change was made to the ducal election procedure, a change that has been characterized by a modern historian as "a milestone in the creation of a new Venetian government."[15] During the election of Doge Silvo, the elites had quietly orchestrated his "spontaneous" selection by the General Assembly. But they could no longer take the chance that the assembly would be so pliable, and so they decided to take the choice out of its hands altogether.[16] The members of the council of wise men determined that, in the words of Andrea Dandolo's chronicle, "to avoid discord," a committee of eleven "virtuous men" would select the man they judged to be the wisest and most qualified to serve as doge and then declare their choice to the assembly.[17] The gathered multitude was still expected to ratify the choice. Sebastiano Ziani, almost certainly the richest man in the city at the time, was the first doge elected under the new procedure.

The electoral reform of 1172 aimed at several different targets. First, it was designed to reduce the unfettered regal pretensions of the doges. Doge Michiel had undertaken the naval expedition against the advice of his councilors.[18] The way to guard against such high-handed action in the future was to select a consensus candidate, one who enjoyed the support of and was beholden to the eleven prominent electors. Such a man was unlikely to go against the will of those who had chosen him. Second, the new procedure targeted the majority of freemen and constituted a significant power grab by the elites. In previous elections, including that of Doge Silvo, the elite had clearly manipulated the General Assembly to carry out its will, but the new electoral process guaranteed that the successful candidate would be one of their own. The 1172 reform thus signaled the undisputed rise to political prominence of the rich merchants, the men who had grown wealthy through Mediterranean trade, in alliance with the older elite families.[19] Third, it diminished the role of the clergy, turning the election of the doge into a secular affair that did not require the prayers and invocations of the clergy.[20] Finally, the change indicated the triumph of Venice over the other communities in the lagoon such as Torcello and Chioggia. From the earliest times, the General Assembly had been a gathering of freemen from throughout the *dogado*. By diminishing the assembly's role, the lesser lagoonal communities were effectively disenfranchised.[21]

The electoral procedure was modified yet again on the death of Doge Ziani in 1178, creating a process that would become known as double election. First, a committee of four "provident men," in the words of the chronicler Andrea Dandolo, were selected who then chose forty men who comprised the electoral committee and selected the doge.[22] The man they chose was Orio Mastropiero, an extremely wealthy man who had been a major lender to the government. This same two-committee election process would be utilized in the future to select members of various councils.[23]

It is difficult to precisely trace the institutional evolution of the commune in these early decades. What we know is that in its earliest form it consisted of a group of wise men who presided over a council of the commune and that they ruled in conjunction with the doge and his *iudices*. How many wise men there were and how they were selected is unknown. By 1187, the government had evolved to encompass two councils: a lesser council composed of six ducal councilors and a greater council of perhaps forty men, as well as the General Assembly of freemen.[24] This is clear from a promise the Procurators of San Marco made that year to compensate those who were willing to lend their ships for a siege of Zara. The procurators stated that they were acting on order of the doge and with "the approval of the *iudices*, and the greater and lesser councils and the attorneys of our commune and people of Venice."[25] Just as it appears that the salt dispute with Padua had served as the impetus for the creation of the very first council, so the ongoing conflict with Zara may have propelled a multiplication of representative bodies. By the end of the twelfth century, Venice was a full-fledged communal regime that was an expression of the elite's collective will and in which the power to act depended in large measure on the consent of councils.

The other facet of Venice's evolution from a dukedom into a commune involved bridling the doge. The commune stripped him of many of the prerogatives commonly associated with monarchy. It limited, for example, his ability to use public funds, offices, and other perks, known as *bona comunis* (public goods), for his personal benefit or that of his family. Similarly, the appointment of officials to Istrian and Dalmatian territories under Venetian domination, although technically the responsibility of the doge, had to have the consent of the councils. The commune did allow the doge to retain certain honorific gifts paid in kind by subject lands but only because they also served communal purposes as tangible expressions of Venetian sovereignty. However, more valuable forms of revenue, like taxes and other duties, went directly into the public coffers for use by the commune itself.[26]

By far the most significant change to the doge's status involved the new requirement that he swear an oath upon entering office. Recall that in the election of Domenico Silvo in 1071 the people had taken an oath to the doge; now the doge swore to the people. Historians debate which doge first took the oath that came to be known as the *promissione* (promise). Some have suggested that it was Polani, although that seems unlikely since there is no evidence that the commune existed until more than a decade into his reign. It was most likely Domenico Morosini in 1148. However, the earliest extant oath is that of Enrico Dandolo, who entered office in 1192. His oath is relatively brief, two and a half pages in a modern print edition. Ducal oaths would grow dramatically longer over time, as clauses were added on the death of each incumbent, as a way of correcting what the commune saw as his shortcomings. The oath that Pietro Gradenigo swore a little less than a century after Dandolo comprises thirty pages in the same edition, while that of Francesco Foscari (elected in 1423) runs to sixty-two pages in its modern print version.[27] Taken together, the ever-evolving oaths offer a kind of running history or moving picture of the dogeship.

The first four clauses of Dandolo's oath outlined his primary responsibilities. He swore to preside over the government and safeguard the honor and profit of the Venetians. He agreed to render justice equitably in accordance with the law and custom and not accept any "gift" (read bribe) regarding a case that came before him. Most of the succeeding clauses were proscriptive. He promised, for example, not to distribute funds without the council's consent; not to select candidates for the patriarchate of Grado, bishoprics, or certain monasteries but instead leave those selections to the appropriate bodies; not to appoint judges without election or notaries without approval of the council or interfere in the administration of various taxes and tariffs. He also agreed not to reveal any matters of state that the council deemed secret. In the penultimate clause, Dandolo swore, "In the matter of an issue that might especially concern the dogeship, we will discharge those concerning which all of the councilors of the Lesser Council will agree with the majority of the Greater Council." This provision was clearly intended to prevent the doge from trying to circumvent the rules of the oath. Any deviation from it would require a unanimous decision by the six members of the Lesser Council and a majority of the Greater. If those thresholds were met, then the change would be understood as the will of the commune. Dandolo also swore to furnish at his own expense ten fully equipped warships.[28]

The initial clauses in Dandolo's oath expressed the traditional duties of a monarch to rule conscientiously, fairly, speedily, and equitably on behalf of his people. All other clauses, except the outfitting of ships, were designed to limit his sphere of action and delimit his capacity to act independently. The men who devised the oath were especially concerned about the doge pursuing an independent foreign policy. This accounts for the clauses regarding communication with foreign leaders and the necessity of maintaining secrecy. Most importantly, the doge was to act in accordance with the will of the Lesser and Greater Councils.

In the rise of the commune, the leading men in Venice did not revolt against the doge; instead, they asserted their dominion over him. In the view of one expert on the Venetian constitution, the parties struck the following bargain: "to the doge the honors; to the commune the power."[29] This is an overstatement, even if the doge retained "certain regal insignia," as the chronicler Boncompagno da Signa noted in 1173.[30] Over the course of the succeeding decades and centuries, doges would continue to exert often quite extensive powers. But Venice's new political structure had been decided. The doge would be the leader of the Venetian commune, not a monarch. Ultimate authority would reside in the councils as the expression and manifestation of the communal will.

The evolution from a dukedom into a commune was accompanied by expansion of the bureaucracy. As Venice's population and economy grew, specialized offices developed, particularly those involved with justice and revenue collection. In ducal Venice, the *iudices*, the small group of men around the doge who made up the ducal court, had been adequate to decide policy and hear legal cases, while wardens (*gastaldi*) had been charged with overseeing other settlements in the lagoon.[31] In communal Venice this system was no longer adequate to meet administrative demands.

Two of the most important new offices—the Avogadori di Comun (Communal or State Attorneys) and the Communal Treasurers—appear in the record for the first time in 1173.[32] This date suggests that some formalization of governmental structures took place following the ouster of Doge Michiel and around the same time the ducal election procedures were changed. Forty years after the creation of the commune, the government was acquiring a more autonomous and rational organization, one divorced from the ducal court. The State Attorneys were responsible for protecting the interests of the commune, while the Treasurers collected fines and tribute. The office of Giustizieri (Justices) also dates from 1173. The Justices were responsible for guaranteeing food supplies, managing prices, and ferreting out fraud in the sale of food products.[33] Still another office, the Judges of the Commune, may have originated a decade before the others and was charged with handling disputes between the state and private persons. It evolved in the thirteenth century into the Giudici al Forestier (Judges of Foreigners) to handle legal cases involving foreigners.[34] This was especially important given the number of foreign merchants in the city. The Salineri di Chioggia (Chioggia Salt Officials), in charge of the revenue generated by salt production, also developed late in the twelfth century.[35]

Still the commune had not yet developed a chancellery or writing office. When documents needed to be drafted, the task was entrusted to priest-notaries, many of whom were chaplains associated with San Marco and served the ducal court.[36] Another position connected to the basilica was that of Procurator of San Marco. The office may be nearly as old as the church itself, although the first man known to have occupied the post was Otto Basilius who in 1152 was identified as the *procurator operis ecclesie sancti Marci* (procurator of the works of the church of San Marco). Basilius was responsible for the administration of the church, including building and maintenance projects (known as the "works"), as well as safeguarding the basilica's revenues and sacred treasures. Procurator Angelo Falier's commissioning the alteration of the Pala d'Oro in 1209 fell under this rubric. Such heavy responsibilities required men of irreproachable character. Accordingly, the procurators quickly assumed fiduciary responsibilities both for the government and private individuals. In 1207 they were maintaining tax census records for the government. Over the centuries the number of Procurators of San Marco would grow from two to six and later nine. The office would rank second only to the dogeship in terms of prestige. Indeed, the men who were selected as procurators were so highly regarded that the post quickly became a stepping-stone to the dogeship.[37] Thus, while San Marco remained the doge's palatine chapel, it was also becoming Venice's state church. Like the city itself, it was undergoing significant transformation in the eleventh and twelfth centuries.

Starting sometime during the reign of Doge Domenico Contarini, the basilica was rebuilt for the third and final time. Work continued under Domenico Silvo and was completed under Vitale Falier. No calamity such as a fire prompted the rebuilding. Instead, the Venetians appear to have been motivated by civic honor and a desire to compete with other Italian cities, most particularly Venice's maritime rival Pisa which began building its cathedral in 1063, the same year as the groundbreaking for the Contarini church.[38]

The new church followed the footprint of the two earlier churches, although an extension was made to the north transept by demolishing the old church of San Teodoro and incorporating its south wall into the new structure. A similar extension was made to the south transept by utilizing an old corner tower of the Ducal Palace. A narthex or atrium was adjoined to the west end; while on the east end two small apses were added on either side of the presbytery. A large crypt was excavated and built to the east of the old one; and the main altar was moved from the central crossing to the presbytery. The most important change was the replacement of the original single wooden dome with five brick domes supported by brick vaulting; they were not adorned with onion-shaped cupolas until the thirteenth century. Even though the church, like its predecessors, was generally modeled on the Apostoleion in Constantinople, it was no longer a true Greek cross with four equidistant arms. Instead, the three apses at the east end and the slight extension of the western arm were designed to accommodate liturgical and processional needs. The exterior was plain brickwork punctuated by windows and niches, although it did include carved or molded friezes with scroll, braid, and animal motifs. Even at this early date San Marco was also being used to display war trophies. The yardarm of a lateen-rigged enemy ship was affixed to a wall near the main entrance.[39] It also became an important site for ducal burials: doges Domenico Silvo, Vitale Falier, Vitale I Michiel, and Ordelaffo Falier were all laid to rest in the newly constructed narthex.

The architect behind the Contarini church was an anonymous Greek master builder who incorporated elements current in Byzantine architecture at the time. However, the church also includes Italian components such as the crypt. And the influence of Western workmen is evident in the brickwork and the decorative friezes.[40] In San Marco, as in so much of Venice, East and West met—in this case in homage to Mark.

Yet while the Contarini church was being built, the Venetians had somehow or other managed to misplace Mark's body. At least that is the story they put forth, known as the *inventio* (rediscovery) of his relics. They came to believe that the saint's relics had been lost amid the mayhem caused by the fire that occurred during the revolt against Pietro IV Candiano in 976. A diligent search conducted during the building of the Contarini church failed to locate them. In desperation, Doge Falier had the bishop of Castello organize a three-day communal fast followed by a procession. During Mass after the procession, one of the basilica's columns moved, a fragrant odor perfumed the church, and Mark's relics revealed themselves. The newly rediscovered remains were kept on display until they were placed in the new crypt during the consecration of the church on October 8, 1094. By the fourteenth century the story circulated that Mark had made his presence known by thrusting his arm through the column.[41]

Why tell such an extraordinary tale? It had to do in part with having Mark conform to the pattern of other medieval saints, namely, martyrdom, followed by translation or transfer, and then rediscovery. There can be little doubt that the consecration of the new basilica required a significant event,

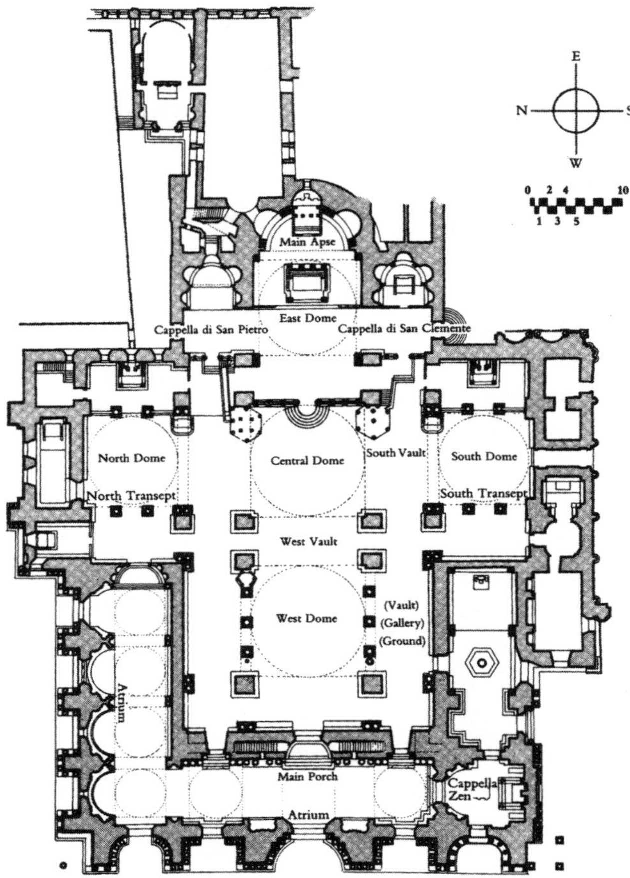

FIGURE 5.2 Plan of Basilica of San Marco, Venice. From Otto Demus, *The Mosaics of San Marco in Venice*, vol. 1, *Text* (Chicago, 1984), 389. Courtesy of the University of Chicago Press.

and the *collocatio* (placement) of the saint's relics in the new crypt fit the bill. By the thirteenth century that installation had been expanded into the story of his apparition and rediscovery. The *collocatio* heralded to the wider world Venice's importance on the eve of the preaching of the First Crusade, while domestically it reaffirmed the link between the doge and the cult of Mark. Yet soon, the commune would appropriate Mark for itself in the banner-consignment image on coins just as it incorporated the doge into the new structures of government. Accordingly, chroniclers expanded the simple installation of the relics in the crypt into the miraculous rediscovery.[42]

In the late twelfth century, the space in front of San Marco underwent a significant amplification to create Piazza San Marco. To do so, a preexisting church dedicated to San Geminiano had to be razed and relocated farther west, and the Rio Batario, a canal that ran across the area at about the halfway point of the present-day Piazza, had to be covered.[43] The twelfth-century demolition of San Geminiano was the impetus for one of the doge's annual processions. Every year he was required to visit the relocated church to ask forgiveness for razing the original. Tradition holds that Doge Sebastiano Ziani contributed some of the land for the enlarged piazza as well as buildings that eventually surrounded it, but this is impossible to verify.[44] San Marco's bell tower, which did double duty as a landmark for returning ships, had been erected during the reign of Domenico Morosini.[45]

Doge Ziani did spearhead a building campaign to give the new communal government an architectural presence suited to its growing stature. A stone quay—the Molo—was built running along the waterfront in front of the Ducal Palace, and sometime after 1177 the two huge granite columns that mark the sea entrance into the Piazzetta and that were eventually adorned with statues of Saints Mark and Theodore were erected.[46] Ziani's initiative also included creating suitable assembly and workspaces for the communal councils and offices. In the late twelfth century, in the area adjacent to San Marco and facing the Piazzetta, the Venetians built a courthouse. Fronting the water, they built a *palatium communis* or council hall. Although little is known about these buildings, they did have ground floor porticos and upper floor loggias. In this way, they were open and inviting as was fitting for buildings designed for public use. This was in stark contrast with the defensive posture of the old Ducal Palace with its fortress towers and thick walls. Architecturally, communal Venice was presenting a different message from that of ducal Venice.[47]

Rialto also underwent significant development in the eleventh and twelfth centuries. The origins of the Rialto market are unknown, although the area's topographical characteristics made it an ideal spot for the exchange of goods. The wide expanse of available space at Rialto was well suited for accommodating the storage and sale of bulky goods like oil, wine, and charcoal, while the curve and narrowness of the Grand Canal at this point made it the logical terminus for seagoing craft and a launch point for riverboats conveying goods to the *terraferma*. In addition, because of the curve in the canal, the distance from Rialto to San Marco is relatively short. For all these reasons, merchants may simply have started congregating and doing business there. From at least the tenth century, the sale of meat was taking place on the far side of the Grand Canal from San Marco, and two prominent families, the Gradenigos and Orios, had residences and rental properties, including butcher shops, there.

The decisive step in the advancement of Rialto as the city's wholesale commercial center occurred when in 1097 the heirless brothers Pietro and Tiso Orio donated to the doge and "to all the people of the Venetian fatherland" a row of shops and the surrounding land at Rialto.[48] Suddenly, a significant amount of property at the growing market was under direct public ownership, and the rental of that property could generate a considerable amount of revenue for the state. Governmental offices concerned with commerce soon began to locate at Rialto rather than San Marco. Already in the twelfth century, the office of weights and measures was located there, as was the mint, which was situated in the parish of San Bartolomeo on the San Marco side of the Grand Canal.[49]

Given the importance of the Rialto market to the economy, it is no accident that it is where the first, and for centuries the only, bridge across the Grand Canal was situated. Some chronicles date the first bridge to the reign of Sebastiano Ziani, but that cannot be proved. It was almost certainly a pontoon bridge that was replaced in the thirteenth century by a more permanent wooden structure resting on pilings.[50]

Rialto is also where the patriarch of Grado Enrico Dandolo, who had been expelled by Doge Polani, built his Venetian residence. He selected a site in the parish of San Silvestro that was almost adjacent to the market and was one of the few parishes in the city under the jurisdiction of the patriarch, not the bishop of Castello. It had the advantage of being close to the centers of economic and political power and yet some distance from the bishop's residence at San Pietro di Castello. Dandolo may also have favored the site since it was located almost directly across the Grand Canal from the Dandolo family compound.[51]

While San Marco and Rialto were coalescing as the centers of political and economic power, the rest of the city was undergoing significant change. As the number of inhabitants grew—one estimate places the population in the twelfth and thirteenth centuries between 70,000 and 80,000—the density of the urban core increased.[52] Empty fields and lots were converted into building sites as fishponds, shoals, salt pans, and other expanses of water were transformed into dryland. Between the tenth and eleventh centuries, approximately thirty parish churches were founded on the tiny islets that make up Venice, joining a nearly equal number that had been established in the preceding centuries. By the end of the twelfth century, as many as seventy parish churches had been built in the city; another 120 churches, both parochial and monastic, dotted the *dogado*.[53] In Venice itself, development was most dense along the Grand Canal, especially in the areas encompassed by the two curves of the canal, roughly corresponding to the San Marco and Santa Croce sections of the city. The growing compactness of the central core meant that further land reclamation and development would largely have to take place on the margins.[54]

The increasing density of the urban space also fostered a new way of conceptualizing and administering the city. By 1084, parishes had acquired agreed on boundaries, and parish residence became a way of identifying the city's inhabitants. This replaced the older method of distinguishing people by their proximity to physical or topographical features or their residence in one of the six natural clusters that made up the original Rialto/Venice settlement. For example, in 1073 Giovanni Lissado had identified himself as residing in the cluster of Luprio, while in 1128 the formerly enslaved Dobramiro was described as a resident of the parish of San Provolo. It is uncertain what prompted this altered perception. Regardless, parish neighborhoods, comprised for the most part of the tiny islets that make up Venice today, became the framework on which the entire ecclesiastical and civic structure of Venetian life hung.[55]

In addition to serving as a crucial element of residents' identity, administrative divisions found their way into the commune's organization. Certainly, by the end of the twelfth century, the seventy-odd parishes had been organized into pairs, each of which was referred to as a *trentacia* (thirtieth). By the early thirteenth century at the latest, members of the Greater Council were being distributed one per *trentacia*. At the same time, the city was organized into larger units known as *sestieri* or sixths. Each *sestiere* (Cannaregio, San Marco, Castello, Santa Croce, San Polo, and Dorsoduro) had the right to select one of the six members of the Lesser Council.[56] Over time many minor bureaucratic positions would also be assigned either by parish or *sestiere*. The topographical equity of this system of apportioning both legislative and administrative power further served to fuse the city and reduce tension and resentment, particularly between the central parishes and those on the fringes.

The same was not true for other towns and settlements in the lagoon. At least until the election of Doge Silvo, men from all parts of the *dogado* had come together to select the doge, but under the new method of distributing seats in the councils by *trentacie* or *sestieri*, the residents of other settlements were disenfranchised. Accordingly, it seems likely that ambitious men in those settlements relocated to Venice, as the patriarch of Grado did, to be close to the center of power. This further contributed to the marginalization of other lagoon settlements. Certain towns were relegated to the status of producers of specialized products—in Chioggia's case salt and fish—while others slowly faded into obscurity.

Nature also played an important role in this reorganization of human habitation and hence governance. Rivers continued their unrelenting deposition of silt. The effect was especially pronounced in the northern part of the lagoon and led to the disappearance of vast stretches of open water and their replacement with mosquito-infested marshes. The insalubrity of that zone contributed to the slow demise of once powerful Torcello.[57] In 1110, silting combined with flooding led the Piave River to shift its course and caused the disappearance of Cittanova. While silting was a gradual process, change could also occur swiftly. A sudden rise in sea level around 1108 forced the abandonment of the old island town of Malamocco and its transfer to higher ground on the Lido. The bishop of Malamocco moved his seat to Chioggia, while the monastery of San Cipriano relocated to Murano. Smaller settlements such as Ammiana and Costanziaco in the vicinity of Torcello also disappeared under the rising waters.[58] The history of these abandoned towns along with those of other lagoon towns that continued to exist was largely erased as well. No chronicles were written to celebrate their glorious pasts. Instead, their histories, like their power, were subsumed into or overshadowed by that of Venice itself.[59]

6

The Fourth Crusade and the Creation of a Mediterranean Empire

TWO MOMENTOUS EVENTS bookend the Venetian thirteenth century: the Fourth Crusade, which resulted in the conquest of Constantinople in 1204, and the Serrata (Closing) of the Greater Council of 1297, which defined the contours of the ruling class. Together, these episodes fundamentally altered the internal structure and nature of Venetian society as well as Venice's relationship to the Mediterranean Sea.

The Fourth Crusade, which began as military pilgrimage to rescue Jerusalem from the Muslims, ended in the sack of the Byzantine capital and creation of the Latin Empire of Constantinople. It also resulted in Venice's acquisition of a maritime dominion that included substantial holdings in Constantinople and Negroponte (Euboea), the strategically vital towns Modon (Methoni) and Coron (Koróni) at the southwestern tip of Greece, and several Aegean islands, including militarily and economically significant Crete. In what must have seemed the blink of an eye, Venice morphed from an Adriatic power into a Mediterranean one and found itself frequently at war with its maritime rivals, especially Genoa. The Venetians suddenly had to deal with all the questions that an empire carries in its wake. The answers would impact not only the possessions but also Venice's domestic politics. Just as important, the Venetians had to come to terms with their new role as rulers of an empire.

Like the Fourth Crusade, the Serrata of 1297 was both an end and a beginning. It marked the culmination of a century of dramatic social change, much of it ushered in by economic growth that resulted from the overseas expansion. The city's population exploded, new men grew wealthy in commerce, and artisans and manufacturers began to make their presence felt. These changes sparked social ferment, new forms of association including guilds and confraternities, and the growing popularity and influence of the mendicant religious orders, such as the Franciscans and Dominicans. Tax riots, the emergence of family-based clienteles, and factionalism eventually culminated in the almost complete exclusion of guildsmen, as representatives of the *popolo*, from political power and the consolidation of a ruling class made up of old and new merchant families who defined themselves as noble. In all these ways, the Serrata marked the end of a century of extraordinary social and political change. At the same time, it marked the beginning of what can properly be called the Venetian Republic.

The social change and population growth of the thirteenth century also resulted in the expansion of Venice at the city's edges—a movement championed by the mendicants. Meanwhile the ruling elite fostered the development of a form of domestic architecture that would remain the characteristic Venetian palace type. This form was capable of accommodating changing stylistic and decorative fashions, at least until the end of the nineteenth century.

All this makes the thirteenth century one of the most decisive centuries in Venice's long history. This chapter tells the story of the Fourth Crusade and its impact on the creation of an image of Venice, both for the Venetians and for others. It also examines the acquisition of Venice's Mediterranean empire as well as trade.

On August 15, 1198, Pope Innocent III called for a new crusade to bring to fruition what the Third Crusade (1189–92) had so conspicuously failed to accomplish, namely, the rescue of Jerusalem from the Muslims. The Holy City had been wrested from Western control by Saladin following the battle at Hattin in 1187. Eighteen years earlier Saladin had toppled Egypt's Fatimid dynasty and followed that up with the conquest of Muslim Syria. The Third Crusade, which was led by Kings Richard I (Lionheart) of England and Philip Augustus of France, and Holy Roman emperor Frederick Barbarossa (who died while on the mission), ended ignominiously with Richard managing only to secure access to Jerusalem for Christian pilgrims and the restitution of Jaffa and other coastal towns to the crusaders.[1]

The crowned heads of Europe largely ignored Innocent's call to take the cross. The monarchs of England and France were preoccupied with war with one another, while Germany was riven by the opposing claims to the imperial title of Philip of Swabia and Otto of Brunswick. Instead, it was Flemish and northern French knights who responded. Their leaders decided that it was best to journey to the Holy Land by sea rather than risk the treacherous overland route favored by many previous crusaders. They needed a fleet, however, and sent a delegation to Venice to arrange transport.

The envoys arrived in Venice in spring 1201 and, following negotiations with Doge Enrico Dandolo and his council, reached an agreement. In exchange for a payment of 85,000 silver marks, Venice would supply transport for 4,500 knights and an equal number of horses, 9,000 squires, and 20,000 foot-soldiers. The Venetians agreed to maintain the men and horses for a year. In addition, they pledged to outfit fifty war galleys at their own expense in return for half of any spoils. Following an emotion-filled Mass in San Marco, the General Assembly approved the undertaking, and a day later the contract was formalized. The leaders also secretly decided that they would first attack Egypt and, after taking Alexandria, turn to Palestine.

The Venetians had committed themselves to a massive undertaking. In the end, in addition to the fifty warships they pledged as their contribution, they outfitted as many as 450 transport vessels, including ones specially designed for the conveyance of war horses. To concentrate on the effort, which has been described as "the largest state project in western Europe since the time of the Romans," the Venetians suspended normal commerce for up to eighteen months.[2] They contracted with private shipyards to build the vessels, gathered supplies, and instituted a parish-based lottery system to recruit the crews to man the fleet. As many as 14,000 men were needed, the equivalent of about half the city's adult male population.

While the Venetians met their contractual requirements, the northern crusaders failed to keep theirs. The trickle of men who began to arrive in early June 1202 never turned into a flood. The shortfall in funds was even worse. Of the 85,000 marks promised, they could come up with only 50,000. The crusaders' commander was Boniface, Marquess of Montferrat, a valorous soldier, scion of a family with connections across Europe, and favorite of both Pope Innocent and Philip of Swabia, the Hohenstaufen claimant to the Holy Roman Empire. Fatefully for the coming crusade, he also had connections to Byzantium since two of his brothers had married Byzantine princesses: one brother had been murdered, while the other had never reaped the material benefits that the marriage promised. While visiting the court of Philip at Christmas, Boniface encountered the Byzantine prince and pretender to the throne Alexius, son of the emperor Isaac II Angelus, who had had been deposed and blinded in 1195 by his brother Alexius III. Philip was married to the pretender Alexius's sister Irene. Prince Alexius lobbied for a show of force by the Westerners that would provoke a palace coup and install him on the throne. But the crusaders did not commit to the enterprise. Neither did Innocent III, whom Alexius visited in the late winter of 1202.

When June 29, the scheduled departure date arrived, the northerners were short of both men and cash and suffering from the unhealthiness of their Lido encampment. They and the Venetians faced a dilemma—disband or proceed. A solution offered itself when Doge Dandolo, with the approval of his councilors, proposed that, if the crusaders would help the Venetians subdue the rebellious Dalmatian city Zara, the Venetians would delay payment of the debt until the anticipated profits from the expedition allowed the crusaders to make good on their obligation. Zara had long thwarted Venice's efforts to dominate completely the eastern shore of the Adriatic. Anxious to get under way, the crusaders agreed. Even the papal legate went along, recognizing that failure to do so would jeopardize the entire undertaking.

During a Mass held in San Marco in early September, Doge Dandolo personally joined the crusade. According to Geoffrey of Villehardouin, Marshal of Champagne and chronicler of the crusade, the doge addressed the assembled Venetians and barons this way:

> Sirs, you are joined with the most valiant men in the world in the greatest enterprise that anyone has ever undertaken. I am old and weak and in need of rest, and my health is failing. But I see that no one knows how to govern and direct you as I do, who am your lord. If you agree that I should take the sign of the cross to protect and lead you, and that my son should remain and guard the land, then I shall go to live or die with you and the pilgrims.[3]

The Venetians assented, and Dandolo took the cross, affixing it to the ducal *corno* (crown). They also agreed that Dandolo's son Raniero would serve as vice-doge in his absence.

Enrico Dandolo is one of the few doges to stand out in the long line of often colorless men who held the ducal office. His fame is due in large measure to the fact that he was likely ninety-five years old when he joined the crusade—and blind. It was not unusual for the Venetians to elect elderly men to the dogeship; indeed, it was their preference. But Dandolo's election at age eighty-five pushed the limits. As for his blindness, it was likely due to a blow to the head that he received in 1175 and not, as one chronicle had it, to a 1172 order by Emperor Manuel Comnenus to have him blinded. Instead, following the concussion, his vision deteriorated to the point that he was very nearly or completely sightless.[4]

The Dandolo family had begun to distinguish itself by the mid-eleventh century. Dandolo's father Vitale was noted for his sagacity and probity. He was one of the eleven electors who selected Sebastiano Ziani as doge. Ziani dispatched Vitale on an unsuccessful mission to Constantinople to secure the release of Venetian hostages. A subsequent mission in 1174 with the same aim proved too much for the ninety-year-old. He died in Constantinople and was buried there. With his death, Enrico assumed family leadership while continuing to pursue his own political career, including ambassadorial missions to Constantinople, Alexandria, and Ferrara.[5]

When Doge Orio Mastropiero died in May 1192, the ducal electors chose Dandolo as his successor. During the first decade of his dogeship, he oversaw the compilation of a civil code consisting of seventy-four statutes that served as the basis for later, more elaborate collections of Venetian law. Dandolo also presided over a reorganization of Venetian currency that introduced the silver *grosso.* During his reign, Venice reached new accords with Verona, Ferrara, Treviso, and the patriarch of Aquileia and continued its efforts to subdue Zara, which was aided in its defiance of Venice by the Pisans. In 1198 a new agreement with Byzantium granted the Venetians several trade privileges.[6] Dandolo's personal familiarity with Constantinople and Alexandria, his experience in treating with the Byzantine emperor and other rulers, his desire to subdue Zara, combined with his forceful personality, would prove crucial to the crusading mission ahead.

According to Robert of Clari, another chronicler of the crusade, when the massive fleet finally set sail in October 1202, the very sea itself was "all a-tremble."[7] A letter from Pope Innocent forbidding an attack Christian Zara reached the crusaders only after they had arrived there and were preparing a siege. Assessing the size of the invading force, the Zarans offered to surrender. However, when some of the northern knights informed them of Innocent's prohibition and their own misgivings about assaulting fellow Christians, the inhabitants decided to resist. Dandolo was adamant that the attack proceed. Zara fell and was pillaged on November 24. Innocent excommunicated the Venetians.

It was customary in this period, when navigation still depended on observation of landmarks and the heavens, to suspend long-distance Mediterranean Sea travel from November to March. Accordingly, the crusaders wintered in Zara. In early January envoys arrived from Philip of Swabia and his brother-in-law the pretender Alexius with an extravagant offer. If the crusaders would depose the usurper Alexius III and place young Alexius on the throne, he

(Alexius) would bring the Greek church into union with Rome thus ending the schism of the two churches, pay the crusaders 200,000 marks, supply a force of 10,000 soldiers to join the enterprise, and station 500 knights in the retaken Holy Land. The envoys also assured the crusaders that the Byzantines would welcome their rescue from Alexius III. After much debate, the offer was accepted, and Innocent's prohibition of the plan suppressed.

In April the crusading force decamped from Zara, but only after the Venetians leveled the town, save for its churches. Alexius the pretender joined the expedition late in the month. Worried that the September 29, 1203, expiration date of the contract with the Venetians was fast approaching, it was agreed that the force would head to Constantinople and remain there no more than a month. The fleet arrived in the Byzantine capital in late June.

It quickly became apparent that the metropolis would not rise up to overthrow Alexius III, who sent envoys to the crusaders with offers of supplies and cash if they would depart for the Holy Land. The offer was refused. In an effort to spark an uprising against the usurper-emperor, the crusaders paraded Alexius the pretender before the walls of the city. This was met with derision by the Greeks, and so on July 5, 1203, an assault was launched. The crusaders decided not to attack the city from the Sea of Marmara or the Bosphorus, where the city walls stretched to the very edge of the water, but rather to secure a beachhead on the north shore of the Golden Horn, the estuary that served as the primary harbor for the Byzantine fleet, since it was protected from the strong currents of the Bosphorus. Near its tip, the shore was guarded by the Tower of Galata to which a chain, designed to prevent the entry of enemy ships into the harbor, stretched. On the first day, the knights were able to capture most of the northern shoreline. The following day, they managed to take the tower, allowing the Venetian galleys to break the chain, destroy the small and decrepit Byzantine fleet, and find safe harbor.

Building on their momentum, the crusaders decided to launch a two-pronged attack. The knights would approach from the land, striking the walls near the Blachernae Palace at the northern tip of the city, while the Venetians would try to overcome the relatively weaker harbor walls along the southwestern shore of the Golden Horn. On July 17 the offensive was launched, and although the knights were rebuffed at the Blachernae, the Venetians managed to secure about a quarter of the towers along the harbor wall. According to Villehardouin, it was Dandolo whose courage proved decisive. He recounts,

> Now may you hear of a strange deed of prowess; for the Doge of Venice, who was an old man, and saw naught (seeing he was blind),

> stood, fully armed, on the prow of his galley, and had the standard of St Mark before him; and he cried to his people to put him on land, or else he would do justice upon their bodies with his hands. And so they did, for the galley was run aground, and they leapt therefrom, and bore the standard of St. Mark before him on the land.[8]

To protect their foothold in the city, the Venetians set a fire, which quickly got out of control and consumed more than 125 acres.

Furious at Emperor Alexius III's perceived cowardice, the Constantinopolitans turned on him. Before they could take their revenge, he took flight, while still claiming to be emperor. The Byzantines did not, however, see it that way. Rather than bestow the emperorship on young Alexius, whom they viewed as a Western and Venetian puppet, they decided to restore his father Isaac II, the brother whom Alexius III had deposed and blinded. Isaac then sent for his son, the pretender, and agreed to honor the extravagant commitments that young Alexius had made at Zara even though he knew his son had overpromised. The diversion to Constantinople appeared to have paid off. The crusade could finally proceed, replenished with men and money.

In the capital itself, events at first appeared to go the crusaders' way. They prevailed upon Isaac to crown Alexius, subsequently known as Alexius IV Angelus, as co-emperor. They received elaborate gifts from the imperial family, including the bestowal of Crete upon Boniface of Montferrat. Even better, Isaac handed over 100,000 of the 200,000 marks pledged by him and Alexius to the crusade. Half went to the Venetians, the other half to the knights who at last were able to clear their original debt to Venice. But relations between Latins and Greeks—already tense because of economic grievances and religious and cultural differences—quickly soured, especially since the crusaders had overstayed the one-month limit originally agreed upon. Alexius IV needed them to remain since his uncle still controlled large portions of the empire and would no doubt try to retake the city once the crusaders left. To keep them in the capital, he promised to pay for an extension of the lease on the Venetian navy for another year, to September 29, 1204.

In August 1203 Greek disgust with the Latins led the inhabitants of the city to attack the Italian merchant communities in the city indiscriminately. In retaliation a group of Westerners set fire to the houses and other properties of many Greeks. The fire consumed 450 acres: fortunes and lives were lost, and tens of thousands of Constantinopolitans were left homeless. The Greeks blamed not only the Latins but also Alexius IV, for bringing this scourge upon them.

To save his neck, Alexius distanced himself from the crusaders, hoping that the arrival of spring would see their departure for Jerusalem, while his promised payments slowed. A delegation of crusaders and Venetians went to see him and demanded in the most impolitic way that he fulfill his obligations. Their effrontery outraged the Greeks, while Alexius's non-reply infuriated the Latins, who launched a series of raids in December 1203 to take what they believed they were owed. In retaliation, the Greeks tried unsuccessfully to destroy the Venetian fleet by sending fire ships across the Golden Horn.

At the same time, a rival to Alexius emerged. Alexius Ducas Mourtzouphlus, a high court functionary, won popular favor by his willingness to challenge the Latins militarily. He seized the initiative and imprisoned Alexius IV. His claim to power was further strengthened by Isaac II's death from natural causes. On February 5, 1204, Ducas was crowned as Alexius V. A meeting between him and Dandolo came to naught in large part because the Latins continued to see Alexius IV (who still owed them 90,000 marks) as the legitimate emperor. So Ducas decided to rid himself of his bothersome predecessor; on February 8 or 9 Alexius IV was strangled. With that, Byzantine commitments to the crusaders, namely, the extension of the contract for the Venetian fleet and the promises Alexius had made at Zara, were nullified.

During a subsequent meeting of the Latins, the clergy who accompanied the crusaders offered them the justification they needed to attack Constantinople, namely, that Ducas was a murderer and the Greek church had again fallen out of union with Rome. In March, the Venetians and crusade leaders agreed that once the city was conquered, the Venetians would receive three-fourths of the booty (to pay off the 150,000 marks they claimed Alexius IV owed them). If the take was greater, the remainder would be divided evenly between the allies. A committee of six Venetians and six northern crusaders would select the new emperor, who would receive a quarter of the lands taken, while the rest would be divided equally between the Venetians and the northerners. A committee of twenty-four (twelve crusaders and twelve Venetians) would distribute offices and fiefs. If the chosen emperor was a crusader, then the Venetians would occupy the patriarchate and vice versa. They agreed to remain in the capital until March 1205 to support the new emperor, who for his part was forbidden to do business with any of Venice's belligerents, especially Pisa and Genoa. Oaths were taken not to violate women or churches and to bring all the booty collected to a common location for equitable distribution.

Based on their earlier experience, the crusaders decided that they would attack the city along the walls of the Golden Horn. On April 8 the assault began but proved unsuccessful. The Byzantines defended their city bravely.

Because of the wind, few Venetian ships were able to affix their flying bridges (platforms suspended high on the masts of the ships by which troops could gain access to the top of the walls) to the towers. Following their retreat, the Latin clergy rallied the dispirited troops with fiery sermons condemning the Greeks as "dogs" and "worse than the Jews," and offering full absolution to those who would take part in the next assault.[9]

It came on Monday April 12. This time the wind was favorable, and two Venetian ships were able to secure their flying bridges to the towers. Another group of attackers, including the chronicler Robert of Clari, secured a toehold on the land between the walls and the water and managed to open one of the city gates. In poured troops and horses. That same night, Alexius V tried to rally the Constantinopolitans to defend the city but to no avail. To most of the city's inhabitants, the struggle appeared to be little more than a contest between rival claimants to the imperial throne: namely, Alexius V as a member of the Ducas family, and the crusaders as defenders of the Angelus family. Finding himself without meaningful support, Alexius V slipped away. At Hagia Sophia a successor, Theodore Lascaris, was chosen, but when he realized that he too lacked the forces necessary to resist the crusaders, he retreated to Nicaea where he established the Nicaean Empire in exile. The Constantinopolitans suddenly found themselves instead at the mercy of a marauding horde. So began the sack of Constantinople.

The magnificence of the four golden horses adorning the façade of San Marco, the most visible booty secured during the rampage, masks the horrifying events that brought the steeds to Venice. For three days, the conventional time soldiers were allotted to sack a vanquished town, the Latins pillaged the capital. Churches, including Hagia Sophia, were denuded and desecrated, relics spirited away, imperial tombs despoiled. Even the body of Justinian the Great was defiled. In the most oft-cited image of the sack, Byzantine official and historian Nicetas Choniates recorded that a prostitute, whom he described as "a woman laden with sins, . . . the handmaid of demons . . . waxing wanton against Christ," sat on the patriarch's throne in Hagia Sophia and also sang obscene songs as she "whirled about and kicked up her heels in dance."[10] The Latins took revenge on the Greeks, raping women and killing men who tried to protect them. Prized works of ancient art were smashed, ancient bronze statues melted down.

Choniates fulminated against the crusaders and condemned them as frauds, writing that "seeking to avenge the Holy Sepulcher, they raged openly against Christ and sinned by overturning the Cross with the cross they bore on their backs."[11] Villehardouin sanitized his account, concluding that "those who before had been poor were now in wealth and luxury."[12] Venetian chronicler Martino da Canal, writing in 1267, omitted the sack entirely from his account since it darkened Venice's reputation.[13]

Once the frenzy passed, a committee of twelve men, six northerners and six Venetians, set about choosing the new Latin emperor. The imperial throne went to Baldwin of Flanders, who received more votes than Boniface of Montferrat and was crowned on May 16, 1204. Boniface got as a consolation prize the provinces in Asia Minor and the Peloponnese (or as the Venetians called it, the Morea) but swapped them for the lordship of Thessalonica. As part of a larger deal, he sold Crete, which he possessed in name only, to the Venetians for 1,000 marks. Venetian Tommaso Morosini became Latin patriarch.

The final division occurred in October. The Venetians got three-eighths of the Byzantine Empire, expressed at the time as one-quarter and half of one-quarter. They took as their portion of Constantinople itself those parts of the city that bordered the Golden Horn, namely, the quays and warehouses that could serve their maritime interests. Outside the capital, they secured a tract of land running from Adrianople to the Sea of Marmara and down the Gallipoli peninsula. In addition, they received the westernmost part of mainland Greece, running from Durazzo to the tip of the Morea where Modon and Coron, later referred to as the "Eyes of the Republic," would become strategic outposts guarding Venetian sea lanes. In the Ionian Sea, Venice got the islands of Corfu, Santa Maura (Lefkada), Cephalonia, and Zante (Zakynthos). In the Aegean, Venice acquired the two tips of Negroponte, and Andros, Salamis, and Aegina.[14]

With Constantinople secured for the Latins, the crusaders believed and the clergy confirmed that their pilgrimage vow had been fulfilled. Rather than continuing on to the Holy Land, they simply went home. After much dithering, Innocent lifted the excommunication against the Venetians. For his part, Dandolo remained in Constantinople to help put in order the newly enriched Venetian community but died the following year. The doge was buried in Hagia Sophia, in the city that also sheltered the remains of his father.[15]

The Fourth Crusade was controversial in the thirteenth century and remains so to this day. The transformation of a war pilgrimage against Muslims into an attack on the Christian cities of Zara and Constantinople offended many, including Pope Innocent, and troubled the consciences of more than a few crusaders. The blame for the diversion has traditionally fallen on the Venetians, Dandolo in particular. That is certainly how Nicetas Choniates understood it. He contends that the doge, whom he called "a sly cheat," planned all along to target Constantinople as revenge for Manuel's 1171 imprisonment of the Venetian community in the empire and confiscation of their properties.[16] According to those who subscribe to this view, the "wily old Dandolo" was able to hoodwink the naïve northern knights as he "stage-managed" events.[17] In this interpretation, Dandolo spared Egypt, where Venice had important trade interests from attack; subdued rebellious Zara; overcame the arrogant Byzantines; and acquired three-eighths of the empire for his homeland.

Others, following Villehardouin's narrative, see the crusade's outcome as the product of a series of miscalculations and bad decisions. The root cause was the original contract whereby the northerners agreed to unrealistic terms, and this led the crusade off course.[18] From this perspective, the fault did not lie with the Venetians, who, as good businessmen, were simply demanding that the crusaders fulfill their contract.

While historians continue to debate what happened and why, the Fourth Crusade unquestionably created an indelible image of the Venetians, one that haunts them to this day. They come across as cynical opportunists, interested only in gain, not God. For centuries, the Venetians, who saw themselves (often rightfully so) as bearing the brunt of the Islamic offensive against Christendom, were criticized by other Westerners as not fully committed to the fight. Even the more sympathetic view of Dandolo and his fellow Venetians presents them as sticklers for upholding the original agreement with the crusaders, casting them as exacting merchants for whom a contract was sacrosanct. Either way, they come across as caricatures of capitalists, interested only in money, not in nobler principles.

This is not, of course, how Venetians of the time saw themselves or the Fourth Crusade. A mosaic floor executed in the church of San Giovanni Evangelista in Ravenna in 1213 depicting the pretender Alexius meeting with Innocent and the section of Martino da Canal's chronicle describing the crusade show that thirteenth-century Venetians viewed themselves as loyal servants of the church and of Innocent, who—in this interpretation—supported and even promoted the diversion to Constantinople in order to put Alexius on the throne. Although Venetians' understanding of what happened would grow more complex in subsequent centuries, the Fourth Crusade remained at the center of their consciousness. Eight paintings depicting episodes from the crusade were executed for the Greater Council Hall in the Ducal Palace between 1578 and 1620 by such artists as Tintoretto and Palma il Giovane.[19]

What does the Constantinopolitan plunder—much of it conspicuously displayed on the basilica of San Marco—say about the Venetians' motivations and their self-image? Throughout its brief existence, the Latin Empire of Constantinople (1204–61) served as a quarry that Venice mined for saints' relics, works of art, and building materials. During the thirteenth century, these war trophies and symbols of domination would be deployed on buildings around Piazza San Marco to present an image of Venice as heir to Byzantium and therefore the New Rome. The immediate message of the relics and the bronze horses was that the crusading Venetians were a pious people who had been performing God's work. After all, like Mark before them, Saint George and Saint John the Baptist, parts of whose bodies the Venetians obtained in the sack, must have sanctioned their transfer to the lagoon.[20] Even the horses, which were only mounted on San Marco during the reign of Doge Ranieri Zeno at midcentury, contained a Christian meaning that resonated in face of the criticism leveled at the Venetians. The stallions, affixed so prominently on the west front of the basilica, represented the Quadriga Domini, the Four Horse Chariot of the Lord, drawn by the four Evangelists.[21] The bones of the saints and the horses affirmed in Venetian minds that theirs had been a pious undertaking.

While determining the conquest's meaning would take time, the Venetians faced more immediate tasks, including determining how to administer the lands that were already in their possession and taking control of those that were not but had been assigned to them. The most pressing problem was Constantinople itself. Before the conquest, the Venetians had entrusted administration of their quarter to private individuals and ecclesiastical institutions, but all that changed with the conquest and Dandolo's death. The Constantinopolitan Venetians could not await instructions from Venice; they had to act quickly, and so they elected Marino Zeno as their podesta or governor, who took the title that Dandolo had been using, namely "Lord [*dominator*] of three-eighths of the Empire of Romania." (Romania was the term the Venetians used to refer to the Byzantine Empire.) He set up an administration modeled on the one in Venice, including a Lesser Council, and informed the home government of his selection. When Pietro Ziani, son of Doge Sebastiano Ziani, was elected to succeed Doge Dandolo, he confirmed Zeno in the post but made clear that islands and territories near the mouth of the Adriatic, including Durazzo and Corfu, would come under direct Venetian control, while other territories gained in the crusade would be under the jurisdiction of the podesta in Constantinople. Ziani also authorized his fellow Venetians to grab whatever Greek islands they wished and hold them hereditarily, with the proviso that they never alienate them to non-Venetians.[22]

When Ottaviano Querini replaced Zeno in 1207 the pattern was established that the podesta would be chosen in Venice, not in Constantinople, and that he would swear an oath of loyalty to the Venetian commune, while the title *dominator* of three-eighths of Romania was transferred to the doge. The new administrative arrangement and ducal title made clear that the Venetian community in Constantinople was subordinate to Venice.[23] This would last until 1261 and the fall of the Latin Empire. From 1268 on, an official known as a *bailo* (rector) became the chief administrator of the Constantinopolitan Venetian community.

The years immediately following the crusade saw Venice stepping cautiously into its new role as an imperial power. That tentativeness supports the view that the Fourth Crusade was not a pre-planned Venetian plot aimed at domination. Indeed, the overwhelming impression from these years is that the Venetians were making decisions on the fly. For example, they entrusted governance of strategically important Durazzo to a governor, who held the title of duke and was accountable to the home government. In Corfu, by contrast, after brief experimentation with a governor, Venice entrusted administration of the island to a group of ten Venetian noble lessees who agreed to defend it. Venice rented Coron and Modon to four leaseholders, although by 1226 it was administering them directly through castellans. Still another arrangement was worked out for Cephalonia, Ithaca, and Zante, where an Orsini count held the islands as a vassal of the doge. On Negroponte, Venice utilized a *bailo* to superintend its possessions.[24]

Doge Ziani's invitation for his countrymen to acquire Greek islands set off a land grab, much of it centered on the Cyclades and Sporades. Marco Sanudo, nephew of Doge Dandolo, took the lead. He secured Naxos, Paros, Milos, and Santorini, establishing himself in 1207 as the Duke of Naxos or of the Archipelago. Others who accompanied him acquired their own enclaves: the island of Andros went to Marino Dandolo; Tinos, Mykonos, Skyros, Skopelos, and Skiathos to Andrea and Geremia Ghisi; Lemnos and Imbros to Filocalo Navigaioso. Marco Venier took Cerigo (Kythira); Iacopo Viaro, Cerigotto (Antikythira); and Leonardo Foscolo the island of Anafi.[25] Some declared themselves vassals of the Latin emperor, others of the doge.

After Constantinople itself, Crete was the biggest prize, but Venice had to fight to gain possession. When Boniface sold the island to Venice, he did not actually control it. It was in the hands of his allies, the Genoese. The Venetians launched an attack in 1207, and it took several years of hard fighting against the Genoese and Cretans to gain control. Genoa did not formally cede the island until 1218.[26]

Crete's importance as the largest Greek island, its economic significance as a major producer of wine, cheese, and fruit, and its strategic location (a jumping off point for ships headed north to Constantinople, east to Lebanon, or south to Egypt), required an altogether different solution to its governance, namely, actual Venetian military colonization. A 1211 document, known as the Concession of the Island of Crete, divided the island into six districts, except for the area around Candia (Heraklion) which would serve as the Venetian capital. These districts in turn were divided into 200 units known as knightships, 132 of which were assigned to mounted soldiers; the remainder were further subdivided into 408 sergeantries and allotted to foot soldiers. The majority of the knightships went to Venetians of distinguished heritage, sergeantries to Venetians and non-Venetians of humbler origin. The men who received these fiefs—the feudatories—were expected to form a militia to defend the island.[27]

Venice decided, however, not to place supervision of the colony in the hands of the feudatories but to direct it from the lagoon. It appointed a chief officer, known as the Duke of Candia, who served a two-year term. Giacomo Tiepolo, the first duke, implemented Venice's military colonization of the island. The duke was assisted by two councilors also chosen in Venice from among the city's most prestigious families. Over time administering such a large territory required the appointment of rectors, chosen in Venice, to supervise Chania and Rethymno, the other large towns on the northern coast of the island. A staff of bureaucrats numbering up to 100 and modeled on offices and courts in the metropole assisted the duke in administering justice.[28]

To tie the interests of the feudatories more closely to Venice, three councils—the Greater Council of Candia, the Council of Feudatories, and the Candiote Senate—were established. The Greater Council focused on military issues regarding the eastern part of the island, while the Council of Feudatories was responsible for carrying out its decisions. The Candiote Senate handled matters regarding defense, taxes and imposts, and religion.[29]

Venice deployed religion and saints to help secure the island. The Venetians converted the old Greek rite cathedral dedicated to Saint Titus into the Latin cathedral and installed a Latin archbishop for the island. The Greek bishops were exiled. Saint Titus was legendarily a pagan who was converted to Christianity by Saint Paul and was ordained the first bishop of Crete. The

Venetian authorities incorporated Titus and his feast day into official church ceremonials and made him the special protector of the Duke of Candia and his government. By promoting Titus's cult, the Venetians asserted their ownership of the island and sought to use him as a bridge between the Greek and Latin communities.[30] But it was not an easy divide to span given the theological and ritual differences between the churches.

Venice's administration of Crete was unique enough that Pope Urban V, writing in 1368, noted Venice's "uncommon dominion" over it.[31] Even so, Venice would endure numerous revolts against its rule throughout the thirteenth and fourteenth centuries.

As is clear, Venice did not have a one-size-fits-all approach to its overseas territories, some of which it acquired through the crusade, others by purchase or military conquest. Instead, it improvised and experimented as the situation and local circumstances demanded. In general, however, Venice was not interested in territory per se but rather in sites that offered strategic or commercial advantages. Even in Crete, Venice's primary focus was on the northern coastal towns that could service its trade routes rather than on the countryside. All told, the Fourth Crusade and its immediate aftermath placed Venice in possession of an overseas empire that served its commercial and naval interests.

Another consequence of the Fourth Crusade was a further significant expansion of Venetian commerce. While it lasted, the Latin Empire of Constantinople offered Venice trade advantages that its rivals Pisa and Genoa could only envy. Although the Pisans and the Genoese (after 1218) were permitted to reconstitute their quarters in Constantinople and resume their old trade privileges, these could not match those of the Venetians, who built a large new warehouse in the city in 1220 to handle increased business.[32] But Constantinople did not retain the unparalleled commercial primacy that it had before the conquest, as other Greek towns siphoned off some of the trade. Venice even reached commercial accords with the despot of Epirus and the emperor of Nicaea, Greek rulers who each hoped to recapture Constantinople and reestablish the Byzantine Empire.[33] It signed another agreement in 1220 with the sultanate of Rūm or Iconium, which controlled the parts of Anatolia that the Seljuk Turks had conquered from Byzantium.[34] Coastal trade around the Aegean and transit trade between Constantinople and Alexandria constituted important components of Venetian business.[35]

Additionally, the collapse of the Byzantine Empire opened the Black Sea, a trade zone that had been largely closed to Westerners before the fall of Constantinople. Egypt continued to be a major trading partner and the primary terminus of the spice trade. Although relations were often tense due to ongoing papal efforts to launch a new crusade to retake the Holy Land, in 1238 the Venetians reached an accord with the sultan that granted the Venetian consul resident in Alexandria jurisdiction in disputes between Latins and established rules for the operation of the two Venetian *fondachi* (warehouse/hostels), which included the right to consume wine within their precincts and for the Venetians to maintain a church. Egypt was not Venice's only North African port of call. Following in the footsteps of Romano Mairano, Venetians were also trading in Bougie and Ceuta, and in 1231 Venice reached a forty-year treaty with the ruler of Tunis where a consul was in residence and a *fondaco* was established. Venice also continued to carry out significant trade with Tyre and Acre in the Crusader States and posted a *bailo* in both places. Venice even had favorable commercial relations with the Muslim rulers in Syria and thus access to Aleppo, Laocidea (Latakia), and Damascus, where bulk items like cotton and soda ash (used in Venice's flourishing glass industry) and choice items such as pearls, precious stones, and pepper could be secured. The Christian kingdom of Lesser Armenia, with major ports at Laiazzo (Yumurtalik) and Korykos, was still another trade partner from whom Venice secured numerous trade privileges including a *fondaco* and church in Mamistra (Mopsuestia). Lesser Armenia was a valuable source of cotton, wool, mohair, iron, lumber, grain, and horses. The many agreements forged with both Christian and Muslim rulers attest to the Venetians' sole concern with obtaining commercial rights and privileges.[36]

Another factor fueling the surge in trade was the growth of Venice's population and of Europe's generally and the concomitant increased demand for goods. Some estimates suggest that the city reached 100,000 souls by the end of the century, Europe as a whole around 78 million. The Greater Council acknowledged Venice's growth early in the fourteenth century when it declared, "Thanks be to God, the city grows and increases continuously."[37] Another component driving demand for Eastern luxury goods was the burgeoning interest in material objects as status symbols. To the already familiar list of spices, silks, and perfumes can be added precious building materials. Churches, monasteries, and palaces in the East became a vast stone-yard from which the Venetians extracted exotic marbles, fragments of antique reliefs and inscriptions, columns, and capitals. When, in 1291 in Coron Venetian trader Giacomo Trevisan sought a loan of 200 hyperpers, he put up as collateral thirty-nine marble columns, four smaller ones, and some marble plaques.[38] Such materials, when incorporated into a Venetian church or private palace, conveyed sophistication and an appreciation for antiquity.

Venetian shipowners also made money transporting Western pilgrims to and from the Holy Land. Most landed at Acre, an important Venetian outpost, from which they could make the short overland journey to Jerusalem. Given its geographical location, Venice was the preferred embarkation point for pilgrims from northern Italy, Austria, Hungary, and Bohemia. While waiting to set sail, pilgrims sought to earn merit for their souls by visiting the many saints' relics housed in the city, especially in San Marco. The ideal pilgrimage itinerary through the basilica, demarcated as it was by Byzantine plunder and Islam-inspired decorative motifs, offered pilgrims a preview of what awaited them in the Holy Land.[39] A service industry developed to accommodate these pilgrim/tourists. Ten of the sixteen hostels/hospices established in Venice before the end of the thirteenth century provided lodging to pilgrims.[40] Before embarking, pilgrims of means purchased straw mattresses and food to supplement the rations allotted onboard, procured information regarding the fees and bribes they would have to pay at holy sites, and perhaps learned a few useful phrases.[41]

What most distinguished thirteenth-century commerce from the earlier period was the growth of trade in bulk items. The population created a huge demand for food, including grain, wine, and olive oil. Venice was supplying not only itself with these materials but also the boom towns of the Po River valley. During a three-month period in 1224, for example, it transported 48,000 liters of oil, 82,000 kilos of figs, and 24,000 kilos of cheese up the Po.[42] The textile industries of those towns also fueled a demand for wool and cotton, which the Venetians were securing in Syria, Lesser Armenia, and elsewhere. Venice itself had a nearly insatiable demand for timber, used for building, the naval industry, and fuel.

Salt remained one of Venice's most lucrative products, which through governmental intervention retained its special place in the economy. Starting in the 1240s Venice began to allow the importation of salt that was produced overseas, labeling it "sea salt" to distinguish it from locally produced salt. Then in 1281 the Greater Council started requiring merchant vessels returning to Venice to carry, based on the calculation of their outbound cargo, a certain quantity of salt as ballast. Because Venice was trying to impose a salt monopoly on neighboring cities in the Po valley, it could then charge a high price for the imported salt and garner a big profit for its merchants on a commodity that otherwise would not have been so lucrative.[43]

In this way, the government subsidized private shipowners who, starting in the early fourteenth century, began building increasingly large round ships called *coche* (cogs) with square sails and stern mounted rudders. The *coche* were easier to defend than the old lateeners. The government benefited as well since during wartime it could commandeer these ships for service to the city. In peacetime, the owners were guaranteed a profit due to the salt subsidy. Another savings derived from the change in rigging: square-rigged ships required just half the manpower of lateen-rigged ones.[44]

A combination of technological innovations—including use of a compass with a magnetized needle, development of port books (listing the distances between landmarks), marine charts called portolans, and traverse tables—fostered in the late thirteenth century adoption of dead reckoning, a method of navigating based on estimating distance traveled and direction. Using it, mariners were no longer dependent on the sun and stars to know the direction in which they were heading and could navigate in winter when clouds, fog, and storms hindered observation of the heavens and landmarks. It became possible to make two round trips a year to the Levant whereas before ships had made one and a half. Previously, ships departing in the fall had had to spend the winter in the East when the Mediterranean was closed to long distance traffic. Now ships leaving in winter could return by the feast of the Ascension in the spring, and ships leaving in summer could make it back in time for Christmas. With two annual round trips, merchants could better meet growing consumer demand.[45]

Like their predecessors of earlier centuries, thirteenth-century Venetian merchants continued to seek new markets and to be jacks-of-all-trades rather than specialists in any one commodity. One such operator was Pietro Viglioni, who drew up his will in Tabriz in Persia where he was acting as agent for several other merchants in 1263. Since he was one of the few, if not the only, Venetians in Tabriz at the time, he requested that, on his death, his goods be consigned to the *bailo* of Acre. The inventory of his merchandise included Western products that he was seeking to sell. These consisted primarily of textiles, including linen from Germany and Lombardy and stanforte cloth from Flanders. He also had in his possession chess and backgammon sets and candelabra carved in Venice from rock crystal. Among the Eastern products he had acquired were sugar (likely from Syria), as well as pearls and precious stones.[46]

The textiles in Viglioni's possession are a salutary reminder of the European side of Venetian trade, which is often overshadowed by the exotic products of the East. As Martino da Canal observed, "Germans and Bavarians, Frenchmen and Lombards, Tuscans and Hungarians and all people who live by trade" came to Venice "to buy goods and transport them to their homelands."[47] An early example of these northern businessmen who frequented Venice was Bernardus Teotonicus, a dealer in precious metals mined in the eastern Alps, Hungary, and Carinthia. Descended from a line of administrators from Munich, Bernardus settled in Venice, helped Frederick Barbarossa secure loans for the Third Crusade, and himself made loans to various German princes. By the time he drafted his will in 1215, he was one of the richest men in the city. Just two years earlier he had paid the highest price yet recorded for a piece of urban real estate, a stone house in San Bartolomeo, the parish where the Merceria, the main commercial street starting at San Marco, intersected with the square near the Rialto bridge.[48]

Although Bernardus was exceptional for his wealth and level of success, other merchants from beyond the Alps were coming to Venice to procure goods from the East and to sell in turn precious metals, furs, and leather. During a colloquy held in 1245 Holy Roman emperor Frederick II remarked that the Venetians earned "great advantage and . . . great gain" from his realm, although he acknowledged that many of his subjects derived in return "great gain from Venice."[49] Merchandise moving north traveled on barges and boats up rivers like the Adige and then on the backs of pack animals along paths and tracks through the Alps.

The extraordinary growth of international commerce in the thirteenth century tends to overshadow a notable increase in mainland property investment by Venetians. With diminishing opportunities for purchase of land within the *dogado* itself, wealthy Venetians looked to the *terraferma*. When nobleman Marco Badoer's heirs divided portions of his estate in 1288, it included land in the countryside around Padua, Treviso, and Ferrara, as well as unusually a fief near Capua in the Kingdom of Sicily bestowed on Marco and his wife Marchesina Ziani (heir of the Ziani fortune) by Charles of Anjou. The properties in the Padovano were situated on the Brenta River and comprised houses, cultivated fields, vineyards, pastureland, mills, and swampland. They included a *castrum* (fort/castle) at Borbiago that Marco's father had built. While the Badoer castle and southern Italian fief conveyed a degree of social prestige, the primary benefit of landholdings outside the *dogado* was practical. In an age of growing food shortages, *terraferma* properties were dependable sources of grain, wine, meat, and firewood, as well as rents from tenant farmers. Many of the treaties worked out with mainland cities included clauses exempting Venetian property holders from the duties normally levied on imported consumables.[50] A century and a half before Venice's conquest of the mainland, Venetian economic exploitation of the Italian hinterland was already well established.

Venice's burgeoning population and trade and its growing maritime empire impacted the city's form and spawned important infrastructure projects. Two in particular—the Fondaco dei Tedeschi (the German Merchants' Warehouse) and the Arsenal—remain prominent landmarks in the cityscape.

The Venetians adopted the *fondaco*—a combination hostel, warehouse, and trading post—from the Middle East and North Africa where such establishments went by various names including *khan*, *caravanserai*, *wakala*, and *funduq*—the latter the Arabic root of the Venetian word *fondaco*. In the thirteenth century the Venetians themselves occupied *fondachi* in several cities including Alexandria, Acre, and Tyre where they traded, stored goods, and maintained their native customs.[51]

Some of the *fondachi* built in Venice served primarily as warehouses. A grain warehouse was constructed at Rialto perhaps during the reign of Sebastiano Ziani. It also served as headquarters for the Ufficiali al Frumento (Grain Officials) who monitored the quantity of grain available in the city, along with its quality, sale, and distribution. Four much larger grain warehouses were begun in 1341 on a tract of land known as Terranova facing the Bacino near the Ducal Palace. They could each store as much as 40,000 bushels of grain.[52] The still extant Fondaco del Megio (Millet Warehouse) on the Grand Canal at San Stae was built in the early fifteenth century; an earlier structure on the site served as a deposit for salt. In the thirteenth and early fourteenth centuries, the commune maintained or rented warehouses for salt throughout the city and at Chioggia. However, the city's 1281 requirement that merchant vessels use sea salt as ballast prompted the commune to build huge salt warehouses in Dorsoduro on the stretch of land leading to what is today the Custom's House Point. They were situated facing the wide Giudecca Canal in order to facilitate loading and unloading of large seagoing vessels.[53]

The Fondaco dei Tedeschi conformed more closely to Middle Eastern prototypes in its multi-functionality. Located in the parish of San Bartolomeo on the San Marco side of the Rialto market, it provided lodging, warehousing, and space for sociability for German merchants in the city. In this the Germans were following the example of other co-nationals who congregated together. In the same decade as the founding of the Fondaco, for instance, merchants from Modena were sharing accommodations at a hostel in the

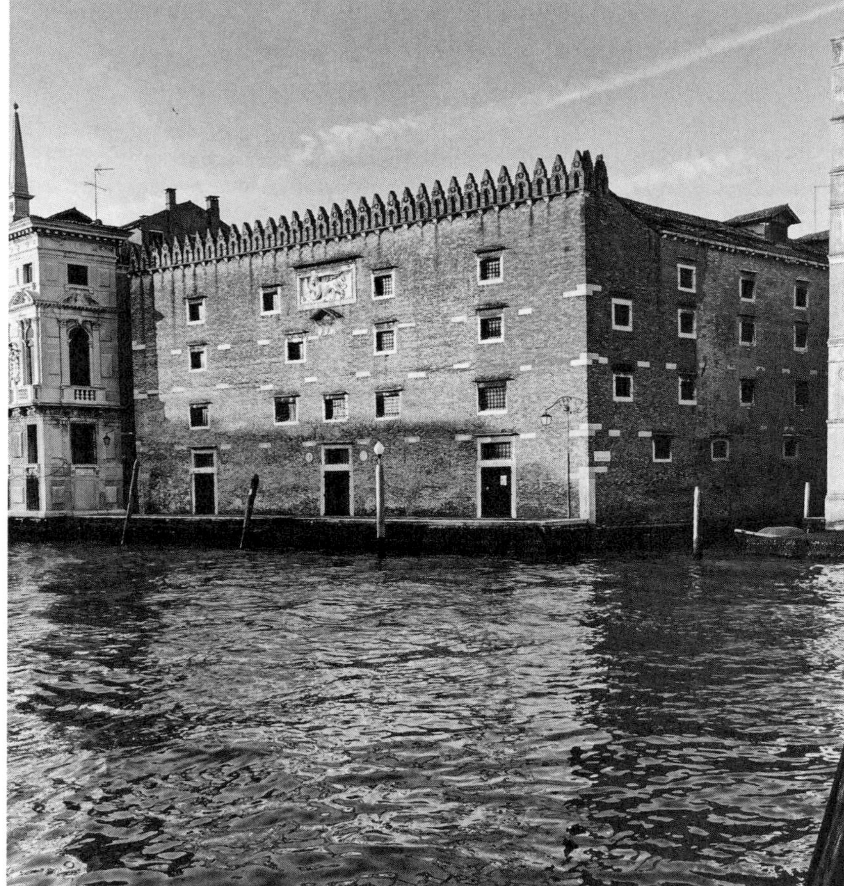

FIGURE 6.1 Fondaco del Megio at San Stae, early fifteenth century, Venice. The utilitarian purpose of the building is clear from the small windows and lack of ornamentation except for the Lion of Saint Mark denoting it as a public property. Photo by the author.

parish of San Giovanni di Rialto run by an innkeeper who was identified as the "hosteler of the Modenese."[54] Even before the creation of the Fondaco, German merchants had been gravitating to San Bartolomeo. In 1222 the commune purchased land nearby in order to expand a preexisting building for the Fondaco. At first, management was leased to a group of German merchants, but in 1268 the government assumed direct supervision by appointing three Visdomini del Fondaco (Vice-lords of the Fondaco) who were assisted by a staff of notaries and brokers who mediated all transactions. The resident German merchants were carefully supervised and their trade activities tightly controlled and subject to political surveillance.[55]

Like the Modenese, merchants from other Italian cities found lodging in the inns concentrated at Rialto and San Marco while pilgrims stayed in the hostels dedicated to them. Taverns offered visitors food, drink, and entertainment in the form of gambling. While pilgrims visited the relics of Mark and other saints housed in the city, some merchants and sailors (and perhaps a few pilgrims as well) sought less-edifying services. In 1260 a woman known only as Lucarda of the parish of San Giovanni Grisostomo had a notary draft her last will and testament. In it, Lucarda mentioned no relations other than her daughter Maria, named as executor and sole beneficiary of her estate. Given her low social status as indicated by her lack of a surname, failure to identify herself as a daughter, wife, or widow, and residence near the Rialto market, it is possible that Lucarda was a prostitute.[56] If so, she is the earliest known practitioner in Venice of a profession that serviced foreign merchants and sailors frequenting Rialto and for which the city would become renowned in later centuries.

The origins of the other great infrastructure project, the state-owned shipyard or Arsenal, remain shrouded in mystery, although the Venetian complex shared affinities with arsenals in both Constantinople and Alexandria. The word *arsenale* (Venetian *darzanà*, *arzanà*, *arzanàl*) derives from the Arabic *dār ṣināʿah* meaning workshop. The first incontrovertible evidence of its existence dates from 1206, making it possible that construction of the huge Fourth Crusade fleet prompted its establishment.

The commune situated the Arsenal in a sparsely populated marshy area in the sestiere of Castello, strategically located near the fortified San Nicolò mouth to the Adriatic and the earliest customs house. Some of the city's salt warehouses were also nearby. The original Arsenal, which corresponded to the section referred to today as the Arsenale Vecchio (Old Arsenal), was quadrangular in form and encompassed an area of approximately eight acres. It was protected by a wall and connected to the Bacino by the Rio dell'Arsenale (Arsenal Canal).

This first Arsenal was not intended to meet the city's shipbuilding needs; privately owned shipyards continued to perform that function. It could not even satisfy the government's military requirements. In the 1220s, for example, the commune contracted with Artico Massario, a private supplier, for 1,000 ash oars. Nevertheless, activity at the Arsenal flourished. In the 1220s the government ordered the dredging of the Rio dell'Arsenale, an indication of its increasing usage. In those same years it hired a notary to keep track of the complex's expenses. By 1265 timber reserves were being stored at the Arsenal in case galleys needed to be built in a hurry. During the next decade

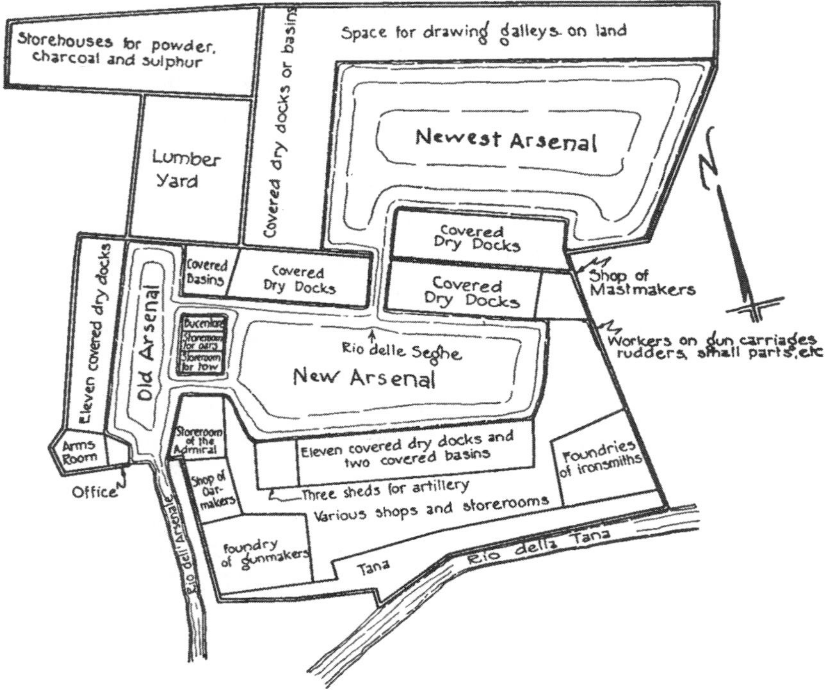

FIGURE 6.2 Plan of the Arsenal around 1560. The original section, the Old Arsenal, is on the left. From Frederic Chapin Lane, *Venetian Ships and Shipbuilders of the Renaissance*, p. 173, Fig. XVIII. © Johns Hopkins University Press. Reprinted with permission of Johns Hopkins University Press.

an armory was added. In 1276 the commune ordered the Patroni all'Arsenale (Lords of the Arsenal), the three noble officials in charge of the complex, to keep at the ready a squadron of four galleys and two other vessels for quick dispatch. The early Arsenal served as a depot for naval stores, a repair yard, and the headquarters of a guard fleet.[57]

The mint comprised another essential component of Venice's commercial infrastructure. It was relocated at some unknown date from San Bartolomeo to a site along the Molo and across the Piazzetta from the Ducal Palace. Judging from a fifteenth-century depiction of the area, the medieval mint comprised two buildings: a three-story one facing the water with shops, and a smaller one-story edifice with a door facing the Piazzetta and Ducal Palace.[58] It was here, starting in 1285, that mint masters began to produce the gold ducat. The government authorized its issue in October 1284 as a delayed response to the introduction in 1252 of gold coins by Genoa and Florence

FIGURES 6.3A AND 6.3B Gold Ducat of Doge Tommaso Mocenigo, 1414–23, obverse and reverse. American Numismatic Society. 1954.237.158.

and as a boon to Venetian merchants purchasing gold mined in Hungary and Transylvania at the Fondaco dei Tedeschi. Composed of 3.545 grams of pure gold, the ducat would retain this standard until the Republic's demise in 1797.[59] Its iconography too would remain unchanged: on the obverse it depicted the kneeling doge receiving the banner from Saint Mark while the reverse showed a blessing Christ enveloped in a mandorla.

Around this time the mint began to be referred to as the Zecca. Previously, the word *moneta* had been used to designate the mint. Zecca derives from the Arabic work *sikka*, meaning a "die." The Venetians' adoption of Arabic words for the Arsenal, *fondachi*, and Mint offers further evidence of the myriad exchanges—in this instance linguistic—between Venice and the Islamic world.[60]

Although its location naturally endowed Venice with undeniable advantages as the nexus of East/West trade, it could not rely on geography alone since several towns along the northern Adriatic enjoyed similar attributes. To maintain its dominant trade position, the commune constantly had to monitor or crush competing cities on the Adriatic and enforce its trade policies on towns in the Italian hinterland. At the same time, Venetian merchants continually had to adapt to changing market conditions and alter the choice of ports they frequented in response to shifting political developments in the wider Mediterranean sphere, developments that were often beyond the city's control.

Venice's acquisition of Durazzo, Corfu, Modon, and Coron in the partition of the Byzantine Empire following the Fourth Crusade makes clear that surveillance and domination of the Adriatic remained its primary concern. In his chronicle, Martino da Canal even went so far as to claim that "in truth, the Adriatic Sea belongs to the dukedom of Venice."[61] The commune's aim was to monopolize trade in the northern Adriatic. The goal was for all merchandise, whether traveling on Venetian or foreign ships, to be brought to Venice for unloading, taxation, and resale. Foreign merchants were encouraged to come to the city, purchase the cargo, and re-export it. The system was designed to ensure that Venice would be the only place where goods could be exchanged and hence an obligatory stop for merchants. Franciscan friar Salimbene di Adam of Parma described the plan this way: "The Venetians bar the river route to the Lombards so that they cannot receive provisions from either Romagna or the March of Ancona, from which they would be able to supply themselves with grain, wine and oil, fish, meat and salt, figs, eggs and cheese, fruit and every kind of merchandise necessary for their life, if the Venetians did not impede it."[62] Venetian merchants profited by serving as the middlemen, while the government secured food supplies for the city as well as revenue through customs duties, brokerage, weighing, packing, and cartage fees. It also garnered the ire of its neighbors.[63]

Venice was able to enforce its staple rights only in the northern stretches of the sea and even there only partially. These rights never extended as far south as Ancona or Apulia, nor did they encompass many of the Dalmatian cities. However, Venice did require that if ships from those places sailed into the northern Adriatic, then they had to unload at Rialto. Allowing these cities to trade among themselves did Venice little harm since the greatest demand for goods and the most profitable markets lay, as Salimbene made clear, with the consumer-hungry towns of the Po River valley accessible by the many rivers emptying into the Adriatic in Venice's backyard. Through various treaties Venice tried to guarantee its access to these river routes. In 1192, for example, Verona promised uninhibited passage to Venetian merchants "by land and water," along the Adige River from Verona to Caverzere; Venice received similar guarantees of free passage along the Adige from Padua in an agreement signed nearly a century later.[64] Where trade really counted—that is, in the Gulf of Venice—the city vigorously strove to enforce its monopoly claim and protect access.

The treaty that Venice reached with Ravenna in 1234 offers a good example of how the city treated its Gulf rivals. Venice forbade Ravenna from transporting pilgrims anywhere except to Venice itself en route to the Holy

Land. The treaty also prohibited Ravenna from exporting wine and grain produced in its surrounding countryside except to Venice. Residents of Ravenna were permitted to import grain, meat, figs, wine, oil and cheese from the Marches and Apulia for their personal use, but any surplus had to be sold exclusively to Venetian merchants, in which case the sellers had to pay customs duties of 20 percent. With this treaty, "the complete dependence of Ravenna [on Venice] was sealed."[65] Venice's 1240 treaty with Ferrara forbade the Ferrarese from allowing merchants to import goods up any branches of the Po or by sea, unless the goods came through Venice.[66] Although the treaties reached with other cities from Ancona to Zara included innumerable variations, the intent was the same.

Venice used a panoply of tactics to enforce its monopoly claims. Merchants from cities that contravened the accords were subject to reprisal; they could have their merchandise confiscated or impounded, and the cities themselves were subject to boycott. Weaponizing salt, Venice sought to cripple its rival Cervia, just as it had destroyed Comacchio in 932. Twice, between 1243 and 1248 and again between 1251 and 1253, Venetian forces occupied Cervia. In a series of treaties signed between 1285 and 1336, Venice drastically limited Cervia's salt production, bought up most of what was produced, and restricted where the rest could be sold. In return, it made annual payments to Cervia's government.[67]

Venetians acting as administrators in *terraferma*, Istrian, and Dalmatian towns pushed policies and issued rulings favorable to Venice. In 1226 a court made up of three Ferrarese arbiters was established to handle disputes between Venetians and Ferraresi, but Venice got to select the arbiters. A 1222 treaty with Aquileia established a Venetian consul in that town; Ravenna had a consul by 1261, Ferrara by the late thirteenth century. For twenty-two years between 1221 and 1302, Venetians served as podestas in Treviso.[68] High church officials offered yet another means of extending Venetian influence. The Querini family acquired property at Papozze in Ferrarese territory in the mid-thirteenth century when Giovanni Querini was serving as bishop of the city.[69]

Venice also built forts and maintained patrols on the Po and Adige rivers to ensure compliance and stop contraband. In 1258 it built a fort named Marcamò on the Po del Primaro, at that time the main branch of the Po. Here the Venetians could monitor and control cargo moving upriver to Ferrara and beyond.[70] When intimidation did not work, Venice resorted to force. In 1331, for example, patrols intercepted a boat carrying salt from Cervia to Ravenna; one of the boatmen was killed and the cargo was dumped into the sea.[71]

At other times Venice engaged in open warfare with nearby cities such as Padua and Ferrara. Given the constantly shifting landscape in the delta regions where rivers and streams changed course frequently, it is not surprising that border disputes dominated relations with Padua.[72] In 1303–4 the Paduans constructed salt pans near Chioggia and built a fort to protect them. They did this, they claimed, in response to Venetian provocations including the building of a tower in Paduan territory and the destruction of landings under Paduan jurisdiction, although their real intent was to gain a foothold in salt production and break the Venetian monopoly. In response, the Venetians built a dike to prevent salt water from reaching Padua's new salt works. The brief conflict that ensued, known as the Salt War, ended in a Venetian victory.[73] The amphibious environment of the lagoons and delta regions of the northern Adriatic, where fixed borders were hard to discern, contributed to these contests over the control of natural resources and trade.

Environmental conditions also made it easy for smugglers to operate. Sparsely inhabited islets in the lagoon and poorly patrolled channels snaking through canebrakes in the deltas offered places to stash goods and run contraband. Judging from laws passed by the Greater Council, foreigners were not the only ones flouting the law. In 1226, the government forbade everyone living in Venice proper or anywhere in the *dogado* from transporting to Padua, Aquileia, Friuli, or Trieste any items, including food, cash, and merchandise, without a license from the doge and the Lesser Council. Doing so would undercut Venice's efforts to enforce its staple rights. Nearly a half century later, the Greater Council prohibited "anyone from Venice" from going to Treviso or Padua to buy German goods. Clearly, some Venetian merchants were seeking to gain advantage over their competitors by purchasing German products without paying the brokerage and other fees imposed at the Fondaco dei Tedeschi.[74] The broad sweep of laws limiting free trade spurred constant efforts to circumvent them.

Ritual, a form of soft power, was another tool Venice used to affirm its control over the Adriatic. The Marriage of the Sea ceremony became one of the most important festive events in the Venetian calendar. The observance probably began around the year 1000 as a simple blessing of the sea and commemoration of Doge Pietro II Orseolo's naval expedition against the Narentan pirates. As a springtime rite, it marked the opening of the sailing season before navigational advances made sea travel safe year-round. By the mid-eleventh century, the bishop was performing the blessing at San Nicolò on the Lido and invoking the protection of Saint Nicholas for the coming season. Venice's Fourth Crusade territorial acquisitions may have prompted a further amplification since, by the mid-thirteenth century at the latest, a marriage rite had been folded into the event. According to Martino da Canal, on the Thursday following Ascension Day, the doge boarded his ceremonial galley and was rowed to the Adriatic where his chaplain blessed the water, and the doge tossed "a ring of gold into the sea."[75]

By the sixteenth century the ceremony had been moved to Ascension Day itself and further expanded to include a procession involving innumerable small watercraft, a Mass, feasting, and parties. Its core message, however, remained unchanged. When the doge cast the ring into the waves, he recited the words, "We wed thee, O sea, as a sign of true and perpetual dominion."[76] In assuming the role of the husband, the doge claimed possession of the (female) sea. Through this "imperial rite"—one in keeping with the city's status as an empire—the doge asserted Venice's dominion over the sea lanes of the Adriatic and warned rival powers to stay out of the city's aquatic backyard.[77]

While Venice worked to assert through action and ritual its staple rights over the Adriatic, after midcentury its merchants had to respond to rapidly shifting political developments in the wider Mediterranean and beyond. The first of these involved the collapse of the Latin Empire of Constantinople, the restoration of the Byzantine Empire, and the loss of the privileged position that Venice had achieved in the Fourth Crusade. The Latin Empire survived as long as it did in large part because of the rivalry between the despot of Epirus and the emperor of Nicaea, Greeks who both claimed to be the legitimate successors to the Byzantine throne. In the end, Nicaea proved the stronger. In 1259, Michael VIII Paleologus was able to defeat the coalition allied against him and followed that up by retaking Constantinople, with Genoese assistance, on July 25, 1261.[78]

Once crowned, Michael rescinded the privileges granted to the Venetians and conferred them on the Genoese. Venice moved quickly to protect Negroponte and Crete and engaged Genoa in naval skirmishes. Michael soon soured on his Genoese allies and tried to reconcile with Venice. An accord was finally reached in 1277 that granted the Venetians a substantial quarter in Constantinople and various trade privileges. Then in 1281 Venice foolishly signed on to a plan by the pope and the king of Sicily Charles of Anjou to restore the Latin Empire. The plan's failure to proceed due to a rebellion against Charles, that placed Sicily in Aragonese hands, left Venice again locked out of Constantinople. The two powers reconciled again in 1285, and Venetian merchants returned to Constantinople.[79]

The Venetians also regained access to the Black Sea where trade accelerated in the second half of the century. This was due to the political stability and trade security, known as the Pax Mongolica (Mongol Peace), that the Mongols were able to impose across a huge swath of territory that extended from China to the frontier with Hungary. Following the death of Genghis Khan in 1227, the lands he had conquered were divided into several different khanates or realms, including the Khanate of the Golden Horde that controlled parts of Hungary, Poland, and southern Russia; the Il-Khanate that comprised much of Persia, Iraq, and parts of Anatolia; the Chaghatai Khanate of Central Asia; and the empire of the Great Khan with its new capital at Khanbalik (Beijing). In 1258, Hulegu, the founder of the Il-Khanate Empire, sacked Baghdad. In 1265, the year of his death, he established Tabriz farther to the north as the capital. The Pax Mongolica opened up a secure trans-Asiatic land route by which spices and other luxury products could make their way to the Black Sea by caravan along the Silk Road. It connected the sea-based Mediterranean trade network with the land-based Eurasian one and offered an alternative to the more traditional southerly routes through Syria/Palestine and Egypt.[80]

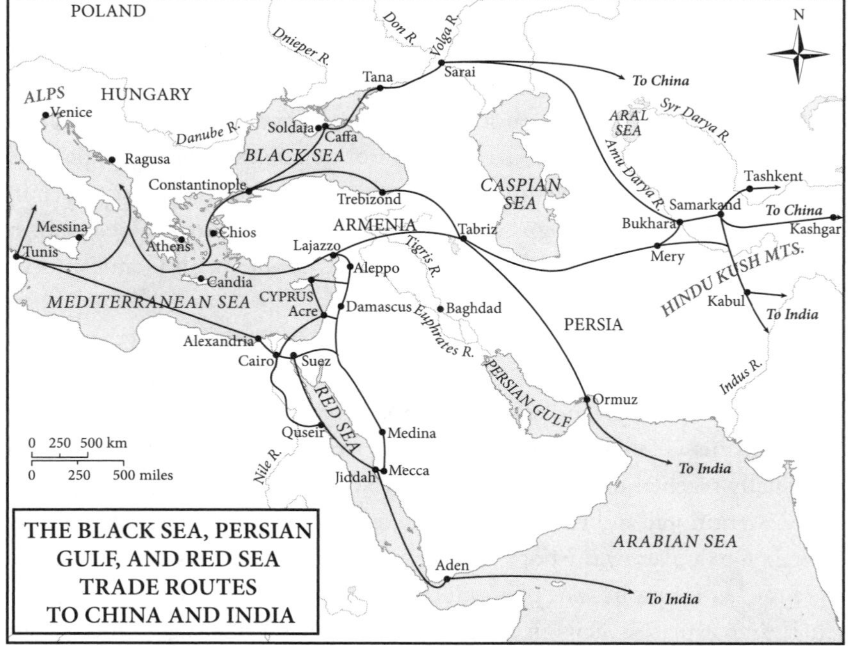

FIGURE 6.4 Black Sea, Persian Gulf, and Red Sea Trade Routes to China and India. Based on Frederic C. Lane, *Venice: A Maritime Republic* (Baltimore, 1973), 71.

Western Europe's "discovery" of the Far East was due in large measure to Marco Polo, Venice's most famous native son. In 1260 Marco's father Nicolò and uncle Maffeo set out from Soldaia (Sudak) on the Crimean Peninsula, the main Venetian outpost in the Black Sea, and made their way east to the capital of the Khanate of the Golden Horde, trading especially in precious stones. When the fall of the Latin Empire of Constantinople in 1261 made their return via the Byzantine capital impossible, they continued east, hoping to return via Tabriz, but that route too was closed due to war. After spending three years in Bokhara, they joined a caravan traveling to China, where they were received at the court of Kublai Khan in his new capital Khanbalik. He asked them to travel home and return with 100 Christian missionaries. After arriving in Laiazzo in Lesser Armenia in 1269, they made their way to Venice.

On their return mission to Kublai Khan in 1271, they took with them Nicolò's seventeen-year-old son Marco and two priests, and after a three-year journey arrived in the court of Kublai Khan minus the priests. For almost two decades, Marco served Kublai Khan, traveling the stretches of his empire. When he finally returned to Venice in 1295, he had been away for nearly a quarter century. Along with marvelous adventures, he had acquired great wealth—hence his nickname Il Milione (the Millionaire) although another theory holds that the sobriquet refers to the million tales he spun of his adventure. He made his fortune in large part by dealing in jewels. Lightweight and highly portable, precious stones were the perfect commodity for such a journey, while the stability that the Mongols had imposed along the Silk Road made their transport secure. In 1295 Marco was in Laiazzo either on business or as part of Venice's war effort against Genoa. There he was captured by the Genoese and imprisoned.[81]

While in prison, Marco met Rustichello da Pisa, a writer of romances, and together they collaborated in composing Marco's book, *Livre des Merveilles du Monde* (The Book of the Wonders of the World). The work was written in French, which had great currency in northern Italy.[82] That Marco, a Venetian, sitting in a Genoese jail, dictated his adventures to Rustichello, a Pisan, who then wrote them up in French, is striking evidence of the fluidity of contacts and cultural interactions in the Mediterranean basin at the time.

Polo's book has been the subject of endless debate. Some have questioned whether he even made it to China, although his descriptions of such things as Chinese currencies and salt production and income from the salt monopoly indicate that he did. As a Venetian, Polo would have been attuned to the nuances of the salt industry. While the book shares characteristics with other merchant manuals, describing, for example, the quality of Turkish carpets, the availability of products including precious stones in Tabriz, and the wares to be had in Hormuz, that was not its primary purpose.[83] Thanks to Rustichello, it was a book of tales of the marvelous sites and customs that Marco experienced on his trans-Asiatic journey. It exponentially expanded Westerners' knowledge of the Far East. As one authority has observed, "Never before or since has one man given such an immense body of new geographical knowledge to the West."[84] One early fifteenth-century Florentine manuscript claims that a copy of Polo's book was kept at Rialto.[85] If true, it is unlikely that merchants consulted the Rialto copy for practical information, but it would have served as a striking advertisement to the reach of Venetian trade in the business heart of the city. As for Marco Polo himself, after being released from prison in 1299, he returned home, married, and had three daughters. He died in January 1323 with an estimated net worth of 10,000 ducats.[86]

Other Venetian merchants followed his steps to China, although their numbers were not great. One such trader was Giovanni Loredan, who ventured there in the early 1330s. He and his brother Paolo made a subsequent journey to India, but Giovanni died before he made it back to Venice. Paolo did return home, having invested in pearls and realized a considerable profit.[87] Members of another Venetian family, the Viglioni, seem to have established themselves for a time in China. Caterina Viglioni, who died in Yangzhou in 1342, may have been a descendant of the Tabriz testator Pietro.[88] However, others contend that she was a member of the Genoese Ilioni family.[89]

Certainly, the Genoese established themselves in the Black Sea before the Venetians did. They had a resident consul in Caffa by 1281. Soldaia was the Venetians' primary center in the region; they dispatched a consul there in 1288. In addition to exporting Asian products that had made their way along the Silk Road to Trebizond, the Venetians trafficked in salted fish and caviar from the coastal waters of the Black Sea; alum from Asia Minor; and furs, honey, wax, grain, and slaves (sent mainly to Muslim lands) from Ukraine and southern Russia.[90]

Marco Polo's presence in Laiazzo in Lesser Armenia in 1295 is indicative of another radical political development to which Venetian traders had to adapt. In 1291 the last remnants of the Crusader States, including Acre, Tyre, and Tripoli, fell to the Mamluk rulers of Egypt. Acre had been a particularly important Venetian stronghold and the source of crucial raw materials for Venice's rapidly growing glass industry. Just four years later, the Mongol rulers of the Il-Khanate or Khanate of Persia converted to Islam. This dislocated the second great trade route to the East, the one that passed through the Persian Gulf up the Tigris River to Baghdad (and after the establishment of the Il-Khanate to Tabriz) and then overland to Syria/Palestine. Venetian merchants responded by turning more of their attention to the Black Sea ports and by shifting their business activities to Christian Lesser Armenia, Famagosta in Cyprus, and Candia in Crete.[91] In the decade before and immediately after the fall of the Crusader States, Venice built an arsenal and improved the port facilities at Candia as Crete took on new importance as a way station to Lesser Armenia and Egypt.[92]

The most southerly trade route, the one that proceeded up the Red Sea to Egypt, continued to flourish. By 1260 the Mamluks had wrested control of Egypt from the Ayyubid dynasty that had ruled Egypt since 1171 and then went on to reconquer Syria from the crusaders.[93] Despite the change of regimes, Egyptian policy remained constant, namely, to deny the Italians direct access to the Red Sea. Instead, Western merchants, the Venetians foremost among them, could only call at Alexandria, where their cargos were surveyed and taxed. While in the city, they were confined to their *fondachi*. There they purchased goods for the voyage home such as spices (especially pepper) and dyes, silk and cotton cloth, porcelains and other items from Egyptian wholesale merchants who had themselves secured the goods at Red Sea ports like Aden from Indian and Arab importers. At Alexandria, two near-monopolies converged: a Muslim one carrying the goods as far as Egypt and a Venetian one transporting them on to western Europe.

The fall of the Latin Empire in Constantinople made Venice's trade with Egypt even more crucial. It has been suggested that in 1261 the Venetians began utilizing the winged lion of San Marco as a symbol of the commune as a "marketing" ploy to ingratiate themselves with the Mamluk Sultan of Egypt Baybars, whose coat of arms sported a feline.[94] Still, as in the Adriatic, the Venetian monopoly in Egypt was never absolute. Venice's main competitor again was Genoa, which also did a thriving business in supplying slaves taken in the Black Sea to the Mamluks. From the Black Sea to north Africa, the Genoese and Venetians vied for trade and political influence. The Pisans competed with both, until they were crushed by Genoa in 1284 at the Battle of Meloria in the Ligurian Sea.

Twice in the thirteenth century, the rivalry between the Venetians and the Genoese turned into outright war.[95] The first (1256–70), sometimes referred to as the War of Saint Sabas, began in Acre. Tension between the merchant communities boiled over, partly the result of a dispute over a house belonging to the Monastery of Saint Sabas that both powers coveted for its location near the harbor. In 1258 an outnumbered Venetian fleet under Lorenzo Tiepolo defeated the Genoese fleet off Acre and took many of its sailors prisoner. But the tide turned against Venice when, in 1261, with Genoese assistance Michael VIII Paleologus restored the Byzantine Empire, revoked Venetian trade privileges, and granted them instead to Genoa in return for Genoese naval support. Even so, the Venetians continued to get the better of the Genoese, defeating them in the Battle of Settepozzi off the Morea in 1263 and again off Trapani in Sicily in 1266, although the Genoese managed to inflict significant damage on Venetian shipping even in the Adriatic. Two events eventually led to a peace. In 1268, Michael soured on his Genoese allies and readmitted the Venetians to Constantinople, and in 1270 Louis IX of France (Saint Louis) pressured the Genoese into signing the Peace of Cremona so that he could employ their fleet for a crusade.

In fact, the peace treaty concluded at Cremona in 1270 settled nothing. Accordingly, the Second Venetian-Genoese War (1294–99), also known as the War of Curzola, grew out of the powers' mutual desire to control Lesser Armenia and the Black Sea. The first engagement off Laiazzo in 1294 led to a crushing defeat for the Venetian fleet and the capture of its crews, including perhaps Marco Polo. Another in September 1298 near Curzola on the Dalmatian coast had the same result: Genoese admiral Lampa Doria's fleet of eighty ships defeated the ninety-vessel Venetian flotilla. But Doria was unable to carry the victory into the Gulf of Venice, and the following year, Domenico Schiavo, a Venetian corsair, led a raid on Genoa itself. Venice took advantage of internecine conflict within the Genoese ruling elite by aligning itself with the Grimaldi headquartered in Monaco, who had been expelled from Genoa by the Doria and Spinola families. The peace that was signed in 1299 in Milan recognized Genoese dominion over the Ligurian Riviera and Venetian control of the Gulf of Venice but did nothing to resolve the underlying competition between the two powers, particularly in the Black Sea.

During the thirteenth century, the Venetian lion emerged from its Adriatic den to become a Mediterranean power, one whose economic reach and naval might extended from Trebizond and Constantinople to Alexandria and Tunis. It also became an imperial power, with significant possessions in the Ionian and Aegean seas. In the process, the basilica of San Marco was transformed into a trophy case. Indeed, after decades in storage at the Arsenal the four gilded bronze horses were finally mounted on the façade of the church during the reign of Doge Ranieri Zeno. The fall of the Latin Empire of Constantinople in 1261 likely provided the impetus for their display on the parapet of the church since, by placing them there, the Venetians could claim that with the return of Byzantium to rule by Greek religious schismatics, a true transfer of power from Rome to Byzantium to Venice had occurred. As Constantinople once had been, so Venice became the New Rome. Only from the Fourth Crusade on did Venice fully lay claim to its Byzantine cultural inheritance. With Constantinople no longer in a position to assert its sovereignty over Venice, the Venetians could finally and fully embrace their Byzantine origins.

This is evident in the systematization of Piazza San Marco that started under Doge Pietro Ziani in the immediate aftermath of the Crusade and concluded with the paving of the Piazza under Doge Zeno in the 1260s. Most of the public buildings surrounding the square were built or refashioned in a similar Romanesque/Byzantine style, with ground floor arcades resting on columns. A pair of square columns from the church of Saint Polyeuctus in Constantinople (referred to today as the Pillars of Acre) were set up flanking the south, Bacino-facing entrance to San Marco. They joined the two monumental granite columns that already adorned the Molo. San Marco itself was embellished with dozens of marble and granite columns, yet more booty looted from Constantinople. The entire Piazza San Marco complex recalled the ancient imperial fora still extant in Constantinople, dotted as they were with porticoes and colossal columns topped with statues. One such column surmounted by a cross included statues of Emperor Constantine and his mother Helen, as well as a porphyry ensemble with four embracing kings, reputed to be the sons of Constantine. Commonly known as the tetrarchs, the group was shipped to Venice following the Fourth Crusade and embedded in the south exterior wall of San Marco, where it remains to this day. Nearby stands a sawed-off porphyry column—the *pietra di bando* (proclamation stone)—from which public decrees were read. It had been used by the Genoese for that same purpose and seized from them during the First Venetian-Genoese war.[96] Carefully planned out and stylistically unified, Piazza San Marco and the smaller Piazzetta leading to the Bacino announced Venice's new imperial standing as a worthy successor to Byzantium.[97]

As the imperial decoration of the Piazza announced, the Venetians began to think of themselves as rulers of an empire. Yet, it was a curious empire, with some lands ruled directly, others by proxy, and still others subject to economic coercion. And their empire lacked an emperor, despite the claim in Doge Pietro Ziani's epitaph that he had no equal "amongst the high born and wise, not even Caesar and Vespasian were they still alive."[98] Instead it was governed by a group of merchant families who during the thirteenth century excluded all others from power and began to define themselves as noble.

7

Society and Politics in the Thirteenth Century

IN DECEMBER 982, Doge Tribuno Menio granted the island of San Giorgio Maggiore to Giovanni Morosini so that he could erect a Benedictine monastery there; at the time, the doge declared that he was doing so with the consent of "our bishops and the leaders (*primatibus*) and people of Venice."[1] Menio and others in the tenth century thought of Venetian society as composed of three main groups: high ecclesiastical officials, prominent laymen, and then everyone else—the people. When Martino da Canal began composing his chronicle in 1267, he offered a strikingly different vision of the Venetian social order. He wrote, "In that beautiful city you can find a great quantity of gentlemen—old, young, and in full maturity—whose nobility merits great praise; and with them merchants who buy and sell and moneychangers, and citizens of every trade; mariners of every kind, and ships for transporting [goods] everywhere and galleys for wreaking havoc on enemies. And in this beautiful city there are many beautiful ladies and maidens and girls—all in abundance and dressed very richly."[2]

Gone from Da Canal's description is any reference to the clergy, even though they continued to play an important role in society. Instead, gentlemen, men who are distinguished by their nobility, come first. They are followed closely by merchants and moneychangers (the earliest bankers), then by artisans and sailors. Last are women, clearly noblewomen, distinguished by their beauty, number, and rich attire. Da Canal does not even mention laboring-class women. But he is alert to the lifecycles of both noblemen and noblewomen. Curiously, Da Canal's portrait of Venetian society includes ships—both merchant vessels and war galleys—almost as living beings and thus a vital part of the community.

The chronicler employs a variety of criteria to characterize Venice's inhabitants: status still counts, some are noble, others are not. So too does profession. Merchants and moneychangers matter in particular; they are named specifically, whereas artisans and sailors are lumped together as practicing "every" trade and being of "every" sort. Even so, they are no longer the undifferentiated "people" of Menio's time but take on identities based on the work they do. Noblewomen are included, even if only to emphasize that they enhance Venice, which is "the most beautiful and pleasing [city] in the world, full of beauty and every good."[3]

The complexity of thirteenth-century Venetian society was due to the large population of nearly 100,000 souls which required a variety of goods and services for its sustenance, and to the economic expansion following the Fourth Crusade, which allowed specialized manufactures to flourish. As the population grew, Venetians were confronted by all the problems that accompany a densely urbanized environment, including policing, hygiene, and issues of transportation and communication. These concerns fostered growth in administration and bureaucracy. As society grew richer and the government more powerful, the struggle to control the levers of authority intensified. Factional infighting among the elites, long an element of Venetian politics, continued to fester, but so too did conflict among various social groups, including old noble families, newly rich merchants, and artisans. The doges allied themselves at times with various of these groups. Yet by the end of the century, the die had been cast. Artisans were excluded from power, while the old nobles and merchants came together in the Serrata, a series of laws passed between 1286 and 1323, to create a regime in which lineage became the principal criterion for Greater Council membership and enfranchisement. The commune was transformed into an aristocratic republic.

In contrast to Da Canal, most chroniclers simply divided Venetian society into *magni et parvi* (big and small) or *maiores et minores* (greater and lesser).[4] Although these broad categories were strikingly imprecise, they reflected the reality on the ground when social distinctions were not yet clearly defined.[5]

This was particularly true for the elite, those referred to as nobles. Any number of factors could lead to someone being considered noble. Antiquity counted. Families, like the Gradenigos, that could trace their forebears to Venice's earliest days were venerated, as were those that had founded parish churches or endowed monasteries.[6] But families were always in danger of failing to produce male heirs and going extinct. Important lineages of earlier centuries like the Orseolos and Partecipazios had already disappeared. The same fate befell the ducal branch of the Zianis in the thirteenth century. Doge Pietro Ziani died in 1229 leaving a son Marco, but when he died without issue, most of the estate passed in 1254 to his sister Marchesina who had married Marco Badoer.[7] Reputation also mattered. Families that had held numerous important offices or had served on military and diplomatic missions were also regarded as noble. However, many noble families, like the Zianis, were noteworthy foremost for their wealth, which they had earned through trade and property investment.[8]

The Badoers are a good example of a noble family that had a venerable history among the city's elite but could not trace their lineage back to Venice's origins. At least four family members witnessed Doge Menio's transfer of San Giorgio Maggiore to Giovanni Morosini in 982. In the eleventh and twelfth centuries Badoers served as *iudices* in the ducal court and on embassies. For a time in the early twelfth century, they occupied important ecclesiastical posts as well, including the patriarchate of Grado and bishopric of Malamocco. The Badoers were significant property holders in the city. An expanse of open water near the parish of San Giacomo dall'Orio was known as the "lacus Badovariorum" (Badoers' pond). They also owned land on the barrier islands, had saltworks near Chioggia, and engaged in commercial activities especially with Byzantium.[9]

In the thirteenth century, the Badoers reached the highest echelons of Venetian society, although none ever attained the dogeship. By this time, the family had divided into two branches, one centered in the parish of San Salvador, the other in San Giacomo dall'Orio. From the latter branch emerged one of the most distinguished men of the period, Marco, son of Giovanni. His success was due in no small measure to his marriage to Marchesina Ziani. Shortly after she received her inheritance, Marco's career soared. He helped lead the war against Ezzelino da Romano, henchman of Emperor Frederick II and lord of the March of Treviso. Badoer served as podesta of Treviso in 1259–1260, and in 1261 as ambassador to Pope Urban IV. In 1264 he was elected to the Greater Council and in 1266 was chosen as Count of Arbe (Rab), the strategically important Croatian island. At this point, he was certainly one of the most influential men in Venice and very likely the richest.[10] After a hiatus during the dogeship of his political opponent Lorenzo Tiepolo, he resumed his political career in the late 1270s and early 1280s, serving in the Lesser Council, Greater Council, and Senate. When he died in 1284, he left behind massive property holdings.

One of Marco's most important legacies to his family was the marriages he arranged for his children. He married his son Marino to Balzanella da Peraga, sole heir to one branch of that powerful Paduan family. Badoero, his second-born son, wed Mabilia da Lendinara, from a family that controlled territory along the Adige River. Daughter Sibilla was married into the noble Polani family. Like other great nobles, Marco Badoer used marriages to secure ties both within Venice and beyond.

Compared to the Badoers who occupied the top rank of society and were indisputably noble, the Zustos was a step below them in antiquity, prestige, distinction, and status. They first made their mark in trade. Like the Badoers they had extensive commercial dealings in the Byzantine Empire in the twelfth century and a variety of real estate holdings in Venice. In 1222, Enrico Zusto sold some property in San Bartolomeo to the commune for construction of the Fondaco dei Tedeschi. The family also owned saltworks near Chioggia.[11]

The Zustos only came to occupy an important place in Venetian political life in the middle and later thirteenth century. Ermolao Zusto served as Duke of Candia in the early 1290s; Marino Zusto served on the court of the Piovego, the tribunal charged with supervision of streets and canals. By the end of the century, the Zustos had achieved a degree of political standing. Members were regularly sitting in the Greater Council and were eventually included in the Serrata itself. Overall, they occupied a more middling position among the Venetian elite than the Badoers.

The rapid economic development that followed the Fourth Crusade created a whole cadre of newly wealthy men, some of whom eventually took their place among the officeholding elite. In the thirteenth century the nobility was very much a "class in the process of formation, relatively open and composite."[12] As merchants made their fortunes, they could move into positions of power, even if they lacked the prestige of older families. At the same time, families could drop out of the top ranks by losing their fortunes. The anonymous author of the *Historia ducum veneticorum* (History of the Doges of Venice) records that Doge Pietro Ziani loaned money to poor nobles so that they could engage in trade and in so doing return "from nothing, to honors and riches."[13]

Many factors set the Venetian nobility apart from mainland nobles. First and foremost, military service was not the distinguishing characteristic of Venetian nobles; elsewhere in medieval Europe nobles constituted the warrior class. Nor was maintenance of a feudal retinue an attribute of the Venetian elite. There is little evidence that feudal ties penetrated the lagoon after the reign of Pietro IV Candiano in the tenth century. Similarly, Venetian nobles were not strongly attached to a particular property or seat, from which they derived their name and identity. They did not build defensive towers like those in San Gimignano and other Italian towns. Although a lineage might possess an urban palace, referred to as the *casa grande*, which family members sought to retain in the male line, individuals felt no compunction about changing residence. At some point Marco Badoer abandoned San Giacomo dall'Orio to take up residence in Santa Giustina, the old stronghold of his wife Marchesina Ziani's family. Ermolao Zusto changed his parish residence at least four times during his life.[14] Landed possessions, fortified palaces, and spatial solidarity did not define the Venetian elite.

Venetian nobles were, however, actively engaged in trade. This too distinguished them from the landholding nobility of mainland Europe, most of whom shunned commerce. The lagoon elite had been trading since Cassiodorus's time. Older families did not look down on newcomers for how they made their money. They might view them as arrivistes lacking antiquity and prestige, but they could not fault them for the source of their wealth. This meant that in the long run, and particularly after the Serrata, the old rich nobles and the new rich merchants were able to coalesce around their common interest in trade.

Noblewomen also participated in trade and lending. In what appears to have been a classic *colleganza* contract, Maria, wife of Enrico Zusto, loaned money to her son Ermolao. The agreement entitled her to three-fourths of the profit. But Maria also made loans beyond the family.[15] Aliphia, widow of Domenico Orio, entered into a *colleganza* with Nicolò da Mula. In her 1252 will she bequeathed him seven lire of the profit that he still owed her. Further evidence of her business acumen is another testamentary bequest. She wanted fifteen lire to be invested as an interest-bearing bank deposit and the proceeds used to help provide a dowry for Aliphia, her namesake and daughter of her servant Maria.[16]

Venetian women enjoyed legal rights including the ability to dispose of their personal property such as their dowries as they pleased, act as legal guardians, assume powers of attorney, and give testimony.[17] Nevertheless, the male ideal of womanhood remained centered on virtue rather than legal or financial ability. In his will of 1287 Uberto Zanasi offered to let his wife continue to live in their home after his death if she would "solemnly swear [herself to] chastity according to the customs of our fatherland." On her death the house was to be offered to another widow as charity, if she could meet the following requirements: she had to be Venetian, over forty, orphaned, honest, childless, heirless, pledged to chastity, and noble.[18]

In another clause in his will Zanasi wrote that after his death he wanted his house rented only to "good and honest men," not to "artisans and weavers."[19] As a new man among the Venetian elite, Zanasi clearly wanted to associate himself and his property with men of reputation and standing and distance himself from craftsmen. This suggests not only the status anxiety of someone who barely ranked among city's elite but also the divide that separated the merchant class from those below them.

It is only in the thirteenth century that those whom Zanasi shunned, artisans and workers, start to become visible, as, for example, in one of the arches of the grand new central portal to San Marco. Constructed in the 1230s, the arch depicts master shipbuilders, wine sellers, butchers, coopers, and other tradesmen hard at work alongside their assistants. Craftsmen had always existed in Venice, but not until the thirteenth century were their numbers great enough for them to appear regularly in notarial acts and other documents. More crucially, guilds formed and began to compile statutes that had to be registered and approved by the Giustizieri Vecchi (Old Justices), the governmental officers charged with guild supervision. Between 1218 and 1330, the Giustizieri Vecchi approved the statutes of fifty-two guilds. Together the statutes offer a vivid but by no means complete portrait of manufacturing and artisanal production in medieval Venice.[20]

FIGURES 7.1a AND 7.1b Principal Portal of the Basilica of San Marco, details of a master blacksmith and his apprentice and a fisherman and his assistant at work, first half of the thirteenth century. Basilica of San Marco, Venice. O. Böhm, Venice.

Many craftsmen supplied the city with the necessities of life. The fishmongers, bakers, and oil- and grain-sellers were all organized into guilds in the thirteenth century. Guilds of other provisioners, such as fruit-sellers and wine porters, came later. The large number of specialized governmental offices concerned with the supply and distribution of food may have retarded or inhibited guild organization in this sector.[21] Clothing was represented by guilds of tailors, doublet-makers, hatters, and cappers as well as by second-hand dealers who sold all manner of clothing and other used items. Cobblers, tanners, and furriers worked with animal skins and pelts. Doctors and barbers provided medical and hygienic services. The huge population growth of the thirteenth century and the resulting building boom provided work for sawyers, joiners, turners, carpenters, stonemasons, and brick makers. Sand suppliers provided sand for filtering rainwater draining into wells. Coopers, box makers, hoop makers, and potters made vessels for cartage and storage; gut-string makers provided twine for packaging. Smiths produced locks, chains, hinges, nails, and other hardware. Painters, in addition to producing religious images, decorated shields, helmets, saddles, small storage boxes, and dinnerware. Mercers or dry goods dealers offered a variety of items in their shops, everything from kerchiefs to pewter tankards to gloves; druggists sold various medicines and the pigments artists used in their paints.[22]

Most artisans and retail shopkeepers serviced the local population rather than producing goods for export. The few manufactures of note in this period were almost all involved in the production of luxury items. Goldsmithing was one. The large amounts of precious metals passing through Venice meant that there was a steady supply of raw materials for this craft. Rock-crystal carvers fashioned clear quartz crystal into buttons, jewels, reliquaries, even eyeglasses.[23] Combmakers produced items for personal adornment. Venice's most famous industry was glassmaking. Its production required the importation of a particular type of sand from near Verona and soda ash from Syria. Glass furnaces required a major capital investment; many were owned by men (and some women) who were not glassmakers themselves. Luxury trades frequently involved partnerships between noble merchants and craftsmen given the large amount of capital investment required to operate and the reliance on overseas trade for raw materials.

Another specialized industry in Venice that operated on a massive scale was shipbuilding, most of it carried out in private shipyards. Large numbers of carpenters and caulkers toiled building merchant vessels and warships. Auxiliary trades included rope- and sailmaking, oarmaking, pitchmaking, and arms production. Venetian blacksmiths could not keep up with the demand for nails, pins, and anchors. Accordingly, the Giustizieri Vecchi oversaw an office of supervisors charged with ensuring the quality of foreign imports.[24] For most of the century, the government forbade the sale of Venetian-built ships to foreigners, but this was changed to allow the sale of vessels over ten years old. By contrast, Venetians were permitted to buy foreign-built ships. Both policies favored the interests of merchants over shipbuilders.[25] Small shipyards dotted Venice and other settlements of the lagoon and produced the small watercraft used for fishing and transportation of people and goods throughout the *dogado* and to the mainland.

Venetian guilds stood apart from their mainland counterparts in many respects. One was the relative weakness of textile manufacturers. In many Italian towns, woolen cloth production was a mainstay of the economy. Of the so-called seven greater guilds of Florence, the Lana (drapers) guild specialized in the production of local cloth and the Calimala (finishers) in the finishing of foreign-made wool imports. In Venice there was a wool guild, but it operated on a much smaller scale than its Florentine counterparts. One hindrance to the industry was environmental, namely, the lack of fresh water for fulling (the cleaning and thickening of cloth). Cloth had to be transported to Treviso, Padua, or Portogruaro for fulling. Dyeing was performed locally; the dyers' guild was one of the earliest established in Venice. There were also guilds of silk weavers and makers of fustian (a mixed cotton and linen cloth). But none of these were mainstays of the thirteenth-century Venetian economy, which remained centered on commerce. Governmental policy was more focused on the importation of woolen cloth than on fostering local production since foreign-made cloth was re-exported to the Middle East and brought significant profit to Venetian merchants.[26]

The government's focus on commerce was reflected in the guilds themselves. In most Italian cities, the leading guilds were made up of great merchants. In Florence, for example, in addition to the guilds of drapers and foreign cloth finishers, the seven greater guilds included the bankers, silk merchants, spice dealers, and furriers as well as the guild of judges and notaries. There and elsewhere, men of such professions, often referred to as the *popolo grasso* (fat people), spearheaded the emergence of the communes, opposing the bishops, administrators, and great landholders who had controlled the towns until then. In Venice, no merchant or banking guilds developed since the government, comprised of merchants, had long pursued policies and issued regulations designed to promote trade. There was no need for guilds of merchants for the simple reason that the government itself acted as one.[27]

Venetian peculiarities also inhibited the formation of a guild of judges and notaries, two other professions influential in the rise of the mainland communes. Venice resisted a full-scale adoption of Roman law, which had been revived in the twelfth century at the University of Bologna to deal with legal matters brought to the fore by the economic and urban renewal then sweeping Europe. In Venice most communal councils enjoyed some judicial authority. There was strong reliance on *arbitrium*, that is, the deciding of cases on the basis not only of written law but also custom and the common sense of the adjudicators. Venetian law was not the domain of highly trained experts in a field of specialized knowledge. Lawyers had a more limited role.[28] Additionally, most of the notaries in Venice were priests, not laymen, and thus ineligible to form or join a guild.

Another difference between Venetian guilds and their mainland counterparts was their sheer number. While Florence had twenty-one guilds and Bologna thirteen, Venice had more than fifty in the same period. Venice had, for instance, three guilds of furriers, each specializing in different kinds of pelts. By allowing craftsmen, known elsewhere as the *popolo minuto* (little people), to fracture in this way, the Venetian merchant/governing class effectively diluted their influence. None of the dozens of guilds was large or powerful enough to exert tremendous pressure on the government. Competition among guilds also weakened them politically since it prevented them from forming a united bloc. The glassmakers and rock-crystal carvers, for instance, warily eyed the others' efforts to imitate their products. Guilds in Venice more closely resembled what were known in Florence as the middling and minor guilds (such as the bakers, carpenters, innkeepers, and vintners) since they tended to be organizations of craftsmen rather than large-scale producers or merchants. In addition, given their strict supervision by the Giustizieri Vecchi, Venetian guilds served both as unions of craftsmen and vehicles of governmental control.[29]

For the most part, the government was content to allow guild officers to regulate themselves, provided they did not challenge the merchants for control of the commune. Most guilds were presided over by a board of officials known as deacons, supervisors, or judges. In many there was a chief officer—the *gastaldus* (warden)—who was assisted by the board. Guild officers had a good deal of power: they adjudicated minor disputes among members, assigned shops and market stalls, and determined eligibility requirements for new entrants. Since they often established electoral procedures, they were able to control who had access to power within the guilds. Most guilds were unions of masters, with workers, including journeymen and apprentices, allowed few rights.[30] Hierarchy was particularly pronounced in industries, like glassmaking, that required large startup capital or importation of raw materials by merchants. These were also industries in which a few great masters controlled the production processes, while many of the individual tasks were performed by semi-skilled or even unskilled laborers. In these trades, the interests of the master employers more closely aligned with those of merchants than with the workers they employed. In other crafts, like stonecutting and ship-caulking, there was no way to increase or accelerate production by dividing workers into accomplished masters and unskilled workers. In those guilds, hierarchy was less pronounced, although masters remained in control.

Even with the extraordinary proliferation of guilds, a substantial portion of the workforce remained outside the guild structure, most notably the huge number of seamen who manned the merchant marine and navy. They were freemen, not slaves. Many were recruited from settlements throughout the lagoon and nearby Istria. Seamen had to be at least eighteen and agree to a fixed term of service. Pay was based on skill and the duties required. Oarsmen were paid less, for example, than sailors who were responsible for tending the sails or handling the rudder. All had to be ready to defend the vessel from attack. Crews enrolled on state-owned ships could count on steadier employment than those in the merchant marine, but the command structure on the former was more hierarchical, with noblemen filling the top positions. On a merchant ship, crewmen had some say over such decisions as how much supplemental cargo to take onboard. During wartime, the city could draft men for service into the navy.[31]

Thirteenth-century maritime service offered certain advantages over enrollment in the guilds. Guild participation normally involved long apprenticeships with no guarantee of ever being able to operate one's own shop. Because maritime service did not require much technical skill, a young man with muscle power but little else could enlist on a ship, learn on the job, and move up the ranks. Since all crewmen were permitted to carry a small amount of cargo, they could also engage in trade and earn extra cash. Through careful observation, even the most unskilled could learn how commerce operated, gain knowledge of merchandise, acquire negotiating skills and business contacts, and become familiar with foreign ports, customs, and languages. More than the guilds, service in the merchant marine offered the possibility of upward social mobility.[32]

In addition to seamen, Venice was filled with many other workers who fell outside guild ranks. Many found work as lower-ranking bureaucrats, performing such jobs as operating the public scales at Rialto, serving as brokers and bailers at the Fondaco dei Tedeschi, or working as patrolmen for the city's police forces. Stevedores, domestic servants, slaves (primarily Russians, Tartars, and various ethnic groups from the Caucasus), canal dredgers, gardeners, prostitutes, and ferrymen did not benefit from guild organization.[33]

At some point, however, the boatmen who worked at fixed *traghetto* (ferry) stations did begin to organize themselves into *scuole* (confraternities). These brotherhoods provided mutual aid to members, including alms to the living, visits to the sick, and burial and prayers for the deceased. Most of Venice's guilds had affiliated *scuole dell'arte* (confraternities of the trade), which predated the guilds by some decades.[34] As religious and social service organizations, the trade confraternities did not intervene in work matters that were the province of the guilds.

Thirteenth-century Venice was also home to a select group of big confraternities, known as *scuole dei battuti* (confraternities of the beaten), after the ritual self-flagellation that members practiced as a way of atoning for both their personal sins and those of society. The first flagellant confraternity was Santa Maria della Carità whose statutes date to December 1260, followed by San Marco, San Giovanni Evangelista, and Santa Maria della Misericordia in 1261.[35] Inspiration for the *scuole dei battuti* came from the religious revival movement including processions of flagellants and calls for penitence that began in Perugia and swept through the towns of Italy in 1260, reaching nearby Padua that November.

The prologue to the statutes of the confraternity of San Giovanni Evangelista captures the pessimism and sense of human wretchedness that inspired its establishment.

> Human frailty itself clearly teaches and shows us how profound are the uncertainties of the present life. For every day man, in his wretchedness, is oppressed with care, overwhelmed by toil and imprisoned in bondage to the Devil. He is always immersed and enmeshed in sin.[36]

The antidotes to this debasement were penitence, charity, and mercy. Members were expected to recite prayers, attend Mass, distribute alms, and participate in processions during which they would flagellate themselves, "in a spirit of peace and humility, and without complaint."[37]

The piety promoted by the flagellant confraternities struck a chord in a rapidly changing Venice. The emphasis on brotherhood, epitomized by the identical hooded gowns that members wore while processing, may have helped smooth over resentments fueled by a society increasingly obsessed with social status. By the 1360s the four *scuole dei battuti* together had around 2,600 members who came from parishes scattered throughout the city and from different social groups. Some members were nobles, most were not. A small percentage were priests. Women were inscribed although they were forbidden to flagellate. After 1476 the flagellant confraternities came to be referred to as the *scuole grandi* (big confraternities). The confraternity of San Rocco, founded in the mid-fifteenth century, joined the ranks of the *scuole grandi* in 1477, and San Teodoro in 1552. The patronage exercised by the six *scuole grandi* would play a prominent role in Venetian cultural, artistic, and musical life.

Long predating the *scuole grandi* were numerous lesser confraternities referred to as *scuole piccole* (little confraternities), most of which were devoted to a particular saint.[38] By 1442 there were as many as 200 of them in the city.[39] Like the big confraternities, the *scuole piccole* were channels for the expression

FIGURE 7.2 Confraternity Brothers in Prayer Before Saint John the Evangelist. Tabernacle on the façade of the Scuola Grande of San Giovanni Evangelista, 1349, Venice. Note the hooded robes the brothers are wearing. Photo by the author.

of both piety and charity, and members came from diverse social backgrounds, but especially from non-elite ones. The solidarity, sense of belonging, and assistance that the *scuole piccole* offered members were especially welcome for the poor and those who lacked extensive kinship-based support networks.[40] Most admitted women, although that often occurred only when a confraternity was in decline. Elected female officers worked in parallel with their male counterparts. All three types of *scuole—dell'arte, piccole, e grandi*—were lay institutions. Although they maintained altars and tombs in churches and engaged priests to say prayers for the dead, they were outside the purview of the church.

Venice was also home to a significant number of religious, both the secular clergy who served in parishes and had responsibility for the cure of souls, and the regular clergy—monks, nuns, and friars who lived in monasteries or friaries, following a *regula* or rule.

Parish priests served as spiritual advisors to their flocks. But their role extended far beyond matters purely spiritual. Indeed, the clergy nearly monopolized the notarial profession in medieval Venice. Consequently, priests were present at such important events in the lives of the laity as the contracting of marriages, exchanging of dowries, and drafting of wills. As notaries, priests were also privy to all sorts of commercial transactions and participated in them themselves. In 1235, for example, Angelo, a priest in the church of San Lio, received from Gabriele Marignoni a loan of ten lire with which to trade.[41] Priests served as clerks in governmental offices, accompanied ambassadors and rectors on overseas missions, and acted as scriveners on merchant vessels. They came from a variety of social backgrounds, most were not nobles.[42] Property owners enjoyed the right to elect their parish priests, so the parish clergy were very much members of the neighborhood.[43] No figures exist for the number of priests and clerics in the thirteenth-century city, but it must have been large. In 1293 the church of San Moisè considered limiting their number, "on account of the multitude of priests and other lesser clergymen [resident]."[44]

Figures are lacking for the regular clergy as well. One survey indicates that by 1300 there were at least sixty Benedictine monasteries in the area encompassing just the Venetian lagoon and Chioggia, not the entire *dogado*. While the twelfth century saw a preponderance of new male houses, the first half of the thirteenth saw an increase in female ones. In Venice itself, Santi Biagio e Cataldo (founded on the Giudecca in 1226) and Santa Maria della Celestia (established in Castello in 1237) joined the much older Benedictine convents San Zaccaria and San Lorenzo.[45] The twelfth century also witnessed the establishment of several priories of canons regular who followed the rule of Saint Augustine. Santa Maria delle Vergini was established in 1219 as a female priory on the initiative of Ugolino di Conti (later pope Gregory IX) and Doge Pietro Ziani and became a bastion of noblewomen. Its privileged position and status as an institution under the special patronage of the doge found ritual expression in a ceremony in which the sitting doge symbolically "married" the incoming abbess.[46]

The mendicant orders, so-called after the begging that characterized the original members, arrived in the thirteenth century. The Franciscans got their first friary in the lagoon when in 1233 Giacomo Michiel donated to them the island San Francesco del Deserto, near Torcello, already the site of a church dedicated to Saint Francis. A year later Giovanni Badoer of San Giacomo dall'Orio gave the Friars Minor a large property in the parish of San Tomà, not far from a church they were already using. Over the following decades, the friars systematically acquired contiguous properties and ponds in this underdeveloped part of the city and in 1250 began to build a new church dedicated to Mary to replace the earlier one. The current large Gothic church, Santa Maria Gloriosa dei Frari, known simply as the Frari, was begun in 1330 and replaced that second church. A third Franciscan friary, San Francesco della Vigna, owed its origins to a bequest from Marco Ziani. As the name indicates, it was built on the site of a vineyard in Santa Giustina.

In 1234, the same year that Badoer donated land to the Franciscans, Doge Giacomo Tiepolo and his government authorized the transfer to the Dominican friars of a low-lying property located on the northern edge of the city between the parishes of Santa Maria Formosa and Santa Marina. Here the Order of Preachers, as the Dominicans were formally known, established its church dedicated to Santi Giovanni e Paolo, commonly referred to as San Zanipolo. Construction on the current church began around 1333.[47] Together Santa Maria Gloriosa dei Frari and San Zanipolo would dominate Venetian religious life, along with San Marco.

Other orders of mendicants established themselves in Venice in the thirteenth century. The Eremitani or Hermits of Saint Augustine (the Austin Friars) first settled in Castello but moved late in the century to a more central location in the parish of Sant'Angelo where they built a church dedicated to Santo Stefano Protomartire. A second Augustinian house, Santa Maria di Nazareth, was set up at midcentury on an island, later known as San Lazzaro after the plague hospital established there in 1423. A third, Sant'Erasmo, was located on another island. The order known as the Brothers of Penitence or Friars of the Sack (Saccati) had a brief tenure in Venice; their friary, Santa

Caterina in Cannaregio, was sold in 1289 and turned into a convent for female Augustinians. The Carmelites appeared late in the century and built Santa Maria del Carmelo, in Dorsoduro, near the parish of Santa Margherita. The Servites who arrived in the early fourteenth century, built their church, Santa Maria dei Servi, in Cannaregio. The only new female order to take root in Venice in the thirteenth century was the Poor Clares. Their convent, first known as Santa Maria Madre di Cristo, later as Santa Chiara, was situated in the parish of Santa Croce and was founded around 1236 with patronage from the Badoers. While testamentary bequests indicate that the piety of the mendicants struck a responsive chord with many Venetians, their most lasting impact derived from their role as pioneers in land reclamation. Notable is their dispersal on the city's periphery, from Cannaregio to Castello, Santa Croce to Dorsoduro.[48]

There is no definitive evidence for a Jewish presence in the city in the thirteenth century or earlier. Some have argued that the name Giudecca, by which the island Spinalonga came to be known, attests to early Jewish settlement there, but this rests on shaky etymological ground. Another theory—that the name derived from the island "of the judged" (*del giudicato*), the place where those who had been found guilty were banished—seems equally dubious. Likely, the only members of minority faiths present in Venice in this period were Jewish and Eastern rite Christian merchants who came to the city to trade but not to take up permanent residence.[49]

Thirteenth-century Venice would have presented a bustling spectacle to those visiting merchants. With its booming trade and growing manufactures, thriving building and land reclamation projects, and burgeoning population, it was very much a city on the make. This activity placed great demands on the commune, which responded by further elaborating and defining its councils and courts and dramatically expanding its administrative apparatus.

During the thirteenth century, the Greater Council emerged as the ultimate organ of governmental authority. Begun in the twelfth century as a council of *sapientes* (wise men), it quickly grew in size and stature. For a time, in the early thirteenth century, it comprised about thirty-five members, one for each of the *trentacie* (thirtieths) into which city's seventy parishes were grouped. But the number of members was not fixed, nor was the process for electing new members. Sitting members selected new ones. Consequently, the number grew as friends, kinsmen, and other supporters were added. Members of other communal councils enjoyed the right to be part of the

Greater Council. Additionally, various magistrates were admitted by virtue of the offices they occupied. This meant that the Greater Council grew from a few dozen members in the early part of the century to about 450 members by 1265. Seating virtually all the powerful families and men in Venetian society, this body held ultimate legislative authority and had the power to grant special favors and pardons.[50]

Two other councils emerged with special competencies. The first was the Quarantia (Council of Forty), which came into being sometime between the last decades of the twelfth and first decades of the thirteenth century. It was comprised of forty men, twenty-five years of age or older, who had previously held high office. They were elected for one-year terms but could be reelected. The Forty served as the court of appeals for both criminal and civil cases. Its portfolio also included supervision of the mint and money and development of financial plans for consideration by the Greater Council. The gravity of the matters it supervised explains why only seasoned officeholders were eligible for it.[51]

The Senate, also known as the Consiglio dei Pregadi, emerged sometime shortly before 1232. It was composed of sixty members elected by the Greater Council for one-year terms, and from 1279 no more than three members of the same family could be senators simultaneously. As with the Forty, the doge and his councilors had the right to attend Senate meetings. So did certain officeholders, such as the State Attorneys when the Senate was dealing with judicial matters. Like the Forty, the Senate enjoyed some appellate powers, but its primary responsibilities encompassed foreign affairs, commerce, and navigation. The Senate authorized the dispatch of ambassadors and supervised their activities. It oversaw the merchant marine: issuing orders and rules for captains and crews, vetting the finances of maritime entrepreneurs, appraising the seaworthiness of merchant vessels, and granting navigation licenses. When vessels or cargo were lost to piracy, shipwreck, or war, it was the Senate that sought to recover the losses. Although both the Greater Council and the Forty enjoyed more prestige and authority in the thirteenth century, the Senate would later increase its power at the expense of the other two.[52]

At the summit of the commune stood the doge. He was assisted by the Lesser or Ducal Council, which was made up of six councilors, one for each *sestiere*, or, failing that, three from each side of the Grand Canal. The apportionment of ducal councilors by *sestiere* and the Greater Council by *trentacie* gave every part of the city a say in communal affairs and checked the forces that could pull the city into competing communities, as had happened in earlier centuries with various settlements in the lagoon. Another potentially dangerous force was family coalitions. Accordingly, no members of the doge's family could serve as ducal councilors, and the six members of the Ducal Council had to come from different lineages. To forestall conflicts of interest, councilors were forbidden to engage in trade or banking while serving.[53]

The ducal councilors were expected to advise the doge and keep an eye on him to ensure that he did not undermine the commune. If there was a disagreement between the doge and his councilors, then, as the Greater Council made clear, "[the matter] will proceed in the way that the councilors will determine."[54] They, not the doge, would have the final word. During interregna, the senior ducal councilor acted as the head of the government, while the councilors initiated the process of electing the next doge.

Together the doge, his six councilors, and the three heads of the Forty constituted the Signoria (Lordship). It formed, in essence, the executive branch of the commune, although in later centuries that role would be assumed by the Collegio (College), which when meeting as the Pien Collegio (Full College) included the Signoria and the Senate *savi* (sages) with special competencies.[55] The Signoria received and dispatched diplomatic communications, supervised the bureaucracy and courts, and heard petitions and appeals. Most important, it initiated most legislation. Members drafted bills that went first to the Senate or Forty for further debate and amendment before being presented to the Greater Council, where a final vote was taken. With the notable exception of the Council of Ten, the primary organs of Venice's republican government were in place by the mid-thirteenth century.

The number of courts and administrative offices also expanded dramatically. These were divided into three broad categories: Palace Offices, Rialto Offices, and Foreign Offices. The Palace Offices, housed at the Ducal Palace, included several courts that emerged out of the old ducal court made up of the doge and his *iudices*. These courts handled a variety of matters such as disputes over dowries (the Giudici del Proprio), minor debts and *colleganze* (the Giudici del Mobile), cases between Venetians and foreigners (the Giudici del Forestier), and property transfers (the Giudici del Esaminador). Other Palace Offices supervised the police, contraband, the Arsenal, currency, and armaments. The Rialto Offices dealt with commercial and financial matters. These included, to name just a few, the Grain Officers, the Supervisors of Brokers, the Supervisors of the Rialto Market, and the Communal Treasurers. The third category, the Foreign Offices, comprised all officials posted outside Venice. While many, like the Duke of Crete and the *bailo* of Alexandria, were stationed in distant lands, others like the podestas of Torcello and Chioggia served in communities within the lagoon itself.[56] By the thirteenth century, a few hundred men were serving as officers or staff in governmental posts both at home and overseas.

The office of Visdomini (Vice-lords) offers a good example of how offices proliferated over the course of the century. One of the oldest positions in Venice, perhaps originating in the ninth century, the Visdomini regulated the import and export trade and collected customs duties. Between 1229 and 1248 the office was divided into three separate offices. The first, the Visdomini dei Lombardi (the Vice-lords of the Lombards), was responsible for assessing duties on merchandise traveling by land or river between Venice and the Italian mainland as far as central Italy. The Visdomini del Mare (Vice-lords of the Sea) controlled duties on goods reaching Venice by sea from other Italian ports as well as Dalmatia and elsewhere along the Adriatic coast. Until 1268 they were also responsible for the Fondaco dei Tedeschi, but that year a separate set of officials was created for it. A different office altogether—the Ufficio Sopra le Merci del Levante (Office over Merchandise from the Levant)—handled merchandise arriving from the East. The third office, the Visdomini di Ternaria (Vice-lords of Oil), collected duties on specific products, such as olive oil, cheese, salted meat, and smoked and salted fish. It ensured that the state's oil reserves were well stocked and supervised the *ternieri*, the retail sellers of oil and fat. Late in the century or early in the next, this office was divided: into the Ternaria Vecchia, in charge of oil imported from the mainland, and the Ternaria Nuova, responsible for oil imported by sea.[57]

As the office split, a total of twelve men served as Vice-lords, with one-year terms of office. Starting in the mid-1280s, the Vice-lords were required to attend certain meetings of the Greater Council. They also had to maintain accounts of the money coming into their coffers, which were regularly audited by the Soprastanti le Ragioni (Supervisors of Accounts), and turn over the cash to the Communal Treasurers. An unknown number of scribes and office-boys assisted each office.

As the government grew in complexity, so too did the need to keep records. By 1205, a chancery had been established within the Ducal Palace; and by 1261 the position of Grand Chancellor was created to oversee the chancery and the secretaries who were assigned to various councils and magistracies. The Grand Chancellor's position was, like the dogeship and procuratorships of San Marco, one of the few with lifetime tenure.[58]

The keeping of systematic records evolved slowly over the course of the century. Between 1223 and 1229 a notary named Wilielmus, described as a "scribe of the ducal court of Venice," kept a paper volume of the deliberations of the Lesser Council.[59] However, many governmental papers continued to be recorded on unbound parchments that were easily misplaced and hard to search. Starting around midcentury, courts and magistracies began maintaining registers of their accounts and actions. The communal councils commenced somewhat later; the Greater Council started keeping registers of its deliberations in 1268; the Forty began doing so a year later. From the 1260s on, the Greater Council ordered various offices to maintain their records under lock and key. In 1283 Doge Giovanni Dandolo set up a commission of five men to distill earlier decisions of the Greater Council into two books, the *Liber comunis* (Book of the Commune) and the *Liber officiorum* (Book of Offices).[60] Even so, there was not at that time an effort to maintain a central governmental archive. Nevertheless, the creation of the chancery and the growing concern with keeping, organizing, and maintaining an easily searchable paper trail reflect a new self-consciousness on the part of the communal government and awareness of its importance.

On October 5, 1276, the Forty passed a law declaring that whenever the Greater Council was in session, "the business of the commune shall have been completely finished and conducted" before taking up issues involving "special persons."[61] This firmly prioritized the public good over private concerns.

Nowhere was the commune's growing interest in its own power and protection of the public good from encroachment by private interests more evident than in its assertion of control over urban space. In previous centuries, most land development projects had been undertaken by private individuals and families, neighbors, or monastic communities. But beginning in the thirteenth century, the commune became more involved in monitoring and controlling the urban environment.[62] In 1224 the Greater Council appointed two men to supervise canals, public streets, and embankments. In 1282 the office was reorganized as the Iudices super Publicis (Judges over Public Things), known in the vernacular as the Giudici del Piovego. They were responsible for all public lands and waters and as a court could impose penalties for usurpations and abuses of public property. From this point on, land reclamation projects had to have communal approval.[63] Some of these projects were vast: in 1303 the government authorized the reclamation of four and a half acres; a few years later it permitted the infilling of an additional eighteen.[64]

As the population expanded and the city became more densely developed, the commune also started monitoring movement and traffic on the canals. It authorized the periodic dredging and deepening of waterways to prevent them from becoming clogged with silt and refuse. Residents on both sides of a canal due for dredging were expected each to pay one-third of the cost, with the government covering the remaining third. Embankments had to kept in good repair. At Rialto, walls and other structures along quays were demolished to facilitate the loading and unloading of cargo. Everywhere, brickmakers and stonecutters were forbidden from blocking canals, basins, and landings with stone or lumber.

Streets began to form an alternative transportation system to canals. Major pedestrian routes developed running roughly parallel to both sides of the Grand Canal, with San Giacomo di Rialto and San Bartolomeo serving as the hubs from which these and other routes fanned out into the city. To keep traffic unencumbered, upper-story projections on houses that overhung streets were prohibited, and existing ones demolished. Starting in 1272 the Merceria was paved, and the buildings along it fitted with gutters to prevent rainwater from dousing pedestrians below.[65] Bridges were built to link parishes, with construction costs shared by the conjoined parishes.

As streets came to rival canals, public access became a pressing matter. Denser development, along with subdivision and sale of houses, meant that property holders could find themselves without legal right-of-way. The principle gradually developed that streets and paths were public property, but the process was often fraught. A sentence issued by the Giudici del Piovego in 1303 concerning a property in the parish of San Maurizio is illustrative. The case involved a vacant lot where once there had been a stagnant pond. The property holders in the parish claimed that the lot, which abutted the church, was public, whereas the parish clergy contended that it belonged to the church. Both sides presented the judges with multiple charters supporting their position: those presented by the parishioners emphasized that the infilled pond adjoined a public street, whereas a charter presented by the parish priest showed that in 1275 the church had granted the right to build on the lot to the Viadro brothers. After reviewing the evidence, the judges ordered a crier to go to the parish and invite anyone with additional information to come forward. When none did, the judges issued their verdict: the lot was "a public and common street that is to be perpetually open and unoccupied to the glory and profit of the church of San Maurizio and the entire commune of Venice and all persons [with property] surrounding that vacant lot and all those of the parish of San Maurizio and all wishing thence to come and go, by day and by night." They also ruled that the embankment or steps at the edge of the lot should be rebuilt and paid for by those whose property adjoined it. In return they could use the landing for transit and loading and unloading goods, just as at any "public and common quay and landing without objection by any man or person."[66] In this case, as in so many others, the public good superseded private interests.

The commune also promoted hygiene and safety. Late in the century, it banished to the Giudecca the noxious tanning of leather and furs. In November 1291 the Greater Council ordered that glassmaking furnaces be moved to Murano to reduce the danger of fire. Errant embers could easily spark a conflagration and sweep through the brick and wood city with devastating results. Large loads of timber that were floated down from the mountains could clog canals and other waterways. They were directed to the Barbaria delle Tole near San Zanipolo on the northern edge of the city or San Nicolò dei Mendicoli on the southern edge. Along with the Arsenal, the lumberyards, tanning workshops, and glassworks formed an industrial cordon on the city's periphery and nearby islands.[67]

Administration of other communities in the lagoon also underwent a significant change. The ducal wardens who had once supervised outlying settlements were replaced by podestas. With this substitution the older conception of relations between center and periphery based a personal/contractual tie to the doge yielded to a territorial conception of the *dogado* and its inhabitants that was impersonal and emphasized vertical ties between Venice and the rest of the *dogado*.[68]

Yet all these rules and regulations would have been meaningless without means of enforcement. Accordingly, the commune developed police forces to patrol the city and impose its will. The Signori di Notte (Lords of the Night) were probably established around midcentury. Six *signori*, one per *sestiere*, were assisted by heavily armed guards who were responsible for safety and public order. They were authorized to confiscate prohibited weapons. The Signori di Notte also protected the city against moral danger. They could fine men for gambling at Rialto or under the portico of San Marco as well as for blaspheming.[69] Since they patrolled on a regular basis, the Signori also helped supervise certain building and reclamation projects and collected infraction fines. Other patrol forces included the Capi di Sestieri (Chiefs of the Sestieri) and the Cinque alla Pace (Five of Peace), who were responsible for ending brawls and fights.[70]

As the city became more densely settled, parishes, most originally built on individual islets, were connected to one another by streets and bridges. Many were dominated by noble families who had founded and financed parish churches and built their grand houses facing the *campo* (field/square) surrounding the church. These noble enclaves included dependent buildings that housed retainers or that were rented to tenants.

During the thirteenth century, domestic architecture underwent a revolution. For the first time, private homes began to be constructed of brick and stone rather than wood. They were built facing the water rather than the *campo* since it was easier to unload cargo and place it in storerooms on the ground floor. This type of palace has been dubbed the *casa-fondaco*. Although *fondachi* had a different function, the name captures the dual function of these palaces as both private dwellings and warehouse spaces.[71]

In some early examples, like the Fondaco dei Turchi, originally built as a private family palace and later turned into a *fondaco* for Turkish merchants, the long side of the structure faced the Grand Canal. Such an orientation had two disadvantages. First, as the population exploded and the competition for access to easily navigable canals grew more intense, water frontage became much more expensive. Second, structures built at the water's edge were susceptible to having their foundations damaged by tidal flow and wave action. Therefore, it became common to turn the short ends of buildings to the water and rear courtyard and extend the structure deep into the lot behind the façade. For these reasons, most Venetian palaces are narrow and long.[72]

FIGURE 7.3 Fondaco dei Turchi Prior to Restoration, originally built as a private family palace, later twelfth to later thirteenth century, Venice. Antonio Perini (1830–79), photographer. DCOW/EUB/Alamy Stock Photo.

These palaces had a long center room, called an *androne*, on the ground floor that ran from the water entrance at the front to the land entrance at the rear, where the courtyard with the well was located. On the first floor directly above the *androne* was an identical room known as the *portego*. The *androne* and *portego* were flanked on each side by narrower rooms. Those on the ground floor served as storage, office, and kitchen space; the rooms on the floor above as bedchambers and other living spaces. The maximum width of any of these parts was determined by the length of the tree trunks used as beams. This too meant that palaces tended to be narrow and long. An exterior staircase in the rear courtyard offered access to the first floor.[73] The weight of these buildings was carried by the four walls running the length of the structure (the two exterior walls and the two dividing the *portego and androne* from the side rooms). The front façade and the façade facing the rear courtyard had minimal weight-bearing functions. Consequently, they could be pierced with windows to allow in light and air. This was important since the long sides of palaces often had no windows if they directly abutted other palaces or overlooked narrow and dank side streets or canals.

Ca' Loredan and Ca' Farsetti on the Grand Canal, which date to the early thirteenth century, are good examples of this new palace type and its waterfront orientation. Like the Fondaco dei Turchi, they still have ground floor porticos that lead to the *androni*; the first-floor façades, with their massed windows, become more or less walls of glass. Eventually, the front portico was dropped since all that was needed was a wide-arched watergate to allow access to the *androne*.

It is easy to discern the interior layout of most Venetian palaces by examining the façades. The grouped windows on the upper floors demarcate the narrow ends of the *porteghi*, while the flanking windows puncturing the brick expanses indicate where chambers and other rooms leading off from the *porteghi* are located. This palace type was so well adapted to Venice's unique environmental conditions and the high demand for waterfront building lots that it endured. It was also easily adaptable to shifting architectural tastes since the front façade could be ornamented differently as styles changed.

Over time the integrity of noble compounds succumbed to the vicissitudes of biology and the real-estate market. Families split into branches or went extinct; houses were divided up; rear courtyards were cannibalized as rows of small apartments were constructed and rented out. Emotional attachment

FIGURE 7.4 Ca' Loredan and Ca' Farsetti, early thirteenth century, Venice. The second and attic floors and balustrades are later additions. Photo by Wolfgang Moroder, distributed under a CC-BY 3.0 license via Wikimedia Commons.

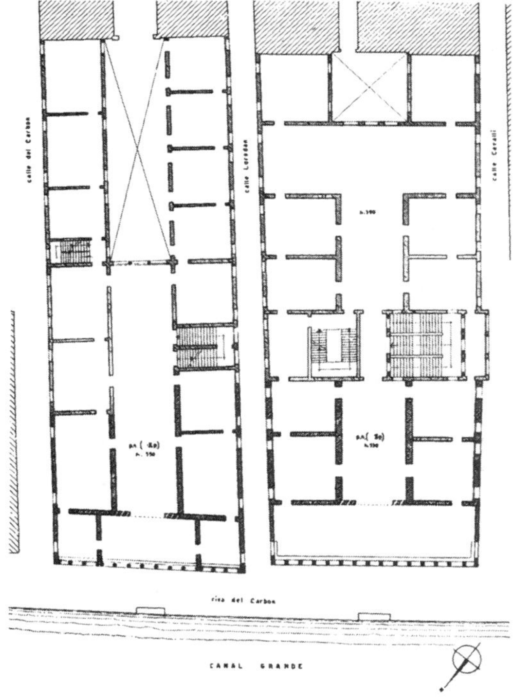

FIGURE 7.5 Plans of the first floors of Ca' Loredan and Ca' Farsetti. The earliest sections fronting the Grand Canal are in darker shading. From Paolo Moretto, *L'edilizia gotica veneziana*, 2nd ed. (Venice, 1978). Courtesy of Filippi Editore, Venice.

to particular parishes weakened as nobles moved around. Laboring-class tenants came to see their noble neighbors not as their patrons or protectors but merely as their landlords.[74]

This breakdown of the parish as the focus of social life was a gradual process. Nevertheless, parishes continued to be important components of administrative and festive life. The Capi di Contrade (Chiefs of the Parishes) had several responsibilities, including enrolling men in the civic militia. Moreover, one of the most important civic festivals in medieval Venice—the Festival of the Twelve Marys—was organized by parish and culminated on February 2, the feast of the Purification of the Virgin.

The Venetians told various stories to explain the origins of the Marys festival. One had it that, either in the ninth or tenth century, while the doge was bestowing dowries on twelve poor girls, pirates from Trieste sneaked into the cathedral of San Pietro where the ceremony was taking place, snatched the girls and their dowry chests, and fled. Venetian men gave chase, caught the pirates at the port of Caorle, still known as the Porto delle Donzelle (Maidens' Port)—on February 2, killed the thieves, and retrieved the brides and their dowries. Another version put the focus on the Virgin Mary, arguing that the entire fracas took place while the Venetians were marking the feast of the Purification.[75]

The Purification of the Virgin had been celebrated in Venice at least since the reign of Pietro Polani in the mid-twelfth century. In its earliest known form, it consisted of a water procession that included the doge and bishop of Castello, linked San Marco and San Pietro, and made its way up the Grand Canal before ending at Santa Maria Formosa, the first Venetian church dedicated to Mary. By the time of Martino da Canal's chronicle, it had changed considerably, organized each year by two parishes. On January 30, the first official day of the fete, men from each of the two designated parishes made separate excursions first to Piazza San Marco where they distributed sweets, wine, and flags to children before making their way to Santa Maria Formosa where they gave gifts to poor girls. The next day, men from one of the parishes reassembled in Piazza San Marco, again distributed flags, and processed with priests, one of whom was dressed as the Virgin, to Santa Maria Formosa to await the procession of the second parish accompanying a priest outfitted as the Archangel Gabriel. Upon meeting, the two costumed priests reenacted the Annunciation. The processions then returned to their home parishes where the houses of nobles displayed twelve wooden statues, the Marys, arrayed in fine robes, jewels, and crowns. Women and men attended separate receptions held in honor of the Marys. The following evening the doge, along with the priests impersonating the Virgin and Gabriel, attended services at Santa Maria Formosa.

The fourth and final day, the Feast of the Purification or Candlemas itself, involved an elaborate water procession, including four boats each carrying three of the wooden Marys accompanied by women from the sponsoring parishes, two boats from the parishes scheduled to host the festival the following year, two more for the clergy and bishop, and yet another bearing forty armed men. The procession made its way from San Pietro to San Marco for another Mass. With the doge's boat joined to the flotilla, the procession traveled up the Grand Canal as far as Rialto before arriving at Santa Maria Formosa for a third Mass. Parties and receptions continued for several more days.

The Marys festival celebrated Venetian military valor in the legendary rescue of the abducted brides. It also glorified marriage and fertility, commended female chastity, and honored the Virgin. The public participation of women in it is notable. But the overriding significance of the festival lay in its ability to unite the individual, constituent communities of Venice. This was best exemplified by the final procession that linked the ecclesiastical focal point at San Pietro with the political center at San Marco and the market at Rialto before ending, in a recollection of Venice's legendary founding on the feast of the Annunciation, at a Marian church.

Martino da Canal describes the festival as proceeding harmoniously and without a hitch. The reality was different: processional routes had to be improvised when low tides made it impossible to reach Santa Maria Formosa by boat, families vied to host the twelve wooden statues, and parishes scrambled to outdo one another in the extravagance of their receptions.[76] At this same time, much bigger battles were taking place, not for the honor of hosting "this junket of wooden women" but to control the government itself.[77]

Every Italian city-state had to decide its form of government and who would have a voice in governmental affairs. The answers were unique to each city and depended on many factors, including the area's natural resources, economic base, kinship structures, family alliances, and long-standing civic traditions. In Florence, for example, the predominance of manufacturing meant that guilds became the basis for political enfranchisement. One had to be a member of a guild to sit in the Florentine councils. In Venice the underlying conditions were different, with the result that heredity became the grounds for participating in the government. It took a century of struggle to arrive at that solution in the Serrata of the Greater Council.

At the end of the twelfth and beginning of the thirteenth centuries, Venetian domestic politics resembled that of most Italian communes.[78] It was characterized by competition and conflict among a few great families. These extremely wealthy oligarchs had a disproportionate say in affairs of state because they subsidized its wars. To resist Frederick Barbarossa, the commune borrowed 1,150 silver marks from twelve subscribers. Two of these were Sebastiano Ziani and Orio Mastropiero; each contributed one-sixth of the total, and each later became doge. This was no accident. These men claimed power based on their subsidies of the state. They were as much financiers as merchants.[79] The new ducal election procedures of 1172, which placed control of the process in the hands of a committee of eleven electors, and those of 1178 with its double election leading to a committee of forty electors, were the means by which the super-rich decided electoral outcomes.

Yet consensus hit a snag in 1229 when Pietro Ziani abdicated after twenty-four years in office. When the committee of forty met to choose his successor, two candidates, Marino Dandolo, nephew of Doge Enrico, and Giacomo Tiepolo, who had a long record of public service, each ended up with twenty votes. A lottery broke the tie. Tiepolo won, and Dandolo conceded. However, when Tiepolo went to see the ailing Ziani, the former doge "spurned" him because of the unorthodox manner of his election.[80] This created a rift between Tiepolo and his followers and Dandolo and his that grew over time.

The Tiepolo party, tended to attract more families that grew wealthy in the aftermath of the Fourth Crusade, while Dandolo's adherents represented the older, more established families. Tiepolo's promulgation of a new law code in 1242, for example, has been seen as an effort by the newly rich to introduce Roman law to Venice. This was opposed by the older oligarchic families who preferred to rely on *arbitrium*, since it accorded more flexibility to judges, did not bind them to a written code, and enabled them to manipulate the law to their advantage.[81]

The factions did not exhibit great differences in foreign policy. One of the biggest concerns during Tiepolo's reign was the challenge posed by Holy Roman emperor Frederick II, who was engaged in a vicious struggle with the pope and against a revived league of Lombard cities. Venice became particularly alarmed when one of his allies, the famously cruel Ezzelino da Romano, aided by German soldiers, took control of the March of Treviso. This jeopardized Venice's commercial relations with nearby *terraferma* cities. Yet both Tiepolo and members of the Badoer family, adherents of the Dandolo faction, favored intervention against Frederick and Ezzelino. Tiepolo's son Pietro was even taken prisoner in Frederick's stunning victory over the Second Lombard League at Cortenuova in November 1237 and suffered the humiliation of being chained to the League's captured war wagon as it was paraded into Cremona. He was imprisoned and later executed.[82] Perhaps fear of Ezzelino's growing power on their border united all Venetians. In her will of April 1256, noblewoman Nicolota Michiel, née Contarini, requested that when the pope formed an alliance against Ezzelino, her executors should use money from her estate to pay for a man to serve for two months in the army arrayed against him. She made this bequest "for the remission of my sins."[83] In the final years of Tiepolo's reign Venice reconciled with Frederick, though not with Ezzelino. Unlike in most Italian cities, adherence to the Guelf (pro-papal) or Ghibelline (pro-imperial) causes never gained much purchase in Venice, nor did it define domestic political struggles.

Tiepolo's base of support extended beyond the new rich merchants to the growing number of artisans in Venice. His popularity and power no doubt alarmed the more conservative members of the merchant elite, who feared ducal might. In a series of changes to the oath of office sworn by his successor Marino Morosini, they corrected what they saw as Tiepolo's abuses of office. Morosini was forbidden, for example, to allow his sons to hold offices in towns outside the *dogado* or Istria. More important still, he could not call the General Assembly without the consent of a majority in the Lesser and Greater Councils. Clearly, the oath correctors were worried that the doge might try to bypass the elites and appeal directly to the assembled citizenry of Venice. In addition, for the first time, the oath outlined a procedure whereby, if all six members of the Lesser Council were in accord with a majority of the Greater Council, a doge could be removed from office.[84]

The tensions roiling Venice's domestic politics reached a crisis point in the 1260s, one of the most turbulent in the city's history. Two contributing factors were the collapse of the Latin Empire of Constantinople in 1261 and the costs of the first Venetian-Genoese War. When in 1266 the government announced that it was raising the tax on grinding grain to pay for paving Piazza San Marco, the "plebs" (the term used by the doge/chronicler Andrea Dandolo) hurled rocks at Doge Renieri Zeno as he tried unsuccessfully to pacify them. They then stormed and plundered the houses of some nobles. Once the fury passed, Zeno had the leaders of the "tumult" (again Dandolo's term) hanged in the Piazza.[85] Responding to an Italy-wide famine in 1268, the government scoured the Mediterranean and Black Sea to secure grain for the city, but high food prices kept the city on edge.[86]

Taxes and periodic food insecurity were not the only sources of popular discontent. The 1260s also witnessed an extraordinary power grab by the commune that reduced the independence of the guilds and made them as much instruments of noble control as expressions of craft self-governance. The newfound popularity of confraternities may have emboldened guildsmen to demand a greater share of power for themselves. But the elites, through the Greater Council, would have none of it. Their first step was an administrative reform. In 1261 they divided the office of the Giustizieri (Justices) into the Giustizieri Nuovi and Vecchi (New and Old Justices). The Nuovi were responsible for overseeing the city's food supplies and regulating taverns, while the Vecchi were placed in charge of the guilds and were responsible for approving their statutes.[87]

The Greater Council followed up this reorganization with four measures in October 1264 intended to cripple the guilds and subordinate them to the merchant-controlled regime. The first required that the guild wardens be changed annually. This was designed to prevent a coherent and effective guild leadership from developing. The second specified that the guild wardens had to accept the statutes that the Giustizieri Vecchi gave them and not make any changes without the Giustizieri Vecchi's approval. This reduced the power of the guilds to legislate. The third forbade the assembly of guild members more than twice a year without the Giustizieri Vecchi's consent. The fourth and final law made it illegal for guildsmen to form any "arrangement, company, armed band or conspiracy by oath, bond, or any other sworn commitment against the honor of the doge, the councils and the commune of the Venetians or against any other person."[88]

These laws were motivated by the merchant elite's fear that through the guilds the *popolo* would develop a cohesive leadership and band together to seize control of the commune. The *popolo* were attempting to do this in communes throughout north and central Italy and succeeded in doing so in Florence in the 1290s. The government-appointed Giustizieri Vecchi transformed the guilds into "instrument[s] of political control" through their "minute regulation of [the guilds'] commercial activity and associative life." For their part, guild officers served as representatives of their members as well as tools of the commune's surveillance.[89] The government's encouragement of the formation of numerous guilds, often in closely related trades, further reduced their strength.

The danger facing the commune in the 1260s was not confined to the *popolo*. In the same year as the popular tax revolt, the Greater Council passed a law forbidding any man either "small or great" from wearing or owning any "shields, blades, helmets, cloaks, banners or other equipment" painted with the coat of arms of "any great man of Venice." Those in possession of such items were to destroy them within fifteen days, and the Signori di Notte were authorized to enforce the order.[90] According to chronicler Andrea Dandolo, the impetus for this law was a tussle in the Piazza between brothers Leonardo and Giovanni Dandolo and Lorenzo Tiepolo, son of former doge Giacomo, in which Tiepolo was wounded.[91] With groups of armed noblemen and their clients roaming the city, the already fragile peace between noble rivals could easily snap.

The danger that Venice would descend into factional warfare was grave enough that after Doge Ranieri Zeno's death in 1268, the ducal councilors advanced a new ducal election procedure. It would remain the standard method for electing doges until the end of the Republic. The process began when all members of the Greater Council were assembled, and wax ballot balls equal to the number of attendees prepared. Thirty of the balls were embedded with a piece of parchment inscribed with the word *lector* (elector). Once the thirty electors were chosen, they gathered in a separate room, and other members of the Greater Council were dismissed. A second lottery then reduced the thirty electors to nine. These nine men then nominated a committee of forty (one had to get seven votes of the nine to be one of the forty). The forty were then pared down by lot to twelve; the twelve nominated twenty-five, the twenty-five were reduced by lot to nine who nominated forty-five; the forty-five were trimmed by lot to eleven; and the eleven nominated a committee of forty-one men that then elected the new doge. The final electoral committee had been changed from forty to forty-one members following the tie that had brought Giacomo Tiepolo to the throne, but the successful candidate had to get twenty-five of forty-one votes to win. The first man chosen under the new procedure was Giacomo Tiepolo's son Lorenzo.[92]

The several rounds of lottery in this new electoral procedure made it nearly impossible for a faction or candidate to manipulate the outcome of the election since it was difficult for a candidate's supporters to survive all the lotteries and secure seats in the final electoral committee. Underscoring the theoretical equality of all members of the Greater Council, the rounds of lottery offered an opportunity, according to beliefs of the time, for God and Saint Mark, in their own mysterious ways, to influence the outcome of the election. But the men who devised this system also understood that the result could not be left entirely to chance or to God. So, they also built several rounds of nomination into the procedure with majorities of the nominators having to agree on who should be included in the next subcommittee. This meant that those who were chosen tended to be consensus candidates, men unlikely to advance diehard partisans for the dogeship. The elaborate ducal election system stifled factionalism and division, while at the same time promoting the nomination of men who were acceptable to a majority of Greater Council members.[93]

Even so, the election of Lorenzo Tiepolo was surely met with consternation by some of the ducal councilors who had devised the new procedures. The *popolo*, by contrast, were jubilant.[94] Residents of neighboring islands and various parishes made their way to the Ducal Palace to honor Tiepolo. One of the most oft-cited passages in Martino da Canal's chronicle recounts the festive processions and displays that the guildsmen mounted for Tiepolo and his wife, the dogaressa. He wrote of the furriers of wild-animal pelts:

> The master furriers of wild-animal pelts bedecked themselves in sumptuous robes of ermine and vair and other precious wild furs and ornamented their apprentices most luxuriously. And they arranged themselves two by two with their banner in the lead and they had excellent marshals, and they were preceded by trumpets and other instruments. And so, they reached the palace and mounted the stairs and there had found their new lord, Messer Lorenzo Tiepolo, the noble doge of Venice. They saluted him most courteously and each wished that God would grant him long life and victory. And Messer the doge returned their greeting with much courtesy, and they all cried out together, "Long live our lord, Messer Lorenzo Tiepolo, the doge." And then they turned around, led by their marshals, and they went as they were arrayed, to visit Madonna the dogaressa [at the Tiepolo palace at Sant'Agostin]. And when they were before her, they saluted their lady, and she returned their greeting with much courtesy.

The master barbers arrived with two armed men on horseback decked out as knights-errant in the company of four damsels whom the knights had "conquered." They asked Tiepolo if there were any in his "court" who wished to challenge them for possession of the damsels. Tiepolo replied that God left it to them to "enjoy their conquest." The combmakers bore cages filled with various species of birds that they released to the delight of the assembled. Several of the guilds came bearing amphoras of wine and silver goblets; the glassmakers carried glass objects, while the goldsmiths adorned their outfits with "pearls, and gold, and silver and rich precious stones, that is sapphires, emeralds, diamonds, topazes, jacinths, amethysts, rubies, jaspers, garnets, and other precious stones."[95]

The guild processions served in part as advertisements of their products and their workmanship. They also revealed the guildsmen's cultural orientation. The barbers' outfitting of two knights-errant indicates that the appeal of chivalric tales was not confined to the elites. It also suggests the barbers' own status aspirations, as they played at noble culture. Most important, the amphoras of wine recalled an older understanding of the dogeship by which various communities in the lagoon and elsewhere were obliged to offer gifts to the doge both for his upkeep and as symbols of their loyalty and subordination to him.

Herein lay the danger for the elites. A doge in alliance with the *popolo* could undermine the growing monopoly on power enjoyed by the merchants. In fact, in the brief oration that Ughetto, a master combmaker, offered Tiepolo during the combmakers' procession, he declared, "Sire, I pray Jesus Christ and his sweet mother and Messer Saint Mark that they give you health and life and victory and that they concede to you to govern all your life in victory and honor the honorable Venetian *popolo*."[96] As one historian has observed, "Never had any doge elicited such insistent enthusiasm on the part of the *popolo* of the parishes and guilds."[97]

Despite the guildsmen's optimism, there is little to suggest that Tiepolo pursued policies that hurt rich merchants or particularly favored artisans. Nevertheless, fear of ducal might and a doge/*popolo* alliance, including recourse to the General Assembly, remained.[98] In May 1269, the Greater Council passed a law that anyone who drew arms in San Marco or the Ducal Palace or its courtyard would be fined 100 lire, or 50 if they did so in Piazza San Marco or the Rialto market. Those who could not pay the penalty would be jailed six months or until they paid. That the latter clause was added demonstrates that it was not aimed solely at the wealthy who could afford the fine. Two months later the council drew up a new list of weapons that it was illegal to carry in the city; it forbade as well as their production by craftsmen. And in 1273 the council banned guildsmen from serving as patrolmen for the Signori di Notte out of fear that they were not fully committed to protecting the commune.[99]

The most telling change came following Tiepolo's death in 1275 in the oath sworn by his successors. In the article dealing with the wardens of guilds, it reiterated sections from previous oaths that forbade the doge without consent of the Lesser and Greater Councils from removing wardens from their posts or creating wardens for trades that had not previously had them. The intent was to prevent the doge from arbitrarily removing leaders of guilds who were not pleasing to him or imposing them on groups that did not have them already. What was new was the second part of the article, barring the doge from calling the wardens to come armed or unarmed to the commune's aid without approval of the ducal councilors. This would forestall any attempt by the doge, in alliance with the guilds, to overthrow the regime as well as prevent the guilds from defending the doge if he were under attack by the merchant nobles.[100]

By 1275 the guilds (and hence the *popolo)* had been effectively eliminated from power. They could not assemble or legislate for themselves without governmental approval; their leaders were barred from holding office for more than a year; and they were forbidden from doing anything that threatened the state. They could not legally take up arms to protect their interests, and all their actions were subject to strict surveillance by the Giustizieri Vecchi. The ruling merchants made sure that artisans and manufacturers would not have the means to advance their own economic interests or political power. Venice resoundingly announced that the *popolo* would not have a direct voice in government.[101]

That did not, however, resolve the issue for the elites. Factionalism remained a concern, as did possible conflict between the older established noble merchants and those who recently had made their fortunes in trade. In many Italian communes, when one faction got the upper hand, it excluded its rivals from power, often exiling them. The most famous Italian exile was the White Guelf Dante Alighieri who was banished from Florence when the rival Black Guelfs came to power. The Venetians managed to escape this fate through the Serrata. In the process, they defined the contours of their ruling class.

The change involved the way in which membership in the Greater Council was determined.[102] The method that was used before the Serrata worked as follows: a few days before Michaelmas (September 29), the Greater Council chose four electors, two from each side of the Grand Canal, who then selected the 100 ordinary members of the Greater Council and the sixty members of the Senate for a one-year term beginning on Michaelmas. Membership in the Greater Council included the 100 elected ordinary members, the sixty senators, the forty members of the Forty, as well as various magistrates and administrators who served ex officio—about 400 to 450 men in total. Additional committees of four electors were created as needed to hold by-elections when vacancies occurred. In essence, selection to be one of the ordinary members of the council rested on the judgement of a tiny number of men—the four electors. To dispel this concern, two proposals put forward in October 1286 would have required that the men selected for membership by the four electors get the approval of some combination of majorities in the Ducal Council, Senate, Forty, or Greater Council; however, the proposal failed to pass. The usual procedure was reaffirmed. Nevertheless, these bills reveal dissatisfaction with the existing system. Factions or family alliances could overly influence a system that relied on only a few men to serve as electors.

These fears were largely laid to rest by a law passed in February 1297 that changed the electoral procedure. It declared that "all those who have served [in the Greater Council] during the past four years should be proposed one by one to the Forty, and whoever shall have twelve or more votes shall be a member of the Greater Council until the Michaelmas and then for one year."[103] It further ruled that anyone who had been in the council during the past four years but was not considered because he was away from Venice at the time could petition the Heads of the Forty to have the Forty vote on his Greater Council membership. In addition, three nominators were to be chosen. When called upon by the doge and his councilors, they were to propose to the Forty the inclusion of men who had not served in the Greater Council during the preceding four years. These nominees too would need to get only twelve positive votes in the Forty. This experimental procedure was to last until Michaelmas 1298, at which point the issue could be revisited. But no change was made. The reelection of those who were already sitting members was taken for granted; the only question involved new members.

The law of February 1297 removed restrictions on the size of the Greater Council. No longer would it be limited to just 100 ordinary members plus those who had the right to sit ex officio or as members of the Senate or Forty. From approximately 450 members in the years prior to 1297, it mushroomed to 1,100 members by 1320.[104] By enlarging the council in this way, the 1297 law reduced the possibility that certain factions or families would be excluded from a voice in governmental affairs. It guaranteed that everyone who was anyone would have a seat. And it offered a means by which new men could be admitted. It lowered the stakes involved in Greater Council elections and thus the political temperature of the city.

Soon, however, the door for the admission of new men began to close. In December 1298, the Greater Council decided that no one was eligible to sit in the Forty unless his father, grandfather, or even more distant male forebears had been members of the Greater Council. This transformed the

Forty into a bastion of the establishment. Families, with a history of service to the commune as members of the Forty, would decide on new Greater Council members for whom the requirements for membership also began to tighten. In March 1300 a law was passed that the ducal councilors could not propose any "new man" (*homo novus*) for admission to the Greater Council unless his candidacy was approved by a majority of the Forty, provided that a quorum of twenty members was present. Sometime between March 1300 and December 1307 the rule was changed again so that new men had to have prior approval by four of the six ducal councilors plus a majority of the Forty. In December 1307 those numbers were raised to five ducal councilors and twenty-five members of the Forty. In March 1310 it was raised to thirty votes in the Forty and a majority in the Greater Council. Finally, by 1315 admission of new men required approval by two-thirds of Greater Council members and three-fourths of the Forty. Whereas in 1297 it had been easy for new men to enter the Greater Council since they had to get only twelve votes of the Forty, by 1315 it had become extremely hard, especially since it required securing the approval of thirty votes in the Forty, the stronghold of the older more established families. Economic difficulties that the city experienced in these years may explain the tightening requirements. Members of the Greater Council were circling the wagons against new admissions.

The value of Greater Council membership also grew since it increasingly became the criterion for eligibility to sit in other councils. The 1298 law restricted membership in the Forty to those whose male ancestors had sat in the Greater Council. In 1311, Greater Council membership became a requirement for election to the Senate. The Greater Council was rapidly becoming the body from which all the other councils and officers of the state derived. If a man was not part of the Greater Council, he was effectively excluded from high office in Venice.

Hereditary right also became associated with membership, although it took more than twenty years to be enshrined in law. There was no mention of heredity in the 1297 law, although ancestry did become a requirement for admission to the Forty in 1298. It is not entirely clear how elections were conducted once the procedure established in 1297 took hold. One chronicle states that on September 11, 1298, it was decided that families that had been admitted a year earlier should continue to participate "without the usual balloting that is done on the feast of Saint Michael."[105] Moreover, if a man qualified, then so did his sons upon reaching the proper age. A statute of 1311 established eighteen as the minimum age for Greater Council membership. Apparently by one means or another, some young men were entering then rather than at the traditional age of twenty-five. An amendment of 1315 required those who wished to be considered for membership at eighteen to register with the Forty. Thus began the centuries-long practice of officially recording the names of those eligible for Greater Council membership. An applicant's male kin had to vouch for him during the registry. Then in 1319 the method for early entry was systematized. A special lottery was created, known as the Barbarella since it was held on Saint Barbara's feast day (December 4). With this provision, noble sons who were properly registered with the government and who won the lottery could enter the council at twenty rather than twenty-five. Finally, on September 27, 1323, the hereditary requirement for council membership was enshrined in law. Noting that previous laws had required candidates for membership to prove they were at least twenty-five years of age but said "nothing about demonstrating their right to be members through the [previous] membership in the Greater Council of their father or grandfather," the new law required proof of age as well as entitlement "to membership on account of their forebears, members of the Council, according to the laws of Venice."[106]

By 1323 then, the contours of the Venetian ruling class had been defined. Participation was based on blood, on membership in one of the approximately 210 families who had been included since 1297.[107] The men who sat in the Council styled themselves as nobles, a status that was formalized. Only Greater Council members and their kin could claim nobility. As the sixteenth-century genealogist of the Venetian nobility, Marco Barbaro, wrote, "The dignity of noble citizens and members of the Great[er] Council was and is one and the same, because there is no one in the Great[er] Council who is not one of our noble citizens."[108] Although the possibility remained for the admission of new men, the entry requirements became so stringent that none passed the test. In 1381, thirty new families were admitted to the Council as reward for their sacrifices during the Fourth Venetian-Genoese War. Following that, the ranks of the nobility closed again (with a few exceptions mostly for foreign notables) until the seventeenth century when, under severe financial pressure and different international circumstances, the government put membership in the Greater Council up for sale.

The term Serrata derives from the Venetian verb *serar* (Italian *serrare*) meaning to lock, tighten, or close. What happened in these years has long been interpreted as both a locking in and a locking out. This is clear from a chronicle, parts of which were written within two generations of the events themselves possibly by nobleman Nicolò Trevisan. The chronicler states, "He [Doge Pietro Gradenigo] wished to reform the Great[er] Council, into which he wished to admit a larger number of families, so that they might be recognized as noble and equal to the others, and not that a few families [only] should be the chief and most revered of the city, taking away [at the same time however] from the citizens and common people [*popolari*] the way that they used to have of being admitted to the Great[er] Council." According to this account, Gradenigo was motived not only by a desire to lock in a greater number of families and ensure their noble status but also by his wish to lock out the *popolo*. The latter impulse was motivated, according to the chronicler, by "the hate which he [Gradenigo] had towards the common people who . . . continued after his election to show their preference for the house of Tiepolo."[109] When Doge Giovanni Dandolo died on November 1, 1289, the *popolo* had demanded that Giacomo Tiepolo, son of doge Lorenzo and grandson of doge Giacomo, be his successor. Another fourteenth-century chronicle reports that on November 22, 1289, the feast of Saint Cecilia, "the *popolo* created a great tumult."[110] But the forty-one electors chose Gradenigo. Why they did so is unclear. The electors may have feared Tiepolo's popularity and wanted to send a message to the *popolo*. It is also possible that they were concerned that the Tiepolo family was creating a ducal dynasty. Regardless, in the Serrata, the *popolo* were effectively locked out of the Greater Council.

Other than the arrival of Mark's relics in the ninth century, the Serrata was arguably the most important event in Venice's history. On one hand, it created the aristocratic regime that ruled the city until its surrender to Napoleon in 1797. Starting in 1297 it is legitimate to describe this regime as a republic. For the next 500 years, between 1,000 and 2,500 noblemen, members of approximately 150 families provided the manpower for governance and rule through councils.[111] Furthermore, Venice came to serve in early modern treatises on politics as an example of the ideal or model republic. During most of this period, monarchy was the most common form of government in both Europe and Asia. One thousand men ruling a city of 100,000 souls surely seemed egalitarian by the standards of the time. Still, it is important to recall that those same 1,000 men also ruled over territories stretching from nearby Murano to far away Crete and Negroponte. The number of inhabitants over whom the Venetian nobles actually ruled numbered in the hundreds of thousands. From that perspective, the regime appears less representative and benign.

The Serrata is also important for how it has been continually reinterpreted. In the wake of the French Revolution and following the end of the Republic in 1797, it came to be viewed as the genesis of a tyrannical, reactionary aristocratic establishment that quashed the aspirations of the people in 1297. Both for what it accomplished and how it has been redeployed for ever-changing political ends, the Serrata was a crucial watershed in Venice's history.

To Venetian noblemen alive in 1300, the future must have appeared bright indeed. Their aristocratic status and right to govern had been guaranteed for themselves and their heirs, trade was strong, and the city had survived its recent war with Genoa. What they could not have known was that in the following decades Venice would face an unprecedented string of crises.

8

The Consolidation of the Patrician Regime

IN DECEMBER 1340, the Greater Council authorized the building of a new council hall. The current one was no longer adequate to meet its needs since the number of members had grown so dramatically because of the Serrata. Recognizing the necessity of having a space that was commensurate with the "fame, honor, and benefit of the city," the council voted to build the new hall above the offices occupied by the Signori di Notte that faced the Bacino. It allocated 9,500 ducats for the hall's construction and another 2,000 ducats for its decoration "in gold and painting."[1] Work was interrupted during the Black Death but must have been completed by 1365 when the government commissioned Paduan painter Guariento di Arpo to execute a huge fresco depicting the *Coronation of the Virgin* on the east wall. Flanking Christ's crowning of Mary were orderly rows of saints positioned at right angles to the heavenly throne. The composition created an equivalence between the celestial court and the assembled Greater Council.[2] An Annunciation adjoined the central coronation image and recalled Venice's legendary founding on March 25. On the side walls, Guariento and his assistants painted scenes of the Peace of Venice of 1177, when Sebastiano Ziani hosted Frederick Barbarossa and Alexander III.

The decision to build a new assembly hall is emblematic of the consolidation of the noble regime that occurred in the roughly four decades following the Serrata. In those years the newly defined noble or patrician ruling class gradually tightened admission standards, making it increasingly difficult for those who had been left out to gain Greater Council membership. At the same time, it modified the requirements for foreigners to acquire Venetian citizenship and, with it, valuable commercial privileges. Policy oscillated between

FIGURE 8.1 Paolo Furlani, *The Venetian Great Council in Session*, c. 1566. Guariento's *Coronation of the Virgin* fresco dominates the tribune wall. Rijksmuseum, Amsterdam, RP-P-1999-86.

openness to foreigners and protectionism, as the patricians sometimes sought to restrict the benefits of international trade to themselves.

The hallmark of that trade was the creation of a system of state-owned merchant galleys operating on established routes. Starting around the turn of the fourteenth century, the government undertook at public expense the construction of a fleet of merchant galleys, which it then auctioned for individual voyages to the highest bidders. The Senate determined the itineraries, set the schedules and kinds of cargo that could be transported, and required that all ships on particular routes sail in convoy. The system was so profitable and successful that it would remain the emblem of Venetian trade and source of great wealth for the patricians until the early sixteenth century.

These years also witnessed other business innovations including widespread adoption of agents or factors who worked on commission, the composition and consultation of merchant manuals, and the proliferation of letter-writing as a means of business communication. Exchange at Rialto was facilitated by the development of banks that allowed merchants to transfer funds between buyers and sellers with just a few strokes of the banker's pen. Shares in Venice's public debt raised through forced loans to the state developed into a recognized form of commercial paper.

In addition, the city's infrastructure was further modified to facilitate trade. Enhancements were made to the Rialto market, although the bulk of the infrastructure improvements occurred around the Bacino. Defense of the port from human and natural enemies took on new urgency as the city tried to prevent the barrier islands from eroding and the port of San Nicolò from silting up.

This was also a period of intellectual consolidation as the nobles created an official culture—one that promoted a vision emphasizing Venice's unique place not only in the world but also in God's plan for it. The building and decoration of the new Greater Council Hall was part of that effort. But it was only part. Especially during the dogeship of Andrea Dandolo, the city undertook a further codification of its laws and developed a distinctive tradition of history-writing. Art, like literature, was also used to document and authenticate Venice's past and portray the city as specially chosen.

The accomplishments of the decades before the Black Death were impressive indeed as the newly minted patrician class consolidated its hold on politics, business, society, and culture. But this period of consolidation did not begin on a triumphant note, as war and conspiracies preceded and fostered it.

The War of Ferrara (1308–13) was a military, diplomatic, and public relations debacle.[3] A succession crisis, triggered by the death of the Marquess of Ferrara Azzo VIII precipitated the war, but its true causes lay in the resentment of neighboring cities provoked by Venice's economic and political hegemony over the entire northern Adriatic. Before his death in January 1308, Azzo had named his natural son Fresco to the throne, bypassing Azzo's brother Francesco. Venice supported Fresco's claim with troops, while pressuring him to grant it significant commercial privileges. Francesco appealed to the papacy for help realizing his claim and offered to hold the city in fief from the pope.

Pope Clement V's representatives worked to rally the Guelf cities, Bologna, Ravenna, and Padua, to his side. But in a preemptive strike, the Venetians forced Fresco, who was facing revolt within Ferrara, to cede the city to them. They took possession of Tedaldo Castle overlooking the Po, while other parts of the town fell into the hands of troops under the command of papal representatives. When a papal legation to Venice was rebuffed and assaulted, Clement placed the Venetians under interdict in October 1308 and authorized widespread seizure of Venetian goods. Interdict was the ultimate pressure tactic and most powerful weapon in the papal arsenal. Venice reacted by seizing complete control of Ferrara and appointing Giovanni Soranzo as podesta.

When the war resumed in spring 1309, Venice found itself facing an alliance that included various towns in Romagna and Emilia, including Bologna, Ravenna, and Cervia, which were only too happy to throw off Venetian commercial domination and join the pontiff's newly declared crusade against the city. Padua, against which Venice had recently fought the Salt War, joined too. When enemy troops managed to capture and destroy Venice's strategically important fort Marcamò, the Venetians had to find a way to bypass the Ferrarese branch of the Po and so allied themselves with the Scaligeri (or Della Scala) lords of Verona. Together they decided to excavate a canal connecting the Adige River with the Ficarolo branch of the Po, thus avoiding the branch flowing past Ferrara. The Venetians also had an ally in the lord of Treviso, who assisted them in putting down the revolt against Venice that had spread to Aquileia and Istria. Zara too was once again seeking to shake off the Venetian yoke. As the conflict dragged on, the Venetian garrison in Ferrara was struck by disease and suffered stunning military defeats, including the loss of a river fleet under the command of Marco Querini that had been sent to provide relief. Venice had lost the war. Protracted peace talks finally resulted in February 1313 in a total papal victory. According to the treaty terms, Venice had to give up all claims to Ferrara, which was officially recognized as a papal possession, and pay an indemnity of 50,000 florins. Just as significantly, the Venetians agreed to use the branches of the Po that passed through Ferrarese territory and not bypass Ferrara by means of the recently built canal to the Adige. In addition, Venetians were not to acquire any more property in Ferrarese territory without papal approval.

Even with these harsh peace terms Venice still managed to secure what really mattered, namely, continued access to the Po via Ferrara. This had never been a war about territory but about protecting Venice's staple rights and control of river traffic. Still, by occupying a *terraferma* city, the Venetians had demonstrated just how far they were willing to go to defend those rights. It also revealed the anger that Venetian economic hegemony provoked in other cities and temporarily made an enemy of the papacy. The Venetians used prose and poetry to repair relations with the pontiff. In 1317 the Greater Council commissioned Bonincontro dei Bovi, a member of the ducal chancery, to write an official account of the Peace of Venice of 1177, and in 1319 it ordered that scenes of the occasion "when the Pope was in Venice with the Lord Emperor [Barbarossa]" be painted in the Chapel of San Nicolò in the Ducal Palace.[4] This was just one of many occasions when the Venetians would place art in the service of diplomacy.

The War of Ferrara was also a precipitating factor in the gravest internal threat yet faced by the newly established patrician regime, the 1310 Querini-Tiepolo Conspiracy.[5] The plot was not the first time the Serrata settlement had been challenged. In 1300 a *popolano* (commoner) named Marino Boccono (or Bocho) led a conspiracy against the regime. Little is known about what occurred. In his *Chronica brevis* (Short Chronicle), written less than half a century after the event, Doge Andrea Dandolo related only that Doge Pietro Gradenigo dealt with a conspiracy aimed at him and the fatherland by Boccono and "his accomplices" and that Gradenigo condemned the traitors to death.[6] The Giustinian chronicle from later in the century added little except to note that the conspirators were quickly captured and hanged between the two columns in the Piazzetta.[7] Writing in the early sixteenth century, chronicler Giovanni Giacomo Caroldo declared that the conspirators were unhappy that the committee of forty-one ducal electors with no *popolano* members had selected Gradenigo as doge and bypassed Giacomo Tiepolo, "who was called the doge by all the *popolo*."[8] At heart, the Boccono conspiracy was an expression of popular discontent against the Serrata and the doge who orchestrated it.

The Querini-Tiepolo Conspiracy represented a much graver challenge to the regime, the most serious in the period of its formation.[9] Unlike the Boccono cabal, it originated within the patriciate itself. The plot, led by noblemen Marco Querini (who resented the treatment he had received after his poor performance in the Ferrarese war) and his son-in-law Baiamonte Tiepolo (grandson of Doge Lorenzo and great-grandson of Doge Giacomo Tiepolo), unfolded on the morning of June 15, 1310, the feast of Saint Vitus. The conspirators had gathered the night before at the Tiepolo palace at Sant'Agostin and the Querini palace at Rialto to prepare their assault on the governmental center at San Marco. In the morning, they crossed the Rialto Bridge, divided into groups, and proceeded toward the Piazza, which they planned to enter from different directions and rendezvous with their fellow conspirator Badoero Badoer, who was bringing reinforcements from Padua. But as Machiavelli would later warn would-be plotters, conspiracies seldom go as planned. Doge Gradenigo had been alerted to the plot and gathered men loyal to the regime, including all the ducal councilors (except Andrea Doro who had joined the conspiracy) in the Piazza and barricaded the entry points. He had also called on the podestas of Chioggia, Torcello, and Murano to send reinforcements. The rebels had lost the element of surprise. To make matters worse, a thunderstorm delayed Badoer's crossing of the lagoon, and Tiepolo's men got bottled up in the Merceria. Marco Querini's troops reached the Piazza alone and were quickly cut down by the doge's forces. The corpses of Querini and his son Benedetto were among those littering the square. Tiepolo's troops abandoned the assault when their standard-bearer was knocked down by a woman named Giustina Rossi who dropped a brick or stone from a window along the Merceria. The men farther back saw the standard topple, lost heart, retreated across the Rialto drawbridge, raised it behind them, and hunkered down at Rialto. In the meantime, the podesta of Chioggia Ugolino Giustinian and his men intercepted and captured Badoer and his forces. When the Chioggian contingent arrived in Venice, the doge ordered the recapture of Rialto. Some of the rebels were killed in fighting at the marketplace. Rather than risk further bloodshed, the government agreed to allow the noble participants, including Baiamonte Tiepolo, to go into exile, while those who were *popolani* were to be shown mercy. After being condemned by the Council of Forty, the imprisoned Badoer and several of his followers were executed. The regime had survived.

With the rebels vanquished, Gradenigo acted quickly to ensure that the government's account of events prevailed. The rebellion was presented as a conspiracy by malcontents rather than what it was—a civil war within the nobility.[10] In letters dispatched to Venetian officials overseas on June 17, Gradenigo noted that they had probably already heard rumors of the great "novelty" that had occurred in the city. He framed it as a contest between good and evil. Comparing Tiepolo implicitly to the devil, Gradenigo described him as "the vilest traitor and seducer of iniquities," who was "ungrateful" for the many honors and dignities the commune had bestowed upon his ancestors. He, his co-conspirator Querini, and their fellow nobles had beguiled many *popolani* into following them and assembled an unsavory coalition of "exiles, foreigners, and rogues." Gradenigo declared that he and his forces had fought "manfully" (unlike the rebels) and, with "the help of God and his evangelist Saint Mark," had prevailed.[11]

That same day, the Greater Council issued a decree banishing Tiepolo and the other noble participants. Tiepolo was exiled to the regions of Dalmatia beyond Zara, but he fled to often rebellious Zara. The banishments applied only to the individuals involved, rather than all members of their patriline. Most non-nobles were, as had been agreed, forgiven if they showed contrition. These punishments were surprisingly lenient given the enormity of the offense. The many marital and commercial ties that linked members of the patriciate together perhaps explain why punishment was not extended to a wider net of kinsmen, or perhaps Gradenigo did not think his position was strong enough to go after entire clans. Regardless, leniency had the salutary effect of not further inflaming tensions within the ruling elite. This is exemplified by what happened to Marco Querini's house at Rialto. As part of Tiepolo's and Querini's punishment, the government ordered their houses razed. Tiepolo's palace at Sant'Agostin was destroyed. But Marco Querini's house at San Matteo di Rialto posed a problem since it was held in *fraterna* not only by him and his brother Pietro, both of whom had participated in the rebellion, but also by a third brother Giovanni, who had not. The government therefore ruled that two-thirds of the palace should be demolished. But, unable to determine the boundaries of the various shares, they decided to purchase Giovanni's part and convert the palace into the offices of the Ufficiali alle Beccherie (Supervisors of Butchershops), the officials responsible for overseeing the city's meat supplies.

The government also realized that the exiles needed monitoring lest they break their confinement, seek allies among Venice's enemies, and foment new trouble. Accordingly, on July 10 it authorized the temporary creation of a special body of ten men who would take over supervision of the conspirators from the Forty. The efficacy of this Council of Ten soon became clear, and it was reauthorized for longer and longer periods until finally in July 1335 the Greater Council voted to make it a permanent organ of the government. In October 1339 the General Assembly added its assent.[12]

The Ten would become over time the most powerful and feared governmental council in Venice. Writing in the early sixteenth century, Marino Sanudo described it as "the most severe magistracy."[13] The dread it inspired was due in large measure to its use of the inquisitorial rather than the accusatorial method when trying those accused of crimes. This meant that it did not have to adhere closely to the steps normally followed by other councils when hearing criminal cases. It could abbreviate them and act in secret, while defendants had no right to legal representation. Additionally, there was no appeal of the Ten's sentences since the Greater Council had given it authority to act on its behalf. Within a decade of the conspiracy, the Ten had also created its own police force.[14]

The rebels who observed the terms of their exile retained their legal rights as citizens. Those who broke the terms lost all protections and were declared "traitors." Their property was confiscated, and bounties placed on their heads. The Ten kept special track of Baiamonte Tiepolo, who continued his machinations. In 1311 he was plotting an expedition against Venice from Padua with some of its leading citizens. In 1325 he was in Zara, where he received emissaries from Bologna. The Ten wrote to the counts of Traù (Trogir), Sebenico (Šebenik), Ragusa (Dubrovnik), and Curzola (Korčula) urging them to capture him. In January 1329 the Ten authorized Doge Giovanni Soranzo and Ferigo Dandolo to use all necessary means to have him killed.[15] Tiepolo must have died soon after, perhaps at the hands of an assassin, since he disappeared from the Ten's deliberations at that point. A few years later, the Ten referred to his spouse as a widow.

In September 1310, the Ten ordered the rebels' wives to leave Venice and the *dogado* and all other subject lands within eight days. They were not permitted to return while their husbands were alive.[16] When, in 1320, the Ten learned that Pietro Querini had been killed, they gave his widow permission to repatriate if she had no sons or daughters by him and was not pregnant; if pregnant, they would decide on the terms of her continuing exile.[17] In this ruling the Ten displayed a notable ambivalence toward traitors' spouses. They saw Querini's wife herself as innocent. But if she was perpetuating his line through pregnancy, then she was somehow culpable. When she remarried, Caterina, widow of Nicolò Querini, was freed of the convent confinement to which she had been restricted.[18] As long as Caterina was associated with her rebel husband, even in widowhood, she remained guilty by association. But once she remarried and came under the legal authority of another man, she was effectively exonerated.

The Ten were not only worried about the biological stain on these women but also that they might share the same political convictions as their male relatives or seek to aid them. For example, an unnamed daughter of the late Pietro Querini was residing at the convent of Santa Maria della Celestia—almost certainly in confinement. In autumn 1322 the Ten ordered the abbess to admonish her not to send or receive letters or "ambassadors" from her brother or any of the other rebels and remind her to "comport herself well." Failure to comply would prompt the Ten to take appropriate action against both her and the convent.[19]

The government also made a show of rewarding *popolani* who had remained loyal. A few well-placed ones were inducted into the Greater Council, while humbler men got minor governmental offices or other special favors. A man named Nigerno, for example, was rewarded with a post with the Giustizieri Nuovi since "on the feast of Saint Vitus [he] fought manfully in the Piazza San Marco against the enemy," while a cutler named Benedetto was given a favorable payment schedule for a fine he had incurred since he was both a Ferrara War veteran and had "comported himself well on the feast of Saint Vitus."[20] Corporate groups also benefited. Members of the confraternity of the Carità and the painters' guild had battled the rebels in Campo San Luca near Rialto. Both groups were given the privilege of hoisting their emblems on a flagpole in the square. But the most famous reward went to Giustina, the woman who had knocked down Tiepolo's standard-bearer. She was given the right to fly the banner of San Marco on the feast of Saint Vitus and other holy days and was assured that the rent she paid her Procurator of San Marco landlords would never be raised on her or her descendants. A small statue of Giustina launching her missile, erected in 1841, marks the spot along the Merceria where it occurred.[21]

Finally, rather than erasing all evidence of the rebellion, the government kept the memory of the rebels' fate alive as a warning to other would-be traitors. In 1364, when Crete was in revolt against the metropole, the Ten decided to erect a column on the site of Tiepolo's razed palace. One of the earliest inscriptions in Venetian dialect, it reads, "This plot of land was Baiamonte's and now, because of his evil betrayal, it has been made common land to frighten others, and forever show all people (the benefits of) good sense."[22]

Even more significantly, just ten days after the plot, the Greater Council proclaimed the feast of Saint Vitus a public holiday to be celebrated annually with a ducal procession to the church of Saint Vitus in Dorsoduro. It also decided to embellish the church. It voted to spend five lire on altar vessels and ordered that the pilasters from Tiepolo's demolished palace be used as victory trophies to adorn the portal of the church.[23]

At least seventy-seven nobles are known to have participated in the plot. They belonged to twenty-eight different families, although thirty-five came from just four: seventeen Querinis, seven Tiepolos, six Badoers, and five Barozzis. Twenty-three members of the clergy also took part, as did an unknown number of *popolani*.[24] Members of each of these groups had their own reasons for joining. For some patricians, it was a way to settle old scores. Marco Querini resented having been blamed for the military debacle at Ferrara, while Baiamonte Tiepolo's father Giacomo was Gradenigo's chief competitor for the dogeship. Some clergymen were upset by the papal interdict and wanted to overthrow the doge who prosecuted the Ferrarese war. Several of the noble participants, especially the Querini, had significant landholdings in Ferrarese territory, while Badoero Badoer was closely tied to landholding magnates around Padua and to the Este of Ferrara. After all, Padua is where Baiamonte Tiepolo tried to organize a second assault on the regime following the rebellion. These patricians with interests on the mainland found common purpose with the elites of *terraferma* cities who resented Venetian commercial hegemony and wrapped themselves collectively in the banner of the Guelf or pro-papal cause. As for the *popolano* participants, some no doubt were clients of the Tiepolos and Querinis and other noble houses who followed their patrons in hope of reward. Others were spurred to join because of their resentment of the Ferrara war in which many laboring-class Venetians had lost their lives. Still others may have seen Tiepolo, heir to a family tradition of popular support, as the man to undo the Serrata, though that was never his intent. If anything, Tiepolo, like other factional or party leaders in late medieval Italian cities, simply wanted to take revenge on his patrician enemies and grab power for himself and his allies. Above all, the Querini-Tiepolo rebellion was a conflict within the ranks of the newly defined Venetian ruling class and a response to the Ferrarese war.

Its most important legacy was the Council of Ten. Within a short time, the council became a central arm of the government. Its ability to act expeditiously was particularly valued, especially in comparison to the considered deliberations of larger governmental bodies like the Senate and Greater Council. Vigilant in its duties, it aggressively investigated threats to the regime, both real and perceived. In 1328 it prosecuted the participants in yet another noble conspiracy against the state—this one led by members of the Barozzi family. Jacopo Querini was an accomplice. The Ten made a show of executing the ringleaders, Jacopo and Marino Barozzi as well as Querini. They were paraded up and down the Grand Canal from San Marco to Santa Croce before being decapitated between the two columns in the Piazzetta. Nonnobles, like the earlier conspirator Marino Boccono, were hanged.[25]

For much of the fourteenth century the Council of Ten was also zealous in its prosecution of seditious speech. In August 1350 it investigated two women, Catarina, otherwise unidentified, and Pencina, wife of Francesco de Florentia. Both women were prosecuted for speaking against the officials who were registering men for the *duodena* (the citizen militia). In August the Ten unanimously sentenced Catarina to spend the balance of the month in jail for what they described as "blasphemies spoken by her against those who ordered [enlistment in] the *duodena*." On September 1 the Ten voted to proceed against Pencina, who had fled the city. She was sentenced, "on account of the dishonest and ugly words that were spoken by her, namely 'that those who inscribed and had inscribed the *duodena* ought to end up just like those of Ca' Barozzi, and that this city ought to sink just like any ship goes under and fire ought to consume it and the magnates who thus rule it.' "[26] The Ten's reach extended far. It investigated words that were uttered on a ship bound for Crete, in Alexandria, even in a Genoese jail.

The Ten played a particularly important role in suppressing popular protests against the patrician regime and thwarting any sort of organizing that might challenge noble rule.[27] In 1328 it forbade anyone from hosting more than four foreigners in his house without first informing the Capi di Sestieri. It frequently investigated clandestine gatherings. The confraternities were of special concern since they brought together large groups of people, mostly non-nobles. From its beginning, the Council of Ten was preoccupied with them. Just two years after the Querini-Tiepolo conspiracy, it prohibited the flagellant confraternities from meeting or parading at night, while clauses forbidding seditious actions were inserted into the confraternities' statutes sometime before 1330. Starting in 1360, all requests to form new confraternities required the Ten's approval.[28]

Petrarch described Venice as standing "solid on a foundation of civil concord."[29] Apologists for the regime continually emphasized that Venice was immune to the civil strife that plagued other Italian cities since the *popolo* willingly accepted their social subordination and exclusion from government. La Serenissima (The Most Serene [Republic]), the name by which Venice came to be known, perfectly captured this carefully cultivated image of concord. Chroniclers and painters systematically commemorated the memory of Giustina Rossi, *La Vecchia del Mortajo* (The Mortar Launching Crone), since she epitomized the image of the patriotic "people [who came] to the defense of the oligarchy which exercised justice and good government on the part of the doge."[30]

Venice's renown for social concord has spawned numerous explanations for why the *popolo* did not revolt. One emphasizes the city's unique topography. The many canals, it is claimed, made it difficult for angry mobs to gather and engage in joint action.[31] Alternatively, it has been argued that the largely self-contained parish-islands in which rich and poor lived "cheek by jowl" fostered harmonious social integration that percolated up to the city at large.[32] Another group of theories argues that institutions such as the guilds, ferry stations, and *scuole piccole* offered a "sense of belonging" to the disenfranchised, along with offices for those who needed an outlet for their ambitions.[33] Social practices, including the cultivation and protection of laboring-class clients by male and female noble patrons, also purportedly promoted good relations.[34] So too did walking, the city's primary means of getting about, since it put people of all classes into frequent contact on the streets.[35] Governmental policies, including the bestowal on loyal subjects of favors and minor bureaucratic offices, the right to petition for redress of grievances, guarantees of bread supplies, the selective exercise of equitable justice, and the awarding of honorific privileges to such groups as the Arsenal workers and the fishermen of San Nicolò dei Mendicoli, also supposedly mitigated the worst aspects of disenfranchisement.[36] More negatively, the city's large police force and its use of show trials and exemplary punishments, especially by the Council of Ten, have been interpreted as cowing the *popolo* into obedience.[37] It has even been suggested that the discipline demanded of ships' crews permeated society and reinforced "clientelism, solidarity, and hierarchy" among Venetians.[38]

Evidence can be marshaled to support each of these theories, but none adequately explains Venetian popular quiescence since similar practices and policies existed in cities such as Florence that were renowned for civil unrest. In fact, the much-vaunted trait does not survive serious scrutiny.[39] The *popolo* frequently displayed their discontent through organized activities such as work slowdowns and riots as well as acts of vandalism, aggression toward minor governmental officials, composition and performance of derogatory songs, use of defamatory language, and defacing of buildings with graffiti. The Ten, along with other governmental bodies, played a central role in erasing evidence of this discontent in order to promote the image of Venice as serene.[40]

With the creation of the Council of Ten, the evolution of Venice's republican governmental councils was complete. When fully fledged, the government comprised five deliberative bodies: the Greater Council, Senate, Forty, the Lesser (or Ducal) Council, and Ten. Nineteenth-century German historian Leopold von Ranke compared the Republic's constitutional structure to the five domes of San Marco, with one larger than the rest.[41] More commonly Venice's governmental structure is imagined as a triangle, with the Greater Council (or sometimes the General Assembly) at its base and the Senate, Forty, Ten, and Lesser Council leading ladder-like to the doge at the apex. Although flawed, this diagram captures the governmental skeleton onto which the flesh of Venetian politics was attached. In the wake of the War of Ferrara and the Querini-Tiepolo Conspiracy, the institutional consolidation of the post-Serrata republican regime was complete. But it was only one part of the larger consolidation taking place in the first half of the fourteenth century.

The dramatic growth of the Venetian economy was evidenced by a building boom. The basis of that strength was international trade, which took on a new dimension with the creation of the system of state-owned merchant galleys traveling in convoy along established routes.[42] In the first decades of the fourteenth century the elements of this new maritime system came together. One component was the development of the great or merchant galley, a hybrid vessel that combined a larger carrying capacity with the speed and defensibility of the light or war galley.

Unlike round ships which relied entirely on wind for propulsion, merchant galleys were triremes, equipped with up to thirty rows of benches on each side separated by a gangway. At each bench sat three oarsmen, pulling separate oars. When the other crew members, including the galley captain, the twenty or so crossbowmen, the sailors needed to handle the rudder and sails, the scribe, carpenter, caulker, cook, captain's manservant, and assorted others are counted, merchant galley crews numbered between 180 and 200 men. (In addition, a ship's cat was aboard to keep rodents in check).[43] This crew size made merchant galleys highly defendable and thus ideally suited for carrying high value, low bulk cargo such as silk cloth, precious metals, and spices. Cargo space was limited; most merchant galleys could carry only about 150 tons in the hold and another fifty tons on deck. By contrast, most round ships or cogs transported between 400 and 600 tons of cargo. Wind remained the merchant galley's primary form of propulsion since it was usually equipped with two or three lateen sails. The oarsmen were deployed to overcome windless stretches, maneuver in and out of ports, outrun enemy ships or pirates, and stay on schedule. The merchant galleys were, "more than almost any other a distinctly Venetian ship, a product molded equally by her shipbuilding craft and her commercial system."[44]

While some merchant galleys were privately built and financed, what made the Venetian system unique was the government's decision to build most of them at public expense and then auction their use for individual voyages to the highest bidders, usually members of one patrician family or syndicates of several patricians. The first state-owned merchant galleys are documented around the turn of the fourteenth century.[45] By assuming the construction costs, the state relieved merchants of one of the most significant expenses of doing business. At the same time, required travel in convoy lowered their protection costs since a convoy of three or four galleys constituted a fighting force of between 600 and 800 men. The government also benefited since in time of war the ships could be converted to military use.[46] These state-owned merchant galleys offered Venetian merchants a competitive edge over rivals from other cities. By contrast, Genoa never built publicly owned vessels, due in large measure to the factionalism and divisions among its elite that frequently tore that city apart. When in the fifteenth century Florence acquired Pisa and decided to compete for Mediterranean trade, it adopted the Venetian model.[47]

The second crucial element of the Venetian system was the establishment of fixed freight lines, which were carefully managed by the government. In March 1321 the Greater Council noted that because of the lack of established rules regarding when ships would sail and the outfitting of galleys, merchants could not plan and so were reluctant to invest their money. In 1303, for instance, a galley operated by Marco Barbo and Andrea da Mosto was forced to wait at Negroponte for another galley so that the two ships could safely sail back to Venice together. Barbo and da Mosto sought damages incurred by the delay. To resolve this sort of problem, in December 1321 the council ordered the Senate to elect five sages, subsequently known as the Savi agli Ordini (Maritime Sages), whose job it was to establish the rules for the armed merchant galleys concerning such matters as the itineraries to be followed, cargo-loading periods, and the number of ships to be deployed for the following sailing season. In this way merchants could plan ahead.[48] With the establishment of these rules and appointment of the Savi agli Ordini, the Senate assumed the major responsibility of overseeing and coordinating Venetian shipping.

The best way to convey a sense of the system and the comprehensiveness of the Senate's control is to quote at length its deliberations for one auction. It was held in May 1340 for the merchant galleys traveling to Constantinople and the Black Sea. On the recommendation of the Savi agli Ordini, the Senate approved the following:

> That in the name of Christ, eight galleys be armed for operation by private individuals for the voyage to Constantinople and the Black Sea. For which the following rules are specified.
>
> That the commune is required to hand over the galleys fully outfitted as is customary. And the said galleys ought to be auctioned at one price for the outward voyage and the return and they cannot be

offered for less than 70 lire di grossi [700 ducats] per ship. And the Lords of the Arsenal must give the best and newest galleys that they have of the usual galleys that are currently in use. And those who win the auction ought to draw lots [to decide who will get which ship] and as the lottery turns out, so that is how the ships will be distributed. And they ought to have a fleet commander with the same salary, commission, and other conditions and cargo rates as in the past year. And those who win the auction of the said galleys are required to pay for them within five months of returning to Venice under penalty of 2 soldi per pound. . . .

That the said galleys ought to be loaded by July 22. And beyond that date no merchandise can be accepted onto a galley under pain of 20 soldi di grossi for every bale or standard chest as it applies to every merchant whose merchandise it is. This does not apply to his personal trunk; the same applies to the galley captain [the winner of the auction] of the ship. And they ought to depart on 25 July under penalty of 40 soldi di grossi for every galley for every day that they remain in port beyond that date. . . .

That of the two convoys of galleys going to Romania and Cyprus, whichever arrives first in Lower Romania [the Morea and southern Aegean] can take on merchandise. But if the two convoys arrive simultaneously in Lower Romania, the Cyprus galleys ought to load first until they reach full capacity and afterward the Romania galleys can load the rest. And if there is merchandise left over from both convoys, it can be loaded onto ships assigned to the Gulf if they happen to be in those parts, and if they are not, the commander can if it seems wise for the safety of his armada, send two or three ships to load the leftover merchandise with the proviso that the commune is not required to make reparations for any merchandise that is ruined on account of [being loaded onto] the said three ships.

That the captains of the said galleys are required to have as many foot soldiers and oarsmen as they had last year. And they can accept up to 50 men per galley from lands under our control as far as Ragusa. And once in Ragusa the fleet commander must do an inspection and those who do not have the required number of crew will be penalized 10 lire for each man they lack. And let it be added to the commander's commission that he is required to do this inspection and exact the said penalty, of which he will receive a quarter just as the commander received last year.

> That [of these eight galleys], three must go to Tana [in the Black Sea] with our merchandise, and if the galley captains cannot agree on which ones ought to go to Tana before the first of July, then they ought to draw lots on that date and whoever draws the lots must go [to Tana]. Truly, if once in Constantinople, it seems to the fleet commander that more ships ought to go to Tana, he should do so and if the galley captains cannot decide, then lots are to be drawn; but the galley of the commander is exempt from the lottery. Of those galleys that make the voyage to Tana, they cannot remain there more than seven days, not counting the arrival or departure days. And during those seven days they are to take onboard the merchants and merchandise of all those who wish to make the journey or to send goods with them and afterward the galleys must return to the commander in Constantinople. And if the fleet commander is not there, they must await him. And the said Tana galleys must, both on the outbound voyage [to Tana] and on the return first load the cargo of our people and only afterward of others if they wish. . . . And one of the merchants traveling to Tana, whoever will seem the best and most sufficient, should be chosen as the commander for the galleys going to Tana. And if he plans to stay in Tana, our consul in Tana, who is leaving his post, should serve as commander of the said galleys until they return to Constantinople. And with the rest of the galleys the commander must go to Trebizond to pick up merchants and merchandise but must not remain there less than eight days, but can stay longer according to custom, not counting the arrival or departure days. And afterwards he ought to come to Constantinople and then with the others from Tana return to Venice.[49]

As these deliberations make clear, the Senate spelled out as many contingencies as possible. On the following day, the auction was held. Only members of the patriciate were eligible to bid. The eight galleys attracted prices ranging from 810 to just over 900 ducats, all above the 700-ducat reserve established by the Senate. The eight *patroni* or winning bidders then had to get Senate approval, and each was required to provide a guarantor for his bid.[50]

Each ship was divided into twenty-four carats or shares that the captain then rented out, although he usually kept several for himself or his syndicate. He was prohibited from favoring certain merchants over others. Similarly, ships in a particular convoy were prevented from competing with one another. All had to observe the same rules regarding loading and unloading, and cargos were distributed equitably. All would share in the gain (or loss) in proportion to their shares. Moreover, privately owned ships were forbidden to call at ports visited by the state convoy for a month before or after the convoy had passed, thus protecting the convoy's monopoly and guaranteeing higher prices for the goods once they reached Venice. Venice's fisc benefited from the customs duties paid on the cargo, which was often valued in the hundreds of thousands of ducats.[51]

Despite occasional losses, the commercial and security advantages of the merchant galley system were so clear that Venice developed seven different freight lines over the course of the fourteenth and fifteenth centuries: Romania/Black Sea, Cyprus/Armenia, Alexandria, Beirut, Flanders/England, Aigues-Mortes, and Barbary. In 1335, a robust year, twenty-six merchant galleys were deployed on the various lines with a total cargo capacity of approximately 3,900 tons.[52] By paying close attention to the international political situation and market conditions, the Senate was able to make annual adjustments regarding destinations, ports of call, and the number of ships allocated to each line. For example, when the Pax Mongolica broke down in the mid-fourteenth century and trade routes shifted south, Venice adjusted by assigning more ships to the Beirut and Alexandria lines. Similarly, the Flanders line was interrupted for a time at midcentury because of the Hundred Years War. By coordinating the timetables of the various lines, based on prevailing winds, the Senate sought to ensure that goods were constantly on the move and not sitting in storage.[53] The Flanders galleys, for example, were timed to depart soon after the arrival of ships from the Levant. The system was organized to take maximum advantage of Venice's vital position at the intersection of Eastern and Western trade routes.[54]

A large majority of patricians took part in the auctions. One detailed study of the auctions held between 1301 and 1453 has identified the names of 1,729 galley captains from 135 different patrician families. Additionally, 261 patricians from seventy-one different families served as fleet commanders on 355 separate voyages. Individual patrician families did not tend to favor one freight line over another. These lines were not a monopoly of the richest patricians or the preserve of a limited number of families.[55]

Except for the occasional disaster, shipping goods on merchant galleys was very secure. In 1401 a Prato merchant's agent in Venice advised the merchant that buying insurance for the goods transported on the galleys would be like "throwing away money"; also, in a 1455 contract that the Medicis of Florence worked out with their partner in Bruges, the Medicis required him to take out insurance on all goods "no matter in what ship it be loaded, with the exception that if he should ship by Florentine or Venetian galleys he may take a risk up to sixty pounds groat (lire di grossi) in each galley and no more."[56]

Nobles were not the only ones to benefit. The twenty-five or thirty ships dispatched annually in the first half of the fourteenth century required between 4,000 and 5,000 crew members, personally hired by captains at Piazza San Marco. The voyages offered employment and allowed crewman a modest opportunity to trade privately. The sailors also got their keep. Their diet generally consisted of pork and bean soup, along with biscuit or hard tack, wine, and cheese. The total daily caloric intake has been estimated to have been about 3,915 calories, which was adequate even given the strenuous nature of the work. Any attempt by a captain to skimp on food for his crew would have been a false economy.[57]

The voyages were long, "not at all like the trip from Rialto to San Marco," as one merchant wrote of the journey to Tana.[58] The average length of trips on the Romania line was 150 days, of which sixty-four were spent in various ports.[59] Fifteenth-century-pilgrim Felix Faber's voyage to the Holy Land on a Venetian pilgrim galley took forty-three days on the out-voyage to Jaffa and seventy for the return.[60] Ships had to stop frequently to take on supplies, especially fresh water. Ships on the Alexandria line, for example, carried around 1,722 gallons of water. Since each barrel took up precious cargo space, they were kept to the minimum. Consequently, ships seldom traveled more than eight or nine days without making a port call.[61] That and the opportunity to trade explains why virtually all the lines followed the same route down the Adriatic, stopping at the many ports along the way such as Pola, Zara, Ragusa, Durazzo, and Corfu. From there the Flanders galleys would turn west, while the lines heading east stopped at Modon, Coron, and Crete before diverging. Because of the prevailing winds, ships returning from Alexandria tended to travel up the coast of Palestine and Syria rather than risk a sea-crossing to Cyprus, Rhodes, or Crete. This also allowed them to take on supplies and continue trading along the way.[62]

Even the freight lines have been offered as a purported source of popular quietude in Venice. One authority has argued that by producing wealth for the patricians and offering employment and small trade opportunities to crewmen, the system "maintained a broad enough distribution of wealth within the Venetian polity to sustain a vivid patriotic consciousness up and down the social scale."[63] However, like other *popolani*, sailors were not immune to expressing their discontent. In January 1353, the Ten prosecuted a group of oarsmen who became verbally abusive over the pay owed them at the end of a voyage.[64] Furthermore, the government forbade oarsmen from forming a guild. But certainly, many in society, including brokers, stevedores, and those engaged in shipbuilding, profited in some measure from the merchant galley system and the continuous flow of merchandise it produced.

While the benefits of the system to rank and file members of Venetian society are debatable, for the patricians, the state-owned galley convoys amounted to a form of welfare for the rich—one that combined state and private initiative. Though they sacrificed their freedom of navigation, they could decide whether to invest in the galleys and, if so, in what commodities.[65] Their investments took place under favorable economic conditions that were guaranteed by the government. In return, the government benefited not only fiscally from the revenue generated by customs duties but also politically since members of the patriciate had a vested interest in supporting a regime that not only guaranteed through the Serrata their monopoly on political power but also their exclusive right to bid on the state-owned merchant galleys.[66] It was a closed circle: the Senate, composed of businessmen, devised a system designed to benefit businessmen. Thus, in the first half of the fourteenth century, the patricians consolidated their hold on the most lucrative sector of the Venetian economy, one that also functioned as a symbolic projection of Venetian power.

Despite the importance of the merchant galleys, round ships and even small vessels remained the workhorses of the merchant marine. In 1418–19 merchant galleys constituted only about one-tenth of the Venetian ships voyaging to Alexandria.[67] In 1423 Doge Tommaso Mocenigo claimed that Venice boasted 300 *navi* (ships), likely meaning ships over 100 tons. It is estimated that about thirty of these round ships were large capacity vessels (400 to 600 tons). In 1449 Venice's merchant marine included thirty-five big tonnage round ships and twenty-eight merchant galleys.[68] Although a merchant galley might carry 100,000 ducats worth of cargo, the value of the freight conveyed on large round ships was not inconsiderable. In the late fifteenth century, individual round ships transported freight valued in the tens of thousands of ducats.[69]

This period also witnessed other business innovations. One was the development of the factor or resident agent.[70] In previous centuries it had been customary for merchants, like Marco Polo, to travel with their goods. The *colleganza* contract required one partner to undertake a journey and trade along the way. By the fourteenth century, it had evolved into a simple loan contract, one that was used primarily by small-time investors for transactions in Venice. International merchants instead relied on companies in which partners each put up portions of the capital but did not necessarily require any of the partners to travel. As Venice acquired colonies or trading posts in foreign lands, Venetians increasingly took up residence in those places, sometimes permanently. In 1333, for instance, Venice acquired a quarter in Tana to which it assigned a consul with a staff of eight, including an interpreter and a chaplain/notary, and four horses. Venetians, noble and non-noble, who moved to locales such as Tana or Alexandria could serve as the agents or factors for merchants headquartered at Rialto.[71] In 1318 the priest Nicolò Bono wrote a long, wide-ranging letter to his friend and fellow priest Felice de Merlis, who was serving as a priest/notary in Laiazzo, in which Bono updated de Merlis on some of their joint commercial ventures: "Item, I received from the said Bertucio the sack of pistachios, which presently was divided into our shares, yours and mine and we had a good return from it."[72] It was no longer necessary to travel to engage in trade; merchants and others could simply send instructions to their agents or friends authorizing them to buy and sell. In a fifteenth-century example, well-known explorer Alvise da Mosto authorized Giovanni Contarini, who was taking a galley to Flanders, to sell three casks of malmsey (a sweet wine from Greece) and some silk handkerchiefs that were loaded on the galley and buy in turn satin and pewter. Concerning the casks, da Mosto wrote Contarini, "kindly sell them in England for the best price you can get, acting with them as you would with your own. For I shall be satisfied with everything you do, because, since we regard each other as true brothers, I am quite certain that you will do with my things as you would with your own."[73] Merchants preferred to rely on kinsmen as their agents. In this particular case, da Mosto sought to guarantee Contarini's good faith by comparing their relationship to that of brothers.

Letters and memoranda were how merchants communicated with their agents and partners overseas. Information and connectedness were essential to business success.[74] As Florentine Leon Battista Alberti advised, it was important for businessmen to have "ink-stained fingers."[75] To be successful, merchants had to constantly send and receive letters since those were the best means, besides collecting "news on the Rialto," of gleaning information regarding gluts and shortages, droughts and floods, exchange rates, wars and other conflicts, all of which could affect supply and demand and thus influence prices.[76] "Write to me," one fourteenth-century merchant wrote to a colleague, "about conditions [on the ground] and the movement of prices so that I can be informed of everything."[77]

One extant letter collection is comprised of sixty-eight missives that merchants wrote to Nicolò Zuchello, nicknamed Pignol, an immigrant from Pisa who established himself in a shop at Rialto and became a naturalized Venetian citizen with the right to engage in overseas commerce. This business correspondence was filled with news about shipments and goods. In October 1345, for instance, Francesco Bartolomei wrote to Zucchello from Crete, "Again I pray that you peddle for me at the current price the malmsey that you still have from last year and don't hold on to it any longer; and from the net profit that you receive from it, send me enough pretty cotton cloth that I can have made from it six bonnets for daytime wear and [send] two crates that are well fitted with good keys for shipping on the galleys . . . if you can."[78] In another letter Francesco wrote from Crete, "Pignol, I pray you for the goodwill that you have for yourself and for me that it please you to send to me on the first ship coming this way 14 arms-lengths *(braccia)* of a very fine cloth of this color like the sample sewn to this letter; get the finest and best color you can, which costs between 40 and 44 grossi a length, but no more and out of love I pray you to do it so that I can be well furnished with it as soon as possible."[79] Another correspondent, Vannino da Firenze, informed Zuchello about the availability and current price of spices in Alexandria.[80]

Merchants also utilized business manuals to provide them with the basic information and skills needed to engage in international commerce. The earliest extant Venetian example is the *Zibaldone da Canal* (Da Canal Commonplace Book), likely compiled by a member of that patrician family in the 1320s or 1330s. Like many merchant manuals, it is a miscellany. About a third of the manuscript is taken up with mathematics problems involving fractions, geometric volume, and area. One exercise asks how the profit from a voyage to Constantinople is to be divided among three partners each of whom invested different sums in the enterprise. Doing such calculations was an essential part of engaging in commerce. Another third of the manuscript comprises mercantile information such as a formulary for comparing currencies, weights, and measures of foreign locales with Venice's. The reader is also instructed how to judge the quality of various spices: "nutmegs: they ought to be big and firm, and no more than a fourth of them ought to be unripe, and that is good; and to the extent that fewer are unripe, that is better. And you want to pierce the shell with a needle, and if it yields water, that is good; and any other way is not worth anything."[81] The *Zibaldone* includes astrological material, medical advice, a brief excerpt from the story of Tristan, two poems in the troubadour tradition, one of which offers advice and moral precepts, the Ten Commandments, and even a four-page chronicle of Venice. The chronicle makes no mention of either the Peace of 1177 or the Fourth Crusade, but does record the arrival of Saint Mark's relics, their "rediscovery" in the eleventh century, and the procuring of the bones of Saint Nicholas. The *Zibaldone* may have been compiled by a schoolboy or a young patrician learning to do business math and just embarking on a career in commerce. But information regarding the conversion of weights and measures would have been essential for merchants who no longer traveled with their goods but stayed home reading the news conveyed to them through letters.

Banking also underwent significant evolution in the fourteenth century. Deposit and transfer banks were located at Rialto, while moneychangers who primarily serviced the retail trade and the needs of pilgrims had their counters (*banchi*) at San Marco. The difference in scale between these two types of banking is evidenced by the value of the bonds that the bankers were required to post according to a 1283 law. Rialto bankers had to put up a 3,000-lire bond, San Marco bankers only 1,000 lire.[82]

The Rialto banks accepted deposits of cash or even goods. In what was referred to as a "regular" deposit, the depositor expected to get back the very same coins or goods as those he or she had deposited. The banker got a fee for what was in essence the safe-deposit box he provided. In the case of an "irregular" deposit, there was no expectation that the depositor would get back the exact same coins; instead, the banker could use the money for various commercial enterprises and pay the depositor interest in return.[83] However, the most important function the Rialto bankers performed was in-bank transfers from what were known as *giro* (gyration) accounts. A buyer simply went to his banker and told him to transfer money from his own account to the seller's. No actual money changed hands; the money simply made a gyration from one account to another. An anonymous French observer writing around 1500 explained, "Individuals leave large sums of money with a banker merely for the convenience, and not to earn interest. Most purchases, sales, and other contracts are paid for in bank, without any counting out of coin but solely in script, for the banker merely debits the buyer's account, and credits that of the seller."[84] These bankers set up their counters around the church of San Giacomo at Rialto in a covered arcade that still bears the name Sottoportico di Banco Giro.

In the first half of the fourteenth century, there were probably eight to ten banks located at Rialto. But banks could fail. There was a rash of bankruptcies in 1340–2 due to fluctuations in the grain trade, speculation in bullion, and disputes with Florence regarding paying for the recent war against the Della Scalas of Verona. Bankers could also be robbed, especially when they transported money home at night. In 1382 several men used a subterfuge to gain access to the home of banker Gabriele Soranzo, who they tied up and robbed. Once caught, the instigator of the plan, Antonio di Nerio from Padua, was dragged through the city and had his hands cut off before being executed and his body quartered in the Piazzetta. Three sections of his corpse were placed on roads leading to mainland towns; the fourth was displayed in front of Soranzo's house before it was moved to Mestre. The warning was clear: foreigners should not come to Venice expecting to commit crimes with impunity.[85]

Rich foreigners, especially rulers of neighboring states, looked to Venice as a place where they could safely stash funds. They did so at the Grain Office, a magistracy with some financial deposit responsibilities, that has been compared to a "Swiss bank" for foreigners and a "quasi-public bank" for Venetians.[86] Some of the participants in the Querini-Tiepolo conspiracy stopped at the Grain Office at Rialto and looted it of cash before proceeding to San Marco.[87] The funds the Grain Office held were considerable. In 1345 it owed grain importers and various depositors 235,938 ducats.[88] Among those who deposited money with the office were Marsilio da Carrara, lord of Padua; Enrico Scrovegni, patron of Giotto's Arena Chapel; Cangrande della Scala, lord of Verona; Luchino Visconti, ruler of Milan, and other Italian and Balkan rulers. By statute, they could only earn 3 percent interest, much less than could be earned in other investments. But given the vagaries of life in these strife-torn polities, deposits at the Grain Office were a safe option.

Venetian citizens who deposited money there earned 4 percent interest. Dowry funds garnered 5 percent. For example, when in 1363 nobleman Domenico Gussoni sold the property that had been put up to guarantee eventual repayment of his wife's dowry, the money from the sale was deposited with the Grain Office.[89] In some instances, portions of the fines levied against rapists were placed with the Grain Office to earn interest and accumulate as eventual dowries for the victims.

Venetians on the whole did not worry that the interest they received on deposits with the Grain Office was usurious and threatened their souls. One exception is Cecilia, widow of Marco della Frescada, who noted in her will that a deposit she was going to make there would eventually earn nearly 100 ducats in interest. Because "this fact is troubling my conscience," she asked her executors, the Procurators of San Marco, to bring the matter before the Lesser Council. Following her death, the council voted to take back the interest owed her and return it to the treasury. In 1404, Pandolfo Malatesta, captain general of Venice's land forces, also suffered pangs of conscience but chose to observe the letter not the spirit of the injunction against ill-gotten gain. He ordered that the interest owed him be restituted to the government. The government then turned around and gifted him the money.[90]

Even more important was Venice's long-term funded debt. Because so many different councils, offices, and magistracies had some financial responsibility, it is difficult to get a clear picture of the government's overall budget. The only figures that exist for the fourteenth and fifteenth centuries are for 1341–2 when the budget was very nearly in balance: the state had income between 670,000 and 685,000 lire a grossi versus expenditures between 670,000 and 745,000 lire.[91] In peacetime the budget could be kept more or less in equilibrium. The problem was the cost of war which led to significant deficits.

To pay for its wars, Venice exacted forced loans. The practice began in 1207, replacing the earlier system by which some of the richest citizens made voluntary loans to the state. By the mid-thirteenth century, however, the government found itself unable to retire the debt, which thus became a permanent feature of the budget. In 1279 the balance on these forced loans (known eventually as the Monte Vecchio or Old Fund) stood at 400,000 lire. The outlays for the Second Venetian-Genoese War caused it to jump to 1,500,000 lire by 1299. It rose even further before being reduced to 1,100,000 lire in 1343. However, by the end of the Fourth Venetian-Genoese War (also known as the War of Chioggia) in 1381, the Monte had mushroomed to 12,300,000 lire.[92]

Loans were based on an assessment, known as the *estimo* (estimate), of individuals' movable and immovable wealth. Then a levy (perhaps 1 percent or less) of the estimate was exacted. Between the mid-thirteenth century and 1381, 259 levies were imposed.[93] Not everyone was subject to these loans. According to the *estimo* of 1379, only those with property worth more than 300 ducats were assessed; in 1379 that amounted to 2,128 individuals (including 1,211 nobles) out of a population of between 80,000 and 100,000 souls. The burden of forced loans fell on the rich, even if there was a vast difference between someone like Federico Corner, the richest man in Venice with an assessment of 60,000 ducats, and the many individuals like the furrier Donato, the cutler Zanin, and noblewomen Catarina Zulian and Filipa Zorzi, all of whom were assessed at 300 ducats.[94]

It is important to remember that these were loans, not taxes. In return, the government paid interest that, until the beginning of the War of Chioggia, amounted to 5 percent per annum paid in regular biannual installments. Shares in the public debt thus became a reliable investment, one producing a modest gain. The government struggled to amortize the debt; and shares were bought and sold on the open market, where their value oscillated above and below par. Shares were used for all sorts of transactions and obligations. For example, a father might fund his daughter's dowry partly with cash and commodities and partly with debt shares. Or a testator might endow Masses or other legacies to be paid for out of shares in the public debt. Zana, wife of Francesco Querini, was well acquainted with how shares in the funded debt operated. In her 1331 will, she wanted her executors to purchase 150 lire of debt shares, interest on which was to be given to her daughter Maria, a nun at San Giovanni Evangelista of Torcello. Zana noted that if the shares were redeemed by the government, then she wanted "the capital" to be reinvested in new shares for Maria's benefit.[95]

Like the state-owned merchant galleys, the public debt benefited patricians first and foremost. In return for (forced) loans to the state, they got a reliable and steady source of interest income. The interest they earned and the funds that were provided to amortize the debt were paid for by customs duties and brokerage fees imposed on foreign merchants and indirect taxes that fell disproportionately on poor consumers.[96] Both the merchant galleys and the funded debt tied patricians' interests more closely to the state's, reinforcing cohesion among patricians and strengthening the regime.[97] The many infrastructure improvements that the government undertook in these years further served international commerce and benefited nobles.

The decision to build the state-owned merchant galleys significantly impacted the city's urban form. It necessitated a huge expansion of the Arsenal, since a 1302 law required that publicly owned ships be built there. At about eight acres, the original Arsenal was far too small to accommodate the construction of several great (merchant) and light (war) galleys per year, in addition to the repair of older ones. In 1325 the government purchased from the monastery of San Daniele a large stretch of open water contiguous to the Arsenal for the expansion. Known as the Arsenale Nuovo (New Arsenal), it added more than thirty-four acres to the complex and quadrupled the overall size of the state shipyard. Ropemaking was concentrated in an adjoining complex known as the Tana; the production of armor, crossbows, and other weapons was situated to the south. The old salt warehouses at San Biagio were converted to grain warehouses, allowing nearby bakeries to produce the biscuits consumed by sailors.[98]

Improvements were also made to the maritime infrastructure of Venice's far-flung overseas possessions. In 1303 the Arsenal at Candia was repaired following an earthquake. In 1319 the government ordered the *bailo* of Negroponte to make repairs to its Arsenal, and a remodeling of the Arsenal at Chania was finished by 1325. The Venetian Arsenal functioned as logistical headquarters for the entire empire and the depot from which all sorts of materials, from oars to nails, rudders to masts, were dispatched throughout the dominions.[99]

Other projects were undertaken around the Bacino and at the port of San Nicolò. In 1312 a lighthouse was added to the tower guarding the seaward side of the mouth at San Nicolò; another tower protected the lagoon side.[100] In 1324 the embankment running from San Marco to Castello, known today as the Riva degli Schiavoni (Dalmatians' Embankment), was paved.[101] This facilitated the loading and unloading of vessels anchored in the Bacino and assessment of customs duties at the Customs House at San Biagio. In 1414 the customs office for goods traveling by sea run by the Visdomini del Mare was moved to a location near the salt warehouses in Dorsoduro (today's Customs House Point). A separate customs office for goods traveling inland and collected by the Visdomini dei Lombardi was set up at Rialto. In 1341 the huge new public granaries at San Marco were begun.[102] Around the same time, construction on the new Greater Council Hall commenced. Taken together, these projects improved the efficiency of port operations and projected an image of the greatness and reach of Venetian trade. Petrarch described the Bacino as "a public harbor for the human race."[103]

Yet Venice's ever changing natural environment threatened the harbor's viability. The barrier islands (*lidi*) protecting the lagoon were eroding, and sand churned up by the sea and silt carried by the mainland rivers were reducing the depth of the lagoon and the mouths, impeding the flow of water and threatening commerce. Throughout the century, the government undertook several efforts to fix these problems. However, no solution proved more than a stopgap in the never-ending effort to control the lagoon's natural features.

Special sages to examine the *lidi* had already been appointed in the 1280s. Some efforts to protect the islands focused on human abuse of the environment. In 1322 the government forbade setting fires on the *lidi* and cutting trees and canes, whose roots helped stabilize the soil. Other regulations prohibited sand removal, except from designated areas. Efforts were also undertaken to protect the islands from the sea's wave action. The shoreline was reinforced with wooden pilings—sometimes placed three-deep. Rocks transported from Istria were dumped between the rows.[104] Recognizing the islands' protective function, the Greater Council declared in 1343 that work on the Lido was "the conservation of the city."[105]

Of more pressing concern was silting that threatened to turn the lagoon into a swamp and close up the mouths leading to the sea. In the 1320s a dike was built to divert the waters of the Fusina branch of the Brenta and several lesser rivers from emptying into the lagoon near Venice and direct them southward so that the water would exit via the mouth of Malamocco. The dike had gates that could be opened and closed as needed. These actions made it possible to dredge the silt and mud that had built up along the old course of the Brenta as it made its way toward the western edge of the city, thereby reducing the danger of malaria by returning these precincts to open water. However, by limiting the amount of fresh water flowing into the lagoon, sea water came to predominate and changed the lagoon's ecosystem.

The reduction of the amount of water flowing down the Giudecca Canal and toward the mouth of San Nicolò created another problem—it became difficult for ships with greater drafts to navigate the port. As a map of Venice from around 1330 indicates, there were two main shipping channels in the vicinity of the city. One entered the lagoon from the sea near Sant'Erasmo and flowed toward Murano; the other entered at San Nicolò and flowed to the Bacino and the Giudecca and Grand Canals. In 1349 the Senate expressed concern that sand from the Sant'Erasmo mouth was clogging up the San Nicolò mouth. It ordered the Sant'Erasmo mouth closed and a channel dredged between the island of Sant'Elena and Castello to divert the flow of water toward San Nicolò. However, by 1355 it became apparent that these efforts had not ameliorated conditions at the San Nicolò mouth and had instead created their own problems. Accordingly, in 1360 the government decided to reopen the Sant'Erasmo mouth and build a breakwater to try to keep the water flowing out of the two mouths separate. It also resolved to stop the diversion of the Brenta and reopen the Fusina branch in the hope that the increased flow moving along the Giudecca canal would scour out the San Nicolò channel. But the benefits were few, and in 1368 the Fusina branch was again closed. At the end of the century, the debate over how to protect the lagoon from silting continued unabated. Managing the hydraulics of the lagoon is one of the seemingly unresolvable constants in the history of Venice.[106] It was complicated by the policies of neighboring cities like Padua, through whose territory the rivers flowed before reaching the lagoon. Those towns had objectives often at odds with those of Venice, including securing the most direct water route to the emporium of Rialto.[107]

Another environmental concern was the availability of wood. Massive amounts were needed to meet the needs not only for land reclamation projects and the building boom, but also for fuel for a burgeoning population and the shipbuilding industry and navy. In its first attempt to deal with a perceived timber shortage, the Greater Council voted in 1350 to give the Arsenal first refusal on naval quality oak for sale in the city.[108] In 1339, in the aftermath of a war against Verona, Venice acquired Treviso and established a kind of protectorate over Padua. Despite the acquisition of its first significant chunk of mainland territory, the war did not mark a significant shift in Venice's attitude toward the *terraferma*, which it continued to view primarily in economic rather than political terms. However, Venice's acquisition of Treviso and surrounding territory did give it direct control over the final stretches of the Piave River, which emptied into the lagoon until the fifteenth century. The Piave was the only river in the region whose watershed could supply all the types of timber needed by Venice.[109] The Republic's efforts to control the natural environment and its first acquisition of *terraferma* lands were driven at least in part, like so much else in the first half of the fourteenth century, by the needs of the merchant galley shipping lines and the city's mercantile elite.

That elite had to decide how widely the benefits of Venice's trade system would be shared. At various times throughout the fourteenth century protectionists within the patriciate tried to restrict access to the benefits to Venetians by, for example, forbidding them from acting as front men for foreign investors. In August 1324 they pushed through a law forbidding any native born or naturalized Venetian from importing goods from the East worth more than the amount of his *estimo* assessment. This was designed to ensure that the importer was not relying on foreign capital and sharing any profits with the (foreign) lender. A new office, the Officium de Navigantibus (Sailing Office), was established to oversee its enforcement. Although intended to prevent an influx of foreign capital, the law hurt smaller patrician investors whose capacity to engage in commerce was severely impeded. The authors of the law tried to prevent it from being overturned, but just a few months later the Senate and Forty did just that. The Officium was revived for a time in the 1330s and again in 1361 before it was finally abolished in 1363, although some restrictions on the amount of capital that foreign-born Venetian citizens could trade with were retained.[110]

The Officium de Navigantibus was only one means by which the patricians sought to restrict the benefits of international trade largely to themselves.

They also did so by erecting steep barriers to Venetian citizenship and the rights and privileges that went with it. The city nonetheless relied on immigration for growth, since deaths outpaced births, as in all medieval and early modern cities.

In the thirteenth century, immigrants could be naturalized after ten years of residence. However, in the aftermath of the Serrata, the prerequisites for citizenship grew more stringent. In 1305 the Greater Council created two categories of naturalized citizenship. In the first, after fifteen years of continuous residence and regular payment of taxes and forced loans, immigrants could acquire what came to be known as citizenship *de intus*, meaning that they had the right to trade locally. The second, known as citizenship *de extra*, earned after twenty-five years residence and payment of taxes, carried the right to engage in wholesale trade, ship goods by sea, and enter the Fondaco dei Tedeschi to make deals with German merchants. In 1314 a requirement that the aspiring citizen live in Venice with his family was added. In other words, only those who fully committed to their new homeland could garner its benefits. Children of these naturalized citizens as well as children of native-born Venetians enjoyed a different citizenship status as *cittadini originarii* (original citizens). Beginning in the fifteenth century that status would become a requirement for holding certain governmental posts as well as leadership positions in the *scuole grandi*. But in the first half of the fourteenth century, with a burgeoning population and booming trade, the regime had little need to incentivize immigration, especially for those who wanted to engage in international commerce.[111]

For some, the lure of citizenship and the privileges it conveyed was irresistible. That was the case for Francesco, son of Bartolomeo, an associate of immigrant Pignol Zucchello who had himself likely already attained naturalized citizen status. Francesco was Sienese and hoped that citizenship would enable him and Zucchello to set up a trading company. In several letters to Zucchello, he laid out the merits of his case. He noted that he had lived with his family six years in Venice itself and another sixteen in Candia and had paid various special imposts, such as one levied in 1327–8 to support Venice's military actions against the Genoese quarter in Constantinople. This led him to believe that, for all intents and purposes, he "should be a citizen of Venice."[112] Both he and Zucchello were counting on the assistance of nobleman Gianni Babilonio to push the bill conferring the privilege. Francesco assured Zucchello that once he received it, they would benefit greatly: "Sir Pignol it seems to me that with the help of God, if my citizenship is attained, we will do very well because it seems to me that you are very adept at selling and I believe that from here [in

Crete] we will always have a good advantage over others so that by all means we will benefit. Let us pray God that the operation happens quickly so that we will be able to earn our profit and good."[113] But before these two native Tuscans could see their plan come to fruition, they succumbed to the bubonic plague.

They were hardly the only Tuscans to immigrate to Venice. The early years of the century saw a large influx of silk manufacturers and workers from Lucca who left their native city when it was overrun by the Ghibelline Uguccione della Faggiuola in 1314. Around sixty arrived in Venice with their families where they settled near Rialto in the parishes of San Bartolomeo, San Giovanni Grisostomo, San Cancian, and Santi Apostoli and set up shops along the Calle della Bissa. Unlike other immigrant communities that dispersed throughout the city over time, these immigrants stayed clustered together.[114]

The Venetian government was happy to accept Lucchesi because they brought with them the skills to promote a lucrative industry that was underdeveloped in the city. It even allowed them to set up a governing body, the Corte della Seta (Silk Court), which was closely modeled on the one in their native city. The equivalent of a guild, the Corte represented silk manufacturers and merchants; artisan silk-workers could also enroll but were subordinate. Dyers, velvet makers, and weavers of silk cloth without a pile (*samitari*) formed separate guilds.

The industry blossomed. Much of the benefit accrued to patrician merchants who imported raw silk from the East. Late in the century, silk accounted for two-thirds of the cargo loaded on ships on the Romania/Black Sea line, worth annually between 130,000 and 200,000 ducats. The raw silk was then transformed into cloth in Venice, most of which was used locally or exported to cities in the Po valley. The leading silk manufacturer/entrepreneurs also prospered. One, Castruccio Saggina, a *cittadino* originally from Lucca, had a 1,000 lire *estimo* assessment in 1379. When in 1390 the Forty and Greater Council granted Saggina permission to return to Lucca without losing his Venetian citizenship rights, they noted that he paid 500 ducats annually in brokerage fees and that his "great [manufacturing] establishment" provided work for "400 poor persons."[115] Many poor women found work spooling thread and other menial tasks associated with silk production.

Between 1310 and 1369, 144 immigrants from Lucca were naturalized, slightly more than a third of them in the 1340s. Like Saggina, some were extraordinarily successful in their adopted city. Bandino Garzoni's 1379 *estimo* assessment of 50,000 lire made him one of the richest men in Venice.[116]

Another was Paolo Paruta who became a *cittadino de extra* in 1352. In 1359 the government used his connections to facilitate a payment of 2,000 ducats to the papacy in Avignon.[117]

In that same year, the Lucchese community in Venice established a confraternity dedicated to the Volto Santo, Lucca's most precious relic. The following year they sought permission to build an oratory at Santa Maria dei Servi. The confraternity was the first of several so-called national confraternities established in Venice to serve the spiritual and social needs of immigrants from particular locales. Late in the century the confraternity resolved to build a hospital of ten small houses for needy members. Castruccio Saggini and his wife Filippina were among the benefactors.[118] National confraternities played a complex role in integrating immigrants into Venetian life. While they offered the sustenance necessary to survive and perhaps even prosper, they reinforced members' identity as belonging to a "foreign" community. Immigrants from Milan and Monza established a *scuola* dedicated to John the Baptist and Saint Ambrose at the Frari just a year after the Lucchesi created their confraternity.

Florentines never immigrated en masse like the Lucchesi, but over the course of the fourteenth and fifteenth centuries, they received the most citizenship grants. Many were involved in the woolen cloth industry. In 1435 the Florentines founded a *scuola* dedicated to the Virgin and John the Baptist at San Zanipolo but soon moved it to the Frari. Many of the most powerful Florentines who took up residence in Venice were merchant/bankers. They handled most of the foreign currency exchange that facilitated trade across distant markets, whereas Venetian bankers concentrated on transfer banking.[119] Since most of these Florentine merchant/bankers spent only a few years in Venice, they usually did not seek or qualify for citizen status. Even so, in the fourteenth century, citizenship grants provided "constant replenishment of the merchant class." Those who sought it were an elite for whom the trade advantages were tangible and worth seeking.[120] Most immigrants did not seek that privileged status since they did not have the means to engage in international trade. They were small-time artisans, sailors, servants, slaves, and other manual laborers. For example, large numbers of German immigrants worked as shoemakers, bakers, and in the woolen cloth industry.[121] Immigrants were often identified in contemporary documents by their place of origin and as "inhabitants" (*habitatores*) of Venice.

One study has identified the names of 2,938 immigrants from the East (which the author of the study defines as southeastern Europe), who came to Venice between 1300 and 1510. Of these 1,210 were from Dalmatia, 932 from Greece, and 637 from Albania. The 159 others came from Georgian,

Hungarian, Bulgarian, Russian, Tartar, Moorish, and Turkish lands. In other words, the vast majority came from the heart of Venice's maritime sphere: the shores of the Adriatic, Ionian, and Aegean seas. It is therefore not surprising that of those whose profession can be identified, 40 percent were employed in activities associated with the sea, 16 percent in artisan trades, and 12 percent in domestic service (or were outright slaves). Those with some status (priests, doctors, notaries, and minor civil servants) were a small minority. Since only 191 women appear in the sample, female domestic servants and slaves are certainly grossly underrepresented. Unlike the Lucchesi, who were political exiles, and the Florentines, who came to gain economic advantage, most of these immigrants came because of "poverty and misery."[122]

They tended to live on the San Marco side of the Grand Canal. For many, religion was a barrier to full assimilation into Venetian society since they observed the Greek rite, which was practiced in certain churches in Castello, near the Arsenal and the city's other maritime industries. The Dalmatians founded a *scuola* dedicated to Saints George and Tryphon in 1451. Like all immigrant groups, those from southeastern Europe contributed to Venetian culture, influencing everything from its cuisine to its language. Several words in Venetian dialect derive from Greek including *carega* (chair; Italian *sedia*), *piron* (fork, Italian *forchetta*), *yaya* (aunt, Italian *zia*), as well as *gondola* and *squero* (boatyard).[123]

One estimate suggests that at the end of the Middle Ages, out of a total population of 100,000 to 110,000 in Venice, between 15,000 and 20,000 and "maybe many more" were born elsewhere.[124] Although it is impossible to assess their cumulative impact, immigrants have been a constant in Venice's history, replenishing and ever transforming Venetian society, economics, and culture.

For the patrician elite at least, the first half of the fourteenth century was also a period of cultural consolidation, whose chief proponent, Doge Andrea Dandolo, helped bring it about through his own literary works and artistic patronage. The fourth member of the Dandolo clan to attain the dogeship, Dandolo was, by Venetian standards, a child prodigy. Born in 1306, he likely received legal training at the University of Padua, supplemented by studies of history, philosophy, and literature. At age twenty-two, he was elected a Procurator of San Marco. Then in 1339, following the death of his distant cousin Doge Francesco Dandolo, he was a contender, along with Bartolomeo Gradenigo and Marino Falier, for the ducal throne. In the end Dandolo threw his support to seventy-six-year-old Gradenigo. After Gradenigo died in December 1342, Dandolo was elected doge at age thirty-six. His youthfulness is striking. His three predecessors were all in their seventies at election. Except for the procuratorship, Dandolo had held few posts of real distinction prior to his elevation. His reputation for learning, eloquence, and courtesy, as well as some electors' distaste for his competitor Falier, likely propelled him into office. But Dandolo's reign was not a happy time for Venice. It was marked by famine, another Zaran revolt, renewed war with Genoa, and the Black Death. Nevertheless, he enjoys a positive posthumous reputation, largely due to his contributions to Venetian culture.[125]

Several of these were in the realm of law. While a procurator, Dandolo produced the *Summula statutorum floridorum Veneciarum* (Summa of the Valid Laws of the Venetians), a compilation of the most important of the Greater Council's decisions that had not been included in Giacomo Tiepolo's 1242 law code. Composed of sections on contracts, testaments, and the juridical order, it was designed to serve as a handbook for magistrates and notaries who were not well versed in the law. A month after his election as doge, Dandolo created a commission of five sages to amend the civic statutes. In 1346 a sixth book was added to Tiepolo's code. That same year saw the completion of two other books: the *Liber albus*, a compilation of treaties and agreements that Venice had made with various Eastern powers since the eleventh century, and the *Liber blancus*, a record of agreements with Italian powers. Dandolo was intent on making the law the foundation of the Venetian state and society.[126]

Dandolo's role as a historian was equally important. While a procurator, he wrote his *Chronica brevis*, a brief compilation of Venetian history that ends with the death of his predecessor Gradenigo. While doge, Dandolo composed, with assistance of the ducal chancery, the chronicle known as the *Chronica per extensum descripta* (Long Chronicle), which begins with Saint Mark's founding of the Aquileian church and concludes in 1280. Dandolo drew on previous chronicles for much of the early chronology. But he also larded the text with numerous documents such as Cassiodorus's letter to the tribunes of the maritime provinces. Given the prestige of the author, both works took on the aura of the official version of Venice's past.

Indeed, Dandolo's chronicles drew together many of the components of the regime's ideology—which has come to be known as the myth of Venice.[127] Like all myths it contains just enough truth to make it plausible but exaggerates various elements to promote the interests of the regime and its beneficiaries. Described most cynically, it is propaganda put forward by those with power in order to perpetuate that power.

As presented in Dandolo's chronicles, the Venetian elite's mythic vision first and foremost presented the idea that Venice was specially favored by God as substantiated by its origins, miraculous aquatic setting, and relationship with Saint Mark. The saint's purported founding of the church at Aquileia bestowed on Venice an apostolic status and a near equivalency with Rome. It was Dandolo who gave definitive form to the *praedestinatio*—Mark's dream-vision of his final resting place and the bountiful city that would arise there.[128] Also like Rome and its founder Aeneas, Venice could trace a Trojan pedigree through the legendary refugee Antenor, who was believed to have founded Padua since Paduans had in turn fled to the lagoon during the barbarian invasions. The other main component of the ideology was the emphasis on Venice's essential freedom. Born in the sea, the city was subject to no secular power, while internally Venetian society was marked by equity and justice.

This latter element helped spawn the idea that Venice was almost preternaturally serene. That was attributed in large part to its form of government. Venetian apologists advanced the idea that the Republic had created the perfect regime, namely, a mixed constitution—an ideal form of government originally propounded by Aristotle and Polybius. The Venetian version received its first known articulation in the Dominican friar Henry of Rimini's treatise on the four cardinal virtues, which was likely composed in the immediate aftermath of the Serrata. Henry argued that the government

> has something of each of the three principal types of constitution. For, in so far as one [the Doge] is set over all, it could be called a kingly regime; in so far as a few of the leading citizens elect the Doge and govern with him . . . it could also be called a regime ruled by the best men; in so far as these leading citizens, ducal electors, councilors and members of the Forty are elected from the whole [Greater] Council, the constitution has something of a popular polity, for there are in the Council not only the greater nobles, but also many of the worthy popolo.[129]

The idea that membership in the Greater Council was synonymous with nobility had not yet fully taken hold when Henry was writing c. 1300 since he still thought the council was made up of both nobles and *popolani*. But by combining the best elements of rule by one, the few and the many—in other words, monarchy, aristocracy, and democracy—Venice had achieved a kind of political perfection. Henry rehearsed many of the other elements of the myth, including that Venetians were "good Catholics and totally free from the taint of heresy," and "deeply loyal to the state," and that "wide freedoms and singular immunities [were] enjoyed, not only by the citizens, but even by the plebeians." The idea that the Venetian Republic had mastered the art of government through its mixed constitution would circulate widely in early modern European political discourse after it was taken up again by nobleman and cardinal Gasparo Contarini in the early sixteenth century.

Many of the elements of Venice's ideology were present from the earliest days. Cassiodorus's letter, for example, advanced the idea of the essential equality of the residents, while John the Deacon wrote of a "golden Venice" situated so extraordinarily in the lagoon and grown so wealthy.[130] In his chronicle, Martino da Canal stated that he was writing so that all the world might know "how the noble city is made and how it has an abundance of all goods and how the lord of Venice, the noble doge, is potent and so that they may know the nobles who reside there and the prowess of the Venetian people."[131] But it was Dandolo who widely publicized these ideas in his long chronicle.

The crucial passage was Dandolo's discussion of the Peace of Venice in 1177 when Doge Ziani mediated the peace between Frederick Barbarossa and Pope Alexander III. The proof was in the various *trionfi* or symbolic objects that Alexander bestowed on Ziani and his successors and that became essential components of ducal processions. These included a white candle, a splendid sword, lead seals, a golden ring (to be used for the marriage of the sea), a plenary indulgence on the feast of the Ascension, an umbrella, silk banners, and silver trumpets. These Alexandrian gifts emphasized Venice's status as a faithful servant of the church, a point that needed stressing following the War of Ferrara. By contrast, Dandolo reported no gifts from Barbarossa since they could have been interpreted as symbols of subordination to the empire and compromised Venice's prized autonomy and freedom. In that vein, where in a diploma dated 992 Holy Roman emperor Otto III spoke of the "fidelity" that Venice showed him, Dandolo substituted the word "legality."[132] The word fidelity, redolent of feudal ties, implied dependence, whereas legality did not. By "giving definitive form to the story [of the Peace of 1177] in his chronicle," Dandolo "pulled together and made available to the men of the government documentation of Venice's original freedom and the legitimacy of its prerogatives."[133] Following Dandolo's death, his chronicle was continued by his Grand Chancellor Benintendi de' Ravegnani, Petrarch's close friend. Dandolo's historical work became a template for Venetian history-writing and served as the model for other chronicles, many of which were composed for individual patrician families.[134] By commissioning chronicles and preserving them in their private libraries, patricians embedded themselves and their families in the city's history.[135]

The parading of the *trionfi* in ducal processions offered a tangible reminder of the ideas they embodied.[136] Art played a similar role as in the depictions of the Peace of 1177 in the chapel of San Nicolò in the Ducal Palace and in the Greater Council Hall. Dandolo also used art to further his vision of Venice and its place in God's plan for the world. His efforts focused on that most central of Venetian spaces, San Marco.

Dandolo undertook three major projects in San Marco. One was the building of a chapel appended to the left transept to house the relics of Saint Isidore. Isidore was a third-century Roman military officer who converted to Christianity and was martyred on the Aegean island Chios. His relics were brought to Venice by Doge Domenico Michiel in 1125 after the Venetians defeated the Egyptian navy off Ascalon and wintered in Chios, where they took Isidore's relics and subsequently deposited them in San Marco. Somehow in the intervening two centuries, the Venetians managed to lose track of Isidore's body, just as they had previously done with Saint Mark. In this case, Isidore was rediscovered by Doge Dandolo, who then had the barrel-vaulted chapel built. Isidore's body was entombed in a sarcophagus at the east end of the chapel. An inscription above relates his arrival from Chios at the behest of Michiel and his rediscovery by Dandolo; mosaics on the sides of the vault illustrate Isidore's life and the relics' triumphal arrival at San Marco.[137] The miraculous rediscovery of Isidore should be understood in the context of the ongoing tension with Genoa, which had controlled Chios since 1261. The publicity afforded to Isidore offered Venice an opportunity to assert its claim to the strategically and commercially vital island. Isidore's rediscovery also provided Dandolo with a chance to emphasize the doge's special patronage rights over San Marco for which he commissioned three liturgical books: a Gospel lectionary, a sacramentary, and an epistolary. The epistolary and lectionary were bound in enameled covers created in Constantinople in the ninth and tenth centuries, respectively, while the sacramentary was encased in a Byzantine style binding produced in Venice in the thirteenth century.[138]

Dandolo's interest in recycling Byzantine enamels is even more apparent in his second major project for the church, the full and final articulation of the Pala d'Oro. On May 20, 1343, just five months into Dandolo's dogeship, the Greater Council voted to donate 400 ducats to the Procurators of San Marco and allow them to use additional money in unclaimed funds in their office for a project to ornament the Pala "for the honor of such a saint [as Mark] and also for the magnificence of the city."[139] The reworking resulted in a spectacular ensemble of Byzantine enamels with rows of angels, apostles, and prophets placed in architectural settings on the lower section surrounding the enthroned Christ and the four Evangelists, as well as scenes from the lives of Christ and Saint Mark, and the upper panel with Michael and six feasts of the *dodekaorton* (the Byzantine cycle of twelve great feasts). The entire assemblage was enclosed in a Gothic frame and encrusted with hundreds of precious and semi-precious gems and pearls. Two inscription plaques placed in the bottom register offer a history of the Pala and its ducal associations. The block on the left explains that when Ordelaffo Falier was "reigning," the Pala was created and then was "renovated" under Pietro Ziani. The right block says that after 1345 under Dandolo and Procurators Marco Loredan and Fresco Querini it was "made new."[140]

Since the Pala was only put on display on feast days, a cover known as the Pala Feriale (everyday screen) was commissioned from the painter Paolo Veneziano and his sons. The upper register depicts Saints Theodore, Mark, and the Virgin on the left flanking the dead Christ, with John the Evangelist, Saints Peter, and Nicholas on the right, all in a half-length mode typical of Byzantine icons. The lower register illustrates seven scenes from the life of Saint Mark, including his apparition to the sailors transporting his relics to Venice, the finding of his relics after they were lost, and pilgrims at Mark's tomb. These narrative scenes are predominantly Byzantine in style but with some Italian elements.[141]

But Dandolo's synoptic vision of Venice and its place in Christian history is most fully on display in the greatest of his San Marco projects, the Baptistery. Unlike the freestanding baptisteries in most Italian cities, San

FIGURE 8.2 Paolo Veneziano and Sons, Pala Feriale, 1345. Museo di San Marco, Venice. Scala/Art Resource, NY.

Marco's baptistery is attached to the church. Also unlike most other cities, San Marco was not the only baptistery in Venice; five churches were designated as *matrici* (mother churches) and could perform baptisms.[142]

The San Marco baptistery comprises an antechamber and two domed bays along the south wing of the atrium, directly adjacent to what was once the seaward entrance to the basilica. The first bay, which is reached by passing through the antechamber, houses the baptismal font; the second contains an altar. The tomb of Doge Giovanni Soranzo who died in 1328 was mounted on the north wall of the antechamber directly opposite the entrance into the Baptistery from the Piazzetta. Since Dandolo had been elected procurator two months before Soranzo's death, he likely had a say in its placement. Soranzo's was the first ducal burial in San Marco in three-quarters of a century and its situation in the direct line of sight of visitors entering the Baptistery emphasized the ducal presence in a space where one was initiated into the Christian (and Venetian) communities.[143]

The iconography of the mosaics in the next two bays vastly extends the message. The dome of the bay housing the baptismal font depicts Christ's charge to the apostles to carry the message of Christianity to the world. Fanning out from the central enthroned Christ are the twelve apostles, each baptizing a catechumen who is immersed in a marble font up to his waist. The mosaicists were careful to depict the baptismal fonts as constructed from different types of marble quarried in the eastern Mediterranean. Inscriptions identify the apostles and where their missions had taken them: Mark to Alexandria, John the Baptist to Ephesus, Jacob to Judea, Philip to Phrygia (Anatolia), Matthew to Ethiopia, Thomas to India, Andrew to Achaia (the Morea and Crete), Peter to Rome, Bartholomew to India, Thaddeus to Mesopotamia, and Matthias to Palestine. The territories outlined in Christ's mission to the apostles coincide closely with Venice's maritime and commercial empire, reinforcing the belief that Venice's commercial activity and eastern colonial empire are sanctioned by God.[144]

The next bay houses the altar. The dome depicts Christ in Glory and the Second Coming. Christ is shown raising both hands in blessing as he welcomes the saved into the Kingdom of Heaven. Against the east wall, behind the altar is the Crucifixion. The crucified Christ is shown flanked by Mark and Mary on the left, John the Evangelist and John the Baptist on the right. Kneeling at the foot of cross, in the space usually occupied by the Virgin, is Dandolo himself, dressed in the ducal ermine cape and the bejeweled ducal *corno*. As he stares intently at his crucified savior, he comprehends the divine plan. As a chronicler writing in the 1360s put it,

"And God through his mercy and divine grace illuminates the mind of each doge, chief and rector of that [Venice], . . . so that his state which has always grown, . . . may [continue to] expand."[145] Dandolo's close associate Grand Chancellor Benintendi de' Ravegnani kneels at the far left while a young patrician kneels on the right. This emphasizes those who count in this newly amalgamated patrician regime. Just as Venice's empire is sanctioned in the Apostles' dome, so its post-Serrata political settlement is solemnized in the Crucifixion mosaic.

Dandolo chose San Marco as the site of his own burial and wanted to be entombed in the main body of the church, but the procurators decided after his death to locate his tomb instead in the baptistery in the bay housing the baptismal font. The tomb chest is adorned with an Annunciation, an enthroned Virgin, and depictions of various saints, including Dandolo's patron Andrew. A recumbent figure of the doge, the first in a long line of ducal tomb effigies, rests atop the chest. The Latin epitaph below the tomb reads in part, "The small space of a cold tomb contains the limbs of that valorous one whom the venerable army of virtues never deserted . . . Andrea, whom the

FIGURE 8.3 *The Crucifixion with Doge Andrea Dandolo at the Foot of the Cross*, mosaic, mid-fourteenth century. Baptistery of San Marco, Venice. Federico Zeri Foundation, Zeri Photo Archive, Bologna.

noble house of Dandolo gave birth to, worthy in every respect of the Venetian state."[146]

Andrea Dandolo was the last doge to be buried in San Marco. One later chronicler records that after his death a law forbidding future ducal burials in the church was promulgated. Such a law has never been found. Perhaps the chronicler was merely expressing the common opinion that this should have been enshrined in law. What seems clear is that Dandolo, through his chronicles and patronage of San Marco, had raised the ducal profile to new heights and endangered the subtle balance of power between various branches of the government.

In the four decades following the Serrata, the patricians consolidated their hold on power. They tightened requirements for new admissions to the Greater Council and manipulated the economy through the creation of the state-galley system to advance their own commercial interests. They defined the role of foreigners and immigrants in Venice's mercantile empire and shaped the infrastructure of the city to facilitate trade. They crafted a vision of a just, bountiful, tranquil, free, and divinely favored Venice that legitimated their rule, and they deployed art to further the message.

9

Calamity and Survival

IN JANUARY 1348 a powerful earthquake shook Venice. An inscription carved in a lunette at the Scuola Grande of Santa Maria della Carità records: "In the year of the Incarnation of our Lord mister Jesus Christ 1347 [Venetian style, that is 1348] on the 25th of January, the feast of the conversion of Saint Paul, around the hour of vespers, there was a big earthquake in Venice and almost all the world; and many tops of bell towers and houses and chimneys toppled as well as the church of San Basegio; and there was such a big fright that almost all the people thought they were going to die, and the earth did not stop trembling for nearly forty days."[1]

In the Middle Ages, people regularly took natural phenomena as portends of events that would change the course of history. Haley's comet, for example, made a pass in 1066, just months before the Norman conquest of England and seemed to foretell great happenings. Its appearance was depicted in the Bayeux tapestry, and the comet's 1301 pass may have been used as the model for the Star of Bethlehem in the *Adoration of the Magi* that Giotto painted in the Arena Chapel in Padua. Venice's earthquake too was portentous. The inscription continues, "and a little after this there began a great mortality and people died from various diseases and for various reasons; some spat blood from their mouths and some got swollen glands [buboes] in their armpits and groin, and some got carbuncles on their flesh; and it seemed that these illnesses took whomever they wished, that is the healthy and the infirm." According to the inscription, the earthquake augured the bubonic plague that carried away perhaps half the population of the city and its dominions.

The Black Death itself ushered in three decades that were among the most calamitous in Venice's history, including a conspiracy to overthrow the state by Andrea Dandolo's successor, a revolt in Crete, and a final showdown with Genoa. The Venice that emerged at the end of the Fourth Venetian-Genoese

War was much changed. And the generation that came of age during that crisis would take the city and its empire to unprecedented political and economic might. This chapter surveys the fourteenth-century catastrophes that tested the mettle of the Venetian regime and people and set them on a new course.

If the Carità inscription is correct and the plague began after forty days of aftershocks, then it must have hit Venice in the middle of March 1348 after arriving via rats on ships loaded with grain returning from the Black Sea.[2] Some experts, however, claim that it reached Venice in early January. Perhaps the chronology presented in the inscription reflected the belief that the earthquake had to foretell the plague's arrival. The inscription captures the terror that accompanied the pandemic and calls to mind Boccaccio's famous account of the plague in Florence in the introduction to the *Decameron.* It continues, "and the people were so frightened that fathers did not want to go to their [ill] sons; or sons to their fathers; and this mortality lasted around six months and it is commonly said that two-thirds of the people of Venice died." It goes on to tell that Piero Trevisan, the chief warden of the confraternity, perished along with ten members of the governing board and more than 300 of the approximately 500 regular members, with the result that "the confraternity was in great ruin."

On March 30, the government took its first official action in response to the crisis.[3] The Greater Council appointed a committee of three noble sages to examine hygienic conditions in the city and report back in a few days with recommendations "for the preservation of health and in order to avoid the corruption of the city." On April 3, based on their recommendation and recognizing that the situation was "extremely dangerous and horrible," the Greater Council voted that the cadavers of hospice residents, the homeless and indigent, and those whose relatives did not want them buried in the city should be transported to two locales in the southern part of the lagoon where there was ample consecrated ground. The council further agreed to pay priests to perform services at the sites, gravediggers to dig trenches at least five feet deep, men to collect the corpses in the city, and boatmen to transport the bodies. The well-to-do could continue to be buried in the city's parish graveyards or monasteries, as was customary, so long as the corpses were covered with five feet of sand and sludge dredged from canals. These requirements were instituted to minimize miasmas, which were thought to be the most likely source of contagion.[4] However, by early May the designated cemeteries had reached capacity, and so burials were authorized at Sant'Erasmo and San Martino di Strada.

In June, the Greater Council forbade foreigners who were ill from coming to the city. Those who disobeyed were to be jailed and fined, and the boats on which they arrived burned. In July, the Senate amplified that measure, adding that all boats approaching Venice were to be examined, and any boatman who transported anyone who was ill or even "seemed ill" was to have his boat burned and spend a month in jail. An exception was made for ambassadors, merchants, and other notables who could still come to the city if they had permission of the doge and his councilors since denying them entry would injure Venice's "honor."[5]

In a further effort to halt the spread, the government ordered that all rotten salami, which could contribute to "corruption of the air," be removed from the city or dumped in the canals.[6] It also forbade the retailing of wine from boats or in taverns except for select taverns that were permitted to remain open at Rialto and San Marco. In the face of mass death, some residents apparently abandoned themselves to hedonistic pleasures, and, according to the Greater Council, uncontrolled drinking was leading to "tumults and homicides."[7]

Others reacted by atoning for their sins. Notarial records show that people hurried to get their earthly affairs in order and looked to the welfare of their eternal souls. Sometime in the first half of April, Marco da ca' da Modena drafted his will. Noting that he was of sound mind, but ill, he made several charitable bequests for the good of his soul, including endowing 1,000 Masses and paying for the completion of a sculpture of the Virgin and Child with Saints Peter and Paul over the portal of the Hospice of Saints Peter and Paul. He left 17 ducats to the hospice's rector to have Mass said daily for a year in honor of the two apostles.[8] Marco de Vorardo drafted his will in May. He endowed sixty Masses in his parish church and wanted a love-feast (a distribution of food and drink) to be held monthly at the church door for four months following his burial. He also wanted cloaks to be distributed to thirty of the "poor little boys and girls who are shoeless and poorly dressed" who lingered near the bridge and public scales at Rialto.[9] A famine in 1347 had prompted an influx of peasants from the mainland in search of food. They became prime victims of the outbreak. But the wealthy and powerful were not immune, and the government faced potential paralysis because nobles had either succumbed to the disease or fled to their *terraferma* estates. In June, the Greater Council noted that "many, many" nobles had died and few of the survivors were attending its meetings. In face of this absenteeism, it lowered the number of attendees needed to attain a quorum in the Forty. Special provisions were made to return the Council of Ten to its normal size.[10] Notaries, other minor officials, even physicians had also fled the city.

By August 1348 the epidemic started to wane. To raise residents' spirits, the Senate passed a measure prohibiting them from wearing mourning garb. Noting that the sight of so many bereaved people was provoking even more sadness and doing nothing to benefit the deceased, it banned the wearing of black and other dark colors and encouraged bright-colored clothing that would "induce full happiness and merriment." Women over fifty were exempt since mourning was old women's work, as were the poor who could afford nothing else.[11]

It is impossible to assess accurately the plague's demographic impact. Historians estimate that the city's pre-plague population of between 110,000 and 120,000 inhabitants (160,000 for the entire *dogado*) was reduced by roughly half in six months. One Paduan chronicler observed that once the plague infected a household, it claimed everyone "right down to the dogs."[12] The psychological impact was compounded by multiple waves after 1348. Almost every year some succumbed, and then with alarming regularity, flareups occurred. In the fourteenth and fifteenth centuries there were mass mortalities in 1361, 1400, 1423, 1478, and 1486. Venice only returned to its pre-plague population in the early sixteenth century.

During the epidemic's height, trade came to a virtual standstill. When the plague returned in 1400, one merchant voiced a sentiment that must have been common in 1348, writing, "Now is not the time to conduct business but instead to get right with God."[13] With business slowed or suspended, revenue from customs duties and other levies dropped. The government halted efforts to amortize the public debt and undertook various cost-cutting measures, including suspending construction of the new Greater Council Hall and diverting funds to pay for the extraordinary expenses associated with the epidemic. It sought to extract more money from Crete and reached a deal with the bishop of Castello regarding the tithe—the death tax—that supported the church. With the huge mortality, the church was in for a windfall. Both the government and individuals were reluctant to see so much money pass to ecclesiastical authorities. The agreement with the bishop did not hold, however, and the issue would remain a point of contention for decades.

The government also needed to get trade moving again and clear the backlog of merchandise that had stacked up in warehouses. In July 1348, the Senate authorized the auction of ten state-owned galleys for voyages to Alexandria, Romania, and Cyprus. Trade resumed quickly. While there were fewer customers, survivors had more disposable income because of the legacies they had received. Within a year revenue was outpacing expenses, and the government was able to resume amortizing the debt and building the Council Hall.

Immigration policy witnessed the biggest change as the government was eager to repopulate the city. In June 1348 with the outbreak ongoing, the Greater Council authorized the Senate to find ways to "induce men to inhabit and restore our city."[14] Various measures were taken to augment the workforce: exiles could be repatriated, debt-prisoners freed, restrictions on guild enrollment eased for both men and women, and entry fees for the guilds waived for two years. The Senate also created incentives to ensure that the fleets were properly manned. Any man who established himself in Venice with his wife and family, paid taxes, and signed on as a sailor or oarsman could carry 300 pounds of merchandise free of charge instead of the previous 50, provided his wife or family remained in Venice. These incentives no doubt helped, but given the reduced workforce, it was likely higher wages that spurred an influx of artisans and laborers. To foster commerce, the government reduced the prerequisites for naturalized citizenship. In August, the Senate decided that for the next two years anyone who wished to do so could obtain *de intus* status simply by registering with the government instead of waiting the traditional fifteen years, and *de extra* status after ten years, instead of twenty-five. Around sixty men took advantage of the latter offer. The government continued to encourage immigration during the 1350s, including to Crete and Negroponte. However, by the 1360s the openness to foreigners ended with the reinstitution of the Officium de Navigantibus and its protectionist trade policies.[15]

With a smaller population, the city's physical growth slowed. Land reclamation efforts were much reduced, with only a few minor projects recommencing around 1360.[16] One small-scale project, partly still visible in Campo Angelo Raffaele, was undertaken on private initiative. On May 28, 1348, merchant Marco Arian, who subsequently died of the plague, composed his last will and testament. In it, he left 300 ducats with the Grain Office for the construction of two wells, one of which was to be in the parish square so that water would be available for the "neighbors," both "the *popolo* and the good men of the parish." Arian wanted his bequest to be commemorated. To this end he ordered that his coat of arms and merchant's mark—the brand with which he stamped his merchandise—be sculpted on the wellhead and his largesse be declaimed at the church door every year on Christmas and Easter. Carved in Istrian stone, the wellhead is inscribed, "July 15, 1349, sir

FIGURE 9.1 Wellhead Donated by Sir Marco Arian, with his merchant mark and dedicatory inscription, 1349. Campo Angelo Raffaele, Venice. Photo by the author.

Marco Arian, son that he was of Sir Antonio Arian of San Raffaele, made me."[17] It offers testimony both to the health concerns—namely, the fear of contaminated water—and the spiritual worries that the Black Death unleashed.

Crisis followed crisis without respite. The 1350s saw Venice facing challenges in the two spheres that had long been at the center of Venetian foreign relations: the Adriatic, where its dominance was contested once again by Dalmatian cities and the Kingdom of Hungary, and the wider Mediterranean, where its protracted rivalry with Genoa continued unabated.

In the Adriatic, Venice's policy remained consistent: to avoid a political vacuum in Dalmatia that would allow an opening for the Croats, Serbs, Bosnians, or Hungarians to control the coastline, and to keep the sea's eastern and western shores from being united under a hostile power. In this period that meant the Angevins who controlled both the Kingdom of Hungary and that of Naples. Venice also strove to limit cooperation among the Dalmatian cities, especially the ever-rebellious Zara, the more compliant Ragusa, and towns such as Sebenico, Traù, and Spalato that had submitted themselves to the Republic in the 1320s. Despite its efforts, Venice found itself engaged in a protracted contest with Hungary that grew worse with the ascension of the Angevin Louis I in 1342. Four years after Louis assumed the throne, Zara again revolted against Venice but was subdued by Pietro Civran, captain general in charge of the navy, and Marino Falier, who supervised the land forces. In the peace that was concluded in December 1346 Venice imposed harsh terms on Zara.

In August 1348 Venice signed an eight-year peace with Louis. But the following month Capodistria rose in revolt, expelling podesta Marco Giustinian and torching his headquarters. Venice again dispatched a combination of naval and land forces, and the city was forced to resubmit in October. In the pact of submission, Doge Dandolo continued to style himself Duke of Dalmatia and Croatia as well as ruler of one-quarter and half of one-quarter of the Roman empire.[18]

Just two years later, on August 6, 1350, Venice declared war on Genoa. The causes of the Third Venetian-Genoese War (1350–55) were rivalry between the two maritime republics over Black Sea trade, control of the Aegean, and transit through the Bosphorus.[19] Indeed, the longer-term conflict is often referred to as the War of the Straits. These two commercial giants also competed to control the grain trade and supply salt to Po valley cities, especially Milan.[20] Provocations on both sides precipitated the war. Following their expulsion from Tana in 1343 by the Tartars, the two parties had agreed not to trade there. But when the Genoese learned that the Venetians had broken the deal by reaching a separate agreement with the khan of the Tartars, their merchants in Caffa tried to forbid Venetian ships from proceeding to Tana. For their part, the Genoese had in 1346 reoccupied Chios, a major producer of gum mastic (sap from the mastic tree with cosmetic, perfume, and culinary uses), as well as Phocaea, an important source of alum, thus cementing their route up the eastern Aegean; the Venetians dominated the western side. Venice had an ally in Byzantine emperor John VI Cantacuzene, who found the Genoese settlement at Pera (Galata) particularly troublesome as it was siphoning off trade from the empire and afforded the Genoese control of the Bosphorus. His goal was to rebuild the Byzantine navy and restore trade to the capital. The alliance with Venice would be his way of humbling the Genoese.

The initial phase of the Third Venetian-Genoese War was fought in the Aegean. A Venetian fleet under Marco Ruzzini attacked a group of fourteen Genoese galleys near Negroponte. However, four Genoese ships managed to escape due to lack of discipline among the newly recruited sailors from Dalmatia and Venice's Greek possessions who replaced men from the plague-decimated *dogado*. The missed opportunity was made worse when the escapees teamed up with other ships sent from Genoa and launched a successful attack on Venetian Negroponte.

Venice realized it needed a much larger fleet, and for that it needed allies. It found them in the Aragonese, who were challenging Genoa for control of Sardinia, and the Byzantines under John VI. Each agreed to contribute ships at its own expense as well as supply others that Venice would subsidize. Venice had the money, but because of the plague losses, it lacked the men necessary to put a large fleet to sea. John also rescinded the commercial privileges the Genoese had been granted in 1261 when the Byzantine empire was restored.

In early summer 1351, the Venetians and Byzantines launched an offensive against the Genoese quarter of Pera, with the emperor attacking from the land and the joint fleet of thirty-two vessels under Nicolò Pisani blockading it from the sea. But on receiving word that a Genoese flotilla of over sixty vessels under Paganino Doria had managed to sail east before an allied fleet of Venetians and Aragonese could stop it, Pisani fled to Negroponte and scuttled his ships to prevent them from being captured. When the Venetian/Aragonese squadron arrived, the Genoese retreated first to Chios, then to Pera. Pisani refloated the ships that he had intentionally sunk and got reinforcements from Aragon. But the approach of winter delayed a new assault on Pera, much to the consternation of John VI who was also troubled by the Ottoman Turks' provisioning of the Genoese with intelligence and supplies.

The navies finally engaged in February 1353 in the Battle of the Bosphorus. Both sides suffered heavy losses—the Venetians 1,500 men—and the fighting proved inconclusive. Pisani, blamed for the failure by the Aragonese and John, left the region with his ships in April. The departure of his Venetian ally forced the emperor to treat with the Genoese. Their peace accord in early May reaffirmed Genoese commercial privileges, strengthened their position at Pera, and confirmed their occupation of Chios and Phocaea. To make matters worse for Venice, the Genoese formed an alliance with Louis I of Hungary. Although Pisani made another appearance in the region late in the year, the theater of war shifted westward.

In the summer of 1353 Pisani assisted the Aragonese in their designs on Sardinia by defeating a Genoese fleet near Alghero off Sardinia's northwestern coast, but Doria eluded him and sailed into the Adriatic. There he attacked Lesina and Curzola in Dalmatia and even Parenzo (Poreč) in Istria, which he burned and despoiled of the relics of Saints Maurus and Eleutherius much to the "ignominy" of the Venetians.[21] Fearing an attack on Venice itself, the Venetians placed a chain across the San Nicolò mouth to prevent enemy ships from entering the Bacino. Louis of Hungary demanded the cession of Dalmatia. Pisani eventually followed Doria to Chios, but the forces failed to engage, and Pisani retreated to winter in Modon and Coron. Since peace negotiations were in the works, the government ordered him to abstain from battle. He prepared his fleet to spend the winter at Porto Longo, a small harbor near Modon. While he kept fourteen galleys on duty guarding the entrance to the harbor, twenty-one others were tied together to pass the winter. Doria's fleet managed to slip past the guard ships and capture all thirty-five Venetian vessels, along with the entire Venetian force of 5,000 men including the humiliated Pisani. Civil strife within Genoa had recently caused the city to surrender to the Visconti of Milan, who orchestrated a peace between the maritime rivals. The agreement finalized on June 1, 1355, reaffirmed the maritime spheres of influence outlined in the peace treaty of 1299 that ended their second war. Both sides also agreed to refrain from sending merchant galleys to Tana for three years. Like the previous peace treaties, it failed to resolve the underlying commercial competition between the combatants.

Nor did it bring about a resolution of the conflict with Louis of Hungary, who won over the count of Gorizia and the patriarch of Aquileia, while Venice's efforts to garner the support of Francesco da Carrara, lord of Padua, failed. In 1356 Louis invaded Dalmatia, then entered Friuli, went on to take Sacile and Conegliano, and laid siege to Treviso. On August 8, 1356, Doge Giovanni Gradenigo died, and Giovanni Delfin, currently serving as commissioner in Treviso, was elected in his place. Denied safe conduct by Louis, he managed to elude Hungarian forces and arrived in Venice on August 25. Serravalle and Asolo were also lost to the Hungarians; and Carrara aided Louis in provisioning his forces. Venice responded with a salt blockade and encouraged the Della Scalas of Verona to move against Carrara.

Under pressure from the pope, Louis reluctantly agreed in April 1357 to a five-month armistice, but hostilities recommenced at its conclusion. Venice found itself trying to protect its interests in Dalmatia and the Trevisano (the area around Treviso), which it briefly considered abandoning. The Hungarians tried unsuccessfully to take several towns close to Venice, including Mestre, but they had more success in Dalmatia, where they took Traù, Spalato, Zara, and other places. After suffering a defeat near Treviso in February 1358, the Venetians decided to seek peace. Louis laid out severe conditions. After much debate and fearing that Genoa might take advantage of their vulnerability and rejoin the fight, the Venetians accepted the terms, which were confirmed on February 18. Venice renounced all claims to Dalmatia and agreed to turn over all towns still in its possession, while for his part Louis promised to surrender his conquests in Istria and the Trevisano. Venice agreed not to support the Dalmatians against the king, while he promised to prevent the region from becoming a haven for pirates. Venice would enjoy freedom of commerce in the towns and ports of the kingdom. Most humiliatingly, the doge had to renounce his title as Duke of Dalmatia and Croatia and style himself instead as "duke of the Venetians et cetera."[22] For the rest of the century Venice would shift its attention to the lower Adriatic and Aegean.[23] A separate peace was signed with Padua in June.

The Third Venetian-Genoese War and war with Louis were in many respects a dry run for the fourth and final struggle with Genoa that began in 1379. These conflicts exploded the public debt. During the Third Venetian-Genoese War those required to make forced loans had to pay 15 percent of their assessed patrimony, and the market value of shares in the debt dropped from 98 to 77 percent. Nevertheless, the government was only a month or two in arrears in making its regular 5 percent interest payments to lenders. Also, in the immediate aftermath of the war, the bank operated by Marino Baffo and Marco Trevisan failed, and interest rates rose. More bank failures followed the peace concluded with Louis and the loss of Dalmatia.[24] The wars also brought to the surface resentment on the part of the *popolo* who were required to serve in the navy and were therefore unable to take advantage of the higher wages being offered for other kinds of work. Also many *popolano* men were taken prisoner or died during the war. In addition, to pay for the wars and continue making interest payments on the public debt, the government raised duties on such basic consumer goods as salt, meat, cheese, and wine. These increases hit the humblest members of society the hardest. Many were resentful that after enduring the plague, they were being asked to sacrifice for a war that benefited first and foremost the patricians' commercial interests. Doge Marino Falier played on these resentments to recruit adherents to his plot to overthrow the regime.

The conspiracy that Falier orchestrated in the final months of the Third Venetian-Genoese War is, quite simply, one of the most confounding episodes in the Republic's history.[25] It seems to defy explanation because it is difficult to imagine anyone more dedicated to governmental service than Falier or better qualified to be doge. Even Petrarch, who was familiar with him, was hard pressed to explain what happened and why.

Born into one of the oldest and most prestigious noble families, Falier began his political career at the highest echelons, serving for several years when he was only in his early thirties on the Council of Ten. Subsequent appointments and posts took him to many parts of the Mediterranean where Venice had interests and provided him with administrative, diplomatic, and military experience. At various times he was podesta in Lesina and Brazza in Dalmatia, as well as in Chioggia, Padua, Treviso, and Serravalle. He oversaw troops during Venice's war against the Della Scalas, served as commander of the Black Sea galleys, directed land forces during Venice's 1345 efforts to put down rebellion in Zara, and was appointed a sage during the war against Genoa. He undertook embassies to Bologna, Dalmatia, Ferrara, Genoa, the Duke of Austria, and the pope in Avignon. While on the papal mission in September 1354, he was elected doge on the first ballot, garnering thirty-five of the forty-one votes.[26] Some later chroniclers report that when he arrived in Venice on October 5, fog prevented him from landing at the usual disembarkation point and forced him instead to make his way between the twin columns in the Piazzetta—the spot where executions were held. This was taken as an ill omen. Petrarch remarked that he entered the palace "on the left foot," the side viewed as sinister or evil.[27]

Falier was also immensely wealthy. Hailing from the family's Santi Apostoli branch, he was actively engaged in commerce and had extensive properties. These included the family palace at Santi Apostoli and other real estate holdings in the city and the Padovano, Ferrarese, and Trevisano. He was made count and lord of Valmareno by the bishop of Ceneda, who also awarded him the castle of Fregona. His first wife, who may have been a Contarini and with whom he had a daughter, died, and in 1335 he married Aluica (Ludovica) Gradenigo, granddaughter of doge Pietro Gradenigo.[28]

When he ascended the ducal throne Falier was nearly seventy, without a direct male heir, and married to a woman who was two or three decades his junior. Soon after taking office, he was apparently mocked as a cuckold. The earliest mention of the incident by a chronicler is extremely cryptic. The author of the so-called chronicle of Enrico Dandolo says simply that Falier suffered "some injuries by some young sons of the gentlemen of Venice."

Falier believed that they had not been punished adequately for the offense.[29] Lorenzo de Monacis writes in his slightly later chronicle that "some adolescent nobles" wrote "ignominious words" in a corner of the Ducal Palace, and that Falier was enraged when the perpetrators got off lightly.[30] By the time Marino Sanudo was writing in the late fifteenth/early sixteenth century, the story had been much elaborated. According to this amplified version, during Fat Thursday celebrations, Michele Steno, who became doge in 1400 but was a young man in 1355, misbehaved during a party that Falier hosted, was called out by the doge, and was publicly humiliated. In revenge, Steno sneaked into the Ducal Palace that night and scribbled on the ducal throne, "Marino Falier doge with the beautiful wife—he maintains her while others enjoy her."[31] This attack on his honor purportedly drove the doge to hatch his plot against the noble regime.

Since the mid-nineteenth century most historians have seen the insult as too trivial to have driven Falier to conspire against the state. Typical is the assessment that, even though the story is "built on the undoubted facts that, soon after his election, some words insulting to the doge were written on a wall in the Ducal Palace . . . this romantic legend carries no conviction because it appears only long after the event."[32] Yet the Dandolo chronicle was composed within a decade of Falier's reign. As for the "undoubted facts," on November 10, 1354, the Council of Forty authorized the State Attorneys to detain and examine those who were responsible for writing the "ugly and shameful [words] that were the cause of great shame and disgrace to the entire city." Ten days later, the Forty sentenced Michele Steno, Pietro Bolani, and Rizzardo Marioni to a few days in jail, while three other nobles were exonerated. The sentence against Steno specified that "outlandish" words had been written "in vituperation of the lord doge and his nephew."[33] The light sentences meted out to the perpetrators and the handling of the case by the Forty rather than the Ten, suggest that it was not taken all that seriously, perhaps because of the offenders' youth. But that does not mean that Falier did not take umbrage at an attack on his manhood and his wife's virtue, even if such insults were not uncommon.[34]

The other proximate cause of the conspiracy was a dust-up between nobleman Giovanni Dandolo, a naval paymaster, and Bertuccio Isarello, *popolano* captain of a merchant ship traveling to Cyprus.[35] Dandolo tried to assign a particular crew member to Isarello; when he refused, Dandolo struck him. Isarello then went and rallied a group of discontented seamen to his side, and they paced about the Piazza in what Dandolo took to be a threatening manner. He complained to the doge, who upbraided Isarello for his behavior. Later, however, Falier summoned Israello and convinced him to join a conspiracy.

The plan they worked out was as follows. Isarello would recruit twenty *popolano* leaders who would each be placed in command of forty men, although only a few of the leaders knew the real goal or of the doge's involvement. On nights preceding the takeover, the leaders would parade around, pretending to be nobles, and hurl sexual insults at the homes of well-to-do commoners as a way of arousing resentment against the nobility. Then on the night of April 15, these bands would assemble at San Marco and the doge would sound the alarm that fifty Genoese galleys were about to breach the port. When the leading nobles rushed to the Palace, they would be massacred. The rebels would then disperse throughout the city crying, "Long live the *popolo*," and slaughter the rest of the nobles and their children. Falier would be declared Lord of the Rod (Signore a Bacheta), the rod being a potent symbol of power, and various offices would be assumed by the *popolo*.

As in the Querini-Tiepolo conspiracy, things did not go as planned. According to some accounts, Falier revealed the plot to his friend Nicolò Zucuol, who pretended to go along, but instead told the rebel leaders that the plan was off. Hearing this and fearing that he would be implicated when things came to light, one of those leaders, a furrier named Vendrame, revealed the plan to nobleman Nicolò Lion who went to Falier and, unaware that the doge was involved, urged him to act. Falier tried to stall but finally was forced to convene the Ducal Council. Nobleman Giacomo Contarini also came forward saying that a seaman had told him of the plot. Investigations followed. Under torture, one of the leaders finally revealed that Falier was in on the conspiracy. The ducal councilors gave orders for nobles throughout the city to gather trustworthy men from their parishes and come defend the Piazza. In the meantime, the ducal councilors alerted the members of the Council of Ten, who gathered to decide their course of action. Given the gravity of the situation and desiring to lend their decisions greater authority, the Ten added twenty men to their deliberations. Known as an *aggiunta* (addition) or in Venetian *zonta*, it was a practice that the Ten would use regularly when deciding particularly weighty cases. On April 16, the Ten ordered a roundup of the leading conspirators. Two of the ringleaders, stonecutter Filippo Calendario and Isarello, were immediately hanged, apparently with bits in their mouths so that they could not cry out and incite spectators to violence. Over the next few days, nine other *popolani* were executed.

On April 17, the Ducal Council, the Ten with its *zonta*, and the State Attorneys met, and the Ten voted to behead Falier on the landing of the staircase leading into the Ducal Palace, the spot where only six months earlier he had sworn his oath of office. The Ten ordered his wealth confiscated but allowed him to dispose of 2,000 lire. In the will he dictated that day, Falier asked his wife to distribute the money to the poor and for pious works. After he was executed, his body (with his head placed at his feet) was displayed in the Ducal Palace before being taken to San Zanipolo for burial in the Falier family tomb.

As in the Querini-Tiepolo revolt, the government acted quickly to control the narrative by informing officials outside Venice of what had occurred. This was done primarily to reassure foreigners of the reliability of Venetian commercial structures and institutions.[36] Lorenzo Celsi, the podesta of Treviso, was informed that Falier had been the "originator and head" of the plot and that the other ringleaders had been handled "without any uproar or disturbance of the citizens."[37] On April 21, the Greater Council elected Giovanni Gradenigo as Falier's successor. Bodyguards were assigned to those who had heard the case against Falier and the notaries who recorded the proceedings. The Ten also acted against men who were peripheral to the conspiracy. They sentenced Bertuccio Falier and Nicoleto, son of Filippo Calendario, to life imprisonment for knowing about the conspiracy but not revealing it. Nicolò Zucuol was permanently exiled to Candia for the same reason. Zanello del Bruno, who was at Isarello's house the night of the conspiracy but claimed that he had been duped into going there, received a one-year prison sentence. Following a call from the government, thirty-one men confessed that they had mobilized but thought they were doing so to defend the regime. They were pardoned, although in December the Ten ruled that none of them could ever serve in responsible positions on any of the state's armed ships. Several men who did not come forward had bounties placed on their heads. Worried that unrest might occur during the upcoming Ascension Day festivities, the Ten ordered reinforcement of police patrols.

Also, as in the aftermath of the Querini-Tiepolo conspiracy, the government rewarded several men who had come to its defense. The Ten proclaimed a solemn procession every April 16 to the chapel of Saint Isidore in San Marco to thank God for his intervention against Falier, just like the one to San Vio to commemorate the triumph over Querini and Tiepolo. In this way, the feast day of the saint in whose chapel Andrea Dandolo had done so much to elevate the visibility of the doge became a warning to future doges to know their place in Venice's mixed government. Petrarch captured the sentiment well when he wrote of Falier and his fate: "Those who are for a time doge I would warn to study the image this sets before their eyes, that they may see as in a mirror that they are leaders not lords, nay not even leaders, but honored servants of the Republic."[38]

Given the many legends that have grown up around Falier and the ways in which later chroniclers embroidered events, it is hard to make sense of what actually happened. This is made more difficult still because the Ten recorded their deliberations about the case in a separate register that was either lost or intentionally destroyed. If the latter, it was part of the government's policy of covering up dissent as a way of burnishing Venice's reputation for serenity. One interpretation is that the plot was, like the Querini-Tiepolo conspiracy, symptomatic of deep divisions within the patriciate, especially over how to prosecute the war with Genoa.[39] But this relies on an overly subtle reading of the evidence in which a small clique of nobles orchestrated a coup against Falier. What is certain is that Falier reacted badly to insults by Steno and others, and his co-conspirators were *popolani*. Many of these *popolano* ringleaders were men of some means. Stonecutter Filippo Calendario owned boats that were used to haul stone for the reinforcement of the barrier islands, and he received several contracts with the government to do so. His son-in-law and co-conspirator Bertuccio Isarello was *nochiero* (mate) and *paron* (captain) on merchant vessels, traded in pepper, and owned houses in the city. Stefano Trivisan was a money-changer, Antonio dalle Binde a scribe for the Visdomini dei Lombardi, Nicolò Doro the owner of a ship. Among the other followers were another *paron* of a ship, a caulker, a notary, a couple of poor seamen, a supervisor of the project to close the Sant'Erasmo mouth, a dyer, and a furrier. Many made their living from the sea and thus acutely felt the sacrifices demanded by the Genoese war. Before the conspiracy Falier had garnered the goodwill of the *popolo* by appointing three non-nobles as captains of war galleys. These commanders inflicted great losses on the Genoese and, in so doing, according to the Enrico Dandolo chronicle, brought "great honor to our city Venice."[40]

Falier and his co-conspirators were drawn together more by discontent than by common goals. While the doge aspired to lordship, his followers wanted to overturn the settlement reached in the Serrata and empower the *popolo*. As Matteo Villani, a Florentine chronicler noted, the conspirators' plan was "to run about the city yelling 'Long live the *popolo*' and make the doge the lord and annul the rule of the council and the gentlemen and assign all offices to the *popolo*."[41] The idea that the doge would make himself leader of the *popolo* was not farfetched. Six years after the conspiracy, the Ten condemned nobleman Jacopo Marango for accusing his fellow nobleman Pietro Giustinian of something similar. Marango exclaimed to Giustinian, "You want to make yourself head of the *popolo*."[42]

The Falier conspiracy reinvigorated the doge/*popolo* alliance that had been such a potent force in thirteenth-century politics when commoners found champions in the Tiepolo family. It occurred at a time when many cities throughout Italy were submitting to one-man rule. Genoa had recently surrendered itself to the Viscontis of Milan, and the Florentine Republic several times placed itself in the hands of a foreign lord. Closer to home were the Della Scalas of Verona, Carraras of Padua, and Estes of Ferrara. These examples likely fueled Falier's desire for lordship. Andrea Dandolo's efforts to elevate the dogeship, and such works of political theory as Fra Paolino's *De regimine rectoris* (On the Rule of the Rector), in which he argued that monarchy was the best form of government, pulled in the same direction. For their part, the *popolo* were unhappy with the sacrifices they were being asked to make in the war. Paduan chronicler Guglielmo Cortusi wrote that Falier wished to be lord and that he offered the *popolo* the possibility of peace with Genoa.[43] These elements coalesced into the perfect storm that was the Falier conspiracy. Had it succeeded, the coalition would likely have quickly sundered since Falier's aim of signorial rule was incompatible with the *popolo*'s ambition to create a popular regime. Ironically, the Falier conspiracy—named after the doge—was the closest Venice ever came to a popular rebellion against the patrician regime. Throughout the 1360s the *popolo* continued to express their displeasure with the government.[44]

The curious fate of Lorenzo Celsi, who ascended the ducal throne in July 1361, six years after Falier's death, offers further proof of the threat that the dogeship continued to pose.[45] An imperious man, Celsi died in July 1365 under what some took to be mysterious circumstances. The nearly simultaneous death of Grand Chancellor Benintendi de' Ravegnani, who at the time was involved in unauthorized negotiations with representatives of the king of Hungary, set off rumors of poisoning. Fueling the speculation were serious accusations made against Celsi that the Ten suppressed after his death. According to one report, Celsi went about preceded by a servant carrying a rod or scepter—something that was particularly inflammatory given Falier's desire to be the Lord of the Rod. A ducal councilor was so incensed by this that he broke the rod and denounced Celsi to the Ten. They ruled on July 30, 1365, that all the papers regarding the accusations against the doge be destroyed and the new doge, Marco Corner, publicly declare in the first meeting of the Greater Council that the rumors that Celsi had acted "against the honor of the commune of Venice" were calumnies.[46] However, corrections made to the ducal oath of office that Corner swore placed significant new limits on ducal power. Among other changes, the doge was forbidden to conduct negotiations or judge cases by himself, was required to keep his personal retainers lodged in the Ducal Palace, and was prohibited from spending more than 100 lire di piccoli on improvements or changes to the palace. The revised oath reiterated that the doge could be removed from office if the six ducal councilors and a majority in the Greater Council agreed and added that the doge could not renounce the dogeship without similar approval. Finally, and most important, the State Attorneys were enjoined to ensure that the doge did not overstep the limits outlined in his oath. The preamble to the decision stated that doges were "continuously" arrogating to themselves powers that violated the oath "to the detriment of the entire city."[47]

The accusations against Celsi, coming as they did so soon after the Falier conspiracy, may well have prompted the government to curb the power of future doges and warn them not to overstep their proper role. The government also made a further example of Falier. The ongoing decoration of the Greater Council Hall included a frieze of ducal portraits, along with the doges' coats of arms and mottos that characterized their reigns. On December 16, 1366, the Ten debated what to do about Falier's portrait. One proposal was that it should be repainted and that he should be shown decapitated with a caption stating that he had been executed for treason. The winning proposal recommended that Falier's portrait and coat of arms be blotted out with blue paint and the inscription "This is the place of Sir Marino Falier who was decapitated for the crime of treason" be painted in white in their stead."[48] Falier's erased portrait offered a salutary reminder to subsequent doges to respect their place in Venice's mixed governmental structure. The erection in 1364 of the inscribed marker at the location of Baiamonte Tiepolo's razed palace and Falier's mutilated portrait offer evidence of fraught domestic politics at midcentury.

Discontent with the regime was not confined to the metropole but extended throughout the empire as centrifugal forces pulled at the bonds between Venice and its dominions. Zara's many revolts against Venice are symptomatic, yet a graver threat came from a Cretan revolt in 1363–6.[49] Previous revolts there had primarily involved Greek nobles (*archontes*). This time was different, however, because it began with the Venetian colonists themselves. Cretans of both Greek and Latin descent and from all walks of life harbored grievances against the government, which they accused of exploiting the island for its own benefit. The capital made many demands of the colonists; they were required to lend military and financial support to

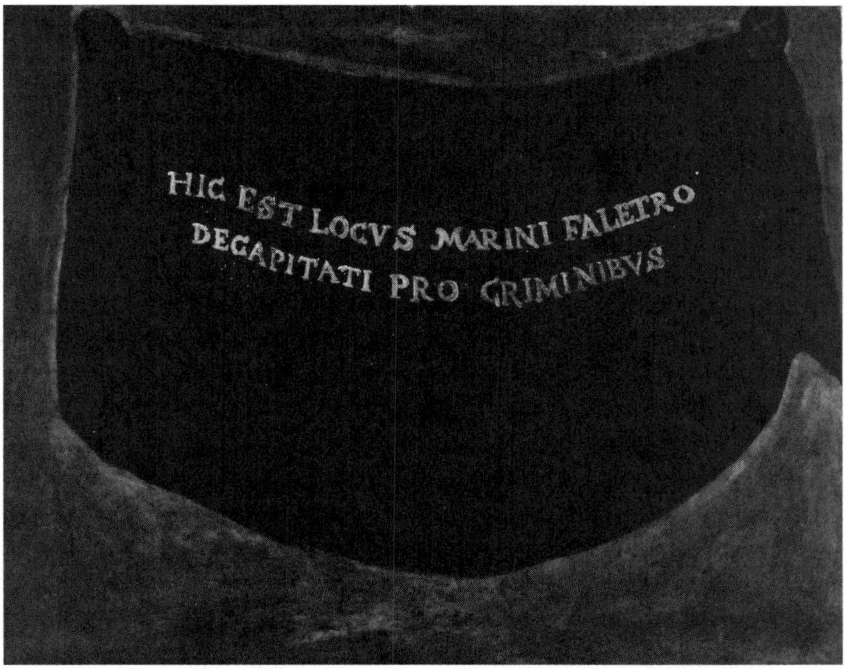

FIGURE 9.2 Domenico Tintoretto, Painted Drapery with Inscription where the portrait of Doge Marino Falier originally stood, late sixteenth century. Greater Council Hall, Ducal Palace, Venice. This version replaced the original, which was destroyed in a 1577 fire. © 2022 Archivio Fotografico—Fondazione Musei Civici di Venezia.

protect not just Crete but Venice's other far-flung possessions. Tight control of the island's substantial agricultural resources particularly rankled. Many feudatories felt excluded from the island's lucrative trade in favor of Venetian merchants and from positions of power in the Cretan government, which were held by administrators dispatched from Venice. At the other end of the social spectrum, peasants resented exploitation at the hands of their feudatory landlords. Religious differences between the locals who adhered to the Orthodox (Greek) faith and the colonists who were Roman Catholic (Latin) exacerbated the situation. Legally, people of Greek descent could be enslaved, while Latins could not. Further complicating matters were intermarriage and assimilation between Venetian feudatories and the *archontes*.

In June 1363 the Venetian Senate imposed new fiscal and military demands. New taxes that were three times more onerous than previous ones were to be partially spent on repairs to Candia's port and wharf. When the Candiote feudatories learned this, they protested, arguing that the improvements were designed primarily to benefit Venetian merchants. When the Duke of Candia, the chief Venetian official on the island, demanded they comply, seventy feudatories met at the Cathedral of Saint Titus to request that a contingent go to Venice to appeal the decision. The duke refused and again demanded they agree to the tax.

The following day a crowd consisting of feudatories, led by members of the Venier and Gradenigo families along with some members of the Cretan noble Kalergis family, townspeople of Candia, and others, attacked the ducal palace, deposed, and imprisoned Duke Leonardo Dandolo and his two councilors as well as other Venetian citizens. The rebellion quickly spread throughout the island. The Venetian rectors of Chania and Rethymno were taken prisoner. The rebels then appointed Marco Gradenigo "governor and rector" of the entire island and named four ducal councilors. In its first action, the new government expanded the religious liberty of the Greek church by lifting restrictions regarding ordination of Orthodox priests. Later in the month, they declared Saint Titus protector of the new government named for him, the Republic of Saint Titus. His standard replaced Saint Mark's and was to be flown on all Cretan ships.

The Venetian government at first tried to mediate, as did Pope Urban V who feared that the revolt would jeopardize a planned crusade to retake Jerusalem. But when mediation failed, the government prepared more forceful action. It placed governors in Negroponte, Coron, and Modon on alert lest the rebellion spread to those places. It also secured the neutrality of Genoa and the king of Cyprus, and exploited rivalries among the *archontes*, winning over opponents of the Kalergis. It then dispatched ten galleys to prevent outside support from reaching the rebels and recruited Veronese mercenary Luchino dal Verme to lead an invasion. Word of the Venetian counterattack led some rebel leaders to abandon the cause, while those who persisted took more radical action. One of the remaining rebels, Leonardo Gradenigo, a former monk from the Latin feudatory family, allied with Milletos, a Greek monk, who spearheaded an effort to murder Latin feudatories outside the capital. Milletos also inspired the peasantry to revolt. At this point the townspeople of Candia and the Latin rebels, fearing the peasants, turned on Milletos, who was tossed from the roof of the ducal palace and slain by the mob below. New divisions broke out in rebel ranks: some wanted to hand the island over to the Genoese, others to surrender to Venice. Leonardo Gradenigo and his followers imprisoned those ready to capitulate and sent a delegation to Genoa, which refused the offer of the island.

In April 1364 the Venetian reconquest began. Dal Verme quickly retook Candia. Marco Gradenigo, head of the rebel government, and two of his four councilors were captured and executed. The other principal towns on the northern coast were retaken as the remaining rebel leaders escaped into the mountainous interior. Other members of the Gradenigo and Venier families were banished from all Venetian lands. But rebellion in the countryside continued under the leadership of the Kalergis family, and the rebels managed to gain control of the western part of the island and make inroads to the east. During a series of campaigns overseen by commissioners, Venetian forces slowly pacified the entire island, gradually tracking down the remaining leaders. The reinstituted Venetian government rewarded those who had remained faithful, restored lands the rebels had expropriated, and exiled permanently some members of the rebel feudatory families. The position Captain of Crete became a permanent fixture of the restored government; he was responsible for protecting the island from external and internal threats and sat on the various governmental councils. Finally, the restored Venetian government instituted an annual procession in honor of Saint Titus to celebrate its triumph over the rebels. Both Latin and Greek clergy were required to participate in celebrating the Cretan saint who had for a time been the protector of the insurgents' regime.[50]

The Revolt of Saint Titus illustrates the difficulty that Venice had managing its most important colony. Settled on the island since the early thirteenth century, some of the oldest Latin feudatory families, many of whom had kinship ties to Greek archontic families, led the revolt. After several generations they had developed an identity that was as much Cretan as Venetian and so, at first in alliance with the townspeople of Candia and peasants, they revolted. The Revolt of Saint Titus highlights a problem that would plague Venice in both its overseas and its acquired mainland dominions—how to bind the inhabitants of those places to the Venetian state while simultaneously milking their lands' resources and denying them participation in the government.

Venetian exploitation of the eastern Mediterranean took many different forms.[51] While Crete was a state-sponsored colony, Cyprus presented a vastly different form of dominion. It was ruled by the French Lusignan family who had received the crown from Richard the Lionheart after he conquered it during the Third Crusade. The kings of Cyprus also laid claim to the extinct Kingdom of Jerusalem and constantly lobbied for renewed crusades to retake the Holy Land. The Venetians, however, were always reluctant crusaders, despite their native son Marino Sanudo the Elder's enthusiastic calls for a crusade at the beginning of the century. Crusades were bad for business.

Cyrus was strategically located and resource rich. Its plantations, largely worked by slave labor, produced sugar cane and cotton while Cypriot salt was prized for its quality. Following the fall of Acre and Tyre, the last Crusader towns, in 1291, Cyprus became an essential trading post and jumping off point for trade with the Levant. In 1366 Venice established the "cotton line"—state-owned galley service dealing exclusively in cotton from Cyprus, Syria, and Egypt. Other galleys were part of the "sugar line."[52] Rivalry with Genoa extended to Cyprus since the Genoese were even better established on the island than the Venetians. In 1374 King Peter II was forced to cede Famagusta to the Genoese, which led the Venetians to shift most of their business activities to Nicosia, although they retained a consul in Famagusta. In 1376 Cyprus ranked fifth behind Alexandria, Spain, Flanders, and Provence among Genoa's trading partners.[53]

The Venetian Corner family's stake in Cyprus was especially notable. Federico Corner, along with his brothers Fantino and Marco, received royal privileges to exploit salt pans and sugar cane plantations. By 1365 the brothers, along with Vito Lion, were operating a "mega-business"—a partnership with an operating capital of more than 83,000 ducats.[54] Cypriot king Peter I stayed as a guest at the Corner family palace in Venice in 1368. By that time, Federico had diversified into finance and loaned the visiting monarch 70,000 ducats. He also loaned 5,000 ducats per year for several years to Peter's widowed sister-in-law Maria de Bourbon and more than 10,000 ducats to the count of Savoy. It was probably in return for the loan to Peter that Fantino and Federico received the villages and adjoining sugar and cotton plantations of Episkopi and Pelendhrakia on the southern coast near Limassol. Federico was knighted by Peter and allowed to display the Lusignan coat of arms on his own emblem. This branch of the Corner family was subsequently known as the Corner-Piscopia after their principal Cypriot estate.[55]

With Fantino stationed in Episkopi and Federico in Venice, the brothers ruthlessly exploited their plantations, commandeering the waters of a nearby river to the detriment of neighboring property holders. The water irrigated the sugar cane fields and powered the mills that crushed the cane and produced the juice that was boiled and crystallized into sugar. The brothers contracted with a Venetian bellfounder to make two huge cauldrons that were sent to Cyprus for use in refining the sugar. The Corner family controlled all stages of the production process. Fantino died in 1372, and Federico's fortunes became more precarious. Genoese raids on Cyprus and the onerous tribute they imposed on the king made it uncertain whether Federico would ever be repaid the loan he had made to the Lusignan royal house, as he noted in his will dated 1378. To repay the loan, the king ceded to him for a time the entire salt production of Cyprus, including the right to ship it overseas. Federico retained his status as the wealthiest man in Venice, according to the *estimo* of 1379. The Cyprus connection brought great wealth and power to the Corners and indirectly to Venice.[56] Federico's son Pietro married Marie d'Enghien of the French house of Brienne, whose dowry included Argos and Nauplion (Nafplio) in the Morea. When Pietro died without heirs, the towns passed into Venetian governmental control—another example of the haphazard way by which Venice acquired its overseas dominions.

Venice's effort to gain yet another Greek possession—Tenedos in the Aegean Sea—was the spark that set off the fourth war with Genoa, known as the War of Chioggia. Tenedos's strategic location at the mouth of the Dardanelles made it much coveted since from that site it was possible to monitor and control maritime traffic to Constantinople and the Black Sea. Daniele di Chinazzo, a chronicler of the War of Chioggia, referred to it as the "mouth and the key to the Black Sea."[57] It was especially vital to Genoa's eastern Aegean shipping lanes.[58] Complicating the picture was the precarious state of the Byzantine empire and the advance of the Ottoman Turks. In Byzantium, Emperor John VI Cantacuzene and his son Matthew fought a civil war against John V Paleologus. John VI allied with Orchan, emir of the Ottoman Turks. The Ottoman emirate was just one of several Turkish principalities contending for power in western Anatolia. The Ottomans were able to occupy much of the old Byzantine province of Bithynia, a vital crossroads between Constantinople and Asia that bordered both the Bosphorus and the Black Sea. John VI married his daughter to Orchan, and the Ottomans assisted him in his successful efforts against John V in Thrace. After the victory, the Ottomans claimed and occupied Gallipoli on the European side of the Dardanelles. In the 1360s, Orchan's son Murad I captured Adrianople (Edirne) and transferred his court there from Asia Minor. This paved the way for the Ottoman conquest of southeastern Europe. Murad defeated the Serbs in 1371, opening Serbia, Macedonia, and Greece to attack, and he did so again at the battle of the Field of Blackbirds at Kosovo in 1389 where he lost his life.[59]

In 1354 John V forced John VI Cantacuzene into retirement. The status of the empire itself was so shaky that the Venetian *bailo* suggested that Venice should take it over before the Ottomans could do so. John V seemed at times to favor the Genoese; in 1355 he affirmed their possession of Chios. A sore point between him and the Venetians was the debt of 30,000 ducats plus interest that his mother Anne of Savoy had incurred in 1343 while acting as regent. The Venetians held the Byzantine crown jewels as surety for the loan but managed to get John to agree to a five-year treaty in 1357. John also appealed to the western powers for help against the Ottoman advance, alarming Venice which had recently restarted trading at Trebizond in the Black Sea. In 1362 the Venetians proposed a league consisting of themselves, Genoa, and Byzantium, but wanted Tenedos in return for 20,000 ducats and the crown jewels. John refused but did renew the treaty with Venice in 1363 for five years and did so again in 1370. A plan later that year to hand over Tenedos to the Venetians fell through. The victory of the Ottomans over the Serbs in 1371, combined with the lack of help from the West, forced John to become a vassal of Murad. When in 1376 the Venetian captain general of the sea, commander in chief of the navy, Marco Giustinian showed up in Constantinople with ten galleys, John not only agreed to renew yet again his treaty with Venice but also to hand over Tenedos in exchange for 30,000 ducats and the crown jewels. Before the Venetians could take possession of it, the Genoese of Pera and the Sultan Murad supported John's son Andronikos's rebellion against his father. John V was imprisoned. Andronikos gave Tenedos to the Genoese and returned Gallipoli to the Turks, who had lost it in 1366. But the residents of Tenedos repelled the Genoese, and Giustinian took possession of the island and appointed Donato Tron as governor. Andronikos retaliated by arresting the *bailo* of Constantinople, attacking Venetian residents, and confiscating their property, while the Genoese went after Venetian shipping. When Genoa protested Venice's occupation of Tenedos, the Venetians replied that it had been sanctioned by their favored claimant to the throne, John V, who was still imprisoned. When in November 1377 Andronikos and the Genoese attacked Tenedos, they were beaten back by Carlo Zeno, a former cleric turned adventurer, who oversaw the island's defense. War was formally declared between the two maritime powers. Support for rival contestants to the Byzantine throne was simply a proxy for the rivalry between Venice and Genoa to control trade in Constantinople and the Black Sea.

In the meantime, Venice had also been fighting against a much closer opponent—Francesco il Vecchio Carrara, lord of Padua. From the moment he took control in 1355, he pushed back against the informal protectorate that Venice had established over Padua starting in 1337 after it was secured from Veronese rule. Venice exercised its influence through an unbroken series of podestas, including Marino Falier. The Venetians even spoke of how the regime in Padua was "our own affair."[60] Francesco il Vecchio abandoned Padua's alliance to Venice, aiming to expand Paduan territory and influence in Friuli and with the patriarch of Aquileia. As a reward for Francesco's support in his attack on Venetian lands in 1356, Hungarian king Louis ceded Belluno and Feltre to him in 1360, thus giving him strategic control over important crossings on the Piave River. For much of the 1360s Venice's attention was diverted east by the revolt in Crete, the imperial rivalries in Constantinople, and the Ottoman expansion into Europe. Francesco used the opportunity to build forts on the frontiers between Venetian and Paduan possessions including those at Castelcarro on the Bacchiglione River near Chioggia. In spring 1372 a brief border war broke out between Padua and Venice. To gain the support of the dukes of Austria, Francesco ceded to them in early 1373 Feltre, Belluno, and the entire Valsugana, the Sugana Valley east of Trent. A major victory by Padua and its Hungarian allies in May was met by an even greater Venetian one in July that forced Francesco to terms. Although several of his possessions were guaranteed by the peace, he had to raze strongholds that he had built on the border, was forbidden to build forts within seven miles of the lagoon, had to pay 250,000 ducats in reparations to Venice, was forced to respect Venice's salt agreements with Padua, and, most humiliating of all, had to go to Venice and declare before the doge his responsibility for the recent war. Venice also prevailed upon Francesco in 1376 to join together to oppose the Duke of Austria's threats to Venetian territory in the Trevisano. In that same year, Louis, Francesco, and the patriarch of Aquileia formed a defensive alliance set to last fifty years. With it, Louis demonstrated his ongoing interest in northeastern Italy.[61]

Soon the eastern Mediterranean and northeastern Italian conflicts conjoined.[62] Shortly after war broke out between Venice and Genoa over Tenedos, Louis signed a treaty with Genoa targeted at Venice. Francesco il Vecchio, the dukes of Austria, the patriarch of Aquileia, and various Friulian prelates all joined the alliance, meaning that Venice was facing enemies on both land and sea. Louis's control of Dalmatia deprived Venice of manpower and other resources that it traditionally gleaned there; Genoa could rely on them instead. Venice countered by allying with Bernabò Visconti, lord of Milan, and Peter II of Cyprus, neither of whom would offer much assistance.

Although the conflict began over Tenedos, the theater of war quickly shifted west. In 1378 Vettor (Vittore) Pisani was named captain general of the sea. Pisani had been present at his uncle's defeat at Porto Longo during the Third Venetian-Genoese war but was acquitted of any responsibility for it. An experienced commander of merchant galleys and a veteran of Venice's quelling of the Cretan rebellion, Pisani was popular with rank-and-file seamen. In 1378 he took a fleet of fourteen galleys—its small size due to the manpower shortage caused by the plague—into the Tyrrhenian Sea where he won a victory at Capo d'Anzio over the Genoese and captured many prisoners. The government ordered him to spend the winter of 1378–9 at Pola in Istria. In May, he was surprised there by a Genoese fleet under Luciano Doria who lured Pisani into a battle that resulted in a disastrous loss. Pisani escaped with a handful of his ships, but many crewmen were killed or taken prisoner, including twenty-four nobles. Francesco il Vecchio da Carrara ordered a procession in Padua in thanksgiving for the victory. When Pisani arrived in Venice, he was tried by the Senate and Forty and convicted for having gone into battle unprepared and fleeing before it was decided. Although the latter charge carried the death penalty, he was sentenced to six months in jail and forbidden to hold any office for five years.[63] In the meantime, the government had dispatched Carlo Zeno with eleven galleys to harass Genoese shipping in the Ligurian Sea.

With Pisani in prison and Zeno off the Ligurian coast, the front door to Venice and the lagoon lay wide open to the Genoese. The back door was unlocked as well. Louis's Hungarian forces, with help from Padua, began a siege of Treviso and burned and sacked territories in the Trevisano, even threatening Mestre. After appearing at the mouth of San Nicolò, the Genoese fleet set about besieging and burning towns around the Gulf of Venice. Flames and smoke from towns burning on the Lido were visible in Venice. Finally, on August 16, 1379 the enemies began a coordinated attack on Chioggia. The Paduans, who had already captured Cavarzere and Loreo, advanced from the south while the Genoese prohibited reinforcements from Venice from reaching the town. The invaders overwhelmed the Venetian defenders, killing more than 850. The podesta of Chioggia Pietro Emo, the captain of the troops Taddeo Giustinian, and the governor of the fort Nicolò Contarini were all taken prisoner. The ensigns of Genoa, Padua, and Hungary were prominently displayed on major buildings throughout Chioggia. Besieged, surrounded, and running low on food and materiel, Venice offered to negotiate, but its envoys were met with the blunt reply, "Return to the Signoria and tell your government that we will not entertain your pleas until we have bridled the horses that stand above San Marco."[64] However, the Genoese offended their Paduan allies by offering to sell Chioggia and its salt works to them for an exorbitant 200,000 ducats. Miffed at the insult, Francesco il Vecchio returned to Padua, taking many of his soldiers with him.

On the ropes, the Venetians somehow found the will to resist. An effort by the Genoese to cross from Chioggia and proceed up the Lido was repelled. Nobles especially rallied to the cause. The ducal councilors each agreed to pay for the outfitting of a galley. The government ordered old cogs and chains be used to block the port of San Nicolò, while forts and stockades were built at strategic locations. Venice enlisted mercenaries to try to break the blockade along mainland roads. Funds were raised through forced loans, and a promise was made to admit to the Greater Council the thirty non-nobles who offered the most money to support the war effort. Orders were given for the civic militia, the *duodena*, to be mobilized. But at this point, old social resentments, like those that had erupted at the time of the Falier conspiracy, came to the fore. Many of the *popolo* refused to report for the galleys or serve under Taddeo Contarini, the captain general. They resented the imprisonment of their hero, Vettor Pisani. As chronicler Daniele di Chinazzo noted, they regarded Pisani as the "chief and father of all the seamen of Venice."[65] Feeling the weight of popular pressure, the government released Pisani. A jubilant crowd greeted him with cries of "Viva Mister Vettor." He admonished them, saying "Be quiet, boys," encouraging them to exclaim instead, "Long live the good Evangelist Mister Saint Mark."[66] Galley enrollment boomed, enough for thirty-four ships. Doge Andrea Contarini personally supervised drills that helped prepare the craftsmen and shopkeepers who had been drafted into service. The doge was named captain general, with Pisani as his right-hand man. Venice's efforts to get its lukewarm ally Milan to attack Genoa from the east languished, although Visconti did agree to close Genoa's reinforcement route to Chioggia through Lombardy.

The plan the Venetians hatched was to besiege Chioggia by cutting it off from support from both land and sea. To accomplish this, in late December 1379 the Venetians set about blocking the deep-water channels that were Chioggia's lifeline with sunken barges and round ships. Knowledge of the topography of the lagoon and skill with small watercraft that could navigate the shallows allowed the Venetians to rebuff Genoese efforts to reopen those channels. Perhaps, as Pisani hoped, Saint Mark had heard the seamen's accolades since on January 1, 1380, Carlo Zeno returned with fourteen galleys. His harassment of Genoese shipping had taken him all over the Mediterranean. He was quickly deployed to Loreo, which he recaptured. This opened an important route for grain and military supplies, especially saltpeter for gunpowder, to be shipped from Lombardy via the Po and Adige rivers to Chioggia. Regina della Scala, wife of Bernabò Visconti, facilitated this opening, motivated as she was by Scaligeri hatred of the Carraras. The arrival in April of a Genoese fleet off Chioggia caused consternation. But Zeno and Pisani refused to engage it, keeping the focus on now-desperate Chioggia where the beleaguered Paduan and Genoese forces were reduced to eating horses, dogs, cats, even rats. On June 24, 1380, Chioggia finally succumbed. Nineteen Genoese galleys fell into Venetian hands as the 4,000 Genoese defenders surrendered.

Venice spent the balance of the summer and fall clearing the Adriatic, while for their part, the Genoese helped the patriarch of Aquileia capture Trieste and continued to hassle Venetian shipping along the Istrian coast. On August 13, Pisani, who had finally been made captain general, died of exhaustion following the Istrian campaign. His entrails were interred in Manfredonia in Apulia where he died; the rest of his body was salted and sealed in a casket to be transported to Venice for burial in the church of Sant'Antonio. Pisani was succeeded as captain general by Zeno. On the mainland, Carrara continued to besiege Treviso. To prevent Treviso from falling to Padua, Venice agreed to hand it over to the Duke of Austria. With that accomplished, peace negotiations began in earnest. They were overseen by the count of Savoy Amadeus VI, who pushed for them since he was worried about Milanese aggression on his eastern border and by the generally unbalanced state of north Italian affairs.

The Peace of Turin was signed on August 8, 1381.[67] Regarding Tenedos, the immediate cause of the war, Venice agreed to consign it within fifty days to Amadeus, who was to oversee the destruction of all forts, walls, and houses on the island, "in such fashion that the place can never be rebuilt or reinhabited."[68] Genoa would foot the bill for the demolition. The island's 4,000 native Greek inhabitants had no voice in the matter but were to be compensated for their losses.

They were eventually relocated to Negroponte and Crete. The goal was to remove Tenedos as a point of contention between the two maritime powers. To that end, both parties also agreed to abstain from trade at Tana for two years. Genoa's special status on Cyprus was affirmed; Famagusta remained their hub for Levantine trade. The Corners' Cypriot properties went unmentioned in the treaty. The treaty affirmed Louis of Hungary's legal claim to Dalmatia and required Venice to pay him an annual indemnity of 7,000 ducats as compensation for the staple rights that it continued to enjoy over the northern Adriatic. Venice insisted that Treviso be ceded to the Duke of Austria rather than Padua, although it agreed that if Carrara gained Belluno, Feltre, and sites on the Piave in the future, he could hold them. He was allowed to keep his forts at Oriago and Castrocarro but had to relinquish

Cavarzere and Moranzane. And he had to pay Venice an indemnity of 50,000 ducats. Regarding the claims of the patriarch of Aquileia, Venice renounced its dominion over Trieste but continued to enjoy exemption from customs duties there. The two parties would refer their disputes over Istria to the pope.

No one except Louis of Hungary could claim much of a victory. Venice had lost Tenedos and Treviso, its first significant Italian mainland possession. Genoa had profited little as well. The stage might have been set for yet another war between the maritime powers except that Genoa rapidly descended into even greater internal civil strife and suffered more than Venice from the decline in Black Sea trade, although its trade in slaves, especially to the Mamluks, remained strong.[69] It would increasingly look to the western Mediterranean, while Venice concentrated on trade with Egypt and the Balkans. In the run up to the war, the Byzantine Empire had been weakened by the struggles of its rival claimants to the throne while the Ottoman Turks grew stronger. During debates about the resettlement of Tenedos's Greek inhabitants, Doge Antonio Venier himself argued that the uninhabited and unguarded island would be ripe for picking by the Turks. Then they would control the Dardanelles. The balance of power in the eastern Mediterranean was shifting rapidly.

The War of Chioggia impacted all aspects of life, but the economic dislocation was especially pronounced. As during the Third Venetian-Genoese war, trade was suspended. So governmental revenue fell dramatically at the very moment that expenses, especially to pay mercenaries, rose dramatically. Noting the "large and many expenses" burdening the government, in April 1379 the Senate ordered the suspension of salaries for noble officeholders and required them to retain only half the emoluments that went with their offices.[70] Non-noble employees had to forfeit half their stipend and emoluments. This created a hardship for poorer nobles and *popolano* bureaucrats who depended on the income the offices afforded them.

To fund the war, the government again relied on forced loans, though this time the sum needed was truly staggering. In 1379, at the beginning of the war the total funded debt was approximately 8,500,000 lire a grossi. That was already a huge increase over the 3,700,000 lire at which it had stood in 1363 at the time of the rebellion in Crete. Yet by 1381 the total had jumped to 12,300,000 lire (around 4,730,000 ducats).[71] Between 1378 and 1381 those who were liable for forced loans had to lend 41 percent of their assessed patrimony. Considering various exemptions, this amounted to approximately one-quarter of their actual patrimony or total wealth.[72] Since many were unable to bear the burden, at one point in 1380 the government allowed one-third of those liable for forced loans to pay just 40 percent of the imposed levies, but in return they had to forfeit a claim to interest-bearing shares or repayment of what they had paid. In effect they were paying a direct tax rather than making a loan. Doge Andrea Contarini was described as "in the greatest extreme in terms of money."[73]

To make matters worse, the value of outstanding debt shares plummeted. By 1379 they stood at just 18 percent of par. And after September 1379 the government was forced to suspend interest payments temporarily. In Venice, the agent of Ludovico Gonzaga, lord of Mantua, described the situation to him this way: "Everyone complains of the impositions which are too great, but they are even more burdened because they are used to making money [from the public debt] not to being weighed down by it."[74] The situation was so grave that some questioned whether the system could survive. In his 1380 will, physician Andrea de Alemanis wrote that if the loan office returned to "its pristine and usual state as it was in peacetime," then he wanted his assets to be sold and the money invested in debt shares. However, "if the loan office is not and does not stand as usual . . . then I want [the money to be used] to purchase properties in or outside Venice."[75] Better to invest in real estate than in increasingly worthless bonds.

The amount of money demanded was so large that many defaulted. In early April 1381 a council of experts assisting with the war effort ordered the names of those who had failed to make the most recent loan of 3 percent be referred to the State Attorneys and the Cazudi (Ital. Caduti [the Fallen]), the officials responsible for tax insolvents, who would then sell off their property. They also recommended that the names of delinquents be read in a session of the Greater Council so that the council's business could be conducted, "with equality."[76] The intent was clear. Knowledge of those who failed in their responsibility to the state should be taken into consideration when the council held elections.

It was not just those who barely qualified for forced loans who found themselves in difficult straits. The wealthy were affected as well. The war considerably impacted Federico Corner, Venice's richest man at the war's start. He was still owed 70,000 ducats by the king of Cyprus, and he himself owed 6,000 ducats to Nicolò II Este, marquess of Ferrara. When Corner died in 1382, his estate was so short of cash that his executors could not pay his outstanding debts or fulfill his bequests, including one for the construction of a chapel in the Frari to house tombs for himself and his brother Marco. The Estes were granted the Corner palace in San Luca as compensation for the money Federico owed them. The palace eventually passed to Taddea d'Este and her husband Francesco Novello da Carrara before being repurchased by the Corner family in 1404.[77]

The Estes did not inhabit the palace since they used another property that the Venetian government had given them as their Venetian residence. It too had changed hands because of the war. In 1309 the palace, later used as the Fondaco dei Turchi, was owned by nobleman Angelo da Pesaro. When his four great-grandsons were unable to pay their forced loans, they were compelled to sell the palace in February 1381 by the Supervisors of War Finances for 10,000 ducats. The government then awarded the palace to Nicolò d'Este who as early as 1364 had been maneuvering for a Venetian residence. The government rewarded him for his loyalty to Venice during the war.[78]

The loss to the Pesaros and Corners of their family palaces exemplifies the social dislocation caused by the war. When Nicolò de Garzoni wanted to buy a property that the Cazudi were selling to cover the forced loans for which his brothers were liable, the Senate noted that Nicolò wished to buy it "for his honor and that of his house and in order that [the property] not fall into the hands of extraneous persons."[79] The war was undoing generations of established neighborhood relationships. The situation was far worse for families whose menfolk died in the war, were injured, or had been taken prisoner since they were both mourning and deprived of income earners. Deserters presented yet another problem. In September 1381 the Greater Council railed against those who "in prosperous times enjoy the benefits of our city and in times of adversity flee."[80] Those who had done so were to be denied the commercial privileges that came with Venetian citizenship. If any of the deserters tried to exercise those privileges, their merchandise was to be treated as contraband. And as it frequently did, the government rewarded residents who had shown special loyalty to the regime.[81]

In the war's aftermath, Venice needed to stimulate the economy and rebuild the population. In 1382 it offered incentives for artisans to establish themselves in the city. It again loosened the requirements for attaining naturalized citizenship, offering *de intus* status after eight years and *de extra* after fifteen. It even made a provision, valid for a year, that foreigners who had lived in Venice during the war, paid all the imposts, and could prove that they had done so could enjoy the privileges of citizenship immediately.[82] It also decided to allow foreigners to purchase property in the city as well as shares of the government debt up to the value of the real estate they had bought. They could even invest an amount equal to the property and bond shares they had purchased in overseas commerce like native Venetians. The goal was to bolster the value of real estate and bonds, both of which had decreased because of the war. Protectionist tendencies again yielded to the need to spur economic recovery.[83]

For the first time in its history, Venice allowed Jews to reside in the city. The shortage of capital meant that nobles were having difficulty paying their debts, merchants did not have the resources with which to trade, and the poor could not secure the small loans that tided them over in hard times. When loans could be secured, interest rates were exorbitant. To alleviate the shortage of money, the government decided in February 1382 to allow anyone, whether Venetian or foreigner, to lend money at a maximum rate of 10 percent interest on pawns and 12 percent on promissory notes. Although the law did not explicitly mention Jews, they overwhelmingly took advantage of the opportunity. Jewish moneylenders were already well established on mainland Italy, including at Mestre. In November 1385 this privilege, now mentioning the Jews, was extended for two more years. But when it came up for renewal again in 1387, the government insisted that the Jews as a group either pay 4,000 ducats annually in tax or lend at lower rates (8 percent on pledges, 10 percent on notes). The Jews chose the latter option, but when it turned out that they were not making many low-interest loans on pledges, the government compelled them in 1388 to honor all requests for loans of 30 ducats or less. Then in 1394, with the money shortage easing, the government ordered the Jews to leave Venice when their *condotta* (contract) ended in 1397. Several Jewish lenders again settled in Mestre. Thereafter they were not permitted in Venice for more than fifteen days at a time. When they did visit, they had to wear a yellow circle on their clothing identifying them as Jews. Thus, for a short time between 1382 and 1397 Jews resided in Venice, although not without incidents. In 1389 they requested that a fence be built around their cemetery on the Lido to protect it from vandalism. Only in the sixteenth century would they be allowed to settle permanently in the city.[84]

The most significant social change was the admission of thirty new men (and their heirs) to the patriciate. In December 1379, during the height of the war, the government had promised that at the end of the conflict thirty non-nobles who had been especially generous and prompt in aiding the war effort would be rewarded with admission to the Greater Council. Many non-nobles assisted in a variety of ways, including paying for oarsmen and bowmen for the galleys, offering their private ships for governmental use, and making voluntary cash and bond contributions. At war's end, the Senate voted in September 1381 on the candidacy of sixty-two men from fifty-eight different families. In some cases, preexisting ties to important noble families were more important than the monetary value of war contributions in determining the winners. Eleven of the thirty successful candidates bore the same last names as patricians. It is likely that they were the illegitimate sons of nobles or members of branches of noble families that had failed to register properly for membership in the Greater Council, perhaps because they were resident in Venice's overseas colonies, especially Crete.[85] Others had worked closely with the government. Grand Chancellor Rafaino de Caresini, who contributed about 500 ducats to the war effort, was among the victors. Other winners included men whose families had immigrated to Venice earlier in the century. A silk merchant who had come to Venice from Lucca, Bandino Garzoni, was naturalized and one of the four richest men in the city. He had married two of his daughters into different branches of the prestigious Morosini family. Bandino died before the election, but two of his sons, Giovanni and Nicolò, gained admission. So did Bartolomeo Paruta, son of immigrants from another Lucchese family.[86] Some of the inductees brought an infusion of capital into a patriciate that had suffered immensely during the war.

The 1381 induction was the last wholesale admission of new men to the patriciate until the mid-seventeenth century. Although its primary purpose was to prompt generous acts of patriotism at a particularly dark moment, it should also be seen in the context of the ongoing popular unrest with the regime, demonstrated most recently by *popolano* support for Vettor Pisani. By peeling off a portion of the well-to-do non-nobles, the nobles effectively reduced the strength of non-noble resistance by coopting potential leaders for the aspiring *popolo*. Additionally, since no one could have known that it would be the last mass admission for centuries, the logical response for non-nobles was to toe the line and hope they would be lucky when the patriciate next opened its ranks. The patricians once again pursued a policy of divide and conquer.

It is unclear what groups within the patriciate advocated most strongly for these new men. It may have been the oldest and most distinguished families, referred to either as the *longhi* (long) clans or *case vecchie* (old houses), who had ruled Venice for centuries.[87] They may have thought that the newly minted patricians would be so awed by their family histories and social prestige that they would easily bend to their wishes. By contrast, members of marginal patrician families, those with few adult males in the Council and extremely modest means, may have feared the competition for remunerative offices that the new members represented. The economic ruination and social disruption caused by the war had heightened noble demand for offices and the accompanying salaries.

The war even accelerated the redefinition of what it meant to be noble. The process began in the 1360s and would only conclude in the 1430s. It moved along two parallel tracks. The first involved an increasingly rigid application of the rules for establishing one's legal right to sit in the Greater Council and the benefits that derived from it. In 1367, for example, a law was passed that offices were not to be awarded by *grazia*, favors, but only through election. It was designed to lessen the ability of the most powerful patricians, particularly members of the *case vecchie*, to exercise patronage by rewarding their friends and clients and instead to benefit minor nobles who depended on regular electoral procedures to garner jobs. Another decision of 1370 was intended to prevent minors from sitting in the Greater Council by requiring a check of their credentials. The second track emphasized the social purity of the nobility. In 1376 it was decided that illegitimate sons of nobles could not sit in the Council even if their parents subsequently married. The legislation was aimed particularly at liaisons between noblemen and women of "debilitating or vile status." Nobility no longer depended "only on the status of father, but also the circumstances of the birth."[88] This decision was most likely promoted by the lesser nobles who were disturbed by intermarriage between old distinguished houses like the Morosinis and upstarts like the Garzonis. The cooptation of thirty new families in 1381 thus heightened concern with social status just as it intensified competition for jobs.

The old idea of nobility based on social prestige and antiquity of service to Venice was giving way to a juridical definition regarding who had a right to sit in the Greater Council and thus access to governmental perquisites. The ruling class was changing "from a simple governing nobility rooted in history into a privileged patriciate."[89] At the same time a quiet political revolution was taking place that ended the *case vecchie*'s centuries-long monopoly of the dogeship. In 1382 Antonio Venier was elected doge. The Veniers were members of what were called the *curti* (short) clans or *case nuove* (new houses). The other were the Barbarigos, Donàs, Foscaris, Grimanis, Grittis, Landos, Loredans, Malipieros, Marcellos, Mocenigos, Moros, Priulis, Trevisans, Trons, and Vendramins.[90] Starting in 1382, these families, along with one or two others, controlled the dogeship until 1612. The reasons for this seismic shift remain obscure although it seems likely that the *case nuove* and the lesser nobles resented the haughtiness of the *case vecchie* and the policies that had led to so many crises. Accordingly, they denied them the city's highest office.

Certainly, the War of Chioggia started a policy debate that would consume Venetian politics for the next forty years. During the war, the attack on the city from both the mainland and the sea had exposed Venice's vulnerability to a two-sided assault. But how the Venetians should respond was unclear. One group advocated a continuation of Venice's long-standing policy of economic domination but political detachment from mainland affairs. For them, the conquest of Treviso and its territories was an aberration. Venice should look instead to its maritime empire, traditional source of its wealth and prestige. Grand Chancellor, chronicler, and newly minted patrician Rafaino de Caresini was a proponent of this view. In his opinion, the sea was the source of Venice's "honors and riches," while only "scandals and mistakes" derived from the mainland.[91] Others believed the only way for Venice to protect itself was to assume direct control of the nearby *terraferma*. In 1388 Venice did retake Treviso. However, in the 1380s and 1390s it also acquired Corfu and Durazzo in the lower Adriatic to compensate for the loss of Dalmatia, as well as more Aegean outposts.[92] The issue of Venice's future sphere of influence remained unresolved.

The city that emerged at the end of the War of Chioggia was much changed. Emblematic was the abolition of the Festival of the Marys, the long-standing celebration with its twelve wooden statues and water processions. During the war the government had suspended the festival as a cost-saving measure, but it was never revived and was instead replaced by a simple ducal procession to Santa Maria Formosa.

The Festival of the Marys had celebrated and embodied an earlier Venice—one comprising many small islets in which a few noble and rich non-noble families served as patrons of their local communities as they outfitted the statues and offered dowries to deserving brides. The festival's processional routes through the city served to bind these local communities together. As Venice became more densely settled and as streets and bridges knitted the city ever more tightly together, parishes lost their sense of community. Inhabitants started to look to city-wide institutions such as the *scuole grandi* and mendicant friaries for their spiritual and social support, and noble males turned increasingly to the central government to exercise influence and patronage activities. The processional shift after the suppression of the festival highlighted this change. It focused on San Marco, the governmental center, and Santa Maria Formosa rather than on a circuit of the city. As this change and the tightening definition of noble status make clear, Venetian society was becoming increasingly centralized and hierarchical, and less communitarian.

The old bonds that had held Venice together were dissolving and being replaced by new ones.[93] The War of Chioggia marks the end of the Venetian Middle Ages, the period when the city was established, its republican governmental form worked out, and its overseas empire acquired. A new amalgam was being forged, and a new period in the city's history—the Renaissance—was taking shape.

PART II

Renaissance Venice

10

The Early Renaissance and the Turn Toward Italy

IN 1423 THE musician Cristoforo de Monte composed a motet celebrating Francesco Foscari's installation as doge in April that year. The text reads,

> Applaud o jewel of the world, o famous crowd of Venice, since, with the accustomed sacred lot, you have made the high doge Italy's star, to whom Jupiter himself, flowering Venus, and sweet Minerva give great gifts; and so that for you the prince would shine from great Olympus, Mercury gave him strength and fostering grace to the people.
>
> Nor should you rejoice less, eminent house of Foscari, since now you shine, Francesco having been made prince. Happy are the countries that the city of the Venetians governs.
>
> Applaud, for a just and pious doge has come to the people, in fourteen hundred and twenty-three *anno domini*, when the sun had been thrice five times through the heavens and was shining upon the horns of the strong bull.[1]

Foscari has often been viewed as the chief proponent of the most important foreign policy change the Venetian Republic ever made: its decision to acquire a large territorial state on the Italian mainland. In a well-known speech Foscari's predecessor purportedly gave on his death-bed, Doge Tommaso Mocenigo cautioned his fellow patricians against electing Foscari as his successor, warning that his advocacy of an aggressive policy of *terraferma* expansion would jeopardize the Venetians' prosperity and reputation and render them "vassals to soldiers," echoing Rafaino de Caresini's earlier admonition that mainland involvement promised nothing but vexation.[2] Although reworked in later decades, the speech, along with two others supposedly delivered by Mocenigo, captures the debate about Venice's future that consumed these years as well as the changes—military, political, economic, and cultural—that the mainland acquisitions brought in their wake.

The second part of de Monte's work offers a reminder of the central place of the family in Venetian politics. According to the composer, Foscari's kin could rejoice in the glory that accrued to them with his election as doge. The third decade of the fifteenth century would witness a further refinement of what it meant to be a noble, with special emphasis placed on the status of noble women. Indeed, noble wives who straddled patrilines—they left their fathers' houses to join their husbands' clans—came to play an important, if unofficial, role in Venetian politics, binding the patriciate together and counterbalancing the forces that threatened to pull it asunder. The tension between familial and individual self-promotion and the common interests of the patriciate remained a constant in Venetian politics. Indeed, the inability of Doge Foscari to disentangle his ducal obligations from his paternal ones would lead in 1457 to one of the most serious constitutional crises in the Republic's history.

Finally, de Monte's references to the Olympian gods reflect the growing importance that classical antiquity came to play in the Venetians' representation of themselves. Byzantium had long been the touchstone of Venetian cultural aspirations, but as the new overlords of mainland towns with distinct and visible Roman pasts and of domains that extended across land and sea, the Venetians had to reimagine their empire. The best model for this was Imperial Rome. Venetian humanists used their knowledge of classical texts to shape an ideology that met the needs of the Venetian ruling class. In architecture and the figurative arts, by contrast, the turn to the West was much more gradual. The Venetians were slow to adopt the classical idiom in building and continued to favor their local Gothic style both in public projects like the expansion of the Ducal Palace and private palaces like Marino Contarini's celebrated Ca' d'Oro (House of Gold). When commissioning paintings, Venetians favored artists like Jacobello del Fiore who worked in the International Gothic idiom. In Venetian minds, localism and cosmopolitanism tussled.

Although Venice had survived the War of Chioggia, it remained vulnerable on both its mainland and maritime fronts. While the danger posed by Byzantine weakness and growing Ottoman Turkish power represented a greater menace in the long run to Venetian prosperity, at the turn of the fifteenth century the more immediate challenge emanated from the mainland and involved Venice's recent enemies, the king of Hungary and the Carraras of Padua. Francesco il Vecchio Carrara continued to be a particularly bothersome thorn in Venice's side. In 1384 he wrested Treviso along with other towns from the Duke of Austria and had designs on Friuli to his east and Verona, under the Scaligeri, to his west. He found an ally in Giangaleazzo Visconti, lord of Milan. They agreed to divide up the Della Scala lands: Visconti would get Verona, and Carrara would have Vicenza. But Visconti took it all for himself and then allied with Venice against Carrara. Francesco il Vecchio was forced to resign in favor of his son Francesco Novello, who in turn had to surrender Padua to Visconti in November 1388 while Venice reclaimed Treviso. But a powerful anti-Visconti coalition allowed Francesco Novello to reestablish Carrara rule in Padua in 1390. Undaunted, he aspired to be more than a mere Venetian satellite.[3]

In March 1400 Venice renewed its peace treaty with Visconti, who was cobbling together a large state that, in addition to towns in Lombardy and the Veneto, included Tuscan cities such as Siena and Pisa, and Perugia in Umbria, effectively encircling Florence. Then Visconti set his sights on Bologna and Padua. He captured Bologna in July 1402, and his forces were attempting to dam the Brenta at Bassano to choke off trade to Padua. Visconti's unexpected death from a fever in September averted the danger. His widow Caterina became regent for her two sons, Giovanni Maria and Filippo Maria.[4]

By the next spring, a new anti-Visconti alliance emboldened Francesco Novello's aspiration to create a state that would run from the Mincio River west of Verona to the edge of the lagoon. In league with Ferrara and Florence, he declared war on Milan in August 1403, while Venice pushed for peace with Milan. On April 8, 1404, Carrara's troops captured Verona and then headed toward Vicenza. But hatred of the Carraras prompted the Vicentines to hand their city over to Venice on April 25, the feast of Saint Mark. For her part, Caterina Visconti ceded to the Venetians Bassano on the Brenta and Belluno and Feltre on the Piave. On June 25 Venice declared war on Padua and ordered its commander at Rovigo to undermine dikes on the Adige River to inundate the southern Padovano. In December it offered bounties for the capture of Francesco Novello and his sons and by March 1405 had made a separate peace with Carrara's ally Nicolò III d'Este, Marquess of Ferrara. Venice's brutal policy toward Verona resulted in that city's surrender in June. Out of options, Francesco Novello offered to sell Padua to Venice but was met with calls for unconditional surrender. As the Venetian grip tightened, ambassadors from Padua surrendered the city in November. Francesco Novello and his sons were taken as prisoners to Venice.[5] Since they had previously been accorded honorary membership in the Greater Council, the Council of Ten tried them as Venetian citizens and condemned them to death as traitors. Francesco Novello's plea to his confessor—"Why do I have to die? Isn't it bad enough that you've taken my lordship and my lands?"—fell on deaf ears.[6] He was beaten and strangled in his cell in the Ducal Palace; his sons were executed the following day.

Venice had taken to heart the lessons learned in the War of Chioggia—its strategic trade routes and access to northern markets were vulnerable to disruption, and its old policy of relying on satellite signorial regimes was no longer adequate to meet the threat posed by the territorial consolidation that was leading to the creation of a few large states on the Italian peninsula. Economic intimidation had worked well when small city-states such as Padua and Ferrara controlled only discrete stretches of strategic rivers, because alternative trade routes could be exploited. But the prospect of a large, unified state bordering the lagoon changed all that. Venice had to secure its control of the rivers that carried goods north and west and moved silt and debris south and east to the lagoon. The lagoon was increasingly in danger of silting up, potentially dooming Venice to the same fate that had befallen Spina, Adria, and Ravenna in the early Middle Ages. Controlling the hinterland would allow Venice to change, if necessary, the course of the rivers. Saint Mark's lion stepped onto the mainland in reaction to new political realities and environmental concerns. Within a few short years it found itself possessing a dominion that extended from the Mincio in the west, almost to the Po in the south, and included major towns such as Padua, Vicenza, and Verona.[7] Like the acquisition of the overseas territories following the Fourth Crusade, the turn to the mainland was not a premeditated move but a make-shift reaction to Francesco Novello's provocations. However, it also meant that there were no longer any minor states to serve as buffers between Venice and Milan.

The War of Chioggia had not resolved the danger posed by the Kingdom of Hungary in Friuli and Dalmatia. In 1409 Ladislaus of Naples renounced his claims to Dalmatia and ceded Zara to Venice in return for 100,000 ducats. This set Venice on a collision course with Sigismund, king of Hungary, who became king of the Romans and hence Holy Roman emperor-elect in 1410. He had a powerful ally in the patriarch of Aquileia. In autumn 1411 the Hungarians invaded Friuli. A Venetian counterattack the following year was only partially successful. A renewed Ottoman threat in the Danube region,

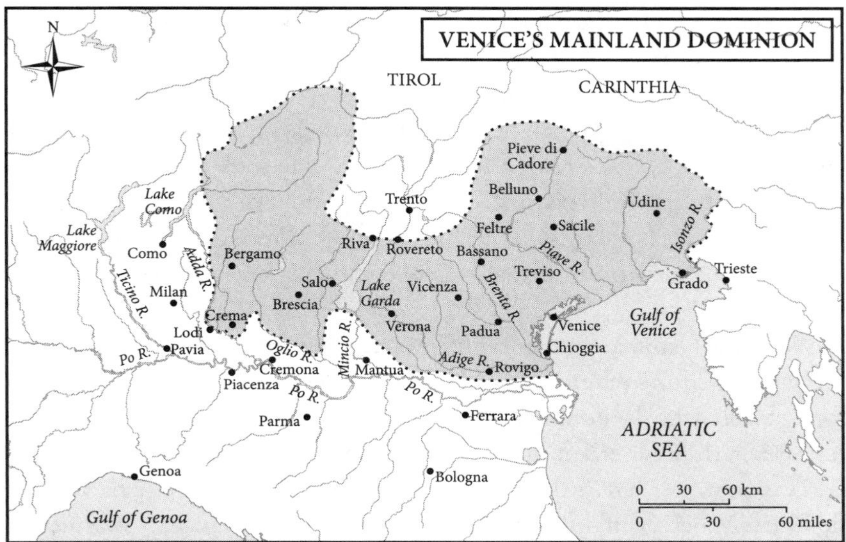

FIGURE 10.1 Venice's Mainland Dominion

schism within the Catholic Church involving rival claimants to the papal throne, and the heretical movement led by John Hus in Bohemia forced Sigismund to agree to a five-year peace in 1413 by which Venice relinquished Feltre and Belluno.[8]

Nevertheless, Sigismund remained a worry. In 1418 the Venetians took Rovereto, a strategically important town on the Adige, in order to protect Veronese territory from a possible imperial invasion. Then in 1419 Sigismund's forces again invaded Friuli. But with Sigismund still distracted by the Hussites, the war went dramatically in Venice's favor as Sacile, Cividale, Prata, Portogruaro, Belluno, Feltre, Udine, Cadore, and Aquileia fell under its control. From there, Venice extended its conquest to Istria and down the Dalmatian and Albanian coasts. Venetian forces under captain of the Gulf Pietro Loredan took possession of the islands Brazza, Lesina, and Curzola and various towns including Traù, Spalato, Cattaro, and Dulcigno (Ulcinj). The patriarch of Aquileia was forced to recognize the loss of Friuli in return for an annual tribute and retention of a few small possessions including San Vito, San Daniele, and Aquileia itself.[9]

In the eastern Mediterranean, the Venetians had also managed to gain significant victories over the Ottomans. In a treaty signed in 1411 between the Republic and Musa, a contender for the sultanate, the Ottomans had agreed not to send warships south or west of Tenedos. However, the new sultan Mehmed I resumed raids on Venetian interests including Negroponte. When in May 1416 a fleet under Pietro Loredan entered the Dardanelles, the Ottomans attacked it near Gallipoli. Loredan scored a stunning victory. In a long letter to the Signoria, he recounted how his troops battled valiantly against the Turks "who fought like dragons."[10] He took special pleasure in executing Giorgio Kalergis, one of the protagonists of the Cretan revolt. It was his "greatest honor" to have had Kalergis "cut to pieces on the poop of my galley."[11] A new treaty signed in 1419 essentially renewed the terms of the 1411 pact.

With the Ottomans temporarily thwarted by their defeat at Gallipoli and Sigismund's efforts rebuffed, it appeared that Venice had finally achieved its foreign policy goals: dominance of the Adriatic, protection of trade routes in the eastern Mediterranean, and establishment of a *terraferma* buffer zone. By 1420, however, a new threat was looming on the horizon, one that would dominate Venetian affairs for the next century, namely, Venice's powerful and restless western neighbor, the Duchy of Milan. As one historian has noted, "If the fourteenth century was the century of conflict with Genoa, in the fifteenth, the contest was with the Lombards" (i.e., Milan).[12]

In the meantime, Venice had to decide how to administer its new *terraferma* dominion. Its treatment of Vicenza, which hyperbolically if inaccurately proclaimed itself the "firstborn of Venice," that is, the first to come under Venetian rule, is illustrative. Long subject to neighboring cities and lords (Padua, the Della Scalas of Verona, and then the Viscontis), Vicenza was governed by a podesta and captain, a Council of Five Hundred, and smaller councils like the eight deputies. According to the articles of submission, Venice assumed full power over Vicenza, but the Vicentine magistracies and councils were retained, and local prerogatives and municipal statutes remained in force. Venice allowed justice in Vicenza to continue to be determined by the *ius commune* or Roman civil law. Venice did dispatch two rectors to administer Vicenza (one as podesta with civil authority, the other as captain in charge of defense), along with a rudimentary staff including a chancellor, chamberlain, and a few others; but local administrators far outnumbered the Venetians, and the two sets of officials often worked in tandem. The municipal councils continued to legislate and elect local officials, and Vicentines continued to monopolize the College of Notaries and shape legal discourse according to local traditions. However, the creation in 1410 of the Auditori Nuovi, magistrates who traveled throughout the *terraferma* to hear appeals, served to limit local autonomy. By the end of the century, the Nuovi's workload was so great that another magistracy, the Auditori Nuovissimi was created to hear minor cases.

Over the course of the fifteenth century, Venice collaborated in the formation of a Vicentine patriciate that excluded guildsmen and tightened citizenship requirements. And after 1404 Venetian nobles monopolized Vicenza's bishopric and the abbacies of its major monasteries.[13]

Venetian intervention was strongest when it came to state security, commerce, the money supply, and defense. Vicentine competition in the production of Venetian luxury goods was forbidden. In times of scarcity the Vicentines were required to sell grain to the capital. The exportation of horses and timber to foreign entities was frequently prohibited and the mining of minerals, especially for gunpowder, was carefully controlled. For their part, the Vicentines could freely transport their goods to Venice for sale; this offered a boost to Vicenza's woolen cloth industry, a sector in which Venice lagged. According to the rules laid out in Vicenza's submission to Venice, the capital garnered all tolls and customs duties; and after 1411 it demanded annual payment of a tax known as the *dadia delle lanze* to support Venice's military. By 1442 the tax amounted to 15,600 ducats per year. Venice monopolized the minting of coins, although some were stamped with the insignia of Vicenza. Venice also periodically imposed forced loans and cash levies, and the Vicentines had to support the garrisoning of fortresses in the territory. The countryside was responsible for billeting cavalry; this was eventually commuted to a flat tax. Overall, the old and new taxes levied by Venice "constituted a massive drain on mainland resources."[14] However, the Council of Ten's constant exhortations that taxes be paid indicate that there was often a disparity between what Venice demanded and what it received. In other areas as well, there was a significant gap between how Venetian administration worked on paper and how it functioned on the ground, especially given the annual turnover of the podesta's staff. While rotation prevented the podesta from becoming corrupted by local Vicentine politics and provided more job opportunities for Venetian nobles, it meant a steep learning curve for each incoming podesta. Just when he got a handle on the local situation, his term of office ended. Outright corruption, absenteeism, and inaction also thwarted centralized governmental control. For example, one captain in the early sixteenth century explained that he could not investigate a riot in nearby Marostica because of the rain; once the rain stopped, he claimed he could not complete the trip because his successor's term would shortly begin.[15] Venice's solution to the problem of ineffectual administration was to confer more authority on the Vicentine commune.

While the general outlines of Venetian administration were the same throughout the mainland and overseas, there were infinite variations, based essentially on the privileges that each city managed to secure in its original pact or act of submission to Venice. The capital did not attempt nor was it capable of creating a uniform system of management and control across its widely scattered realm. While, for example, most cities had a rector (or podesta) and captain, the chief official in Friuli, which was dominated by feudal lords, was a lieutenant. What this meant in practice was that local communities and entities could maneuver to protect their privileges and they could bargain, via embassies, complaints, protests, and appeals, for some measure of power for themselves.

In all this, the Venetians exhibited a failure of imagination and would continue to do so until the very end of the Republic. Unlike the ancient Romans, they could not move beyond a city-state mentality and conceive of their empire as a unified entity. They did, beginning in 1404, extend citizenship *de intus* to inhabitants of subject territories on the *terraferma* and Dalmatia (the Vicentines received it in 1406), meaning that peoples from those lands had the right to trade in Venice, invest in governmental bonds, and buy property in the capital, but not the benefits in international trade conferred by citizenship *de extra*. In practice, most residents of the *terraferma* and overseas dominions were labeled and considered foreign subjects and given no say in the central government. There was no thought of extending membership in the Greater Council to the elites of the provincial cities. A proposal put forth in 1411 to allow nobles from Zara to help administer subject cities on the *terraferma*, in Istria, and Dalmatia, was rejected.[16] Bureaucratic posts remained beyond the reach of Venice's subject peoples as well.

The epitaphs of doges Michele Steno (d. 1414) and Tommaso Mocenigo (d. 1423) illustrate how slowly the Venetians reconciled themselves to their new role as lords of a vast mainland realm. The inscription on the tomb of Steno, who presided over the acquisition of Padua, Vicenza, and Verona, contains no mention or even allusion to those events. The sole commemoration of these acquisitions was the display on his tomb of the keys and seal of Padua, which delegates from Padua presented to him at the time of the city's submission. Mocenigo's epitaph, by contrast, refers to Loredan's victory over the Ottomans at Gallipoli and the humbling of the Hungarians. It also notes the acquisition of Friuli, Treviso, Feltre, Ceneda, Cattaro, Spalato, and Traù and concludes by observing that "his worthy mind approaches heaven, wearied by his country's triumphs."[17]

The Venetians' struggle to integrate the *terraferma* into a vision of themselves was due in large measure to the ad hoc and contingent way in which they had acquired it. Going in with no plan, they "produced no theory of the mainland state," or for that matter of the overseas one.[18] Instead they deployed a variety of metaphors when speaking about their subject lands and relations between the capital (the *dominante*) and the dominion. They emphasized in some cases that the subject lands had voluntarily submitted themselves to Venetian rule. This had advantages for both sides: it helped absolve the Venetians of the charge that they were rapacious and intent on conquest; and it painted the subject cities in a positive light as a way of garnering favorable treatment. In 1471 Doge Cristoforo Moro declared that the Vicentines "are especially worthy to be treated liberally, for before the citizens of all other cities, they came to give themselves and their city . . . into the hands and power of our Dominion, uncoerced by force of arms."[19] Both ruler and ruled also utilized familial metaphors to characterize their relationship, with the Venetians in the role of parents, their subjects as children, although the Paduans in 1449 tried to equalize relations by referring to the parties as "brothers born of the same parents."[20] Comparisons to the body were also deployed with Venice as the head, the subject cities and territories as the limbs.

The best model for empire was ancient Rome, but the Venetians moved slowly in that direction since other towns could legitimately claim Roman descent, and Venice could not. For political reasons, Venice also had to maintain its distance from the Holy Roman Empire of which these mainland cities were theoretically a part. One congenial argument was that Venice was reconstituting the ancient Roman province of Venetia.[21] The more powerful image of Venice as the New Rome would develop only slowly until in the sixteenth century it became the predominant Venetian representation of itself. Modern-day students of Venice have been equally hard-pressed to characterize the Venetian state, given its pluralistic and composite nature. It has recently been described, not especially convincingly, as a commonwealth.[22]

Having reached the natural boundary of the Veneto demarcated by the Mincio River, the Venetians had to decide whether to cross it and move into Lombardy. The actions of Filippo Maria Visconti, son of Giangaleazzo, supplied the answer. His efforts to reconstitute the state created by his father again threatened Florence, which sent three embassies to Venice seeking an alliance of the two republics against Milan. Finally, in December 1425 the Venetians agreed to a ten-year pact: each pledged to field armies composed of 8,000 cavalry and 3,000 infantry, while Venice also promised to outfit a large Po River fleet, whose expense the Florentines would share. Florence would get lands wrested from Visconti in Tuscany and Romagna, Venice those in

Lombardy. Genoa, then under Visconti control, would be restored to independence. Venice created a special Council of One Hundred to oversee the war effort, despite opposition to its creation.[23]

Events in the First Venetian/Visconti War moved rapidly. The captain general of Venice's land forces was the condottiere Francesco Bussone, known as Carmagnola, who until recently had been in Visconti's service and was married to one of his relations. Nobleman Francesco Bembo oversaw the Po River fleet. Carmagnola moved against Brescia, while Bembo threatened Cremona and Pavia. When the Duke of Savoy allied with Venice, Visconti faced enemies on his eastern, western, and southern fronts. In November Brescia fell; and a peace, mediated by the pope's representative, was concluded on December 30. Known as the Peace of Venice, it brought Brescia, as well as territory on the Lake Garda riviera, into Venetian possession.[24]

The peace turned out to be little more than a mid-winter pause. Soon Visconti was scoring victories around Parma and Mantua and moved against Brescello on the Po. Carmagnola failed to counter these attacks despite repeated pleas from the Senate to do so. It was Bembo's fleet that retook Brescello. During the summer Carmagnola continued to dally, ignoring pleas to cross the Adda River and take the fight to Visconti. Finally, in October his army, numbering 18,000 cavalry and 8,000 foot soldiers, did score a major victory against the Milanese army comprised of 12,000 cavalry and 6,000 infantry at Maclodio, southwest of Brescia. As a reward, Venice gave Carmagnola (who had previously been granted honorary membership in the Greater Council) a palace on the Grand Canal as well as a villa in the Bresciano. Rather than follow up the victory by striking Milan, Carmagnola conducted mopping-up operations and then went into winter quarters. A peace agreement was hammered out in May 1428. The Peace of Ferrara largely reiterated the terms of the Peace of Venice with one important difference: Visconti had to cede Bergamo and the surrounding Bergamasco to Venice. These two brief wars had added Brescia and Bergamo to the Venetian dominion and brought it within forty miles of Milan itself.[25]

By January 1431 the parties were at war once again when Carmagnola attacked Lodi on the western side of the Adda, after which he again dithered. The Senate dispatched Pietro Loredan, captain general of the sea, to make trouble for Visconti in the waters around Genoa. In June the Po fleet suffered a crushing defeat near Cremona; some blamed Carmagnola, who failed to help the doomed river forces. But this rout was balanced by Loredan's victory against the Genoese in August. Nevertheless, as Carmagnola's biographer observes, the mercenary had begun the 1431 Lombard campaign at the head of a large and well-equipped army and ended it "without having risked a battle, without having taken a fort, without having added a handful of land to the conquests of the years 1426–8."[26] He did, however, rush troops to Friuli in the autumn to counter an attack by the Hungarians. To spur Carmagnola to action in Lombardy and bring the war to a conclusion, the Senate twice considered but failed to approve a measure to offer him Milan itself as a reward.[27] At the same time, Venice tried to immunize itself against claims that it was the aggressor by asserting that it was acting not out of "ambition for dominion" but rather for the "health and conservation of honor and of our state and the liberty of Italy."[28]

Carmagnola allowed an opportunity to take Soncino slip through his fingers. Increasingly suspicious of his intentions and concerned that he was colluding with Visconti, the Ten set a trap. They summoned him to the capital purportedly for consultation. An unsuspecting Carmagnola arrived in Venice on April 7, 1432. Once at the Ducal Palace he was met by what he took to be an honor guard of eight nobles. The doors to the palace were locked. He was escorted to a room where he awaited the arrival of the doge. After some time, he was informed that Foscari had taken ill and that the meeting was postponed until the following morning. In the meantime, his personal retainers had been told that their master would be dining with the doge and were dismissed from the palace. At this point Carmagnola decided to return to his Grand Canal palace and await the next day's colloquy. As he made his way downstairs, he was told, according to Marino Sanudo, "Signor Count, come this way along the corridor of the prisons." When his escorts pointed him toward the prison door, he responded, "This is not the way," and they replied, "This is indeed the right way." He exclaimed, "I see all too well that I am dead."[29]

Under torture, Carmagnola confessed. The Ten convicted him on May 5 of treason. He was beheaded with three strokes of the ax between the two columns of the Piazzetta. Chronicler Antonio Morosini judged that he died "rather devoutly."[30] After a mix-up by which his body was taken to San Francesco della Vigna, it was interred, according to his wishes, at the Frari. His properties and palace on the Grand Canal were confiscated; his wife, the countess, agreed to lodge at the convent of Santa Maria delle Vergini. In August 1433 she was allowed to transfer to the mainland, but by April 1434 she and her daughters had escaped to Milan.

Carmagnola's life is a lesson in the pitfalls that Venice faced in attempting to organize the military protection of its mainland realm. Venice had decided, like the other Italian states, to entrust its defense to mercenary companies rather than to citizen armies, but then it failed to find a way to control the captains it placed at their helm. They devised a system of long-distance supervision by the Senate, including control of the budget, and direct oversight by noble commissioners (*provveditori*). But the captains and commissioners often clashed over strategy and other issues. The problems eased somewhat as more nobles gained experience working with the mercenary captains.[31]

The egos and ambitions of the condottieri further complicated matters. In an age of territorial consolidation, they had to find a place for themselves in the rapidly diminishing interstices of regional power. This was not a problem for mercenary captains like the Gonzagas of Mantua and the Estes of Ferrara, who were already rulers of independent states. It was more so for upstarts like Carmagnola and Francesco Sforza who aspired to realms of their own. Carmagnola's entrapment and execution by the Ten did, however, send a powerful message that mercenary captains were expected to subordinate their interests to those of Venice. His beheading sent "a salutary shock to his fellow captains and eventual successors."[32]

Even with Carmagnola's death, the war dragged on until the Second Peace of Ferrara was signed in April 1432. It essentially restored the status quo ante bellum. One of the factors pushing Visconti toward peace was the growing rapprochement between Venice and the emperor-elect Sigismund, a warming facilitated by pope Eugenius IV (Venetian Gabriele Condulmer) who finally crowned Sigismund Holy Roman emperor in May 1432. The peace was followed by a major reshuffling of alliances and personnel across Italy. In Florence the Medicis (headed by the banker Cosimo) were expelled in September 1433, although they were recalled a year later. The condottiere Francesco Sforza abandoned Visconti and took up service for Eugenius, while Erasmo da Narni, better known as Gattamelata, left papal service and signed on with Venice. By autumn 1434 Sforza had contracted with the Veneto-Florentine League. And in August 1435 Venice and Sigismund agreed to a ten-year alliance. As part of the agreement, Sigismund promised to invest the doge as imperial vicar of all Venice's *terraferma* lands, save Vicenza and Verona. This legitimated Venetian claims to sovereignty over its mainland realm and inserted Venice into the still-lively system of feudal obligations and privileges. It helped solidify Venice's control over the Roman-founded mainland cities that had been ruled for the most part by signorial regimes imbued with strong feudal/chivalric traditions.[33]

The goal of Venice and its allies was encirclement of Milan. That seemed within reach when in May 1436 Genoa, which had recently thrown off the

Visconti yoke, joined the League. This move effectively increased the strategic importance of Lombardy and meant the burden of the struggle would fall to Venice, not Florence. The Fourth Venetian-Visconti war began to heat up in 1437. Venice and Genoa called for an all-out assault on Milan, while Florence wanted the army to concentrate its efforts in Tuscany where Sforza was operating. The year 1438 began with Milan again on the offensive. Still more worrisome for the League was Sforza's decision to switch sides when Visconti promised him his only child, his illegitimate daughter Bianca, in marriage. That put him in line to inherit the duchy itself. Venice's former commander Gonzaga also joined the Milanese side. He was promised Verona and Vicenza once they were seized from Venice. This left Venice's flank exposed. The Milanese captain Nicolò Piccinino laid siege to Brescia, which was defended by its rector, nobleman and humanist Francesco Barbaro, while Gonzaga moved into the Veronese. Gattamelata managed to save his army by marching through the mountains north of Lake Garda—humanist Giovanni Pontano compared it to Hannibal's crossing of the Alps—and was rewarded with the title captain general.[34]

During winter 1438–9 the Venetians performed an extraordinary feat in their effort to relieve beleaguered and besieged Brescia. The only safe way to get supplies to the city was via Lake Garda but access to the lake was blocked by Milanese forces patrolling the Mincio. So the Venetians adopted an audacious plan concocted by Cretan engineer/shipwright Nicolò Sorbolo to transport the needed ships over the mountains from the Adige to the lake. The fleet, including many small vessels and between two and five galleys, traveled up the Adige, was hauled overland by oxen; ascended Mount Baldo along a specially constructed causeway; and was lowered by ropes, pulleys, and cables into the lake below. All this took place in the dead of winter. The spectacle of ships traversing the snow-covered mountains symbolized Venetian determination, engineering skill, and power.[35] A subsequent victory on the lake was commemorated in the sixteenth century in a ceiling painting in the Greater Council Hall by the workshop of Tintoretto.

The return of Sforza to the Venetian side after Visconti repeatedly delayed the promised marriage to Bianca temporarily restored the initiative to the Venetians. The Venetians promised him Mantua, Cremona, or, if he should cross the Adda, Milan itself. But the tide turned just as quickly when in November 1439 Verona was betrayed to the enemy, although Gattamelata and Sforza managed to retake it. Momentum kept swinging back and forth in large part because the goals of the various parties, including allies, were so varied and their forces too evenly matched for any side to win a definitive victory. The 1439 campaign was also Gattemelata's last; he suffered a debilitating stroke in December before dying in January 1443. Buried at the Santo, the church dedicated to Saint Anthony in Padua, Gattamelata was commemorated by Donatello with the most famous equestrian statue of the Italian Renaissance.[36]

As the war dragged on, Venice did make one more significant territorial gain. In early 1441, it annexed Ravenna, exiling to Crete the last member of its Da Polenta ruling family. This move south of the Po and into papal territory threatened relations with both Ferrara and the pope and again laid Venice open to the charge of harboring imperialist intentions. Venetians such as contemporary chronicler Giorgio Dolfin claimed instead that the people of Ravenna freely placed themselves under Venetian rule "with benevolence and love."[37] Peace was finally reached in November 1441. It was largely orchestrated by Sforza, who less than a month before had finally married Bianca Visconti and received Cremona as her dowry. The treaty restored territories to their status at the time of the Second Peace of Ferrara (1433) and designated the Adda River as the border between Venetian and Milanese possessions. Genoa was declared independent from Milan. This was the second war in which Venice

FIGURE 10.2 Donatello, *Equestrian Statue of Gattamelata*, 1453. Piazza del Santo, Padua. The condottiere is shown wielding the baton or rod of command. Scala/Art Resource, NY.

had failed to make any territorial gains, except for the acquisition of Ravenna which was not directly related to the war.[38]

The peace did nothing to stabilize the ever-shifting alliances and conflicts among the various powers as all awaited Filippo Maria's death and eventual disposition of the Duchy of Milan. He died in August 1447. Before any of the interested parties could act, the Milanese decided they had had enough of princely rule and proclaimed their state a republic under the protection of the city's patron Saint Ambrose. They named Sforza their captain general but then, after a series of mind-boggling reversals, he succeeded in having himself declared lord of Milan in March 1450. A major shift of alliances followed. Florence and Pope Nicholas V were pleased by Sforza's success since he seemed best able to block further Venetian expansion. Cosimo de' Medici, Venice's former ally, warned that it was essential that "the Venetians not become the lords of Italy."[39] For their part, the Venetians formed an alliance with Alfonso, king of Naples, aimed at dismembering Milan. The stage was set for the final act in this more than quarter century of nearly continuous warfare.[40]

The conflict resumed in 1452 as Alfonso concentrated his efforts in southern Tuscany, and the Venetians undertook a new thrust across the Adda. As a countermeasure, the Florentines and Sforza encouraged the Frenchman René of Anjou to pursue his claims to the Neapolitan throne. In the end, financial exhaustion, coupled with the shock of the fall of Constantinople to the Ottomans in May 1453, propelled the quest for a lasting peace. Recriminations were especially pronounced in Venice where critics complained that the focus on the West had led to the final collapse of the Byzantine Empire. Peace talks convened in October under the auspices of Pope Nicholas V but dragged on for months. Meanwhile Sforza and Venice conducted separate negotiations that finally resulted in the Peace of Lodi officially promulgated in April 1454. The treaty restored to Venice Sforza's conquests in the Bresciano and Bergamasco and ceded it the city of Crema, while Venice was to encourage its allies to restore lands that they had taken from Sforza. Milan retained its rights over the Adda. This was followed in August by an agreement between Venice, Florence, and Milan to form a league to last twenty-five years. Often anachronistically dubbed the Concert of Italy, this amounted to a mutual non-aggression pact. Allies were encouraged to join. Bologna did so quickly; others moved more slowly; Alfonso of Naples finally signed on in 1455.[41]

The Peace of Lodi and the subsequent Italian League have often been characterized as prototypes for the kind of balance-of-power configurations that dominated Europe through the Cold War. Likewise, the need to maintain the delicate equilibrium required for the League to work provided additional impetus for the development of novel diplomatic practices, such as the dispatch of resident ambassadors.[42] Venice would become especially renowned for the sophistication of its diplomatic apparatus and maneuvering. But the peace was first and foremost a demonstration of "the sterility of conflict among the major Italian powers."[43] Three decades of nearly non-stop aggression had revealed that none of the major powers was in a position to dominate the entire peninsula: the peace recognized *de iure* what was a *de facto* balance of power. It was also designed to minimize the threat of intervention by the French, who had claims to both Milan and Naples, and the Holy Roman Emperor.[44]

The incessant *terraferma* wars had a pronounced effect on Venice. They changed the city's military preparedness. Although Venice had made sporadic use of mercenary forces as early as the fourteenth century, their employment became a fixture of governance as the city had to field a permanent army near the borders, a function the old citizen militia was unable adequately to meet. The recourse to mercenaries, along with all the other associated costs of war, dramatically drove up expenses and prompted a desperate search for revenue. To raise money the government relied not only on long-standing practices such as increasing customs duties, taxing rents, and withholding or reducing interest payments on forced loans, but also new ones such as taxing the new *terraferma* possessions and instituting in 1439 a tax known as the *boccatico* that was assessed on houses or hearths and from which few, except the most destitute, were exempt. However, the *boccatico* largely failed, yielding a paltry 1,000 ducats per year. Just a few months later, the government decided to return to the system of forced loans for those with the qualifying income; those who did not meet that threshold would pay the *boccatico*. The 1440-1 period was particularly bad: twenty-three forced-loan levies were imposed, amounting to a tax of about 30 percent of assessed wealth. Interest payments were suspended, and shares of the funded debt fell to 20 percent of face value. By 1454 the situation was so dire that the system of forced loans was abandoned in favor of a variety of revenue-generating measures, including new taxes on the *terraferma* and on Jews living on both the mainland and overseas.[45]

The wars also accelerated a reshuffling of power among the various governmental councils. This was due in part to the need for faster and more efficient decision-making. It typically took thirty days for news to reach Venice from Constantinople and as many as sixty from Alexandria, so councils were typically responding to outdated information. Furthermore, it took an equally long time for their decisions to reach their destination. Rulings did not require speed because they could not be instituted speedily. By contrast, it only took three days for news to reach Venice from Milan. In an emergency, couriers could make the journey in as little as one day. News could travel between Venice and Padua in eight hours.[46] The timetable for decision-making accelerated accordingly. In this, most of Venice's rivals on the peninsula had an advantage since they were princely regimes in which decisions could be quickly made by the ruler in consultation with a small group of close advisors. By comparison, Venice's slow-moving deliberative bodies, especially the Greater Council, could prove a liability. Venice responded in two ways. The short-lived experiment with the Council of One Hundred (it was abolished in 1428) was one attempt to create a body that could expeditiously prosecute the wars. The longer-term response was to concentrate power in the Senate and especially the Ten. This came at the cost of the Greater Council, which no longer served as the city's premier deliberative body. The Greater Council's lopsided vote not to renew the One Hundred (170 in favor of renewal, 320 opposed, and 49 abstentions) offers one measure of the consternation over the council's loss of power.[47] Even its primary duty to hold elections for other governmental bodies and administrative posts faced infringement by the Senate. The mainland wars accelerated the bifurcation of the nobility into orders of rich and poor, with the Greater Council functioning as a stronghold of the poorer nobles.

The newly acquired *terraferma* possessions, along with those in the overseas dominions—dubbed, respectively, the *stato da terra* (land state) and the *stato da mar* (maritime state)—required a lot of personnel to administer them. Most of these offices rotated annually, a few biennially. This was a godsend for poorer nobles, who depended on these positions for income. Indeed, the demand for an ever-greater number of jobs was one impetus for the move onto the *terraferma*. Competition for offices became so great that it led to some egregious examples of electoral corruption. In 1433 the Ten uncovered a plot by more than three dozen nobles to rig elections. Chronicler Giorgio Dolfin wrote that it was designed "to destroy the government of Venice."[48]

Even when legitimately elected, officeholders, especially those tapped as rectors of cities in the dominion, posed other threats. They might treat these positions as sinecures, become too cozy with the people they were sent to govern, or act in their own, rather than Venice's, interest. The government tried to counteract these dangers. Noting that rectors and others were giving self-aggrandizing speeches when assuming and leaving office, the Senate ordered in 1425 that they were to say only that they accepted or consigned the office, "in the name of the illustrious Signoria of Venice."[49] Two years later, the Senate forbade rectors from wearing mourning clothes except in the case of the deaths of their immediate relatives, instead requiring them to wear bright and "cheerful" colors. In both instances, the Senate wanted to emphasize that officeholders were representatives of the state, not individual noble families.[50] All told, the dramatic expansion of Venice's dominion on both the mainland and overseas placed new stresses on the city's republican traditions.

One reason Venice survived these challenges as well as it did was the continuing strength of its overseas trade and the wealth generated by it. One galley on the Romania line alone might transport between 70,000 and 100,000 ducats' worth of goods; and in these decades, Venice was regularly dispatching up to twenty-four merchant galleys along its various freight lines. In 1412 the Aigues-Mortes line was initiated with stops at Naples, Pisa, and various ports along the southern coast of France and eastern coast of Spain. The Barbary line was added in 1436, with regular calls at Syracuse, Tunis, Granada, and Valencia. When it was interrupted, the Senate created in 1460 the *muda del trafego*, which carried North African merchants and products, such as leather goods, olive oil, fish, and coral, from Barbary to Alexandria. In addition, hundreds of privately owned vessels plied the seas.[51] These decades constituted a high point for Venetian trade as the city stood at the nexus of trade routes stretching from northern Europe to the Far East.[52] The extraordinary wealth generated helped carry Venice through the wars. The city also profited from the Ottomans remaining primarily a land-based power in this period.

Even so, the Ottomans posed a growing threat to Venice's well-being as they closed in on the ever-shrinking Byzantine Empire. In 1423 they set their sights on Thessalonica and invaded the Morea. In desperation, Andronicus, despot of Thessalonica and brother of Emperor John VIII, offered the city to Venice with the proviso that the Venetians respect Thessalonica's statutes and customs. The Venetians, fearing for the fate of Negroponte as well as Coron and Modon, accepted and justified the annexation by claiming (unabashedly) that they had agreed to it "for the honor of the Christian faith and not out of ambition for dominion."[53] At the same time, they tried to explain to Sultan Murad II that they had taken over the city only to prevent it from falling into rival Christian hands. The co-emperor John's journey to Venice and Sigismund in the autumn to reconcile the two powers who were most directly threatened by the Ottomans came to nothing. In early 1424 John's aged father Emperor Manuel II reached an accord in which he agreed to pay the Turks an annual tribute of 100,000 hyperpers for the Morea. Sanudo, writing several decades after the fact, judged this agreement harshly, declaring, "Thus the Morea was turned into a tax farm of the Turk."[54] The Venetians played a double game throughout, offering encouragement but little else to the Byzantines, while trying not to antagonize the Ottomans. They lost Thessalonica in 1430; their seven-year occupation of the city cost them an estimated 700,000 ducats. In September of that year, they reached a new treaty with the sultan, who agreed to respect Venice's control of the seas south and west of Tenedos. That same year they renewed their treaty with the emperor John and negotiated with the Mamluk sultan of Egypt over the terms of the spice trade. The failed attempt to hold Thessalonica taught them that they needed to concentrate on protecting trade rather than expanding their territorial possessions in the eastern Mediterranean.[55]

This explains Venice's ambivalent attitude toward the disastrous Crusade of Varna. In 1439 at the Council of Florence, Pope Eugenius IV managed to bring an end to the schism between the Latin and Greek churches. The emperor John believed that the reward for this reconciliation should be a crusade against the Ottomans. For this he gained the support of the pope, the Duke of Burgundy, Serbian despot George Brankovic, and Ladislaus III, king of Hungary and Poland, as well as the half-hearted support of the Venetians, who agreed to supply some of the ships for the fleet. Alvise Loredan was named captain of the Venetian contingent. The plan was for land forces to move from Hungary and the fleet to sail from Venice. Murad, preoccupied with problems in Anatolia, faced danger on two fronts and for a time bought off Brankovic and Ladislaus. When at papal urging the crusade resumed, the sultan dealt it a fatal blow at Varna on the Black Sea in November 1444. Both Ladislaus and the papal representative were killed. The Crusade of Varna was "the last attempt by western Christendom to drive the Turks out of Europe."[56] Eugenius hurled invectives against his fellow Venetians for not fully supporting the effort. For their part, the Venetians scurried to repair relations with Murad and his son and eventual successor Mehmed II. And in 1448 they renewed for what turned out to be the final time their treaty with Byzantium. The Varna crusade seemed to confirm the Western Christian view of the Venetians as shameless opportunists since they had used the crusade to shore up their possessions along the coasts of Montenegro and Albania. For their part, the Venetians continued to see themselves as the bulwark against the Ottoman advance.[57]

The final act in the protracted drama that was the obliteration of the Byzantine Empire began in 1451 when Mehmed II, who had his eyes set on the conquest of Constantinople, succeeded his father.[58] The Venetians responded with sympathy to the pleas for aid from Constantine XI Paleologus, who had assumed the Byzantine throne two years earlier, but did little else. They claimed that they could assist only as part of a unified Western effort. Among the excuses they offered was renewed war in Italy. But when in August 1452 Mehmed completed constructing the fortress of Rumeli Hisar on the European side of the Bosphorus and proclaimed that all ships passing through the straits had to pay a toll and get permission to proceed, the Venetians took note that Mehmed controlled access not just to Constantinople but to the Black Sea. When a Venetian merchantman captained by Antonio Rizzo transporting barley from the Black Sea to Constantinople refused to stop that November, he and his crew were captured and executed. At this point, the large colony of Venetian merchants resident in Constantinople voted to cast their lot with that of the Byzantines. Giovanni Minotto, the *bailo*, forbade all Venetian ships currently in harbor to depart.

When news of what was happening reached Venice in February 1453, the Senate authorized the construction of two more war galleys, and the Greater Council elected Jacopo Loredan, son of the victor at Gallipoli in 1416, as captain general of the sea. But he received his commission only in May and was told to proceed to Tenedos, along with the galleys stationed in Corfu and Crete, to assess the situation. Accompanying him was Bartolomeo Marcello, Venice's ambassador to the sultan. Venice was hampered by outdated news, since in April the siege of Constantinople by Mehmed's army of 160,000 soldiers had already begun. Resident Venetians assumed major roles in the city's defense: *bailo* Minoto was placed in charge of the defenses of the Blachernai Palace, while Venetian ships patrolled the port and Golden Horn, which was protected by a chain stretched across to Galata. When the Ottomans carried seventy-two vessels around the chain, Leonardo di Chio, archbishop of Mytilene, compared this extraordinary feat to the Venetians' own 1438 portage of ships over the mountains to Lake Garda. The final assault began on the morning of May 29. Both sides fought valiantly, until the Ottomans were able to breach the walls and take the city. Emperor Constantine died fighting. *Bailo* Minotto, his son, and several other Venetians were captured and beheaded; others were held for ransom. Although several Venetian and Cretan galleys managed to escape, the financial losses were huge. Dolfin estimated that the Venetians lost 200,000 ducats, the Cretans 100,000. Modern estimates place the figure closer to half a million.[59]

Letters announcing the disaster reached Venice on June 29 when the Greater Council was in session. Their reading set off recriminations and lamentations. Dolfin observed that some "mourned for their fathers, others for their sons, others for their brothers, and others for their goods."[60] In fact, the government acted quickly to repair relations with Mehmed and resume trade. Bartolomeo Marcello was ordered to continue his diplomatic mission to the sultan, although the Senate decided, "given recent events," that the value of the gifts he was proffering should be increased from 500 to 1,200 ducats.[61] He was even told to offer the old treaties that Venice had made with Byzantium as models for a new commercial accord. Hedging their bets, the Venetians also opened negotiations with Ibrahim Bey, ruler of the Karamanid emirate in southeastern Anatolia who was hostile to the Ottomans, to see if it would be possible for the Romania line galleys to trade through his lands. They also strengthened their defense of the Morea and Negroponte.

The fall of Constantinople, which Sanudo described as "the worst news for all of Christendom," sent shock waves through Europe.[62] The psychological effect was particularly pronounced in Venice, which began life as a Byzantine outpost and then conquered the city in 1204. For centuries the Venetians had garnered riches from the empire, taken up residence there, and drawn cultural inspiration from Constantinople's art and architecture. The conquest prompted the exodus of Greek refugees, including scholars like Cardinal Basilio Bessarion, who contributed to the advancement of Greek studies in Italy. Yet the extinction of the Byzantine Empire did not fundamentally alter the balance of power in the eastern Mediterranean since by the time Byzantium succumbed, it was but a shadow of its former self. What it did do was bring into sharp focus the stark reality of Ottoman expansion and call into question the wisdom of Venice's policy of *terraferma* aggrandizement. Had the Venetians not been so focused on events in the West, some contended, they would have better understood the reality of what was happening in the East.

During these same decades, especially in the 1420s and 1430s, the Venetians redefined the nature of their polity and clarified the criteria for noble status. The trend on both counts was toward greater hierarchy and exclusivity. Regarding the polity, two decisions completed the exclusion of the *popolo* from any formal role in government. The first was taken in 1403 when the Full College rejected a proposal to allow one *cittadino originario* family to be admitted to the Greater Council every time a noble family went extinct.[63] The goal was to rejuvenate the nobility whose numbers were diminishing as families died out. Indeed, the family of Michele Steno, the reigning doge at the time, went extinct on his death; that of his wife, noblewoman, and dogaressa Maria Gallina disappeared shortly thereafter. By failing to allow this proposal to advance, the Full College reinforced the exclusivity of the nobility, which continued to transform itself into an aristocracy and distance itself from the *cittadini originarii*.

The second decision was taken twenty years later, in 1423, when on the death of Doge Tommaso Mocenigo, the correctors of the ducal oath of office made their recommendations to the Greater Council. Among the changes they advocated was one that stripped the old General Assembly of its last vestiges of power. The Assembly could no longer even rubber-stamp legislation. Additionally, the question was posed: what would happen if the Assembly failed to acclaim the chosen ducal candidate? To avoid that unnerving possibility, the Greater Council ruled that the Assembly would be convened only to be informed of but not confirm the results of ducal elections.[64]

A telling shift in nomenclature accompanied these changes. The old name of the polity, the *comune Veneciarum* (commune of the Venetians), with its connotation of widespread participation, was utilized less and less. In its place the Latin term *dominium* (dominion) or the Venetian term *signoria* (lordship) was substituted. (As we have seen, the latter could also refer to the Ducal Council composed of the doge, the six ducal councilors, and the three heads of the Forty.) In 1462 this change was formalized when the Greater Council ruled that in the ducal oath of office, all uses of *comune Veneciarum* be eliminated in favor of *dominium Veneciarum*. No longer a city-state with a fictional equality among its male citizens, Venice was understood to be a dominion, a regional-state composed of rulers and ruled, nobles and their subjects.[65]

The growing aristocratization of the nobility also found expression in a series of laws that have been described as a Second Serrata and "the definitive closing of the patriciate."[66] First, the Greater Council sought in 1414 to immunize itself against men of uncertain paternity. To do this, it required that only young men whose fathers were or had been members of the Greater Council could register for the Barbarella, the annual lottery that allowed winners to enter the Greater Council at twenty rather than the normal age of twenty-five. If alive, fathers were expected to enroll their sons for the lottery with the State Attorneys, who were required to keep a registry of the entrants. The notebook in which the names were kept became the first official list of noble families and included 164 houses. Not until a full century after the original Serrata did the government finally begin taking an active part in documenting membership in the nobility, a trend that would culminate in 1506 in the official register of noble births known as the *Libro d'Oro* (Golden Book). In 1430 the government sought to prevent further infiltration by requiring men whose fathers had failed to register them for the Barbarella but who then tried to enter the council automatically at age twenty-five be scrutinized by the State Attorneys, who had to record their findings in yet another register documenting proof of age. Increasingly governmental procedures, records, and rituals became the determinants of noble status.[67]

At the same time, an effort was made to further differentiate nobles from the *popolo* and minimize disparities within the nobility itself. This was achieved through a series of laws passed between 1420 and 1430 regarding marriage. These laws affected both women and men. In 1420 the Senate set a 1,600-ducat limit on dowries. This intervention was prompted by dowry inflation, which was making it difficult for fathers to arrange marriages for their daughters. According to the preamble, the siphoning of so much money into dowries was impoverishing sons and forcing fathers to place their daughters unwillingly in convents or condemn them to spinsterhood as well as to the risks of sexual dishonor should they be seduced. An exception was made for daughters of *popolani*, but not *cittadini*, who could enjoy dowries up to 2,000 ducats. This allowed nobles to profit from infusions of capital from exceptionally wealthy commoners while at the same time discouraging marriages between nobles and *cittadini*, those who came closest to storming the ramparts of noble status. Two other laws were aimed at defending against infiltration from the very bottom ranks of society. The first refused noble status to the children of noblemen and enslaved women and erected nearly insurmountable barriers for children of marriages with servants or women of "vile" status. The second required the State Attorneys to verify the identity of mothers as well as fathers when determining eligibility for the Greater Council.[68]

Together these laws regarding marriage "constituted an enormous escalation of state supervision over the social and political order" and redefined what it meant to be noble.[69] They also brought more sharply into focus life-cycle stages, especially the passage from adolescence into adulthood for males and from maidenhood to wifehood for females. Overseeing all this were husbands and fathers whose role as *patresfamilias* (male heads of household) took on new importance as they supervised and educated their wives and children and attempted to inculcate in them the values that furthered the material interests of the patriline and steer them clear of threats to family honor.

There were various ways to live as a nobleman in fifteenth-century Venice. One path followed a well-prescribed curriculum vitae. Boys received a basic education in reading, writing, and numeracy, which they attained either through the services of a tutor or by attending private schools run by grammar teachers and abacus masters. Basic literacy in the vernacular and Latin and the ability to handle the kind of mathematical problems found in the *Zibaldone da Canal* were considered sufficient for careers in commerce and governance.[70] In 1446 the government established the Scuola di San Marco (School of Saint Mark) to train boys in the new humanist-inspired curriculum if they were destined for careers in the chancery.

With a rudimentary education in hand, the young patrician embarked on what was certainly the most important part of his training, a kind of apprenticeship in commerce and governance. Teenage boys and young men in their twenties sometimes accompanied their fathers or other male relatives on commercial travels to acquire trading skills and contacts and become familiar with the geography and peoples in Venice's vast trade network. Sons might also accompany their fathers to administrative posts or on diplomatic missions. In 1437, for example, Pietro Loredan received permission to take his adult son Jacopo, already an officeholder, with him on what turned out to be an unsuccessful trip to convince the condottiere and Marquess of Mantua Gianfrancesco Gonzaga to remain in Venetian service.[71]

In adolescence, young patrician men inhabited a liminal space poised between boyhood and adulthood. Some engaged in rowdy or even criminal behavior as they tested their elders and the limits of manhood. As an adolescent Doge Michele Steno was among the youths who taunted Marino Falier as a cuckold, and Doge Foscari's son Lorenzo was among those prosecuted for illegally entering the convent of Santa Maria delle Vergini on the day of the new abbess's consecration.[72] Such youthful transgressions seldom had long-term consequences and may even have been viewed as demonstrations of blossoming virility. At the same time, the Barbarella lottery served to acculturate youths to future careers in politics as they and their families anxiously waited to learn whether they had won the right to enter the Greater Council early.[73]

Regardless of the lottery, the next stage was often marriage and entry into political office. Most marriages were arranged, usually by the fathers of the bride and groom, and had little to do with compatibility or affection, although some fathers did try to gauge the enthusiasm of their children for married life. Instead, arranged marriages had everything to do with establishing or cementing political, commercial, and social bonds. The dowry inflation that the Senate tried (unsuccessfully) to control is an indicator of just how much was at stake in matrimony. At the beginning of the century the average age at marriage for males was twenty-six and a half years; by the end of the century, it had risen to thirty-three and a half.[74] Once settled into married life, many nobles began their climb up the *cursus honorum* that, for the lucky few, culminated in procuratorships of San Marco or even the dogeship.

The climb was often agonizingly slow. It was regulated in part by age requirements for specific offices. Starting in 1431, candidates had to be thirty-two to be eligible for the Senate, forty for the Ten. Other positions, like Capo di Sestiere and Savio agli Ordini, were understood to be entry-level ones to which younger men could be elected and in which poorer nobles often stalled. There was an unwritten rule that young men ought to be patient and bide their time. The 1433 electoral conspiracy was an expression of youthful resentment at this exclusion. Only after years of experience could most patricians aspire to higher offices, while men from the most powerful families often did not begin their political careers until they were in their early fifties and could leap-frog past their humbler colleagues. The dogeship itself was, with few exceptions, the preserve of the truly elderly. The average age at election in the fifteenth and sixteenth centuries was seventy-two.[75] This contrasts with the youthfulness of many doges of the Middle Ages and most princely states and suggests the degree to which Venice had become a gerontocratic regime. This preference for rule by the aged has been cited as one reason for the deliberateness of Venetian decision-making and the Republic's essential conservatism. Incapacity or death ended most careers. The idea of retirement seems hardly to have existed, although there was the notion that old age was a good time to consider the fate of one's soul. As he left the Ducal Palace after his removal from office, Doge Foscari reportedly remarked that he and his old friend Marino Memmo ought to "go together by boat and enjoy ourselves in visiting the monasteries."[76]

Many patrician males did not adhere to this model, however. Over 40 percent of patrician males in the fifteenth century never married, Doge Tommaso Mocenigo among them.[77] This trend would grow even more pronounced in later centuries as families tried to preserve their wealth by limiting the number of heirs. Some noblemen remained bachelors out of a preference for a life of study and prayer. Others' primary erotic interest was homosexual. In 1406 the Ten investigated a large homosexual ring involving fifteen nobles and eighteen non-nobles; and in 1454 the Ten restricted the number of guests who could be invited to dinners, lamenting that of late it had become the dangerous habit for "old men, youths, and middle-aged men" to socialize together. There is even some evidence of a flourishing gay subculture.[78] But dowry inflation was likely the primary reason there were so many bachelors. As fathers gave larger marriage portions to certain daughters and relegated others to convents or spinsterhood, the pool of marriageable girls declined. Similarly, fathers may have hesitated to marry their daughters to men whose patrimony was being diverted into dowries for their sisters. In one respect, Doge Mocenigo was exceptional; most bachelor patricians never reached the higher echelons of government and simply played a supporting role in the noble regime.[79]

Other noblemen, like Marino Contarini, eschewed politics altogether. Unlike his father Antonio and brother Andrea, who both had illustrious careers culminating in procuratorships of San Marco. Marino devoted himself to commerce and never held political office. But what really captured his interest and imagination from 1421 to the mid-1430s was the building of his splendid Ca' d'Oro.[80]

Contarini's contemporary, nobleman Andrea Barbarigo, also devoted himself to trade and forswore political office. Barbarigo began his career in virtual poverty after his father Nicolò was fined a ruinous 10,000 ducats for abandoning one of the vessels in the merchant fleet he was commanding as they returned from Alexandria. Starting with only 200 ducats, Barbarigo was able to rebuild the family fortune, through diligence and hard work and by taking advantage of every available opportunity. He got an early boost when he was awarded the position of *balestriere alla popa* (archer of the quarterdeck), a military post on merchant galleys that paid wages and allowed the right to carry cargo duty free. Intended for impoverished noblemen, the position was yet another form of welfare for patricians. Barbarigo also relied heavily on his uncle and cousins, holders of Cretan knighthoods, to further his business ventures. He trafficked in Cretan wine and cheese. He and his brother even inherited a sergeantry in Crete, which they sold. He profited as well from the friendship of banker Francesco Balbi, at whose bank Barbarigo was often overdrawn, and of Vittore, Alban, and Giovanni Capello, Venetians active in London, who eventually became his brothers-in-laws. By the time of his death, Barbarigo was worth between 10,000 and 15,000 ducats. In one respect he differed completely from Marino Contarini since he did not own real estate in Venice, preferring instead to rent a house in the parish of San Barnaba. He did buy an estate at Montebelluna, between Bassano and Treviso, that provided a summer escape, refuge from the plague, and probably some rents and agricultural produce. On his death, Cristina, his widow and mother of his young sons, purchased for 1,400 ducats eight-ninths of the house in San Barnaba that they had been renting, effectively shielding from the vagaries of commerce some of the capital Barbarigo had worked so hard to accumulate.[81]

Cristina's decision underscores the important role noblewomen played in patrician society. One factor in Barbarigo's success was the financial assistance he received from his mother and wife. His initial capital of 200 ducats was a gift from his mother, while Cristina brought a huge dowry of 4,000 ducats, far above the limit established by the Senate. Barbarigo also had good relations with Cristina's widowed mother, for whom he performed various services, and with Cristina's maternal aunt, Cristina da Canal, who lent him money. Marino Contarini likewise profited greatly from marriage. His first wife, Soradamor Zeno, had a dowry of 2,400 ducats. In 1412 Marino bought the old Zeno family palace in Santa Sofia from Soradamor's sister and brother-in-law for 3,200 ducats. He tore down the old building and used the site for Ca' d'Oro. After Soradamor's death, he married Lucia, daughter of Giorgio Corner and widow of Giovanni Foscari.

The prominent role women played in patrician society was due in good measure to their ability to dispose of their dowries as they saw fit. This gave them a degree of power or at least influence as they dangled the prospect of legacies and gifts before possible heirs.[82] Yet noble women did much more than that. Positioned between patrilines and nurturing both practical and affectionate ties to their natal and marital families, women bound the patriciate together. The 1411 will of Soradamor Zeno highlights this role. Counting the birth families of the women listed in her will, Soradamor noted ties to at least seven different patrician families.[83]

Noblewomen often maintained affectionate bonds with female relations in monastic houses. Soradamor asked to be buried in the habit of the nuns of Sant'Andrea where her mother was living; and in May 1417, Giovanna Dandolo, described as a *conversa* (a lay sister) and "procuratoress" of the convent, acknowledged a bequest of 50 ducats and candles that Soradamor had left the convent.[84] She was likely Soradamor's aunt. Some abbesses and prioresses commanded prestige and authority. They were in touch with the world of power politics, especially given the Ten's habit of confining the wives of traitors to convents. As partial recompense for providing lodging for Carmagnola's widow, the convent of the Vergini "insistently" petitioned the Ten to be awarded a brocaded silk cloth that Carmagnola had loaned to various churches in Brescia on solemn feast days. They wanted it to adorn the high altar of their church. The Ten acceded unanimously to their request.[85] Nuns, especially in the wealthiest convents, were themselves important art patrons. As abbess of San Zaccaria, Doge Foscari's sister Elena undertook a renovation of the church's chancel for which she and the other female officeholders commissioned three altarpieces to adorn the space at a total cost of 1,874 ducats.[86]

Of course, Renaissance Venice was no paradise for patrician women. They had no direct political power and were largely confined to the household, neighborhood, parish churches, and convents, although many did cultivate patronage ties to humble residents of their neighborhoods at a time when men were increasingly turning to the state to garner favors for their clients. Soradamor, for instance, asked in her will that 1 ducat each be given to thirteen "poor women." Noblewomen's field of activity was also bound by strict notions of chastity and honor, while they were simultaneously threatened with sexual molestation or at least the importuning of men. Some suffered physical abuse.[87] Many were also un- or under-educated. Little is known about how patrician girls learned what they did; some were taught to read in the vernacular by their mothers; others may have studied alongside their brothers if the family engaged a private tutor. Much of their education would have been practical, as they learned to sew, embroider, and manage the household. Unlike males whose *cursus honorum* was tied to politics, the life cycle of women not destined for the nunnery was marked by changes in their marital and reproductive status as they transitioned from maidenhood to bridehood, motherhood to mature wifehood, and finally widowhood.

The work and family life of artisans differed markedly from those of nobles as a few examples make clear. When he drew up his will in 1442, Giovanni Bon, the master stonecarver whom Marino Contarini employed at Ca' d'Oro, left 100 ducats to his wife, which included her dowry.[88] Compare that to the 2,400 ducats that Soradamor received as her marriage portion. Even more startling is the agreement of the 1430s that Giovanni and his son Bartolomeo reached with the Salt Office to build the Porta della Carta, the new entryway into the Ducal Palace replete with multiple sculptures. The Bons were to be paid 1,700 ducats for their work, and they had to supply some of the stone.[89] Like the Bons, painter Jacobello del Fiore stood at the top of his profession. In 1415 he was warden of the painters' guild. He married twice. His first wife's dowry was 200 ducats; his second wife's at least 500 ducats.[90] Most artisan women had considerably smaller dowries.

The Bons' wills also illustrate how different artisan family life was from that of nobles. They had a much more limited range of family relations: Giovanni named Bartolomeo as his sole executor, while Bartolomeo named his wife Maria and two men, who were not related to him, as his fiduciaries.[91] Artisans seldom had support from a vast kinship network. The statutes of the used-clothing dealers required members to escort relatives of deceased brothers to burial, "if the deceased has [any relatives]."[92] For this reason, the marital bond took on added significance, especially as husbands and wives both contributed to the family's economic well-being, sometimes running their trades or shops side by side. In many crafts, especially involving textiles, women performed the less skilled and often tedious tasks, like reeling and winding silk. However, other guilds, like the mercers and combmakers, had female members. In 1396 Sentucia, an armorer, sold four helmets to the Ten to help resupply their armory.[93] She may have owned her own shop or perhaps she continued to operate her deceased husband's shop until a male heir came of age. Artisans who failed to produce heirs could adopt. Jacobello del Fiore adopted two boys, Ercole and Matteo, perhaps in hope that they would perpetuate his artistic legacy. In his will, he left his drawings and pigments to Ercole, should he wish to follow in his adoptive father's profession.[94] The more limited range of kin available to artisans also explains why many of them relied upon guilds and *scuole piccole* for assistance with dowries, nursing care, and burial.[95]

Little is known about schooling among artisans. Certainly, some masters and shopkeepers received at least enough education to keep accounts, as did some women. The autograph will of Maria, wife of a barber, is organized like the page of a ledger. In it she noted that her husband refused to give her a receipt for her dowry.[96] Apprenticeships could range from as little as one and a half years for fustian workers to eight years for glassmakers, although most guilds mandated apprenticeships between four and seven years. This means that most youths would have reached a level of technical expertise in their mid- to perhaps late teens. The evidence for when artisans married is sparse, although among the *popolo* sexual relations often preceded marriage. This may have been due to less restrictive notions of female honor among artisans as well as the need to delay marriage until the man had established himself in his trade and the woman had accumulated a dowry.

The wills of Soradamor Zeno and Giovanni Bon also offer insights into the thousands of men and women who did not enjoy the advantages of guild membership and occupied the lowest ranks of society. In addition to the bequest of 1 ducat each for thirteen poor women, Soradamor left ten ducats to Margarita, her own wetnurse, and three ducats to Lena, the wetnurse of her daughter Samaritana. For his part, Bon called for the manumission of Antonio his enslaved but only after Antonio had lived and worked with Bon's son Bartolomeo for another ten years. For some males, domestic service or slavery offered a vehicle, albeit a difficult one, to a skilled trade. By contrast, for vast numbers of women (both free and unfree) household service was a way of life. Wetnurses like Margarita occupied a privileged place in the hierarchy of domestic laborers. They received higher wages than most servants; and given the nature of their work, they sometimes formed long-lasting emotional bonds with their charges.[97] When Margarita acknowledged receipt of her bequest from Soradamor, she described her as her "milk-daughter."

Girls began domestic service as early as age seven. In the fifteenth century, female servants earned on average just 7 ducats per year, although they also got room and board. Nevertheless, at that rate it could take years for them to earn enough for a dowry, which for servants then averaged around 65 ducats. Bequests from masters and mistresses and grants from charitable institutions helped. For that reason, female servants and slaves had an incentive to comply with their masters' wishes. Yet this also meant that they were vulnerable to sexual exploitation by males of the household. Their illegitimate offspring usually ended up in an orphanage for adoption by a family that needed added hands, and so the cycle would continue.

The enslaved suffered doubly for having been wrenched from their homes and, if they came from non-Christian or sometimes even Greek Orthodox backgrounds, from being forcibly converted to Latin Christianity. Men who were enslaved enjoyed a slightly higher status than their female counterparts; many served as gondoliers for their masters. The lucky ones might even receive a boat as a legacy, and once manumitted secure a post at one of the city's ferry stations. Giovanni the Ethiopian, formerly enslaved by the noble Capello family, rose to be warden of the San Felice ferry station.[98] Presumably, after working side by side with his masters, the Bons' enslaved man Antonio acquired the skills to be a stonecarver himself. Yet examples of enslaved persons escaping or servants attempting to poison their masters indicate just how desperate their lives often were.[99] In 1393 the enslaved on a ship at Tana revolted, killing the ship's captain, scribe, and many other crew members. The vessel was transporting around 200 slaves, well above the legal limit set to guarantee ship security.[100]

The city had an insatiable demand for unskilled labor. When in 1454 the Council of Ten was organizing fire brigades, it estimated that there were more than 1,000 porters in the city who loaded and unloaded cargo and hauled necessities such as firewood, charcoal, wine, and flour.[101] Some poor women worked as prostitutes. They often found themselves in the financial and emotional clutches of pimps or more commonly female brothel keepers, the preferred managers of Venice's public house of prostitution. Many lived in grinding poverty. The estate of one prostitute, Agnes from Ljubljana, consisted of little more than one silver belt and 10 ducats.[102]

Immigrants filled much of Venice's need for labor. The promise of decent wages drew many to the city. A stonemason/architect from Milan wrote in 1461 that in Venice, "they pay twice what they pay in Milan."[103] Servants came overwhelmingly from the Veneto, Lombardy, Dalmatia, and Albania, lands at least partially under Venetian rule. Many prostitutes came from Germany. Peasant women made frequent commutes to the city from the nearby *terraferma* or neighboring islands to sell chickens, eggs, and other farm produce. While immigration was the norm, there was also a steady if less well-noted emigration. In fact, when the wetnurse Margarita claimed her legacy from Soradamor's estate, she and her cobbler husband had moved to Bologna. Venetian masons found employment in Ferrara working on that city's cathedral.[104] Anastasia, a brothel-keeper from Venice, relocated to Pavia to manage the public brothel there.[105]

Although for many immigrants the promise of a better life in Venice remained a chimera, there were nonetheless spectacular examples of upward mobility. Because they were not locked into the guild system with its rigid rules regarding entry into the profession and the number of shops and employees that masters could keep, freed slaves, like Giovanni the Ethiopian, oarsmen, and others had some possibility of social advancement.

Such was the case for Michael of Rhodes, an exact contemporary of Marino Contarini and Andrea Barbarigo.[106] While his name (Michali) indicates his Greek origins, nothing is known about him before he signed on in Manfredonia as an oarsman with Venice's Gulf or Guard fleet, for which he would have earned around 3 ducats per month. After three years in the Gulf fleet, Michael served as an oarsman on one of the Flanders merchant galleys. Then began his progress up the ranks. His first promotion was to the post of *proder* (prow-end rower). Then for five years he served as the *nochiero* on ships in both the Guard fleet and Flanders merchant galleys. The *nochiero* was armed with a bow, had other unspecified duties, dined at the captain's table, and slept in a bed, unlike the oarsmen who slept at their benches. Michael next advanced to the job of *paron*, the duties of which included provisioning the galley, directing sailors, and managing the ropes, sails, and anchors, and then to *homo da conseio*, a post that included navigational responsibilities and commanded a salary of 80 ducats per voyage. In 1421 he became a *comito*, the highest ranking non-noble officer on a guardship. A year later he attained the top rank open to a non-noble officer, that of *armiraio*, or adjutant to the captain of the entire fleet. These higher positions were filled through election by the College and thus depended on garnering the votes of the noble members of that body. During his career Michael traveled on merchant voyages to London, Flanders, Tana, Alexandria, Albania, Apulia, Trebizond, Aigues-Mortes, Constantinople, Moncastro, and Cyprus. In 1443 the Greater Council named him one of the eleven weighers at the steelyard, a position he took up in January 1445 when a vacancy came open. These jobs, which carried a small stipend, were a reward for service to the Republic and a recognition of need.

Michael married three times. His first wife Dorotea died in 1415, his second wife Cataruccia in 1436, and his third Menegina outlived him. At the time of his death, he had no living children; his son Teodorino had died in 1422. In a brief codicil to his will dated 1445, Michael noted that he "remained in the greatest poverty."[107] He was in financial straits when he died, and he was childless despite three marriages, indicating just how difficult it was for immigrants to succeed and establish their families in Venice. He clearly did not profit greatly from the opportunities he had to carry cargo aboard the ships on which he served. He may not have had either the interest or the aptitude for trade or may have been simply unlucky.

All of this is known about Michael because he compiled a book. Likely he did so as a kind of resumé as he stood for election to various shipboard posts. Much like the *Zibaldone da Canal*, Michael's book is a miscellany. It contains a long section on mathematical problems; another on the calendar, zodiac, and constellations; navigational instructions for different routes; instructions on constructing galleys and other ships; prayers; and assorted other materials. Written in the vernacular in a clear hand, the text contains color illustrations, including drawings of ships and tools. A coat of arms with the letter "M" may offer a clue to Michael's unrealized social aspirations. His book offers a unique window into the world of immigrants and seamen in fifteenth-century Venice, as well as evidence of a growing appreciation for practical knowledge.

At the time Michael was writing his book, humanism was coming into full flower in Venice. The humanists concerned themselves with mundane matters, not composing esoteric philosophical or theological tracts but treatises on topics such as politics, family life, and notions of nobility. They found a congenial model for their concerns in the writings of the ancient Greeks and Romans who also responded to an urban environment. Linguistic emulation of antiquity became a hallmark of the movement. In comparison with Florence and nearby Padua, humanism got a late start in Venice where it came to be dominated by patrician writers who, unsurprisingly, celebrated their native city.[108]

One of the first to do so was Francesco Barbaro whose distinguished political career, including his captaincy of Brescia during the Milanese siege, culminated in a procuratorship of San Marco. Born into an old noble family, Barbaro enrolled in the University of Padua where he studied Greek. His most famous work, *De re uxoria* (On Marriage) was written in 1415 as a wedding gift to Cosimo de' Medici's brother Lorenzo. The tract is divided into two sections. The first explores the nature of marriage and selection of a wife. The purpose of marriage is the procreation of children, whose virtue is a direct result of that of their parents. Noble parents produce noble offspring who in their turn become the leaders of the state, the veritable "walls" of the city.[109] For this reason, the nobleman must take care to select a wife who is both virtuous and nobly born. These were the very concerns that the patriciate was debating in the legislation of the Second Serrata. Barbaro's entire treatise constitutes "a defense of the principle of noble descent."[110]

The second half takes up wifely duties, which Barbaro summarizes as "love for her husband, modesty of life, and diligent and complete care in domestic matters."[111] A woman's first duty is obedience to her husband. The moderation that the wife observes in all aspects of her life blossoms into love between spouses, which itself forms "a pattern of perfect friendship."[112] She is responsible for managing the household. "What," Barbaro asks, "is the use of bringing home great wealth unless the wife will work at preserving, maintaining, and utilizing it?"[113] In one of many references to classical Greece, Barbaro states that like Pericles, who attended to the affairs of Athens, wives should attend to their households, especially the servants; when the servants receive firm but kind treatment, they will return to the household loyalty and gratitude. In a particularly telling insight into patrician attitudes toward those beneath them on the social scale, Barbaro compares loyal servants to the ancient Athenian Xanthippus's faithful dog.

Yet marriage was not in the cards for many patrician males, and in the second half of the century Barbaro's eighteen-year-old grandson Ermolao composed a defense of celibacy, *De coelibatu*. While he sees marriage as essential to civic and republican life, it poses an impediment to those who wish to pursue solitude and study. Barbaro advocates a non-monastic celibacy, which frees its followers from public and familial duties and allows them to pursue the life of the mind. But Barbaro himself was not able completely to escape administrative responsibilities. In the end, he defied the patrician ideal of obedience to the Republic by accepting without Senate confirmation (indeed in defiance of the Senate's choice) Pope Innocent VIII's nomination of him to the patriarchate of Aquileia. Although an extreme example, Barbaro illustrates how heavily the burdens of patrician manhood rested on some noble shoulders.[114]

The defense of nobility found an even stronger proponent in the work of another noble humanist, Lauro Querini. His work was a response to Florentine humanist Poggio Bracciolini's treatise entitled *De nobilitate* (On Nobility), in which the Tuscan argued that nobility is a matter of virtue acquired through education, not birth; of nurture, not nature. Its thesis represented a direct challenge to Venice's hereditarily established ruling class. A member of that elite, Querini held only one office before settling permanently in Crete. In 1449 he composed his own *De nobilitate* in which he countered Bracciolini. Relying on the notion of the Great Chain of Being, Querini argued that everything in the universe—animals, plants, inanimate objects, and of course humans—is arranged in a hierarchy of excellence. Nobility and, with it, the capacity for virtue derive from nature. "From noble and excellent parents, noble and excellent children are necessarily born." Correspondingly little can be expected of the common folk who "burst forth from some stormy and fetid sewer."[115]

Querini also argues that nobility emanates from one's birthplace. Carefully eliding his own ancestors' participation in the Querini-Tiepolo conspiracy, he argues that "without sect, without faction, without any division. No other republic ever, no empire, no kind of city, so long endured as a harmony of minds of one accord . . . without domestic discord as long as has excellent Venice. For now, for more than one thousand years, the gods willing, she has ruled in just empire with virtue and dignity the greater part of Italy and nearly the whole of the Mediterranean Sea."[116] In this way, his tract also becomes a defense of Venice against those who see it as the aggressor in Italian politics. Querini's work attempts to reconcile two contrasting views of Venice: one as a beacon of liberty to the rest of Italy, much like the ancient Roman Republic; the other as an overweening empire ruling over land and sea on the model of the Roman Empire.

Following the death of Visconti and Milan's short-lived return to republican rule, some, including Francesco Barbaro, questioned Venice's aggressive stance toward its neighbors. One who took up the challenge of defending the city against foreign detractors was Paolo Morosini in his treatise *Defensio venetorum ad Europae principes contra obtrectatores* (Defense of the Venetians to the Princes of Europe Against Its Detractors). He was responding to claims that Venice was not active enough in taking on the Ottomans and countering the calumnies of its critics, who impugned the city's nobility. Against the charge that Venetian nobles' blood was not true blue, Morosini argued that they descended from three different groups of ancient nobles, including the Paphlagonians of Troy, who fled to the lagoons in antique times to preserve their liberty. As to the criticism that they were sullied by their engagement in trade, he countered that the barren wasteland to which they escaped, meager in resources, drove them to commerce, which was born not out of avarice but necessity. Indeed, their engagement in trade serves all the world as they transport "from nearly all encircling shores, at . . . [their] own cost and peril" both things necessary and pleasant. They have "by their earnest labors acquired innocent wealth."[117] And when Venice has conquered, it has been to safeguard itself or the freedom of others or the church. Venice's participation in the Fourth Crusade, for example, was aimed at the heterodox Greeks and driven by its desire to place the rightful incumbent on the imperial throne. The charge that the Venetian nobles were not truly noble especially stung since the ideals of chivalry still dominated the courts of Europe. Venice also stood apart because of its republican form of government.

Accordingly, the city's government was another favorite topic of the Venetian humanists including Querini. His *De republica* (On the Republic), a work much influenced by Aristotle's *Politics*, is a defense of aristocratic rule. Households in which fathers rule are microcosms of the polity that can take the form of monarchy, aristocracy, or democracy. Of these, Querini judges aristocracy the best. "Liberty therefore," he declares, "exists in that the noble rule, but the people confirm their choices: in a certain sense, they rule, although they do not hold office."[118] In the ideal city, virtue is pursued, rather than wealth, since both immoderate wealth and poverty can lead to discord. The goal is harmony and concord born of moderation.

Venetian humanists clearly struggled to defend republicanism in a world where monarchs were the norm, just as they vacillated between the models of republican and imperial Rome. Querini dedicated *De republica* to "Francesco Foscari the best prince" and declared that just as ancient times had produced Caesars and Augustuses, so his own age had produced Foscari, a man in no way inferior to those rulers.

The awkward positioning of the doge—a prince at the apex of a republic—is also evident in the works of Giovanni Caldiera, a *cittadino originario*. In his treatise *De concordantia poetarum, philosophorum et theologorum* (On the Concordance of the Poets, Philosophers, and Theologians), the narrator travels through several mythical realms and assigns a place of honor to Doge Foscari, who is under the special protection of the goddess Respublica. Foscari, sitting at the throne of Respublica and surrounded by other members of the government organized by rank, greets the traveler with an oration praising Venice's wealth and achievements as well as its aristocracy, "which resembles supercelestial government and imitates the form of divine institutions."[119] The context is clearly hierarchical.

In his trilogy, *De virtutibus* (On the Virtues), *De oeconomia* (On the Economy) and *De Politia* (On the Polity), composed in 1463 and dedicated to Doge Cristoforo Moro, Caldiera portrays the doge as a veritable monarch. A kind of philosopher-king, the doge seeks advice from the other organs of government, but it is his innate sense of right, his moral compass, that guides the polity. There is one exception to this ducally controlled government, namely, the Council of Ten, which tolerates "nothing threatening to the republic."[120]

As a group, Venetian humanists of the first half of the fifteenth century, most of whom were themselves patricians, supplied the theoretical underpinnings for noble rule, Venetian expansion, and republicanism. They emphasized the moral basis of Venetian hegemony and the city's piety, downplayed internal division, and affirmed that Venetian minds were, as Querini claimed, "of one accord." Hardest to reconcile were the contrasting republican and imperial legacies of ancient Rome as well as the position of the doge as the princely ruler of a republican regime.

While the language, ideas, and images of ancient Greece and Rome suffused humanist writing in the first half of the fifteenth century, in architecture and painting the Venetians still largely resisted the lure of the classical world. They continued to favor instead the local Gothic style, which combined Western and Islamic elements. This is especially evident in the Ducal Palace itself.

By the 1420s the old courthouse that stood between the communal palace facing the Bacino and San Marco was in a ruinous state. The Greater Council voted in 1422 to tear it down and construct a new building that would run along the Piazzetta and meet the communal palace at a right angle. In this way the Ducal Palace became a U-shaped complex, with the ducal apartment and Piazzetta wings forming the sides and the communal palace wing the base of the U. Oversight of the project was entrusted to the Salt Office.[121] Construction would be delayed by a serious outbreak of plague, and once begun in 1424, would continue for many years.

When deciding on the architectural style of the new wing, the Salt Officers made a conservative choice. They decided to match it to the communal wing, in which the weight of the upper floors is carried by squat columns with simple Gothic arches. The colonnade above consists of narrow ogee arch bays, with each column of the bays culminating in a quatrefoil. The huge expanse of solid wall above is broken by large windows as well as the central balcony and is lightened by the lozenge pattern of red, white, and a few gray marble

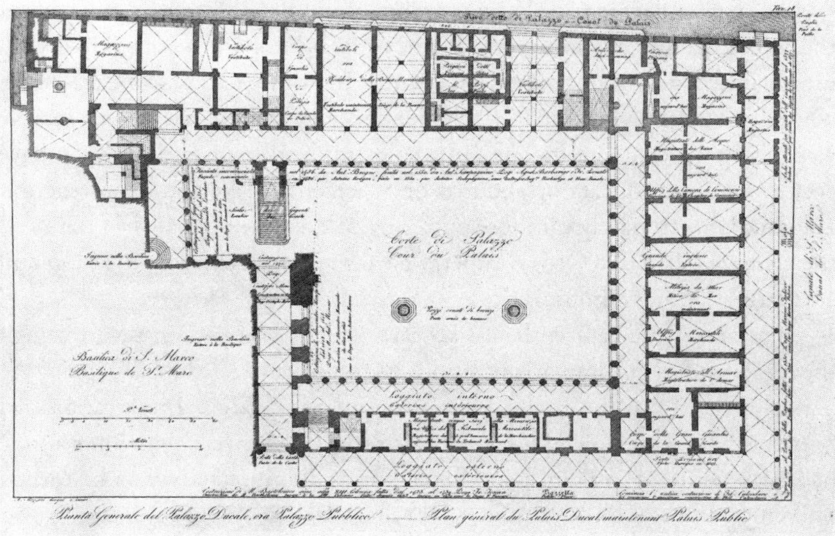

FIGURE 10.3 Ground Floor Plan of the Ducal Palace. From L. Cicognara, A. Diedo and G. Selva, *Le fabbriche e i monumenti cospicue di Venezia*, vol. 1, Venice, 1838. Special Collections Research Center, Syracuse University Libraries.

tiles. The lozenge design recalls a decorative pattern imported to Anatolia by the Seljuk Turks in the eleventh century, while the fanciful crenellation calls to mind buildings in the Levant.[122]

In domestic architecture, too, the Venetians continued to prefer the Gothic style. The basic building type pioneered in the twelfth and thirteenth centuries did not change. Rather, Gothic decorative elements were applied to the façade. This was taken to the extreme in Contarini's Ca' d'Oro, whose façade is completely clad with marble and stone veneers. Contarini may have intended the palace to be a memorial to his deceased wife Soradamor since ornamental bits, including Veneto-Byzantine friezes taken from the old Palazzo Zeno that occupied the site, were embedded vertically in the façade. (Plate 3) Much of the work was entrusted to the workshops of Matteo Raverti, a Milanese sculptor, and Giovanni Bon. Raverti created the two six-bay loggias on the first and second floors on the left side of the façade. The quatrefoils of the first-floor loggia echo those of the Ducal Palace, while the second-floor loggia displays the influence of German and French stonemasons then working in Milan. Bon designed the ground-floor arcade, the single-light windows and balconies on the right side of the façade, the cornice, and the fanciful crenellation. What made Ca' d'Oro a showstopper was its surface decoration. Various architectural details, such as the balls at the top of the crenellation, were gilded, while other parts were painted with ultramarine made from crushed lapis lazuli. The white Istrian stone was made whiter still by applying a coat of white lead paint, and the red Verona marble was oiled to accentuate its hue. This colorful detailing is estimated to have cost around 300 ducats or about 7 or 8 percent of the total construction amount. Unfortunately, all those glittering colors have been lost to time and the elements. In Ca' d'Oro, symmetry gave way to decorative profusion and Contarini's desire to impress.[123]

That is not the case with Ca' Foscari, which impresses instead through sheer size and by its dramatic position. Its façade is visible looking down the Grand Canal from the Rialto Bridge toward San Marco. The location had previously been occupied by the Palace of the Two Towers, which for a time had been awarded to Francesco Sforza, but was confiscated when he turned on Venice. In 1453 the government sold the palace to raise money for the war effort. The buyer, eighty-year-old Doge Foscari, razed the old palace and built his new one, likely intending it for his grandsons and as a monument to the Foscari family.[124]

The massive red-brick four-story façade, which sits on a foundation of white Istrian stone is nearly square. The corners of the façade are defined by alternating blocks of Istrian stone, the top by a substantial cornice of the same material, while horizontal bands called stringcourses mark the floors. The palace boasts two *piani nobili*, each with an eight-light window; the quatrefoils on the second floor echo the loggia of the Ducal Palace. Surmounting that window is a frieze with a helmet topped by a lion of Saint Mark and putti on each side presenting the Foscari coat of arms. The top floor has a four-light window with crossed inflected arches. Unlike Ca' d'Oro, the placement of the windows allows one to discern the interior layout, which is traditional and comprises central *porteghi* with smaller rooms on each side. In his guide to Venice, written fifty years after its construction, Marino Sanudo singled out only two palaces on the Grand Canal for mention: Giorgio (Zorzi) Corner's palace at San Samuele and Ca' Foscari. In *The Stones of Venice*, nineteenth-century aesthete and art critic John Ruskin described it as "the noblest example in Venice of the fifteenth-century Gothic."[125]

In addition to serving as a monument to his family and a rebuke to Sforza, Doge Foscari may also have intended his palace as a challenge to his ally turned enemy Cosimo de' Medici who was in the process of building Palazzo Medici. However, in Venice, the impact of the other innovations occurring in Florence, especially in painting, was attenuated. Giotto's revolutionary Scrovegni

FIGURE 10.4 Ca' Foscari, mid-fifteenth century, Venice. O. Böhm, Venice.

Chapel frescoes in Padua had had a negligible impact on Venetian painters who continued to look to Byzantium both stylistically and iconographically. From the 1370s on the International Gothic style, strongly influenced by artists from Verona, central Italy, and Bohemia and emphasizing rich decorative detail and ornately carved and gilded frames, came to predominate. Gentile da Fabriano's sojourn in Venice between 1408 and 1414 and that of Pisanello of Verona (before 1414 to 1422), both of whom executed now lost frescoes in the Ducal Palace, had an important impact.

Jacobello del Fiore's triptych of Justice executed for the Giudici del Proprio is emblematic of Venetian International Gothic. (Plate 4) A figure of Justice was appropriate for a work destined for the magistracy that adjudicated property disputes. The artist combined elegant swaying movement and gilded embossed gesso to create a work that captured the complex iconography of the Republic. The central panel shows a seated figure of Justice holding sword and balance, flanked by two lions, themselves recalling the throne of Solomon as well as Saint Mark. The side panels depict archangels Michael and Gabriel, the latter the messenger of the Annunciation, another evocation of Venice and its legendary founding on that day.[126] Indeed, the Venetians took 1421, the year the painting was made, to be the one-thousandth anniversary of the city's establishment. Justice thus transmogrifies into Venice itself.

The brief sojourns in Venice of the Florentines Paolo Uccello and Andrea del Castagno helped introduce linear perspective and classical forms into Venetian art. The building in the background of the *Death of the Virgin* mosaic in the Chapel of the Madonna (or Mascoli Chapel) in San Marco is a classicizing triumphal arch, and the composition is arranged according to linear perspective. The two figures on the left are clearly based on a cartoon by del Castagno. Antonio Vivarini and Giovanni D'Alemagna's triptych *Virgin and Child and Four Latin Doctors*, commissioned for the Scuola Grande of the Carità, utilizes the one-point linear perspective pioneered by Florentine Filippo Brunelleschi to create the walled enclosure in which the Virgin and saints are located. However, the figures themselves, as well as the thrones and stalls before which they are assembled, remain Gothic in sensibility, and it all seems to partake of the world of Ca' d'Oro.[127]

Ca' Foscari also served as a challenge to the Council of Ten, which had forced Doge Foscari's only surviving son Jacopo into permanent exile in Crete.[128] The story of the two Foscaris—the doge and his son—is certainly tragic. When Foscari was elected doge in 1423, he had five sons. However, by 1438 all but Jacopo had died. Unlike most patrician youths, Jacopo received an up-to-date education and corresponded with humanist luminaries. But the lot of ducal sons was not easy since the ducal oath of office forbade them from holding office or engaging in trade. Nevertheless, the celebrations that the doge staged for Jacopo's marriage to Lucrezia Contarini had all the trappings of a princely affair, including sumptuous banquets and jousts in which troops of mercenary captains participated. The extravagant wedding gifts that the doge showered on Lucrezia included a necklace valued at 8,000 ducats that had recently been worn by Amadea, daughter of the Marquess of Montferrat, who married King James II of Cyprus. The jewels thus had royal associations. Perhaps out of boredom or a desire to appear important, in 1445 Jacopo allowed himself to get caught up in a bribery scheme in which he received gifts and money from various lords including Sforza and, most damning of all, Filippo Maria Visconti, Venice's sworn enemy.

From foreign princes' point of view, it made sense to try to influence Venetian policy via the doge's kinsmen. After all, in princely states, a ruler's relatives were often among his closest advisors. Foreign potentates clearly did not understand the limitations on ducal power or how the Venetian republican regime operated. During the War of Chioggia, for example, Ludovico Gonzaga, the Marquess of Mantua's agent in Venice, had to inform him that "not even the doge or his council" could keep the promise to pay interest on the marquess's shares in the public debt. Instead, Gonzaga's only recourse was to petition the Senate.[129] But blame for the bribery scheme lay with Jacopo for accepting the gifts. Even Giorgio Dolfin, a Foscari partisan, said that Jacopo committed these acts, "not thinking of God or the honor of his fatherland."[130] Jacopo was tried by the Council of Ten and exiled to Treviso. Then in 1447 with a final showdown with Sforza looming, the Ten, worried that the doge was too preoccupied with Jacopo's exile and not giving his full attention to matters of state, allowed Jacopo to repatriate.

Yet Jacopo's problems were only beginning. In late 1450 he was accused, wrongly it seems, of murdering one of the members of the Ten who had tried him for collusion with Visconti. Even under torture, he refused to confess. Uncertain what to do, the Ten exiled him to Crete, in part so they could focus on more pressing matters and in part to humble Foscari and his son. The doge's decision to build his new magnificent family palace should be viewed against the backdrop of the humiliation that he and his son had endured.

The final act in the tragedy of Jacopo Foscari began in June 1456 when the Ten again tried him for communicating with foreign princes, including Sforza and even the Ottoman sultan. The Ten retrieved Jacopo from Crete for interrogation and rejected a proposal by Jacopo Loredan, one of the chiefs of the Ten and son of Foscari's old rival Pietro, to behead Jacopo. They voted instead to return him to exile in Crete. Jacopo pleaded with his father to allow him to stay, but the doge responded, "Jacopo, go and obey the wishes of the city and don't seek anything more."[131] He died on Crete in January 1457. The doge's own quasi-regal actions, including the extravagant wedding he staged for his son, the building of Ca' Foscari, and the adornment of the new entryway to the Ducal Palace, the Porta della Carta, with a life-size statue of himself kneeling before the lion of Saint Mark, may have convinced Jacopo that as a ducal son he could push the limits. The Ten reminded him he could not.

In a final humiliation, the Ten decided in October 1457 to remove Foscari from the ducal throne. They claimed, with some justification, that his extreme old age, coupled with despair over Jacopo's death, were causing him to neglect matters of state and so voted to urge him as "a good Prince and true *Pater Patriae* (Father of the Fatherland)" to renounce the dogeship.[132] Yet when a delegation from the Ten conveyed the message to him, Foscari responded that "it was not the business of the Council of Ten to provide for this matter, but rather the Greater Council."[133] He saw the request for what it was: a power play by the Ten, especially Jacopo Loredan. By urging a vote in the Greater Council, the doge clearly hoped that the poorer nobles would put the brakes on this unprecedented step by the most powerful men in the patriciate. In the end, the members of the Ten determined that they did indeed have the right to depose the doge and voted to have the delegation return and inform Foscari that he had eight days to vacate the Ducal Palace. Outmaneuvered, Foscari renounced the dogeship on October 23, 1457. Many in the city were outraged saying, "This should not have been the reward for so many efforts and troubles that he suffered on behalf of the Republic."[134] The Ten voted to investigate those, including nobles, who protested its actions. On November 1, All Saints' Day, Foscari died. With their hypocrisy on full display, the Ten and Full College voted to accord him a ducal funeral.

The funeral oration was delivered by humanist Bernardo Giustinian. He used the occasion to present a defense of Venice's *terraferma* expansion, arguing that Venice had accepted its destiny to protect the freedom of Italy. Enumerating the cities that had come under Venice's control during Foscari's reign, Giustinian declared, "These [cities], Francesco, are your monuments, the fruits of your labors by which the splendor of your name is rendered immortal."[135] He glossed over the divisions within the patriciate that had brought about Foscari's removal from office.

The deposition of Francesco Foscari reveals much about Venetian politics at mid-century. Years of warfare and the accompanying financial sacrifices had opened fissures within the patriciate: some cleavages were based on family alliances like the rivalry between the Loredans and the Foscaris; others were founded on wealth and power like the contest between the influential nobles of the Ten and Senate and the lesser nobles of the Greater Council. The power grab by the Ten should be seen in the context of the creation of the mainland state, the necessity for faster decision-making, and the consolidation of a few large states on the Italian peninsula. Venice was no longer a city-state with a communal form of government, distant colonial possessions, and a relatively homogeneous ruling class. It had become a regional-state with a complex bureaucracy, maritime and *terraferma* interests under threat from both other Italian states and overseas powers, and a socially and economically stratified ruling class. At the center of this struggle was a debate over the nature and character of the dogeship itself, a perennial issue in Venetian politics. Princely power was on the rise throughout the Italian peninsula. Even republican Florence found itself increasingly under the sway of the Medicis, who functioned in the fifteenth century as disguised princes. The fate of the two Foscaris reaffirmed the doges' subordination to the councils of state. It should also be understood against the backdrop of Venetian patrician family relations and the importance nobles attached to kinship ties. The tragedy for Doge Foscari was that he was never able to reconcile his conflicting roles as *paterfamilias* and *Pater Patriae*. His inability to choose between the city and his son led to his ruin.

The power grab by the Ten represented one of the gravest constitutional crises that the Republic ever faced, a challenge to the dogeship as well as the entire system of checks and balances. Under mounting pressure, the Ten took steps to reform itself a year later and reestablish some equilibrium among the various deliberative bodies. First, the Ten agreed that it could not intervene in matters (like the deposition of a doge) that concerned the ducal oath of office and that were properly the responsibility of the Greater Council. Second, it restricted the ability of its heads to issue orders, commissions, and letters without the full authority of the entire council. Third, the Ten decided not to institute penalties that deprived a convicted man's kinsmen from holding certain offices or serving as judges as it had done in the past. It noted that it was not proper to deny members of the nobility the privileges that their "noble origins and liberty and the laws of the city of Venice" conferred on them.[136] This was a restatement of the essential equality of all members of the ruling class, regardless of their wealth, prestige, or family connections.

Even so, the aggrandizement of the Ten continued unabated. In 1468 the Greater Council again tried to rein it in. In a vote of 450 to 166 with 110 abstentions, the Council reiterated the traditional competencies of the Ten, namely, treason and conspiracies against the state, sodomy, and supervision of the *scuole*, but it otherwise prohibited the Ten from expanding its jurisdiction, especially warning the Ten's heads to observe those limits.[137] The divided vote underscores yet again the deep divisions between the smaller councils filled by the more powerful nobles and the bulk of poorer ones who hoped to maintain the authority of the Greater Council.

Although the laws of 1458 and 1468 constituted major reforms, they by no means resolved the issue of executive authority in the Venetian Republic.

The problem would persist as the demands of international politics continued to push toward concentrating power in an ever-narrower circle of men. In response, several of Foscari's successors in the dogeship would continue to strive for an ever more princely dogeship, one heavily imbued with Roman imperial associations. That was just one of many challenges facing the Republic in the turbulent decades ahead as international politics and the "discovery" of new worlds humbled the ambitions of the Venetian lion.

11

Taming the Lion

IN 1516 VITTORE Carpaccio completed a painting for the office of the State Treasurers at Rialto. (Plate 5) The artist depicted a winged and haloed lion of Saint Mark, bestriding land and sea and displaying with his right front paw the gospel book with the words of Mark's *praedestinatio* inscribed thereon. The lion's left front paw is firmly planted on the sandy shore of a small beach. The land rises to the left as the littoral yields to a rocky escarpment, with a heavily wooded forest beyond. The landscape serves as a cipher for Venice's mainland dominion that extends from the shoreline of the lagoon to the Alps. The lion's rear paws float on the tranquil waters of the Bacino. On the horizon, Carpaccio offers a stunning depiction of the city. The governmental center at San Marco is visible on the left, between the forest and the lion's head. The Ducal Palace, basilica of San Marco, campanile, and recently constructed Torre dell'Orologio (clocktower) that marks the entry to the Merceria are all rendered in exquisite detail. The fully outfitted *bucintoro* (doge's ceremonial galley), an allusion to Venice's ducal regime, is anchored on the Molo, along with smaller vessels. A gondola glides past. The right side of the horizon portrays Venice's maritime strength. Just above the lion's rump is the fortress that protects the San Nicolò entrance to the lagoon. On the right, three large carracks (multi-masted merchant vessels) are making their way to the custom's house, with a galley docked in front. A fourth carrack is anchored near the walled monastery of San Giorgio Maggiore with its tall and slender bell tower. At the top of the canvas, clouds are yielding to a clement sky, while the coats of arms of the treasurers who commissioned the work are at the bottom.

Carpaccio's painting was both nostalgic and prophetic. Completed just a few years after Venice had seen its mainland empire vanish and its overseas trade dominance challenged, the painting seemed to recall a time when the Venetians could boast of ruling both land and sea, as in an inscription on an image of Saint Mark's lion in Rovereto: "I am the lion, of whom no one in the world possesses a vaster empire. The land obeys me; the sea obeys me."[1] By 1516 such leonine haughtiness seemed misplaced, if not foolhardy. At the same time, Carpaccio's masterwork points to how the Venetians would come to understand and present themselves to the world after being humbled. They would continue to take pride in their possessions on land and sea and their still vibrant economy, but more important, they would celebrate their republican government and the miracle that was the city itself, constructed as it was in a fragile amphibious environment.

This chapter explores the diplomatic, military, economic, and governmental challenges Venice faced between 1460 and 1530, when it fought two major wars with the Ottomans and conflicts both great and small on the Italian peninsula. Technological innovations in the use of artillery and ships' rigging dramatically altered commercial vessels and how wars were fought. By 1530, the age of the state-owned merchant galleys was nearly over. Ottoman naval supremacy in the eastern Mediterranean and the opening of the Atlantic by the Portuguese displaced Venice from its role as the chief trade intermediary between East and West. The nobles reacted to these changes by erecting the final set of barriers distinguishing themselves from the rest of the city's inhabitants. At the same time, divisions within the ruling class, between richer and poorer nobles, between those who favored mainland or maritime interests, and between young and old became ever more pronounced. Emergency provisions enacted during the Cambrai Wars undermined the notions of equity and moderation that had been the hallmarks of the patrician ethos.

Over these decades, Venice adjusted its horizons. At the beginning of the period, it seemed to many observers that Venice was on the cusp of achieving hegemony in Italy. As Borso d'Este, Duke of Ferrara, warned in 1451, "The Venetians, who are immortal, will without difficulty become rulers of Italy."[2] He understood that the leadership continuity afforded by their republican regime allowed them to maintain a policy consistency unachievable in princely regimes, including the papacy, where the death of the prince or pope could result in abrupt changes of course. Venice's republican government, by contrast, appeared unwavering or, as Borso said, immortal. He expressed the widely held view that the Venetians aspired to the *imperio d'Italia*, the rulership of Italy.

The Venetians, for their part, objected to such an assessment. They argued instead that they were protecting the *libertà d'Italia*, which they defined as the independence of smaller states and freedom of the peninsula from foreign intervention. They believed as well that they constituted the chief Christian defense against the Ottomans. To retain their position as a world-class power, they needed to marshal all their resources, and so they adopted a more synoptic vision of their dominions as they continued to transform their polity from a city-state into a regional-state or indeed into something even grander as was gradually happening in France, Spain, England, and the Ottoman Empire. But forces beyond Venice's control thwarted these efforts. The Ottomans effectively reconstituted the dominion of the Byzantine Empire, as they turned the eastern Mediterranean and Black Seas into Ottoman lakes. For their part the Portuguese opened the Atlantic world to Europeans.[3] By 1530, the Hapsburgs were the predominant power in Italy, but the peninsula was just one part of their vast empire that stretched from Palermo to Amsterdam, from Milan to Mexico City. Caught in a vise between the Hapsburg and Ottoman behemoths, between two gunpowder empires of vast scale, Venetians could do little but try to protect their hold on the Adriatic, maintain a neutral stance, present themselves to the world as the model republic, and extol their miraculous city, product of both God and man.

Although the Peace of Lodi of 1454 and the subsequent Italian League brought an end to the nearly constant warfare that had marked the previous three decades, it did nothing to halt the jockeying among the various Italian states or their ambitions. Venice remained preoccupied with the powerful Duchy of Milan on its western border, but also faced new threats to its supremacy in the Adriatic and northern Ionian Seas. The Ottomans were contesting Venetian control over the eastern shores of these waterways, while Florence, Naples, and the papacy sought to undercut Venetian commercial domination of the western shores. As a manufacturing center, Florence was constantly seeking ways to get its goods to consumers in the eastern Mediterranean. Its takeover of Pisa and construction of a merchant galley fleet were part of that effort. But Florence also recognized the potential of Adriatic ports such as Ancona as possible outlets from which to ship its goods to the East. The Kingdom of Naples posed graver challenges. Its control of Apulia, the heel of the Italian boot, meant that it could hamper Venetian shipping through the Strait of Otranto. Furthermore, the perennial royal dream of launching a reconquest of the now-defunct Byzantine empire kept alive Venetian fears that both shores of the Adriatic might come under a single hostile power. Papal nepotism also threatened Venetian interests. Pontiffs saw their elevation as an opportunity to enrich their kinsmen and carve out territories, especially in Romagna and the Marches, for them to rule. Alexander VI's efforts to promote the interests of his son Cesare Borgia are the best-known example. If properly outfitted with infrastructure and favorable customs policies, the coastal cities of the States of the Church, including Cervia, Rimini, Pesaro, and Ancona, could challenge Venice's Adriatic commercial hegemony.

Accordingly, Venetian policy in these decades was to assert tighter control over the western shore of the sea. In 1441 Venice annexed Ravenna, but its port and the canal that linked it to the Po had long since silted up. Then in 1463 Domenico Malatesta, condottiere and lord of Cesena, sold salt-rich Cervia to Venice for an annual payment of 4,000 ducats and 200 sacks of salt.[4] Venice coveted Cervia since salt produced there was being clandestinely exported to cities in Romagna, undercutting Venetian efforts to maintain its salt monopoly. The humanist pope Pius II (Aeneas Silvius Piccolomini) fulminated against this transgression into papal dominions, accusing the Venetians of being one with "thieves and robbers" and warning them, "You think your republic will last forever. It will not last forever nor for long . . . a mad state cannot long stand."[5] Reversing Cassiodorus's ancient claim that the lagoon's watery environment promoted virtue, Pius argued instead that it rendered the Venetians subhuman. "What," he asked, "do fish care about law? As among brute beasts aquatic creatures have the least intelligence, so among human beings the Venetians are the least just and the least capable of humanity, and naturally, for they live on the sea and pass their lives in the water; they use ships instead of horses; they are not so much companions of men as of fish and comrades of marine monsters."[6] Venice sought to limit papal and Neapolitan influence over Romagna and the Marches. It supported Sigismondo Malatesta, lord of Rimini, in his struggle against Alfonso of Naples and Pius II, who wanted to create dominions for his Piccolomini relations in Malatesta lands.

Pius's antipathy toward the Venetians was fueled in part by their lukewarm response to his 1458–9 call for a crusade to recover Constantinople and the Balkans from the Ottomans. After conquering Constantinople, the Ottomans under Mehmed II had seized most of the islands in the northern Aegean as well as Trebizond on the Black Sea, conquered Serbia, taken possession of the Morea, and in 1463 were attacking Bosnia. Evacuees from Dalmatia, Albania, and Greece were making their way to Venice, establishing "national" confraternities like San Giorgio degli Schiavoni and San Gallo degli Albanesi, and contributing to the Hellenization—or better yet, neo-Byzantinization—of Venetian culture and architecture in this period. Another refugee was Saint

George. When the Senate learned that his head, as a holy relic, was kept on the island of Aegina off the coast of the Morea, which was under Ottoman threat, it ordered Vettor Capello, captain general of the sea, to secure the relic and bring it to Venice for safekeeping at the monastery of San Giorgio Maggiore. Once it arrived safely in Venice, the Senate and the abbot of San Giorgio each agreed to contribute 100 ducats for the repair of fortifications on Aegina as partial recompense for the loss of the relic.[7] As the fleeing Saint George evidently knew, the Venetians and the Ottomans, with their lands abutting, seemed destined for a showdown. However, when it came to Pius's proposed crusade, the Venetians feared that other parties would renege on their promises of aid and that they would be left to face the Ottomans alone.

Venice chose to look to potential allies such as Mathias Corvinus, king of Hungary and Croatia, and Albanian leader Scanderbeg, both of whom were also directly threatened by the Ottoman advance. On July 28, 1463, Venice declared war on the Ottomans, the first of seven wars the two would fight.[8] Aiming to retake the Morea, it dispatched 5,000 infantry and 800 cavalrymen under the command of Bertoldo d'Este, with Alvise Loredan serving as captain general of the sea. With lightning speed and the support of the local Greeks, the Venetians quickly captured most of the Morea. They laid siege to Corinth and rebuilt the Hexamilion, the wall first constructed in the fifth century CE across the isthmus of Corinth to protect the Morea from invasion from the north. At the ceremony inaugurating the wall's refurbishment, a banner with Saint Mark's lion and a cross inscribed with the words "in hoc signo vinces" (in this sign conquer) fluttered in the wind. The slogan recalled Emperor Constantine I's vision of the cross before the Battle of the Milvian Bridge in 312 CE. The banner asserted the Venetians' status as heirs to Constantine and Venice's role as the new Byzantium.[9] For his part, Venice's ally Corvinus retook much of Bosnia.

However, Ottoman reinforcements soon reversed the tide. When Bertoldo d'Este was wounded during the siege of Corinth and died, Venetian resolve evaporated. By the end of 1463 they had lost the greater part of the Morea except Modon and Nauplion. At this point, the Venetians decided to support Pius's crusade. Doge Cristoforo Moro reluctantly agreed to lead the Venetian forces in person. But when the contingent of twenty-four galleys finally arrived at Ancona to launch the expedition, Pius was gravely ill. He died on August 14, 1464, just three days after the Venetians' arrival. With its leader gone, the enterprise was abandoned.

In the meantime, the war dragged on. Venice sought allies in Anatolia and beyond as a way of forcing Mehmed to fight on two fronts. Then in 1470 the Ottomans secured a stunning victory by conquering Negroponte, Venice's most important outpost in the eastern Aegean. The Ottoman fleet was so huge that one eyewitness reported that "the sea looked like a forest."[10] Against this Ottoman fleet numbering around 400 vessels, including 100 war galleys, Nicolò Canal, captain general of the sea, commanded only thirty-five war galleys. As the Ottomans built a pontoon bridge across the narrow Euripus strait separating Negroponte from the Greek mainland in order to convey troops to the island, Canal retreated to Crete to recruit more ships. When he returned with fifty-two galleys, he let an opportunity to attack the ill-guarded Ottoman fleet slip. The Ottomans overran Negroponte on July 12, 1470, taking the town's women and children prisoner and killing the men, including the *bailo* Paolo Erizzo. The losses on the part of the victorious Ottomans were also huge. When news of the debacle reached Venice, everyone was shocked. Chronicler Domenico Malipiero said of the disaster, "Now it well seems that Venetian greatness has been laid low and our haughtiness extinguished."[11] On his return to Venice, Canal was tried and exiled. Pietro Mocenigo assumed the post of captain general. The Venetians considered the commercial loss of Negroponte so grave that in talks with Mehmed II the following year they offered to buy it back for 250,000 ducats.[12]

Venice also faced the Ottoman menace much closer to home. Various bands of semi-regular light cavalry, who lived primarily off plunder, brought the war to Friuli. In 1472 they crossed the Isonzo River and threatened Udine before retreating with a large capture of animals. The next year they reached the Tagliamento River. In response, Venice constructed earthen-work defenses on the western shore of the Isonzo. The fleet under Pietro Mocenigo raided cities along the coast of Anatolia and tried unsuccessfully to destroy the Ottoman Arsenal at Gallipoli. While besieging the castle of Sighun (Syedra), the taunts of the defenders echoed Pius II's in what had become a commonplace insult. They yelled from the battlements, "Go, Venetians, to rule over the sea and the fishes!"[13] In their continuing effort to draw Mehmed's attention east, the Venetians renewed their overtures to the Karamanids and the Turkoman ruler Uzun Hasan, whose realm included much of present-day Iran, Iraq, eastern Anatolia, and Azerbaijan. Yet just when it appeared that their combined forces might carry out an attack on Constantinople itself, the Venetian fleet under Mocenigo abandoned the enterprise to safeguard Venice's interests in Cyprus. Through Venetian noblewoman Caterina Corner's marriage to James II, king of Cyprus, in 1468, Venice had established a protectorate over the island. Venice needed to defend the widowed and pregnant Caterina (and its own commercial interests) against a rival claimant to the throne supported by Naples and Savoy. Mocenigo returned to Cyprus in February 1474 in the aftermath of a failed coup against Caterina and then made his way to Venice, after defending Scutari (Shkodër) from an Ottoman siege. He was elected doge in December 1474 and died only fourteen months later. His tomb in San Zanipolo, by the Lombardo family of sculptors, celebrates him as a warrior. He stands armored and wearing the ducal *corno* atop his sarcophagus on which is depicted the siege of Scutari and the restoration of Caterina Corner to power following the attempted coup.

While Mocenigo was on his first mission to Cyprus, Mehmed dealt a serious defeat to Uzun Hasan. Once Mehmed had again secured his eastern border, he turned his troops on Albania. New and more serious attacks were also launched in Friuli, as the defenses erected by the Venetians proved incapable of stopping them. In 1477 the Ottomans crossed the Tagliamento and raided the countryside around Pordenone, Sacile, and elsewhere. The 1478 incursions were graver still. The invaders made off with 8,000 prisoners and 10,000 head of livestock, laying waste to the countryside around Gorizia.[14] As the war dragged on, so did diplomatic efforts to secure a peace. A treaty was finally concluded through the efforts of Venice's *cittadino* secretary Giovanni Dario in January 1479. For Venice the terms were sobering. It had to surrender Scutari and Croia (Krujë) in Albania, Lemnos and Negroponte in the Aegean, and Brazzo di Maina (the Mani peninsula) on the Morea. It agreed to pay an indemnity of 100,000 ducats to the sultan and an annual tribute of 10,000 for the privilege of trading in his lands. In return it got the right to maintain a *bailo* in Constantinople. Good commercial relations resumed soon thereafter. As a sign of goodwill, Venice acceded to Mehmed's request for a painter to be sent to him by dispatching Gentile Bellini to Constantinople, where he executed portraits of the sultan and decorated some rooms in the Seraglio, the living quarters of Mehmed's harem.[15] The war effectively expelled Venice from the Aegean Sea (except for the Duchy of Naxos), while the Ottomans were better established than ever along the shores of the Ionian.

The war revealed above all that the Ottomans had become the predominant naval power in the Aegean and Black Seas. During the first half of the century, Venice had been able to stall the Turkish advance because the Ottomans remained predominantly a land-based power. But once Mehmed conquered Constantinople, he embarked on an effort to build up his navy and a new harbor for his warships.[16] The mismatch between the Ottoman and Venetian navies at Negroponte signaled the shift. In addition, firearms and artillery were changing the nature of warfare on both land and sea. As the Senate observed in 1498, "the present wars are being decided more by bombards and artillery than by men-at-arms."[17] The Ottomans were highly advanced in this arena. Firearms posed a particular threat to heavy cavalry who were increasingly replaced by light cavalry. Venice looked to *stradioti*, light cavalry recruited from Albania and Greece. The 1477 Ottoman invasion of Friuli also demonstrated the inadequacy of the defensive earthenworks that had been constructed on the Isonzo following the attacks earlier in the decade. In response Venice decided to concentrate its troops in strongholds from which they could be deployed and utilize local conscripted militias. A major enclosed compound was built at Gradisca on the Isonzo. Refugees from Scutari were settled there.[18] On the sea, light (war) galleys were vulnerable to cannonades, and their narrow decks made it difficult to outfit them with artillery. But cannons could be mounted on round ships and great (merchant) galleys. Nevertheless, light galleys remained the principal warships in the Mediterranean until the end of the sixteenth century on account of their speed and maneuverability.

Above all else, Venice needed to increase the size of its war fleet to something approaching 100 light galleys to match the Ottoman threat. But the Arsenal as it was then configured was inadequate to the task of maintaining that number as well as approximately twenty merchant galleys. Hence in 1473 the Senate decided to enlarge the Arsenal by adding a new section that came to be known as the Arsenale Novissimo. Work progressed slowly. The Novissimo added another twenty acres, bringing the size of the entire complex to approximately sixty acres. An effort was also made to centralize and coordinate the activities required for the navy around the Arsenal. Foundries for forging cannons were built, along with warehouses for the storage of saltpeter and gunpowder. In 1500 a Scuola dei Bombardieri (School for Artillerymen) was established to train gunners. The diverse activities concentrated in and around the Arsenal also required greater administrative oversight and coordination.[19] In the 1460s and early 1470s Venice also made improvements to its Arsenals at Candia, Corfu, Negroponte, Chania, and Rethymno.

All this required huge outlays of money. Venice was appropriating about 100,000 ducats annually to the Arsenal alone.[20] But as usual, it was the cost of war that exploded the deficit. Malipiero estimated that the war against the Ottomans was costing 1,200,000 ducats a year.[21] In order to raise money, the Senate decided in 1463 that it would institute a new system of direct taxation, known as the *decima* (tithe or tenth). It empowered a board of nine noblemen to conduct a citywide survey of all properties, including houses, fishponds, and mills in the *dogado*, and estimate how much each would yield annually if rented out. Income and rents on *terraferma* properties were also assessed.

Ecclesiastical properties and incomes were not exempt, nor was interest on the old Monte shares. Merchandise was to be taxed, as were rents from shops, gold imported from Barbary, even the income derived from the rental of jewelry. Jews living on the *terraferma* were to pay an annual tax of 3,000 ducats; those in the *stato da mar* would owe 2,000.[22] The Senate justified this new tax scheme, which carried no promise of reimbursement, by declaring that it was more equitable and fairer than the old forced loans, was necessary for the "preservation of our state," and was being instituted "in the name of Jesus Christ."[23] The latter reason and the necessity of making war on the Ottomans justified the taxation of ecclesiastics. Like the monarchs of Europe, the Republic was seeking ways to get its hands on the church's revenue.

During the war against the Ottomans, the *decima* was imposed nearly forty times, raising on average between 70,000 and 80,000 ducats each time. However, forced loans were not completely abandoned. In 1482 a new forced loan fund, known as the Monte Nuovo, was instituted, but with a difference. Assessments were based on the *decima*. In any given year, the first two impositions of the *decima* were considered direct taxes and the funds would not be returned. Subsequent impositions in that year were considered loans and credited to the Monte Nuovo, which paid 5 percent interest. The Monte Nuovo had an initial cap of 550,000 ducats, although by the first decade of the sixteenth century the cap had risen to 3 million ducats. This shifted the weight of taxation from trade onto property, which reflected the war-torn economy. Malipiero noted that for the year 1475, "the city has no trade and money doesn't flow and imposts aren't paid."[24] Towns on the *terraferma* also contributed to the war effort in both money and kind; in 1470 Padua offered 6,000 bushels of biscuits for the navy. In return, Venice gave the elites of those cities a large degree of control over local matters. Overall, the war compelled the government to tap new revenue sources in a more systematic and intrusive way. This was just one of the changes that the shifting international situation was forcing on the government.

The peace accord with the Ottomans allowed the Venetians to turn their attention once again to the western shore of the Adriatic.[25] Ironically it was Mehmed's intervention there that prompted the shift. In July 1480 his fleet sailed from Valona in Albania and occupied Otranto. Like Justinian's campaign in the sixth century, this was intended as a first step in a Constantinopolitan reconquest of Italy. Mehmed's overtures for an alliance with Venice were spurned, as were calls by the pope and Naples for Venice to join a crusade to drive the Ottomans from Otranto. Having recently made peace with Mehmed, the Venetians did not want to jeopardize their revival of trade in Ottoman realms. Besides, they had no interest in seeing either the Ottomans or Neapolitans establish themselves on both Adriatic shores. The crisis was averted when in May 1481 Mehmed died while fighting the Persians in Asia Minor. The Ottomans withdrew from Otranto, which was retaken by Ferrante of Naples. But the episode revealed to the Venetians that they needed to gain greater control over the ports of Apulia. A more immediate challenge much closer to home occurred when Ercole d'Este tried to free Ferrara (and the lower Po) from Venetian economic hegemony.

In his attempt to do so, Ercole hassled Venetian merchants trading in Ferrara and facilitated the smuggling of salt, in contravention of Venice's monopoly.[26] He had the support of his father-in-law Ferrante of Naples, who was allied at the time with Florence and Milan. Pope Sixtus IV sided with Venice since he was trying to carve out territories in the Marches and Romagna for his relatives, a move Ercole opposed. Sixtus also had designs on the Neapolitan throne for his nephew Girolamo Riario, who was made an honorary member of the Venetian Greater Council in 1481. In return for a free hand in those realms, Venice could have Ferrara as well as ports in Apulia. Venetian public opinion was riled up when the Bishop of Ferrara's vicar excommunicated the Venetian consul who had arrested a priest for debts. Over the protests of both Sixtus and the bishop, Ercole refused to lift the excommunication. Although some members of the Senate advised caution, other nobles as well as many *popolani* wanted action. According to Malipiero, never had a decision to go to war met with "so much agreement."[27] The Monte Nuovo was instituted at this time to help pay the anticipated expenses. In a letter that Doge Giovanni Mocenigo sent to Venetian governors, he described the war as "most just and honorable."[28] But to Venice's many enemies it seemed to confirm their view that the Venetians were still intent on the domination of Italy.

The Venetians began their attack on Ferrara on May 1, 1482, when they launched an assault with land forces, led by the condottiere Roberto da Sanseverino, and a 400-vessel river fleet that included many small craft manned by crews recruited from the city and lagoon. Venice scored some early successes, taking the region north of the Po known as the Polesine and the town of Rovigo. At sea the navy was raiding the Apulian coastline and in November won a major battle at Argenta. By the end of the year, Sixtus had become wary of Venetian success and reached a peace accord with Naples, Milan, and Florence. He threatened the Republic with interdict if it did not accede to his requests to come to terms. When he finally issued the interdict, Venice refused to publish it and pushed for a church council to be summoned. The Great Schism of earlier in the century (the contest between rival claimants to the papal throne) had fueled the conciliar movement, the belief that a council of all the leading churchmen ought to preside over the church. It was intended as a check on papal monarchy.

The land war moved into the Bresciano and Bergamasco, while the navy managed to take Gallipoli in Apulia. With so many allies arrayed against it, Venice considered calling in the support of the sultan, as well as of the king of France and the Duke of Orleans, who had claims to the throne of Naples and the Duchy of Milan, respectively. But financial exhaustion and Milan's wariness of French intervention finally resulted in the Peace of Bagnolo in October 1484. Venice had to renounce its efforts to claim Ferrara, while papal lordship of the city was reaffirmed; Venice surrendered Gallipoli and other sites it had taken in Apulia to Ferrante. But it retained its commercial privileges in Ferrara and got possession of Rovigo and, much to the consternation of Ercole, the Polesine. Thus, despite its cost, the war added a significant new chunk of territory to the *stato da terra*. The interdict was lifted by Sixtus's successor, Innocent VIII, in February 1485. The tournament that was held in Venice to celebrate the end of the war marked the last major occasion when such military displays were used to mark important events in the city's civic life. As the city grew more densely settled, horses became both a nuisance and a threat and finally were banned. Centuries earlier than elsewhere, the age of horsepower passed into history.[29]

Just two years later Venice was involved in a brief war at the northern extreme of its *terraferma* dominion, the War of Rovereto.[30] This time its opponent was the archduke of Austria, Sigismund, of the house of Hapsburg, who controlled the county of Tyrol. Border disputes at the northern end of Lake Garda, along with conflicts over mineral and timber rights, aggravated relations in the region. When Sigismund had Venetian merchants who were traveling to a fair at Bolzano arrested and their goods confiscated, violating treaty rights, Venice declared war in spring 1487. The Republic's forces had an early advantage and marched nearly to Trent, but a counterattack led to the loss of Rovereto in May and its recovery in July. During combat in August, Venice's captain, Roberto da Sanseverino died, along with many of his men. But the Austrians were unable to pursue their advantage. Under pressure from Holy Roman emperor Frederick III and Pope Innocent VIII, the parties came to terms in November. Little had been accomplished, except that this war, like the Ferrarese one, reinforced the image of Venice as an aggressor intent on expanding its dominion.

Two years later Venice decided that it needed to formalize its hold on Cyprus, a territory that dwarfed its interests in south Tyrol. When noblewoman Caterina Corner (or Cornaro) married King James II of Cyprus, she was officially adopted by the doge.[31] Until her death in 1510 she was referred to in official Venetian documents as the "adopted daughter of the doge" or, more frequently, as the "daughter of the Republic." This appellation apparently assuaged King James's concern that he had besmirched his honor by not marrying into another royal house. In the end Venice got the better deal because when James died in July 1473, followed by his infant son and heir just thirteen months later, Caterina's designation as Venice's adoptive daughter strengthened the Republic's claim to the island, since fathers had legal control over their daughters. For the next fifteen years, Caterina ruled in her own right, styling herself queen of Jerusalem, Cyprus, and Armenia. But officials sent from the metropole kept close watch on her, as did her brothers. She chafed at the interference writing, (employing the royal 'we') that commissioner Giovanni Soranzo had "for our person . . . so little estimation or reputation that it was as if we were his serving girl."[32]

By 1488 Venice had had enough with its sometimes recalcitrant "serving girl" and decided to annex the island directly, prompted by fear that the Ottomans were about to invade Mamluk Egypt and concern that Caterina might succumb to one of several suitors, such as Alfonso, son of King Ferrante of Naples. The prospect that Cyprus might fall into Neapolitan hands drove the Ten to send the captain general of the sea to persuade Caterina to leave Cyprus. They promised that she could retain her royal title and enjoy an 8,000-ducat annuity. Emphasizing the kinship bond that had been established by her adoption, the Ten beseeched her to "acknowledge and give way to most faithful parental counsel and our deliberation."[33] Caterina's brother Zorzi finally convinced her to accede in January 1489. She departed Famagusta in March. Thirty years after these events, Venice's ambassador to English king Henry VIII heard the complaint, echoing a now familiar trope that "the Venetians are fishermen . . . who are expert in seizing what belongs to others and had taken something from all the potentates of the world."[34]

In Cyprus's case the aggrieved potentate was the Mamluk sultan of Egypt Qa'it Bay since the island was after 1426 legally a Mamluk dependency that owed an annual tribute of 5,000 ducats. Ambassador Pietro Diedo was able to mollify the sultan's indignation by emphasizing the common threat that both faced from the Ottomans, strategically deploying gifts, and assuring him that the tribute that Cyprus owed would continue to be paid. In this way, Venice added the third largest island in the Mediterranean (after Sicily and

FIGURE 11.1 Gentile Bellini, *Portrait of Caterina Corner*, c. 1500. Museum of Fine Arts, Budapest, Hungary. Photo by Yelkrokoyade, distributed under a CC BY-SA 3.0 license via Wikimedia Commons.

Sardinia) to its dominion. Its annexation helped compensate for the losses it had suffered in the Aegean.

As for Caterina, she received a triumphal entry into Venice in June, where she was feted by Doge Agostino Barbarigo. But once those festivities ended, the government faced the tricky problem of permanently hosting one of its noblewomen who was also a queen. By its very nature, her status threatened the patrician ideals of equality and *mediocritas* (material moderation) that were at the heart of the city's republican ethos. The matter was further complicated by the extraordinary wealth and growing power of Caterina's brother

Zorzi, who was knighted by the doge in recognition of his help in pressuring her to leave Cyprus. A solution to the Caterina problem was found when on June 20, she was officially designated "Lady of Asolo," a small hill town of 1,000 persons northwest of Treviso, where she was accorded full regalian rights, except that she could not give refuge to criminals or abrogate Venice's salt monopoly. Caterina established her court there and passed her time with hunts, games, and other entertainments, all the while reminding the government of her status as its adoptive daughter. She also continued to advocate for her former Cypriot subjects. Court life at Asolo is commemorated in Pietro Bembo's *Gli Asolani* (The People of Asolo), a dialogue on the nature of love. Caterina died on July 10, 1510. Her tomb in the church of San Salvador, which dates from the 1580s, is part of a celebration of the Corner family and its many cardinalships, including one that Zorzi bought for his son Marco for 15,000 ducats.[35] It includes a relief sculpture of her surrendering the crown of Cyprus to the doge. In the opposite transept Marco is depicted receiving his cardinal's hat from Alexander VI. The tomb reinterprets Caterina's reluctant removal as the patriotic act of a faithful daughter of the Republic. The scene would also be depicted in a ceiling painting in the Greater Council Hall where Caterina is the only historical woman commemorated in that space. The annexation of Cyprus came at a propitious time for Venetian commercial interests in the eastern Mediterranean and offers yet another example of the myriad methods by which Venice expanded its dominion, while Caterina's life offers further evidence of the fraught position of women in patrician society. Although she demonstrated some agency and advocated for herself, in the end her interests were subordinated to those of her natal and adoptive families, the Corners and the Republic.

The international situation became infinitely more complicated when in 1494 French monarch Charles VIII invaded Italy, bringing an end to the forty years of relative stability that had settled over the peninsula following the Peace of Lodi.[36] Charles intended to assert an Angevin claim to the Neapolitan throne, which he believed had been usurped by Alfonso II of the Spanish house of Aragon following his father Ferrante's death in January. Charles planned to use the Neapolitan kingdom as the jumping off point for a reconquest of Constantinople from the Ottomans and Jerusalem from the Mamluks. Despite Charles's promise of a Christian crusade, Pope Alexander VI opposed the mission since he feared a powerful French presence to his south. Also opposed were Siena, Florence, and Bologna. The man pushing for

French intervention was Ludovico Sforza, known as Il Moro, regent for his nephew Gian Galeazzo, the titular Duke of Milan and Alfonso's son-in-law. If the Aragonese could be forced out of Naples, Ludovico could depose his nephew and claim Milan for himself. The Venetians were characteristically non-committal. Charles was offering them Apulian ports in return for their support. But they were cautious since the proposed crusade could destabilize the situation in both the southern Adriatic and eastern Mediterranean.

Charles's invasion commenced in September 1494 when he entered Italy at the head of a huge army, including thousands of Swiss mercenaries. He stopped at Milan, where Ludovico had already proclaimed himself duke, having poisoned his nephew Gian Galeazzo. Charles then traveled to Tuscany where Piero II de' Medici surrendered several strategic towns to him. This infuriated the Florentines, who forced Piero into exile for acceding to Charles's demands. Passing through Rome, Charles entered Naples. Alfonso II fled to Sicily, abdicating in favor of his son Ferrante II. Charles's success shocked the Italians. In just a few months, the rulers of Milan, Florence, and Naples had all been overthrown.

Charles again urged the Venetians to join him in his proposed crusade to retake Constantinople, promising them Apulian ports and cities that they had lost in Albania and Greece. He needed their navy if his crusade was to have any hope of success. The Venetians waffled. If the enterprise failed, they would be the ones to bear the brunt of Ottoman anger. If it succeeded, their interests in the old Byzantine empire would be subordinated to those of France. As Malipiero noted, "It is dangerous to align oneself with such a great king, who with our help could become our neighbor."[37]

The Venetians were not alone in concluding that Charles was a threat. Ludovico Sforza, France's erstwhile ally, had reached the same conclusion. He had good reason to be nervous since Charles's retinue included the Duke of Orleans, who had a claim to the Duchy of Milan through a past Visconti marriage. The Florentines resented that Charles had not restored the cities that he had taken. In July 1495, the league that formed against him, including Venice, met his army at Fornovo near Parma. Venetian forces made up the bulk of the army facing the French. The battle resulted in no clear winner, and Charles was able to retreat, departing Italy by the end of the year.

All the while the Venetians were angling for greater control over Apulia. They made a 200,000-ducat loan to Ferrante II. In return they got control of Monopoli, Brindisi, Otranto, and other towns that were to be restored to Ferrante when he repaid the loan. But as Philippe de Commynes, the French diplomat, wrote, "I don't believe that they have any intention of returning them, as is their custom with cities that, like these in this part of the gulf [the Adriatic] are useful to them; and in this way they are the true owners of the gulf."[38] The Venetians seemed to be the only ones who had gained any real advantage from Charles's expedition. It was hard to disagree with Venice's opponents who believed that the lion was on a rampage.

Yet it was about to be tamed. The new French king Louis XII was preparing a campaign to avenge Ludovico Sforza's betrayal of Charles VIII. In a reversal, the Venetians allied with Louis in the Treaty of Blois signed in February 1499. They wanted to grab Cremona from the Milanese and were promised that the border between Milan and their territory would be the Adda River. They also wanted French assistance in their upcoming conflict with the Ottomans. By September, Cremona was in their hands. Sforza, hoping to force Venice into war on two fronts, informed Ottoman sultan Bayezid II that it was a propitious time to attack the Venetians. The Florentines were urging the same. In June 1499 an Ottoman fleet of around 260 vessels made its way toward the Morea to assist the army in its assault on the Venetian-held town of Lepanto. The Venetian fleet, comprising ninety-five vessels including forty-four war galleys, twelve merchant galleys, and around two dozen carracks, was under the command of wealthy financier Antonio Grimani.[39] The fleets engaged on August 12 near Zonchio, off the Greek coast. When two large Venetian round ships and a Turkish carrack ended up in a conflagration exacerbated by gunpowder stored on board, the Venetian commanders failed to obey orders, and the Turkish fleet was able to retreat to Zonchio. In further engagements on August 20, 22, and 25, disorder and disobedience again crippled the Venetian cause. Domenico Malipiero, who was present, explained that everything proceeded from "too little love for Christianity and the fatherland, from too little heart, too little order, and too little [regard for] reputation."[40] The Turkish fleet proceeded to Lepanto, which succumbed.

When news of the disaster reached Venice, the Senate elected Melchiorre Trevisan the new captain general of the sea and ordered Grimani repatriated in chains. According to Malipiero, children and the *popolo* (the pairing suggests nobleman Malipiero's social prejudices) cursed him with the cry, "Antonio Grimani, the ruin of the Christians."[41] Fearing that his house would be sacked, Grimani's sons moved spices stored there to monasteries for safekeeping. After being tried by the Greater Council, Grimani was exiled to the island of Cherso (Cres). He eventually escaped and made his way to Rome, where his son Domenico was a cardinal and the newly elected patriarch of Aquileia. As the war continued, Zonchio, Modon, and Coron all fell to the Turks. The latter two, the "eyes of the Republic," had long served as early warning posts near the junction of the Ionian and Adriatic seas. But Venice did manage to gain Cephalonia and Santa Maura. In September, the Turks invaded Friuli, again crossing the Isonzo after meeting little resistance from the local militias that Venice had organized or the defenses that had been erected. The following year, Leonardo da Vinci inspected the fortifications along the Isonzo and recommended the construction of retaining ponds and other projects that could turn the river itself into a weapon.[42] The bulk of Venice's professional forces were engaged in Lombardy.

Venice's poor performance during the war was partly due to the changing nature of naval warfare as vessels propelled by oars had to be integrated with ships like carracks that depended entirely on wind propulsion and with the increasing use of artillery. The recruitment of crewmen was also an issue. Other navies faced similar logistical challenges. Venice's problems were compounded by its propensity for choosing commanders, like Grimani, who were better known for their financial acumen and political connections than their expertise at sea.[43]

Peace was finally secured in 1503 through the efforts of nobleman Andrea Gritti and the *cittadino* secretary Zaccaria de' Freschi. Venice had to give up Santa Maura and pay an annual tribute for Zante. But at least Zante and Cephalonia could assume the lookout role that Modon and Coron had formerly played. Venice also retained its trade privileges in the Ottoman empire and its *bailo* in Constantinople. Nevertheless, the 1499–1503 war marked "the point of no return" for Venice's *stato da mar* and the moment when it "lost its maritime supremacy."[44] Although the Republic would continue to hold many territories until its demise in 1797, the period of overseas expansion had largely come to an end and its navy would face increasingly formidable opponents. As the scale of its foes increased, Venice had to adjust its ambitions and horizons.

Only in retrospect did the full significance of the war against the Turks become clear. Yet contemporaries immediately grasped the importance of news that reached Rialto in July 1501, in the middle of the war. That month, the Venetians learned from Pietro Pasqualigo, their ambassador in Portugal, that six Portuguese ships laden with spices had returned to Lisbon from India after rounding the Cape of Good Hope. Banker and diarist Girolamo Priuli records that everyone in Venice was "stupefied that in the present day a new route had been found" and that this was "the worst news that the Venetian Republic could ever have gotten other than the loss of its freedom." Priuli calculated that for every ducat invested, the Portuguese had recouped 100 and that for this reason, "the King of Portugal will be able to call himself the King of Money because everyone will go to that country to get their spices and the money will remain in Portugal." He had no doubt that "the Hungarians, Germans, Flemish, and French and all northerners who used to come to Venice to buy spices with their money, will all turn instead to Lisbon since it is closer to their lands and transportation is easier, and indeed they will get a better deal, because Portugal will import it all." Given the many customs duties and other surcharges that the Mamluks and Venetians imposed on spices, the Portuguese could easily "sell at a much better price." Adding insult to injury, Portuguese king Manuel I had even told Pasqualigo that the Venetians could now come to Lisbon to get their spices.

At first, Priuli says, "many still believed that this news couldn't be true." Others thought the cost would be too great, since of the thirteen vessels that had set out on the voyage, only six had returned safely. Some hoped that the Portuguese would be unable to find crews because they would be terrified of such a treacherous journey. Still others thought that the Mamluk sultan would find a solution since, once spices stopped arriving in Alexandria and Syria, he too would suffer great financial loss. Priuli apologized to his readers for going on so long about the matter but explained that the news was of such significance "to our fatherland" that he had gotten carried away.[45]

By September the Venetians learned that Portuguese spices had reached Bruges and Antwerp, while hope that the voyage would be too treacherous to become routine was dashed when four more Portuguese vessels completed it in September 1502. Rather than being too dangerous, "the voyage to India" was, as Priuli noted, "most easy."[46] The new route was also calamitous news for Venice's spice trade partner, the Mamluk sultan Qansuh al-Ghawri, since he saw the supply of spices for sale to the Venetians, Genoese, Catalans, and others slow to a trickle. Turning on the Venetians, he confiscated their goods and tried to force them to buy the spices available in Egypt at extremely high prices. Benedetto Soranzo was sent on a mission to urge the sultan to act against the Portuguese and lower the prices he was charging the Venetians but was unsuccessful. The entire matter was so serious that in December 1502, the Ten decided to convene a special *zonta* of fifteen men whenever it discussed the spice trade. When the Ten dispatched another ambassador, Bernardino Giova, to the sultan in 1504, his instructions were to encourage him to send emissaries to India to dissuade the rulers there from trading with the Portuguese and apply pressure by reminding him that the Portuguese were inviting the Venetians to procure spices in Lisbon.[47]

Although it was deleted from Giova's final commission, the Ten and the spice *zonta* even contemplated urging al-Ghawri to build a canal that would link the Red Sea to the Mediterranean, an early modern version of the Suez Canal. Giova was to tell the sultan that such a waterway could be built "very easily and quickly" and protected by forts at either end so that only those whom the sultan wished to do so could pass through. With this canal, the sultan would be able to move galleys between the two seas and drive the Portuguese from the region, resulting in greater security and benefit to his realm. Giova was warned to tread lightly for fear that the sultan would take umbrage at the proposal, which he might construe as redounding more to Venice's benefit than his own and posing a danger to his realm.[48] In the end, the Ten erred on the side of caution and dropped these recommendations altogether from Giova's commission. But the fact that the building of a Suez Canal was contemplated in the early sixteenth century indicates that the Venetians were frightfully aware of the danger that the Atlantic world posed to the Mediterranean one and were searching for a way to mitigate the damage. It also reflected Venetian expertise in hydraulics and hydrology gained through management of the *terraferma* river systems and lagoon.

Al-Ghawri did try to drive the Portuguese from the Arabian Sea but failed because his ships could not compete against Portuguese gunpower. His navy suffered a major defeat in the Battle of Diu (1509). But Portuguese king Manuel I undercut his own price advantage by maintaining a crown monopoly on pepper rather than allowing private traders to find the free-market price. He needed the revenue to pay for his conquests in India and protect the fleets carrying the spices. The Ottomans' conquest of Egypt in 1517 changed the equation since they were in a position, unlike the Mamluks, to challenge Portuguese naval might. In their effort to combat the Ottomans, the Portuguese allied with the Persians. Consequently, a large quantity of spices made its way up the Persian Gulf and to Aleppo and Beirut. At the same time, illicit sales of spices to Arabian merchants by Portuguese officials in India allowed spices to continue to find their way into the Red Sea and then to Alexandria. Despite the dire predictions following the Portuguese circumnavigation, the Venetians were again able to procure significant amounts of spices in both Syria and Egypt in a kind of informal economic alliance with the Ottomans and in so doing compete with the Portuguese. Indeed, by the middle decades of the century they were importing nearly the same quantity of spices as they had before the Portuguese venture. But their earlier quasi-monopoly was irrevocably gone. They were just one of many suppliers of spices to Europe.[49]

The Portuguese circumnavigation of Africa was part and parcel of the opening of the Atlantic and the European encounter with the New World. The Venetians played a modest role in these endeavors since their orientation was toward the eastern Mediterranean, unlike the Genoese who had been largely driven from that zone and so increasingly looked westward. Notable exceptions were nobleman Alvise da Mosto and the *cittadino de extra* Giovanni Caboto (or Cabot) and his son Sebastiano.[50]

Alvise da Mosto, commonly referred to as Cadamosto, followed the career pattern typical of many Venetian noblemen. Forced to rebuild the family fortune after his father's disgrace, he began by serving as an agent for merchant-nobleman Andrea Barbarigo. Like Barbarigo, he received assistance from the government in establishing himself when he was chosen as an archer of the quarterdeck for the Alexandria and Flanders galleys. When in 1454 a ship on which he was sailing was forced to seek shelter at Cape Saint Vincent in Portugal, he met Prince Henry the Navigator and decided to join a small ship belonging to Henry that was making a journey down the west coast of Africa. Along the coast of Senegal, he traded horses and woolen cloth for slaves and parrots. For each horse he got between nine and fourteen slaves. His ship joined up with two others, one of which was captained by the Genoese Antoniotto Usodimare, and went in search of gold. The convoy "discovered" the Gambia River but was unsuccessful in landing because of local hostility. It then returned to Portugal.

In 1456, Da Mosto outfitted at his own expense a ship that, together with two others, headed again toward the Gambia. Near Cap-Vert in present-day Senegal they were blown off course and were perhaps the first Europeans to reach the Cape Verde Islands. Returning to the coast, they sailed up the Gambia but failed to find gold. They continued to explore along the coast, going as far south as the Geba River but had to turn back when they reached a linguistic barrier that their interpreters could not traverse. Da Mosto's second journey marked the southernmost point along the coast of west Africa that European explorers had yet reached. After a few more years in Portugal, Da Mosto returned to Venice and married. Although he continued to engage in trade, he also held numerous governmental posts.

Alvise da Mosto's reputation rests less on his discoveries than on his description of them in his *Navigazioni* (Navigations), written in the 1460s after his return to Venice. True to his merchant roots, Da Mosto filled his account with quantitative information but also offered descriptions of the flora, fauna, people, customs, and foods he encountered. He wrote, "Truly in comparison with our own [places], those that I saw and came to know could be called another world."[51] His account, first published in 1507, would be republished in many later editions and translations. The great nineteenth-century German geographer Carl Ritter said that Da Mosto's treatise brought to a European audience knowledge of the Senegambia region of Africa, much as Marco Polo's *Livre des merveilles du monde* had of Asia.[52]

Giovanni Caboto's place of origin remains uncertain, he had resided in Venice for at least fifteen years when he earned *de extra* citizenship in 1476. While traveling in the eastern Mediterranean he grew familiar with the spice routes and became convinced, following Columbus's first voyage, that a westerly voyage could carry one to China and Japan. Sometime in the 1480s he transplanted to Spain and then ultimately to England. With financial backing from English merchants in Bristol and Italian merchants in London, Caboto received privileges from Henry VII authorizing him to sail in search of this new route. A first expedition in 1496 failed. The second on the ship *Matthew* departed in spring 1497 with a crew of a few as twenty. It made landfall in June somewhere on the coast of North America, likely either in Newfoundland or Cape Breton Island. He planted the flag of Henry and, according to a letter written by Venetian Lorenzo Pasqualigo from London, the banners of Saint Mark and the pope. After some exploration of the coastline, the *Matthew* returned to Bristol in just over two weeks, owing to favorable winds. Caboto believed that he had reached eastern Asia or, as he said, "the land of the Great Kahn."[53] The outcome of a third voyage that comprised five vessels remains in dispute. Some contend that Caboto died during the trip, others that he returned successfully after leaving behind friars to establish a mission in North America.

Caboto's son Sebastiano was born in Venice and thus enjoyed citizenship by birth. In 1508–9 he led an English expedition to find the Northwest Passage but was halted by ice, probably in Hudson Bay. He then explored the coastline of North America, traveling perhaps as far south as the Chesapeake Bay before returning to England. Finding Henry VIII less amenable to exploration than his father Henry VII, Sebastiano took his services to Spain where he served as pilot major for decades. At one point, he appealed to the Ten, seeking Venetian support to find the Northwest Passage. But his petition was rejected.

Although Alvise da Mosto and Giovanni and Sebastiano Caboto certainly played a role in the opening of the Atlantic world to European trade and settlement, none did so in the service of Venice. These new realms were simply too far removed from Venice's traditional sphere of influence to garner much interest from the Republic. Where Venice did play an outsized role was in the diffusion of knowledge about the discoveries via the new medium of print, of which the Republic was in the forefront.[54]

While the Atlantic world created an opening for some Venetian products like glass beads, which were employed in the slave trade in Africa and the fur trade in North America, on balance it hurt Venice's economy not only by short-circuiting the spice routes but also by offering new sources for goods such as sugar and cotton that the Venetians either produced themselves in Cyprus or imported from the Middle East. The Portuguese began growing sugar cane in the Madeira Islands in the 1420s and later in the Canary and Cape Verde Islands and could sell it to consumers in northern Europe more cheaply than the Venetians. Exchanges went both ways. For example, in the mid-sixteenth century Venetian dyers started using New World cochineal, obtained from insects in Mexico, as an alternative to kermes (derived from insects native to the Mediterranean region) as a crimson dye for cloth. Another New World native, maize, eventually became an important component of Veneto agriculture and polenta a staple of the diet, particularly of the peasantry and urban poor.

The short-term crisis in the spice trade also prompted an administrative adjustment. In 1507 the Senate created a committee known as the Cinque Savi alla Mercanzia e Navigazione (Five Sages Concerning Commerce and Navigation) to make recommendations to the College regarding trade. It was made permanent in 1517. Yet there was no way to turn the clock back to when Venice enjoyed undisputed commercial dominance. The Age of Discovery had created new routes and competitors while other structural changes rendered obsolete the venerable system of state-owned merchant galleys operating on fixed freight lines.

Numerous factors contributed to the breakdown of the merchant galley system.[55] Constant delays in the regular departure and arrival of various lines undermined investor confidence. Some delays were due to the Arsenal's inability to produce or outfit the necessary vessels on time. The number of merchant galleys declined from thirty-two in 1504 to just nine in 1518.[56] Recruitment of oarsmen and other qualified sailors grew more difficult. Plague, corsairs, and competition from the Portuguese, Flemish, English, and smaller powers like Ancona and Ragusa also took their toll. The wars with the Ottomans and those caused by the French invasions prompted more frequent requisitioning of the merchant galleys for wartime use. As rival navies grew larger, Venice had to divert the merchant galleys to the navy, further undermining their commercial dependability. Some lines became dangerous or unprofitable. The Aigues-Mortes line was suspended in 1495, while the Flanders/England line operated only six times between 1516 and its termination in 1533. Divisions within the patriciate opened between those who believed the maintenance of commerce was essential and those who emphasized mainland defense. Some patricians believed Venice's future lay on the *terraferma*; others, like Girolamo Priuli, thought it continued to rest on eastern commerce. He lamented that his fellow nobles had abandoned the hard life of overseas business travel in favor of a *terraferma*, that is, villa, lifestyle, that, in his view, made them soft and lascivious.[57]

The development of artillery and changes in ship rigging contributed to the decline of the merchant galley system as well. With their low-sitting decks, merchant galleys were especially vulnerable to gunfire. This deprived them of the strategic advantage that had made them the preferred (and in some instances required) form of transport for precious cargo. Round ships well outfitted with cannons were highly defensible and increasingly secure from attack.[58] Around the turn of the sixteenth century, the addition of topsails, foresails, and mizzens rendered round ships, like carracks, much more maneuverable and "as safe for most long voyages as the galleys."[59] Accordingly, in 1514 the Senate began allowing round ships to transport spices from Beirut and Alexandria. The salaries for the large crews of oarsmen required on merchant galleys put the merchandise they carried at a price disadvantage since the sailors' pay had to be recouped. Great or merchant galleys did retain an important role in sixteenth-century Mediterranean naval warfare in part because having all the oarsmen on a bench pull a single oar, rather than multiple oars, increased their propulsion and boosted the size of the fighting force they carried.

Failure of individual ship captains to follow the orders of convoy commanders became chronic as they placed their individual interests over those of the group. The concentration of ships in the hands of fewer and fewer rich families exacerbated this problem. In 1520, for example, Girolamo Priuli and his brother Lorenzo controlled nearly all the shares in a state-owned galley sailing to Alexandria while between 1494 and 1529 just thirty patricians played an outsized role as captains, guarantors, and shareholders in merchant galleys.[60] In Domenico Malipiero's estimation, "full warehouses were fighting with empty ones and individual interests with those of the public."[61] When commerce came to be regarded as an individual activity rather than a cooperative enterprise, the entire system, which had done so much to foster solidarity within the patriciate and project Venetian political and commercial might abroad, collapsed.[62] After 1534 Beirut and Alexandria were the only lines still operating. The final state merchant galley sailed in 1569. The age of great galleys as merchantmen and the freight lines had passed, as had Venice's economic domination of the eastern Mediterranean.

The peace reached with the Ottomans in 1503 allowed the Venetians to return their attention to Italy. Venice took advantage of the chaos created by the deaths of Pope Alexander VI in 1503 and his son Cesare Borgia in 1507 to occupy some of the territory that Cesare had carved out for himself in the Marches and Romagna. Faenza, Rimini, and Fano all offered themselves to Venice in part to gain protection from the Duke of Ferrara and the Florentines. But when Giuliano della Rovere became Pope Julius II, he demanded that the cities be restored to the papacy. Venice surrendered Fano and offered to hold the others as papal vicariates. But Julius was not satisfied. A staunch proponent of ecclesiastical power, he wanted to rein in various prerogatives including the nomination of bishops and taxation of the clergy that the Republic had arrogated to itself. When in 1507 Venice offered refuge to Giovanni II Bentivoglio, the former ruler of Bologna whom Julius had ousted, as well as to Giovanni Sforza, ruler of Pesaro, who was in rebellion against him, Venice completed its alienation of Julius.

Around the same time, it made an enemy of the Holy Roman emperor Maximilian I of the Hapsburg dynasty who already harbored grievances against Venice. When he began to amass troops along Venice's northern border in anticipation of marching to Rome to be crowned emperor, the Republic refused him passage through its territory. When hostilities broke out, the Venetians won a victory over the imperial forces at Pieve di Cadore and then moved east, wresting Pordenone, Gorizia, Trieste, and Fiume from imperial control. After centuries of effort, the Venetians gained complete command of the territory surrounding the Gulf of Venice. A treaty ending the hostilities was reached in June 1508. The Venetians' quick military victory over Maximilian gave them a mistaken sense of security, as did confidence in their diplomatic ability to play one rival power off another.[63]

With this the stage was set for one of the worst existential crises that the Republic ever faced, one that rivaled in gravity the War of Chioggia. Just six months after signing the peace with Venice, Maximilian, along with his rivals, the kings of France and Spain, agreed in the city of Cambrai in northern France in December 1508 to form an anti-Venetian alliance dubbed the League of Cambrai. Its goal, according to Maximilian, was "to put an end to the losses, injuries, robberies, and damages that the Venetians have caused . . . [and to] extinguish like a fire, the insatiable greed of the Venetians and their thirst for dominion."[64] Each of the parties and future signatories would be rewarded with territories that the Venetians had snatched from them. The emperor would reclaim the Veneto, Friuli, and Istria; the king of France would take Bergamo, Brescia, Cremona, and other lands that had once been part of the Duchy of Milan. Apulian ports occupied by Venice were to be returned to the Kingdom of Naples, while the pope would again take possession of Ravenna, Cervia, Rimini, and other lands in the States of the Church. The king of Hungary could reclaim all Dalmatia, and the Duke of Savoy Cyprus. The Duke of Mantua would be awarded some territories in Lombardy, the Duke of Ferrara would have Rovigo and the Polesine.[65] Over the next few months, Venice tried to peel away some of the allies, but to no avail. If the league accomplished its goals, the dismemberment of Venice's *stato da terra* would be complete. In April 1509 Doge Leonardo Loredan exhorted members of the Greater Council that, to win God's favor in the upcoming war, they had to condemn blasphemy and sodomy. They also needed to render justice equitably, conduct fair elections without politicking, and pay their taxes. He warned, "If we lose, we will lose a beautiful state; there will no longer be a Greater Council, we will no longer be a free city, as we are now."[66]

In April 1509 Julius II placed Venice under interdict. By then, 40,000 French forces had already crossed the Adda, and war was under way. Venice's commanders were Nicolò Orsini, count of Pitigliano, designated captain general, and Bartolomeo d'Alviano, serving as governor general. Although the Venetians quickly retook Treviglio, which had been seized by the French, on May 14 they suffered a terrible defeat at Agnadello where they lost half their troops. D'Alviano was captured, along with the army's artillery. Brescia, Verona, and Vicenza all refused to open their gates to Pitigliano's retreating forces. The French occupied Brescia and waited for the emperor's forces to take Verona, Vicenza, and Padua, as agreed to in the terms of the league.

Letters announcing the Agnadello debacle arrived on May 15 as the *savi* were meeting. According to Marino Sanudo, who was at the Ducal Palace at the time, "all began to weep and lament, or to put it better, to lose [control of] themselves. . . . [T]hey were like dead men."[67] Over the next few days, the city's mood worsened. Doge Loredan appeared, to Sanudo, "more dead than alive."[68] Fearing for the city's internal security, the final days of the Ascension fair were canceled. In the following weeks, Venice made frantic offers to various league members to get them to renounce the alliance while more of the *terraferma* was conquered. Verona, Vicenza, and Padua all fell into imperial hands. The local civic elites were happy to reclaim the authority that the Venetians had taken from them, while the peasantry and *popolo* constituted a force of resistance. Only Treviso held out. What was left of Venice's forces took up position at Mestre. In what seemed like the blink of an eye, the *stato da terra* had evaporated. As Machiavelli put it in *The Prince*, the Venetians "lost in a single battle what it had taken them 800 years to acquire with so much effort."[69]

In July, under the leadership of commissioner Andrea Gritti, Padua was retaken. In celebration and as thanksgiving for the divine favor shown, the Senate ordered that an annual procession be held to the church of Santa Marina, the saint on whose feast day Gritti had accomplished the reconquest.[70] The Venetian forces then had to withstand an imperial effort to retake Padua. In a desperate search for allies, Venice approached the Ottoman sultan for a loan and troops and asked both him and the Mamluk ruler to curtail certain types of commerce with Venice's enemies.[71] Negotiations continued as territories were won and lost. Finally, in February 1510 Venice was able to pry Julius II from the league by promising, among other things, to surrender many of its ecclesiastical privileges, allow freedom of movement in the Gulf of Venice to papal subjects, and downgrade the authority of its official in Ferrara. These latter two represented important concessions concerning Venice's long-standing position as the staple port of the northern Adriatic and arbiter of Po River traffic. Julius acceded to the alliance because he had become increasingly worried about the French who were strongly supported by the Duke of Ferrara with whom he had various grievances, including over the salt monopoly in the States of the Church.

With much of the Romagna in French hands, Julius organized the Holy League in 1511. It was comprised of Venice, Spain, the papacy, and England (Henry VIII signed on in order to gain territory in northern France). By the end of the year the French had lost the Duchy of Milan, but they continued to hold various cities, including Brescia. The Medicis were restored in Florence. Yet when Julius engineered a new alliance with Maximilian aimed at securing Verona, Vicenza, and Padua for the empire, Venice shocked by allying with France in the Treaty of Blois of March 1513. Louis would guarantee the Veneto cities to Venice, while the Venetians would help him reclaim the Duchy of Milan. But the French troops performed poorly when confronted by Swiss pikes, and soon Padua was again under siege. Enemy artillery was even positioned at the edge of the lagoon, and the sound of shelling could be heard in Venice. The nearby *terraferma* was on fire. A letter recovered from the body of a fallen enemy soldier stated that where the imperial army passed, all that was left was "smoke and ash." The writer exaltingly proclaimed that not "since the time of Frederick Barbarossa" had an emperor advanced so far toward Venice.[72] Around this time, German court painter Albrecht Altdorfer and his assistants created a series of miniatures illustrating the triumphs of Maximilian. One, entitled *The Great Venetian War*, shows the *terraferma* aflame and overrun by imperial troops, while the lion of Saint Mark with a rat-like tail glances back in fright at the mainland as it desperately paddles across the lagoon to the safety of Venice. Nothing contrasts more sharply with Carpaccio's confident lion.[73] As during the War of Chioggia, all that protected the city from invasion was its location in the waters of the lagoon. The Venetians suffered another serious defeat at La Motta in October, but the exhausted enemy forces did not take advantage of the victory. They went instead into winter quarters.

When Louis died in January 1515, he was succeeded by his son-in-law Francis I, who by also taking the title Duke of Milan revealed where his ambitions lay. In September 1515 Francis and the Venetians won a decisive victory, causing Massimiliano Sforza to renounce the dukedom of Milan. The emperor gathered his troops and again entered Italy but quickly changed his mind and returned to Germany. In May 1516 Brescia finally came back into Venetian hands. In the autumn of 1516 peace was arranged between France and soon-to-be Holy Roman emperor Charles of Burgundy, heir to Ferdinand of Aragon. Pope Leo X reconciled with France, and eventually Maximilian made peace with Francis as well in the Peace of Brussels, according to which Venice had to give up its claim to Cremona. A treaty between Venice and the empire in 1518 saw the restitution to the Republic of the lands on the *terraferma* that it had lost, except Rovereto, Gradisca, and Gorizia. With these few exceptions, the Venetian *stato da terra* was restored to the status quo ante bellum.

Palma il Giovane's *Allegory of the League of Cambrai* in the Ducal Palace reimagined the war as a Venetian triumph. It depicts angels bearing the laurels of victory toward Doge Loredan, who directs the allegorical figure of Venice with sword in hand and a diminutive and not particularly ferocious lion of Saint Mark charging toward Europa's bull on which is mounted a figure bearing a shield emblazoned with the coats of arms of Venice's enemies. Despite being executed in the 1590s, the painting captured the city's hubris in the years immediately following the war. Venice continued to grab territory as circumstances allowed and sought to maintain its status as a major player. Yet growing Hapsburg power was soon to demonstrate just how misplaced those aspirations were and how idealizing Palma's retrospective painting was.

In June 1519 Charles, ruler of the Netherlands and Burgundy and king of Castille and Aragon, was elected Holy Roman emperor. His lands included

FIGURE 11.2 Palma il Giovane, *Allegory of the League of Cambrai*, late sixteenth century. Senate Hall, Ducal Palace, Venice. Photo by Didier Descouens, distributed under a CC-BY-SA-4.0 license via Wikimedia Commons.

Naples, Sicily, and Sardinia and, by virtue of the Neapolitan connection, a claim to the Duchy of Milan. He also controlled the Spanish lands in the New World and the gold and silver they yielded. His European realms encircled France. Over the next several decades, he and Francis I would fight a series of wars for domination of Europe, largely fought on Italian soil. Venice too was in danger of encirclement by Charles. If he could realize his claim to Milan, then the Republic would be surrounded to its east, north, and west by Hapsburg dominions. In addition, as ruler of Naples, Charles would have some control over the lower Adriatic. Even though French control of Milan represented a danger to Venice, it paled compared to that posed by Charles's possession of the duchy. Accordingly, Venice and France were natural allies in their opposition to Charles. Most of the leading Venetian politicians of the period, including Andrea Gritti and Gasparo Contarini, were pro-French.

When Charles became emperor, Venice was still allied with France according to the Treaty of Blois. In 1522 the French were forced from Milanese territory, but Charles did not move to retake the Veneto. In July 1523 Venice switched sides again, allying with Charles, but saw no action in the famous Battle of Pavia in February 1525 in which Francis was captured by imperial forces. In the Holy League of Cognac, agreed to in May 1526, Venice again allied with France and the papacy under Clement VII (Giulio de' Medici). One of the new alliance's goals was to restore the Duchy of Milan to the Sforza family. There followed the Sack of Rome in May 1527 by imperial troops, many of whom were Lutherans. Venetian forces, mindful of protecting the *stato da terra* above all else, failed to offer any meaningful support to the besieged pope. Indeed, in that moment of papal weakness, Venice reverted to its policy of seizing territory. Ravenna and Cervia again offered themselves to Venice—offers that were gladly accepted. Venetian forces fighting with the French against the emperor in the Kingdom of Naples also retook several Apulian ports. Venice also ignored the agreement it had been forced to sign with Julius II by imposing forced loans on the clergy. Things did not go well for the French in their attempts to retake Naples and Milan. Yet Charles had his own problems with which to contend. A huge Ottoman army was advancing toward Vienna. Clement reached an accord with Charles in June 1529 by which the Medicis were restored to power in Florence under a kind of Hapsburg protectorate and Francesco II Sforza was recognized as Duke of Milan. Clement promised to crown Charles as Holy Roman emperor and to invest him with the Kingdom of Naples. Then in August 1529 Francis reached a separate peace with Charles at Cambrai in which he renounced his claims to Milan and Naples. The Venetians were shocked by Francis's perfidy. As Sanudo put it, "The whole state, upon hearing such bad news, remained astounded, seeing so great a betrayal by the king of France."[74]

Both of Venice's erstwhile allies had abandoned it. Isolated, Venice agreed to the terms of the more general Peace of Bologna concluded in December 1529. It surrendered Cervia, Ravenna, and the Apulian ports, thus returning its dominions to where they had stood in 1517. The Hapsburgs became the predominant power in Italy, controlling Naples and having strong influence over the papacy, Florence, and Milan, which was ruled by Francesco II Sforza, brother of the deposed Massimiliano. Venice found itself in a vise. Its possessions were situated between two superpowers: the Hapsburgs and the Ottomans.[75] Indeed, it sits nearly at the midpoint between Madrid and Constantinople. While in 1517 Venice still aspired to great power status, by 1530 its position as a second-rank power was recognized by all. The pope and Francis failed to even consult with the Republic when they treated with Charles.

The Venetians, understanding their newly reduced stature, acted quickly to ingratiate themselves to Charles and rewrite the past. Doge Andrea Gritti urged Gasparo Contarini, ambassador to Charles, to remind him that "we [Venetians] shall always embrace all honorable and reasonable conditions for peace with his Imperial Majesty, to whom we are naturally most inclined."[76] More astonishing still, when Contarini met with Charles's representatives in Bologna in November he declared "that the Signoria did not take up arms against the emperor is certain . . . that Venice did not go to war to obtain anything is evident. . . . It is obvious that there is no equality between the emperor and the Signoria, and no relation between our Republic and the greatness and power of the emperor."[77] In this new formulation of itself, Venice was no longer a raging lion intent on the *imperio d'Italia* but rather a peaceable republic, meekly protecting its interests.[78] Its days of going in search of new territories on the peninsula were over. Instead, its stance on the *terraferma* would become one of defense and armed neutrality.[79] To that end it embarked on a program of modernizing the fortifications of its mainland cities.

The geopolitical changes and economic challenges that Venice faced between 1463 and 1530 placed tremendous strain on the city's political system, especially on the nobility's cohesion. Divisions of wealth, family, policy, governmental and legal authority as well as worldview became more pronounced. There had always been discord and dissension within the ruling elite, but the new fissures appeared more severe and consequential. However, it is also possible that the unusually detailed insights into the rough-and-tumble politics of this period offered by the voluminous eyewitness accounts of Girolamo Priuli, Marino Sanudo, and others foster the impression that this period's fractures were unusual. Unique or not, these tumultuous years strained the very principles and practices of Venetian republicanism.[80]

One of the issues that again came to the fore was the perennial problem of ducal overreach. Doges' efforts to increase their prestige and that of their families continued unabated. Few doges seem to have heeded the lesson of Doge Foscari's removal from office. Nicolò Tron minted a coin emblazoned with his portrait, as was customary among princely rulers in other states. Leonardo Loredan got his son elected a Procurator of San Marco after illegally altering the statutes that forbade the practice. An anonymous poster had Loredan mouthing the words, "I don't care [about anything] so long as I can fatten myself and my son Lorenzo."[81] The consecutive dogeships of Marco and Agostino Barbarigo proved especially problematic. That Agostino succeeded his brother Marco raised yet again the long-dormant prospect of a hereditary dogeship, although the brevity of Marco's reign likely explains why the electors found Agostino an acceptable successor. But Agostino's haughtiness rankled. He required visitors to kneel in his presence and kiss his hand, challenging republican sensibilities and the notion of the doge as simply the *primus inter pares*, the first among equals.

A fire in the Ducal Palace in 1483 offered the Barbarigo brothers an extraordinary opportunity for self-promotion. The wing housing the ducal apartments was severely damaged. In the fire's aftermath, the interior courtyard façade was redecorated to reflect "antiquarian grandiosity."[82] The most spectacular feature was a new staircase designed by Veronese stonemason Antonio Rizzo, which completed the triumphal entryway into the palace and made the ducal apartments the focal point of the palace's access system. The summit of the staircase became the spot where, from 1485 on, doges received the *corno* during the ducal coronation ceremonies. The staircase culminates in a triumphal arch made up of three rounded arches that stand out from the pointed arches along the rest of the first-floor loggia. Marco Barbarigo commissioned the staircase, but Agostino saw it through. Elaborately and elegantly carved, it celebrated Agostino and Venice's new "Augustan" age. It included portraits of the doge himself and of Aristotle and Alexander, symbols of the learning and military skill required of a leader. Agostino's name was inscribed in different places on the monument, as was the Barbarigo coat of arms. He was proclaimed by fawning writers as the "Prince of my new Rome" and compared to such classical and mythological figures as Brutus, Camillus, even Ulysses. The inscription on the double tomb monument that Agostino erected for himself and Marco at Santa Maria della Carità celebrated the military triumphs of his dogeship.[83]

On his death, Barbarigo's arrogance, nepotism, openness to bribery, and illicit dealings led to renewed efforts to control the doges. The traditional correction of the ducal oath of office incorporating new clauses prohibiting the abuses of the previous doge was deemed insufficient. A board of three men, known as the Tre Inquisitori sopra il Doge Defunto (Three Inquisitors Regarding the Dead Doge), was instituted to investigate the deceased doge's actions and levy fines on his heirs. Sanudo, usually a stickler for constitutional propriety, was appalled that Barbarigo's dirty laundry was aired in a meeting of the Greater Council attended by 1,200 noblemen, allowing word of it to seep out to the *popolo* and causing "indignity to the state." He thought the matter should have been dealt with in the Ten.[84] But Domenico Morosini who wrote his *De bene instituta republica* [On the Well-Constituted Republic] as a

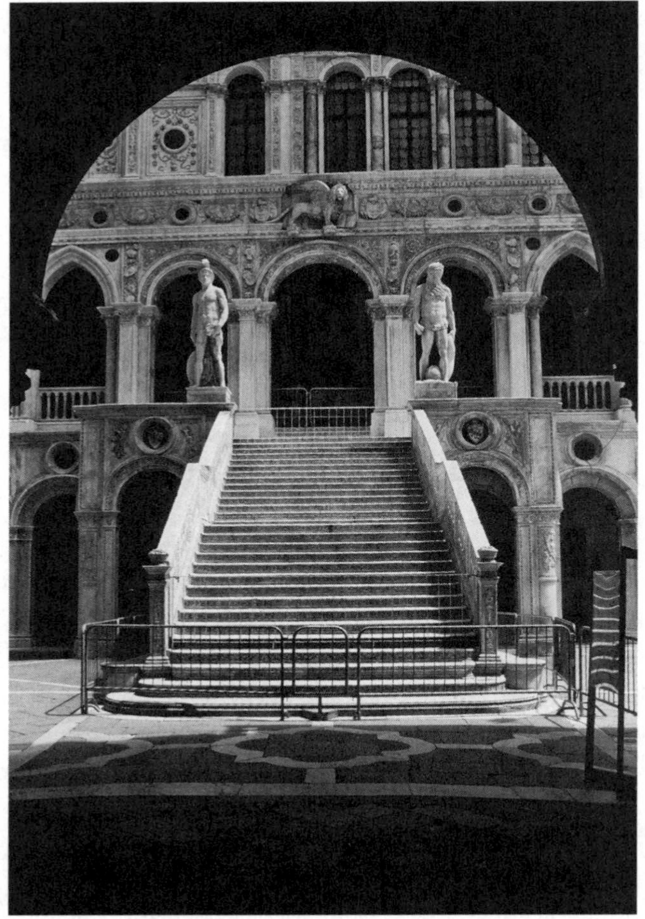

FIGURE 11.3 Scala dei Giganti, late fifteenth century. Ducal Palace, Venice. Scala/Art Resource NY.

prescription for curing some of the Republic's ills, wanted to go even further. He suggested that inquests into doges' behavior be held every five years *during* their reigns.[85] Another effort to cut the doges down to size occurred in 1544 when two huge statues of Mars and Neptune were placed atop the Barbarigo staircase, thereafter known as the Scala dei Giganti (the Giants' Staircase). These symbols of Venetian might on sea and land dwarfed the men who at that very spot became the Republic's temporary custodians.[86]

One commonplace notion bandied about at the time was that the doge was "a mere tavern sign," that is, little more than an advertisement for the state, its trademark, a figurehead.[87] Yet the reigns of Agostino Barbarigo's successors, Leonardo Loredan and Andrea Gritti, show how wrong that viewpoint was and how they were not inhibited by the posthumous inquisition into Barbarigo's actions. Loredan abused his office by getting his son elected a procurator. He also violated his oath by speaking privately with ambassadors rather than sticking to carefully scripted noncommittal responses prepared in consultation with the College. The ambassador from Mantua reported that on one occasion Loredan whispered to him, "Be certain that I and my following will do all we can for the marquess."[88] Gritti was one of the *savi* who objected to Loredan's action, but when he became doge, he too conferred

FIGURE 11.4 Titian, *Portrait of Doge Andrea Gritti*, c. 1546–8. National Gallery of Art, Washington. Courtesy of National Gallery of Art, Washington. Samuel H. Kress Collection.

privately with ambassadors. In a dispute during Gritti's reign over how the captain of a fleet was to be selected, nobleman Leonardo Emo reminded his colleagues that "we live under a republic, not a lord, and everything needs to be done by ballot."[89] Titian's well-known portrait of Gritti brilliantly captures the doge's imperious nature.

The political rehabilitation of Antonio Grimani, who reigned briefly between the dogeships of Loredan and Gritti, illustrates the growing role of money and foreign connections in Venetian political life. After being exiled for the naval debacle at Zonchio and escaping to Rome, Grimani was permitted to return in 1509 during the League of Cambrai and quickly reassumed important offices. When Loredan died in 1521, Grimani and Zorzi Corner were the leading contenders. Both had sons who were cardinals, were part of the tight circle of men who monopolized the most important civic offices, especially the Ten and College, and were referred to as the *primi di la terra* (the first ones of the city).[90] In the end, the electors chose Grimani, who at eighty-seven was the oldest man ever elected doge.

The intense rivalry between the Corners and Grimanis is just one example of the many fissures within the patriciate. The competition between the *case vecchie* and *nuove* was pronounced. Some patrician families had strong connections in papal Rome; others did not. These were fights among men with money, power, and influence. Generational conflict also divided the patriciate especially as younger men (the *giovani*) chafed at having to bide their time to assume higher office. But given Venice's predilection for rule by the elderly, men in their fifties sometimes qualified as *giovani*. The difference was partly one of style and willingness (or unwillingness) to accept long-standing rules and precedents.[91] The biggest gap was between the *primi di la terra* and the growing number of middling and poor patricians who relied on governmental jobs for a living.

Over the course of the fifteenth century the patriciate experienced a demographic boom. Sanudo notes that in 1493 the number of patricians stood at 2,600 men, of whom between 1,400 and 1,500 regularly attended sessions of the Greater Council. When important matters such as election of a new Procurator of San Marco were on the agenda, the number of attendees swelled to 1,800 or more. Those who did not attend were, according to Sanudo, either serving in administrative posts outside the city, engaged in business overseas, or simply not interested in politics.[92]

The number of offices for the Greater Council to fill had grown dramatically, increasing by two-thirds from the beginning to the end of the fifteenth century. According to one count, there were 434 such posts in 1400, 576 in 1437, and 765 by 1493.[93] The pressure to secure such jobs by poor nobles created a situation ripe for politicking and outright corruption.

The intricate method by which elections were held provided ample opportunities for influence peddling. The first stage was the nomination procedure. All eligible members of the Greater Council in attendance on a given day participated in a lottery to determine who would sit on one of four nominating committees composed of nine members each. Those committees then met separately to select their nominees for whatever posts were scheduled for election that day. With four nominees for each position in place, the Greater Council then proceeded to the election itself. Each candidate was voted on separately and whoever received the greatest number of votes, provided he got a majority vote of those in attendance, was elected. This four-hand method—the term "hand" was used to denote the nominating committees—was employed for elections to important offices. Some minor offices used only two "hands," meaning council members voted on two candidates chosen by two nominating committees.[94] Complicating matters further, the Senate could exercise its right to put forward its own nominee to a post who then had an advantage over the four-hand nominees in that he had the backing of the *primi di la terra*.[95] Especially during the war years, the Senate and the Ten also appropriated some election prerogatives to themselves, further increasing divisions within the patriciate.

The term for electoral corruption was *broglio* (Venetian *brogio*). The section of the Piazzetta nearest the Ducal Palace became known as the Broglio or the Piazza del Broglio since that was where patricians promenaded as they made connections and cut deals. A perennial issue in the Republic, *broglio* became more pronounced as the demographic pressure on the patricians increased. Some practices constituted what would today be considered electioneering or campaigning, others outright fraud and corruption. The line between the two is often hard to discern.[96] Examples of the former include trying to influence nominating committees by watching as ballot balls were cast, directly asking for votes, and refusing to observe the rules that forbade kinsmen from being present when relatives were up for election. Patricians often traded favors, nominating colleagues to offices with the expectation that the support would be reciprocated. Noblemen distributed handbills advertising their candidacies as members entered the Greater Council. Others used hand signals or applauded when a candidate's name was read. Would-be officeholders tried to ingratiate themselves to the more powerful by congratulating them on their electoral victories. Dinner parties, weddings, baptisms, and other social occasions provided other opportunities for gaining support. According to Malipiero, Zorzi Corner used his daughter's wedding to entertain hundreds of guests who were then "easily bent to his desires and attend to his requests."[97] Blatantly illegal activities included drawing more than one lottery ball from the electoral urns, casting more than one ballot, using counterfeit ballots balls, and buying votes. Of the latter Sanudo complained, "votes are being bought for money. Everyone knows it; it is evident that he who does not have a group of poor gentlemen to whom it is necessary to give money before nomination and then again once elected, cannot win any office that counts."[98] The practice of selling votes became commonplace enough that a group of enterprising poor noblemen, dubbed *sguizari* (Switzers) by Sanudo after the famed Swiss mercenaries, organized to sell their votes as a bloc. They were well coordinated and developed a series of signals, such as stroking their beards, to alert members how to vote.[99] The widespread practice of *broglio* seems a perversion of republican ideals. Yet it points to just how important officeholding had become to patricians—not only for those who needed the salaries but also for those who wanted offices for power and prestige. The politicking associated with *broglio* may also have had a positive effect by giving ambition an institutional form, creating cohesion within the patriciate and tying patricians and their interests (and those of their rivals) more closely to the state. As Priuli darkly observed, "A wolf never eats the flesh of another wolf."[100] *Broglio* greased the wheels of government or, in a metaphor more apt for Venice, unfurled the ship of state's sails.

Officially, however, *broglio* was a perversion of the system, and efforts were made to squelch its influence. Countless laws were passed (and promptly ignored) aimed at ending abuses. In 1517 a new magistracy, the Censori (Censors), was created to deal with electoral corruption. Suspended in 1521, it was reinstituted in 1524 in large part because of Doge Gritti's support. Over time, the Censors' mandate came to include enforcement of rules against betting on elections and other forms of gambling and such diverse matters as crimes committed by domestic servants, including gondoliers.[101]

Another attempt to limit electoral corruption was the creation in 1492 of a new style of ballot box designed to guarantee the secrecy of voting. The old voting method had utilized yay and nay ballot boxes that made it easy to see how members had voted. The new urns had three sections (yay, nay, abstain). The voter placed his hand, which was hidden from view by a collar affixed to the top, into the urn and dropped his ballot ball into the appropriate section. Moreover, the new ballot balls were fashioned from cloth rather than metal so that there was no sound to help listeners discern into which section ballots had been dropped. Of course, malfeasants soon found ways to circumvent these urns as well.[102]

Contemporaries were convinced that corruption increased after Agnadello. Priuli complained that "laws were defeated along with Venetian forces."[103] The formation of the League of Cambrai and the Agnadello rout undermined Venetians' confidence in themselves. Many took these debacles as God's punishment for their maladministration of justice and proclivity for luxury and immorality. Priuli adhered to the long-standing view that the turn to the mainland was the root cause of Venice's problems—that turning away from overseas trading voyages and opting instead for time at their country villas, had made nobles soft and effeminate. Various attempts were made to win back divine favor. Processions were held to seek God's assistance, and alms were distributed to win his goodwill. Efforts were made to reduce immoral conduct, especially the violation of nuns. A new magistracy, the Provveditori sopra le Pompe (Commissioners Concerning Pomp), was created in 1512 "to placate the anger of Our Lord."[104] The commissioners quickly issued rules limiting luxury spending on clothing, home decor, and parties. Three examples: women were forbidden to wear pearl necklaces valued at more than 100 ducats; no more than 150 ducats could be spent ornamenting a single room; and pheasant could not be served at wedding parties. Although the primary goal of these rules was to enforce morality, they were also designed to prevent the rich from moving their assets into commodities like jewels that were not easily taxable.[105]

As always, military expenditures placed huge fiscal demands on the government as revenue from the mainland and customs duties slowed. War was costly, and the government sought to economize. Salaries were suspended throughout the war, and attempts were made to cut waste. For example, an investigation was launched into a rumor that Titian had been paid 700 ducats for two paintings not yet begun for the Greater Council Hall, when others were willing to do the work for 250 ducats. Titian clarified the situation but also agreed to accept a reduced price for the work.[106] Pardons for crimes could be obtained for cash.

The government also began auctioning offices, a practice that undermined the very principles of republicanism. The process began gradually with a decision in 1510 to sell minor scribal, notarial, and other posts in the bureaucracy for which nobles were ineligible. In that same year, however, the Ten declared that it would admit up to ten men to the Senate in return for loans of 2,000 ducats apiece. Seven got in. In 1514 the Ten began allowing noblemen less than twenty-five years of age to enter the Greater Council in return for loans of 100 ducats each. Some 300 men took advantage of that offer. Suddenly a loan to the state could guarantee early admission to the Council. A year later, the same amount of money could gain a patrician early entry into the Forty. As Sanudo complained, "The Council of Ten will sell anything in order to get money."[107] In 1516, even a procuratorship of San Marco could be gained with a voluntary loan to the state. A year before that, "the most shocking measure of this kind was adopted."[108] It was decided that prior to elections, the names of those who had loaned money to the state would be published, which would obviously favor their victories. Although these measures were abolished at the end of the war, the practice of auctioning offices was revived during the wars between Francis I and Charles V. The theoretical equality of all members of the patriciate was being sacrificed to mammon.

Moreover, the rich found ways to get around the laws. Many who were in tax arrears, including Andrea Gritti, still got elected to important posts even though tax delinquency was supposed to disqualify a man from officeholding. Others got exemptions from the laws prohibiting luxury spending. More than anything else, the wars contributed to a further bifurcation of the nobility into orders of rich and poor, with a small clique of extremely rich families tightly controlling the levers of government and concentrating their power in the Ten and College. To make matters worse, the decline of the state merchant galley system made it increasingly difficult for poor nobles to relaunch their families. As increasing numbers of youths entered the Greater Council and Senate through voluntary loans, the Ten and its zonta, College, Signoria, and State Attorneys—around seventy men—appropriated even greater decision-making powers to themselves. In 1505, one member of the Ten presumptuously referred to himself and his colleagues as "the seventeen pillars of the state."[109] In 1524 the College's *savi* could be reelected without experiencing a period of ineligibility for having recently served. Sanudo lamented that this and other laws were "creating permanent members of the College."[110] The inner elite was becoming a closed and exclusive group. Just as in the fourteenth century the Senate had replaced the Greater Council as the most important governmental body, so the Senate's authority and prestige were being eclipsed by even smaller and more exclusive committees. This was done partly to maintain secrecy, since news readily leaked out of the enlarged Senate, and partly to keep power in the hands of experienced elders.

The declining influence of the Greater Council and Senate in favor of the Ten and College was symptomatic of a shift in Venice's governing principles from an emphasis on equality to one on authority. Since the Serrata, the nobles had touted the essential equality of all members. The State Attorneys epitomized this since they worked to see that all nobles were subject to the law, that it was applied vigorously, and that appeals were heard. As various crises stacked up and the Ten acquired greater power, its rapid inquisitorial trial method and the absence of an appeals process further cemented its authority. The move toward oligarchy was accompanied by a new conception of the scope and focus of government. But in a sleight of hand, the elites couched these innovations as conservatism, as a return to the customs of the ancestors.[111]

In these times of significant economic difficulties and political tensions, the patricians further refined the criteria for membership in the Greater Council and hence noble status in what has been termed the Third Serrata. The new rules made "marriage, birth, and wifehood the pivotal elements in the new patrician order."[112] As dowry inflation grew worse, causing patrician families to limit the number of noble marriages, the incidence of bastards fathered by unmarried nobles grew. Efforts by these same men to get their illegitimate sons admitted to the Greater Council threatened the status and honor of the entire noble class. The solution lay in new controls on marriage and birth. In 1505 the Senate instituted a requirement that all patrician marriage contracts be registered with the State Attorneys, making the couples' status and that of their parents part of the official record. Less than a year later, the Ten followed up with a law that required noble fathers to register the births of their sons within eight days, and parish priests to inform the State Attorneys of all patrician baptisms. This information, including the first and last names of the mothers, was recorded in the *Libro d'oro* (Golden Book). Entry into the nobility was no longer defined by admission to the Greater Council in young adulthood, but by birth itself. With the *Libro d'oro,* the patriciate was definitively transformed into an aristocracy based on birth. A further refinement occurred in 1526 when the Ten determined that noble marriages had to be registered with the State Attorneys. This erected a further bulwark against illegitimate infiltrators. In the words of the preamble, the law was intended to guarantee "the honor, peace, and preservation of our state."[113] Patricians got the message. The percentage who married outside their class was extremely low—only about 4 percent.

The final legislative act in the Third Serrata was the Senate's 1535 decision to limit dowries to 4,000 ducats. This was designed to address problems that had come to the fore following the War of the League of Cambrai and the Portuguese circumnavigation. The first was the growing gap between rich and poor patricians. By limiting dowries to 4,000 ducats, the senators hoped to prevent extremely rich patricians, often synonymous with the *primi di la terra*, from contracting marriages only among themselves.[114] The second was Venice's loss of commercial primacy. The aim was to rekindle the entrepreneurial spirit among young patricians and revive the economy. Noting that "our young men no longer engage in business in the city or overseas commerce or any other praiseworthy enterprise, instead they put all their hopes on their wives' extravagant dowries," the Senate trusted that the dowry limit would revive the spirit of mercantile enterprise that had allowed the city to prosper.[115]

These were pipedreams. The clock could not be turned back to when the Mediterranean predominated over the Atlantic or when the patricians collectively secured their fortunes through the state-owned merchant galley system. Even so, sixteenth-century Venice would continue to be a powerhouse, although its economic might would increasingly be based on manufacturing and industry rather than trade.

12

The Industrial and Ceremonial City

THE BIRD'S-EYE VIEW of Venice in 1500 created by Jacopo de' Barbari is perhaps the most famous image of the city ever made. Endlessly reproduced, it is often taken as an accurate representation of the city at the beginning of the sixteenth century. It is not. Some buildings are distorted. The Ducal Palace appears to be approximately half as tall as it is wide, when it should be a third. Many bell towers are depicted as taller than they really are. Other buildings and canals are omitted entirely or radically truncated, and many of the minor buildings are simply generic placeholders. The scale of the cityscape is not consistent.[1]

Yet dwelling on these inaccuracies is to miss the point of why the image was created. Produced just months before the Portuguese disrupted the spice trade, it was intended to celebrate Venetian greatness, especially the city's commercial supremacy, and disseminate that fame to a discerning and privileged buying public. The key to its meaning is the two colossal Gods—Mercury and Neptune—and their accompanying inscriptions, which together create a vertical line that focuses the viewer on Piazza San Marco. Mercury, god of commerce and communication, declares, "I Mercury shine favorably on this above all other emporia," while Neptune, god of the sea, responds, "I Neptune reside here, smoothing the waters at this port." Immediately below Mercury is the locative form of the word Venice [VENETIE] (meaning "At Venice") and below the date MD (1500).[2] At Venice in 1500, the viewer is to understand, commerce flourishes and tranquil waters abide. The imaginary line linking Mercury and Neptune cuts through the clocktower, the entryway to the Merceria, further reinforcing the mercantile message. The outsized ships surrounding Neptune and the Arsenal's detailed rendering underscore Venice's trade greatness and naval might, as do the personifications of the winds that propel vessels. Conspicuously missing is the Lion of Saint Mark, except as

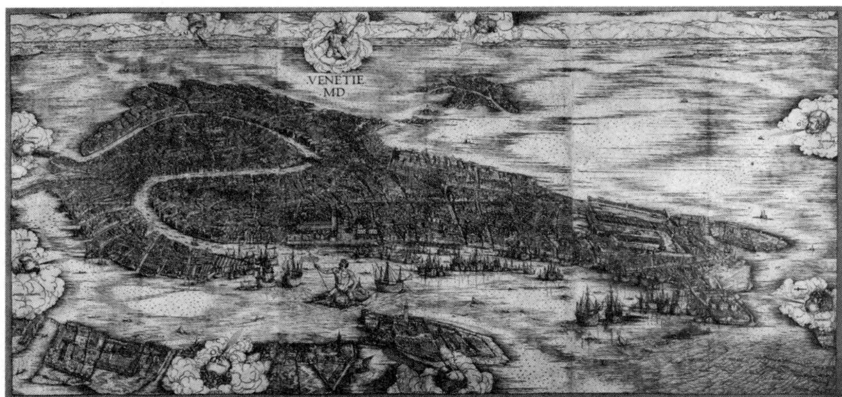

FIGURE 12.1 Jacopo de' Barbari, *Bird's–Eye View of Venice*, 1500. Minneapolis Institute of Art, The John R. Van Derlip Fund.

a tiny detail on the clocktower and one of the columns in the Piazzetta. In De' Barbari's vision, Venetian glory derives not from its saintly protectors but from human ingenuity and activity.

How was the view created? It is unlikely that it was based on measurements taken with ropes and scientific instruments. Instead, it was probably produced by compiling a series of preliminary drawings made from bell towers throughout the city to give it the bird's-eye perspective. The image has two registers with different viewpoints. The main register, which takes up most of the print, shows Venice itself and the nearby islands: San Giorgio Maggiore and the Giudecca at the bottom, Murano and some smaller islands at the top. Venice is presented as if tilted upward and viewed from the south, from a location corresponding roughly to the bell tower of San Giorgio Maggiore. The second register occupies a narrow strip at the top. Here the viewpoint is from near the ground. Torcello, Burano, and Mazzorbo appear as thin strips situated in the distant lagoon. Beyond is the mainland plain, then the pre-Alps and a few high peaks of the Alps proper. Four towns are identified on the *terraferma*: Mestre, Marghera, and Treviso on the flatlands, Serravalle (later, along with Ceneda, renamed Vittorio Veneto) in the pre-Alps. Numerous generic buildings dot the *terraferma*, creating the impression of a prosperous and populous land. Together the surrounding waters and the mountains provide a bulwark for "this most excellent" of cities.[3]

The print and original woodblock plates for this image tell of a vast collaboration. The impresario behind it was the Nuremburg merchant and Venetian resident Anton Kolb, who in 1500 petitioned the College for the right to export copies of the view, which were to cost 3 ducats each, without paying any customs duties. Kolb emphasized the project's difficulty and novelty, which had taken three years to realize. The petition declared that the drawing took "incredible skill," while its translation into "the new art of printing [in] a form of such large dimensions and the difficulty of the overall composition" required great "mental subtlety." In the end, the government granted him a four-year copyright but denied the customs exemption.[4]

The drawing and overall design were the work of De' Barbari, who was born in Venice around 1450. It required combining individual sketches into a coherent whole. De' Barbari would have entrusted the actual carving to cutters who translated the design onto six large blocks made of pear wood. Each of the six blocks was itself made up of several smaller blocks which were fastened together by dovetailing. The wood had to be perfectly seasoned to prevent warping, and knots and other imperfections were filled with pegs. The blocks then were treated with multiple applications of paraffin and linseed oil. The design was copied onto a sheet of paper that had been rendered nearly transparent by brushing it with varnish. This copy was applied in reverse to the blocks to guide the carvers. The carvers recreated the reversed design on the blocks using a variety of knives and chisels. Once the carving was complete, the plates could be printed. This required another set of skilled craftsmen and a variety of other materials, including a press, ink, and large sheets of paper. The entire process required, as Kolb noted, incredible skill, especially in aligning the blocks properly. The format was huge; the extant prints measure approximately 4.42 feet by 9.25 feet. It was a monumental work and achievement—the product not only of De' Barbari and Kolb but also dozens of suppliers and workmen who furnished the necessary materials, tools, labor, and skill to bring it to fruition.

De' Barbari's view serves as a fitting introduction to this chapter since it was first and foremost a manufactured product. In the second half of the fifteenth and early sixteenth centuries Venice became an industrial giant, producing a plethora of goods and employing thousands of workers. Printing was just one of these industries but of vital importance not only for the profits it generated and the workers it employed but also because it allowed the city to become arguably the leader in the new information technology of the age. Venice developed into a center of communication and information, disseminating images and texts to many parts of the world and in numerous languages. The industrial evolution that Venice underwent at this time helped its economy weather the trade vicissitudes it experienced due to the Ottomans and Portuguese.

The new medium of print also allowed the Venetians to disseminate information about the city itself. In this period, the city and especially its republican government became an object of study and the subject of books and treatises. Marino Sanudo not only kept a detailed diary of daily happenings in the city but also wrote a kind of guide to the city. Others composed histories. In 1516 the government appointed its first official historiographer, whose job was to disseminate the authorized version of Venice's past. Painters, including Gentile Bellini, Giovanni Mansueti, and Vittore Carpaccio, also replicated and celebrated Venice, most famously in the series of canvases executed for the Scuola Grande of San Giovanni Evangelista. Like De' Barbari's view, many of these images emphasized the everyday and mundane. Architecture and urban renewal projects likewise offered opportunities for the Venetians to project images of themselves and reimaginings of the city's past.

Many of these found literal embodiment in rituals and ceremonies. Processions and other observances had long been a means by which Venetians communicated various precepts and fostered a sense of community. But they took on new splendor. The governmental calendar was filled with required ducal outings, ambassadorial receptions, and commissions of captains general of both land and sea. Ducal inaugurations and funerals symbolically conveyed the Republic's unwritten constitution, while the arrivals and departures of provincial governors and rectors were ways for Venice to communicate its values to its subject peoples and, occasionally, for the subjects to respond.[5] Print played its role by reproducing for posterity images of important ritual occasions.

The industrial boom that Venice underwent was partly due to the availability of raw materials from the mainland and greater integration of the mainland's economy with the city's. The government asserted its control over two essential resources: timber and water. In these decades, the Venetians increasingly came to see the city and the *stato da terra* as an interconnected whole. This was most evident in new understandings of hydrology and efforts to protect the lagoon by diverting various silt-laden rivers away from it. De' Barbari's map is evidence of this more synoptic vision. The *terraferma* and mountains are essential elements of the print, providing a frame for the image. Without the upper register, the image loses coherence and orientation. The *terraferma* anchors the city. Driven from the Aegean and challenged by the Atlantic world, the Venetians looked to the mainland as never before.

Patents offer one measure of the city's success in fostering manufacturing and technical innovation. In the final quarter of the fifteenth century, the Senate issued thirty-three patents for various industrial techniques and devices. That number jumped dramatically in the sixteenth century to 577 patents. Since privileges could also be issued by the Provveditori di Comun (Commissioners of the Commune) who had some jurisdiction over trade and certain guilds, one estimate places the number of patent applications in the late fifteenth and sixteenth centuries at nearly 1,000. The silk industry alone saw approximately forty patents issued for everything from spinning machines to cloth printing equipment, to new dyeing techniques.[6]

Textiles were one driver of Venice's industrial awakening. Starting in the mid-fifteenth century, the merchant-controlled government adopted a protectionist policy that fostered local woolen manufacturing, long left to other cities. Many nobles profited from this new interest, even owning wool shops. The city's ability to import wool of varying quality from northern Europe, the Mediterranean, and its own mainland territories meant that Venice could meet the needs of different markets. It produced lower-quality cloth for export to the Levant and higher quality for Italian consumers.[7]

The wool guild stated in 1423 that it was producing 3,000 bolts of cloth per year (a bolt measured 4 to 4.5 feet in width and 90 to 113 feet in length); that figure may have doubled by the 1460s.[8] Then the industry entered a crisis phase that corresponded with the War of the League of Cambrai and the Italian wars. In 1516, only 1,310 bolts were produced. A boom followed. Mid-century output was around 11,000 bolts per annum. Production continued to climb until it peaked in 1602 (28,729 bolts) before going into a slow decline over the course of the seventeenth century.[9]

The woolen cloth industry employed thousands of men and women. One estimate from 1537 puts the number of workers at 5,800 including seasonal workers.[10] Many were immigrants from Lombardy but some also came from the Veneto and the Balkans. The industry was concentrated in the *sestiere* of Santa Croce. In the 1410s, the Purgo, the office that maintained quality controls, was constructed along the Rio Marin in the parish of San Simeon Profeta, while near San Rocco were large sheds for stretching cloth. Many of the workers lived in this section of the city.

The mainland cities had their own traditions of sheep breeding and woolen cloth production. Sanudo claimed that the Veronese countryside produced the best wool in Italy.[11] But as Venetian production grew in the sixteenth century, output in Verona, Vicenza, and Padua declined, though it continued to flourish in Bergamo. The decline in sheep raising on the *terraferma* was partially compensated for by a huge increase in sericulture. Already in the fifteenth century, much of the area around Vicenza was devoted to mulberry trees and raising silkworms, serving, as Doge Agostino Barbarigo declared in 1488, as "the main aliment and source of employment for our people of Vicenza," especially women.[12] In that same year the Venetian government forbade the export of mulberry trees from anywhere in its dominion. By the mid-sixteenth century the *stato da terra* was producing over 300,000 pounds of raw silk materials per year.[13] Much of the spinning of raw silk into thread occurred in Vicenza and Verona. Most of the thread was then exported outside the Venetian state after paying duties. Despite resistance from the Venetian *setaioli* (silk cloth manufacturers), who claimed that weaving was a monopoly of the capital, the Veronese won the right to weave black velvets in the 1550s and the Vicentines, Brescians, and Bergamasques did so a few years later. The weaving of other types of silk fabrics followed, whether officially sanctioned or not.

In the fifteenth century, silk manufacturing in the capital already had, unlike wool, a distinguished history, beginning with the arrival in the fourteenth century of political refugees from Lucca. In policy, however, the government vacillated between protectionism and free trade. As for the importation of raw silk, the government was forced, in the end, to favor free trade since it was competing with other European powers for supplies from Syria, Greece, and the Balkans. For semi-finished products like thread, the *setaioli* and spinners had differing interests. The *setaioli* wanted freedom to import thread from elsewhere, notably the *terraferma* cities, while the spinners sought to protect their profession from outside competition.

One of the Venetian silk industry's strengths was its ability to meet the demands of a wide variety of consumers from Emperor Charles V's wife, Isabel of Portugal, who ordered six bolts of Venetian satin in 1532, to Francesco di Antonio, a wool weaver who in 1565 owned silk sleeves, doublets, trousers, and a black silk hat.[14] Silk cloth was used on litters and gondolas, for banners, umbrellas, sheets, curtains, cushions, book covers, and other items. As a diplomatic tool, it was often gifted to ambassadors and visiting dignitaries. When Vincenzo Gradenigo went as *bailo* to Constantinople, he took with him a cornucopia of gifts including 3.5 kilometers of fabrics.[15] These gifts served to advertise the quality of Venetian production and generate further demand.

The government divided silk cloth into five distinct categories, from cloth commissioned for personal, domestic use to the finest cloths that were exhibited to foreigners at a trade show, known as the *paragon* (comparison), located along the Ruga del Paragon (Paragon Street) at Rialto. Here an elite clientele could compare samples of the best Venetian production. Medium-quality cloth constituted another category, as did cloth produced exclusively for export (often to the Levant), and yet another for sale only at the Fondaco dei Tedeschi.[16] The sixteenth century saw an explosion of new colors and a growing taste for black as well as the gradual acceptance of fabrics made from silk mixed with flax, cotton, or wool. The silk manufacturers and dyers were constantly torn between preserving quality standards and the reputation of Venetian silk and the changing tastes and budgets of consumers. Large numbers of men and women found employment in the silk industry. In the 1550s, master weavers alone are estimated to have numbered around 1,200.[17] The production of cotton cloth, by contrast, was less important since it had to compete against German-made wares. However, cotton was used widely in the production of sails.[18]

Dyeing was an essential ancillary industry with a long history in Venice. The earliest statutes of the dyers' guild date to 1243. The guild and government waged a constant battle against counterfeiting since dyeing was highly susceptible to fraud. Dyers could cut corners by using cheaper dyes intended to imitate finer ones or dyeing woven cloth rather than unwoven thread. Both practices threatened the reputation of Venetian output. When in 1453 the State Attorneys prosecuted two *setaioli* for palming off cheaper brazilwood-dyed silk cloth as kermes-dyed, they noted that it resulted in "great damage to the buyers and great shame for this Republic."[19] At the same time, regulations frequently had to be adjusted to technological innovations and changing market conditions. Greater flexibility was allowed in the dyeing of cheaper grades of cloth than prestigious ones.

Venice's easy access to dyeing agents from both Asia and the Levant, as well as New World alternatives, meant that dyers were constantly developing new tints, and this fostered growth. But the city's environment posed obstacles. One was the lack of fresh water. Salt water's chemical properties can affect the reaction of dyes. Accordingly, much of the rinsing of dyed cloth was relegated to the edges of the lagoon where sweet river water was more abundant. Another problem was water pollution caused by the chemicals used in dyeing. The government tried to push most dyeing to the city's edges.[20]

The absence of ready supplies of fresh water was an even greater liability for the tanning and leather trades since the chemical reaction caused by salt water made it extremely difficult to skin carcasses without causing tears in the hides.[21] For this reason, these activities tended to take place on the *terraferma*. But Venice imported large quantities of skins, furs, and leather. Shoemakers were major consumers of leather. Venice also developed several crafts specializing in the production of luxury leather products. Among these were the *cuoridori*, artisans who produced and worked gilded leather and were enrolled as a branch of the painters' guild. In the sixteenth century there were more than seventy workshops engaged in this craft, generating as much as 100,000 ducats in business per annum.[22] The printing revolution created a sizable demand for gilded leather book covers and bindings. Leather also had military and naval uses. It was fashioned into helmets, applied to oars and ship masts, and made into wineskins for crewmen.

If textiles constituted a major component of industrial output, so did shipbuilding. At the Arsenal it achieved an unmatched level of organization and supervision given the navy's and merchant marine's importance to the city's fortunes.[23] Managers at the Arsenal proliferated. At the apex stood the three Lords of the Arsenal. As part of their compensation, each was awarded one of three houses, evocatively named Paradiso, Purgatorio, and Inferno, located near the entrance to the Arsenale Vecchio. Such proximity facilitated their supervisory role and allowed them to react quickly in emergencies. In the fifteenth century three noble Provveditori all'Arsenale (Commissioners of the Arsenal) were added. By the mid-sixteenth century, top management at the Arsenal included the Ammiraglio all'Arsenale (Admiral of the Arsenal), a position dating to the late fourteenth century, who was the overall superintendent of the complex, the foremen (*proti*) shipwright, caulker, oar maker, and mast maker, the arms steward, and the chief bookkeeper.[24] Each had many assistants working under him. The admiral, for example, supervised thirteen warehouse managers and a mistress of the sailmakers, who oversaw in turn twenty-five female sailmakers. The chief bookkeeper's staff included three other bookkeepers, four or five pages, three paymasters, four doorkeepers, forty-two night-watchmen, a bell ringer, a clock keeper, and a wine steward and his twelve assistants who distributed wine to the workers.[25] The Lords of the Arsenal, commissioners, admiral, and foremen, in consultation with the College and Senate, set the agenda for the complex.

The bulk of the Arsenal's skilled employees worked as shipwrights, caulkers, or oar makers. Hundreds of porters hauled raw and finished materials around the worksite, while masons repaired the Arsenal's miles of walls and other structures, smiths forged and repaired tools, and sawyers finished lumber. The Arsenal also employed rope makers, pulley makers, cannon founders, powder makers, and shield and sword makers, to name a few.[26] The complex included not only dry and wet docks but also specialized workshops and warehouses. The oar makers' workshop was so big that the Greater Council met there in

1577 when a fire in the Ducal Palace rendered its hall temporarily unusable.[27] The thread used for sails was stored in the thread warehouse. The Arsenal had room for 116 galleys, some in dry docks, others under roofed wet docks. In 1504 the Arsenal had thirty-two merchant galleys, twelve in or ready for use and twenty under construction. It also had eighty-three light or war galleys, twenty-eight in use, fifty-five under construction, and five so-called *galee bastarde* or hybrids of great and light galleys. In 1559, the navy comprised six great galleys, 120 light galleys, and ten *galee bastarde,* either in service or being built.[28] New ships were built in batches, and it often took a long time for them to be brought to completion. While some workers constructed the new ships, others repaired older vessels or prepared rigging and other fittings.

The Arsenal was designed for speed and efficiency. At its best, it resembled a production line. As ships made their way from the docks toward the exit on the Rio dell'Arsenale, they were outfitted with masts and other fittings, as well as weapons, ropes, and other supplies. In 1436 Castilian writer and traveler Pero Tafur described the process.

> And as one enters the gate [of the Arsenal] there is a great quay on either side with the canal in the middle, and on one side are windows opening out of the buildings of the Arsenal, and the same on the other side, and out came a galley towed by a boat, and from the windows they handed out to them, from one the cordage, from another the bread, from another the arms, and from another the balistas and mortars, and so from all sides everything which was required, and when the galley had reached the end of the canal all the men required were on board, together with the complement of oars, and it was equipped from end to end. In this manner there came out ten galleys, fully armed, between the hours of three and nine. I know not how to describe what I saw there, whether in the manner of its construction or in the management of the workpeople, and I do not think there is anything finer in the world. If the Venetians desired to show their strength, the enemies of the Faith in those parts would not, in my opinion, have a single ship at sea, still less on the coast, nor would they dare to match themselves against such a powerful enemy.[29]

Demonstrations like the one Tafur witnessed served two purposes. They honed the workmen's skills and allowed management to look for bottlenecks and inefficiencies. And they advertised to foreigners Venice's naval might with the goal of discouraging potential enemies.

But in its everyday operations, the Arsenal was plagued by the theft of materiel by workers, low productivity, tardiness, and slipshod work. Since the master shipwrights, caulkers, and oar makers who were enrolled on its rosters were guaranteed employment, they had little incentive to do their best. Elderly craftsmen who had passed their peak productivity and had difficulty finding work in private shipyards took advantage of the guaranteed employment.[30]

In 1559 the Arsenal employed 600 shipwrights, 300 caulkers, and sixty oar makers, although many more were listed on the rosters as eligible to work there.[31] It was around this time that the workforce reached its peak. The *dogado* was dotted with private yards where shipbuilding also took place, though the number employed is unknown. These shipyards produced large tonnage round ships (over 100 tons) and smaller vessels, including long ships, river vessels, and the many types of smaller watercraft used throughout the lagoon. However, between the early fifteenth century and the mid-sixteenth century, the production of smaller vessels (on both sides of the 100-ton mark) went into serious decline. Some production moved to shipyards located along rivers around Padua, Treviso, and in Friuli. Places in the eastern Adriatic, like Ragusa and Curzola, became important producers of ships due to their easy access to timber.[32] The construction of large merchantmen continued in Venice, as did the building of gondolas and other canal boats for city use. By the end of the century, however, even the production of large round ships declined dramatically.

Closely tied to shipbuilding, at least at the Arsenal, were the metallurgical industries and the production of weaponry. Founders cast artillery and cannonballs; other workmen constructed the carriages on which cannons were mounted. Refiners produced saltpeter and gunpowder. Outside the Arsenal, founders worked iron, copper, bronze, and precious metals. The Jewish Ghetto established in 1516 derived its name from a copper foundry that was located in that remote corner of the city. The Venetian word for founding (*gettare*) morphed into *geto* or ghetto. The capital's production of metalware had to compete with *terraferma* refiners, who had easier access to fuel and raw materials, and ironware coming from Germany where ore was mined. Much metalwork had practical uses (as armor, swords, kitchenware, hardware, and bells), but bronze was also highly prized as a medium for sculptors who produced life-size statues as well as statuettes and medals.[33]

It was in the production of luxury items (including the finest silk cloth) that Venetian manufacturers really excelled.[34] They were aided by the access to exotic or rare raw materials offered by the city's location at the nexus of trade networks. Goldsmiths, silversmiths, and jewelers could procure not only the base metals of their trade but also precious and semi-precious stones, pearls, coral, and rock-crystal. Sugar refiners and confectioners looked to suppliers in Cyprus, Crete, Sicily, and North Africa. Soapmakers needed huge amounts of imported olive oil as well soda ash from Syria and Egypt. In 1489 the government forbade soap production except in the capital.[35] Raw wax was imported from Greece and the Balkans and refined and whitened for candles, both for domestic use and export. Cosmetic makers relied on some of the same ingredients as the dyers, while perfumers used musk imported

FIGURE 12.2 Christoph Krieger, engraver, *Woman Dyeing Hair*. From Cesare Vecellio, *Degli abiti antichi et moderni di tutto il mondo* (Venice, 1598). Rijksmuseum, Amsterdam.

from central Asia. The blond hair immortalized in Titian's female figures was achieved by women first washing their hair in a soda-water solution that had been boiled with a kind of thistle and then drying it in the sun, while wearing a specially contrived hat that allowed the hair to bleach but the skin not to tan.[36] Paintings were also luxury items, even if the run-of-the-mill devotional subjects churned out by icon painters would not have cost much. While the most prestigious artists like Titian worked primarily on commission, there was a market for ready-made pictures in Venice. The 240 enrollees in the painters' guild in 1530 offer some sense of the scale of the industry, as does the presence in Venice of *vendicolori* (color-sellers), merchants who specialized in selling pigments to artists.[37]

Two luxury industries stand out: glassmaking and printing. It was during the fifteenth century that Venice became the world's glassmaking center.[38] The fame of Venetian glass rested in large measure on the development of a nearly colorless transparent glass (*cristallino*) that was produced by first combining silica with sodium carbonate and then adding manganese oxide. The molten material was then blown or shaped. Glassmakers could add metal oxides and salts to create various colors.[39]

Venice derived its silica from quartz pebbles found in abundance in the Ticino and Adige Rivers that were heated and then pulverized by dunking them in cold water or milled into powder. In the early fifteenth century, nobleman Stefano Michiel was utilizing mills along the Sile River near Treviso to crush pebbles.[40] Sodium carbonate was produced from vegetable ashes, the best of which came from Syria and Egypt. In the late fifteenth century, Venice was importing as much as 1,750 tons of this ash annually.[41] While Muranese glassmakers carried their knowledge of *cristallino* manufacturing to other towns, the government was able to protect the industry from competitors by forbidding the export of ash. Although raw materials were one secret to Murano's success, another was the glassblowers' skill in fashioning and decorating their wares. Glassmaker Angelo Barovier has long been credited with inventing *cristallino* around 1450. It seems more likely that he simply perfected some of the techniques that had been evolving over the past two centuries and that his workshop was especially skilled at fashioning and decorating the vessels it produced. Within a decade, at least four Murano glassworks were manufacturing *cristallino*.[42]

Murano glassmakers developed other types of innovative glass in the fifteenth and sixteenth centuries as well. These included *calcedonio*, a marbled glass that imitated chalcedony, a category of semi-precious stones, including agate. *Lattimo* or milk glass, an opaque white glass made by the addition of tin oxide, resembled porcelain. It could be decorated with colored enamels to illustrate mythological scenes, religious subjects, or, in the case of wedding goblets, idealized male and female portraits. *Filigrana* was created when white glass rods were embedded in *cristallino* to create an elegant straight or lattice pattern. A visit to Murano became an obligatory stop for visitors to Venice. Milanese pilgrim Pietro Casola visited there in 1494 and remarked, "All the beautiful glass vessels that are sent all over the world are made here."[43]

While Murano's renowned luxury products commanded the highest prices, the island also made a huge variety of utilitarian objects including flasks, jugs, ampules, drinking glasses, plates, lamps, beads, and eyeglasses. Venetian glass beads dating from before Columbus's arrival in the New World have been found in Arctic Alaska; they probably made their way east along the Silk Road and were then carried across the Bering Strait.[44] The industry produced prodigious amounts of small round or diamond shaped disks that were soldered into metal lattices to form windows. Over 140,000 of these glass disks were exported to Krakow in the first half of the sixteenth century for use in Wawel Castle.[45] Venetian glass was also in high demand in the Mamluk sultanate.[46] Late in the sixteenth century, the glassmakers mastered the art of making highly reflective mirrors by applying a coating of tin/mercury alloy to panes that had been blown and then stretched. Although modest in size, Venetian mirrors dominated the market until they were overtaken by French competitors in the seventeenth century who developed techniques to create much bigger mirrors.[47]

At the beginning of the sixteenth century there were around twenty glassworks on Murano; at midcentury, the number stood at around thirty-six.[48] Each had a host of men working in it, including the glassmasters who had several assistants. As in so many Venetian industries, glassmaking evolved into several separate guilds, specializing in different products. These included the glassmakers' guild, the bead-makers, the window makers, a guild for the local sale of everyday glassware, and the mirror makers' guild. Women found work finishing and stringing beads.

In addition to its privileged access to raw materials, Venice's luxury industries benefited from the availability of investment capital and the city's ability to attract the required man- and womanpower. This was especially true for printing.[49] Paper mills on the *terraferma*, particularly in the Valle del Toscolano on the western side of Lake Garda, supplied much of the paper, which accounted for about half the cost of producing a book. By the end of the fifteenth century, there were twenty-three paper mills there.[50] The city had access not only to artisans who had the technical skills required to cast and set the type pieces, operate the presses, and bind the books, but also people with the intellectual training to edit, translate, and proofread. Together they made Venice the center of the European book trade and an information hotspot.[51]

Venice's long-standing commercial ties to Germany may explain printing's early arrival in the city. Johann von Speyer (Giovanni da Spira) is usually credited with bringing the new technology to Venice from Mainz, although there were other printers in the Veneto at about the same time. In Venice, von Speyer published editions of Cicero's letters and Pliny's *Natural History*. In September 1469, he received a five-year monopoly on the new technique from the College. But when he died in 1470, so did the privilege. His brother Wendelin took over the press and published ten new titles that year, but without a monopoly, he soon faced competitors—eleven within three years.[52] The most important were German Christoph Valdarfer and Frenchman Nicholas Jenson, who would become the premier Venetian publisher of this early period.

Although many of the early books were published with intellectual, diplomatic, or political agendas in mind—for example, a translation of Cardinal Bessarion's tracts against the Turks—the commercial possibilities soon became apparent. In 1471 Jenson published medical and law texts that found a market at the University of Padua and elsewhere. Capital fostered growth as well. The Priuli and Agostini banking families had ties to the printing industry. In one instance the Agostinis facilitated the purchase of eighty-six bales of paper valued at 731 ducats.[53] Venice's trade connections facilitated the production of necessary materials like ink. According to one account, the ingredients to make ink included "linseed oil, turpentine, Greek pitch, black pitch, marcasite, cinnabar, rosin, solid and liquid varnish, gall, vitriol, and lac."[54] Already in 1476-7 Venice was home to twenty presses.[55] When Jenson allied with several of his competitors in 1480, the new company had working capital of nearly 10,000 ducats and within a year published twenty titles.[56] By the end of the century well over a million books had been printed in the city.

Technological changes further propelled the industry as printers found ways to reproduce mathematical figures such as geometrical shapes, musical notation, and frontispieces, the latter previously having been consigned to miniaturists to execute by hand. Foreign printers flocked to the city where they found a favorable environment. In 1492 the government issued its first copyright. As production increased, prices fell. Missals and breviaries cost around 3 lire; psalters a couple of soldi, about the cost of half a bushel of flour.[57] Bookshops sprouted up, especially along the Merceria, while itinerant sellers hawked their wares around the city.

The most famous Venetian printer was Roman humanist Aldus Manutius, who arrived in Venice around 1490 with the goal of publishing many of the Greek classical texts.[58] Venice's thriving Greek community provided a valuable resource on which he could draw, while Bessarion's bequest of his library to the Republic offered manuscripts for study. In 1495 Aldus formed a company with Piero Francesco Barbarigo, son of Doge Marco, and the printer Andrea Torresani. Within three years, the press had published nearly the entire corpus of Aristotle. Aldus also branched out into Latin and Italian works, perhaps to make up for mediocre Greek text sales. Then in 1501 he unveiled the two innovations on which his fame still rests: the octavo format and italic font. The octavo was a pocket-size book that was easily portable and manageable, while italic print (*corsivo* in Italian) imitated cursive handwriting and facilitated reading. Aldus also made liberal use of punctuation marks, as he expanded his list. By the time of his death, his publishing house had produced around 130 editions. Torresani continued to publish, concentrating on medical texts by Galen, Hippocrates, and others. Another printing establishment founded by two immigrants from Crete, Zaccaria Kalergis and Nicolò Vlastos, also produced some works in Greek. Their project was promoted by Anna Notaras, daughter of the last *megas doux* (naval commander) of the Byzantine empire and a central figure in Venice's Greek expatriate community.

The most prolific publisher in the subsequent period was Lucantonio Giunta, a Florentine who began publishing in Venice in 1489 with profit in mind. For this reason, a little more than half the works he published were religious texts, including seventy-three editions of breviaries for such places as Mantua, Passau, and Salzburg, and sixty editions of missals for churches in, among others, Aquileia, Messina, Valencia, Augsburg, and Majorca.[59] His publishing house would continue operation until 1657.

Following a slowdown during the Cambrai and Italian wars, Venetian publishing entered its period of greatest flourishing. Between 1526 and 1550 it is estimated that three-quarters of all the books published in Italy emanated from Venice.[60] The relative freedom of the city allowed for the publication of books by Protestant reformers such as Martin Luther and Philip Melanchthon and libertines like Pietro Aretino. In 1515 Daniel Bomberg of Antwerp received from the Senate a ten-year privilege to publish texts in Hebrew. And in 1537 Alessandro Paganino published the Quran in Arabic. Ten years later an Italian translation appeared. Works also appeared in Spanish, Armenian, Old Church Slavonic, and Croat (using the Cyrillic alphabet).

One estimate suggests that, at its height, printing employed around 1,500 persons. Some of the publishing houses were family concerns where women worked. In his will of 1517 Bernardino Benali noted that his wife's niece Angela "served me for four years painting figures, binding books, and preparing paper for printing," while her sister Laura oversaw the entire enterprise of "printing images."[61] Typographer Johann von Speyer's widow Paola had a relationship with another printer following von Speyer's death, married another man involved in the book trade, and was herself a partner in the company formed in 1480 by Jenson. She brought capital, know-how, and valuable connections to other printers and patrons to these later relationships.[62]

In addition to books, Venetian printers published a flood of ephemeral material such as broadsheets, small pamphlets, and flyers that were printed on cheap paper. Worried about the declining quality of Venetian books, the Senate approved a bill in 1537 designed to force printers to use high-quality paper. Exempt, however, were "minor things that sold up to the sum of 10 *soldi* apiece."[63] Such inexpensive works provided an entryway into literacy for the unlearned, as many of them contained poems, songs, and other genres that were recited or sung by street performers, like Nicolò di Aristotile de' Rossi, a native of Ferrara. Known by his stage name Lo Zoppino, he combined publishing, printing, bookselling, and performing; had a shop in the parish of San Fantin; opened another in Ravenna with his son; and circulated throughout towns of north and central Italy. In 1510 he was tried by the Signori di Notte for having performed a *frottola* (a secular song) in Ferrara that the Venetian government took to be "in vituperation of the Venetian state." Performed during the War of the League of Cambrai, it warned the Venetians that "the latest move that you have made with your men towards Ferrara with great fury will bring you new woe."[64] After spending a few months in jail, Zoppino published Venturino of Pesaro's poem "Laude della Serenissima cità de Venetia" (Praise of the Most Serene City of Venice). The ability to respond quickly to market demand, public opinion, and political pressure was characteristic of the cheap print publishers.

As Zoppino's example shows, the changes brought about by the printing industry extended into the religious, social, cultural, and political spheres. In an economic sense, printing was part of the larger industrial transformation taking place in Venice at this time, a transformation that made up for the ebb in overseas trade. As one authority notes, the rise of the Via del libro (Book Road) compensated at least somewhat for the decline of traffic along the Via delle spezie (Spice Road).[65] Manufacturing in all its forms meant that Venice continued to be an economic powerhouse well into the sixteenth century.

The city's industrial development was due in no small measure to its control of the *terraferma* and its resources. Timber and water were especially important. Wood was of course used in the shipbuilding and construction industries but also for fuel to heat homes, cook food, and fire the furnaces that produced glass, refined sugar and wax, and smelted iron, copper, and other metals. Waterpower drove mills for everything from grinding grain to pulverizing pebbles for glass and fulling woolen cloth. In addition, the city had to import fresh water for drinking and other domestic uses. As demand for these resources grew, a more integrated vision of the city and the *terraferma* developed, one that resulted in more direct intervention by the government on the *terraferma* and prioritized the needs of the metropole.[66] Writers and painters emphasized the interconnectedness of the two realms.[67]

In the mid-fifteenth century, the Venetian government adopted an active approach to the management of mainland forests and the flow of timber and fuel to the capital. Previously, reliant on the market to guarantee supplies, in 1458 it created the Provveditori alle Legne (Firewood Commissioners) to root out corruption, establish favorable tariffs, and maintain better inventories of supplies. A few years later, recognizing the Ottoman empire's growing naval might and the possibility that Venice might quickly need to respond, the Senate turned its attention to the high-grade timber that was essential to the Arsenal and established public forest preserves. In 1463 it took its first tentative step in that direction. It reached an agreement with the ruling council of Pieve di Cadore, a town north of Belluno that had been under Venetian rule since 1420, that Venice would have special access to a large community forest of fir trees that were ideal for ship masts in the territory known as the Vizza di Cadore. The agreement did not supersede local rights. In December 1471 the Senate voted to confiscate a set of oak-rich community forests located in the hills north of Treviso, known as the Bosco del Montello (the Montello Forest), and placed them under the Provveditori all'Arsenale for exclusive use by the shipyard. As the law proclaimed, no one "shall cut or have cut timber of any sort in that forest for any reason except the needs of our Arsenal."[68] Violators could not appeal their convictions. The Arsenal's demand for high-quality oak drove the Republic's forest policy. As one Arsenal employee wrote in 1596, "Without oak there is no Arsenal, [and] without the Arsenal, there is no preeminence, no stability, no security, no liberty, and consequently, no life."[69] The creation of public forests altered the relationship between the capital and inhabitants of the mainland. Eventually the Republic established over forty reserves, which became known collectively as Saint Mark's Forests.[70]

Nonetheless, the issue of fuel wood remained. In 1476 the Senate approved a set of bills regarding community forests that, among other things, mandated rotational harvesting, forbade sale of community forest lands, prohibited pasturing animals in the forests or the setting of fires (for clearing), and expanded the city's firewood warehouses near the Arsenal. Over time restrictions on such activities as charcoalmaking were added. These rules were eventually extended to private and church-owned woodlands as well. And in 1531 the Ten ordered owners to reforest 8 percent of any land they had clear-cut.[71] Local communities often resented these restrictions for placing the capital's needs over theirs, but "the Venetians had become—in theory at least—the masters of all forests in their domain."[72]

All this required management and some degree of technical knowledge. When the government undertook systematic surveys of its forest resources in the sixteenth century, it entrusted them to a new magistracy known as the Provveditori sopra Boschi (Forest Commissioners) who were usually former Arsenal commissioners and whose mandate lasted only until the survey was completed. They did not concern themselves with firewood. Instead, their job was to compile information regarding the status of various species in state forests, community forests, and privately owned lands. They did so for the first time in 1569 when nobleman Nicolò Surian and his team presented their survey of virtually every oak tree on the mainland, except the area around Brescia. Furthermore, they categorized the trees according to their age, size, and suitability for various uses. Subsequent surveys were compared with this one, so the government could track change over time. Forest policy shifted from rooting out abuses to actively managing forests to guarantee sustainability.[73]

Even more than timber, water directly affected the capital due to the ongoing threat of siltation. The mainland's agricultural and industrial uses of water had to be balanced against the commercial interests of Venice and the long-term viability of the lagoon itself. As with wood, the needs of the capital took priority. In this period the Venetians began to see the waters of the lagoon not as beneficent but as threatening. In 1463 they complained, "As everyone can see, the lagoons are getting narrower and are filling with earth and the city is suffering great damage because of this."[74] With much of the northern part of the lagoon already heavily silted, efforts concentrated in the southern lagoon. The complex interplay of the rivers and the lagoon forced the Venetians to see the mainland and lagoon as one hydrologic system.[75]

One of the first to study forest and water together was nobleman Marco Corner. In 1441 he was commissioned along with two other patricians to inspect mainland forests along the Sile, Piave, and Tagliamento rivers in order to find new sources of fuel. At the end of his mission, he composed a treatise on his findings entitled *Sopra i boschi* (On Forests). In it he argued that the shortage of firewood in the capital was partly the result of deforestation along the riverbanks and their tributary streams, which led to both increased siltation of the lagoon and the clogging of the channels by which firewood was transported to the city. In other words, the rivers, lagoon, and forests were one ecosystem. For Corner the solution was twofold: dredge the streams to increase their flow and reforest the stream banks.[76]

Corner continued to ponder the problems facing the lagoon. In 1460 he authored a treatise entitled *Della laguna* (On the Lagoon) in which he recounted various projects, beginning in the twelfth century with Padua's efforts to protect its lands by diverting the Brenta toward Venice. Three years earlier he himself had proposed redirecting the Brenta at the village of Stra and routing it toward Brondolo near Chioggia. This proposal was rejected in favor of a less radical plan that redirected it toward Malamocco. The fresh water needs of the city, combined with the economic interests of mill owners along the Brenta, thwarted his solution. Yet even this redirection and other less radical river diversions had consequences. The diminution of river water entering the lagoon increased tidal flow, which raised the salinity of the lagoon, had ripple effects on flora and fauna, and increased the susceptibility to seasonal high-tide flooding. Sanudo recorded in his diary that on March 29, 1511, "water overflowed the embankments [along the canals] most greatly and at my house there was more than a foot of water in the courtyard, and many wells were ruined."[77] By the middle of the sixteenth century, a consensus had developed that the Brenta and Bacchiglione should be channeled out of the lagoon to the south, while the Piave and Sile should be rerouted out of the lagoon to the north. This work would only be fully accomplished in 1610 with the completion of the Brenta Novissima, which carried the Brenta and Bacchiglione away from Chioggia, and in 1685 with the diversion of the Piave to Cortelazzo.[78]

Land reclamation projects in the areas bordering the estuary also affected the lagoon's fragile equilibrium. As nobles increasingly converted their liquid wealth into mainland property, there was a strong incentive to reclaim swampland and convert it to profitable agricultural use. But as dikes and levees were erected to protect the reclaimed land, they impeded the ability of the tides to disperse into and then drain from those marshy areas. The reduced tidal flux lessened the natural cleansing produced by the outgoing tide and increased the possibility of flooding as the incoming sea water had nowhere to go but up.

The conflict between private land reclamation and maintaining an expansive lagoon with porous boundaries found spokesmen in Alvise Corner and Cristoforo Sabadino. An eccentric figure, Corner (whose effort to be recognized as noble was rejected) resided in Padua, where he presided over a circle of artists and intellectuals.[79] He was a strong advocate of land reclamation efforts, telling the Venetian government that its *terraferma* dominion held more than half a million *campi* (fields) of swampland capable of being reclaimed.[80] One *campo* was approximately three-quarters of an acre.[81] To protect Venice itself, he proposed building embankments that would completely surround it and the Giudecca, turning it into a city in the midst of a lake. He may have been inspired by descriptions and maps of Tenochtitlan, the Aztec capital.[82] Sabadino, in contrast, thought that reclamation was interfering with nature, exacerbating silting, and destroying the lagoons. He claimed that the northern section of the lagoon, the section near the Sile and Piave was "as good as lost."[83] He compared the entire lagoon to the human body, with Venice as its heart and the tidal flow as its food, "which she receives every six hours, and throws back after six hours."[84]

Like the concern for timber, the problems posed by managing the lagoon and land reclamation resulted in new magistracies and more sweeping governmental powers. In earlier centuries, various courts and magistracies had been responsible for different elements of the hydraulic and hydrologic systems: lagoon, barrier islands, and rivers. It also became common for commissions of sages to be appointed to tackle these issues. In 1501 the Ten made the Savi alle Acque (Water Sages) a permanent body; in 1530 three executors, the Esecutori alle Acque, (Water Executors) were added.[85] In 1556 the government regularized the office of the Provveditori sopra i Beni Inculti (Commissioners of Uncultivated Natural Resources) that had been established in 1545. They were given jurisdiction over irrigation and land reclamation projects, asserting public ownership of all waterways.[86] Just as Venice had affirmed its control over mainland forests, so now it claimed ownership of all mainland waterways, a principle that had been established in the lagoon centuries earlier. Water and wood were too important to be left to private interests.

Maps functioned as symbolic projections of Venetian power over the mainland and its resources. In 1460 the Ten ordered the creation of maps of the city's dominions, likely the "earliest state-sponsored maps" created in Europe.[87] Maps were also utilized to manage the Republic's forest reserves. The bird's-eye view of the beech forest at Cansiglio in Angelo Badoer's 1638 survey shows the Lion of Saint Mark near the center of the image. The

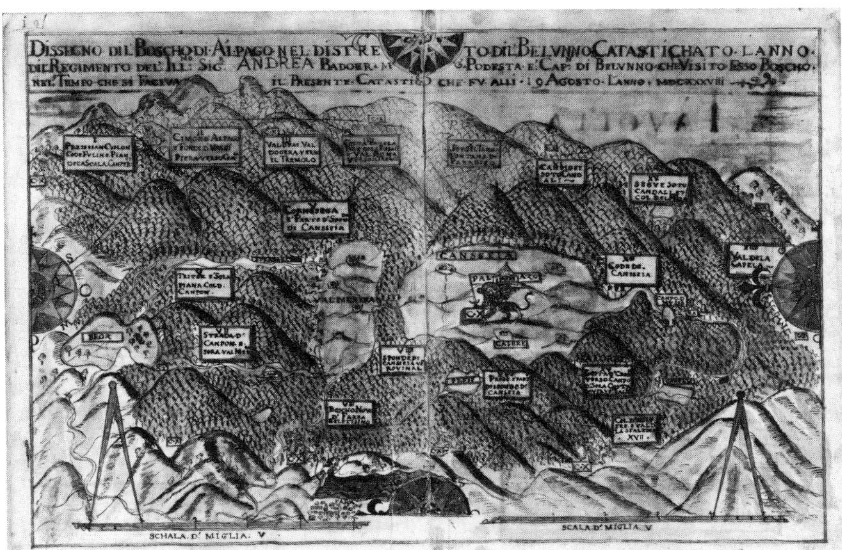

FIGURE 12.3 Andrea Badoer, *View of the Cansiglio Forest Reserve*, 1638. Archivio di Stato di Venezia, Provveditori e Sopraprovveditori alle Legne e Boschi, reg. 150bis, disegno 19, Venice. Archivio di Stato di Venezia.

seventeen placards indicate the sections of the forest that were to be rotationally harvested.

Architecture and art were other instruments of hegemony and control. Towns throughout the dominion were adorned with clock and bell towers asserting the capital's control of time, while banners of Saint Mark hoisted atop flagpoles affirmed Venetian sovereignty. Plaques celebrating Venetian rectors' terms of office demonstrated the metropole's juridical and administrative reach.[88]

Defense too came to be understood in territory-wide terms. In 1536 Doge Gritti's military advisor, Captain General Francesco Maria della Rovere, described the *terraferma* dominion as a "city-fortress" in which the principal cities functioned as "bastions" and the mountains and rivers as the "curtains that link and secure all this land."[89] Architect Michele Sanmicheli wrote that Padua and Treviso could be considered "suburbs [borghi] of this city [Venice], which together with them forms one body."[90] Yet Venetian authority was never uniform nor absolute, especially in the Bresciano and Bergamasco, where the economic pull of Milan and Genoa was strong.[91] If Crete was Venice's uncommon dominion, the *terraferma* was its patchwork one.

In addition to advocating the encirclement of Venice with walls, the eccentric Alvise Corner also had a grand plan that, if implemented, would have fundamentally altered the Bacino. First, he wanted to erect in the Piazzetta a fountain fed by waters from the Sile or Brenta. Although the fountain would offer much-needed fresh water to the city, Corner was primarily interested in its aesthetic function as a "marvel."[92] Second, he planned to construct an artificial island in the middle of the channel separating the Molo and San Giorgio Maggiore. The island was to be adorned with trees, streets, and a loggia and serve as a place for relaxation. The third and most spectacular proposal was a Roman-style theater in the channel separating the Customs House Point from the Giudecca. As he observed, "This edifice will be easily seen when one is standing in Piazza San Marco, and it will be a very beautiful view and an edifice of a type that is no longer found in any other city."[93] Corner had long had an interest in the theater and commissioned the Veronese architect Giovanni Maria Falconetto to design a loggia and odeon for performances in Padua. Angelo Beolco, known as Ruzzante, actor and playwright, was part of Corner's Paduan circle, and Corner himself may have helped establish one of the *compagnie della calza* (stocking companies) that staged plays and other entertainments. Although Corner's scheme for the Bacino was never realized, it highlights the growing importance of festivity, ceremonial, and antiquity in the life of the Republic. The architectural, artistic, and urban transformations that Venice experienced in these years were partly a response to the challenges that the city faced in wake of the political and economic changes in Italy and the wider Mediterranean. As the Venetians saw their political influence and economic clout diminish, they reimagined their history, with the city itself becoming an object of glorification.

Rituals, ceremonies, and processions had always been part of Venice's civic life.[94] In the later fifteenth and sixteenth centuries the Venetians placed even greater attention on the staging of processions and other celebrations than it had in the Middle Ages. The festive calendar became ever more crowded both with annual events and one-off occasions including ducal installations and funerals, victory celebrations, and visits by foreign dignitaries. Although the government and church still took the lead, the *scuole grandi* and the *compagnie della calza* played a significant role in these events. Ritual occasions offered opportunities for the Venetians to enact different aspects of their religious, social, and political life.

The message of the Corpus Christi (or Domini) celebration was overwhelmingly religious.[95] The Venetians represented themselves as a pilgrim community in quest of the Heavenly Jerusalem. It was a movable feast held on the first Thursday after Trinity Sunday. On that day, the doge entered San Marco, made confession, and watched as a lengthy procession, composed of guildsmen, clergy, and members of the *scuole grandi* and of the *scuole piccole* dedicated to the Eucharist, passed through the basilica after having wound its way around the Piazza. The doge and patriarch then made their own procession accompanied by senators, each of whom escorted a foreign pilgrim who was about to embark for Jerusalem. In the afternoon, another procession made its way to the church of Corpus Domini. The honor accorded the departing pilgrims emphasized Venice's preeminent role in the pilgrimage trade as well as the city's position as the gateway to the East.

Starting in the early sixteenth century, floats with tableaux vivants began to be incorporated into the Corpus Christi processions. One year, the Scuola Grande of San Rocco presented three Old Testament scenes. Other *scuole* outfitted children as angels, while the Dominicans of San Zanipolo presented a tableau of Adam and Eve, as well as the various orders of friars. A model ship came next, adorned with silver-plate and a caption reading, "For the faith and the fatherland."[96] Other times, the Venetians used floats to send explicitly political messages supporting the Republic's stance in various conflicts and disputes.

Unlike the piety of the Corpus Christi celebrations, Carnival incorporated rowdier, more socially charged, and potentially disruptive messages. Extending from December 26 to Fat Tuesday, Carnival combined elite and popular elements. On Fat Thursday, the government staged in the Piazzetta the ritual slaughter of a bull and twelve pigs by members of the blacksmiths' guild, while on that same day in the Senate a group of senators, in the presence of the doge, shattered twelve model castles. Both events commemorated a twelfth-century victory over the patriarch of Aquileia. Reforms enacted in the 1520s by the Ten eliminated the senators' demolition derby and reduced the public slaughter to one bull in order to bring greater dignity to the occasion.[97]

Official rites were only one aspect of Carnival season. Games, animal tortures, mummeries, fireworks, and other spectacles also took place, with the *compagnie della calza* taking the lead in many of these festivities. Overseen by the Ten, each company was made up of twenty-five youths from the wealthiest and most powerful patrician families who were identified by the colorful stockings they wore.[98] The *compagnie* sponsored parties and other celebrations often to honor distinguished foreign guests.[99] For Carnival the companies commissioned plays from such writers as Ruzzante and Arentino and stage sets from artists like Titian and Giorgio Vasari. Sanudo wrote on February 3, 1515, "The city is in the grandest festive mood.... [T]hree comedies were put on by three *compagnie* . . . then there were fetes in various courtyards and masquerades throughout the city."[100] For that Carnival season, the Immortali staged the ancient Roman playwright Plautus's *Miles Gloriosus* (The Vainglorious Knight). During the intermission, the buffoon Zuan Polo performed his own "new comedy" in which he played a necromancer who conjured up a vision of Hell filled with devils and fire. Into the Inferno descended the God of Love who returned with a chorus of dancing eunuchs, followed by a group of nymphs who performed a song accompanied by the beating of hammers against an anvil fashioned as a heart. After Plautus's play ended, the Judgment of Paris was reenacted. All of it was, in Sanudo's opinion, "a beautiful thing, at which there were a lot of people who count." These included many elderly patricians, fashionable patrician women, the sons of Doge Loredan, and the French ambassador.[101] The nymphs' pounding of the anvil and Paris's awarding of the golden apple to Venus were unsubtle references to sexual intercourse, one of the predominant themes of Carnival. Sanudo noted that one performance of a rustic comedy by Ruzzante and Menato (Marc'Aurelio Alvarotto) was "very lascivious with very dirty words . . . the whole ending was about fooling around and cuckolding husbands"[102] Carnival never sparked a riot in Venice as it did in some places, partly due to the Ten's vigilance and the banning of masqueraders carrying weapons in 1518.[103] However, high politics did sometimes intrude. Francis I's capture by Charles V at the Battle of Pavia did not halt Carnival 1525, but Sanudo reported, "There has been little masking, so that it seems as if the city is mourning."[104]

Domestic politics took center stage in the solemnity and strict regulation of ducal processions, which contrasted with the misrule of Carnival. According to Matteo Pagan's engraving *The Procession of the Doge on Palm Sunday*, it proceeded as follows. Standard-bearers, criers, trumpeters, servants of foreign ambassadors, fife and other players, and the squires and cavalier of the doge led the procession. Next came the canons of San Marco, followed by the patriarch accompanied by a crucifix. Immediately behind him marched servants carrying a huge white candle and the ducal coronation crown. Secretaries were next, followed by the ducal chaplain, squires bearing the ducal faldstool and cushion, and then the grand chancellor. The ballot boy of ducal elections immediately preceded the doge, who was sheltered by his umbrella bearer. Foreign ambassadors, the ducal sword-bearer, and members of the Signoria brought up the rear. According to some accounts, the last portion of the procession comprised many important officeholders, including the heads of the Ten, State Attorneys, censors, and others arranged by office, followed by ordinary members of the Senate.[105]

FIGURE 12.4 Matteo Pagan, *Procession of the Doge*, section 2, c. 1555–60. Rijksmuseum, Amsterdam.

The ducal procession encapsulated the government's admixture of princely and republican elements. The ducal *trionfi* (the candle, umbrella, sword, trumpets, etc.) recalled the 1177 Peace of Venice when these items were purportedly awarded to Doge Ziani by Pope Alexander III. The inclusion of foreign ambassadors emphasized the doge's status as a prince and highlighted the Republic's international standing. At the same time, the cortege incorporated the principal components of the city's republican regime: *cittadino* chancery members and noble officeholders. The ballot boy's participation reminded onlookers and the doge himself that his was an elective office, and that he was merely the first among equals.[106]

The procession did not, however, fully replicate Venetian society. The *popolo* had no role, except as servants of the doge, nor did the guilds or *scuole*. Women had no place, not even the dogaressa. Pagan's etching shows women observing the procession from mezzanines and first floor windows. Since they had no official political role in the government, they had no standing in the parade. Barely visible behind the figures in the procession is an assortment of male spectators, many of whom sport the short tunics and leggings of the laboring classes. The old men visible in the background behind the doge are a particularly rambunctious bunch who appear to be joyously proclaiming the doge's arrival. Also visible are several turbaned men and others whose costumes signify them as foreigners. In this respect, Pagan got things right: the ducal procession was meant to be a lesson in Venetian governance both for the governed and outsiders. Moreover, his etching, yet another product of the printing press, spread the message even to those who would never attend the event in person. In their rituals and ceremonies, the Venetians were working out for themselves and others the meaning and significance of their city.

In Pagan's etching, Piazza San Marco serves as the backdrop. Although some progresses continued to make their way to destinations throughout the city and lagoon, the Piazza enjoyed pride of place. Indeed, the Piazza encapsulated the city. It was no longer necessary, as it had been in the Middle Ages during the Festival of the Marys, to incorporate various parishes and outlying islands in processions since all authority, both real and symbolic, centered on San Marco.[107] Even so, in the second half of the fifteenth century and the first three decades of the sixteenth, the city did undergo significant physical transformation. Although expansion slowed, except at its edges particularly in Cannaregio and on the Giudecca, the city became still more densely developed, and canals and streets continued to be systematized and regularized.[108] Many structures were built (or rebuilt) in newer architectural styles that reflected the city's evolving sense of itself and its past.

Unlike the Florentine revival of ancient art and architecture, the Venetians again looked East—to their touchstone Byzantium as well as the *stato da mar*. The fall of Constantinople in 1453 and the Ottoman's westward advance reinforced Venice's sense of itself as the heir to Byzantium and by proxy to antiquity. Refugee Greek intellectuals from Constantinople, Cardinal Bessarion first among them, actively promoted this stance. Bessarion did so by collecting as many ancient Greek texts as he could, growing his library to more than 1,000 manuscripts. In 1468 he donated it to the basilica of San Marco.[109] Bessarion's bequest, together with the large Greek exile community, Venice's anti-Ottoman stance, and Aldus's program of publishing ancient Greek texts, made the city "the center of Hellenism in western Europe."[110] In painting, Giovanni Bellini's half-length Madonnas consciously recalled Byzantine icons.[111] Writing to Doge Cristoforo Moro in 1468, Bessarion noted that when Greeks arrived in Venice, "they feel they are entering another Byzantium."[112]

Venice's Byzantine-tinged approach to antiquity was evident architecturally. Its newfound role as the heir and protector of the classical inheritance was

PLATE 1 The lagoon near Torcello looking north. The green pre-Alps and snowcapped Alps are visible in the distance. Stephen Fleming/Alamy Stock Photo.

PLATE 2 Pala d'Oro following fourteenth-century modifications, 1342–45. Basilica of San Marco, Venice. Photo by Daperro, distributed under a Creative Commons Attribution-Share Alike 4.0 International license via Wikimedia Commons.

PLATE 3 Ca' d'Oro, begun 1421, Venice. Photo by Wolfgang Moroder, distributed under a CC-BY-3.0 license via Wikimedia Commons.

PLATE 4 Jacobello del Fiore, *Justice with the Archangels Michael and Gabriel*, 1421. Gallerie dell'Accademia, Venice. Scala/Ministero per i Beni Culturali e le Attività Culturali/Art Resource, NY.

PLATE 5 Vittore Carpaccio, *Lion of Saint Mark*, 1516. Ducal Palace, Venice. Cameraphoto Arte, Venice/Art Resource, NY.

PLATE 6 Gentile Bellini, *Procession in Piazza San Marco*, 1496. Gallerie dell'Accademia, Venice. Erich Lessing/Art Resource, NY.

PLATE 7 Giambattista Tiepolo, *Allegory of Marriage of Ludovico Rezzonico and Faustina Savorgnan*, commissioned 1758. Ca' Rezzonico, Venice. Photo by Didier Descouens, distributed under a CC-BY-SA-4.0 license via Wikimedia Commons.

PLATE 8 Giovanni Borghesi, *Bombardment of Venice from July 29 to August 22, 1849*, 1849. Museo Correr, Gabinetto dei Disegni e delle Stampe, St. PD 8234 gr. © 2022 Archivio Fotografico—Fondazione Musei Civici di Venezia.

appropriately showcased at the entryway to the Arsenal from which warships sailed to battle the Ottomans. The gateway was built in 1460 in the form of a triumphal arch and is attributed to Antonio Gambello. It was modeled on the ancient Arch of the Sergians in Pola, yet another example of how the Venetians looked eastward for inspiration. Its style deviates from the Sergian Arch, however, in utilizing four free-standing smooth granite columns that culminate in Byzantine style "basket" capitals, all reminiscent of San Marco. The Arsenal portal is an amalgam of the Roman and Byzantine worlds and a fitting symbol of Venice's double inheritance.[113]

Venice's new stance was also evident in the churches that were built or remodeled in these years. They include San Zaccaria, San Giovanni

FIGURE 12.5 Attributed to Antonio Gambello, Gateway to the Arsenal, 1460, Venice. Matthias Süßen, creator QS: P170,Q5908707075 (https://commons.wikimedia.org/wiki/File:Venice_Arsenale-msu-2021-5226-.jpg), distributed under a CC-BY-SA-4.0 license via Wikimedia Commons.

Grisostomo, Santa Maria Formosa, San Salvador, San Giobbe, and Santa Maria dei Miracoli. The latter two, uncharacteristically for Venice, show Tuscan influence, but nevertheless also harken to Venice's Byzantine legacy. San Giobbe, an Observant Franciscan church, was patronized by Doge Cristoforo Moro, who was buried in the chancel. The triumphal arch that frames the chancel and the dome above it suggest Florentine influence on Pietro Lombardo, the architect of the church's interior.[114] But San Marco was the prototypical domed church in Venice. What is more, San Giobbe had come to possess the relics of a saint that were being threatened by the Ottomans in Bosnia. Bessarion unhesitatingly identified them as those of the Evangelist Luke, despite papal protests that there were in fact the relics of Saint Luke of Steiris. Thus Venice claimed to have rescued the bones of two of the four Evangelists from the clutches of the Muslims.[115]

Lombardo built Santa Maria dei Miracoli in the 1480s to house a miracle-working image of the Madonna. This small barrel-vaulted church with a domed altar at the east end recalls the Chapel of the Virgin in San Marco (the Mascoli chapel) as well as early Christian sarcophagi from Ravenna, even if the orders of the exterior show the influence of the Baptistery in Florence.[116] The rich marble cladding on all four exterior walls as well as the disks of porphyry and serpentine marble, which Sanudo thought were "worked in the antique style," also recalled the ducal basilica.[117] These same types of materials would be used to decorate Ca' Dario, the palace on the Grand Canal built for *cittadino* secretary and diplomat Giovanni Dario.

More forthrightly Byzantine are the parish churches Santa Maria Formosa and San Giovanni Grisostomo, both of which are centralized Greek-cross churches with three aspe chapels at the east end. Bergamasque architect Mauro Codussi took as his model Veneto-Byzantine churches of the Middle Ages like San Giacomo di Rialto and San Giacomo dall'Orio. Venice's Byzantine inheritance would again be recalled in the church of San Salvador at the Rialto terminus of the Merceria. The cornerstone of the rebuilt church was laid on March 25, 1507, the feast of the Annunciation, the date of Venice's legendary establishment.[118] San Salvador's first architect was the native Venetian Giorgio Spavento. Tullio Lombardo would eventually take over. With its central dome and four smaller ones, plus the succession of three domes over the nave, it recalls San Marco's modified Greek-cross plan.

In 1485, fire destroyed the Scuola Grande of San Marco. In that same year the relics of Saint Roch (San Rocco in Italian) arrived in the city. A confraternity dedicated to Roch, the patron saint of plague sufferers, was founded in 1478 when Venice was again struck by the disease. San Rocco attained *scuola grande* status in 1489. San Teodoro, adjacent to San Salvador, achieved that rank in 1552, bringing the number of *scuole grandi* to six. In the later fifteenth century, they began competing on building projects and painted narratives in their meeting rooms.

The Scuola Grande of San Marco decided to decorate its hall with a cycle that recounted Saint Mark's evangelizing efforts in Alexandria. The first painting to be executed was Gentile Bellini's *Saint Mark Preaching in Alexandria*, completed by his brother Giovanni in 1507. Gentile's painting seeks to evoke the East, with its depiction of well-known Alexandrian monuments including the column of Diocletian (also known as Pompey's Tower) and the city's famous lighthouse, which also served as the inspiration for Codussi's reworking in white Istrian stone of the campanile of San Pietro di Castello. The huge basilica that dominates the scene is the temple of the pagan god Serapis, whose cult will be undone by Mark's evangelizing. Accordingly, the temple prefigures San Marco itself.[119]

Vittore Carpaccio's cycle at the Scuola of San Giorgio degli Schiavoni is a hodgepodge. It includes scenes from the lives of Saints George and Tryphon to whom the confraternity is dedicated as well as Saint Jerome, a Dalmatian. The cycle, executed between 1502 and 1507, may have commemorated the arrival of George's relics in Venice in 1499. The scenes of Saint George slaying the dragon take place in Silena in Libya. Like Bellini, Carpaccio creates an oriental land- and cityscape by using known monuments such as Cairo's Bab al-Futuh gate and Jerusalem's Dome of the Rock, as well as date palm trees. Both Gentile's *Mark Preaching* and Carpaccio's *George and the Dragon* were executed shortly after Venice saw its stake in the Alexandrian spice trade disrupted by the Portuguese and when the Balkans were under threat from the Ottomans. They harken back to when Venice and Christianity were ascendant in the East.[120]

The action in the most famous cycle of all, which predates the oriental turn of the paintings at San Marco and San Giorgio, takes place in Venice itself. The cycle created between 1494 and 1505 (or 1510) for the Scuola Grande of San Giovanni Evangelista recounts the miracles performed by the confraternity's most precious possession, a fragment of the True Cross it received in 1369 from Philippe de Mézières, Grand Chancellor of Crete. The series, created by five artists, has a remarkable coherence.[121] It begins with Lazzaro Bastiani's *Donation of the Relic*, which takes place in the nave of the church of San Giovanni Evangelista with the confraternity's meeting hall clearly visible.

The other canvases depict various miracles performed by the relic. The best known is Gentile Bellini's *Procession in Piazza San Marco.* (Plate 6) It details the procession that occurred annually on April 25, Mark's feast day. As the members of the confraternity pass with their precious relic at the opposite end of the Piazza from the church, Brescian merchant Jacopo de' Salis drops to his knees and prays for the relic's intercession on behalf of his son who has fractured his skull. The other confraternities have already completed their circuit of the Piazza and are grouped on the left while the ducal procession is just proceeding from the right. The miracle of de' Salis's son being healed is overshadowed by the basilica itself. The message is that this is a city where the miraculous is commonplace. Other canvases in the cycle commemorate sites in Venice where the relic performed other miracles: the bridges at San Lorenzo and San Lio, a private home in San Polo, and a loggia at the Patriarchal Palace at Rialto. In *Healing of the Possessed Man* the miracle takes place amid the hubbub of the marketplace as gondoliers ferry passengers to their appointments, Turkish merchants conduct business underneath the loggia where noblemen gather, and processing members of the confraternity reach the summit of the bridge. The meaning is clear: one does not need to travel to the Holy Land to experience miracles; they occur in Venice—the new Byzantium, the new Jerusalem.[122]

The Rialto so carefully depicted by Carpaccio in the *Healing of the Possessed Man* in 1494 was devastated by fire twenty years later. The flames were fanned by the Bora, the fierce wind from the northeast, and aided by a brutal cold snap that caused the canals to freeze, making it difficult to get water to battle the flames. Sanudo, who witnessed the blaze, criticized shop-owners and others who were more interested in saving their stock than fighting the conflagration. He especially blamed the *popolo* who, in his opinion, "were quicker to busy themselves with looting than with protecting Rialto."[123] The records of dozens of magistracies that had their headquarters at Rialto were destroyed. In the end, Sanudo declared that it "looked like the fall of Troy and the sack of Padua, which I myself witnessed," and that it "was the most dreadful and horrifying thing that was ever seen in Venice or anywhere else."[124]

Nine years earlier another fire destroyed the medieval Fondaco dei Tedeschi on the opposite side of the Grand Canal. The building was replaced by a structure that, with its five-arched portico and two side blocks, harkened back to medieval *fondachi* like the Fondaco dei Turchi. The sparseness and severity of the exterior architectural detailing was made up for by frescos executed by Giorgione and Titian. Titian's portrayal of Judith or Justice (or Venice) with sword in hand, a decapitated head at her feet, and an onlooking German soldier would have reminded the German merchants residing at the Fondaco of Venice's commitment to fair dealing. Indeed, an image of a man named Zuan Favro who had been condemned by the Ten for running contraband was painted on the side facing San Bartolomeo as a lesson to malefactors.[125]

The Rialto fire offered an opportunity to reorganize the market. Four plans were submitted: some favored reconstructing the site as it had been before the fire, others advocated a complete reimagination and amplification of the space. The most radical was that of Fra Giocondo, a Veronese friar and humanist, who wanted the new Rialto to be a perfect square with four entryways and a central piazza with various loggias that would evoke an ancient Greek agora. In the end, the constricted nature of the site and preexisting property rights prevailed, and a conservative reconstruction overseen by Antonio Abbondi (known as Scarpagnino) was approved. Within twenty years Rialto was reconstructed much as it had been before, although masonry vaults replaced flammable wooden beams.[126]

At Piazza San Marco, a fire in 1512 prompted the rebuilding of the Procuratie Vecchie. The rebuilt block consists of a covered arcade with shops, above which rise two floors of apartments. It is topped by crenellation. The new building largely replicates the medieval one built during the dogeship of Pietro Ziani, despite the use of Tuscan piers and Corinthian capitals. The overall effect evokes Venice's Byzantine heritage. Austerity and adherence to local traditions were the architectural response to the Cambrai crisis.[127]

Once the wars were over and the Peace of Bologna signed, Venice went in search of both renewal and a new identity.[128] The impresario of this *renovatio* (renewal) was Doge Gritti.[129] One of his most ambitious projects was an overhaul of the city's statutes, which would have required that judges have technical legal expertise rather than rely on common sense (*arbitrium*).[130] Gritti pushed for a reorganization of the state's *terraferma* defenses and for more sophisticated accounting systems. He also tried to eliminate the more indecorous elements of Carnival. Gritti patronized the Observant Franciscans' church San Francesco della Vigna and built nearby his austere family palace, which exemplified the ideal of noble self-effacement.[131]

At the same time, he sought to increase the dignity of the state and the Republic's reputation. He had a hand in hiring Flemish composer Adrian Willaert as the *maestro di capella* (choir master) for San Marco. Willaert was especially famed for his use of multiple choirs, which became a distinguishing feature of Venetian music. It was well suited both to the layout of San Marco, with its galleries that could serve as choir lofts, and the requirements of Venetian ceremonies and processions. Willaert began a tradition of musical composition and performance at San Marco that would flourish throughout the sixteenth century and beyond, even as organists like Andrea Gabrieli and his nephew Giovanni came to replace choir masters as the preeminent composers of polychoral works for the basilica.[132]

The Sack of Rome in 1527 and the collapse of the last Florentine republic in 1530 led to a diaspora of artists and intellectuals, many of whom looked to Venice as a safe haven. The satirical and often scurrilous writer Pietro Arentino was among them. Just as the fall of Constantinople in 1453 had led to the imagining of Venice as "another Byzantium," so the Sack of Rome called for the establishment of a "New Rome." Gritti and the architects he patronized, including Jacopo Sansovino and Michele Sanmicheli, took up the task and gave the city, especially the buildings clustered around Piazza San Marco, a convincing Roman look as the city on the Tiber became the model for Venice.

In the late fifteenth and early sixteenth centuries a number of writers made Venice the subject of their works, just as painters were doing with their canvases. Indeed, the Venetians were almost obsessively auto- or self-referential.[133] As the city's political clout diminished, its cultural significance increased, and the Venetian ruling elites were determined to write their history the way they wanted it portrayed.

In the last quarter of the fifteenth century, Bernardo Giustinian, ambassador and Procurator of San Marco, composed *De origine urbis Venetiarum* (On the Origins of Venice), published posthumously in 1493. Written in the years surrounding the War with Ferrara and the accompanying papal interdict, it offers a glimpse at how the Venetian ruling elite viewed their city in its most expansionist phase and before its humbling at Agnadello. Covering the first four centuries of Venice's history, Giustinian goes beyond the chronicle tradition of history writing exemplified by Martino da Canal and Andrea Dandolo and gives his work a humanist slant. Using classical historians as his models, Giustinian writes in an elegant Latin and subjects his sources, including Cassiodorus, one of his preferred authorities, to scrutiny. Venice's origins were threefold: the founding of San Giacomo at Rialto on March 25, 421; the flight of refugees from Attila; and the transfer of the capital to Rialto after Pepin's defeat. The work becomes a justification of Venetian policy and the elites who direct it. In Giustinian's view Venice has been from its origins peaceful in its intentions, orthodox in its faith, and generous in its treatment of subject people. The desire for freedom is at the heart of its existence. In an invented speech before Charlemagne, a Venetian representative proclaims, "Our ancestors migrated to these lagoons for the sake of safety and liberty."[134]

In another imagined speech Giustinian has an early inhabitant of the lagoon counter Padua's protest that the Venetians have seized the mouths of rivers in the area, saying, "Certainly, a people which in the beginning has found a place empty of inhabitants and owners, may take it for itself and live there by the best law of nations and of nature."[135] In a barren and uninhabited land, the Venetians created their own nation, one not subject to others. The lagoons were, in Giustinian's words, "inviolate and intact almost as certain holy places," and "left as kinds of boundaries between . . . Emperors."[136] When Venice did act, it did so in self-defense. Central to Venice's beginning was its relationship to Mark. Its access to the holy was not mediated via the papacy, making Venice's origins superior to those of Rome and Florence because its birth was sanctioned by God.

Shortly before Giustinian's work appeared, the *Rerum Venetiarum ab urbe condita libri XXXIII* (Thirty-Three Books on Things Venetian from the Foundation of the City) by Marcantonio Coccio Sabellico was published. Originally from near Rome, Sabellico taught for many years in Udine. Escaping the plague raging in Venice in 1485, he retreated to Verona where in just fifteen months he composed his history, which he dedicated to Doge Marco Barbarigo and the Senate. Although he was never named the Republic's official historiographer, the first holder of that post was instructed to begin his work where Sabellico's left off.[137]

Hastily compiled, Sabellico's work raided earlier chronicles but repeated errors, especially when dealing with Venice's early history. Yet his work was well received as evidenced by the rewards granted him by the Republic. The reason for this success was that Sabellico compared Venice favorably to ancient Rome and celebrated the Venetian commitment to freedom. Although Rome attained greater imperial status, Venice was superior "in the inviolability of its laws, the impartiality of its justice, its integrity and the sanctity of its constitution."[138] His contention that Venice's imperial policy in the middle years of the fifteenth century was pursued in the name of liberty found a receptive patrician audience, as did his justification of the recent war with Ferrara. Sabellico followed up this history with two other works, one on the site of Venice, another on its magistracies.

Ten years after Sabellico's death and having rebounded from the disaster of Agnadello, the Venetians named an official historiographer to celebrate and justify the city's recent history. They chose nobleman Andrea Navagero who was learned in Latin and Greek, had collaborated with Aldus Manutius in his editions of various Latin authors, and was an accomplished politician sent on important diplomatic missions for the Republic. In the bill of January 1516 creating the post of state historiographer, the Ten declared that "reputation is one of the fundamental principles of every state" and needs to be preserved for posterity. However, it is not served by "compendious and uncertain, mottled and coarse chronicles and annals" but by "certain, authentic, elegant and florid histories" by which the truth is made "more illustrious."[139] This is especially true for states that have endured "arduous and difficult undertakings and avoided the greatest dangers." It is the job of the "best patricians" to see that this is done. With the Ten's law, "the writing of the history of Venice became an affair of state."[140] But in the end, Navagero never wrote a word, at least according to Sanudo. Others declared that on his death he ordered burned what he had written.

Sanudo had special reason to be annoyed by Navagero's lack of productivity and the 200-ducat annuity he received, since he himself aspired to be state historiographer. But his pedantic and scolding personality and his probable homosexuality likely explain his lackluster career.[141] But at least Sanudo was prolific. At age eighteen he wrote an account of his inspection tour of the *terraferma*. Nine years later he began composing his *Vite dei dogi* (Lives of the Doges) which covered the years 1423–94. He also wrote a commentary on the war of Ferrara and a history of Charles VIII's descent into Italy.[142] His best-known works are his chronicle/guidebook *De origine, situ, et magistratibus urbis venetae ovvero la città di Venetia* and his diary. His goal in all his work was "to make known for eternity our Venetian state."[143] Unlike the others, he wrote in the vernacular, which he recognized meant that his writings would "be read more willingly by everyone than any other."[144]

Sanudo's *De origine*, intended for patricians and foreigners alike, offers an introduction to the origins, site, and government of Venice. Unlike the learned histories of Giustinian and Sabellico, it leads the reader on a tour of the city and gives thumbnail sketches of offices and magistracies. Sanudo catalogues the city's parishes *sestiere* by *sestiere,* its monasteries, the bodies of saints and other relics, the ferry stations, the various coins produced by the Mint, the species of fish sold at Rialto, the doges, the streets at Rialto, and "the notable things one shows to [visiting] lords in Venice."[145] Like Carpaccio's *Healing of the Possessed Man*, Sanudo's work is filled with endless details since "the slice of life in all its fullness signified uncontrived authenticity."[146]

Sanudo's "eyewitness style" is most apparent in his voluminous diary (fifty-eight volumes in its modern print edition), a mine of information on all aspects of Venetian life between 1496 and 1533.[147] As he admitted, "I was continually in the public squares investigating every occurrence, no matter how minimal, however unimportant it was."[148] Only by recording everything did he think he could capture the essence and excellence of "my most dear fatherland" and get at "the truth."[149] In 1515 he was given special access to governmental records in the chancery with the proviso that anything he published first had to be approved by the heads of the Ten.[150] Finally in 1531 the Ten awarded him a stipend of 150 ducats per annum so that he could continue his diary. In return, Sanudo had to agree to give it to the Ten on his death and provide access to Pietro Bembo, who had been chosen to succeed Navagero as the Republic's official historian. Sanudo had again been passed over.

Unlike Sanudo, Bembo was a well-connected cosmopolitan who enjoyed a European-wide reputation. In the late 1490s he began composing his dialogue, *Gli Asolani*, set in the court of Caterina Corner, and a few years later began work on *Prose della volgar lingua* (Prose in the Vernacular Tongue), which did not appear until 1525. In it he argued that the Tuscan dialect of Dante, Petrarch, and Boccaccio was the proper language for vernacular prose. It was part of a peninsula-wide debate about language, itself a proxy for a debate about Italian identity. Bembo took minor clerical orders for the income and eventually set up a household in Padua with his companion Ambrogina Faustina della Torre, known as La Morosina, with whom he had three children. In 1539 he became a cardinal and in 1543 bishop of Gubbio.[151]

Bembo worked on his history of Venice from his appointment as historiographer in 1530 until his death. He completed twelve books that cover the period from 1494 to 1513, ending with the election of Pope Leo X. He considered himself an unlikely choice to continue Venice's history, admitting that he had never contemplated writing history, especially since his life was so far removed from the rough and tumble of politics. Yet his international reputation as a stylist recommended him. He took as his models the commentaries of Julius Caesar and Livy's Roman history. His mission, according to the Ten's charge, was to preserve for posterity "the honor and glory of our State." It was also to serve as a guide to those governing; by studying past events they might better "foresee" the future.[152] The Republic's goal was no longer to extend its dominion but to exercise prudence and survive, as it had done through the Cambrai and Italian wars.

It fell to Gasparo Contarini to explain that survival. In so doing he enshrined Venice as the model republic. His treatise *De magistratibus et republica Venetorum* (On the Magistracies and Republic of the Venetians) has been described as an "ideological *summa* of the Venetian ruling oligarchs."[153] Born in 1483, Contarini studied at the School of Rialto and the chancery School of San Marco before continuing his education at the University of Padua where he moved in a circle of men, foremost among them Tommaso

Giustinian, in search of a more intense spirituality. Unlike Giustinian, who opted for the monastic life, Contarini believed salvation could also be attained by engagement with the world. From 1521 to 1525 he served as Venice's ambassador to Charles V and was in Bologna when peace was finally concluded in 1530. Named a cardinal by Paul III, he was the papal legate at the 1541 Colloquy of Regensburg, which tried unsuccessfully to restore religious unity to Christendom. Contarini's compromise position on the nature of salvation via faith and good works was rejected by both Luther and the pope. He died the following year.[154]

Contarini wrote *De magistratibus* starting in the early to mid-1520s, although it was not published until 1543. Intended as an introduction for foreigners to the government of Venice, it is composed of five books. Like other paeans to Venice, it begins with remarks on the city's marvelous location and the surfeit of available goods. But the real marvel is its form of government, which surpasses even those of antiquity. He then dissects and describes Venice's republican regime. Book One treats the Greater Council; Book Two the dogeship; Book Three the Senate, Ten, and certain tribunals; the fourth discusses various magistracies; and the fifth examines matters including governance of the *terraferma*. Most important, Contarini revives the idea of Venice as the prime example of a mixed constitution, one that combines monarchic, aristocratic, and democratic elements. Contarini's regime is unabashedly aristocratic, and he contends that it has always been so. The people who fled Attila were men from the mainland who were "superior to the others in nobility and wealth" and were escaping "the devastation brought to Italy."[155]

Contarini sees the *popolo* as represented by the Greater Council to which all nobles are members, even those who have been reduced to poverty. Only nobles are citizens of the Republic. The *popolo* have no role in governance except for some *cittadini originarii* who have been entrusted with certain offices in the chancery. The *popolo* are discussed instead in the context of the *scuole grandi* and guilds. Offices in these institutions satisfy their "desire for honor."[156] Despite their exclusion from politics, they remain happy with their lot, given the moderation and commitment to justice of those who govern them. He explains that the absence of rebellion by the ruled "has not been achieved by force, armed garrisons, or a well-fortified citadel, but rather by a just and balanced system of government, such that the people obey the nobility of their own accord and do not wish for any revolution, while retaining a strong affection towards the nobility."[157] This is true not only in the city but also among the *terraferma* subjects.

For Contarini, the monarchic, aristocratic, and democratic elements of government combine in a perfect harmony that translates into happy lives for Venice's inhabitants.[158] Despite his picture of near perfection, Contarini was aware of the danger that lurked even in a state as seemingly stable as Venice. He noted, "Nature so works that nothing can be perpetual among men, but all things . . . require restoration."[159] He was particularly concerned that certain young nobles no longer prioritized the common good over their private interests. Contarini supported Gritti's program of renewal, which called for an even greater role for the very best men, as embodied in the Ten and its *zonta*. His treatise was both descriptive, offering a picture of Venetian governance, and prescriptive, calling for the nobles to exercise again their inherent virtue. Most important, *De magistratibus* created an image of Venice and its ruling class as peaceful, just, wise, and stable, an image that the Venetians would perpetuate for centuries and that they came to believe surpassed even the greatness of ancient Greece and Rome. That idealized image obscured the realities of life for the 96 percent of the populace that did not belong to the nobility. Those throngs of people lived out their lives in this "New Rome," displaced this time not to the shores of the Bosphorus but to the northwest coast of the Adriatic Sea.

13

Late Renaissance Venetian Society

IN FEBRUARY 1543 the Senate issued a rule decrying an outrageous practice that was setting a "bad example" and causing "scandals." What rankled the senators was the "excessive number of whores (*meretrici*) in this our city" going about "openly in the streets and churches" so finely clothed that "our noble and citizen women have been confused with them, the good with the bad, and not only by foreigners but also by those who live here, because there is no difference of dress." To stop this affront, the Senate limited the gold, silver, silk, and jewels that prostitutes could wear and the fabrics with which they could decorate their homes. It explained that it was taking this action to curb these indignities, placate God, and end the prostitutes' excessive expenditures.[1]

Sixty-four years later, the Health Commissioners sent out instructions to parish priests who were responsible for compiling census data. The commissioners informed them that they were to place a "0" in the box for the number of male servants in artisan households. Some of the completed forms show that the priests either did not read the instructions carefully or were baffled by them since they initially listed male servants in artisan households and they had to go back and change the forms to conform to the instructions.[2]

These examples illustrate just how difficult it was to define the contours of late Renaissance Venetian society and fit members into preestablished categories. Prostitutes were mistaken for noblewomen, and priests were asked to enter data that was demonstrably wrong. The authorities were fighting a futile battle as they attempted to impose their vision of the social order and pigeonhole an expanding and ever-changing population into fixed categories with impermeable boundaries.

The authorities struggled mightily because the sixteenth century was such a dynamic period of societal change. Venice experienced rapid population growth followed by a huge decline. The increase had many roots, including an influx of foreign merchants and immigrant laborers engaged in manufacturing, torrents of refugees escaping famine on the mainland and the Ottoman advance in Venice's overseas possessions, and the permanent (though always provisional) admission of Jews into Venice. Census data document the demographic rise. From an estimated 115,000 inhabitants (excluding the outlying islands and other locales in the *dogado*) in 1509, the population rose to 129,971 in 1540 and 168,627 in 1563. A devastating outbreak of the plague in 1575–7 caused the population to drop to 134,871 in 1581. Rapid recovery followed with the city reaching its all-time peak of 188,970 in 1607. But the plague's return in 1630–1 carried off an estimated 90,000 (including in the *dogado*). By 1633 the city was reduced to 102,243 inhabitants.[3]

This chapter explores the lives of the people behind these statistics—their workaday activities, sexual and family relations, social networks, political influence, and pious and religious affiliations. While generalizations about a subject this broad are hazardous, the late Renaissance appears to have been an age of anxiety as Venetians grappled with the fluctuations they experienced. As inhabitants adjusted to these changes, they struggled to judge who was Venetian and who was not. Venice was not unique in this, as peoples across Europe and the Mediterranean contended with the larger forces impinging on their lives, including the Protestant Reformation and the Catholic response to it, and encounters with other cultures in the New World.

In the late Renaissance, *cittadini*, both original and naturalized, comprised one of the most dynamic elements of Venetian society. According to the detailed census data from 1563 they (men, women, boys, and girls) made up 8 percent of the population. What percentage were original citizens and what percentage were naturalized citizens is not clear.

Although the precise criteria for original citizenship remained ill-defined, various bureaucratic posts began to be reserved for them beginning in the fifteenth century. By 1478, only they could take up careers in the chancery, and positions of responsibility in the *scuole grandi* and important hospitals also became nearly their exclusive preserve. In the sixteenth century the procedures for establishing original citizenship status and its benefits were formalized. Starting in 1538 those who wanted to enter the chancery had to prove to the State Attorneys their status using, as the legislation stated, the same "form and procedure followed in proofs of nobility."[4] The process of definition culminated in 1569 with a law that only original citizens could hold intermediate offices in the bureaucracy. Aspirants had to prove to the State Attorneys that they, their fathers, and their grandfathers had been born in Venice and were the issue of legitimate marriages. To document this, the State Attorneys began keeping a register of those who qualified, whereas several different magistracies had previously been able to certify original citizenship status. The State Attorneys' register, the *Libro d'argento* (Silver Book), played the same role in authenticating original citizenship status that the *Libro d'oro* did in detailing noble status. The 1569 law did not, however, transform original citizens into a closed caste in the same way the Serrata did for the nobility over time. New men continued to enter the ranks as they met the qualifying criteria.[5]

Venice's original citizens have often been described as a sort of secondary nobility. Certainly, that is how many thought of themselves. A chronicle dated 1540 listing notable citizen families bears the revealing title *Cronica di tutte le antiche e nobili famiglie de' cittadini venetiani che non sono del Maggior Consiglio* (Chronicle of All the Ancient and Noble Families of Venetian Citizens Who Are Not of the Greater Council).[6] In their private documents, original citizens sometimes ascribed to themselves the same honorifics (*nobel homo, nobel madonna, clarissimus*) as did patricians. In so doing they were associating themselves with their social superiors and distancing themselves from the *popolo*.

An applicant for original citizenship was disqualified if he, his father, or his grandfather had ever practiced a manual trade or been retail sellers, both of which were deemed vile "mechanical arts." Three professions, however, escaped the manual labor disqualifier: owners of glass furnaces, furriers of wild animal pelts, and goldsmiths.[7] When in 1584 the sons of Zuane Stefani applied, they were questioned about their father's profession. Their reply that he sold wine at both wholesale and retail caught the examiners' attention. They were then asked if their father personally had ever sold at retail, even whether he wore an apron when doing so. Recognizing the repercussions of a wrong answer, the sons replied that he did not sell the retail wine himself but left that menial task to his assistants.[8] As the question about the apron (and as the Senate's prohibition of certain outfits for prostitutes) indicates, clothing was an important marker of status and identity. Marino Sanudo observed that both original citizens and nobles wore long black robes with wide sleeves that marked their honorable civil status.[9]

One subset of original citizens was illegitimate noble offspring. Original citizens interacted with nobles on a regular basis, especially in the chancery, which employed around eighty personnel. Noble magistrates, who rotated in and out of posts, relied on these citizen secretaries to know the institutional rules and procedures, locate essential documents and legal precedents, and generally train incoming officeholders.[10] Some secretaries specialized in the translation of coded dispatches from ambassadors and war commissioners. Since many noblemen were interested only in the prestige that went with officeholding and not with the work itself, the expertise of the citizen bureaucrats was critical. On diplomatic missions, noble ambassadors interacted very closely with their secretaries. Under certain circumstances, secretaries, such as Zaccaria de' Freschi, were themselves entrusted with treaty negotiations. Original citizens also monopolized lesser posts as notaries, scriveners, accountants, bookkeepers, and cashiers serving various governmental offices. In these roles they were able to influence policy, especially its implementation, and in this way participate in the Republic's politics.[11]

Socializing with nobles extended beyond the workplace, especially for members of the chancery. Some original citizens married their daughters into noble houses while others made alliances with naturalized or other original citizen families. Marriages with nobles guaranteed their grandchildren the right to noble status. The rituals associated with marriage, baptism, and death offered opportunities to strengthen mutual ties of obligation and affection. In 1504 Zaccaria de' Freschi married his daughter Samaritana to Melchiore della Nave, citizen and merchant. In the Freschi family memoir—the compilation of which was itself an act of family social promotion—the wedding festivities were carefully recorded. The bride came to Santa Maria Formosa accompanied by fifers and twenty matrons dressed in gold-shot silk. She was bedecked in a gown of the "most precious crimson velvet" and adorned with golden jewels. A who's who of noblemen attended the event, including the son of sitting doge Leonardo Loredan, Zorzi Corner, and future doge Andrea Gritti. An elegant banquet with music and dancing lasted into the night.[12]

Original citizens also used cultural patronage to distinguish themselves socially. The Amadi family, the original owners of a miracle working image of the Madonna, were instrumental in seeing that Santa Maria dei Miracoli was built to house it. In their family memoir, Angelo Amadi recorded that when the church was officially founded on May 2, 1481, he placed a medal in the first pilaster to the left of the main door. It included his image with the inscription "Angelus de Amatis" on one side and the Amadi family crest on the other.[13]

Yet it was through their control of offices in the *scuole grandi* that original citizens (and some naturalized citizens) were able to exercise patronage on a massive scale. In the sixteenth century, these great confraternities evolved as the egalitarian impulse on which they had been founded gave way to the creation of internal orders of rich and poor among members, with the wealthy distributing charity to their poorer brethren. Increasing amounts of money were spent on pomp and display as the confraternities competed with one another in the building and decoration of larger and ever more elaborate meeting halls.[14] The Scuola Grande of the Misericordia employed Jacopo Sansovino to build a new headquarters that, in the words of two authorities, was "an absurdly oversized idea, quite unrelated to the resources of the Scuola" and hence never completed—an "unhappy monument to frustrated grandeur."[15]

If original citizens were vital to the government's operation and drivers of a good portion of the city's cultural patronage, naturalized citizens were "among the principal protagonists" of Venice's economic revival in the second half of the sixteenth century.[16] Between 1534 and 1622 the Senate awarded 278 privileges of citizenship to 325 men, who met the residency and tax-responsibility requirements. In 190 cases, the applicants' place of origin is known: 128 came from Venice's *stato da terra* (ninety from Bergamo and its environs), eighteen from the *stato da mar* (eight from Cyprus), thirty from other Italian states (seven each from Genoa and Milan), and fourteen from other places in Europe including six Swiss, three Germans, and two Flemings.[17] They were merchants, shopkeepers, and artisans, although the artisans were owners of workshops, not mere laborers. Textile merchants and producers predominated, not surprising given the growth of the wool and silk industries in this period. In his application Alvise Pocobello noted that he had produced 5,662 bolts of cloth between 1572 and 1586. Nevertheless, the viability of his application was in doubt since he had not paid taxes during his twenty-six years as a resident in Venice. But his marriage into the noble Pizzamano family swung matters in his favor. Another textile manufacturer, the Bergamasque Gian Antonio Zois, had continued to produce cloth even during the plague of the 1570s. By so doing, his application noted, he had helped "the industry and the poor of this city."[18] Over time, citizenship also became associated with certain professions that were considered honorable, such as medicine and the law. Many physicians especially used ownership of books and familiarity with classical culture to acquire cultural legitimacy.[19]

In this period only one woman applied for naturalized citizenship.[20] Yet as wives, mothers, and widows, women played an important role in the lives of citizen families. Applicants for naturalization often emphasized that they had married native Venetians, while the requirement of legitimate birth also increased (as it did among the patriciate) women's importance. Although there was no hard and fast rule, there was some tendency for merchant citizens to marry among themselves and chancery families to do the same. The hold of the *fraterna*, the joint inheritance by brothers, remained strong especially among prominent citizen families as did the practice of channeling sons and daughters into various livelihoods. For example, each generation of the Ziliol family tracked one or more sons into commerce, others into the bureaucracy, and still others into ecclesiastical careers. Ziliol daughters were married into other citizen families or the families of Venetian and Paduan nobles or placed in convents.[21]

A striking example of upward social mobility and respectability is that of mercer Bartolomeo Bontempelli. Born in the Bresciano in 1538, he emigrated to Venice and eventually operated two shops, the Chalice and the Moon, with a working capital of 6,000 ducats. But that was only a small portion of his wealth, as he owned iron mines north of Belluno worth tens of thousands of ducats. He attained full citizenship in 1579. He served on the governing board of the mercers' guild several times in the late 1560s and early 1570s and was its warden in 1582. But much of his energy and generosity was channeled into charity. He served on the board of the Scuola Grande of San Rocco and gifted 36,000 ducats toward the construction of the Hospital of the Mendicanti to which he also bequeathed an additional 100,000 ducats. In the church of San Salvador, he, along with his brother, appear in an altarpiece painted by Sante Peranda.[22]

The Cuccinas, who had immigrated from Bergamo to Venice, were another prominent naturalized citizen family. In Venice the brothers Zuanne and Girolamo, who continued to hold their assets in *fraterna* and to maintain a joint household, amassed a substantial fortune based on wool and eventually expanded into luxury goods such as mirrors. Like Bontempelli, they were also active in San Rocco. After renting housing for many years, they purchased in the mid-1540s a property on the Grand Canal. But they did not begin construction on their new family palace until 1558, and it was not completed until 1566, by which time both had died and Girolamo's sons Alvise and Antonio, also linked in *fraterna*, took up residence. Girolamo's third son, who was not part of the *fraterna*, married Marina Surian, whose father eventually became grand chancellor. Alvise developed a close relationship with painter Paolo Veronese, who decorated the family chapel in San Francesco della Vigna and then executed in the early 1570s a cycle of four paintings for the *portego* of the new palace. Alvise, his wife Zuanna di Mutti, and their many children are at the center of one canvas, the *Cuccina Family Presented to the Madonna and Child*. They are accompanied by the three theological virtues, Faith, Hope, and Charity. At the far right a female servant carries the couple's youngest son. In the gap between her and the others appears a glimpse of the family palace. Alvise's recently deceased brother Antonio is shown with Faith taking his hand. The entire group is depicted before the family chapel in San Francesco della Vigna. The painting links the living and the dead across generations. Zuanna's stunning dress serves as an advertisement for the Cuccinas' textile manufacturing interests, while its striking red color references her natal family's deep involvement in the importation of cochineal from the New World.[23] The Cuccina family story is one of dramatic economic and social advancement achieved through hard work and astute artistic and architectural patronage.

Cittadino Andrea Odoni also used cultural patronage as a tool. Son of an immigrant from Milan who partnered with nobleman Piero Orio in the lucrative collection of the city's wine tax, Odoni used his modest palace, with its frescoed façade and his collection of antique and contemporary sculptures and fragments, to project an image of refinement and discernment.[24]

The heterogeneity of the *cittadini*, their lack of fixity as a social group, is also evidenced by their attitude toward the patriciate. Some were regime loyalists and grateful for the benefits they received from it. Scipione Ziliol wrote in his will of 1589, "I order all my nephews always to hold in reverence all the Venetian nobility, and serve them even with the sacrifice of their lives, not only because they merit it, but also because our family is more obliged to them than any other family in Venice on account of the numerous benefits and favors that they have done for us . . . and [I order] that they [my

FIGURE 13.1 Paolo Veronese, *The Cuccina Family Presented to the Madonna and Child*, 1571. Gemäldegalerie Alte Meister, Staatliche Kunstsammlungen Dresden. Photograph: Hans Peter Klut/Elke Estel. Via Google Arts & Culture.

nephews] love and serve them perpetually, as their true and natural lords."[25] Others, especially some of the oldest citizen families, resented their exclusion from the patriciate at the time of the Serrata. During the Cambrai wars, Emperor Maximilian tried to lure what he called the *popolo*—although he especially meant the *cittadini*—to his side by promising them that if he took possession of Venice and its lands, "in the future you will share the government of the city of Venice with the others, and that they will not exclude you from it as they have done in the past."[26] In contrast to Scipione Ziliol, his grandnephew Alessandro thought the patricians, whom he refused to call nobles but referred to instead as "those of the [Greater] Council," were stingy in granting rights of citizenship since they did not want to share the regime's benefits with others. In his *Le due corone della nobiltà veneziana* (The Two Crowns of the Venetian Nobility), he claimed that there were two kinds of gentlemen in Venice: the "noble gentlemen," who were members of the Greater Council, and the "citizen gentlemen." He reversed Gasparo Contarini's formulation of Venetian society. Contarini argued that it was composed of two elements—the nobles and the *popolo*—with the latter subdivided into the "more honorable part" and the rest. Ziliol retained the twofold division but divided the nobility in two: gentlemen of the Greater Council and gentlemen *cittadini*.[27]

The *popolo* remained an amorphous group, divided along ethnic, workplace, and neighborhood lines. The 1563 census listed 127,746 persons (75 percent of the population) as "artisans." For many, guilds continued to provide institutional foci for their lives. Guilds kept proliferating, from around fifty in the early fourteenth century to 142 in 1773.[28] So too did subdivisions within guilds based on the products they produced. The shoemakers' guild, for example, had three branches: the shoemakers proper, the cobblers, and the makers of clogs. Divisions within the turners' guild were based on the raw materials—ivory, wood, or brass—that members worked. In some cases, these divisions eventually led to the formation of separate guilds, with the impetus for independence coming from within rather than the government.[29] Membership in some guilds numbered in the hundreds. In 1530, 242 ironsmiths were enrolled in the guild's confraternity.[30] Others such as the charcoal porters, numbered only in the teens. Street names such as Calle dei Fabbri (Smiths' Alley) and Merceria (Mercer's Way) commemorate the professional concentrations along certain thoroughfares or in specific neighborhoods.

Guild proliferation meant that there were many opportunities for artisan men to hold positions of modest power within their trades. Guild officials were responsible for protecting guild privileges while the government through the Giustizia Vecchia was primarily concerned with prosecuting guildsmen who failed to observe religious holidays, manipulated prices, or cheated consumers by using scant measures. Proliferation also created inter-guild conflict as crafts sought to protect their institutional and market boundaries. The manufacture of mirrors with painted frames was the source of dispute between the painters' and mirror-makers' guilds; the retailing of nails divided the ironsmiths and mercers.[31]

The guilds remained closely tied to their affiliated religious confraternities. The ironsmiths' guild even used its *scuola* at San Moisè to store charcoal bought in bulk on the Riva del Carbon (Charcoal Quay) at Rialto and distribute it to members.[32] Confraternities with a purely religious orientation continued to thrive and constituted another central element of popular life. One estimate suggests that circa 1500 there were about ninety devotional confraternities in the city; another seventy-nine were added in the first half of the century, many of them focused on veneration of the Eucharist.[33] Another innovation of the sixteenth century was *sovvegni*, societies based on the idea of self-help. Enrollees paid an entry fee and weekly dues and after a set period were eligible for assistance if misfortune struck. Some of the *sovvegni* were affiliated with preexisting confraternities or guilds. As with the guilds, the impetus to form new confraternities came largely from the *popolo* themselves and indicates how important the impulse to band together was for workers, many of whom were immigrants.

However, the laboring classes' primary source of support remained kin. Most of their households were presided over by a married couple. According to one survey spanning 1589 to 1607, most couples lived alone or with their children. Around a third had others dwelling with them, such as siblings, in-laws, or widowed parents. Yet sixteenth-century Venice was also chock-full of single people, both unmarried and widowed. Parish records indicate that a little more than a quarter of the population (many of whom were children) fell into this category.[34] On reaching adulthood—signified by marriage—most working Venetians established their own households. Usually they rented their lodgings, which generally consisted of two or three rooms, and were furnished in a simple and utilitarian manner. Very few could afford to purchase property.[35] The presence of looms in the dwellings of textile workers indicates that they often labored and lived in the same cramped quarters, as did other artisans.[36] Consequently, taverns, barbershops, and even pharmacies became places of sociability where news about politics and religion, along with gossip, was exchanged.[37]

Many factors including neighborhood ties, common background, and shared occupation figured in the selection of spouses. These often-arranged marriages produced many satisfying unions, but there were also disastrous liaisons. However, since the Catholic Church held that willing consent was essential to marriage, the patriarch's court, which had jurisdiction over marriage, did provide a way for some Venetians to separate from their spouses or have their marriages annulled. Coercion and failure to consummate a marriage were both grounds for annulment. In 1584, for example, Lucrezia Balatini, daughter of a boatman, went to the court to have her marriage annulled because she claimed that her husband, Francesco Revedin, a weaver, was impotent. She testified that whenever they tried to have sex, "his member stands up, but when he tries, it immediately goes limp."[38] Francesco countered that Lucrezia had engaged in adultery and gotten pregnant by another man and that she wanted the annulment so she could marry her lover. The case's outcome is unknown. Physical abuse, neglect, or outright cruelty were grounds for separation. Paola da Venezia petitioned to separate from her husband, a fuller named Jacobo Furlano, since according to her and her neighbors in Santa Margherita, he beat and starved Paola, all the while dissipating her dowry of 137 ducats on drink, gambling, and prostitutes. One neighbor who lived in the same building testified that her mother had taken pity on Paola and given her food.[39] While the outcome of this case is also unknown, it shows that under extreme circumstances abused women had some legal recourse. Although it would have taken great courage to stand up to prevailing attitudes about wifely duties and female submission, women could challenge an institution central to both church and state.[40]

The reliance on neighbors as witnesses attests to the role that neighborhood ties played in laboring class lives.[41] Such bonds provided another layer of support for those at poverty's edge. Many of the *scuole piccole* had a local focus. People living in the parishes near the Arsenal frequently chose marital partners from the same parish, sometimes even the same street or courtyard.[42] The fishermen of San Nicolò dei Mendicoli and Angelo Raffaele formed a unique community with their own general assembly, board of governors, and *gastaldo grande* (chief warden), who was elected for life and invested by a secretary at the Ducal Palace with the symbol of his office.[43]

Neighborhood bonds were also at the heart of one of Venice's great rivalries, that between residents in the western (landward) side of the city, who took their nickname Nicolotti from San Nicolò dei Mendicoli, and the Castellani, from the seaward side including the *sestiere* of Castello in the eastern reaches of the town, and parts of Cannaregio and Dorsoduro. This rivalry was institutionalized in a series of battles staged on bridges throughout the city. The bridges' narrowness served to focus antagonism as the factions struggled to gain control of the spans. The two most popular bridges were in San Marziale and San Barnaba and became known as the Ponti dei Pugni or Ponti della Guerra (Fist or War Bridges). The factions included close-knit fighting squads composed for the most part of men from the city's poorest peripheral areas. Originally fought with long sticks and some protective clothing, these contests had evolved by the end of the sixteenth century into a series of one-on-one boxing matches followed by a melee known as the *frotta* in which squads of fighters continually stormed the bridge until the losing side exhausted its reinforcements. Injuries and even drownings as participants tumbled into the canals were part and parcel of the battles. Such reveries were a way for marginalized men to win honor for themselves and their neighborhoods and assert their identity. They also represented popular resistance to the dominant noble culture and power of the state, which had grown more pronounced and centralized during the sixteenth century.[44]

FIGURE 13.2 Gabriele Bella, *Combat on the Ponte dei Pugni*, first half seventeenth century. Galleria Querini Stampalia, Venice. Cameraphoto Arte, Venice /Art Resource NY.

The bridge battles were not, however, exclusively popular affairs. While most erupted spontaneously, others were staged, usually for the benefit of foreign dignitaries. When Henry III of France visited in July 1574, he lamented that the battle he witnessed "was too small to be a real war and too cruel to be a game."[45] Great international rivalries reverberated on humble Venetian bridges. French diplomats supported the Castellani because the Spanish envoy favored the Nicolotti.[46] Noblemen and women, *cittadini*, and even priests followed the battles like modern-day sporting events, cheering from balconies and boats, betting on the results, and feting victors. Battles were staged as part of the coronation celebrations for Dogaresse Zilia Dandolo in 1557 and Morosina Morosini in 1597. The Ten, unsuccessful in its efforts to suppress the battles, in the end simply tried to impose a modicum of control over them.

Nowhere was intermingling of rich and poor, noble and *popolano* more intimate or intense than in households employing servants. In the minds of the 1563 census takers at least, servants stood apart from other members of the *popolo*; they were included in the households of their masters and mistresses. The 12,908 servants counted in the census constituted 7.65 percent of the total population. By 1642 they accounted for 8.49 percent of Venice's reduced population of 120,307 souls. Female servants outnumbered males nearly two to one.

Yet the number of servants in individual households was never very large. Foreigners were struck by what poor figures Venetian gentlemen cut in comparison to those of their own countries. Frenchman Michel de Montaigne observed that "a train of valets is of no use to us at all here, for everyone goes around by himself," while Englishman Thomas Coryat noted that Venetian nobles had no "gallant retinue of servants."[47] Indeed households with even ten servants were rare. One large household was that of the grand chancellor Andrea Surian; its twenty-four members included four male and eight female servants.[48] Nevertheless, the employment of at least one male servant was an unmistakable marker of (and nearly a prerequisite for) high status since most served as private gondoliers. In support of Agostin Agostini's petition for original citizenship, witnesses reported not only that he had co-owned a ship with nobleman Francesco Morosini, possessed real estate on the mainland and in Venice, and had factors who managed the dirty work of his wool business, but also that he "kept a gondola with two gondoliers."[49] Enslaved black Africans were especially prized as personal retainers and became important status symbols.[50] The tasks assigned within households to free and unfree retainers were often indistinguishable, although the enslaved lacked the ability of their free counterparts to simply leave a cruel master.

Relations between masters and servants ran the gamut from loving to hostile. Some masters and their female servants formed long-term sexual and emotional relationships. In his will of 1518 Antonio Zorzi left his house and its furnishings as well as his shares in the Mint, to "my most loving wife who is not my wife but my slave, who always struggled to make a living with me."[51] While the relationship between Zorzi and his enslaved ended well, it likely started with her sexual exploitation. Adolescent serving girls were constantly vulnerable to sexual abuse by their masters and other males in the household. A few like the enslaved Ursa were lucky. Ursa's mistress, Lorenza de Zanobi, stated in her will that she wanted Ursa to be freed upon her death and assume the role of "rectoress" of the hospice for poor women that Lorenza and her husband had established.[52] The widow turned gold-thread merchant Lucia ab Auro freed Benvenuta dalla Tana, her enslaved, whom she had taught to spin gold thread and then made her business partner.[53] Giovan Battista Peranda, the child of two servants, was the beneficiary of a generous bequest from his parents' master, studied medicine at the University of Padua, and eventually served as advisor to the College of Surgeons.[54]

Masters expected obedience and loyalty. According to the prevailing elite ideology which viewed households as microcosms of the polity, failure of servants to obey was tantamount to rebellion and might be met with a severe beating or dismissal. Male servants sometimes struck back by publicly humiliating their masters, using foul language, or vandalizing their masters' property, especially their gondolas.[55] In his book *La piazza universale di tutte le professioni del mondo* (The Universal Piazza of All the Professions of the World), Tommaso Garzoni declared that boatmen took after Charon, the ferryman of the River Styx, saying that they were "the devil's kind."[56]

A servant girl who became pregnant might well find herself tossed onto the streets and resorting to prostitution. Renaissance Venice was renowned for the trade, which encompassed different categories of sex workers. At the top of the profession were courtesans, women who cultivated an image of refinement and sexual allure. They surrounded themselves with luxury objects and mastered talents such as music-making and the art of conversation. As a group, they earned an international reputation, and an assignation with them was often an obligatory part of a visit to the city for elite foreign male visitors. A 1565 guidebook known as the *Catalogo di tutte le principali et più honorate cortigiane di Venezia* (List of All the Principal and Most Honored Courtesans of Venice) included information about their fees and how to contact them.

Many courtesans came from respectable backgrounds where they acquired the requisite learning and sophistication. One such figure was Julia Lombardo, née Leoncini, whom Sanudo described as the "sumptuous whore" (*somtuosa meretrize*).[57] Lombardo almost certainly numbered among the *cittadini* since her father was a draper and her grandfather a physician. She used her considerable talents to support herself and her invalid sister Angelica. The inventories taken of their possessions in their home in Santi Apostoli offer a glimpse into the lavish material world of courtesans and the fantasies of opulence that were part and parcel of their image and trade. The furnishings, including books, objets d'art, a portrait of Dante, twenty-eight paintings, a gilded bed, a harpsichord, and a brass and glass chandelier, projected an aura of learning and refinement. Coffers and chests were filled with carpets, linens, and clothing. Among Julia's clothes were eight "women's shifts in the style of men." Later in the century, it became common for courtesans to cross-dress, which allowed them greater freedom to move about the city and may have titillated certain clients.[58]

The luxury objects with which courtesans surrounded themselves were intended to enhance their allure. Yet ultimately it was their sexual expertise that mattered. A satirical catalogue of Venice's courtesans described Lucrezia Squarcia as a "goddess of crude acts."[59] Venice's most renowned courtesan, Veronica Franco, straightforwardly declared, "I, well taught in such matters, know how to perform so well in bed that this art exceeds Apollo's by far, and my singing and writing are both forgotten by the man who experiences me in this way, which Venus reveals to people who serve her."[60]

Courtesans' quest for reputation and respectability is evident not only in their literary pursuits but also in the tomb in San Francesco della Vigna that Julia's sister Angelica commissioned for them following Julia's death. San Franceso della Vigna was the most fashionable church in early sixteenth-century Venice, thanks to its patronage by Doge Gritti. Although Julia was accorded burial in the church, the tomb inscription reads: "Angelica Leoncini and her sister prepared this perpetual site."[61] Just as Sanudo refused to honor Julia by calling her a courtesan—using instead the more vulgar *meretrice*—so the authorities would only go so far in allowing commemoration of a woman who so openly violated patriarchal norms.

Below the courtesans came the *meretrici*, the run-of-the-mill prostitutes. By the early modern period, the authorities no longer sought to confine prostitution to licensed brothels like those long established near Rialto. Older women continued to take the lead as entrepreneurs in the industry. They organized their recruits into brothels, known by the loaded term *scolette*, which evokes both schools and confraternities. The procuresses also provided other services, offering shelter to unmarried pregnant women who needed a place to hide their condition from wagging tongues, and finding employment as wet nurses for those who had recently given birth.[62] But the prostitutes were often seriously indebted to their brothel managers and frequent victims of violence and disease.

Many women turned to prostitution as their family circumstances changed. If a woman's husband left, lost his job, or died, she might look to sex work to make ends meet. Immigrant women provided a steady stream of new recruits. The most destitute—new arrivals from the mainland fleeing famine and poverty and those ravaged by diseases like syphilis—literally lived on the streets where they plied their trade. Landlords, tavern keepers, launderesses, used-clothing dealers, boatmen, and others all profited in various ways from prostitution.

The world of the courtesans and prostitutes intersected with other forms of sexual activity, many of which came under the umbrella term sodomy. These so-called crimes against nature included anal intercourse among men, anal intercourse with women including wives and prostitutes, and bestiality. In the fourteenth and much of the fifteenth century, Venice differed from most other polities in prosecuting the active partner in homosexual male intercourse more aggressively than the passive partner. The passive partner usually was punished with a jail term, corporal punishment, and perhaps exile, while the active partner was executed and his remains burned.[63] But over time the differentiation in prosecution and punishment of active and passive partners declined, and by the seventeenth century the authorities were much less concerned with sodomy, except when it involved force or violence.[64] Schools, barbershops, secluded porticos, and dinner parties were some of the places where same-sex contact was initiated (or so the authorities worried). The clergy accounted for nearly a fifth of the cases prosecuted in the seventeenth century. While many same-sex encounters were fleeting, there were also long-term relationships, especially among nobles and other elites.[65] The elite's changing marital patterns and cultural factors may account for this, though such long-term relationships may simply have been more likely to come to the authorities' attention than those among *popolano* men.[66] Few cases of female same-sex relations have been uncovered, in part because they did not threaten patrician family concerns and reputations the way male same-sex relations did and because male authorities had a difficult time conceiving of lesbian sex.[67] In one recorded example, in 1631 a nun at the convent of San Sepolcro denounced a servant named Pasqua who worked at the convent for "engaging in shameful acts with one of the said nuns, such as touching her breasts and doing other things that out of modesty I will skip over."[68]

Many Venetians turned to magic and its practitioners to bind lovers to them and remedy other problems. When nobleman Marco Dandolo married courtesan Andriana Savorgnan in a private ceremony that defied the new regulations concerning marriage issued by the Council of Trent, as well as conventions regarding suitable matches for noblemen, the Dandolo clan denounced Savorgnan in the patriarch's court. They claimed that she had used magic to ensnare the hapless Marco and bind him to her. Witnesses reported that Andriana had previously been privately married to another nobleman, Filippo da Canal, and on another occasion had procured from a witch a concoction to poison the wife of a different potential marital partner.[69] No less a figure than courtesan Veronica Franco was denounced to the Inquisition for resorting to magic to reveal who had stolen goods from her home. The ritual involved using holy water, blessed candles, a basin of water, and other objects so that a "White Angel" would reveal the culprit. Her accuser also claimed that she used various incantations to "make certain Germans who have been frequenting her house fall in love with her" and that she failed to attend Mass and ate meat on prohibited days, signs of Protestant sympathies.[70] Through skillful redirection of the inquisitor's questions and support from powerful patrons, Franco escaped the more serious allegation of heresy, admitting only to allowing the water ritual to take place in her house.[71] While expertise in magic constituted a form of power and source of income for marginal women, their authority in such matters and the efficacy of magic in general were widely accepted at all levels of society well into the seventeenth century.[72] So too was the power of poor women who claimed or were believed to be receiving visions from God. In 1523 Sanudo reported that a woman in San Barnaba, the sister of a turner, was experiencing ecstasies.[73]

One group that saw a marked drop in status and living standards in the sixteenth century was oarsmen. When the merchant galley lines declined and then ceased altogether, a vast pool of steady jobs disappeared. So did the opportunity for oarsmen to carry merchandise for trade. During peacetime, the war fleet was demobilized, further limiting employment possibilities. In 1519 the Senate cut the base pay for oarsmen from 12 lire per month to 8 but was forced to raise it again to 10 in 1524, where it stayed for the rest of the century, despite rising prices. In addition, the quantity and quality of onboard rations declined, as did the prospects of garnering booty from captured enemy ships.[74]

At a time when most other Mediterranean powers were relying on galley slaves, it became increasingly difficult for Venice to outfit its warships with volunteers, forcing it to turn to conscription. Some of the crewmen were drafted from the *stato da terra*, although these landlubbers' lack of preparation for the rigors of life at sea proved problematic. *Terraferma* men were expected to fill about half the required positions, while the government began conscripting residents of the capital for the rest. No longer relying on the parish-based system of *duodene*, the government began demanding in 1539 that every guild, *scuola grande*, and ferry-station supply a quota of oarsmen. When the lists were revised in 1595, the eligible conscripts numbered 23,000.[75] While poorer guildsmen and boatmen often had to serve in person, it became common for members of the richer guilds and the *scuole grandi* to hire substitutes by offering bonuses. Clever recruits were able to collect several bonuses and then abscond without serving.

To remedy the situation Venice began to use convicts, who were chained to their benches. This approach was advocated by nobleman Cristoforo da Canal who claimed that Venice's comfortable standard of living meant that only "pressing need" would ever cause Venetian residents to volunteer for the galleys. In addition, he argued that the governors of Venice's mainland and overseas dominions who were reluctant to punish wrongdoers with corporal punishment, such as the loss of limbs, would be "more prompt and eager to sentence criminals . . . if they had to condemn them harmlessly to the chain itself." He improbably added that "this would make the prisoners very happy, and would further the public interest without impeding justice."[76] In 1545, Da Canal personally took command of the first war galley rowed by convicts. Of the 140 ships that Venice mobilized for the War of Cyprus, sixteen were manned by prisoners who served under miserable conditions.[77]

The difficult circumstances in which the *galleoti* (free galley oarsmen) found themselves led to frequent protests over their wages, which were often in arrears. In 1509, for example, oarsmen from the galley *Pisana* went to the Ducal Palace to complain of their failure to be paid.[78] Arsenal workers were also quick to act on grievances. In 1569, 300 Arsenalotti grabbed their tools and stormed Piazza San Marco protesting a reduction in their pay for Saturday afternoons. When the heads of the Ten failed to satisfy their demands, they surged into the College. Doge Pietro Loredan managed to defuse the situation. Some of the leaders were arrested but released after six months.[79] When in 1581 the Arsenalotti learned that they would be deprived of a day's pay, at a time when the city was suffering famine and bread prices were skyrocketing, they again went to the College to complain. Doge Nicolò da Ponte's words failed to assuage their anger. As they left in frustration, one of the protesters, named Bongerolamo, yelled, "There is nothing for it, brothers, but to go and plunder the public granary." They went to the grain warehouses at Terranova and made off with many bushels of flour. The Ten acted quickly and had Bongerolamo and several others, including two boatmen, arrested. Two days later Bongerolamo was hanged; five others were sentenced to the galleys, the two boatmen for ten-year terms. The Ten even forbade the mariners' confraternity to give Bongerolamo a proper burial.[80]

Unrest among the *galleoti* and Arsenalotti was just one manifestation of popular discontent. The *popolo* were politically aware and found a variety of ways to make their opinions known. In his diary, Marino Sanudo noted several times when various laws and actions were met with "the murmuring of the city."[81] The city awoke one morning in April 1532 to graffiti that had been scrawled around Piazza San Marco. One declared, "O people, destroy the tyrants."[82] Another proclaimed, "O people, wake up for now is the time" and next to it the words, "Tyrants, cruel ones, soon you will regret [your ways]." The Ten quickly dispatched men to erase the offending words.[83]

The *popolo* demonstrated their political feelings in heightened fashion during ducal funerals and elections. In 1570, their plan to throw bread at the corpse of Doge Pietro Loredan, whom they blamed for high bread prices, forced the funeral procession's quick re-routing.[84] During the 1595 funeral of Doge Pasquale Cicogna, a crowd made up of youths and the *popolo* started shouting "Viva, viva Marino Grimani," their choice as Cicogna's successor. Decades before, Grimani's father Girolamo, known for his avarice, had had to withdraw his candidacy for the dogeship when a crowd started chanting, "If you make Grimani doge, we will feed him to the dogs!"[85] Well aware of his father's fate, Marino cultivated a reputation for largesse. The Spanish ambassador described him to Philip II as "effectively a father of the poor."[86] As the conclave to elect Cicogna's successor dragged on, the *popolo* (and some *cittadini*) staged demonstrations in Grimani's favor, and the slogan, "Viva Grimani, who will have large loaves of bread baked" resounded.[87] When an attempted attack on the Ducal Palace occurred, Leonardo Donà withdrew his candidacy, and Grimani was elected on the seventy-first ballot.

The celebrations soon led to looting and more disorder, which Grimani defused with even more extravagant acts of munificence. The coronation of his wife Morosina Morosini as dogaressa in 1597 provided yet another opportunity for Grimani to burnish his image as the advocate of the poor. Much of the ephemeral architecture created for the festivities celebrated abundance and liberality. In 1612, Grimani's successor, the frugal and austere Leonardo

Donà, was taunted during the annual ducal procession to Santa Maria Formosa with the old refrain, "Viva, viva Doge Grimani, father of the poor." Donà was so traumatized by the experience that he refused to participate in any public processions during the final six months of his reign.[88] As these examples demonstrate, non-nobles had ways to make their political feelings known, and in Grimani's case they even helped determine the outcome of a ducal election. They did so again in 1676 when *popolano* rioters mobilized by noble patrons had the election of Giovanni Sagredo annulled by the Greater Council, and Alvise Contarini elected in his stead.[89] The *popolo* were not passive and contented subjects but political actors who could transform Piazza San Marco into contested space and influence policy.[90] In spite of its well-honed image, the Republic's much touted serenity was always contingent and fragile.

One subset of the *popolo* was comprised of those unable or judged unwilling to work. The 1563 census data give the number of poor and beggars as 539 and the number of hospital inmates (listed under the category of the religious) as 1,479. It is unclear how the census takers determined who was poor or a beggar, although they probably meant those who were considered legitimate, licensed beggars. Tricksters and fakes, like Giacomo Antonio of Vicenza, who pretended "to have the shakes, with a bloodstained cap on his head, and yet . . . is robust and healthy," or Venetian Giovanni Francesco, who paraded around with a severed arm hung around his neck, although officials found him to be "perfectly fit and . . . defrauding good Christians to the detriment of the truly needy," were difficult to track down and survey.[91] Even so, the number of beggars in the census appears artificially low.

Yet at times during the sixteenth century, throngs of the desperate, fleeing war, violence, famine, and disease flooded the city. The War of the League of Cambrai and Italian Wars brought an influx of refugees, as did the 1463–79 war with the Ottomans, when many fled the Turkish advance. Worse still were the terrible harvests in 1527 and 1528 when peasants from the *terraferma* swamped the city. In December 1527, Sanudo offered this wrenching account: "Every evening in Piazza San Marco and on the streets and at Rialto little children cry out 'Bread, I am dying of hunger and the cold' . . . and in the morning some are found dead under the portico of the Ducal Palace."[92] The 1527 dearth ushered in decades of famines that struck as frequently as every five or ten years. A combination of factors—including a swelling population in the city, short-term environmental calamities such as floods and droughts on the *terraferma*, and longer-term climate change (the Little Ice

Age)—were at the root of the problem. The famines in the last two decades of the century were the most devastating as they affected the Mediterranean as a whole. Normally Venice was able to use its fleet to procure grain from afar to replenish its warehouses, but that became impossible, especially as Constantinople acquired Egyptian grain to feed its own population. In December 1588, the Senate declared, "Everywhere there are vast numbers of paupers who go through the city begging and interrupting the prayers and offices of the church."[93] Seen in this light, the *popolo*'s concern with bread during Doge Grimani's election comes into focus. One estimate suggests that 70 percent of the population depended on price-controlled bread.[94] To make matters worse, syphilis arrived in Venice in 1495–6.[95] And plague continued its periodic visits, peaking in the devastating outbreak of 1575–7 and its harrowing return in 1630–1.

Traditional Venetian charity was geared to those who did not have the capacity to provide for themselves: the infirm, aged, widows, orphans, and those with disabilities like blindness. They were considered part of the community and deemed respectable. Numerous institutions were organized to meet their needs, including the many hospices and hospitals run by the guilds, *scuole*, and government.[96] Among these was the Ospedale dei Crociferi. Founded in the twelfth century as a hospital for pilgrims and the poor, it had evolved by the beginning of the fifteenth century into a home for poor women. Its building was modified to accommodate twelve small apartments, one for each resident, as well as an oratory that was redecorated by Palma il Giovane with the patronage of Doge Pasquale Cicogna. The residents were required to attend Mass every Sunday and genuflect every morning in front of the altar of the Madonna in the oratory; they were to "give thanks to her and pray God for the well-being of our most Illustrious Signoria, the liberty and preservation of the monastery [of the Crociferi], and for the souls of those who have arranged things so well."[97] This obligation encapsulated the reciprocity and paternalism that were at the heart of conventional charity and society more generally. In return for material assistance, the poor were expected to pray for their benefactors. According to the standards of the time, the worthiest recipients of charity were the shame-faced poor, who, having fallen from high station, were ill-equipped to earn wages and were to be aided as inconspicuously as possible to lessen their humiliation. It would also spare the regime the embarrassment of publicly acknowledging that some of its members had been brought low.[98] There was, however, no notion of eliminating the causes of poverty. Jesus's injunction, "you will always have the poor with you" (Matthew 26: 11), was a given.

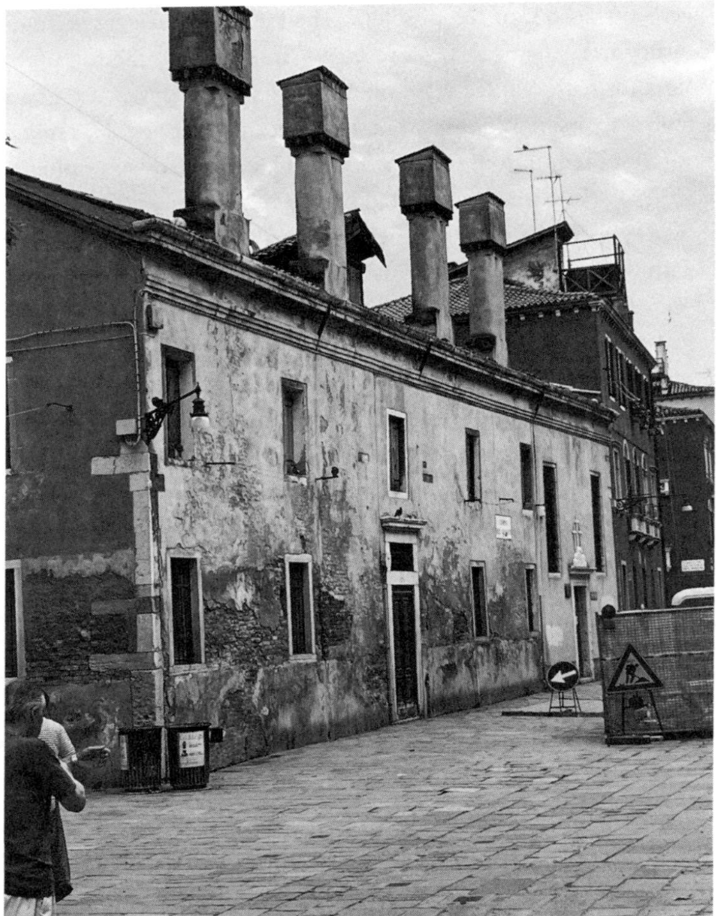

FIGURE 13.3 Hospice of the Crociferi, sixteenth century. Campo dei Gesuiti, Venice. The hospital was rebuilt following a fire in 1514 and renovated again late in the century. Photo by the author.

Conventional charity was able to care for a substantial number of these traditional poor. At least fifty-five hospices and hospitals were founded in the fifteenth and sixteenth centuries.[99] The government sponsored programs like the *poveri al pevere* (pepper-poor) by which a small tax levied originally on pepper and then on additional products was used to support aged mariners.[100] In addition, individuals offered posthumous assistance to persons they knew. One testator noted that he continued to maintain his servant Donna Anzola, even though she had gone blind and could no longer serve, and requested that his sister continue to look after Anzola "out of charity and out of love of the

Lord and me."[101] Even the poor distributed charity.[102] Margarita, a widowed immigrant from Friuli, bequeathed a pair of sheets and a small painted box "to the orphan Francesco who lives in the house of Cecilia near me."[103]

When long-established charitable practices proved unable to meet acute and widespread needs, assistance had to be organized on a larger scale. The great influxes of the poor and ill created moral, political, and logistical problems for the authorities, made worse by the fact that unlike the traditional poor, who were considered respectable, familiar, and local, these poor were judged to be abject, anonymous, and foreign.

The plague provided a sort of dry run for the new initiatives. When it returned in 1423, carrying off more than 15,000 of the city's 85,000 inhabitants, the government decided to build a plague hospital on the island of Santa Maria di Nazareth close to the Lido, which became known as the Lazzaretto Vecchio. Anyone infected was to be immediately transferred to the hospital for care by a staff that included a prior, one or more physicians, and nurses.[104] When the disease recurred in 1468 the government decided to build another establishment, the Lazzaretto Nuovo, near the island of Sant'Erasmo, to quarantine those who had been cured as well as those who were suspected of infection. In 1486 a new magistracy, the Provveditori alla Sanità (Health Commissioners) was established to deal with the ongoing curse. The commissioners had broad jurisdiction over sanitation, food, cemeteries, and prostitutes—all perceived vectors of contagion. Ships coming from places where there were outbreaks of the plague were quarantined in Istria, and health certificates were required for entry into Venice. Within the city, deaths had to be reported, wells maintained, canals cleared, and the clothing and other personal effects of those suspected of having plague burned or cleansed. In 1556 the Sopraprovveditori alla Sanità (Superior Health Commissioners) were created. These commissioners had authority even over *terraferma* governors. And in 1598 the Senate created the Provveditore Generale per la Peste (Commissioner General for the Plague) who was responsible for the entire *terraferma*. During the plague of 1630-1, the *terraferma* was divided into three zones, each with a Provveditore Generale.[105] The plague was another factor compelling the Venetians to think of the city and *terraferma* as interrelated.

But it was the influx of refugees that provided the impetus to help the new category of unknown poor. Displaced persons fleeing the 1463–79 war with the Ottomans prompted the Senate to order the erection of a tent at Sant'Antonio and shipments of bread there so that the exiles would have food and shelter. Then in December 1474, in thanksgiving for the salvation of Scutari from the Ottomans, the Senate ordered the building of a permanent refuge at Sant'Antonio, known as the Ospizio di Messer Gesù Cristo, although it evolved over time into a hospice for aged mariners.[106]

The spread of syphilis and the famine of 1527-8 led to the creation of larger hospitals. The Incurabili, the hospital for syphilitics, was inspired by Gaetano da Thiene, a member of the reforming Oratory of Divine Love, noblewomen Maria Malipiero and Marina Grimani, and nobleman turned religious Girolamo Miani, one of the founders of the Company of the Servants of the Poor (Somascans). The donation of a piece of property at Santo Spirito along the Zattere led to a permanent headquarters that by 1525 was already serving 150 patients. In 1522 the Senate ordered beggars infected with syphilis to enter the hospital.[107]

The famine of 1527-8 prompted Miani to take some of the suffering into his own home and place others at a small hospital near San Zanipolo. This evolved into the hospital of the Derelitti (Destitute), where at first the number of deaths was prodigious. Sanudo reported that 115 died there in March 1528, 137 in April. Over time, Miani was able to equip the young residents with the skills to earn a living. According to a 1542 report of the overseers, the hospital tended to the needs of widows, orphans, wards, and the sick.[108]

The famine of 1527-8 also led to more coercive laws. In March 1528 the Senate ordered vagabonds to enter one of several locales where they were to be supplied with straw beds. If they refused, they were to be imprisoned, publicly flogged, and expelled from the city. Ferry operators were advised to warn passengers of the new rules; if they failed to do so, they would have their boats burned, an example of how even humble Venetians were expected to help implement policy.[109] To pay for all this, a special tax was to be assessed and collected at the parish level. This was followed in April 1529 by the most important piece of legislation regarding the poor ever enacted by the Republic. It distinguished between local poor and foreign poor and ordered the immediate return of the latter to their place of origin. As for the native poor, those who were disabled and had a home were to stay there and look to their parish priests for help. Those without a home were to enter hospices. Able-bodied men were to sign on with the navy, where they would be paid half the regular seaman's salary, or they could learn a trade. Each guild was encouraged to take on three or four as apprentices and maintain them while they learned the craft. Parish priests were to find appropriate work for poor women, while abbesses were asked to give refuge to girls of good reputation. The poor were not to change parishes, and parish committees made up of two nobles, one citizen, and one *popolano* were to oversee the parish poor. The repressive measures embodied in these laws constituted a new element in

Venetian attitudes toward the poor.[110] The 1545 famine led to further efforts to manage charity at the parochial level.

The challenges of the sixteenth century transformed Venetian attitudes toward the poor and how charity was organized. The Incurabili and Derelitti were the first of what came to be known as the *ospedali grandi* (big hospitals), followed in 1595 by the Mendicanti and the restructured Pietà. The Mendicanti was established to deal with the ongoing problem of beggars. Children taken into its care were to be assigned gainful work, such as spinning or domestic service for girls and craft apprenticeships or naval service for boys. Adults and others who were unable to work would be looked after. It soon housed nearly 400 inmates.[111] Like the Derelitti it was located near San Zanipolo. The Pietà was founded in the mid-fourteenth century to deal with abandoned children. Originally located near San Francesco della Vigna, it moved in the early sixteenth century to its permanent location on the Riva degli Schiavoni. In 1535 the Greater Council placed it in charge of all the city's foundlings. It farmed out many of its charges to wet nurses throughout the city. By the mid-sixteenth century it was providing care for between 800 and 1,200 children.[112] The four big hospitals (Derelitti, Incurabili, Mendicanti, and Pietà), together with the poor laws, tried to care for the sick, see to the welfare and education of children, and limit begging to authorized beggars.

These hospitals were soon joined by a host of other new institutions specializing in the care of particular groups: the Fraternity of the Poveri Vergognosi, founded in 1537 to assist the shame-faced poor; the Casa delle Zitelle (House for Unmarried Maidens), to save young girls from falling into prostitution by preparing them for marriage or the convent; the Casa del Soccorso (Aid House) for prostitutes who wished to leave the profession; the Convertiti (Shelter for Repentant Women) for former prostitutes who wished to take religious vows; and the Catecumeni (House for Catechumens) to promote conversion to Christianity, especially for captured Turks. The emphasis of many of these institutions indicates how females, especially unmarried ones, threatened family strategies and inheritance patterns at the heart of patrician domination.[113] Courtesan Veronica Franco had advocated the creation of an institution like the Soccorso. Given that prostitutes desiring to abandon the sex trade were ineligible to enter the Zitelle and that "it is difficult . . . for them to persuade themselves to pass, in a moment, from such a licentious existence to so strict and austere a way of life as that of the Convertiti," Franco noted that they had no option in their great need but to continue to sell themselves and even "the virginity of their own innocent daughters."[114] In addition to administering charity and reinforcing gender norms, these institutions, along with the great hospitals, reshaped Venice's topography. All were located either on the city's periphery or nearby islands such as the Giudecca, where undeveloped land was available. Confining the infirm, poor, and fallen to the fringes fit with Doge Gritti and others' efforts to give the city center, particularly San Marco and Rialto, a more decorous and resplendent aura.

The city's population increasingly encompassed thousands of immigrants. French emissary to Venice Philippe de Commynes famously said of Venice in the late fifteenth century, "Most of their people are foreigners."[115] Some—for example, Netherlandish merchants—came as temporary sojourners, although a few stayed and became naturalized citizens.[116] Others, like porters from the mountain valleys in the Bergamasco, came seasonally, while the enslaved had no choice in their transfer to Venice. Some immigrants integrated quickly into Venetian life; others stuck close to their fellow immigrants.[117] The authorities recognized the benefits and liabilities of a workforce comprised of significant numbers of non-natives. On one hand, immigrants offered a steady supply of cheap labor. On the other, differences could lead to tension and conflict. As the Ten noted in 1447, the Italian-born fustian workers wished to form their own *scuola*, separate from the *scuola* of the German-born workers on account of the "disparity of customs" between the two.[118] In his *Piazza universale*, Tommaso Garzoni noted how Bergamasque porters clung so tenaciously to their dialect that they were nearly incomprehensible to others and were portrayed as comic figures by Renaissance playwrights.[119]

Of the many partially integrated immigrant groups, the Greeks and the Jews were both distinguished by religion. One force pushing Greek immigration was the Ottoman advance, as when the fall of Nauplion and Monemvasia to the Turks in 1540 created a wave of refugees. Most Greeks came seeking work, which they secured in various trades, especially those associated with maritime industries.[120] Those with more education and skills found employment in the city's thriving printing industry. The community also included a small minority of wealthy merchants, some of whom married into the patriciate, as well as captains of the stratiotes, light cavalry mercenary chiefs, whose families intermarried. It is estimated that as many as 4,500 Greeks were living in Venice at the end of the sixteenth century.

Language and religion set the Greeks apart from their fellow residents. Most Greeks were Uniates, that is, they followed their own liturgy and practices but accepted the authority of the pope. For a long time, they lacked an institutional focus for their collective religious lives. Their efforts to establish a Greek-rite church met with resistance until 1470, when the Ten authorized services in a chapel in the church of San Biagio. Nearly thirty years later, the Ten approved a petition put forward by the Greek community (*Università*) to establish a *scuola* dedicated to Saint Nicholas at San Biagio. In the petition, the Greeks noted that they had "striven at every opportunity to meet the needs of Your Serenity, where they thought it a glorious thing to spill their blood for the expansion of your state" and that other "nations" including the Dalmatians and Albanians had already been granted the right to form *scuole*.[121] The Ten approved the petition but capped membership at 250 males, with no limit on the number of female members. Membership was not, however, based on religious affiliation. San Nicolò dei Greci included both Greek- and Latin-rite members. Like other Venetian *scuole*, San Nicolò's leadership grew more exclusive over time, although by the late sixteenth century, representation on its board was distributed proportionally among various regional groups, including Cretans and Cypriots.

In 1511 a group of stratiote captains petitioned the Ten to establish a Greek-rite church. Observing that at San Biagio, Greek and Latin services commingled, the cemetery was hopelessly overcrowded with their bones being mixed with those "of galleymen, porters and other low creatures," and that even the Ottomans allowed houses of worship for their Christian subjects, the stratiotes asked permission to purchase land for a church to be dedicated to Saint George, the patron of soldiers.[122] Three years later the Ten approved their petition with the proviso that the Greeks continue to accept papal supremacy. In 1526 they purchased land in the parish of Sant'Antonin. Begun in 1539, San Giorgio dei Greci was completed in 1573 and the bell tower thirty years later. Although the Greeks had a church of their own, it was not accorded full parochial rights.

The primary opponents to the establishment of a Greek-rite church were the patriarchs of Venice, who were worried about encroachments on their jurisdiction. In 1451 Pope Nicholas V had abolished the old patriarchate of Grado, uniting it with the bishopric of Castello to create the patriarchate of Venice. When the pope removed San Giorgio from the patriarch's control, Patriarch Girolamo Querini excommunicated the Greeks. In 1577 the Cretan Gabriele Seviros (already the metropolitan of Philadelphia in Asia Minor) was appointed Greek metropolitan of Venice (with jurisdiction over the Greek rite inhabitants of Venice's Ionian island possessions and Dalmatia), a move that garnered opposition from the ecumenical patriarch of Constantinople. The Venetian Republic intervened, affirmed the status of the Venetian metropolitan (who retained the title the metropolitan of

Philadelphia), and entrusted his election, pending Senate approval, to the board of the *scuola* of San Nicolò. However, consecration of the new metropolitan remained the prerogative of the ecumenical patriarch.[123] Henceforth, Venice was home to two high churchmen: the Latin patriarch of Venice and the Greek metropolitan.

Like most immigrant communities, the Greeks were integrated into many aspects of Venetian life, but in other ways retained their own tastes and style. In 1597 the building committee at San Giorgio awarded the design for a mosaic to decorate the apse of the church to prolific native Venetian painter Jacopo Palma il Giovane. But when the mosaic was unveiled, many in the community thought that its style "did not conform to our rite" and wanted instead a work executed "in the old style and the devout Greek manner." The mosaic, reworked by Cretan immigrant Tomio Bathàs, retains aspects of Palma's design, blending Western and Greek elements.[124] Immigrants from sixteenth-century Crete included several talented icon painters, El Greco (Domenikos Theotokopoulos), among them.[125]

For much of the fifteenth century, Jews could come to Venice only for brief periods of time and could not openly practice their faith or establish synagogues. The government was especially worried about the possibility of sexual relations with Christians and extended the yellow badge or headwear requirement to Jewish women. In both Venice's *stato da terra* and *stato da mar*, Jews enjoyed greater freedom.[126]

Financial needs prompted by the Cambrai and Italian wars finally brought the Jews permanently to Venice. In return for payments and loans to the state, they were again allowed to lend money in the city as well as engage in the secondhand trade. But pressure from zealous Christians, especially the clergy, prompted the Senate in March 1516 to order that all Jews in the city be segregated in a section of Cannaregio known as the Ghetto Nuovo (New Ghetto), a patch of land that had been reclaimed from the surrounding marshes by the dumping of waste from the nearby state-owned copper and bronze foundry, which was located on the adjacent island known as the Ghetto Vecchio (Old Ghetto). When founding activities were moved to the Arsenal, the two islets were auctioned to private investors. The Ghetto Nuovo eventually came into the hands of the Da Brolo family who built rental housing there.[127]

The Senate ordered the existing tenants to move out and authorized the owners to charge the new Jewish tenants a third more in rent. (Jews were forbidden to own real estate anywhere in the city.) Gates were built at the entrances to the islet and manned by four Christian guards. Walls were added to completely seal off the area, and two boats, paid for by the Jews, patrolled the perimeter night and day. The contract for settlement had to be periodically renewed, with the government each time exacting higher payments and adding more restrictive clauses. It did not really want Jews living in the city but was compelled to allow this as a way of offering pawn-brokerage services to the poor. The Senate acknowledged as much when in 1553 it declared that "this Council has permitted the Jews to dwell in our dominions for the sole purpose of preventing Christians from lending on usury in violation of both the divine and the civil laws."[128] By 1591, the number of pawnshops was capped at three and the official interest-rate set so low (5 percent) as to render it unprofitable. Subvention of moneylending services became the collective responsibility of the Jewish community, in essence the tax they paid for being granted the right to stay in Venice. Almost every time the contract came up for renewal, so too did calls for the Jews' expulsion from the city, as when Sanudo declared, "Our forefathers had never wanted Jews to be traders with stores in this city, but only to buy, sell, and go away."[129]

But they stayed and the Ghetto expanded. Due to major shifts in trade patterns and the diaspora of Jews throughout the Mediterranean, Jewish merchants came to play an ever-greater role in international trade, especially with the Ottoman Balkans. To secure a bigger share of that trade and fend off competition from Ancona and Ragusa, Venice decided in 1541 to make space in the Ghetto Vecchio for Levantine Jewish merchants, who were Sephardic and subjects of the Ottoman empire. It too was walled off and gated. Then in 1573 the government offered safe-conduct to Marranos, Portuguese, Spanish, and other Jews who had been forced to convert to Christianity but who often continued secretly to practice their faith, enabling them to come to Venice, engage in commerce, and live as Jews. Its proponent, Jew Daniel Rodriga, touted the benefits of their admission to Venetian trade and the fisc; he referred to these newcomers as Ponentine (Western) Jews as a way of avoiding religiously charged terms like Marranos. With their connections to the Jewish community in Amsterdam, the Ponentines helped link Venice to an important new center of world commerce. Rodriga was also central in establishing a new trade line between Venice and Spalato and hence to the European provinces of the Ottoman empire, including Constantinople itself. The charter of 1573 marked the first time that a group of non-Venetians was granted many of the same trade privileges as Venetians without having to wait twenty-five years to be declared naturalized citizens. When in 1630 the Jews explained to the government that even more Jewish traders would take up residence if additional space were made available, the Senate responded in 1633 with an order that another stretch of land be annexed to the Ghetto Nuovo. It came to be referred to as the Ghetto Nuovissimo (Newest Ghetto).[130]

The government thus recognized three different categories of Jews based on the charters they received: the moneylenders, referred to as the Tedeschi since many were originally from Germany (Ashkenazi) and which included a subset known as the Italiani; and the Ponentines and the Levantines who were merchants. Although originally relegated to different parts of the Ghetto, over time the residential distinction disappeared. With few exceptions, only the dead escaped confinement to the Ghetto; the Jewish cemetery was located on the Lido. At its height, the Ghetto is estimated to have been numbered between 2,500 and 3,000 souls, although some estimates go as high as 5,000. Population density was much higher there than in other parts of the city, leading to the construction of buildings whose height pushed structural limits and with many more floors than was typical. In the mid-seventeenth century, a Loredan remarked, "Four to eight Christians would take up the space occupied by twenty Jews."[131]

Life in the Ghetto took on its own form and character. Eventually several synagogues were established, including the Scuola Grande Tedesca, the Scuola Levantina, and Scuola Ponentina. There were also yeshivas and, starting in the late sixteenth century, confraternities that undertook charitable work or were devoted to worship. Venetian Jews had their own form of self-government known as the Università degli Ebrei, which consisted of Large and Small Assemblies. The Large Assembly, around 125 members in the early seventeenth century, was composed of adult men whose tax assessment was 12 ducats or more. Each of the three ethnic groups making up the Jewish community, the Tedeschi, Ponentines, and Levantines, was guaranteed representation in the Small Assembly, which also included two members from Jewish communities on the mainland since those communities had to help support the Ghetto's financially struggling pawnshops. In 1616 the number of members of the Small Assembly, which was responsible for everyday governance of the Ghetto and relations with the Republic, was lowered from eleven to seven. It oversaw the Ghetto's infrastructure, licensed food preparers, and issued sumptuary regulations. Infractions were punished with fines or excommunications that had to be issued (and rescinded) by rabbis, who otherwise played no formal role in community governance. A banking committee oversaw the pawnshop charter and operations, and a tax assessment committee rounded out the community's governmental structure. The Venetian government's Ufficiali al Cattaver had jurisdiction over the Ghetto Nuovo and the task of limiting interaction between Christians and Jews. The Cinque Savi alla Mercanzia supervised the Ghetto Vecchio and mercantile matters involving the Jews. The Sopraconsoli dei Mercanti oversaw the pawnshops.[132]

Despite the physical separation created by the Ghetto, Venetian Christians and Jews interacted in a variety of ways. Jewish physicians ministered to their Christian patients, and Jewish musicians and dancers went to Christian homes to teach and perform. Christians found employment in the Ghetto as bookkeepers, porters, menial assistants in the printing of Hebrew books, and domestic servants. Others went there to gamble. Rabbi Simon Luzzatto claimed in his *Discorso circa il stato de gl'Hebrei, et in particolar dimoranti nell'inclita città di Venetia* (Discourse on the Situation of the Hebrews and in Particular on Those Living in the Illustrious City of Venice) that "they [the Jews] do not seem burdensome or threatening to any estate or order within the city." This was due, in his view, to the low interest rate that pawnshops were allowed to charge and to prohibitions on Jews joining guilds, engaging in manufacturing, or owning property. Nevertheless, a special canal known as the Canal degli Ebrei had to be dug in 1668 so that funeral corteges could avoid a previous route to the Lido cemetery that had taken them under a bridge at San Pietro di Castello where Christian children regularly pelted the passing processions with rocks.[133]

Rabbi Leon Modena's autobiography documents arbitrary intrusions by governmental authorities and the anxious atmosphere in which the Jews continually lived. In 1634, for example, Modena's hope that a book he had written would find its way into print saw a significant delay when the Cattaver shut down the print shop for six months.[134] On another occasion the entire Ghetto was sealed and a house-by-house search conducted to find two Jews who had received 70,000 ducats in goods and cash that had been stolen by some Christians from a shop in the Merceria. As Modena noted, "The outcry against and contempt for all Jews on the part of everyone in the city—nobles, citizens, and commoners—increased as usual. For when one individual committed a crime, they would grow angry at the entire community."[135] When Modena's *Historia de gli riti hebraici* (History of Jewish Rites) was published in 1637 in Paris, he worried that it contained passages that would get him in trouble with the Inquisition.[136] In this case, his fears were largely unfounded, and soon he was writing that, as a result of his revised 1638 Venice edition, "on my account, many friars have spoken well of the Jews while preaching in their churches."[137] Modena's emotional roller-coaster conveys the constant apprehension and uncertainty under which the Jews lived.

While much is known about immigrants to Venice, it is hard to gauge how many Venetians emigrated to other locales. Certainly, foreign governments encouraged highly skilled Venetian artisans like glassmakers and shipwrights to settle in their lands to foster economic development. Other residents with particularly strong Protestant convictions fled the Inquisition and settled in lands more amenable to their religious views. Still others left in search of adventure or to escape the confines of family and homeland. Leon Modena's son Isaac, for example, lived for a time in Brazil, although he eventually returned to Venice.

Many Venetians, especially merchants, spent time in foreign lands. In some cases, their numbers were large enough to constitute a veritable community. The best-known example is the Venetians of Constantinople. The community comprised the officially recognized "nation," that is, the diplomatic corps and merchant houses, as well as a much larger unofficial nation, made up primarily of persons who were Venetian subjects from the *stato da mar*. The headquarters of the community was the embassy. The *bailo*, who functioned as chief diplomat, defender of Venetian commercial interests, arbitrator of disputes, protector of Latin-rite Christians, and redeemer of captured slaves, was assisted by a staff of up to 100, including his secretary and under-secretary, accountant, several dragomans (interpreters), physician, chaplain, boys studying to be dragomans, and servants. The dragomans were deeply embedded in Constantinopolitan society and might be either Venetian or Ottoman subjects.[138] Also, servants were not necessarily Venetian subjects; a few were even Muslims.[139] Janissaries performed guard and other duties, and a large contingent of couriers, many from Montenegro, kept mail flowing between the two capitals.

Resident merchants with full Venetian citizenship constituted the other element of the officially recognized Venetian Constantinopolitan nation. By the late sixteenth century very few were nobles; most were naturalized citizens. Venetian subjects, especially from places like Crete, also traded under the protection of Saint Mark's flag, as did some non-Venetian and Ottoman subjects, even though the practice was technically illegal since they were not actually citizens.[140] But increased trade and customs revenue trumped legal niceties. Some of these men even served on the merchant Council of Twelve that advised the *bailo*.

To this small group of officially recognized Venetians can be added several thousand other Venetian subjects, be they natives of the mother city or from its mainland or overseas dominions. Some found work in Constantinople as artisans or petty traders; others were enslaved persons captured by the

Ottomans; others still were exiles from Venice and its lands who were attracted in part by the *bailo*'s ability to commute sentences and issue safe-conducts that allowed them to return home for a time. Exiles could prove useful. For example, the Arsenal worker Gregorio di Giana, who had been banished from Venice for murder, was sent by the *bailo* to spy on Ottoman shipbuilding.[141] The number of Greek Venetians, that is people from Venice's *stato da mar*, living in Constantinople was especially large. One patrician wrote, "So many Levantine subjects are in this city . . . that I remain truly amazed."[142] They went there in search of work or to escape harsh conditions in Venice's colonial possessions.

Constantinopolitan Venetians were not isolated from their Muslim and Jewish neighbors. Commerce brought Venetians and Ottomans together, as when Tommaso Bonastori and Hasan Çelibi concluded a deal by touching "their hands two times saying that the bazaar [i.e., sale] was done."[143] Friendships based on mutual benefit and genuine affection developed especially between the embassy staff and Ottoman officials. And Venetian officials and merchants who resided in the city often formed completely licit (according to local law) temporary marriages with Ottoman Christian women.[144] Andrea Gritti famously fathered three sons by his Greek concubine. Opponents of his candidacy for the dogeship railed that "one who has three bastard sons in Turkey should not be made doge."[145] Venetians in Constantinople were a heterogenous lot composed of "Venetians born, Venetians made, non-Venetians, Greek-Venetians, and even Ottoman subjects."[146]

In London, by contrast, the number of Venetians could be counted on one hand. In the 1560s merchant Innocenzo Lucatelli handled business for some of his fellow Venetians, but he went bankrupt in 1570 when the war over Cyprus dried up the supply of products, such as sweet wines, raisins, and oil, that the Venetians traditionally imported to England.[147] As the English themselves moved into the Mediterranean (the Levant Company was chartered in 1580), the number of Venetian merchants residing in London in 1592 shrank to just a single man.[148]

In Venice and elsewhere there was the need for persons who could straddle religious, mercantile, political, imperial, and cultural divides. Dragomans and brokers are good examples. Venice had long employed brokers at the Fondaco dei Tedeschi to arrange deals between German and Venetian speakers. As a sign of the growing importance of trade with the Ottomans in the later sixteenth century, Venice increased the number of brokers assigned to deal with Turkish merchants from fifteen or twenty in 1587 to more than thirty by 1621.[149] A number were Turks or Jews who had converted to Christianity, or Christians, like Michele Summa di Santo, who had been enslaved and embraced Islam and then reconverted on his return to Venice.[150] The formerly enslaved who returned to their native lands and religion often possessed the linguistic and cultural skills to cross divides and even to switch loyalties as circumstances dictated.[151] Dragomans and brokers also proved valuable as spies and informants, although there was always the danger that they were double agents.

In 1621 the Venetian government created a *fondaco* for Ottoman Muslims, the Fondaco dei Turchi. Since the late 1570s Muslim merchants had been lodging at an inn near Rialto managed by a Greek broker named Francesco Lettino. The site selected for the new *fondaco* was the great medieval palace on the Grand Canal that the Pesaro family had been forced to sell following the War of Chioggia and that subsequently served as the residence of several ambassadors. The Fondaco dei Turchi, as it came to be known, shared characteristics both with the Fondaco dei Tedeschi and the Jewish Ghetto. Like the former, it provided lodging and storage space for sojourning merchants; like the latter it was intended to limit contact between persons of different religions. Windows were walled up, doors locked at night, and guards posted. Among the rules that the Cinque Savi issued was this: "The said doorkeepers shall not allow either women or beardless persons who may be Christians to enter the exchange house at any time, on pain of fitting punishment."[152] The board feared sexual contact between Muslim men and Christian women and the potential enslavement of boys. The ambiguity of the term "Turks" meant that, for several decades, Persian Muslims, those who lived under the rule of the Safavid dynasty, were exempt from residing at the Fondaco but were forced to transfer there in 1662. The term "Levantines," which gained traction in the seventeenth century, likewise masked the often-deep differences that existed among those lumped into that category.[153] This hodgepodge left the government and everyday Venetians struggling to identify people, even though the categories could have profound political, economic, and religious implications.

This confusion partially explains the popularity in sixteenth-century Venice of costume books that illustrated and sometimes described the clothing or outfits worn by persons from various locales around the world.[154] Seeing the costumes of persons from other places also "seems to have sharpened the focus on local identities."[155] The most famous Venetian example of the genre is Cesare Vecellio's *De gli habiti antichi, et moderni di diverse parte del mondo libri due* (Two Books on the Clothes Both Ancient and Modern of Various Parts of the World). The 1590 edition includes more than 400 illustrations, the 1598 version more than 500. The book begins with sixty illustrations of Venetians of various social ranks and occupations, starting with the doge. Yet the growing market for new fashions and styles, combined with the production of cheap textiles that imitated more expensive ones and the thriving secondhand market that allowed the less wealthy to acquire the hand-me-downs of the elites, undermined the ability of fashion to unmistakably signal social status. The Magistrato alle Pompe's efforts to regulate dress often proved for naught.

Thus, despite the effort by writers, governmental officials, and religious leaders to establish fixed identities, reality confounded them. Borders, especially in places like the Balkans, were uncertain, ill-defined, or constantly shifting. For this reason, they were seldom included on printed maps.[156] This was even more the case at sea where projections of power were as variable as the waves. And people converted from one religion to another with startling regularity. They did so for all sorts of reasons: out of conviction, to gain economic advantage, to win friends and patrons, or to escape old enemies, family pressures, or unhappy marriages. Something as simple as changing one's costume or hairstyle could change one's perceived identity.[157] This sense of movement, malleability, and lack of fixity was not confined to border or contact zones but extended everywhere, even to the metropole itself. Well-to-do immigrants from the *terraferma* became naturalized Venetian citizens, freed slaves became rectoresses of hospices, Jews became Christians and then returned to Judaism, enslaved persons "turned Turk" and then reconverted to Christianity, and respectable young women transformed themselves into worldly courtesans. As much as apologists for the regime and census-takers liked to imagine society as comprising neat and orderly categories all serenely in equilibrium, in real life, identities were far messier and more changeable.[158] The inability to keep order, maintain boundaries, and make reality correspond to preconceived notions explains why the sixteenth century was an age of anxiety as Venetian officialdom struggled mightily to gain tighter control over all aspects of life.

The one group whose identity remained stable until the mid-seventeenth century was the nobility. Even this found expression in dress. The long black gown that older male patricians wore symbolized the gravity of their governmental and familial responsibilities as well as the Republic's supposed stability. In his treatise on color, Venetian Lodovico Dolce explained that elite males favored black because, in addition to signaling virility and temperance, "[it] shows . . . firmness, because this color cannot change into another."[159] Here was the sartorial expression of how Venetian noblemen wished the world to be. Body language also conveyed station. Commentators recommended that patrician men adopt a gait that made it appear as if they were gliding, an effect enhanced by their robes nearly reaching the ground.[160]

Nonetheless, the nobility was undergoing change, especially as the number of noblemen declined from 2,435 in 1563 to 1,660 in 1631.[161] The plagues of the 1570s and 1630s partially account for the loss. Some 300 noblemen died in the plague years 1575–6.[162] The other factor, likely the crucial one, was that as a group, nobles began to restrict the number of marriages they contracted. No matter how many sons and daughters a family had, it would allow only one or two to marry. The *fraterna* certainly conditioned noblemen to this form of self-sacrifice, provided it advanced family interests. Unmarried brothers could enter the church or simply remain bachelors. By restricting the number of heirs, families guarded against dispersal of the patrimony. At the same time, fideicommissum or entailing (the creation of a fixed line of property inheritance) also became common as noble testators increasingly decreed that their property should pass undivided and unalienated through an established order of male succession. Nobleman Domenico Contarini explained in 1596 that he was establishing an entail "because I want [my possessions] to remain perpetually in our family, because I wish that the hard work done by our ancestors, with so much sweat, should not go for naught."[163] Doge Leonardo Donà created an entail in his will of 1609 requiring unmarried Donà brothers to leave their estates to their surviving brothers and after that to their nephews.[164] The strategy of limiting marriages worked. In the sixteenth century 51 percent of marriage-age nobles remained single; in the seventeenth century 60 percent did.[165]

Limiting the number of sons who married also meant the number of noble daughters who could marry also declined. Furthermore, while noble males had incentives to marry *cittadini* or *terraferma* nobles (they could garner sizable dowries and their children would still be noble), no such inducements existed for women. As the number of marriages declined, dowries rose, soaring as high as 30,000 ducats.

Most of the girls who were not destined for marriage were sent to convents, whether they had a religious vocation or not.[166] The 1563 city census indicates that there were 2,134 nuns in the city, comprising 1.26 percent of the total population. By the end of the sixteenth century there were more than fifty convents in Venice and the surrounding lagoon.[167] Prospective nuns had to bring a sort of dowry, but the amount was considerably lower than what was required for marriage. In the early seventeenth century, the figure was set at 1,000 ducats, although parents could also choose to pay 60 ducats per annum throughout the girl's lifetime.[168] Social distinctions invaded convent walls. Some convents, like San Zaccaria, continued to be the preserve of the city's elite families, while others, like San Iseppo, where only half the nuns were noble, were less prestigious.[169] Within convents, stark differences existed between choir nuns, who took full vows, were consecrated, and held offices within the establishment, and *converse* (lay sisters), who took only a simple vow and performed the menial tasks that kept the convent running, including acting in some instances as the choir nuns' personal servants.[170] Nuns from wealthy families often kept in their cells such accoutrements of noble life as clothing, "shameless paintings, dogs, [and] birds" and insisted on being addressed as "Signora."[171] In poor convents, nuns lived in dire poverty, suffering from the cold and damp and surviving on meager rations. Nuns could supplement their income, maintain their networks outside the convent, affirm their (secular) social status, and demonstrate creativity by producing handiwork such as lace and embroidery, baking biscuits and cakes, concocting medicines, or even chronicling the histories of their convents.[172] Convent life had its compensations. Women could exercise considerable power as prioresses or abbesses, cultivate their minds with books, stage plays and make music, or simply bask in a largely male-free environment.

The nobles' changing marriage patterns and inheritance practices were spurred by a desire to conserve wealth since the other great change affecting the nobility was a shift in their economic activities and entrepreneurial enterprises. The long-held view that patricians grew risk-averse and so abandoned dicey trade in favor of lower yielding landholding and rent collection is exaggerated.[173] Many nobles continued to invest in trade and lucrative maritime insurance and own merchant vessels. But landholding also made economic sense. With growing populations in both the city and its mainland dominion, the price of agricultural products, especially cereals, rose.[174] The Little Ice Age that gripped Europe and was particularly pronounced in the late sixteenth and seventeenth centuries contributed to higher grain prices. While Venetian nobles used the opportunity to invest in land reclamation and agriculture on the *terraferma*, rival merchants in the Dutch Republic took the opposite approach and increased their share of international commerce.[175]

The Barbarigo family offers a precocious example of the growing interest in land. When Andrea Barbarigo died in 1449, his sons were still young boys and so the trustees of the estate moved much of his capital into real estate. His widow purchased the palace that the family had been renting while the other trustees purchased land at Carpi di Castagnaro in the lower Veronese. Andrea's son Nicolò showed only passing interest in international trade but devoted considerable energy to improving the Carpi estate. The property, which was located on the right bank of the Adige, was susceptible to flooding and required significant reclamation work that involved filling in land, channeling waters, and most difficult of all, assuring that the reclaimed land drained properly. Once land had been reclaimed, dikes needed to be maintained, channels kept free of debris and silt, and problem areas monitored to prevent nature from undoing what had been accomplished. Through great effort, Nicolò was able to transform terrain that had been swampy and suitable only for pasturage into fertile fields for the cultivation of grain, vines, and flax. He also reached new contractual accords with the peasants who worked the land, creating better housing for them, and constructing structures such as storage sheds for hay and a dovecote.[176]

In compensation, the Carpi estate was an important source of income for Nicolò—second only to properties in Crete. Just as important, it freed his family from dependency on the urban food market. In 1516, for example, a year when the estate suffered from predations of war, the Barbarigos nevertheless received from it wine, millet, sorghum, beans, vinegar, small animals like chickens and rabbits, and linen.[177] The property would continue to increase in value in the following generation. Between 1518–26 and 1572, income from the estate tripled.[178]

In addition to improving the land and organizing management of the estate, Nicolò built a house on the property. He chose a site where the Veronese noble Dal Verme family had previously headquartered the administrative center for their extensive Carpi properties, enabling him to take advantage of its lordly associations.[179] The brick house included several features designed to display the Barbarigos' social rank, including loggias, balconies, a surrounding garden, and a portal adorned with marble.[180] So valued was this home that in his will Nicolò forbade his sons from selling it, unless they could find a property less susceptible to flooding. He enjoined them "to prize it dearly together with the other estates, those in the Trevisano, and the government bonds of the old and new series, since commercial activity does not succeed as it used to."[181]

Nicolò Barbarigo's land reclamation efforts, interest in agriculture, and construction of a substantial house at Carpi foreshadowed the Venetian nobility's turn to the land and the importance that villas and summer sojourns at them—known as *villeggiatura*—would play in their lifestyle. An estimated eighty-four villas were built in the Veneto in the fifteenth century and a

FIGURE 13.4 Andrea Palladio, Villa Barbaro at Maser, begun c. 1560. Photo by Marcok, distributed under a CC-SA-3.0 license via Wikimedia Commons.

whopping 257 in the sixteenth.[182] Andrea Palladio became the premier architect of these summer estates, building one, for example, for Giorgio Corner, grandnephew of Caterina.[183] Modeling them on the villas of ancient Rome, Palladio created complexes that not only allowed their owners to indulge in the leisure activities that defined an aristocratic lifestyle but that also met the demands of a working farm. Palladio's villa for Daniele Barbaro, who became patriarch of Aquileia in 1550, and his brother statesman Marcantonio at Maser in the Trevisano is a well-known example. The interior decoration by Veronese and the nymphaeum, inspired by the Villa Giulia in Rome, announced the refinement of the owners, while the coat of arms on the front façade pediment proclaimed their identity to passersby. The two side pavilions, topped with dovecotes, served as work areas. They were joined to the main block by an arcade that offered storage space for farm machinery. The cultural cachet of *villeggiatura* legitimated economic investment in agriculture as the merchants of Venice transformed themselves into aristocratic landlords.[184]

The effort by the government, church, and charitable institutions to assign the city's inhabitants to fixed and immutable categories and roles often came at a deep psychological cost, particularly for women. On the surface, worldly courtesan Veronica Franco and nun Arcangela Tarabotti, who spent most of her life in the Benedictine convent Sant'Anna in Castello, could not have been more different; but they shared a common fate of being brilliant women whose free will was hemmed in by the demands and expectations of Venetian patriarchy.

Both came from the middle ranks of Venetian society. Veronica Franco's father Francesco was an original citizen; her mother, Paola Fracassa, was also a courtesan, though not as accomplished as her daughter. It was almost certainly Paola who led Veronica into prostitution. Veronica married a doctor, but they soon separated. Her six children were all born to different fathers. Tarabotti was born Elena Cassandra but took the name Arcangela in the convent. Her parents, Stefano Tarabotti and Maria Cadena, had numerous children. Some of the girls married; others remained single. Arcangela, the eldest, was sent to live at Sant'Anna at age eleven on account of her lameness, which, in her father's view, made her unsuitable for the competitive marriage market. She bitterly resented her forced monachization.

Parental decisions thus propelled Franco and Tarabotti into lives that they likely would not have chosen for themselves. Franco mastered the art of being a courtesan. Yet in a letter to a friend who was thinking of making her daughter one, Franco offered a devastating critique of the possibility. She noted that she had been willing to help the girl enter the Casa delle Zitelle "in such a way that you can marry her decently." First, she was blunt in gauging the girl's chances of success as a courtesan, judging her neither beautiful nor quick-witted enough to master the role. Second, she offered a baleful assessment of the very profession in which she excelled, noting that even if the girl had the requisite looks and skills, she would end up in "a life that always turns out to be a misery." Franco recounted the pitfalls that lay ahead including the danger of robbery, physical assault, and "dreadful contagious diseases." Most wrenching of all was her assessment of the courtesan's life, doomed as she was "to eat with another's mouth, sleep with another's eyes, move according to another's will, obviously rushing toward the shipwreck of your mind and your body—what greater misery?"[185] Franco, who in her poetry presented herself as sexually in control, reveals herself to have been subject to her clients' whims and threats.

That same lack of free will is what provokes Tarabotti's fierce ire in her treatise *Tirannia paterna* (Paternal Tyranny), later published as *La semplicità ingannata* (Innocence Betrayed).[186] She condemns fathers "who out of pure greed and social ambition dedicate innocent babes in the womb to a living Hell—for that is what the cloister means for nuns forced to live there."[187] Tarabotti laments the lot of women who are relegated to the cloister, "not through their own choice but through another's determination, imposed on those bodies and souls."[188] She argues that if men were truly interested in honoring God, they would offer up their "most beautiful and virtuous daughters." Instead, like Cain, they are grudging in their gifts and proffer those who are "most repulsive and deformed: lame, hunchbacked, crippled, or simple-minded." Marshalling a nautical image, she notes that convents are like a "ship's bilge."[189]

Tarabotti extends her critique to the Venetian Republic and its self-proclaimed role as a beacon of liberty. She asks,

> What else is it but deep ingratitude when that country under the special protection of the Virgin Mary, that country which once triumphed against the uprising of Baiamonte Tiepolo by means of a woman [the reference is to Giustina Rossi who felled the rebels' standard-bearer], finds itself engaged in degrading, deceiving, and denying liberty to its own young girls and women more than any other kingdom in the world?[190]

Tarabotti turns Venetian self-celebration on its head as *Paternal Tyranny* becomes a lamentation for lost liberty.

Franco and Tarabotti share one final characteristic. Both gained at least a modicum of control over their lives through writing. By means of letters, poetry, and treatises, the two engaged with the growing group of intellectuals, overwhelmingly male, who animated Venetian public conversation. Within the strict limits imposed on them, they were able to fashion identities for themselves. As Tarabotti forthrightly and rebelliously declared from behind the walls of Sant'Anna, "I myself am a layperson."[191] She made that visible for as long as she could by refusing to cut her hair, as nuns were required to do.

The celebrated courtesan and unhappy nun are reminders of how much was sacrificed on the altar of patrician rule. The interests of all groups in Venetian society, including elite women's, were subordinated to those of the noblemen who sat in the Greater Council and a small group of male citizens, both naturalized and native-born, who partook to some degree in the political and commercial power of the city.

14

Roman Venice and the End of the Renaissance

IN 1538, FLORENTINE sculptor and architect Jacopo Sansovino (born Jacopo Tatti) began work on the loggia at the foot of the bell tower of San Marco. Like many artists and intellectuals, Sansovino sought refuge in Venice following the Sack of Rome. Appointed *proto* (superintendent of buildings) for the Procurators of San Marco just two years after his arrival, he oversaw a remodeling of the Piazza and Piazzetta, construction of a new Mint, erection of the elegant Marciana library, projects at Rialto, and private palaces.[1] More than any other figure, the architect gave visual expression to Doge Andrea Gritti's program of renovation, the reimagining of the city following the difficult years of the Cambrai and Italian wars. Yet unlike earlier Venetian renovations or renaissances that harkened back to Ravenna and Byzantium, this one was unabashedly Roman. For the first time, the Venetians fully embraced the architectural vocabulary of the ancient world but gave it a local twist. They made Venice Roman.

The Loggetta was completed in 1545. The most sculptural of Sansovino's designs, it richly conveys how the Venetian ruling elite thought of themselves and their polity at midcentury. Sansovino fashioned the Loggetta, where patricians met to talk politics, to resemble a triumphal arch. Aligned with the Porta della Carta, it extends into the Piazza the triumphal entryway that terminates in the triumphal arch at the summit of the Scala dei Giganti. The Loggetta's sculptural decoration offers a primer on Venetian dominion and rule. The bronze statues in the niches between the columns represent Pallas Minerva, Mercury, Apollo, and Peace. The first two symbolize the wisdom of the ruling elite and their eloquence, which translates into action; the latter two represent the singularity of Venetian law and liberty, and the city's love of peace and concord. On the upper level, Venice's mainland and overseas dominions are rendered. In the central panel Venice as Justice sits on her lion throne surrounded by river gods symbolizing the *stato da terra*. The *stato da mar* is represented in the side panels. On the left, Jupiter, who according to myth was raised on Crete, stands in for that island; on the right, Venus, who emerged from Cypriot waters, represents Venice's other great insular possession.[2] The Loggetta's message is clear: the wisdom of Venice's ruling class has made the city peaceful, wise, and prosperous and extended its dominion on both land and sea. Its architecture recalls imperial Rome, but the exuberant use of red, white, and green marbles situates it firmly within the long Venetian tradition of utilizing colorful decorative materials.[3]

Other architects active in sixteenth-century Venice, including Michele Sanmicheli, Andrea Palladio, Sebastiano Serlio, and Vincenzo Scamozzi, also helped adapt the architecture of the classical world, while painters, especially Paolo Veronese, situated some of their most important painted subjects in architectural settings that evoked the glory of antiquity. Venice's renowned printing press also played its part. Serlio published his *Regole generali di architettura sopra le cinque maniere de gli edifici* (General Rules of Architecture Concerning the Five Styles of Buildings) in 1537, while in 1556 Daniele Barbaro published an Italian translation of and commentary on the ancient Roman

FIGURE 14.1 Jacopo Sansovino, Loggetta, 1538–45. Piazza San Marco, Venice. Photo by Wolfgang Moroder, distributed under a CC-BY 3.0 license via Wikimedia Commons.

architect Vitruvius's *De architectura* (Ten Books of Architecture) which he followed up a year later with an emended Italian translation and commentary and a Latin edition that included illustrations by Palladio.[4]

The Loggetta's figure of Peace captured in bronze Venice's effort to reframe itself following the 1530 Treaty of Bologna. For the next two centuries that stance would translate into a policy of armed neutrality as the city tried to thread the needle between the Hapsburg and Ottoman empires. Neutrality was not so much a programmatic statement as a necessity forced on the Republic by the high cost of competing militarily with the two superpowers.[5] Only a handful of times over the next century would Venice find itself at war: twice with the Ottomans and twice with Hapsburgs. In Europe, the religious upheaval sparked by the Protestant Reformation prompted a severe reaction by the Catholic church exemplified by the militancy of the Council of Trent (1545–63). The papacy's effort to impose its will on the remaining Catholic states—a policy often in tune with the interests of the Hapsburgs—met resistance in Venice, which tried to blunt papal interference in its internal affairs yet embarked on its own program of internal surveillance and discipline. Further exacerbating tension between the papacy and the Republic were questions regarding the Adriatic. The conflict came to a head in the Interdict Crisis of 1606–7 when Venice presented itself as the defender of liberty against a papacy bent on exerting overweening power. Not surprisingly, such struggles rankled the political dynamic within the patriciate as it pitted some of the richest families with strong papal connections against others who advocated vigorous resistance to the papacy and Hapsburgs and promoted an indigenous, traditional Venetian piety. This resulted in two separate efforts to rein in the power of the Ten.

In the sixteenth century, Venice reimagined itself in the image of ancient Rome but also actively resisted contemporary papal Rome. Ambivalence regarding that twofold Roman influence reflected Venice's diminished position in the Mediterranean and European power constellations.

As the statesman Luca Tron declared in a 1519 Senate meeting, "the world has changed," and Venice needed to adjust.[6] Tron was addressing the city's need to adapt to shifting trade routes. But the separate betrayals of Venice by Francis I and Pope Clement VII in 1529, followed by the Peace of Bologna that rendered the Hapsburgs the predominant power in Italy, forced Venice to modify its military and diplomatic stance as well. In the sixteenth century, the choice was no longer between war and peace, but, as its commander Sforza Pallavicino declared in 1575, between war and "greater danger" and "lesser danger."[7] Given this, the policy Venice settled on was one of non-entanglement. Alliances were dangerous and could turns allies' enemies into Venice's enemies or commit the city to wars that were not in its direct interest. Worse still, given its rivals' size and resources, victory was unlikely.

Such a policy did not come without costs. The mainland dominion was surrounded to the east, north, and west by Hapsburg possessions and remained physically vulnerable to invasion. The *terraferma*'s geographical configuration exacerbated the problem from a military point of view. As one commander observed to the doge in 1579, "Your state being long and narrow can truthfully be described as nothing but frontier, and thus is more likely to be cut into and divided by whoever wants to attack it than had it been of any other shape."[8] To defend this vulnerable land and discourage enemies, the Republic embarked on building ambitious and costly fortifications. In 1542 a new office, the Provveditori alle Fortezze (Commissioners of Forts), was established.[9] In 1543 the fortifications of Chioggia and Venice itself were bolstered. Sanmicheli designed the fortress of Sant'Andrea to protect the San Nicolò entrance to the lagoon. In the 1580s, work was carried out on fortifications at Bergamo and Brescia, and in 1593 the decision was made to construct a new fort at Palma (known as Palmanova) in Friuli. Ostensibly built to protect against an Ottoman incursion, its primary purpose was to deter aggression by the archduke of Austria. Building citadels in the mainland cities came with its own political cost since locals were responsible for up to a third of the expense, and many resented the surveillance and control symbolized by these strongholds.

Protection of the *stato da mar* presented a different set of problems. Trying to update the defenses of all the overseas possessions was fiscally impossible. Instead, the capital chose to concentrate on a few bases, including Zara, Corfu, and Crete, the first two for their strategic importance, Crete for its economic value.[10] Still, it is unclear whether by the sixteenth century the mercantile benefit derived from the overseas territories justified the cost of their maintenance.[11] The policy of neutrality better fit the needs of the booming industrial and agricultural sectors of the Venetian economy than those of maritime trade.[12]

More than fortifications, Venice relied on its navy. Divided into five squadrons, it had approximately thirty active-duty galleys to protect the seas running from the Gulf of Venice to Crete. Crete was responsible for outfitting an additional four galleys. In theory an additional 100 warships were kept in Arsenal reserve for wartime mobilization. If the shape of the *terraferma* dominion made it vulnerable to attack, the contours of the *stato da mar* presented other difficulties. Venice stood at one extreme of its vast and elongated expanse, making it difficult to get men, materiel, and payrolls where they were needed. For centuries Venice's position had made it the ideal location for exchange between the Mediterranean and central Europe, but in the new international configuration of power, this situation proved highly hazardous.[13]

One incident exemplifies how little room Venice had to maneuver and how neutrality came at an economic cost. In the 1580s, Philip II, king of Spain and of Naples, offered the Venetians the opportunity to load spices in Lisbon and ship them through Venice for distribution to central Europe, as the city had done for centuries before the Portuguese circumnavigation of Africa. Philip made the overture because Dutch and English pirates, as well as the 1576 sack of Antwerp, part of his possessions in the Spanish Netherlands, were making it impossible for him to get spices to their intended markets. But the Venetians declined the proposal since it might jeopardize their generally good trade relations with the Ottomans and tie their own fortunes too tightly to those of Hapsburg Spain. It would also alienate the Hapsburgs' archenemy, France.[14]

Nevertheless, four times between 1530 and 1630 Venice went to war.[15] The first occurred in 1537 when the Ottoman sultan Suleiman I the Magnificent attacked Corfu. At the time, he was teamed up with Francis I of France in an anti-Hapsburg alliance. Venice's refusal to join their alliance provoked the Corfu assault, which proved unsuccessful. The Ottomans withdrew and turned instead to a year-long siege of Nauplion in the Morea. Desperate for allies who could help match the Ottoman navy, Venice, "a sea power with insufficient power at sea," allied in February 1538 with the papacy and Charles V. The Republic agreed to supply two-sixths of the fleet and troops, the pope one-sixth, and Charles the rest.[16] The Genoese Andrea Doria was named overall commander.

Given the partners' differing priorities, the Holy Alliance, as it was known, was doomed to failure. Charles was primarily concerned with protecting the seas around Sicily and the north African coast, a region over which the Ottomans had begun to exert influence following their seizure of Egypt from the Mamluks in 1517. The corsair Hayreddin Barbarossa had consolidated his hold on parts of the Maghrib. Suleiman named him grand admiral of the Ottoman navy in 1534. Soon he was launching attacks on Sicily and in 1537 on Otranto. When the two war fleets finally met at Prevesa, south of Corfu, in September 1538, the Ottomans emerged victorious. Efforts by the alliance to take the forts surrounding the Gulf of Prevesa were unsuccessful; and when

Hayreddin's fleet was finally lured into battle, the opposing forces were so spread out (and Doria so hesitant to risk his fleet) that full engagement was impossible. Doria's successful follow-up attack on Ottoman-held Castelnovo near Cattaro resulted in further Venetian disillusionment with its allies since Doria refused to hand the outpost over to them in territory that was indisputably within their sphere of influence.

The war dragged on until October 1540 when Venice reached a separate peace with the Ottomans. The agreement had been delayed by French spies who kept the sultan apprised of just how much the Venetians were willing to concede. In the humiliating settlement, Venice surrendered Nauplion, Malvasia, and the Cyclades islands (except Tinos); agreed to pay annual tribute for Zante and Cyprus; and also paid an indemnity of 300,000 ducats. A new boundary gave the Ottomans access to the Adriatic at locations not far from Zara. In recompense, the Venetians retained commercial access to Egyptian and Syrian ports. The war revealed the strategic significance of Corfu and, most important, that allies were of little use when their objectives were not parallel. As one commentary on the war noted, "The art of peace and quiet is the very nutriment and conservation of this Republic and the troubles of war its poison and ruin."[17] For the next thirty years Venice and the Ottomans remained at peace, enjoying mutually beneficial commercial relations.

In that interval Ottoman expansion westward was halted when they failed to capture Malta in 1565. Henceforth they largely directed their naval operations to North Africa and the eastern Mediterranean, with the goal of protecting the all-important trade route linking Constantinople and Alexandria, vital to supplying the capital with grain. They had captured Rhodes in 1522. Yet Venetian Cyprus and Crete still posed significant challenges to Ottoman domination of the eastern waters of the Middle Sea.

Matters came to a head when the Ottomans demanded Cyprus in March 1570. Six months earlier a massive explosion at the Arsenal had fueled unfounded fears of a Turkish plot. By September the Ottomans had taken Nicosia and were laying siege to Famagusta. Once again desperate for allies, Venice approached Philip II of Spain and Pope Pius V, who both agreed to assist, although no formal alliance was finalized. France, wracked by internal religious conflict and hesitant to jeopardize good relations with the Ottomans, did not join, nor did Holy Roman emperor Maximilian II of the Austrian Hapsburgs. Overtures to the Persians also failed. A large Venetian, Spanish, and papal fleet finally assembled at Crete, but disagreement among the commanders led to delays. The overall commander was Marcantonio

Colonna, the pope's man. Philip's contingent was captained by Gian Andrea Doria, Venice's by Girolamo Zane. Doria especially was hesitant to engage and was more concerned with returning west to protect the waters around Sicily and southern Italy. The fleet finally made a purposeless foray around Rhodes. By this point Nicosia had fallen, and the Ottomans were continuing to besiege Famagusta. With winter approaching, the fleet returned without having engaged the enemy.

The following May a formal alliance known as the Holy League was concluded. For their part the Ottomans had been attacking Crete and then Zante and Cephalonia. Fearful of being trapped in the Adriatic, the Venetian contingent, under Sebastiano Venier, rendezvoused with the allies at Messina in August. It was a formidable force, made up of 208 light galleys, six galleasses (merchant galleys redesigned to carry more cannonry and deliver broadsides) and supply ships. The Venetian contribution was half the light galleys and all the galleasses. In the meantime, the Ottomans were ravaging the Dalmatian coast. The Senate pleaded with Venier to convince the allies to come to Venice's defense, saying, "The enemy is penetrating the very vitals of our state."[18] The defenses of the Lido were beefed up out of fear of an Ottoman attack. After an unsuccessful Ottoman assault on Corfu, the two navies met near Lepanto in the Gulf of Patras on October 7, 1571.

With the fleets in battle formation, Venice's galleasses were moved to the front to soften up the Ottoman fleet with cannonades. But once the enemy maneuvered past them, they were largely useless. The battle assumed the centuries-old Mediterranean tradition of hand-to-hand combat fought on the decks of ships that were bunched together—as conveyed by Andrea Michieli's depiction of the battle in the Ducal Palace. At the center of the swarm were the Venetian, papal, and Spanish flagships. In the end the League prevailed, due in part to the galleasses, its troops' heavier armor, and greater reliance on arquebuses (muzzle-loaded long guns). Many of the Ottoman soldiers still used bows and arrows. It was sadly a slaughter: the Ottomans lost approximately 30,000 men, including their commander Müezzinzade Ali Pasha, to the League's 9,000. Untold numbers were wounded, among them Miguel de Cervantes, who later wrote *Don Quixote*. The allies divided up 117 captured Ottoman galleys.

It took eleven days for the victory annunciation to reach Venice, carried by a ship appropriately named *Angel Gabriel*. The city erupted into celebrations that lasted for months—with the ringing of bells, the lighting of bonfires, the staging of processions and displays, and the celebrating of Masses, including polychoral works likely composed by San Marco's choirmaster

FIGURE 14.2 Andrea Michieli, il Vicentino, *Battle of Lepanto*, c. 1600. Sala dello Scrutinio, Ducal Palace, Venice. Wikimedia Commons.

Andrea Gabrieli. The text of one of Gabrieli's works seems to have fit the occasion perfectly, declaring, "Blessed be the Lord of Hosts. . . . Our armies have fought in the name of the Lord. God has sustained us in battle and won over His enemies."[19] Guilds put on displays, as did the Germans at the Fondaco dei Tedeschi. Painters produced allegories of the victory, while broadsheets commemorated the celebrations. Although Lepanto did not change the balance of power—the Ottomans were able to assemble a formidable new fleet the following year—, it proved to Westerners that the Ottoman advance was not inexorable.

Unbeknown to the victors, two days before Lepanto, Famagusta had succumbed to the Ottoman siege. Caterina Corner's old kingdom of Cyprus was lost. Nevertheless, plans were made for another fleet to assemble the next summer and take the fight to the Ottomans in their home waters, although little came of that campaign, and the new pope, Gregory XIII, was less bellicose than his predecessor. Prospects for the 1573 campaign were even more ambitious, with Venice being asked to supply a staggering 130 galleys. While this was being organized, Venice was secretly negotiating with the sultan. A separate peace, orchestrated by the Ten but opposed by many in the Senate, was agreed to in March. Again, the terms were humiliating. While the Ottomans kept Cyprus, both parties agreed to return most of the other conquered territories to their ante bellum status. Venice again owed an indemnity of 300,000 ducats, and the tribute for Zante was increased from 500 to 1,500 ducats. Commercial relations between Venice and the Ottomans were once again renewed and confiscated merchant ships returned. The Republic justified the decision to its allies by pleading its ongoing vulnerability to invasion in Friuli and the financial sacrifices it had made. It claimed that it had spent 12 million ducats on the war effort. When Venice's ambassador to

Spain, Leonardo Donà, reported informing Philip II of the separate peace, he interpreted the king's enigmatic smile as his way of saying, "In short, you've done it, just as everyone told me you would."[20] Venice's action reinforced once again foreigners' view of the Republic as mercenary and opportunistic. Yet as in the previous war, plans for a full-scale war against the Ottomans were thwarted by the conflicting interests of Spain and Venice.

The next two wars to interrupt Venice's policy of neutrality occurred in Italy and again involved the Republic in power plays among European monarchs. The first was the War of Gradisca (1615–18), which was in some ways the latest iteration of the centuries-old threat posed to Venice by Milan, now firmly under Spanish control. Venice was supporting the Duke of Savoy in his effort to secure Montferrat, which bordered Milan to the west. Venice, fearful that the Spanish Hapsburgs might use the occasion to drive east into Venetian Lombardy, increased troops and inspected fortresses along the Mincio River. But the greater danger was posed by Ferdinand II, archduke of Inner Austria, who for years had turned a blind eye to the Uskok pirates.

The Uskoks (the name means fugitive) were refugees from the Ottoman invasion of Hungary and Croatia. From Segna (Senj) on the Croatian coastline north of Zara, they wantonly attacked passing ships, many of them Venetian.[21] Using small boats that could travel as much as 100 miles in a single night, they were nearly impossible to catch and did not hesitate to pursue galleys. From one of their bases on the island of Brazza, they kept watch over the mouth of the Narenta River. To protect trade with the Ottoman Balkan hinterland, including the all-important Spalato route, Venice stationed a squadron of ships in the region under the command of a capitano contro Uscocchi (captain against the Uskoks). By the early seventeenth century, it was spending 200,000 ducats a year in the effort to thwart these "gangsters of the Illyrian seas," who were operating where the Venetian, Hapsburg, and Ottoman empires intersected.[22]

Ferdinand's support of the Uskoks was part of his effort to assert Austrian control over the Gulf of Trieste, thereby challenging Venice's claims to the northern Adriatic and eastern Friuli. Austria already held Gradisca and Gorizia and had designs on Capodistria and Marano. In August 1615 the Venetian offensive began. By the end of the year both Trieste and Gradisca had been isolated from their resupply routes. The war then settled into stalemate in part because Venice again became concerned not only with the possibility of a Spanish thrust into Lombardy but also of a naval advance into the Adriatic by the Spanish viceroy of Naples. By August 1617 the Venetians even believed a conspiracy was afoot to attack Venice itself, led by the Spanish ambassador, Alonso de la Cueva y Benavides, the Marquess of Bedmar.[23] The war hobbled along until a peace arranged in June 1618 called for joint Austrian and Venetian operations to disband and destroy the Uskoks. Finances and difficulties in recruiting soldiers had again proved to Venice the virtue of neutrality.[24]

The lesson was taught a final time in the War of Mantuan Succession (1628–31). It was precipitated by the death in 1627 without a legitimate heir of Vincenzo II, Gonzaga, ruler of the duchies of Mantua and Monferrat and the last in the direct line of Gonzaga descent. Three men claimed the inheritance: Charles, Duke of Nevers, who had married into the Gonzaga family; Charles Emmanuel I, Duke of Savoy; and Ferrante II Gonzaga, Duke of Guastalla (a duchy near Mantua). Nevers was supported by France, Ferrante by Emperor Ferdinand II, whose wife was the sister of the last Gonzaga duke and by Spain. Charles of Nevers was declared the rightful heir in January 1628. Soon a coalition of the Spanish and Piedmontese laid siege to Casale, the capital of Monferrat, although a French army descended into Italy and managed to break the siege.

Venice agreed to support Nevers and join an anti-Hapsburg coalition of France, Nevers's Mantua, and the pope. The plan was for France to protect Casale, Venice to guard Mantua. Yet by late 1629 Ferdinand's imperial troops had entered Italy and started laying siege to Mantua. Doge Nicolò Contarini was a strenuous advocate of the war, but Venetian troops performed badly at Valeggio in the spring. Their retreat to Peschiera left the Veneto open to an imperial invasion. Ferdinand's army conquered Mantua and sacked the city in July 1630. But any follow-up into Venetian territory was thwarted by the plague, which was decimating the troops, and by the emperor's need to relocate them to counteract Swedish king Gustavus Adolphus's invasion of Germany. The plague had also reached Venice, where by September hundreds were dying daily.

The treaties that ended the conflict revealed Venice's greatly diminished international standing. Its delegation did not even arrive at the peace talks until they had already been concluded in October 1630. Charles of Nevers was confirmed as ruler of Mantua and Monferrat, while Savoy and Ferrante of Guastalla received minor concessions. The Republic was completely excluded from follow-up talks that resulted in the Treaty of Cherasco in June 1631, which confirmed Nevers's position and France's growing international role.

Over the course of a century then, Venice had engaged in four wars and come out badly in each, losing significant territory including Cyprus in the *stato da mar* and adding nothing to the *stato da terra*. The wars exposed the

Republic's difficulty in recruiting, training, and disciplining its armies and navy. Like all previous wars, these forced the city into years of deficit spending. The Cyprus war cost about 3 million ducats annually at a time when ordinary revenues averaged 2 million. Even in peacetime, the costs of defense were enormous. In 1618 they amounted to 2,700,000 ducats, or three-quarters of all spending.[25] In addition to indirect taxes, the city relied on direct imposts to raise funds, some of which were considered loans and thus paid interest. At the end of the Cyprus War the Republic annually was paying out 700,000 ducats in interest payments alone.[26] In 1577 the decision was made to amortize the Mint debt in the hope that the restituted money would reinvigorate commerce, but investors were leery. In his will of 1558, Marcantonio Grimani cautioned his executors that, if the Monte del Sussidio (created during the Italian wars) was eliminated, the money should be put into some "cautious, sufficient, and secure" investment.[27] For many that meant land on the *terraferma* or investments in the credit market. By the 1590s Venice had eliminated virtually all the debt funds, including the Monte Novissimo, the Monte del Sussidio, even the Monte Vecchio. However, the War of Mantuan Succession again raised the debt to more than 8 million ducats. Servicing it cost half a million ducats a year.[28]

The wars were part of larger structural and geopolitical changes quickly undermining Venice's historical strength, namely, its role as intermediary between East and West.[29] These changes included a decline in Venetian shipping, increased English and Dutch competition for trade, a growing disconnect between the ruling elite and commerce, the concomitant prioritizing of territorial defense over commerce, and the contestation of Venice's claims to Adriatic sovereignty.

Venice's shipbuilding industry and merchant marine underwent substantial change at the end of the sixteenth century. After centuries of resisting foreign-built ships, Venice began to allow its merchants to rent or buy foreign ships, particularly northern European ones that were cheaper than locally built ones. Their design also meant they were faster, could be used for both commerce and war, and could sail in winter, giving them a competitive advantage. For centuries Venice had enjoyed the advantage of its merchant galleys quickly converting from commercial to wartime use and vice versa. Now the navy and merchant marine diverged.[30] Galleys continued to be used in warfare since the Ottomans also relied on galleys. But, except for the all-important Venice/Spalato trade route that utilized galleys (due to the threat of piracy), trade operated primarily on full-rigged carracks.[31] The ubiquity of pirates also drove up the cost of doing business as the expense of maritime insurance, contracted on Calle della Sicurtà (Security Lane) at Rialto, rose.

Just as significantly, Venice faced competition in the Mediterranean from the English and Dutch. The English especially made a play for trade with the Ottomans. Previously Levantine goods had made their way to England via Venice. In the 1580s the English established the Venice and Turkey Companies, which merged in 1592 to form the Levant Company. The salary of the English ambassador to the sultan was even paid by the company rather than the government. Soon the English were able to undercut Venice's vital textile trade with the Ottoman empire by counterfeiting Venetian cloth and selling it more cheaply than the original. As one observer noted, "There was nobody [in Constantinople] who wanted to buy Venetian cloth save at a much lower price than before."[32] The English gained another advantage with the establishment of peace with Spain in 1604, which made it safer for their ships to pass through the Strait of Gibraltar. By the 1620s the English share of Ottoman trade was nearly double Venice's.[33]

Another example of English penetration into Venice's trading sphere involved currants and raisins produced on the Ionian islands of Cephalonia and Zante. As Venetian merchant Zuan Domenego de Lazarini noted in 1578, traditionally several Venetian ships had annually transported huge quantities of raisins and currants to England.[34] Having elbowed their way into this lucrative trade, the English were also encroaching on the Cretan wine trade.

Venice's Greek-island subjects were willing accomplices in this English takeover. English pirates found safe haven along the coast of these islands, where the locals were happy to sell them supplies and purchase plunder. As farmers converted from producing grain (much of which supplied the Venetian navy) to growing more lucrative raisins and currants, the English filled the gap by supplying the islands with cereals. When there was a brief social rebellion on Zante in 1628, the English managed to remain in the good graces of all the parties involved. Prominent Greek merchant families in Zante played an important role in linking London to the islands and connecting English merchants to the Mediterranean-wide trade network of Jewish merchants.[35] Farther afield, both the English and Dutch East Indian Companies were able to exploit more effectively the Cape passage to India than had the Portuguese, further undermining the remaining routes that brought spices to the eastern shores of the Mediterranean. In 1675 the Venetians finally stopped sending a consul to Aleppo, an important intersection of Ottoman trade routes, since the volume of business had declined so greatly.[36]

Venice's response to all this was backward looking and inadequate to changing circumstances. The imposition of tariffs as a way to continue funneling traffic through its harbor proved unsuccessful. Venice refused to declare itself a free port, like Livorno. Had it done so, the English and Dutch would have happily shipped goods to Germany via Venice since it was cheaper than transporting them via Gibraltar. But Venice failed to play the "geography card."[37] Failure to adapt resulted from two separate causes. The first concerned the patriciate's own withdrawal from direct involvement in international trade. By the end of the sixteenth century, patricians owned only about one in ten Venetian ships.[38] Those merchants actively engaged in international trade, namely, *cittadini*, Greek subjects, and Jewish resident traders, were not part of the decision-making process or were at best bit players in it. Unlike centuries past, Venetian decision-makers were often out of touch with the realities of trade on the ground.[39]

Second, decision-making revolved around politics and the need to defend what was an increasingly indefensible overseas empire. Venice was spending huge amounts of money to maintain the *stato da mar*, which in return was contributing only about a tenth of the government's revenue. Meanwhile the *stato da terra* generated around 40 percent and saw increasing economic integration with the capital.[40] Venice had the opportunity to reimagine its empire as a constellation of commercial hubs and in so doing further both its own economic interests and those of its subject peoples. But it continued instead to prioritize the capital.[41]

Competitors even began to challenge Venice's claims to Adriatic sovereignty, the very foundation of Venetian might. These included the Archdukes of Austria, the papacy which in 1593 had declared Ancona a free port, and to a lesser extent the Ottomans. According to Roman law, the sea was a common good over which no nation could claim possession. But Venice had never adopted Roman law. For centuries Venice had based its claim to the Adriatic on long usage and the 1177 Peace of Venice by which, according to some accounts, Pope Alexander III had given to Doge Ziani the gold ring with which to marry the sea.[42] But what was given could also be taken back. Venice's successful effort in 1510 to lure the papacy away from the League of Cambrai by granting freedom of navigation in the Gulf to papal subjects created another impediment to Venetian claims, even though Venice acted as if the concession had never been made once the crisis passed. The popes did not forget.

It fell to Paolo Sarpi, Servite friar and legal advisor to the Republic, to make anew Venice's case for control of the Adriatic. Sarpi composed two treatises on the subject. For him dominion of the Gulf was both a natural right and a historical one, having been "born along with the Republic, [then] augmented and maintained with virtue, blood, and treasure."[43] He did not credit the claim that the privilege had been ceded to Venice by Pope Alexander III in 1177. Rather, as the papal ambassador to Venice wrote in 1598, the Venetians argued that Alexander merely "confirmed what they already possessed."[44] As for the doctrine of freedom of the seas, Sarpi said the sea, like the land, was divided among nations; and the Adriatic was not, in fact, an ocean but was "closed and limited"—in other words, an inland sea, over which Venice enjoyed jurisdiction and possession.[45] Tintoretto's *Venetia Maris Adriaci Regina* (Venice Queen of the Adriatic Sea) in the Senate Hall mirrors Sarpi's claim that Venice's right to the Adriatic is natural and immemorial, not the result of a papal privilege. In the painting the Gods bear various fruits of the sea including coral to Queen Venice. Andrea Spinelli's 1539 bronze medal *Regina Maris Adriaci* (Queen of the Adriatic Sea) uses the model of ancient Roman coinage to affirm Venetian sovereignty over the Adriatic.[46] Venice sits on a lion throne and holds the scales of justice and

FIGURE 14.3 Andrea Spinelli, *Regina Maris Adriaci*, bronze medal, reverse, 1539. Courtesy of the National Gallery of Art, Washington. Samuel H. Kress Collection.

a cornucopia. There is armor to her left and a fully manned galley on her right. That Venice was compelled to defend its claim to the Adriatic in print, paint, and bronze indicates the precarity of its hold on the Adriatic and how reduced its position among the Mediterranean and European powers had become.

Venice's policy of neutrality depended on massive defense spending as well as the assiduous gathering of intelligence by diplomats, informers, and spies. The city was a major center for the dissemination of information and a diplomatic and espionage hotspot, a veritable "*fondaco* of news."[47] And it was a trusted one. When word of the 1525 Battle of Pavia reached the pasha in Istanbul, he did not apprise the sultan until he had confirmed the information from Venetian sources. According to Pietro Bragadin, "the pasha believes news coming out of Venice and nowhere else."[48]

Ambassadors' most important duty was to gather intelligence useful to their home governments by any means necessary. After serving as ambassador to Milan, humanist Ermolao Barbaro wrote in his treatise *De officio legati* (On the Office of Ambassador) that the legate's job was to "do, say, advise, and think" whatever advanced the interests of his state.[49] England's long-serving ambassador to the Republic, Henry Wotton, declared that "an ambassador is an honest man sent to lie abroad for the good of his country."[50] The constant stream of letters and dispatches that Venetian ambassadors composed kept the home government abreast of current events, while the *relazioni* (final reports) that they presented orally on their return educated senators about everything from the economy to the geography and customs of foreign states. Ambassadors gathered some of this information themselves but also relied on paid and unpaid informers, whose viewpoints and agendas inflected these summary reports.[51] Rectors and governors in Venice's widespread mainland and overseas dominions were also official sources of intelligence. In addition, the Ten and the Inquisitori di Stato (State Inquisitors) fielded their own spies who operated independently of ambassadors and rectors. In 1504, the Ten and its spice *zonta* sent Lunardo da Ca' Masser to Lisbon to gather news about the spice trade there.[52] Merchants had long served as unofficial information gatherers. A bevy of others—exiles hoping for a pardon, informants seeking cash, those who disagreed with the policies of their own governments—were also willing to pass along information.

Spying was tricky and dangerous. Letters were hidden in shoes, sewn into clothing, or buried in the ground. Cryptography was widely used. One method deployed merchant vocabulary to mean something else entirely since business letters, which flowed abundantly to Rialto, seemed innocuous. Andrea Gritti had used this technique when he was a merchant in Constantinople. When he wrote, for example, that someone who was "in prison for debts would be released in June," that was code for "the Turkish fleet will sail in June." During the War of Cyprus, Jewish spy Caim Saruch used the same approach: "sacks of cotton" denoted "Turkish *fuste* [galleys]."[53] Other codes substituted numbers for names (M31 equaled France, M33 England) or used random letters and numbers that required a key to decipher.[54] Until 1547 Venice used one key for all its diplomats; subsequently it used different ones for different locales and changed them regularly. The chancery staff included secretaries who were expert at devising codes and breaking those of foreign governments. In 1569 the papal nuncio to Venice warned his correspondents not to allow letters to be intercepted since "here there are secretaries who with the greatest ease understand everything."[55] Invisible ink was also employed. During the War of Cyprus, the *bailo* in Constantinople, Marcantonio Barbaro, got permission to write home and inserted messages in invisible ink between the lines.[56] The government also concocted schemes to sabotage infrastructure, unleash deadly biological agents, and assassinate enemies.[57]

Foreign governments employed the same practices and methods to gather information from and about Venice. The Spanish ambassador, Alfonso de la Cueva, Marquess of Bedmar, suspected in 1617 of plotting against the Republic, maintained a stable of spies and informants. Venice's ambassador to Madrid, Pietro Priuli, broke up one of his networks through counterespionage efforts. To foil leaks, the Republic forbade noblemen from talking with foreign ambassadors, but to little avail. The city's dense built environment and the intersection of various social circles at dinners, Mass, official receptions, and other occasions offered plentiful opportunities for information to be gathered and transmitted. And some Venetians could be bought. Bedmar suborned nobleman Domenico Bollani, bishop of Chania. In 1591, Girolamo Lippomano, *bailo* to Constantinople, was accused of passing state secrets to Spain. While being extradited home for prosecution, he met a mysterious end. As the ship on which he was traveling neared the Lido, he went to urinate off the deck but fell into the sea and drowned.[58] An even more horrible case involved nobleman and seasoned diplomat Antonio Foscarini who the Ten arrested on April 8, 1622, for having had unauthorized contact with foreigners and divulging state secrets. On April 13 he was found guilty and a week later was strangled in his prison cell. His body was then publicly exposed between the two columns of the Piazzetta. However, a few months later it came to light that he had been falsely accused and was publicly exonerated. Many saw his case as an example of what they considered the Ten's unchecked power.[59]

Venice was such an important center of espionage because, despite its diminishing role as a trade intermediary between Europe and the eastern Mediterranean, it remained a nexus for the transmission of intelligence between the two spheres. The Spanish especially depended on Venice for reliable information about the Ottomans, while the English and Dutch hoped that the Republic might take up the Protestant cause. The papacy, concerned with Adriatic navigation and the spread of Protestantism, counted on its nuncios in Venice to keep it abreast of developments in both arenas.

The government was obsessed with secrecy, as exemplified by the inquisitorial trial procedure utilized by the Ten and the maintenance of secret archives.[60] In 1536, the papal nuncio stated that it was easier "to hope to extract a secret from Heaven than from them [the Venetians] when they want to keep one."[61] A 1542 Senate law declared, "One of the principal concerns in the governance of states is secrecy without which no matter can be pursued to its desired end."[62] This was, in part, a public relations ploy, designed to project an image of the Republic as almost preternaturally unified in its goals and free of the factionalism and interest groups that crippled other states.[63]

Additionally, secrecy instilled fear and served as an instrument of political and social control. To this end, in September 1539 the Ten created a new body, the Inquisitori sopra la Propalazione dei Segreti (Inquisitors over the Spreading of Secrets), that was renewed annually. Established to put an end to the "disgraceful" leaking of information regarding "the most important matters dealt with in our secret Councils," the magistracy was temporarily abolished in 1582, but revived a year later under the name State Inquisitors.[64] From 1588 on, one of the three inquisitors had to be a ducal councilor, the other two members of the Ten. All three had to agree to pass a sentence. Closely tied to the Ten, the inquisitors over time assumed primary responsibility for state security and many other matters.[65]

The creation of the State Inquisitors was just one of many efforts in the sixteenth century to exert tighter control over almost all aspects of life in the city and its dominions. Foreigners were put under greater surveillance. In 1583 the government began requiring them to register on their arrival and present that registration to those with whom they sought lodging.[66] In the 1520s the Provveditori sopra Monasteri (Commissioners of Monasteries) was created to supervise female religious houses but expanded to include enforcement of enclosure by which outsiders were prohibited from entering convents and nuns from leaving. In 1569 the Ten ordered the commissioners and patriarch to carry out inspections of nunneries and seal up unauthorized points of access and egress. Several convents vigorously resisted these encroachments on their already limited freedom.[67] The Provveditori sopra gli Ospedali (Commissioners of Hospitals), established in 1561, supervised administration of hospitals and other pious foundations and oversaw the ransoming of subjects enslaved by the Turks. In 1565 the office of Provveditori sopra la Giustizia Vecchia (Commissioners over the Old Justices) granted nobles more supervision of the guilds. The Provveditori sopra i Beni Comunali (Commissioners of Common Lands), regularized in 1574, dealt with, as their name indicates, common lands and protected them from usurpation; while the Provveditori sopra i Beni Inculti (Commissioners of Uncultivated Lands) [1556] superintended land reclamation and irrigation projects. Numerous other magistracies were instituted to handle fiscal, monetary, defense, and myriad other matters.[68]

Two new magistracies that exerted an outsized influence stand out: the Esecutori contro la Bestemmia (Executors Against Blasphemy), created in 1537, and the Tre Savi all'Eresia (Three Sages on Heresy), instituted in 1547. The Esecutori were established by the Ten and followed their inquisitorial rite. Their mandate rapidly expanded beyond blasphemy to encompass a wide range of offenses against social order, including bad behavior in churches, gambling, insults to nobles, and rape preceded by false promises of marriage. Aimed primarily at offenses by the *popolo*, the Esecutori represented a powerful effort at social control, even going so far as to define the limits of acceptable speech.[69] Their jurisdiction extended to the subject territories and Venetian ships in foreign parts. In the government's view, protecting God and the saints from insult was essential to maintaining proper social boundaries on earth.[70] Printed proclamations and plaques erected throughout the city engraved with the Esecutori's orders served to extend their reach into every corner of the city.[71] This program of purification "reflected the republic's insecurity in an age of war and crisis."[72]

The spread of heresy, fomented by the Protestant Reformation, was a special concern. Following the failure of the Protestants and Catholics to reach a compromise at the 1541 Colloquy of Regensburg, Catholic hardliners gained the upper hand and convinced Pope Paul III in July 1542 to establish the Roman Inquisition. That same year he also gave official recognition to the Jesuit order. Venice was perceived to be a potential hotbed of reform due to the large number of Germans and other foreigners in the city as well as the presence of high-profile Protestant sympathizers in Venetian lands, such as Pier Paolo Vergerio, bishop of Capodistria. Fearing papal interference with its sovereignty, Venice resisted admitting the Inquisition but eventually relented. When it did, it gave it a distinctly Venetian twist, building into the tribunal some of the checks and balances characteristic of Venetian republican rule. Specifically, it called for the appointment of lay advisors, the Tre Savi all'Eresia, who together with the patriarch, father inquisitor, and papal legate would oversee the tribunal and its proceedings. The ducal decree establishing the Tre Savi in April 1547 made clear that their job was to be present at the tribunal's proceedings, guarantee that "appropriate sentences are passed upon those who are found guilty," and keep the government informed "of everything that happens."[73] Venice had long seen itself as a bulwark of Christianity, exemplified by its close association with Saint Mark and the Virgin, vibrant confraternal piety, and ongoing confrontation with Islam. At the same time, it was zealous in protecting its traditions and ecclesiastical privileges, known as immunities, and resisting papal encroachment. The two powers even differed over the goals of the Inquisition: while the papacy was primarily concerned with extirpating heresy, the Republic was mainly interested in preserving public order.[74]

A major source of conflict between the two was Venice's printing industry. Books and reading were at the very heart of Protestantism and its idea of a priesthood of all believers. Printed books were one of the primary means by which reform spread and hence a major papal concern. At the same time, the Republic was intent on protecting this key sector of its economy. These two impulses see-sawed back and forth. The printers, with the backing of the College, resisted Paul IV's 1559 Index of Prohibited Books that included the entire corpus of works of more than 550 authors including Erasmus and Machiavelli. But with the growing strength of the Counter Reformation, opposition grew more difficult, and for much of the 1560s the goals of Venice and the papacy regarding printed books aligned. This rapprochement was aided by the disturbing revelation that several young patricians had converted to Protestantism and by the religious fervor that would lead to the creation of the Holy League during the War of Cyprus. The printers adapted to the new mood by printing more religious texts. But when the bookmen found themselves locked out of the publication of new canonical texts of the breviary, missals, and catechism—an economic windfall for those who did win the privilege—the Republic for financial reasons again took their side.[75] Fear of competition from bookmen in Rome and Turin also drove Venice and the papacy apart. Venice resisted promulgation of the index published by Pope Clement VIII in 1596, although a compromise was reached that gave the state more control over it.

The Inquisition's pursuit of heretics likewise waxed and waned. In Venice those accused of heresy adhered in varying degrees to three strains of heterodox belief: evangelism, Anabaptism, and millenarianism. The papal nuncio Giovantonio Facchinetti warned the government that heretics were Venice's "hidden enemies."[76] Just as during the 1560s the Inquisition and government aligned regarding the book trade, so the decade from 1565 to 1574 was the most active in the pursuit of heretics.

One of those ensnared by the inquisitorial fervor was Paolo Veronese. In 1573 he appeared before the tribunal regarding a painting of the *Last Supper* he had recently completed for the refectory of San Zanipolo. The meal takes place under a grandiose classical loggia beyond which is Veronese's imagined Jerusalem townscape. While a haloed Jesus sits front and center surrounded by his disciples, the scene is the very antithesis of Leonardo's subdued *Last Supper*. It is a riot of activity as waiters scurry about, the steward oversees the meal, a young black retainer chases away a dwarf jester holding a parrot, two German halberdiers sample the food and wine, and, directly in front of Jesus, a cat taunts a dog by reaching for a bone. The Inquisitors questioned Veronese about the appropriateness of these figures. The painter defended himself by claiming that he had added them "for ornament" and that they did not occupy the space under the loggia where the supper proper was taking place. The Inquisitors replied, "Do you not know that in Germany and other places infected with heresy they are accustomed, by means of outlandish paintings full of indecencies and similar devices, to abuse, mock and pour scorn on the things of the Holy Catholic Church?" Veronese played dumb, declaring, "I did not think of such important things." The inquisitors decided that he should "correct and amend" the painting within three months at his own expense. In the end, he simply changed the name from the *Last Supper* to the *Feast in the House of Levi*.[77]

In the early 1580s Venice again became concerned with the effects that pursuing heretics would have on commerce and potential Protestant allies like England and the Dutch Republic. The papal nuncio Alberto Bolognetti lamented the Venetians' toleration of Protestants in the city declaring that "they [the Venetians] only ask them not to cause any public scandal, permitting them to live as they wish in their own homes."[78] Following a brief return to rigor with the election of Pasquale Cicogna as doge in 1585, including the drowning of several persons who had relapsed into heresy, Rome

FIGURE 14.4 Paolo Veronese, *Feast in the House of Levi*, 1573. Gallerie dell'Accademia, Venice. Photograph by Oakenchips, distributed via Wikimedia Commons.

and Venice again diverged.[79] With the near disappearance of heresy in the city, the Inquisition turned its attention to witchcraft.

The debate over whether to ally the Venetian state with the policies of the papacy exacerbated the already significant fissures within the patrician ruling class. The most serious of these remained that between rich and poor patricians, but also significant was the split between those who regularly sat in the most powerful councils and those who could never hope to do so. Since smaller bodies like the Ten and College controlled the information that the larger councils received and their ability to debate policy, many patricians felt they were being denied knowledge of affairs of state.[80]

Yet there were also divisions among the wealthy and powerful. One bloc comprised the *papalisti* (papal ones), like the Grimanis and Corners, whose fortunes were tied closely to positions in the church. They could spend vast sums to secure ecclesiastical benefices and maintain cardinalate households in Rome and, in the process, bring the Venetian church more in line with the Counter Reformation. Their great wealth also allowed them to purchase procuratorships of San Marco and buy early entry into the Senate and Greater Council.[81] The ephemeral architecture created by Vincenzo Scamozzi for the 1597 coronation of Doge Marino Grimani's wife Morosina Morosini included a barge with a grand triumphal arch celebrating the many offices, including ecclesiastical posts, held by the Grimani and Morosini families. Although Dogaressa Morosini had to swear to obey the clauses of the ducal oath of office pertaining to ducal wives, her coronation procession appeared more royal than republican. Leonardo Donà particularly opposed the conferral of the Golden Rose, a papal honor, on Grimani's wife.[82] By contrast, bachelor Dona's own installation as doge in 1606 was austere. He was one of the leading members of another bloc of families who continued to promote the ethos of *mediocritas* that had long sought to keep aristocratic display in check. These families celebrated the Venetian church's autonomy from Rome and the Republic's indigenous religious traditions.[83]

Disagreement over how to rebuild the Ducal Palace following the devastating fire of 1577 captures this tension. One proposal evidenced by a drawing attributed to Palladio advocated rebuilding the Palace in the classical style, including a central entryway in the form of a triumphal arch. Had this plan been adopted, the palace would have complemented Sansovino's library across the Piazzetta and his other Romanizing projects. In the end, the decision was made to maintain the building's distinctive Venetian Gothic style or, as one chronicler put it, to rebuild it "neither more nor less than as it was before." In this way, the restored Ducal Palace continued to celebrate Venice's independence and local traditions.[84] The growing divisions within the patriciate resulted in part from the "impossibility of reconciling Tridentine [Council of Trent] reform with Venetian tradition."[85]

Other divisions also plagued the patriciate. Some, such as that between the *case vecchie* and *case nuove*, were centuries old. Others were relatively recent. The fund-raising decision taken in the lead-up to Lepanto to allow young patricians to enter the Greater Council at eighteen in return for 200 ducats brought an influx of young men (the *giovani*) into the patriciate, producing some degree of generational conflict with the old (the *vecchi*).

But such names were by and large simply labels, and, on important domestic and foreign policy matters, often counted for little.[86] The real fault lines lay between those nobles who felt excluded from the most important councils and members of the Ten and College. There were those who believed that power should be narrowly held and others who thought that this created an oligarchy of officeholders and argued instead that offices should be broadly shared.[87] With respect to policy, opinions within the patriciate differed markedly regarding how Venice should confront its rapidly diminishing international position. Some were lukewarm on neutrality. They advocated closer ties to England, the Dutch Republic, and France as a way of counterbalancing Spanish power in Italy. They feared that Venice would end up like other minor states such as Genoa and Lucca. They also resisted papal intervention in internal affairs and were wary of Jesuit meddling. At the same time, they were pious Catholics. Men of this opinion gathered in a kind of salon that met at the palace of Andrea and Nicolò Morosini in the parish of San Luca. Not standing on ceremony and attracting an eclectic mix of clergy and laymen, nobles, *cittadini*, and foreigners, members of the salon, known as the Ridotto Morosini, advocated inquiry and the kind of truth-seeking represented by thinkers like Montaigne. Sarpi, future doges Donà and Nicolò Contarini, and even Galileo Galilei frequented it.[88]

These divisions led to the 1582-3 effort to rein in the Ten.[89] A big source of discontent among rank-and-file patricians was the Ten's frequent appointment of *zonte* (supernumerary members), which had the effect of permanently enlarging this most powerful council. For critics, this epitomized the tendency toward oligarchy. Another bone of contention was the Ten's penchant for secrecy. It had secretly negotiated the end to both recent wars with the Ottomans, usurping a traditional Senate responsibility. The arrogance of the Ten's secretaries also rankled, as did the council's seeming arbitrariness in enforcing certain laws.

Matters came to head in October 1582 when it was time to elect members of the *zonta* for the following year. Over the course of several sessions, the Greater Council refused to elect the requisite number of *zonta* members. Finally, after rancorous debate, a bill was approved in late December that restored to the Senate many of the powers the Ten had arrogated to itself while reaffirming the Ten's competency in state security. And in January 1583 the *zonta* was abolished in practice when the Greater Council again refused to elect the required number of members.[90] With many matters of state back in the hands of the Senate, concern grew about the potential divulging of state secrets. This prompted the revival and regularization of the State Inquisitors. Writing to King Henry III, French ambassador Hurault de Maisse declared, "The business seems to be settled although not all are content with it."[91] Yet matters were not settled. The laws passed in 1582-3 were hardly likely to restore the equilibrium between councils and between rich and poor nobles that had been almost two centuries in the making. Accordingly, another attempt to limit the Ten's power followed.

It took place in 1628 and more dramatically than the first brought out the division between rich and poor, *papalisti* and others.[92] The poorer nobles resented the light sentences given to malefactors from rich and powerful families, the inquisitorial procedure that appeared arbitrary to those on the outside, and the perceived power of the Ten's secretaries. To critics the 1622 execution of the falsely accused Antonio Foscarini epitomized the Ten's abuses.

The election of Giovanni Corner as doge precipitated the showdown. After his election, Corner twice got approval from the Signoria for his sons to continue to sit in the Senate, a clear violation of long-standing laws designed to limit ducal sons' power and a signal that the rules did not apply to the rich. Then in 1626 Pope Urban VIII tapped another of Corner's sons, Federico, to be a cardinal. Shortly thereafter, he was appointed bishop of Vicenza. Yet in that same year, the Ten banished poor nobleman Carlo Querini from Venice and its territories and stripped him of his nobility for soliciting ecclesiastical favors. Different standards applied to different men.

Taking the lead against these abuses was Raniero Zeno, newly elected head of the Ten. He launched an all-out attack on Corner and wanted the State Attorneys to investigate how his sons had been allowed to remain in the Senate. The English ambassador to Venice Isaac Wake wrote, "Wee have a kind of civil warre betwixt this doge and one Renier Zen, a principall senator."[93] Zeno continued his attacks on the doge in the Greater Council. Then one night he was assaulted and gravely wounded. Corner's youngest son was found guilty of the crime and banished, but he took refuge in Ferrara under the protection of his cardinal brother. The papal ambassador was unhappy that the assassination attempt had not succeeded, writing, "If Zeno had been killed, there would not be half the uproar that runs through the city or the public resentment."[94]

Once recovered, Zeno staged a carefully choreographed return, traveling by gondola from his house in San Geremia to the Piazza. He entered San Marco, heard Mass, and then prostrated himself at the tomb of Saint Isidore. Recently, two merchants had secured Isidore's head from Chios. While many in the College were hesitant to reward the merchants for their sacred theft, Zeno supported the idea. Manipulation of the saints and their relics remained a useful tool for ambitious politicians. Once back in the Ten, Zeno made clear that he wanted the Greater Council to annul Corner's sons' ecclesiastical appointments.[95] In a preemptive strike, the Ten ordered Zeno's arrest. Finding that he had already fled, they banished him and placed a bounty on his head.

Zeno's supporters in the Greater Council fell back on the tactic used in 1583, refusing to fill vacancies to the Ten and Ducal Council. They elected one of Zeno's staunchest opponents to a minor post on an island near Crete, refusal of which would result in a fine, as a way of removing him from the city. At this point the rich nobles capitulated by agreeing in late August to appoint a committee of five correctors to oversee another reform of the Ten. The poorer nobles wanted the three heads of the criminal branch of the Council of Forty, which represented their interests, to be made members of the Ten and wanted as well for the powers of the Ten and its secretaries to be delimited. They disliked that the inquisitorial procedure had been extended to the Esecutori contro la Bestemmia and the Provveditori sopra Monasteri. However the rehabilitated Zeno's growing megalomania cost him support, and in the end the changes were modest and of little effect: the Esecutori, Provveditori sopra Monasteri, and the secretaries were to be elected by the Senate, not the Ten. The Ten would still hear cases involving nobles but could not annul laws passed by the Greater Council.

Twenty years earlier those nobles who wanted change and opposed papal power had achieved a great victory, one that did much to secure the image of the Venetian Republic in Old Regime Europe. By the 1590s the policies of the papacy and the Venetian government regarding the Inquisition and Index had diverged. What was at stake was the papacy's ability to intervene in other states' business and the independence of those states to manage their own affairs and protect their interests. In 1595 Paolo Paruta, who had recently returned from an ambassadorship to Rome, diagnosed the problem in his report to the Senate. He wrote, "The Roman pope can be considered in terms of the two persons he incorporates: that is, as head and universal pastor of all Christendom, and vicar of Christ and true successor of Peter in the Catholic and Apostolic Church; and then as a temporal prince who holds a state in Italy." He went on to note that "the popes have sometimes been accustomed to take up spiritual weapons even for differences over temporal things."[96]

Those "temporal things" were the source of many conflicts between the Republic and the papacy. One involved the Patriarchate of Aquileia. When Venice intervened in territory that was under the jurisdiction of the patriarch, claiming that it had conquered that territory in 1420, Patriarch Giovanni Grimani referred the question to Pope Gregory XIII who declared that he had the right to decide the matter. The issue was particularly sensitive for Venice since the Archdukes of Austria also had interests in the region. The papacy and Venice were also disputing claims to the town of Ceneda. Papal control of Ferrara (gatekeeper to the Po) and possible papal annexation of Urbino (a Venetian military recruitment ground) were much bigger points of contention, as were Adriatic navigation rights.[97] Jesuit-run schools and the openness of the University of Padua to non-conformist thought were also in dispute.

Two issues finally precipitated a showdown: clerical immunity from criminal prosecution by the state and the rapid growth of ecclesiastical property on the *terraferma*, which meant that significant amounts of land and tax revenue were escaping the Republic's control. In 1605 the Ten arrested two *terraferma* clerics for crimes including sexual misconduct and homicide. Paul V protested, saying that these men needed to be handed over to ecclesiastical courts. He also demanded the Republic rescind two recent laws forbidding the construction of churches, hospitals, and other charitable institutions and alienation of lands to ecclesiastics. If Venice failed to comply, he threatened to excommunicate members of the Senate and place Venice and its dominions under interdict. In the age of Counter Reform, the fundamental question behind the interdict was this: was it possible to be Catholic without being papist?[98]

Venice's response was rapid and unequivocal. After papalist doge Marino Grimani died on Christmas Day 1605, the Greater Council elected Leonardo Donà in early January.[99] The same month it elected Sarpi as the government's Consultant in Theology and Canon Law. Leading the Venetian charge were two men deeply opposed to the Counter Reformation church and committed to protecting the Republic from papal overreach. On April 17 the pope did as he had threatened, excommunicating the doge, Senate, and "their supporters and accomplices" and placing Venetian lands under interdict unless the government capitulated within twenty-four days.[100] Donà complained to the papal nuncio that the Republic was being "denigrated and vituperated in the Theater of the World which is the Roman Curia."[101] When the deadline passed, Venice responded by declaring the pope's action "null and of no value and thus invalid."[102] The Republic refused to publish the interdict and expelled those clergy, especially the Jesuits, who withheld the sacraments.

The showdown dragged on for nearly a year as Sarpi and the Venetians transformed a relatively technical dispute over jurisdiction into a debate over papal power. It took the form of a pamphlet war—"an all-out battle over political communication."[103] The Republic put tremendous pressure on the clergy to toe the party line and relied on public actions and rituals to bolster support among the urban populace. The patriarch of Venice continued to celebrate Mass and ordain clergy, Donà publicly attended divine services, and processions replete with floats created by the *scuole grandi* drove home the Venetian position. One float in the 1606 Corpus Christi procession depicted Christ and the Pharisees with the motto, "Render unto Caesar the things that are Caesar's and unto God the things that are God's." Another depicted a young Doge Donà being blessed by Saint Mark.[104] Adherence was much less pronounced on the *terraferma*. Venice feared that disagreement there might invite rebellion or invasion, especially from Philip III of Spain's Milan. Fortunately for Venice, the Austrian Hapsburgs, Philip's cousins, were not in a position at the time to get involved. Venice's strongest proponent among foreign powers was James I of England, who could offer little more than moral support from afar. Venetian ambassadors everywhere were instructed to make the Republic's case and emphasize that the pope's actions threatened every secular state. Donà explained to the Spanish ambassador that the goal of the pope was "to subordinate all princes to his power even in lay matters."[105]

Both France and Spain followed events closely, calculating how they might use them to increase their influence in Italy. When a Spanish attempt at mediation failed, Henry IV of France commissioned two French cardinals to find a resolution since the papacy and Venice were the two biggest obstacles to complete Spanish domination of the peninsula. It was not in France's interest to have them at odds. The interdict ended on April 21, 1607, with a diplomatic compromise in which neither side admitted error, and both claimed victory. Cardinal François de Joyeuse gave a quick blessing absolving the Republic (thereby allowing the pope to claim that Venice had repented), while Venice retained the laws about ecclesiastical property, continued to claim penal jurisdiction over the clergy, and refused to readmit the Jesuits, although it did hand over the two criminal clergy whose arrest had led to the crisis. While both sides could claim to have won, on balance the victory went to Venice, as papal claims to universalism were dealt a blow. It was the last time the papacy used interdict as a weapon. Nevertheless, the pope was not placated. When Sarpi survived a near-fatal knife attack just weeks after the interdict ended, he famously remarked that he recognized the "style" of the Roman curia, punning on the word "styletto." The would-be assassins fled to the Papal State.[106]

The Interdict of 1606-7 was more important for its impact than for its resolution of the technical issues that precipitated it. First, the Interdict Crisis undermined the image of Venice as an avaricious, predatory regime, a view of Venice and its policies that began with the Fourth Crusade, and replaced it with a view of Venice as a state that protected its own interests boldly. Second, it secured for the Republic a fundamental place in European discussions regarding sovereignty, a central concern to Old Regime monarchs who were still in the process of unifying and centralizing their states and negotiating the counterclaims and demands of representative assemblies. Sarpi, for one, brooked no limits on Venice's sovereignty, writing, "He who imposes laws and obligations on him [a prince] deprives him of the essence of a prince, even if he possesses the whole of Asia."[107] Venice's capacity to survive such onslaughts as the League of Cambrai, the Ottomans, and the interdict made it appear to many political writers that the Venetians possessed an almost unique political wisdom that rivaled or even superseded that of the ancients. Accordingly, much discussion focused on the qualities the Venetians cultivated that allowed them to maintain concord at home and peace overseas. The patricians were celebrated for their supposed civic mindedness and willingness to sacrifice for the state. The image of Venice as an aristocratic republic—a view congenial to elites throughout Europe—supplemented the idea of Venice as the model of a mixed constitution popularized by Contarini. Venice was thought to display flexibility and pragmatism that was much admired. Exemplary were the writings of official historiographer Paolo Paruta who argued that the Venetians' "great glory" lay not in the size of their territory but in "good governance of the city and true knowledge of themselves."[108] The interdict helped secure for Venice a fundamental place in "the political education of Europe" over the next 200 years.[109]

Yet the theoretical discussions of Venice and its constitution generated by the interdict obscure the nobility's failure in the aftermath of the interdict to redirect and revitalize Venetian republicanism. The crisis presented the government with a dilemma: on one hand, it sought to deny the interdict's very existence by prohibiting its publication; on the other, it needed to rally public support to its side. Communicating with the populace threatened the long-standing policy of secrecy, one of the keys to the nobility's monopoly on power. They believed that only they should be privy to the arcane rules of governance and secrets of state. But the news could not be contained and was discussed throughout the city, including in pharmacies and barbershops, and aided by cheap print. As one writer noted, "I hear plebeian men who discuss it [excommunication] with substance and in conformity with their intelligence and capacity."[110] Once the interdict ended, the government sought to stifle continued discussion. By resuming the policy of secrecy and the aristocratic monopoly on power, they failed to take advantage of a growing public sphere just as they had traditionally resisted opening the Greater Council to newcomers.[111] At the same time, the two corrections of the Ten failed to heal the rift between rich and poor patricians or truly foster ways to share governance more evenly.

Despite Doge Donà and his supporters' reputation as challengers of the status quo, their agenda was fundamentally conservative. To the pretensions of the Counter Reformation papacy, they offered not a program of renewal but rather continued adherence to Venice's long-standing formulation of church/state relations and local religious practices. During the interdict they were defending not just Venetian claims to sovereignty but also the "sacrality of the State" itself, epitomized by veneration of Mark and the Virgin and the city's vibrant confraternal piety.[112] In a moment ripe for change, Venetian aristocrats, *case vecchie* and *nuove*, *giovani* and *vecchi*, *papalisti* and not, opted for versions of the status quo. A century after the Portuguese circumnavigation of Africa and the defeat at Agnadello, the patriciate had settled into a conservatism—military, political, and economic—that would characterize the regime until the end of the Republic.

All the while the city's urban form continued to evolve. At midcentury, Cristoforo Sabbadino developed an ambitious town plan. He wanted to enlarge the city by extending land reclamation especially at the eastern reaches of Cannaregio and in Dorsoduro near Santa Marta, and by nearly doubling the Giudecca by increasing it to the south. These projects would create new land for housing, terminals for ferry traffic to the mainland, and an industrial zone on the Giudecca. Sabbadino also wanted to completely encircle the city with a wide embankment that would serve as a kind of ring road and build a bridge across the Grand Canal at Corpus Domini that would allow one to walk the city's entire circumference. The embankment would include thirty-six bridges over internal canals debouching into the lagoon. Finally, two large new canals running parallel to the city—one along its northern border, the other behind the Giudecca—would help increase the tidal flow and further cleanse the city. Only part of Sabbadino's plan was implemented in the early modern period, namely, the Fondamenta Nuove, the section of the exterior embankment on the city's northern border and the Zattere, on the southern one. More than anything else, the plan was designed to define the borders of city and lagoon, to delineate land and water. It was also in keeping with the synoptic vision that recognized the links between *terraferma* land reclamation projects, the hydrology of the lagoon, and the morphology of the city.[113]

Adding to the city's Roman veneer, the *papalisti* in particular built huge new family palaces on the Grand Canal: the Corners at San Maurizio and the Grimanis at San Luca. Doge Donà, by contrast, built his "sober and laconic" palace, the epitome of *mediocritas*, on the Fondamenta Nuove.[114] Palladio, a Paduan who cut his architectural teeth in Vicenza, never enjoyed in Venice the same success with secular commissions as Sansovino. He failed to win appointment as *proto*, the Republic's semi-official architect. He had more success with ecclesiastical projects, even designing the façade for Sansovino's Observant Franciscan church San Francesco della Vigna. If Sansovino redefined the Piazza and Piazzetta, Palladio bestowed grandeur on the Bacino by rebuilding the church of San Giorgio Maggiore.[115] The façade composed of two classical temple fronts, one superimposed on the other, reveal the church's interior configuration of a central nave and two side aisles. The dramatic use of Istrian stone with no voids to interrupt the whiteness gives the church a "luminosity" as it appears almost to float in the Bacino.[116]

FIGURE 14.5 Andrea Palladio, San Giorgio Maggiore, begun 1566, Venice. Photo by Wolfgang Moroder, distributed under a CC-BY 3.0 license via Wikimedia Commons.

The interior is suffused with light. Palladio wrote, "Of all the colors, none is more proper for churches than white, since the purity of the color, as of life itself, is particularly satisfying to God."[117]

In 1576 Palladio finally received a major state commission. In that year the Senate pledged 10,000 ducats for construction of a temple dedicated to Christ the Redeemer to serve as thanksgiving for ending the terrible plague that was ravaging the city. It further vowed that every year on the anniversary of the plague's cessation the doge would make a pilgrimage to the church. The Giudecca was chosen since the wide canal separating it from Venice proper created an appropriately arduous pilgrimage route, one that would be traversed annually via a bridge of boats specially assembled for the occasion. Situated facing the city, Santissimo Redentore, like San Giorgio Maggiore, deploys a series of superimposed temple fronts but, unlike the Benedictine church, the ones at the Redentore serve to conceal such building elements as the buttresses. The pediments seem almost to hoist in place the huge dome, surmounted by a statue of Christ the Redeemer. From a distance the church appears centrally planned as was conventional for pilgrimage churches, although it is, in fact, a Latin cross. The interior reflects how the architect had absorbed both the influence of ancient Roman architecture and the innovations of Donato Bramante. In the end, the church cost more than 60,000 ducats.[118]

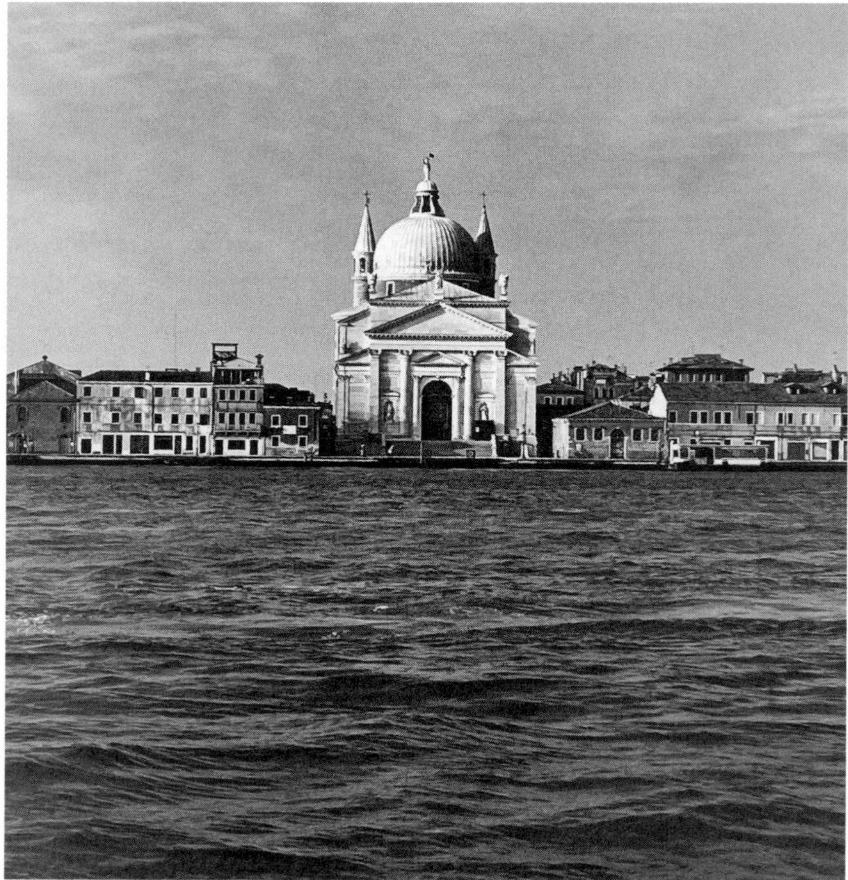

FIGURE 14.6 Andrea Palladio, Santissimo Redentore, begun 1577, Venice. Photo by the author.

A third building, the church for the maidens' hospital of the Zitelle begun in 1581, evidences a strong Palladian influence even if Palladio himself was only tangentially involved in its construction. The façade is flanked by the two wings of the hospital, all in Istrian stone. Facing the Piazza, the façade is notable for its large semi-circular thermal window, inspired by the windows of the baths (*termae*) of ancient Rome, while similar windows over the side chapels allowed the girls at the Zitelle to observe the divine services from behind grilles. Built on a centralized plan, the church is topped by a dome with a lantern and two domed towers.[119] The Zitelle, along with San Giorgio Maggiore and the Redentore, comprised Palladio's notable redefinition of the Bacino and Giudecca canal.

Palladio was unsuccessful, however, in realizing some of his other projects. His plan to rebuild the Ducal Palace in the classical style was rejected, as was his design, submitted in the mid-1550s, for the new Rialto Bridge. A design by Sansovino was chosen, although it failed to be realized. Finally, in 1588 the foundation for the new stone bridge to replace the wooden one was laid. The commission went to the Salt Office's appropriately named *proto*, Antonio da Ponte. Consisting of a single great arch, the new bridge was a masterpiece of engineering (and a costly one), while the incorporation of double rows of shops connected at the summit by arches maintained the bridge's traditional commercial function. The mounting of sculptures of the Archangel Gabriel and the Virgin on opposite sides of the span created a frisson as vessels passing under the bridge were intercepted by the angelic message launched across the Grand Canal at the very spot where legendarily, on the feast of the Annunciation, the city was founded.[120]

The Senate invoked Mary's protection and the city's Annunciation Day foundation when in October 1630 it again vowed to build a church—this one to be called Santa Maria della Salute (Holy Mary of Health and/or Salvation)—as a way of appeasing God's wrath and bringing an end to another outbreak of plague. The doge and Senate pledged, as they had when building the Redentore, to make an annual pilgrimage to the church on the anniversary of the day on which the city was declared plague-free, "in perpetual memory of the public gratitude for this great benefit."[121] They allocated 50,000 ducats to the project.

Native Venetian architect Baldassare Longhena won the competition to design and build the church. Its iconography seems to have begun as a statement of the *giovani*'s adherence to traditional Venetian religiosity with special emphasis on local saints, but as executed, the Salute soon fell in line with Counter Reformation church architecture and ornament, just as the *giovani* party itself faded away.[122] The site the government selected was a spectacular one, near the Customs House at the tip of Dorsoduro where the Grand and Giudecca Canals converge into the Bacino. The massive circular votive church that Longhena designed with its major and minor domes and twin bell towers required driving 1,156,627 wooden poles into the *caranto*.[123] The design drew inspiration from early Christian churches in Ravenna and Rome and also evoked elements of Byzantine architecture, including San Marco itself.[124] Longhena also incorporated Palladian features such as thermal windows on the lesser façades. The building committee's requirement, which Longhena fulfilled, that only the main altar be visible on entering the church and that the others be revealed as pilgrims circumambulated, endowed the

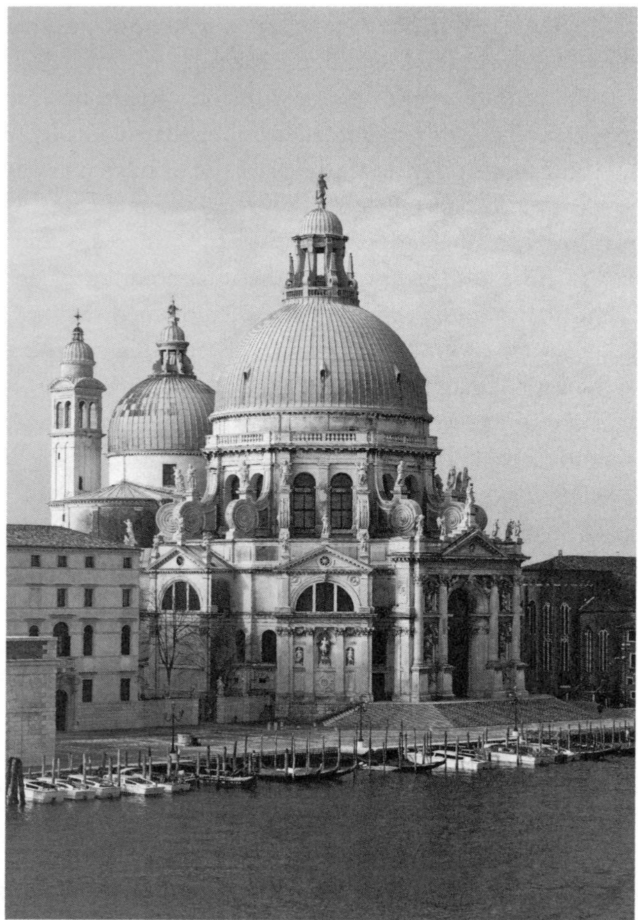

FIGURE 14.7 Baldassare Longhena, Santa Maria della Salute, begun 1631, Venice. Photo by Wolfgang Moroder, distributed under a CC-BY 3.0 license via Wikimedia Commons.

Salute with a theatrical quality.[125] The building also served to unify the monumental domed churches around the Bacino. It stands at the center of an imaginary semicircle with San Marco, San Giorgio, and the Redentore located at almost equal distances on the edges of the circle.[126] Atop the principal dome, Mary brandishes the baton wielded by captains general of the sea, while Mark on the lesser dome mans a rudder. Here at the confluence of waters, the Republic's heavenly protectors steer the ship of state.[127]

The cornerstone of the Salute was intended to be laid on Annunciation Day 1631, although it did not actually occur until April 1. This was to be yet another symbolic rebirth of the city. The effects of this refoundation, however, were more attenuated. Although Venice had managed to recover from the plague of the 1570s, after the 1630 epidemic, the economy failed to recover fully. Trade and manufacturing moved to other lands, and the city's clout in international affairs continued to diminish. The great age of Renaissance Venice had come to an end. For 250 years, from the end of the War of Chioggia in 1381 to the plague of 1630, not only had Venice continued to function as a major trade intermediary between East and West, but had also developed into a manufacturing powerhouse, as well as the capital of a large mainland and overseas empire. It became the leader in the new medium of print and home to an extraordinary school of painters. The inability to sustain those strengths into the seventeenth century and beyond has often been described, in keeping with the rise and fall narrative that has long dominated Venetian history, as a decline. Yet it is more accurate to say that Venice was finding new strengths and assuming new roles in Old Regime Europe.

PART III

Old Regime Venice

15

The Transformative Seventeenth Century

IN 1662 GIACOMO dell'Angelo's opera *Cleopatra* had its debut at the Teatro San Salvatore. In the prologue to this *dramma per musica*, as the still nascent musical genre was known, Jupiter addressed the topic of the Cretan war that had been raging between Venice and the Ottomans since 1645. He exclaimed,

> What's this? Will the furor of haughty, tempestuous Mars always triumph? And will the happy torch of peace never shine in the bosom of fair Adria? But what peace? What peace? To arms, rage on, Venetian heroes, against the wicked Ottoman. . . . Crete is mine, let that be enough. I have come down only to lend you my thunderbolts, and just as I struck the wicked giants with them, so do I mean to reduce the Thracians [Ottomans] to ashes.

Poetry tries to temper Jupiter's bellicosity, saying,

> Supreme mover, check your fury. Do not, no, do not disturb the serenity of the tranquil Venetian breast. . . . Behold the Venetian heroes collected in the fair circle of this new Theater, who await from our music sweet solace for their heavy thoughts.[1]

In 1662 hearts were indeed heavy since the War of Candia, as the Venetians called the war for Crete, would remain at an impasse until 1669 when they finally were forced to cede the island, their most precious overseas possession, after having held it for 450 years. Although they would stage one last heroic military venture, the reconquest of the Morea, in the 1680s, they would see that triumph come to naught in the 1718 Peace of Passarowitz. Thereafter Venice would be largely an Adriatic power, much as it had been in the earliest centuries of its existence. Yet there as well Venice faced a new challenger—Hapsburg Austria. Imperial Austria emerged over the course of the seventeenth century as the leading power on the Italian peninsula. Accordingly, Venice found its fate inextricably tied to Austria's—a situation that would persist until the city and its former mainland territory were incorporated into the newly unified Kingdom of Italy in 1866.

The reduction of Venice to an Adriatic power was just one of many changes that the city and Republic experienced during the seventeenth century. Transformation best describes the processes that marked the era commonly known as the Old Regime, spanning the seventeenth and eighteenth centuries but with elements that persisted until Venice became part of Italy. Adjustments occurred in virtually all aspects of life. For the first time since 1381 the nobility opened itself to new members. At the same time many nobles adopted the ethos and ethics, even the fashions, of the European aristocracy. Around 1670, following several decades of stagnation, Venetian manufacturing regained its footing, and the city and *terraferma* continued as important centers of industrial production. Much of this success came at the expense of male workers who saw avenues to guild advancement close, as female workers and immigrants who supplied cheaper labor kept Venetian manufactured products competitive.

Venice's image changed too. Although it continued to serve for some as the model republic, others saw it as the premier example of a secretive, oligarchic, even tyrannical regime. Venice came to be perceived as a libertine city, a place where sexual freedom, gambling, violence, and other predilections could be indulged. The habit of wearing masks for six months a year seemed to symbolize the ability to remain anonymous or shift one's identity in a world fixated on station and birth. Libertinism found its intellectual foundations in the free-thinking of the University of Padua, in essence Venice's state university, and in the city's flourishing academies. Several members of the Accademia degli Incogniti (Academy of the Unknowns) were involved in the evolution of the most innovative art form of the period—opera. As Poetry's admonition to Jupiter makes clear, opera was the medium that allowed seventeenth-century Venetians to process the changes taking place around them and, quite literally, give them voice. By contrast, painting stagnated as artists recycled the themes and styles of the great sixteenth-century triumvirate Titian, Veronese, and Tintoretto. But collecting and the art market flourished, as did writing about the Venetian school of painting. Architecture blossomed too.

Several churches were redesigned in the grand Baroque style of Longhena and others, while magnificent private palaces were built by noble families old and new. Although little land was reclaimed from the lagoon, the outfitting of squares with up-to-date church façades endowed the cityscape with a theatrical quality, as if these refurbished spaces were themselves stage sets for some *dramma per musica*. Venice itself was represented on the stage in the prologue to Vincenzo Nolfi's 1642 opera *Bellerofonte*, with set designs by Giacomo Torelli. As a model of the Piazzetta emerged from the sea, Innocence, Astrea (goddess of Justice), and Neptune intoned,

> City wise, rich and noble over any the world admires, Sparta, Athens, and Stagira are but a modest shadow of your greatness. Henceforth the ages to come will see Heaven, swollen with light, rush to your shores as a river to pay you tribute.[2]

As if gazing in a mirror, Venetian audiences saw themselves and their city reflected on the operatic stage. Little wonder then that opera became

FIGURE 15.1 Giovanni Giorgi, *Harbor in the City of Patera with a View of Venice, Prologue*, in *Il Belloferonte (1642)*, engraving. From Giacomo Torelli, *Apparati scenici per lo teatro Nuovissimo di Venetia* (Venice, 1644). Collection of the McNay Art Museum. Gift of the Tobin Endowment.

the medium through which they sought to make sense of their rapidly transforming world.

During most of the seventeenth century, Venice tried to adhere to its policy of armed neutrality as it steered a course between the Hapsburgs and France, a rivalry that took on new life with the rise of the French Bourbon dynasty and touched on territories bordering the Republic. Venice did side with France when the Spanish occupied the Valtelline, a mountainous region north of Bergamo providing a vital link between Spanish Milan and the Holy Roman Empire, until the two superpowers agreed to demilitarize the territory. The Venetians again allied with France during the War of Mantuan Succession (1628–31). France won the peace that secured Mantua for the French claimant to the duchy, thereby giving the Bourbons an indirect foothold in northern Italy. Otherwise, Venice played virtually no part in the Thirty Years War that ended in 1648 with the Peace of Westphalia, a settlement that signaled France's European ascendancy.

Venice's focus for the rest of the century was on the Ottomans and their challenge to its possessions in the eastern Mediterranean, the Ionian Sea, and Dalmatia.[3] This eventually drew Venice and Austria closer due to their common threat from the Ottomans, while, for his part, Louis XIV allied at times with the Ottomans as a way of hassling his Hapsburgs rivals. The grueling War of Candia (1645–69) was precipitated when in 1644 the Maltese attacked a ship carrying members of the sultan's harem returning from a pilgrimage to Mecca that had taken refuge on Crete during a storm. This incident offered the Ottomans the casus belli they needed to attack the island, the last major impediment to their complete control of the sea lanes linking Constantinople, Syria, and Egypt. In June 1645 the Ottomans assailed Chania, which they captured by mid-July. By the end of the following year, they had taken most of Crete except for Sitia, the islands of Spinalonga and Gramvousa at Crete's eastern and western extremes, and Venice's capital at Candia. One reason for the Ottoman success was the feeble resistance mounted by Cretan locals who resented Venice's corrupt administration and subordination of the Orthodox faith.[4]

The Ionian Sea and Dalmatia constituted a second war theater. Fearing an Ottoman advance up the Adriatic, Venice went so far as to bolster its defenses on the Lido and in Friuli. The war went much better in this arena because Venice's naval might, strong fortifications, local militias, and, unlike on Crete, a local population favorable to Venetian rule made it possible to defend the

FIGURE 15.2 Italy and the Western Balkans c. 1700

thin strip of land along the coast that constituted the Republic's dominions. In 1648 Venice conquered Clissa (Klis), which was vital to protecting Spalato.

With most of Crete in Ottoman hands, the war settled into a grueling siege of Candia, which meant that the Aegean became a third theater of war. Venice had to resupply the beleaguered city by sea and at the same time disrupt Ottoman communication with the island. To this end, the Venetian navy tried to keep the enemy fleet bottled up in the Dardanelles and even sought, in 1657, to launch an assault on Constantinople itself. Its navy scored some stunning victories but to no avail. Both sides were intransigent. For Venice, control of Crete was a matter of pride and prestige, not just economic interest. Legally the island was considered a *regno* or kingdom, possession of which placed Venice among the crowned heads of Europe.[5] When in 1658 the Venetians rejected a peace proposal that would have required them to give up Crete, the government wrote to its secretary Giovanni Battista Ballarino in Constantinople stating that to do so would be to repudiate "the obligation we have to God, natural reason, [and] regard for religion; nor certainly can we abandon the most ancient and most just possession that we hold."[6] For their part, the Ottomans chafed at Venice's refusal to surrender. When Alvise Contarini was dispatched in 1649 to congratulate Sultan Mehmet IV on his ascension to the throne and the Ottomans learned that he was not coming to cede Clissa and Crete, they refused his passport, strangled his interpreter, and jailed the *bailo* Giovanni Soranzo and secretary Ballarino.[7] Prison awaited nobleman Giovanni Capello too when he went to Constantinople in 1653 to negotiate peace.[8]

Venice had few allies. The Dutch, English, and French were unwilling to jeopardize their growing commercial ties with the Ottoman Levant. Beginning in 1657 Pope Alexander VII did provide some modest assistance in Crete and Dalmatia once the Venetians agreed to readmit the Jesuits, who had been expelled during the interdict. But the Ottomans had problems too since they found themselves fighting on several fronts. They had to defend against the Hapsburgs and the Kingdom of Poland in far-flung borderlands including Transylvania, Wallachia, and Moldavia, and against Muscovy in the Crimean Khanate and the Cossack Sech.[9] In 1660, France did an about-face and sent money and troops to help Venice, but that expedition too came to naught, as did Venetian proposals that Crete be divided between the two contenders. In 1665 the Holy Roman Empire and the Ottomans signed an accord after an Ottoman thrust toward Vienna was repelled near Graz in July 1664, bringing peace to Hungary.

By 1667, after twenty-two years of conflict, the war neared its denouement. The Ottoman grand vizir Ahmed Koprulu sent 70,000 troops to prepare a final siege of Candia, which was heavily fortified and defended by 6,000 Venetian troops and 400 cannons. Francesco Morosini was installed as Venice's captain general of the sea. As the attention of Europe focused on the struggle—cast as yet another crusade—various rulers and entities, including the Duke of Savoy, the pope, and the Knights of Malta, offered Venice some modest support of money, troops, and ships. Louis XIV allowed French nobles who were anxious for, as Marcantonio Giustinian wrote from Paris in 1668, "heroic actions" to come to Candia's aid.[10] The Ottoman besiegers made various assaults on the town, using tunnels and mines to weaken its massive defenses. From May to November 1667 alone the Ottomans made thirty-two different attempts and exploded more than 600 mines. Venetian losses in that period numbered 3,200 fighters, Ottoman ones a staggering 20,000.[11] But infighting among the allies hampered the defense, and the French troops departed after their last unsuccessful sortie. The Maltese left as well.

By August 1669, Morosini concluded that surrender was his only option. He negotiated the treaty without authorization from the home government, and under the circumstances, the terms was surprisingly lenient. The defenders were able to depart Candia with more than 300 cannons and other munitions, saints' relics (among them Saint Titus's head), and other sacred objects, including an icon of the Virgin, the Panagia Mesopanditissa (Mediator of All), which was incorporated into the high altar of the Salute. Venice was even able to retain Suoda, Gramvousa, and Spinalonga as resupply stations for its merchant fleet, along with its conquests in Dalmatia including Clissa. So concluded a war that cost Venice thousands of lives, among them those of 280 nobles, and millions of ducats. When Morosini returned to Venice, he was put on trial for exceeding his authority in arranging the surrender but was acquitted. One of his defenders noted that Candia had become a veritable Hell with an "unceasing vomiting of fire" and that, even though the island had in the end been lost, the Venetians had won for themselves "the most celebrated glory that fame had ever announced with its sonorous trumpet."[12]

Morosini was also the chief protagonist in Venice's next conflict with the Ottomans, known as the First War of the Morea, which has been described as Venice's "last colonial adventure."[13] When in 1683 the Ottomans pushed toward Vienna, Venice remained neutral. A year later Venice joined the anti-Ottoman league formed by Austria that included the pope, Poland, and eventually Russia, all the while recognizing that Austrian gains might threaten its dominion of the Adriatic. Venice's astounding success in this war was due in no small measure to the Ottomans having to fight on a front that stretched from Poland to southern Greece. Venice's first action was to seize the island of Santa Maura in the Ionian Sea. Morosini then decided on a reconquest of the Morea which turned into a romp across the Peloponnesus as stronghold after stronghold fell into Venetian hands until the troops crossed the isthmus at Corinth and settled into a siege of Athens. Most of the city was taken, although Ottoman troops held out on the Acropolis. Then, in one of the darkest moments in history, a Venetian projectile went astray, hitting the Parthenon, which the Ottomans were using as a munitions depot, setting off a catastrophic explosion. Morosini is reputed to have exclaimed, "Oh Athens . . . how you are reduced."[14] On September 29, 1687, the Ottomans surrendered.

Once in possession of the mount, Morosini further contributed to its ruin. He attempted to remove a Neptune sculpture from the west pediment of the Parthenon and, perhaps in imitation of the Fourth Crusaders, "the reliefs of two most beautiful horses." But when his workmen tried to remove the works, "everything came crashing down from that extraordinary height," and he abandoned the enterprise. But he noted, "I have decided to take a lioness, done in beautiful fashion, although damaged in the head which, however, can be perfectly repaired with a similar piece of marble that I intend to send off with it."[15]

The Venetians settled into winter quarters before an anticipated spring assault on Negroponte. When Doge Marcantonio Giustinian died in March 1688, Morosini, whom the Senate had voted to commemorate with a bronze bust and honor with the sobriquet "the Peloponnesian," was elected in his place. Still, he remained on the warfront. Not since the Middle Ages had a doge personally commanded Venetian forces. At this point, however, the offensive stalled; Morosini's troops were unable to retake Negroponte. Louis XIV's thrust into the Palatinate gave the Ottomans a respite as Emperor Leopold I turned his attention to the west. After the 1689 campaign season proved unsuccessful, Morosini returned to Venice. Still the war sputtered along, with the Venetians unable to make much headway. An effort to retake Crete failed miserably. To regain the initiative, a reluctant Morosini was drafted by an overwhelming vote in the Greater Council to reassume command. The elderly hero died on January 6, 1694, while strengthening Venetian fortifications in the Morea. At the end of the year, a Venetian effort to take Chios also failed. The great Venetian counteroffensive had run out of steam.

By contrast, Leopold's league, commanded by Eugene of Savoy, won a massive victory over the Ottomans at Zenta in Serbia in September 1697, which paved the way for the Treaty of Carlowitz signed in January 1699. According to the treaty, Venice retained the Morea, the seven Ionian islands, the Cretan fortresses Suda and Spinalonga, the Aegean islands Aegina and Tinos, and other possessions in Dalmatia, Albania, and Montenegro. For the first time as well, the treaty made no mention of Venice paying tribute to the sultan for such possessions as Zante. Leopold secured Hungary as well as the parts of Transylvania, Croatia, and Slavonia that his troops had occupied. Venice fared well in the treaty, Austria better. Ominously for Venice, the emperor signed the peace even before the Republic gave its final approval.[16]

Venice celebrated its victory by redesigning the space in front of the fifteenth-century Arsenal gateway. A patio was created leading to the entrance and adorned with sculptures of Neptune and Mars, Justice and Plenty. The redesign also commemorated Morosini and his triumphs. The bronze flagpole base depicted him as Neptune, while the bronze doors sported his family coat of arms and various tokens of victory. The sculpted lioness seized from the Acropolis, along with two others Morosini had plundered in Greece, were installed to flank the expanded entryway. In its moment of accomplishment, the Republic rehearsed time-honored symbols of Venetian military and economic might and deployed lions to allude to Mark's continuing favor.[17]

The triumph, however, was short-lived. Within two years of Carlowitz, war broke out between Louis XIV and Austria over succession to the Spanish throne. According to the Peace of Utrecht (1713) that ended that conflict, Louis's grandson became king of Spain. Austria gained control of Milan and Mantua as well as Sardinia, and its claim to Naples was recognized. At the same time Russia was stirring up rebellion against the Ottomans among Balkan adherents of the Greek Orthodox faith. After a rebel leader took refuge in Venetian-held Cattaro, the Ottomans declared war on Venice in December 1714. So began the Second War of the Morea (1714–8). This time it was the Ottomans' turn to romp across the peninsula. In just over three months, the entire Morea was lost, along with Tinos in the Aegean, Cerigo and Cerigotto strategically located between the Morea and Crete, and Suda and Spinalonga on Crete itself. The Ottoman success alarmed both Austria and Pope Clement XI, who managed to cobble together an anti-Ottoman league.

In July 1716 a huge Ottoman force under the command of pasha Djanum Khoja Mehemed set its sights on Corfu. If he could seize it, the Ottoman fleet could navigate up the Adriatic and attack Austria from the rear. But a month later, imperial forces under Eugene of Savoy scored a major victory at Petrovaradin and then took Belgrade. When news of that victory reached the besiegers on Corfu, they lost heart, and Venetian forces under the command of Matthias Johannes von Schulenburg were able to expel them from the island. In the peace treaty that followed at Passarowitz in July 1718, Venice lost the Morea, Tinos, and Aegina, but retained its possessions in Dalmatia, Albania, and the Ionian islands, including Santa Maura. It was a humiliating defeat for Venice. For their part, the Austrians got the banat of Temesvar (a military province that straddled present-day Romania, eastern Serbia, and southeastern Hungary), western portions of Wallachia and Serbia, and northern Bosnia. Just a month later, the anti-Ottoman league that had been orchestrated by Clement XI fell apart when Philip V of Spain set his sights on Sicily. In the peace worked out in 1720, he had to cede Sicily to Austria; the Duke of Savoy gained Sardinia and with it a royal title. Austria had grown in strength and had more reason than ever to challenge Venetian control of the Adriatic. According to Carlo Ruzzini, one of Venice's most distinguished diplomats, the growing influence of Austria and Savoy on the Italian peninsula constituted great "novelties" from which might arise "new conjunctures [that will] render them [Austria and Savoy] greater yet."[18] These words proved prophetic.

One constitutional consequence of the First War of the Morea was yet another restriction on ducal power. After Morosini's death, revisions to the ducal oath of office made it difficult for doges personally to command troops. But efforts at ducal aggrandizement by the great families that competed for the office continued. Morosini's successor, Silvestro Valier, had his wife Elisabetta Querini crowned dogaressa, even though a 1640s law had abolished the practice. And in July 1700 a law forbade outgoing dogaresse from wearing their crown (modeled after the ducal *corno*) or receiving ambassadors during ducal interregna.[19] There were further technical "corrections" to the power of the Ten in the second half of the century that were designed to rein in its power, but that had the effect of increasing the influence of the State Inquisitors.[20]

Like previous conflicts, the wars played havoc with Venice's finances. Between 1641 and 1679, the state debt increased sixfold to more than 46 million ducats. In 1668 alone, the defense of Candia cost 4,392,000 ducats.[21] Various time-honored methods were deployed to raise money: taxes and duties were raised; offices put up for sale; and early admissions to the Greater Council granted in return for cash payments. The desperate need for funds led to the momentous decision to open the ranks of the Greater Council to newcomers. The way this happened shows the nobility's reluctance to take this fateful step. It began when news spread that certain non-noble families were each willing to pay 60,000 ducats (enough to subsidize 1,000 infantry) in return for entry into the Council. A Senate proposal to admit five families under these terms failed, and the decision was left to the Greater Council, where the bill was introduced on March 4, 1646.[22]

The proposal sparked a vigorous debate, with Giacomo Marcello speaking in favor, Angelo Michiel against. Marcello argued that losing the maritime empire on account of financial considerations would lead to a decline in Venetian prestige. He also worried how those rich citizens who sought membership would react if the bill failed. Even though he supported the idea, he still distinguished between those who were born noble and those who earned admission due to special circumstances. For his part, Michiel rejected the proposal on grounds that true nobility was based on birth, not lucre. "One can never be noble by force of gold," he declaimed, "who was not born of good blood, and does not acquire it [nobility] with fine and brave deeds." The arguments echoed the fifteenth-century debate between Venetian Lauro Querini and Florentine Poggio Bracciolini over whether nature or nurture constituted nobility, although the dispute had moved within the Venetian nobility. Michiel further argued that the war's territorial losses were nothing compared to the damage that Venice—what he called "this unstained Virgin"—would suffer were it to prostitute itself by selling privileges of nobility. He feared that Venice would lose face with the other European nobility. Yet his position too was ambiguous since he seemed to hold out the possibility that men of courage and virtue might somehow earn nobility. Michiel carried the day. The Greater Council rejected the bill with 366 votes in favor, 528 opposed, and 140 abstentions.[23]

In June 1646 the logjam broke when Giovanni Francesco Labia, a rich *cittadino* merchant who had been lobbying for the admission of a few wealthy families, offered 100,000 ducats: 60,000 in cash, 40,000 in Mint deposits. He was admitted by a *grazia* or special bill. This became the procedure by which seventy-five families were admitted to the nobility between 1646 and 1669. Relying on *grazie* indicates just how reluctant the nobility was to open its ranks.[24] It never approved a blanket bill authorizing new admissions; rather, each candidate was judged on a case-by-case basis. The need for cash during the First War of the Morea led to forty further admissions between 1684 and 1704 and a few more in 1717–8 during the Second War of the Morea.

Who were the admittees? Of the seventy-five War of Candia entrants, seventeen were *terraferma* nobles, fourteen chancery secretaries, four lawyers, and forty-one wealthy merchants. *Terraferma* nobles and secretaries were the easiest for established nobles to accept because the former had ancient pedigrees and centuries of living nobly, the latter because they were already an integral part of the government with long-standing ties to the nobility. Some rich merchants, like the Widmanns (metal merchants originally from Augsburg) and the Bergonzis (silk merchants), had been orchestrating their social advancement for years via business contacts and other links to the nobles and careers in the church.[25] Others, like the Zolios, pork butchers from Verona, the Contentis, and Riccis, felt the sting of snobbery. The Contentis were described as having made the leap "from the counter of their own shop to the hall of the Greater Council."[26] One anonymous writer asked, "What type of manners do we believe they [the new entrants] have brought with them, the majority of whom were workers in the guilds [and] shops, oil dealers and merchants of vile trades?"[27]

Not all admittees jumped at the opportunity to join. The Ottobonis, a *cittadino originario* family, are a case in point. As grand chancellor Marco Ottoboni had reached the pinnacle of success; his son Marcantonio was a Senate secretary, two other sons were running the family villa, and another, Pietro, had embarked on an ecclesiastical career that would culminate with his election as Pope Alexander VIII in 1689. When the Ottobonis learned in 1645 that the Labias, Widmanns, and others had put out feelers about admission, they concluded that it would be a "great dishonor" for them not to seek it too since this would be taken as a sign of "hatred toward the Prince, baseness of spirit due to avarice, and demerit for the family which does not wish to be aggregated."[28] But they also knew that assembling the cash would be difficult, and it led to conflict among the brothers. In the end the Ottobonis put themselves forward and were approved by a vote of 923 to 39 with 6 abstentions.[29] Marco had to renounce the grand chancellorship but got the government to agree to pay for his eventual funeral. Peer pressure as much as anything led the Ottobonis to advance their case for admission, while the divisions that their aggregation caused within the family illustrate the sometimes-fraught internal workings of *fraternas*.

New families complicated the already complex dynamic within the nobility. The anonymous author of the 1669 treatise *Della nobiltà veneta* (On Venetian Nobility) divided the patriciate into six categories: twenty-four "old" families connected to the city's origins; "new" families who, in spite of the label, could trace their nobility back 700 or 800 years; the "newest" families that were added in 1381 at the end of the War of Chioggia; the Greeks, that is Venetian nobles who had been resident on Crete but returned to the city when that island fell; those who had been awarded membership as an honor; and the newly aggregated.[30] How these various groups interacted and allied varied. Some rich and distinguished nobles would have nothing to do with the inductees. In her 1688 will Cecilia Corner stated that she wanted her daughter to marry someone from a "*casa grande* and not one of those made gentlemen by means of money."[31] Other old families willingly married their sons to inductees' daughters in exchange for dowries often worth tens of thousands of ducats. It is estimated that between 1646 and 1684, 11 million ducats were transferred from the admittees to state coffers and old patrician families.[32] Nevertheless, the new men found themselves excluded from the most prestigious and important governmental offices until they started to align with the "Greeks" and poor nobles to gain election to such councils as the Forty, which included the right to sit in the Senate ex officio. At that point, the rich nobles started to peel away some of the richest new men by seeing that they got elected to castellanies and other posts.[33]

In a letter Antonio Ottoboni wrote to his son Pietro instructing him how to navigate Venetian politics, he divided the nobility into three groups: the great, the middling, and the lowly. The great, he warned Pietro, would be hostile to him because he was equal to them in wealth, the middling envious of his riches, the lowly obliged to "beg for his vote" in their quest for offices with stipends. Under the circumstances, Pietro would need to exhibit "a perpetual reverence toward the great, an affable familiarity with the middling, and a loving brotherliness toward the lowly." He would have to "render himself gracious to everyone."[34]

While the need for money was the explicit motive for opening the nobility, the declining number of nobles was the implicit one since it became increasingly difficult to fill all governmental posts. The demographic drop was notable. Whereas there had been 2,520 noblemen in 1550, by 1645 their number had declined to 1,620. The new admissions raised the total to 1,710 in 1719 but a precipitous decline followed. When the Republic ended in 1797, there were only 1,090 noblemen.[35] The new members only temporarily stemmed the demographic plunge. Of the 130 or so new families admitted between 1646 and 1718, fully thirty-seven had gone extinct by 1775, among them the Ottobonis.[36]

The family strategies of preserving wealth primarily by limiting marriages and entailing property gained greater momentum in the seventeenth century. In the sixteenth century 82 percent of only sons married; in the seventeenth century 65.3 percent did.[37] This was a recipe for family extinction. Often the unmarried were destined for the church. But rich noble families monopolized the greatest church offices; one estimate suggests that 95 percent of the richest bishoprics in the Republic's lands were held by patricians.[38] Many women, noble and otherwise, suffered the fate of being unwanted, unloved, and uneducated. A notable exception was Elena Corner Piscopia, child prodigy and illegitimate daughter of Gianbattista Corner Piscopia. Given the label Oraculum septilingue (Seven Language Oracle), Corner Piscopia studied at the University of Padua and became the first woman to receive a university degree.[39]

The poorest noble families suffered the most. Not only were they unable to contract marriages, but they also had to compete against one another for meager-paying governmental jobs. Many had incomes considerably below 100 ducats a year, less than some artisans. This was true of nearly a quarter of the nobles in the *sestiere* of Dorsoduro, who became known as the Barnabotti, after the parish of San Barnaba where many of them lived.[40] Many resorted to selling their votes since "noble poverty and corruption traveled in convoy."[41] In 1619 the government established the Academy of Nobles on the Giudecca to educate noble boys whose parents paid less than 20 ducats in the *decima*. They were to be taught reading, writing, and arithmetic and prepared for careers in the government or navy. A similar academy was established in Padua. In a speech given at its inauguration, Baldassare Bonifaccio exhorted the attendees, saying, "It is true that you are born to command . . . only the common virtues are required of the people; but heroic virtues are demanded of you, who are the sons of heroes."[42] The Paduan academy closed in 1642, and it is unclear how successful the Venetian one was in fulfilling its mission.

The opening of the Greater Council thus highlighted and exacerbated the festering division between the rich powerful nobles and the rank and file. A decade before the War of Candia even started, a sumptuary law had been enacted that restricted the use of robes with wide sleeves to the highest officeholders, while other nobles had to wear tight sleeves.[43] For the less powerful, such outward signs of difference galled. Then late in the century, seasoned politician, diplomat, and official historiographer Giovanni Battista Nani went so far as to claim that while nobles were equal in status, they were not in rank or office. He declared, "Among us we are all treated as equals, and with equal titles: 'Sir such and such' and 'Sir such and such'; but one is referred to as 'Councilor,' another as a member of the Council of Ten."[44] Among the richest and most powerful families, special emphasis was placed on noble blood, as Michiel's speech against aggregation made clear. At mid-century Francesco Pisani went so far as to say that the patriciate included thirty "princes of the blood" (a term redolent of royalty) and 100 or so gentlemen, while "all the rest are plebs."[45] The various schemes for making distinctions among the nobility (the six ranks of *Della nobiltà veneta*, the three grades of Ottoboni's letter, Pisani's princes of the blood, gentlemen, and plebs) indicate that the theoretical equality that had once fostered patrician solidarity and cohesion was in the past.

Noble lifestyle and values were also changing as the merchant patriciate of the Renaissance evolved into an aristocracy, as they increasingly entailed property and passed several months at their mainland villas. This is also apparent in increased emphasis on military service, which had long been a characteristic of the European aristocracy. For Venetian nobles this meant the navy, where captaining a ship became a way for men of rich noble families to exhibit their natural superiority, fitness for command, and heroism. For poor nobles and newly aggregated ones, military service was a vehicle of social acceptance.[46] The Ottoman wars are replete with examples of extraordinary valor. To take one example, in 1657 Captain General Lazzaro Mocenigo pursued an Ottoman fleet up the Dardanelles. Suddenly an onshore cannon hit the powder store on Mocenigo's ship, setting off an explosion that caused one of the masts to topple and kill him. The assault ended as the other ships in his squadron scrambled to recover the flag, lantern, papers, cash, and body of the captain general from the burning vessel. As Giovan Battista Nani wrote of Mocenigo in his 1688 *Historia della Repubblica Veneta* (History of the Venetian Republic), "He believed that everything ceded in the face of courage, nature obeyed, and fortune itself lent a hand to strong men."[47]

Noblemen reveled in their sacrifices for the state and were fulsome in their self-glorification. Carlo Pisani wrote in 1694, "After I had the happy chance to risk my life in the most dangerous attack on Valona . . . I tried on many occasions to demonstrate the qualities of a devout and loyal citizen." In 1698 he was still eager for opportunities to acquire for himself, "even at the cost of blood, the glory of public gratitude."[48] Antonio Barbaro, who had a mixed record of military service, chose to commemorate his deeds in stone. He bequeathed 30,000 ducats for the reworking of the façade of Santa Maria Zobenigo (also known as Santa Maria del Giglio) by the architect Giuseppe Sardi, as a monument to himself and his brothers. Barbaro stands in full armor above the portal and below a giant version of the family coat of arms accompanied by figures of Fame, Honor, Virtue, and Wisdom. Statues of his four brothers dressed in robes denoting their offices fill the niches on the ground floor. Reliefs of naval battles grace the bases of the upper columns, depictions of fortified towns under Venetian possession fill the lower ones. The façade was intended to commemorate Barbaro for posterity, a task made even more important since neither he nor his brothers produced any male heirs, and this branch of the family died with them.[49]

Lavish spending on churches and family palaces came to be viewed as a service to the Republic and represented a further renunciation of the old ideal of republican modesty. Santa Maria di Nazareth (commonly known as the Scalzi) was designed by Longhena and patronized by Benedetto Soranzo, although the façade was the work of Giuseppe Sardi and financed by newly aggregated nobleman Girolamo Cavazza. The extravagant church of San Moisè was bankrolled by the Venetian Cypriot Fini family, while bequests by

FIGURE 15.3 Giuseppe Sardi, Façade of Santa Maria Zobenigo (or del Giglio), begun 1678, Venice. Francesco Turio Böhm, Venice.

merchant Jacopo Galli paid for completion of the façades of San Salvador and San Teodoro.[50] Longhena also designed palaces for a number of families, including the Widmanns, Bellonis, Basadonnas, Bons, and Pesaros. Ca' Pesaro, commissioned by future doge Giovanni Pesaro, was particularly lavish with its Grand Canal façade notable especially for its diamond-shape rustication on the ground floor and free-standing columns on the *piano nobile*. The palace Longhena designed for the Bon family was not finished before his death, but in 1712 the building was acquired by the aggregated noble Rezzonico family and finished by architect Giorgio Massari.[51] These architectural projects embellished the city and honored the families that patronized them.

In its effort to raise money for the War of Candia the government also began selling fiefs with signorial and jurisdictional rights. Most of these were purchased by new nobles like Giovanni Francesco Labia who, just two years after buying his way into the nobility for 100,000 ducats, acquired the fiefdom of Frattesina in the Polesine for 180,000 ducats, or the Giovanellis, merchants originally from Bergamo who bought a fief at Morengo that conveyed the title of count.[52] The new nobles were buying status, acquiring in one fell swoop the patina of antiquity and prestige. Older patrician families did not participate in this fiefdom rush since many of them, such as the Corners at Asolo and Foscaris at Zellarino, already enjoyed feudal rights. Beginning in 1586 the government tried to gain greater control over its feudatories by establishing the Provveditori sopra Feudi (Commissioners of Fiefs) who were charged with monitoring feudal rights and requiring pledges of loyalty since these private jurisdictions impinged on the state's sovereignty.[53]

Less serious but no less telling were other indicators of the status stampede. One was title inflation, which was not confined to the nobility. Opera librettist Giovan Francesco Busenello wrote a satirical poem in which he noted that *cittadini* wanted to be addressed as "Most Illustrious," merchants as "Most Renowned," even porters as "Magnificent Signor."[54] Another was men's adoption of French fashion, namely, the frockcoat, waistcoat, breeches, and silk stockings. This ensemble replaced the ankle-length toga that had long served as the nobles' uniform.[55]

A less savory side of the new noble lifestyle was a penchant for violence. It was particularly pronounced among *terraferma* nobles, so much so that the Sindici Inquisitori in *Terraferma* (Auditor Inquisitors on the *Terraferma*) were responsible for prosecuting noble malefactors and bandits, the plague of the mainland.[56] In Venice itself, noblemen utilized *bravi* (hired thugs) who accompanied and aided them in the deployment of violence to indulge their passions. This was primarily a phenomenon among younger noblemen who chose to distance themselves from respectable society and the political hierarchy. *Bravi*, like prostitutes, sold and gave themselves "over to the will of another."[57] Nobles who employed *bravi* tended to be the politically marginal, and for them violence, often aimed at women, itself became a form of power. Generally, poorer nobles did not employ *bravi* for the simple reason that they could not afford them. Yet for a subset of the nobility, violence, extortion, and sexual aggression became a way of life.

Bravi were just one of many phenomena that contributed to the reputation of seventeenth-century Venice as a libertine city. On one hand, libertinism meant a propensity for indulging the appetites, and engaging in licentiousness, frivolity, and wastefulness. On the other, it represented freedom, broke down social barriers, allowed for the free exchange of ideas, and fostered new institutions and art forms.

Sexual adventuring was one manifestation of Venetian libertinism. Although the city had long been famous for its courtesans, this became more pronounced in the Old Regime. The ubiquity of prostitution was widely remarked by upper-class visitors, who were partly drawn to the city for its sexual undercurrents. Homosexual and pederastic impulses were also indulged, as was a celebration of all things obscene. In 1650 Antonio Rocco, a Benedictine monk who studied at the University of Padua and lectured on moral philosophy in Venice, published his novella *Alcibiade fanciullo a scuola* (The Schoolboy Alcibiades). In his novella, modeled on a Socratic dialogue, the tutor Filotimo uses a variety of arguments to convince his student Alcibiades to surrender to his sexual importuning.[58] In the preface to his libretto for the opera *Alcibiade* of 1680, Aurelio Aureli offered an unconvincing justification for the ribaldry of the work, when he wrote, "You will enjoy a few lascivious though restrained actions, composed by me with the sole aim that you learn to shun them, and not to imitate them."[59]

One of the men who denounced Rocco to the Inquisition reported that he and others often gambled at Rocco's home in San Moisè. Gambling was a major pastime in Old Regime Venice and another manifestation of its freewheeling style. Most betting involved card games, although bookmakers at Rialto specialized in wagers on elections. Gaming took place in private homes, public gambling parlors called *ridotti*, social clubs also referred to as *ridotti* or by a new term *casinò*, and even in boats. In these venues, fortunes were won and lost. Gambling was sometimes accompanied by drunkenness, prostitution, and violence. Since gambling debts were illegal, creditors might resort to force to collect what they were owed. In 1628 the Senate complained to the Ten that the *ridotti* precipitated "grave losses, the deviation and ruin of the young and families, incredible disturbances of houses, property, [and] good manners, with a too evident risk of scandals."[60] Partly to gain greater control of the situation, certain *ridotti*, like one at San Moisè, eventually received official sanction.

Gambling was seen as a test of character. Admired was the nobleman who showed self-restraint as he watched thousands of ducats vanish with a poorly played hand. In an age given to excess and conspicuous display, what better way to display stoic indifference than by wasting a fortune? France's ambassador wrote of the *ridotti*, "To see in how much tranquility and gravity very considerable sums are lost is really so very extraordinary, that one would almost think this is a school to learn the art of behaving one's self with moderation in the alternatives of fortune."[61] Reputations, not just patrimonies, were won and lost in the *ridotti*.

Gambling parlors were also where noblemen made connections and socialized. But *ridotti* were neither exclusively noble nor male. Here nobles and commoners, Venetians and foreigners, Christians and Jews, men and women came together.[62] One factor that made such mixing possible was mask wearing. Noblemen wore a long black cape known as the *tabaro*, while shielding their faces with a white mask called the *bauta*. Some women adopted a smaller black mask known as the *moretta*, that was held in place by clenching it with the teeth. Masking soon became the norm in Venice, worn by all social classes. Masks created an atmosphere of plausible deniability and anonymity, although contemporary testimony indicates that people knew exactly who was

FIGURE 15.4 Giuseppe de Gobbis, *The Ridotto*, c. 1760, oil on canvas. The San Diego Museum of Art, Gift of Anne R. and Amy Putnam and commemorating the Silver Jubilee Celebration of the Fine Arts Society. www.sdmart.org. There are several versions of this painting. This one is attributed to Pietro Longhi's principal assistant. It captures the highly charged atmosphere in casinos.

who. Under these circumstances a nobleman could accept with aplomb losses to his social inferiors. Masks also allowed men of high station who had fallen on hard times to save face while begging.[63] Rather than upending the social hierarchy, the *tabaro* and *bauta* protected the dignity of noblemen and the aura of modesty associated with noblewomen.

All these elements of Venetian libertinism came together, especially in foreigners' eyes, in Carnival. Antonio Persio, a supporter of the pope during the 1607 interdict, went so far as to refer to the Venetians (*Venetiani*) as Venutians (*Veneriani*) [followers of Venus]. Meant as an indictment, his comment was an unintended acknowledgment of Venice's long-standing association with the Goddess of Love.[64] Carnival attracted throngs of foreign visitors drawn to balls, masquerades, *commedia dell'arte* performances, bull-baitings, acrobatics, high-wire feats, fireworks, and, of course, prostitution and gaming. Yet governmental surveillance and denunciation of those who went too far kept Carnival excess within limits. Even so, later moralizers often condemned the frivolity of Carnival as both a symptom and a cause of the Republic's demise.[65]

Yet such condemnations missed Venetian libertinism's other elements. It was associated with freedom of thought and immunity from the rigorous censorship and reach of the Roman Church, made easier by the expulsion (until 1657) of the Jesuits from the Republic's lands. The pursuit of pleasure actually "served to heighten the Republic's reputation for unmatched freedom and political wisdom."[66] Libertinism meant liberty.

In the 1590s the University of Padua was home to two influential professors: Galileo Galilei and Cesare Cremonini. As a professor of mathematics, Galileo advocated observation and scientific experimentation, while as a professor of moral philosophy, Cremonini pursued Aristotelianism to its logical limits. Their rivals were the faculty at Padua's alternative school, the Jesuit College, who practiced the brand of Aristotelianism pioneered by Thomas Aquinas in the thirteenth century, which was concerned primarily with reconciling Aristotle's philosophy with Christian theology. From the church's point of view, it was Cremonini, not Galileo, who posed the greater threat since he denied the soul's immortality. For him, body and soul were inextricably linked. Physical desires were natural and could be pursued without fear of God's wrath since on the death of the body, the soul too expired. The philosopher reportedly composed an epitaph for himself that epitomized his view: "Hic iacet totius Cremonini" (Here lies all of Cremonini).[67] Galileo and Cremonini were founding members in 1599 of the Accademia dei

Ricoverati, which served to diffuse their brand of philosophical skepticism to many leading Venetians and Paduans.

Cremonini's philosophical libertinism found its greatest institutional support in the Accademia degli Incogniti, founded in 1630 by powerful nobleman Giovanni Francesco Loredan. Academies had by this time become an important element of intellectual and social life throughout Italy, including Venice and its dominions, and even in minor urban centers. They often adopted fanciful names (the Aspirants of Conegliano, the Unanimous of Salò), devised emblems, and drafted elaborate rules, creating micro-republics. Emphasis was placed on the art of conversation as members discussed and wrote on a range of topics both serious and frivolous, with particular stress on verbal agility and improvisation. Prized was the ability to argue any side of an argument—a trait that inculcated an attitude of questioning and skepticism. Some academies sponsored theatrical productions or concerts. The Filarmonici of Verona gathered weekly to make music. Few were dedicated to scientific inquiry. The Immobili (Unmoved) of Venice opposed Copernicus's theories. The academies became yet another way for the elites to distinguish themselves by demonstrating their virtuosity, while Venice's *terraferma* rectors viewed them as an antidote to noble violence.[68]

Loredan's Incogniti, dedicated as its motto declared "To the Unknown God," was by far the most important and influential academy in Venice. It included more than a hundred members, both Venetian and foreign, and scores of writers and intellectuals enjoyed some association with it. For instance, Loredan's patronage led to the publication of Rocco's *The Schoolboy Alcibiades.* The Incogniti combined "conservative patriotism and *libertinismo*" as "they moved seamlessly from the patriotic to the erotic."[69] This is exemplified by Ferrante Pallavicino, a Parma native, Lateran canon, personal secretary to Loredan, frequenter of prostitutes, and prolific writer. He won the favor of the Venetian government when in 1635 he published *Il Sole ne' pianeti, cioè le grandezze della Serenissima Republica di Venezia* (The Sun in the Planets, that is the Greatness of the Most Serene Republic of Venice). In his novella *Il corriero svaligiato* (The Postman Robbed), he attacked the Barberini papacy, Jesuits, the Inquisition, and Spain. The Senate repeatedly resisted papal pressure to have him arrested. Among his other writings was his rabidly anti-Jesuitical *La retorica delle puttane* (The Rhetoric of Whores) in which an aged prostitute instructs a young initiate in the profession. Ingeniously modeled on a Jesuit schoolbook, it drew parallels between the rhetorical skills of the Society of Jesus and the beguiling tricks of prostitutes. The work also served as an apology for the naturalness of sexual pleasure, in line with Cremonini's brand of Aristotelianism. When Venice became too dangerous, Pallavicino tried to escape to France but was apprehended in papal Avignon and executed in 1644 at age twenty-eight.[70]

If Pallavicino was one planet orbiting around Loredan, "the arbiter of taste in mid-seventeenth-century Venice," another was Arcangela Tarabotti, whose brother-in-law was a member of the Incogniti.[71] Pallavicino's vicious misogyny in *Il corriero svaligiato* provoked Tarabotti's rage, prompting her to claim that it was "just as well he was put to death before the book's publication."[72] Tarabotti's relationship with Loredan was also fraught. While he praised her writing and assisted with its publication, the two disagreed over Loredan's own *Life of Adam*, prompting her to lay the blame for humankind's fall on Adam not Eve. Whether a genuine rift developed between them or they were only engaged in the kind of intellectual play characteristic of academic debate remains unclear.[73] Regardless, by combining politics and pleasure, libertinism offered an intellectual justification for Venice's antagonistic stance toward the Roman Church and Hapsburgs and a rationale for its republican institutions and the free exchange of ideas, facilitated by the city's presses.

All the elements of libertinism came together in the creation of a novel art form—*dramma per musica*. Opera first emerged in the private courtly spheres of Medicean Florence and papal Rome but took on its form and identity in mid-seventeenth-century Venice.[74] Crucial to its success was a new building type, the *teatro all'italiana*, which included open seating on the parterre surrounded by multiple floors of closed boxes radiating in a semicircle from the stage. These boxes were rented by the season or even longer and provided space that was simultaneously public and private. Under pressure from the Jesuits, the Ten had shut down two theaters in the 1580s, concerned not only about the bawdiness of the plays performed in them but also the licentious behavior taking place in the boxes. After the Jesuits were expelled and the interdict defied, the stops were out. The dark private boxes of the theaters regained their reputation as the perfect venue for assignations. In fact, the Sant'Aponal theater, the first opera house, which opened in 1637 with the opera *Andromeda*, had a box reserved "for the women," that is, courtesans.[75]

Theaters were privately run by noble owners, including members of the Tron, Grimani, and Zane families, who sold seasonal subscriptions. Between 1637 and 1678, nine different theaters operated in Venice, staging at least 150 operas, the work of almost forty librettists and twenty composers, including Claudio Monteverdi.[76] An entertainment industry was born as theater owners competed with one another for the services of impresarios and artists as well as designers who created ever more elaborate stage sets and special effects. The opera season coincided with Carnival, which meant that theater owners could rely on both locals and foreigners for subscriptions. Opera became one of the major draws in Venice's emerging tourism industry as entertainment became commercialized. After seeing *Ercole in Lidia* in 1645, Englishman John Evelyn said of opera, "It is one of the most magnificent and expensive diversions the wit of men can invent."[77] In a half century of frenetic activity and creativity, opera's conventions (the three-act format, da capo arias, recitatives, and star singers, especially the *prima donna*) were birthed in Venice.

Given their centrality to Venetian intellectual life in this period, it is not surprising that the Incogniti played a role in opera's development. Several of its members were librettists. Loredan himself wrote a play *La forza d'amore* (The Power of Love) that bears striking resemblance to a libretto and was even referred to as an "opera scenica."[78] In 1640 a group of Incogniti members built a brand new theater, called appropriately enough the Novissimo, which was reserved for the presentation "only [of] heroic operas in music, not plays."[79] *La finta pazza* (The Feigning Madwoman), by librettist Giulio Strozzi, composer Francesco Sacrati, scenic designer Giacomo Torelli, and starring soprano Anna Renzi, was the first work performed when the theater opened in January 1641. With the aid of the Incogniti's formidable publicity machine, *La finta pazza* became opera's first smash hit. It and other works were memorialized in post-production publications, one of which declared,

> Venice, always and on every occasion extraordinary, and never tired of displaying her greatness, has discovered the remarkable also in virtuoso entertainment, having introduced a few years ago the presentation in music of grand drama with such sets and stage machines that they surpass all belief; and what the richest treasuries can produce only with difficulty (and only rarely) in royal halls, here we see easily achieved with private resources.[80]

The writer linked private enterprise, republican government, Venetian patriotism, and opera.

Another reason for opera's extraordinary success was its ability to engage current political affairs and social concerns and allow audiences to tap into wells of emotions that such issues precipitated. In addition to the Ottoman wars, the changing marital patterns of the nobles, including shifting gender roles, found voice on the operatic stage. One side effect of the new patrician family strategies was greater attentiveness to personal feelings, as fathers tried to decide which of their children were temperamentally fit or unfit for marriage. As audiences watched the family dramas of the Julio-Claudian emperors of ancient Rome and mythical characters on stage, they saw reflections of their own family dynamics.[81] Maiolino Bisaccioni, a member of the Incogniti, used the example of the character Deidamia's madness in *La finta pazza* to exhort fathers when "raising their children, to provide for them and foresee the dangers they face."[82]

With the readmission of the Jesuits in the 1650s and the Republic's growing alliance with Rome and the Austrian Hapsburgs, Venice's libertine moment began to fade. Opera changed in response. No longer were the most dramatic arias assigned to characters like the virago Messalina, wife of the emperor Claudius, but instead they were written for chaste and lamenting women. The politically dangerous and sexually charged female voice was muted. In one particularly telling example of the new conservatism, noble brothers Giovanni Carlo and Vincenzo Grimani canceled the opera *Eliogabolo* by librettist Aurelio Aureli and composer Francesco Cavalli, which was set to open the 1667-8 season at their Teatro Santi Giovanni e Paolo and substituted a different version with a score by Giovanni Antonio Boretti. At the end of Cavalli's version the tyrannical Heliogabulus is murdered and his virtuous cousin assumes power. In the revised version, Heliogabulus regrets his misdeeds, repents, and co-rules with his cousin—all in line with the readmitted Jesuits' emphasis on repentance. Another disturbing scene in Cavalli's *Eliogabolo* was its depiction of the emperor's creation of an all-female senate of prostitutes that distributes political appointments. This struck too close to home for Venetian nobles who had sold admission to the Greater Council. In the revised version, the Senate scene was cut from 152 to just seven lines. Under pressure from the Grimanis, *Eliogabolo* was rewritten to reflect the more conservative atmosphere that had taken hold in Venice. In a 1687 restaging the title was changed to *L'Eliogabolo rifformato col titolo del vitio depresso e la virtù coronata* (Heliogabulus Reformed with the [sub]title Vice Overthrown and Virtue Crowned).[83]

As the fate of *Eliogabolo* indicates, Venice's associations with Venus and its reputation for libertinism—long a source of pride and symbol of the city's freedom—also became fodder for critics who saw the city as a corrupt, diseased, and enfeebled regime. Sparked by the Interdict Crisis, foreign writers developed a strong counternarrative to Venice's encomiastic tradition. One of the most famous of these works was the 1612 *Squitinio della libertà veneta* (Investigation of Venetian Liberty), most likely the work of Alfonso de la Cueva, Marquess of Bedmar. It set out to refute Venice's claim of exemption from imperial jurisdiction and its much-vaunted internal freedom. By citing evidence from the early Middle Ages, the author asserted that Venice had indeed at times acknowledged its obedience to the emperor. As for its domestic liberty, the Serrata of the Greater Council had rendered the majority of Venetians mere "subjects," since it was the nobles who held "the reins of governance."[84]

The latter theme was also developed by French diplomat Nicholas Amelot de la Houssaye in his *Histoire du gouvernement de Venise* (History of the Government of Venice) published in 1677 in both French and English and in 1695 in Dutch. According to him, Venice's famed libertinism was a political tool of the nobles, used to render the people obedient. He wrote, "The Senate keeps the people content by letting them live in laziness and debauchery... this licentious life they call freedom." The clergy too are permitted to live dissolute lives, which has the salutary effect of discrediting them in the eyes of the people, while courtesans keep young nobles, who might otherwise develop "ideas dangerous to the State," occupied. He compared courtesans to leeches that are applied to those who "have too much blood." Even sodomy is tolerated; only the powerless are prosecuted for this crime. The author condemned Venice's political institutions and policies. Terror and suspicion keep everyone in line, including the doge, who is little more than a "captive." In foreign affairs, Venice "conquers the enemy with ruses rather than force." While Venetians are schooled in intrigues and *broglio*, they are ignorant of the rest of the world and mistakenly maintain the view that their government "ought to serve as the rule and model for all others."[85]

In face of such criticism, Venetian writers and artists continued to put forward a celebratory vision of the city and its timeless, stable government. A caption in a bird's-eye view of the city published by Stefano Scolari in 1696 described Venice as the "hobbler of time, tamer of years, conqueror of centuries."[86] However, city views themselves were changing as the bird's-eye view began to be replaced by panoramic views or topographical maps like that published by Vincenzo Coronelli in 1696, with eight pages of toponyms. Increasingly engravers like Luca Carlevarijs produced images of individual palaces, churches, and squares in what has been described as a "fragmentation" of Venice's pictorial image.[87]

If the seventeenth century saw a burst of creativity in music, the same cannot be said of painting. Local artists of this period tended to imitate the great sixteenth-century masters, while many of the most popular living painters, like Domenico Fetti, Bernardo Strozzi, and Jan Liss, were foreigners. The conservatism of seventeenth-century painting is attributable in some measure to art's function as a status symbol and means of demonstrating cultural superiority.[88] Those asserting their place in society aspired to own a Titian or at least a work that imitated or even copied a Titian. This impulse fueled a mania for collecting. In their palaces, collectors displayed paintings along with medals, coins, precious stones, natural curiosities, and antiquities. According to one count, in 1660 the city was home to at least seventy-five notable collections.[89] While the older and most distinguished noble families showed a preference for works by the established "old masters," some newly aggregated nobles like the Widmanns and Rezzonicos also bought those by living painters like Luca Giordano.

The demand for paintings created a lively art market as well as a need for experts and middlemen who could provide appraisals and advise clients on their purchases. Paintings were a sound investment and attracted all sorts of dealers. One was Simon Giogalli, a wealthy merchant who married two of his daughters to recently aggregated nobles. His major business dealings involved importing olive oil from Apulia and supplying precious metals to the Mint. But he also trafficked in the paintings of Salvator Rosa and Giordano. He sold six paintings by Giordano to the Elector of Bavaria for 2,000 thalers (3,000 ducats), half of which was to be paid in cash, half in gunpowder.[90] On his death he had twenty-seven works by Rosa in his house. Giogalli combined business acumen with an awareness of what works clients coveted and his own knowledge of artistic trends.

Marco Boschini also served as a middleman and estimator in the picture trade. He was, even more than Giogalli, a jack-of-all-trades. He worked as an engraver (producing engravings of opera sets and a currency conversion table), painter, broker, restorer, miniaturist, and merchant dealing in imitation pearls and seed-beads, even serving as warden of the glass beadmakers' guild.[91] Best known as the chronicler of Venetian painting, he published his *La carta del navegar pittoresco* (The Chart of Pictorial Navigation) in 1660.[92]

Written in Venetian dialect, the *Carta* is a poem of more than 5,370 quatrains presented as an imaginary dialogue between a Venetian senator and a professor of painting. They move around the city looking at works of art. Unlike earlier chroniclers of painting Carlo Ridolfi and Giorgio Vasari, Boschini prioritizes artistic creativity over imitation of nature. For him it is the effect that painting creates that takes priority. For this reason, in the famous debate over the superiority of sculpture or painting, known as the *Paragone*, he comes down decisively on the side of painting that can "trick the eye."[93] Color is crucial for its ability to express emotion. His resistance to system and love of inventiveness and wordplay echo the Incogniti as when he says of Veronese's *Feast in the House of Levi*, "Oh what a great thing to make nothingness into everything!"[94] Boschini moved in Incogniti circles. He sought Loredan's help in correcting his text and prefaced the *Carta* with Loredan's letter praising him for having guided his Venetian ship "through the Sea of Glory and berthed it at the Port of Immortality."[95] Boschini's work is of a piece with the freewheeling, inventive, theatrical spirit of Venetian culture in the mid-seventeenth century. Boschini himself praised the freedom of his native city, writing, "In sum, the Venetian style bears with it the same liberty that everyone who lives in this City bears, the Fatherland that keeps coercion at bay."[96]

The cultural vibrancy of the seventeenth century belies the notion of decline that has long characterized this period, especially regarding the economy. Yet even here, the idea of some ineluctable deterioration fails to account for the dramatic transformations that occurred in trade and especially manufacturing. Population figures alone challenge the picture of a catastrophic collapse. At the beginning of the century Venice was the fourth largest city in Europe; at mid-century it still ranked eighth. Simply feeding, clothing, and housing such a large population required formidable economic resources. One estimate suggests that providing for sustenance alone generated around 5,400,000 ducats in commerce annually.[97]

This is not to say that trade did not undergo significant shocks. The middle decades of the century were especially difficult as Venetian merchants continued to lose market share to competitors from England, France, and the Netherlands. Several factors contributed, in addition to the northern "invasion" of the Mediterranean markets. The Thirty Years War caused severe dislocations and stifled demand in Germany, the traditional outlet for Venetian goods imported from the Levant. At the other terminus of Venice's trade routes, devaluation of the Ottoman currency put Venetian merchants who traditionally relied on barter with their Ottoman counterparts (exchanging goods for goods) at a disadvantage compared with merchants from northern Europe who paid with cash. The devaluation meant that the northerners could purchase more with their much sought-after gold and silver.[98] Piracy and the Ottoman wars increased Venice's transaction costs as merchant ships needed greater protection. Venetian merchants had to pay more than their competitors to insure their cargo. In 1671, Venetians were paying between 8 and 10 percent insurance rates compared to the 5 percent Dutch merchants were paying.[99] The long duration of the War of Candia indicates the degree to which Venetian/Ottoman trade had slackened. Neither side saw the loss of business between them as reason enough to warrant a speedy resolution of the conflict.[100]

Venice did try to increase commerce during the war. In 1652 the city declared itself a free port. This exemption from customs duties continued until 1684. While the war lasted, the government allowed foreign-flagged ships to carry merchandise to Venice from the Levant. The end of the century witnessed something of a revival of commerce. In 1693, twenty-five Venetian ships called at Smyrna (Izmir).[101] Indeed, the volume of trade at the end of the century equaled trade a century earlier, indicating Venice's decline was only relative to the rise of other powers. In 1687 Venice was still the fourth largest importer of Levantine goods to Europe, significantly ahead of Genoa and Livorno.[102]

What did change was the composition of Venice's merchant class. Englishman Richard Lassels writing in 1670 was particularly struck by the presence of foreign merchants. He wrote of Piazza San Marco, "In this Piazza I found alwaies a world of strangers perpetually walking and talking of bargains and traffick, as Greeks, Armenians, Albanians, Slavonians, Polonians, Jewes, and even Turks themselves; all in their several habits, but all conspiring in this one thing, to sell dear and buy cheap."[103] The number of Jews in Venice swelled following the admission of the Ponentine Jews in 1589, and by 1654 Jews made up 3 percent of the city's population. And in 1621 the Senate cleared the way for the establishment of the Fondaco dei Turchi.

Agriculture also presents a mixed picture, although it too improved in the second half of the century. After the sixteenth-century population growth had created a favorable environment for investment in agriculture and land reclamation, the first decades of the seventeenth century saw a reversal of these trends. Falling population due to the plagues of the 1570s and 1630s led to decreased demand for food and a marked slowing of reclamation projects. However, by the 1640s the pendulum began to swing in the other direction.[104] Population growth and the War of Candia led to an increased need for food and a return to profitability in the agricultural sector. To raise money for the war effort, the government increased the sale of common lands; between 1646 and 1727 almost half of all common lands were sold. Venetian nobles purchased nearly 40 percent, while slightly less than 7 percent was purchased by the communes that traditionally had enjoyed use of these resources, thereby hurting the peasants.[105]

The peasantry paid the price in other ways as well. Not all reclaimed lands or water resources were put to agricultural use. In the Vicentino, water courses often served the needs of grain, paper-, and sawmills. The pressure to produce grain also meant less land was devoted to grazing. Venice imported much of its meat from Hungary. The resulting lack of manure and exhaustion of the soil led to lower yields. Maize became the predominant grain of the Venetian *terraferma*, accounting for fully half of all cereal production by the mid-eighteenth century.[106]

Although maize predominated, there was some agricultural specialization. Rice was cultivated in parts of the Veronese and Vicentino, hemp in the countryside around Montagnana and Cologna, vines in the zone between San Bonifacio and Soave, transhumance, bee-keeping, and chestnut harvesting in the pre-Alps and high plateaus. The fertile soil of the lagoon islands, enriched by sedimentary deposits of crustaceans, continued to provide produce for the metropole.[107] On balance, renewed interest in agricultural investment, the purchase of common lands, and specialization of production suggest that Venice was one of the first states to emerge from the recession that gripped most of Europe in the seventeenth century.[108]

Revival in the later decades of the century is also evident in manufacturing, although success in this sphere came at a steep cost for a large segment of the *popolo*. This is apparent from two trends across industries. First, numerous guilds tightened requirements for admission to mastership, meaning that many apprentices and journeymen no longer had a path to upward mobility within the guilds. Second, several industries increasingly relied on the low-cost, non-guild labor of women, children, and recent immigrants in what has been described as a "proletarianization" of the workforce.[109]

The tightening of mastership ranks was widespread. In 1615, for example, the journeymen wool shearers filed a petition in which they complained that "many of us have worked in this trade for twenty-five or thirty years or even more, and when we are ready to enter the mastership, we find ourselves in such difficulty with those who don't allow us to succeed because they limit [membership in] the guild to their own few and to their sons."[110] The same was true in several of the guilds involved in the glass industry and in printshops where regular contracts for apprentices and journeymen became rare. This was part and parcel of the protection of privileges, characteristic of Old Regime Europe. The separation of the labor force from management was especially pronounced at the Arsenal, where the workforce evolved from one made up of highly skilled workmen who could also find employment in private shipyards into a less skilled workforce performing repetitive, "factory-style" tasks.[111] As in other industries, the gap between Arsenal managers and workers widened. A side effect of the tightened restrictions was an aging of the guild workforce as the flow of younger workers slackened.[112]

The other trend was greater reliance on non-guild labor altogether, much of it supplied by women. The silk industry flourished in the last three decades of the century, with the number of weavers increasing from around 700 in the 1670s to 1,200 by the end of the century. One estimate suggests that perhaps as much as 10 percent of the city's population earned its livelihood from silk. Women worked as warpers, spoolers, and weavers; the weavers were paid a weekly salary rather than by the piece. Only in 1753 were female weavers allowed to enroll in the guild.[113] The industry also made significant use of children, some as young as seven.[114] Glass manufacturing too relied heavily on women who performed much of the work of making glass beads in their own homes. Another process, the finishing of small glass mirrors, became the specialty of immigrants from the town of Maniago in Friuli, an example of "hyper-specialization" of immigration itself.[115] The cheap labor that women and immigrants provided helped keep Venice's glass industry competitive as it moved from blown glass products to semi-worked ones like beads, windowpanes, and mirrors. But the reliance on cheap non-guild labor across the economy contributed to a dismal standard of living for a large portion of the *popolo* who often lived in dire conditions. It is estimated that in 1661 a third of Venice's population was living on charity or in wretched housing.[116]

Some industries shifted production to the *terraferma*, the woolen cloth industry being a prime example. After reaching its peak in 1602, the Venetian woolen cloth industry went into a steady decline, with output dropping about 1.4 percent per annum between 1602 and 1655. Even so, through the early 1650s, it was still usually producing more than 10,000 bolts of cloth a year.[117] The biggest cause of decline was falling demand for Venetian woolen cloth in the Levant due to the War of Candia and Levantine consumers' preference for woolen fabrics produced by the French and Dutch. Starting around 1670 the Venetian woolen cloth industry again began to expand but was concentrated in places like Padua and Bergamo where labor was cheaper, raw materials closer at hand, and waterpower readily available. Venetian producers found themselves losing out to their *terraferma* counterparts, although often there were connections between businessmen in both places.[118] In other instances, the *terraferma* offered complementarity rather than competition. Venice's printing industry, for instance, profited from the availability of cheap paper provided by papermills in the stream-rich countryside around Treviso and Vicenza.[119] Similarly the success of Venice's thriving silk industry explains the agricultural expansion of mulberry trees and sericulture. More than ever before, the seventeenth century witnessed the development of a regional economy with some industries and tasks headquartered on the *terraferma*, others in Venice itself, although workers in Venice paid a heavy price for this shift.[120]

While seventeenth-century Venetian industries have long been accused of stagnation and failure to innovate, there is considerable evidence that they and even guilds readily adapted to the changing tastes of consumers and sought out new markets. The silk industry, for example, began to imitate the hugely popular silk fabrics being produced in Lyons while continuing to make the expensive luxury fabrics that had long been Venice's specialty. Printers shifted to producing missals and breviaries, for which there was huge demand. Wool manufacturers began to produce cloth in imitation of their French and Dutch competitors in the Levant market. And in the glass industry, the overtaking of blown glass by semi-worked glass was an adaptation to market demand. In a stunning example of triple exploitation, low-labor-cost female bead-makers produced a product that was central to both the African slave trade and the North American fur trade. In 1723, the *Dictionnaire universel de commerce* (Universal Dictionary of Commerce) by Jacques and Philemon Savary observed that 1.2 tons of glass imitation pearls could purchase 612 slaves along the Angolan coast and that Venetian beads were well suited to trade with "the savages of Canada and the Negroes of Guinea."[121]

Finally, tourism took on increasing economic importance. No longer a transporter of pilgrims to the Holy Land, Venice itself became an obligatory

FIGURE 15.5 Venetian Glass Trade Beads, eighteenth to twentieth century. Collection of the Smithsonian National Museum of African American History and Culture, Gift of Oprah Winfrey.

stop on the Grand Tour, part of the required curriculum vitae for gentlemen, especially from England. Richard Lassels is a good example of this new tourist type. His Venetian sojourn included many features familiar to modern-day visitors such as tours of San Marco, the Ducal Palace, and Rialto, a visit to the glass factories on Murano, and attendance at a sermon in the Ghetto. Unlike many Grand Tourists, Lassels did not discuss the city's famed courtesans or casinos, both major draws.[122] Less reticent was Charles Baldwyn who declared in 1712, "I think their whole City may well be term'd the Brothell house of Europe, and I dare say virtue was never so out of countenance or vice so encouraged in any part of the World and I believe not in any age as at this time at Venice."[123] Lassels did, however, acknowledge the Incogniti, which he described as an "Academy of wits," and remarked that some years earlier he had met "the noble and ingenious [Francesco] *Loredano*, whose witty books make him famous over all the Academies of *Italy* and *Europe*."[124]

Lassels was also not the only visitor to be struck by the myriad of nationalities seen and the babel of languages heard in Venice, where the world seemed to be on display and many felt they had already left Europe for the Orient. In 1645, John Evelyn noted that the doges' robes of state "are very particular, after the eastern fashion," while those who wished to learn about other nations had to go no "farther than *Venice*." In 1782 William Beckford opined, "I cannot help thinking Saint Mark's a mosque."[125] Foreigners eroticized, exoticized, and Orientalized Venice.[126] In the seventeenth century the city's time-honored role as the meeting place of East and West assumed new cultural meaning.

Often condemned as a period of torpor and decline, the Venetian seventeenth century was instead a period of creativity, adaptation, and transformation. As Venice's international political and economic preeminence was eclipsed by others, the city and the *terraferma* became ever more tightly linked as an integrated regional economy. More significantly, Venice assumed cultural leadership, especially in the realms of music and free thought, and as a place for foreigners in particular to escape the strictures of religion and society. While Venice worked to burnish its traditional image as the ideal republic and its role as an international entrepot, the contours of a new image emerged, one that would predominate in the centuries that followed. Venice, the sturdy, stable, model republic gradually yielded to one famous for Carnival, masking, opera, and libertinism and infamous for surveillance and repression. Both were soon to be swept away by a storm named Napoleon.

16

Reform, Revolution, and the End of the Republic

IN THE 1750S a ferocious battle erupted in Venice. Unlike earlier centuries, it was not over ducal power, family rivalries, or discontent among poor nobles; instead, it was over the direction comic theater was taking. The protagonists were the lawyer-turned-playwright Carlo Goldoni, son of a pharmacist, and his fellow Venetian, writer Carlo Gozzi, the child of nobles.[1] Since returning to Venice in 1748 and contracting with impresario Girolamo Medebach whose company was performing at the Teatro Sant'Angelo, Goldoni had churned out dozens of original comedies as well as librettos for operas, cantatas, and intermezzi. In 1750 alone, Goldoni debuted sixteen new plays. Goldoni's prodigious output was not what rankled Gozzi. It was the form, content, characters, and even the language he employed.

Goldoni was intent on revolutionizing comedy, which for nearly two centuries had been dominated by the *commedia dell'arte* performance style in which actors and actresses usually wearing masks and costumes representing stock characters (such as Arlecchino, Pulcinella, Pantalone, and Il Dottore) bawdily improvised their way through scenarios involving love, jealousy, and old age. During the fourteen years Goldoni spent working in Venice, first at Teatro Sant'Angelo and later at the Vendramin family's Teatro San Luca, he dropped the masks, had his actors perform fully scripted works rather than improvise, developed emotionally complex male and female characters reacting to everyday situations, and composed some plays in Venetian dialect. His works were far removed from the noble milieu and featured *cittadino* and *popolano* characters encountering real-life problems.

Goldoni's intent was to present a theatrical experience that was "honest and instructive."[2] In his play *Il teatro comico* (The Comic Theater), the character Orazio (the stand-in for the author) declares,

> for our consolation, not only has any wicked custom been removed from people but so has any scandal from the stage. One no longer hears obscene words, dirty puns, dishonest dialogues. One no longer sees dangerous jests, indecorous gestures, lewd scenes, to set a bad example. Young girls can attend it without fear of learning immodest or malicious things.[3]

Goldoni's project for an edifying theatrical experience owed much to the Enlightenment, the philosophical movement emanating from France that promoted the belief that philosophical inquiry could lead to the betterment of society. Goldoni moved in circles sympathetic to Enlightenment ideals, composed a comedy *Le donne curiose* (The Curious Women) about a Masonic lodge, and counted Voltaire among his admirers.[4] He advocated the ethics of merchants and petty shopkeepers. Although the pursuit of profit drove these characters, happiness was the goal, and sincerity its sign. Siding with the new against the old, one of the characters in *Il sior Todero brontolon* (Grumpy Signor Todero) declares, "What's needed is a good heart, above all a good heart. Love your neighbor, hold dear your kin, justice for all, charity to all."[5] For Goldoni, virtue knew no class distinction. As café proprietor Ridolfo states in *La bottega del caffè* (The Coffeehouse), "I'm in an honest line of trade of the artisan class that is dignified, clean, and civil." In *La famiglia dell'antiquario* (The Antiquarian's Family), the merchant Pantalone advises his daughter, who is married to a nobleman, "Be modest, patient, good, and then you too will be noble, rich, and respected."[6] Goldoni's plays implicitly challenged the patrician monopoly on social and political power and supposed virtue. As Pantalone in *The Curious Women* declares, "Birth does not make the gentleman, good deeds do."[7]

Nobleman Gozzi was incensed. He was a member of the Accademia Granelleschi, part of whose mission was to defend Italian language and literature against innovation, especially that coming from France. He and other members of the Granelleschi launched scathing attacks on, in Gozzi's words, Goldoni's "diarrhea of dramatic works."[8] He criticized him for populating his plays with working-class characters who had the audacity to speak in Venetian dialect, employing actors who abandoned improvisation and performed without masks, and, most of all, placing all his characters, be they noble or common, on the same ethical plane.

Gozzi got revenge by teaming up with actor Antonio Sacchi, a well-known Arlecchino who, like several *commedia dell'arte* actors, had had a difficult time adjusting to Goldoni's style. In January 1761 Gozzi premiered his *L'amore delle tre melarance* (The Love of Three Oranges) at Teatro San Samuele in which the old comic characters returned, masked and engaging in slapstick. The play was a huge success, and Gozzi followed it up in 1762 with other fabulous tales including *Il re cervo* (The Stag King) and *Turandot.* Gozzi wanted to restore the old order in the theater and bolster it in society. As an enslaved girl recounts in the play *Zeim, re de' geni* (Zeim, King of the Genies),

> He [a wise old man] told me that sacred, inscrutable Providence had planned everything, and that the position of great men was a wonder of God. . . . [R]espect the great ones, love them, and however heavy your state may be to you, do not be envious of them.[9]

In other words, know your place. Audiences voted with their feet, abandoning Teatro San Luca and packing San Samuele. Vanquished in Venice, Goldoni retreated to France, where he sustained himself in part as a pensioner of the Bourbon court.

The conflict between Goldoni and Gozzi is emblematic of the struggle for reform in eighteenth-century Venice. There was certainly much talk of reform, and initiatives were taken in many spheres. But on balance the results were meager.[10] Resistance to change came primarily from nobles like Gozzi, who were stubbornly intent on protecting their privileges. Tellingly, the one arena where significant reform did occur—the suppression of monasteries and selling of their lands—succeeded precisely because it benefited nobles and helped ameliorate the national debt.

Reform particularly foundered in the political sphere. On the international front, the Republic clung to neutrality, refusing time and again to take sides in the standoff between Bourbon France and Hapsburg Austria. Domestically, great noble families resisted efforts to relieve the poverty of their fellow nobles, while the Ten arrested figures like Angelo Querini and Giorgio Pisani who advocated change. Additionally, patricians remained resistant to sharing power with *terraferma* notables. Consequently, when Napoleon's army invaded the Veneto in 1796-7, the mainland dominion simply dissolved as it had during the Cambrai crisis three centuries earlier.

With the French army threatening at the lagoon's edge, the Greater Council voted itself out of existence on May 12, 1797.

The end of the Republic ushered in dramatic change as three different regimes controlled Venice in just eighteen years: the revolutionary Democratic Municipal Government (May 1797–January 1798), the first Austrian domination (January 1798–January 1806), and the Napoleonic Kingdom of Italy (January 1806–April 1814). These years witnessed a turnover in Venice's ruling elite; impoverishment of the city; suppression of monasteries, parish churches, confraternities, and guilds; abolition of the Ghetto; and plundering of some of the city's most important treasures, including San Marco's horses. The most lasting effects of these years were a reorganization and reimagining of the cityscape.

A visual analogy of the failed project of reform in eighteenth-century Venice is the façade of the church of San Stae and the abutting goldbeaters' confraternity hall. When a competition was held to design the façade of the reconstructed church in 1709, twelve different plans were submitted. In the end, Domenico Rossi's neo-Palladian design was selected, which included just a few Baroque elements such as the broken pediment over the door. One of Rossi's competitors, Giovan Giacomo Gaspari, offered a fully Baroque scheme. As recompense for his loss, Gaspari was commissioned to design the adjoining *scuola*. It is one of the few façades in Venice veering toward the Rococo.[11] The juxtaposition of these two notions of proper architecture is an index of the ambivalence that the elites had toward change and their lack of clear direction. This resulted in the destruction of the Republic, a topic that, as the city's last official historiographer Francesco Donà predicted, has stirred as much interest (and elicited as many myths and emotions) as the founding of the city.[12]

Unlike most of Europe, Venice had no royal court to attract writers, artists, intellectuals, and others seeking patronage and power.[13] Instead there existed numerous venues to which people were drawn and where they could engage in intellectual debate, arrange sexual liaisons, trade gossip, review the latest scientific or geographic discoveries, and discuss politics. Through informers, spies, and secret denunciations, the Ten and State Inquisitors worked to tamp down unauthorized political discussion. Some matters appeared serious. In February 1765, for example, one of their agents noted an exchange of gestures between the Austrian ambassador's wife and a masked man during an opera at Teatro San Cassiano. The masker fixed his gaze on the ambassador's wife

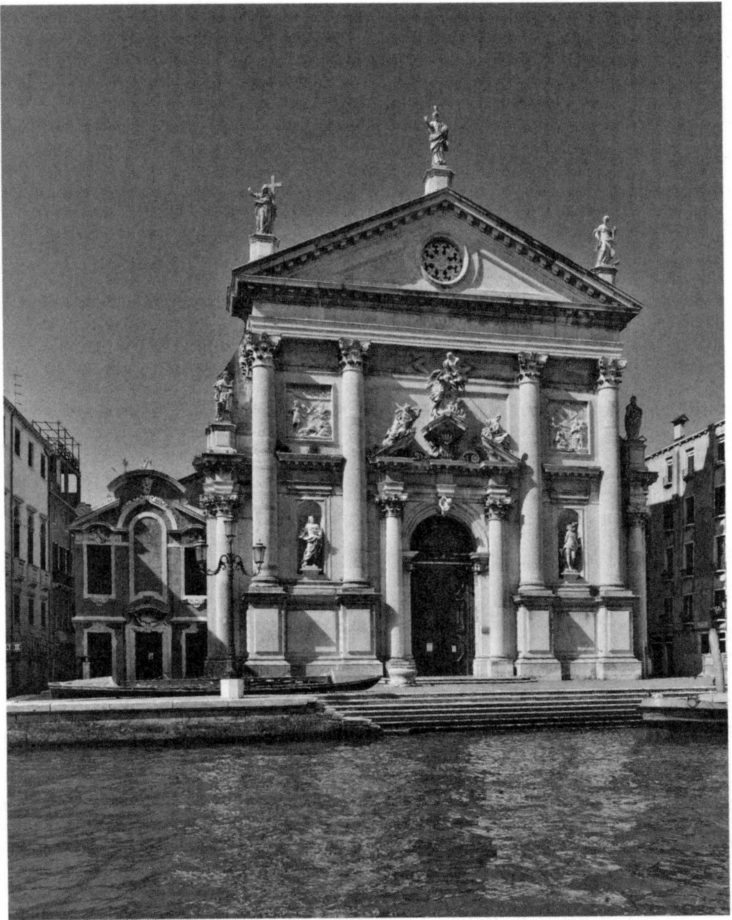

FIGURE 16.1 Domenico Rossi, Church of San Stae, and Giovan Giacomo Gaspari, Goldbeaters' Confraternity Hall, begun c. 1709. San Stae, Venice. Photo by Wolfgang Moroder, distributed under a CC-BY 3.0 license via Wikimedia Commons.

and touched his mask. But the agent reported, "I was unable to understand the significance of this signal."[14] Others appeared trivial, as when another agent reported on events of August 11, 1747. He wrote, "This evening around 5 p.m., the nobleman Marco Antonio Corner was seen under the arcade of the Procuratie Vecchie wearing a silk *velada* [long coat] of undulating violet hues and a grey wig."[15] More than at any time in the past, state secrets and political debate escaped the Ducal Palace and entered public space. Agents reported that a group of men at a café near Rialto "spoke publicly about the most secret business of the Senate," while in another café a cleric "advanced expressions that were disrespectful toward the patrician class."[16]

Coffeehouses epitomized the new venues for sociability, conversation, and debate. Gozzi's brother Gasparo wrote in the biweekly *L'Osservatore veneto* (Venetian Observer) that coffeehouses were the best school for learning everything from geography and current events to the character and foibles of humankind. He praised them as antidotes to melancholy, writing, "If he [a solitary man] goes out of his house and finds friends and acquaintances who reason about this and about that, they shake him up; and little by little his intellect is cleared, and the weight of his heart is lightened."[17]

The first coffeehouse opened in Piazza San Marco in 1683. By the middle of the eighteenth century there were more than 200 in the city. Some, like Venice Triumphant (also known as Florian), were richly appointed and catered to a refined clientele. Others were modest establishments with a socially varied customer base.[18] Like everything else in eighteenth-century Venice, cafes came under surveillance as possible sites of gambling, prostitution, sexual rendezvous, and espionage. The government sought unsuccessfully to prohibit women from frequenting them, partly to prevent scandal but also to stifle their engagement with current events. Poet-abbot Angelo Maria Barbaro described female habitues of casinos as "New-fangled Machiavellis discussing politics, in casinos and cafes, on the bed and bidet, concocting new systems, As legislatresses assessing the Republic, displacing the Senators."[19] In his *Principi di una amministrazione ordinata e tranquila* (Principles of a Calm and Ordered Administration), nobleman Giacomo Nani lamented the social mixing in cafes, which had the effect of "eclipsing every difference of rank and putting all men on the same footing."[20]

In coffeehouses patrons read newspapers and journals, another means by which Venetians engaged in debate. A letter published in the *Gazzetta urbana veneta* (Venetian City Gazette) so incensed one female coffeehouse reader that she published a rebuttal.[21] Over the course of the century, the Republic saw the publication of hundreds of periodicals, newsletters, news summaries, literary reviews, anthologies, and scientific journals. The city's tradition as a center of printing, its role as an international crossroads, and its relatively lenient censorship facilitated the boom that made Venice, especially in the first half of the century, the "undisputed capital of Italian journalism."[22]

Journals reflected the agendas of their editors. Giuseppe Baretti used his short-lived fortnightly to rail against bad taste and mores and defend the church and established social order. Gasparo Gozzi sought to reach a wider audience in his *Gazzetta veneta*, which began publication in 1760 with a similarly conservative bent. He filled it with moralizing tales and allegories, theater reviews, business news, and advertisements. His second journal, *Il Mondo morale* (The Moral World), failed because of its heavy-handed preaching. He found the right formula in *L'Osservatore veneto* with its short essays and articles. The more reform-minded also used periodicals to disseminate advances in medicine, natural science, commerce, and agriculture. Freemason and Sarpi apologist Francesco Griselini used his *Giornale d'Italia* (Italian Journal) to diffuse Enlightenment ideals. Domenico Caminer's *L'Europa letteraria* (Literary Europe) presented articles first published elsewhere in Europe.[23] Caminer's daughter Elisabetta was an even more forthright supporter of ideas emerging from France and used the journal to publicize the work of Voltaire and Jean Jacques Rousseau and defend Goldoni's comic style. Under her direction and in collaboration with Vicentine Giovanni Scola, the journal, which her father had renamed the *Giornale enciclopedico* (Encyclopedic Journal), pushed the limits of censorship and placed itself at the forefront of reformed thought. In the process, Caminer herself became a leading figure in the city in the latter half of the century.[24]

Women also played an important role as *salonnières* (salon hostesses). Besides Caminer, the most influential was Caterina Dolfin, daughter of impoverished nobles who became a poet and in 1755 married nobleman Marcantonio Tiepolo. A year into the marriage she began a notorious affair with Andrea Tron, known as "el paròn" (the boss), one of the richest and most powerful politicians of the period and an advocate of the Venetian version of enlightened despotism. Dolfin attracted to her salon a coterie of conservative voices. Her marriage to Tiepolo was annulled in 1772, and she married Tron in 1773, the same year in which he was elected Procurator of San Marco. She used her position as "Procuratoress" to influence her husband and dispense patronage. Around this same time, she began an intense friendship with a much younger Milanese duke, Gian Galeazzo Serbelloni. Dolfin's reputation, along with a feud with *cittadino* secretary Pier Antonio Gratarol, likely prevented Tron's election as doge in 1778.[25] Other notable *salonnières* were Isabella Teotochi Albrizzi and Giustina Renier Michiel.

Theaters, piazzas, shops, concerts, festivals, receptions, and academies offered other opportunities for encounters, discussion, and opportunities to be seen. Concerts by all-female musicians at the city's four *ospedali grandi* were much in vogue in the first half of the century. Best known was the Hospital of the Pietà, where Antonio Vivaldi first worked as a violin teacher in 1703. In 1723 the Pietà's board of governors contracted with him to supply two concertos per month. Over the next six years they paid Vivaldi for over

140. Many attendees found the female voices emanating from behind screens irresistible. Rousseau, serving as secretary to the French ambassador, was enthralled, writing, "There are motets during vespers, for a large chorus and orchestra, composed and directed by the greatest masters of Italy, performed from the grated galleries uniquely by girls under the age of twenty. I had no notion of anything so voluptuous, so touching as this music: the richness of the art, the exquisite taste of the singing, the beauty of the voices." After importuning a friend to introduce him to the singers, he was shocked to discover that many had some disfigurement that limited their marriage prospects and explained their ongoing presence in the hospital. He wrote that his friend "presented me to one after another of these celebrated singers, whose voices and names alone were known to me. . . . Almost every one of them had some notable defect. My tormenter laughed at my cruel surprise."[26]

Ambassadors and members of their staffs like Rousseau were an important component of the city's social life, although they attracted special surveillance by the State Inquisitors. Given Venice's increasingly marginal role in the power politics of international affairs, diplomats made the social circuit in search of intelligence.[27] Other attendees were there to be seen, none more so that Giacomo Casanova, an exaggerated example of how public space could be exploited to achieve notoriety and celebrity. One contemporary scathingly described him as "one of those phenomena in the civil atmosphere whose brightness we cannot account for."[28] His association with Venice is wildly out of proportion to his real significance.

Along with music, painting and architecture flourished. After the stasis of the seventeenth century, painting blossomed. Giambattista Tiepolo and his son Giandomenico drew inspiration from Veronese but infused his style with pastel colors, illusionistic perspective, and a Rococo sensibility. Giambattista enjoyed the patronage of some of the rich families added to the nobility in the seventeenth century, including the Rezzonicos and Labias. His ceiling painting in Ca' Rezzonico's Salon of the Allegory celebrating the marriage of Ludovico Rezzonico and Faustina Savorgnan, who appear in the guise of ancient gods, is a tromp l'oeil masterpiece. (Plate 7) However, the Rococo found its fullest expression in the decorative arts, especially lacquered commodes and chests, and the elaborately carved and often ebonized chairs, gueridons, and candelabra of Andrea Brustolon.[29] Working in a completely different style from the Tiepolos, Pietro Longhi eschewed the grandiose and focused instead on intimate scenes of everyday life, as in his painting *The Faint.* Rosalba Carriera, the only well-documented Venetian female artist, specialized in pastel portraits of the well-to-do.

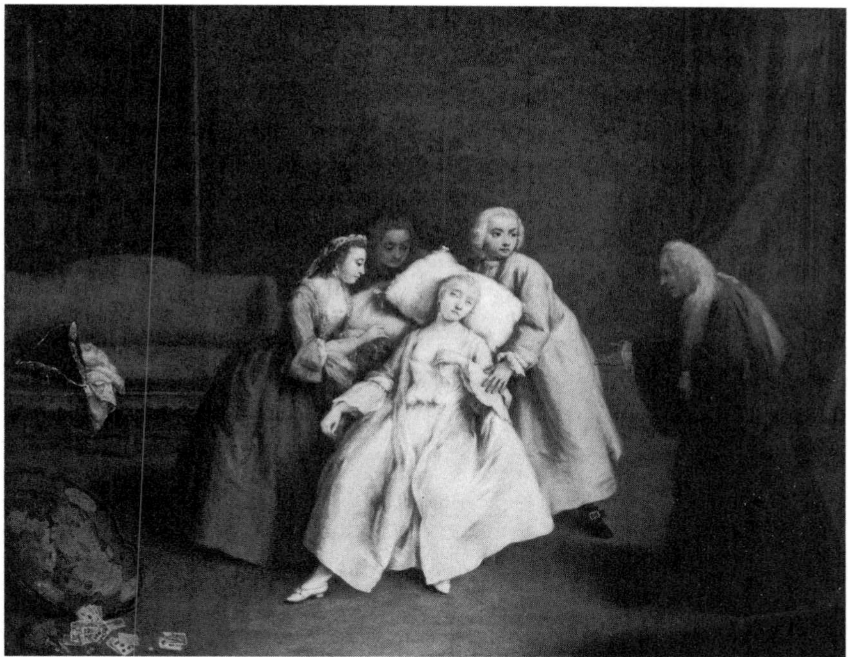

FIGURE 16.2 Pietro Longhi, *The Faint*, c. 1744. Courtesy of the National Gallery of Art, Washington. Samuel H. Kress Collection.

Veduti (view paintings) represent the other important strand in eighteenth-century painting, especially as practiced by Giovanni Antonio Canal, known as Canaletto, and Francesco Guardi. Canaletto's depictions of important monuments, civic festivals, and more mundane spaces like a stonemason's yard at San Vitale, at first appear to be accurate depictions of events and places. Yet his works were highly manipulated, and the Venice he depicted—industrious yet placid, with persons from all social ranks going about their appointed tasks—subtly promoted the venerable notion of Venice as the model republic and a serene society. Joseph Smith, the British consul in Venice from 1744 to 1760, served as Canaletto's agent and created a market for his paintings among British Grand Tourists, who took home with them not only Canaletto's *veduti* but also the Palladian ideal of the country house.[30]

Guardi's atmospheric canvases, characterized by quick brushwork, differed markedly from Canaletto's crisp images. In many of Guardi's works, buildings and figures are dwarfed by the waters of the lagoon and brooding skies as he seeks to capture the play of light. Works like *Gondola on the Lagoon* are

FIGURE 16.3 Francesco Guardi, *Gondola on the Lagoon*, 1765. Museo Poldi Pezzoli, Milan. Via Google Arts & Culture.

nearly monochromatic. Unlike Canaletto, who was interested in conveying an image of Venice, Guardi was intent on capturing a mood.[31]

Although Rococo triumphed in the decorative arts and palace and church interiors, neo-classicism was the preferred style in ecclesiastical and domestic architecture.[32] A fine example of the latter is the church of San Simeon Piccolo. Designed by Giovanni Scalfarotto, it draws on many influences, including the Pantheon in Rome for the porch, Longhena's Salute for the giant dome, and Palladio's Tempietto at the Villa Barbaro at Maser. San Simeon Piccolo together with the church of the Scalzi served to demarcate the western entryway to the Grand Canal in much the same way San Marco and the Salute did at the canal's other terminus.[33] Other neo-classical churches include Santa Maria del Rosario or the Gesuati (with a Giambattista Tiepolo ceiling) and Santa Maria Maddalena. Palazzo Grassi and the diminutive Palazzo Mangilli-Valmarana designed by Antonio Visentini for Consul Smith are examples of neo-classical domestic palaces. Finally, Gianantonio Selva realized the austere façade of the new Teatro La Fenice with its Corinthian portico and statues of Music and Dance below masks of Comedy and Tragedy. Bronze letters commemorate the noble consortium that built the theater and the date of its completion (1792).

As the Grand Tourists buying up Canaletto's canvases illustrate, eighteenth-century Venice's reputation increasingly relied on its role as a cultural center.

Following the advice of the custodian of the Marciana library that "the precious and abundant body of public paintings is, perhaps, the rarest ornament of this powerful republic," the Ten in 1773 voted to protect paintings in public places. The following year a survey of significant paintings was prepared for the government.[34] And when in 1752 official state historiographer Marco Foscarini published the first volume of his *Della letteratura veneziana* (On Venetian Literature), the Ten agreed to accept it as part of the canon of state historiography. Previously, writers of Venice's official history had recounted the Republic's military and political exploits. As even the Ten recognized, Venice's claim to greatness had shifted to the cultural sphere, despite efforts to restore the city through reform.[35]

Although there was a flurry of reform in the late 1760s, the list of major accomplishments is short.[36] Two areas of concern were agriculture and trade. A series of bad harvests spurred a movement for the diffusion of new agricultural knowledge. To this end a chair in agronomy was created in 1761 at the University of Padua, and in 1764 the *Giornale d'Italia spettante alla scienza naturale e principalmente all'agricoltura, alle arti, ed al commercio* (Italian Journal Regarding Natural Science and Principally Agriculture, Trades, and Commerce) began publication. In 1768 the decision was made to create agricultural academies in the *terraferma* cities under the supervision of the Deputazione all'Agricoltura and a superintendent of agriculture, a post held by geologist and secretary of the Agricultural Academy of Vicenza, Giovanni Arduino.[37] Five years later a veterinary college was established at Padua. Despite this, Veneto agriculture remained committed to traditional practices and the grape/mulberry/grain triad, in part because Venice's prodigious demand for beef (around 18,000 cattle were slaughtered at the abattoir at San Giobbe in 1792 alone) was met by Hungarian herds that were driven over the Alps or transported on *manzere* (beef-boats) traveling between Venice and Zara.[38] In that same year, an Azienda Boschiva (Forest Agency) was established to manage the Republic's forest resources on the basis of advanced technical principles. Yet rivalries among magistracies with traditional competency over forests created roadblocks to change.[39]

Reform was also fitful in commerce. Advocates of free trade were opposed by those who advocated mercantilism (governmental control of the economy) and the protection of privileges. Maritime trade faced numerous challenges including Barbary piracy and competition from major Mediterranean freeports including Marseilles, Livorno, Naples, and Messina as well as lesser Adriatic ones such as Ancona (promoted by the papacy) and Trieste and Fiume (supported by Austria). In 1736 Venice opted to retain its tariff system and decided to rely instead on heavily armed ships known as *navi atte* (fit ships) that could protect themselves from pirates and to promote better seamanship through the creation of nautical schools on Corfu in 1734 and in Venice in 1739.[40]

Another initiative foundered on the shoals of the Republic's internal politics. In 1763 the Cinque Savi alla Mercanzia proposed the creation of a Chamber of Commerce, an idea first floated fifty years earlier. The goal was to foster a "national vision" by creating a board of twenty-four members representing eighteen geographic trading zones and six leading sectors of the economy. However, conservative elements of the nobility managed to have the Chamber scuttled in 1768.[41] So too Venice failed to establish joint-stock companies like England's East India Company, although the Jewish merchant Isaac Treves created a Baltic company to exchange Mediterranean goods for raw materials from Russia and Denmark.[42]

Many of the leading merchants and manufacturers were Jews from such families as Treves, Jacur, Luzzatto, and Bonfil. This sparked resentment among their Christian competitors. In 1771 the Senate backed by the Tron faction forbade Jewish merchants from trafficking in olive oil from Corfu; opponents saw this as a limitation on free trade, an ideal of the Physiocrats, a group of Enlightenment economic thinkers. The renewal of the Jews' *condotta* in 1777 included harsh provisions that, among others, prohibited them from owning property outside the Ghetto, engaging in manufacturing activities, or holding state contracts. Furthermore, Jews were forbidden to live in *terraferma* towns lacking designated Ghettos. These strictures further damaged the economy. Some were removed in the 1788 *condotta*, the final one in the Republic's history.[43]

Shipping prospered during periods of conflict between the great powers when Venice's neutrality gave it a competitive advantage, particularly from 1746 to 1751 and again from 1777 to 1781, roughly corresponding to the War of Austrian Succession and the American Revolutionary War. Commerce in the latter period was also facilitated by peace treaties that the Republic reached with the rulers of Barbary (Algeria and Tunisia in 1763, Tripoli in 1764, Morocco in 1765) in which it agreed to pay large indemnities to gain customs advantages and freedom from piracy. In this way, Venice's merchants could finally take advantage of the Republic's long-standing peace with the Ottomans. However, the city remained a minor commercial player. At century's end Venice had the third largest merchant marine in the Mediterranean (behind France and Naples) but controlled only around 1.78 percent of European global trade.[44]

The same conflict between those advocating free trade and open markets and those intent on protecting privileges played out in efforts at guild and customs reform. There was much talk of opening the guilds or abolishing them altogether as the traditional systems of production gave way to new forms of organization and practice. But little was accomplished other than a systematic survey of the guilds, while the disenfranchisement of laborers in favor of merchant/entrepreneur masters continued. Notably in 1782 the guild of silk weavers—workers whom reformer Andrea Memmo described as "stupid people" and an "undisciplined race"—was dissolved.[45] The crunch felt by laborers in the baking industry led them to strike.[46] Proposals were also put forward to replace the complicated system of customs duties with just two: one based on consumption, the other on trade. Yet reform occurred only in 1794 when all internal customs within the Republic were abolished.

Oher areas show the same pattern—much talk of reform, committees organized, reports written, and discussions held, but fitful results. This was especially true in the law. An effort was made to revise the civil and penal codes, but revisions only of the Feudal and Maritime codes were realized.[47] Education fared somewhat better, with changes to both primary and secondary education. In 1774-5 primary schools were set up in every *sestiere*, and a free secondary school was established in the old Jesuit community after the order was abolished by papal decree in 1773. During the century, various plans were also put forward for reform of the University of Padua, such as abolishing some professorships in traditional fields and creating new ones, offering lectures in Italian as well as Latin, and closing certain colleges. One innovation was the creation in 1779 of the Accademia Patavina di Scienze, Lettere, ed Arti (Paduan Academy of Science, Letters and Arts), a forum for research.[48]

Innovations in public health and welfare included the creation of a school of obstetrics (1770), publication between 1762 and 1781 of Pietro Orteschi's *Giornale di medicina* (Journal of Medicine), and a large-scale smallpox inoculation program. However, efforts at penal reform and the consolidation of poor relief into one centralized institution faltered.[49] Urban improvements did, however, get successfully carried out. In 1723 the brick pavement of Piazza San Marco was replaced with gray stone from the Euganean Hills, ornamented with a white Istrian stone geometric pattern created by architect Andrea Tirali. Nine years later the decision was made to illuminate the city with oil lamps.[50] And between 1737 and 1782 the Republic constructed massive sea walls known as the *murazzi* to protect the fragile shoreline of the barrier islands, replacing earlier wooden palisades backfilled with rocks. Huge blocks of Istrian stone were bound together to provide the foundation for walls, which were sloped to lessen the impact of waves. A special waterproof mortar, made with volcanic ash (*pozzolana*) imported from south-central Italy, was used to bind the stones together, and breakwaters were added. In the end the *murazzi* extended over three miles, protecting stretches of the barrier islands from the Lido to Chioggia. They complemented the system of dikes on the landward side of the lagoon that regulated the inflow of fresh water and represent the culmination of the Republic's centuries-long effort to protect its amphibious environment.[51]

The religious sphere is the one arena where reform had a significant impact. For a time, relations between the Republic and the papacy improved, as evidenced by Pope Clement XII's canonization in 1731 of medieval doge Pietro I Orseolo. But relations soured again over the age-old question of the patriarchate of Aquileia. Pressured by Empress Maria Teresa, Benedict XIV abolished the patriarchate, which had jurisdiction over bishoprics in both Venetian and Austrian territory, and replaced it with two archbishoprics: one in Udine for the Republic's lands, the other in Gorizia for Austria's holdings in Friuli. Although Venice resisted and for a time broke off diplomatic relations with the papacy, the solution had the advantage of aligning the political and ecclesiastical borders between Venice and the empire and removing at least one pretext for Austrian interference in Friuli and Istria, thereby protecting Venice's neutrality. To secure an end to the diplomatic stalemate, the Republic agreed to implement its recent treaty with the papacy regarding the boundaries and navigational rights over the branch of the Po known as Po di Goro. As a bonus, the Republic laid claim to the old patriarchal enclaves San Vito and San Daniele that had been exempt from its jurisdiction and gained control over nomination to the bishoprics of Caorle, Chioggia, and Torcello. However, Venice had shown itself to be at the mercy of international players. One contemporary, nobleman Andrea Querini, wrote, "I hope to God that these are not signs of a mortal illness."[52]

If nothing else, the conflict over Aquileia revived the Sarpian stance on church/state relations that would bear fruit during significant ecclesiastical reform in the 1760s, in part because of Andrea Tron's support. The Senate created in 1766 the Deputazione ad Pias Causas (Deputation on Pious Trusts) to survey the issue. In their report, the deputies found that although the clergy constituted only around 2 percent of the Republic's population, they controlled massive amounts of property. Acting on these data, the Senate forbade further alienation of property to the church, prohibited entry into monasteries that supported themselves primarily through begging, established twenty-one as the minimum age to enter monastic life, and called for the abolition of monastic houses that did not have the means to support at least twelve members. The result was a reduction in the number of regular clergy from 7,770 in 1766 to 4,265 in 1790 and, more significantly still, a massive sell-off by the Deputazione of around 28,000 acres, much of it fertile agricultural land in the Padovano and Trevisano, that garnered nearly 6 million ducats.[53]

In yet another example of the Republic subsidizing the rich, the state agreed to accept as payment for the auctioned land old state bonds at their face rather than their current market value, which varied between 40 and 60 percent of par. Among those who took advantage was nobleman Andrea Querini, one of the three members of the Deputazione, who purchased around 6,400 acres, quintupling his family's real estate holdings.[54] This operation also helped bail out the state's finances since in 1767 the Republic had for the first time set the price of old bonds at their current market value, causing investors to lose faith in the national debt. The millions of ducats garnered from the auction of ecclesiastical property were put into a fund referred to as the *Deposito Nuovissimo* (Newest Deposit), helping to restore faith in the Republic's credit and increasing significantly the share of the debt held by religious and charitable institutions.[55] Although the Deputazione's actions resulted in real changes in the ecclesiastical sphere, the motives behind it included the Venetian tradition of asserting state control over the church, Enlightenment skepticism regarding religion, the investment interests of rich noble families, and concern with shoring up state finances. That confluence explains why in this arena significant reform succeeded.

In almost all these areas of reform, the government increasingly looked to technical experts for advice, men who had highly specialized knowledge based on advanced scientific, technical, or legal expertise or who were adept at statistics, accounting, and administration. This represented a move away from the traditional reliance on noble officeholders. In an increasingly complex world, the arm-chair patrician administrator was rapidly being rendered obsolete.[56]

Reform faltered completely in the political arena. Failure to modify the Republic's governmental structure or alter the composition of its ruling class were major reasons for its collapse in 1797. The short-lived Chamber of

Commerce had been instituted to rectify the lack of a "national vision" when establishing economic policy, yet the absence of such a vision was even more glaring in politics, where the right to political enfranchisement remained bound to the solution reached in the Serrata. That settlement had worked well when Venice was a city-state with distant overseas possessions and a state-run commercial galley system that could revive flagging patrician fortunes, but it had already begun to founder in the early sixteenth century as Venice's commercial power declined and the *terraferma* assumed a larger role in the state's overall health. Granted, in the seventeenth century Venice opened membership in the Greater Council, and some mainland notables were admitted, but their inclusion in an outmoded governmental system did nothing to redistribute power between the capital and its dominions. In addition, the now centuries-old division of the nobility into rich and poor, powerful and powerless grew even more pronounced in the eighteenth century as a small group of men, who dominated the positions of Savi del Consiglio (the Savi Grandi) and relied increasingly on special committees to handle problems, monopolized power over the Republic's roughly 2.8 million inhabitants. For example, the three men who were appointed to the Deputazione ad Pias Causas held those posts for six consecutive years, a break with the tradition of frequent office rotation and a striking example of the concentration of power in a few hands, although this is explained at least in part by the decreasing number of nobles who could shoulder the expense of major offices.[57] Lack of political imagination, fear of change, and failure of the elite to adapt or relinquish power inhibited the formation of a common identity (between rich and poor nobles and between Venetian and provincial elites) that might have allowed the Republic to survive as a minor state in the interstices of the greater ones. In 1770 Francesco Pesaro wrote to his fellow nobleman Giovanni Querini, "The thing that saddens me, as you know, is that Venice doesn't lack for men who are in love with novelty [*novità*]. The worst thing that could possibly happen would be some change in our internal [governmental] system."[58] As his words make clear, there were advocates for constitutional change, but they ran into stiff opposition from those intent on protecting their privileged position.

Several proposals for political reform were put forward early in the century, but none gained traction. Two were designed to reduce the ever-widening gap between rich and poor patricians. Elderly politician and official historiographer Pietro Garzoni diagnosed the problem when he observed that when rich families intermarried, it simply concentrated wealth even more densely and widened the gap between rich and poor patricians which was "harmful to symmetry and good governance."[59] Accordingly in March 1723 the Deputati alla Provvigion del Denaro (Deputies for the Provision of Money) put forward a proposal suggested by the Savi Grandi, Garzoni among them, that when a noble house went extinct, one-third of its wealth should devolve to the state. This would help reduce the public debt and slow the accumulation of riches in just a few hands. It passed on a divided vote in the Senate. Less than two weeks later the decision was rescinded as rich nobles and even poor ones (who hoped that windfall legacies might miraculously land in their laps) mobilized against the measure.[60]

Another proposal for change was put forward by Nicolò Donà in the 1730s. He too diagnosed the Republic's problem as division within the patriciate, which he classified into four categories: the *grandi* or magnates (who held the highest offices), the well-to-do (who could afford costly posts), the "mechanics" (members of the Forty and holders of lucrative magistracies), and the plebeians (nobles without power or income who lived off charity). These differences were a hindrance to the proper functioning of an aristocracy. He recommended reducing the number of plebeians by tightening marriage requirements for those inscribed in the Golden Book. This would decrease the number of men sitting in the Greater Council from 1,400 to between 800 and 1,000. He also wanted to dilute the power of the *grandi* by forcing certain super-rich families to split into multiple branches and proposed that Senate seats, the six Savi Grandi posts, and the three State Attorney positions be distributed proportionally among the various groups. Donà's proposal was not even taken up for consideration, but he had acutely diagnosed the problems within the ranks of the patriciate.[61]

It fell to Veronese nobleman Scipione Maffei to suggest a solution to the unequal distribution of power between provincials and the capital. Lamenting that "the cities and people [of the *terraferma*] are kept in a state of full subordination" and excluded from any participation in governance or society, Maffei proposed in 1736 that twenty mainland families with impeccable noble credentials be admitted to the Greater Council as representatives of various *terraferma* cities and districts. Likewise, he wanted provincial councils to become more representative of their territories. Like Donà's proposal, Maffei's failed to be taken up for consideration.[62] Giacomo Nani believed that the men in charge of the ship of state only wanted to "manage the current, stay on track, and not shift course."[63] According to French political philosopher Charles-Louis de Secondat, Baron de Montesquieu, Venice had "two great enemies"—"fear and avarice."[64]

In the second half of the century, efforts at political reform moved from theory to practice through new attempts to institute "corrections" to the power of the Ten and State Inquisitors. The first and most dramatic took place in 1761-2 when a group of patricians coalesced around State Attorney Angelo Querini, who wanted to check the ever-growing power of those two institutions. He was viewed by some as the spokesman for the middling-rank nobles of the Forty. But in a preemptive strike the Ten arrested Querini and confined him without trial to a Veronese jail. Relying on a tactic used in previous conflicts, the Greater Council failed to approve candidates for posts in the Ten until a committee of five Correctors was created. The five included three conservatives, Marco Foscarini among them, and two in the Querini camp. Due in part to a speech by Foscarini, who was elected doge two months later, the effort to rein in the State Inquisitors was defeated in a vote of the Greater Council on March 16, 1762.[65] Reform had failed, as had the effort to restore internal equilibrium between the various patrician groups. One modern analysis claims that the Republic "died" on that fateful day in March 1762.[66]

The second correction grew out of Boss Andrea Tron's push for strong state action, especially in the economic sphere. His power was so great that some mocked that the "Re-pubblica" (the public thing) had become the "Re-trona" (the Tron thing). In 1774 his push for the state to take over the postal service led to complaints that Tron and the Senate were interfering in matters that were the Forty's responsibility. This seemingly minor matter reignited debate about the power of the Savi Grandi and demands by poor nobles for assistance to ameliorate their situation. An unwieldy coalition of those opposed to Tron forced the appointment of a new committee of Correctors. The results were mixed. Among the changes made were the closing of the public gambling establishment at San Moisè that had ruined many families; increased salaries for various governmental offices; some strengthening of the Senate at the expense of the Savi and College; and the decision to open membership in the Greater Council to up to forty *terraferma* families that could demonstrate that they had enjoyed noble status for at least four generations and had an annual income of at least 10,000 ducats.[67] What is significant about the last measure is that for the first time the decision to admit new members to the Greater Council was based on the demographic decline of the nobility rather than fiscal needs. Proponents argued that shrinking membership in the Council concentrated power in the hands of a few. Corrector Alvise Emo warned that declining numbers would lead to oligarchy, that "a small number of the great and powerful, in the shortest amount of time, would exclude completely the much more numerous little guys, who would not be able to resist the force and violence of the former."[68] The city was in such a state of agitation that the Ten tried to limit political discussion in cafes and casinos.[69]

A third correction followed soon thereafter and focused on the concerns of the poorest nobles led by Carlo Contarini, who in a dramatic address bemoaned the sorry state of the people reduced by the high cost of food and other essentials, and Giorgio Pisani, who proposed redistributing land to poor noble families. After much maneuvering, the creation a new board of Correctors was decided upon in May 1780. Electoral shenanigans prevented Contarini from being seated, although Pisani was. In the meantime, Pisani's partisans had secured his election as a Procurator of San Marco and in late May he triumphally took up his post. To some it appeared that Venice was veering toward demagoguery or even revolution.[70] Reaction came quickly. Just days after entering the procuratorship, the State Inquisitors arrested Pisani and imprisoned him first in Verona and later in Brescia. Contarini was confined to prison in Cattaro. In the end the third correction only confirmed for many the tyranny of the Ten and State Inquisitors.[71]

All three corrections, despite the controversy they provoked, amounted to little more than tinkering around the edges. None sought to extend power to new groups in society or truly bridge the divide between the capital and its dominions. Conservation of the nobility's privileges and monopoly on power triumphed and made Venice susceptible to radical change. An index of how enfeebled the Republic had become is that only ten families sought admission to the Greater Council following the correction of 1774-5, even though allowance had been made for forty new families.[72] The benefits of membership in the Venetian nobility no longer seemed worth the effort.

The inertia demonstrated in domestic politics extended to foreign affairs, where the Republic stubbornly clung to neutrality, a rationalization of its diminished place in the world.[73] This "politics of peace" was simultaneously a "fear of politics," that is, a decision to avoid engagement.[74] Such a stance was based on necessity, lack of will, and fiscal constraints—on the elite not wanting to be taxed—with the result that the government did not have the resources necessary to defend the realm properly.[75] The reduced *stato da mar* dominions also were producing an ever smaller portion of the government's revenue. In previous centuries, the Republic's naval strength could compensate for military weakness in other areas. In the eighteenth century that was no longer the case.[76] Ominously too, the Russians had made their entry into the Mediterranean. In their conflict with the Ottomans, they were stirring up discontent among the Ottomans' (and the Venetians') Greek Orthodox subjects.

Venice depended for protection of the *stato da terra* on an army of approximately 14,000 infantry, 2,000 cavalry, and local militiamen numbering 30,000, numbers barely adequate for a defensive stance. The government failed to reorganize the military in any significant way, stalled as it was in a system that was an inheritance of the piecemeal acquisition of the mainland in the fifteenth century.[77] The Republic avoided direct involvement in the Wars of Polish Succession (1733–38) and Austrian Succession (1740–48) but suffered destructive troop movements through its territory by French, Piedmontese, and Austrian forces.[78] It survived precisely because it was insignificant and could still play the powers off one another. The wars resulted in Austria gaining possession of Tuscany (it already controlled Lombardy and Mantua), a Bourbon being installed in the duchy of Parma and Piacenza, and the king of Sardinia/Piedmont acquiring territory up to the Ticino River. Should the balance of power be broken, however, Venice's survival would be in jeopardy. Already at midcentury, possible annexation of the Republic's lands had been floated by the Austrians in the negotiations leading up to the treaty ending the War of Austrian Succession.[79] And in the 1780s, Russia and Austria contemplated divvying up the Republic's remaining overseas possessions.[80]

The French Revolution of 1789 and the rise of Napoleon spelled the Republic's doom. As the Revolution and reaction against it spread across Europe, Venice continued to maintain its neutrality, trying desperately not to antagonize France or Austria. There is little evidence that events in France awakened revolutionary sentiments either in the capital or its dominions, although the State Inquisitors were on the lookout. Venice resisted repeated calls to join an anti-French coalition, comprised of Austria, England, Russia, Sardinia, and others, fearing that doing so would provide a pretext for Austria to make further incursions into its dominions. Even when the French abolished their monarchy in September 1792, declared a republic, and invaded Savoy and Nice, Venice remained noncommittal and, in the process, alienated all sides. France was annoyed that the Republic allowed Austrian troops to traverse its territory to reach Mantua, collaborated with Austrian Milan in halting the spread of revolutionary impulses, and allowed French noble emigres to take refuge in its lands. At the same time, the antirevolutionary allies saw nothing but hypocrisy in Venice's refusal to close its embassy in Paris (even though the ambassador had fled to London). Worse still, its decision to accept the credentials of the French Republic's chargé to

Venice, thereby giving diplomatic legitimacy to the new regime, rankled. The Venetians offered the feeble excuse that when his credentials were presented, news of Louis XVI's execution had not yet reached the lagoon.[81] It seemed a repeat of the run-up to Cambrai when Venice played subtle diplomatic games and earned the distrust of all. Otherwise, the Savi were paralyzed, unable even to prepare for an armed defense of the Republic against invasion or home-grown revolutionary fervor. They hoped instead for a miracle to salvage the situation. Following the radical revolutionary Maximilien Robespierre's fall in July 1794, ending the so-called Reign of Terror, and French victories in Belgium, Holland, and elsewhere, Venice made some gestures toward France, dispatching nobleman Alvise Querini as ambassador to Paris. And in January 1796 the Senate voted to expel future king Louis XVIII from his refuge in Verona, a bone of contention with France led by the Directory (1795–99), named after the five directors who constituted the executive branch of the government.

Two months later the Directory placed Napoleon Bonaparte in command of the ill-prepared and ill-equipped 45,000 strong Armée d'Italie. The plan was for Napoleon's forces to keep the Piedmontese bottled up, while to the north the principal army battled Austria and its German allies in the main war theater. Unexpectedly, Napoleon quickly defeated the Piedmontese, who ceded Nice and Savoy in April. He entered Milan in May. With Mantua serving as the main Austrian stronghold, Venice suddenly found its *terraferma* lands at the center of the fight. To oversee the situation, Venice named Nicolò Foscarini Provveditore Generale (General Commissioner) of the *terraferma* but failed to supply him with adequate military forces or equipment. The Austrians occupied Peschiera and Chiusa to protect their lines of communication across the Alps, while Napoleon took Crema. Both occupying armies requisitioned food, supplies, and services, displaced families, and terrorized the locals. In a meeting with Venetian army officers, Napoleon alternatively flattered the Venetians (evoking the "long friendship" of the two republics) and menaced, reminding them among other things of their having harbored "the king of Verona" [Louis XVIII].[82] Threatened with war, Venice ceded Verona to Napoleon on June 1, 1796.

For the next several months, the conflict centered on Napoleon's siege of Austrian Mantua. In Venice, the government opted for a plan to defend the capital but not the mainland, with one patrician evoking an anachronistic image of Venice as a "maritime and commercial city that cannot exist without its overseas possessions, like it can without the *terraferma*."[83] It rejected a French overture for a Mediterranean alliance composed of France, Spain,

Venice, and the Ottomans. On February 2, 1797, Mantua fell to Napoleon, while in Venice, Carnival went on as usual. Nobleman Francesco Lippomano observed, "It is a pleasure to see the people [acting] as if there weren't any troubles in the world and everything were proceeding happily."[84]

On March 16 Napoleon defeated the Austrians in the Battle of the Tagliamento and continued his drive toward Vienna. At the same time Bergamo and Brescia declared their independence from Venice and established provisional municipal revolutionary governments. The rural inhabitants of the mountain valleys of the Bergamasco and Bresciano remained loyal to Venice and fought against these urban "Jacobins." To maintain the rest of the *terraferma* and win back what had been lost, some in the government proposed extending power to *terraferma* nobles, as Scipione Maffei had suggested six decades earlier, but the idea came to naught. Venice again refused Napoleon's offer of an alliance, one that would protect him from rearguard action as he pushed toward Vienna but would have placed the Republic at war with both Austria and England. Instead, led by anti-French Savio Grande and Procurator of San Marco Francesco Pesaro, the Senate tried to buy Napoleon off with a 250,000 ducat per month stipend for six months in exchange for allowing the Republic to suppress the "democratic insurgents."[85]

However, on April 18, Napoleon reached a peace accord with the Austrians at Leoben. Unbeknownst to the Venetians, according to the terms of the agreement France would receive Belgium and the left bank of the Rhine as well as Mantua and the Duchy of Milan. Austria would increase its territory in Istria and Dalmatia and receive the Venetian *terraferma*. Venice would be compensated with some lands seized from the papacy in Emilia and Romagna. Knowing that peace was in the works, three days earlier Napoleon had given the Venetians an ultimatum, requiring them within twelve hours to declare whether they were at war with France. The government, divided between those who wanted to fight and those who wished to stall, reacted by appointing two deputies to meet the Corsican. On April 17, Verona rebelled against the French, in what came to be known as the "Veronese Easter" and received assistance from Venetian forces. The Republic had openly come out against the French, who quickly retook Verona, as Vicenza and Padua also fell into their hands. By April 29, their forces had reached the edge of the lagoon.

On April 20, the Venetians had handed Napoleon an even better pretext for war. When the French military vessel *Liberateur d'Italie* (Liberator of Italy) tried to enter the San Nicolò mouth on the Lido, the commander of the fortress of Sant'Andrea, Domenico Pizzamano, opened fire, sinking the ship and killing its crew, including its commander Jean-Baptiste Laugier. On April 25 at Graz, Napoleon gave Venetian emissaries Francesco Donà and Lorenzo Giustinian-Lolin a list of demands (such as dismissing the English ambassador) and, in a chilling reference to Venice's origin story, warned that he would be "an Attila to the Venetian state."[86] Then on the first of May at Palmanova, Napoleon informed Donà and Giustinian-Lolin that France was now at war with Venice, although they concluded an armistice the very next day. With the agreement of Leoben in mind (namely, the eventual handover of the Veneto to Austria) and wanting it to appear that the government of Venice had willingly reformed itself and not been taken by force of arms, Napoleon entrusted orchestrating the Republic's surrender to Joseph Villetard.

For their part, the Savi Grandi had already decided no longer to convene the Senate and entrusted decision-making to a committee of forty-two, made up of the Signoria, current and former Savi, the heads of the Ten, and State Attorneys. Tellingly, Giovanni Zusto, the commissioner entrusted with defense of the lagoon and barrier islands, was not included, an indication that decision-makers no longer intended to resist.[87] On May 9, Villetard detailed Napoleon's demands, including that a provisional municipal government be established, Venice's navy be placed under joint command of the French and the new municipal government, and French troops be invited into the city to ceremonially take command of all strategic sites.[88] Accordingly, on May 12, 1797, the Greater Council assembled for the final time, not even reaching the required 600-member quorum. Doge Ludovico Manin urged acceptance of Napoleon's latest ultimatum. When shots were heard outside (as it turned out, a salute by departing Dalmatian soldiers), the assembled nobles hurried to vote. The resolution passed with 512 yeas, 20 nays, and 5 abstentions. The Republic was no more. Unaware of what had transpired, many of the *popolo* continued to rally in the streets, shouting "Viva San Marco."[89]

Four days later, Donà, Giustinian-Lolin, and Luigi Alvise Mocenigo signed a peace accord with Napoleon that recognized the dissolution of the Greater Council, the end of Venice's hereditary aristocracy, and the sovereignty of "the union of all the citizens."[90] Secret articles also spelled out the payment of 3 million *tornesi* that would be made to the paymaster of the Armée d'Italie in three installments, the handover of naval supplies worth an additional 3 million *tornesi*, and three ships of the line and two frigates. Venice also agreed to consign twenty paintings and 500 manuscripts chosen by Napoleon.[91] In return, he promised that his troops would protect lives and property and that the Venetian public debt would be honored, as would the stipends and other subsidies provided to poor, property-less nobles. In other words, the representatives traded the Republic's independence for a guarantee that the wealth of rich nobles, namely, their stake in the national debt and especially their mainland estates, would be safeguarded from confiscation by Napoleon's army, while poor nobles would continue to receive their pensions.[92] In their last official transaction, the nobles traded Saint Mark's Republic for financial guarantees.

The end of the Republic can be attributed, on one hand, to the patricians' lack of political will and imagination. During the eighteenth century, they had repeatedly refused to modify the constitution to better reflect new elements of society, trim from their ranks poor nobles who formed the elite's political clienteles, or extend power to *terraferma* notables. As the policy of neutrality indicates, they were unwilling to take risks and continued to protect their privileges until time ran out. On the other hand, it is important to recognize that they were operating from a position of weakness, ruling a minor state caught in the vise of greater ones. How could they possibly reverse changes in geopolitics that had been in motion since the turn of the sixteenth century? To create a truly defensible minor state—one without natural borders but strategically positioned at the top of the Adriatic Sea—would have required greater financial sacrifices than they were willing to make and concession to *terraferma* notables of a real voice in political decision-making in order to create a genuinely cohesive regional state. In the end they sacrificed political power for their *terraferma* properties. For a final time, the patricians used their monopoly on power to protect their economic interests and, in so doing, allowed their anachronistic city-state form of government to pass into history.

On May 16 a proclamation was issued in the name of the "Most Serene Prince" declaring that power had been transferred to the new Democratic Municipal Government. A manifesto issued that same day named the members of the new municipal assembly. The government now consisted of sixty delegates, with a president, vice president, four secretaries, and eight committees. To ease tensions within the city, the French had pushed for former doge Manin to be offered the presidency, but the idea was rejected. Assembly members included ex-patricians, merchants, professionals, clergy, military men, and even some representatives of the *popolo*, such as the warden of the Nicolotti. Three were Jews. During the summer, twenty additional delegates were added to the assembly as representatives of Cavarzere, Torcello, Murano, Mestre, Pellestrina, Loreo, Chioggia, Gambarare, and Oriago, a modified version of the old *dogado*.[93]

In the few short months of its existence, the Democratic Municipal Government enacted liberal reforms aimed at dismantling old privileges and asserting equality (of males). Nobility was suppressed, coats of arms and titles were forbidden. As patrician Andrea Querini remarked in late 1797, "I am now a subject, and can be ordered about."[94] The entailing of property, one of the primary means by which nobles had accumulated and preserved wealth, was abolished.[95] In July, Jews were emancipated from confinement in the Ghetto and were granted the same juridical rights as others, including the freedom to buy property, enter the military, and attend public schools. Plans were also drawn up for educational, penal, police, and judicial reforms, including replacement of the hated inquisitorial procedure. The mentally ill, who had long been under the purview of the Ten, were moved to a hospital on the island of San Servolo.[96]

Although some effort was made to emphasize continuity with the Republic by including former patricians in the government, assuming the defunct Republic's public debt, and engaging the clergy in public celebrations, a stronger impulse was to affirm a radical break with the past and reeducate the populace in liberty, equality, and fraternity. As had happened in France, this involved reimagining space and time, erasing the former Republic's symbols of power, and rewriting history. The new government's Committee on Public Instruction, which included two ex-patricians and two clergymen, was charged with this task.

One profoundly unsettling change was substitution of the French revolutionary calendar for the Gregorian one; weeks, hours, and minutes were organized on the decimal system in this "Year One of Italian Liberty." Space too had to be reworked. The plan was to abolish the *sestieri* and divide the city into eight more or less co-equal sections, several of whose names alluded to their principal urban function: Marina (Sea)—the area around the Arsenal; Legge (Law)—the San Marco precinct; Spettacoli (Spectacles)—the theater district; Educazione (Education); Commercio (Commerce); Pesca (Fishing)—San Nicolò to Santa Marta; Rivoluzione (Revolution); and Viveri (Victuals). Although not a section, the Ghetto was to be renamed Reunione (Reunion).[97]

Piazza San Marco was rechristened Piazza Grande and reclaimed for democracy. The main event took place on June 4 (16 Pratile, according to the revolutionary calendar). The centerpiece was a liberty tree. Banners adorned the space, and as bands played and processions marched, the president of the assembly, Angelo Talier, gave a speech referencing the Cassiodorian image of Venice's original inhabitants who, "animated by the fire of virtue, preferred true equality and liberty to every other comfort and pleasure, submitting even to the lack of healthy waters and fertile earth."[98] The festivities culminated with the burning of the Golden Book and ducal insignia as the president intoned, "May the vain and imposing titles scatter themselves to the winds . . . may perfidy and political suspicion stay far from us forever, which, after having imposed on us the hateful and detestable aristocratic yoke, replaced our calm of spirit with the fear of hired spies."[99] Over the next several months, such symbols of the old regime as statues of doges, coats of arms, and sculpted lions of Saint Mark were systematically defaced or destroyed, the Porta della Carta offering a prime example with its doge and lion group removed and demolished. In Portobuffolé near Treviso the inscription on the book in Mark's lion's paws was changed from the traditional "Pax tibi Marce evangelista meus" (Peace to You Mark My Evangelist) to "Diritti e doveri dell'uomo e del cittadino" (Rights and Duties of Man and Citizen).[100]

After the festivities in San Marco, the dignitaries attended the opera at La Fenice. The opera presented that night, *La morte di Mitridate* by librettist Antonio Simeone Sografi and composer Nicola Zingarelli, was changed to fit the new political situation. The 1796 rendition had had "a quasi-happy ending" with Mithridates's death greeted with sorrow by his subjects and defeat of the invading Romans. In the version staged at La Fenice, Mithridates, the tyrannical king of Pontus, is portrayed as even more barbaric and suffers a ghastly death as shouts of Roman victory resound in the distance and the chorus sings "Viva la libertà!"[101]

Just as operatic ancient history was rewritten to bolster the new order, so too was Venetian history, including the central event in the Republic's past, the Serrata, and the subsequent Querini-Tiepolo Conspiracy. This especially involved the rehabilitation of Baiamonte Tiepolo, who was portrayed as a democrat seeking to turn back the oligarchs' Serrata power grab. Sografi composed an "Azione Teatrale, Democratica" (Democratic Theater Action) to portray these events. As he wrote to the Committee on Public Instruction, "The uniting of the two epochs would be of no little instruction to the people. I speak of the closing of the Maggior Consiglio [Greater Council] of 1296 [*sic*] and the Conspiracy of Baiamonte in 1310."[102] An engraving by Francesco del Pedro of Luigi Sabelli's drawing in the series *Fasti veneti, o collezione de' più illustri fatti della Repubblica veneziana insino a Bajamonte Tiepolo* (Venetian Events or Collection of the Most Illustrious Deeds of the Venetian Republic up to Baiamonte Tiepolo) published in Venice in 1796-7 depicts Tiepolo preparing to leave the body-strewn Piazza at the end of his revolt, as the defenders of the regime approach. Iconographically, the figure of Tiepolo is complex: his armor renders him like an ancient Roman freedom fighter while his stance, especially the positioning of his sword, calls to mind the avenging Archangel Michael. As in Mark's lion at Portobuffolé, Christian and revolutionary imagery conjoin. The caption explains how through the actions of the doge (namely the Serrata), "the good people" were "defrauded of their most sacred and precious rights." Oligarchy overthrew primitive democracy.

Another outstanding issue was Venice's relationship to its former *terraferma* dominions. In June, Napoleon organized the mainland territories into seven units modeled on French *départments*. The new revolutionary municipal governments of the mainland cities were determined to avoid falling anew under Venetian control. In July representatives from Belluno, Vicenza, Padua, Verona, and Treviso convened in Bassano and decided to

FIGURE 16.4 Francesco del Pedro, *Bajamonte Tiepolo sottraendosi dalla vendetta aristocratica*, 1796–7. From *Fasti veneti o collezione de' più illustri fatti della Repubblica veneziana insino a Bajamonte Tiepolo* (Venice, 1797), plate 29. O. Böhm, Venice.

seek admission to the Cisalpine Republic that Napoleon had created south of the Po, with its capital at Milan.[103] Negotiations dragged on until the question was rendered moot by the Treaty of Campoformido (or Campo Formio) between Austria and France that was signed on October 17 and ended the War of the First Coalition (1792–7).

The treaty concluded Venice's brief revolutionary interval. In the preceding months, the French and Austrians had been picking over the carcass of the former Republic: the French seizing the Ionian islands, the Austrians Istria and Dalmatia in keeping with what had been decided at Leoben. By the terms of Campoformido, the French also acquired the Austrian Netherlands (essentially Belgium), the left bank of the Rhine, Venice's old *terraferma* possessions west of the Adige that had been incorporated into the Cisalpine Republic, and recognition of the new Ligurian Republic (Genoa and surrounding lands) that Napoleon had created. In addition to Istria, Austria claimed Dalmatia as far south as Cattaro, Venice's *terraferma* possessions east of the Adige and north of the Po, and the city itself. The peace proved to be little more than a truce once the War of the Second Coalition (1798–1802) erupted in fall 1798.[104]

In November 1797 Venice's Democratic Municipal Government began to wind down its activities while seeking to maintain public order. French troops started to depart, and politically compromised members of the municipal government, ardent revolutionary poet Ugo Foscolo among them, emigrated to the Cisalpine Republic. The French took with them everything that was salvageable from the Arsenal (artillery, gunpowder, ships) and destroyed the rest. They carted away numerous paintings, including Veronese's *Wedding Feast at Cana* from the refectory at San Giorgio Maggiore and hundreds of manuscripts as agreed to in May.[105] To the Venetians' chagrin, they also took the horses of San Marco, which was not part of the agreement, and burned the doge's ceremonial galley. On January 18, 1798, the last French troops left as Austrian soldiers began to occupy the city, although the Austrian commander decided to maintain his headquarters in Padua. As Austrian officials made their way down the Grand Canal, bells clanged and shouts of "Long live the Emperor, long live Francis II, our liberator" resounded.[106]

The period known as the First Austrian Domination saw a concerted effort to undo most of the changes instituted by the Democratic Municipal Government. One of the first things Austrian commander Olivier Remigius, Count of Wallis, did was abolish the governmental system the French had established in both Venice and the Veneto and declare Venice the capital of the new Austro-Veneto state under the rule of a Governo Generale which answered to Vienna. In late February, 900 patricians assembled in the Ducal Palace to swear allegiance to Francis, a ritual undoing of the abolition of the Republic. The city and *dogado* were to be managed by a Congregation of Noble Delegates who would handle such matters as waters and streets, censuses, food, and the militia. Several prominent noblemen were appointed to posts in the government: Andrea Querini Stampalia was placed in charge of the Arsenal; Zuanne Zusto and Girolano Ascanio Molin (former State Inquisitors and heads of the Ten) led the police. The conservative Francesco Pesaro, who had taken refuge in Austria, returned as Extraordinary Commissary and set out to purge those who had been pro-French. But on his death in 1799, the Austrians began to assume more posts, to the detriment of former patricians. Increasingly the criterion for participation in government was property-holding rather than noble status. Clearly, the Austrians did not intend to reset the clock to before the Republic ended. The years of the first Austrian domination were difficult ones, with troop movements, battles, and requisitions in the Veneto, and economic hardships in the city. In the December 1805 Treaty of Pressburg between Austria and France, France received Istria, Dalmatia, Venice, and the Veneto. The latter two were then incorporated into the Kingdom of Italy that Napoleon created in 1805 and that also included Savoy, Lombardy, Friuli, South Tyrol, the Trentino, and the Marches.[107] Napoleon, who had become emperor of France in 1804, assumed the title king of Italy, although the kingdom with its capital in Milan was governed by Viceroy Eugène de Beauharnais, Napoleon's stepson.

Venice's interval as part of the Kingdom of Italy saw the abolition or suppression of many of the former Republic's institutions as well as lasting and significant changes to the city's urban form. When incorporated into the kingdom, Venice and the Veneto were divided into seven departments most named after bodies of water. The department encompassing Venice was called Adriatico. Each department had as its chief official a prefect, none of whom were locals. Venice's first prefect was a Milanese, the second from Novara. With this pattern, Napoleon planned to disrupt regional identities and loyalties and institute administrative homogeneity. Each prefect was assisted by a Council of the Prefecture and by a seldom convened General Council, all of which ultimately answered to the minister of the interior of the kingdom in Milan. The prefectures were subdivided into vice-prefectures, districts, and communes. In Venice, local government was made up of a municipal Council of Savi (later called the Communal Council) serving under an executive known as the podesta. That post was held from 1806 to 1811 by ex-patrician Daniele Renier who had held high office during the Republic and served in the Congregation of Noble Delegates under the Austrians. Former patrician Bartolomeo Gradenigo, who had also occupied many posts in the Republic and been a member of the Congregation of Noble Delegates, succeeded him. The choice to collaborate in the various governments that ruled Venice in this period was sometimes motivated by ideological agreement with the regimes' goals but more often by simple pragmatism.[108] Napoleon created a top-down administrative system in which local decisions could be overruled by the central government in Milan. In the centuries-old competition between Venice and Milan, the latter seemed to have triumphed. The structure Napoleon put in place dealt a further blow to Venice's claim to rule over the *terraferma* and its role as a capital city. From 1809 on, Istria, Dalmatia, Carinthia, and Croatia were organized as the Illyrian Provinces, answering directly to France.[109]

Some effort was made to restart the economy, which was suffering severely from the English naval blockade aimed at French-controlled territories. The Chamber of Commerce was relaunched. In addition, institutions were set up to promote scientific and cultural revival. In 1810, Ateneo Veneto (Venetian Athenaeum) was created, as was the Reale Istituto Nazionale, renamed in 1838 the Istituto Veneto di Scienze, Lettere ed Arti (Venetian Institute of Science, Letters, and Arts). These organizations provided means for bourgeois elites to move into positions of political and cultural power.[110] Ateneo Veneto was open to Jews. In 1807 the Accademia di Belle Arti was reinstituted as the Reale Accademia di Belle Arti (Royal Academy of Fine Arts). But both Venetians and *terraferma* residents bore a heavy burden of taxation and conscription into military service. Of the estimated 27,000 men from the Kingdom of Italy who participated in Napoleon's disastrous Russian campaign, only a tiny fraction survived.[111]

One of the biggest impacts of the Napoleonic years was on the cityscape. On January 9, 1807, Viceroy de Beauharnais created the Commissione all'Ornato (Design Commission). Its five members included Antonio Diedo, secretary of the Accademia di Belle Arti, and Gianantonio Selva, architect of La Fenice and the moving force behind many of the subsequent projects. Specifically, it was charged with devising a plan "for the symmetrical betterment of buildings fronting streets; and the enlargement and straightening of the streets themselves."[112] In other words, the commission was to impose on Venice a coherent, rationalized neo-classical vision, in keeping with that being realized in Paris. This differed markedly from the labyrinth of narrow winding streets and canals that had emerged ad hoc during the Middle Ages in response to Venice's unique natural conditions.[113]

Eleven months later, on December 7, 1807, a decree with twelve rubrics was issued outlining a broad plan for a relaunch of the city, designed above all to reclaim Venice's maritime and commercial traditions.[114] The first rubric added a number of communes previously assigned to other departments to Adriatico; the last recommended further systematization of the Brenta and Bacchiglione river courses. The island of San Giorgio Maggiore was declared a freeport and was to be equipped with warehouses. The decree called for the appointment of a chief engineer to oversee projects regarding the port, both ordinary maintenance work and new projects such as creation of a rear gateway into the Arsenal and dredging of a deep shipping channel to the Malamocco mouth. The prefect was placed in charge of the magistracy of health, and all charitable and welfare institutions (hospitals, orphanages, hospices, etc.) were to be under the direction of a Congregation of Charity, composed of "upright and zealous citizens" who would volunteer their services. A general hospital was to be established at Santa Maria Maggiore, and the number of parishes reduced from sixty-nine to forty. The design rubric called for creation of a municipal cemetery on the island of San Cristoforo between Venice and Murano, illumination of the city with oil lamps, extension of the Riva degli Schiavoni, creation of public gardens with promenades and paths in the far reaches of Castello, and "another grandiose promenade" on the Giudecca.[115] Other rubrics outlined sources of the city's revenue.

Only some of these projects were realized. To facilitate its freeport status, San Giorgio Maggiore was furnished with a quay and two lighthouses. To improve access to the new public gardens, the Rio di Sant'Anna was filled in to create a wide street dubbed Via Eugenia in honor of the viceroy. To make way for the gardens, several monasteries were razed along with a sailors' hospice, the church of San Nicolò di Bari, and other buildings.[116] The church and monastery of San Cristoforo were torn down to create the municipal cemetery. Elsewhere in the city private houses, parish churches, *scuole*, and monasteries were demolished. In 1810 the number of parishes was further reduced from forty to thirty. During the rule of the French, sixty monasteries and convents in the patriarchate and more than 340 *scuole* (except those dedicated to the Most Holy Sacrament) were suppressed—a stunning blow to the old order of society.[117] Many of the best paintings were hauled off to Milan, while gold and silver altar furnishings were melted down. Other paintings, along with sculptures, wooden choir stalls, and other paraphernalia, were sold off, some used as firewood. Three years earlier San Marco had been designated the city's cathedral church, thus transferring the seat of the patriarchate from San Pietro di Castello. The chapters of the two churches were combined and the office of *primicerio* (chief priest) of San Marco abolished. The patriarch was installed in Ca' Corner at San Maurizio until a new Patriarchal Palace could be built adjoining the basilica. The dioceses of Torcello and Caorle were abolished and joined to Venice's.[118]

With the creation of the Porta Nuova (New Gate) on the northeastern side of the Arsenal, the naval functions of the Bacino diminished, although it remained the center of merchant marine activity. The French also militarized the lagoon, stationing troops at twenty-nine scattered installations, and planned a parade ground on the Giudecca that was never realized.[119] To facilitate all this, a vast survey or census of the urban fabric, known as the Catasto Napoleonico, was compiled, with each property numbered, catalogued, and keyed to accompanying registers and indices. This operation served to "homogenize" the cityscape, erasing its historical and cultural dimensions and facilitating interventions.[120]

Some of the most radical changes occurred in Piazza San Marco, although these projects were not part of the 1807 decree. The viceroy decided to create a Royal Palace by repurposing the Procuratie Nuove, on the Piazza's south side. However, the new residence and governmental center needed an appropriately grandiose entryway. To this end, he had the ancient church of San Geminiano at the west end of the Piazza demolished and replaced with what is known as the Napoleonic wing. The new wing housed a monumental staircase and ballroom. A large bronze "N" (for Napoleon) was mounted in the center of the top floor. Beauharnais also tore down the medieval grain warehouses at Terranova behind the Procuratie Nuove facing the Bacino to make way for the Giardini Reali (Royal Gardens), reserved for the royal household's private use. The Marciana library was turned into the viceroy's private residence, while the library itself, along with the Chamber of Commerce and other offices, were moved to the Ducal Palace. A bronze semi-nude colossus of Napoleon was erected in the Piazzetta. It was paid for by merchants to commemorate the creation of the San Giorgio Maggiore freeport.[121] The effect of all these changes was to "marginalize" the Ducal Palace and reorient the Piazza to its western, Napoleonic, royal wing.[122]

When Napoleon's fortunes turned following his ill-fated invasion of Russia, Italy again became a battlefield as Austrian troops pushed the viceroy's troops out of the Veneto. For several months, from October 1813 to April 1814, Venice found itself blockaded by the English by sea and the Austrians by land. On April 6 Napoleon abdicated and ten days later the viceroy and

Austrians reached an armistice. On April 19, Austrian troops began to reoccupy the city. A year later, on May 3, 1815, representatives of the various Veneto provinces swore fealty to Francis I, emperor of Austria. According to the terms hammered out in the Congress of Vienna in June 1815, the Kingdom of Lombardy-Venetia became part of the Austrian Empire, with Milan and Venice as co-capitals. In that same year, the horses of San Marco were removed from the Arc de Triomph du Carrousel in Paris and ceremonially returned to Venice. A new and difficult chapter in Venice's history had begun.

An essay published in February 1816 in the *Gazzetta privilegiata di Venezia* recalled the pleasures of Carnivals long past with their "immense, ever-swirling vortex of disguised, masked people . . . an ordered disorder." It continued, "To the consequent moral breakdown was added every physical corruption and misery, first convulsing and then destroying the delicious happiness now lost."[123] In this way the destruction of the Republic was recast not as a failure of political leadership on the part of the patricians, nor as a missed opportunity to meet head-on the challenges of a changing world, but as the result of moral decay. Such an interpretation exonerated those in power of responsibility and cast a nostalgic if moralizing eye on times past.

Something of the same is evident in a series of 104 pen-and-ink drawings entitled *Divertimenti per li regazzi* (Amusements for Children) that Giandomenico Tiepolo produced in 1797. In them a tribe of Pulcinellas cohabitate with regular Venetians and engage in everyday activities.[124] But the series takes a political turn when some Pulcinellas are arrested, imprisoned, tried, and exiled by men identifiable by their bicorn hats as French. On one sheet Pulcinellas uproot a Liberty Tree, while on the following sheet a group of them cavort riotously in a tavern. Painted on the wall behind them is Saint Mark's lion with two V's superimposed one on the other—shorthand for "Evviva" (Long live). Read with the lion, they create the slogan "Long live San Marco," an exclamation the French had outlawed.[125] Produced in the year the Republic ended, this image recalled a bygone world, one so far removed from reality as to be irretrievable.

Along with William Wordsworth's melancholic sonnet "On the Extinction of the Venetian Republic" (1802) and musings like those in the *Gazzetta privilegiata di Venezia*, Tiepolo's images served to establish an ongoing vision of Venice as a surreal city lost to time and marked by death and decay, a view congenial to the sensibilities and emphases of the movement known as Romanticism that captivated Europeans in the first half of the nineteenth

FIGURE 16.5 Giandomenico Tiepolo, *Tavern Scene* from pen and ink series *Divertimenti per li regazzi*, 1790s. Cleveland Museum of Art Photographic Library Collection, Department of Image Collections, National Gallery of Art, Washington, DC.

century and persisted well into the twentieth. However, that nostalgia for a lost world obscures the profound changes that Venice experienced in the nineteenth century as its economy shifted gears, new elites emerged, and the cityscape was transformed to meet the needs of industry and tourism. The urban changes introduced between 1797 and 1814 already pointed in those new directions, although elements of the Old Regime, especially the emphasis on hierarchy and authority, persisted while the Austrians controlled the city and until Venice joined a unified Italy in 1866.

17

Austrian Venice, 1815–1866

JANUARY 11, 1846, was one of the most momentous if lesser known dates in Venice's history. On that day, the bridge linking the city by rail to the mainland officially opened. Encompassing 262 arches of brick and Istrian stone, the bridge stretched a mile and a half from Marghera to a station near the entryway to the Grand Canal. Fourteen years later a new terminal was built, with the church of Santa Lucia demolished to provide the site. The railway bridge represented a dramatic rupture with Venice's past. It ended thirteen centuries of physical separation from mainland Europe, isolation that had been the bulwark of the Republic's military defense, basis of its claim to political sovereignty, and one fount of the inhabitants' collective identity. At the same time, the bridge profoundly shaped Venice's future. Its construction led to a radical reorientation of the city—"spinning it around" as it were—so that what had once been the back door became the primary entryway.[1]

The construction of the railway bridge offers a fitting introduction to the years 1815–66 since it played a role in many of the most important developments of the period, which is traditionally subdivided into the Second Austrian Domination (1815–48), the Revolutionary Republic (1848–49), and the Third Austrian Domination (1849–66). First and foremost, the bridge figured in long-term plans to revive Venice's economy after the devastation of the Napoleonic era. By linking Venice to Milan, the railway, known as the Ferdinandea after Emperor Ferdinand of Austria, was intended to draw trade back to the city and away from rivals Genoa and Trieste, the latter favored by Vienna. Second, the railway was advocated by a new industrial bourgeoisie, including many Jews, who in the nineteenth century largely replaced former patricians as Venice's civic elite. Third, construction of the railway became part of the national unification project, known as the Risorgimento, that consumed Italians in the first half of the century. Just as the rail lines physically linked cities, so Venetians, Milanese, and others established contacts that were mobilized to throw off the Austrian yoke. The rail project evolved from a money-making venture into a nation-making one.[2] Fourth, the railway and the subsequent urban restructuring of Venice prompted a vigorous debate about the place of industrialization in the city's future and inspired many, including not a few foreigners, to imagine Venice as a city that defied modernization and offered an alternative to it. Finally, the railway facilitated the rapid growth of tourism, which gained an expanded role in Venice's economy and physical evolution. Only the most prescient of those who attended the bridge's inauguration could have imagined where the span would lead.

The Kingdom of Lombardy-Venetia, created in 1815, was one, albeit a crucial, part of the Austrian empire, which included at least eleven different national groups. Emperor Francis I and his chancellor Klemens von Metternich feared that nationalism and liberalism would rend their multi-ethnic empire asunder. In what almost seems a replay of the Hapsburg/Valois rivalry of the sixteenth century, Austria's goal was to block France; and Italy was again central to that effort. Metternich himself declared, "It is on the river Po that we defend the Rhine."[3] The keys to Austria's defense were the four fortresses known as the Quadrilateral: Verona, Legnago, Peschiera, and Mantua, the first three of which were in the Veneto, meaning that any conflict would inevitably involve Venetia. This explains why the Austrians maintained a large military presence there. Ideologically the regime emphasized obedience to emperor and church. Francis I responded to the salutations of Ateneo Veneto by declaring, "I don't ask of you sciences, I ask of you religion and morality, [and] faithful submission to my person."[4] In keeping with this conservative bent, neo-classicism remained the preferred style in art. Its leading practitioner was the sculptor Antonio Canova, who enjoyed European renown, while Lorenzo Santi's coffeehouse in the Royal Gardens is an example of the continuing vogue for neo-classicism in Venetian architecture under Austrian rule.[5]

The Austrians devised a complex governmental structure for Lombardy-Venetia. At the summit was the viceroy, a position held from 1818 to 1848 by Francis I's brother Rainer, who divided his time between the royal villa at Monza and the Villa Pisani at Strà. But the viceroyalty was much less powerful than it had been in the Napoleonic Kingdom of Italy. Real power was exercised by the governors, one in Milan, the other in Venice, and their cabinets. Lombardy and Venetia were subdivided into provinces (Venetia had

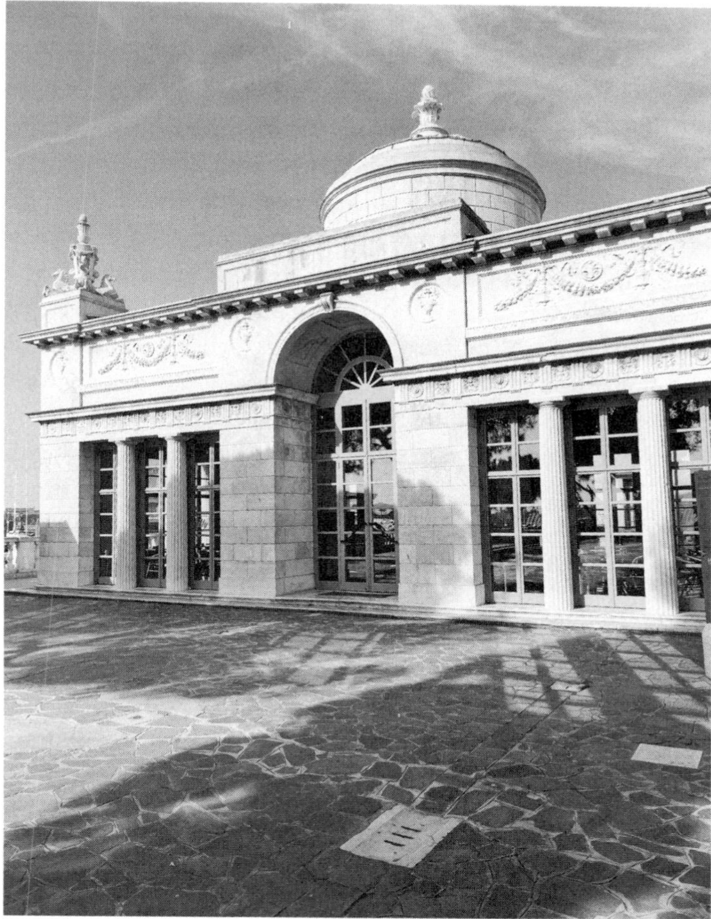

FIGURE 17.1 Lorenzo Santi, Coffeehouse in the Royal Gardens, 1830s, Venice. Photo by the author.

eight). Consultative bodies called "congregations" at the regional and provincial levels, manned by those who met high property qualifications, had little real power. Provincial capitals and other cities had communal councils whose members were chosen by cooptation. Venice's council had sixty members. Its executive was comprised of the mayor, known as the podesta, who was chosen by the emperor from a list of three candidates submitted to him, and a cabinet of assessors. The podesta's term of office was three years and renewable. Communes exercised control over public health, welfare, schools, buildings, streets, and waters, while Vienna maintained a tight grip over military and police powers. But the imperial administration neglected the navy, a liability for

Venice and its Arsenal. All major policy and personnel decisions, including selection of bishops and archbishops, emanated from the imperial court.[6] Very few residents of Venetia advanced to the highest echelons of the imperial bureaucracy, and none of Venetia's governors were natives or even Lombards.[7]

Austria inherited from France a devastated Venice. Writing more than two decades after the Austrians had retaken the city, Metternich's wife Countess Melanie Zichy-Ferraris commented that although from a distance the city presented "a grandiose spectacle," up close, "the first impression is of sadness, because so many houses are in ruin."[8] Indeed the 1810s and '20s were the nadir of the city's fortunes. While in 1790, the city had 136,803 inhabitants, by 1813 the number had dropped to 115,000. Under the Austrians the slide continued: from 100,556 in 1823 to 98,638 in 1830, and finally to a low of 93,545 in 1838 before beginning to rebound.[9] Disease, hunger, war, and emigration all took their toll.

Other figures illustrate the economic and social devastation. Whereas in 1797 Venice had 10,884 persons engaged in wholesale and retail trade, by 1825 the number was 3,628. Over the same period the number of artisans declined from 6,200 to 2,442 and Arsenal workers from 3,302 to 773. Gondoliers in the employ of families dropped from 2,854 to just 297.[10] As the figures for merchants and Arsenal workers suggest, trade and port activities were especially hard hit. Between 1816 and 1820, Venetian exports to the Levant declined by half after having already suffered severely late in the previous century. Such maritime traffic as did exist was largely traffic within the Adriatic, with Venice serving as little more than an ancillary port to Trieste.[11] Manufacturing languished as well, with exports hindered by tariff barriers between Venetia and Lombardy that remained in place until 1822 and between Venetia and Tyrol until 1825. In 1814 only four glassworks were operating on Murano. Additionally, artisans no longer had the employment opportunities and social protections offered by guilds. The steep drop in the number of privately employed gondoliers demonstrates that service sector jobs also dried up as the old ruling class, with its conspicuously consumptive lifestyle, was swept away. Despite the dire economic situation, the Austrians refused to place price controls on necessities and imposed a heavy tax burden on such basics as bread, wine, flour, rice, and butter, as well as a kind of stamp tax (for stamped paper) and in the countryside a personal tax. Although Lombardy-Venetia represented only one-eighth of the empire's territory and one-seventh of its population, it bore one-fourth of the tax burden.[12]

Much of Venice's population lived in wretched poverty. Between 1797 and 1824 the number of persons sheltered in hospitals and other charitable institutions mushroomed from 1,446 to 4,919, but those who lived at the edge of disaster numbered in the tens of thousands.[13] Disease was rife. In the poorest parishes, one in three infants died before age one, and half by age five. Substandard housing and poor hygiene meant that illnesses easily swept through the city. Even hospitals offered no refuge. An 1836 cholera outbreak carried off 421 of the 592 inmates of the Casa di Ricovero (Poor House) housed at the old hospital of the Derelitti while a maize-heavy diet left people susceptible to pellagra.[14] Poor harvests such as occurred in 1816–7 and 1846–7 brought people to the edge of starvation and in the latter period to revolt. As one Austrian official astutely noted, "The price of polenta is a barometer of the public mood."[15]

Although the Austrians mapped out an admirable system of public education largely manned by parish priests and designed to create good imperial subjects, only half the populace was literate in 1869. In the fishermen's parish of Angelo Raffaele the literacy rate dropped to a mere 20 percent of men, even less of women.[16] Poverty limited the physical and imaginative horizons of the poorest residents. People tended to live and die within a restricted geographical area, often not moving from the parish where they had been born. French writer and *salonnière* Madame de Staël wrote that some had never been to Piazza San Marco and that for most the sight of a horse would have been a "true marvel."[17]

Physically too the city was in a parlous state. Housing was worst for the poor, with many living in single rooms without toilet facilities, although Venice was hardly unique in that regard. Waste was left in the streets or dumped into canals.[18] The Napoleonic razing of churches, monasteries, and hundreds of private palaces continued under the Austrians with such losses as the parish churches of Santa Marina, San Basegio, San Boldo, and Sant'Angelo, and the monasteries of Santa Maria dei Servi and the Celestia.[19] Countess Metternich was right to declare the city "in ruin."

At the summit of society, social dislocation was just as pronounced as at the bottom. The period from 1797 to approximately 1820 took a heavy toll on former patricians. Both poor and moderately wealthy nobles suffered the loss of salary-paying jobs and other forms of welfare the Republic had offered. Even the rich found themselves burdened with massive debts that led to a huge sell-off of landed property, both *terraferma* estates and palaces in the city. The richest ex-patricians sold the most. Inheritance laws enshrined in the Austrian civil code accelerated the dispersal of family fortunes as they required testators to leave at least half their estate in equal shares to all their children, daughters as well as sons, and allowed entail only on the half of the estate that the testator could dispose of as he or she pleased,. These changes decreased the incentives for the centuries-old practice of *fraterna*. The four Querini Stampalia brothers continued to live together until 1808 when they went their separate ways. In some families like the Donà, the practice of restricting marriages came to an end.[20] Even so, the class's demographic decline continued. Between 1797 and 1846 another fifty families went extinct. The last Dandolo died in 1875. Patrimonies were sold off. Giovanni Filippo Barbarigo's collection of paintings, including works by Titian, was sold to the czar of Russia for the Hermitage collection.[21] Antiques dealers did a thriving business in nineteenth-century Venice.

According to the procedures established by the Austrians, former patricians could pay a tax that conferred the status of "count." For an even higher fee they could enjoy the appellation "prince" of the Austrian empire. Only two, an Erizzo from an old ducal family and a Giovanelli from a family that had bought its way into the patriciate during the War of Candia, chose that option.[22] But many poor and even moderately wealthy former patricians could not afford the tax and simply blended into the ranks of the bourgeoisie or even the *popolo*.[23] However, a small number of families continued to prosper and maintain a degree of social and political power. Former patricians monopolized the office of podesta under the Austrians.

A new civic elite emerged during this period made up of rich bourgeoisie, many of whom bought up much of the real estate the nobles sold. In the great land transfer of this period, 63 percent of sellers were patricians, but they constituted only 19 percent of buyers. By contrast, the bourgeoisie represented 24 percent of sellers but 54 percent of buyers. Jews made up 2 percent of sellers and 7 percent of buyers.[24] In many instances acquisition of significant property-holdings was an important element of the new elite's social ascent. Many were also heavily involved in commerce and manufacturing and were among the first to recognize the possibilities offered by steam power.

Members of this new elite came from a variety of backgrounds. The Papadopolis were wealthy immigrants from Corfu who came to Venice in the last years of the Republic to engage in trade and banking. By 1830 theirs was the most important banking house in Venice. Spiridione Papadopoli, born in 1822, became co-president of the city's major insurance company and was involved in mining ventures. His brother Giovanni was a railroad pioneer. The family purchased and redesigned several patrician palaces and mainland estates as well as land that had once belonged to the convent of Santa Croce which they transformed into an English style Romantic garden.[25]

Another leading figure of the new elite was Giuseppe Reali. Like the Papadopolis, he had a diverse investment portfolio including a sugar refinery and candle and cream of tartar manufacturing facilities in the city, and brick-making and silk-spinning plants on the mainland. He was vice president of the company constructing the Milan/Venice railway and served as president of the Chamber of Commerce. In 1847 he extolled the possibilities that the project for a Suez Canal offered Venice declaring, "Venetian commerce fell into decay because the sea route around the Cape of Good Hope closed the land route to the Indies. This route is about to be reopened: steamships have indeed already opened it; this then is our 'good hope.'"[26] Like the Papadopolis, he bought a former patrician palace, that of the Corrers at Santa Maria della Fava. And he successfully navigated the 1848 revolution against the Austrians and their subsequent return.[27]

One novel characteristic of Venice's nineteenth-century elite was the presence of a significant number of Jews who, after centuries of exclusion from power, constituted what has been described as a "ruling class in reserve."[28] Among the most prominent were brothers Giacomo and Isacco Treves, sons of Iseppo Treves, the first president of the Chamber of Commerce, and Benedetta Bonfil, sole heir to her father's commercial fortune. The brothers in turn got a large inheritance from their parents and maintained an active banking business. Following the failed revolution of 1848-9 (of which they were supporters), they invested in numerous infrastructure projects, including the Milan/Venice railroad. During the 1820s they purchased significant rural and urban lands, including Ca' Barozzi at San Moisè which Giacomo, a major patron of the arts, decorated with works of Canova, among others.[29] When the family was ennobled by the emperor in 1835, it assumed the surname Treves de' Bonfili.[30]

Other Jewish members of the new Venetian elite included Jacopo Levi, Leone Pincherle, Cesare della Vida, and Isacco Pesaro Maurogonato. Not at the same level were members of the Sullam family, who quickly took advantage of the opportunities following 1797 for Jews to purchase property. In the 1830s Giuseppe Sullam innovated in rice cultivation on the family's properties in the Po delta, winning in 1856 a gold medal from the Istituto Veneto di Scienze, Lettere ed Arti for his land improvement projects.[31] Under the Austrians, Jews were still subject to discriminatory measures; they were denied the right to hold most governmental posts or to sit in the provincial, central, or municipal congregations and were forbidden to be pharmacists and notaries.[32] As wealthy Jews moved out of the Ghetto, the old Jewish quarter was left as one of the poorer and more abject parts of the city.[33]

Members of the liberal professions such as physicians, professors, clerks, and lawyers comprised other elements of the new civic elite. However, lawyers felt aggrieved that the inquisitorial method introduced in the Austrian legal code forbade them from defending their clients in courtroom procedures.[34] They would, not surprisingly, assume an outsized role in the 1848-9 revolution. Although coffeehouses remained important venues for the new bourgeoisie to meet and socialize, institutions such as the Chamber of Commerce, Istituto Veneto, and Ateneo Veneto became loci for the diffusion of scientific, technical, and literary knowledge as well as sites of social and political power. The Istituto was refounded in 1838 by the emperor. Its fellows came from throughout Venetia, with scientists predominating over those in literature. It awarded annual prizes in agriculture and science. Ateneo Veneto's membership was dominated by the liberal professions. Unlike the Istituto, which was more aligned to the regime, Ateneo Veneto played an important role in the Revolution of 1848-9.[35] Although the Chamber of Commerce and Ateneo Veneto were open to Jews, women were excluded. But several influential women such as Giustina Renier Michiel continued to host salons that brought together guests with diverse backgrounds and points of view.

Starting in the 1830s, Venice began to emerge from the economic slump of the preceding three decades. Bowing to Venetian pressure, in 1830 the Austrians extended freeport status from San Giorgio Maggiore to the entire city. This was designed to help Venice compete with Trieste and other Adriatic freeports. But it had little immediate effect.[36] More important to the city's transformation and revival were new industries and technologies related to railways, steam power, and gas lighting. In 1837 the Società Ferroviaria (Railroad Company) was created to manage and finance the rail line to Milan that would be completed twenty years later. But in 1842, rails linked Mestre with Padua, in 1846 (the year the bridge opened) Padua and Vicenza were connected, and three years later Vicenza was linked with Verona.[37]

For the railroad to give the necessary jolt to the economy, improvements also needed to be made to the city's port facilities. Because of the various diversions of the Brenta, water flow into the lagoon was not sufficient to scour out the silt and sand that were accumulating around the main shipping entry to the lagoon at Malamocco. Work to remedy this problem was overseen by engineer Pietro Paleocapa and included the construction of two breakwaters finished in 1857. The channel's depth increased to nearly thirty feet which it mantained for a century. Another infrastructure issue that would not be solved until after Venice's unification with Italy and construction of the Maritime Station was managing the transfer of goods from ship to rail. Since the railroad did not extend to the Bacino or the Giudecca Canal, goods had to be offloaded from ships onto small boats and then onloaded to trains, a costly and time-consuming effort. Venice also made little headway in steam-driven traffic on the Po since Vienna favored steamship operators from Trieste.[38]

The introduction of gas lighting was another significant infrastructure project. After much debate about its safety and technical issues, a contract for this lighting was signed in 1839 with an installation date by 1843. The gasworks themselves needed to be located on the periphery. San Francesco della Vigna was selected.[39] There was greater resistance to the idea of bringing fresh water to the city via an aqueduct since some feared that a hostile power could blockade this source of drinking water. In addition to the companies organized to build and operate the railway and gasworks, other corporations of the period include the insurer Assicurazioni Generali Austro-Italiche, founded in 1831 and headquartered in Trieste but with a Venetian office to service Venetia, and the import/export company Società Veneto Commerciale, established in 1839. Thanks to the latter's efforts, products such as coffee, sugar, and cotton began to reach Venice from North and South America.[40]

Not surprisingly, the first area to be illuminated by gaslight was Piazza San Marco with the goal of enticing tourists to linger in the evening in the cafes around the square. Tourism grew substantially even before completion of the railway. In 1844, 112,644 tourists visited, nearly equaling the number of residents.[41] Although some came for the city's decaying artistic treasures, more came to enjoy gambling, opera, and the therapeutic and recreational possibilities of bathing/swimming. In 1833 a floating bathhouse was erected in the Bacino on the recommendation of Tommaso Rima, a physician at the Civic Hospital who advocated bathing therapy.[42]

Growth of the tourism industry was facilitated by the large number of former patrician palaces that could be converted to hotels as well as by the low wages that workers in the hospitality industry commanded given the city's high unemployment rate.[43] In the 1820s, hotelier Giuseppe Dal Niel relinquished his old establishment, the Leon Bianco at Rialto, and moved to the Dandolo palace on the Riva degli Schiavoni, which came to be known by his nickname, Danieli. His move was part of a general shift of hotels from the industry's traditional center at Rialto to the area around San Marco, which offered bathing opportunities, easy access to La Fenice and cafes in Piazza San Marco, and promenades along the Riva degli Schiavoni to the Public Gardens.[44] Further draws to tourism were the Romantic fascination with ruins and decay as well as Venice's (seeming) resistance to modernization and its resultant appeal as an antidote to the problems of industrialization.[45] At the same time, its uniqueness complicated the question of how this most singular of cities could participate in the push toward Italian national unification.

The so-called black legend of the Venetian Republic, the idea that the aristocratic regime maintained power through terror perpetrated by the Ten and State Inquisitors and their coterie of informers, spies, and assassins, enjoyed its greatest popularity in the first half of the nineteenth century, in large part due to the 1819 publication of Frenchman Pierre Daru's *Histoire de la République de Venise* (History of the Venetian Republic).[46] This terrifying image of the Republic gained wider circulation through such works as Lord Byron's plays *Marino Faliero* and *The Two Foscari*, about the disgraced and deposed doges of the fourteenth and fifteenth centuries. Falier's story was turned into an opera by Gaetano Donizetti (*Marino Faliero*), Foscari's by Giuseppe Verdi (*I due Foscari*). In Byron's play, Jacopo Foscari's wife rails against blind obedience to the Ten, saying, "Your torturing instruments have made ye seem the beings of another and worse world!"[47] What was viewed as the "infamy" of Venice's past, combined with its history as a colonial power and exploiter of its *terraferma* dominions, seemed to many to set the city apart from a common Italian heritage, making it difficult to imagine how Venice could be integrated into a unified Italian state.[48]

Yet there were those in the city, including Nicolò Tommaseo and Daniele Manin, who had that precisely as their aim. Tommaseo was born in Sebenico in 1802, studied law at Padua, began a career as a linguist and journalist, and was an adherent of liberal Catholicism. Late in 1847 he presented a damning attack on Austrian censorship in a speech at Ateneo Veneto.[49] Manin was born in Venice in 1804 into a family that had converted in 1759 from Judaism to Catholicism. His paternal grandfather Samuele Medina was sponsored at the baptismal font by Ludovico Manin, who would be the last doge of Venice. As was common, Medina took his sponsor's surname as his own. Daniele, a child prodigy, enrolled at the University of Padua at age fourteen, where he studied law, graduating in 1821. Ten years later he used uprisings in the papal territories in central Italy and the duchies of Parma and Modena to try to spark an overthrow of the Austrians in Venice. It came to nothing. He practiced law in Mestre and Venice, making his home in the parish of San Paternian in a house he rented from banker Giacomo Treves.[50]

Manin cut his political teeth in the debates over construction of the Milan/Venice railway. Among the Venetian shareholders in the company were Giuseppe Reali, Giacomo Treves, and Spiridione Papadopoli, to whose family Manin was related by marriage. However, a major dispute ensued over the railway line's Lombardy stretch since many of the leading Milanese and Venetian backers favored a link between Brescia and Milan that bypassed Bergamo for a direct lowland route through Treviglio. The Bergamasques and several Austrian investors favored the more northerly route. Manin and the engineer Paleocapa were part of a delegation that went to Milan to strategize for the southern path. When it appeared that the Bergamo faction would prevail, Manin launched an effort to attract additional shareholders who would back Treviglio, and at a shareholders' meeting in April 1842 that decision was affirmed. Although Manin lost a subsequent fight when he opposed a governmental takeover of the project, he had gained valuable contacts in Milan and the Veneto. Just as important, the railway issue had become a matter of public debate.[51] Indeed, industrialization's potential to link traditionally separate regions by rail and steam power helped fuel the drive toward unification.[52] The Austrians were adamantly opposed to linking Lombardy-Venetia to other Italian states, seeing this as potentially promoting Italian nationalism and unification.[53]

Having found his calling, in 1847 Manin coordinated a petition requesting that the emperor funnel trade with India through Venice, instead of Trieste, and link Venice by rail to Innsbruck. He addressed Ateneo Veneto on the importance of revitalizing Venetian commerce and helped organize the visit of British free trade advocate Richard Cobden as part of a push to remove trade barriers within Italy. In September, the ninth annual meeting of the Italian Scientific Congress convened in Venice, bringing attendees from throughout the peninsula together to make contacts, exchange ideas, and advance the nationalist cause. One pro-Austrian diarist lamented that the meeting had "awoken the city and the state." In the agronomy sessions, delegates took great delight in criticizing the quality of the *patate* (potatoes) harvested that year, potatoes being slang for Germans.[54]

Literature and the arts also fueled national feelings. The Austrians were compared to the Goths, Vandals, and Huns.[55] Such references particularly resonated in Venice, which traced its origins to the barbarian invasions of the early Middle Ages. Yet it was not always clear whether references to national feeling encompassed Italy or only Venice and its former dominions. The salon hosted by Giustina Renier Michiel, who was related to the Republic's last two doges, cultivated anti-Austrian sentiments. Michiel said of herself, "Above all else I am most Venetian (*venezianissima*)." In her most important writing, a history of the origins of Venetian festivals, she wrote that their purpose had been to instill in "every Venetian that he had a fatherland . . . and that it was he himself who formed and sustained it."[56] The Venetians did express sympathy for the Lombards, also suffering under the Austrian yoke.[57]

Opera played a conspicuous role in instilling patriotic fervor. During the 1847-8 season, performances of Verdi's *Macbeth* created an uproar at La Fenice when the character Malcolm declared, "He who does not hate the land of his birth, let him take up arms and follow me," and the chorus responded, "Our betrayed fatherland calls us, in tears. Brothers! Let us run to rescue the oppressed!" The police tried in vain to discover which audience members had in frenzies of emotion tossed bouquets of red, white, and green flowers onto the stage.[58] (The Italian tricolor of red, white, and green emerged at the time of the French Revolution as a counterpart to the French blue, white, and red one.)

Despite these patriotic sentiments, there was no agreement on how unification might be achieved since Italy remained a hodgepodge of states. Absolute monarchies predominated. The Kingdom of the Two Sicilies (formerly the Kingdom of Naples) was under the Spanish Bourbons; the Kingdom of Sardinia, encompassing Sardinia, Piedmont, and the former Republic of Genoa, was ruled by the House of Savoy from Turin. The duchies of Parma, Modena, and Tuscany were absolutist satellites of Austria. The papal territories, including Ferrara and Bologna, had their own form of absolutist governance. One model for unification was that espoused by Genoese Giuseppe Mazzini, an ardent republican and democrat who called for expelling foreign rulers and uniting Italy as a democratic republic. A more moderate scheme was known as Neo-Guelfism, by which a federation of independent states would be formed under leadership of the pope. The third plan, advocated by the House of Savoy, involved picking off various states and provinces and annexing them to the Kingdom of Sardinia.

Events soon swept Europe into revolution. Poor harvests in 1845 and 1846 led to food shortages and skyrocketing prices. In Venice, the price of wheat and maize doubled, and some businesses went bankrupt. The situation was more dire in the countryside. The Austrian government's failure to reduce taxes, tardiness in forbidding the export of foodstuffs, and failure to fix the price of bread stoked resentment. The election of Pius IX in June 1846 and his granting of several liberal reforms fueled the Neo-Guelf cause, enthusiasm for national unity, and expulsion of the Austrians.[59]

In this highly charged atmosphere Tommaseo gave his speech at Ateneo Veneto attacking censorship. Just days later Manin presented a wide-ranging petition demanding a large degree of autonomy for Lombardy-Venetia while

FIGURE 17.2 The Unification of Italy. The dates indicate when various states became part of the Kingdom of Italy.

Tommaseo devised his own set of demands. On January 18, 1848, both were arrested. Two weeks earlier Austrian troops had fired on protesters in Milan. With emotions running high, the ancient popular factions—the Nicolotti and Castellani—publicly made peace, with Mayor Giovanni Correr attending a celebratory banquet. Carnival was abandoned, and a group of well-to-do citizens including the mayor offered to post bond for Manin. Agitation spread to *terraferma* cities and the countryside.[60]

Events were spiraling out of control elsewhere in Italy and Europe. In late January, Ferdinand II of the Kingdom of the Two Sicilies was forced to grant a constitution; Pope Pius IX, the grand duke of Tuscany, and even Charles Albert, king of Sardinia (Piedmont), followed suit. In late February, French king Louis Philippe abdicated, and the Second Republic was established. Austria's turn at revolution came in March: Metternich was dismissed, and the emperor agreed to a constitution. When news reached the lagoon of events in Vienna, a crowd forced the city's civilian governor, Hungarian Aloys Palffy, to release Manin and Tommaseo. In his haste to do so, Palffy made one of the great Freudian slips in history, ordering the release of Ludovico Manin, the long-deceased last doge, rather than Daniele. Regardless, revolution was afoot.

On March 18 a skirmish in Piazza San Marco between Austrian troops and laboring-class Venetians and students from Padua resulted in eight Venetian deaths and led Manin and others to demand permission from Palffy to form a civic guard. Its creation gave Manin a military force of 2,000 men over which the Austrians had no control. Women too were eager to join but in the end were relegated to nursing the wounded and sewing uniforms.[61] When news reached Venice that Milan was in revolt, and rumors circulated that the Austrians were planning to reinforce their hold on the weapons-rich Arsenal, Manin decided to act. The Arsenal workers had already taken matters into their own hands and killed their hated chief supervisor. On March 22 Manin and members of the civic guard seized control of the Arsenal. When Austrian reinforcements (many of whom were Italians) arrived to reassert order, the Italians among them mutinied and joined the revolution while in Piazza San Marco, the civic guard commandeered the cannons stationed there. In the late afternoon Manin arrived in the Piazza on the shoulders of his supporters where he declared, "We do not thereby mean to separate ourselves from our Italian brothers. Rather we will form one of those centers which must bring about the gradual fusion of Italy into one. *Viva la Repubblica! Viva la libertà! Viva San Marco!*"[62] Bibliophile and scholar Emanuele Cicogna wrote in his diary that just as the old Republic had been founded on March 25, the feast of the Annunciation, so the new democratic republic was created under the Virgin's auspices on March 22.[63]

In the meantime, the municipal government of Mayor Correr representing bourgeois interests had gotten Palffy and military governor Ferdinand Zichy to agree to surrender the city and had itself tried to assume power, but popular enthusiasm forced it to declare Manin president of the new provisional Venetian republic. Revolution also spread to the mainland where the peasantry hoped for tax relief and formed their own rural guards, while cities created provisional governments. However, the Austrians retained control of Verona and the other fortresses of the Quadrilateral, as well as the navy.

Manin filled his cabinet with members of the bourgeoisie, including Paleocapa at Interior, Pincherle at Commerce, and Tommaseo at Culture and Education. The government put forth a program dedicated to equality before the law, respect for property, and freedom of thought and press. There was an explosion of newspapers, with at least seventy-eight published in 1848–9, including forty-three dailies.[64] Tommaseo pushed moral reform. Nobles were permitted to retain their titles, while merchants were won to the Republic's side when it signaled its intention to promote free trade. The Papadopolis and Treveses responded by pledging money to support the civic guard. To retain popular support, the government reduced the price of salt and ordered items pawned at the Monte di Pietà (the official pawn shop) worth less than 4 lire to be restituted for free. This amounted to 100,000 items, powerful testimony to the poverty that gripped much of the population.[65] But the government erred in allowing the troops who had mutinied against the Austrians to return to their homes, thereby depriving itself of a core of well-trained professional soldiers.

It took some persuading for the provisional governments of the *terraferma* cities to join the new provisional Republic since memories of the old Republic's exploitation lingered. One flier circulating in Padua exclaimed, "It is not we who have cried 'Viva San Marco'; that cry awakes in us only the memory of misery and fear." Manin assured them that "the provinces . . . will form with us a single family without any disparity of rights" and promised a justly apportioned constituent assembly.[66] By early April, all the cities had joined, save Austrian-controlled Verona. The peasantry eagerly supported the new government, lured in part by the elimination of the personal tax and reduction of the salt tax. But the fate of the new Republic was soon to be determined by events beyond its borders.

As so many times in its past, Venice's fate was intertwined with Milan's, where the liberal nobility had a stronger hold than the republicans. Fearful that Milan, like France, would be swept by a republican tide, these nobles looked to Charles Albert of Savoy as their savior. When revolution broke out in Milan on March 18, the republicans at first had the upper hand, but they let the opportunity slip when they agreed that the future political settlement would be decided only when the war against the Austrians was won. Mazzini, who arrived in Milan in early April, adopted the same position. This failure of nerve gave Charles Albert the cover he needed to aid northern Italy in expelling the Austrians and create a kingdom of northern Italy in what became known as the First Italian War of Independence (March 1848–August 1849).

Caught between his republican ideals and a united front against Austria, Manin opted for the latter, deciding that further decisions about the form of government should await the war's end. Tommaseo disagreed, but Manin carried the day. This position had three significant consequences: first, it precluded the military intervention of republican France to combat the Austrians, since the French would be aiding the monarchists in Piedmont. Second, Manin's decision to delay further elaboration of the government alienated the *terraferma* cities who perceived the Venetians as making decisions unilaterally, again raising the specter of Venetian domination. Finally, by relying on monarchist military aid, the Venetian government neglected to form its own national army with contingents from the provinces, thus preventing it from harnessing popular enthusiasm for defense on the *terraferma*. The provisional government opted instead to limit its efforts "only to the arming and defense of Venice and its estuary."[67] Also, many peasants who had enthusiastically enrolled in rural civic guards were disillusioned by Venice's failure to supply them adequately with arms or address their grievances against landlords.

The first military encounters in the area around Vicenza showed how unprepared Venetian forces were against Austria's professional soldiers. Austrian general Laval Nugent was charged with invading the Veneto from the east and uniting with Field Marshall Josef Radetzky in Verona, who was being threatened by Piedmontese forces from the west. On April 22 Udine fell; within days most of Friuli followed. On the political front, Charles Albert made clear his attitude toward republicanism. On April 18 he wrote to the pope that "our greatest enemies are not the [Austrian] imperial soldiers but the anti-religious republican party."[68] He was not going to risk his forces to aid Venetia unless Lombardy-Venetia would fuse with Piedmont in a kingdom with Milan as its capital.

Differences of opinion caused a split in the Venetian cabinet, with Manin and Tommaseo opposed to fusion with Piedmont and others favoring it. The provincial cities adopted the fusionist position since Venice had done so little to provide for their military defense. Meanwhile, the military situation worsened. On May 9 the Austrians won a major battle, opening the way for Nugent to link up with Radetzky in Verona. The Venetians had contributed nothing to the battle, leading one Lombard officer to write, "It is almost as if the Venetians are not sons of the same benign and pious Italian mother, and do not feel the same obligation to fight for the holy cause and independence."[69] The remark echoed the age-old complaint that the Venetians were only out for themselves. When Lombardy held a plebiscite on fusion, the vote went overwhelmingly in favor; only a tiny minority wanted to postpone the political settlement until the end of the war. The Veneto provincial towns quickly organized plebiscites of their own and in early June, Venetia (minus Venice and the lagoon) voted the same.

Manin's provisional government was increasingly isolated, with a counterrevolutionary tide having already swept Naples. Pressure mounted on Manin's government since many felt that its republican intransigence was preventing Charles Albert from sending troops into the Veneto. One Neapolitan wrote that Venice had "retarded and compromised the Risorgimento."[70] For his part, Manin feared that Charles Albert would trade Venetia for Lombardy, as Napoleon had done at Campoformio. But Manin was increasingly isolated, with his cabinet favoring fusion. The decision was made to elect a special assembly from Venice and the *terraferma* to decide the course of action. For the most part the Venetian popular classes continued to support Manin, while most of the bourgeoisie favored fusion, even if it meant that Venice would lose its status as a capital city.

During the June elections, 193 delegates to the special assembly were chosen. In the meantime, the Austrian military offensive had succeeded in capturing Vicenza. Padua and Treviso soon surrendered. With the financial and military situation increasingly dire, the assembly convened on July 3. Fearing civil war in the city if fusion was rejected, Manin gave a speech urging support, declaring, "Let us show that today we are neither royalists nor republicans but that we are all citizens."[71] On July 4, 1848, by a vote of 127 to 6 the assembly approved fusion, and Venice joined Charles Albert's kingdom of upper Italy. But Manin refused to be part of the government created to rule until fusion was achieved.

The timing of the vote could not have been worse since in late July Radetzky defeated Charles Albert's forces at Custozza, and on August 7 the king signed an armistice ceding Lombardy and Venetia, including Milan and Venice, to Austria in return for an agreement not to cross the Ticino River into Piedmontese territory. When the news reached Venice, sentiment was for resistance. On August 11, Manin again seized the initiative, refused to re-establish the provisional Republic, and declared that in two days a new government would be elected; until then, however, he would govern. What emerged on August 13 was a triumvirate consisting of Manin, Colonel

Giovanni Battista Cavedalis in charge of the army, and Admiral Leone Graziani commanding the navy. In the months that followed, the Mazzinians pressured Manin to create a new republican state, but the triumvir had become increasingly fearful of social unrest and on October 3 had republican leaders banished from Venice. Reali wrote, "He [Manin] is no longer the man of 22 March."[72] Furthermore, Manin's hope for French intervention came to naught, save for four French ships that remained stationed in Venice, lessening the effectiveness of an Austrian blockade.

In November, hardliner Felix Schwarzenberg became Austria's prime minister. He intended to crush Venice's determined resistance. Austrian forces in the Veneto numbered around 21,000, while the Venetians had managed to cobble together a force of more than 19,000. Its navy remained weak, especially as it lacked steamships. As Tommaseo acidly observed, "The former queen of the seas . . . became a slave-girl, and the winged lion no more than a water rat."[73] Finances were precarious as the government issued "patriotic [paper] money" and later "communal [paper] money." It even considered using some of the city's artistic treasures as security for an international loan, although the idea was nixed for fear that default would cost the city a significant portion of its cultural patrimony.[74] In January 1849 elections were held for a new Venetian assembly, and on March 7 Manin was appointed president. On the ides of March, Charles Albert again declared war on Austria but a week later suffered a crushing defeat at Novara and abdicated in favor of his son Victor Emmanuel II. The Piedmontese fleet withdrew from Venetian waters. On April 2 the Venetian assembly declared itself ready to resist, and Manin was given unlimited power. The five-month-long death agony of the revolutionary Republic began.

In early May the Austrians attacked Fort Marghera. After a heroic three-week resistance, the Venetians had to abandon it. To protect the city, the Venetians destroyed five arches of the railway bridge and stationed artillery on the middle of it to respond to Austrian fire. Over Manin's objections, a military commission was established to oversee the city's defense. Venice's only glimmer of hope was Hungary, which was also in revolt against Vienna. In the meantime, the city was feeling the full weight of the siege. Food was running short, and prices were soaring. Resentment toward the rich, who wanted surrender, increased. Reali, president of the Chamber of Commerce, asked for but was denied permission to leave Venice. To make matters worse, in late July Austria started bombarding the city, although most of the shells were solid projectiles not explosives. Nevertheless, a thousand bombs a day were raining down, with Castello the only part of the city out of range. (Plate 8) When word spread that the patriarch advocated surrender, the Querini-Stampalia palace where he was staying was attacked by a crowd. Other rioters wanted to move on to the Hotel Danieli, where many ex-patricians had taken up residence out of reach of Austrian shelling. Cholera swept through the city, killing at its height hundreds a day. Still the Venetians held out, displaying both grit and gallows humor. One beggar who collected Austrian cannon balls (for reuse by the defenders) joked, "Look, look, what Radetzky has given me in alms," while others declared that "we will hold out to the last polenta."[75]

With the situation increasingly dire, on August 5 the assembly gave Manin full authority "to act in the way in which he considers most suitable for the honor and salvation of Venice."[76] He was soon informed that the city would run out of bread by August 24. When he learned that the Hungarians had surrendered, he knew it was time to follow. The Austrians offered surprisingly lenient terms: forty leading citizens as well as officers who were subjects of the emperor and had fought against him were allowed to leave the city. The patriotic money was to be removed from circulation and the communal money's face value reduced by half. The Austrians also promised no reprisals. On August 27 their troops occupied Piazza San Marco. The following day, a ship carried Manin, Tommaseo, and other leaders of the revolution into exile. Venice's final incarnation as an independent polity had come to an end. Manin died in Paris in 1857.

While the revolutionary Republic's stand was heroic, it failed, as had the old one, in not resolving the Venice/*terraferma* divide. Despite Manin's assurances that representation in the assembly would be proportional, inhabitants of the mainland still believed that the capital was not giving adequate attention to their need for defense. Manin, a product of the city, had little experience with or understanding of the hinterland. His great strength, namely, his ability to unite and inspire a large portion of the Venetian population of all social classes and paternalistically renew in them a sense of their Venetianness, was at the same time his and the revolution's downfall, that is, the age-old inability to move beyond a municipal perspective. As Austria's crushing of an isolated Venice showed, what amounted to a city-state was inadequate to meet the demands of war in the industrial age.[77]

Manin's was also a bourgeois revolution—despite his widespread and unwavering popular support. The bourgeoisie had chafed at their subordination to Austrian officialdom and seized the opportunity to grab power for themselves.[78] But Manin and the other leaders were too wary of popular unrest to give the working classes full voice. Cicogna wrote in his diary in March 1849, "Manin, although he holds the whip hand over the Venetian rich and poor alike, is nevertheless afraid whenever the people gather together."[79] Similar fear was especially pronounced in the countryside where rural landowners, including many Venetian bourgeoisie, had too much at stake to grant the peasantry needed reforms. In this way as well, the revolutionaries lost the *terraferma*.

In the revolution's aftermath, resentment of Venice's Austrian overlords only grew stronger. When the Austrians returned, the office of viceroy was abolished, and power was assumed by Radetzky in his position as civilian and military governor-general. He resided in Verona, headquarters of the military, and was assisted by two councils. In Venice, the commune continued with Giovanni Correr as podesta in addition to assessors and the communal council. However, the government was saddled with the debts that the revolutionary Republic had assumed. Furthermore, most offices were filled by men who were decidedly pro-Austrian, which had not necessarily been the case before the revolution.[80]

During the Third Austrian Domination, the Catholic Church assumed an ever more important role in supporting the regime. Patriarch Giacomo Monico declared in 1850 that there could be no accord between Catholicism and liberalism, "between light and dark."[81] He allowed the Jesuits to return, while the construction of a new patriarchal palace in the neo-classical style abutting San Marco on the Piazzetta dei Leoncini signaled the patriarch's increasingly prominent role in civic affairs.[82] Designed by Lorenzo Santi, the palace was the last major architectural intervention in the San Marco complex.

The patriarchs acted with the Austrian authorities in instituting an even more repressive regime, smothering freedom of speech and press. Patriarch Angelo Francesco Ramazzotti presided over a provincial church council that affirmed papal primacy and based theological training on Thomism. Patriarch Giuseppe Luigi Trevisanto called Catholicism "the surest support of monarchs," punished priests of a liberal bent, and had Ernest Renan's *Vie de Jésus* (Life of Jesus), an examination of the historical Jesus, publicly burned in Campo San Zulian.[83]

Throughout the Third Domination, the atmosphere in the city remained tense. The Austrians were on the lookout for unrest, while the Venetians found ways to express their resistance. On March 22, 1857, the ninth anniversary of the revolution, a tricolor flag was clandestinely raised in Piazza San Marco. The complexity of the knot led investigators to conclude that the culprit had to be either a seaman or an Arsenal worker. On that flimsy evidence, a perpetrator was identified, arrested, and sentenced to five years in jail.[84] During the Second War of Italian Independence (April–July 1859), which pitted France and Piedmont/Sardinia against Austria, a proclamation was issued signed by the Austrian field commander Ferencz Gyulai warning that territories giving assistance to the Italian cause would be burned and torched. Numerous copies of the proclamation were clandestinely altered, replacing Gyulai's name with Attila's.[85]

Venetians also kept their social distance from the Austrian occupiers. The boxholders at the prestigious La Fenice opted to keep the theater shuttered between 1859 and 1866, while the coffeehouses and bandstands in the Piazza became contested spaces. Café Quadri was the preferred coffeehouse of the Austrians and their supporters, Specchi of the Italian nationalists, and Florian of tourists and neutrals.[86] With the Second War of Independence in the offing, the Venetians began boycotting Austrian military band concerts, abandoning the Piazza as soon as the music started.[87] Many Venetians retreated into private social circles. Starting in 1852 the Austrians sought to break that hold by encouraging Carnival and festivals like the Redentore, but this effort faltered as war neared.[88]

Economically, the city was once more in serious difficulty, as the population declined by approximately 8,000 residents between 1846 and 1857. On their return, the Austrians again limited the freeport to San Giorgio Maggiore, although they lifted that restriction in 1851; beginning in 1855 commerce began to show some modest gains. However, the brief Second Italian War of Independence—which resulted in Lombardy's annexation to Piedmont and the subsequent unification of all Italy save the Papal State and Venetia to the Kingdom of Italy—dealt a severe blow. Although the railway line had just recently been completed, Venetian commerce was cut off from Milan; and the Austrians, fearing they might soon lose Venetia as well, redirected trade to Trieste. One statistic will suffice: between 1860 and 1865 the percentage of empty cargo space on ships leaving the port of Venice increased from 36 percent to 42 percent.[89]

For Venice to prosper economically, it needed to modernize and transform its infrastructure. Most of the urban redevelopment that took place in this period was designed to overcome the bottleneck created by the problematic linkage between the port and the railway. Some of the more radical plans would have irreparably altered the cityscape had they been adopted. One called for extension of the rail line along the Giudecca to a terminal located on San Giorgio Maggiore. Another envisioned the railway terminating at the Customs House point near the Salute with an "Entrepot" or commercial center between San Basilio and the Giudecca.[90]

With the railway station and the Giudecca Canal assuming new commercial importance, it became imperative to improve pedestrian traffic flow to those areas from the city's administrative center at San Marco. To do this, two problems needed to be solved: streets needed to be widened, and canals, especially the Grand Canal, needed bridges. Rialto remained the only bridge across the Grand Canal. Pressure mounted to better link Dorsoduro (and the Zattere/Giudecca Canal area) to San Marco. Plans for a drawbridge or even a tunnel under the Grand Canal were rejected in favor of a cast iron bridge, constructed by the English firm of Alfred Neville to traverse the canal between San Vitale and the Accademia. The bridge's parts were cast in England and transported to Venice for assembly. This first Academia Bridge dating to 1854 spanned the 275-foot width of the canal without underlying supports that could impede canal traffic. In 1863, to improve pedestrian traffic to the Zattere and Giudecca Canal, the canal running along the south side of the Carità (Accademia) complex and through the parish of Sant'Agnese was filled in, creating a *rio terà* (filled canal) and thus a much wider street. In 1858 Neville built another iron bridge at the other end of the Grand Canal near the church of the Scalzi to facilitate pedestrian traffic between the *sestiere* of Santa Croce, Rialto, and the train station. In that same year, Neville established a foundry in Venice that supplied the materials for iron bridges over secondary canals, along with handrails, gaslight fixtures, balustrades, and other ironware.[91]

In addition, streets and even some bridges were widened, especially at Rialto and San Marco. Between 1854 and 1856 Campo San Bartolomeo at the foot of the Rialto Bridge on the San Marco side of the canal was enlarged.[92] Near San Marco, the Ponte della Paglia was widened to improve access to the promenade along the Riva degli Schiavoni.[93] The drive to improve the city's infrastructure continued unabated following Venice's unification with Italy.

These projects signaled a fundamental shift in the Venetian attitude toward water. Through the middle of the fifteenth century, water had been viewed positively as Venice's very lifeblood, like a system of veins and arteries bringing prosperity to the city. Then, starting in the late fifteenth century, water (both riverine and marine) began to be perceived as a problem, leading to silting of the lagoon and clogging of ports. This prompted efforts to preserve the vitality of the arterial system by diverting rivers and dredging harbors. In the nineteenth century, water came to be viewed neither as a benefit nor as a problem but as an obstacle impeding transportation and communication.[94] It was no longer something to be managed or controlled but overcome, either by spanning it or, more radically still, by infilling. Some critics, like Paleocapa, worried about the side effects of these changes on the city's internal transportation needs as well as its sewage system, which depended on the rhythmic flow of the tides. He wrote, "The canals of Venice should be considered just like roads for vehicles in cities on the mainland."[95] Others fretted that these changes would undermine Venice's unique appeal to tourists.

Tourism continued to develop with a growing number of hotels, although many were still modest establishments. In 1863 Maria Bauer Grünwald expanded her fourteen-room Hotel Stella d'Oro into a nearby building with a modest capital investment of 7,715 Austrian lira.[96] Recreational bathing and spa treatments remained big tourist draws. The railway allowed for therapeutic mud from the thermal hot springs at Abano in the Euganean Hills near Padua to be shipped to Venice twice daily—an example of the city's ongoing exploitation of mainland natural resources.[97] In the early 1850s Giovanni Busetto, nicknamed Fisola, a Pellestrina native and self-made man who had grown rich carrying out major works projects, proposed a huge recreational complex extending along the Riva degli Schiavoni from the Prisons to the Public Gardens. The plan included a large hotel, shopping, a theater, beer gardens, coffeehouses, romantic gardens, and a Neptune Plaza. But the project was vetoed since the complex would have architecturally overpowered the Piazzetta and hindered military communication between the Piazza and Arsenal.[98] Thwarted in this project, Busetto shifted his focus to the Lido, where he opened a bathing establishment in 1857 with a restaurant, pharmacy, changing rooms, and other facilities. Before the railway bridge was built, he had organized a four-man rowed waterbus system to carry passengers between Mestre and Venice. He subsequently launched regularly scheduled steamboat service to carry passengers from the Riva degli Schiavoni to Santa Maria Elisabetta on the lagoon side of the Lido and a horse-drawn omnibus to transport them from there to the beach.[99] So began the shift of recreational facilities to the Lido.

Some foreign visitors, particularly Romantics, lamented the effects that industrialization and modernization were having on the cityscape since Venice seemed to offer an escape from the problems of the modern world. American consul to Venice William Dean Howells recalled that "being newly from a land where everything, morally and materially, was in good repair, I rioted sentimentally on the picturesque ruin."[100] *Frankenstein* author Mary Shelley, writing of the railway bridge, said that it was "impossible not to repine by this innovation. . . . [T]he bridge will rob it [Venice] of its romance."[101] Englishman John Ruskin, aesthete and author of the *The Stones of Venice*, worried that Venice was taking on the aspect of Birmingham or Liverpool.[102] He was startled by Baverian Friedrich Christian Oexle's conversion of the former church of San Girolamo into a steam-powered flour mill and its campanile into a smokestack.[103]

Ruskin's moral and aesthetic attachment to Venice's pre-Renaissance past meant that he soon found himself at the center of a debate over modernization versus tradition, restoration versus conservation. His chief opponent was French architect Eugène Viollet-le-Duc, also an admirer of Venetian Gothic style. Viollet-le-Duc, working in France, thought that buildings, even ancient ones, could be completed, improved even. He wrote, "To restore a building is not to preserve, to repair or rebuild it, it is to reconstitute it in a more complete state than it could have been at a given moment."[104] To this end, he replaced work that bore the ravages of time, scrubbed buildings clean of grime, and added architectural details he thought should have been there in the first place. His central spire for Notre Dame de Paris and the northern-style caps he added to the rampart towers at Carcassonne are prime examples of his "improvement" of the originals.

Ruskin, by contrast, revered signs of age and was content to leave buildings as they were, or at most to stabilize them. He wrote, "it is *impossible*, as impossible as to raise the dead, to restore anything that has ever been great and beautiful in architecture."[105] In Venice, Viollet-le-Duc's approach was being followed by Giambattista Meduna who oversaw restorations of Ca' d'Oro and the north face of San Marco itself. Writing of San Marco, Ruskin observed, "Off go all the glorious old weather stains, the rich hues of the marble which nature, mighty as she is, has taken ten centuries to bestow."[106] The premier Venetian example of Viollet-le-Duc's approach was Federico Berchet's radical restoration of the Fondaco dei Turchi in the 1860s. He tore down the old building and then reconstructed it, adding elements the original never possessed, and cladding the façade with marbles, some recycled from San Marco itself. The result was a building that was neither fish nor fowl, neither medieval nor completely nineteenth century. Despite projects like this, Ruskin had succeeded in bringing the debate about Venice's past, present, and future to the world's attention.[107]

While Berchet's restoration of the Fondaco was taking place, the final steps in uniting Venice to Italy occurred. This was the result of the brief Third War of Italian Independence fought for six weeks during the summer of 1866. The Kingdom of Italy, with the sanction of Emperor Napoleon III of France, and Prussia, under minister Otto von Bismarck, formed an alliance against Austria, forcing it into a two-front war. In addition to gaining Venetia, the

FIGURE 17.3 Fondaco dei Turchi following Federico Berchet's radical restoration, 1860s, Venice. Photo by Wolfgang Moroder, distributed under a CC-BY 3.0 license via Wikimedia Commons.

Italians hoped to take Trieste. However, the Italian army and navy both performed poorly, the latter suffering a significant defeat in the Adriatic near Lissa (Vis). The Prussian army fared better, beating the Austrians decisively at the Battle of Sadowa in early July. When Austria and Prussia agreed to an armistice, they pressured the Italians to make peace as well. According to the final treaty signed at Vienna in early October, Austria ceded Venetia and Friuli (but not Gorizia, Trieste, the Trentino, or Istria) to Napoleon III, who then handed them over to Italy. (The Austrians refused to make the transfer directly to the Italians.) Italy had to pay Austria an indemnity and assume Lombardy-Venetia's outstanding public debt. On October 19, the formal transfer from France to Italy took place in the Hotel Europa, and a plebiscite was organized for late October to further legitimate it. The proposition was simple: "We certify our union to the Kingdom of Italy under the constitutional monarchy of King Victor Emmanuel and his successors." The results were as follows: 647,246 men from Venetia, Friuli, and Mantua voted yes; 69 no. On November 7, 1866, King Victor Emmanuel II made his triumphal entry into Venice to rejoicing and acclaim.[108]

Venice's unification with the Kingdom of Italy marked the final step in the protracted end of the Venetian Old Regime. Napoleon's conquest of the city in 1797 was the central event in that process since the city lost its role (except for a brief revival in 1848-9) as an independent state and the nobility saw the end of its monopoly on political power. Other groups and institutions including guilds, monasteries, confraternities, and *cittadini* lost their privileged status as well. Yet under the Austrians several privileges were restored, the church became more powerful, and former patricians retained some of their clout, at least as evidenced by their monopoly of the office of mayor, despite the rise of a new bourgeois elite. Jews still were denied certain rights and little changed for women. As Manin's popularity with all social classes indicates, Venetians still harbored an attachment to their municipality (and Republic), and they remained unable to integrate it and the Veneto into a cohesive whole. Deeply attached to their city and its republican past, they only slowly came to accept their place in the Italian nation-state. Their fate was not in their own hands but was decided by great powers to their east and west.

PART IV

Modern and Contemporary Venice

18

Italian Venice, 1866–1920

LOOKING FROM THE Zattere to the Giudecca, past the Palladian-inspired façade of the Zitelle and Palladio's masterpiece the Redentore, a stretch of low-slung buildings is punctuated by the neo-Gothic bulk of the Molino Stucky, the Stucky flour mill. Begun in 1895 to replace an earlier mill complex, the Molino was designed by German architect Ernst Wullekopf for Giovanni Stucky, offspring of a Venetian mother and Swiss father. The architect adorned what was essentially a utilitarian industrial building with Gothic fripperies including crenellation and a turreted corner tower. Although from certain angles the structure recalls the waterfront grain warehouses at San Marco destroyed during the Napoleonic era, in both size and style the Molino seems out of place. The plan to build it met resistance. Yet the economic advantages of the site—including a large tract of underutilized land, easy approach via the Giudecca Canal for grain-laden cargo ships, and the promise of work for a city teeming with the underemployed—overcame objections. In 1901 the mill engaged 194 workers. In 1910 one of them assassinated Stucky at the Santa Lucia railway station.[1]

The Molino and the issues of industrialization, urban development, unemployment, social unrest, and aesthetics it raised epitomize the myriad questions Venice faced in the years between its unification with Italy in 1866 and the conclusion of the First World War. Some concerned the city's role in the new Italian state. Was Venice to partake fully in the increasing industrialization of northern Italy or would tourism and traditional high-end luxury crafts dominate its economy? If the city chose industrialization, then what place would Venice hold in relationship to other Italian ports, especially its ancient rival Genoa? Different questions involved the legacy of Venice's republican past. Which telling of that past—Venice the hedonistic Carnival city or the Adriatic imperial power—would predominate in forging the city's

FIGURE 18.1 Molino Stucky viewed from the Zattere. The Maritime Station is on the right. The smokestacks in the distance are part of the Porto Marghera industrial complex. Photo by the author.

future? And how could that past be utilized in the Italian national project? Who would have a voice in answering these questions? Would the melded old-patrician and new-bourgeois elite retain power, or would the benefits of economic growth be extended to the thousands of working-class Venetians who still lived in appalling poverty and whose cheap labor fueled economic development? And would foreigners, who played an outsized role in projecting Venice's image to the world, have any influence in determining its future, especially regarding conservation versus modernization? Finally, could the ancient city and lagoon sustain increased industrial development, or would heavy industry need to be relocated? The questions surrounding Venice's incorporation into Italy were daunting. And in the short-term, the answers helped pave the way for fascism.

The first issue facing the Venetians upon unification was reestablishing the city's commercial base. The city had suffered grievously when the Austrians promoted Trieste as the principal Adriatic port. It was also handicapped by Milan's preference for Genoa as the maritime outlet for its formidable industrial production. A number of prominent figures, among them the prefect of the province of Venice Luigi Torelli hoped the Suez Canal, which officially opened in November 1869, would jumpstart the economy and restore the city's time-honored role as an East/West trade hub.[2] In anticipation of the canal's opening, the Scuola Superiore di Commercio (Higher Business

School) was created in 1868 to prepare young men for business careers and provide the personnel, including consular officials, needed to manage the promised takeoff. Anticipating increased trade with the East, instruction was offered not only in modern European languages including Greek, but also Arabic, Turkish, and Persian. Japanese was added in 1873.[3] In 1867 the city also conducted negotiations with the Egyptian shipping company Azizieh to establish regular steamship service between Venice and Alexandria, although in the end the parties failed to reach an accord. This was an early chapter in a decades-long and largely unsuccessful effort to create vibrant steamship lines linking Venice to Egypt, India, and beyond. Here too Venice was thwarted by competition from Trieste-based Lloyd's Adriatico and Genoa-based Navigazione Italiana.[4] Despite initial optimism, the fruits of Suez failed to materialize, at least in the short-term.

Foreign competition was only one factor hampering Venice's economic development. In 1874 the city lost its freeport status as part of a move by the national government to create a level playing field for all Italian ports. More problematic was the inadequacy of Venice's infrastructure, specifically the bottleneck in transferring goods from ships using the Bacino to the railway at Santa Lucia. To solve this, work began in 1869 on the new Maritime Station located on reclaimed land bordering the Giudecca Canal at Santa Marta. When it opened in 1880, the station featured new docks, warehouses, and administrative offices as well as an extension of a branch rail line for the easy transfer of goods from ship to train. Improvements also continued on the mouth at Malamocco. Once those were completed, work began on the San Nicolò mouth. It was dredged to a depth of thirty-six feet to allow the passage of larger vessels, and a deeper channel was created to the Bacino and Giudecca Canal. In time it again replaced Malamocco as the primary entryway into the lagoon.[5]

Venice's lack of rail connections to other parts of Italy and through the Alps, other results of Austrian neglect, further hindered growth. When the Veneto joined Italy in 1866, only Sardinia ranked below it in terms of linear rail miles per square mile and last in terms of rail development relative to population. Between 1873 and 1911, 770 miles of railway were built, compared to 270 in the preceding period. By 1911, the Veneto possessed one of the most heavily developed rail systems of any region in Italy.[6] Even so, that development did not optimize Venice's growth. Although the international and national lines centered on Venice, local lines radiated from Padua, so growing manufactures in the hinterland were imperfectly connected to the port. Tensions once again surfaced between the Venetian leaders' lack of regional vision and the provincial elites' determination not to be subject yet again to Venetian hegemony. Consequently, Venice never assumed the supremacy over the Veneto that Milan did over Lombardy or Turin over Piedmont. Padua, Vicenza, and Verona developed as vibrant local centers.[7]

Nevertheless, the Maritime Station spurred industrial development, especially on the Giudecca and in Dorsoduro and Santa Croce. The Giudecca was home not only to the Stucky flour/pasta manufacture, but also the watchmaking company A. Junghans, whose 112 workers produced 55,000 watches a year, and the shipbuilding Società Veneta di Navigazione a Vapore (Venetian Steamship Company). In 1882 the textile manufacturing plant Cotonificio Veneziano (Venetian Cotton Factory) began operations close by the Maritime Station. Within five years it had more than 900 employees and in 1911 accounted for a quarter of Italy's textile exports.[8] The Manifattura Tabacchi, a state-owned cigar and cigarette factory, opened in 1876 and eleven years later had over 1,700 workers. The Neville foundry/steam engine plant was sited near San Rocco before transferring in 1905 to the Giudecca. In 1887 it employed 400.[9] Elsewhere in the city were industries producing such items as liquors, jams, soap, cement, sulfur, starch, and leather.[10] Essential service industries, like the gasworks and the city's new aqueduct bearing freshwater from the mainland, were situated near the rail station and Maritime Station as well. Much of the capital for the new heavy industries was provided by foreigners or Italians from outside Venice.

The area around the Arsenal remained a shipbuilding center, with the F. Layet company producing ships and heavy machinery including steam engines. Nearby Sant'Elena was home to one branch of Vincenzo Breda's shipbuilding and construction company.[11] The Arsenal itself underwent significant transformation. The basins of the Arsenale Nuovo and Novissimo were combined to create a large new wet dock. Offices were reorganized, two new refitting basins built, and a hydraulic crane capable of lifting 150 tons installed. In 1916 an internal railway was added. Between 1869 and 1913, thirty warships, including two submarines, were constructed there.[12]

In addition to heavy industry, Venice remained a center in the production of luxury items, most of which were either exported or sold to tourists. Glassmaking took pride of place, with the production of glass beads for worldwide export its major component. In 1869 there were forty-two companies with fifty-two plants employing more than 2,300 persons on Murano.[13] Other sectors of the industry produced the tesserae for mosaics, which were much in vogue as architectural ornament, as well as chandeliers, tableware, and art glass. The Salviati and Barovier companies, founded in 1859 and 1896, respectively, were leaders in the field. Salviati strategically located its showroom/workshop across the Grand Canal from some of the leading tourist hotels. Luxury fabrics were another industry whose traditional techniques were revived in the 1870s and '80s. Their importance was boosted when Spanish designer Mariano Fortuny established himself in Venice. The city and islands became renowned for lacemaking. In 1872 the Scuola Professionale del Merletto (Professional Lace-Making School) opened on Burano and by 1882 had 320 workers. Michelangelo Jesurum established his own lace-making operation at Pellestrina on the eponymous barrier island. These manufactures offered a counterpoint to the heavy (and heavily polluting) industries springing up near the Maritime Station and Arsenal and were spurred by many of the same impulses as the Arts and Crafts movement elsewhere in Europe. In 1872, Michelangelo Guggenheim established the Scuola Veneta d'Arte Applicate alle Industrie (Venetian School for the Arts Applied to Industry).[14]

The list of new industries is impressive and its impact on the cityscape significant. Between 1880, when the Maritime Station opened, and 1906, when Venice ranked second only to Genoa as Italy's busiest harbor, port traffic grew 385 percent.[15] Yet its relative importance needs to be kept in perspective. There was a huge differential between imports and exports, the former far outpacing the latter. According to a report by the Chamber of Commerce, in 1909 two-thirds of outgoing ships were doing so with their cargo holds completely empty.[16] Moreover, while Venice was importing bulky items, especially coal, it was exporting lightweight products like glass and textiles. Another measure of the degree to which Venice still lagged was in terms of mechanization. Of the top ten Italian cities with a population over 150,000 in 1911, Venice ranked eighth in steam-produced horsepower per capita.[17] Finally, Venice's industrial products had a hard time competing on the international market, while the Veneto's agricultural products, especially grain were not even competitive on the national level.[18] Progress had been made in improving the economy, but problems persisted.

Another issue was the poverty and misery that still plagued thousands of Venetians. Some of the photographs of Venetian life taken by Carlo Naya in the 1860s and 1870s capture the destitution of the Venetian working class. For example, his image of the Corte dell'Olio in the parish of San Martino shows two blacksmiths laboring in the background while a woman draws water from the courtyard wellhead. Two children in filthy clothing sit on the ground staring at the camera, while women of varying ages stand in a doorway engaged in conversation. One of the women smiles at the camera, as does a woman perched on the staircase. The crumbling plaster of the stairway and broken stones around the well suggest the city's physical decay. Although obviously posed by Naya, the image illustrates the centrality of courtyards to working-class life. By contrast, Piazza San Marco, the Piazzetta, Molo, and increasingly the Lido beach resorts were spaces for elite socializing.[19]

Between 1871 and 1911 the city's population increased from 131,000 inhabitants to 161,000, although that 23 percent growth rate was lower than the rate in almost every other major Italian city. One inhibiting factor was the lack of adequate housing, exacerbated by the inability to increase building

FIGURE 18.2 Carlo Naya, *Corte dell'Olio in San Martino*, mid- to late-nineteenth century. O. Böhm, Venice.

height given the weight-bearing limitations of foundations comprised of tree trunks driven into the mud.[20] Much of the existing housing was substandard. Inspectors reported on the abode of Carmela Lombardo, who was unable to work because of eye disease. She lived in what they described as a windowless, humid, stinking cubbyhole, slept on a sack without a blanket, and dressed in rags. They commented that calling her abode a "pigsty" was too charitable and that she had to pay four lire per month rent to live there.[21] A survey in 1909 judged 3,534 of the city's 23,325 dwellings uninhabitable, the majority being ground floor spaces that were humid, susceptible to flooding, and poorly ventilated. A staggering 10,746 (46 percent of all houses) did not having running water, a number that soared to 70 percent in Castello.[22] Diseases like cholera flourished under such conditions, and the rate of infant mortality (188 deaths per 1,000 births in 1900–4) exceeded that of impoverished Naples (154 deaths per 1,000 births).[23]

While industrialization brought more employment opportunities, it did not result in a significant increase in per capita income. One factor favoring Venice's economic development was the low wage rate paid to many workers, especially women and children. The only professional career open to women was elementary school teaching, but that was beyond the reach of most working-class women. Thousands of them found work instead in the Cotonificio and Manifattura Tabacchi. In 1870 the cigar factory employed 1,365 women and 128 men. Seven years later women and girls constituted almost 78 percent of the cotton mill's workforce. Since the cigar factory was state owned, women made slightly higher wages there than elsewhere and worked an eight-hour day rather than the typical ten- or even sixteen-hour shift. Large numbers of women also worked in factories like the Stucky mill, the Junghans watch-making plant, the Baschiera match factory, and the workshop that sisters Eulalia and Amelia Dorigo operated where glass beads were woven into mourning crowns for export to France.[24]

Many thousands of other women worked at home as bead-stringers or lacemakers. Groups of women sitting together in courtyards stringing beads was a common sight, often eliciting comment from foreign tourists. John Singer Sargent painted *The Bead-Stringers* (c. 1880–2), in which two beautiful young women in simple but immaculately clean clothing perform their task while other women in the background do the same. No image could contrast more sharply with Naya's photos of working-class life. The glass manufacturers hired women known as *mistre* (mistresses) who farmed the beads out to women they knew and periodically collected the finished work. Entrepreneurs in their own right, the *mistre* recruited new employees by teaching young girls the necessary skills, created networks of reliable workers, and even set up small loan-making operations. The bead-stringers themselves were very poorly paid, earning on average 30 to 50 cents a day or about the price of a kilo of bread. The three-month-long summer glassmaking hiatus also meant that work was seasonal.[25]

Venetian lacemaking began as a project by politician Paulo Fambri, with the support of noble patronesses Andriana Marcello and Maria Ghigi Giovannelli, to revive the craft as a way for women to supplement the income of their fishermen husbands. Drawing on the knowledge of an elderly woman who still knew how to make a type of lace known as *punto in aria,* they set up a school in 1872 that soon had 300 students. Entering at age twelve, girls spent six years at the school, earning nothing for their work, and graduating with the title "mistress." They could then continue in the workshop and, after marriage, work from home.[26] Countess Marcello sought commissions from her well-connected friends and boasted that since the school's founding, the rate of illegitimate births on Murano had declined.[27] The project's goal was to combine "entrepreneurship and welfare, economy and ethics," although in 1901 one socialist critic and women's rights advocate, teacher Emilia Mariani, offered a much darker depiction of the monotonous, eye-straining work, for which women were paid by the piece.[28] Michelangelo Jesurum imitated the model on Pellestrina where 2,500 women out of a total population of 7,000 did lacemaking. On both islands, they were little more than cogs in the wheels of a great lacemaking machine.

Women found employment in dozens of other jobs as seamstresses, domestic servants, food sellers, and prostitutes. Many worked as laundresses, starchers, and ironers supporting hotels in the city's constantly expanding tourism sector, earning as little as 20 to 50 cents a day for grueling fifteen- to sixteen-hour shifts in humid and stifling laundries.[29] Among male workers, jobs in the gasworks and railway increased, as did employment at the Arsenal. Broadly speaking, men's jobs shifted from working with wood to working with metal.[30] The number of gondoliers declined when the system of *vaporetti* (small steamships) was installed in 1881 to provide Venice's version of omnibus service.

The inauguration of *vaporetti* prompted a strike by gondoliers, who rightly saw them as a threat to their livelihood. Their action was one example of worker organization and agitation that gained momentum from the late 1870s on. In 1884 and again in 1901 the predominantly female workers at the Manifattura Tabacchi staged strikes. At the time, one of the women complained that although she was in poor health, she was being denied the paltry disability benefits that one was entitled to only after thirty-five years of work. She declared, "For many years you used up my flesh and now you're claiming my bones as well."[31] During a 1904 strike, the women occupied the plant and clashed with police. Since many of them were illiterate, they used different color beans when voting whether to strike with a final tally of 823 yes to 13 no. The results were met with the cry "Long live the resistance. Long live the strike." One of the strike's leaders, Pina Argentin, declared that the labor action was motivated not "by material but by moral" concerns and that the women, who were subject to heavy surveillance, wished to be treated as "donne oneste" (honorable/honest women). When the strike ended, the women wanted to march back to work together singing the "Workers' Hymn."[32] The bead-stringers struck for forty days in 1904, parading through the city in groups, singing and dancing as they went, dispersing when confronted by the police, only to regroup. Much of their anger was directed at the *mistre* who distributed work. The strikers attacked their storerooms and equipment. In the end, the bead-stringers secured a 30 percent increase in their compensation.[33] Women at the Baschiera match factory and the Cotonificio also struck. Although female mobilizing could garner support from men, as when Pina Argentin's husband met calls that he rein in his wife by responding that she was simply doing her duty, their actions also provoked resentment from some of their male counterparts. When women at the Arsenal secured a raise, the men said it was more appropriate to give raises to young men. And when female workers at the Cotonificio secured a reduction of their workday from twelve to eleven hours, the men demanded the twelve-hour shift be reinstated.[34]

The 1904 strikes, including a general strike that year, were the culmination of several decades of increasing worker association and organization, part of a trend toward the awakening of public life following Unification. For workers, this took the form of mutual aid societies, the first of which were organized in 1866, including those of tailors, shoemakers, compositors/typographers, Arsenal workers, Muranese bead-makers, and fishermen of Angelo Raffaele. In some respects, these organizations resembled the guilds and *scuole* of old. The bead-makers' organization was dedicated to San Nicolò and offered aid to the sick and disabled as well as death benefits, while the Angelo Raffaele fishermen tried to secure the old banner of the Nicolotti from their parish priest. The societies also pursued economic demands. The shoemakers and tailors sought to protect their livelihoods against mechanization, the tailors and typographers to create wage standards. By 1868 the number of societies had grown to fifteen with 3,375 members; by 1878 it had increased to nineteen. Many had honorary elite members who supported the organizations financially and acted as intermediaries in labor disputes.[35] Another form of organization was the *casse peote* (protector funds), essentially micro-credit organizations that loaned money to members, many of whom were women, who used the savings to finance festivities.[36]

Over time, the mutual aid societies became more politicized and militant, assisting those who had been fired for insubordination and providing strike funds. Resistance leagues, which emerged in the 1880s, were comprised solely of workers. The league created by the masons and carpenters in 1888 pushed for reduced work hours and wage increases and declared that the goal was for "capital [to] pass into the service of the workers."[37] However, these organizations remained largely trade specific, not bringing together workers from different professions.

Established in 1892, the Camera del Lavoro (Chamber of Work) pushed for workers to unite regardless of occupation to demand higher wages and better working conditions. A report by the Camera to the city government, which provided some of the funding, referred to members as *compagni* (comrades) not *confratelli* (brothers). Despite the language, the leaders of the movement initially did not advocate class conflict; rather they wanted to put the brakes on laissez-faire capitalism and viewed strikes as a last resort. Socialists eventually came to prevail in the Camera, which in 1904 organized a general strike. From 1906 to 1910 the Camera had its headquarters in Campo Santa Margherita, securing that square's reputation as a hotbed of working-class solidarity and sociability. By 1913 the Camera consisted of thirty-three sections with 4,631 male and 300 female members.[38] Venice's Socialist Party was established in 1893 although it was riven by divisions between maximalists like Elia Musatti and moderates like Angelo Vianello, owner of the Capon Inn at Santa Margherita.[39]

Societies and organizations supported by the Catholic Church offered an alternative to worker associations, which were widely viewed as anti-clerical. Pius IX, during whose rule the Papal State was finally annexed to Italy, was an ardent opponent of liberalism and modernism. In 1868, the papacy issued the decree *Non expedit* forbidding Catholics from participating in parliamentary elections as a way of protesting the annexation and convened the First Vatican Council, which promulgated the doctrine of papal infallibility. Venice's patriarch, Giuseppe Luigi Trevisanato, a native of the Giudecca, adhered to the papal line. In 1867 the newspaper *Il Veneto cattolico* (The Venetian Catholic) began publication; its name was subsequently (and tellingly) changed to *La Difesa* (The Defense).[40]

But the real leader of the Venetian Catholic movement was lawyer and politician Count Giovanni Battista Paganuzzi. In 1874 he convened the Opera dei Congressi (Congress of [Italian] Catholics) in Venice, serving as its president from 1889 to 1902. Paganuzzi later declared that the meeting had been announced three years earlier on the anniversary of the Battle of Lepanto to wage war on "modern Muslims," namely, liberals who opposed the clergy.[41] The Opera's purpose was to promote catechization and religious festivals, do good works, pay tithes to the papacy, and support Catholic publications. Parish committees and youth groups were organized to promote its agenda. Patriarch Domenico Agostini pushed for other Catholic organizations to fall in line under its leadership. As a result, "Venice became for many decades a major national fulcrum of . . . Catholic reaction."[42]

The Camera del Lavoro was instituted and received a governmental subsidy during the mayoralty of the strongly anti-clerical leftist Riccardo Selvatico. A year earlier suffrage had been extended to more men, and election of the mayor became the communal council's prerogative. Most previous mayors had been moderately conservative members of former patrician families; Selvatico's immediate predecessor was Lorenzo Tiepolo. Trained in the law but primarily a playwright, Selvatico launched initiatives to improve the lives of working-class Venetians such as abolishing the city flour tax and lowering the cost of *traghetti* (the ferry service across the Grand Canal). His administration worked to expand education for girls and improve medical services. It launched a program to build *case popolari* (public housing projects) and put forward in 1891 the Piano Regolatore e di Risanamento (Regulatory and Rehabilitation Plan) that called for major urban improvements including a new sewer system, better distribution of drinking water, regular dredging of canals, additional street widening, and a prohibition on ground floor housing. Selvatico's coalition believed that better housing, health, and education would improve the lives of ordinary Venetians.[43]

However, the project with the greatest long-term impact was the creation of the international art exhibition that came to be known as the Biennale. Conceived during conversations at Café Florian, the exhibition opened in April 1895. Mounted in a pavilion in the Public Gardens, it was an immediate success, drawing 224,000 visitors its first year.[44] The Biennale established Venice as a center of contemporary art at a time when debate was raging about the respective roles of industry and tourism in the city's future.

In addition to his support of the Camera del Lavoro, Selvatico's anti-clericalism led to other actions that aroused the church's ire and ultimately led to his downfall. His administration forbade the recitation of prayer in city-run schools. In 1892 it erected a statue of Paolo Sarpi by Emilio Marsili in Campo Santa Fosca near where in 1607 papal agents had tried to assassinate the Republic's theological advisor. Venice's patriarch from 1894 to 1903, Giuseppe Sarto (subsequently Pope Pius X) was rabidly anti-socialist and anti-modernist. Sarto worked to topple Selvatico's regime by orchestrating an alliance of conservatives and moderates that beat Selvatico's block of radicals and socialists and elected Filippo Grimani as mayor.[45] Referred to as the *sindaco d'oro* (golden mayor), Grimani, descendant of three doges, presided over the city for nearly a quarter century, from 1895 to 1919. The coalition that kept him in power overcame the Catholic/lay divide and combined traditional conservatives with an increasingly nationalist right.[46] Grimani was mayor during the First World War and helped launch the industrial complex at Porto Marghera.

Seven years into Grimani's mayoralty, on July 14, 1902, San Marco's ancient bell tower collapsed. Fissures had appeared days earlier, and in advance of the catastrophe, the Piazza had been cleared. When the venerable structure buckled, only Sansovino's Loggetta and the corner of the Marciana Library suffered damage. The collapse was captured on camera, and the international press reported the calamity. The same day, Grimani's government vowed to rebuild the campanile "*dov'era, com'era*" (where it was, as it was). This would become the catchphrase for many subsequent rebuilding projects in Venice.[47] The bell tower's collapse, the international reaction to it, and debates over how to rebuild it signal the extent to which Venice stood at a crossroads.

One vision of Venice's future emphasized already successful industrialization and transformation of significant portions of the historic cityscape. The other banked on tourism and championed preservation of Venice's unique physical, architectural, and cultural ambiance. Many critics lamented the wholesale destruction of (often admittedly dilapidated) buildings, the continued infilling of canals, the partial demolition of other buildings to construct wider streets with perfectly aligned façades (for example, the streets Strada Nova, 22 Marzo, and 2 Aprile), the creation of a pool known as the Bacino Orseolo near the far end of Piazza San Marco in order to ameliorate the condition of a particularly fetid canal, and demolition of the church of San Paternian with its unique hexagonal bell tower.[48] Although many of these projects benefited industry by improving communication and transportation, they also served tourism by creating a pedestrian "walking ring," facilitating visitors' access to portions of the city adjacent to San Marco and Rialto.[49]

A full-fledged tourism industry developed with standardized tours, guidebooks like Baedeker's aimed at different nationalities and cultural interests, fixed rates for gondola service, and guides proficient in all the major European languages. Tourism employed huge numbers of working-class Venetians as chambermaids, porters, waiters, and beach attendants. Patriarch Sarto decried how tourism had reduced Venetians to sycophants begging for tips, saying that the city's shield should no longer depict Mark's lion with the *Pax tibi Marce* inscription but rather an outstretched hand with the words "Your good graces, Sir."[50] Complicating matters, tourism work was seasonal and subject to the vicissitudes of international politics and natural disasters. Thomas Mann's *Death in Venice* depicts the 1911 cholera outbreak that authorities and hoteliers sought to downplay to protect profits.

Mann's protagonist Gustav von Aschenbach passes his holiday at one of the grand hotels on the Lido, only making daytime excursions into Venice. In 1904 German novelist Hermann Hesse wrote from the Lido, "The sun and the sea are much more important than all of history."[51] The shift of tourism from the historic center to the Lido continued to accelerate after Unification. In 1883 the Lido accommodated 160,000 overnight stays; by 1907 that number had ballooned to 3.5 million. In 1883 the independent municipality of Malamocco was suppressed and annexed to Venice. With the rise of tourism, the resident population of the Lido doubled from 1,840 inhabitants in 1881 to 3,582 in 1911, although most resided at Santa Maria Elisabetta, disembarkation point for the beach resorts, rather than Malamocco.[52] In 1899 a large military reserve was transferred to the Venetian government, opening new tracts of the island for development, and soon plans were being made for impressive new luxury hotels, the Hotel des Bains and Hotel Excelsior.[53] In 1906 the Compagnia Italiana Grandi Alberghi (CIGA) [Italian Great Hotel Company] was formed with major backing from the Banca Commerciale Italiana and private investors, including Alberto Treves de' Bonfili, Nicolò Papadopoli Aldobrandini, and Giuseppe Volpi.[54] Mayor Grimani's government also backed residential development of the Lido. The Lido resorts appealed to a well-heeled international clientele, who enjoyed the beach facilities, sailing, golf, tennis, and equestrian sports.

While foreign visitors, especially writers and intellectuals, took advantage of modern facilities on the Lido, they simultaneously "fetishized" the historic center in its picturesque dilapidation.[55] The theme of death perdured as the city prompted meditations on mortality and modern ills.

Foreigners were not alone in this. Many locals decried urban redevelopment and modernizing improvements. Among the most vocal was historian and writer Pompeo Molmenti who asked in an 1883 essay, "Who wants to reduce Venice to a boring monotonous modern city, with wide thoroughfares driven through areas of artistic delectation?" He later argued that Venice "is not only an Italian glory, it is the artistic patrimony of the civilized world."[56] Many around the globe concurred, celebrating not just the major tourist sites but also quaint out-of-the-way canals and squares, as well as picturesque "natives" like the bead-stringers, that made the city seem exotic, Oriental even. If the Ruskin/Viollet-le-Duc debate had been about conservation versus restoration, its terms had shifted to preservation versus modernization.

The overall effect was to discourage architectural innovation and set Venice on the path to becoming a museum city, even though, as in the case of the rebuilt campanile, the pledge *dov'era, com'era* did not prevent the installation of elevators and artificial weathering of new bricks to make them appear old. Neo-Gothic and other examples of the local vernacular remained the preferred styles for new buildings, although there were occasional concessions to current trends. The building Guido Sullam designed near the Bacino Orseolo displayed the influence of Art Nouveau (known in Italy as *stile Liberty*). An even more inventive example is the Casa de Maria (also referred to as the Casa dei Tre Oci [House of Three Eyes]) that artist Mario de Maria built on the Giudecca. Neo-Gothic with Liberty elements, it features three *piano nobile* windows formed by exaggerated curved arches, with each window opening onto a small balcony with a semi-circular wrought-iron balustrade. Giuseppe Torres's charming Casa Torres on the Rio del Gaffaro near Piazzale Roma is Neo-Byzantine with a hint of Secession, the avant-garde style originating in Austria and Germany. Architects had a freer hand on the Lido, where a number of houses were built in the Art Nouveau style, Sullam's Villa Monplaisir being the finest example.[57]

Despite the architectural conservatism, the Biennale's extraordinary success kept the city from becoming a cultural backwater. By 1907 the exhibition had expanded from ten to twenty-three rooms, and in that year the Belgians built their own pavilion. Germany, Great Britain, and Hungary followed suit in 1909, and an exhibition in 1910 presented works by Auguste Renoir and Gustav Klimt, one of the leaders of the Secession art movement. The Galleria d'Arte Moderna, which opened in 1908 at Ca' Pesaro, also helped secure Venice's place in the international art world.[58] Still, modernism and further tampering with Venice's urban fabric faced strong headwinds. This

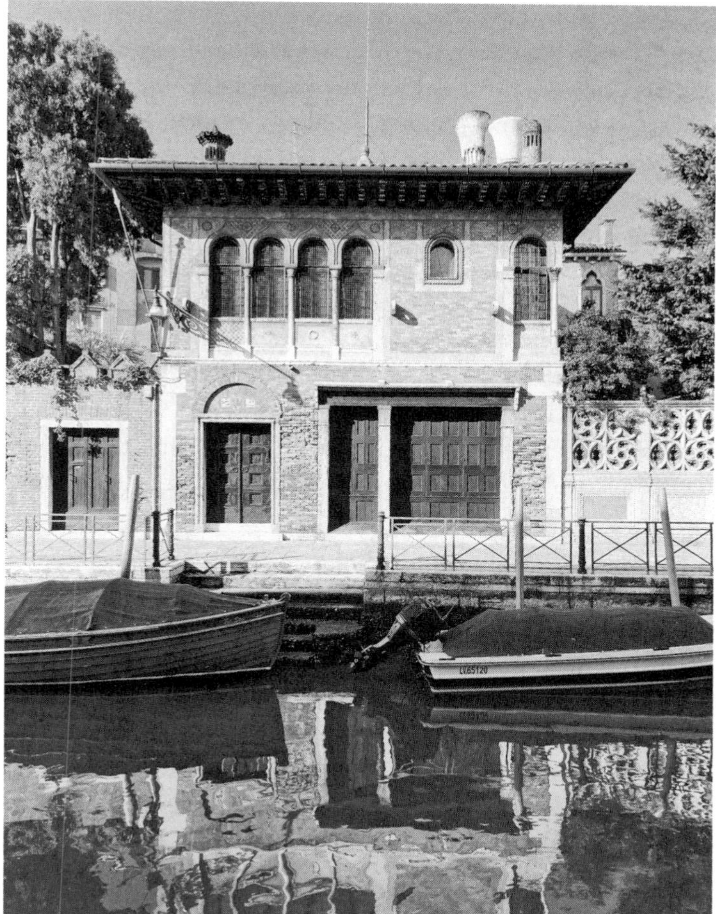

FIGURE 18.3 Giuseppe Torres, Casa Torres on the Rio del Gaffaro, 1905–7. Photo by the author.

would lead a group of new industrialists to look to the mainland for the city's economic future, thereby protecting the historic center from wholesale destruction and encouraging the development of "Greater Venice."[59]

For these industrialists, Venice's economic growth depended on exploitation of the mainland's natural resources along with renewed hegemony over the Adriatic. This meant a new engagement with the *terraferma* and invocation of the old Republic's imperial past. The key figures were Giuseppe Volpi and Piero Foscari, a distant relative of the fifteenth-century doge. They got political and administrative backing from Grimani's administration, while the writer Gabriele D'Annunzio provided the ideological window-dressing.

Volpi has been described as the most "influential Venetian of the twentieth century" and Venice's "last doge."[60] Born to a lesser Bergamasque noble family, he abandoned the study of law at the University of Padua for a career in business. He turned his attention to the Balkans where he and Foscari set out to exploit Montenegro's timber and mineral resources. With the help of connections between the Italian and Montenegrin royal families, they secured an Italian monopoly on tobacco manufacture, formed the Sindicato Italo-Montenegrino and the Compagnia di Antivari to build new port facilities at Antivari (Bar) and link Antivari to the Vienna/Constantinople rail line. Looking to Turkish markets, Volpi created in 1907 the Società Commerciale d'Oriente. His knowledge of the region made him valuable to the Italian government in diplomatic negotiations with Turkey. By combining business, politics, and diplomacy, Volpi recalled Venetian merchants of old.[61] At the same time, Volpi had his hand in Venice's tourism industry as a partner in CIGA, the luxury hotel conglomerate. In these endeavors, he enjoyed financial backing from the Banca Commerciale Italiana, whose Venetian director, the naturalized Pole Giuseppe Toeplitz, was Volpi's close ally. Other associates included the Ferrara-born Vittorio Cini, engineer Achille Gaggia, and old-money families like the Papadopolis.[62]

While the Balkan and Turkish interests reactivated Venice's centuries-old ties to the former *stato da mar*, Volpi also turned his attention to exploiting the water resources of the mainland, the old *stato da terra*, to generate hydroelectric power. He began modestly by acquiring facilities in Cividale, Palmanova, Oderzo, and Motto di Livenza. In 1905 he formed the Società Adriatica di Elettricità (SADE), expanding his interests to include generating plants on the Brenta and Adige rivers. Over time SADE came to control the production and distribution of electric power throughout northeast Italy as far as Bologna and down the eastern Adriatic coast to Apulia.[63]

While Volpi supplied business acumen, Foscari brought a strident nationalism to their joint endeavors. Born in 1865 into a down-and-out noble family, Foscari embarked on a career in the navy, participating in the brutal suppression of rebels in Mogadischu. In 1897 he married wealthy heiress Elisabetta Widmann Rezzonico, thereby securing his fortune and allowing him to abandon his military career and enter politics. He became a leading proponent of irredentism, the view that certain territories that were predominantly ethnically Italian were "irredento" (unredeemed) because they had failed to be included in Italy at Unification, and this needed to be rectified. Many of these territories, such as Trent and the Trentino, either bordered the Veneto or, like Istria and Dalmatia, had once been subject to the Venetian Republic. In this way, proponents of irredentism could easily turn the Republic's past to their nationalist agenda.[64] In 1903 Foscari became the first president of the Associazione Trento-Trieste, which was agitating for the incorporation of those cities into Italy, while his business interests in the Balkans fit seamlessly into the wider political program of reasserting the Adriatic's status as an "Italian lake."[65] He was president of the local section of the Lega Navale Italiana, which promoted interest in the sea and nautical activities, and participated in the first two meetings of the Associazione Nazionalista Italiana (Italian Nationalist Association). His activities got him banned from Hapsburg lands.[66]

With his literary talents, showmanship, and scandalous affairs with actress Eleanora Duse and the extravagantly eccentric Marchesa Luisa Casati, D'Annunzio brought panache to the irredentist cause.[67] Born in Pescara in 1863, he found in Venice fertile ground for his imagination and politics. It became the setting for some of his best-known works. His 1908 play *La Nave* (The Ship) is set in the sixth century when Venice and especially the Arsenal teem with primordial democratizing energy. The ship of the title is launched to cries of "Il Mondo! Il Mondo! Arma la Nave grande" (The World! The World! Arm the great ship).[68] The play premiered in Rome before King Victor Emmanuel III and Queen Elena and had its Venetian opening at La Fenice on April 25, 1909, the feast of Saint Mark. The Venetian performances were sponsored by Foscari's Lega Navale, and D'Annunzio presented his manuscript of the play to Mayor Grimani. The author referred to his work as "an Adriatic tragedy" and wrote that the sea belonged to Italy as "the moral and material inheritance of Venice."[69]

The coalition that coalesced around Grimani accommodated Catholic and lay, old-school right-wingers and new nationalists, guardians of tradition (like Molmenti) and innovators (like Volpi and Foscari) and was staunchly anti-socialist. In the run-up to World War I, these men as a group redefined Venetianness as "industrialist, navalist, irredentist, and imperialist."[70]

When World War I began, Italy was part of the Triple Alliance, along with Germany and Austria-Hungary, yet its irredentist claims to the Trentino and Trieste meant it had little incentive to enter the war on the side of the Central Powers. Many in Italy advocated neutrality. In Venice this included the old guard comprising the Chamber of Commerce and hotel owners who feared the loss of their eastern European clientele. The Socialists favored neutrality as well. In contrast, Foscari and some other members of the new industrialist cohort were pushing for intervention on the side of the Triple Entente (France, England, and Russia).[71] As Foscari put it, war signaled that "we can save Dalmatia!"[72] In the end, the interventionists triumphed, as Italy agreed in April 1915 to enter on the side of the Entente. In return, Italy was promised on successful conclusion of the conflict the Trentino, Alto Adige (or South Tyrol), Istria, including Trieste, northern Dalmatia, Zara, and a protectorate over Albania. Italy declared war on Austria-Hungary in May 1915 and Germany in the summer of 1916.

Fighting took place in the mountains of the Alto Adige and along the Isonzo River where, as in the trenches of northern Europe, the war settled into a grueling stalemate. However, in October 1917, the Austrians, aided by German reinforcements, delivered a crushing defeat to the Italians at Caporetto (Kobarid), forcing them to fall back to the Piave and bringing the war to Venice's backyard.

For some time, the city had already been feeling the war's effects. Even before war was declared, tourism dried up, as the hoteliers had feared, trade came to a standstill, refugees flocked to the city, unemployment spiked, and the price of food rose. There were protests and riots in September 1914 and March 1915. Many of the protesters were young men, but women participated as well, including many lacemakers and bead-stringers who worked from home and were excluded from claiming public assistance since they did not qualify as heads of household.[73] In May 1915, Admiral Paolo Emilio Thaon di Revel assumed military authority over the city even as Grimani continued as mayor. Nightly blackouts were imposed, the ports blocked, and martial law instituted. Foscari organized anti-aircraft units with defenders stationed on the city's rooftop terraces. The first aerial bombardment occurred on May 24, 1915, with strikes near the Arsenal and the gasworks at Santa Marta. On May 26, the horses of San Marco were moved to the Ducal Palace for safekeeping, and the church's façade was covered with protective sandbags.

Over the course of the war, Venice suffered forty-two air raids, resulting in fifty-two civilian deaths, eighty-four injuries, and significant property damage. Piazza San Marco, the Arsenal, and the train station were frequent targets. On October 25, 1915, bombs went astray from the station, hitting the nearby church of the Scalzi, and destroying Giambattista Tiepolo's fresco *The Translation of the Holy House of Loreto.* Photos show the nave filled with rubble. During one week in August 1916, more than 200 bombs fell on the city. The Cotonificio went up in flames.[74] Scarcity and high prices grew worse. Even fishing was forbidden. One sixty-five-year-old boatman, who was described as "most wretched," suffering heart problems, and living off the charity of his sister, was fined for selling mollusks in Cannaregio.[75] Anti-war sentiment grew.

The Italian army's defeat at Caporetto plunged Venice into the darkest period of the war. Although the civic authorities hoped the city would be declared off limits because of its cultural patrimony, and the Austrian authorities inquired whether Venice should be considered an "open city" and thus exempt from attack, Admiral Thaon di Revel refused to renounce the city's strategic importance as the base for northern Adriatic naval operations.[76] Accordingly, the decision was made to evacuate civilian inhabitants. Between November 1917 and April 1918, the population declined from nearly 114,000 to little more than 40,000, many leaving at public expense. They were sent in groups to cities across northern and central Italy. Almost 7,000 were relocated to Genoa and its hinterland, several hundred inhabitants of Murano to Teramo.[77] Industries, including shipbuilding, transferred as well, some never to return. For those Venetians who remained, simply getting by became extremely difficult, with thousands dependent on rations and charity. When the war finally ended, reentry was no easier. Those who had stayed were perturbed, demanding to receive the same subsidies as those who had been evacuated and were being repatriated.[78]

After various attempts by the Austrians to break through the Piave front, the Italians won a decisive victory at Vittorio Veneto on October 30, 1918. Two days later the Italian navy defeated the Austro-Hungarian fleet at Pola (Pula). The Italian army reached Trent, and on November 3, the Italians attacked Trieste from the sea. On that same day, an armistice was signed between Italy and Austria-Hungary, by which the Austrians agreed to withdraw from Alto Adige, Trent, Trieste, Istria, and Dalmatia. However, when the final settlement was worked out at the Paris Peace Conference, Italy got less than it believed it had been promised when it entered on the side of the Entente. It obtained Trent and Alto Adige, Trieste, and Istria; but at the insistence of US president Woodrow Wilson, most of Dalmatia went instead to the new Kingdom of the Serbs, Croats, and Slovenes since it was ethnically Slav. One sticking point was Fiume, which was assigned to the new Slavic kingdom but was ethnically predominantly Italian. D'Annunzio lambasted the agreement as a "mutilated victory." He declared on April 25, 1919, to a crowd gathered in Piazza San Marco to celebrate the feast of Saint Mark that while the peace had closed Mark's book on Italy's Dalmatian ambitions, "if we will reopen it, we will reopen it to the page where it is written with the blood of Montello [site of a battle], with the blood of Vittorio Veneto, . . . *Victory to you Mark, Victory to you complete Italy*."[79]

In Venice, agitation for the restitution of these lands that had formerly been part of the Republic was intense. In June 1918, the city government, along with the Dante Alighieri and Trento e Trieste irredentist associations, agreed to donate to Fiume a sculpted winged lion of Saint Mark even though that city had never been part of the Republic.[80] At the same assembly to which D'Annunzio spoke and that was celebrating the reinstallation of the horses on the façade of the basilica after their wartime removal, Mayor Grimani declared that "the Adriatic people on the propitious day of Saint Mark . . . in the name of his most sacred right and purest blood claim the union to the fatherland of Istria with Fiume and Dalmatia with Spalato, swearing solemnly the indissoluble pact of Italian fraternity."[81] In September, D'Annunzio took matters in his own hands, leading an expeditionary force to Fiume and seizing the city. When the Italian government refused to accept Fiume, and negotiations and a plebiscite failed to deliver the results he desired, D'Annunzio declared the Italian Regency of Carnaro (named after the surrounding gulf) and himself its leader. The 1920 Treaty of Rapallo between Italy and the Kingdom of the Serbs, Croats, and Slovenes temporarily resolved the impasse by declaring the Free State of Fiume, but in the Treaty of Rome of January 1924, Fiume was annexed to Italy. D'Annunzio is credited with instituting in the Regency of Carnaro prototypes of fascist rule, including the fascist (or Roman) salute and the torture of dissidents by forcing them to drink castor oil.[82] The imperial and Adriatic legacy of the Venetian Republic thus played a significant role in the promotion of fascism as a national movement.

Volpi was something of a latecomer to fascism, joining the party in 1923 and serving as Mussolini's minister of finance from July 1925 to July 1928. But during the First World War, Volpi and his business associates achieved their goal of setting Venice on the path to becoming a modern, integrated industrial port and raking in huge profits for themselves in the process. The capital value of SADE alone increased from before to after the war, by an extraordinary 958 percent (accounting for the changing value of the lira).[83] The new industrial port complex was not located in the historic center but on the mainland at Marghera. Its development arguably had a far greater long-term impact on the city than the war itself, although the war fostered the confluence of state, financial, and industrial interests that made Porto Marghera possible.

The development of Marghera was the fulfillment of the idea that first began with the creation of the Maritime Station, namely, the efficient integration of maritime shipping, industry, and railways. However, by the beginning of the century, the station was proving inadequate to meet the growing volume of trade, and debate began over whether to expand port facilities and industry in the historic center or at the lagoon's mainland edge.[84] In 1904 Foscari gave a talk at Ateneo Veneto entitled *Il porto di Venezia nel problema adriatico* (The Port of Venice in [the context of] the Adriatic Problem) proposing the need for new port facilities at Bottenighi, a small village on the nearby mainland, not far from the slightly larger village of Marghera. He countered objections by the Chamber of Commerce and other interests, declaring, "Wherever is the lagoon, there is Venice."[85] By 1907, the Bottenighi plan had gotten approval from the national Ministry of Public Works. It included significant tax breaks, the right to expropriate land by eminent domain, and other benefits. In 1909, work began with the dredging of a deeper channel from the Maritime Station to Bottenighi since initially the plan was for the *terraferma* port to be a subsidiary of the station, handling bulky material like coal, which represented nearly two-thirds of port activity. The first harbor at Bottenighi, dubbed Porto Marghera, was finished in 1916.[86] In a very real sense Venice was returning to its origins near the early medieval center of Malamocco before the Partecipazi doges moved the capital to Rialto.

The idea of complementing the new port facilities with industrial development was Volpi's and had the advantage from his point of view of utilizing SADE's hydroelectric generating capacity, which at the time outpaced demand. In February 1917, Volpi commissioned engineer E. Coen Cagli (who had designed the port at Antivari in Montenegro) to develop a project to augment the new port at Marghera with an industrial zone and a residential neighborhood. Volpi put together a syndicate of companies and private backers involved in shipbuilding, railroads, steel, chemicals, and heavy machinery, as well as the Banca Commerciale Italiana.[87] The residential neighborhood was to be capable of housing 25,000 inhabitants, most of whom were expected to be transplants from the rural Veneto. It was thought these predominantly male workers would be easier to control, were more accustomed to hard work, and could be paid lower salaries than workers from Venice who were schooled in union organizing and strikes.[88]

Volpi's "masterpiece" was the agreement that was signed on July 23, 1917, between the company he had formed, the Società Porto Industriale di Venezia (The Industrial Port of Venice Company), the national government, and the city government of Grimani.[89] It authorized construction of the new

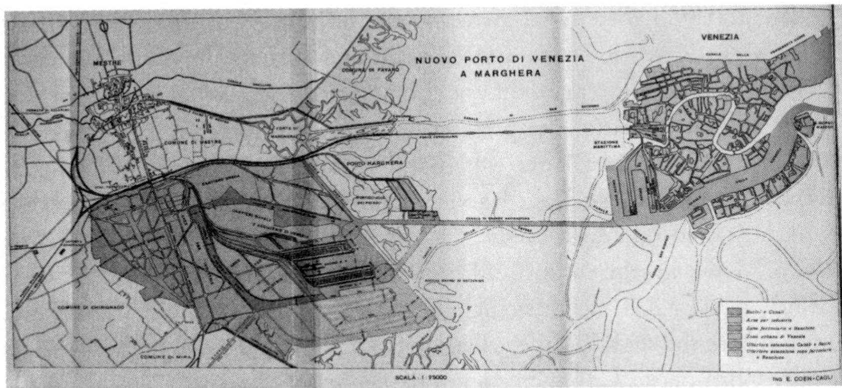

FIGURE 18.4 E. Coen-Cagli, *New Port of Venice at Marghera*. The plan shows the channel linking the Maritime Station and Giudecca Canal with the new piers and industrial complexes at Porto Marghera. The planned residential neighborhood is on the far left. From E. Emmer, "Il nuovo porto di Venezia," *Rivista mensile della città di Venezia*, vol. 1, no. 2 (February 1922), unpaginated foldout map. Courtesy of the University of California, Berkeley.

industrial port of Venice at Marghera, reimbursement for the costs, cession to the company of the necessary land (which the company could then sell to interested industries), and assumption by the city of the infrastructure costs of the proposed residential neighborhood.[90] Traditionalists in the Chamber of Commerce were not happy. Neither was Roberti Galli, a politician from Chioggia, who wrote, "To Mestre the roast, to Venice the smoke"; in other words, Mestre (and Marghera) would enjoy the benefits of the meal, Venice the costs.[91]

A subsequent agreement in August 1926, signed by Volpi in his role as minister of finance, exempted the Società Porto Industriale as well as the other industries in the complex from taxes on their goods and infrastructure. A ministerial decree of earlier in the year allowed the industries at Marghera to utilize their own port personnel for the loading and offloading of ships, bypassing the traditional union of port workers who commanded higher salaries. Thus, the development of Marghera definitively resolved the old problem of moving goods between ship and rail and promised huge profits for its investors, while passing on the costs to the public.[92] Venetian patricians of old would no doubt have approved of Volpi's marshaling of state support in favor of his private interests, just as they had done with the state-owned galley system. World War I imbued the project with national significance, and the new port quickly became a success. By 1928, fifty-five industries were located there, employing 4,880 workers, and the volume of activity at the port of Venice surpassed that of Trieste.[93]

The long-term impacts for Venice of Porto Marghera's development are inestimable. On one hand, by relocating heavy industry to the mainland, it saved the historic center from becoming the object of indiscriminate modernization.[94] On the other, it created a new disjunction between the city and *terraferma*, even though Venice was to annex Marghera, bringing the territory under the city's jurisdiction. Additionally, the lagoon itself was reimagined. It came to be seen as something to be traversed as quickly as possible, by train or by car, rather than as an integral part of life.[95] Unforeseen at the time were the environmental consequences that would later become alarmingly evident. The deep-water shipping channels to the port as well as the reclamation of tidal wastes at the lagoon's edge and their transformation into built-up industrial zones changed the hydrologic equilibrium of the lagoon, increasing inflow while allowing nowhere for the water to go but up, thereby contributing to more frequent and damaging high tides.[96] Furthermore, Galli's quip about Mestre getting the roast and Venice the smoke took on new meaning as air pollution from the heavy industries on the mainland contributed to poor air quality in Venice that damaged human health and the historic center's artistic patrimony.

With the building of Porto Marghera, historic Venice had made its choice. Its twentieth-century future would count on tourism, not heavy industry.

19

Fascist and Cold War Venice

ONE OF THE most moving sculptures in Venice is Augusto Murer's *La Partigiana* (The Female Partisan), commemorating women who struggled against the fascists during World War II. Cast in bronze, the sculpture depicts a woman, hands bound, whose lifeless body is drifting to shore. Although the sculpture is the work of Murer, himself a member of the Resistance, its base and display are the creation of Carlo Scarpa, the most acclaimed architect of twentieth-century Venice. To support the work, he designed a concrete platform covered with bronze intended to rise and fall with the tide so that the body would appear to float. However, the mechanism has seldom functioned properly; the sculpture is often partially submerged and covered with algae. In the foreground Istrian stone cubes placed at various heights create a modernist version of a craggy shoreline. The ensemble is visible through a break in the wall along the Riva dei Sette Martiri (Seven Martyrs' Embankment), an extension of the Riva degli Schiavoni, which was built during the fascist era and christened in 1937 as the Riva dell'Impero (Imperial Embankment) in honor of Italy's recent conquest of Ethiopia. In 1946 it was renamed in memory of seven political prisoners who were executed by the Germans in August 1944 along the walkway in retribution for the disappearance of a German soldier who, as it later turned out, had fallen drunk into the lagoon and drowned. Hundreds of residents were forced to witness the executions.

Murer's *La Partigiana* was not the first sculpture to commemorate Resistance women in Venice. In 1957 a strikingly different work was unveiled in the Public Gardens. Leoncillo Leonardi's neo-Cubist statue in painted ceramic depicted a woman with a red kerchief and a rifle slung over her shoulder marching determinedly forward. It too was mounted on a base designed by Scarpa. But the statue's red kerchief caused consternation among those who thought it gave too much credit to the Communists' role in the Resistance, so

FIGURE 19.1 Augusto Murer, sculptor, and Carlo Scarpa installation design, *La Partigiana*, 1960s. Fondamenta dei Sette Martiri, Venice. Neil Setchfield/Alamy Stock Photo.

the artist replaced it with a copy wearing a brown bandana. On July 27, 1961, the work was destroyed by a bomb detonated by neo-fascists. That prompted the commissioning of Murer's sculpture, which was dedicated on April 25, 1969, Saint Mark's Day and Italy's National Liberation Day.[1]

The complex history of *La Partigiana* and its predecessor brings together a range of issues that gripped Venice from the conclusion of World War I to the end of the Cold War. These include the rise of fascism and its impact on the city, Venice's admittedly minor role in World War II, the fate of Venetian Jews under the fascists and Nazis, and the political and social alignments of the post-war period. The sculptures and Scarpa's pedestals also speak to the ongoing debate in these decades regarding whether and how to integrate modernism into the cityscape. Finally, the *Partigiana*'s frequent submersion due to rising sea level is emblematic of the city's growing environmental vulnerability.

The years following the First World War witnessed in Venice, as elsewhere in Italy, labor agitation, the rise of mass parties, and the birth of fascism. The immediate post-war period was marked by rampant inflation, with the price of food and heat skyrocketing. Unions again became active. There were several labor actions, including a general strike in July 1919. Parties began to organize for the 1919 elections for the national Chamber of Deputies, the first with universal manhood suffrage. The Socialists urged women to supply their men with cards with the Socialist slate "and spur them on November 16 to do their duty: condemn the war, vindicate the 10 million dead, assure a future of peace to all the mothers of the world!"[2] Two mass parties did extremely well: the Socialists scored a major victory garnering 50.4 percent of the vote in Venice, while the Catholic Partito Popolare Italiano (Italian Popular Party), a fusion of right, center, and left, got 16.2 percent. The Liberal-Democratic coalition, comprising the Democratic Socialists and Partito Liberale (Liberal Party) and representing the groups that had ruled liberal Italy for the past several decades, garnered 17.1 percent and 16.4 percent of the vote, respectively, for a total of 33.5 percent. But it suffered from the defection of Catholics to the Partito Popolare. Support for the Socialists was strongest in the working-class districts of Dorsoduro, S. Croce, Castello, and Marghera, weakest in the middle-class strongholds of San Marco and the Lido. In the Veneto the votes were more evenly divided between the three; in Italy overall, the Socialist and Popular parties gained as the Liberal-Democratic coalition began to splinter.[3]

For many veterans and those who had lost loved ones in the war, the Socialists' condemnation of the conflict as the fruit of bourgeois imperialism was a slap in the face. They were attracted to new organizations that defended the war at a time when Venice was in the thrall of D'Annunzio's irredentism. In April 1919 a Venetian Fascio di Combattimento (Fighting Band) was organized, inspired by the Milanese one formed a month earlier by Benito Mussolini.[4] Within a year, the city witnessed violent clashes between fascists and socialists. In July 1920 when socialists marched into Piazza San Marco shouting "Down with the bourgeoisie," they were corralled by fascists. In the melee shots were fired and a grenade detonated, resulting in seventeen injured onlookers. The Socialist newspaper *Secolo Nuovo* lamented that "the proletariat must not enter Piazza San Marco," which had become the province of "the bourgeoisie, of parasites of all sorts and of the exploiters of women."[5] When local communal elections were held in late October 1920, the Socialists lost to a coalition of liberals, nationalists, fascists, and Catholics. Physician Davide Giordano became the new mayor, following Filippo Grimani's quarter-century in office.

Worker agitation and strikes continued into 1920, although disagreements within Socialist ranks led to schism and foundation of the Venetian branch of the Italian Communist Party. The fascists were also deeply divided between adherents of Pietro Marsich and those of Giovanni Giuriati. Marsich was the more radical of the two. An avid nationalist and devotee of D'Annunzio, his newspaper *Italia Nuova* carried the subtitle "The Voice of Fascism and Fiume-ism."[6] He condemned the Treaty of Rapallo, which spelled the end of the poet's Fiume state, the Regency of Carnaro; was contemptuous of traditional parliamentary politics; and never himself stood for election. This led him to clash with Mussolini, who had uneasy relations with D'Annunzio and had come to realize that the way to gain power was to undermine it from within. Marsich's radicalism caused many petty shopkeepers and bureaucrats to abandon his position in favor of Giuriati, who himself shifted his support from D'Annunzio to Mussolini and won a seat in the national Chamber of Deputies in the May 1921 election. When Marsich left the party in spring 1922, it opened the way for industrialist Giuseppe Volpi, who had favored the Treaty of Rapallo and reconciliation with the Kingdom of the Serbs, Croats and Slovenes (Yugoslavia), to align with the fascists. With his implicit sanction, it became acceptable for the Venetian elites and bourgeoisie to embrace fascism.[7] The two leading city newspapers, the *Gazzetta di Venezia* and *Gazzettino*, quickly fell in line. The fascists, who had created their own labor union organizations, also began to make some headway, winning over certain groups within the working class.[8]

Intimidation and violence remained central to their program. In November 1921, a new group, the Cavalieri della Morte (Knights of Death), ransacked the local Communist Party headquarters. Two months earlier they had assaulted socialist Girolamo Li Causi. Another victim of fascist intimidation was socialist Anita Mezzalira, who worked at the tobacco factory and was the first woman in Venice to hold a labor union office.[9] When Mussolini seized power in the March on Rome in October 1922, the Socialist social club in Mestre was attacked by fascist squads.[10] Between 1919 and 1922 there were around 200 violent incidents involving the fascists and their opponents in Venice and the surrounding area, resulting in eleven deaths.[11]

In the 1921 national election for the Chamber of Deputies, Socialists in Venice again came in first, with 46.1 percent of the votes; the Communists garnered 3.5 percent. The Catholic Popular Party got only 10.3 percent, the right-wing National Alliance, which included the fascists and liberals 27.4 percent. In the Veneto the three groups got nearly equal shares of the vote. Yet any characterization of "Red" Venice surrounded by a "White" (Catholic/right) Veneto is only partially correct, since Socialists and Communists got at least 50 percent of the vote in Belluno, Padua, Vicenza, and Verona.[12] However less than a year after becoming prime minister in October 1922, Mussolini changed the electoral system so that any party receiving at least 25 percent of the vote would be awarded two-thirds of the seats in Parliament. In the April 1924 national elections for the Chamber of Deputies, the three leftist parties again came in first in Venice, with 40.5 percent, but the Fascists got 36.5 percent. In the Veneto, the Fascists won 45.6 percent of the vote; in Italy as a whole, they won 64.9 percent.[13] This was the last competitive election until after World War II, although even it was conducted against the backdrop of years of fascist intimidation. As for the local administration, Giordano remained mayor until 1923; the following year he was named Commissario Straordinario (Special Administrator).[14] He was succeeded by men who were appointed rather than elected to the top post and who bore the title podesta, as during Austrian rule. In addition, the city continued to expand by means of annexation. Marghera was incorporated into the city in 1917, Pellestrina in 1923, Murano and Burano in 1924, Mestre and several other villages in 1926. The fascists were firmly in control of what was known as "Greater Venice." Yet the triumph of fascism did little to alter the composition of the Venetian ruling elite. Many old liberals, industrialists like Volpi and Cini, along with Patriarch Pietro La Fontaine simply accommodated themselves to the change in regime.[15]

At the same time, fascism acquired a Venetian tint. While many of the same institutions and organizations were deployed in the city as elsewhere in Italy, the old Republic's maritime and imperial traditions and pretensions, as well as its festivals and customs, were adapted to promote the fascist vision. Volpi especially worked to make Venice a showcase for the fascist totalizing state, a program that simultaneously benefited his hotel interests.[16]

Once in power, the fascists set about dismantling the hallmarks of democratic society: political parties and trade unions were suppressed, the press coopted, freedom of assembly and speech curtailed. In addition to assuming editorial control of the two major newspapers, the fascists colonized the city's major charitable institutions, including the umbrella organization the Congregazione di Carità (Charity Committee), the Civic Hospital, the orphanages, and asylums for the poor and destitute. In 1931 the Ente Opere Assistenziali (Charitable Works Entity) was created to oversee assistance. During the Great Depression, it organized soup kitchens and other forms of welfare. Charity became another means of control since only those who were judged worthy by neighborhood committees were awarded *libretti di assistenza* (welfare booklets) entitling them to food, fuel, and other necessities.

Fascist women did a lot of the legwork as *visitatrici* (visitresses) who called at the homes of the poor to assess their needs as well as their compliance. These more than 250 *visitatrici* were described at the time as the means by which the regime could "penetrate the lowliest social strata," while charity itself was seen as "the means to the goal of defending the race" and "the instrument for the propagation of the principles of fascist ethics."[17] In many ways, the fascists were replicating the patron/client relationships that were a historic hallmark of Venetian charity. The only alternative organizations countenanced were those sponsored by the Catholic church. At the church of San Stae, for example, Masses for the poor were held. Attendees received material aid in return for sitting through religious lessons.[18]

Throughout Italy, the fascists sought to focus people's social lives, from childhood on, around party-sponsored associations and events. By far the most important was Opera Nazionale Dopolavoro (usually referred to simply as Dopolavoro [Afterwork]). From its Venetian headquarters in the Ducal Palace, it organized sporting events, clubs, excursions, open-air film screenings, and even dog and flower shows. Special emphasis was placed on reviving nautical traditions and Adriatic aspirations. Swimming, sailing, and rowing lessons were offered, competitions held, and outings organized. A Maritime Day in July 1927 took 5,000 passengers on eight ships for a low-cost excursion to Trieste; two weeks later 1,500 Triestini visited Venice. Elsewhere in Italy, Dopolavoro organized tours of important World War I sites including stops in Venice, thus helping to integrate the city into stories of national wartime sacrifice.[19]

In 1934, Dopolavoro decided to revive the Festival of the Marys, which had been abolished in 1379 during the War of Chioggia. It too had an imperial cast as the original festival celebrated the rescue of brides kidnapped by Adriatic rivals. In the revived event, twelve betrothed couples were chosen and feted first with a procession by boat to San Pietro where they were married. Then they traveled by water to San Marco, where Patriarch La Fontaine gave them his benediction. Afterward, the newlyweds dispersed to their respective *sestieri* for a meal; the one for the couples from Castello was held in the neighborhood's fascist headquarters. Everything, including the brides' wedding gowns and men's suits, was provided at no cost. Additionally, the couples were given linens, furniture, and tableware to set up house. These were provided by party and city officials, Dopolavoro, the Fascist Merchants' Union, and the CIGA hotel chain.[20] The festival promoted marriage and fecundity as part of Mussolini's program of growing the population. In 1927 he had declared, "If we decrease . . . we won't make an empire, we'll become a colony!"[21] The local press provided extensive coverage. The *Rivista di Venezia* declared that "across the centuries, the wisdom of the ancient Venetians re-entwines with the clear vision which Benito Mussolini, Duce of the new Italy, has."[22]

The fascists also sought to control important cultural institutions like Istituto Veneto and Ateneo Veneto. Giovanni Bordiga, an old school liberal who joined the Fascist Party in 1925, was secretary of the Istituto, board member and president of the Fondazione Querini Stampalia, director of the university's School of Architecture, and president of the Biennale four times in the 1920s. Some liberals held on for a time. Enrico Catellani, a Jewish lawyer, was president of Istituto Veneto from 1919 to 1921 and then president from 1926 to 1928 of Padua's Accademia Galileiana. However, following passage in 1938 of the so-called race laws against Jews, he was expelled from the Istituto and two years later from his teaching post in Padua.[23]

Venice's Museum of Naval History, created in 1919, was a new cultural institution that glorified Italy's naval triumphs and bonded the present to the Republic's past.[24] In 1938, celebrations commemorating the twentieth anniversary of the First World War Battle of the Piave, when Italian forces defeated the Austro-Hungarian army, included a royal visit and the launching of seven new submarines and a torpedo boat. Most of the ships were named for naval heroes of the ancient Republic, including Fourth Crusade Doge Enrico Dandolo. Each ship had a "godmother"—among them Countesses Costanza Mocenigo, Marisa Marcello, and Carola Nani from old patrician families, as well as the wife of the prefect.[25] During his blessing of the ships' flags, Patriarch Adeodato Piazza declared that while Saint Mark had once protected the Republic, he now guarded "the fortunes of Italy." Although Mark's lion book bore a message of peace, the cleric warned, "Let nobody disturb him, lest his legs become vises of steel and his roar the sound of cannon fire."[26] In 1938 one of Venice's major tourist attractions, the Regata Storica Reale (Royal Historical Regatta), was renamed the Regata Imperiale (Imperial Regatta).[27]

Other cultural initiatives of the 1930s included the launch of the Museum of the Venetian Eighteenth Century at Ca' Rezzonico and the Glass Museum on Murano, as well as an enlargement of the Museum of the Risorgimento. However, the Biennale continued to be the city's premiere cultural event. In 1930, the year in which Volpi became president of the exhibition, the king signed a law making it permanent. The ongoing success of the Biennale led to the creation of a music festival beginning in 1930, a theater festival in 1934, and, most important, a film festival in 1932. The latter was held at the Hotel Excelsior on the Lido until a permanent screening hall was inaugurated later in the decade. Adjacent to it was the new municipal casino, which also operated at the Excelsior while its headquarters was being constructed. These initiatives, especially the film festival that attracted matinee idols and burnished the Lido's image as the fashionable playground of the rich and famous, made money for Volpi as vice president of the CIGA chain and promoted his vision of a double-sided Greater Venice with the island city and Lido thriving on culture and tourism and Porto Marghera on industrial and commercial might. In 1934 Volpi hosted Mussolini and Hitler at the Biennale, putting a seal on his "dogeship" of the city.[28]

The years of fascist rule also left their mark on the cityscape. The church of Santa Maria della Vittoria on the Lido, intended as a memorial to the soldiers who died in World War I, was designed by Giuseppe Torres. It mirrored in Art Deco fashion the church of the Salute and visually tied the Lido to the Bacino.[29] Most of the major projects undertaken were linked to transportation. Nicelli Airport, designed in the Art Deco style, opened on the Lido in 1934. Its interior was decorated with Futuristic *aeropitture* (aeropaintings), with their disorienting airborne perspective. By the outbreak of World War II, Nicelli was accommodating 4,000 flights and more than 23,000 passengers annually.[30] Venice's chief engineer Eugenio Miozzi oversaw the replacement of the nineteenth-century Scalzi and Accademia iron bridges: the former with a stone span; the latter with what was supposed to be a temporary wooden bridge that still stands. He also supervised the creation of the Rio Nuovo (New Canal) designed to provide a shortcut for water traffic from the train station and the motor vehicle circle at Piazzale Rome to San Marco and the major tourist hotels. Its construction involved cutting through the Papadopoli Gardens and widening stretches of existing canals before intersecting the Grand Canal at Ca' Foscari. The most contested project was the decision to build a span parallel to the railway bridge for motor vehicle traffic. The debate over it was nearly as ferocious as the one regarding construction of the rail bridge. Giuriati, for one, thought that it would deliver another blow to Venice's maritime orientation.[31] But in the end, those in favor of modernization prevailed, and the bridge—reassuringly built of brick and Istrian stone and named the Ponte del Littorio (Lictor's Bridge and later renamed Liberty Bridge)—opened on Saint Mark's Day 1933. Piazzale Roma, a large cul-de-sac, was built so that incoming traffic could turn around and was equipped with an Art Deco car park designed by Miozzi.

At the opposite end of the bridge Porto Marghera boomed. In 1922 the Vittorio Emanuele Channel linking the Maritime Station and Porto Marghera opened. As the industrial zone grew, the number of industries housed there more than tripled from 1922 to 1928. The primary sectors were chemicals, shipbuilding, petroleum refining, and aluminum production.[32] The pace of development quickened with the end of the Great Depression and Italy's embarkation on overseas military adventures and colonial expansion. By the outbreak of World War II, there were more than seventy industries at Marghera, employing around 19,000 workers.[33] However, port activities continued to show a deficit, with more goods arriving than departing. A large percentage of imports were made up of raw materials like coal, petroleum, and cereals.[34]

Marghera's workforce was drawn overwhelmingly from rural territory within fifteen miles of the complex—a distance that could be traversed by workers commuting by bicycle. Consequently, the residential zone at Marghera did not develop as planned since workers returned to their rural abodes after work. In 1932, less than 9 percent of the workers were residing in the town. Nearby Mestre's urban development far outstripped Marghera's since those workers at Marghera who moved closer, mostly chose to live there. In 1936, while Marghera counted around 7,300 inhabitants, Mestre had expanded to 31,000. Unlike Marghera's garden-city plan, Mestre's development was random and chaotic.[35]

Some of Mestre's residents had been displaced from their homes in Venice, especially after rent-control was lifted in 1923.[36] A large percentage of the island city's residents continued to live in poverty as old industries like bead- and lacemaking declined along with Arsenal shipbuilding. In 1931, more than 13,000 Venetians were unemployed.[37] Nevertheless, the city continued to be a magnet for immigrants arriving from places where life was even harder. Many came from Cadore or Friuli. The Friulians would gather on Sundays, their day off, in Campo San Bartolomeo, which they referred to as "San Bartolonostro" (Our Saint Bartolo).[38] Housing remained a huge problem that the regime tried in some measure to relieve by building public housing on the city's periphery in places like Santa Marta, Sant'Elena, and the Giudecca. There was also an effort to remove those who opposed the fascist regime to new settlements on the mainland that, despite their elegant, invented names (Ca' Emiliani, Ca' Brentelle, Ca' Sabbioni), were little more than barracks.[39]

Given the conditions in which many working-class Venetians languished, it is not surprising that alcohol consumption was in 1921 the highest of any city in Italy. It is estimated that there was one establishment selling alcohol for every 163 inhabitants.[40] As World War II approached, Venice was a tale of two cities. While the rich sipped champagne in swanky bars or hobnobbed in salons presided over by the likes of Countess Annina Morosini and Volpi's wife Nerina, the poor sought escape in hole-in-the-wall *osterie* (taverns) where they downed cheap wine and shots of grappa.[41]

The reaction of Venetians to fascism and its dictates was complicated. While some embraced it wholeheartedly, others resisted. Anti-fascist graffiti might suddenly appear on walls, and in a few places in Castello and on the Giudecca, dissidents dared to meet clandestinely and voice slogans like "Down with the King! Down with Fascism!" Many more Venetians found ways to live with the regime, bend the rules, and get on with their lives.[42] One working-class woman explained her and her husband's decision to grow their family this way: "Not because I wanted to take heed of the 'Duce's orders' [to increase Italy population], but because we wanted to give a little brother to B who was always asking us for one."[43]

When World War II came, it left Venice largely untouched physically since it was among the places that both the Allies and Axis powers sought to safeguard from bombing. Nevertheless, fear of aerial attack haunted inhabitants since the building of underground air raid shelters was impossible.[44] Even Marghera got off relatively lightly. Although some industrial plants suffered significant damage, for many others the destruction was comparatively minor. A report from June 1945 estimated that repairs could be completed in as little as four months.[45]

Psychologically, the war was harder, made worse by food scarcities and high costs. One letter writer lamented that although shop windows still put on "beautiful" displays, "no one can buy anything due to the high prices."[46] The uncertain fate of male family members dragooned into military service also weighed heavily. The 1942 Biennale and the Film Festival bore little resemblance to the lives of ordinary Venetians.[47] As early as 1941 the police were worried about growing discontent. In February around 200 women descended on the prefecture protesting the failure to distribute lard as promised; the prefect defused the situation by authorizing its substitution with cooking oil. Over the following months, other food demonstrations, which the police chief dismissively characterized as "little womanly protests" took place on the *terraferma* and at Chioggia.[48] Worker discontent also grew. In autumn 1942 there was a strike at a plant in Marghera.[49] The Communist and Socialist parties quietly began to reconstitute themselves, and by 1943 worker discontent had only increased. Catholic Action, the umbrella organization for various church-related groups, quickened its activities. When Mussolini was overthrown by the Fascist Grand Council in July 1943 and imprisoned, leaders from all three groups spoke at spontaneous celebrations in Piazza San Marco.[50]

On September 12, Mussolini was rescued from imprisonment by German troops, a day after German forces occupied Venice. Mussolini's newly constituted Italian Social Republic, also known as the Republic of Salò (September 1943–May 1945), was little more than a German puppet. It was headquartered in Salò on the western shore of Lake Garda in territory that had once been part of the Venice's *stato da terra*. Because some components of the new government (including the film industry) were headquartered in Venice, the city's population grew. Removed from the war front (although towns like Padua and Treviso suffered significant war damage) and filled with officials, spies, actors, and prostitutes, life went on much as before.[51]

Venice's unique topography made concerted action difficult and limited Resistance fighters' ability to wage guerilla warfare.[52] An attempt to kidnap the Japanese ambassador, for example, had to be called off at the last minute. Instead, members organized actions to sow disquiet and garner maximum propagandistic effect. The best known was the so-called Beffa del Goldoni (Mockery at the Goldoni) of March 1945 when, during a performance at the Teatro Goldoni, armed and masked members of the Resistance interrupted the play, declared the imminent downfall of Mussolini and Hitler, and tossed leaflets into the crowd of governmental officials and German soldiers before vanishing.[53]

When Mussolini was overthrown in Rome in July 1943, Volpi tried unsuccessfully to escape to Switzerland. A second attempt also failed. Eventually he was arrested by the German Schutzstaffel (SS) and imprisoned but was released and took refuge in Switzerland. His associate, Vittorio Cini, was also arrested and sent to Dachau but was able, with his son Giorgio's help, to buy his way out and likewise flee to Switzerland. At the same time, Cini and Volpi began funneling money to the Resistance, which allowed them after the war to avoid any consequences for their collaboration with the Fascist regime. Volpi died in 1947 and did not have time to rehabilitate his reputation.[54] This was not true for Cini who outlived him by thirty years and created a major cultural institution on the island of San Giorgio Maggiore, the Giorgio Cini Foundation.[55] Having supported the fascist program and expressed both racist and anti-Semitic feelings, Patriarch Piazza suddenly and wholly condemned fascism at a Te Deum for the liberation of Venice in May 1945.[56]

The relative mildness of the war in Venice did not extend to the city's Jewish community. In 1938 there were 1,471 Jews in the city, who were, for the most part, fully integrated into Venetian life. Even before promulgation of the racial laws in that year, intolerance had reared its ugly head as anti-Semitic graffiti began to appear, along with renewed articulations of the blood libel, the defamatory claim that Jews utilized the blood of Christians in their rituals. Patriarch Piazza accused the Jews of deicide. When the racial laws were issued, many Jews lost their jobs and their place in society. The forty-five Jewish fellows of Ateneo Veneto were expelled. Eventually Jews had their radios confiscated and were forbidden to use libraries or even the Lido beaches. When the German occupation began, the situation grew more dire. Many Jews left the city finding shelter in the countryside or with friends. In September, Giuseppe Jona, president of the Jewish community, committed suicide rather than supply a list of community members to the authorities. On December 5, 1943, the order came for Venice's Jews to be arrested; 163 were rounded up (and four others subsequently). They were first housed at a

FIGURE 19.2 Arbit Blatas, *Monument Commemorating Venetian Jewish Victims of the Holocaust*, detail, 1980. Campo del Ghetto Nuovo, Venice. One of seven panels comprising the memorial, this one depicts a figure being executed by firing squad. Photo by the author.

concentration camp near Modena and then sent to Auschwitz, where they all perished. During the balance of the war another ninety Venetian Jews were arrested and murdered. Among the victims was Venice's chief rabbi Adolfo Ottolenghi.[57] A memorial consisting of seven bronze reliefs by the Lithuanian artist Arbit Blatas in the Ghetto Nuovo unveiled in 1980 commemorates the victims and the atrocities suffered by the community.

Once the German retreat began, members of the Resistance found themselves in a delicate position since they did not want to give the withdrawing enemy an excuse to take revenge by destroying Venice's artistic treasures or sabotaging the industries at Marghera. Patriarch Piazza negotiated a conditional surrender, and on April 28, 1945, Allied forces entered the city.[58] On May 7, all German forces throughout Europe unconditionally surrendered (the forces in Italy having done so on May 2). Thus began the Cold War era, one of the most consequential in Venice's history.

In the election of 1946 for the city council, the first in which women could vote, the Communists and Socialists together garnered thirty-two of the sixty seats, the Christian Democrats twenty-three, minor parties the remaining five. Communist Giovanni Battista Gianquinto became mayor, a position he held until 1951. Among the members of his government was Anita Mezzalira, the union activist persecuted by the fascists who became the first woman to hold a municipal governmental office.[59] In the June referendum of that same year, both Venice and the Veneto voted to abolish the monarchy and establish a republic. In Venice, 62.3 percent of voters favored the republic, in the Veneto 58.4 percent, in Italy as a whole, 54.3 percent. However, by 1948, as the Cold War and "Red Scare" heated up, and as old conflicts between church and state, local versus national attachments, and city and countryside reemerged, a swing to the right and toward the Christian Democrats began. Other contributing factors included the Catholic Church's emergence from the fascist era with its institutions largely intact and nearby Yugoslavia's communist regime, which controlled lands that had once been part of the Venetian Republic. In that year's elections for the national Chamber of Deputies, the Christian Democrats garnered 50.4 percent of the vote in Venice; 60.5 percent in the Veneto. They captured the mayorship in 1951 and retained it until 1975.[60] The end of the war did not result in a significant transformation of Venice's ruling elite as Catholics allied with "reformed" fascists—united in Cold War anti-communism.[61] Angelo Roncalli (future Pope John XXIII) was, like his predecessors, strongly anti-modernist and opposed to an alliance with the Socialists during his reign as patriarch from 1953 to 1958.

Politics aside, the story of Venice in the 1950s and '60s is of the industrial boom at Porto Marghera and the accompanying residential growth of Mestre as well as the demise of industry in the old island city and the dramatic expansion of tourism there. From 1949 to 1955 industrial production at Porto Marghera increased an astonishing 150 percent.[62] A Second Industrial Zone was built, which involved the reclamation of 2,471 additional acres of marshland at the lagoon's edge.[63] A second wharf was also added to the complex. This expansion was financed much as before, with public funds paying for the bulk of the infrastructure.[64] The primary focus of the Second Zone was on the production of petrochemicals and plastics; the major firms Edison and Montecatini merged in 1966 to form Montedison. Also, Venice finally benefited, as had been predicted in the nineteenth century, from the Suez Canal since, as the northernmost Mediterranean port, it was ideally situated for the importation of Middle Eastern oil to Western Europe. Accordingly, expansion involved the dredging of a new and deeper channel for oil tankers from the Malamocco mouth to Marghera. The original plan, first articulated in 1930, was for tankers to use the San Nicolò mouth and pass through the Bacino. However, a fire aboard a tanker that was undergoing repairs on the Giudecca in 1951 led to the rerouting.[65] The Canale dei Petroli (Petroleum Tanker Channel) was completed in 1968 not long before the 1973 oil crisis that undercut support for Porto Marghera. In the still heady early 1960s, plans were underway for the creation of a Third Industrial Zone that would have involved the reclamation of another 7,413 acres of marshland, of which nearly half was accomplished before plans for the Third Zone were shelved.[66] Yet as a post-war commercial port, Venice never challenged Genoa's lower-cost supremacy. Genoa enjoyed the advantage of geographical proximity and rail links to Milan and Turin, the latter the headquarters of leading automaker Fiat.[67]

As industrial Marghera grew, so did the number of workers, from over 20,000 in 1949, to 30,000 in 1960, to its peak of 40,000 in 1965. However, it began to decline in the 1970s, and by 1981 the workforce had dropped to 26,000.[68] The immediate post-war period saw worker agitation and union organizing. Yet, by the mid-1950s, unrest subsided as employment opportunities grew, only to roar back in 1968 when, for example, 15,000 Montedison workers marched on Mestre disrupting rail- and roadways, as issues of workplace safety—prompted by dangerous chemical leaks—became concerns. In 1973 the head of the Inspectorate of Work ordered that all workers at Marghera be supplied with gas masks. One employee was photographed going to work carrying a placard reading, "Masks for the smokestacks not the workers."[69] Industries were forced to make some concessions on wages, hours, and workplace safety.[70] Marghera also hosted extremist cells. The radical left terrorist group Red Brigades assassinated both Director Giuseppe Taliercio and Vice-Director Sergio Gori of the petrochemical division of Montedison, as well as Alfredo Albanese, head of the Venetian anti-terrorism unit.[71] The power of the unions started to diminish as Marghera's workforce began to shrink, although each announcement of a plant closure was met with demonstrations and protests.[72]

As Porto Marghera grew, so did Mestre. In addition to workers commuting to Marghera, much of Mestre's growth came from residents of the old island city who wanted to escape deplorable housing conditions, others who were forced to move as buildings were converted into shops, and others who simply wished to enjoy modern conveniences available on the mainland including motorbikes and automobiles.[73] So began Venice's demographic collapse, which has continued to the present. In 1951 the city reached a population of 174,969 residents.[74] Ten years later the number had dropped by nearly 37,000, and the city lost another 29,000 in the 1960s. According to the 1971 census, there were 108,987 residents. By contrast between 1953 and 1973 Mestre grew by almost 67,000, eclipsing the old city's population by nearly 20,000.[75] Most who left were members of the petite bourgeoisie or workers who were young or middle-aged, leaving Venice with an aging population more sharply divided between rich and poor. As one Venetian said, "For an old person to move to Mestre, that is death."[76] What newcomers found there was a Wild West of construction with little urban planning and a focus on apartment living rather than on pedestrian streets and public squares as in the island city.[77]

The exodus was also due to the final collapse of Venetian manufacturing as the city's economy became a tourism "monoculture."[78] Many industries were no longer competitive or viable. The Molino Stucky closed in 1954, the Cotonificio in 1960. Other industries followed. When in the early 1960s the new Marco Polo airport (built on 600 acres of reclaimed marshes) opened on the mainland, Nicelli on the Lido fell into disuse; many of its service and maintenance workers moved to the mainland to be near Marco Polo.[79] Other industries like lace- and bead-making continued their decline, even as the female workers continued to garner miserable wages. One bead-stringer testified, "I worked my whole life and didn't earn even 5 cents of a pension."[80] One bright spot in the 1950s was the production of art glass, with groundbreaking practitioners like Paolo Venini and Archimede Seguso, but the 1960s would see renewed pressure on the glass industry.[81]

The harshest blow of all, both in terms of civic pride and jobs, was dealt at the Arsenal, as the naval complex still employed around 3,000 personnel. In 1956 the Ministry of Defense announced that it was moving the command center for the Northern Adriatic to Ancona and decommissioning the Arsenal as a military installation. The usually divided factions of the city came together in what Patriarch Roncalli called an "accord of souls" to challenge the decision. In the end they were able temporarily to save around 1,100 jobs but not to reverse the ruling or stop the decline.[82] After more than a millennium, Venice was no longer the naval epicenter of the Adriatic.

The picture was completely different in the tourism sector. After the war, a concerted effort was made to get the city's cultural attractions up and running again. The 1948 Biennale was one of the most consequential. Its embrace of modernism included exhibitions of the work of Marc Chagall and Pablo Picasso, as well as the collection of American heiress Peggy Guggenheim. The following year Guggenheim took up residence in the city. These events and subsequent Biennales generated fierce debates over abstraction versus Social Realism that were heavily tinged with Cold War politics.[83] The city also sought to extend the tourist season beyond the traditional summer months and continued to attract royal, intellectual, and Hollywood A-listers. However, the real change during this period was the growth of mass tourism. Already in 1956 the Chamber of Commerce noted that travel had been transformed from an "individual luxury phenomenon" into a "mass phenomenon" and that between March and October the number of tourists exceeded 2 million. These were tourists whose visits were short—down by 1961 to an average stay of only 2.25 days—and whose budgets were tight, which meant they spent less on hotels and meals. The other big change was the decline of the luxurious Lido seaside resorts and the rapid growth of budget accommodations, including camping at the beaches on Cavallino, the barrier island/peninsula. The mid-August holiday in 1960 saw 50,000 tourists staying there, most of them foreigners, many from Austria.[84]

If modernism in painting was welcome at the Biennale, it continued to meet resistance in architecture, where it threatened to alter Venice's revered cityscape. Three giants of twentieth-century architecture failed to see their Venetian projects realized. Frank Lloyd Wright's design for a palace on the Grand Canal for the Masieri family failed to win approval. Le Corbusier's plan for a civic hospital in Cannaregio and Louis Kahn's conference and art center on the Biennale grounds also ran into opposition and were never built.

The projects that succeeded—among them extensions of the Hotel Bauer-Grünwald at San Moisè and the Hotel Danieli on the Riva degli Schiavoni, the bank building for the Cassa di Risparmio di Venezia at San Paternian, and the SADE office building on the Rio Nuovo—are hardly masterpieces and continue to generate opprobrium. The most acclaimed interventions were by Carlo Scarpa, but tellingly they were modest in scale and focused primarily on interiors, namely, the Olivetti showroom in Piazza San Marco and the ground floor and garden of the Palazzo Querini-Stampalia (1963). In the latter, as in his setting for the *Partigiana* sculpture, Scarpa played with water, channeling the tidal flow that regularly floods the ground floor interior and constructing a variegated walkway above it.[85] However, three years after its completion Venice was struck by a high tide that no channel could contain, inflicting a natural disaster of unparalleled proportion.

The terrible flood of November 4, 1966, which the Venetians refer to as "the big water" (*acqua granda*), resulted from a confluence of meteorological, geological, and astronomical factors. In the preceding days, heavy rain fell across north and central Italy causing rivers to overflow their banks. In Tuscany, the raging Arno devastated Florence. The many rivers, great and small, that debouche near Venice became engorged. Normally their flow would be carried safely out to sea. However, a low-pressure system meant that a strong sirocco was blowing, increasing wave action and tidal flow moving up the bathtub-shaped Adriatic and impeding the outflow of river water. Compounding the situation was a spring tide, a regularly occurring high tide caused by the alignment of the earth, sun, and moon. Consequently, when the high tide arrived, augmented as it was by the storm surge, it pushed up against the massive quantity of water coming from the rivers. Unable to disperse, the water could only rise. Normally high tides last six hours and then recede. The sirocco, however, prevented the recession. When the next high tide arrived twelve hours later, it compounded the situation, creating a high tide on top of the still un-receded previous high tide. The water rose to 6.36 feet above average sea level as measured by a gauge near Santa Maria della Salute. Venice was inundated for over twenty hours.[86]

The city was plunged into darkness and isolation as water knocked out the electrical grid and telephone lines which, after an exceptional high tide in 1953, had been raised to what at the time was believed to be a safe height. Garbage, fuel oil, the household belongings of those unfortunate enough to live in ground floor apartments, and dead animals, especially rats, floated in the noxious stew. Some worried that the waves crashing against the columns of the Ducal Palace would bring it down. Books were drenched at the Marciana library, photographic plates at the Cini Foundation, precious historical documents at the State Archives at the Frari. Boats were battered and came unmoored, gondolas were swamped. One photograph of the aftermath shows a *caorlina*—a kind of large flat-bottomed vessel often used for fishing—beached in the middle of a street in the parish of San Giacomo dall'Orio.[87] Miraculously, no one drowned, and most of the city's paintings, mounted high on altars and walls, were spared. Slower to show its effects was the salt water that overtopped foundations of impermeable Istrian stone, seeping into the bricks and marble of which the city is built, corroding and undermining buildings from within.

The situation was equally dire elsewhere in the lagoon. The ferocious wind and waves overwhelmed the *murazzi*, the old Republic's seawalls. Malamocco was inundated, Pellestrina isolated. The Lido beaches eroded. Cabanas were strewn about like matchsticks. On the Cavallino peninsula and nearby island of Sant'Erasmo, which was under six feet of water, orchards and truck farms were destroyed, their fertile soils were sown with salt, and livestock drowned. No place was spared.[88]

FIGURE 19.3 November 1966 Flood in Piazza San Marco. Wikimedia Commons.

As news of the disaster spread around the globe, the international community mobilized. The British organized Venice in Peril, the Americans the Committee to Rescue Italian Art (later changed to Save Venice), the French the Comité pour la Sauvegarde de Venise. In total, more than thirty countries pledged support. The fate of Venice was becoming a worldwide concern. In 1969 UNESCO (United Nations Educational, Scientific, and Cultural Organization) issued a report diagnosing and recommending solutions to the city's ills. Yet the individual national committees devoted themselves, for the most part, to the repair and restoration of specific buildings or works of art. Tackling the causes of Venice's environmental problems lay beyond their mandate, legal jurisdiction, or financial resources.[89]

As for the Italians, especially the Venetians, they immediately sought to explain the disaster. Venetians had grown accustomed to periodic *acque alte* of moderate height and adjusted their lifestyle accordingly—donning "high water" boots, tramping across risers strategically placed on low-lying streets, raising the floors of ground-level apartments, or abandoning them altogether. Most of the blame fell squarely on Porto Marghera. Critics argued that the deepening of the lagoon mouths to accommodate larger vessels and creation of the Petroleum Tanker Channel greatly increased the volume and velocity of water entering the lagoon, destabilizing a centuries-old equilibrium. In addition, the reclamation of the thousands of acres of coastal marshes to create the industrial zones at Marghera created a hardscape where once there had been swamps. Blame was also leveled at the many fish farms in the lagoon whose banks likewise interfered with dispersal of the water. It is estimated that from the beginning of the nineteenth century to 1980, the lagoon's surface area had been reduced by a third. Rather than gradually spreading over a wide expanse of intertidal flats, the surf came up against earthen and concrete barriers. Others argued that over-tapping by industries of aquifers accelerated natural subsidence and made the city vulnerable to rising sea level due to global warming. The failure for decades to dredge canals in Venice and the infilling of others were also cited as having had a deleterious impact on lagoonal hydraulics.[90] In just seven centuries then, the threat to the lagoon had been turned on its head. Whereas in 1300 the danger had been that the rivers would cause the lagoon to silt up and become dry land, now the risk was that the lagoon would be swallowed up by the sea.[91]

The arguments regarding solutions were even more acrimonious and fraught than those about the causes of the catastrophe, involving tales of governmental inaction and corruption, technical studies, special laws, bureaucratic maneuvering, and international pressure.[92] Essentially, the proposed solution to *acqua alta* came down to two different approaches, one technological, the other cultural.[93] The technological solution, which ultimately carried the day, relied on creating mobile gates lying on the seafloor at the barrier island mouths that could be raised when a high tide was approaching in order to cut the lagoon off from the Adriatic. It became known as MOSE (Modulo Sperimentale Elettromeccanico—Experimental Electromechanical Model) after the prototype gate put in place in 1988 for testing. Plagued by huge cost overruns, bribery, and corruption, the project only became operational in autumn 2020. In typical Venetian fashion, the for-profit conglomerate placed in charge of the project known as Consorzio Venezia Nuova (the New Venice Consortium) enjoyed a virtual monopoly and, by law, the right to retain a significant percentage of the tax dollars allotted to the project.[94] Another initiative, known as Insula (Island), controlled by the city and utility companies sought to mitigate flooding by dredging canals, repairing building foundations, and raising sidewalks throughout the city.[95]

Critics of the mobile submerged dikes, which were cleverly named after Moses who parted the waters of the Red Sea, argued that the dikes would have to be raised so frequently due to rising sea levels that they would do more harm than good by interfering with the twice daily tidal flushing of the lagoon and in so doing trap pollutants in the estuary. The solution posed by Italia Nostra (Our Italy), a leading environmental group, relied instead on restoring the lagoon's natural balance, although it begs the question what is "natural" since Venetians have been tampering with the lagoon for centuries. They advocated reducing the depth of the lagoon mouths, building jetties to slow the speed of water entering them, restoring to marsh the reclaimed lands at Porto Marghera, opening fish farms to tidal flow, and banning oil tankers from the lagoon altogether.[96] Not surprisingly, the huge profits to be made by building the mobile gates eventually carried the day.

The impact of the 1966 flood extended far beyond debates over a solution to *acqua alta*. It accelerated the exodus of residents from the old city, driving out those who could no longer abide the constant threat of flooding. Indeed, although the 1966 flood was exceptional, many Venetians had tired of the less devastating but more periodic minor *acque alte*. The flood also heightened environmental awareness, which had already been aroused in 1963 when a huge landslide crashed into the lake behind a hydroelectric dam at Vajont near Belluno, sending a gigantic wave of water and debris into the valley below, destroying four villages and taking 2,000 lives. Geologists had warned of the danger, but the economic interests of business prevailed.[97] Increasing recognition of the toxicity of the chemical plants operating at Porto Marghera also raised environmental consciousness. Workers offered harrowing accounts of worksites fouled with chemical dust and other pollutants and the resulting illnesses and deaths. One laborer told a union organizer, "If I had a son, I wouldn't want him to come [to work] here under any circumstances. Here one dies and that's it, here one dies."[98] Studies documented high levels of air pollution as well as heavy metals contaminating the lagoon floor. The Vajont dam catastrophe, the *acqua granda*, and increasing cancer rates illuminated the true costs of Volpian industrial development. Together environmental concerns, the oil crisis of the early 1970s, and a changing global economy accelerated the decline of industries at Marghera and the concomitant loss of jobs. By 2002 there were fewer than 13,000 positions at the once thriving site, down to around 10,000 in 2017.[99]

Suddenly, Marghera, which many had seen as the solution to Venice's problems, especially its economic dependence on tourism, came to be viewed as the enemy.[100] This was replaced by a new appreciation for the lagoon and its fragile ecosystem. In 1975 the Vogalonga (Long Row), an annual rowing marathon that carries participants through vast stretches of the lagoon, was created. Venetians were rediscovering their watery roots and turning their backs on the idea of Greater Venice. In 1979 the first of several unsuccessful referendums was held aimed at dissolving the union of Venice and Mestre/Marghera. One commentator even went so far as to suggest that Venice once again become a kind of autonomous city-state, in his words a revived "Most Serene Republic," linked to Italy in much the same manner as the Vatican.[101]

Unlike some periods in its history, there is no single event that marks the end of the Cold War era in Venice, especially since many of the issues raised in the 1970s and '80s such as environmentalism, Porto Marghera's industrial decline, and questioning the concept of Greater Venice continue to be concerns. The collapse of the Berlin Wall and the breakup of the Soviet bloc did, however, bring in their wake in the early 1990s a political corruption scandal throughout Italy that upended the political party system that had dominated Italy since 1946 and paved the way for new political organizations and the identity crisis that marks Venice today.

The fate of the horses of San Marco offers a telling coda to the era. In the late 1970s, the horses were removed from the façade of the church for restoration. During the repair it was discovered that acid rain was causing severe damage to the ancient sculptures, which are made primarily of copper covered with gilt. To preserve the horses, the decision was made to protect them from the elements by mounting them in a gallery inside the basilica and replace them with copies on the façade.[102] In this way, industrial pollution accomplished what Napoleon and World War I bombing raids could not, that is, permanent displacement of a powerful symbol of the ancient Republic's imperial past. Venice's future appeared just as fraught.

20

Global Venice

ONE OF THE more recent additions to Venice's infrastructure is the elegant, sweeping Calatrava bridge (officially Il ponte della Costituzione—Constitution Bridge). Designed by the acclaimed Spanish architect Santiago Calatrava and inaugurated in 2008, the bridge traverses a narrow and not very grand section of the Grand Canal and links Piazzale Roma with the embankment leading to the train station. It was commissioned to create a convenient pedestrian way for tourists arriving at Piazzale Roma by car, bus, or ship to begin the walk to Rialto and San Marco.

Although beautiful—its gentle curve has been compared to the asymmetrical hull of a gondola—Calatrava's bridge has proved controversial and impractical.[1] Not surprisingly, its modernist design provoked objections from traditionalists. After disability activists protested its inaccessibility, a "pod" was installed to transport the disabled, but this was plagued with technical difficulties and subsequently dismantled. Even the able-bodied have found using the bridge challenging since the tempered glass pavement is slippery when it is raining or simply wet with condensation in the ever-humid city. In response to almost daily falls, plans were made in 2020 to replace the glass with stone. The bridge offers an example of what happens when someone not intimately familiar with Venice's unique pedestrian and environmental conditions intervenes in the city's infrastructure while trying to pay tribute to the city's association with glass.[2]

The bridge epitomizes the central Venetian dynamic of the past several decades, namely, the conflict between globalization's impact on the city—most obviously in mega-tourism—and the retreat into localism as a reaction to it. Mass tourism has affected everything from housing to local traditions and customs, infrastructure, and the environment. It has led to further domination of the real estate market by wealthy foreigners and cultural

FIGURE 20.1 Santiago Calatrava, Constitution Bridge, 2008, Venice. Photo by the author.

institutions and to an influx of low-wage immigrant labor. Venetians have responded with plans to slow or at least tame the tide of tourists and limit their environmental impact. Globalization has contributed as well to the rise of right-wing parties, like the Liga Veneta (Venetian League) and Lega Nord (Northern League), that are fueled by anti-immigrant sentiment and economic anxiety. Referendums to dismantle Greater Venice by separating the island city from Mestre likewise evidence a retreat into hyper-localism on both sides of the lagoon.

At heart is the question, who has the right to determine Venice's future? Or, more simply, who owns Venice? The global claim was staked in 1987 when UNESCO named Venice and its lagoon a World Heritage Site. The prestigious UN designation declared the city notable for its "authenticity," downplaying the degree of change by describing it as having retained "the formal and spatial characteristics present in the Middle Ages and the Renaissance with a few later additions due to landfills and land reclamation."[3] Venetians are forced into a reactive mode by this global encroachment, while at the same time becoming ever more dependent on the travel industry.

The most important phenomenon of recent decades has been the exponential growth of tourism. Between 1990 and 2020, the number of visitors to Venice grew by at least 150 percent, from approximately 10 million a year to around 25 million. Low-cost airlines, private accommodation rentals through online websites, and a new clientele composed of the growing middle classes of China, India, and other Asian countries with disposable income have dramatically augmented the traditional flow of European and North American tourists. Nearly half of the visitors are "day-trippers." Some stay at inexpensive accommodations on the mainland, while an increasing number (1.6 million in 2019) are cruise ship passengers who disembark for just a few hours and tour only San Marco and Rialto on organized excursions.[4] Their impact is especially heavy because, although they crowd the tourist hot spots, degrading those sites through wear and tear, they do not spend money on hotels and restaurants like overnight guests. During certain times of the year, the number of tourists per day easily exceeds the number of Venetian residents, which in 2022 dropped to just below 50,000.[5]

The disastrous Pink Floyd concert during the Redentore festival in 1989—when thousands of fans descended on the city, damaged monumental buildings, and left tons of garbage strewn around the Piazza and Molo—epitomized Venice's tourism imbalance.[6] Cruise ships became another symbol of tourism overload. These gigantic vessels famously dwarfed the city as they made their way through the Bacino and down the Giudecca Canal. They affected not only the wave action and water flow of the lagoon but also the city's air quality as their engines billowed fumes even when docked. Environmentalists were also concerned about the possibility of accidents, as happened in 2019 when MSC cruise liner *Opera*, which weighs over 65,000 tons and can carry more than 3,400 passengers and crew, slammed into a riverboat and the quay near the Maritime Station, injuring four.[7] Commercial traffic almost completely abandoned the station as its facilities were modified to accommodate the cruise ship industry.[8] In August 2021 the Italian government, under pressure from UNESCO, which threatened to put the city on its "World Heritage in Danger" list, banned large cruise ships from the Bacino and Giudecca Canal. They now berth at a temporary site at Porto Marghera, although some advocate new permanent piers on the Lido.[9] Others will dock at Chioggia.

Venice's dependence on tourism has only grown greater as the industrial decline of Marghera has continued. Dow Chemical closed its plant in 2006, followed by Montedison in 2009.[10] Before his death, Vittorio Cini himself pushed for heavy industry to be moved away from Venice and toward the

FIGURE 20.2 Cruise Ship on the Giudecca Canal approaching San Giorgio Maggiore, 2015. Don Mammoser/Alamy Stock Photo.

Po industrial zones around Ravenna and Ferrara; his proposal represented a reversal of the shift of economic power from Ravenna to Venice in the eighth and ninth centuries.[11] Ironically, one of the firms that has remained viable at Marghera is Fincantieri, which specializes in building cruise ships. However much of its workforce is supplied by immigrants from Asia rather than locals.[12]

The volume of visitors has significantly impacted the city's infrastructure. To relieve the congestion of motor vehicle traffic at Piazzale Roma, the Tronchetto complex was built on reclaimed land. Originally planned as a multi-purpose service center, it is essentially a large carpark and since 2010 has been equipped with a shuttle train that carries passengers between it, the cruise ship docks near the Maritime Station, and Piazzale Roma. The city has also created express *vaporetto* lines to whisk tourists to their preferred destinations and reduce overcrowding on the "local" routes. And to accommodate high-end tourists' shopping demands, the Fondaco dei Tedeschi at Rialto, which had housed the city's main post office, was transformed into a glitzy shopping mall operated by a Hong Kong–based luxury retailer.

Around the turn of the twenty-first century Venice had more than 200 hotels offering approximately 12,000 beds. By 2019 that number had doubled, if hotels in Mestre are included in the count.[13] The Molino Stucky factory complex was adapted into the Hilton Molino Stucky Venice Hotel, and more and more buildings and even small islands in the lagoon have been converted into hotels and resorts. At the same time the number of bed and breakfast options offered through such online platforms as Airbnb has exploded. Investors have purchased properties and converted them into vacation rentals that garner significantly more income by renting to tourists on a nightly basis than renting to residents long-term.[14] Along with the purchase of second homes in the city by foreigners and other Italians, vacation rentals have exacerbated the city's perennial housing shortage and the phenomenon of locals being priced out of the market. Graffiti on a wall near San Basilio in 2019 expressed the anger and frustration of those in danger of being displaced. It read, "Qui siamo e qui restiamo! No gentrification!" (Here we are and here we're staying! No gentrification!)

Cultural institutions in line with Giuseppe Volpi's vision of the island city focused on tourism and the arts have also been expanding and buying up key real estate. The Biennale has made increasing use of space at the Arsenal, while French billionaire and contemporary art collector François Pinault purchased the rights to operate Palazzo Grassi and was awarded a thirty-year lease on the Customs House near the Salute, which he transformed into exhibition space that opened in 2009. A sculpture entitled *Boy with Frog* that Pinault commissioned from California sculptor Charles Ray was installed at the Custom's House Point but provoked such widespread opposition that it was replaced by a replica of the nineteenth-century lamppost that had previously stood there. One critic of the sculpture's removal took it as evidence of Venice's "administrative cowardice" and "cultural darkness," further proof of the city's ongoing resistance to modernist interventions in the cityscape.[15] Also in Dorsoduro, the Peggy Guggenheim Collection, taken over following her death by the New York–based Solomon R. Guggenheim Foundation, has significantly expanded its holdings by acquiring buildings formerly housing apartments at the rear of Guggenheim's Palazzo Venier dei Leoni.

The University of Venice Ca' Foscari and the Istituto Universitario Architettura Venezia (IUAV), the architecture school, have also increased their urban footprints. IUAV converted the Cotonificio into space for its programs, while Ca' Foscari developed a large dormitory at Santa Marta. The former abattoir at San Giobbe currently houses Ca' Foscari's department of economics. The university's enrollment has increased more than tenfold since the early 1950s to more than 20,000 students in 2022.[16] Venice International University, a joint project of Ca' Foscari, IUAV, and other European, North American, and Asian universities, has taken over and restored the former

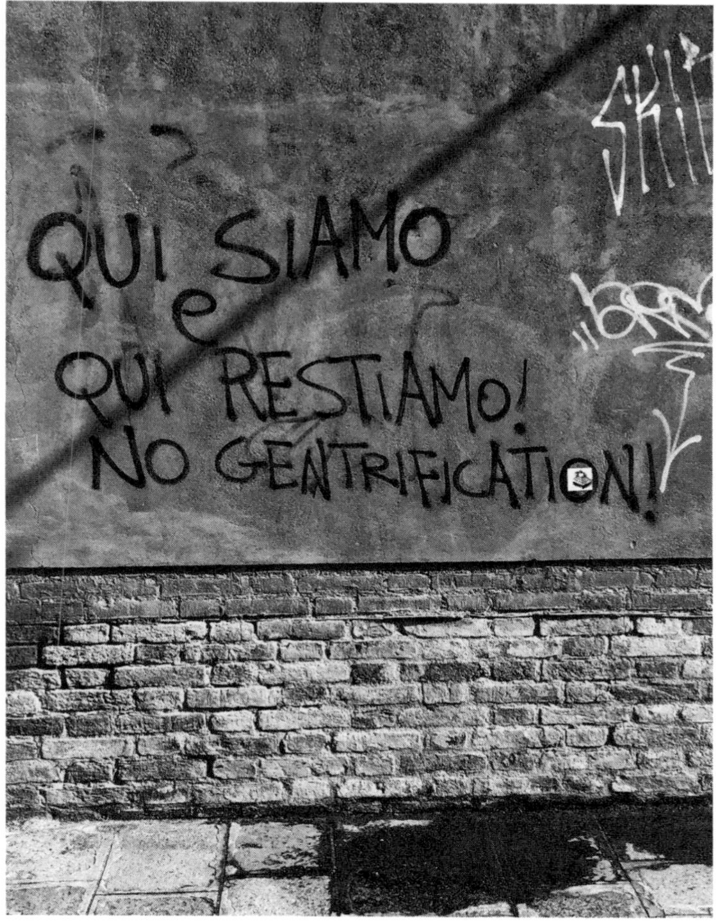

FIGURE 20.3 Grafitti near the Maritime Station, 2019. It is written in Italian, not Venetian dialect. Photo by the author.

mental asylum on the island of San Servolo. Students are among the many "city users," including daily commuters from Greater Venice, outlying *terraferma* towns, and settlements in the lagoon. In the early 1990s, daily commuters numbered over 27,000. They, like tourists and the tide, sweep in and out of the city each day.[17]

The growth of tourism and decline of the resident population have combined to empty out many of the small businesses and shops catering to non-tourist needs and replace them with stores selling Carnival masks and other souvenirs, most of which are not locally produced.[18] Supermarkets have supplanted specialized food stores to better serve tourists, many of whom stay in apartments where they can prepare meals. A declining population also means there is less demand for hardware stores, barbers and hairdressers, fabric stores, cobblers, bakers, and other shops and artisans meeting residents' everyday needs. The stretch of streets running from the Accademia delle Belle Arti to the Guggenheim is perhaps an exaggerated example of how shops and services have been replaced by private art galleries and bars.

The Covid-19 pandemic exposed the vulnerability of an economy focused almost exclusively on tourism. During the first ten months of 2020, tourism dropped by approximately 80 percent, and many businesses shuttered their doors, some forever. This prompted a good deal of discussion about diversifying an economy overly dependent on "free time" as Venetians struggle once again to reimagine the future.[19] Some have proposed that Venice specialize in "clean" information technology.

Although the full deployment of the MOSE flood barriers has intermittently protected the city from *acqua alta* since autumn 2020, the city remains environmentally fragile and vulnerable. Even before the system was deployed, some critics claimed that the planners' underestimation of global warming and accompanying sea-level rise would render the mobile water-gates obsolete before the end of the twenty-first century.[20] Environmental concerns, including the danger of oil spills and other accidents, have led to calls to remove all tankers from the lagoon. Water and air pollution, the cleanup of toxic substances on the lagoon floor, and the deleterious effects of *moto ondoso* (motorboat wave action) on the lagoon shoreline and building foundations remain critical issues.

Another aspect of Venice's globalization is appropriation of its image by international capital. This is hardly new. In the 1960s clever advertising executives for Coca Cola devised a scheme to spread corn in Piazza San Marco in the shape of the company's name and then snapped a photo of the Piazza's famous pigeons gobbling up the corn and spelling out "Coca Cola." The image, a mainstay of bars throughout Italy for years, was an advertising coup. Absolut Vodka replicated the stunt in the Piazzetta in the 1990s when the pigeons were enticed to recreate that company's distinctive bottle, the centerpiece of its advertising campaign.[21] Companies also garner good publicity by underwriting exhibitions and restoration projects and plastering their logos on the accompanying catalogs and scaffolding. In its most extreme form, appropriation becomes replication. Parts of the Piazza have been recreated for the Italian Pavilion at Disney World in Florida, while the Las Vegas Sands Company has created casino-resorts dubbed "The Venetian" with such signifiers as the Campanile and Ducal Palace at Las Vegas and

Macau. Concern over Venice's image prompted Mayor Massimo Cacciari in the late 1990s to consider trademarking the city's name.[22]

Another contemporary phenomenon also with deep roots in Venice's past is immigration. For more than 1,500 years Venice has drawn those seeking work and escape from poverty. The end of the Cold War and fall of the Iron Curtain led to an influx of immigrants from Eastern Europe to the city that continues to the present. Many new arrivals are women who, as in the past, find employment as domestic workers, caregivers, and prostitutes.[23] Many of today's immigrants come from Venice's traditional catchment area around the Adriatic, namely, the Balkans, especially Albania.[24] Yet there are also immigrants from farther afield, including China, Southeast Asia, and North and sub-Saharan Africa. Many of the Asian newcomers find jobs in restaurants or sweatshops, the Africans as itinerant street sellers. Like those of old, today's immigrants are easy prey for criminals and frequent victims of sexual abuse and economic exploitation. Few are residents of the island city. They too commute daily from the mainland.

The economic, social, cultural, and environmental issues facing twenty-first-century Venice—many the consequences of or exacerbated by globalization—are daunting. The solutions are equally so. No single authority exists to adjudicate the competing claims of those who believe they have a stake in determining Venice's future. Within Italy, the municipal, regional, and national governments all jostle for power and to control funds flowing into the city. Their bureaucratic specialization and lack of collaborative strategy are highlighted by such legislation as a 1984 so-called Special Law for Venice that assigned responsibility over the lagoon's hydrology to the national government and pollution control to the regional, as if the two were not interconnected.[25] Overlapping interests have led to inefficiency and corruption, as when Mayor Giorgio Orsoni, along with numerous others, was arrested in 2014 for taking kickbacks associated with the MOSE project. International organizations like Save Venice and Venice in Peril also believe their monetary support gives them a voice in the decision-making process. According to UNESCO, its management plan for Venice as a World Heritage Site received the approval of twenty-one "responsible bodies" and "local organizations" with representation on its steering committee.[26] However, in 2019 it warned that "lack of an integrated management system for the site" put Venice's "'Outstanding Universal Value,' the hallmark of every World Heritage property, in peril."[27] UNESCO has at times threatened to move Venice to its list of places in danger, which would be a public relations disaster. Because of Venice's allure, the entire global community believes it should have a say in the city's future. Yet even this is not novel. In the eighteenth century, Johann Wolfgang von Goethe wrote of traveling around the city by gondola: "I was now suddenly a co-sovereign of the Adriatic Sea, like every Venetian when he reclines in his gondola."[28] Where else do tourists claim to be co-owners of the place they are visiting?

The impact of globalization has fueled a variegated localist response. The most visible has been the rise of the Liga Veneta, founded in 1979, which in its most extreme form has called for independence of the Veneto from Italy and less radically for greater federalism and autonomy. The movement has maintained a strong cultural attachment to the traditions of the Venetian Republic and to the most distinctive marker of Venetian/Veneto identity, the dialect, which some adherents have even falsely claimed is a distinct language. In 1989 the Liga joined forces with Lega Lombarda, its Lombard counterpart, in a union known as Lega Nord. Under Umberto Bossi, the Lega Nord advocated the creation of an independent country Padania, named after the Po, consisting of the Veneto, Lombardy, and Piedmont. At the same time the Venetian separatist movement suffered a succession of internal fractures and schisms.[29] In May 1997, one group, the Veneto Serenissimo Governo (Most Serene Venetian Government), used the bicentenary of the Republic's demise to stage a "coup" by floating a sport-utility vehicle tricked-out as a tank to the Piazza and commandeering the bell tower. They proclaimed, "Today the Serene Republic of Venice is reborn," describing the ancient Republic as "an ornament of Europe" and, in a throwback to Crusader rhetoric, "a bulwark of Christianity."[30] The eight perpetrators—none from the historic city itself—were quickly subdued. The seizure was a public relations sensation; it received international coverage but was a political dead end. However, during the 1990s, Liga Veneta, the regional affiliate of Lega Nord, received between 10 and 20 percent of the votes in national elections and captured the mayoralty of Treviso and control of several provincial assemblies, although support was weaker in Venice itself. It also began to draw support from former voters for the Partito Comunista Italiano since, like the Communist Party, the Liga represented a party of belonging.[31]

Initially the movement was fueled by economic anxiety and antipathy toward southern Italians. Many of its adherents believed that jobs were being lost to immigrants from the south and their lives tyrannized by southern (i.e., Roman) bureaucrats. Furthermore, they argued that money from the richer north of Italy was being siphoned off to support the poorer south. With time, the anti-immigrant stance shifted its focus to foreigners, especially North

Africans and Middle Easterners, and promoted "local" traditions, including cuisine.[32] In one famous poster Lega Nord proclaimed, "Si alla polenta, no al cous cous" (Yes to polenta, no to couscous). Luca Zaia, Lega Nord politician and president of the Veneto region since 2010, has attacked multiculturalism declaring, "He who wishes to live in our territory must also know the laws, the values, the culture, the language, the faith and respect them."[33] Despite ongoing internal squabbles and defections, the Lega Nord has been the Veneto region's leading party in various regional and national elections, essentially replacing the defunct Christian Democrats. It has adopted much of the anti-modernist stance of the right-wing faction of the Catholic Church and captured various mayoralties.[34]

Yet the Lega remains an ideological mishmash, although greater autonomy continues to be a central tenet. Its strongholds are in the pre-Alps. Venice, including Mestre, has never been a bastion of adherence, although here too there are significant variations, with support increasing from traditionally left-leaning trade unionists.[35] In the 2020 communal elections, personally popular center-right Mayor Luigi Brugnaro, who had Lega backing, won reelection, defeating the center-left candidate in the historic city, the estuary (lagoon), and the mainland. While his victory on the mainland was by more than 30 percentage points, in the historic city, he won by only 3.[36]

Those electoral preferences highlight the ongoing division between the historic island city and Mestre, Marghera, and the other parts of the mainland and lagoon incorporated into what has been officially since 2014 the Metropolitan City of Venice, which incorporates forty-four separate communes or civic governments, extending along the Adriatic from the Tagliamento River in the east to Cavarzere in the south.[37] It incorporates much of the old *dogado* (except for the stretch from the Tagliamento to Grado), although it extends farther inland than the duchy did. Discontent with the union of Venice and Mestre as one commune has resulted in five referendums (1979, 1989, 1994, 2002, and 2019) calling for separation and the creation of two distinct city governments. In the first three, votes for separation rose from 27.6 percent to 42.2 percent to 44.4 percent. The referendums of 2002 and 2019 failed to reach the necessary quorums and were declared invalid. Of the 22 percent of eligible voters who cast ballots in the 2019 referendum—a highly self-selected group—66 percent favored separation.[38]

The arguments and alliances on both sides are complex. Those in favor of ongoing union argue that the problems facing Venice are immense and, in the words of one unionist, "you don't resolve big problems by creating two smaller [city] councils."[39] Pollution, for example, remains a central concern, and opponents of separation contend that only by working together can the city and mainland solve the issue since pollutants do not respect political boundaries. As Venetians have understood for centuries, *terraferma* and lagoon are inextricably linked. Proponents of separation focus on the added costs to Mestre's residents and businesses of such practical matters as garbage collection in Venice, but also contend that the two cities have distinctive identities and ways of life. Comedian and politician Beppe Grillo, an advocate of separation in the 2019 referendum, declared that the cities "represent two radically different civilizations, one on the land and the other on water."[40] The group Mestre Mia (My Mestre) promotes "mestrinità" (Mestreness). It too argues that Venice and Mestre are "intrinsically two, with distinct identities and missions" and that the "unitary" approaches of the past have failed.[41] Venetians' sense of superiority can also grate as when a foreign art expert declared that "the Terraferma cities offer nothing to the tourist."[42] In many ways, the Venice/Mestre question is the Veneto/Italy question writ small, that is, a retreat into localism in the face of intractable problems.

For their part, many residents of the historic city also take refuge in their identity, in their sense of "venezianità" (Venice-ness). This takes many forms, including speaking in dialect (a means of self-identification and defense against the tourist onslaught) and the local newspaper the *Gazzettino*'s assiduous chronicling of tourists' boorish behavior. One higher end restaurant actively discourages tourists with warnings such as "No lasagne, no pizza, no menú turistico" and has mockingly created its own sign directing them toward Piazzale Roma and the train station, declaring that it charges 2.5 euros or 5,000 lire [*sic*] for information. Even the decision to rebuild La Fenice *dov'era, com'era* (where it was, as it was) following the 1996 fire that destroyed it can be taken as an affirmation of Venetian tradition and identity and resistance to modernism and change. Worse still, when residents do take the initiative or try to reinvigorate their local customs, as when in 1979 they revived Carnival after decades or 1975 when they began the Vogalonga to celebrate the Venetian style of rowing and lagoon life, they quickly find these activities coopted by the tourism industry.[43] Venetians rightly have a love/hate relationship with the visitors whom they ridicule but whose financial support they simultaneously depend upon. In the words of one newspaper editor, "Since we're the most beautiful city in the world, everyone has to take care of us."[44] In the modern age, *venezianità* is defined largely against the backdrop of mega-tourism. Yet every retreat into localism itself becomes prey to tourism's unrelenting grasp.

The tourist economy is just the latest stage in Venice's long and complicated history. That history, as this book has shown, is marked not only by the perennial struggle to forge a living in a tidal lagoon but also by the need to adapt to changes of regional, Mediterranean, and global dimensions that were often beyond the Venetians' ability to control. Sometimes the Venetians responded to these challenges aggressively, as when they filled the political vacuum left in the wake of Byzantium's retreat from northern Italy and asserted their control over the northern Adriatic, humbling rival cities in the process; or again when, after initial hesitation, they created a *terraferma* regional-state as a counterweight to those created by Florence, Milan, and other Italian powers. They even made the truly consequential decision, partly in order to protect the historic city's touristic value, to compete with Genoa for twentieth-century economic might and to tap the potential of hydroelectric power and fossil fuels by relocating heavy industry to Porto Marghera. At other times, they failed to meet the challenge as when they refused—stuck as they were in a city-state mentality—to extend full citizenship and political participation to the inhabitants of their mainland and overseas dominions, or when they lapsed into a stultifying policy of neutrality, unable to choose between the vestiges of their colonial empire and their mainland territories—a policy that left them an enemy to all and a friend to none. Hesitation also characterizes the Venetians' attitude toward their own cityscape. Although truly significant changes have been made—especially to accommodate the transportation needs of the tourism industry—the mantra remains *dov'era, com'era.* Venetians are unwilling to embrace modernism fully—out of fear that to do so will undercut the city's touristic appeal and their own love for its extraordinary beauty.

Oftentimes Venice and the Venetians seem trapped by that beauty and by the myths and legends that have grown up around the city.[45] Those myths served their purposes. Some, like Saint Mark's premonitory dream while awash in the lagoon and the story of the flight from Attila into a barren landscape, endowed the city's inhabitants with a belief in their predestination to greatness and supremacy. They were, they believed, God's chosen people. Others, like the legends surrounding the Peace of Venice of 1177, worked to establish Venice's claims to the Adriatic Sea and to sovereignty and immunity from the powers of emperor and pope. The notion that Venice was a serene society, undisturbed by rivalry within the ruling elite or by tension between various orders of society, raised doubts in enemies' minds about the wisdom of attacking a united city and internally made challenging the regime all the more difficult. The idea that the Venetians had found the key to political perfection in a mixed government of monarchic, aristocratic, and democratic elements supported a male patrician regime that disenfranchised the vast majority of the city's inhabitants. And finally, the perception that time had passed Venice by became the basis of its appeal to tourists.

Other myths and legends—many as old as the Fourth Crusade and the League of Cambrai—that the Venetians had a preternatural aptitude for business, were double-dealing Machiavels, reigned through terror, reveled in a hedonistic lifestyle, or were suspect Christians essentialized the Venetians, endowing them with what were perceived to be unalterable traits. Usually put forward by Venice's enemies and opponents, they served as denigrating explanations for Venetian economic, political, and cultural might.

All these myths, both those advanced by the Venetians themselves and those put forward by their opponents, obscure the realities that underlay living in an amphibious environment. They rob the Venetians themselves of the credit they deserve for forging an existence in such an inhospitable locale. The work of living in the lagoon is never finished. Even today embankments need to be rebuilt, canals dredged of silt, sea walls reinforced, and mobile gates maintained. Food and water have to be imported and a means found to pay for them. If salt was once the source of Venetian riches, tourists, for good or for ill, are today's font of wealth.

Most of all such legends and images, especially of Venice's various "Golden Ages" in politics, business, art, and culture, give too much credit to the elites of various sorts—the Dandolos, Palladios, Titians, Sarpis, Manins, Volpis, and others of Venice's past. They obscure the agency of the hundreds of thousands of the city's inhabitants who did the truly hard work of forging the city by manning the fleets, loading and unloading the merchant vessels, driving the pilings that supported great churches, dredging the canals of their muck, nursing the ill, burying the dead, stringing glass beads, sewing sails, grinding pigments for artists' paints, cleaning hotel rooms, working in factories steeped in toxic chemicals, and selling trinkets to tourists. De-romanticizing Venice does not strip it of its power. It makes the achievements of the lagoon city and of all Venetians more fascinating and remarkable still.

Any attempt to prognosticate beyond Venice's near-term future is a fool's errand. Just as those living even a generation or two earlier could not have foreseen the Serrata, the rounding of the Cape of Good Hope, Napoleon's conquest, or the rise of Porto Marghera, so it is impossible to discern what the next significant phase in the city's history will be. It is certain, however, to leave its own indelible mark on the cityscape. Nevertheless, two constants have shaped Venice over time: its strategic location at the northern tip of the

Adriatic Sea with abundant natural resources, and its ongoing association and identification with Saint Mark. It seems safe to hazard that both will influence the future, that Venetians will continue to draw on the potential of their amphibious environment and persist in identifying with their saintly protector. In geological terms, however, Venice's fate is easier to discern since ultimately the northern Adriatic Sea is doomed.[46] For many future millennia there will continue to be alternating periods of glaciation and sea level rise. Yet in the end sedimentation and tectonic overriding will transform the northern Adriatic into dry land. In an ironic reversal of the Atlantis legend, Venice, the lagoon city, will become landlocked. *Pax tibi Marce.*

Acknowledgments

This book is the product of a vast collaboration. In writing it, I have been in dialogue with generations of scholars who have explored Venice and its past. I thank them for their brilliant contributions to Venetian scholarship in general and to this book in particular. At the same time, I am aware that much has been left out of this study. Some scholars will search in vain for discussion of their important research or recognition of their published work. I can only apologize in advance. The research on Venice is far too extensive for one study to encompass it all.

There are, nevertheless, certain people whom I gratefully acknowledge because they answered a particular question, helped with a thorny translation, or pointed me in a significant direction. These include John L. (Andy) Andronica, Patricia Fortini Brown, Linda Carroll, Michael Ebner, Joanne Ferraro, Kate Ferris, Wayne Franits, Frederick Ilchman, James Johnson, Bob Korn, Kate Lowe, Luca Molà, Debra Pincus, Meredith K. Ray, Sarah Gwyneth Ross, and Alan Stahl. Pamela O. Long and Monique O'Connell undertook the herculean task of reading the original manuscript and offered numerous suggestions for its improvement. I am deeply grateful and indebted to them both. My dear Venetian friends Michela Dal Borgo and Sandro Bosato offered their usual hospitality, support, and goodwill over the course of many stays in Venice. Annie, the Labrador, provided constant companionship while I was writing and offered an excuse for much needed walks after I had spent too many hours sitting in front of the computer.

I also wish to thank the archives and libraries I relied upon and whose services were essential, especially during the Covid pandemic. I gratefully acknowledge the staffs of the Archivio di Stato di Venezia, the Biblioteca Civico Correr, the Biblioteca Nazionale Marciana, Dumbarton Oaks, the Library of Congress, and the Interlibrary Loan and Special Collections departments of the Syracuse University library. An especially warm thank you is extended to the wonderful staff of the research library at the National Gallery of Art, Washington. In the Department of Image Collections at the NGA, Gregg Most and Missy Lemke help track down the Pulcinella image by Giandomenico Tiepolo. In Venice, Francesco Turio Böhm was gracious and selfless as usual in providing essential images from the amazing Böhm photo archive. Yale University Press allowed me to reproduce several passages from my biography of Doge Francesco Foscari (*The Likeness of Venice: A Life of Doge Francesco Foscari, 1373–1457,* New Haven, 2007).

At Oxford University Press, I am much indebted to my editor Susan Ferber, who approached me about undertaking this project, and whose dedication and eagle eye has made it a much better book. I warmly thank her and the rest of the staff at the press.

Finally, this book is dedicated to my grandniece and grandnephews. I hope they find something as fulfilling in their lives as the study of Venice has been in mine. It is dedicated as well to the memory of my relative Mary Josephine Vaccaro—"Cousin Mary"—who, although she died when I was barely a teenager, had a profound influence on an impressionable youth.

Abbreviations

ASV	Archivio di Stato di Venezia
AT	*Ateneo Veneto*
AV	*Archivio Veneto*
BNM	Biblioteca Nazionale Marciana
DBI	*Dizionario biografico degli italiani* (entries also available online at: www.trecanni.it/biografico/index.html#)
DM	Consiglio dei Dieci, Deliberazioni miste
MC	Maggior Consiglio
NAV	*Nuovo Archivio Veneto*
n.s.	new series
NT	Notarile Testamenti
PSM	Procuratori di San Marco
RQ	*Renaissance Quarterly*
RV	J. R. Hale, ed. *Renaissance Venice* (London: Faber and Faber, 1973).
SCIV	Vittore Branca, ed. *Storia della civiltà veneziana*, 3 vols. (Florence: Sansoni Editore, 1979).
SCUV	*Storia della cultura veneta,* 6 vols in 10 tomes, (Vicenza: Neri Pozza Editore, 1976-86).
SM	Senato, Deliberazioni miste
SMar	Senato, Deliberazioni mar
SS	Senato, Deliberazioni secrete
SV	*Studi Veneziani*
SV Mare	*Storia di Venezia: Temi: Il Mare,* 1 vol. (Rome: Istituto della Enciclopedia Italiana, 1991)
SVOC	*Storia di Venezia dalle origini alla caduta della Serenissima,* 8 vols. (Rome: Istituto della Enciclopedia Italiana, 1992-98)
SVON	*Storia di Venezia: L'Ottocento e il Novecento,* 3 vols. (Rome: Istituto della Enciclopedia Italiana, 2002)
VR	John Jeffries Martin and Dennis Romano, eds. *Venice Reconsidered: The History and Civilization of an Italian City-State, 1297-1797* (Baltimore: Johns Hopkins University Press, 2000)

Notes

INTRODUCTION

1. For Petrarch's multiple references to Venice as "another world," see Lino Lazzarini, "Francesco Petrarca e il primo umanesimo a Venezia," in *Umanesimo europeo e umanesimo* veneziano, edited by Vittore Branca (Florence, 1963), 71; Francesco Sansovino, *Delle cose notabili che sono in Venetia*. Libri II (Venice, 1565), 3 verso; Hans Christian Andersen, *What the Moon Saw and Other Tales*, trans. H. W. Dulcken (London, 1866), 24; Alexander Herzen, *My Past and Thoughts: The Memoirs of Alexander Herzen*, trans. Constance Grant and Humphrey Higgens, 4 vols. (New York, 1968), 3: 1455.
2. For good summaries of the building process, see Élisabeth Crouzet-Pavan, *'Sopra le acque salse': espaces, pouvoir et société à Venise à la fin du Moyen Âge*, 2 vols. (Rome, 1992), 1: 57–139 and, more briefly, Élisabeth Crouzet-Pavan, "Toward an Ecological Understanding of the Myth of Venice," *VR*, 39–64.
3. Nelli-Elena Vanzan Marchini, *Venezia civiltà anfibia* (Sommacampagna, 2009).
4. Martin da Canal, *Les Estoires de Venise: cronaca veneziana in lingua francese dalle origini al 1275*, ed. Alberto Limentani (Florence, 1972), 4–7.
5. Dante, *Inferno*, Canto 21.
6. Alberto Tenenti, "The Sense of Space and Time in the Venetian World of the Fifteenth and Sixteenth Centuries," *RV*, 21–2.
7. The Fourth Crusade was central in creating stereotypes about the Venetians. See Donald E. Queller and Thomas F. Madden. *The Fourth Crusade: The Conquest of Constantinople*, 2nd ed. (Philadelphia, 2000).
8. Dennis Romano, "The Gondola as a Marker of Station in Venetian Society," *Renaissance Studies* 8 (1994): 359–74; Filippo De Vivo, "Walking in Sixteenth-Century Venice: Mobilizing the Early Modern City," *I Tatti Studies in the Italian Renaissance* 19 (2016): 115–41.
9. Quoted in Dennis Romano, *Housecraft and Statecraft: Domestic Service in Renaissance Venice, 1400–1600* (Baltimore, 1996), 227–8.
10. Edward Muir, *Civic Ritual in Renaissance Venice* (Princeton, 1981).

11. The steps leading to both churches created the sense they were on hilltops as was common for pilgrimage churches. Such churches were also usually located outside city walls. See Deborah Howard, *The Architectural History of Venice*, rev. ed. (New Haven, 2002), 203–4, and Tracy E. Cooper, *Palladio's Venice: Architecture and Society in a Renaissance Republic* (New Haven, 2005), 236–7.
12. Robert C. Davis, *The War of the Fists: Popular Culture and Public Violence in Late Renaissance Venice* (New York, 1994).
13. Juergen Schulz, *The New Palaces of Medieval Venice* (University Park, 2004), 18–9.
14. Paul Hills, *Venetian Colour: Marble, Mosaic, Painting and Glass, 1250–1550* (New Haven, 1999).
15. Hills, *Venetian Colour,* 136–9.
16. The inhabitants eventually relocated to the Lido and created the present-day town of Malamocco. Sauro Gelichi, Margherita Ferri, and Cecilia Moine, "Venezia e la laguna tra IX e X secolo: strutture materiali, insediamenti, economie," in *The Age of Affirmation: Venice, the Adriatic, and the Hinterland between the 9th and 10th Centuries*, ed. Stefano Gasparri and Sauro Gelichi (Turnhout, 2017), 103–6.
17. Margaret L. King, *Venetian Humanism in an Age of Patrician Dominance* (Princeton, 1986), xvii–xix.
18. Morris Bishop, trans., *Letters from Petrarch* (Bloomington, 1966), 234.
19. David Rosand, *Myths of Venice: The Figuration of a State* (Chapel Hill, 2001), 80–81.
20. Most famously Gasparo Contarini gave definitive form to the idea that Venice had combined the three forms of good government: monarchy, aristocracy, and democracy. See Gasparo Contarini, *De magistratibus et republica venetorum* (Paris, 1543), now available in a modern translation as Gasparo Contarini, *The Republic of Venice: De magistratibus et republica venetorum*, ed. Filippo Sabetti, trans. Giuseppe Pezzini and Amanda Murphy (Toronto, 2020).
21. Caroline Anastasia Wamsler, "Picturing Heaven: The Trecento Pictorial Program of the Sala del Maggior Consiglio in Venice," PhD diss., Columbia University, 2006, 197.
22. Robert Finlay, "The Venetian Republic as a Gerontocracy: Age and Politics in the Renaissance," *Journal of Medieval and Renaissance Studies* 8 (1978): 157–78.
23. King, *Venetian Humanism*, 174–205.
24. Cited in Catherine Wendy Bracewell, *The Uskoks of Senj: Piracy, Banditry, and Holy War in the Sixteenth-Century Adriatic* (Ithaca, 1992), 28.
25. See, especially, John Pemble, *Venice Rediscovered* (Oxford, 1995).
26. Perhaps most famously, the three volumes of Pompeo Molmenti's *La storia di Venezia nella vita privata* (1st ed., 1880; 7th ed., Trieste, 1973), carry the subtitles *La Grandezza*, *Lo Splendore*, and *Il Decadimento* (The Greatness, The Splendor, and The Decay). Another three-volume work is the *Storia della civiltà veneziana* edited by Vittore Branca under the auspices of the Cini Foundation (Florence, 1979). It does, however, include several chapters on the post-Republic period. The rise and fall narrative is also evident in John Julius Norwich's *A History of Venice* (New York, 1982). He wrote a separate history of Venice in the nineteenth century

(*Paradise of Cities: Venice in the 19th Century* [New York, 2003]). The massive Treccani/Enciclopedia Italiana fourteen-volume *Storia di Venezia* (Rome:1992–2002) groups the first eight volumes under the subtitle *Dalle origini alla caduta della Serenissima* (From the Origins to the Fall of the Serenissima); three under the subtitle *L'Ottocento e il Novecento* (The Nineteenth and Twentieth Centuries); and three under *Temi* (Themes). The history of Venetian art has followed a similar narrative with the apogee judged to have been reached in the sixteenth century by Titian, Veronese, and Tintoretto followed by decline in the seventeenth century and a brief revival under Tiepolo, Guardi, and Canaletto in the eighteenth. Several recent surveys both academic and popular downplay the rise and fall theme but devote considerably less attention to the post-Republic period. See Elizabeth Horodowich, *A Brief History of Venice: A New History of the City and Its People* (Philadelphia, 2009); Joanne M. Ferraro, *Venice: History of the Floating City* (Cambridge, 2012); and Thomas F. Madden, *Venice: A New History* (New York, 2012). The same is true of Frederic C. Lane's classic *Venice: A Maritime Republic* (Baltimore, 1973). Other surveys essentially stop at the end of the Renaissance. These include Garry Wills, *Venice: Lion City: The Religion of Empire* (New York, 2001); Robert Crowley, *City of Fortune: How Venice Ruled the Seas* (New York, 2011); and Élisabeth Crouzet-Pavan, *Venice Triumphant: The Horizons of a Myth*, trans. Lydia G. Cochrane (Baltimore, 2002). Giuseppe Gullino's survey (*Storia della repubblica veneta* [Brescia, 2011]), includes several rises and declines and concludes with Venetia's incorporation into Italy in 1866. Crouzet-Pavan's *Venice. VIe-XXI siècle* (Paris, 2021) appeared too late to be considered in this study.

27. Cesco Chinello, "Foscari, Piero," *DBI* 49 (1997): 338–40.
28. The so-called "myth of Venice" figures widely (but not in a particularly helpful way) in Venetian historiography. I have largely avoided the term preferring to frame the ideas embodied in the myth as ideology or propaganda. For useful introductions, see James S. Grubb, "When Myths Lose Power: Four Decades of Venetian Historiography," *Journal of Modern History* 58 (1986): 43–94; Muir, *Civic Ritual*, 13–61. For its manifestation in art, see Rosand, *Myths of Venice*.

CHAPTER 1

1. Marin Sanudo il Giovane, *De origine, situ et magistratibus urbis Venetae ovvero La città di Venetia (1493–1530)*, edited by Angela Caracciolo Aricò (Milan, 1980), 9–13.
2. Muir, *Civic Ritual*, 70–2.
3. P. Gatto and L. Carbognin, "The Lagoon of Venice: Natural Environment Trend and Man-Induced Modification," *Hydrological Sciences—Bulletin—des Sciences Hydrologiques* 26 (1981): 380–1; John Keahy, *Venice Against the Sea: A City Besieged* (New York, 2002), 21–6.
4. Sandra Donnici et al., "The Caranto Paleosol and Its Role in the Early Urbanization of Venice," *Geoarchaeology: An International Journal* 26 (2011): 514–43.

5. Francesco Sansovino, *Venetia città nobilissima et singolare con le aggiunte di Giustiniano Martinioni*, reprint of 1663 edition in 2 vols. (Venice, 1968), 1: 278.
6. *The Geography of Strabo*, trans. Horace Leonard Jones, 8 vols. (Cambridge, MA, 1917–1949), 2: 309 (Strabo, *Geography*, Bk. 5: 1:5.)
7. In the early Middle Ages, they formed one lagoon. But silting and land reclamation eventually led to their division into separate bodies of water.
8. For these dynamics, Antonio Brambati, "Modificazioni costiere nell'arco lagunare dell'Adriatico settentrionale," *Studi Jesolani* 27 (1985): 13–47.
9. Gian Giacomo Zille, "L'ambiente naturale," in *Storia di Venezia*, 2 vols. (Venice, 1957–58), 1: 47–55; Frank K. McKinney, *The North Adriatic Ecosystem: Deep Time in a Shallow Sea* (New York, 2007).
10. Giorgio Bellavitis and Giandomenico Romanelli, *Venezia* (Rome/Bari, 1985), 5; Antonio Brambatti et al., "The Lagoon of Venice: Geological Setting, Evolution, and Land Subsidence," *Episodes* 2003, DOI: 10.18814/epiiugs/2003/v26i3/020.
11. Bellavitis and Romanelli, *Venezia*, 26.
12. For an excellent summary of these dynamics as they applied to the salt industry in the southern part of the lagoon, see Jean-Claude Hocquet, "Ambiente lagunare, cultura salinara a Chioggia e variazioni del livello marino alla fine del Medioevo," *AV* 6th series 8 (2014): 7–27.
13. Hannelore Zug Tucci, "Pesca e caccia in laguna," *SVOC* 1: 491–514.
14. *Venezia e le sue lagune*, 2 vols. in 4 parts (Venice, 1847), vol. 2, part 1, 540–1.
15. Polybius, *The Histories*, trans. W. R. Paton, revised Frank W. Walbank and Christian Habicht, 6 vols. (Cambridge, MA, 2010–12), 1: 301 (Bk. 2, ch. 14).
16. Juergen Schulz, "The Origins of Venice: Urbanism on the Upper Adriatic Coast," *SV* n.s. 61 (2010), 32–4.
17. Paolo Diacono, *Storia dei Longobardi* (Mariano del Friuli, 1990), 62–3.
18. Andrea Castagnetti, "La pianura veronese nel Medioevo: la conquista del suolo e la regolamentazione delle acque," in *Una città e il suo fiume: Verona e l'Adige*, ed., Giorgio Borelli, 2 vols. (Verona, 1977), 1: 38.
19. Zille, "L'ambiente naturale," 13–5.
20. Schulz, "Origins of Venice," 56.
21. Schulz, "Origins of Venice," 18–32.
22. Lellia Cracco Ruggini, "Acque e lagune da periferia del mondo a fulcro di una nuova 'civiltas,'" *SVOC* 1: 11–32.
23. Luciano Bosio, "Dai Romani ai Longobardi: vie di comunicazione e paesaggio agrario," *SVOC* 1: 175–91.
24. Bosio, "Dai Romani ai Longobardi," 191.
25. Bosio, "Dai Romani ai Longobardi," 192–201.
26. For Pliny's reference to the Seven Seas, see Pliny, *Natural History*, trans. H. Rackham, 10 vols. (Cambridge, MA, 1944–62), 2: 87–9 (Pliny, *Natural History*, Bk. 3, ch. 16).
27. Ruggini, "Acque e lagune," 46.

28. Herodian, *Herodian*, trans. C. R. Whittaker, 2 vols (Cambridge, MA, 1969–70), 2: 259 (Bk. 8, ch. 2).
29. Giovanni Uggeri, "La laguna e il mare," *SVOC* 1: 160–6.
30. For the account, see Andrea Dandolo, *Chronica per extensum descripta aa. 46–1280 d. C.*, edited by Ester Pastorello, *Rerum Italicarum Scriptores* 2nd series, vol. 12, pt. 1 (Bologna, 1938), 10.
31. Giuseppe Cuscito, "La chiesa aquileiese," *SVOC* 1: 367–70; Giorgio Fedalto, *San Marco da Aquileia a Venezia: saggi su terre e chiese venete* (Verona, 2014), 11–77.
32. Karen E. McCluskey, *New Saints in Late-Mediaeval Venice, 1200–1500: A Typological Study* (London, 2020), 56–7.
33. Cuscito, "La chiesa aquileiese," 378–9. For Aquileia more generally, Bruna Forlati Tamaro et al., *Da Aquileia a Venezia: una mediazione tra l'Europa e l'Oriente dal II secolo a. C. al VI secolo d. C.* (Milan, 1980).
34. Ruggini, "Acque e lagune," 54–7.
35. Ruggini, "Acque e lagune," 57–61.
36. Cuscito, "La chiesa aquileiese," 379–86.
37. Cuscito, "La chiesa aquileiese," 381.
38. Bosio, "Dai Romani ai Longobardi," 201–3.
39. Flavius Magnus Aurelius Cassiodorus, *Variae*, Bk. 12, letter 26. See the edition of the *Varie* [*sic*] by Andrea Giardina, Giovanni Alberto Cecconi, and Ignazio Tantillo, 6 vols. (Rome, 2015), 5: 112–3.
40. Cassiodorus, *Variae*, Bk. 12, letter 22; see Giardina et al., *Varie*, 5: 104–7.
41. Cassiodorus, *Variae*, Bk. 12, letter 24, with further instructions in letter 23; Giardina et al., *Varie*, 5: 106–11. For its characterization as the "first historical notice of Venice," see the marginal note to the translation of the letters by Thomas Hodgkin, *The Letters of Cassiodorus, being a condensed translation of the Variae Epistolae of Magnus Aurelius Cassiodorus Senator*, trans. Thomas Hodgkin (London, 1886), 515. I have used, with modifications, Hodgkin's translation.
42. Carlo Guido Mor, "Aspetti della vita costituzionale veneziana fino alla fine del X secolo," *SCIV* 1: 85–7.
43. For this reading of the letters, see Lellia Ruggini, *Economia e società nell'"Italia d'annonaria": rapporti fra agricoltura e commercio dal IV al VI secolo d.C.* reprint (Bari, 1995), 335–49; and Ruggini, "Acque e lagune," 67–72.
44. Antonio Niero, "Culto dei santi da Grado a Venezia," *Studi Jesolani* 27(1985): 163–86.

CHAPTER 2

1. Andrea Ninfo et al., "The Map of Altinum: Ancestor of Venice," *Science* 325, no. 5940 (July 2009): 577; Paolo Mozzi et al., "The Roman City of Altinum, Venice Lagoon, from Remote Sensing and Geophysical Prospection," *Archaeological Prospection* 23 (2016): 27–44, DOI: 10.1002/arp.1520.

2. Sanudo, *De origine*, 11.
3. Diego Calaon, "La *Venetia maritima* tra il VI e il IX sec.: mito, continuità e rottura/ Venetika (*Venetia maritima*) med. 6. in 9. stoletjem: Mit, kontinuiteta in zaton," in *Dalla catalogazione alla promozione dei beni archeologici/Od katalogiziranja do promocije arheoloških dobrin* (Regione del Veneto, 2014), 60.
4. Ruggini, "Acque e lagune," 73–9; Roberto Cessi, "Da Roma a Bisanzio," in *Storia di Venezia*, 2 vols. (Venice, 1957–8), 1: 350–88.
5. See Roberto Cessi, ed., *Documenti relativi alla storia di Venezia anteriore al Mille*, 2 vols. (Padua, 1940–2), 1: doc. 8, pp. 14–9.
6. Not to be confused with present-day Malamocco on the Lido, where the inhabitants of the earlier Malamocco eventually resettled. Gelichi, Ferri, and Moine, "Venezia e la laguna," 103–6.
7. Bosio, "Dai Romani ai Longobardi," 201–3.
8. Agostino Pertusi, "L'iscrizione torcellana ai tempi di Eraclio," *Bolletino dell'Istituto di Storia della Società e dello Stato Veneziano*, 4 (1962): 9–38.
9. Mor, "Aspetti della vita costituzionale veneziana," 85–7; Stefano Gasparri, "The First Dukes and the Origins of Venice," in *Venice and Its Neighbors from the 8th to 11th Century: Through Renovation and Continuity*, ed. Sauro Gelichi and Stefano Gasparri (Leiden, 2018), 8–9.
10. Massimiliano Pavan and Girolamo Arnaldi, "Le origini dell'identità lagunare," *SVOC* 1: 409–27.
11. Diacono, *Storia dei Longobardi*, 76–7.
12. Ruggini, "Acque e lagune," 76–7. For the so-called throne of Saint Mark, see the catalog, *The Treasury of San Marco Venice* (Milan, 1984), 98–105.
13. Daniela Rando, *Una chiesa di frontiera: le istituzioni ecclesiastiche veneziane nei secoli VI–XII* (Bologna, 1994), 13–41.
14. Pavan and Arnaldi, "Origini dell'identità," 439–40.
15. Pavan and Arnaldi, "Origini dell'identità," 447–8.
16. Gasparri, "The First Dukes," 10–19.
17. Donald M. Nicol, *Byzantium and Venice: A Study in Diplomatic and Cultural Relations* (Cambridge, 1988), 10–1.
18. Pavan and Arnaldi, "Origini dell'identità," 436.
19. Pavan and Arnaldi, "Origini dell'identità," 438.
20. Pavan and Arnaldi, "Origini dell'identità," 439. The authors say the Brenta not Bacchiglione, but only later was the former diverted to this locale.
21. Cessi, *Documenti relativi*, 1: no. 30, p. 49.
22. Gelichi, Ferri, and Moine, "Venezia e la laguna," 84.
23. The existence of a castle has been questioned by Sauro Gelichi, "Castles on the Water? Defenses in Venice and Comacchio During the Early Middle Ages," in *Fortified Settlements in Early Medieval Europe: Defended Communities of the 8th–10th Centuries*, ed. Neil Christie and Hajnalka Herold (Oxford, 2016), 266.
24. Rando, *Una chiesa di frontiera*, 21–7.

25. Nicol, *Byzantium and Venice*, 12–4; Gherardo Ortalli, "Il ducato e la 'civitas Rivoalti': tra carolingi, bizantini e sassoni," *SVOC* 1: 725–7.
26. Gasparri, "The First Dukes," 25. For the following narrative of events, see Ortalli, "Il ducato e la 'civitas Rivoalti,'" 725–32; Agostino Pertusi, "L'impero Bizantino e l'evolvere dei suoi interessi nell'Alto Adriatico," *SCIV* 1: 56–8; Nicol, *Byzantium and Venice*, 14–9.
27. Gelichi, Ferri, and Moine, "Venezia e la laguna," 105.
28. Ortalli, "Il ducato e la 'civitas Rivoalti,'" 732.
29. Albert J. Ammerman et al., "Beneath the Basilica of San Marco: New Light on the Origins of Venice," *Antiquity* 19, no. 360 (2017): 1626.
30. Ortalli, "Il ducato e la 'civitas Rivoalti,'" 734; Giovanni Lorenzoni, "Espressioni d'arte: i principali monumenti architettonici," *SVOC* 1: 871–5.
31. Calaon, "La *Venetia maritima*," 57–8.
32. For the wood bridges, Wladimiro Dorigo, *Venezia romanica: la formazione della città medioevale fino all'età gotica*, 2 vols. (Sommacampagna, 2003), 1: 155; for the first stone bridge, see Bartolomeo Cecchetti, "La vita dei veneziani fino al secolo XIII," *AV* 2 (1871): 68.
33. Diego Calaon, *Quando Torcello era abitata* (Venice: 2013), 75.
34. Bellavitis and Romanelli, *Venezia*, 20; Gelichi, Ferri, and Moine, "Venezia e la laguna," 93, 101–2.
35. Elisa Corrò, Cecilia Moine, and Sandra Primon, "Setting the Scene: The Role of Saint'Ilario Monastery in Early Medieval Venice in Light of Recent Landscape Studies," in *Venice and Its Neighbors from the 8th to 11th Century: Through Renovation and Continuity*, ed. Sauro Gelichi and Stefano Gasparri (Leiden, 2018), 116–41.
36. Bellavitis and Romanelli, *Venezia*, 25–6.
37. Crouzet-Pavan, *"Sopra le acque salse,"* 2: map 2 (unpaginated). The reliability of church foundation dates remains highly debated.

CHAPTER 3

1. Marco Pozza, "Particiaco, Agnello," *DBI* 81 (2014): 470–72.
2. The best edition of Giustiniano's will is in Luigi Lanfranchi and Bianca Strina, eds., *Ss. Ilario e Benedetto e S. Gregorio* (Venice, 1965), doc. 2, pp. 17–24.
3. Silvia Carraro, "*Dominae in claustro:* San Zaccaria tra politica, società e religione nella Venezia altomedievale," *Reti Medievali Rivista* 20 (2019): 373–404.
4. Corrò, Moine, and Primon, "Setting the Scene," 116–41.
5. Gina Fasoli, "Comune Veneciarum," *SCIV* 1: 265.
6. Patrick J. Geary, *Furta Sacra: Thefts of Relics in the Central Middle Ages* rev. ed. (Princeton, 1990), 92–3.
7. Geary, *Furta Sacra*, 88–90; Giovanni De Vergottini, "Venezia e l'Istria nell'Alto Medioevo," *SCIV* 1: 75.

8. Luigi Lanfranchi, ed., *S. Giorgio Maggiore*, 4 vols. (Venice, 1968–1986), 2: doc. 1, p. 20.
9. Geary, *Furta sacra*, 91.
10. Geary, *Furta sacra*, 91–2.
11. John Osborne, "Politics, Diplomacy and the Cult of Relics in Venice and the Northern Adriatic in the First Half of the Ninth Century," *Early Medieval Europe* 8 (1999): 369–86.
12. Rando, *Una chiesa di frontiera*, 60–5.
13. Otto Demus, *The Church of San Marco in Venice: History, Architecture, Sculpture* (Washington, 1960), 67.
14. Michela Agazzi, *Platea Sancti Marci: i luoghi marciani dall'XI al XIII secolo e la formazione della piazza* (Venice, 1991), 13–20.
15. Giorgio Ravegnani, "Insegne del potere e titoli ducali," *SVOC* 1: 829–30.
16. Ravegnani, "Insegne del potere," 838–46.
17. Nicol, *Byzantium and Venice*, 45–7.
18. Chiara Provesi, "Le due mogli di Pietro IV Candiano (959–976): le donne e i loro gruppi parentali nella Venezia del X secolo," *Reti Medievali Rivista* 16 (2015): 21–51.
19. Rando, *Una chiesa di frontiera*, 54–60, 65–72. Rando, however, downplays the role of ecclesiastical posts in creating dynasties.
20. Andrea da Mosto, *I dogi di Venezia nella vita pubblica e privata* (Florence, 1983), 38–47.
21. The following is based on the reconstructions of Ortalli, "Il ducato e la 'civitas Rivoalti,'" 761–80; Roberto Cessi, "Politica, economia, religione," in *Storia di Venezia* 2: 205–25.
22. Stefano Gasparri, "Venezia fra l'Italia bizantina e il regno italico," in *Venezia: itinerari per la storia della città*, ed. Stefano Gasparri, Giovanni Levi, and Pierandrea Moro (Bologna, 1997), 61–82; Veronica Ortenberg West-Harling, "'Venecie due sunt': Venice and Its Grounding in the Adriatic and North Italian Background," in *Italia, 888–962: una svolta*, ed. M. Valenti and C. Wickham (Turnhout, 2013), 237–64.
23. For the pact, see Cessi, *Documenti relativi*, 2: doc. 47, pp. 81–5.
24. Giovanni Diacono, *Istoria Veneticorum*, ed. and trans. Luigi Andrea Berto (Bologna, 1999), 162–3.
25. It is referred to by architectural historians as the Orseolo church. For the Partecipazio and Orseolo churches, see Demus, *Church of San Marco in Venice*, 63–70.
26. Chiara Provesi, "Il conflitto tra Coloprini e Morosini: una storia di fiumi, di terre e di persone," in *The Age of Affirmation*, ed. Gasparri and Gelichi, 177–213.
27. Provesi, "Conflitto tra Coloprini e Morosini," 178–9.
28. Nicol, *Byzantium and Venice*, 39–42.
29. For the events, Ortalli, "Il ducato e la 'civitas Rivoalti,'" 739–80; Frederic C. Lane, *Venice: A Maritime Republic* (Baltimore, 1973), 23–8; Ermanno Orlando, *Venezia e il mare nel Medioevo* (Bologna, 2014), 16–26.

30. For the island count, which also includes eighty-two rock shelves above sea level, see Sabine Florence Fabijanec, "Fishing and the Fish Trade on the Dalmatian Coast in the Late Middle Ages," in *The Inland Seas: Towards an Ecohistory of the Mediterranean and the Black Sea*, ed. Tonnes Bekker-Nielsen and Ruthy Gertwagen (Stuttgart, 2016), 369.
31. Francesco Borri, "Captains and Pirates: Ninth Century Dalmatia and Its Rulers," in *The Age of Affirmation*, ed. Gasparri and Gelichi, 11–37.
32. Gelichi, "Castles on the Water?," 268–70.
33. De Vergottini, "Venezia e l'Istria," 76–80.
34. Gino Luzzatto, "L'economia veneziana nei suoi rapporti con la politica nell'Alto Medioevo," *SCIV* 1: 97–8; Gelichi, "Castles on the Water?," 273.
35. Rando, *Una chiesa di frontiera*, 73.
36. Pertusi, "L'impero bizantino," 57–8.
37. Giovanni Gorini, "La monetazione," in *Da Aquileia a Venezia*, ed. Tamaro et al., 740–2; Ortalli, "Il ducato e la 'civitas Rivoalti,'" 748; Michael McCormick, *Origins of the European Economy: Communications and Commerce, A.D. 300–900* (Cambridge, 2001), 366–7.
38. David Jacoby, "Venetian Commercial Expansion in the Eastern Mediterranean, 8th–11th Centuries," in *Byzantine Trade, 4th–12th Centuries*, ed. M. Mandell Mango (Farnham, 2009), 374.
39. Carlo Beltrame, "On the Origin of Ship Construction in Venice," in *The Age of Affirmation*, ed. Gasparri and Gelichi, 131–2.
40. L. Lanfranchi and G. G. Zille, "Il territorio del ducato veneziano dall'VIII al XII secolo," in *Storia di Venezia* 2: 5–8.
41. Beltrame, "On the Origin of Ship Construction," 131–2; Lillian Ray Martin, *The Art and Archeology of Venetian Ships and Boats* (College Station, 2001), 172–3.
42. Gino Luzzatto, *Storia economica di Venezia dall'XI al XVI secolo* (Venice, 1961), 7–8.
43. Martin, *Art and Archeology of Venetian Ships*, 172–3.
44. McCormick, *Origins of the European Economy*, 545–7.
45. Jacoby, "Venetian Commercial Expansion," 373–5; Luzzatto, "L'economia nei suoi rapporti," 98; McCormick, *Origins of the European Economy*, 369–84.
46. Cessi, *Documenti relativi*, 2: doc. 41, pp. 70–4.
47. McCormick, *Origins of the European Economy*, 759–77, 780 (quotes on 776, 780); and Michael McCormick, "New Light on the 'Dark Ages': How the Slave Trade Fueled the Carolingian Economy," *Past and Present* 177 (2002): 17–54, esp. 46ff.
48. Annamaria Pazienza, "Venice Beyond Venice. Commercial Agreements and *Pacta* from the Origins to Pietro II Orseolo," in *The Age of Affirmation*, ed. Gasparri and Gelichi, 150–6.
49. Gerhard Rösch, *Venezia e l'impero, 962–1250: i rapporti politici, commerciali e di traffico nel periodo imperiale germanico* (Rome, 1985), 34–5; Gerhard Rösch, "Mercatura e moneta," *SVOC* 1: 555.

50. Cessi, *Documenti relativi*, 2: doc. 89, pp. 182–4; Rösch, "Mercatura e moneta," 555–6; Pazienza, "Venice Beyond Venice," 167–70.
51. Liudprand of Cremona, *The Complete Works of Liudprand of Cremona*, trans. Paolo Squatriti (Washington, 2007), 272.
52. Sante Bartolami, "L'agricoltura," *SVOC* 1: 466–78.
53. Jean-Claude Hocquet, "Le saline," *SVOC* 1: 515–48.
54. Beltrame, "On the Origin of Ship Construction," 135; Pazienza, "Venice Beyond Venice," 174–6.
55. Cessi, *Documenti relativi*, 2: doc. 61, pp. 115–21; also Lanfranchi, *S. Giorgio Maggiore*, 2: doc. 1, p. 19.
56. Stefano Gasparri, "Dagli Orseolo al comune," *SVOC* 1: 795–6.
57. Mor, "Aspetti della vita costituzionale," 1: 85–93; Cessi, "Politica, economia, religione," 252–3; Gasparri, "Venezia fra l'Italia," 61–5; Andrea Castagnetti, *La società veneziana nel Medioevo I: dai tribuni ai giudici* (Verona, 1992); Andrea Castagnetti, "Famiglie e affermazione politica," *SVOC* 1: 619–28, 637.
58. Cessi, "Politica, economia, religione," 253–4; Zug Tucci, "Pesca e caccia," 508–11; Vittorio Lazzarini, "Escusati del dogado veneziano," *Atti dell'Istituto Veneto di Scienze, Lettere ed Arti, Parte Seconda, Classe di Scienze Morali e Lettere* 105 (1947): 75–85.

CHAPTER 4

1. Raimondo Morozzo della Rocca and Antonino Lombardo, eds., *Documenti del commercio veneziano nei secoli XI–XIII*, 2 vols. (Turin, 1940), 1: doc. 49.
2. Morozzo della Rocca and Lombardo, *Documenti del commercio*, 1: doc. 51.
3. Morozzo della Rocca and Lombardo, *Documenti del commercio*, 1: docs. 65, 67–69.
4. Morozzo della Rocca and Lombardo, *Documenti del commercio*, 1: docs. 164, 179, 290, 292, 298, 300, 301.
5. Lane, *Venice: A Maritime Republic*, 50.
6. Marco Pozza, "I proprietari fondiari in terraferma," *SVOC* 2: 664–5.
7. Louise Buenger Robbert, "Domenico Gradenigo: A Thirteenth-Century Venetian Merchant," in *Medieval and Renaissance Venice*, ed. Ellen E. Kittell and Thomas F. Madden (Urbana, IL, 1999), 34–35. The careers of Dobramiro, his son, and grandsons are also related in Silvano Borsari, *Venezia e Bisanzio nel XII secolo: i rapporti economici* (Venice, 1988), 109–16. See also Stanley Chojnacki, "In Search of the Venetian Patriciate: Families and Factions in the Fourteenth Century," *RV*, 73.
8. Robbert, "Domenico Gradenigo," 35.
9. Morozzo della Rocca and Lombardo, *Documenti del commercio*, 1: doc. 58.
10. Robert S. Lopez, *The Commercial Revolution of the Middle Ages, 950–1350* (Englewood Cliffs, 1971).
11. Morozzo della Rocca and Lombardo, *Documenti del commercio*, 1: doc. 69.
12. Morozzo della Rocca and Lombardo, *Documenti del commercio*, 1: doc. 420.

13. Morozzo della Rocca and Lombardo, *Documenti del commercio*, 1: doc. 13. A translation may be found in Robert S. Lopez and Irving W. Raymond, eds., *Medieval Trade in the Mediterranean World: Illustrative Documents Translated with Introductions and Notes* (New York, 1990), 176–7.
14. Gino Luzzatto, "Il patrimonio privato di un doge del secolo XIII," in Gino Luzzatto, *Studi di storia economica veneziana* (Padua, 1954), 79–87.
15. Gerhard Rösch, "Lo sviluppo mercantile," *SVOC* 2: 142.
16. Adolfo Sacerdoti, "Le colleganze nella practica degli affairi e nella legislazione veneta," *Atti del Reale Istituto Veneto di Scienze, Lettere ed Arti* 59, pt. 2 (1899–1900): 1–45.
17. Dennis Romano, *Markets and Marketplaces in Medieval Italy c. 1100 to c. 1440* (New Haven, 2014), 153–220.
18. Morozzo della Rocca and Lombardo, *Documenti del commercio*, 1: doc. 446; also translated in Lopez and Raymond, *Medieval Trade*, 187–8. For the *fraterna*, James C. Davis, *A Venetian Family and Its Fortune, 1500–1900: The Donà and the Conservation of Their Wealth* (Philadelphia, 1975), 6–8.
19. Gerhard Rösch, "Le strutture commerciali," *SVOC* 2: 443–6.
20. Da Canal, *Les Estoires de Venise*, 4.
21. Rösch, *Venezia e l'impero*, 140–3.
22. Lopez and Raymond, *Medieval Trade*, 115; William D. Phillips Jr., *Slavery from Roman Times to the Early Transatlantic Trade* (Minneapolis, 1985), 63, 97–106; Jeffrey Fynn-Paul, "Empire, Monotheism and Slavery in the Greater Mediterranean Region from Antiquity to the Early Modern Era," *Past and Present* 205 (2009): 3–40.
23. Michel Mollat, "Aux origines de la précocité économique et sociale de Venise: l'exploitation du sel," in *La Venezia del Mille* (Florence, 1965), 197.
24. Hocquet, "Le saline," 515–48; Irmgard Fees, *Ricchezza e potenza nella Venezia medioevale: la famiglia Ziani* (Rome, 2005), 158–71.
25. Lane, *Venice: A Maritime Republic*, 46.
26. For these rentals, see Luigi Lanfranchi, ed., *Famiglia Zusto* (Venice, 1955), ix, n. 2. For anchors as part of dowries, see Luzzatto, *Storia economica*, 16.
27. Renard Gluzman, *Venetian Shipping from the Days of Glory to Decline, 1453–1571* (Leiden, 2021), 198–206, quote 206.
28. McCormick, *Origins of the European Economy*, 795.
29. For Mairano's career, Reinhard Heynen, *Zur Entstehung des Kapitalismus in Venedig*, reprint of 1905 ed. (New York, 1971), 86–120; Lane, *Venice: A Maritime Republic*, 52–3; Borsari, *Venezia e Bisanzio*, 116–30; Rösch, "Lo sviluppo mercantile,"146–50; and the relevant charters in Morozzo della Rocca and Lombardo, *Documenti del commercio*.
30. David Jacoby, "The Venetian Quarter of Constantinople from 1082 to 1261," in *Novum millennium: Studies on Byzantine History and Culture Dedicated to Paul Speck*, ed. Claudia Sode and Sarolta Takács (Aldershot, 2001), 154–6.

31. For the text of the chrysobull, Marco Pozza and Giorgio Ravegnani, eds., *I trattati con Bisanzio, 992–1198* (Venice, 1993), 35–45; for analysis of it, Nicol, *Byzantium and Venice*, 59–63.
32. Orlando, *Venezia e il mare*, 31.
33. Nicol, *Byzantium and Venice*, 60.
34. M. E. Martin, "The Chrysobull of Alexius I Comnenus to the Venetians and the Early Venetian Quarter in Constantinople," *Byzantinoslavica* 39 (1978): 19–23; David Jacoby, "The Expansion of Venetian Government in the Eastern Mediterranean Until the Late Thirteenth Century," in *Il* Commonwealth *veneziano tra 1204 e la fine della Repubblica: identità e peculiarità*, ed. Gherardo Ortalli, Oliver Jens Schmitt, and Ermanno Orlando (Venice, 2015), 74–83.
35. Nichol, *Byzantium and Venice*, 53.
36. Quoted in Agostino Pertusi, "Venezia e Bisanzio nel secolo XI," *SCIV* 1: 182. For an overview of the Adriatic in this period, Alain Ducellier, "L'Adriatique du IXe au XIIIe siècle," in *Histoire de l'Adriatique*, ed. Pierre Cabanes et al. (Paris, 2001), 173–89.
37. Gasparri, "Dagli Orseolo al comune," 801–6; Nichol, *Byzantium and Venice*, 53–64.
38. Rösch, *Venezia e l'impero*, 37–8; Gasparri, "Dagli Orseolo al comune," 806–8.
39. Nichol, *Byzantium and Venice*, 68–71.
40. Nichol, *Byzantium and Venice*, 71–4; Steven Runciman, "L'intervento di Venezia nella prima alla terza Crociata," in *Venezia dalla Prima Crociata alla Conquista di Costantinopoli del 1204* (Florence, 1965), 1–22.
41. Twentieth-century investigations concluded that the Baresi and the Venetians possess parts of the same body, although the Venetians must content themselves with fragments, whereas the Baresi possess some larger bones. Whether the bones are really those of Nicholas will remain, it seems, a matter of faith. See Maria Pia Pedani, *Venezia porta d'Oriente* (Bologna, 2010), 36.
42. Geary, *Furta sacra*, 94–103.
43. Muir, *Civic Ritual*, 97–101.
44. Nichol, *Byzantium and Venice*, 75–81.
45. Jacoby, "Venetian Quarter," 156–8.
46. Nicol, *Byzantium and Venice*, 81–92.
47. Pedani, *Venezia porta d'Oriente*, 243–6.
48. Nichol, *Byzantium and Venice*, 92–3.
49. Rösch, *Venezia e l'impero*, 39–41; Giorgio Ravegnani, "Tra i due imperi. L'affermazione politica nel XII secolo," *SVOC* 2: 44–9.
50. Roberto Cessi, "La diversione del Brenta ed il delta ilariana nel sec. XII," *Atti del Reale Istituto Veneto di Scienze, Lettere ed Arti* 80 pt. 2 (1920–1): 1225–43; Remy Simonetti, *Da Padova a Venezia nel Medioevo: terre mobili, confini, conflitti* (Rome, 2009), 64–8.
51. Rösch, *Venezia e l'impero*, 41; Muir, *Civic Ritual*, 160–4.
52. Luzzatto, *Storia economica*, 29.

53. Ravegnani, "Tra i due imperi," 56–65.
54. Dandolo, *Cronica per extensum descripta*, 264.
55. Patricia Fortini Brown, *Venetian Narrative Painting in the Age of Carpaccio* (New Haven, 1988), 85–6, 259–60, 261–5, 272–9; Muir, *Civic Ritual*, 103–19.
56. Rösch, *Venezia e l'impero,* 41–4.
57. For the following account of events, see Nichol, *Byzantium and Venice*, 92–123; Ravegnani, "Tra i due imperi," 49–56, 65–74.
58. Nicol, *Byzantium and Venice*, 99.
59. Thomas F. Madden, "Venice's Hostage Crisis: Diplomatic Efforts to Secure Peace with Byzantium between 1171 and 1184," in *Medieval and Renaissance Venice*, ed. Kittell and Madden, 96–108.
60. Nicol, *Byzantium and Venice*, 111.

CHAPTER 5

1. Cited in Holger A. Klein, "Refashioning Byzantium in Venice, ca. 1200–1400," in *San Marco, Byzantium, and the Myths of Venice*, ed. Henry Maguire and Robert S. Nelson (Washington, 2010), 194.
2. Demus, *Church of San Marco*, 23–5.
3. David Buckton and John Osborne, "The Enamel of Doge Ordelaffo Falier on the *Pala d'Oro* in Venice," *Gesta* 39 (2000): 43–9.
4. Agostino Pertusi, "Quedam regalia insignia: ricerche sulle insegne del potere ducale a Venezia durante il Medioevo," *SV* 7 (1965): 64–82; for a contrasting view, Roberto Cessi, "L'investiture ducale," *Atti dell'Istituto Veneto di Scienze, Lettere ed Arti, Classe di Scienze Morali, Lettere ed Arti* 126 (1967–8): 251–94, esp. 282–3.
5. Chris Wickham, *Sleepwalking into a New World: The Emergence of Italian City Communes in the Twelfth Century* (Princeton, 2015).
6. Tino's account in Luigi Andrea Berto, ed., *Testi storici veneziani (XI–XIII secolo): Historia ducum Venetorum, Annales Venetici breves, Domenico Tino, Relatio de electione Dominici Silvi Venetorum ducis* (Padua, 2000) 101–5.
7. Pertusi, "Quedam regalia insignia,"67–72.
8. Gasparri, "Dagli Orseolo al comune," 795–8.
9. Gasparri, "Dagli Orseolo al comune," 798, n. 37.
10. Roberto Cessi, ed., *Deliberazioni del Maggior Consiglio di Venezia*, reprint in 3 vols. (Bologna, 1971), 1: 235–6.
11. Cessi, "Politica, economia, religione," 2: 377–9.
12. Cessi, "Politica, economia, religione," 2: 379.
13. In 1054, in what is known as the Great Schism, the Latin Catholic Church and the Greek Orthodox Church had formally split over that question as well as over various theological disagreements and ritual practices.
14. Cessi, "Politica, economia, religione," 379–80; Rando, *Una chiesa di frontiera*, 173–84, 197–8; Gasparri, "Dagli Orseolo al comune," 816–7.

15. Thomas F. Madden, *Enrico Dandolo and the Rise of Venice* (Baltimore, 2003), 57.
16. Fasoli, "Comune Veneciarum," 274.
17. Dandolo, *Chronica per extensum descripta*, 259.
18. For a different interpretation, see Madden, *Enrico Dandolo*, 53–4.
19. Gasparri, "Dagli Orseolo al comune," 818–9.
20. Gasparri, "Dagli Orseolo al comune," 820.
21. Andrea Castagnetti, "Il primo comune," *SVOC* 2: 101–2; Ermanno Orlando, *Altre Venezie: il dogado veneziano nei secoli XIII e XIV (giurisdizione, territorio, giustizia e amministrazione)* (Venice, 2008).
22. Dandolo, *Chronica per extensum descripta*, 266.
23. Castagnetti, "Il primo comune," 95.
24. Fasoli, "Comune Veneciarum," 275.
25. Castagnetti, "Il primo comune," 95.
26. Giuseppe Maranini, *La costituzione di Venezia*, reprint of 1927–31 edition in 2 vols. (Florence, 1974), 1: 117–8; Ravegnani, "Insegne del potere," 836.
27. Dandolo's oath is printed in Gisella Graziato, ed., *Le promissioni del doge di Venezia dalle origini alla fine del Duecento* (Venice, 1986), 1–4; Gradenigo's at 132–63. Dieter Girgensohn, ed., *Francesco Foscari: promissione ducale 1423* (Venice, 2004).
28. I largely follow the English translation of Dandolo's oath in Madden, *Enrico Dandolo*, 96–8.
29. Maranini, *La costituzione di Venezia*, 1: 118.
30. Pertusi, "Quedam regalia insignia," 84, 121.
31. Andrea Castagnetti, "Insediamenti e 'populi,'" *SVOC* 1: 592–6.
32. Castagnetti, "Il primo comune," 117.
33. Giovanni Monticolo, *L'ufficio della Giustizia Vecchia a Venezia dalle origini sino al 1300* (Venice, 1892).
34. Castagnetti, "Il primo comune," 116–8.
35. Michael Knapton, "La finanza pubblica," *SVOC* 2: 376.
36. Marco Pozza, "La cancelleria," *SVOC* 2: 349–50.
37. Reinhold C. Mueller, "The Procurators of San Marco in the Thirteenth and Fourteenth Centuries: A Study of the Office as a Financial and Trust Institution," *SV* 13 (1971): 105–220.
38. Architectural historians refer to the third church as the Contarini church. Demus, *Church of San Marco*, 70–105; Howard, *Architectural History*, 19–24.
39. Demus, *Church of San Marco*, 89.
40. Demus, *Church of San Marco*, 97–100.
41. Demus, *Church of San Marco*, 12–4.
42. Demus, *Church of San Marco*; Muir, *Civic Ritual*, 86–8.
43. The church of San Geminiano was moved westward to where the Napoleonic wing of the buildings surrounding the Piazza, the wing opposite San Marco, stands today. The ill-fated church was razed a second time by Napoleon's stepson and viceroy of Italy Eugène de Beauharnais in 1810.

44. Agazzi, *Platea Sancti Marci*, 79–89.
45. Ennio Concina, *A History of Venetian Architecture*, trans. Judith Landry (Cambridge, 1998), 47.
46. Agazzi, *Platea Sancti Marci*, 83.
47. Agazzi, *Platea Sancti Marci*, 84.
48. The donation charter is printed in Samuele Romanin, *Storia documentata di Venezia*, 3rd ed. in 10 vols. (Venice, 1972–5), 1: 284–5.
49. Robert Cessi and Annibale Alberti, *Rialto: l'isola, il ponte, il mercato* (Bologna, 1934), 21–9; Alan M. Stahl, *Zecca: The Mint of Venice in the Middle Ages* (Baltimore, 2000), 8.
50. Cessi and Annibale, *Rialto*, 163–4.
51. Schulz, *New Palaces*, 92–5.
52. Alfredo Stussi, "La lingua," *SVOC* 2: 783.
53. Wladimiro Dorigo, "Le espressioni d'arte: gli edifici," *SVOC* 2: 814.
54. Crouzet-Pavan, "*Sopra le acque salse*"; Wladimiro Dorigo, *Venezia romanica: la formazione della città medioevale fino all'età gotica* 2 vols. (Venice, 2003).
55. Cessi, "Politica, economia, religione," 2: 324–5.
56. Castagnetti, "Il primo comune," 98.
57. Élisabeth Crouzet-Pavan, *La mort lente de Torcello: histoire d'une cité disparue* (Paris, 1995).
58. Cessi, "Politica, economia, religione," 352; Bellavitis and Romanelli, *Venezia*, 31.
59. Élisabeth Crouzet-Pavan, "Venice and Torcello: History and Oblivion," *Renaissance Studies* 8 (1994): 416–27; Gherardo Ortalli, "I cronisti e la determinazione di Venezia città," *SVOC* 2: 778–80.

CHAPTER 6

1. The following largely reflects the account in Queller and Madden, *Fourth Crusade*.
2. Queller and Madden, *Fourth Crusade*, 17.
3. Geoffrey of Villehardouin, *The Chronicle of the Fourth Crusade and the Conquest of Constantinople*, in *Memoirs of the Crusades by Villehardouin and De Joinville*, trans. Frank Marzials, reprint of 1908 edition (Westport, CT, 1983),16–7 (with slight changes to the translation).
4. Madden, *Enrico Dandolo*, 63–8, 85–6.
5. Madden, *Enrico Dandolo*, 63–89.
6. Madden, *Enrico Dandolo*, 105–16.
7. Robert of Clari, *The Conquest of Constantinople*, trans. Edgar Holmes McNeal, reprint of 1936 ed. (Toronto, 1996), 43.
8. Villehardouin, *Chronicle*, 42.
9. Robert of Clari, *Conquest of Constantinople*, 94.
10. Niketas Choniates, *Oh City of Byzantium, Annals of Niketas Choniates*, trans. Harry J. Magoulias (Detroit, 1984), 315.

11. Choniates, *City of Byzantium*, 316.
12. Villehardouin, *Chronicle*, 64–5.
13. Da Canal, *Estoires de Venise*, 60–1.
14. Giorgio Ravegnani, "La Romània veneziana," *SVOC* 2: 184.
15. Madden, *Enrico Dandolo*, 191–4.
16. Choniates, *City of Byzantium*, 295. See also Alfred J. Andrea, "Essay on Primary Sources," in Queller and Madden, *Fourth Crusade*, 310.
17. Nicol, *Byzantium and Venice*, 136.
18. Andrea, "Essay on Primary Sources," 301.
19. Thomas F. Madden, "The Venetian Version of the Fourth Crusade: Memory and the Conquest of Constantinople in Medieval Venice," *Speculum* 87 (2012): 311–44.
20. Nichol, *Byzantium and Venice*, 182–7.
21. Michael Jacoff, *The Horses of San Marco and the Quadriga of the Lord* (Princeton, 1993).
22. Nichol, *Byzantium and Venice*, 153–5.
23. Nichol, *Byzantium and Venice*, 154.
24. Nichol, *Byzantium and Venice*, 155–8; Monique O'Connell, *Men of Empire: Power and Negotiation in Venice's Maritime State* (Baltimore, 2009), 18–9.
25. Ravegnani, "La Romània veneziana," 197–200; Raymond-Joseph Loenertz, *Les Ghisi: dynastes vénitiens dans l'archipel, 1207–1390* (Florence, 1975), 27.
26. Ravegnani, "La Romània veneziana," 195–6.
27. Sally McKee, *Uncommon Dominion: Venetian Crete and the Myth of Ethnic Purity* (Philadelphia, 2000), 31–50.
28. McKee, *Uncommon Dominion*, 26–31.
29. McKee, *Uncommon Dominion*, 50–6.
30. Maria Georgopoulou, *Venice's Mediterranean Colonies: Architecture and Urbanism* (Cambridge, 2001), 115–8.
31. Quoted in McKee, *Uncommon Dominion*, 19.
32. Orlando, *Venezia e il mare*, 77.
33. Nichol, *Byzantium and Venice*, 159–65.
34. Pedani, *Venezia porta d'Oriente*, 43.
35. David Jacoby, "Thirteenth-Century Commercial Exchange in the Aegean: Continuity and Change," in *Change in the Byzantine World in the Twelfth and Thirteenth Centuries*, ed. Ayla Ödekan, Engin Akyürek, and Nevra Necipoğlu (Istanbul, 2010), 187–94.
36. Gerhard Rösch, "Il 'gran Guadagno,'" *SVOC* 2: 233–48; Orlando, *Venezia e il mare*, 80–6.
37. ASV, MC, Deliberazioni, register 17 (Spiritus), fol. 9r. (August 19, 1326). Quoted in Luzzatto, *Storia Economica*, 41, but with the incorrect date of August 17.
38. Patricia Fortini Brown, *Venice and Antiquity: The Venetian Sense of the Past* (New Haven, 1996), 59.

39. Thomas E. A. Dale, "Cultural Hybridity in Medieval Venice: Reinventing the East at San Marco after the Fourth Crusade," in *San Marco, Byzantium, and the Myths of Venice*, ed. Henry Maguire and Robert S. Nelson (Washington, 2010), 189.
40. Franca Semi, *Gli 'ospizi' di Venezia* (Venice, 1983), 50.
41. Pedani, *Venezia porta d'Oriente*, 28–35; David Jacoby, "Evolving Routes of Western Pilgrimage to the Holy Land, Eleventh to Fifteenth Century: An Overview," in *Unterwegs im Namen der Religion II/On the Road in the Name of Religion II*, ed. Klaus Herbers and Hans Christian Lehner (Stuttgart, 2016), 75–97.
42. Rösch, "Il 'gran Guadagno,'" 257.
43. Jean-Claude Hocquet, *Le sel et la fortune de Venise*, 2 vols. (Villeneuve d'Ascq, 1978–9) and summarized in Jean-Claude Hocquet, "Capitalisme marchand et classe marchande à Venise au temps de la Renaissance," *Annales E.S.C.* 34 (1979): 279–304.
44. Frederic Chapin Lane, *Venetian Ships and Shipbuilders of the Renaissance* (Baltimore, 1992), 35–53; Ruthy Gertwagen, "Characteristics of Mediterranean Ships in the Late Medieval Period (13th–15th Centuries CE), in *Splendour of the Medieval Mediterranean: Art, Culture, Politics, Navigation, and Commerce in the Mediterranean Maritime Cities (13th–15th Centuries)*, ed. X. B. Alter and J. Alemany (Barcelona, 2004), 543–61; Ruthy Gertwagen, "Nautical Technology," in *A Companion to Mediterranean History*, ed. Peregrine Horden and Sharon Kinoshita (Chichester, 2014), 154–69.
45. Frederic C. Lane, "The Economic Meaning of the Invention of the Compass," *American Historical Review* 68 (1963): 605–17; Lane, *Venice: A Maritime Republic*, 118–24.
46. Alfredo Stussi, "Un testamento volgare scritto in Persia nel 1263," *L'Italia Dialettale* 25 (1962), 23–37; David Jacoby, "La Venezia d'oltremare nel secondo Duecento," *SVOC* 2: 274.
47. Da Canal, *Estoires de Venise*, 38–9.
48. Wolfgang von Stromer, "Bernardus Teotonicus e i rapporti commerciali tra la Germania meridionale e Venezia prima della istituzione del Fondaco dei Tedeschi," *Centro Tedesco di Studi Veneziani. Quaderni* 8 (1978): 3–33.
49. Da Canal, *Estoires de Venise*, 116.
50. Marco Pozza, *I Badoer: una famiglia veneziana dal X al XIII secolo* (Abano Terme, 1982), 60–4; Pozza, "I proprietari fondiari."
51. Ennio Concina, *Fondaci: architettura, arte, e mercatura tra Levante, Venezia, e Alemagna* (Venice, 1997); Deborah Howard, *Venice and the East: The Impact of the Islamic World on Venetian Architecture, 1100–1500* (New Haven, 2000), 120–31.
52. Fabien Faucheron, *Nourrir la ville: ravitaillement, marchés et métiers de l'alimentation à Venise dans les derniers siècles du Moyen Âge* (Rome, 2014), 492.
53. Dorigo, *Venezia romanica*, 1: 418–25.
54. Cessi, *Deliberazioni del Maggior Consiglio*, 1: 146.

55. Dorigo, *Venezia romanica*, 1: 406; Giorgio Zordan, *I visdomini di Venezia nel sec. XIII (Ricerche su un'antica magistratura finanziaria)* (Padua, 1971), 567–705.
56. Fernanda Sorelli, ed., *'Ego Quirina': testamenti di veneziane e forestiere (1200–1261)* (Rome, 2015), lxxii, 173.
57. Lane, *Venetian Ships and Shipbuilders*, 129–30; Dorigo, *Venezia romanica*,1: 410–8; Ennio Concina, *L'Arsenale della Repubblica di Venezia* (Milan, 2006), 11–23.
58. Stahl, *Zecca: The Mint of Venice*, 28–40, 281–6.
59. Frederic C. Lane and Reinhold C. Mueller, *Money and Banking in Medieval and Renaissance Venice*, vol. 1, *Coins and Moneys of Account* (Baltimore, 1985), 276–85.
60. Howard, *Venice and the East*, 22.
61. Da Canal, *Estoires de Venise*, 332–3.
62. Cited in Rösch, "Il 'gran Guadagno,'" 254.
63. For the staple, Lane, *Venice: A Maritime Republic*, 57–65; Giovanni Soranzo, *L'antico navigabile Po di Primaro nella vita economica e politica del delta padano* (Milan, 1964), 26–55; Faucheron, *Nourrir la ville*, 328–403; Georg Christ, "The Venetian Coast Guards: Staple Policy, Seaborne Law Enforcement, and State Formation in the 14th Century," in *Merchants, Pirates, and Smugglers: Criminalization, Economics, and the Transformation of the Maritime World (1200–1600)*, ed. Thomas Heeboll-Holm, Philipp Höhn, and Gregor Rohmann (Frankfurt, 2019), 269–96.
64. Ermanno Orlando, "Venezia, l'Adige e la viabilità fluviale nel Basso Medioevo," in *Il fiume, le terre, l'immaginario: l'Adige come fenomeno storiografico complesso*, ed. V. Rovigo (Rovereto, 2016), 105 (for quote), 110.
65. Rösch, *Venezia e l'impero*, 189–91.
66. Soranzo, *L'antico navigabile Po*, 33.
67. Jean-Claude Hocquet, "Monopole et concurrence à la fin du Moyen Age. Venise e les salines de Cervia (XIIe-XVIe siècles)," *SV* 15 (1973): 21–133; Jean-Claude Hocquet, *Venise e le monopole du sel: production, commerce et finance d'une république marchande*, 2 vols. (Venice, 2012), 1: 83–95.
68. Trevor Dean, "Venetian Economic Hegemony: The Case of Ferrara, 1220–1500," *SV* n.s. 12 (1986): 57, 74 n. 107; Élisabeth Crouzet-Pavan, "Venise e le monde communal: recherches sur les podestats vénitiens 1200–1350," *Journals des Savants* (1992, no. 2): 308–10; Faugeron, *Nourrir la ville*, 332.
69. Dean, "Venetian Economic Hegemony," 86–7.
70. Dean, "Venetian Economic Hegemony," 63–74; Lane, *Venice: A Maritime Republic*, 62.
71. Hocquet, *Venise e le monopole*, 1: 90.
72. Orlando, *Altre Venezie*, 130.
73. Orlando, *Altre Venezie*, 130–3; Simonetti, *Da Padova a Venezia*, 151–4.
74. Cessi, *Deliberazioni del Maggior Consiglio*, 1: 165–6; 2: 62.
75. Da Canal, *Estoires de Venise*, 250–1.
76. Sansovino, *Venetia città nobilissima*, 501.

77. Muir, *Civic Ritual*, 127.
78. Nicol, *Byzantium and Venice*, 166–78.
79. Nicol, *Byzantium and Venice*, 178–82, 188–216.
80. Nicola Di Cosmo, "The Black Sea Emporia and the Mongol Empire: A Reassessment of the Pax Mongolica," *Journal of the Economic and Social History of the Orient* 53 (2010): 83–108; David Jacoby, "Western Commercial and Colonial Expansion in the Eastern Mediterranean and the Black Sea in the late Middle Ages," in *Rapporti mediterranei, pratiche documentarie, presenze veneziane: le reti economiche e culturali (XIV–XVI secolo)*, ed. Gherardo Ortalli and Alessio Sopracasa (Venice, 2017), 3–49.
81. The literature on Polo is vast. A good introduction is John Larner, *Marco Polo and the Discovery of the World* (New Haven, 1999). For his family and business ventures, David Jacoby, "Marco Polo, His Close Relatives, and His Travel Account: Some New Insights," *Mediterranean Historical Review* 21 (2006): 193–218.
82. Martino da Canal wrote in his chronicle, "The French language runs throughout the world." Da Canal, *Estoires de Venise*, 2–3. See also Lorenzo Renzi, "Il francese come lingua letteraria e il franco-lombardo. L'epica carolingia nel Veneto," *SCUV* 1: 563–89.
83. For the argument that he never went to China, see Frances Wood, *Did Marco Polo Go to China?* (London, 1995); for the salt industry, see Hans Ulrich Vogel, *Marco Polo Was in China: New Evidence from Currencies, Salts, and Revenues* (Leiden, 2012).
84. Larner, *Marco Polo and the Discovery of the World*, 97.
85. Romano, *Markets and Marketplaces*, 157.
86. Jacoby, "Marco Polo," 206.
87. Robert Sabatino Lopez, "European Merchants in the Medieval Indies: The Evidence of Commercial Documents," *Journal of Economic History* 3 (1943): 174–80; Ugo Tucci, "Mercanti veneziani in Asia lungo l'itinerario Poliano," in *Venezia e l'Oriente*, ed. Lionello Lanciotti (Florence, 1987), 317–21.
88. Francis A. Rouleau, SJ, "The Yangchow Latin Tombstone as a Landmark of Medieval Christianity in China," *Harvard Journal of Asiatic Studies* 17 (1954): 346–65.
89. R. S. Lopez, "I successori di Marco Polo e la febbre della seta," in *Marco Polo, Venezia e l'Oriente*, ed. Alvise Zorzi (Milan, 1981): 289–90.
90. Jacoby, "Western Commercial and Colonial Expansion"; Hannah Barker, *The Most Precious Merchandise: The Mediterranean Trade in Black Sea Slaves, 1260–1500* (Philadelphia, 2019).
91. Jacoby, "Western Commercial and Colonial Expansion"; Lane, *Venice: A Maritime Empire*, 67–85; Janet L. Abu-Lughod, *Before European Hegemony: The World System AD 1250–1350* (New York, 1989).
92. Georgopoulou, *Venice's Mediterranean Colonies*, 66, 78.
93. Pedani, *Venezia porta d'Oriente*, 14.
94. Pedani, *Venezia porta d'Oriente*, 14–6.

95. For these wars, Romanin, *Storia documentata*, 2: 187–97, 237–43; Lane, *Venice: A Maritime Republic*,73–9; 82–5; Roberto Cessi, *Storia della Repubblica di Venezia* (Florence, 1981), 242–6, 255–7, 264–6.
96. Brown, *Venice and Antiquity*, 19–20.
97. Juergen Schulz, "La piazza medievale di San Marco," *Annali di Architettura* 4–5 (1992–3): 134–56; Agazzi, *Platea Sancti Marci*, 133–58.
98. Schulz, "La piazza medievale," 148; translation from Brown, *Venice and Antiquity*, 18.

CHAPTER 7

1. Cessi, *Documenti relativi*, 2: doc. 61, pp. 115–21; also Lanfranchi, *S. Giorgio Maggiore*, 2: doc. 1, p. 19.
2. Da Canal, *Estoires de Venise*, 4–7.
3. Da Canal, *Estoires de Venise*, 4–5.
4. See the numerous examples in Giorgio Cracco, *Società e stato nel Medioevo veneziano (sec. XII–XIV)* (Florence, 1967).
5. For an introduction, see Fernanda Sorelli, "La società," *SVOC* 2: 509–48.
6. See Marino Zorzi and Susy Marcon, eds., *Grado, Venezia, i Gradenigo: catalogo della mostra* (Mariano del Friuli, 2001), especially the essays: Gherardo Ortalli, "Grado e i Gradenigo. Vicende e ruoli alla radici della civiltà veneziana" (27–40), and Giuseppe Gullino, "Una famiglia nella storia: i Gradenigo" (131–53).
7. Fees, *Richezza e potenza*, 45–54.
8. Gerhard Rösch, *Der venezianische Adel bis zur Schließung des Großen Rats: zur Genese einer Führungsschicht* (Sigmaringen, 1989); Fees, *Ricchezza e potenza*, 375–83.
9. Pozza, *I Badoer*, 19.
10. Pozza, *I Badoer*, 56.
11. Lanfranchi, *Famiglia Zusto*.
12. Sorelli, "La società," 515.
13. Berto, *Testi storici veneziani*, 82.
14. Lanfranchi, *Famiglia Zusto*, xiii, n. 1.
15. Lanfranchi, *Famiglia Zusto*, xviii–xix, n. 1.
16. Sorelli, *"Ego Quirina,"* 98–101. For such interest-bearing deposits, see Reinhold C. Mueller, *The Venetian Money Market: Banks, Panics, and the Public Debt, 1200–1500* (Baltimore, 1997), 12–13.
17. Fernanda Sorelli, "Diritto, economia, società: condizioni delle donne a Venezia nei secoli XII–XIII," *AV* 6th series 3 (2012): 19–40. See also, Linda Guzzetti, "Gli investimenti delle donne veneziane nel Medioevo," *AV* 6th series 3 (2012): 41–66.
18. ASV, PSM de Citra, Busta 127, loose parchment number 906. Also cited in Giuseppina De Sandre Gasparini, "La pietà laicale," *SVOC* 2: 942.
19. Also cited in Giorgio Cracco, *Un "Altro mondo": Venezia nel Medioevo, dal secolo XI al secolo XIV* (Turin, 1986),104.

20. Giovanni Monticolo, ed., *I capitolari delle arti veneziane sottoposte alla Giustizia e poi alla Giustizia Vecchia dalle origini al MCCCXXX*, 3 vols. (Rome, 1896–1914).
21. Faugeron, *Nourrir la ville*.
22. Giorgetta Bonfiglio Dosio, "Le arti cittadine," *SVOC* 2: 578–95.
23. Monticolo, *Capitolari delle arti veneziane*, 3: 133–4.
24. Monticolo, *Capitolari delle arti veneziane*, 3: 153–5.
25. Ugo Tucci, "L'impresa marittima: uomini e mezzi," *SVOC* 2: 649.
26. Luzzatto, *Storia economica di Venezia*, 122.
27. Luzzatto, *Storia economica di Venezia*, 116–7; Lane, *Venice: A Maritime Republic*, 103–9.
28. Andrea Padovani, "La politica del diritto," *SVOC* 2: 303–29; Andrea Padovani, "Curie ed uffici," *SVOC* 2: 335–8.
29. Richard C. Mackenney, *Tradesmen and Traders: The World of the Guilds in Venice and Europe, c.1250–c.1650* (Totowa, NJ, 1987), 9.
30. Dennis Romano, *Patricians and Popolani: The Social Foundations of the Venetian Renaissance State* (Baltimore, 1987), 66–76.
31. Tucci, "L'impresa marittima," 627–59.
32. Tucci, "L'impresa marittima," 651.
33. For the ethnicity of slaves, see Barker, *The Most Precious Merchandise*, 52.
34. For a 1213 bequest by the precious metal dealer Bernardus Teotonicus to "my confraternity of the goldsmiths," see Von Stromer, "Bernardus Teotonicus e i rapporti commerciali," 14.
35. Lorenza Pamato, *Le scuole di battuti di Venezia (1260ca–1401)*, Dottorato di Ricerca, University of Padua, 1999, 13–4.
36. Quoted in Brian Pullan, *Rich and Poor in Renaissance Venice: The Social Institutions of a Catholic State, to 1620* (Cambridge, MA, 1971), 40.
37. Pullan, *Rich and Poor*, 51.
38. Gasparini, "La pietà laicale," 945; Daniela Rando, "Aspetti dell'organizzazione della cura d'anime a Venezia nei secoli XI–XII," in *La chiesa di Venezia nei secoli XI–XIII*, ed. Franco Tonon (Venice, 1988), 71, n. 92.
39. Francesca Ortalli, *"Per salute delle anime e delli corpi:" scuole piccole a Venezia nel tardo Medioevo* (Venice, 2001), 183.
40. For mercy as their central aspect, Richard Mackenney, *Venice as the Polity of Mercy: Guilds, Confraternities, and the Social Order, c. 1250–c. 1650* (Toronto, 2019).
41. Morozzo della Rocca and Lombardo, *Documenti del commercio veneziano*, 2: doc. 701, pp. 233–4.
42. Romano, *Patricians and Popolani*, 91–102.
43. Rando, "Aspetti dell'organizzazione," 65.
44. Gasparini, "La pietà laicale," 955, n. 31.
45. Giovanni Spinelli, "I monasteri benedettini fra il 1000 ed il 1300," in *La chiesa di Venezia nei secoli X–XIII*, ed. Franco Tonon (Venice, 1988), 109–33. See also

Gabriele Mazzucco, ed., *Monasteri benedittini nella laguna veneziana: catalogo della mostra* (Venice, 1983).

46. Antonio Fabris, "Esperienze di vita comunitaria: i canonici regolari," in *Monasteri benedittini*, ed. Mazzucco, 73–107. For the marriage, K. J. P. Lowe, *Nuns' Chronicles and Convent Culture in Renaissance and Counter-Reformation Italy* (Cambridge, 2003), 243–57.
47. Fernanda Sorelli, "I nuovi religiosi. Note sull'insediamento degli ordini mendicanti," in *La chiesa di Venezia nei secoli XI–XIII*, ed. Franco Tonon (Venice, 1988), 135–52; and Fernanda Sorelli, "Gli ordini mendicanti," *SVOC* 2: 905–27.
48. Sorelli, "Gli ordini mendicanti." For their urbanistic influence, Crouzet-Pavan, *"Sopra le acque salse,"* 1: 97–116.
49. Riccardo Calimani, *The Ghetto of Venice: A History* (New York, 1987), 1–5.
50. Maranini, *La costituzione*, 1: 207–41.
51. Maranini, *La costituzione*, 1: 262–312.
52. Maranini, *La costituzione*, 1: 262–312; Enrico Besta, *Il senato veneziano (origini, costituzione, attribuzioni e riti)* (Venice, 1899).
53. Maranini, *La costituzione*, 1: 241–62.
54. Maranini, *La costituzione*, 1: 253–4.
55. Maranini, *La costituzione*, 2: 297–383.
56. Cessi, *Storia della Repubblica*, 271–5.
57. Giorgio Zordan, *I visdomini di Venezia nel sec. XIII (Ricerche su un'antica magistratura finanziaria)* (Padua, 1971).
58. Pozza, "La cancelleria."
59. It still exists and is published in Cessi, *Deliberazioni del maggior consiglio*, 1: 1–231; Pozza, "La cancelleria," 359.
60. Both are published in Cessi, *Deliberazioni del maggior consiglio*, 2: 1–361.
61. Cessi, *Deliberazioni del maggior consiglio*, 2: 86, act 33.
62. Crouzet-Pavan, *"Sopra le acque salse,"* 1: 57–370.
63. Bianca Lanfranchi Strina, ed., *Codex Publicorum (Codice del Piovego)*, 2 vols. (Venice, 1985–2006).
64. Juergen Schulz, "Urbanism in Medieval Venice," in *City States in Classical Antiquity and Medieval Italy*, ed. Anthony Molho, Kurt Raaflaub, and Julia Emlen (Stuttgart, 1991), 422.
65. Crouzet-Pavan, *"Sopra le acque salse,"* 1: 220–21.
66. Strina, *Codex Publicorum*, 435–53.
67. Crouzet-Pavan, *"Sopra le acque salse,"* 1: 107, 243–63; 2: 690, 741–50.
68. Orlando, *Altre Venezie*, 11.
69. Cessi, *Deliberazioni del maggior consiglio*, 2: 211.
70. Crouzet-Pavan, *"Sopra le acque salse,"* 2: 263–89; Guido Ruggiero, *Violence in Early Renaissance Venice* (New Brunswick, 1980), 3–17.
71. Howard, *Architectural History*, 31–8; Concina, *History of Venetian Architecture*, 55–67.

72. Schulz, *New Palaces*, 18–9.
73. Schulz, *New Palaces*, 17.
74. Crouzet-Pavan, *"Sopra le acque salse,"* 1: 496–503.
75. Crouzet-Pavan, *"Sopra le acque salse,"* 1: 527–66; Muir, *Civic Ritual*, 135–56.
76. Romano, *Patricians and Popolani*, 122–3.
77. The phrase is Muir's (Muir, *Civic Ritual*, 153).
78. Cracco, *Società e stato*; Lane, *Venice: A Maritime Republic*, 91–5; 103–14; Cracco, *Altro mondo*, 73–112.
79. Cracco, *Altro mondo*, 59.
80. Dandolo, *Chronica per extensum descripta*, 292.
81. Padovani, "La politica del diritto," 322.
82. Marco Pozza, "Tiepolo, Giacomo," *DBI* 95 (2019): 336–9.
83. Sorelli, *"Ego Quirina,"* 131.
84. Graziato, *Promissione del doge*, 23–39.
85. Dandolo, *Chronica per extensum descripta*, 314.
86. Da Canal, *Estoires de Venise*, 324.
87. Monticolo, *L'ufficio della Giustizia Vecchia*.
88. Dosio, "Le arti cittadine," 591–2; Richard Mackenney, "The Guilds of Renaissance Venice: State and Society in the *Longue Durée*," *SV* n.s. 34 (1997): 15–43. A full text of the anti-conspiracy clause is in Monticolo, *I capitolari*, 2: 146. I follow with slight changes the translation in Mackenney, *Traders and Tradesmen*, 25.
89. Dosio, "Le arti cittadine," 594–5.
90. Cessi, *Deliberazioni del maggior consiglio*, 2: 212.
91. Dandolo, *Chronica per extensum descripta*, 314.
92. Da Canal, *Estoires de Venise*, 270–83.
93. Åsa Boholm, *The Doge of Venice: The Symbolism of State Power in the Renaissance* (Gothenburg, 1990), 122–4.
94. For Tiepolo's dogeship, Cracco, *Società e stato*, 243–65.
95. Da Canal, *Estoires de Venise*, 284–305.
96. Da Canal, *Estoires de Venise*, 303.
97. Cracco, *Altro mondo*, 97.
98. Cracco, *Società e stato*, 261–2.
99. Cessi, *Deliberazioni del maggior consiglio*, 2: 213, 215, 259–60.
100. Graziato, *Promissioni del doge*, 90.
101. For *popolo* as a political category, Claire Judde de Larivière and Rosa M. Salzberg, " 'Le peuple est la cité': l'idée de *popolo* e la condition des popolani à Venise (XVe-XVIe siècles)," *Annales: Histoire, Sciences Sociales* 68 (2013–4): 1120–3.
102. The following account follows: Frederic C. Lane, "The Enlargement of the Great Council of Venice," in *Florilegium Historiale: Essays Presented to Wallace K. Ferguson*, ed. J. G. Rowe and W. H. Stockdale (Toronto, 1971), 236–74; and Gerhard Rösch, "The *Serrata* of the Great Council and Venetian Society, 1286–1323," *VR*, 67–88. For the Serrata laws, Benjamin G. Kohl, "The Serrata of the

Greater Council of Venice, 1282–1323: The Documents," in *Venice and the Veneto During the Renaissance: The Legacy of Benjamin Kohl*, ed. Michael Knapton, John E. Law, and Alison A. Smith (Florence, 2014), 3–34.

103. Kohl, "The Serrata of the Greater Council," 15–6.
104. Lane, "The Enlargement of the Great Council," 245.
105. Lane, "The Enlargement of the Great Council," 262–3, n. 4.
106. Kohl, "The Serrata of the Greater Council," 31–2.
107. Chojnacki, "In Search of the Venetian Patriciate," 55.
108. Quoted in Rösch, "The *Serrata* of the Great Council," 69.
109. Quoted in Lane, "The Enlargement of the Great Council," 239.
110. Roberto Cessi and Fanny Bennato, eds., *Venetiarum Historia vulgo Petro Iustiniano Iustiniani Filio Adiudicata* (Venice, 1964), 194.
111. The extinction of certain families explains how the number of 210 families declined to approximately 150.

CHAPTER 8

1. ASV, Maggior Consiglio, Deliberazioni, Register 17 (Spiritus), fols. 114r-v.
2. Andrew Martindale, "The Venetian Sala del Gran Consiglio and its Fourteenth-Century Decoration," *Antiquaries Journal* 73 (1993): 92.
3. On the war, see Giovanni Soranzo, *La guerra fra Venezia e la Santa Sede per il dominio di Ferrara (1308–1313)* (Città di Castello, 1905); Gian Maria Varanini, "Venezia e l'entroterra (1300 circa–1420)," *SVOC* 3: 173–5.
4. Quoted in Brown, *Venice and Antiquity*, 34. For the painted cycle, see Brown, *Venetian Narrative Painting*, 259–60.
5. Romanin, *Storia documentata*, 3: 21–39; Lane, *Venice: A Maritime Republic*,114–7; Nelli-Elena Vanzan Marchini, "La congiura imperfetta," in *La congiura imperfetta di Baiamonte Tiepolo*, ed. Nelli-Ėlena Vanzan Marchini (Caselle di Sommacampagna—Verona, 2011), 13–30.
6. Andrea Dandolo, *Chronica brevis aa.46–1342d.C.*, ed., Ester Pastorello, *Rerum Italicarum Scriptores*, XII, pt. 1 (Bologna, 1938), 370.
7. Cessi and Bennato, *Venetiarum historia vulgo Petro Iustiniano*, 205.
8. Giovanni Giacomo Caroldo, *Istorii Venețiene*, ed. Serban V. Marin, 5 vols. (Bucharest, 2008–2012), 2: 111.
9. Fabien Faugeron, "L'art du compromise politique: Venise au lendemain de la conjuration Tiepolo-Querini (1310)," *Journal des Savants* (July–December 2004): 358.
10. Daniele Dibello, "La stabilità delle istituzioni veneziane nel Trecento. Aspetti politici, economici e culturali nella gestione della congiura di Marino Falier," *Reti Medievali Rivista* 19 (2018): 85–129, esp. 116.
11. It appears in the same edition as Dandolo's *Chronica per extensum descripta* and his *Chronica brevis*, 375–6.

12. For the first five registers of the Ten with appendices of its enabling legislation, see Ferruccio Zago, ed., *Consiglio dei Dieci: deliberazioni miste*, 3 vols. (Venice, 1962–1993). See also Romanin, *Storia documentata*, 3: 40–60; Maranini, *Costituzione di Venezia*, 2: 387–490; Guido Ruggiero, "The Ten: Control of Violence and Social Disorder in Trecento Venice," PhD diss., University of California at Los Angeles, 1972; Guido Ruggiero, *Violence in Early Renaissance Venice*, 6–13.
13. Sanudo, *De origine, situ et magistratibus*, 98.
14. Ruggiero, *Violence*, 1–2, 12–39.
15. Zago, *Consiglio dei Dieci*, 2: 12 (act 20), 132 (act 387).
16. Zago, *Consiglio dei Dieci*, 1: 6–7 (act 5).
17. Zago, *Consiglio dei Dieci*, 1: 64 (act 137).
18. Zago, *Consiglio dei Dieci*, 1: 86 (act 215) and 111 (act 297).
19. Zago, *Consiglio dei Dieci*, 1: 130 (act 354).
20. ASV, MC, Deliberazioni, register 10 (Presbiter), fols. 27v, 36v.
21. In 1468 one of her descendants successfully petitioned the Ten to roll back a rent increase. Romanin, *Storia documentata*, 3: 30, and esp. n. 27.
22. The original reads, "De Baiamonte fo questo terreno, e mo per lo so iniquo tradimento se posto in chomun, per altrui spavento per mostrar a tutti senpre seno." For the transcription and translation, see Ronnie Ferguson, *Venetian Inscriptions: Vernacular Writing for Public Display in Medieval and Renaissance Venice* (Cambridge, 2021), 174–77. Pictures of the column also reproduced in Fabien Faugeron, "Quelques réflexions autour de la conjuration de Baiamonte Tiepolo: des réalités socio-politiques à la fabrication du mythe (1297–1797)," in *Venise 1297–1797: la république des Castors*, ed. Alessandro Fontana and George Saro (Fontenoy Saint-Cloud, 1997), 73–9.
23. ASV, MC, Deliberazioni, Register 10 (Presbiter), fols. 36v, 128v.
24. Faugeron, "L'art du compromise politique," 374–7.
25. Zago, *Consiglio dei Dieci*, 2: 101 (act 292), 102 (act 297), 117 (act 334).
26. Zago, *Consiglio dei Dieci*, 3: 31 (acts 58–9), 33–4 (acts 65–6).
27. Dennis Romano, "Popular Protest and Alternative Visions of the Venetian Polity, c. 1260 to 1423," in *Popular Politics in an Aristocratic Republic*, ed. Van Gelder and Judde de Larivière, 22–44.
28. Lia Sbriziolo, "Per la storia delle confraternite veneziane: dalle deliberazioni miste (1310–1476) del Consiglio dei Dieci: le scuole dei battuti," in *Miscellanea Gilles Gerard Meersseman*, 2 vols. (Padua, 1970) 2: 715–63; Lia Sbriziolo, "Per la storia delle confraternite veneziane: dalle deliberazioni miste (1310–1476) del Consiglio dei Dieci. *Scolae comunes,* artigiane e nazionali," *Atti dell'Istituto Veneto di Scienze, Lettere ed Arti* 126 (1967–8): 405–42; William B. Wurthmann, "The Council of Ten and the *Scuole Grandi* in Early Renaissance Venice," *SV* n.s.18 (1989): 15–66.
29. Petrarch, *Lettere senili*, book IV, n. 3. Quoted in Bishop, *Letters from Petrarch*, 234.
30. Fabien Faugeron, "Quelques réflections," 57–8.

31. Giovanni Botero, *The Reason of State*, trans. P. J. and D. P. Waley (New Haven, 1956), 109. See also Maartje van Gelder, "Protest in the Piazza: Contested Space in Early Modern Venice," in *Popular Politics in an Aristocratic Republic*, ed. Van Gelder and Judde de Larivière, 129–30.
32. Lane, *Venice: A Maritime Republic*, 11–2.
33. Lane, *Venice: A Maritime Republic*, 165–6.
34. Romano, *Patricians and Popolani*, 119–40.
35. Luca Pes, "Le classi popolari," *SVON* 1: 771–7.
36. Romano, *Patricians and Popolani*, 7–9; Davis, *War of the Fists*.
37. Ruggiero, *Violence*.
38. Claire Judde de Larivière, *Naviguer, commercer, gouverner: économie maritime et pouvoirs à Venise (XVe–XVIe siècles)* (Leiden, 2008), 46–7. For the effects of naval discipline, William H. McNeill, *Venice: The Hinge of Europe, 1081–1797* (Chicago, 1974), 261, n. 65. In the early modern period, it was argued that required service on the galleys for convicts would rehabilitate them and prepare them to be productive members of society. Andrea Viaro, "La pena della galera, la condizione dei condannati a bordo delle galere veneziane," in *Stato, società e giustizia nella Repubblica veneta (sec. XV–XVIII)*, 2 vols. ed. Gaetano Cozzi (Rome, 1980), 1:426–7.
39. See the various essays in Van Gelder and Judde de Larivière, eds., *Popular Politics in an Aristocratic Republic*.
40. Romano, "Popular Protest and Alternative Visions."
41. Leopold von Ranke, *Venezia nel Cinquecento con un saggio introduttivo di Ugo Tucci* (Rome, 1974), 150–1.
42. For a summary with extensive bibliography, see Judde de Larivière, *Naviguer, commercer*, 13–25.
43. Benjamin Arbel, "Daily Life on Board Venetian Ships: The Evidence of Renaissance Travelogues and Diaries," in *Rapporti mediterranei, pratiche documentarie, presenze veneziane: le reti commerciali e culturali (XIV-XVI secolo)*, ed. Gherardo Ortalli and Alessio Sopracasa (Venice, 2017), 202.
44. Lane, *Venetian Ships and Shipbuilders*, 1–34, quote 13.
45. Doris Stöckly, *Le système de l'incanto des galées du marché à Venise (fin du XIIIe-milieu du XVe siècle)* (Leiden, 1995), 10, n. 13; Jacoby, "Western Commercial and Colonial Expansion," 34.
46. Alberto Tenenti, "Le film d'un grand système de navigation: les galères marchandes vénitiennes, XIV–XVI siècles," *Annales ESC* 16 (1961); 83–6; Adolfo Sacerdoti, "Note sulle galere da mercato veneziane nel XV secolo," *Bollettino dell'Istituto di Storia della Società e dello Stato Veneziano* 4 (1962): 80–105; Frederic C. Lane, "The Merchant Marine of the Venetian Republic," in *Venice and History: The Collected Papers of Frederic C. Lane* (Baltimore, 1966), 143–62; Frederic C. Lane, "Merchant Galleys, 1300–34: Private and Communal Operation," in Lane, *Venice and History*, 193–226; Stöckly, *Le système de l'incanto*; Jean-Claude Hocquet, "I meccanismi dei traffici," *SVOC* 3: 529–616; Bernard Doumerc, "Gli armamenti marittimi," *SVOC* 3: 617–640; Bernard

Doumerc, "Le galere da mercato," *SV Mare*, 357–95. And on Venetian policy toward pirates and corsairs, Irene B. Katele, "Piracy and the Venetian State: The Dilemma of Maritime Defense in the Fourteenth Century," *Speculum* 63 (1988): 865–89.

47. Michael E. Mallett, *The Florentine Galleys in the Fifteenth Century* (Oxford, 1967).
48. Doumerc, "Gli armamenti marittimi," 624–5.
49. François-Xavier Leduc, ed., *Venezia-Senato: deliberazioni miste: registro XIX (1340–1341)* (Venice, 2004), 42–5.
50. Leduc, *Venezia-Senato*, 45–6.
51. Lane, *Venetian Ships and Shipbuilders*, 26.
52. Stöckly, *Le système de l'incanto*, 97; Judde de Larivière, *Naviguer, commercer*, 66–7; Lane, "The Merchant Marine," 144.
53. Georg Christ, "Quelques observations concernant la navigation vénitienne à Alexandrie à la fin du Moyen Âge," in *Venise et la Méditerranée*, ed. Sandro G. Franchini et al. (Venice, 2011), 60–2.
54. Lane, "Fleets and Fairs"; Stöckly, *Le système de l'incanto*, 94.
55. Stöckly, *Le système de l'incanto*, 283–4.
56. Quotes in Lane, *Venetian Ships and Shipbuilders*, 26, n. 44; and Lopez and Raymond, *Medieval Trade in the Mediterranean World*, 209–10.
57. Lane, "Diet and Wages of Seamen in the Early Fourteenth Century," in Lane, *Venice and History*, 263–8.
58. Raimondo Morozzo della Rocca, ed., *Lettere di mercanti a Pignol Zucchello (1336–1350)* (Venice, 1957), 17.
59. Stöckly, *Le système de l'incanto*, 178.
60. John H. Pryor, *Geography, Technology, and War: Studies in the Maritime History of the Mediterranean, 649–1571* (Cambridge, 1988), 51.
61. Pryor, *Geography*, 75–85.
62. Pryor, *Geography*, 24–101.
63. McNeill, *Venice: The Hinge*, 64.
64. Zago, *Consiglio dei Dieci*, 3: 69–75 (acts 163–75), also 78–80 (acts 186, 192, 194).
65. Stöckly, *Le système de l'incanto*, 89.
66. McNeill, *Venice: The Hinge*, 62–4.
67. Claire Judde de Larivière, "Entre gestion privée et contrôle public: les transports maritime à Venise à la fin du Moyen Âge," *Histoire Urbaine* 12 (2005): 57–68; Christ, "Quelques observations, 57–60.
68. Gluzman, *Venetian Shipping*, 234, esp. n. 4.
69. Lane, *Venice: A Maritime Republic*, 338; Gluzman, *Venetian Shipping*, 228. We can look forward to the results of Nicola Carotenuto's research on private shipping in this period.
70. Lopez and Raymond, *Medieval Trade in the Mediterranean World*, 212–20.
71. Francisco Apellániz, "Venetian Trading Networks in the Medieval Mediterranean," *Journal of Interdisciplinary History* 44 (2013): 157–79.
72. Andreina Bondi Sebellico, ed., *Felice de Merlis: prete e notaio in Venezia ed Ayas (1315–1348)* 3 vols. (Venice, 1973–2012), 1: xxxiii.

73. Lopez and Raymond, *Medieval Trade in the Mediterranean World*, 381–2.
74. Georg Christ, "Beyond the Network—Connectors of Networks: Venetian Agents in Cairo and Venetian News Management," in *Everything Is on the Move: The Mamluk Empire as a Node in (Trans-)Regional Networks* (Göttingen, 2014), 27–59.
75. Leon Battista Alberti, *The Family in Renaissance Florence: A Translation by Renée Neu Watkins of I Libri della famiglia by Leon Battista Alberti* (Columbia, SC, 1969), 197.
76. The quote is from Shakespeare's *The Merchant of Venice*, act 3, scene 1. Franz-Julius Morche, "The Letters of Others: Marino Morosini and His Curious Newssheet on the Battle of Maclodio (1427)," in *Cultures of Empire: Rethinking Venetian Rule, 1400–1700: Essays in Honour of Benjamin Arbel*, ed. Georg Christ and Franz-Julius Morche (Leiden, 2020), 90–122.
77. Tucci, *Venezia e dintorni*, 6.
78. Morozzo della Rocca, *Lettere di mercanti*, 45.
79. Morozzo della Rocca, *Lettere di mercanti*, 59.
80. Morozzo della Rocca, *Lettere di mercanti*, 109.
81. Stussi, *Zibaldone*, 76; *Merchant Culture* (Dotson translation), 128.
82. Mueller, *Venetian Money Market*, 27–8.
83. Mueller, *Venetian Money Market*, 10–11.
84. Mueller, *Venetian Money Market*, 6 [I have made one minor change.]
85. Mueller, *Venetian Money Market*, 76.
86. Mueller, *Venetian Money Market*, 359.
87. Mueller, *Venetian Money Market*, 363.
88. Mueller, *Venetian Money Market*, 363–4.
89. Mueller, *Venetian Money Market*, 397.
90. Mueller, *Venetian Money Market*, 423–4.
91. Michael Knapton, "La dinamica delle finanze pubbliche," *SVOC* 3: 478.
92. Knapton, "La dinamica," 500.
93. Mueller, *Venetian Money Market*, 459–66.
94. The *estimo* is printed in Gino Luzzatto, ed., *I prestiti della Repubblica di Venezia (sec.XIII–XV)* (Padua, 1929), 138–95.
95. Sebellico, *Felice de Merlis*, 2: 39.
96. Mueller, *Venetian Money Market*, 455.
97. Luzzatto, *Storia economica di Venezia*, 116.
98. Concina, *L'Arsenale della Repubblica*, 25–43.
99. Concina, *L'Arsenale della Repubblica*, 32–3.
100. Donatella Calabi, "Fortezze e lidi," *SV Mare*, 111.
101. Élizabeth Crouzet-Pavan, "Sviluppo e articolazione della città," *SVOC* 3: 741.
102. Concina, *History of Venetian Architecture*, 81.
103. Quoted in Concina, *History of Venetian Architecture*, 82.
104. Bartolomeo Cecchetti, "La vita dei Veneziani nel 1300," *AV* 28 (1884): 281–96; 29 (1885), 9–25; Bellavitis and Romanelli, *Venezia*, 53–66.

105. ASV, MC, Deliberazioni, register 17 (Spiritus), fol. 130v.
106. Cecchetti, "La vita dei Veneziani"; Bellavitis and Romanelli, *Venezia*, 53–66.
107. Simonetti, *Da Padova a Venezia*, 9, 64–5.
108. Karl Appuhn, *A Forest on the Sea: Environmental Expertise in Renaissance Venice* (Baltimore, 2009), 51.
109. Appuhn, *Forest on the Sea*, 28.
110. Roberto Cessi, "L''Ufficium de Navigantibus' ed i sistemi della politica commerciale veneziana nel sec. XIV," *NAV* n.s. 63 (1916): 106–46; Lane, *Venice: A Maritime Republic*, 140.
111. Reinhold C. Mueller, *Immigrazione e cittadinanza nella Venezia medievale* (Rome, 2010).
112. Morozzo della Rocca, *Lettere di mercanti*, 48.
113. Morozzo della Rocca, *Lettere di mercanti*, 115.
114. Luca Molà, *La comunità dei Lucchesi a Venezia: immigrazione e industria della seta nel tardo Medioevo* (Venice, 1994), 30.
115. Molà, *La comunità*, 301–2.
116. Molà, *La comunità*, 55, 280.
117. Molà, *La comunità*, 91 n. 55.
118. Molà, *La comunità*, 102–3.
119. Mueller, *Venetian Money Market*, 256.
120. Andrea Zannini, *Venezia città aperta: gli stranieri e la Serenissima, XIV-XVIII sec.* (Venice, 2009), 37.
121. Ermanno Orlando, *Migrazioni mediterranee: migranti, minoranze e matrimoni a Venezia nel Basso Medioevo* (Bologna, 2014); Philippe Braunstein, *Les Allemands à Venise (1380–1520)* (Rome, 2016).
122. Brunehilde Imhaus, *Le minoranze orientali a Venezia, 1300–1510* (Rome, 1997), quote 412.
123. Imhaus, *Le minoranze*, 406.
124. Zannini, *Venezia città aperta*, 40.
125. Giorgio Ravegnani, "Dandolo, Andrea," *DBI* 32 (1986): 432–40.
126. Ravegnani, "Dandolo, Andrea," 434; Claudio Finzi, "Scritti storico-politici," *SVOC* 3: 825–64; Girolamo Arnaldi and Lidia Capo, "I cronisti di Venezia e della Marca Trevigiana," *SCUV* 2: 272–337.
127. Gina Fasoli, "Nascita di un mito," in *Studi storici in onore di Gioacchino Volpe*, 2 vols. (Florence,1958), 1: 445–79.
128. Dandolo, *Chronica per extensum descripta*, 10.
129. David Robey and John Law, "The Venetian Myth and the 'De republica veneta' of Pier Paolo Vergerio," *Rinascimento* ser. 2, 15 (1975): 54–6; I follow with some modifications the translation by Law in *Medieval Italy: Texts in Translation*, ed. Katherine L. Jansen, Joanna Drell, and Frances Andrews (Philadelphia, 2009), 515–6.
130. Fasoli, "Nascita di un mito," 455.

131. Da Canal, *Estoires de Venise*, 2–3.
132. Cited in Girolamo Arnaldi, "La cancelleria ducale fra culto della 'legalitas' e nuova cultura umanistica," *SVOC* 3: 879–80.
133. Fasoli, "Nascita di un mito," 474.
134. Arnaldi and Capo, "I cronisti di Venezia," 304.
135. James S. Grubb, "Memory and Identity: Why Venetians Didn't Keep *Ricordanze*," *Renaissance Studies* 8 (1994): 375–87.
136. Muir, *Civic Ritual*, 103–19.
137. Klein, "Refashioning Byzantium," 193–225.
138. Klein, "Refashioning Byzantium," 200–6.
139. ASV, MC, Deliberazioni, register 17 (Spiritus), fol. 130v. Some earlier studies give the old pagination: fol. 129v.
140. Klein, "Refashioning Byzantium," 196–200.
141. Giuseppe Fiocco and Rona Goffen, "Le pale feriali," in *La pala d'oro: il Tesoro di San Marco*, ed. H. R. Hahnloser and R. Polacco (Venice: 1994), 163–84. For the nexus of artistic styles in fourteenth-century painting in Venice and its colonies, see Michele Bacci, "Veneto-Byzantine 'Hybrids': Towards a Reassessment," *Studies in Iconography* 35 (2014): 73–106.
142. The five were San Marco, San Pietro di Castello, San Silvestro, Santa Maria Formosa, and Santa Maria Zobenigo. Rivalry between the patriarch of Grado at San Silvestro, the bishop at San Pietro, and the *primicerio* (chief priest) at San Marco perhaps explains this unusual division of baptismal responsibilities.
143. Debra Pincus, "Andrea Dandolo (1343–1354) and Visible History: The San Marco Projects," in *Art and Politics in Late Medieval and Early Renaissance Italy: 1250–1500*, ed. Charles M. Rosenberg (Notre Dame, 1990), 191–206.
144. Debra Pincus, "Venice and Its Doge in the Grand Design: Andrea Dandolo and the Fourteenth-Century Mosaics of the Baptistery," in *San Marco, Byzantium, and the Myths of Venice*, ed. Maguire and Nelson, 262.
145. Roberto Pesce, ed., *Cronica di Venexia detta di Enrico Dandolo* (Venice, 2010), 4. For a different version from a different manuscript, see Debra Pincus, "Hard Times and Ducal Radiance: Andrea Dandolo and the Construction of the Ruler in Fourteenth-Century Venice," *VR*, 102–3.
146. Quoted and translated in Debra Pincus, *The Tombs of the Doges of Venice* (Cambridge, 2000), 138–43.

CHAPTER 9

1. Full transcription in *Venezia e la peste 1348/1797* (Venice, 1979), 81–2; in Stussi, "La lingua," *SVOC* 3: 917; and in Ronnie Ferguson, *Le iscrizioni in antico volgare delle confraternite laiche veneziane: edizione e commento* (Venice, 2015), 45.
2. Monica H. Green, "The Four Black Deaths," *American Historical Review* 125 (2020): 1606.

3. For what follows, Mario Brunetti, "Venezia durante la peste del 1348," *AT* 32 (1909), pt.1: 289–311, pt. 2, 5–42; the essays by Reinhold C. Mueller in *Venezia e la peste*; and Alberto Tenenti, "Le 'temporali calamità,'" *SVOC* 3: 27–49.
4. ASV, MC, Deliberazioni, register 17, fol. 155v.
5. It seems unlikely that ambassadors and others were allowed to enter if they showed signs of illness, but the law is unclear. Ermanno Orlando, ed., *Venezia-Senato: deliberazioni miste: registro XXIV (1347–1349)* (Venice, 2007), 332–4.
6. Orlando, *Venezia-Senato*, 334–5.
7. ASV, MC, Deliberazioni, register 16, fol. 156r.
8. Sebellico, *Felice de Merlis*, 2: 115–9.
9. Sebellico, *Felice de Merlis*, 2: 124–6.
10. ASV, MC, Deliberazioni, register 16, fol. 156v.
11. Orlando, *Venezia-Senato*, 366–7.
12. Cited in Reinhold C. Mueller, "Aspetti sociali ed economici della peste a Venezia nel Medioevo," in *Venezia e la peste*, 73.
13. Mueller, "Aspetti sociali," 74.
14. ASV, MC, Deliberazioni, register 17, fol. 157r.
15. Mueller, *Immigrazione e cittadinanza*, 24–7.
16. Crouzet-Pavan, "Sviluppo e articolazione," 768–73.
17. Cited in Reinhold C. Mueller, "Catalogo: dalla reazione alla prevenzione," in *Venezia e la peste*, 80.
18. Bariša Krekiċ, "Venezia e l'Adriatico," *SVOC* 3: 51–62.
19. Jacoby, "Western Commercial and Colonial Expansion," 29–31.
20. For what follows: Nicol, *Byzantium and Venice*, 212–95; Krekiċ, "Venezia e l'Adriatico," 51–86; Michel Balard, "La lotta contro Genova," *SVOC* 3: 87–126; Bernard Doumerc, "La construction d'un empire (1298–1396)" in *Histoire de l'Adriatique*, ed. Pierre Cabanes et al. (Paris, 2001), 203–39; Benjamin G. Kohl, *Padua Under the Carrara, 1318–1405*, (Baltimore, 1998) 89–114; and Federico Pigozzo, *Treviso e Venezia nel Trecento: la prima dominazione veneziana sulle podesterie minori (1339–1381)* (Venice, 2007), 3–41.
21. Cessi and Bennato, *Venetiarum historia vulgo Petro Iustiniano*, 240.
22. Cessi and Bennato, *Venetiarum historia vulgo Petro Iustiniano*, 253.
23. Orlando, *Venezia e il mare*, 124.
24. Mueller, *Venetian Money Market*, 140–45, 467.
25. For what follows: Vittorio Lazzarini, *Marino Faliero: avanti il dogado, la congiura, appendici* (Florence, 1963); Giorgio Ravegnani, *Il traditore di Venezia: vita di Marino Falier doge* (Bari-Rome, 2017).
26. Giorgio Ravegnani, "Falier, Marino," *DBI* 44 (1994): 429–38.
27. Cited in Lazzarini, *Marino Faliero*, 124.
28. Ravegnani, "Falier, Marino."
29. Pesce, *Cronica di Venezia detta di Enrico Dandolo*, 144.

30. Lorenzo de Monacis, *Chronicon de rebus venetis ab U.C. ad annum MCCCLIV*, ed. Flaminio Corner, *Rerum Italicarum Scriptores*, ser. 1, tome 8 (Venice, 1758), 316.
31. Cited in Lazzarini, *Marino Faliero*, 137.
32. Lane, *Venice: A Maritime Republic*, 183.
33. Lazzarini, *Marino Faliero*, 259–60.
34. One night in 1388 two noblemen affixed to a bridge near the Dalle Boccole family palace two large bunches of horns—symbols of cuckoldry—along with scurrilous words about the wife and mother-in-law of Giovanni dalle Boccole. Lazzarini, *Marino Faliero*, 153.
35. Lazzarini, *Marino Faliero*, 158.
36. Dibello, "La stabilità delle istituzioni veneziane," 85–129, esp. 111.
37. Lazzarini, *Marino Falier*, 186.
38. Francesco Petrarca, *Epistolae de rebus familiaribus et variae*, ed. Giuseppe Fracassetti, 3 vols. (Florence, 1859–63), 2: 540–41. It is letter 9 of book 19. I follow with slight modification the translation in Lane, *Venice: A Maritime Republic*, 181.
39. Giovanni Pillinini, "Marino Falier e la crisi economica e politica della metà del '300 a Venezia," *AV* ser. V, 84 (1968): 45–71; Giovanni Pillinini, "I 'popolari' e la 'congiura' di Marino Falier," *Annali della Facoltà di Lingue e Letterature Straniere di Ca' Foscari* 9 (1970): 63–71
40. Pesce, *Cronica di Venezia detta di Enrico Dandolo*, 143.
41. Cited in Lazzarini, *Marino Faliero*, 247.
42. Zago, *Consiglio dei Dieci*, 3: 281 (act 729).
43. Lazzarini, *Marino Faliero*, 100–1.
44. Romano, "Popular Protest."
45. For Lorenzo Celsi, see Romanin, *Storia documentata*, 3: 167–70; Da Mosto, *I dogi*, 130–35; Laura Ginnasi, "Celsi, Lorenzo," *DBI* 23 (1979): 475–78.
46. ASV, DM, register 6, fol. 31r.
47. ASV, MC, Deliberazioni, register 19, fols. 110r-v.
48. ASV, DM, register 6, fol. 48r. Following the 1577 fire in the Ducal Palace, the painting was reworked, and the wording changed slightly to read, "This is the place of Marino Falier who was decapitated for crimes." See also Wamsler, "Picturing Heaven," 245–83.
49. For the revolt, see, among others, Freddy Thiriet, "Sui dissidi sorti tra il comune di Venezia e i suoi feudatari di Creta nel Trecento," in Freddy Thiriet, *Études sur la Romanie greco-vénitienne (Xe–XVe siècles)* (London, 1977), VI: 699–712; J. Jergerlehner, "Die Aufstand der kandiotischen Rittershaft gegen das Mutterland Venedig, 1363–65," *Byzantinische Zeitschrift* 12 (1903): 78–125; Silvano Borsari, "I Veneziani nelle colonie," *SVOC* 3: 142–6; Sally McKee, *Uncommon Dominion*.
50. Maria Georgopoulou, "Late Medieval Crete and Venice: An Appropriation of Byzantine Heritage," *Art Bulletin* 77 (1995): 487.

51. Freddy Thiriet, "Problemi dell'amministrazione veneziana nella Romania, XIV–XV sec.," in *Études sur la Romanie greco-vénitienne (Xe–XVe siècles)* (London, 1977), 14: 773–82.
52. Jacoby, "Western Commercial and Colonial Expansion," 36.
53. Benjamin Arbel, "Roots of Poverty and Resources of Richness in Cyprus Under Venetian Rule," in *Ricchi e poveri nella società dell'Oriente Grecolatino*, ed. Chryssa A. Maltezou (Venice, 1998), 351–60; David Jacoby, "The Venetians in Byzantine and Lusignan Cyprus: Trade, Settlement, and Politics," in *La* Serenissima *and La* Nobilissima: *Venice in Cyprus and Cyprus in Venice*, ed. Angel Nicolaou-Konnari (Nicosia, 2009), 59–100.
54. Schulz, *New Palaces*, 199.
55. Gino Luzzatto, "Capitalismo coloniale nel Trecento," and "Sindicati e cartelli nel commercio veneziano dei secoli XIII e XIV," in Gino Luzzatto, *Studi di storia economica veneziana* (Padua, 1954), 117–23, 195–200; Lane, *Venice: A Maritime Republic*, 141–6; Schulz, *New Palaces*, 196–201; Jacoby "Venetians in Byzantine and Lusignan Cyprus," 75, 84.
56. Benjamin Arbel, "The Venetian Domination of Cyprus: *Cui bono?*," in *La Serenissima and La Nobilissima: Venice in Cyprus and Cyprus in Venice*, ed. Angel Nicolaou-Konnari (Nicosia, 2009), 45–55.
57. Daniele di Chinazzo, *Cronica de la guerra da Veniciani a Zenovesi*, ed. Vittorio Lazzarini (Venice, 1958), 20.
58. Freddy Thiriet, "Venise et l'occupation de Ténédos au XIVe siècle," in *Études sur la Romanie greco-vénitienne (Xe–XVe siècles)* (London, 1977), II: 219–45; Ruthy Gertwagen, "Venice, Genoa and the Fights over the Island of Tenedos (Late Fourteenth and Early Fifteenth Century," *SV* n.s. 67 (2013): 35–87.
59. For the Byzantine background to the war, Nichol, *Byzantium and Venice*, 246–316.
60. For the phrase "protectorate" and the Latin quote, see Varanini, "Venezia e l'entroterra," 186.
61. Kohl, *Padua Under the Carrara*, 101–31.
62. For summaries of the war and the Peace of Turin, see Nicol, *Byzantium and Venice*, 317–22; Kohl, *Padua Under the Carrara*, 205–22; Lane, *Venice: A Maritime Republic*, 189–96; Steven A. Epstein, *Genoa and the Genoese, 958–1528* (Chapel Hill, 1996), 236–42.
63. Giuseppe Gullino, "Pisani, Vittore," *DBI* 84 (2015): 242–45.
64. The Paduan chronicler Gatari quoted in Kohl, *Padua Under the Carrara*, 210.
65. Di Chinazzo, *Cronica de la guerra*, 148.
66. Di Chinazzo, *Cronica de la guerra*, 58.
67. For illustrative documents of the war and treaty, Archivio di Stato di Venezia, *Dalla guerra di Chioggia alla pace di Torino, 1377–1381: catalogo: mostra documentaria 29 giugno–27 settembre* 1981(Venice, 1981).
68. Quoted in Nichol, *Byzantium and Venice*, 318.

69. Barker, *That Most Precious Merchandise*.
70. Partial transcription in Archivio di Stato, *Dalla guerra di Chioggia*, 36–7.
71. Frederic C. Lane, "The Funded Debt of the Venetian Republic, 1262–1482," in Lane, *Venice and History*, 88.
72. Mueller, *Venetian Money Market*, 461.
73. Luzzatto, *I prestiti*, 200–01; clxiii–clxiv.
74. Luzzatto, *I prestiti*, clxvii–clxviii.
75. Archivio di Stato, *Dalla guerra di Chioggia*, 74.
76. Archivio di Stato, *Dalla guerra di Chioggia*, 74.
77. Schulz, *New Palaces*, 187–204.
78. Schulz, *New Palaces*, 133–57.
79. Luzzatto, *I prestiti*, 207–8, clxxi.
80. Archivio di Stato, *Dalla guerra di Chioggia*, 84.
81. Archivio di Stato, *Dalla guerra di Chioggia*, 83–5.
82. Mueller, *Immigrazione e cittadinanza*, 28; Molà, *La communità*, 57.
83. Reinhold C. Mueller, "Effetti della guerra di Chioggia sulla vita economica e sociale di Venezia (1378–1381)," in Reinhold C. Mueller, *Venezia nel tardo Medioevo: Late Medieval Venice/Economia e società: Economy and Society*, ed. Luca Molà, Michael Knapton, and Luciano Pezzolo (Rome, 2021), 125–6.
84. Reinhold C. Mueller, "Les prêteurs juifs de Venise au Moyen Âge," in Mueller, *Venezia nel tardo Medioevo*, 307–33; Benjamin Ravid, "The Legal Status of the Jews of Venice to 1509," *Proceedings of the American Academy for Jewish Research* 54 (1987):169–202.
85. Stanley Chojnacki, "La formazione della nobiltà dopo la Serrata," *SVOC* 3: 700–04.
86. Molà, *La communità*, 55–6.
87. For the names of these families, see Robert Finlay, *Politics in Renaissance Venice* (New Brunswick, 1980), 92, n. 110.
88. For both quotes, see Chojnacki, "La formazione della nobiltà," 690.
89. Chojnacki, "La formazione della nobiltà," 715.
90. Finlay, *Politics in Renaissance Venice*, 92, n. 110.
91. Rafaino de Caresini, *Chronica AA. 1343–1388*, ed. Ester Pastorello, *Rerum Italicarum Scriptores*, 2nd series 12, pt. 2 (Bologna, 1922), 58.
92. Orlando, *Venezia e il mare*, 124.
93. Dennis Romano, "Charity and Community in Early Renaissance Venice," *Journal of Urban History* 11 (1984): 63–82; Romano, *Patricians and Popolani*, 119–58.

CHAPTER 10

1. Latin text and translation in Julie E. Cumming, "Music for the Doge in Early Renaissance Venice," *Speculum* 67 (1992): 336. I follow her translation with minor variations.

2. Cited in Dennis Romano, *The Likeness of Venice: A Life of Doge Francesco Foscari, 1373–1457* (New Haven, 2007), 30.
3. Kohl, *Padua Under the Carrara*, 224–69.
4. Kohl, *Padua Under the Carrara*, 318–29.
5. Kohl, *Padua Under the Carrara*, 329–34.
6. Kohl, *Padua Under the Carrara*, 335.
7. For the environment, see Gullino, *Storia della repubblica veneta*, 62–3.
8. Michael E. Mallett, "La conquista della terraferma," *SVOC* 4: 189–90.
9. Gaetano Cozzi and Michael Knapton, *Storia della Repubblica di Venezia: dalla Guerra di Chioggia alla riconquista della terraferma* (Turin, 1986), 22–3.
10. Giuseppe Gullino, "Le frontiere navali," *SVOC* 4: 30–1. Also Camillo Manfroni, "La battaglia di Gallipoli e la politica veneta-turca (1381–1420), *AT* 25, no. 2 (1902): 3–34 and 129–69.
11. An excerpt in Romanin, *Storia documentata*, 4: 54–6. See also Manfroni, "La battaglia," 147.
12. Gullino, *Storia della repubblica veneta*, 90.
13. For this and what follows, James S. Grubb, *Firstborn of Venice: Vicenza in the Early Renaissance State* (Baltimore, 1988).
14. Grubb, *Firstborn of Venice*, 119.
15. Grubb, *Firstborn of Venice*, 154–5.
16. Giuseppe Gullino, "L'evoluzione costituzionale," *SVOC* 4: 362–3.
17. For the full epitaphs, see Romano, *Likeness of Venice*, 15, 34.
18. Grubb, *Firstborn of Venice*, 14.
19. Grubb, *Firstborn of Venice*, 17.
20. Grubb, *Firstborn of Venice*, 26.
21. Grubb, *Firstborn of Venice*, 27.
22. Gherardo Ortalli, Oliver Jens Schmitt, and Ermanno Orlando, eds., *Il* Commonwealth *veneziano tra 1204 e la fine della Repubblica: identità e peculiarità* (Venice, 2015).
23. Romano, *Likeness of Venice*, 64–8.
24. Romano, *Likeness of Venice*, 68–70.
25. Romano, *Likeness of Venice*, 70–4.
26. Antonio Battistella, *Il conte Carmagnola: studio storico con documenti inediti* (Genoa, 1889), 310.
27. Romano, *Likeness of Venice*, 98–102.
28. ASV, SS, register 12, fols. 52v–53r (December 28, 1431).
29. Marin Sanudo il Giovane, *Le vite dei dogi: 1423–1474, I tomo (1423–1457)*, ed. Angela Caracciolo Aricò (Padua, 1999), 590–91.
30. Andrea Nanetti, ed., *Il codice Morosini: il mondo visto da Venezia (1094–1433)*, 4 vols. (Spoleto, 2010), 3: 1592.
31. Michael E. Mallett and John R. Hale, *The Military Organization of a Renaissance State: Venice c. 1400 to 1617* (Cambridge, 1984), 153–80.

32. Mallett and Hale, *Military Organization*, 37.
33. Romano, *Likeness of Venice*, 119–28.
34. Romano, *Likeness of Venice*, 132–41.
35. Sanudo, *Le vite dei dogi, tome 1*, 291–2; Mallett and Hale, *Military Organization*, 98–9.
36. Romano, *Likeness of Venice*, 154–8.
37. BNM, It. Cl. VII 794 (8503), Zorzi (Giorgio) Dolfin, "Cronica," fols. 387v–388r. [Hereafter Dolfin, "Cronica."]
38. Romano, *Likeness of Venice*, 158–60, 168–71.
39. Cited in *Storia di Milano*, vol. 6, *Il Ducato Visconteo e la Repubblica Ambrosiana (1392–1450)* (Milan, 1955), 416.
40. Romano, *Likeness of Venice*, 205–11, 224–8.
41. Romano, *Likeness of Venice*, 255–61.
42. Giovanni Soranzo, *La lega italica (1454–1455)* (Milan, 1924), 123–67; Garrett Mattingly, *Renaissance Diplomacy* (Boston, 1955), 76–7; Giovanni Pillinini, *Il sistema degli stati italiani, 1454–1494* (Venice, 1970), 38–59.
43. Alan Ryder, *Alfonso the Magnanimous: King of Aragon, Naples and Sicily (1396–1458)* (Oxford, 1990), 290.
44. Cessi, *Storia della Repubblica*, 391.
45. Mueller, *Venetian Money Market*, 464–8; 528–9; Luciano Pezzolo, "La finanza pubblica: dal prestito all'imposta," *SVOC* 5: 703–14.
46. Pierre Sardella, *Nouvelles et spéculations a Venise au début du XVIe siècle* (Paris, 1948), 56–7.
47. ASV, MC, Deliberazioni, register 22, fol. 78v (May 17, 1428).
48. Dolfin, "Cronica," fol. 363v. For the conspiracy, Romano, *Likeness of Venice*, 109–13.
49. ASV, SM, register 55, fol. 102r (March 24, 1425).
50. ASV, SM, register 56, fol. 120v (August 20, 1427).
51. Stöckly, *Le système de l'incanto*, 93–176; Lane, *Venice: A Maritime Republic*, 337–42; Bernard Doumerc, "Il dominio del mare," *SVOC* 4: 143–5.
52. Maurizio Scarpari, "Alcune osservazioni su una moneta veneziana del XV secolo trovata a Canton," *SV* n.s. 3 (1979): 343–50.
53. ASV, SS, register 8, fol. 111v (July 7, 1423).
54. Sanudo, *Vite dei dogi, I tomo*, 25.
55. Romano, *Likeness of Venice*, 57–61, 85–6; Nicol, *Byzantium and Venice*, 373.
56. Nichol, *Byzantium and Venice*, 384.
57. Nichol, *Byzantium and Venice*, 381–9.
58. For what follows, Nichol, *Byzantium and Venice*, 391–407; Romano, *Likeness of Venice*, 23–44.
59. Dolfin, "Cronica," fol. 434v; Mueller, *Venetian Money Market*, 212–3.
60. Dolfin, "Cronica," fols. 434r-v.
61. ASV, SMar, register 4, fol. 201v (July 12, 1453).
62. Sanudo, *Vite dei dogi, I tomo*, 487.
63. Cozzi and Knapton, *Storia della Repubblica*, 118.

64. ASV, MC, Deliberazioni, register 22, fol. 56r. Giovanni Fiastri, "L'assemblea del popolo a Venezia come organo costituzionale dello stato," *NAV* 25 (1913):5–48.
65. Cozzi and Knapton, *Storia della Repubblica*, 100–1.
66. Stanley Chojnacki, "Social Identity in Renaissance Venice: The Second *Serrata*," *Renaissance Studies* 8 (1994): 358.
67. Chojnacki, "Social Identity," 343–50.
68. Chojnacki, "Social Identity," 350–1.
69. Chojnacki, "Social Identity," 351–2.
70. Paul F. Grendler, "The Organization of Primary and Secondary Education in the Italian Renaissance," *Catholic Historical Review* 71 (1985): 185–205.
71. ASV, SS, register 14, fols. 29v-30r, 51r, 74v (acts dated April 9, August 11, and November 26, 1437).
72. ASV, Avogaria di Comun, Raspe, register 3638, fols. 47r-48r.
73. Stanley Chojnacki, *Women and Men in Renaissance Venice: Twelve Essays on Patrician Society* (Baltimore, 2000), 227–43.
74. Chojnacki, *Women and Men*, 195.
75. Finlay, *Politics in Renaissance Venice*, 125.
76. Dolfin, "Cronica," fol. 448v.
77. Chojnacki, *Women and Men*, 249.
78. Guido Ruggiero, *The Boundaries of Eros: Sex Crime and Sexuality in Renaissance Venice* (New York, 1985), 109–45. For the dinner-party restriction, ASV, DM, register 14, fol. 197v.
79. Chojnacki, *Women and Men*, 244–56.
80. Richard J. Goy, *The House of Gold: Building a Palace in Medieval Venice* (Cambridge, 1992).
81. Frederic C. Lane, *Andrea Barbarigo: Merchant of Venice, 1418–1449* (Baltimore, 1944).
82. Chojnacki, *Women and Men*, 132–52.
83. Her will is found in ASV, NT, busta 946, will number 132, dated September 15,1411.
84. ASV, PSM de Citra, busta 269bis, Commissaria of Marin Contarini, loose parchment dated May 28, 1417.
85. ASV, DM, register 11, fol. 53v.
86. Romano, *Likeness of Venice*, 137–8.
87. For a non-noble example, Maria Francesca Tiepolo, ed., *Domenico prete di S. Maurizio: notaio in Venezia (1309–1316)* (Venice, 1970), 159–60 (act 204).
88. ASV, NT, busta 797 (notary Tomaso Pavoni), will n. 270.
89. Romano, *Likeness of Venice*, 148–9.
90. Gino Fogolari, "Iacobello del Fiore e la sua famiglia (nuovi documenti)," *AV* 5th series, 34–5 (1944): 33–50.
91. Bartolomeo's will in ASV, NT, Busta 821 (notary Rosso), n. 24.
92. Monticolo, *Capitolari delle arti veneziane*, 2: 482.
93. ASV, DM, register 8, fol. 31v.

94. Michele Caffi, "Giacomello del Fiore: pittore veneziano del sec. XV," *Archivio Storico Italiano* 4th ser. 6 (1880): 412.
95. Romano, *Patricians and Popolani*, 56–63.
96. Linda Guzzetti, "Donne e scrittura a Venezia nel tardo Trecento," *AV* 5th ser. 152 (1999): 24.
97. Romano, *Housecraft and Statecraft*, 165, 200.
98. Dennis Romano, "The Gondola as a Marker of Station in Venetian Society," *Renaissance Studies* 8 (1994): 371.
99. Romano, *Housecraft and Statecraft*, 218–20.
100. ASV, SM, register 42, fol. 136r. Also discussed in Barker, *Most Precious Merchandise*, 169. She uses, however, the old pagination for the register.
101. ASV, DM, register 15, fols. 23v–24r.
102. Paula C. Clarke, "The Business of Prostitution in Early Renaissance Venice," *RQ* 68 (2015): 454, n. 146.
103. J. R. Spencer, "The Ca' del Duca in Venice and Benedetto Ferini," *Journal of the Society of Architectural Historians* 29 (1970): 5.
104. Dean, "Venetian Economic Hegemony," 81.
105. Clarke, "Business of Prostitution," 449–50.
106. Pamela O. Long, David McGee, and Alan M. Stahl, eds., *The Book of Michael of Rhodes: A Fifteenth-Century Maritime Manuscript*, 3 vols. (Cambridge, MA, 2009).
107. Long, McGee, and Stahl, *Book of Michael of Rhodes*, 2: 616–7.
108. King, *Venetian Humanism*. For their use of anti-Semitic tropes, see Stephen Bowd, "Civic Piety and Patriotism: Patrician Humanists and Jews in Venice and its Empire," *RQ* 69 (2016): 1257–95.
109. King, *Venetian Humanism*, 94.
110. King, *Venetian Humanism*, 94.
111. See the translation of the second half of the treatise, in Benjamin G. Kohl and Ronald G. Witt, eds., *The Earthly Republic: Italian Humanists on Government and Society* (Philadelphia, 1978), 189–228, quote 192.
112. Kohl and Witt, *Earthly Republic*, 196; King, *Venetian Humanism*, 96.
113. Kohl and Witt, *Earthly Republic*, 216.
114. Margaret L. King, "Caldiera and the Barbaros on Marriage and the Family: Humanist Reflections on Venetian Realities," *Journal of Medieval and Renaissance Studies* 6 (1976): 19–50; Chojnacki, *Women and Men*, 244–56.
115. King, *Venetian Humanism*, 122.
116. King, *Venetian Humanism*, 123.
117. King, *Venetian Humanism*, 137. The second quotation contains King's words, not Morosini's.
118. King, *Venetian Humanism*, 129.
119. King, *Venetian Humanism*, 116.

120. King, *Venetian Humanism*, 111.
121. Giambattista Lorenzi, *Monumenti per servire alla storia del palazzo ducale di Venezia ovvero serie di atti pubblici dal 1253 al 1797, pt. 1: dal 1253 al 1600* (Venice, 1868), 58–9.
122. Howard, *Architectural History*, 90–6.
123. Howard, *Architectural History*, 103–6; Goy, *House of Gold*.
124. Romano, *Likeness of Venice*, 245–53.
125. Sanudo, *De origine, situ et magistratibus*, 20–1; John Ruskin, *The Stones of Venice*, 3 vols. (New York, 1860), 3: 309.
126. Rosand, *Myths of Venice*, 19–36.
127. John Steer, *A Concise History of Venetian Painting* (New York, 1970), 36–41.
128. For what follows, see Romano, *Likeness of Venice*.
129. Luzzatto, *I prestiti*, clv–clvi.
130. Dolfin, "Cronica," fols. 402r-v.
131. Dolfin, "Cronica," fols. 444r-v.
132. ASV, DM, register 15, fol. 139v (October 21, 1457).
133. Dolfin "Cronica," fol. 448v.
134. Dolfin, "Cronica," fols. 448v-449r.
135. Bernardo Giustiniano, "Orazione recitata da Bernardo Giustiniano nell'esequie del doge Francesco Foscari," in *Orazioni, elogi e vite scritte da letterati veneti patrizi in lode di dogi, ed altri illustri soggetti*, ed. Girolamo Ascanio Molin, 2nd ed., 2 vols. (Venice, 1798): 2: 53–4.
136. ASV, DM, register 15, fols. 163r-v (acts dated October 25, 1458).
137. ASV, MC, Deliberazioni, register 23, fols. 82v–83r (September 18, 1468).

CHAPTER 11

1. Marino Sanudo, *Itinerario per la Terraferma veneziana*, ed. Gian Maria Varanini (Rome, 2014), 330.
2. Cited in Nicolai Rubinstein, "Italian Reactions to Terraferma Expansion in the Fifteenth Century," *RV*, 206.
3. Molly Greene, "The Early Modern Mediterranean," in *A Companion to Mediterranean History*, ed. Peregrine Horden and Sharon Kinoshita (Chichester, West Sussex, 2014), 96–8.
4. Soranzo, *L'antico navigabile Po*, 92.
5. Pius II, *Memoirs of a Renaissance Pope: The Commentaries of Pius II: An Abridgment*, ed. Leona C. Gabel, trans. Florence A. Gragg (New York, 1959), 304. A new translation of the complete commentaries is being published by Margaret Meserve and Marcello Simonetta in the series *The I Tatti Renaissance Library* by Harvard University Press.
6. Pius II, *Memoirs of a Renaissance Pope*, 301–2.

7. ASV, SMar, register 7, fol. 79v, 20 August 1462; Ennio Concina, *Tempo novo: Venezia e il Quattrocento* (Venice, 2006), 179. Note, however, that Concina's archival reference for the fortification repairs (n. 231) is incorrect. I have been unable to locate the original Senate deliberation.
8. The wars consumed the years 1463–79, 1499–1503, 1537–1540, 1570–1573, 1645–1669, 1684–1699, and 1714–1718. Three earlier conflicts took place in 1416–9, 1422–30, and 1444 (the Crusade of Varna). For the political narrative of the Venetian-Ottoman war, see the essays in *SVOC* 4 by Giuseppe Gullino, "Le frontiere navali" (13–111), Bernard Doumerc, "Il dominio del mare" (113–180), Michael E. Mallett, "La conquista della Terraferma" (181–244), and Michael E. Mallett, "Venezia e la politica italiana, 1454–1530" (245–310); and Romanin, *Storia documentata*, 4: 223–370. See also Franz Babinger, *Mehmed the Conquerer and His Time* (Princeton, 1978), and for the role of the Balkans, James D. Tracy, *Balkan Wars: Habsburg Croatia, Ottoman Bosnia, and Venetian Dalmatia, 1499–1617* (Lanham, MD, 2016), 29–49.
9. Concina, *Tempo novo*, 43.
10. The letter by Girolamo Longo is reported in Domenico Malipiero, *Annali veneti dall'anno 1457 al 1500*, 2 vols. *Archivio Storico Italiano* 7 (1843–4): 1: 51. See also Margaret Meserve, "News from Negroponte: Politics, Popular Opinion, and Information Exchange in the First Decade of the Italian Press," *RQ* 59(2006): 440–80.
11. Malipiero, *Annali veneti*,1: 58–9.
12. Gullino, "Le frontiere navali," 71.
13. Coriolano Cippico, *The Deeds of Commander Pietro Mocenigo in Three Books*, trans. Kiril Petkov (New York, 2014), 44.
14. Malipiero, *Annali veneti*, 1: 120.
15. Elizabeth Rodini, *Gentile Bellini's Portrait of Sultan Mehmed II: Lives and Afterlives of an Iconic Image* (London, 2020).
16. Babinger, *Mehmed the Conquerer*, 213–4.
17. Cited in Mallett and Hale, *Military Organization*, 83.
18. Mallett and Hale, *Military Organization*, 91.
19. Lane, *Venetian Ships*, 137–45; Concina, *L'Arsenale della Repubblica di Venezia*, 65–83.
20. Lane, *Venetian Ships*, 139.
21. Malipiero, *Annali veneti*, 1: 66.
22. Luciano Pezzolo, "La finanza pubblica," *SVOC* 5: 713–9.
23. For an English translation of the enabling legislation, see David Chambers and Brian Pullan, eds., *Venice: A Documentary History, 1450–1630* reprint (Toronto, 2001), 137–9.
24. Malipiero, *Annali veneti*, 1: 108.
25. Mallett, "Venezia e la politica italiana," 259.
26. For the War with Ferrara, Romanin, *Storia documentata*, 4: 292–304; Soranzo, *L'antico navigabile Po*, 78–86; Michael E. Mallett, "Venice and the War of Ferrara,

1482–84," in *War, Culture and Society in Renaissance Venice: Essays in Honour of John Hale*, ed. David S. Chambers, Cecil H. Clough, and Michael E. Mallett (London, 1993), 57–72; Trevor Dean, "After the War of Ferrara: Relations Between Venice and Ercole d'Este, 1484–1505," in *War, Culture and Society in Renaissance Venice: Essays in Honour of John Hale*, 73–98.

27. Malipiero, *Annali veneti*, 1: 257.
28. Cited in Romanin, *Storia documentata*, 4: 295.
29. Mallett and Hale, *Military Organization*, 209.
30. Romanin, *Storia documentata*, 4: 309–13; Cozzi and Knapton, *Storia della Repubblica*, 71; Philippe Braunstein, "Les entreprises minières en vénétie au XVe siècle," *Melanges d'Archéologie et d'Histoire de l'École Française de Rome* 77 (1965): 529–607.
31. For what follows: Holly Hurlburt, *Daughter of Venice: Caterina Corner, Queen of Cyprus and Woman of the Renaissance* (New Haven, 2015).
32. Hurlburt, *Daughter of Venice*, 85.
33. Hurlburt, *Daughter of Venice*, 105.
34. Hurlburt, *Daughter of Venice*, 110.
35. Giuseppe Gullino, "Corner, Marco," *DBI* 29 (1983): 255–57.
36. For the following narrative, see Romanin, *Storia documentata*, 5: 7–110; Cozzi and Knapton, *Storia della Repubblica*, 73–86; Innocenzo Cervelli, *Machiavelli e la crisi dello stato veneziano* (Naples, 1974); Gullino, "Le frontiere navali," 86–95; Mallett, "Venezia e la politica italiana," 276–82.
37. Malipiero, *Annali veneti*, 1: 329.
38. Cited in Cozzi and Knapton, *Storia della Repubblica*, 79.
39. For the fleet size, see Frederic C. Lane, "Naval Actions and Fleet Organization, 1499–1502," *RV*, 149. For slightly larger estimates of both fleets, see Ovidia Cristea, "Venice Confronting the Ottoman Empire: A Struggle for Survival," in *The Ottoman Conquest of the Balkans: Interpretations and Research Debates*, ed. Oliver Jens Schmitt (Vienna, 2016), 273.
40. Malipiero, *Annali veneti*, 1: 179.
41. Malipiero, *Annali veneti*, 1: 182. Alfredo Viggiano, "Il processo al capitano generale da mar Antonio Grimani," in *Les procès politiques (XIVe–XVIIe siècle)*, ed. Yves-Marie Bercé, 251–72 (Rome, 2007).
42. Francesco Savorgnan di Brazza, "Leonardo da Vinci in Friuli e il suo progetto di fortificazione dell'Isonzo," *Atti della Accademia di Udine* 5th series, vol. 13 (1933-4): 5–21.
43. Lane, "Naval Action," 146–73.
44. "Point of no return," see Orlando, *Venezia e il mare*, 184; "lost its maritime supremacy," see Lane, "Naval Actions and Fleet Organization," 146.
45. Girolamo Priuli, *I diarii di Girolamo Priuli*, ed. Arturo Segre and Roberto Cessi, *Rerum Italicarum Scriptores*, 2nd series, tome 24, pt. 3 in 4 vols. (Città di Castello and Bologna, 1921-41), 2: 153–7.

46. Priuli, *Diarii*, 2: 242.
47. The commission was originally to Francesco Teldi and is published in Romanin, *Storia documentata*, 4: 388–91. However, the commission eventually went to Giova. See R. Fulin, "Il canale di Suez e la Republica di Venezia (MDIV)," *AV* 2 (1871): 194.
48. For a transcript of the deleted instructions, Fulin, "Il canale di Suez," 195–6. Apparently, they had considered the idea previously as well.
49. Frederic C. Lane, "The Mediterranean Spice Trade: Its Revival in the Sixteenth Century," in Lane, *Venice and History*, 25–34; Lane, *Venice: A Maritime Republic*, 290–92.
50. For what follows, Ugo Tucci, "Mercanti, viaggiatori, pellegrini nel Quattrocento," *SCUV*, 3/II: 335–53; Ugo Tucci, "Da Mosto (Cadamosto, Ca' da Mosto), Alvise," *DBI* 32 (1986): 369–73; Ugo Tucci, "Caboto," *DBI* 15 (1972): 702–23; Evan T. Jones and Margaret M. Condon, *Cabot and Bristol's Age of Discovery: The Bristol Discovery Voyages, 1480–1508* (Bristol, 2016).
51. Cited in Tenenti, "Venetian Sense of Time and Space," 29.
52. As cited in Tucci, "Da Mosto (Cadamosto, Ca' da Mosto), Alvise," 372.
53. Cited in Tucci, "Mercanti, viaggiatori", 347.
54. Elizabeth Horodowich, *The Venetian Discovery of America: Geographic Imagination and Print Culture in the Age of Encounters* (Cambridge, 2018).
55. Judde de Larivière, *Naviguer, commercer*.
56. Judde de Larivière, *Naviguer, commercer*, 83.
57. Priuli, *Diarii*, 4: 48–55.
58. Lane, *Venetian Ships and Shipbuilders*, 41.
59. Lane, *Venetian Ships and Shipbuilders*, 28.
60. Doumerc, "Il dominio del mare,"175; Judde de Larivière, *Naviguer, commercer*, 140–3.
61. Cited in Bernard Doumerc, "La crise structurelle de la marine vénitienne au XVe siècle: le problème du retard des Mude," *Annales ESC* 40 (1985): 616.
62. Claire Judde de Larivière, "The 'Public' and the 'Private' in Sixteenth-Century Venice: From Medieval Economy to Early Modern State," *Historical Social Research/Historische Sozialforschung* 37 (2012): 85.
63. Mallett and Hall, *Military Organization*, 64.
64. Cited in Romanin, *Storia documentata*, 5: 136.
65. Cozzi and Knapton, *Storia della Repubblica*, 91.
66. Marino Sanuto, *I diarii di Marino Sanuto*, ed. Rinaldo Fulin et al., 58 vols. (Venice, 1879-1903), 8: 117.
67. Sanuto, *Diarii*, 8: 248.
68. Sanuto, *Diarii*, 8: 266.
69. "dove in una sola battaglia persero quello che in ottocento anni, con tanta fatica, avevano acquistato." Niccolò Machiavelli, *Il principe*, ch. 12. And see Cervelli, *Machiavelli e la crisi*, 331–41.

70. The Senate law is printed in Sanuto, *Diarii*, 14: 420–1.
71. Romanin, *Storia documentata*, 5: 168–9.
72. The letter is recorded in Sanudo, *Diarii*, 17: 183–6. On the sound of artillery, Sanudo, *Diarii*, 17: 147.
73. James R. Jewitt, "Liberty on the Lagoon: Venetian Images of the Red Sea, 1480–1530," in *Formations of Identity: Society, Politics, and Landscape*, ed. Floyd Martin and Eileen Yanoviak (Newcastle upon Tyne, 2016), 1–2.
74. Sanuto, *Diarii*, 51: 322. The translation is from Elisabeth G. Gleason, "Confronting New Realities: Venice and the Peace of Bologna, 1530," *VR*, 175. See also Robert Finlay, "Fabius Maximus in Venice: Doge Andrea Gritti, the War of Cambrai, and the Rise of Hapsburg Hegemony, 1509–1530," *RQ* 53 (2000): 1004.
75. Finlay, "Fabius Maximus in Venice."
76. Quoted in Gleason, "Confronting New Realities," 177–8.
77. Gleason, "Confronting New Realities, 178.
78. Gleason, "Confronting New Realities," 179–80.
79. Mallett and Hale, *Military Organization*, 215.
80. For the chroniclers and their motivations, Christiane Neerfeld, *'Historia per la forma di diaria': la cronachistica veneziana contemporanea a cavallo tra il Quattro e il Cinquecento* (Venice, 2006).
81. Cited in Finlay, *Politics in Renaissance Venice*, 120.
82. Concina, *History of Venetian Architecture*, 146.
83. The tomb no longer exists. For the classical references, David S. Chambers, *The Imperial Age of Venice, 1380–1580* (London, 1970), 26; for the tomb inscription, Filippo Nani-Mocenigo, "Testamento del Doge Agostino Barbarigo," *NAV* n.s. 17 (1909): 241.
84. Sanuto, *Diarii*, 4: 181–4. Parts are translated in Chambers and Pullan, *Venice: A Documentary History*, 73–4.
85. Gaetano Cozzi, "Authority and the Law in Renaissance Venice," *RV*, 302–3.
86. Michelangelo Muraro, "La scala senza giganti," in *De artibus opuscula XL: Essays in Honor of Erwin Panofsky*, ed. Millard Meiss (New York, 1961), 350–70.
87. Mario Brunetti, "Il doge non è 'segno di taverna,'" *NAV* 33 (1917): 351–55.
88. Cited in Finlay, *Politics in Renaissance Venice*, 112; Mario Brunetti, "Due dogi sotto inchiesta: Agostino Barbarigo e Leonardo Loredan," *Archivio Veneto-Tridentino* 7 (1925): 278–329.
89. Sanuto, *Diarii*, 50: 149.
90. Finlay, *Politics in Renaissance Venice*, 26.
91. Finlay, *Politics in Renaissance Venice*, 124–41.
92. Sanudo, *De origine, situ et magistratibus*, 146.
93. Andrea Zannini, "L'impiego pubblico," *SVOC* 4: 438.
94. Contarini, *The Republic of Venice*, 21–8.
95. Finlay, *Politics in Renaissance Venice*, 207–8.
96. Donald E. Queller, *The Venetian Patriciate: Reality Versus Myth* (Urbana, 1986), 51–112; Finlay, *Politics in Renaissance Venice*, 196–226.

97. Malipiero, *Annali veneti*, 2: 704; also cited and translated in Finlay, *Politics in Renaissance Venice*, 204.
98. Sanuto, *Diarii*, 54: 7.
99. Finlay, *Politics in Renaissance Venice*, 200–1.
100. Cited in Finlay, *Politics in Renaissance Venice*, 219.
101. Finlay, *Politics in Renaissance Venice*, 208–15; Romano, *Housecraft and Statecraft*, 54–9.
102. Finlay, *Politics in Renaissance Venice*, 202.
103. Cited in Finlay, *Politics in Renaissance Venice*, 205.
104. Cited in Felix Gilbert, "Venice in the Crisis of the League of Cambrai," *RV*, 278.
105. Gilbert, "Venice in the Crisis," 279. See also Giulio Bistort, *Il magistrato alle pompe nella Republica di Venezia: studio storico* (Venice, 1912).
106. Sanuto, *Diarii*, 21: 425–6. See also G. B. Cavalcaselle and J. A. Crowe, *Tiziano, la sua vita e i suoi tempi con alcune notizie della sua famiglia*, 2 vols. (Florence, 1877-8), 2: 130–2.
107. Sanuto, *Diarii*, 20: 446. Also cited in Finlay, *Politics in Renaissance Venice*, 173.
108. The words are Gilbert's. Gilbert, "Venice in the Crisis," 285.
109. Cited in Cozzi, "Authority and the Law," 308. The doge and six ducal councillors often met with the Ten, hence the 17 "pillars."
110. Cited in Cozzi, "Authority and the Law," 333.
111. Cozzi, "Authority and the Law," 333.
112. Stanley Chojnacki, "Identity and Ideology in Renaissance Venice: The Third *Serrata*," *VR*, 267.
113. Chojnacki, "Identity and Ideology," 280.
114. Chojnacki, "Identity and Ideology," 282.
115. Chojnacki, "Identity and Ideology," 281.

CHAPTER 12

1. For the view, see Juergen Schulz, "Jacopo de' Barbari's View of Venice: Map Making, City Views, and Moralized Geography Before the Year 1500," *Art Bulletin* 60 (1978): 425–74; also the essays in Giandomenico Romanelli et al., eds., *A volo d'uccello: Jacopo de' Barbari e le rappresentazioni di città nell'Europa del Rinascimento* (Venice, 1999), especially, Giuseppe Trassari Filippetto, "Tecnica xilografica tra Quattrocento e Cinquecento: 'Il nuovo stile,'" 53–57; and Bronwen Wilson, *The World in Venice: Print, the City, and Early Modern Identity* (Toronto, 2005), 23–69.
2. Schulz, "Jacopo de' Barbari's View," 468, 473.
3. The phrase is from Sanudo, *Diarii*, 29: 567.
4. Schulz, "Jacopo de' Barbari's View," 473. I follow the translation in Chambers and Pullan, *Venice: A Documentary History*, 373.
5. Claire Judde de Larivière, *La révolte des boules de neige: Murano face à Venise, 1511* (Paris, 2014).

6. Luca Molà, *The Silk Industry of Renaissance Venice* (Baltimore, 2000), 189.
7. Walter Panciera, *L'arte matrice: i lanifici della Repubblica di Venezia nei secoli XVII e XVIII* (Treviso, 1996); Andrea Mozzato, ed., *La mariegola dell'arte della lana di Venezia (1244–1595)*, 2 vols. (Venice, 2002).
8. Andrea Mozzato, "The Production of Woolens in Fifteenth- and Sixteenth-Century Venice," in *At the Centre of the Old World*, ed. Lanaro, 80–1. For the size of a bolt, see Panciera, *L'arte matrice*, 367 (under definition of *panni alti*). The standard for silk was similar with bolts running 95 to 114 feet in length in the fifteenth century but growing to between 125 and 146 feet in length by the 1530s (personal communication from Luca Molà).
9. Domenico Sella, "The Rise and Fall of the Venetian Woolen Industry," in *Crisis and Change in the Venetian Economy*, ed. Brian Pullan (London, 1968), 109–10.
10. Mozzato, "Production of Woolens," 85.
11. Cited in Edoardo Demo, "Wool and Silk. The Textile Urban Industry of the Venetian Mainland (15th–17th Centuries), in *At the Centre of the Old World*, ed. Lanaro, 220.
12. Molà, *Silk Industry*, 220.
13. Molà, *Silk Industry*, 236.
14. Molà, *Silk Industry*, 90–1.
15. Luca Molà, "Venetian Luxury Gifts for the Ottoman Empire in the Late Renaissance," in *Global Gifts: The Material Culture of Diplomacy in Early Modern Eurasia*, ed. Zoltán Biedermann, Anne Gerritsen, and Giorgio Riello (Cambridge, 2018), 59.
16. Molà, *Silk Industry*, 96–105.
17. Molà, *Silk Industry*, 267.
18. Salvatore Ciriacono, "Industria e artigianato," *SVOC* 5: 550–2.
19. Molà, *Silk Industry*, 113.
20. Molà, *Silk Industry*, 107–37.
21. Ciriacono, "Industria e artigianato," 557.
22. Molmenti, S*toria di Venezia nella vita privata*, 2: 172.
23. For the bibliography of the Arsenal, see Antonio Lazzarini, *Boschi, legnami, costruzioni navali: l'Arsenale di Venezia fra XVI e XVIII secolo* (Rome, 2021), 22, n. 22.
24. Franco Rossi, "L'Arsenale: i quadri direttivi," *SVOC* 5: 593–639; Lane, *Venetian Ships and Shipbuilders*, 146–75.
25. Lane, *Venetian Ships and Shipbuilders*, 161–3.
26. Ciriacono, "Industria e artigianato," *SVOC* 5: 540.
27. Lane, *Venetian Ships and Shipbuilders*, 166.
28. Lane, *Venetian Ships and Shipbuilders*, 242.
29. See Pero Tafur, *Travels and Adventures, 1435–1438*, ed. and trans. Malcolm Letts (London, 1926), 170. For clarity I have made a few modifications to the translation.

30. Robert C. Davis, *Shipbuilders of the Venetian Arsenal: Workers and Workplace in the Preindustrial Age* (Baltimore, 1991).
31. Lane, *Venetian Ships and Shipbuilders*, 243.
32. Lane, *Venetian Ships and Shipbuilders*, 117, 120.
33. Ciriacono, "Industria e artigianato," 561–2; Victoria Avery, *Vulcan's Forge in Venus's City: The Story of Bronze in Venice, 1350–1650* (Oxford, 2011).
34. Ciriacono, "Industria e artigianato," 562–79.
35. Ciriacono, "Industria e artigianato," 567.
36. Franco Brunello, *Arti e mestieri a Venezia nel Medioevo e Rinascimento* (Vicenza, 1980), 178–9.
37. Louisa C. Matthew, "Were there Open Markets for Pictures in Renaissance Venice?," in *The Art Market in Italy 15th–17th Centuries: il mercato dell'arte in Italia secc. XV–XVII*, ed. Marcello Fantoni, Louisa C. Matthew, and Sara F. Matthews-Grieco (Modena, 2003), 255; Julia A. DeLancey, "'In the Streets Where They Sell Colors:' Placing *Vendicolori* in the Urban Fabric of Early Modern Venice," *Wallraf-Richartz-Jahrbuch* 72 (2011): 193–232.
38. Francesca Trivellato, "Murano Glass, Continuity and Transformation (1400–1800), in *At the Centre of the Old World*, ed. Lanaro, 50. See generally, Luigi Zecchin, *Vetro e vetrai di Murano: studi sulla storia del vetro*, 3 vols. (Venice, 1987–1990).
39. Trivellato, "Murano Glass," 151.
40. David Jacoby, "Raw Materials for the Glass Industries of Venice and the Terraferma: About 1370–about 1460," *Journal of Glass Studies* 35 (1993): 75.
41. Jacoby, "Raw Materials," 70.
42. Jacoby, "Raw Materials," 89.
43. Pietro Casola, *Viaggio a Gerusalemme di Pietro Casola*, ed. Anna Paoletti (Alessandria, 2001), 98.
44. Michael L. Kunz and Robin O. Mills, "A Precolumbian Presence of Venetian Glass Trade Beads in Arctic Alaska," *American Antiquity* 86 (2021), 395–412.
45. Ciriacono, "Industria e artigianato," 569.
46. Benjamin Arbel, "The Last Decades of Venice's Trade with the Mamluks: Importations into Egypt and Syria," *Mamluk Studies Review* 8 (2004): 56–8.
47. For the glass cargo from one shipwreck, see Astone Gasparetto, "The Gnalič Wreck: Identification of the Ship," *Journal of Glass Studies* 15 (1973): 79–84; Irena Lazar and Hugh Willmott, *The Glass from the Gnalić Wreck* (Koper, 2006); Irena Lazar, "The Glass from the Gnalić Wreck and Its Glass Cargo," *Vjesnik za arheolgiju i historiju dalmatinsku Split: Arheološki muzei* 108 (2015): 1–13. It remains uncertain if all the glass was produced on Murano. For evidence of the wreck of a ship likely traveling from Constantinople to Venice around 1580, see Carlo Beltrame, Sauro Gelichi, and Igor Miholjek, *Sveti Pavao Shipwreck: A 16th Century Venetian Merchantman from Mljet, Croatia* (Oxford, 2014).
48. Ciriacono, "Industria e artigianato," 575.

49. For much of what follows, Marino Zorzi, "Dal manoscritto al libro," *SVOC* 4: 817–958.
50. Ivo Mattozzi, "Le radici, il tronco, e le diramazioni della produzione cartaria nella Valle delle Cartiere di Toscolano," *La Bibliofilia* 118 (2016): 394.
51. Peter Burke, "Early Modern Venice as a Center of Information and Communication," *VR*, 389–419.
52. Martin Lowry, *Nicholas Jenson and the Rise of Venetian Publishing in Renaissance Europe* (Oxford, 1991), 94.
53. Lowry, *Nicholas Jenson*, 83–5, 130.
54. Horatio F. Brown, *The Venetian Printing Press* (London, 1891), 25.
55. Lowry, *Nicholas Jenson*, 152.
56. Lowry, *Nicholas Jenson*, 165.
57. Zorzi, "Dal manoscritto," *SVOC* 829, 887.
58. Martin Lowry, *The World of Aldus Manutius: Business and Scholarship in Renaissance Venice* (Ithaca, 1979).
59. Zorzi, "Dal manoscritto," 911–2.
60. Zorzi, "Dal manoscritto," 918.
61. Zorzi, "Dal manoscritto," 929–30. For excerpts from the will, see Bartolomeo Cecchetti, "La pittura a stampa di Bernardino Benalio," *AV* n.s. 33, pt. 1 (1887): 538–9. For more on women as producers and consumers of printed material, Tiziana Plebani, "Ricami di ago e di inchiostro: una ricchezza per la città (XVI secolo), *AV* 6th series 3 (2012): 97–115.
62. Lowry, *World of Aldus Manutius*, 18–9.
63. Rosa Salzberg, *Ephemeral City: Cheap Print and Urban Culture in Renaissance Venice* (Manchester, 2014), 28.
64. Massimo Rospocher, "'In vituperium status veneti': The Case of Niccolò Zoppino," *The Italianist* 34 (2014): 349–61, quote on 351.
65. Vittore Branca, "L'umanesimo veneziano e l'arte del libro," *Revue des Études Italiennes* n.s. 27 (1981): 327.
66. Alfredo Viggiano, "Il Dominio da terra: politica e istituzioni," *SVOC* 4: 564–5. Alfredo Viggiano, *Governo e governati: legittimità del potere ed esercizio dell'autorità sovrana nello Stato veneto della prima età moderna* (Treviso, 1993), 225–6.
67. Sandra Toffolo, *Describing the City, Describing the State: Representations of Venice and the Venetian Terraferma in the Renaissance* (Leiden, 2020), 240; Jodi Cranston, *Green Worlds of Renaissance Venice* (University Park, PA, 2019), 2–3.
68. Appuhn, *Forest on the Sea*, 94.
69. Quoted in Lazzarini, *Boschi, legnami, costruzioni navali,* 11.
70. Appuhn, *Forest on the Sea*, 109, 111.
71. Appuhn, *Forest on the Sea*, 122, 139.
72. Appuhn, *Forest on the Sea*, 143.
73. Appuhn, *Forest on the Sea*, 205–6; Lazzarini, *Boschi, legnami, costruzioni navali*, 101.

74. Élisabeth Crouzet-Pavan, "La maturazione dello spazio urbano," *SVOC* 5 :43.
75. Crouzet-Pavan, "La maturazione," 37–45; Crouzet-Pavan, "Toward an Ecological Understanding," 49–53.
76. Salvatore Ciriacono, *Building on Water: Venice, Holland and the Construction of the European Landscape in Early Modern Times* (New York, 2006), 106–9; Appuhn, *Forest on the Sea*, 58–74.
77. Sanudo, *Diarii*, 12: 89.
78. Ciriacono, *Building on Water*, 116–7.
79. Emilio Menegazzo, "Alvise Cornaro: un veneziano del Cinquecento nella terraferma padovana," *SCUV* 3/II: 514–5; Ciriacono, *Building on Water*, 113–5.
80. Giuseppe Gullino, "Corner, Alvise," *DBI* 29 (1983): 142–6.
81. For the area of a Veronese *campo*, see Piergiovanni Mometto, *L'azienda agricola Barbarigo a Carpi* (Venice, 1992), 4.
82. Manfredo Tafuri, *Venice and the Renaissance*, trans. Jessica Levine (Cambridge, MA, 1989), 151–8.
83. Tafuri, *Venice and the Renaissance*, 142.
84. Tafuri, *Venice and the Renaissance*, 155–6.
85. Pietro Cangiano, "Dal magistrato del proprio al magistrato alle acque: competenze e giusrisdizione," in *Laguna, fiumi, lidi: cinque secoli di gestione delle acque nelle Venezie* (Fieso d'Artico, 1985), 877–86.
86. Ciriacono, *Building on Water*, 33.
87. ASV, DM, register 15, fol. 198r (February 27, 1459mv); Concina, *Tempo novo*, 35–6; P. D. A. Harvey, *The History of Topographical Maps: Symbols, Pictures and Surveys* (London, 1980), 58–61; quote from John Marino, "Administrative Mapping in the Italian States," in *Monarchs, Ministers and Maps: The Emergence of Cartography as a Tool of Government in Early Modern Europe*, ed. David Buisseret (Chicago, 1992), 6. The law is now transcribed and translated in Karen-edis Barzman, "Spatial Histories of Early Modern Borderlands: A Case Study of Novigrad in Venetian Dalmatia (16th–18th CS.) / Prostorna Povijest Ranonovovjekovnog Pograničnog Područja: Studija Slučaja Novigrada U Miletačoj Dalmaciji (16. – 18. ST.)," in *800 Years Since the Restoration of the Roman Tower and the First Appearance of Novigrad in Written Sources / 800 Godina od Obnove Rimske Kule i Prvog Spomena imena Novigrad u Pisanim Izvorima*, ed. Zlatko Begonja and Ante Uglešić (Zadar, 2021), 93, n. 15. Barzman notes that the decree apparently also pertained to the *stato da mar*.
88. Guido Zucconi, "Architettura e topografia delle istituzioni nei centri minori della Terraferma (XV e XVI secolo)," *SV* n.s. 17 (1989): 28; Viggiano, "Il Dominio da terra," 541–3.
89. Manfredo Tafuri, "'Renovatio urbis Venetiarum': il problema storiografico," in *"Renovatio Urbis": Venezia nell'età di Andrea Gritti (1523–1538)*, ed. Manfredo Tafuri (Rome, 1984), 18.
90. Ennio Concina, "Ampliar la città: spazio urbano, 'res publica' e architettura," *SVOC* 6: 255.

91. Michael Knapton, *Una repubblica di uomini: saggi di storia veneta*, ed. Andrea Gardi, Gian Maria Varanini, and Andrea Zannini (Udine, 2017), 248.
92. Tafuri, *Venice and the Renaissance*, 151.
93. Tafuri, *Venice and the Renaissance*, 146.
94. For ritual, see Muir, *Civic Ritual*; Federica Ambrosini, "Cerimonie, feste, lusso," *SVOC* 5: 441–520; Matteo Casini, *I gesti del principe: la festa politica a Firenze e Venezia in età rinascimentale* (Venice, 1996).
95. Muir, *Civic Ritual*, 223 -30.
96. Sanudo, *Diarii*, 56: 285–6; Muir, *Civic Ritual*, 227.
97. Muir, *Civic Ritual*, 156–81.
98. Lionello Venturi, "Le compagnie della calza (sec. XV–XVI)," *NAV* 16 (1908): 161–221; 17 (1909): 140–233; Matteo Casini, "The 'Company of the Hose': Youth and Courtly Culture in Europe, Italy and Venice," *SV* n.s. 63 (2011): 133–53.
99. Matteo Casini, "A Compagnia della Calza in January 1475," in *Reflections on Renaissance Venice: A Celebration of Patricia Fortini Brown*, ed. Blake de Maria and Mary Frank (Milan, 2013), 55–61.
100. Sanudo, *Diarii*, 19: 418.
101. Sanudo, *Diarii*, 19: 443.
102. Sanudo, *Diarii*, 37: 559–60. I follow closely but not exactly the translation in Marin Sanudo, *Venice: Città Excelentissima: Selections from the Renaissance Diaries of Marin Sanudo*, ed. Patricia H. Labalme and Laura Sanguineti White, trans. Linda L. Carroll (Baltimore, 2008), 523–4.
103. Sanudo, *Diarii*, 25: 248.
104. Sanudo, *Diarii*, 37: 560; Sanudo, *Venice: Città Excelentissima*, 529.
105. Muir, *Civic Ritual*, 189–211.
106. Edward Muir, "The Doge as *Primus inter Pares*: Interregnum Rites in Early Sixteenth-Century Venice," in *Essays Presented to Myron P. Gilmore*, ed. Sergio Bertelli and Gloria Ramakus (Florence, 1978), 145–60.
107. Muir, *Civic Ritual*, 154.
108. Crouzet-Pavan, "La maturazione."
109. For the donation letter, see Lotte Labowsky, *Bessarion's Library and the Biblioteca Marciana: Six Early Inventories* (Rome, 1979), 147–9.
110. Zorzi, "Dal manoscritto al libro," 870.
111. Rona Goffen, "Icon and Vision: Giovanni Bellini's Half-Length Madonnas," *Art Bulletin* 57 (1975): 487–518.
112. For the letter, see Chambers and Pullan, *Venice: A Documentary History*, 357–8.
113. Ennio Concina, "Dal Medioevo al primo Rinascimento: l'architettura," *SVOC* 5: 206–10; Howard, *Architectural History*, 120; Debra Pincus, "Venice and the Two Romes: Byzantium and Rome as a Double Heritage in Venetian Cultural Politics," *Artibus et historiae* 26 (1992): 101–14.
114. Howard, *Architectural History*, 128–30; Janna Israel, "Burial *alguno honore*: Doge Cristoforo Moro's Break from Ducal Burial Convention at the Church of San

Giobbe," in *The Tombs of the Doges of Venice from the Beginning of the Serenissima to 1907*, ed. Benjamin Paul (Rome, 2016), 375–407.

115. Concina, "Dal Medioevo," 216.
116. Howard, *Architectural History*, 132.
117. Sanudo, *De origine, situ et magistratibus*, 26.
118. For the church as a refoundation of Venice, see Tafuri, *Venice and the Renaissance*, 17–23.
119. Brown, *Venetian Narrative Painting*, 203–9.
120. Brown, *Venetian Narrative Painting*, 209–16.
121. Brown, *Venetian Narrative Painting*, 137.
122. Brown, *Venetian Narrative Painting*, 135–64.
123. Sanudo, *Diarii*, 17: 462. I follow, with some changes, the translation in Sanudo, *Venice: Cità Excelentissima*, 346.
124. Sanudo, *Diarii*, 17: 462; Sanudo, *Venice: Cità Excelentissima*, 347.
125. Michelangelo Muraro, "The Political Interpretation of Giorgione's Frescoes on the Fondaco dei Tedeschi," *Gazzette des Beaux Arts* series 6, 86 (1975): 183. Muraro attributes the fresco to Giorgione. Also Serena Romano, "Giuditta e il Fondaco dei Tedeschi," in *Giorgione e la cultura veneta tra '400 e '500* (Rome, 1981), 113–25.
126. Cessi and Alberti, *Rialto*, 83–121; Donatella Calabi and Paolo Morachiello, *Rialto: le fabbiche e il ponte* (Turin, 1987), 41–60.
127. Howard, *Architectural History*, 149–53.
128. Tafuri, "'Renovatio urbis Venetiarum': il problema storiografico," 12.
129. See the various essays in *'Renovatio urbis.'*
130. Gaetano Cozzi, "La politica del diritto nella Repubblica di Venezia," in *Stato, società, e giustizia nella Repubblica Veneta (sec. XV–XVIII)*, 2 vols., ed. Gaetano Cozzi (Rome, 1980), vol. 1, esp. 122–52.
131. Patricia Fortini Brown, *Private Lives in Renaissance Venice* (New Haven, 2004), 35–41.
132. Deborah Howard and Laura Moretti, *Sound and Space in Renaissance Venice: Architecture, Music, Acoustics* (New Haven, 2009).
133. Gino Benzoni, "Scritti storico-politici," *SVOC* 4: 757.
134. Cited in Patricia H. Labalme, *Bernardo Giustiniani: A Venetian of the Quattrocento* (Rome, 1969), 301.
135. Labalme, *Bernardo Giustiniani*, 280.
136. Labalme, *Bernardo Giustiniani*, 300.
137. Franco Gaeta, "Storiografia, coscienza nazionale e politica culturale nella Venezia del Rinascimento," *SCUV* 3/I: 65–75.
138. Chambers and Pullan, *Venice: A Documentary History*, 359.
139. Gaeta, "Storiografia," 79.
140. Gaeta, "Storiografia," 81.
141. Finlay, *Politics in Renaissance Venice*, 257.
142. Sanudo, *Venice: Città excellentissima*, xxv–xxx.
143. Sanudo, *De origine, situ, et magistratibus*, 6.

144. Sanudo, *Diarii*, 21: 485 (translation by Carroll in Sanudo, *Venice: Città excellentissima*, xxix.)
145. Sanudo, *De origine, situ, et magistratibus*, 62.
146. Brown, *Venetian Narrative Painting*, 91.
147. The phrase "eyewitness style" is Brown's. Brown, *Venetian Narrative Painting*, 95.
148. Sanudo, *De origine, situ, et magistratibus*, xv; Sanudo, *Venice: Città excellentissima*, xxviii.
149. Sanudo, *De origine, situ, et magistratibus*, xv.
150. Gaeta, "Storiografia," 80–1.
151. Carlo Dionisotti, "Bembo, Pietro," *DBI* 8 (1966), 133–51.
152. Gaeta, "Storiografia," 87.
153. Angelo Ventura, "Scrittori politici e scritture di governo," *SCUV* 3/III, 532.
154. Elisabeth G. Gleason, *Gasparo Contarini: Venice, Rome, and Reform* (Berkeley, 1993).
155. Gasparo Contarini, *De magistratibus et republica venetorum* (Paris, 1543), 3–4. I follow mostly the translation in Contarini, *The Republic of Venice*, 9.
156. Contarini, *De magistratibus*, 109–10; Contarini, *The Republic of Venice*, 101.
157. Contarini, *De magistratibus*, 113; Contarini, *The Republic of Venice*, 104.
158. For the possible influence of Thomas More, author of *Utopia*, on Contarini, see Felix Gilbert, "Religion and Politics in the Thought of Gasparo Contarini," in *Action and Conviction in Early Modern Europe: Essays in Memory of E. H. Harbison*, ed. T. K. Rabb and J. E. Seigel (Princeton, 1969), 114–5.
159. Contarini, *De magistratibus*, 104. Here I follow the translation in William J. Bouwsma, *Venice and the Defense of Republican Liberty* (Berkeley, 1968), 153.

CHAPTER 13

1. Chambers and Pullan, *Venice: A Documentary History*, 127.
2. Museo Civico Correr, Ms. Donà dalle Rose 351, fascicle for the parish of San Polo, entries for the households of Dominico calegher, Dominico tentor, and others; fascicle for the parish of San Ubaldo, entries for the households of Salvador galliner and Zuan Maria botter; fascicle for the parish of Sant'Aponal, entries for the households of Constantin capeler and Iacomo bombaser.
3. Daniele Beltrami, *Storia della popolazione di Venezia dalla fine del secolo XVI alla caduta della Repubblica* (Padua, 1954), 59; Romano, *Housecraft and Statecraft*, 106–7.
4. Andrea Zannini, *Burocrazia e burocrati a Venezia in età moderna: i cittadini originari (sec. XVI–XVIII)* (Venice, 1993), 44.
5. Zanini, *Burocrazia e burocrati*, 45–7.
6. James S. Grubb, "Elite Citizens," *VR*, 348; James S. Grubb, ed., *Family Memoirs from Venice (15th–17th Centuries)* (Rome, 2009), xxiii, n.47.
7. Zannini, *Burocrazia e burocrati*, 75–6.
8. Zannini, *Burocrazia e burocrati*, 71.

9. Cited in Grubb, *Family Memoirs*, xxiv, but without a citation to the original.
10. The same was true of dragomans. See E. Natalie Rothman, *The Dragoman Renaissance: Diplomatic Interpreters and the Routes of Orientalism* (Ithaca, 2021), 74–9.
11. Claire Judde de Larivière, "Political Participation in Renaissance Venice," in *Popular Politics in an Aristocratic Republic*, ed. Van Gelder and Judde de Larivière, 78–82.
12. Grubb, *Family Memoirs*, 249–50. For a full English translation of the festivities surrounding the marriage of Samaritana's sister, see Chambers and Pullan, *Venice: A Documentary History*, 263–6.
13. Grubb, *Family Memoirs*, 14.
14. Patricia Fortini Brown, "Honor and Necessity: The Dynamics of Patronage in the Confraternities of Renaissance Venice," *SV* n.s. 14 (1987): 179–212.
15. The first quote is from Deborah Howard, *Jacopo Sansovino: Architecture and Patronage in Renaissance Venice* (New Haven, 1975), 102; the second from Brown, "Honor and Necessity," 207.
16. Anna Bellavitis, *Identité, marriage, mobilité sociale: citoyennes et citoyens à Venise au XVIe siècle* (Rome, 2001), 36.
17. Bellavitis, *Identité, marriage*, 43, 53.
18. Bellavitis, *Identité, marriage*, 57.
19. Sarah Gwyneth Ross, *Everyday Renaissances: The Quest for Cultural Legitimacy in Venice* (Cambridge, MA, 2016), 47–51.
20. Bellavitis, *Identité, marriage*, 314.
21. Bellavitis, *Identité, marriage*, 282.
22. Pullan, *Rich and Poor*, 81–2, 101–2, 368; Mackenney, *Tradesmen and Traders*, 110; Mackenney, *Venice as the Polity of Mercy*, 231–2.
23. For analysis of the painting, see Blake de Maria, *Becoming Venetian: Immigrants and the Arts in Early Modern Venice* (New Haven, 2010), 143–59.
24. Monika Schmitter, *The Art Collector in Early Modern Italy: Andrea Odoni and His Venetian Palace* (Cambridge, 2021).
25. Quoted in Bellavitis, *Identité, marriage*, 295–6.
26. Chambers and Pullan, *Venice: A Documentary History*, 271–2.
27. Bellavitis, *Identité, marriage*, 307–10.
28. Andrea Zannini, "Conflicts, Social Unease, and Protests in the World of the Venetian Guilds (Sixteenth to Eighteenth Century)," in *Popular Politics*, ed. Van Gelder and Judde de Larivière, 219.
29. James E. Shaw, *The Justice of Venice: Authorities and Liberties in the Urban Economy, 1550–1700* (Oxford, 2006), 111–2.
30. Mackenney, *Venice as the Polity of Mercy*, 135.
31. Shaw, *Justice of Venice*, 110.
32. Mackenney, *Venice as the Polity of Mercy*, 129.
33. Mackenney, *Venice as the Polity of Mercy*, 196.

34. Monica Chojnacka, *Working Women in Early Modern Venice* (Baltimore, 2001), 1–25.
35. Paola Pavanini, "Abitazioni popolari e borghesi nella Venezia Cinquecentesca," *SV* n.s. 5 (1981), 96; Isabella Palumbo-Fossati, "L'interno della casa dell'artigiano e dell'artista nella Venezia del Cinquecento," *SV* n.s. 8 (1984): 109–53.
36. Pavanini, "Abitazioni popolari," 112–3.
37. Rosa Salzberg, "Spaces of Unrest? Policing Hospitality Sites in Early Modern Venice," in *Popular Politics*, ed. Van Gelder and Judde de Larivière, 105–28; Filippo De Vivo, "Pharmacies as Centres of Communication in Early Modern Venice," *Renaissance Studies* 21 (2007): 505–21.
38. Joanne M. Ferraro, *Marriage Wars in Late Renaissance Venice* (New York, 2001), 86.
39. Ferraro, *Marriage Wars*, 125.
40. Joanne M. Ferraro, "Female Agency, Subjectivity, and Disorder in Early Modern Venice," in *Popular Politics in an Aristocratic Republic*, ed. Van Gelder and Judde de Larivière, 158–75.
41. Claire Judde de Larivière, "Sense of Neighbourhood (*Vicinanza)* in Sixteenth-Century Venice," in *The Experience of Neighbourhood in Medieval and Early Modern Europe*, ed. Bronach C. Kane and Simon Sandall (London, 2022), 48–60.
42. Davis, *Shipbuilders of the Venetian Arsenal*, 89–91.
43. Roberto Zago, *I Nicolotti: storia di una comunità di pescatori a Venezia nell'età moderna* (Abano Terme, 1982), 58, 103; Robin Quillien and Solène Rivoal, "Boatmen, Fishermen, and Venetian Institutions: From Negotiation to Confrontation," in *Popular Politics*, ed. Van Gelder and Judde de Larivière, 197–216.
44. Davis, *War of the Fists*, 45, 127.
45. Davis, *War of the Fists*, 47.
46. Davis, *War of the Fists*, 139.
47. Romano, *Housecraft and Statecraft*, 227–8.
48. Romano, *Housecraft and Statecraft*, 95.
49. Zannini, *Burocrazia e burocrati*, 74.
50. Kate Lowe, "Black Gondoliers and Other Black Africans in Renaissance Venice," *RQ* 66 (2013): 412–52.
51. Romano, *Housecraft and Statecraft*, 201.
52. Alberto Stelio de Kiriaki, *La beneficenza di ricovero a Venezia nel passato e nei nostri tempi. Ricordo per l'anno 1900* (Venice, 1900), 181–2.
53. Paula Clarke, "Le 'mercantesse' di Venezia nei secoli XIV e XV," *AV* 6th series 3 (2012): 74–5.
54. Ross, *Everyday Renaissances*, 170–71.
55. Romano, "The Gondola as a Marker of Station," 359–74.
56. Tommaso Garzoni, *La piazza universale di tutte le professioni del mondo* (Venice, 1595), 869. It was first published in 1585.
57. Cathy Santore, "Julia Lombardo: 'Somtuosa Meretrize': A Portrait by Property," *RQ* 41 (1988): 44.

58. Margaret F. Rosenthal, "Clothing, Fashion, Dress, and Costume in Venice," in *Companion to Venetian History*, ed. Dursteler, 914.
59. Santore, "Julia Lombardo," 51.
60. Veronica Franco, *Poems and Selected Letters*, ed. and trans. Ann Rosalind Jones and Margaret F. Rosenthal (Chicago, 1998), 69.
61. Santore, "Julia Lombardo," 52.
62. Joanne M. Ferraro, "Making a Living: The Sex Trade in Early Modern Venice," *American Historical Review* 123 (2018): 47; Clarke, "Business of Prostitution."
63. Ruggiero, *The Boundaries of Eros*, 109–45.
64. Gabriele Martini, *Il 'vitio nefando' nella Venezia del Seicento: aspetti sociali e repressione di giustizia* (Rome, 1988), 54–6, 112.
65. Martini, '*Vitio nefando*,' 114–5.
66. Martini, '*Vitio nefando*,' 113, 131.
67. Judith C. Brown, *Immodest Acts: The Life of a Lesbian Nun in Renaissance Italy* (New York, 1985).
68. Martini, '*Vitio nefando*,' 115–6.
69. Guido Ruggiero, *Binding Passions: Tales of Magic, Marriage, and Power at the End of the Renaissance* (New York, 1993), 29–33.
70. Margaret F. Rosenthal, *The Honest Courtesan: Veronica Franco, Citizen and Writer in Sixteenth-Century Venice* (Chicago, 1992), 167.
71. Rosenthal, *Honest Courtesan*, 176.
72. Ruth Martin, *Witchcraft and the Inquisition in Venice, 1550–1650* (Oxford, 1989), 234.
73. Sanudo, *Diarii*, 33: 562.
74. Lane, *Venice: A Maritime Republic*, 364–9; Frederic C. Lane, "Wages and Recruitment of Venetian Galeotti, 1470–1580," *SV* n.s. 6 (1982): 15–43.
75. Chambers and Pullan, *Venice: A Documentary History*, 293.
76. Chambers and Pullan, *Venice: A Documentary History*, 99–101.
77. Lane, *Venice: A Maritime Republic*, 369; Alberto Tenenti, *Cristoforo da Canal: la marine vénitienne avant Lépante*. Paris: S.E.V.P.E.N., 1962; Viaro, "La pena della galera," 377–430.
78. Finlay, *Politics in Renaissance Venice*, 48.
79. Lane, *Venetian Ships and Shipbuilders*, 188.
80. For two different accounts of what occurred, see Chambers and Pullan, *Venice: A Documentary History*, 289–91.
81. Finlay, *Politics in Renaissance Venice*, 53.
82. Sanudo, *Diarii*, 56: 76.
83. Sanudo, *Diarii*, 56: 78.
84. Maartje van Gelder, "The People's Prince: Popular Politics in Early Modern Venice," *Journal of Modern History* 90 (2018): 258.
85. Van Gelder, "People's Prince," 263–4.
86. Van Gelder, "People's Prince," 269.

87. Van Gelder, "People's Prince," 274.
88. Van Gelder, "People's Prince," 289.
89. Jean Georgelin, *Venise au siècle des lumières* (Paris, 1978), 686–93.
90. Van Gelder, "Protest in the Piazza."
91. Pullan, *Rich and Poor*, 302–3.
92. Sanudo, *Diarii*, 46: 380.
93. Pullan, *Rich and Poor*, 360.
94. Ivo Mattozzi, "Il politico e il pane a Venezia (1570–1650): calmieri e governo della sussitenza," *Società e Storia* 20 (1983): 280–1.
95. Laura J. McGough, *Gender, Sexuality, and Syphilis in Early Modern Venice: The Disease that Came to Stay* (Houndmills, Basingstoke, 2011).
96. Dennis Romano, "L'assistenza e la beneficenza," *SVOC* 5: 355–406.
97. Silvia Lunardon, ed., *Hospitale S. Marie Cruciferorum: l'ospizio dei Crociferi a Venezia* (Venice, 1985), 156.
98. Pullan, *Rich and Poor*, 229.
99. Romano, "L'assistenza e la beneficenza," 366.
100. Pullan, *Rich and Poor*, 214–5.
101. ASV, NT, busta 372, notary Donati Viti, protocol, fols. 11v–14r, will number 14.
102. Ioanna Iordanou, "Pestilence, Poverty and Provision: Re-evaluating the Role of the *Popolani* in Early Modern Venice," *Economic History Review* 69 (2016): 801–22.
103. ASV, NT, busta 595, notary Giovanni Lombardo, protocol, fol. 17r.
104. *Venezia e la peste*, 365.
105. *Venezia e la peste*, 97–156.
106. Pullan, *Rich and Poor*, 213–15.
107. Pullan, *Rich and Poor*, 235–8.
108. Pullan, *Rich and Poor*, 262.
109. Quillien and Rivoal, "Boatmen, Fishermen," 204.
110. Pullan, *Rich and Poor*, 252–4.
111. Pullan, *Rich and Poor*, 370.
112. Pullan, *Rich and Poor*, 207.
113. Ferraro, "Female agency," 163.
114. Pullan, *Rich and Poor*, 392.
115. Philippe de Commynes, *Memorie*, trans. Maria Clotilde Daviso di Charvensod (Turin, 1960), 442.
116. Maartje van Gelder, *Trading Places: The Netherlandish Merchants in Early Modern Venice* (Leiden, 2009).
117. Gigi Corazzol, *Livelli stipulati a Venezia nel 1591: studio storico* (Pisa, 1986), 77.
118. Braunstein, *Les Allemands à Venise*, 673, n. 240.
119. Garzoni, *Piazza universale*, (1605 ed.), 801.
120. For their marriage patterns, see Orlando, *Migrazioni mediterranee*, 344–8; Ersie Burke, *The Greeks of Venice, 1498–1600: Immigration, Settlement, and Integration* (Turnhout, 2016), 33.

121. Chambers and Pullan, *Venice: A Documentary History*, 333–4.
122. Chambers and Pullan, *Venice: A Documentary History*, 334–6.
123. Efstathios Birtachas, "Un 'secondo' vescovo a Venezia: il metropolita di Filadelfia (secoli XVI–XVIII)" in *I Greci a Venezia: atti del convegno internazionale di studio, Venezia, 5–7 novembre 1998*, ed. Maria Francesca Tiepolo and Eurigio Tonetti (Venice, 2002): 103–21.
124. Panayotis K. Ioannou, "Palma il Giovane e Giovanni Bilivert nella collezione dell'Istituto Ellenico di Venezia," *Thesaurismata* 32 (2002): 153–65.
125. Nano Chatzidakis, *From Candia to Venice: Greek Icons in Italy, 15th–16th Centuries* (Athens, 1993).
126. Rena N. Laurer, *Colonial Justice and the Jews of Venetian Crete* (Philadelphia, 2019).
127. Donatella Calabi, "The 'City of the Jews,'" in *The Jews in Early Modern Venice*, ed. Robert C. Davis and Benjamin Ravid (Baltimore, 2001), 31–49; Donatella Calabi, *Venezia e il Ghetto: cinquecento anni del "recinto degli ebrei"* (Turin, 2016); Dana E. Katz, *The Jewish Ghetto and the Visual Imagination of Early Modern Venice* (Cambridge, 2017).
128. Benjamin Ravid, "The Venetian Government and the Jews," in *Jews of Early Modern Venice*, ed. Davis and Ravid, 12.
129. Quoted in Benjamin Arbel, "Jews in International Trade: The Emergence of the Levantines and Ponentines," in *Jews of Early Modern Venice*, ed. Davis and Ravid, 73.
130. Ravid, "Venetian Government," 14–20.
131. Quoted in Brian Pullan, *The Jews of Europe and the Inquisition of Venice, 1550–1670* (Totowa, NJ, 1983), 158.
132. David J. Malkiel, "The Ghetto Republic," in *Jews of Early Modern Venice*, ed. Davis and Ravid, 117–42.
133. For the Luzzatto quote, Pullan, *Jews of Europe*, 159; for the Canal degli Ebrei, Calabi, "'City of the Jews,'" 48–9.
134. Mark R. Cohen, ed., *The Autobiography of a Seventeenth-Century Venetian Rabbi: Leon Modena's* Life of Judah (Princeton, 1988), 141.
135. Cohen, *Autobiography*, 144.
136. Cohen, *Autobiography*, 147.
137. Cohen, *Autobiography*, 151. The 1638 Venice edition bore the title *Historia de riti Hebraici: vita & osservanze degl'Hebrei di questi tempi.* The full title of the 1637 Paris edition is *Historia de gli riti Hebraici: dove si ha'breve, e total relatione di tutta la vita, costume, riti et osservanze, de gl'Hebrei di questi tempi.*
138. Rothman, *Dragoman Renaissance*, 20–79. For redemptions of the enslaved, Andrea Pelizza, *Riammessi a respirare l'aria tranquilla: Venezia e il riscatto degli schiavi in età moderna* (Venice, 2013).
139. Eric R. Dursteler, *Venetians in Constantinople: Nation, Identity, and Coexistence in the Early Modern Mediterranean* (Baltimore, 2006), 38.
140. On the role of non-citizens in trade, Apellániz, "Venetian Trading Networks."

141. Dursteler, *Venetians in Constantinople*, 71.
142. Dursteler, *Venetians in Constantinople*, 80.
143. Dursteler, *Venetians in Constantinople*, 171.
144. Dursteler, *Venetians in Constantinople*, 95–8.
145. Sanudo, *Diarii*, 34: 158, cited in Robert Finlay, "Al servizio del Sultano: Venezia, i Turchi e il mondo cristiano, 1523–1538," in *'Renovatio Urbis,'* ed. Tafuri, 79.
146. Dursteler, *Venetians in Constantinople*, 184.
147. G. D. Ramsay, "The Undoing of the Italian Mercantile Colony in Sixteenth Century London," in *Textile History and Economic History: Essays in Honour of Miss Julia de Lacy Mann*, ed. N. B. Harte and K. G. Ponting (Manchester, 1973), 37.
148. Ugo Tucci, "The Psychology of the Venetian Merchant in the Sixteenth Century, *RV*, 348.
149. Giorgio Vercellin, "Mercanti turchi e sensali a Venezia," *SV* n.s. 4 (1980): 63.
150. Vercellin, "Mercanti turchi," 49. For Michele Summa di Santo, see Maria Pia Pedani, *The Ottoman-Venetian Border (15th–18th Centuries)* (Venice, 2017), 119.
151. For the permeability of borders in this period, see Barzman, "Spatial Histories of Early Modern Borderlands."
152. Chambers and Pullan, *Venice: A Documentary History*, 352.
153. E. Natalie Rothman, *Brokering Empire: Trans-Imperial Subjects Between Venice and Istanbul* (Ithaca, 2012), 240–47.
154. Rosenthal, "Clothing, Fashion, Dress," 894.
155. Wilson, *The World in Venice*, 74.
156. Wilson, *The World in Venice*, 71.
157. For an example, see Stephen Ortega, *Negotiating Transcultural Relations in the Early Modern Mediterranean: Ottoman-Venetian Encounters* (Farnham, 2014), 17–8.
158. See also Rothman, *Brokering Empire*, 114–21.
159. Quoted in Rosenthal, "Clothing, Fashion, Dress," 921.
160. De Vivo, "Walking in Sixteenth-Century Venice," esp. 137–8.
161. They also numbered 2,570 in 1513, 2,435 in 1563, and 2,000 in 1620. Sources: James C. Davis, *The Decline of the Venetian Nobility as a Ruling Class* (Baltimore, 1962), 58, and note 3 above for the 1563 census. In 1563 nobles (men, women, and children) constituted 4.5 percent of the total population.
162. Davis, *Decline of the Venetian Nobility*, 56.
163. Davis, *Decline of the Venetian Nobility*, 69–70.
164. Davis, *Venetian Family and its Fortune*, 87.
165. Davis, *Decline of the Venetian Nobility*, 72.
166. Jutta Gisela Sperling, *Convents and the Body Politic in Late Renaissance Venice* (Chicago, 1999).
167. Mary Laven, *Virgins of Venice: Broken Vows and Cloistered Lives in the Renaissance Convent* (New York, 2002), 248–51.

168. Laven, *Virgins of Venice*, 41.
169. Laven, *Virgins of Venice*, 52.
170. Laven, *Virgins of Venice*, 8.
171. Laven, *Virgins of Venice*, 6, 51. I have changed "dishonest" to "shameless" to clarify the meaning.
172. Bartolomea Riccaboni, *Life and Death in a Venetian Convent: The Chronicle and Necrology of Corpus Domini, 1395–1436*, ed. and trans. Daniel Bornstein (Chicago, 2000); Lowe, *Nuns' Chronicles*, 78–94.
173. For the traditional view, Brian Pullan, "Occupations and Investments of the Venetian Nobility in the Middle and Late Sixteenth Century," *RV*, 379–408.
174. Judde de Larivière, *Naviguer, commercer*, 123–77.
175. Dagomar Degroot, *The Frigid Golden Age: Climate Change, the Little Ice Age, and the Dutch Republic, 1560–1720* (Cambridge, 2018).
176. Mometto, *L'azienda agricola Barbarigo*.
177. Mometto, *L'azienda agricola Barbarigo*, 137, n. 7.
178. Mometto, *L'azienda agricola Barbarigo*, 141.
179. Mometto, *L'azienda agricola Barbarigo*, 7–9.
180. Mometto, *L'azienda agricola Barbarigo*, 107.
181. Lane, *Andrea Barbarigo*, 38.
182. Bruce Boucher, *Andrea Palladio: The Architect in His Time* (New York, 1994), 61.
183. Boucher, *Andrea Palladio*, 118.
184. Giuseppe Gullino, "Quando il mercante construì la villa: le proprietà dei Veneziani nella Terraferma," *SVOC* 6: 877.
185. Franco, *Poems and Selected Letters*, 37–40.
186. Meredith K. Ray, "Letters and Lace: Arcangela Tarabotti and Convent Culture in *Seicento* Venice," in *Early Modern Women and Transnational Communities of Letters*, ed. Julie R. Campbell and Anne R. Larsen (Farnham, 2009), 45–73.
187. Arcangela Tarabotti, *Paternal Tyranny*, ed. and trans. Letizia Panizza (Chicago, 2004), 41.
188. Tarabotti, *Paternal Tyranny*, 57.
189. Tarabotti, *Paternal Tyranny*, 66.
190. Tarabotti, *Paternal Tyranny*, 38.
191. Tarabotti, *Paternal Tyranny*, 65.

CHAPTER 14

1. Howard, *Jacopo Sansovino*.
2. Sansovino, *Venetia città nobilissima*, 1: 307–8.
3. Howard, *Jacopo Sansovino*, 28–35.
4. Margaret Muther d'Evelyn, *Venice and Vitruvius: Reading Venice with Daniele Barbaro and Andrea Palladio* (New Haven, 2012).
5. Mallett and Hale, *Military Organization*, 5.

6. Sanudo, *Diarii*, 27: 456–7.
7. Quoted in Mallett and Hale, *Military Organization*, 218.
8. Quoted in Mallett and Hale, *Military Organization*, 412.
9. Mallett and Hale, *Military Organization*, 409, 436.
10. Dragoş Cosmescu, *Venetian Renaissance Fortifications in the Mediterranean* (Jefferson, NC, 2016).
11. Mallet and Hale, *Military Organization*, 460.
12. Lane, *Venice: A Maritime Empire*, 392.
13. Alberto Tenenti, *Piracy and the Decline of Venice, 1580–1615*, trans. Janet and Brian Pullan (Berkeley, 1967), 123.
14. Innocenzo Cervelli, "Intorno alla decadenza di Venezia: un episodio di storia economica ovvero un affare mancato," *Nuova Rivista Storica* 50 (1966): 596–642; Domenico Sella, "L'economia," *SVOC* 6: 668–9.
15. The narrative of these wars derives from Romanin, *Storia documentata*, 6: 7–49, 182–237; 7: 30–81, 194–242; Gaetano Cozzi, *Il doge Nicolò Contarini: ricerche sul patriziato veneziano agli inizi del Seicento* (Venice, 1958), 149–95; 285–304; Mallett and Hale, *Military Organization*, 221–47; Gaetano Cozzi, "Venezia dal Rinascimento all'età barocca," *SVOC* 6: 3–125.
16. The phrase comes from Mallett and Hale, *Military Organization*, 230.
17. Quoted in Romanin, *Storia documentata*, 6: 49, n. 41.
18. Quoted in Mallett and Hale, *Military Organization*, 238.
19. Iain Fenlon, *The Ceremonial City: History, Memory and Myth in Renaissance Venice* (New Haven, 2007), 179.
20. Quoted in Richard Mackenney "'A Plot Discover'd?': Myth, Legend, and the 'Spanish' Conspiracy Against Venice in 1618," *VR*, 189.
21. Tenenti, *Piracy and the Decline*. However, the Venetians also saw some advantage in the Uskoks raids against the Ottomans since they helped slow the Turks' expansion in the Adriatic. See Bracewell, *The Uskoks of Senj*, 176–9.
22. The phrase is Tenenti's (*Piracy and the Decline*, 14); Maria Fusaro, *Political Economies of Empire in the Early Modern Mediterranean: The Decline of Venice and the Rise of England, 1450–1700* (Cambridge, 2015), 124.
23. Mackenney, "'A Plot Discover'd.'"
24. Tracy, *Balkan Wars*, 337–46.
25. Luciano Pezzolo, "La finanza pubblica," *SVOC* 6: 717.
26. Pezzolo, "La finanza pubblica," 728.
27. Pezzolo, "La finanza pubblica," 734.
28. Lane, *Venice: A Maritime Republic*, 402.
29. Sella, "L'economia," 693.
30. But private vessels could be requisitioned for military use. Judde de Larivière, *Naviguer, commercer*, 269–70.
31. Lane, *Venice: A Maritime Republic*, 348.
32. Quoted in Tenenti, *Piracy and the Decline,* 60.

33. Fusaro, *Political Economies*, 79.
34. Fusaro, *Political Economies*, 51–2.
35. Fusaro, *Political Economies*, *passim*.
36. Bruce Masters, *The Origins of Western Economic Dominance in the Middle East: Mercantilism and the Islamic Economy of Aleppo, 1600–1750* (New York, 1988), 14. See also Ugo Tucci, *Mercanti, navi, monete nel Cinquecento veneziano* (Bologna, 1981), 95–143.
37. Sella, "L'economia," 697–700.
38. Sella, "L'economia," 686; Judde de Larivière, *Naviguer, commercer*, 293–310.
39. Fusaro, *Political Economies*, 174–9.
40. Pezzolo, "La finanza pubblica," 716–7.
41. Fusaro, *Political Economies*, 304, 351.
42. Sansovino, *Venetia città nobilissima*, 501. I follow the translation in Muir, *Civic Ritual*, 124 but with significant modifications.
43. Quoted in Cessi, *Storia della Repubblica*, 601.
44. Mario Brunetti, "Le istruzioni di un nunzio pontificio a Venezia al suo successore," in *Scritti storici in onore di Camillo Manfroni* (Padua, 1925), 376. For conflicts between Venice and the pope over diversions of branches of the Po near the Venice/Ferrara border with implications for Adriatic trade, see Benvenuto Cessi, "Il taglio del Po a Porto Viro," *NAV*, n.s. 30, pt. 2 (1915): 319–68.
45. Cessi, *Storia della Repubblica*, 601. See also Alberto Bin, *La Repubblica di Venezia e la questione adriatica, 1600–1620* (Rome, 1992); Pedani, *The Ottoman-Venetian Border*, 83–95; De Vivo, "Historical Justifications."
46. Wolfgang Wolters, "L'autocelebrazione della Repubblica nelle arti figurative," *SVOC* 6: 488–9.
47. Paolo Preto, *I servizi segreti di Venezia: spionaggio e controspionaggio ai tempi della Serenissima* (Milan, 2016), 87.
48. Preto, *Servizi segreti*, 88.
49. Ermolao Barbaro, *De coelibati, De officio legati*, ed. Vittore Branca (Florence, 1969), 159.
50. Preto, *Servizi secreti*, 197.
51. Filippo De Vivo, "How to Read Venetian Relazioni," *Renaissance and Reformation/Renaissance et Réforme* 34 (2011), 25–59.
52. Preto, *Servizi secreti*, 218.
53. Preto, *Servizi secreti*, 269.
54. Preto, *Servizi secreti*, 271.
55. Preto, *Servizi secreti*, 272.
56. Preto, *Servizi secreti*, 281.
57. Paolo Preto, "La guerra segreta: spionaggio, sabotaggi, attentati," in *Venezia e la difesa del Levante: da Lepanto a Candia 1570–1670* (Venice, 1986), 79–85.
58. Preto, *Servizi secreti*, 76–8.
59. Roberto Zago, "Foscarini, Antonio," *DBI* 49 (1997): 361–65.

60. Filippo De Vivo, *Information and Communication in Venice: Rethinking Early Modern Politics* (Oxford, 2007), 48–53; Besta, *Senato*, 102–8.
61. Preto, *Servizi secreti*, 56.
62. Preto, *Servizi secreti*, 55.
63. De Vivo, *Information and Communication*, 40–5.
64. Romanin, *Storia documentata*, 6: 58–9. I follow the translation in Chambers and Pullan, *Venice: A Documentary History*, 81.
65. Maranini, *La costituzione di Venezia*, 2: 473–90; Maria Francesca Tiepolo, ed., *Archivio di Stato di Venezia*, in *Guida Generale degli Archivi di Stato Italiani*, 4 vols. (Rome, 1994), 4: 902–3; De Vivo, *Information and Communication*, 33–6.
66. Alfredo Viggiano, "Giustizia, disciplina e ordine pubblico," *SVOC* 6: 852–3; Salzberg, "Spaces of Unrest," 112.
67. Laven, *Virgins of Venice*, xxv, 88–90, *passim*; Lowe, *Nuns' Chronicles*, 190–200.
68. Maranini, *La costituzione*, 2: 179–91; Alfredo Viggiano, "Politics and Constitution," in *Companion to Venetian History*, ed. Dursteler, 62–5.
69. Renzo Derosas, "Moralità e giustizia a Venezia nel '500-'600: gli esecutori contro la bestemmia," in *Stato, società e giustizia nella Repubblica Veneta (sec. XV–XVIII)*, ed. Gaetano Cozzi (Rome, 1980), 431–528; Elizabeth Horodowich, *Language and Statecraft in Early Modern Venice* (Cambridge, 2008), 56–90.
70. Gaetano Cozzi, "Religione moralità e giustizia a Venezia: vicende della magistratura degli esecutori contro la bestemmia (secoli XVI–XVIII)," *AV* n.s. 29 (1991): 7–95 esp. p. 31.
71. Horodowich, *Language and Statecraft*, 65–9.
72. Laven, *Virgins of Venice*, 101.
73. Chambers and Pullan, *Venice: A Documentary History*, 229.
74. John Jeffries Martin, *Venice's Hidden Enemies: Italian Heretics in a Renaissance City* (Berkeley, 1993), 63.
75. Paul F. Grendler, *The Roman Inquisition and the Venetian Press, 1540–1605* (Princeton, 1977), esp. 180.
76. Martin, *Venice's Hidden Enemies*, 184.
77. Partial transcription in Chambers and Pullan, *Venice: A Documentary History*, 232–6.
78. Martin, *Venice's Hidden Enemies*, 191.
79. Martin, *Venice's Hidden Enemies*, 69–70.
80. De Vivo, *Information and Communication*, 25–45.
81. Pezzolo, "La finanza pubblica," 722.
82. Cassini, *I gesti del principe*, 45–6.
83. Paolo Prodi, "Chiesa e società," *SVOC* 6: 312, 328–9.
84. Giangiorgio Zorzi, *Le opere pubbliche e i palazzi privati di Andrea Palladio* (Venice, 1965), 157.
85. Prodi, "Chiesa e società," 332.
86. Giacomo Fassina, "Factiousness, Fractiousness or Unity? The Reform of the Council of Ten in 1582–1583," *SV* n.s. 54 (2007): 89–117.

87. Cessi, *Storia della Repubblica*, 581.
88. Cozzi, *Il doge Nicolò Contarini*, 1–52.
89. Martin Lowry, "The Reform of the Council of Ten, 1582–3: An Unsettled Problem?," *SV* 13 (1971): 275–310.
90. Romanin, *Storia documentata*, 6: 254–8; Maranini, *Costituzione di Venezia*, 2: 412–31; Viggiano, "Giustizia, disciplina e ordine pubblico," 825–61.
91. Chambers and Pullan, *Venice: A Documentary History*, 82.
92. Romanin, *Storia documentata*, 7: 143–68; Cozzi, *Il doge Nicolò Contarini*, 229–83.
93. Cozzi, *Il doge Nicolò Contarini*, 247.
94. Cozzi, *Il doge Nicolò Contarini*, 250.
95. Cozzi, *Il doge Nicolò Contarini*, 255.
96. William J. Bouwsma, *Venice and the Defense of Republican Liberty: Renaissance Values in the Age of the Counter Reformation* (Berkeley, 1968), 260.
97. Cozzi, "Venezia dal Rinascimento all'età barocca," 75–82.
98. Franco Gaeta, "Venezia da 'stato misto' ad aristocrazia 'esemplare,'" *SCUV* 4/ II: 465.
99. Federico Seneca, *Il doge Leonardo Donà: la sua vita e la sua preparazione politica prima del dogado* (Padua, 1959).
100. Chambers and Pullan, *Venice: A Documentary History*, 225–7.
101. Bouwsma, *Venice and the Defense*, 373.
102. Cozzi, "Venezia dal Rinascimento all'età barocca," 83.
103. De Vivo, *Information and Communication*, 159.
104. Bouwsma, *Venice and the Defense*, 389–90.
105. Bouwsma, *Venice and the Defense*, 393–4.
106. Lane, *Venice: A Maritime Republic*, 398.
107. William J. Bouwsma, "Venice and the Political Education of Europe," *RV*, 448.
108. Maria Luisa Doglio, "La letteratura ufficiale e l'oratoria celebrativa," *SCUV*, 4/ I: 172–3.
109. Bouwsma, "Venice and the Political Education," 445–66.
110. De Vivo, *Information and Communication*, 242.
111. De Vivo, *Information and Communication*, 246–8.
112. Prodi, "Chiesa e società," 328–9; Anthony Wright, "Republican Tradition and the Maintenance of 'National' Religious Traditions in Venice," *Renaissance Studies* 10 (1996): 405–16.
113. Tafuri, *Venice and the Renaissance*, 184–91.
114. Tafuri, *Venice and the Renaissance*, 188.
115. Cooper, *Palladio's Venice*, 109–45.
116. Howard, *Architectural History*, 198–9.
117. Howard, *Architectural History*, 200.
118. Howard, *Architectural History*, 203–7; Cooper, *Palladio's Venice*, 229–57.
119. Cooper, *Palladio's Venice*, 281–5.
120. Cessi and Alberti, *Rialto*, 170–223; Calabi and Morachiello, *Rialto*, 186–300.

121. Vittorio Piva, *Il tempio della Salute eretto per voto de la repubblica veneta XXVI–X–MDCXXX* (Venice, 1930), 29.
122. Howard, *Architectural History*, 215.
123. Quoted in Howard, *Architectural History*, 216.
124. Andrew Hopkins, *Santa Maria della Salute: Architecture and Ceremony in Baroque Venice* (Cambridge, 2000).
125. Rudolf Wittkower, "S. Maria della Salute," *Saggi e Memorie di Storia dell'Arte* 3 (1963): 49.
126. Wittkower, "S. Maria della Salute," 43.
127. Antonio Niero, "I templi del Redentore e della Salute: motivazioni teologiche," in *Venezia e la peste*, 297–8.

CHAPTER 15

1. Cited and translated in Ellen Rosand, *Opera in Seventeenth-Century Venice: The Creation of a Genre* (Berkeley, 1991), 147.
2. Rosand, *Opera in Seventeenth-Century Venice*, 134–5.
3. For the wars with the Ottomans, Romanin, *Storia documentata*, 7: 169–367; 8: 7–41; *Venezia e la difesa del Levante: da Lepanto a Candia,1570–1670* (Venice, 1986); Kenneth M. Setton, *Venice, Austria and the Turks in the Seventeenth Century* (Philadelphia, 1991); Gaetano Cozzi, "Dalla riscoperta della pace all'inestinguibile sogno di dominio," *SVOC* 7: 3–104.
4. Piero del Negro, "La milizia," *SVOC* 7: 520.
5. Cozzi, "Dalla riscoperta," 27, 29.
6. Romanin, *Storia documentata*, 7: 308.
7. Romanin, *Storia documentata*, 7: 286.
8. Romanin, *Storia documentata*, 7: 297.
9. McNeill, *Venice: The Hinge of Europe*, 182–3.
10. Cozzi, "Dalla riscoperta," 41.
11. Romanin, *Storia documentata*, 7: 316.
12. Romanin, *Storia documentata*, 7: 328.
13. Mario Infelise, "L'ultima crociata," in *Venezia e la guerra di Morea: guerra, politica e cultura alla fine del '600*, ed. Mario Infelise and Anastasia Stouraiti (Milan, 2005), 9. For a survey of the war, see Sergio Perini, "Venezia e la guerra di Morea (1684–1699)," *AV* 5th series, 153 (1999): 45–91.
14. Romanin, *Storia documentata*, 7: 343.
15. Setton, *Venice, Austria and the Turks*, 340.
16. Stefano Andretta, *La Repubblica inquieta: Venezia nel Seicento tra Italia ed Europa* (Rome, 2000), 169–200.
17. Concina, *History of Venetian Architecture*, 264–5; Concina, *L'Arsenale*, 185–6.
18. Cozzi, "Dalla riscoperta," 96.
19. Romanin, *Storia documentata*, 7: 357.

20. Cozzi, "Dalla riscoperta," 13–21.
21. Luciano Pezzolo, "L'economia," *SVOC* 7: 421; Romanin, *Storia documentata*, 7: 319.
22. Dorit Raines, "Strategie d'ascesa sociale e giochi di potere a Venezia nel Seicento: le aggregazioni alla nobiltà," *SV* n.s. 51 (2006): 286–7.
23. Davis, *Decline of the Venetian Nobility*, 107–9.
24. Raines, "Strategie," 288.
25. Raines, "Strategie," 290.
26. Raines, "Strategie," 284, n. 24.
27. Raines, "Strategie," 284.
28. Antonio Menniti Ippolito, *Fortuna e sfortune di una famiglia veneziana nel Seicento: gli Ottoboni al tempo dell'aggregazione al patriziato* (Venice, 1996), 35.
29. Ippolito, *Fortuna e sfortune*, 59, 61.
30. Roberto Sabbadini, *L'acquisto della tradizione: tradizione aristocratica e nuova nobiltà a Venezia (sec. XVII–XVIII)* (Udine, 1995), 58.
31. Quoted in Federica Ambrosini, "Penombre femminili," *SVOC* 7: 305–7.
32. Raines, "Strategie," 312.
33. Sabbadini, *L'acquisto della tradizione*, 68.
34. Sabbadini, *L'acquisto della tradizione*, 69–70.
35. Davis, *Decline of the Venetian Nobility*, 58.
36. Davis, *Decline of the Venetian Nobility*, 118.
37. Davis, *Decline of the Venetian Nobility*, 72.
38. Antonio Menniti Ippolito, "'Sudditi d'un altro stato?' Gli ecclesiastici veneziani," *SVOC* 7: 331.
39. Renzo Derosas, "Corner, Elena Lucrezia," *DBI* 29 (1983): 174–79.
40. Laura Megna, "Grandezza e miseria della nobiltà veneziana," *SVOC* 7: 162–3.
41. Megna, "Grandezza e miseria," 175.
42. Quoted in Pullan, *Rich and Poor*, 409–10. And see Luigi Zenoni, "Per la storia della cultura in Venezia dal 1500 al 1797: l'Accademia dei Nobili alla Giudecca (1619–1797)" in *Miscellanea di Storia Veneta edita per cura della R. Deputazione Veneta di Storia Patria* ser. III, 9 (1916): 1–272.
43. Cozzi, "Dalla riscoperta," 11.
44. Cozzi, "Dalla riscoperta," 20.
45. Quoted in Sergio Zamperetti, "Patriziato e giurisdizioni private," *SVOC* 7: 220.
46. Del Negro, "La milizia," 509–14.
47. Battista Nani, *Historia della Republica Veneta, Parte Seconda* (Venice, 1686), 329.
48. Quoted in Alberto Tenenti, "La navigazione," *SVOC* 7: 566–7, n. 134.
49. Megna, "Grandezza e miseria," 188.
50. Martina Frank, "Spazio pubblico, prospetti di chiese e glorificazione gentilizia nella Venezia del Seicento. Riflessioni su una tipologia," *Atti dell'Istituto Veneto di Scienze, Lettere ed Arti, Classe di Scienze Morali, Lettere ed Arti* 144 (1985–6): 109–26.
51. Howard, *Architectural History*, 223–7.

52. Zamperetti, "Patriziato e giurisdizioni private," 205.
53. Zamperetti, "Patriziato e giurisdizioni private," 211–20.
54. Andrea Zannini, "La presenza borghese," *SVOC* 7: 267.
55. James H. Johnson, *Venice Incognito: Masks in the Serene Republic* (Berkeley, 2011), 144.
56. See Gaetano Cozzi, *Repubblica di Venezia e stati italiani: politica e giustizia dal secolo XVI al secolo XVIII* (1982), 181–5; Claudio Povolo, *L'intrigo dell'onore: poteri e istituzioni nella Repubblica di Venezia tra Cinque e Seicento* (Verona, 1997).
57. Jonathan Walker, "*Bravi* and Venetian Nobles, c. 1550–1650," *SV* n.s. 36 (1998): 106.
58. James Grantham Turner, *Schooling Sex: Libertine Literature and Erotic Education in Italy, France, and England, 1534–1685* (Oxford, 2003), 88–105; Giorgio Spini, *Ricerca dei libertini: la teoria dell'impostura delle religioni nel Seicento italiano* (Florence, 1950), esp. 154–57.
59. Rosand, *Opera in Seventeenth-Century Venice*, 59.
60. Jonathan Walker, "Gambling and Venetian Noblemen, c. 1500–1700," *Past and Present* 162 (1999): 37. I have modified the quote for readability.
61. Walker, "Gambling and Venetian Noblemen," 60, again with minor modifications for readability.
62. For Leon Modena's addiction to gambling, Cohen, *Autobiography*, 41.
63. The phrase is borrowed from Johnson, *Venice Incognito*, ch. 13 (entitled "Saving Face"), which gives examples of begging while masked.
64. Eugene J. Johnson, "The Short, Lascivious Life of Two Venetian Theaters, 1580–85," *RQ* 55 (2002): 955–6.
65. Johnson, *Venice Incognito*, 218.
66. Wendy Heller, *Emblems of Eloquence: Opera and Women's Voices in Seventeenth-Century Venice* (Berkeley, 2003), 51.
67. Edward Muir, *The Culture Wars of the Late Renaissance: Skeptics, Libertines, and Opera* (Cambridge, MA, 2007), 55.
68. Gino Benzoni, "Le accademie," *SCUV* 4/I: 131–62.
69. Heller, *Emblems of Eloquence*, 49, 51.
70. Muir, *Culture Wars*, 63–107.
71. Heller, *Emblems of Eloquence*, 53.
72. Tarabotti, *Paternal Tyranny*, 147.
73. Heller, *Emblems of Eloquence*, 52–8.
74. Rosand, *Opera in Seventeenth-Century Venice*, 1.
75. Jonathan E. Glixon and Beth L. Glixon, "Oil and Opera Don't Mix: The Biography of S. Aponal, a Seventeenth-Century Venetian Opera Theater," in *Music in the Theater, Church and Villa: Essays in Honor of Robert Lamar Weaver and Norma Wright Weaver*, ed. Susan Parisi (Warren, MI, 2000), 137. See also Eugene J. Johnson, *Inventing the Opera House: Theater Architecture in Renaissance and Baroque Italy* (Cambridge, 2018), 205–26.
76. Rosand, *Opera in Seventeenth-Century Venice*, 3.

77. Rosand, *Opera in Seventeenth-Century Venice*, 107.
78. Heller, *Emblems of Eloquence*, 78.
79. Rosand, *Opera in Seventeenth-Century Venice*, 89.
80. Rosand, *Opera in Seventeenth-Century Venice*, 104.
81. Dennis Romano, "Commentary: Why Opera? The Politics of an Emerging Genre," *Journal of Interdisciplinary History* 36 (2006): 401–9.
82. Rosand, *Opera in Seventeenth-Century Venice*, 57.
83. Mauro Calcagno, "Censuring *Eliogabolo* in Seventeenth-Century Venice," *Journal of Interdisciplinary History* 36 (2006): 355–77.
84. *Squitinio della liberta veneta* (Mirandola, 1612), 75.
85. All quotations from Amelot de la Houssaye are cited in Gaeta, "Venezia da 'stato misto' ad aristocrazia 'esemplare,'" 491–3.
86. Juergen Schulz, "The Printed Plans and Panoramic Views of Venice (1486–1797)," *Saggi e Memorie di Storia dell'Arte* 7 (1970): 74.
87. Bellavitis and Romanelli, *Venezia*, 125.
88. Maurice Aymard, "Conclusions," in *At the Centre of the Old World*, ed. Lanaro, 373.
89. Krzysztof Pomian, "Antiquari e collezionisti," *SCUV* 4/I: 533.
90. Ugo Tucci, *Un mercante veneziano del Seicento: Simon Giogalli* (Venice, 2008), 256–7.
91. Marco Boschini, *La carte del navegar pitoresco*, ed. Anna Pallucchini (Venice, 1966), x n. 5, xi; Francesca Trivellato, *Fondamenta dei vetrai: lavoro, tecnologia e mercato a Venezia tra Sei e Settecento* (Rome, 2000), 240.
92. Lionello Puppi and Ruggero Rugolo, "'Un'ordinaria forma non alletta.' Arte, riflessione sull'arte e società," *SVOC* 7: 657–62.
93. Boschini, *Carta del navegar*, 86.
94. Boschini, *Carta del navegar*, 381.
95. Boschini, *Carta del navegar*, 11.
96. Boschini, *Carta del navegar*, 98.
97. Pezzolo, "L'economia," 374–82.
98. Luca de Biase, "Immagini delle città e delle campagne tra la metà del XVI e la fine del XVII secolo," *SCUV* 4/I, 653. Domenico Sella, *Commerci e industrie a Venezia nel secolo XVII* (Rome, 1961), 29–34.
99. Lane, *Venice: A Maritime Republic*, 419.
100. McNeill, *Venice: The Hinge of Europe*, 152.
101. Pezzolo, "L'economia," 400.
102. Pezzolo, "L'economia," 399.
103. Richard Lassels, *The Voyage of Italy*, 2 vols. (Paris, 1670), 2: 403–4.
104. Salvatore Ciriacono, "Investimenti capitalistici e colture irrigue: la congiuntura agricola nella terraferma veneta (secoli XVI e XVII) in *Atti del Convegno: Venezia e la terraferma attraverso le relazioni dei rettori*, ed. Amelio Tagliaferri (Milan, 1981), 149–51.
105. Beltrami, *Saggio di storia dell'agricoltura*, 46–8.

106. Beltrami, *Saggio di storia dell'agricoltura*, 21–30; De Biase, "Immagini delle città," 640.
107. De Biase, "Immagini delle città," 634–42.
108. Ciriacono, "Investimenti capitalistici," 151–2.
109. Trivellato, *Fondamenta dei vetrai*, 124, n. 34, 186.
110. Quoted in Brian Pullan, "Poveri, mendicanti e vagabondi (secoli XIV–XVII)" in *Storia d'Italia Annali I: dal feudalesimo al capitalismo* (Turin, 1978), 1032–3.
111. Davis, *Shipbuilders of the Venetian Arsenal*, 45.
112. Richard Tilden Rapp, *Industry and Economic Decline in Seventeenth-Century Venice* (Cambridge MA., 1976), 83–6.
113. Walter Panciera, "The Industries of Venice in the Seventeenth and Eighteenth Centuries," in *At the Centre of the Old World*, ed. Lanaro, 192–3.
114. Marcello della Valentina, "The Silk Industry in Venice: Guilds and Labour Relations in the Seventeenth and Eighteenth Centuries," in *At the Centre of the Old World*, ed. Lanaro, 134–6.
115. Trivellato, *Fondamenta dei vetrai,* 156–7.
116. Pullan, "Poveri, mendicanti e vagabondi," 994–5. For a general discussion of the growth of inequality and its relationship to the fiscal demands of the state, with an emphasis on the Venetian *terraferma*, see Guido Alfani and Matteo di Tullio, *The Lion's Share: Inequality and the Rise of the Fiscal State in Preindustrial Europe* (Cambridge, 2019).
117. Panciera, *L'arte matrice*, 42–3.
118. Panciera, *L'arte matrice*, 16–21; Panciera, "Industries of Venice," 188–90.
119. Ivo Mattozzi, "Intraprese produttive in Terraferma," *SVOC* 7: 463.
120. Panciera, "Industries of Venice," 190.
121. Trivellato, *Fondamenta dei vetrai,* 242–3.
122. Robert C. Davis and Garry R. Marvin, *Venice: The Tourist Maze: A Cultural Critique of the World's Most Touristed City* (Berkeley, 2004), 30–51.
123. Bruce Redford, *Venice and the Grand Tour* (New Haven, 1996), 56.
124. Lassels, *Voyage of Italy*, 2: 425–6.
125. John Evelyn, *Diary and Correspondence*, 4 vols. (London, 1854), 1: 197; John Pemble, *Venice Rediscovered* (Oxford, 1995), 118 (for Beckford).
126. Davis and Marvin, *Venice: Tourist Maze,* 48.

CHAPTER 16

1. Franco Fido, *Nuova guida a Goldoni: teatro e società nel Settecento* (Turin, 2000); Franco Fido, "Carlo Goldoni," *SCUV* 5/I:309–35; Giorgio Padoan, "L'impiego civile di Carlo Goldoni," *Lettere Italiane* 35 (1983): 421–56; John Louis DiGaetani, *Carlo Gozzi: A Life in the 18th Century Venetian Theater, an Afterlife in Opera* (Jefferson, NC, 1999); Alberto Beniscelli, "Gozzi, Carlo," *DBI* 58 (2002): 240–47.
2. Quoted in Lucia Strappini, "Goldoni, Carlo," *DBI* 57 (2001): 581–92.

3. Quoted in Ricardo Bigi de Aquino, "Eighteenth-Century Theatrical Reform in Goldoni's 'Il Teatro Comico' and Moratín's 'La Comedia Nueva,'" *Mediterranean Studies* 12 (2003): 150.
4. Piero del Negro, "Carlo Goldoni e la massoneria veneziana," *Studi Storici* 43 (2002): 411–9.
5. *Sior Todero brontolon*, act 2, scene 14, my translation. See Carlo Goldoni, *Tutte le opere di Carlo Goldoni*, 14 vols. (Milan, 1935–48), 8: 102.
6. *La bottega del caffè*, act 2, scene 2 [Goldoni, *Tutte le opere*, 3: 38]; *La famiglia dell'antiquario*, act 1, scene 19 [Goldoni, *Tutte le opere*, 2: 911]. Translations are by James Johnson in *Venice Incognito*, 162–3.
7. *Le donne curiose*, act 2, scene 13. [Goldoni, *Tutte le opere*, 4: 898.]
8. Quoted in Johnson, *Venice Incognito*, 158.
9. Quoted in Ted Emery, "Carlo Gozzi in Context," in Carlo Gozzi, *Five Tales for the Theatre*, ed. and trans. Albert Bermel and Ted Emery (Chicago, 1989), 6.
10. Gianfranco Torcellan, "Un problema aperto: politica e cultura nella Venezia del '700," *SV* 8 (1966): 493–513.
11. Concina, *History of Venetian Architecture*, 267–8; Howard, *Architectural History*, 237–8.
12. Francesco Donà, *Esatto diario di quanto è sucesso dalli 2 sino a 17 maggio 1797 nella caduta della veneta aristocratica repubblica* (Basel, 1797), 3.
13. Marco Fincardi, "I luoghi delle relazioni sociali," *SVON* 1: 490.
14. Johnson, *Venice Incognito*, 52.
15. Johnson, *Venice Incognito*, 147.
16. Johnson, *Venice Incognito*, 125.
17. Gasparo Gozzi, "Elogio delle botteghe di caffè," in *Prose varie di Gasparo Gozzi* (Milan, 1849), https://www.rodoni.ch/busoni/bibliotechina/autoriinrete/gasparogozziprose.pdf, pp. 120–22.. I follow the translation in Larry Wolff, *Paolina's Innocence: Child Abuse in Casanova's Venice* (Stanford, 2012), 80.
18. Danilo Reato, *La bottega del caffè: i caffè veneziani tra '700 e '900* (Venice, 1991), 26.
19. See Bianca Tamassia Mazzarotto, *Le feste veneziane: i giochi popolari, le cerimonie religiose e di governo* (Florence, 1980), 132; I follow partly the translation in Johnson, *Venice Incognito*, 20.
20. Johnson, *Venice Incognito*, 151.
21. Johnson, *Venice Incognito*, 151.
22. Marco Cuaz, "Giornali e gazzette," *SCUV* 5/I: 119.
23. Cuaz, "Giornali e gazzette," 122–27.
24. Cesare de Michelis, "Caminer, Elisabetta," *DBI*, 17 (1974): 236–41.
25. Madile Gambier, "Dolfin, Caterina," *DBI* 40 (1991): 465–69.
26. Quoted in Wolff, *Paolina's Innocence*, 214–5.
27. Marino Berengo, "Il problema politico-sociale di Venezia e della sua terraferma," *SCIV* 3: 153.

28. Quoted in Nicola Vinovrški, "Casanova: A Case Study in Celebrity in 18th Century Europe," *Historical Social Research/Historische Sozialforschung* Supplement 32 (2019): 106.
29. Anna Maria Spiazzi, Massimo De Grassi, and Giovanna Galasso, eds., *Andrea Brustolon, 1662–1732, "Il Michelangelo del legno"* (Milan, 2009); and, more generally, Giuseppe Morazzoni, *Il mobile veneziano del '700* (Milan, 1927).
30. Davide Dotti, "Precursori e protagonisti del vedutismo veneziano settecentesco," in *Lo splendore di Venezia: Canaletto, Bellotto, Guardi e i vedutisti dell'Ottocento*, ed. Davide Dotti (Milan, 2016), 10–31.
31. André Chastel, "Il Settecento veneziano nelle arti," *SCIV*, 3: 225.
32. Howard, *Architectural History*, 234–260; Concina, *History of Venetian Architecture*, 267–89.
33. Bellavitis and Romanelli, *Venezia*, 152.
34. Krzysztof Pomian, *Collectors and Curiosities: Paris and Venice, 1500–1800* (Cambridge, 1990), 186–92.
35. Franco Venturi, *Settecento riformatore*, vol. 1, *Da Muratori a Beccaria* (Turin, 1969), 289–92.
36. Much of what follows is drawn from Paolo Preto, "Le riforme," *SVOC* 8: 83–142.
37. Piero del Negro, "Introduzione," *SVOC* 8: 64–8.
38. Walter Panciera, *La Repubblica di Venezia nel Settecento* (Rome, 2014), 59; Karl Appuhn, "Ecologies of Beef: Eighteenth-Century Epizootics and the Environmental History of Early Modern Europe," *Environmental History* 15 (2010): 268–87.
39. Lazzarini, *Boschi, legnami*, 262–76.
40. Massimo Costantini, "Commercio e marina," *SVOC* 8: 561; Lane, *Venice: A Maritime Republic*, 419.
41. Romanin, *Storia documentata*, 8: 102–3; Ferruccio Zago, ed., *Documenti relativi alla istituzione in Venezia della prima camera del commercio (1713–1768)* (Venice, 1964).
42. Salvatore Ciriacono, *Olio e ebrei nella Repubblica Veneta del Settecento* (Venice, 1975), 62.
43. Calimani, *The Ghetto of Venice*, 238–47; Panciera, *La Repubblica*, 74–5.
44. Costantini, "Commercio e marina," 603–8.
45. Quoted in Della Valentina, "The Silk Industry in Venice," 140.
46. Paolo Preto, "'Lo sciopero dei 'lavoranti-pistori' a Venezia nel 1775 e 1780-82," in *Non uno itinere: studi storici offerti dagli allievi a Federico Seneca*, ed. Federica Ambrosini et al. (Venice, 1993), 241–63.
47. Preto, "Le riforme," 115.
48. Preto, "Le riforme," 125–8.
49. Preto, "Le riforme," 128–30.
50. Manlio Brusatin, *Venezia nel Settecento: stato, architettura, territorio* (Turin, 1980), 219; Salvatore Ciriacono, "Il governo del territorio," *SVOC* 8: 624–5.

51. Vanzan Marchini, *Venezia civiltà anfibia*, 56–62; Salvatore Ciriacono, "Management of the Lagoon and the Urban Environment in 18th-Century Venice," *Water History* 10 (2018): 148–9.
52. Del Negro, "Introduzione," 38–48 (quote on 48).
53. Giuseppe Gullino, "Il giurisdizionalismo dello stato veneziano: gli antichi problemi e la nuova cultura," in *La chiesa di Venezia nel Settecento*, ed. Bruno Bertoli (Venice, 1993), 30.
54. Giuseppe Gullino, "Venezia e le campagne," *SVOC* 8: 679–82.
55. Gullino, "Il giurisdizionalismo," 30–32.
56. Viggiano, "Politics and Constitution," 80–1.
57. Gullino, "Il giurisdizionalismo," 29; Volker Hunecke, "Il corpo aristocratico," *SVOC* 8: 403–21; Volker Hunecke, *Il patriziato veneziano alla fine della Repubblica: demografia, famiglia, ménage* (Rome, 1997), 27.
58. Quoted in Madile Gambier, "I carteggi privati dei Querini. Spunti di vita domestica e familiare," in *I Querini Stampalia: un ritratto di famiglia nel Settecento veneziano*, ed. Giorgio Busetto and Madile Gambier (Venice, 1987), 94.
59. Quoted in Del Negro, "Introduzione,"19. See also Piero del Negro, "Proposte illuminate e conservazione nel dibattito sulla teoria e la prassi dello stato," *SCUV* 5/II: 129–31.
60. Del Negro, "Introduzione," 19–20.
61. Del Negro, "Proposte illuminate," 131–5.
62. Del Negro, "Proposte illuminate," 135–7.
63. Del Negro, "Introduzione," 10.
64. Del Negro, "Introduzione," 18.
65. For this correction, see Romanin, *Storia documentata*, 8: 70–94.
66. Georgelin, *Venise au siècle des lumières*, 804.
67. Romanin, *Storia documentata*, 8: 130–9.
68. Quoted in Hunecke, *Patriziato veneziano*, 18.
69. Romanin, *Storia documentata*, 8: 175; Preto, "Le riforme," 96.
70. Preto, "Le riforme," 98.
71. Romanin, *Storia documentata*, 8: 160–79.
72. Hunecke, *Patriziato veneziano*, 47, 394.
73. Bellavitis and Romanelli, *Venezia*, 133.
74. Berengo, "Il problema politico-sociale," 152.
75. Sergio Perini, *La difesa militare della terraferma veneta nel Settecento* (Sottomarina, 1998), 153–64.
76. Cessi, *Storia della Repubblica*, 741.
77. Perini, *Difesa militare*, 48–56, 175.
78. Del Negro, "Introduzione," 21–4; 31–7.
79. Panciera, *La Repubblica*, 47.
80. Piero del Negro, "La fine della Repubblica aristocratica," *SVOC* 8: 193.

81. Del Negro, "La fine," 203, 215.
82. Del Negro, "La fine," 226–7.
83. Del Negro, "La fine," 231.
84. Del Negro, "La fine," 236.
85. Del Negro, "La fine," 244.
86. Romanin, *Storia documentata*, 10: 87.
87. Del Negro, "La fine," 252.
88. Romanin, *Storia documentata*, 10: 117.
89. Giovanni Scarabello, "La municipalità democratica," *SVOC* 8: 271.
90. Romanin, *Storia documentata*, 10: 139–40.
91. Romanin, *Storia documentata*, 10: 140–1.
92. For Doge Manin's property holdings, see Georgelin, *Venise au siècle des lumières*, 493–502.
93. Scarabello, "La municipalità democratica," 273–8.
94. Quoted in Valentina Dal Cin, *Mondo nuovo: l'élite veneta fra rivoluzione e restaurazione (1797–1815)* (Venice, 2019), 331.
95. Preto, "Le riforme," 131.
96. Preto, "Le riforme," 132.
97. Giandomenico Romanelli, *Venezia Ottocento: materiali per una storia architettonica e urbanistica della città nel secolo XIX* (Rome, 1977), 18–22.
98. Martha Feldman, "Opera, Festivity, and Spectacle in 'Revolutionary' Venice: Phantasms of Time and History," *VR*, 230–1 with slight modification of the translation.
99. Feldman, "Opera, Festivity, and Spectacle," 232 with slight modification of the translation.
100. Reproduced in Scarabello, "La municipalità democratica," 318.
101. Feldman, "Opera, Festivity, and Spectacle," 233–47.
102. Feldman, "Opera, Festivity, and Spectacle," 226–7.
103. Scarabello, "La municipalità democratica," 300–1.
104. Scarabello, "La municipalità democratica," 285–93.
105. The painting is still in the Louvre.
106. Scarabello, "La municipalità democratica," 344–9.
107. Giovanni Scarabello, "Da Campoformido al Congresso di Vienna: l'identità veneta sospesa," *SCUV* 6: 1–11.
108. Dal Cin, *Il mondo nuovo*, 345.
109. Scarabello, "Da Campoformido," 11–18; Eurigio Tonetti, "Il comune prima dell'Unità," *SVON* 1: 45–9.
110. Fincardi, "Luoghi," 495–6.
111. David Laven, *Venice and Venetia under the Habsburgs, 1815–1835* (Oxford, 2002), 121.
112. Romanelli, *Venezia Ottocento*, 111.

113. Romanelli, *Venezia Ottocento*, 42–3.
114. Romanelli, *Venezia Ottocento*, 489–500.
115. Romanelli, *Venezia Ottocento*, 494.
116. Romanelli, *Venezia Ottocento*, 116 n. 39.
117. Laven, *Venice and Venetia*, 167–8.
118. Silvio Tramontin, "Sguardo d'insieme su novant'anni di storia," in *La chiesa veneziana dal tramonto della Serenissima al 1848*, ed. Maria Leonardi (Venice, 1986), 16–7; Giandomenico Romanelli, "Venezia e la sua chiesa nell'età Napoleonica" in *La chiesa veneziana dal tramonto della Serenissima al 1848*, ed. Maria Leonardi (Venice, 1986), 66–7.
119. Concina, *History of Venetian Architecture*, 292.
120. Bellavitis and Romanelli, *Venezia*, 176.
121. Romanelli, *Venezia Ottocento*, 89.
122. Bellavitis and Romanelli, *Venezia*, 176.
123. Johnson, *Venice Incognito*, 217–8.
124. Johnson, *Venice Incognito*, 218–9.
125. Johnson, *Venice Incognito*, 228.

CHAPTER 17

1. The phrase "spinning it around" is John Julius Norwich's. See his *Paradise of Cities: Venice in the 19th Century* (New York, 2003), 92.
2. Adolfo Bernardello, *La prima ferrovia fra Venezia e Milano: storia della imperial-regia privilegiata strada ferrata Ferdinandea Lombardo-Veneta* (Venice, 1996), 224; Piero del Negro, "Il 1848 e dopo," *SVON* 1: 118.
3. Quoted in Laven, *Venice and Venetia*, 80.
4. Quoted in Giuseppe Gullino, "Istituzioni di cultura," *SVON* 2: 1071.
5. Luigi Coletti, "L'arte dal neoclassicismo al romanticismo," *SCIV* 3: 289–97.
6. Tonetti, "Il Comune prima dell'Unità," 49–60; Michele Gottardi, "Da Manin a Manin: istituzioni e ceti dirigenti dal '97 al '48," *SVON* 1: 76–95; Franco della Peruta, "Il Veneto nel Risorgimento fino al 1848," in *Venezia e l'Austria*, ed. Benzoni and Cozzi, 383–90.
7. Laven, *Venice and Venetia*, 88.
8. Quoted in Alvise Zorzi, *Venezia Austriaca, 1798–1866*, 2nd ed. (Gorizia, 2000), 61.
9. Renzo Derosas, "La demografia dei poveri. Pescatori, facchini e industrianti nella Venezia di metà Ottocento," *SVON* 1: 718; and Casimira Grandi, "Assistenza e beneficenza," *SVON* 2: 871.
10. Grandi, "Assistenza e beneficenza," 871; Zorzi, *Venezia Austriaca*, 59.
11. Massimo Costantini, *Porto, navi e traffici a Venezia, 1700–2000* (Venice, 2004), 86–7.
12. Della Peruta, "Il Veneto nel Risorgimento fino al 1848," 390; Laven, *Venice and Venetia*, 104–19.

13. Grandi, "Assistenza e beneficenza," 871.
14. Grandi, "Assistenza e beneficenza," 888.
15. Giulio Monteleone, "La carestia del 1816–1817 nelle province venete," *AV* series 5, 86–7 (1969): 33. And see Alessandro Fadelli, "Quando la gente moriva per le strade dalla fame: riflessi demografici e sociali della grande carestia del 1816–1817 nel Friuli occidentale," *Atti dell'Accademia San Marco di Pordenone* 19 (2017): 721–61.
16. Derosas, "Demografia dei poveri," 733.
17. Derosas, "Demografia dei poveri," 734.
18. Derosas, "Demografia dei poveri," 730–2.
19. Zorzi, *Venezia Austriaca*, 60–1.
20. Davis, *A Venetian Family and Its Fortune*, 143–56; Renzo Derosas, "Aspetti economici della crisi del patriziato veneziano tra fine Settecento e primo Ottocento," *Cheiron* 12–13 (1989–90): 30.
21. Zorzi, *Venezia Austriaca*, 233–46.
22. Zorzi, *Venezia Austriaca*, 234.
23. Dal Cin, *Il mondo nuovo*, 347–8.
24. Derosas, "Aspetti economici," 21.
25. Riccardo Martelli, "Papadopoli," *DBI* 81 (2014)—online version only, see [https://www.treccani.it/enciclopedia/papadopoli_%28Dizionario-Biografico%29/].
26. Quoted in Paul Ginsborg, *Daniele Manin and the Venetian Revolution of 1848–49* (Cambridge, 1979), 50.
27. Zorzi, *Venezia Austriaca*, 248–9.
28. Mario Isnenghi, "I luoghi della cultura," in *Storia d'Italia. Le regioni dall'Unità a oggi. Il Veneto*, ed. Silvio Lanaro (Turin, 1984), 319, n. 6.
29. Martina Massaro, "Giacomo Treves dei Bonfili, profile di un collezionista," *AT* 3rd series 13/II (2014): 47–68.
30. Paolo Pellegrini, "Treves de' Bonfili, Alberto Isacco," *DBI* 96 (2019): 708–11.
31. Antonio Lazzarini, "Possidenti e bonificatori ebrei: la famiglia Sullam," *SVON* 1: 607–9.
32. Zorzi, *Venezia Austriaca*, 292.
33. Gadi Luzzatto Voghera, "Gli ebrei," *SVON* 1: 625, 633.
34. Andrea Zannini, "Vecchi poveri e nuovi borghesi," in *Venezia e l'Austria*, ed. Benzoni and Cozzi, 187–8.
35. Gullino, "Istituzioni di cultura," 1051–80.
36. Costantini, *Porto, navi*, 87–91.
37. Gino Luzzatto, "L'economia veneziana dal 1797 al 1866," *SCIV* 3: 275–6; Bernardello, *La prima ferrovia*.
38. Costantini, *Porto, navi*, 91–101.
39. Sergio Barzizza, "Il gas a Venezia. La prima volta del 'nuovo,' le contraddizioni di sempre," *Cheiron* 12–13 (1989–90): 147–58.
40. Luzzatto, "L'economia veneziana dal 1797," 274–5.
41. Ginsborg, *Daniele Manin*, 32.

42. Andrea Zannini, "La costruzione della città turistica," *SVON* 2: 1125.
43. Zannini, "Vecchi poveri," 179–80.
44. Zannini, "La costruzione," 1124–30.
45. Zannini, "La costruzione," 1131.
46. Claudio Povolo, "The Creation of Venetian Historiography," *VR*, 491–519.
47. Romano, *The Likeness of Venice*, 342–58, quote on 345–6.
48. Mario Infelise, "Venezia e il suo passato. Storie miti 'fole,'" *SVON* 2: 982–4.
49. Ginsborg, *Daniele Manin*, 66–7; Del Negro, "Il 1848 e dopo," 123–5.
50. Ginsborg, *Daniele Manin*, 53–5.
51. Ginsborg, *Daniele Manin*, 53–8; Del Negro, "Il 1848 e dopo," 116–21.
52. Feliciano Benvenuti, "Venezia da patria a nazione: un percorso," in *Venezia e l'Austria*, ed. Benzoni and Cozzi, 485.
53. Ginsborg, *Daniele Manin*, 52–3.
54. Ginsborg, *Daniele Manin*, 67–9, quote on 69.
55. Irene Schrattenecker, "Il potere delle immagini. Gli inni patriottici. I canti popolari e le stampe della rivoluzione del 1848," in *Venezia e l'Austria*, ed. Benzoni and Cozzi, 464.
56. Filippini, "Figure, fatti e percorsi," 465.
57. Laven, *Venice and Venetia*, 226.
58. Ginsborg, *Daniele Manin*, 72; Carmelo Alberti, "Teatro, musica e stagione teatrale," *SVON* 2: 1037.
59. Ginsborg, *Daniele Manin*, 58–67.
60. The narrative of the Revolution follows Ginsborg, *Daniele Manin;* and Del Negro, "Il 1848 e dopo."
61. Filippini, "Figure, fatti e percorsi," 467–9.
62. Ginsborg, *Daniele Manin*, 101.
63. Del Negro, "Il 1848 e dopo," 142.
64. Giovanni Pillinini, "La pubblicistica veneziana nel 1848–49," in *Venezia e l'Austria*, ed. Benzoni and Cozzi, 438.
65. Ginsborg, *Daniele Manin*, 117.
66. Ginsborg, *Daniele Manin*, 121–2.
67. Ginsborg, *Daniele Manin*, 159.
68. Ginsborg, *Daniele Manin*, 185.
69. Ginsborg, *Daniele Manin*, 202.
70. Ginsborg, *Daniele Manin*, 224.
71. Ginsborg, *Daniele Manin*, 250.
72. Ginsborg, *Daniele Manin*, 277.
73. Ginsborg, *Daniele Manin*, 301.
74. Ginsborg, *Daniele Manin*, 304.
75. Zorzi, *Venezia Austriaca*, 103.
76. Ginsborg, *Daniele Manin*, 357.
77. Del Negro, "Il 1848 e dopo," 167; Ginsborg, *Daniele Manin*, 369–70; Benvenuti, "Venezia da patria a nazione," 490–1.

78. Del Negro, "Il 1848 e dopo," 167; Brigitte Mazohl-Wallnig, "L'Austria e Venezia," in *Venezia e l'Austria*, ed. Benzoni and Cozzi, 15.
79. Ginsborg, *Daniele Manin*, 267.
80. Tonetti, "Il comune prima dell'Unità," 67.
81. Giovanni Vian, "La chiesa," in *Venezia e l'Austria*, ed. Benzoni and Cozzi, 122.
82. Concina, *History of Venetian Architecture*, 300–1.
83. Giovanni Vian, "La Chiesa Cattolica e le altre Chiese cristiane," *SVON* 1: 655–8.
84. A. Pilot, "Venezia dal 1851 al 1866 nei diari inediti del Cicogna" *NAV* 32, pt. 1 (1916): 410–11, 414, 416.
85. Pilot, "Venezia dal 1851 al 1866," 426.
86. William Dean Howells, *Venetian Life*, 2nd ed. (New York, 1867), 17–26.
87. John Rosselli, "La vita musicale a Venezia dal 1815 al 1866," in *Venezia e l'Austria*, ed. Benzoni and Cozzi, 44–5.
88. Fincardi, "I luoghi delle relazioni sociali,"502–3; Roselli, "La vita musicale," 45.
89. Costantini, *Porto, navi*, 95–101.
90. Bellavitis and Romanelli, *Venezia*, 180–1, figs. 180–1 [*sic*].
91. Romanelli, *Venezia Ottocento*, 215–26; 281–91; Margaret Plant, *Venice: Fragile City, 1797–1997* (New Haven, 2002), 146–9.
92. Bellavitis and Romanelli, *Venezia*, 188.
93. Plant, *Venice: Fragile City*, 148.
94. Costantini, *Porto, navi*, 96–7.
95. Plant, *Venice: Fragile City*, 148.
96. Adolfo Bernardello, "Iniziative economiche, accumulazione e investimenti di capitale (1830–1866)," *SVON* 1: 593.
97. Romanelli, *Venezia Ottocento*, 317.
98. Romanelli, *Venezia Ottocento*, 315–24; Plant, *Venice: Fragile City*, 149–50.
99. Zannini, "Vecchi poveri," 189–91; Zannini, "La costruzione," 1139; Bernardello, "Iniziative economiche," 594–5.
100. Howells, *Venetian Life*, 37.
101. John Pemble, *The Mediterranean Passion: Victorians and Edwardians in the South* (Oxford, 1987), 172.
102. John Ruskin, *Ruskin in Italy: Letters to His Parents, 1845*, ed., Harold I. Shapiro (Oxford, 1972), 198–9.
103. Adolfo Bernardello, "Il molino a vapore di S. Girolamo a Venezia (1840–1870)," *Atti dell'Istituto Veneto di Scienze, Lettere ed Arti, Classe di Scienze Morali, Lettere, ed Arti* 154 (1995–6): 257; Bernardello, "Iniziative economiche," 578–9.
104. Plant, *Venice: Fragile City*, 133.
105. Quoted in Pemble, *Venice Rediscovered*, 131.
106. Ruskin, *Ruskin in Italy*, 201.
107. Pemble, *Venice Rediscovered*, 134–65.
108. Zorzi, *Venezia Austriaca*, 140–53 (referendum wording on 149). For a firsthand account of the festivities, see Letizia Pesaro Maurogonato, *Il diario di Letizia (1866)*, edited by Mario Isnenghi (Verona 2004).

CHAPTER 18

1. For the Molino, Howard, *Architectural History*, 275–6; for the number of employees, Giovanni Luigi Fontana, "L'economia," *SVON* 2: 1444.
2. Nico Randeraad, "I prefetti e la città nei primi decenni postunitari," *SVON* 1: 210–11.
3. Danilo Bano, "La Scuola Superiore di Commercio," *SVON* 1: 549–66.
4. Andrea Cafarelli, *Il leone ferito: Venezia, l'Adriatico e la navigazione sussidiata per le Indie e l'Estremo Oriente (1866–1914)* (Rome, 2014), esp. 19–47.
5. Romanelli, *Venezia Ottocento*, 432–40; Massimo Costantini, "Dal porto franco al porto industriale," *SV Mare*, 902.
6. Guido Zucconi, "La cultura degli ingegneri: acque e strade ferrate all'indomani dell'annessione," *SCUV* 6: 640–45.
7. Zucconi, "Cultura degli ingegneri," 645–50; Wladimiro Dorigo, "Venezia e il Veneto," in Lanaro, ed., *Storia d'Italia, Il Veneto*, 1046–7.
8. R. J. B. Bosworth, *Italian Venice: A History* (New Haven, 2014), 39; Maria Teresa Sega and Nadia Maria Filippini, *Manifattura Tabacchi. Cotonificio Veneziano* (Padua, 2008), 97–9, 101, 105–6.
9. Fontana, "L'economia," 1445.
10. Fontana, "L'economia," 1446.
11. Fontana, "L'economia," 1445.
12. Ennio Concina, "La casa dell'Arsenale," *SV Mare*, 203–6; Bellavitis and Romanelli, *Venezia*, 228.
13. Pes, "Le classi popolari," 779–80.
14. Plant, *Venice: Fragile City*, 176–80.
15. Maurizio Rebershak, "Filippo Grimani e la 'nuova Venezia,'" *SVON*, 1: 330.
16. Costantini, "Dal porto franco," 899.
17. Pes, "Le classi popolari," 783.
18. Costantini, "Dal porto franco," 902.
19. Fincardi, "I luoghi delle relazioni sociali," 509.
20. Pes, "Le classi popolari," 783.
21. Leopoldo Magliaretta, "La qualità della vita," in *Venezia*, ed. Franzina, 336–7.
22. Reberschak, "Filippo Grimani," 336; Gianni Riccamboni, "Cent'anni di elezioni a Venezia," *SVON* 2: 1190.
23. Derosas, "La demografia dei poveri," 727.
24. Maria Teresa Sega, "Lavoratrici," *SVON*, 2: 830–1; Pes, "Le classi popolari," 780.
25. Sega, "Lavoratrici," 831.
26. Sega, "Lavoratrici," 822–3.
27. Lidia A. Sciama, *A Venetian Island: Environment, History and Change in Burano* (New York, 2003), 175.
28. Sega, "Lavoratrici," 823.
29. Sega, "Lavoratrici," 837.

30. Pes, "Le classi popolari," 782.
31. Sega, "Lavoratrici," 844.
32. Sega, "Lavoratrici," 844, 848.
33. Sega, "Lavoratrici," 848–9.
34. Sega, "Lavoratrici," 845, 848.
35. Renato Camurri, "Istituzioni, associazioni e classi dirigenti dall'Unità alla Grande guerra," *SVON* 1: 250; Pes, "Le classi popolari," 790–91.
36. Fincardi, "I luoghi delle relazioni sociali," 506–8.
37. Pes, "Le classi popolari," 791.
38. Pes, "Le classi popolari," 794–7.
39. Bosworth, *Italian Venice*, 66–9.
40. Vian, "La Chiesa cattolica," 664.
41. Sergio Apruzzese, "Paganuzzi, Giovanni Battista," *DBI* 80 (2014): 270–2.
42. Vian, "La Chiesa cattolica," 668–9; Silvio Tramontin, "Il movimento cattolico," in *La chiesa veneziana dal 1849 alle soglie del Novecento*, ed. Gabriele Ingegneri (Venice, 1987), 165–88; Bosworth, *Italian Venice*, 31 (quote).
43. Camurri, "Istituzioni, associazioni," 270–3; Bellavitis and Romanelli, *Venezia*, 210–24; Tiziana Agostini, "Selvatico, Riccardo," *DBI* 91 (2018): 840–43.
44. Rodolfo Pallucchini, "Significato e valore della 'Biennale' nella vita artistica veneziana e italiana," *SCIV* 3: 389–91; Plant, *Venice: Fragile City*, 215–19.
45. Vian, "La Chiesa cattolica," 669–74; Annibale Zambarbieri, "Il patriarca Sarto," in *La chiesa veneziana dal 1849 alle soglie del Novecento*, ed. Gabriele Ingegneri (Venice, 1987), 129–63.
46. Mario Isnenghi, "Introduzione," *SVON* 2: 1154.
47. Plant, *Venice: Fragile City*, 234–8.
48. Deborah Howard (*Architectural History*, 290) says the tower was hexagonal; Alvise Zorzi (*Venezia scomparsa*, 2 vols. [Milan, 1982], 2: 380) says pentagonal; Giulio Lorenzetti (*Venice and Its Lagoon: Historical-Artistic Guide* [Trieste, 1975, 518]) says octagonal. An illustration by eighteenth-century artist Giovanni Grevembroch shows it was a hexagon. Reproduced in Avery, *Vulcan's Forge*, 233.
49. Zannini, "La costruzione," 1141.
50. Zambarbieri, "Il patriarca Sarto," 131.
51. Zannini, "La costruzione," 1144.
52. Maurizio Reberschak, "L'economia," in *Venezia*, ed. Franzina, 248–9.
53. Plant, *Venice: Fragile City*, 214–5, 228, 257–8.
54. Reberschak, "Filippo Grimani," 339.
55. The term is Plant's (*Venice: Fragile City*, 209).
56. Plant, *Venice: Fragile City*, 209, 211.
57. Howard, *Architectural History*, 277–80; Concina, *History of Venetian Architecture*, 306–14; Plant, *Venice: Fragile City*, 239–44.
58. Pallucchini, "Significato e valore della 'Biennale,'" 391–95; Plant, *Venice: Fragile City*, 244–50.

59. Concina, *History of Venetian Architecture*, 314.
60. Bosworth, *Italian Venice*, 98.
61. Sergio Romano, *Giuseppe Volpi: industria e finanza tra Giolitti e Mussolini* (Milan, 1979), 8.
62. Maurizio Reberschak, "Gli uomini capitali: il 'gruppo veneziano' (Volpi, Cini e gli altri)," *SVON* 2: 1256–61.
63. Reberschak, "Gli uomini capitali," 1258–60.
64. Luca Pes, "Il fascismo adriatico," *SVON* 2: 1321.
65. Camurri, "Istituzioni, associazioni," 240.
66. Chinello, "Foscari, Piero," 338–40.
67. Judith Mackrell, *The Unfinished Palazzo: Life, Love and Art in Venice* (London, 2017).
68. Plant, *Venice: Fragile City*, 251.
69. Gino Damerini, "Venice, D'Annunzio e l'ultima guerra per l'unità d'Italia," *SCIV* 3: 377–9.
70. Isnenghi, "Introduzione," 1155.
71. Bruna Bianchi, "Venezia nella Grande guerra," *SVON* 1: 358–62.
72. Bosworth, *Italian Venice*, 86.
73. Bianchi, "Venezia nella Grande guerra," 357.
74. Bianchi, "Venezia nella Grande guerra," 364. A commemorative book produced in the Fascist era is filled with photos of the damage suffered from the various air raids. Giovanni Scarabello, *Il martirio di Venezia durante la grande guerra e l'opera di difesa della marina italiana* (Venice, 1933).
75. Bianchi, "Venezia nella Grande guerra," 371–2.
76. Bianchi, "Venezia nella Grande guerra," 386–7.
77. Bianchi, "Venezia nella Grande guerra," 387, 390, 401.
78. Bianchi, "Venezia nella Grande guerra," 406.
79. Italics in original. Damerini, "Venice, D'Annunzio e l'ultima guerra," 384.
80. Pes, "Il fascismo adriatico," 1322.
81. Pes, "Il fascismo adriatico," 1321.
82. Martin Clark, *Modern Italy, 1871–1995*, 2nd ed. (London, 1996), 204–5.
83. Reberschak, "Gli uomini capitali," 1262.
84. Fontana, "L'economia,"1448.
85. Chinello, "Foscari, Piero."
86. Reberschak, "Gli uomini capitali," 1263; Fontana, "L'economia," 1448–50.
87. Santo Peli, "Le concentrazioni finanziarie industriali nell'economia di guerra: il caso di Porto Marghera," *Studi Storici* 16 (1975): 182–204.
88. Bianchi, "Venezia nella Grande guerra," 407; Sega, "Lavoratrici," 855.
89. The phrase "masterpiece" is Dorigo's. See Wladimiro Dorigo, *Una legge contro Venezia: natura, storia, interessi nella questione della città e della laguna* (Rome, 1973), 163.
90. Reberschak, "Gli uomini capitali," 1262–3; Costantini, "Dal porto franco,"910–11.
91. Peli, "Concentrazioni finanziari," 195.

92. Costantini, "Dal porto franco," 910–11.
93. Costantini, "Dal porto franco," 910–11; Reberschak, "Gli uomini capitali," 1264.
94. Concina, *History of Venetian Architecture*, 314.
95. Fontana, "L'economia," 1455; Costantini, "Dal porto franco," 906–7.
96. Costantini, "Dal porto franco," 906.

CHAPTER 19

1. Bosworth, *Italian Venice*, 158–61; also https://www.iveser.it/2018/07/25/monumento-alla-partigiana-murer/.
2. Riccamboni, "Cent'anni di elezioni," 1195.
3. Riccamboni, "Cent'anni di elezioni," 1197–8; Renato Camurri, "La classe politica nazionalfascista," *SVON* 2: 1375. More generally, see Clark, *Modern Italy*, 203–13.
4. Pes, "Il fascismo adriatico," 1317.
5. Bosworth, *Italian Venice*, 115.
6. Pes, "Il fascismo adriatico," 1330.
7. Bosworth, *Italian Venice*, 117–9.
8. Camurri, "La classe politica," 1396–7; Riccamboni, "Cent'anni di elezioni," 1205, 1210.
9. Nadia Maria Filippini, "Storia delle donne: cultura, mestieri, profili," *SVON* 3: 1650–1.
10. Bosworth, *Italian Venice*, 119–20.
11. Camurri, "La classe politica," 1368.
12. Riccamboni, "Cent'anni di elezioni," 1206–8.
13. Riccamboni, "Cent'anni di elezioni," 1212–3.
14. Stefano Arieti, "Giordano, Davide," *DBI* 55 (2001): 259–62.
15. Camurri, "La classe politica," 1395; Bosworth, *Italian Venice*, 119.
16. Kate Ferris, *Everyday Life in Fascist Venice, 1929–40* (Houndmills, 2012), 86.
17. Alessandro Casellato, "I sestieri popolari," *SVON* 2: 1612.
18. Casellato, "I sestieri popolari," 1611–3; Camurri, "La classe politica," 1406–7.
19. Marco Fincardi, "Gli 'anni ruggenti' dell'antico leone: la moderna realtà del mito di Venezia," *Contemporanea* 4 (2001): 445–74; Marco Fincardi, "I fasti della 'tradizione': le ceremonie della nuova venezianità," *SVON* 2: 1494–9.
20. Ferris, *Everyday Life*, 90–9.
21. Ferris, *Everyday Life*, 92.
22. Ferris, *Everyday Life*, 95–6.
23. Camurri, "La classe politica," 1408.
24. Fincardi, "Gli 'anni ruggenti,'" 457.
25. Ferris, *Everyday Life*, 109–19.
26. Ferris, *Everyday Life*, 117.
27. Ferris, *Everyday Life*, 89.

28. Ernesto Brunetta, "Figure e momenti del Novecento politico," in *Venezia*, ed. Franzina, 178–82; Plant, *Venice: Fragile City*, 294–306.
29. Concina, *History of Venetian Architecture*, 322.
30. Bosworth, *Italian Venice*, 111–3.
31. Camurri, "La classe politica," 1406–18.
32. Reberschak, "Gli uomini capitali," 1264–6.
33. Reberschak, "L'economia," 256–60.
34. Fontana, "L'economia," 1466–78.
35. Fontana, "L'economia," 1466, 1479–81.
36. Casellato, "I sestieri popolari," 1607.
37. Fontana, "L'economia," 1463–4; Filippini, "Storia delle donne," 1632–3.
38. Casellato, "I sestieri popolari," 1599.
39. Casellato, "I sestieri popolari," 1615–6.
40. Casellato, "I sestieri popolari," 1594.
41. Filippini, "Storia delle donne," 1633–9.
42. Casellato, "I sestieri popolari," 1604; Ferris, *Everyday Life*, 198.
43. The names of the interviewees were replaced with initials. Ferris, *Everyday Life*, 105.
44. Emilio Franzina, "Il 'fronte interno' sulle lagune: Venezia in guerra (1938–1943)," *SVON* 3: 1701–3.
45. Brunetta, "Figure e momenti," 194.
46. Franzina, "Il 'fronte interno,'" 1728.
47. Bosworth, *Italian Venice*, 164–5.
48. Franzina, "Il 'fronte interno,'" 1730.
49. Brunetta, "Figure e momenti," 184–5.
50. Brunetta, "Figure e momenti," 189; Raffaele Liucci, "Il '43–'45," *SVON* 3: 1754.
51. Liucci, "Il '43–'45," 1745–51; Bosworth, *Italian Venice*, 174–5.
52. Liucci, "Il '43–'45," 1743.
53. Liucci, "Il '43–'45," 1758–9.
54. Bernard Poulet, *Volpi, Prince de la Venise moderne* (Paris, 2017).
55. Reberschak, "Gli uomini capitali," 1282–4.
56. Gianantonio Palladini, "Clero e laicato nella dramma della Resistenza," in *La chiesa di Venezia dalla seconda guerra mondiale al concilio*, ed. Bruno Bertoli (Venice, 1997), 78–80.
57. Simon Levis Sullam, "Gli ebrei a Venezia nella prima metà del Novecento," *SVON* 3: 1673–81.
58. Liucci, "Il '43–'45," 1759–60.
59. Filippini, "Storia delle donne," 1655.
60. Riccamboni, "Cent'anni di elezioni," 1218–40.
61. Brunetta, "Figure e momenti," 197–225; Mario Isnenghi and Silvio Lanaro, "Un modello stanco," in *Il Veneto*, ed. Lanaro, 1069–71.
62. Bosworth, *Italian Venice*, 192.
63. Franco Mancuso, "La laguna e le isole," *SVON* 3: 2362.

64. Reberschak, "L'economia," 277.
65. Leopoldo Pietragnoli and Maurizio Reberschak, "Dalla ricostruzione al 'problema' di Venezia," *SVON* 3: 2251.
66. Mancuso, "La laguna," 2362.
67. Costantini, *Porto, navi*, 132.
68. Reberschak, "L'economia," 277–8, 283; Gilda Zazzara, "La disparition de l'Italie industrielle: Porto Marghera en Vénétie," *Revue d'histoire* 20–21 (2019): 151.
69. Brunetta, "Figure e momenti," 205, 213–6; Cesco Chinello, "Storia operaia di Porto Marghera," *SVON* 3: 2307.
70. Bosworth, *Italian Venice*, 209.
71. Luca Pes, "Gli ultimi quarant'anni," *SVON* 3: 2420.
72. Chinello, "Storia operaia," 2306–17.
73. Fontana, "L'economia," 1480–1; Pes, "Gli ultimi," 2410–14.
74. Its record high was 188,970 in 1607. See Andrea Zannini, "Un censimento inedito del primo Seicento e la crisi demografica ed economica di Venezia," *SV* n.s. 26 (1993): 87–116.
75. Reberschak, "L'economia," 269–70; Pes, "Gli ultimi," 2408.
76. "Mock Funeral for Venice Dramatizes the Flight of Residents from City's Heart," *New York Times*, November 15, 2009, Section A, p. 18, https://www.nytimes.com/2009/11/15/world/europe/15venice.html—accessed 2/17/2021.
77. Sergio Barizza, "Mestre, la città del Novecento," *SVON* 3: 2345–50; Pes, "Gli ultimi," 2414.
78. Costantini, *Porto, navi*, 138.
79. Reberschak, "L'economia," 274; Mancuso, "La laguna," 2380.
80. Quoted in Nadia Maria Filippini, "Organizzazione del lavoro, ruoli sociali e familiari nei racconti delle infilaperle (1910–1950)," in *Perle e impiraperle: un lavoro di donne a Venezia tra '800 e '900* (Venice, 1990), 31.
81. Plant, *Venice: Fragile City*, 319–22; Magliaretta, "La qualità della vita," 366.
82. Pietragnoli and Reberschak, "Dalla ricostruzione," 2246–9.
83. Plant, *Venice: Fragile City*, 314–9; Nancy Jachec, "Anti-Communism at Home: Europeanism Abroad: Italian Cultural Policy at the Venice Biennale, 1948–58," *Contemporary European History* 14 (2005): 193–217.
84. Pietragnoli and Reberschak, "Dalla ricostruzione," 2251–3.
85. Plant, *Venice: Fragile City*, 342–54; Howard, *Architectural History*, 285–93; Concina, *History of Venetian Architecture*, 323–30.
86. Keahey, *Venice Against the Sea*; Plant, *Venice: Fragile City*, 355–8.
87. Reproduced in Keahey (see insert photo gallery) but mistakenly labeled a *carolina*.
88. Account of the flood reconstructed from Bosworth, *Italian Venice*, 202–4; Keahey, *Venice Against the Sea*, 10–12, 104–13.
89. Bosworth, *Italian Venice*, 206; Keahey, *Venice Against the Sea*, 117–53; Plant, *Venice: Fragile City*, 362–4.

90. Gatto and Carbognin, "The Lagoon of Venice"; Chinello, "Storia operaia," 2306–7; Plant, *Venice: Fragile City*, 356.
91. Gatto and Carbognin, "The Lagoon of Venice," 389.
92. Keahey, *Venice Against the Sea*, 211–59.
93. Keahey, *Venice Against the Sea*, 257.
94. Keahey, *Venice Against the Sea*, 124, 159–60, 212.
95. Keahey, *Venice Against the Sea*, 193–210.
96. Keahey, *Venice Against the Sea*, 258.
97. Maurizio Reberschak, ed., *Il grande Vajont*, 2 vols. (Longarone, 1983).
98. Quoted in Gilda Zazzara, "I cento anni di Porto Marghera (1917–2017)," *Italia Contemporanea* 284 (2017): 223–4.
99. Costantini, *Porto, navi*, 135, n. 30; Zazzara, "La disparition," 160.
100. On the symbolic significance of Marghera, see Laura Cerasi, *Perdonare Marghera: la città del lavoro nella memoria post-industriale* (Milan, 2007).
101. Sandro Meccoli, "Salvare Venezia: da chi?," *Meridiani* 1 (1988): 64–7; Pes, "Gli ultimi," 2401–2.
102. Ottavio Vittori and Anna Mestitz, *Four Golden Horses in the Sun*, trans. James A. Gray (New York, 1976).

CHAPTER 20

1. Plant, *Venice: Fragile City*, 432.
2. For other proposed glass bridges, see Plant, *Venice: Fragile City*, 400–1.
3. UNESCO website: https://whc.unesco.org/en/list/394—accessed February 8, 2021.
4. Davis and Marvin, *Venice: The Tourist Maze*, 105; Anna Momigliano, "Venice Tourism Could Never Be the Same. It Could Be Better," *New York Times*, July 2, 2020.
5. *The Guardian*, August 10, 2022.
6. Davis and Marvin, *Venice: The Tourist Maze*, 244.
7. Alessio Perrone, "Venice Cruise Ship Crash: Four Injured as MSC Opera Liner Hits Dock and Tourist Boat," *The Independent*, June 2, 2019, https://www.independent.co.uk/news/world/venice-cruise-ship-crash-boat-canal-italy-giudecca-victims-a8940456.html.
8. Costantini, "Dal porto franco al porto industriale," 912; Plant, *Venice: Fragile City*, 431.
9. Gaia Pianigiani and Emma Bubola, "Italy's Government to Ban Cruise Ships from Venice," *New York Times*, July 13, 2021, https://www.nytimes.com/2021/07/13/world/europe/venice-italy-cruise-ship-ban.html—accessed August 25, 2021.
10. Bosworth, *Italian Venice*, 210, 233.
11. Plant, *Venice: Fragile City*, 407.
12. Zazzara, "La disparition," 159.

13. Davis and Marvin, *Venice: Tourist Maze*, 112; "Tourismo, Anno Zero. L'ultimo record ed ora un modello tutto da ricostruire," *La Nuova di Venezia e Mestre*, February 10, 2021.
14. "La sfida impossibile di trovare una casa a Venezia se sei veneziano. Vince l'affitto ai turisti," *La Nuova di Venezia e Mestre*, February 2, 2021.
15. "Venice Plans to Evict 'Boy with Frog,'" *New York Times*, May 2, 2013.
16. Pes, "Gli ultimi," 2427.
17. Pes, "Gli ultimi," 2429.
18. Davis and Marvin, *Venice: Tourist Maze*, 272–82.
19. "Tourismo, Anno Zero."
20. "Venice Flood Barriers Scheme 'Will Soon Be Obsolete,'" *The Independent*, April 16, 2014, https://www.independent.co.uk/news/world/europe/venice-flood-barriers-scheme-will-soon-be-obsolte-9263236.html.
21. Plant, *Venice: Fragile City*, 419.
22. "Death of Venice," *The Guardian*, July 17, 1999; Davis and Marvin, *Venice: Tourist Maze*, 282–92.
23. Joanna Kostylo, "Sinking and Shrinking City: Cosmopolitanism, Historical Memory and Social Change in Venice," in *Post-Cosmopolitan Cities: Explorations of Urban Coexistence*, ed. Caroline Humphrey and Vera Skvirskaja (New York, 2012), 188–9.
24. Wolff, *Paolina's Innocence*, 266.
25. Plant, *Venice: Fragile City*, 389.
26. UNESCO, World Heritage List, "Venice and Its Lagoon," https://whc.unesco.org/en/list/394—accessed February 12, 2021.
27. "UNESCO closely monitoring ongoing threats to Venice World Heritage site," October 14, 2019, https://whc.unesco.org/en/news/2043–accessed February 12, 2021.
28. Quoted in Wolff, *Paolina's Innocence*, 256.
29. Francesco Jori, *Dalla Liga alla Lega: storia, movimenti, protagonisti. Prefazione di Ilvo Diamanti* (Venice, 2009).
30. Bosworth, *Italian Venice*, 228–33; Plant, *Venice: Fragile City*, 455–6.
31. Jori, *Dalla Liga alla Lega*, x.
32. Paolo Barcella, "Percorsi leghisti: dall'antimeridionalismo alla xenofobia," *Meridiana* 91 (2018): 95–119.
33. Quoted in Giovanni Miccoli, "Chiesa e Lega Nord," *Studi Storici* 53 (2012): 241.
34. Miccoli, "Chiese e Lega Nord," 241–3; Alessandro Casellato and Gilda Zazzara, "Un viaggio nel Veneto *agro*," in *Veneto agro. Operai e sindacato alla prova del leghismo (1980–2010)*, ed. Alessandro Casellato and Gilda Zazzara (Mestre-Treviso, 2010), 19–60.
35. Casellato and Zazzara, "Un viaggio."
36. https://elezioni2020.comune.venezia.it—accessed February 17, 2021.
37. Gianfranco Perulli, *Venezia città metropolitana* (Venice, 2018), 5–7.

38. https://campaignforalivingvenice.org/2019/11/22guide-to-the-referendum-for-separation-of venice-and-mestre—accessed February 16, 2021.
39. Hannah Roberts, "After Floods, Venice Eyes Autonomy," *Politico*, November 28, 2019, https://politico.eu/article/venice-floods-autonomy-referendum/—accessed February 16, 2021.
40. Roberts, "After Floods, Venice Eyes Autonomy."
41. https://www.mestremia.it/idee-per-mestre/#mestre-venezia—accessed February 16, 2021.
42. The words are Plant's. See Plant, *Venice: Fragile City*, 435.
43. Davis and Marvin, *Venice: Tourist Maze*, 237–60.
44. "Mock Funeral for Venice Dramatizes Flight of Residents from City's Heart," *New York Times*, November 14, 2009, https://www.nytimes.com/2009/11/15/world/europe/15venice.html—accessed February 17, 2021.
45. The myth of serenity and uniqueness persists. In late 2022, the *Gazzettino* reported that Police Commissioner Maurizio Mascopinto argued that Venice, unlike most cities, is so safe that one could walk around the city wearing a Rolex. See *Il Gazzettino*, December 29, 2022. At the same time, the newspaper consistently runs stories about how the city has been invaded by purse-snatchers.
46. McKinney, *North Adriatic Ecosystem*, 250.

Bibliography

Abu-Lughod, Janet L. *Before European Hegemony: The World System AD 1250–1350*. New York: Oxford University Press, 1989.

Agazzi, Michela. *Platea Sancti Marci: i luoghi marciani dall'XI al XIII secolo e la formazione della piazza*. Venice: Comune di Venezia, 1991.

Agostini, Tiziana. "Selvatico, Riccardo." *DBI* 91 (2018): 840–43.

Alfani, Guido, and Matteo Di Tullio. *The Lion's Share: Inequality and the Rise of the Fiscal State in Preindustrial Europe*. Cambridge: Cambridge University Press, 2019.

Alberti, Carmelo. "Teatro, musica e stagione teatrale." *SVON* 2: 1019–50.

Alberti, Leon Battista. *The Family in Renaissance Florence: A Translation by Renée Neu Watkins of I Libri della famiglia by Leon Battista Alberti*. Columbia: University of South Carolina Press, 1969.

Ambrosini, Federica. "Cerimonie, feste, lusso." *SVOC* 5: 441–520.

Ambrosini, Federica. "Penombre femminili." *SVOC* 7: 301–23.

Ammerman, Albert J. et al. "Beneath the Basilica of San Marco: New Light on the Origins of Venice." *Antiquity* 91, no. 360 (2017): 1620–9.

Andersen, Hans Christian. *What the Moon Saw and Other Tales*. Trans. H. W. Dulcken. London: George Routledge and Sons, 1866.

Andrea, Alfred J. "Essay on Primary Sources." In Donald E. Queller and Thomas F. Madden. *The Fourth Crusade: The Conquest of Constantinople*, 2nd ed., 299–318. Philadelphia: University of Pennsylvania Press, 2000.

Andretta, Stefano. *La Repubblica inquieta: Venezia nel Seicento tra Italia ed Europa*. Rome: Carocci Editore, 2000.

Apellániz, Francisco. "Venetian Trading Networks in the Medieval Mediterranean." *Journal of Interdisciplinary History* 44 (2013): 157–79.

Appuhn, Karl. "Ecologies of Beef: Eighteenth-Century Epizootics and the Environmental History of Early Modern Europe." *Environmental History* 15 (2010): 268–87.

Appuhn, Karl. *A Forest on the Sea: Environmental Expertise in Renaissance Venice*. Baltimore: Johns Hopkins University Press, 2009.

Apruzzese, Sergio. "Paganuzzi, Giovanni Battista." *DBI* 80 (2014): 270–72.

Arbel, Benjamin. "Daily Life on Board Venetian Ships: The Evidence of Renaissance Travelogues and Diaries." In *Rapporti mediterranei, pratiche documentarie, presenze veneziane: Le reti commerciali e culturali (XIV–XVI secolo)*. Edited by Gherardo Ortalli and Alessio Sopracasa, 183–219. Venice: Istituto Veneto di Scienze, Lettere, ed Arti, 2017.

Arbel, Benjamin. "Jews in International Trade: The Emergence of the Levantines and Ponentines. In *Jews of Early Modern Venice*. Edited by Davis and Ravid, 73–96.

Arbel, Benjamin. "The Last Decades of Venice's Trade with the Mamluks: Importations into Egypt and Syria." *Mamluk Studies Review* 8 (2004): 37–86.

Arbel, Benjamin. "Roots of Poverty and Resources of Richness in Cyprus Under Venetian Rule." In *Ricchi e poveri nella società dell'Oriente Grecolatino*. Edited by Chryssa A. Maltezou, 351–60. Venice: Ellenico Institouto, 1998.

Arbel, Benjamin. "The Venetian Domination of Cyprus: *Cui bono?*" In *La Serenissima and La Nobilissima: Venice in Cyprus and Cyprus in Venice*. Edited by Angel Nicolaou-Konnari, 45–55. Nicosia: Bank of Cyprus Cultural Foundation, 2009.

Archivio di Stato di Venezia. *Dalla guerra di Chioggia alla pace di Torino, 1377–1381: catalogo: mostra documentaria 29 giugno–27 settembre 1981*. Venice: Archivio di Stato di Venezia, 1981.

Arieti, Stefano. "Giordano, Davide." *DBI* 55 (2001): 259–62.

Arnaldi, Girolamo. "La cancelleria ducale fra culto della 'legalitas' e nuova cultura umanistica." *SVOC* 3: 865–88.

Arnaldi, Girolamo, and Lidia Capo. "I cronisti di Venezia e della Marca Trevigiana." *SCUV* 2: 272–337.

Avery, Victoria. *Vulcan's Forge in Venus's City: The Story of Bronze in Venice, 1350–1650*. Oxford: Oxford University Press, 2011.

Aymard, Maurice. "Conclusions." In *At the Centre of the Old World*. Edited by Lanaro, 367–76.

Babinger, Franz. *Mehmed the Conquerer and His Time*. Princeton: Princeton University Press, 1978.

Bacci, Michele. "Veneto-Byzantine 'Hybrids': Towards a Reassessment." *Studies in Iconography* 35 (2014): 73–106.

Balard, Michel. "La lotta contro Genova." *SVOC* 3: 87–126.

Bano, Danilo. "La Scuola Superiore di Commercio." *SVON* 1: 549–66.

Barbaro, Ermolao. *De coelibati, De officio legati*. Edited by Vittore Branca. Florence: Olschki, 1969.

Barcella, Paolo. "Percorsi leghisti: dall'antimeridionalismo alla xenofobia." *Meridiana* 91 (2018): 95–119.

Barker, Hannah. *The Most Precious Merchandise: The Mediterranean Trade in Black Sea Slaves, 1260–1500*. Philadelphia: University of Pennsylvania Press, 2019.

Bartolami, Sante. "L'agricoltura," *SVOC* 1: 461–89.

Barzizza, Sergio. "Il gas a Venezia. La prima volta del 'nuovo,'" le contraddizioni di sempre." *Cheiron* 12–13 (1989–90): 147–58.

Barzizza, Sergio. "Mestre, la città del Novecento." *SVON* 3: 2325–57.

Barzman, Karen-edis. "Spatial Histories of Early Modern Borderlands: A Case Study of Novigrad in Venetian Dalmatia (16th–18th CS.) / Prostorna Povijest Ranonovovjekovnog Pograničnog Područja: Studija Slučaja Novigrada U Miletačoj Dalmaciji (16.–18. ST.)." In *800 Years Since the Restoration of the Roman Tower and the First Appearance of Novigrad in Written Sources / 800 Godina od Obnove Rimske Kule i Prvog Spomena imena Novigrad u Pisanim Izvorima*. Edited by Zlatko Begonja and Ante Uglešić, 86–145. Zadar: University of Zadar Press, 2021.

Battistella, Antonio. *Il conte Carmagnola: studio storico con documenti inediti*. Genoa: Stabilimento Tip. e Lit. dell'Annuario Generale d'Italia, 1889.

Bellavitis, Anna. *Identité, marriage, mobilité sociale: citoyennes et citoyens à Venise au XVIe siècle*. Rome: École Française de Rome, 2001.

Bellavitis, Giorgio and Giandomenico Romanelli. *Venezia*. Rome and Bari: Laterza, 1985.

Beltrame, Carlo. "On the Origin of Ship Construction in Venice." In *The Age of Affirmation: Venice, the Adriatic, and the Hinterland between the 9th and 10th Centuries*. Edited by Stefano Gasparri and Sauro Gelichi, 129–46. Turnhout: Brepols, 2017.

Beltrame, Carlo, Sauro Gelichi, and Igor Miholjek, *Sveti Pavao Shipwreck: A 16th Century Venetian Merchantman from Mljet, Croatia*. Oxford: Oxbow Books, 2014.

Beltrami, Daniele. *Saggio di storia dell'agricoltura nella Repubblica di Venezia durante l'età moderna*. Venice: Istituto per la Collaborazione Culturale, 1955.

Beltrami, Daniele, *Storia della popolazione di Venezia dalla fine del secolo XVI alla caduta della Repubblica*. Padua: CEDAM, 1954.

Beniscelli, Alberto. "Gozzi, Carlo." *DBI* 58 (2002): 240–47.

Benvenuti, Feliciano. "Venezia da patria a nazione: un percorso." In *Venezia e l'Austria*. Edited by Benzoni and Cozzi, 475–94.

Benzoni, Gino. "Le accademie." *SCUV* 4/I: 131–62.

Benzoni, Gino. "Scritti storico-politici." *SVOC* 4: 757–88.

Benzoni, Gino, and Gaetano Cozzi, eds. *Venezia e l'Austria*. Venice: Marsilio, 1999.

Berengo, Marino. "Il problema politico-sociale di Venezia e della sua terraferma." *SCIV* 3: 151–63.

Bernardello, Adolfo. "Iniziative economiche, accumulazione e investimenti di capitale (1830–1866)." *SVON* 1: 567–601.

Bernardello, Adolfo. "Il molino a vapore di S. Girolamo a Venezia (1840–1870)." *Atti dell'Istituto Veneto di Scienze, Lettere ed Arti, Classe di Scienze Morali, Lettere, ed Arti* 154 (1995–6): 257–90.

Bernardello, Adolfo. *La prima ferrovia fra Venezia e Milano: storia della imperial-regia privilegiata strada ferrata Ferdinandea Lombardo-Veneta*. Venice: Istituto Veneto di Scienze, Lettere ed Arti, 1996.

Berto, Luigi Andrea, ed. *Testi storici veneziani (XI–XIII secolo): Historia ducum Venetorum, Annales Venetici breves, Domenico Tino, Relatio de electione Dominici Silvi Venetorum ducis*. Padua: CLEUP, 1999.

Besta, Enrico. *Il senato veneziano (origini, costituzione, attribuzioni e riti)*. Venice: A Spese della Società, 1899.

Bianchi, Bruna. "Venezia nella Grande guerra." *SVON* 1: 349–416.

Bigi de Aquino, Ricardo. "Eighteenth-Century Theatrical Reform in Goldoni's 'Il Teatro Comico' and Moratín's 'La Comedia Nueva.'" *Mediterranean Studies* 12 (2003): 133–53.

Bin, Alberto. *La Repubblica di Venezia e la questione adriatica, 1600–1620*. Rome: Il Veltro, 1992.

Birtachas, Efstathios, "Un 'secondo' vescovo a Venezia: il metropolita di Filadelfia (secoli XVI–XVIII)." In *I greci a Venezia: atti del convegno internazionale di studio, Venezia, 5–7 novembre 1998*. Edited by Maria Francesca Tiepolo and Eurigio Tonetti, 103–21. Venice: Istituto Veneto di Scienze, Lettere ed Arti, 2002.

Bistort, Giulio. *Il magistrato alle pompe nella Republica di Venezia: studio storico*. Venice: Regia Deputazione Veneta di Storia Patria, 1912.

Boholm, Åsa. *The Doge of Venice: The Symbolism of State Power in the Renaissance*. Gothenburg: IASSA, 1990.

Borri, Francesco. "Captains and Pirates: Ninth Century Dalmatia and Its Rulers." In *The Age of Affirmation: Venice, the Adriatic, and the Hinterland Between the 9th and 10th Centuries*. Edited by Stefano Gasparri and Sauro Gelichi, 11–37. Turnhout: Brepols, 2017.

Borsari, Silvano. *Venezia e Bisanzio nel XII secolo: i rapporti economici*. Venice: Deputazione di Storia Patria Editrice, 1988.

Borsari, Silvano. "I Veneziani nelle colonie." *SVOC* 3: 127–58.

Boschini, Marco. *La carte del navegar pitoresco*. Edited by Anna Pallucchini. Venice: Istituto per la Collaborazione Culturale, 1966.

Bosio, Luciano. "Dai Romani ai Longobardi: vie di comunicazione e paesaggio agrario." *SVOC* 1: 175–208.

Bosworth, R. J. B. *Italian Venice: A History*. New Haven: Yale University Press, 2014.

Botero, Giovanni. *The Reason of State*. Trans. P. J. and D. P. Waley. New Haven: Yale University Press, 1956.

Boucher, Bruce. *Andrea Palladio: The Architect in His Time*. New York: Abbeville Press, 1994.

Bouwsma, William J. *Venice and the Defense of Republican Liberty: Renaissance Values in the Age of the Counter Reformation*. Berkeley: University of California Press, 1968.

Bouwsma, William J. "Venice and the Political Education of Europe." *RV*, 445–66.

Bowd, Stephen. "Civic Piety and Patriotism: Patrician Humanists and Jews in Venice and its Empire." *RQ* 69 (2016): 1257–95.

Bracewell, Catherine Wendy. *The Uskoks of Senj: Piracy, Banditry, and Holy War in the Sixteenth-Century Adriatic*. Ithaca: Cornell University Press, 1992.

Brambati, Antonio. "Modificazioni costiere nell'arco lagunare dell'Adriatico settentrionale." *Studi Jesolani* 27 (1985): 13–47.

Brambatti, Antonio et al. "The Lagoon of Venice: Geological Setting, Evolution, and Land Subsidence" *Episodes* 2003. DOI: 10.18814/epiiugs/2003/v26i3/020.

Branca, Vittore. "L'umanesimo veneziano e l'arte del libro," *Revue des Études Italiennes* n.s. 27 (1981): 325–33.

Braudel, Fernand. *La Méditerranée et le monde méditerranéen à l'époque de Philippe II*, 2nd ed. in 2 vols. Paris: A. Colin, 1966.

Braunstein, Philippe. *Les Allemands à Venise (1380–1520)*. Rome: École Française de Rome, 2016.

Braunstein, Philippe. "Les entreprise minières en vénétie au XVe siècle." *Melanges Archéologie et d'Histoire de l'École Française de Rome* 77 (1965): 529–607.

Braunstein, Philippe. "Confins italiens de l'Empire: nations, frontières et sensibilité européenne dans la seconde moitié du XVe siècle." In *La conscience européenne aux XVe et XVIe siècles*, 35–48. Paris: Collection de l'École Normale Supérieure de Jeunes Filles 22, 1982.

Brown, Horatio F. *The Venetian Printing Press*. London: J. C. Nimmo, 1891.

Brown, Judith C. *Immodest Acts: The Life of a Lesbian Nun in Renaissance Italy*. New York: Oxford University Press, 1985.

Brown, Patricia Fortini. "Honor and Necessity: The Dynamics of Patronage in the Confraternities of Renaissance Venice." *SV* n.s. 14 (1987): 179–210.

Brown, Patricia Fortini. *Private Lives in Renaissance Venice*. New Haven: Yale University Press, 2004.

Brown, Patricia Fortini. *Venetian Narrative Painting in the Age of Carpaccio*. New Haven: Yale University Press, 1988.

Brown, Patricia Fortini. *Venice and Antiquity: The Venetian Sense of the Past*. New Haven: Yale University Press, 1996.

Brunello, Franco. *Arti e mestieri a Venezia nel Medioevo e Rinascimento*. Vicenza: N. Pozza, 1980.

Brunetta, Ernesto. "Figure e momenti del Novecento politico." In *Venezia*. Edited by Franzina, 152–225.

Brunetti, Mario. "Il doge non è 'segno di taverna.'" *NAV* 33 (1917): 351–55.

Brunetti, Mario. "Due dogi sotto inchiesta: Agostino Barbarigo e Leonardo Loredan." *Archivio Veneto-Tridentino* n.s. 7 (1925): 278–329.

Brunetti, Mario. "Le istruzioni di un nunzio pontificio a Venezia al suo successore." In *Scritti storici in onore di Camillo Manfroni*, 369–79. Padua: A. Draghi, 1925.

Brunetti, Mario. "Venezia durante la peste del 1348." *AT* 32 (1909): pt.1: 289–311, pt. 2:5–42.

Brusatin, Manlio. *Venezia nel Settecento: stato, architettura, territorio*. Turin: Einaudi, 1980.

Buckton, David, and John Osborne. "The Enamel of Doge Ordelaffo Falier on the *Pala d'Oro* in Venice." *Gesta* 39 (2000): 43–9.

Burke, Ersie. *The Greeks of Venice, 1498–1600: Immigration, Settlement, and Integration*. Turnhout: Brepols, 2016.

Burke, Peter Burke. "Early Modern Venice as a Center of Information and Communication." *VR*, 389–419.

Cafarelli, Andrea. *Il leone ferito: Venezia, l'Adriatico e la navigazione sussidiata per le Indie e l'Estremo Oriente (1866–1914)*. Rome: Viella, 2004.

Caffi, Michele. "Giacomello del Fiore: pittore veneziano del sec. XV." *Archivio Storico Italiano* 4th series 6 (1880): 402–33.

Calabi, Donatella. "The 'City of the Jews.'" In *The Jews of Early Modern Venice*. Edited by Davis and Ravid, 31–49.

Calabi, Donatella. "Fortezze e lidi." *SV* Mare, 111–34.

Calabi, Donatella. *Venezia e il Ghetto: cinquecento anni del "recinto degli ebrei."* Turin: Bollati Boringhieri, 2016.

Calabi, Donatella, and Paolo Morachiello. *Rialto: le fabbiche e il ponte*. Turin: Einaudi, 1987.

Calaon, Diego. *Quando Torcello era abitata*. Venice: Regione del Veneto, 2013.

Calaon, Diego. "La *Venetia maritima* tra il VI e il IX sec.: mito, continuità e rottura/ Venetika (*Venetia maritima*) med. 6. in 9. stoletjem: Mit, kontinuiteta in zaton." In *Dalla catalogazione alla promozione dei beni archeologici/Od katalogiziranja do promocije arheološki dobrin*, 53–66. Mestrino: Regione del Veneto, 2014.

Calcagno, Mauro. "Censuring *Eliogabolo* in Seventeenth-Century Venice." *Journal of Interdisciplinary History* 36 (2006): 355–77.

Calimani, Riccardo. *The Ghetto of Venice: A History*. New York: M. Evans, 1987.

Camurri, Renato. "La classe politica nazionalfascista." *SVON* 2: 1355–1438.

Camurri, Renato. "Istituzioni, associazioni e classi dirigenti dall'Unità alla Grande Guerra." *SVON* 1: 225–303.

Cangiano, Pietro. "Dal magistrato del proprio al magistrato alle acque: competenze e giurisdizione." In *Laguna, fiumi, lidi: cinque secoli di gestione delle acque nelle Venezie*, 877–86. Fieso d'Artico: La Press, 1985.

Caresini, Rafaino de. *Raphayni de Caresinis, cancellarii Venetiarum Chronica aa. 1343-1388*. Edited by Ester Pastorello. *Rerum Italicarum Scriptores*, 2nd series, vol. 12, pt. 1. Bologna, N. Zanichelli, 1922.

Caroldo, Giovanni Giacomo. *Istorii Venețiene*. 5 vols. Edited by Serban V. Marin. Bucharest: Archivele Nationale ale României, 2008–2012.

Carroro, Silvia. "*Dominae in claustro:* San Zaccaria tra politica, società e religione nella Venezia altomedievale." *Reti Medievali Rivista* 20 (2019): 373–404.

Casellato, Alessandro. "I sestieri popolari." *SVON* 2: 1581–1621.

Casellato, Alessandro, and Gilda Zazzara. "Un viaggio nel Veneto *agro*." In *Veneto agro. Operai e sindacato alla prova del leghismo (1980–2010)*. Edited by Alessandro Casellato and Gilda Zazzara, 19–60. Mestre-Treviso: Istresco, 2010.

Casini, Matteo. "A Compagnia della Calza in January 1475." In *Reflections on Renaissance Venice: A Celebration of Patricia Fortini Brown*. Edited by Blake de Maria and Mary Frank, 55–61. Milan: 5 Continents, 2013.

Casini, Matteo. "The 'Company of the Hose': Youth and Court Culture in Europe, Italy and Venice." *SV* n.s. 63 (2011): 133–53.

Casini, Matteo. *I gesti del principe: la festa politica a Firenze e Venezia in età rinascimentale*. Venice: Marsilio, 1996.

Casola, Pietro. *Viaggio a Gerusalemme di Pietro Casola*. Edited by Anna Paoletti. Alessandria: Edizioni dell'Orso, 2001.

Cassidorous. *The Letters of Cassiodorus– Being a Condensed Translation of the Variae Epistolae of Magnus Aurelius Cassiodorus Senator*. Trans. Thomas Hodgkin. London: Frowde, 1886.

Cassiodorus, Flavius Magnus Aurelius. *Varie*. Edited by Andrea Giardina, Giovanni Alberto Cecconi, and Ignazio Tantillo. 6 vols. Rome: L'Erma di Bretschneider, 2014–5.

Castagnetti, Andrea. "Famiglie e affermazione politica." *SVOC* 1: 613–44.

Castagnetti, Andrea. "Il primo comune." *SVOC* 2: 81–130.

Castagnetti, Andrea. "Insediamenti e 'populi.'" *SVOC* 1: 577–612.

Castagnetti, Andrea. "La pianura veronese nel Medioevo: la conquista del suolo e la regolamentazione delle acque." In *Una città e il suo fiume: Verona e l'Adige*, 2 vols. Edited by Giorgio Borelli, 2: 33–138. Verona: Banca Popolare di Verona, 1977.

Castagnetti, Andrea. *La società veneziana nel Medioevo I: dai tribuni ai giudici*. Verona: Libreria Universitaria Editrice, 1992.

Cecchetti, Bartolomeo. "La pittura a stampa di Bernardino Benalio," *AV* n.s. 33, pt. 1 (1887): 538–9.

Cecchetti, Bartolomeo. "La vita dei veneziani fino al secolo XIII." AV 2 (1871): 63–123.

Cecchetti, Bartolomeo. "La vita dei Veneziani nel 1300." *AV* 28 (1884): 281–96; 29 (1885), 9–25.

Cerasi, Laura. *Perdonare Marghera: la città del lavoro nella memoria post-industriale*. Milan: Francoangeli, 2007.

Cervelli, Innocenzo. "Intorno alla decadenza di Venezia: un episodio di storia economica ovvero un affare mancato." *Nuova Rivista Storica* 50 (1966): 596–642.

Cervelli, Innocenzo. *Machiavelli e la crisi dello stato veneziano*. Naples: Guida Editori, 1974.

Cessi, Benvenuto. "Il taglio del Po a Porto Viro." *NAV* n.s. 30, pt. 2 (1915): 319–68.

Cessi, Roberto. "Da Roma a Bisanzio." In *Storia di Venezia*, 2 vols. 1: 179–401. Venice: Centro Internazionale delle Arti e del Costume, 1957–8.

Cessi, Roberto, ed. *Deliberazioni del Maggior Consiglio di Venezia*. Reprint in 3 vols. Bologna: Forni Editore, 1971.

Cessi, Roberto, ed. *Documenti relativi alla storia di Venezia anteriore al Mille*, 2 vols. Padua: Gregoriana, 1940–2.

Cessi, Roberto. "La diversione del Brenta ed il delta ilariana nel sec. XII." *Atti del Reale Istituto Veneto di Scienze, Lettere ed Arti* 80 pt. 2 (1920–1): 1225–43.

Cessi, Roberto. "L'investiture ducale." *Atti dell'Istituto Veneto di Scienze, Lettere ed Arti, Classe di Scienze Morali, Lettere ed Arti* 126 (1967–8): 251–94.

Cessi, Roberto. "Politica, economia, religione." In *Storia di Venezia*, 2 vols. 2: 67–476. Venice: Centro Internazionale delle Arti e del Costume, 1957–8.

Cessi, Roberto. *Storia della Repubblica di Venezia*. Florence: Giunti Martello, 1981.

Cessi, Roberto. "L' 'Ufficium de Navigantibus' ed i sistemi della politica commerciale veneziana nel sec. XIV." *NAV* n.s. 63 (1916): 106–46.

Cessi, Roberto, and Annibale Alberti. *Rialto: l'isola, il ponte, il mercato*. Bologna: Nicola Zanichelli, 1934.

Cessi, Roberto, and Fanny Bennato, eds. *Venetiarum Historia vulgo Petro Iustiniano Iustiniani Filio Adiudicata*. Venice: Deputazione di Storia Patria per le Venezie, 1964.

Chambers, David S. *The Imperial Age of Venice, 1380–1580*. London: Thames and Hudson, 1970.

Chambers, David, and Brian Pullan, eds. *Venice: A Documentary History, 1450–1630*. Reprint. Toronto: University of Toronto Press, 2001.

Chastel, André. "Il Settecento veneziano nelle arti." *SCIV* 3: 219–26.

Chatzidakis, Nano. *From Candia to Venice: Greek Icons in Italy, 15th–16th Centuries*. Athens: Foundation for Hellenic Culture, 1993.

Chinello, Cesco. "Foscari, Piero." *DBI* 49 (1997): 338–40.

Chinello, Cesco. "Storia operaia di Porto Marghera." *SVON* 3: 2279–2323.

Chojnacka, Monica. *Working Women in Early Modern Venice*. Baltimore: Johns Hopkins University Press, 2001.

Chojnacki, Stanley. "La formazione della nobiltà dopo la Serrata." *SVOC* 3: 641–725.

Chojnacki, Stanley. "Identity and Ideology in Renaissance Venice: The Third *Serrata*." *VR*, 263–94.

Chojnacki, Stanley. "In Search of the Venetian Patriciate: Families and Factions in the Fourteenth Century." *RV*, 47–90.

Chojnacki, Stanley. "Social Identity in Renaissance Venice: The Second *Serrata*." *Renaissance Studies* 8 (1994): 341–58.

Chojnacki, Stanley. *Women and Men in Renaissance Venice: Twelve Essays on Patrician Society*. Baltimore: Johns Hopkins University Press, 2000.

Choniates, Niketas. *Oh City of Byzantium, Annals of Niketas Choniates*. Trans. Harry J. Magoulias. Detroit: Wayne State University Press, 1984.

Christ, Georg. "Beyond the Network—Connectors of Networks: Venetian Agents in Cairo and Venetian News Management." In *Everything Is on the Move: The Mamluk Empire as a Node in (Trans-)Regional Networks*. Edited by Stephan Conermann, 27–59. Göttingen: V & R Unipress, 2014.

Christ, Georg. "Quelques observations concernant la navigation vénitienne à Alexandrie à la fin du Moyen Âge." In *Venise et la Méditerranée*. Edited by Sandro G. Franchini et al., 55–74. Venice: Istituto Veneto di Scienze, Lettere ed Arti, 2011.

Christ, Georg. "The Venetian Coast Guards: Staple Policy, Seaborne Law Enforcement, and State Formation in the 14th Century." In *Merchants, Pirates, and Smugglers: Criminalization, Economics, and the Transformation of the Maritime World (1200–1600)*. Edited by Thomas Heeboll-Holm, Philipp Höhn, and Gregor Rohmann, 269–96. Frankfurt: Campus Verlag, 2019.

Ciriacono, Salvatore. *Building on Water: Venice, Holland and the Construction of the European Landscape in Early Modern Times*. New York: Berghahn Books, 2006.

Ciriacono, Salvatore. "Il governo del territorio." *SVOC* 8: 613–49.

Ciriacono, Salvatore. "Industria e artigianato." *SVOC* 5: 523–92.

Ciriacono, Salvatore. "Investimenti capitalistici e colture irrigue: la congiuntura agricola nella terraferma veneta (secoli XVI e XVII). In *Atti del Convegno: Venezia e la terraferma attraverso le relazioni dei rettori*. Edited by Amelio Tagliaferri, 123–58. Milan: Giuffrè, 1981.

Ciriacono, Salvatore. "Management of the Lagoon and the Urban Environment in 18th-Century Venice." *Water History* 10 (2018): 141–61.

Ciriacono, Salvatore. *Olio e ebrei nella Repubblica Veneta del Settecento*. Venice: Deputazione di Storia Patria per le Venezie, 1975.

Cippico, Coriolano. *The Deeds of Commander Pietro Mocenigo*. Trans. Kiril Petkov. New York: Italica Press, 2014.

Clari, Robert of. *The Conquest of Constantinople*. Trans. Edgar Holmes McNeal. Reprint of 1936 ed. Toronto: University of Toronto Press, 1996.

Clark, Martin. *Modern Italy, 1871–1995*, 2nd ed. London: Longman, 1996.

Clarke, Paula C. "The Business of Prostitution in Early Renaissance Venice." *RQ* 68 (2015): 419–64.

Clarke, Paula. "Le 'mercantesse' di Venezia nei secoli XIV e XV." *AV* 6th series 3 (2012): 67–84.

Cohen, Mark R. ed. *The Autobiography of a Seventeenth-Century Venetian Rabbi: Leon Modena's* Life of Judah. Princeton: Princeton University Press, 1988.

Coletti, Luigi. "L'arte dal neoclassicismo al romanticismo." *SCIV* 3: 289–300.

Cosmescu, Dragoş. *Venetian Renaissance Fortifications in the Mediterranean*. Jefferson, NC: McFarland, 2016.

Concina, Ennio. "Ampliar la città: spazio urbano, 'res publica' e architettura." *SVOC* 6: 253–73.

Concina, Ennio. *L'Arsenale della Repubblica di Venezia*. Milan: Electa, 2006.

Concina, Ennio. "La casa dell'Arsenale." *SV Mare*, 147–210.

Concina, Ennio. *Fondaci: architettura, arte, e mercatura tra Levante, Venezia, e Alemagna*. Venice: Marsilio, 1997.

Concina, Ennio. *A History of Venetian Architecture*. Trans. Judith Landry. Cambridge: Cambridge University Press, 1998.

Concina, Ennio. "Dal Medioevo al primo Rinascimento: l'architettura." *SVOC* 5: 165–306.

Concina, Ennio. *Tempo novo: Venezia e il Quattrocento*. Venice: Marsilio, 2006.

Contarini, Gasparo. *De magistratibus et republica venetorum*. Paris: Ex officina Michaëlis Vascosani, 1543.

Contarini, Gasparo. *The Republic of Venice: De magistratibus et republica venetorum*. Edited by Filippo Sabetti. Trans. Giuseppe Pezzini and Amanda Murphy. Toronto: University of Toronto Press, 2020.

Cooper, Tracy E. *Palladio's Venice: Architecture and Society in a Renaissance Republic*. New Haven: Yale University Press, 2005.

Corazzol, Gigi. *Livelli stipulati a Venezia nel 1591: studio storico*. Pisa: Giardini, 1986.

Corrò, Elisa, Cecilia Moine, and Sandra Primon. "Setting the Scene: The Role of Saint'Ilario Monastery in Early Medieval Venice in Light of Recent Landscape Studies." In *Venice and Its Neighbors from the 8th to 11th Century: Through Renovation and Continuity*. Edited by Sauro Gelichi and Stefano Gasparri, 116–41. Leiden: Brill, 2018.

Costantini, Massimo. "Commercio e marina." *SVOC* 8: 555–612.

Costantini, Massimo. "Dal porto franco al porto industriale." *SV Mare*, 879–914.

Costantini, Massimo. *Porto, navi e traffici a Venezia, 1700–2000*. Venice: Marsilio, 2004.

Cozzi, Gaetano. "Authority and the Law in Renaissance Venice." *RV*, 293–345.

Cozzi, Gaetano. "Dalla riscoperta della pace all'inestinguibile sogno di dominio." *SVOC* 7: 3–104.

Cozzi, Gaetano. *Il doge Nicolò Contarini: ricerche sul patriziato veneziano agli inizi del Seicento*. Venice: Istituto per la Collaborazione Culturale, 1958.

Cozzi, Gaetano. "La politica del diritto nella Repubblica di Venezia." In *Stato, società, e giustizia nella Repubblica Veneta (sec. XV–XVIII)*. 2 vols. Edited by Gaetano Cozzi, 1: 17–152. Rome: Jouvence, 1980–85.

Cozzi, Gaetano. "Religione moralità e giustizia a Venezia: vicende della magistratura degli esecutori contro la bestemmia (secoli XVI–XVIII)." *AT* n.s. 29 (1991): 7–95.

Cozzi, Gaetano. *Repubblica di Venezia e stati italiani: politica e giustizia dal secolo XVI al secolo XVIII*. Turin: Einaudi, 1982.

Cozzi, Gaetano. "Venezia dal Rinascimento all'età barocca." *SVOC* 6: 3–125.

Cozzi, Gaetano, and Michael Knapton. *Storia della Repubblica di Venezia: dalla Guerra di Chioggia alla riconquista della terraferma*. Turin: UTET, 1986.

Cracco, Giorgio. *Un "Altro mondo": Venezia nel Medioevo, dal secolo XI al secolo XIV*. Turin: UTET, 1986.

Cracco, Giorgio. *Società e stato nel Medioevo veneziano (sec. XII–XIV)*. Florence: Olschki, 1967.

Cranston, Jodi. *Green Worlds of Renaissance Venice*. University Park: Pennsylvania State University Press, 2019.

Cristea, Ovidia. "Venice Confronting the Ottoman Empire: A Struggle for Survival (Fourteenth-Sixteenth Centuries)." In *The Ottoman Conquest of the Balkans*. Edited by Oliver Jens Schmitt, 265–79. Vienna: Verlag der Österreichischen Akademie der Wissenschaften, 2016.

Crouzet-Pavan, Élisabeth. "La maturazione dello spazio urbano." *SVOC* 5: 3–100.

Crouzet-Pavan, Élisabeth. *La mort lente de Torcello: histoire d'une cité disparue*. Paris: Fayard, 1995.

Crouzet-Pavan, Élisabeth. *"Sopra le acque salse": espaces, pouvoir et société à Venise à la fin du Moyen Âge*, 2 vols. Rome: École Française de Rome, 1992.

Crouzet-Pavan, Élisabeth. "Sviluppo e articolazione della città." *SVOC* 3: 729–82.

Crouzet-Pavan, Élisabeth. "Toward an Ecological Understanding of the Myth of Venice." *VR*, 39–64.

Crouzet-Pavan, Élisabeth. "Venice and Torcello: History and Oblivion." *Renaissance Studies* 8 (1994): 416–27.

Crouzet-Pavan, Élisabeth. *Venice Triumphant: The Horizons of a Myth*. Trans. Lydia G. Cochrane. Baltimore: Johns Hopkins University Press, 2002.

Crouzet-Pavan, Élisabeth. "Venise e le monde communal: recherches sur les podestats vénitiens 1200–1350." *Journals des Savants* (1992, no. 2): 277–315.

Crowley, Roger. *City of Fortune: How Venice Ruled the Seas*. New York: Random House, 2011.

Cuza, Marco. "Giornali e gazzette," *SCUV* 5/I: 113–29.

Cumming, Julie E. "Music for the Doge in Early Renaissance Venice." *Speculum* 67 (1992): 324–64.

Cuscito, Giuseppe. "La Chiesa aquileiese." *SVOC* 1: 367–408.

Da Canal, Martin. *Les Estoires de Venise: cronaca veneziana in lingua francese dalle origini al 1275*. Edited by Alberto Limentani. Florence: Olschki, 1972.

Dal Cin, Valentina. *Il mondo nuovo: l'élite veneta fra rivoluzione e restaurazione (1797–1815)*. Venice: Edizioni Ca' Foscari, 2019.

Dale, Thomas E. A. "Cultural Hybridity in Medieval Venice: Reinventing the East at San Marco after the Fourth Crusade." In *San Marco, Byzantium, and the Myths of Venice*. Edited by Henry Maguire and Robert S. Nelson, 151–91. Washington: Dumbarton Oaks, 2010.

Damerini, Gino. "Venice, D'Annunzio e l'ultima guerra per l'unità d'Italia." *SCIV* 3: 373–86.

Da Mosto, Andrea. *I dogi di Venezia nella vita pubblica e privata*. Florence: Giunti Marzocco, 1983.

Dandolo, Andrea. *Chronica brevis aa.46–1342d.C.* Edited by Ester Pastorello. *Rerum Italicarum Scriptores*, 2nd series, vol. 12, pt. 1. Bologna: Zanichelli, 1938.

Dandolo, Andrea. *Chronica per extensum descripta aa. 46–1280 d.C.* Edited by Ester Pastorello. *Rerum Italicarum Scriptores*, 2nd series, vol. 12, pt. 1. Bologna, Zanichelli, 1938.

Davis, James C. *The Decline of the Venetian Nobility as a Ruling Class*. Baltimore: Johns Hopkins University Press, 1962.

Davis, James C. *A Venetian Family and Its Fortune, 1500–1900: The Donà and the Conservation of Their Wealth*. Philadelphia: American Philosophical Society, 1975.

Davis, Robert C. *Shipbuilders of the Venetian Arsenal: Workers and Workplace in the Preindustrial Age*. Baltimore: Johns Hopkins University Press, 1991.

Davis, Robert C. *The War of the Fists: Popular Culture and Public Violence in Late Renaissance Venice*. New York: Oxford University Press, 1994.

Davis, Robert C., and Garry R. Marvin. *Venice: The Tourist Maze: A Cultural Critique of the World's Most Touristed City*. Berkeley: University of California Press, 2004.

Davis, Robert C., and Benjamin Ravid, eds. *The Jews of Early Modern Venice*. Baltimore: Johns Hopkins University Press, 2001.

Dean, Trevor. "After the War of Ferrara: Relations Between Venice and Ercole d'Este, 1484–1505." In *War, Culture and Society in Renaissance Venice: Essays in Honour of John Hale*. Edited by David S. Chambers, Cecil H. Clough, and Michael E. Mallett, 73–98. London: Hambledon Press, 1993.

Dean, Trevor. "Venetian Economic Hegemony: The Case of Ferrara, 1220–1500." *SV* n.s. 12 (1986): 43–98.

De Biase, Luca. "Immagini delle città e delle campagne tra la metà del XVI e la fine del XVII secolo." *SCUV* 4/I: 625–56.

De Commynes, Philippe. *Memorie*. Trans. Maria Clotilde Daviso di Charvensod. Turin: Einaudi, 1960.

Degroot, Dagomar. *The Frigid Golden Age: Climate Change, the Little Ice Age, and the Dutch Republic, 1560–1720*. Cambridge: Cambridge University Press, 2018.

DeLancey, Julia A. "'In the Streets Where They Sell Colors': Placing *Vendicolori* in the Urban Fabric of Early Modern Venice." *Wallraf-Richartz-Jahrbuch* 72 (2011): 193–232.

Della Peruta, Franco. "Il Veneto nel Risorgimento fino al 1848." In *Venezia e l'Austria*. Edited by Benzoni and Cozzi, 383–99.

Della Valentina, Marcello. "The Silk Industry in Venice: Guilds and Labour Relations in the Seventeenth and Eighteenth Centuries." In *At the Centre of the Old World*. Edited by Lanaro, 109–42.

Del Negro, Piero. "Il 1848 e dopo." *SVON* 1: 107–86.

Del Negro, Piero. "Carlo Goldoni e la massoneria veneziana." *Studi Storici* 43 (2002): 411–19.

Del Negro, Piero. "La fine della Repubblica aristocratica." *SVOC* 8: 191–262.

Del Negro, Piero. "Introduzione." *SVOC* 8: 1–80.

Del Negro, Piero. "La milizia." *SVOC* 7: 509–31.

Del Negro, Piero. "Proposte illuminate e conservazione nel dibattito sulla teoria e la prassi dello stato." *SCUV* 5/II: 123–45.

De Maria, Blake. *Becoming Venetian: Immigrants and the Arts in Early Modern Venice*. New Haven: Yale University Press, 2010.

De Michelis, Cesare. "Caminer, Elisabetta." *DBI* 17 (1974): 236–41.

Demo, Edoardo. "Wool and Silk. The Textile Urban Industry of the Venetian Mainland (15th–17th Centuries). In *At the Centre of the Old World*. Edited by Lanaro, 217–43.

De Monacis, Lorenzo. *Chronicon de rebus venetis ab U.C. ad annum MCCCLIV.* Edited by Flaminio Cornaro. *Rerum Italicarum Scriptores*, 1st series, vol. 8. Venice: Remondini 1758.

Demus, Otto. *The Church of San Marco in Venice: History, Architecture, Sculpture*. Washington: Dumbarton Oaks, 1960.

Derosas, Renzo. "Aspetti economici della crisi del patriziato veneziano tra fine Settecento e primo Ottocento." *Cheiron* 12–13 (1989–90): 11–61.

Derosas, Renzo. "Corner, Elena Lucrezia." *DBI* 29 (1983): 174–9.

Derosas, Renzo. "La demografia dei poveri. Pescatori, facchini e industrianti nella Venezia di metà Ottocento." *SVON* 1: 711–70.

Derosas, Renzo. "Moralità e giustizia a Venezia nel '500–'600: gli esecutori contro la bestemmia." In *Stato, società e giustizia nella Repubblica Veneta (sec. XV–XVIII)*. 2 vols. Edited by Gaetano Cozzi, 1: 431–528. Rome: Jouvence, 1980–85.

De Vergottini, Giovanni. "Venezia e l'Istria nell'Alto Medioevo." *SCIV* 1: 71–83.

D'Evelyn, Margaret Muther. *Venice and Vitruvius: Reading Venice with Daniele Barbaro and Andrea Palladio*. New Haven: Yale University Press, 2012.

De Vivo, Filippo. "Historical Justifications of Venetian Power in the Adriatic." *Journal of the History of Ideas* 64 (2003): 159–76.

De Vivo, Filippo. "How to Read Venetian Relazioni." *Renaissance and Reformation/ Renaissance et Réforme* 34 (2011): 25–59.

De Vivo, Filippo. *Information and Communication in Venice: Rethinking Early Modern Politics*. Oxford: Oxford University Press, 2007.

De Vivo, Filippo. "Pharmacies as Centres of Communication in Early Modern Venice." *Renaissance Studies* 21 (2007): 505–21.

De Vivo, Filippo. "Walking in Sixteenth-Century Venice: Mobilizing the Early Modern City." *I Tatti Studies in the Italian Renaissance* 19 (2016): 115–41.

Diacono, Giovanni. *Istoria Veneticorum*. Edited and translated by Luigi Andrea Berto. Bologna, Zanichelli, 1999.

Diacono, Paolo. *Storia dei Longobardi*. Reprint of Basel 1532 edition and Venice 1548 Italian translation. Mariano del Friuli: Edizioni della Laguna, 1990.

Dibello, Daniele. "La stabilità delle istituzioni veneziane nel Trecento. Aspetti politici, economici e culturali nella gestione della congiura di Marino Falier." *Reti Medievali Rivista* 19 (2018): 85–129.

Di Chinazzo, Daniele. *Cronica de la guerra da Veniciani a Zenovesi*. Edited by Vittorio Lazzarini. Venice: Deputazione di Storia Patria per le Venezie, 1958.

Di Cosmo, Nicola. "The Black Sea Emporia and the Mongol Empire: A Reassessment of the Pax Mongolica." *Journal of the Economic and Social History of the Orient* 53 (2010):83–108.

DiGaetani, John Louis. *Carlo Gozzi: A Life in the 18th Century Venetian Theater, an Afterlife in Opera*. Jefferson, NC: McFarland, 1999.

Dionisotti, Carlo. "Bembo, Pietro." *DBI* 8 (1966): 133–51.

Doglio, Maria Luisa. "La letteratura ufficiale e l'oratoria celebrativa." *SCUV* 4/I: 163–87.

Donà, Francesco. *Esatto diario di quanto è successo dalli 2 sino a 17 maggio 1797 nella caduta della veneta aristocratica repubblica*. Basel: n.p., 1797.

Donnici, Sandra et al. "The Caranto Paleosol and its Role in the Early Urbanization of Venice," *Geoarchaeology: An International Journal* 26 (2011): 514–43.

Dorigo, Wladimiro. *Una legge contro Venezia: natura, storia, interessi nella questione della città e della laguna*. Rome: Officini Edizioni, 1973.

Dorigo, Wladimiro. *Venezia romanica: la formazione della città medioevale fino all'età gotica*. 2 vols. Sommacampagna: Cierre, 2003.

Dorigo, Wladimiro. "Venezia e il Veneto." In *Storia d'Italia. Le regioni dall'Unità a oggi. Il Veneto*. Edited by Lanaro, 1037–65.

Dosio, Giorgetta Bonfiglio. "Le arti cittadine." *SVOC* 2: 577–626.

Dotson, John E. trans. *Merchant Culture in Fourteenth Century Venice: The Zibaldone da Canal*. Binghamton, NY: Medieval and Renaissance Texts and Studies, 1994.

Dotti, Davide. "Precursori e protagonisti del vedutismo veneziano settecentesco." In *Lo splendore di Venezia: Canaletto, Bellotto, Guardi e i vedutisti dell'Ottocento*. Edited by Davide Dotti, 10–31. Milan: Silvana Editoriale, 2016.

Doumerc, Bernard. "Gli conquisti marittimi." *SVOC* 3: 617–640.

Doumerc, Bernard. "La construction d'un empire (1298–1396)." In *Histoire de l'Adriatique*. Edited by Pierre Cabanes et al., 203–39. Paris: Éditions du Seuil, 2001.

Doumerc, Bernard. "La crise structurelle de la marine vénitienne au XVe siècle: le problème du retard des Mude." *Annales ESC* 40 (1985): 605–23.

Doumerc, Bernard. "Il dominio del mare." *SVOC* 4: 113–80.

Doumerc, Bernard. "Le galere da mercato." *SV Mare*, 357–395.

Ducellier, Alain. "L'Adriatique du IVe au XIIIe siècle." In *Histoire de l'Adriatique*. Edited by Pierre Cabanes et al., 107–99. Paris: Éditions du Seuil, 2001.

Dursteler, Eric R. ed. *A Companion to Venetian History, 1400-1797*. Leiden: Brill, 2013.

Dursteler, Eric R. *Venetians in Constantinople: Nation, Identity, and Coexistence in the Early Modern Mediterranean*. Baltimore: Johns Hopkins University Press, 2006.

Emery, Ted. "Carlo Gozzi in Context." In Carlo Gozzi, *Five Tales for the Theatre*. Edited and translated by Albert Bermel and Ted Emery, 1–19. Chicago: University of Chicago Press, 1989.

Epstein, Steven A. *Genoa and the Genoese, 958–1528*. Chapel Hill: University of North Carolina Press, 1996.

Evelyn, John. *Diary and Correspondence*. 4 vols. London: H. Colburn, 1854.

Fabijanec, Sabine Florence. "Fishing and the Fish Trade on the Dalmatian Coast in the late Middle Ages." In *The Inland Seas: Towards an Ecohistory of the Mediterranean and the Black Sea*. Edited by Tonnes Bekker-Nielsen and Ruthy Gertwagen, 369–86. Stuttgart: Franz Steiner Verlag, 2016.

Fabris, Antonio. "Esperienze di vita comunitaria: i canonici regolari." In *La chiesa*. Edited by Tonon, 73–107.

Fadelli, Alessandro. "Quando la gente moriva per le strade dalla fame: riflessi demografici e sociali della grande carestia del 1816–1817 nel Friuli occidentale." *Atti dell'Accademia San Marco di Pordenone* 19 (2017): 721–61.

Fasoli, Gina. "Comune Veneciarum." *SCIV* 1: 263–78.

Fasoli, Gina. "Nascita di un mito." In *Studi storici in onore di Gioacchino Volpe*. 2 vols. 1: 445–79. Florence: Sansoni, 1958.

Fassina, Giacomo. "Factiousness, Fractiousness or Unity? The Reform of the Council of Ten in 1582–1583." *SV* n.s. 54 (2007): 89–117.

Faugeron, Fabien. "L'art du compromise politique: Venise au lendemain de la conjuration Tiepolo-Querini (1310)." *Journal des Savants* (July–December 2004): 357–421.

Faucheron, Fabien. *Nourrir la ville: ravitaillement, marchés et métiers de l'alimentation à Venise dans les derniers siècles du Moyen Âge*. Rome: École Française de Rome, 2014.

Faugeron, Fabien. "Quelques réflexions autour de la conjuration de Baiamonte Tiepolo: des réalités socio-politiques à la fabrication du mythe (1297–1797)." In *Venise 1297–1797: La république des Castors*. Edited by Alessandro Fontana and George Saro, 36–79. Fontenoy Saint-Cloud: ENS Editions, 1997.

Fedalto, Giorgio. *San Marco da Aquileia a Venezia: saggi su terre e chiese venete*. Verona: Mazziana, 2014.

Fees, Irmgard. *Ricchezza e potenza nella Venezia medioevale: la famiglia Ziani*. Rome: Il Veltro, 2005.

Feldman, Martha. "Opera, Festivity, and Spectacle in 'Revolutionary' Venice: Phantasms of Time and History." *VR*, 217–60.

Fenlon, Iain. *The Ceremonial City: History, Memory and Myth in Renaissance Venice*. New Haven: Yale University Press, 2007.

Ferguson, Ronnie. *Le iscrizioni in antico volgare delle confraternite laiche veneziane: edizione e commento*. Venice: Marcianum Press, 2015.

Ferguson, Ronnie. *Venetian Inscriptions: Vernacular Writing for Public Display in Medieval and Renaissance Venice*. Cambridge: Legenda, 2021.

Ferraro, Joanne M. "Female Agency, Subjectivity, and Disorder in Early Modern Venice." In *Popular Politics in an Aristocratic Republic*. Edited by Van Gelder and Judde de Larivière, 158–75.

Ferraro, Joanne M. "Making a Living: The Sex Trade in Early Modern Venice." *American Historical Review* 123 (2018): 30–59.

Ferraro, Joanne M. *Marriage Wars in Late Renaissance Venice*. New York: Oxford University Press, 2001.

Ferraro, Joanne M. *Venice: History of the Floating City*. Cambridge: Cambridge University Press, 2012.

Ferris, Kate. *Everyday Life in Fascist Venice, 1929-40*. Houndmills: Palgrave Macmillan, 2012.

Fiastri, Giovanni. "L'assemblea del popolo a Venezia come organo costituzionale dello stato." *NAV* 25 (1913): 5–48.

Fido, Franco. "Carlo Goldoni." *SCUV* 5/I: 309–55.

Fido, Franco. *Nuova guida a Goldoni: teatro e società nel Settecento*. Turin: Einaudi, 2000.

Filippetto, Giuseppe Trassari. "Tecnica xilografica tra Quattrocento e Cinquecento: 'Il nuovo stile.'" In *A volo d'uccello: Jacopo de' Barbari e le rappresentazioni di città nell'Europa del Rinascimento*, 53–57. Venice: Arsenale, 1999.

Filippini, Nadia Maria. "Figure, fatti e percorsi di emancipazione femminile (1797–1880)." *SVON* 1: 453–88.

Filippini, Nadia Maria. "Organizzazione del lavoro, ruoli sociali e familiari nei racconti delle infilaperle (1910–1950)." In *Perle e impiraperle: un lavoro di donne a Venezia tra '800 e '900*, 28–46. Venice: Arsenale, 1990.

Filippini, Nadia Maria. "Storia delle donne: cultura, mestieri, profili." *SVON* 3: 1623–62.

Fincardi, Marco. "Gli 'anni ruggenti' dell'antico leone: la moderna realtà del mito di Venezia." *Contemporanea* 4 (2001): 445–74.

Fincardi, Marco. "I fasti della 'tradizione': le ceremonie della nuova venezianità." *SVON* 2: 1485–1522.

Fincardi, Marco. "I luoghi delle relazioni sociali." *SVON* 1: 489–512.

Finlay, Robert. "Al servizio del Sultano: Venezia, i Turchi e il mondo Cristiano, 1523–1538." In *'Renovatio Urbis': Venezia nell'età di Andrea Gritti (1523-1538)*. Edited by Manfredo Tafuri, 78–118. Rome: Officina Edizioni, 1984.

Finlay, Robert. "Fabius Maximus in Venice: Doge Andrea Gritti, the War of Cambrai, and the Rise of Hapsburg Hegemony, 1509–1530." *RQ* 53 (2000): 998–1031.

Finlay, Robert. *Politics in Renaissance Venice*. New Brunswick: Rutgers University Press, 1980.

Finlay, Robert. "The Venetian Republic as a Gerontocracy: Age and Politics in the Renaissance." *Journal of Medieval and Renaissance Studies* 8 (1978): 157–78.

Finzi, Claudio. "Scritti storico-politici." *SVOC* 3: 825–64.

Fiocco, Giuseppe, and Rona Goffen. "Le pale feriali." In *La pala d'oro: il Tesoro di San Marco*. Edited by H. R. Hahnloser and R. Polacco, 163–84. Venice: Canal and Stamperia, 1994.

Fogolari, Gino. "Jacobello del Fiore e la sua famiglia (nuovi documenti)." *AV* 5th series, 34–5 (1944): 33–50.

Fontana, Giovanni Luigi. "L'economia." *SVON* 2: 1439–83.

Franco, Veronica. *Poems and Selected Letters*. Edited and translated by Ann Rosalind Jones and Margaret F. Rosenthal. Chicago: University of Chicago Press, 1998.

Frank, Martina. "Spazio pubblico, prospetti di chiese e glorificazione gentilizia nella Venezia del Seicento. Riflessioni su una tipologia." *Atti dell'Istituto Veneto di Scienze, Lettere ed Arti, Classe di Scienze Morali, Lettere ed Arti* 144 (1985–6): 109–26.

Franzina, Emilio. "Il 'fronte interno' sulle lagune: Venezia in guerra (1938–1943)." *SVON* 3: 1685–1739.

Franzina, Emilio, ed. *Venezia*. Rome-Bari: Laterza, 1986.

Fulin, R. "Il canale di Suez e la Republica di Venezia (MDIV)." *AV* 2 (1871): 175–213.

Fusaro, Maria. *Political Economies of Empire in the Early Modern Mediterranean: The Decline of Venice and the Rise of England, 1450–1700*. Cambridge: Cambridge University Press, 2015.

Fynn-Paul, Jeffrey. "Empire, Monotheism and Slavery in the Greater Mediterranean Region from Antiquity to the Early Modern Era." *Past and Present* 205 (2009): 3–40.

Gaeta, Franco. "Storiografia, coscienza nazionale e politica culturale nella Venezia del Rinascimento." *SCUV* 3/I: 1–91.

Gaeta, Franco. "Venezia da 'stato misto' ad aristocrazia 'esemplare'." *SCUV* 4/II: 437–94.

Gambier, Madile. "I carteggi privati dei Querini." In *I Querini Stampalia: un ritratto di famiglia nel Settecento veneziano*. Edited by Giorgio Busetto and Madile Gambier, 89–95. Venice: Fondazione Scientifica Querini Stampalia, 1987.

Gambier, Madile. "Dolfin, Caterina." *DBI* 40 (1991): 465–69.

Garzoni, Tommaso. *La piazza universale di tutte le professioni del mondo*. Venice: Vincenzo Somasco, 1595.

Gasparetto, Astone. "The Gnalič Wreck: Identification of the Ship." *Journal of Glass Studies* 15 (1973): 79–84.

Gasparini, Giuseppina De Sandre. "La pietà laicale." *SVOC* 2: 929–61.

Gasparri, Stefano. "Dagli Orseolo al comune." *SVOC* 1: 791–826.

Gasparri, Stefano. "The First Dukes and the Origins of Venice." In *Venice and Its Neighbors from the 8th to 11th Century: Through Renovation and Continuity*. Edited by Sauro Gelichi and Stefano Gasparri, 5–26. Leiden: Brill, 2018.

Gasparri, Stefano. "Venezia fra l'Italia bizantina e il regno italico." In *Venezia: itinerari per la storia della città*. Edited by Stefano Gasparri, Giovanni Levi, and Pierandrea Moro, 61–82. Bologna: Mulino, 1997.

Gasparri, Stefano, and Sauro Gelichi, eds. *The Age of Affirmation: Venice, the Adriatic, and the Hinterland between the 9th and 10th Centuries*. Turnhout: Brepols, 2017.

Gatto, P., and L. Carbognin. "The Lagoon of Venice: Natural Environment Trend and Man-Induced Modification," *Hydrological Sciences—Bulletin—des Sciences Hydrologiques* 26 (1981): 379–91.

Geary, Patrick J. *Furta Sacra: Thefts of Relics in the Central Middle Ages*. Revised ed. Princeton: Princeton University Press, 1990.

Gelichi, Sauro. "Castles on the Water? Defenses in Venice and Comacchio during the Early Middle Ages." In *Fortified Settlements in Early Medieval Europe: Defended Communities of the 8th–10th Centuries*. Edited by Neil Christie and Hajnalka Herold, 263–76. Oxford: Oxbow, 2016.

Gelichi, Sauro, Margherita Ferri, and Cecilia Moine. "Venezia e la laguna tra IX e X secolo: strutture materiali, insediamenti, economie." In *The Age of Affirmation: Venice, the Adriatic, and the Hinterland Between the 9th and 10th Centuries*. Edited by Stefano Gasparri and Sauro Gelichi, 79–128. Turnhout: Brepols, 2017.

Georgelin, Jean. *Venise au siècle des lumières*. Paris: École des Hautes Études en Sciences Sociales, 1978.

Georgopoulou, Maria. "Late Medieval Crete and Venice: An Appropriation of Byzantine Heritage." *Art Bulletin* 77 (1995): 479–96.

Georgopoulou, Maria. *Venice's Mediterranean Colonies: Architecture and Urbanism* Cambridge: Cambridge University Press, 2001.

Gertwagen, Ruthy. "Characteristics of Mediterranean Ships in the Late Medieval Period (13th–15th Centuries CE)." In *Splendour of the Medieval Mediterranean: Art, Culture, Politics, Navigation, and Commerce in the Mediterranean Maritime Cities (13th–15th Centuries)*. Edited by David Abulafia, X. B. Alter, and J. Alemany, 543–61. Barcelona: Lunwerg Editores, 2004.

Gertwagen, Ruthy. *"Nautical Technology."* In *A Companion to Mediterranean History*. Edited by Peregrine Horden and Sharon Kinoshita, 154–69. Chichester: John Wiley, 2014.

Gertwagen, Ruthy. "Venice, Genoa and the Fights over the Island of Tenedos (Late Fourteenth and Early Fifteenth Century)." *SV* n.s. 67 (2013): 35–87.

Gilbert, Felix. "Religion and Politics in the Thought of Gasparo Contarini." In *Action and Conviction in Early Modern Europe: Essays in Memory of E. H. Harbison*. Edited by Theodore K. Rabb and Jerrold E. Seigel, 90–116. Princeton: Princeton University Press, 1969.

Gilbert, Felix. "Venice in the Crisis of the League of Cambrai." *RV*, 274–92.

Ginnasi, Laura. "Celsi, Lorenzo." *DBI* 23 (1979): 475–78.

Ginsborg, Paul. *Daniele Manin and the Venetian Revolution of 1848–49*. Cambridge: Cambridge University Press, 1979.

Girgensohn, Dieter, ed. *Francesco Foscari: promissione ducale 1423*. Venice: La Malcontenta, 2004.

Giustiniano, Bernardo. "Orazione recitata da Bernardo Giustiniano nell'esequie del doge Francesco Foscari." In *Orazioni, elogi e vite scritte da letterati veneti patrizi in lode di dogi, ed altri illustri soggetti*. 2nd ed. in 2 vols. Edited by Girolamo Ascanio Molin, 2: 21–59. Venice: Tipografia di Antonio Curti, 1798.

Gleason, Elisabeth G. "Confronting New Realities: Venice and the Peace of Bologna, 1530." *VR*, 168–84.

Gleason, Elisabeth G. *Gasparo Contarini: Venice, Rome, and Reform*. Berkeley: University of California Press, 1993.

Glixon, Jonathan E., and Beth L. Glixon. "Oil and Opera Don't Mix: The Biography of S. Aponal, a Seventeenth-Century Venetian Opera Theater." In *Music in the Theater, Church and Villa: Essays in Honor of Robert Lamar Weaver and Norma Wright Weaver*. Edited by Susan Parisi, 131–44. Warren, Michigan: Harmonie Park Press, 2000.

Gluzman, Renard. *Venetian Shipping from the Days of Glory to Decline, 1453–1571*. Leiden: Brill, 2021.

Goffen, Rona. "Icon and Vision: Giovanni Bellini's Half-Length Madonnas." *Art Bulletin* 57 (1975): 487–518.

Goldoni, Carlo. *Tutte le opere di Carlo Goldoni*. 14 vols. Milan: Mondadori, 1935–48.

Gorini, Giovanni. "La monetazione." In *Da Aquileia a Venezia: una mediazione tra l'Europa e l'Oriente dal II secolo a. C. al VI secolo d. C.* Edited by Bruna Forlati Tamaro et al., 695–749. Milan: Libri Scheiwiller, 1980.

Gottardi, Michele. "Da Manin a Manin: istituzioni e ceti dirigenti dal '97 al '48." *SVON* 1: 75–105.

Goy, Richard. *The House of Gold: Building a Palace in Medieval Venice*. Cambridge: Cambridge University Press, 1992.

Gozzi, Gasparo. "Elogio delle botteghe da caffè." In *Prose varie di Gasparo Gozzi*. Milan: Dalla Società Tipografica de' Classici Italiani, 1849, 120–2. Accessed from https://www.rodoni.ch/Busoni/bibliotechina/autoriinrete/gasparogozziprose.pdf.

Grandi, Casimira. "Assistenza e beneficenza." *SVON* 2: 865–903.

Graziato, Gisella, ed. *Le promissioni del doge di Venezia dalle origini alla fine del Duecento* Venice: Il Comitato Editore, 1986.

Green, Monica H. "The Four Black Deaths." *American Historical Review* 125 (2020): 1601–31.

Greene, Molly. "The Early Modern Mediterranean." In *A Companion to Mediterranean History*. Edited by Peregrine Horden and Sharon Kinoshita, 91–108. Chichester, West Sussex: Wiley, 2014.

Grendler, Paul F. "The Organization of Primary and Secondary Education in the Italian Renaissance." *Catholic Historical Review* 71 (1985): 185–205.

Grendler, Paul F. *The Roman Inquisition and the Venetian Press, 1540–1605*. Princeton: Princeton University Press, 1977.

Grubb, James S. "Elite Citizens." *VR*, 339–64.

Grubb, James S. ed. *Family Memoirs from Venice (15th–17th Centuries)*. Rome: Viella, 2009.

Grubb, James S. *Firstborn of Venice: Vicenza in the Early Renaissance State*. Baltimore: Johns Hopkins University Press, 1988.

Grubb, James S. "Memory and Identity: Why Venetians Didn't Keep *Ricordanze*." *Renaissance Studies* 8 (1994): 375–87.

Grubb, James S. "When Myths Lose Power: Four Decades of Venetian Historiography." *Journal of Modern History* 58 (1986): 43–94.

Gullino, Giuseppe. "Corner, Alvise." *DBI* 29 (1983): 142–46.

Gullino, Giuseppe. "Corner, Marco." *DBI* 29 (1983): 255–57.

Gullino, Giuseppe. "L'evoluzione costituzionale." *SVOC* 4: 345–78.

Gullino, Giuseppe. "Una famiglia nella storia: i Gradenigo." In *Grado, Venezia, i Gradenigo: catalogo della mostra*. Edited by Marino Zorzi and Susy Marcon, 131–53. Mariano del Friuli: Edizioni della Laguna, 2001.

Gullino, Giuseppe. "Le frontiere navali." *SVOC* 4: 13–111.

Gullino, Giuseppe. "Il giurisdizionalismo dello stato veneziano: gli antichi problemi e la nuova cultura." In *La chiesa di Venezia nel Settecento*. Edited by Bruno Bertoli, 23–38. Venice: Studium Cattolico Veneziano, 1993.

Gullino, Giuseppe. "Istituzioni di cultura." *SVON* 2: 1051–80.

Gullino, Giuseppe. "Pisani, Vittore." *DBI* 84 (2015): 242–45.

Gullino, Giuseppe. "Quando il mercante construì la villa: le proprietà dei Veneziani nella terraferma," *SVOC* 6: 875–924.

Gullino, Giuseppe. *Storia della repubblica veneta*. Brescia: Editrice La Scuola, 2010.

Gullino, Giuseppe. "Venezia e le campagne." *SVOC* 8: 651–702.

Guzzetti, Linda. "Donne e scrittura a Venezia nel tardo Trecento." *AV* 5th ser. 152 (1999): 5–31.

Guzzetti, Linda. "Gli investimenti delle donne veneziane nel Medioevo." *AV* 6th ser. 3 (2012): 41–66.

Harvey, P. D. A. *The History of Topographical Maps: Symbols, Pictures and Surveys*. London: Thames and Hudson, 1980.

Heller, Wendy. *Emblems of Eloquence: Opera and Women's Voices in Seventeenth-Century Venice*. Berkeley: University of California Press, 2003.

Herodian. *Herodian*. Trans. C. R. Whittaker. 2 vols. Cambridge, MA: Harvard University Press, 1969–70.

Heynen, Reinhard. *Zur Entstehung des Kapitalismus in Venedig*. Reprint of 1905 ed. New York: B. Franklin, 1971.

Herzen, Alexander. *My Life and Thoughts: The Memoirs of Alexander Herzen*. Trans. Constance Grant and Humphrey Higgens. 4 vols. New York: Alfred A. Knopf, 1968.

Hills, Paul. *Venetian Colour: Marble, Mosaic, Painting and Glass, 1250–1550*. New Haven: Yale University Press, 1999.

Hocquet, Jean-Claude. "Ambiente lagunare, cultura salinara a Chioggia e variazioni del livello marino alla fine del Medioevo." *AV* 6th series 8 (2014): 7–27.

Hocquet, Jean-Claude. "Capitalisme marchand et classe marchande à Venise au temps de la Renaissance." *Annales E.S.C.* 34 (1979): 279–304.

Hocquet, Jean-Claude. "I meccanismi dei traffici." *SVOC* 3: 529–616.

Hocquet, Jean-Claude. "Monopole et concurrence à la fin du Moyen Age. Venise e les salines de Cervia (XIIe-XVIe siècles)." *SV* 15 (1973): 21–133.

Hocquet, Jean-Claude. "Le saline." *SVOC* 1: 515–48.

Hocquet, Jean-Claude. *Le sel et la fortune de Venise*. 2 vols. Villeneuve d'Ascq: Université de Lille III, 1978–9.

Hocquet, Jean-Claude. *Venise e le monopole du sel: production, commerce et finance d'une république marchande*. 2 vols. Paris: Belles Lettres, 2012.

Hopkins, Andrew. *Santa Maria della Salute: Architecture and Ceremony in Baroque Venice*. Cambridge: Cambridge University Press, 2000.

Horodowich, Elizabeth. *A Brief History of Venice: A New History of the City and Its People*. Philadelphia: Running Press, 2009.

Horodowich, Elizabeth. *Language and Statecraft in Early Modern Venice*. Cambridge: Cambridge University Press, 2008.

Horodowich, Elizabeth. *The Venetian Discovery of America: Geographic Imagination and Print Culture in the Age of Encounters*. Cambridge: Cambridge University Press, 2018.

Howard, Deborah. *The Architectural History of Venice*. Revised ed. New Haven: Yale University Press, 2002.

Howard, Deborah. *Jacopo Sansovino: Architecture and Patronage in Renaissance Venice*. New Haven: Yale University Press, 1975.

Howard, Deborah. *Venice and the East: The Impact of the Islamic World on Venetian Architecture, 1100–1500*. New Haven: Yale University Press, 2000.

Howard, Deborah, and Laura Moretti. *Sound and Space in Renaissance Venice: Architecture, Music, Acoustics*. New Haven: Yale University Press, 2009.

Howells, William Dean. *Venetian Life*. 2nd ed. New York: Hurd and Houghton, 1867.

Hunecke, Volker. "Il corpo aristocratico." *SVOC* 8: 359–429.

Hunecke, Volker. *Il patriziato veneziano alla fine della Repubblica: demografia, famiglia, ménage*. Rome: Jouvence, 1997.

Hurlburt, Holly. *Daughter of Venice: Caterina Cornaro, Queen of Cyprus and Woman of the Renaissance*. New Haven: Yale University Press, 2015.

Imhaus, Brunehilde. *Le minoranze orientali a Venezia, 1300–1510*. Rome: Il Veltro, 1997.

Infelise, Mario. "L'ultima crociata." In *Venezia e la guerra di Morea: guerra, politica e cultura alla fine del '600*. Edited by Mario Infelise and Anastasia Stouraiti, 9–19. Milan: Franco Angeli, 2005.

Infelise, Mario. "Venezia e il suo passato. Storie miti 'fole.'" *SVON* 2: 967–88.

Iordanou, Ioanna. "Pestilence, Poverty and Provision: Re-evaluating the Role of the *Popolani* in Early Modern Venice." *Economic History Review* 69 (2016): 801–22.

Ioannou, Panayotis K. "Palma il Giovane e Giovanni Bilivert nella collezione dell'Istituto Ellenico di Venezia." *Thesaurismata* 32 (2002): 153–65.

Isnenghi, Mario. "Introduzione." *SVON* 2: 1153–80.

Isnenghi, Mario. "I luoghi della cultura." In *Storia d'Italia. Le regioni dall'Unità a oggi. Il Veneto*. Edited by Lanaro, 231–406.

Isnenghi, Mario, and Silvio Lanaro. "Un modello stanco." In *Storia d'Italia. Le Regioni dall'Unità a oggi. Il Veneto*. Edited by Lanaro, 1069–85.

Israel, Janna. "Burial *alguno honore*: Doge Cristoforo Moro's Break from Ducal Burial Convention at the Church of San Giobbe." In *The Tombs of the Doges of Venice from the Beginning of the Serenissima to 1907*. Edited by Benjamin Paul, 375–407. Rome: Viella, 2016.

Jachec, Nancy. "Anti-Communism at Home: Europeanism Abroad: Italian Cultural Policy at the Venice Biennale, 1948–58." *Contemporary European History* 14 (2005): 193–217.

Jacoby, David. "The Venetians in Byzantine and Lusignan Cyprus: Trade, Settlement, and Politics." In *La* Serenissima *and La* Nobilissima: *Venice in Cyprus and Cyprus in Venice*. Edited by Angel Nicolaou-Konnari, 59–100. Nicosia: Politistiko Idryma Trapezēs Kypru, 2009.

Jacoby, David. "Evolving Routes of Western Pilgrimage to the Holy Land, Eleventh to Fifteenth Century: An Overview." In *Unterwegs im Namen der Religion II/On the Road in the Name of Religion II*. Edited by Klaus Herbers and Hans Christian Lehner, 75–97. Stuttgart: Franz Steiner Verlag, 2016.

Jacoby, David. "The Expansion of Venetian Government in the Eastern Mediterranean until the Late Thirteenth Century." In *Il* Commonwealth *veneziano tra 1204 e la fine della Repubblica: identità e peculiarità*. Edited by Gherardo Ortalli, Oliver Jens Schmitt, and Ermanno Orlando, 73–106. Venice: Istituto Veneto di Scienze, Lettere ed Arti, 2015.

Jacoby, David. "Marco Polo, His Close Relatives, and His Travel Account: Some New Insights." *Mediterranean Historical Review* 21 (2006): 193–218.

Jacoby, David. "Raw Materials for the Glass Industries of Venice and the Terraferma: About 1370–about 1460." *Journal of Glass Studies* 35 (1993): 65–90.

Jacoby, David. "Thirteenth-Century Commercial Exchange in the Aegean: Continuity and Change." In *Change in the Byzantine World in the Twelfth and Thirteenth*

Centuries. Edited by Ayla Ödekan, Engin Akyürek, and Nevra Necipoğlu, 187–94. Istanbul: Vehbi Koç Vakfi, 2010.

Jacoby, David. "Western Commercial and Colonial Expansion in the Eastern Mediterranean and the Black Sea in the late Middle Ages." In *Rapporti mediterranei, pratiche documentarie, presenze veneziane: le reti economiche e culturali (XIV-XVI secolo)*. Edited by Gherardo Ortalli and Alessio Sopracasa, 3–49. Venice: Istituto Veneto di Scienze, Lettere ed Arti, 2017.

Jacoby, David. "Venetian Commercial Expansion in the Eastern Mediterranean, 8th–11th Centuries." In *Byzantine Trade, 4th–12th Centuries*. Edited by M. Mandell Mango, 371–91. Farnham: Ashgate, 2009.

Jacoby, David. "The Venetian Quarter of Constantinople from 1082 to 1261." In *Novum Millenium: Studies on Byzantine History and Culture Dedicated to Paul Speck*. Edited by Claudia Sode and Sarolta Takács, 153–70. Aldershot: Ashgate, 2001.

Jacoby, David. "La Venezia d'oltremare nel secondo Duecento." *SVOC* 2: 262–302.

Jacoff, Michael. *The Horses of San Marco and the Quadriga of the Lord*. Princeton: Princeton University Press, 1993.

Jansen, Katherine L., Joanna Drell, and Frances Andrews, eds. *Medieval Italy: Texts in Translation*. Philadelphia: University of Pennsylvania Press, 2009.

Jergerlehner, J. "Die Aufstand der kandiotischen Rittershaft gegen das Mutterland Venedig, 1363–65." *Byzantinische Zeitschrift* 12 (1903): 78–125.

Jewitt, James R. "Liberty on the Lagoon: Venetian Images of the Red Sea, 1480–1530." In *Formations of Identity: Society, Politics, and Landscape*. Edited by Floyd Martin and Eileen Yanoviak, 1–18. Newcastle upon Tyne: Cambridge Scholars Publishing, 2016.

Johnson, Eugene J. *Inventing the Opera House: Theater Architecture in Renaissance and Baroque Italy*. Cambridge: Cambridge University Press, 2018.

Johnson, Eugene J. "The Short, Lascivious Life of Two Venetian Theaters, 1580–85." *RQ* 55 (2002): 936–68.

Johnson, James H. *Venice Incognito: Masks in the Serene Republic*. Berkeley: University of California Press, 2011.

Jones, Evan T., and Margaret M. Condon. *Cabot and Bristol's Age of Discovery: The Bristol Discovery Voyages, 1480–1508*. Bristol: Cabot Project Publications, 2016.

Jori, Francesco. *Dalla Liga alla Lega: storia, movimenti, protagonisti. Prefazione di Ilvo Diamanti*. Venice: Marsilio, 2009.

Judde de Larivière, Claire. "Entre gestion privée et contrôle public: les transports maritime à Venise à la fin du Moyen Âge." *Histoire Urbaine* 12 (2005): 57–68.

Judde de Larivière, Claire. *Naviguer, commercer, gouverner: économie maritime et pouvoirs à Venise (XVe–XVIe siècles)*. Leiden: Brill, 2008.

Judde de Larivière, Claire. "Political Participation in Renaissance Venice." In *Popular Politics in an Aristocratic Republic*. Edited by Van Gelder and Judde de Larivière, 69–87. London: Routledge, 2020.

Judde de Larivière, Claire. "The 'Public' and the 'Private' in Sixteenth-Century Venice: From Medieval Economy to Early Modern State." *Historical Social Research/ Historische Sozialforschung* 37 (2012): 76–94.

Judde de Larivière, Claire. *La révolte des boules de neige: Murano face à Venise, 1511*. Paris: Fayard, 2014.

Judde de Larivière, Claire. "Sense of Neighbourhood (*Vicinanza*) in Sixteenth-Century Venice." In *The Experience of Neighbourhood in Medieval and Early Modern Europe*. Edited by Bronach C. Kane and Simon Sandall, 48–60. London: Routledge, 2022.

Judde de Larivière, Claire, and Rosa M. Salzberg. "'Le peuple est la cité': l'idée de *popolo* e la condition des popolani à Venise (XVe–XVIe siècles)." *Annales: Histoire, Sciences Sociales* 68 (2013–4): 113–40.

Katele, Irene B. "Piracy and the Venetian State: The Dilemma of Maritime Defense in the Fourteenth Century." *Speculum* 63 (1988): 865–89.

Katz, Dana E. *The Jewish Ghetto and the Visual Imagination of Early Modern Venice*. Cambridge: Cambridge University Press, 2017.

Keahy, John. *Venice Against the Sea: A City Besieged*. New York: St. Martin's Press, 2002.

King, Margaret L. *Venetian Humanism in an Age of Patrician Dominance*. Princeton: Princeton University Press, 1986.

Kiriaki, Alberto Stelio de. *La beneficenza di ricovero a Venezia nel passato e nei nostri tempi. Ricordo per l'anno 1900*. Venice: Tipografia all'Orfanotrofio (Gesuati), 1900.

Klein, Holger A. "Refashioning Byzantium in Venice, ca. 1200–1400." In *San Marco, Byzantium, and the Myths of Venice*. Edited by Henry Maguire and Robert S. Nelson, 193–225. Washington: Dumbarton Oaks, 2010.

Knapton, Michael. "La dinamica delle finanze pubbliche." *SVOC* 3: 475–528.

Knapton, Michael. "La finanza pubblica." *SVOC* 2: 371–408.

Knapton, Michael. *Una repubblica di uomini: saggi di storia veneta*. Edited by Andrea Gardi, Gian Maria Varanini, and Andrea Zannini. Udine: Forum, 2017.

Kohl, Benjamin G. *Padua Under the Carrara, 1318–1405*. Baltimore: Johns Hopkins University Press, 1998.

Kohl, Benjamin G. "The Serrata of the Greater Council of Venice, 1282–1323: The Documents." In *Venice and the Veneto During the Renaissance: The Legacy of Benjamin Kohl*. Edited by Michael Knapton, John E. Law, and Alison A. Smith, 3–34. Florence: Firenze University Press, 2014.

Kohl, Benjamin G., and Ronald G. Witt. *The Earthly Republic: Italian Humanists on Government and Society*. Philadelphia: University of Pennsylvania Press, 1978.

Kostylo, Joanna. "Sinking and Shrinking City: Cosmopolitanism, Historical Memory and Social Change in Venice." In *Post-Cosmopolitan Cities: Explorations of Urban Coexistence*. Edited by Caroline Humphrey and Vera Skvirskaja, 170–93. New York: Berghahn, 2012.

Krekić, Bariša. "Venezia e l'Adriatico." *SVOC* 3: 51–85.

Kunz, Michael L. and Robin O. Mills. "A Precolumbian Presence of Venetian Glass Trade Beads in Arctic Alaska." *American Antiquity* 86 (2021): 395–412.

Labalme, Patricia H. *Bernardo Giustiniani: A Venetian of the Quattrocento*. Rome: Edizioni di Storia e Letteratura, 1969.

Labowsky, Lotte. *Bessarion's Library and the Biblioteca Marciana: Six Early Inventories*. Rome: Edizioni di Storia e Letteratura, 1979.

Lanaro, Paola, ed. *At the Centre of the Old World: Trade and Manufacturing in Venice and the Venetian Mainland, 1400–1800*. Toronto: Centre for Reformation and Renaissance Studies, 2006.

Lanaro, Silvio, ed. *Storia d'Italia: Le regioni dall'Unità a oggi. Il Veneto*. Turin: Einaudi, 1984.

Lane, Frederic C. *Andrea Barbarigo: Merchant of Venice, 1418–1449*. Baltimore: Johns Hopkins University Press, 1944.

Lane, Frederic C. "The Economic Meaning of the Invention of the Compass." *American Historical Review* 68 (1963): 605–17.

Lane, Frederic C. "The Enlargement of the Great Council of Venice." In *Florilegium Historiale: Essays Presented to Wallace K. Ferguson*. Edited by J. G. Rowe and W. H. Stockdale, 236–74. Toronto: University of Toronto Press, 1971.

Lane, Frederic C. "The Funded Debt of the Venetian Republic, 1262–1482." In Lane, *Venice and History*, 87–98.

Lane, Frederic C. "The Mediterranean Spice Trade: Its Revival in the Sixteenth Century." In Lane, *Venice and History*, 24–34.

Lane, Frederic C. "Naval Actions and Fleet Organization, 1499–1502." *RV*, 146–73.

Lane, Frederic C. *Venice: A Maritime Republic*. Baltimore: Johns Hopkins University Press, 1973.

Lane, Frederic C. *Venice and History: The Collected Papers of Frederic C. Lane*. Baltimore: Johns Hopkins University Press, 1966.

Lane, Frederic Chapin. *Venetian Ships and Shipbuilders of the Renaissance*. Reprint. Baltimore: Johns Hopkins University Press, 1992.

Lane, Frederic C. "Wages and Recruitment of Venetian Galeotti, 1470–1580." *SV* n.s. 6 (1982): 15–43.

Lane, Frederic C., and Reinhold C. Mueller. *Money and Banking in Medieval and Renaissance Venice*, vol. 1, *Coins and Moneys of Account*. Baltimore: Johns Hopkins University Press, 1985.

Lanfranchi, Luigi, ed. *Famiglia Zusto*. Venice: Il Comitato Editore, 1955.

Lanfranchi, Luigi, ed. *S. Giorgio Maggiore*. 4 vols. Venice: Il Comitato Editore, 1968–1986.

Lanfranchi, Luigi, and Bianca Strina, eds. *Ss. Ilario e Benedetto e S. Gregorio*. Venice: Il Comitato Editore, 1965.

Lanfranchi, L. G., and G. Zille. "Il territorio del ducato veneziano dall'VIII al XII secolo." In *Storia di Venezia*. 2 vols. 2:1–65. Venice: Centro Internazionale delle Arti e del Costume, 1957–8.

Larner, John. *Marco Polo and the Discovery of the World*. New Haven: Yale University Press, 1999.

Lassels, Richard. *The Voyage of Italy*. 2 vols. Paris: Vincent du Moutier, 1670.

Lauer, Rena N. *Colonial Justice and the Jews of Venetian Crete*. Philadelphia: University of Pennsylvania Press, 2019.

Laven, David. *Venice and Venetia Under the Habsburgs, 1815–1835*. Oxford: Oxford University Press, 2002.

Laven, Mary. *Virgins of Venice: Broken Vows and Cloistered Lives in the Renaissance Convent*. New York: Penguin, 2002.

Lazar, Irena. "The Glass from the Gnalić Wreck and Its Glass Cargo." *Vjesnik za arheolgiju i historiju dalmatinsku Split: Arheološki muzei* 108 (2015): 1–13.

Lazar, Irena, and Hugh Willmott. *The Glass from the Gnalić Wreck*. Koper: Založba Annales, 2006.

Lazzarini, Antonio. *Boschi, legnami, costruzioni navali: l'Arsenale di Venezia fra XVI e XVIII secolo*. Rome: Viella, 2021.

Lazzarini, Antonio. "Possidenti e bonificatori ebrei: la famiglia Sullam." *SVON* 1: 603–17.

Lazzarini, Lino. "Francesco Petrarca e il primo umanesimo veneziano." In *Umanesimo europeo e umanesimo veneziano*. Edited by Vittore Branca, 63–92. Florence: Sansoni, 1964.

Lazzarini, Vittorio. "Escusati del dogado veneziano." *Atti dell'Istituto Veneto di Scienze, Lettere ed Arti, Parte Seconda, Classe di Scienze Morali e Lettere* 105 (1947): 75–85.

Lazzarini, Vittorio. *Marino Faliero: avanti il dogado, la congiura, appendici*. Florence: Sansoni, 1963.

Leduc, François-Xavier, ed. *Venezia-Senato: deliberazioni miste: registro XIX (1340–1341)*. Venice: Istituto Veneto di Scienze, Lettere ed Arti, 2004.

Liucci, Raffaele. "Il '43–'45." *SVON* 3: 1741–66.

Liudprand of Cremona. *The Complete Works of Liudprand of Cremona*. Trans. Paolo Squatriti. Washington: Catholic University of America Press, 2007.

Loenertz, Raymond-Joseph. *Les Ghisi: dynastes vénitiens dans l'archipel, 1207–1390*. Florence: Olschki, 1975.

Long, Pamela O., David McGee, and Alan M. Stahl, eds. *The Book of Michael of Rhodes: A Fifteenth-Century Maritime Manuscript*. 3 vols. Cambridge, MA: MIT Press, 2009.

Lopez, Robert S. *The Commercial Revolution of the Middle Ages, 950–1350*. Englewood Cliffs: Prentice Hall, 1971.

Lopez, Robert S. "European Merchants in the Medieval Indies: The Evidence of Commercial Documents." *Journal of Economic History* 3 (1943): 174–80.

Lopez, Robert S. "I successori di Marco Polo e la febbre della seta." In *Marco Polo, Venezia e l'Oriente*. Edited by Alvise Zorzi, 289–90. Milan: Electa, 1981.

Lorenzetti, Giulio. *Venice and Its Lagoon: Historical-Artistic Guide*. Trans. John Guthrie. Trieste: Edizioni Lint, 1975.

Lorenzi, Giambattista. *Monumenti per servire alla storia del palazzo ducale di Venezia ovvero serie di atti pubblici dal 1253 al 1797, pt 1: dal 1253 al 1600*. Venice: Tipografia Marco Visentini, 1868.

Lorenzoni, Giovanni. "Espressioni d'arte: i principali monumenti architettonici." *SVOC* 1: 865–92.

Lowe, Kate. "Black Africans in Renaissance Venice." *RQ* 66 (2013): 412–52.

Lowe, K. J. P. *Nuns' Chronicles and Convent Culture in Renaissance and Counter-Reformation Italy*. Cambridge: Cambridge University Press, 2003.

Lowry, Martin. *Nicholas Jenson and the Rise of Venetian Publishing in Renaissance Europe*. Oxford: Blackwell, 1991.

Lowry, Martin. "The Reform of the Council of Ten, 1582–3: An Unsettled Problem?" *SV* 13 (1971): 275–310.

Lowry, Martin. *The World of Aldus Manutius: Business and Scholarship in Renaissance Venice*. Ithaca: Cornell University Press, 1979.

Lunardon, Silvia, ed. *Hospitale S. Marie Cruciferorum: l'ospizio dei Crociferi a Venezia*. Venice: IRE, 1985.

Luzzatto, Gino. "Capitalismo coloniale nel Trecento." In Gino Luzzatto. *Studi di storia economica veneziana*, 117–23. Padua: CEDAM, 1954.

Luzzatto, Gino. "L'economia veneziana dal 1797 al 1866." *SCIV* 3: 267–77.

Luzzatto, Gino. "L'economia veneziana nei suoi rapporti con la politica nell'Alto Medioevo," *SCIV* 1:95–106.

Luzzatto, Gino. "Il patrimonio privato di un doge del secolo XIII." In Gino Luzzatto, *Studi di storia economica veneziana*, 79–87. Padua: CEDAM, 1954.

Luzzatto, Gino, ed. *I prestiti della Repubblica di Venezia (sec. XIII-XV)*. Padua: Libreria Editrice A. Draghi, 1929.

Luzzatto, Gino. "Sindicati e cartelli nel commercio veneziano dei secoli XIII e XIV." In Gino Luzzatto, *Studi di storia economica veneziana*, 195–200. Padua: CEDAM, 1954.

Luzzatto, Gino. *Storia economica di Venezia dall'XI al XVI secolo*. Venice: Centro Internazionale delle Arti e del Costume, 1961.

Luzzatto Voghera, Gadi. "Gli ebrei." *SVON* 1: 619–48.

McCluskey, Karen E. *New Saints in Late-Mediaeval Venice, 1200–1500: A Typological Study*. London: Routledge, 2020.

McCormick, Michael. "New Light on the 'Dark Ages': How the Slave Trade Fueled the Carolingian Economy." *Past and Present* 177 (2002): 17–54.

McCormick, Michael. *Origins of the European Economy: Communications and Commerce, A.D.300–900*. Cambridge: Cambridge University Press, 2001.

McCough, Laura J. *Gender, Sexuality, and Syphilis in Early Modern Venice*. Houndmills, Basingstoke: Palgrave Macmillan, 2011.

McKee, Sally. *Uncommon Dominion: Venetian Crete and the Myth of Ethnic Purity* Philadelphia: University of Pennsylvania Press, 2000.

Mackenney, Richard. "The Guilds of Renaissance Venice: State and Society in the *Longue Durée*." *SV* n.s. 34 (1997): 15–43.

Mackenney, Richard. "'A Plot Discover'd?': Myth, Legend, and the 'Spanish' Conspiracy against Venice in 1618." *VR*, 185–216.

Mackenney, Richard C. *Tradesmen and Traders: The World of the Guilds in Venice and Europe, c.1250–c.1650*. Totowa, NJ: Barnes and Noble, 1987.

Mackenney, Richard. *Venice as the Polity of Mercy: Guilds, Confraternities, and the Social Order, c. 1250–c. 1650*. Toronto: University of Toronto Press, 2019.

McKinney, Frank K. *The Northern Adriatic Ecosystem: Deep Time in a Shallow Sea*. New York: Columbia University Press, 2007.

Mackrell, Judith. *The Unfinished Palazzo: Life, Love and Art in Venice*. London: Thames and Hudson, 2017.

McNeill, William H. *Venice: The Hinge of Europe, 1081–1797*. Chicago: University of Chicago Press, 1974.

Madden, Thomas F. *Enrico Dandolo and the Rise of Venice*. Baltimore: Johns Hopkins University Press, 2003.

Madden, Thomas F. "The Venetian Version of the Fourth Crusade: Memory and the Conquest of Constantinople in Medieval Venice." *Speculum* 87 (2012): 311–44.

Madden, Thomas F. *Venice: A New History*. New York: Viking, 2012.

Madden, Thomas F. "Venice's Hostage Crisis: Diplomatic Efforts to Secure Peace with Byzantium Between 1171 and 1184." In *Medieval and Renaissance Venice*. Edited by Ellen E. Kittell and Thomas F. Madden, 96–108. Urbana: University of Illinois Press, 1999.

Magliaretta, Leopoldo. "La qualità della vita." In *Venezia*. Edited by Franzina, 323–80.

Malipiero, Domenico. *Annali veneti dall'anno 1457 al 1500*. 2 vols. *Archivio Storico Italiano* 7 (1843–4).

Malkiel, David J. "The Ghetto Republic." In *Jews of Early Modern Venice*. Edited by Davis and Ravid, 117–42.

Mallett, Michael E. "La conquista della terraferma." *SVOC* 4: 181–244.

Mallett, Michael E. *The Florentine Galleys in the Fifteenth Century*. Oxford: Clarendon Press, 1967.

Mallett, Michael E. "Venezia e la politica italiana, 1454–1530." *SVOC* 4: 245–310.

Mallett, Michael E. "Venice and the War of Ferrara, 1482–84." In *War, Culture and Society in Renaissance Venice: Essays in Honour of John Hale*. Edited by David S. Chambers, Cecil H. Clough, and Michael E. Mallett, 57–72. London: Hambledon Press, 1993.

Mallett, Michael E., and John R. Hale. *The Military Organization of a Renaissance State: Venice c. 1400 to 1617*. Cambridge: Cambridge University Press, 1984.

Mancuso, Franco. "La laguna e le isole." *SVON* 3: 2359–92.

Manfroni, Camillo. "La battaglia di Gallipoli e la politica veneta-turca (1381–1420)." *AT* anno 25, vol. 2 (1902): 3–34 and 129–69.

Maranini, Giuseppe. *La costituzione di Venezia*. Reprint of 1927–31 edition in 2 vols. Florence: La Nuova Italia, 1974.

Marino, John. "Administrative Mapping in the Italian States." In *Monarchs, Ministers and Maps: The Emergence of Cartography as a Tool of Government in Early Modern Europe*. Edited by David Buisseret, 5–25. Chicago: University of Chicago Press, 1992.

Martelli, Riccardo. "Papadopoli." *DBI* 81 (2014). Online version: [https://www.treccani.it/enciclopedia/papadopoli_%28Dizionario-Biografico%29/].

Martin, John Jeffries. *Venice's Hidden Enemies: Italian Heretics in a Renaissance City.* Berkeley: University of California Press, 1993.

Martin, Lillian Ray. *The Art and Archeology of Venetian Ships and Boats.* College Station: Texas A&M Press, 2001.

Martin, M. E. "The Chrysobull of Alexius I Comnenus to the Venetians and the early Venetian Quarter in Constantinople." *Byzantinoslavica* 39 (1978): 19–23.

Martin, Ruth. *Witchcraft and the Inquisition in Venice, 1550–1650.* Oxford: Blackwell, 1989.

Martindale, Andrew. "The Venetian Sala del Gran Consiglio and Its Fourteenth-Century Decoration." *Antiquaries Journal* 73 (1993): 76–124.

Martini, Gabriele. *Il 'vitio nefando' nella Venezia del Seicento.* Rome: Jouvence, 1988.

Massaro, Martina. "Giacomo Treves dei Bonfili, profile di un collezionista." *AT* 3rd series 13/II (2014): 47–68.

Masters, Bruce. *The Origins of Western Economic Dominance in the Middle East: Mercantilism and the Islamic Economy of Aleppo, 1600–1750.* New York: New York University Press, 1988.

Matthew, Louisa C. "Were There Open Markets for Pictures in Renaissance Venice?" In *The Art Market in Italy 15th–17th Centuries: il mercato dell'arte in Italia, secc. XV-XVII.* Edited by Marcello Fantoni, Louisa C. Matthew, and Sara F. Matthews-Grieco, 253–61. Modena: Franco Cosimo Panini, 2003.

Mattingly, Garrett. *Renaissance Diplomacy.* Boston: Houghton Mifflin, 1955.

Mattozzi, Ivo. "Intraprese produttive in terraferma." *SVOC* 7: 435–78.

Mattozzi, Ivo. "Il politico e il pane a Venezia (1570–1650): calmieri e governo della sussitenza." *Società e Storia* 20 (1983): 271–303.

Mattozzi, Ivo. "Le radici, il tronco, e le diramazioni della produzione cartaria nella Valle delle Cartiere di Toscolano." *La Bibliofilia* 118 (2016): 389–408.

Mazohl-Wallnig, Brigitte. "L'Austria e Venezia." In *Venezia e l'Austria.* Edited by Benzoni and Cozzi, 3–20.

Mazzucco, Gabriele, ed. *Monasteri benedittini nella laguna veneziana: catalogo di mostra.* Venice: Arsenale, 1983.

Meccoli, Sandro. "Salvare Venezia: da chi?" *Meridiani* 1 (1988): 64–7.

Megna, Laura. "Grandezza e miseria della nobiltà veneziana." *SVOC* 7: 161–200.

Menegazzo, Emilio. "Alvise Cornaro: un veneziano del Cinquecento nella terraferma padovana." *SCUV* 3/II:513–38.

Menniti Ippolito, Antonio. *Fortuna e sfortune di una famiglia veneziana nel Seicento: gli Ottoboni al tempo dell'aggregazione al patriziato.* Venice: Istituto Veneto di Scienze, Lettere ed Arti, 1996.

Menniti Ippolito, Antonio. "'Sudditi d'un altro stato?' gli ecclesiastici veneziani," *SVOC* 7: 325–65.

Merchant Culture in Fourteenth Century Venice: The Zibaldone da Canal. Trans. John E. Dotson. Binghamton, NY: Medieval and Renaissance Texts and Studies, 1994.

Merkel, Ettore. "Un problema di metodo: la 'Dormitio virginis' dei Mascoli." *Arte Veneta* 27 (1973): 65–80.

Meserve, Margaret. "News from Negroponte: Politics, Popular Opinion, and Information Exchange in the First Decade of the Italian Press." *RQ* 59 (2006): 440–80.

Miccoli, Giovanni. "Chiesa e Lega Nord." *Studi Storici* 53 (2012): 237–44.

Molà, Luca. *La comunità dei Lucchesi a Venezia: immigrazione e industria della seta nel tardo Medioevo*. Venice: Istituto Veneto di Scienze, Lettere ed Arti, 1994.

Molà, Luca. "Venetian Luxury Gifts for the Ottoman Empire in the Late Renaissance." In *Global Gifts: The Material Culture of Diplomacy in Early Modern Eurasia*. Edited by Zoltán Biedermann, Anne Gerritsen, and Giorgio Riello, 56–87. Cambridge: Cambridge University Press, 2018.

Molà, Luca. *The Silk Industry of Renaissance Venice*. Baltimore: Johns Hopkins University Press, 2000.

Mollat, Michel. "Aux origines de la précocité économique et sociale de Venise: l'exploitation du sel." In *La Venezia del Mille*, 198–202. Florence: Sansoni, 1965.

Molmenti, Pompeo. *La storia di Venezia nella vita privata*. 7th ed. in 3 vols. Trieste: LINT, 1973.

Mometto, Piergiovanni. *L'azienda agricola Barbarigo a Carpi*. Venice: Il Cardo, 1992.

Monteleone, Giulio. "La carestia del 1816–1817 nelle province venete," *AV* series 5, 86–7 (1969): 23–86.

Monticolo, Giovanni, ed. *I capitolari delle arti veneziane sottoposte alla Giustizia e poi alla Giustizia Vecchia dalle origini al MCCCXXX*. 3 vols. Rome: Istituto Storico Italiano, 1896–1914.

Monticolo, Giovanni. *L'ufficio della Giustizia Vecchia a Venezia dalle origini sino al 1300* Venice: A Spese della Società, 1892.

Mor, Carlo Guido. "Aspetti della vita costituzionale veneziana fino alla fine del X secolo." *SCIV* 1: 85–93.

Morazzoni, Giuseppe. *Il mobile veneziano del '700*. Milan: Casa Editrice d'Arte Bestetti & Tumminelli.

Morche, Franz-Julius. "The Letters of Others: Marino Morosini and His Curious Newssheet on the Battle of Maclodio (1427)." In *Cultures of Empire: Rethinking Venetian Rule, 1400–1700: Essays in Honour of Benjamin Arbel*. Edited by Georg Christ and Franz-Julius Morche, 90–122. Leiden: Brill, 2020.

Morozzo della Rocca, Raimondo, ed. *Lettere di mercanti a Pignol Zucchello (1336–1350)* Venice: Comitato per la Pubblicazione delle Fonti Relative alla Storia di Venezia, 1957.

Morozzo della Rocca, Raimondo and Antonino Lombardo, eds. *Documenti del commercio veneziano nei secoli XI–XIII*. 2 vols. Turin: Editrice Libraria Italiana, 1940.

Morris, James (Jan). *The World of Venice*. New York: Pantheon Books, 1960.

Mozzato, Andrea, ed. *La mariegola dell'arte della lana di Venezia (1244–1595)*.2 vols. Venice: Comitato per la Pubblicazione delle Fonti Relative alla Storia di Venezia, 2002.

Mozzato, Andrea. "The Production of Woolens in Fifteenth- and Sixteenth-Century Venice." In *At the Centre of the Old World*. Edited by Lanaro, 73–107.

Mozzi, Paolo, et al. "The Roman City of Altinum, Venice Lagoon, from Remote Sensing and Geophysical Prospection." *Archaeological Prospection* 23 (2016): 27–44 [DOI: 10.1002/Arp.1520].

Mueller, Reinhold C. "Aspetti sociali ed economici della peste a Venezia nel Medioevo." In *Venezia e la Peste*, 71–6.

Mueller, Reinhold C. "Catalogo: dalla reazione alla prevenzione." In *Venezia e la Peste*, 77–92.

Mueller, Reinhold C. "Effetti della guerra di Chioggia sulla vita economica e sociale di Venezia (1378–1381)." In Reinhold C. Mueller. *Venezia nel tardo Medioevo: Late Medieval Venice/Economia e società: Economy and Society*. Edited by Luca Molà, Michael Knapton, and Luciano Pezzolo, 115–26. Rome: Viella, 2021.

Mueller, Reinhold C. *Immigrazione e cittadinanza nella Venezia medievale*. Rome: Viella, 2010.

Mueller, Reinhold C. "Les prêteurs juifs de Venise au Moyen Âge." In Reinhold C. Mueller. *Venezia nel tardo Medioevo: Late Medieval Venice/Economia e società: Economy and Society*. Edited by Luca Molà, Michael Knapton, and Luciano Pezzolo, 307–33. Rome: Viella, 2021.

Mueller, Reinhold C. "The Procurators of San Marco in the Thirteenth and Fourteenth Centuries: A Study of the Office as a Financial and Trust Institution." *SV* 13 (1971): 105–220.

Mueller, Reinhold C. *The Venetian Money Market: Banks, Panics, and the Public Debt, 1200–1500*. Baltimore: Johns Hopkins University Press, 1997.

Muir, Edward. *Civic Ritual in Renaissance Venice*. Princeton: Princeton University Press, 1981.

Muir, Edward. *The Culture Wars of the Late Renaissance: Skeptics, Libertines, and Opera*. Cambridge, MA: Harvard University Press, 2007.

Muir, Edward. "The Doge as *Primus inter Pares*: Interregnum Rites in Early Sixteenth-Century Venice." In *Essays Presented to Myron P. Gilmore*. Edited by Sergio Bertelli and Gloria Ramakus, 145–60. Florence: La Nuova Italia, 1978.

Muraro, Michelangelo. "The Political Interpretation of Giorgione's Frescoes on the Fondaco dei Tedeschi." *Gazzette des Beaux Arts* series 6, 86 (1975): 177–84.

Muraro, Michelangelo. "La scala senza giganti." In *De artibus opuscula XL: Essays in Honor of Erwin Panofsky*. Edited by Millard Meiss, 250–70. New York: New York University Press, 1961.

Muraro, Michelangelo. "The Statutes of the Venetian *Arti* and the Mosaics of the Mascoli Chapel." *Art Bulletin* 43 (1961): 263–74

Nanetti, Andrea, ed. *Il codice Morosini: il mondo visto da Venezia (1094–1433)*. 4 vols. Spoleto: Centro Italiano di Studi sull'Alto Medioevo, 2010.

Nani, Battista. *Historia della Republica Veneta, Parte Seconda*. Venice: Combi e la Noù, 1686.

Nani-Mocenigo, Filippo. "Testamento del Doge Agostino Barbarigo." *NAV* n.s. 17 (1909): 234–61.

Neerfeld, Christiane. *'Historia per la forma di diaria': la cronachistica veneziana contemporanea a cavallo tra il Quattro e il Cinquecento*. Venice: Istituto Veneto di Scienze, Lettere ed Arti, 2006.

Nicol, Donald M. *Byzantium and Venice: A Study in Diplomatic and Cultural Relations*. Cambridge: Cambridge University Press, 1988.

Niero, Antonio. "Culto dei santi da Grado a Venezia." *Studi Jesolani* 27(1985): 163–86.

Niero, Antonio. "I templi del Redentore e della Salute: motivazioni teologiche." In *Venezia e la peste*, 294–8.

Ninfo, Andrea et al. "The Map of Altinum: Ancestor of Venice." *Science* 325, no. 5940 (July 2009): 577 [DOI 10.1126/science.1174206].

Norwich, John Julius. *A History of Venice*. New York: Knopf, 1982.

Norwich, John Julius. *Paradise of Cities: Venice in the 19th Century*. New York: Doubleday, 2003.

O'Connell, Monique. *Men of Empire: Power and Negotiation in Venice's Maritime State*. Baltimore: Johns Hopkins University Press, 2009.

Orlando, Ermanno. *Altre Venezie: il dogado veneziano nei secoli XIII e XIV (giurisdizione, territorio, giustizia e amministrazione)*. Venice: Istituto Veneto di Scienze, Lettere ed Arti, 2008.

Orlando, Ermanno. "Dalmatians and Slavs in Venice During the Late Middle Ages: Between Integration and Assimilation." In *Towns and Cities of the Croatian Middle Ages: The City and the Newcomers*. Edited by Irena Benyovky Latin and Zrinka Pešorda Vardič, 283–96. Zagreb: Croatian Institute of History, 2020.

Orlando, Ermanno. *Migrazioni mediterranee: migranti, minoranze e matrimoni a Venezia nel Basso Medioevo*. Bologna: Mulino, 2014.

Orlando, Ermanno, ed. *Venezia-Senato: deliberazioni miste: registro XXIV (1347–1349)*. Venice: Istituto Veneto di Scienze, Lettere, ed Arti, 2007.

Orlando, Ermanno. "Venezia, l'Adige e la viabilità fluviale nel Basso Medioevo." In *Il fiume, le terre, l'immaginario: l'Adige come fenomeno storiografico complesso*. Edited by V. Rovigo, 99–122. Rovereto: Edizioni Osiride, 2016.

Orlando, Ermanno. *Venezia e il mare nel Medioevo*. Bologna: Mulino, 2014.

Ortalli, Francesca. *"Per salute delle anime e delli corpi": scuole piccole a Venezia nel tardo Medioevo*. Venice: Marsilio, 2001.

Ortalli, Gherardo. "I cronisti e la determinazione di Venezia città." *SVOC* 2: 761–82.

Ortalli, Gherardo. "Il ducato e la 'civitas Rivoalti': tra carolingi, bizantini e sassoni," *SVOC* 1: 725–90.

Ortalli, Gherardo. "Grado e i Gradenigo. Vicende e ruoli alla radici della civiltà veneziana." In *Grado, Venezia, i Gradenigo: catalogo della mostra*. Edited by Marino Zorzi and Susy Marcon, 27–40. Mariano del Friuli: Edizioni della Laguna, 2001.

Ortalli, Gherardo, Oliver Jens Schmitt, and Ermanno Orlando, eds. *Il* Commonwealth *veneziano tra 1204 e la fine della Repubblica: identità e peculiarità*. Venice: Istituto Veneto di Scienze, Lettere ed Arti, 2015.

Ortega, Stephen. *Negotiating Transcultural Relations in the Early Modern Mediterranean: Ottoman-Venetian Encounters*. Farnham, Surrey: Ashgate, 2014.

Osborne, John. "Politics, Diplomacy and the Cult of Relics in Venice and the northern Adriatic in the first half of the ninth century." *Early Medieval Europe* 8 (1999): 369–86.

Padoan, Giorgio. "L'impiego civile di Carlo Goldoni." *Lettere Italiane* 35 (1983): 421–56.

Padovani, Andrea. "Curie ed uffici." *SVOC* 2: 331–47.

Padovani, Andrea. "La politica del diritto." *SVOC* 2: 303–29.

Palladini, Gianantonio. "Clero e laicato nella dramma della Resistenza." In *La chiesa di Venezia dalla seconda guerra mondiale al concilio*. Edited by Bruno Bertoli, 69–85. Venice: Edizioni Studium Cattolico Veneziano, 1997.

Pallucchini, Rodolfo. "Significato e valore della 'Biennale' nella vita artistica veneziana e italiana." *SCIV* 3:387–402.

Palumbo-Fossati, Isabella. "L'interno della casa dell'artigiano e dell'artista nella Venezia del Cinquecento." *SV* n.s. 8 (1984):109–53.

Pamato, Lorenza. *Le scuole di battuti di Venezia (1260ca–1401)*. Dottorato di Ricerca. University of Padua, 1999.

Panciera, Walter. *L'arte matrice: i lanifici della Repubblica di Venezia nei secoli XVII e XVIII*. Treviso: Fondazione Benetton Studi Ricerche/Canova Editrice, 1996.

Panciera, Walter. "The Industries of Venice in the Seventeenth and Eighteenth Centuries." In *At the Centre of the Old World*. Edited by Lanaro, 185–214.

Panciera, Walter. *La Repubblica di Venezia nel Settecento*. Rome: Viella, 2014.

Pavan, Massimiliano, and Girolamo Arnaldi. "Le origini dell'identità lagunare." *SVOC* 1: 409–56.

Pavanini, Paola. "Abitazioni popolari e borghesi nella Venezia cinquecentesca." *SV* n.s. 5 (1981): 63–126.

Pazienza. Annamaria. "Venice Beyond Venice. Commercial Agreements and *Pacta* from the Origins to Pietro II Orseolo." In *The Age of Affirmation: Venice, the Adriatic, and the Hinterland between the 9th and 10th Centuries*. Edited by Stefano Gasparri and Sauro Gelichi, 147–76. Turnhout: Brepols, 2017.

Pedani, Maria Pia. *The Ottoman-Venetian Border (15th–18th Centuries)*. Venice: Edizioni Ca' Foscari, 2017.

Pedani, Maria Pia. *Venezia porta d'Oriente*. Bologna: Mulino, 2010.

Peli, Santo. "Le concentrazioni finanziari e industriali nell'economia di guerra: il caso di Porto Marghera." *Studi Storici* 16 (1975): 182–204.

Pelizza, Andrea. *Riammessi a respirare l'aria tranquilla. Venezia e il riscatto degli schiavi in età moderna*. Venice: Istituto Veneto di Scienze, Lettere ed Arti, 2013.

Pellegrini, Paolo. "Treves de' Bonfili, Alberto Isacco." *DBI* 96 (2019): 708–11.

Pemble, John. *The Mediterranean Passion: Victorians and Edwardians in the South*. Oxford: Clarendon Press, 1987.

Pemble, John. *Venice Rediscovered*. Oxford: Oxford University Press, 1996.

Perini, Sergio. *La difesa militare della terraferma veneta nel Settecento*. Sottomarina: Il Leggio, 1998.

Perini, Sergio. "Venezia e la guerra di Morea (1684–1699)." *AV* 5th series, 153 (1999): 45–91.

Pertusi, Agostino. "L'impero Bizantino e l'evolvere dei suoi interessi nell'Alto Adriatico." *SCIV* 1: 51–69.

Pertusi, Agostino. "L'iscrizione torcellana ai tempi di Eraclio." *Bolletino dell'Istituto di Storia della Società e dello Stato Veneziano*. 4 (1962): 9–38.

Pertusi, Agostino. "Quedam regalia insignia: ricerche sulle insegne del potere ducale a Venezia durante il Medioevo." *SV* 7 (1965): 3–123.

Pertusi, Agostino. "Venezia e Bisanzio nel secolo XI." *SCIV* 1: 175–98.

Perulli, Gianfranco. *Venezia città metropolitana*. Venice: Supernova, 2018.

Pes, Luca. "Le classi popolari." *SVON* 1: 771–801.

Pes, Luca. "Il fascismo adriatico." *SVON* 2: 1313–54.

Pes, Luca. "Gli ultimi quarant'anni." *SVON* 3: 2393–2435.

Pesaro Maurogonato, Letizia. *Il diario di Letizia (1866)*. Edited by Mario Isnenghi. Verona: Edizioni Novacharta, 2004.

Pesce, Roberto, ed. *Cronica di Venexia detta di Enrico Dandolo*. Venice: Centro di Studi Medievali e Rinascimentali 'E. A. Cicogna,' 2010.

Petrarch (Francesco Petrarca). *Letters from Petrarch*. Trans. Morris Bishop. Bloomington: Indiana University Press, 1966.

Pezzolo, Luciano. "L'economia." *SVOC* 7: 369–433.

Pezzolo, Luciano. "La finanza pubblica." *SVOC* 6: 713–73.

Pezzolo, Luciano. "La finanza pubblica: dal prestito all'imposta." *SVOC* 5: 503–51.

Phillips, William D. *Slavery from Roman Times to the Early Transatlantic Trade*. Minneapolis: University of Minnesota Press, 1985.

Pietragnoli, Leopoldo and Maurizio Reberschak. "Dalla ricostruzione al 'problema' di Venezia." *SVON* 3: 2225–77.

Pigozzo, Federico. *Treviso e Venezia nel Trecento: la prima dominazione veneziana sulle podesterie minori (1339–1381)*. Venice: Istituto Veneto di Scienze, Lettere ed Arti, 2007.

Pillinini, Giovanni. "Marino Falier e la crisi economica e politica della metà del '300 a Venezia." *AV* ser. V, 84 (1968): 45–71.

Pillinini, Giovanni. "I 'popolari' e la 'congiura' di Marino Falier." *Annali della Facoltà di Lingue e Letterature Straniere di Ca' Foscari* 9 (1970): 63–71.

Pillinini, Giovanni. "La pubblicistica veneziana nel 1848–49." In *Venezia e l'Austria*. Edited by Benzoni and Cozzi, 437–50.

Pillinini, Giovanni. *Il sistema degli stati italiani, 1454–1494*. Venice: Libreria Universitaria Editrice, 1970.

Pilot, A. "Venezia dal 1851 al 1866 nei diari inediti del Cicogna." *NAV* 32, pt. 1 (1916): 397–480.

Pincus, Debra. "Andrea Dandolo (1343–1354) and Visible History: The San Marco Projects." In *Art and Politics in Late Medieval and Early Renaissance Italy: 1250–1500*. Edited by Charles M. Rosenberg, 191–206. Notre Dame: Notre Dame University Press, 1990.

Pincus, Debra. "Hard Times and Ducal Radiance: Andrea Dandolo and the Construction of the Ruler in Fourteenth-Century Venice." *VR*, 89–136.

Pincus, Debra. *The Tombs of the Doges of Venice*. Cambridge: Cambridge University Press, 2000.

Pincus, Debra. "Venice and Its Doge in the Grand Design: Andrea Dandolo and the Fourteenth-Century Mosaics of the Baptistery." In *San Marco, Byzantium, and the Myths of Venice*. Edited by Henry Maguire and Robert S. Nelson, 245–71. Washington: Dumbarton Oaks, 2010.

Pincus, Debra. "Venice and the Two Romes: Byzantium and Rome as a Double Heritage in Venetian Cultural Politics." *Artibus et Historiae* 26 (1992): 101–14.

Pius II (Aeneas Silvius Piccolomini). *Memoirs of a Renaissance Pope: The Commentaries of Pius II: An Abridgment*. Edited by Leona C. Gabel. Trans. Florence A. Gragg. New York: Putnam, 1959.

Piva, Vittorio. *Il tempio della Salute eretto per voto de la repubblica veneta XXVI-X-MDCXXX*. Venice: Libreria Emiliana Editrice, 1930.

Plant, Margaret. *Venice: Fragile City, 1797–1997*. New Haven: Yale University Press, 2002.

Plebani, Tiziana. "Ricami di ago e di inchiostro: una ricchezza per la città (XVI secolo). *AV* 6th series 3 (2012): 97–115.

Pliny. *Natural History*. Trans. H. Rackham. 10 vols. Cambridge, MA: Harvard University Press, 1944–62.

Polybius. *The Histories*. Trans. W. R. Paton. Revised Frank W. Walbank and Christian Habicht. 6 vols. Cambridge MA: Harvard University Press, 2010–12.

Pomian, Krzysztof. "Antiquari e collezionisti." *SCUV* 4/I: 493–547.

Pomian, Krzysztof. *Collectors and Curiosities: Paris and Venice, 1500–1800*. Cambridge: Polity Press, 1990.

Poulet, Bernard. *Volpi, Prince de la Venise moderne*. Paris: Éditions Michel de Maule, 2017.

Povolo, Claudio. "The Creation of Venetian Historiography." *VR*, 491–519.

Povolo, Claudio. *L'intrigo dell'onore: poteri e istituzioni nella Repubblica di Venezia tra Cinque e Seicento*. Verona: Cierre, 1997.

Pozza, Marco. *I Badoer: una famiglia veneziana dal X al XIII secolo*. Abano Terme: Francisci Editore, 1982.

Pozza, Marco. "La cancelleria." *SVOC* 2: 349–69.

Pozza, Marco. "Particiaco, Agnello." *DBI* 81 (2014): 470–72.

Pozza, Marco. "I proprietari fondiari in terraferma." *SVOC* 2: 661–80.

Pozza, Marco. "Tiepolo, Giacomo." *DBI* 95 (2019): 636–9.

Pozza, Marco, and Giorgio Ravegnani, eds. *I trattati con Bisanzio, 992–1198*. Venice: Il Cardo, 1993.

Preto, Paolo. "La guerra segreta: spionaggio, sabotaggi, attentati." In *Venezia e la difesa del Levante: da Lepanto a Candia 1570–1670*, 79–85. Venice: Arsenale, 1986.

Preto, Paolo. "Le riforme." *SVOC* 8: 83–142.

Preto, Paolo. " 'Lo sciopero dei 'lavoranti-pistori' a Venezia nel 1775 e 1780–82." In *Non uno itinere: studi storici offerti dagli allievi a Federico Seneca*. Edited by Federica Ambrosini et al., 241–63. Venice: Stamperia di Venezia, 1993.

Preto, Paolo. *I servizi segreti di Venezia*. Milan: Il Saggiatore, 1994.

Priuli, Girolamo. *I diarii di Girolamo Priuli*. Edited by Arturo Segre, Roberto Cessi, et al. *Rerum Italicarum Scriptores*, tome 24, pt. 3 in 4 vols. Città di Castello: S. Lapi, 1912–41.

Prodi, Paolo. "Chiesa e società." *SVOC* 6: 305–39.

Provesi, Chiara. "Il conflitto tra Coloprini e Morosini: una storia di fiumi, di terre e di persone." In *The Age of Affirmation: Venice, the Adriatic, and the Hinterland between the 9th and 10th Centuries*. Edited by Stefano Gasparri and Sauro Gelichi, 177–213. Turnhout: Brepols, 2017.

Provesi, Chiara. "Le due mogli di Pietro IV Candiano (959–976): le donne e i loro gruppi parentali nella Venezia del X secolo." *Reti Medievali Rivista* 16 (2015): 21–51 [DOI 10.6092/1593-2214/470].

Pryor, John H. *Geography, Technology, and War: Studies in the Maritime History of the Mediterranean, 649–1571*. Cambridge: Cambridge University Press, 1988.

Pullan, Brian. *The Jews of Europe and the Inquisition of Venice, 1550–1670*. Totowa, NJ: Barnes and Noble, 1983.

Pullan, Brian. "Occupations and Investments of the Venetian Nobility in the Middle and Late Sixteenth Century." *RV*, 379–408.

Pullan, Brian. "Poveri, mendicanti e vagabondi (secoli XIV–XVII)." In *Storia d'Italia Annali I: dal feudalesimo al capitalismo*, 981–1047. Turin: Einaudi, 1978.

Pullan, Brian. *Rich and Poor in Renaissance Venice: The Social Institutions of a Catholic State, to 1620*. Cambridge, MA.: Harvard University Press, 1971.

Puppi, Lionello, and Ruggero Rugolo. "'Un'ordinaria forma non alletta.' Arte, riflessione sull'arte e società." *SVOC* 7: 595–699.

Queller, Donald E. *The Venetian Patriciate: Reality Versus Myth*. Urbana: University of Illinois Press, 1986.

Queller, Donald E., and Thomas F. Madden. *The Fourth Crusade: The Conquest of Constantinople*. 2nd ed. Philadelphia: University of Pennsylvania Press, 2000.

Quillien, Robin, and Solène Rivoal. "Boatmen, Fishermen, and Venetian Institutions: From Negotiation to Confrontation." In *Popular Politics in an Aristocratic Republic*. Edited by Van Gelder and Judde de Larivière, 197–216.

Raines, Dorit. "Strategie d'ascesa sociale e giochi di potere a Venezia nel Seicento: le aggregazioni alla nobiltà." *SV* n.s. 51 (2006): 279–317.

Ramsay, G. D. "The Undoing of the Italian Mercantile Colony in Sixteenth Century London." In *Textile History and Economic History: Essays in Honour of Miss Julia de Lacy Mann*. Edited by N. B. Harte and K. G. Ponting, 22–49. Manchester: Manchester University Press, 1973.

Randeraad, Nico. "I prefetti e la città nei primi decenni postunitari." *SVON* 1: 205–24.

Rando, Daniela. "Aspetti dell'organizzazione della cura d'anime a Venezia nei secoli XI–XII." In *La chiesa*. Edited by Tonon, 53–72.

Rando, Daniela. *Una chiesa di frontiera: le istituzioni ecclesiastiche veneziane nei secoli V--XII*. Bologna: Mulino, 1994.

Rapp, Richard Tilden. *Industry and Economic Decline in Seventeenth-Century Venice*. Cambridge, MA: Harvard University Press, 1976.

Ravegnani, Giorgio. "Dandolo, Andrea." *DBI* 32 (1986): 432–40.

Ravegnani, Giorgio. "Falier, Marino." *DBI* 44 (1994): 429–38.

Ravegnani, Giorgio. "Insegne del potere e titoli ducali." *SVOC* 1: 829–46.

Ravegnani, Giorgio. "La Romània veneziana." *SVOC* 2: 183–232.

Ravegnani, Giorgio. *Il traditore di Venezia: vita di Marino Falier doge*. Bari: Laterza, 2017.

Ravegnani, Giorgio. "Tra i due imperi. L'affermazione politica nel XII secolo." *SVOC* 2: 33–79.

Ravid, Benjamin. "The Legal Status of the Jews of Venice to 1509." *Proceedings of the American Academy for Jewish Research* 54 (1987): 169–202.

Ravid, Benjamin. "The Venetian Government and the Jews." In *Jews of Early Modern Venice*. Edited by Davis and Ravid, 3–30.

Ray, Meredith K. "Letters and Lace: Arcangela Tarabotti and Convent Culture in Seicento Venice." In *Early Modern Women and Transnational Communities of Letters*. Edited by Julie R. Campbell and Anne R. Larsen, 45–73. Farnham: Ashgate, 2009.

Reato, Danilo. *La bottega del caffè: i caffè veneziani tra '700 e '900*. Venice: Arsenale, 1991.

Reberschak, Maurizio. "L'economia." In *Venezia*. Edited by Franzina, 227–98.

Reberschak, Maurizio. "Filippo Grimani e la 'nuova Venezia.'" *SVON* 1: 323–47.

Reberschak, Maurizio, ed. *Il grande Vajont*. 2 vols. Longarone: Comune di Longarone, 1983.

Reberschak, Maurizio. "Gli uomini capitali: il 'gruppo veneziano' (Volpi, Cini e gli altri)." *SVON* 2: 1255–1311.

Redford, Bruce. *Venice and the Grand Tour*. New Haven: Yale University Press, 1996.

Renzi, Lorenzo. "Il francese come lingua letteraria e il franco-lombardo. L'epica carolingia nel Veneto." *SCUV* 1: 563–89.

Riccaboni, Bartolomea. *Life and Death in a Venetian Convent: The Chronicle and Necrology of Corpus Domini, 1395–1436*. Translated and edited by Daniel Bornstein. Chicago: University of Chicago Press, 2000.

Riccamboni, Gianni. "Cent'anni di elezioni a Venezia." *SVON* 2: 1183–1254.

Robbert, Louise Buenger. "Domenico Gradenigo: A Thirteenth-Century Venetian Merchant." In *Medieval and Renaissance Venice*. Edited by Ellen E. Kittell and Thomas F. Madden, 27–48. Urbana: University of Illinois Press, 1999.

Robey, David, and John Law. "The Venetian Myth and the 'De republica veneta' of Pier Paolo Vergerio." *Rinascimento* 2nd ser. 15 (1975): 3–59.

Rodini, Elizabeth. *Gentile Bellini's Portrait of Sultan Mehmed II: Lives and Afterlives of an Iconic Image*. London; I. B. Tauris, 2020.

Romanelli, Giandomenico. *Venezia Ottocento: materiali per una storia architettonica e urbanistica della città nel secolo XIX*. Rome: Officina Edizioni, 1977.

Romanelli, Giandomenico. "Venezia e la sua chiesa nell'età Napoleonica." In *La chiesa veneziana dal tramonto della Serenissima al 1848*. Edited by Maria Leonardi, 61–78. Venice: Edizioni Studium Cattolico Veneziano, 1986.

Romanelli, Giandomenico et al., eds. *A volo d'uccello: Jacopo de' Barbari e le rappresentazioni di città nell'Europa del Rinascimento*. Venice: Arsenale, 1999.

Romanin, Samuele. *Storia documentata di Venezia*. 3rd ed. in 10 vols. Venice: Filippi, 1972–5.

Romano, Dennis. "L'assistenza e la beneficenza." *SVOC* 5: 355–406.

Romano, Dennis. "Charity and Community in Early Renaissance Venice." *Journal of Urban History* 11 (1984): 63–82.

Romano, Dennis. "The Gondola as a Marker of Station in Venetian Society." *Renaissance Studies* 8 (1994): 359–74.

Romano, Dennis. *Housecraft and Statecraft: Domestic Service in Renaissance Venice*. Baltimore: Johns Hopkins University Press, 1996.

Romano, Dennis. *The Likeness of Venice: A Life of Doge Francesco Foscari, 1373–1457*. New Haven: Yale University Press, 2007.

Romano, Dennis. *Markets and Marketplaces in Medieval Italy c. 1100 to c. 1440*. New Haven: Yale University Press, 2014.

Romano, Dennis. *Patricians and Popolani: The Social Foundations of the Venetian Renaissance State*. Baltimore: Johns Hopkins University Press, 1987.

Romano, Dennis. "Popular Protest and Alternative Visions of the Venetian Polity, c. 1260 to 1423." In *Popular Politics in an Aristocratic Republic*. Edited by Van Gelder and Judde de Larivière, 22–44.

Romano, Dennis. "Commentary: Why Opera? The Politics of an Emerging Genre." *Journal of Interdisciplinary History* 36 (2006): 401–9.

Romano, Serena. "Giuditta e il Fondaco dei Tedeschi." In *Giorgione e la cultura veneta tra '400 e '500*. 113–25. Rome: DeLuca, 1981.

Romano, Sergio. *Giuseppe Volpi: industria e finanza tra Giolitti e Mussolini*. Milan: Bompiani, 1979.

Rosand, David. *Myths of Venice: Figurations of the State*. Chapel Hill: University of North Carolina Press, 2001.

Rosand, Ellen. *Opera in Seventeenth-Century Venice: The Creation of a Genre*. Berkeley: University of California Press, 1991.

Rösch, Gerhard. "Il 'gran Guadagno.'" *SVOC* 2: 233–62.

Rösch, Gerhard. "Mercatura e moneta." *SVOC* 1: 549–73.

Rösch, Gerhard. "The *Serrata* of the Great Council and Venetian Society, 1286–1323." *VR*, 67–88.

Rösch, Gerhard. "Le strutture commerciali." *SVOC* 2: 437–60.

Rösch, Gerhard. "Lo sviluppo mercantile." *SVOC* 2: 131–54.

Rösch, Gerhard. *Venezia e l'impero 962–1250: i rapporti politici, commerciali e di traffico nel periodo imperiale germanico*. Rome: Il Veltro, 1985.

Rösch, Gerhard. *Der venezianische Adel bis zur Schließung des Großen Rats: zur Genese einer Führungsschicht*. Sigmaringen: J. Thorbecke, 1989.

Rosenthal, Margaret F. "Clothing, Fashion, Dress, and Costume in Venice." In Dursteler, *Companion to Venetian History*, 889–928.

Rosenthal, Margaret F. *The Honest Courtesan: Veronica Franco, Citizen and Writer in Sixteenth-Century Venice*. Chicago: University of Chicago Press, 1992.

Rospocher, Massimo. "'In vituperium status veneti': The Case of Niccolò Zoppino." *The Italianist* 34 (2014): 349–61.

Ross, Sarah Gwyneth. *Everyday Renaissances: The Quest for Cultural Legitimacy in Venice*. Cambridge, MA: Harvard University Press, 2016.

Roselli, John. "La vita musicale a Venezia dal 1815 al 1866." In *Venezia e l'Austria*. Edited by Benzoni and Cozzi, 37–51.

Rossi, Franco. "L'Arsenale: i quadri direttivi." *SVOC* 5: 593–639.

Rothman, E. Natalie. *Brokering Empire: Trans-Imperial Subjects Between Venice and Istanbul*. Ithaca: Cornell University Press, 2012.

Rothman, E. Natalie. *The Dragoman Renaissance: Diplomatic Interpreters and the Routes of Orientalism*. Ithaca: Cornell University Press, 2021. [https://doi.org/10.7298/fxrs-fn65].

Rouleau, Francis A. "The Yangchow Latin Tombstone as a Landmark of Medieval Christianity in China." *Harvard Journal of Asiatic Studies* 17 (1954): 346–65.

Rubinstein, Nicolai. "Italian Reactions to Terraferma Expansion in the Fifteenth Century." *RV*, 197–217.

Ruggiero, Guido. *Binding Passions: Tales of Magic, Marriage, and Power at the End of the Renaissance*. New York: Oxford University Press, 1993.

Ruggiero, Guido. *The Boundaries of Eros: Sex Crime and Sexuality in Renaissance Venice*. New York: Oxford University Press, 1985.

Ruggiero, Guido. "The Ten: Control of Violence and Social Disorder in Trecento Venice." PhD diss., University of California at Los Angeles, 1972.

Ruggiero, Guido. *Violence in Early Renaissance Venice*. New Brunswick: Rutgers University Press, 1980.

Ruggini, Lellia Cracco. "Acque e lagune da periferia del mondo a fulcro di una nuova 'civilitas.'" *SVOC* 1: 11–102.

Ruggini, Lellia. *Economia e società nell'"Italia d'annonaria': rapporti fra agricoltura e commercio dal IV al VI secolo d.C.* Reprint. Bari: Edipuglia, 1995.

Runciman, Steven. "L'intervento di Venezia nella prima alla terza Crociata." In *Venezia dalla Prima Crociata alla Conquista di Costantinopoli del 1204*, 1–22. Florence: Sansoni, 1965.

Ruskin, John. *Ruskin in Italy: Letters to His Parents, 1845*. Edited by Harold I. Shapiro. Oxford: Clarendon Press, 1972.

Ruskin, John. *The Stones of Venice*. 3 vols. New York: John Wiley, 1860.

Ryder, Alan. *Alfonso the Magnanimous: King of Aragon, Naples and Sicily (1396–1458)*. Oxford: Clarendon Press, 1990.

Sabbadini, Roberto. *L'acquisto della tradizione: tradizione aristocratica e nuova nobiltà a Venezia (sec. XVII–XVIII)*. Udine: Istituto Editoriale Veneto Friulano, 1995.

Sacerdoti, Adolfo. "Le colleganze nella practica degli affairi e nella legislazione veneta." *Atti del Reale Istituto Veneto di Scienze, Lettere ed Arti* 59, pt. 2 (1899–1900): 1–45.

Sacerdoti, Adolfo. "Note sulle galere da mercato veneziane nel XV secolo." *Bollettino dell'Istituto di Storia della Società e dello Stato Veneziano* 4 (1962): 80–105.

Salzberg, Rosa. *Ephemeral City: Cheap Print and Urban Culture in Renaissance Venice*. Manchester: Manchester University Press, 2014.

Salzberg, Rosa. "Spaces of Unrest? Policing Hospitality Sites in Early Modern Venice." In *Popular Politics in an Aristocratic Republic*. Edited by Van Gelder and Judde de Larivière, 105–28.

Sansovino, Francesco. *Delle cose notabili che sono in Venetia, libri II*. Venice: Francesco Rampazetto, 1565.

Sansovino, Francesco. *Venetia città nobilissima et singolare con le aggiunte di Giustiniano Martinioni*. Reprint of 1663 edition in 2 vols. Venice: Filippi Editore, 1968.

Santore, Cathy. "Julia Lombardo: 'Somtuosa Meretrize': A Portrait by Property." *RQ* 41 (1988): 44–83.

Sanudo, Marino. *Itinerario per la Terraferma veneziana*. Edited by Gian Maria Varanini. Rome: Viella, 2014.

Sanudo, Marin il giovane. *De origine, situ et magistratibus urbis Venetae ovvero La città di Venetia (1493–1530)*. Edited by Angela Caracciolo Aricò. Milan: Cisalpino-Goliardica, 1980.

Sanudo, Marin il giovane. *Le vite dei dogi: 1423–1474, I tomo (1423–1457)*. Edited by Angela Caracciolo Aricò. Padua: Editrice Antenore, 1999.

Sanudo, Marin. *Venice: Cità Excelentissima: Selections from the Renaissance Diaries of Marin Sanudo*. Edited by Patricia H. Labalme and Laura Sanguineti White. Trans. Linda L. Carroll. Baltimore: Johns Hopkins University Press, 2008.

Sanuto (Sanudo), Marino. *I diarii di Marino Sanuto*. Edited by Rinaldo Fulin et al. 58 vols. Venice: F. Visentini, 1879–1903.

Sardella, Pierre. *Nouvelles et spéculations a Venise au début du XVIe siècle*. Paris: Librairie Armand Colin, 1948.

Savorgnan di Brazza, Francesco. "Leonardo da Vinci in Friuli e il suo progetto di fortificazione dell'Isonzo." *Atti della Accademia di Udine* 5th series 13 (1933–4): 5–21.

Sbriziolo, Lia. "Per la storia delle confraternite veneziane: dalle deliberazioni miste (1310–1476) del Consiglio dei Dieci. *Scolae comunes,* artigiane e nazionali." *Atti dell'Istituto Veneto di Scienze, Lettere ed Arti* 126 (1967–8): 405–42.

Sbriziolo, Lia. "Per la storia delle confraternite veneziane: dalle deliberazioni miste (1310–1476) del Consiglio dei Dieci: le scuole dei battuti." In *Miscellanea Gilles Gerard Meersseman*. 2 vols. (Padua: Antenore, 1970) 2: 715–63.

Scarabello, Giovanni. *Il martirio di Venezia durante la grande guerra e l'opera di difesa della marina italiana*. Venice: Tipografia del Gazzettino Illustrato, 1933.

Scarabello, Giovanni. "Da Campoformido al Congresso di Vienna: l'identità veneta sospesa." *SCUV* 6: 1–20.

Scarabello, Giovanni. "La municipalità democratica." *SVOC* 8: 263–356.

Scarpari, Maurizio. "Alcune osservazioni su una moneta veneziana del XV secolo trovata a Canton." *SV* n.s. 3 (1979): 343–50.

Schmitter, Monika. *The Art Collector in Early Modern Italy: Andrea Odoni and His Venetian Public*. Cambridge: Cambridge University Press, 2021.

Schrattenecker, Irene. "Il potere delle immagini. Gli inni patriottici. I canti popolari e le stampe della rivoluzione del 1848." In *Venezia e l'Austria*. Edited by Benzoni and Cozzi, 451–74.

Schulz, Juergen. "Jacopo de' Barbari's View of Venice: Map Making, City Views, and Moralized Geography Before the Year 1500." *Art Bulletin* 60 (1978): 425–74.

Schulz, Juergen. *The New Palaces of Medieval Venice*. University Park: Pennsylvania State University Press, 2004.

Schulz, Juergen. "The Origins of Venice: Urbanism on the Upper Adriatic Coast." *SV* n.s. 61(2010): 15–56.

Schulz, Juergen. "La piazza medievale di San Marco." *Annali di Architettura* 4–5 (1992–3): 134–56.

Schulz, Juergen. "The Printed Plans and Panoramic Views of Venice (1486–1797)." *Saggi e Memorie di Storia dell'Arte* 7 (1970): 7–182.

Schulz, Juergen. "Urbanism in Medieval Venice." In *City States in Classical Antiquity and Medieval Italy*. Edited by Anthony Molho, Kurt Raaflaub, and Julia Emlen, 419–45. Stuttgart: Franz Steiner Verlag, 1991.

Sciama, Lidia A. *A Venetian Island: Environment, History and Change in Burano*. New York: Berghahn, 2003.

Sebellico, Andreina Bondi, ed. *Felice de Merlis: prete e notaio in Venezia ed Ayas (1315–1348)*. 3 vols. Venice: Comitato per la Pubblicazione delle Fonti Relative alla Storia di Venezia, 1973–2012.

Sega, Maria Teresa. "Lavoratrici." *SVON* 2: 803–63.

Sega, Maria Teresa, and Nadia Maria Filippini. *Manifattura Tabacchi. Cotonificio Veneziano*. Padua: Il Poligrafo, 2008.

Sella, Domenico. *Commerci e industrie a Venezia nel secolo XVII*. Venice: Istituto per la Collaborazione Culturale, 1961.

Sella, Domenico. "L'economia." *SVOC* 6: 651–711.

Sella, Domenico. "The Rise and Fall of the Venetian Woolen Industry." In *Crisis and Change in the Venetian Economy*. Edited by Brian Pullan, 106–26. London: Methuen, 1968.

Semi, Franca. *Gli 'ospizi' di Venezia*. Venice: Edizioni Helvetia, 1983.

Setton, Kenneth M. *Venice, Austria and the Turks in the Seventeenth Century*. Philadelphia: American Philosophical Society, 1991.

Shaw, James E. *The Justice of Venice: Authorities and Liberties in the Urban Economy, 1550–1700*. Oxford: Oxford University Press, 2006.

Simonetti, Remy. *Da Padova a Venezia nel Medioevo: terre mobili, confini, conflitti*. Rome: Viella, 2009.

Sohm, Philip L. "Pietro Longhi and Carlo Goldoni: Relations Between Painting and Theater." *Zeitschrift für Kunstgeschichte* 45 (1983): 256–73.

Soranzo, Giovanni. *L'antico navigabile Po di Primaro nella vita economica e politica del delta padano*. Milan: Vita e Pensiero, 1964.

Soranzo, Giovanni. *La guerra fra Venezia e la Santa Sede per il dominio di Ferrara (1308–1313)*. Città di Castello: S. Lapi, 1905.

Sorelli, Fernanda. "Diritto, economia, società: condizioni delle donne a Venezia nei secoli XII–XIII." *AV* 6th series 3 (2012): 19–40.

Sorelli, Fernanda, ed. *"Ego Quirina": Testamenti di veneziane e forestiere (1200–1261)*. Rome: Viella, 2015.

Sorelli, Fernanda. "I nuovi religiosi. Note sull'insediamento degli ordini mendicanti." In *La chiesa*. Edited by Tonon, 135–52.

Sorelli, Fernanda. "Gli ordini mendicanti." *SVOC* 2: 905–27.

Sorelli, Fernanda. "La società." *SVOC* 2: 509–48.

Spencer, John R. "The Ca' del Duca in Venice and Benedetto Ferini." *Journal of the Society of Architectural Historians* 29 (1970): 3–8.

Sperling, Jutta. *Convents and the Body Politic in Late Renaissance Venice*. Chicago: University of Chicago Press, 1999.

Spiazzi, Anna Maria, Massimo De Grassi, and Giovanna Galasso, eds. *Andrea Brustolon, 1662–1732, "Il Michelangelo del legno."* Milan: Skira, 2009.

Spinelli, Giovanni. "I monasteri benedettini fra il 1000 ed il 1300." In *La chiesa*. Edited by Tonon, 109–33.

Spini, Giorgio. *Ricerca dei libertine: la teoria dell'impostura delle religioni nel Seicento italiano*. Florence: Editrice "Universale di Roma," 1950.

Squitinio della liberta veneta. Mirandola: Apresso Giovanni Benincasa, 1612.

Stahl, Alan M. *Zecca: The Mint of Venice in the Middle Ages*. Baltimore: Johns Hopkins University Press, 2000.

Steer, John. *A Concise History of Venetian Painting*. New York: Praeger, 1970.

Stöckly, Doris. *Le système de l'incanto des galées du marché à Venise (fin du XIIIe–milieu du XVe siècle)*. Leiden: Brill, 1995.

Storia di Milano. vol. 6. *Il Ducato Visconteo e la Repubblica Ambrosiana (1392–1450)*. Milan: Fondazione Treccani degli Alfieri, 1955.

Strabo. *The Geography of Strabo*. Trans. Horace Leonard Jones. 8 vols. Cambridge, MA: Harvard University Press, 1917–1949.

Strappini, Lucia. "Goldoni, Carlo." *DBI* 57 (2001): 581–92.

Strina, Bianca Lanfranchi, ed. *Codex Publicorum (Codice del Piovego)*. 2 vols. Venice: Il Comitato Editore, 1985–2006.

Stussi, Alfredo. "La lingua." *SVOC* 2: 783–802.

Stussi, Alfredo. "Un testamento volgare scritto in Persia nel 1263." *L'Italia Dialettale* 25 (1962): 23–37.

Stussi, Alfredo, ed. *Zibaldone da Canal: manoscritto mercantile del sec. XIV*. Venice: Comitato per la Pubblicazione delle Fonti Relative alla Storia di Venezia, 1967.

Sullam, Simon Levis. "Gli ebrei a Venezia nella prima metà del Novecento." *SVON* 3: 1663–84.

Tafur, Pero. *Travels and Adventures, 1435–1438*. Edited and translated by Malcolm Letts. London: George Routledge and Sons, 1926.

Tafuri, Manfredo. "'Renovatio urbis Venetiarum': il problema storiografico." In "*Renovatio Urbis": Venezia nell'età di Andrea Gritti (1523–1538)*. Edited by Manfredo Tafuri, 9–55. Rome: Officina Edizioni, 1984.

Tafuri, Manfredo. *Venice and the Renaissance*. Cambridge, MA: MIT Press, 1989.

Tamaro, Bruna Forlati et al. *Da Aquileia a Venezia: una mediazione tra l'Europa e l'Oriente dal II secolo a. C. al VI secolo d. C.* Milan: Libri Scheiwiller, 1980.

Tamassia Mazzarotto, Bianca. *Le feste veneziane: i giochi popolari, le cerimonie religiose e di governo*. Florence: Sansoni, 1980.

Tarabotti, Arcangela. *Paternal Tyranny*. Edited and translated by Letizia Panizza. Chicago: University of Chicago Press, 2004.

Tenenti, Alberto. *Cristoforo Da Canal: la marine vénitienne avant Lépante*. Paris: S.E.V.P.E.N., 1962.

Tenenti, Alberto. "Le film d'un grand système de navigation: les galères marchandes vénitiennes, XIV–XVI siècles." *Annales ESC* 16 (1961): 83–6.

Tenenti, Alberto. "La navigazione." *SVOC* 7: 533–67.

Tenenti, Alberto. *Piracy and the Decline of Venice, 1580–1615*. Berkeley: University of California Press, 1967.

Tenenti, Alberto. "Le 'temporali calamità.'" *SVOC* 3: 27–49.

Tenenti, Alberto. "The Sense of Time and Space in the Venetian World of the Fifteenth and Sixteenth Centuries." *RV*, 17–46.

Thiriet, Freddy. "Problemi dell'amministrazione veneziana nella Romania, XIV–XV sec." In Freddy Thiriet, *Études sur la Romanie greco-vénitienne (Xe-XVe siècles)*, XIV: 773–82. London: Variorum Reprints, 1977.

Thiriet, Freddy. *Délibérations des assemblées vénitiennes concernant la Romanie*, Tome I, 1160–363. Paris: Mouton, 1964.

Thiriet, Freddy. "Sui dissidi sorti tra il comune di Venezia e i suoi feudatari di Creta nel Trecento." In Freddy Thiriet, *Études sur la Romanie greco-vénitienne (Xe–XVe siècles)*, VI: 699–712. London: Variorum Reprints, 1977.

Thiriet, Freddy. "Venise et l'occupation de Ténédos au XIVe siècle." In Freddy Thiriet, *Études sur la Romanie greco-vénitienne (Xe–XVe siècles)*, II: 219–45. London: Variorum Reprints, 1977.

Tiepolo, Maria Francesca, ed. *Archivio di Stato di Venezia*. In *Guida Generale degli Archivi di Stato Italiani*, 4: 857–1148. Rome: Ministero per i Beni Culturali e Ambientali, 1994.

Tiepolo, Maria Francesca, ed. *Domenico prete di S. Maurizio: notaio in Venezia (1309–1316)*. Venice: Comitato per la Pubblicazione delle Fonti Relative alla Storia di Venezia, 1970.

Tiepolo, Maria Francesca, and Eurigio Tonetti, eds. *I Greci a Venezia: atti del convegno internazionale di studio, Venezia, 5–7 novembre 1998*. Venice: Istituto Veneto di Scienze, Lettere ed Arti, 2002.

Toffolo, Sandra. *Describing the City, Describing the State: Representations of Venice and the Venetian Terraferma in the Renaissance*. Leiden: Brill, 2020.

Tonetti, Eurigio. "Il Comune prima dell'Unità." *SVON* 1: 45–73.

Tonon, Franco, ed. *La chiesa di Venezia nei secoli XI–XIII*. Venice: Edizioni Studium Cattolico Veneziano, 1988.

Torcellan, Gianfranco. "Un problema aperto: politica e cultura nella Venezia del '700." *SV* 8 (1966): 493–513.

Tracy, James D. *Balkan Wars: Habsburg Croatia, Ottoman Bosnia, and Venetian Dalmatia, 1499–1617*. Lanham, MD: Rowman and Littlefield, 2016.

Tramontin Silvio. "Il movimento cattolico." In *La chiesa veneziana dal 1849 alle soglie del Novecento*. Edited by Gabriele Ingegneri, 165–88. Venice: Edizioni Studium Cattolico Veneziano, 1987.

Tramontin, Silvio. "Sguardo d'insieme su novant'anni di storia." In *La chiesa veneziana dal tramonto della Serenissima al 1848*. Edited by Maria Leonardi, 11–23. Venice: Edizioni Studium Cattolico Veneziano, 1986.

The Treasury of San Marco, Venice. Milan: Olivetti, 1984.

Trivellato, Francesca. *Fondamenta dei vetrai: lavoro, tecnologia e mercato a Venezia tra Sei e Settecento*. Rome: Donzelli, 2000.

Trivellato, Francesca. "Murano Glass, Continuity and Transformation (1400–1800)." In *At the Centre of the Old World*. Edited by Lanaro, 143–84.

Tucci, Hannelore Zug. "Pesca e caccia in laguna." *SVOC* 1: 491–514.

Tucci, Ugo. "Caboto." *DBI* 15 (1972): 702–23.

Tucci, Ugo. "Da Mosto (Cadamosto, ca' da Mosto), Alvise." *DBI* 32 (1986): 369–73.

Tucci, Ugo. "L'impresa marittima: uomini e mezzi." *SVOC* 2: 627–60.

Tucci, Ugo. *Un mercante veneziano del Seicento: Simon Giogalli*. Venice: Istituto Veneto di Scienze, Lettere ed Arti, 2008.

Tucci, Ugo. *Mercanti, navi, monete nel Cinquecento veneziano*. Bologna: Mulino, 1981.

Tucci, Ugo. "Mercanti veneziani in Asia lungo l'itinerario Poliano." In *Venezia e l'Oriente*. Edited by Lionello Lanciotti, 307–21. Florence: Olschki, 1987.

Tucci, Ugo. "Mercanti, viaggiatori, pellegrini nel Quattrocento." *SCUV* 3/II: 335–53.

Tucci, Ugo. "The Psychology of the Venetian Merchant in the Sixteenth Century." *RV*, 346–78.

Tucci, Ugo. *Venezia e dintorni: evoluzioni e trasformazioni*. Rome: Viella, 2014.

Turner, James Grantham. *Schooling Sex: Libertine Literature and Erotic Education in Italy, France, and England, 1534–1685*. Oxford: Oxford University Press, 2003.

Uggeri, Giovanni. "La laguna e il mare." *SVOC* 1: 149–174.

Van Gelder, Maartje. "The People's Prince: Popular Politics in Early Modern Venice." *Journal of Modern History* 90 (2018): 249–91.

Van Gelder, Maartje. "Protest in the Piazza: Contested Space in Early Modern Venice." In *Popular Politics in an Aristocratic Republic*. Edited by Van Gelder and Judde de Larivière, 129–57.

Van Gelder, Maartje. *Trading Places: The Netherlandish Merchants in Early Modern Venice*. Leiden: Brill, 2009.

Van Gelder, Maartje, and Claire Judde de Larivière, eds. *Popular Politics in an Aristocratic Republic: Political Conflict and Social Contestation in Late Medieval and Early Modern Venice*. London: Routledge, 2020.

Vanzan Marchini, Nelli-Elena. "La congiura imperfetta." In *La congiura imperfetta di Baiamonte Tiepolo*. Edited by Nelli-Elena Vanzan Marchini, 13–30. Caselle di Sommacampagna (Verona): Cierre, 2011.

Vanzan Marchini, Nelli-Elena. *Venezia civiltà anfibia*. Sommacampagna (Verona): Cierre, 2009.

Varanini, Gian Maria. "Venezia e l'entroterra (1300 circa–1420)." *SVOC* 3: 159–236.

Venezia e la difesa del Levante: da Lepanto a Candia, 1570–1670. Venice: Arsenale, 1986.

Venezia e la peste 1348–1797. Venice: Marsilio, 1979.

Venezia e le sue lagune. 2 vols. in 4 parts. Venice: Antonelli, 1847.

Ventura, Angelo. "Scrittori politici e scritture di governo." *SCUV* 3/III: 513–63.

Venturi, Franco. *Settecento riformatore*, vol. 1, *Da Muratori a Beccaria*. Turin: Einaudi, 1969.

Venturi, Lionello. "Le compagnie della calza (sec. XV–XVI)." *NAV* n.s. 16 (1908): 161–221; 17 (1909): 140–233.

Vercellin, Giorgio. "Mercanti turchi e sensali a Venezia." *SV* n.s. 4 (1980): 45–78.

Vian, Giovanni. "La chiesa." In *Venezia e l'Austria*. Edited by Benzoni and Cozzi, 103–27.

Vian, Giovanni. "La Chiesa Cattolica e le altre Chiese cristiane." *SVON* 1: 649–709.

Viaro, Andrea. "La pena della galera, la condizione dei condannati a bordo delle galere veneziane." In *Stato, società e giustizia nella Repubblica veneta (Sec. XV–XVIII)*. 2 vols. Edited by Gaetano Cozzi, 1:377–430. Rome: Jouvence, 1980

Viggiano, Alfredo. "Il Dominio da terra: politica e istituzioni." *SVOC* 4: 529–75.

Viggiano, Alfredo. "Giustizia, disciplina e ordine pubblico." *SVOC* 6: 825–61.

Viggiano, Alfredo. *Governo e governati: legittimità del potere ed esercizio dell'autorità sovrana nello stato veneto della prima età moderna*. Treviso: Edizioni Canova, 1993.

Viggiano, Alfredo. "Politics and Constitution." In Dursteler, *Companion to Venetian History*, 47–84.

Viggiano, Alfredo. "Il processo al capitano generale da mar Antonio Grimani." In *Les procès politiques (XIVe–XVIIe siècle)*. Edited by Yves-Marie Bercé, 251–72. Rome: École Française de Rome, 2007.

Villehardouin, Geoffrey of. *The Chronicle of the Fourth Crusade and the Conquest of Constantinople*. In *Memoirs of the Crusades by Villehardouin and De Joinville*. Trans. Frank Marzials. Reprint of 1908 edition. Westport, CT: Greenwood Press, 1983.

Vinovrški, Nicola. "Casanova: A Case Study in Celebrity in 18th Century Europe." *Historical Social Research/Historische Sozialforschung* Supplement 32 (2019): 99–120.

Vittori, Ottavio, and Anna Mestitz. *Four Golden Horses in the Sun*. Trans. James A. Gray. New York: International Fund for Monuments, 1976.

Vogel, Hans Ulrich. *Marco Polo Was in China: New Evidence from Currencies, Salts, and Revenues*. Leiden: Brill, 2012.

Von Ranke, Leopold. *Venezia nel Cinquecento con un saggio introduttivo di Ugo Tucci.* Rome: Istituto della Enciclopedia Italiana, 1974.

Von Stromer, Wolfgang. "Bernardus Teotonicus e i rapporti commerciali tra la Germania meridionale e Venezia prima della istituzione del Fondaco dei Tedeschi." *Centro Tedesco di Studi Veneziani. Quaderni* 8 (1978): 3–33.

Walker, Jonathan. "*Bravi* and Venetian Nobles, c. 1550–1650." *SV* n.s. 36 (1998): 85–113.

Walker, Jonathan. "Gambling and Venetian Noblemen, c. 1500–1700." *Past and Present* 162 (1999): 28–69.

Wamsler, Caroline Anastasia. "Picturing Heaven: The Trecento Pictorial Program of the Sala del Maggior Consiglio in Venice." PhD diss., Columbia University, 2006.

West-Harling, Veronica Ortenberg. "'Venecie due sunt': Venice and Its Grounding in the Adriatic and North Italian Background." In *Italia, 888–962: una svolta*. Edited by M. Valenti and C. Wickham, 237–64. Turnhout: Brepols, 2013.

Wickham, Chris. *Sleepwalking into a New World: The Emergence of Italian City Communes in the Twelfth Century*. Princeton: Princeton University Press, 2015.

Wills, Garry. *Venice: Lion City: The Religion of Empire*. New York: Simon and Schuster, 2001.

Wilson, Bronwen. *The World in Venice: Print, the City, and Early Modern Identity.* Toronto: University of Toronto Press, 2005.

Wittkower, Rudolf. "S. Maria della Salute." *Saggi e Memorie di Storia dell'Arte* 3 (1963): 31–54.

Wolff, Larry. *Paolina's Innocence: Child Abuse in Casanova's Venice*. Stanford: Stanford University Press, 2012.

Wolters, Wolfgang. "L'autocelebrazione della Repubblica." *SVOC* 6: 469–513.

Wood, Frances. *Did Marco Polo Go to China?* New York: Routledge, 1995.

Wright, Anthony. "Republican Tradition and the Maintenance of 'National' Religious Traditions in Venice." *Renaissance Studies* 10 (1996): 405–16.

Wurthmann, William B. "The Council of Ten and the *Scuole Grandi* in Early Renaissance Venice." *SV* n.s.18 (1989): 15–66.

Zago, Ferruccio, ed. *Consiglio dei Dieci: deliberazioni miste*. 3 vols. Venice: Comitato per la Pubblicazione delle Fonti Relative alla Storia di Venezia, 1962–1993.

Zago, Ferruccio, ed. *Documenti relativi alla istituzione in Venezia della prima camera del commercio*. Venice: Poligrafiche Venete Ommassini e Pascon, 1964.

Zago, Roberto. "Foscarini, Antonio." *DBI* 49 (1997): 361–65.

Zago, Roberto. *I Nicolotti: storia di una comunità di pescatori a Venezia nell'età moderna.* Abano Terme: Francisci, 1982.

Zambarbieri, Annibale. "Il patriarca Sarto." In *La chiesa veneziana dal 1849 alle soglie del Novecento*. Edited by Gabriele Ingegneri, 129–63. Venice: Edizioni Studium Cattolico Veneziano, 1987.

Zamperetti, Sergio. "Patriziato e giurisdizioni private." *SVOC* 7: 201–23.

Zannini, Andrea. *Burocrazia e burocrati a Venezia in età moderna: i cittadini originari (sec. XVI-XVIII)*. Venice: Istituto Veneto di Scienze, Lettere ed Arti, 1993.

Zannini, Andrea. "Conflicts, Social Unease, and Protests in the World of the Venetian Guilds (Sixteenth to Eighteenth Century)." In *Popular Politics in an Aristocratic Republic*. Edited by Van Gelder and Judde de Larivière, 217–38.

Zannini, Andrea. "La costruzione della città turistica." *SVON* 2: 1123–49.

Zannini, Andrea. "L'impiego pubblico." *SVOC* 4: 415–63.

Zannini, Andrea. "La presenza borghese." *SVOC* 7: 225–72.

Zannini, Andrea. "Vecchi poveri e nuovi borghesi." In *Venezia e l'Austria*. Edited by Benzoni and Cozzi, 169–94.

Zannini, Andrea. *Venezia città aperta: gli stranieri e la Serenissima, XIV–XVIII sec.* Venice: Marcianum Press, 2009.

Zannini, Andrea. "Un censimento inedito del primo Seicento e la crisi demografica ed economica di Venezia." *SV* n.s. 26 (1993): 87–116.

Zazzara, Gilda. "I cento anni di Porto Marghera (1917–2017)." *Italia Contemporanea* 284 (2017): 209–36.

Zazzara, Gilda. "La disparition de l'Italie industrielle: Porto Marghera en Vénétie." *Revue d'histoire* 20–21 (2019): 146–60.

Zecchin, Luigi. *Vetro e vetrai di Murano*. 3 vols. Venice: Arsenale, 1987–1990.

Zenoni, Luigi. "Per la storia della cultura in Venezia dal 1500 al 1797: l'Accademia dei Nobili alla Giudecca (1619–1797)." In *Miscellanea di Storia Veneta edita per cura della R. Deputazione Veneta di Storia Patria* ser. III, 9 (1916): 1–272.

Zille, Gian Giacomo. "L'ambiente naturale." In *Storia di Venezia*. 2 vols. 1: 1–76. Venice: Centro Internazionale delle Arti e del Costume, 1957–8.

Zordan, Giorgio. *I visdomini di Venezia nel sec. XIII (Ricerche su un'antica magistratura finanziaria)*. Padua: CEDAM, 1971.

Zorzi, Giangiorgio. *Le opere pubbliche e i palazzi privati di Andrea Palladio*. Venice: N. Pozza, 1965.

Zorzi, Alvise. *Venezia Austriaca*. Gorizia: Libreria Editrice Goriziana, 2000.

Zorzi, Alvise. *Venezia scomparsa*. 2 vols. Milan: Electa, 1982.

Zorzi, Marino. "Dal manoscritto al libro." *SVOC* 4: 817–957.

Zorzi, Marino, and Susy Marcon, eds. *Grado, Venezia, i Gradenigo: catalogo della mostra*. Mariano del Friuli: Edizioni della Laguna, 2001.

Zucconi, Guido. "Architettura e topografia delle istituzioni nei centri minori della Terraferma (XV e XVI secolo)." *SV* n.s. 17 (1989): 27–49.

Zucconi, Guido. "La cultura degli ingegneri: acque e strade ferrate all'indomani dell'annessione." *SCUV* 6: 625–50.

Index

For the benefit of digital users, indexed terms that span two pages (e.g., 52–53) may, on occasion, appear on only one of those pages.

Note: Figures are indicated by an italic f following the page